North Carolina grade 7
HOLT SCIENCE & TECHNOLOGY

Teacher Edition WALK-THROUGH

Student Edition CONTENTS IN BRIEF

HOLT, RINEHART AND WINSTON
A Harcourt Education Company
Orlando • **Austin** • New York • San Diego • Toronto • London

Support for everyone in your classroom— including you.

Holt Science & Technology North Carolina reflects current curriculum developments and includes the strongest skills-development strand of any middle school science series.

DESIGNED FOR NORTH CAROLINA.

- Scope sequence follows the **North Carolina Standard Course of Study.**
- Correlations to the **North Carolina Standard Course of Study** are found in each chapter of the *Teacher Edition,* in the **Lesson Plans,** and on the **Test Generator.**
- Two pages of *Standardized Test Preparation* at the end of the chapter helps students prepare for the **End-of-Grade Test.**
- The *North Carolina Test Prep Workbook* allows students to take pretests in the *End-of-Grade Test* format.

STUDENTS OF ALL ABILITIES RECEIVE THE READING HELP AND TAILORED INSTRUCTION THEY NEED.

- The *Student Edition* is accessible with a clean, easy-to-follow design and highlighted vocabulary words.
- Inclusion strategies and different learning styles are addressed to support all learners.
- **Comprehensive Section** and **Chapter Reviews** and **Standardized Test Preparation** allow students to practice their test-taking skills.
- **Reading Comprehension Guide** and **Guided Reading Audio CDs** help students better understand the content.

A FLEXIBLE LABORATORY PROGRAM HELPS STUDENTS BUILD IMPORTANT INQUIRY AND CRITICAL-THINKING SKILLS.

- The laboratory program includes labs in each chapter, labs in the **LabBook** at the end of the text, six different lab books, and **Lab Videos.**
- All labs are teacher-tested and rated by difficulty in the *Teacher Edition,* so you can be sure the labs will be appropriate for your students.
- A variety of labs, from **Inquiry Labs** to **Skills Practice Labs,** helps you meet the needs of your curriculum and work within the time constraints of your teaching schedule.

INTEGRATED TECHNOLOGY AND ONLINE RESOURCES EXPAND LEARNING BEYOND CLASSROOM WALLS.

- An **Online Edition** or **CD-ROM Version** of the student text lightens your students' load.

- **SciLinks,** a Web service developed and maintained by the National Science Teachers Association (NSTA), contains current prescreened links directly related to the textbook.

- **Brain Food Video Quizzes** on videotape and DVD are game-show style quizzes that assess students' progress and motivate them to study.

- The **One-Stop Planner®** CD-ROM with **ExamView®** Test Generator contains all of the resources you need including an *Interactive Teacher Edition,* worksheets, customizable lesson plans, **Holt Calendar Planner,** a powerful test generator, **Lab Materials QuickList Software,** and correlations to the **North Carolina Standard Course of Study.**

Inquiry Labs

Study Guide

Includes
- **Section Reviews**
- **Chapter Reviews**

North Carolina 7
HOLT SCIENCE & TECHNOLOGY

CHAPTERS

1 The World of Earth Science
2 Maps as Models of the Earth
3 Minerals of the Earth's Crust
4 Rocks: Mineral Mixtures
13 Exploring the Oceans
14 The Movement of Ocean Water
15 The Atmosphere

North Carolina 7
HOLT SCIENCE & TECHNOLOGY

One-Stop Planner®
with Test Generator

CD-ROM for Macintosh® and Windows®

Printable
Teaching Resources
Special Needs Resources

Customizable
Lesson Plans
Holt Calendar Planner
PowerPoint® Presentations

Video
At the Click of a mouse!

Powerful
Test Generator
Lab Materials QuickList
Holt PuzzlePro
Interactive Teacher Edition

HOLT RINEHART AND WINSTON

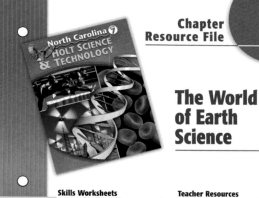

Chapter Resource File **1**

The World of Earth Science

North Carolina 7
HOLT SCIENCE & TECHNOLOGY

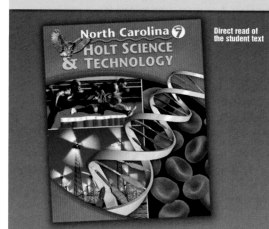

Guided Reading Audio CD Program

North Carolina 7
HOLT SCIENCE & TECHNOLOGY

Direct read of the student text

The skills students need for science success

A WELL-DESIGNED TEXT MAKES SCIENCE ENGAGING AND ACCESSIBLE.

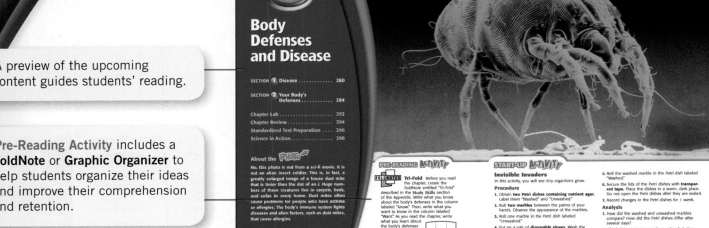

A preview of the upcoming content guides students' reading.

Pre-Reading Activity includes a **FoldNote** or **Graphic Organizer** to help students organize their ideas and improve their comprehension and retention.

An engaging photo and hands-on **Start-Up Activity** motivate students.

Objectives and **Terms to Learn** help focus students' attention and develop reading skills.

Accessible navigation engages students with outline-style headings, content grouped into small chunks, and text that doesn't break between pages.

Reading Strategy gives students additional reading guidance with a **Reading Organizer, Prediction Guide, Discussion, Paired Summarizing, Brainstorming,** or **Mnemonics Tip.**

Key Terms are highlighted in yellow and defined in the margin to develop students' vocabulary skills.

Reading Check allows students to check their understanding at least once every two-page spread. Answers are found in the **Appendix.**

Visuals are engaging and closely related to the text narrative.

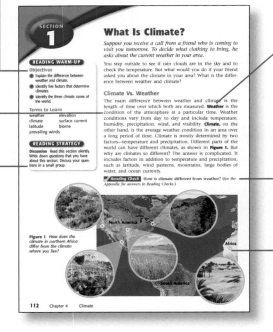

RELEVANT AND EXCITING FEATURES PROMOTE STUDENTS' INTEREST.

Science in Action grabs students' attention with three short articles and online extensions.

Current Science connects students to interesting online articles from **Current Science**® magazine.

SciLinks refers students to the NSTA Web site for up-to-date links, information, and activities.

CROSS-DISCIPLINARY FEATURES CONNECT SCIENCE TO OTHER SUBJECTS.

Math Practice and **Math Focus** help build students' math skills.

Connection shows how science relates to social studies, language arts, or other sciences.

Writing skills are developed and highlighted throughout the program, including in the **Science Journal**.

Social Studies, Language Arts, and **Math Activity** are included in the **Science in Action** feature at the end of every chapter.

LABS AND ACTIVITIES MAKE LEARNING HANDS-ON.

Internet Activity sends students online for a variety of projects, such as creating scientist biographies and writing articles.

Quick Lab and **School to Home Activity** require few materials and reinforce science concepts.

Chapter Lab includes **Inquiry, Model-Making**, and **Skills Practice labs**. Additional labs are located in the **LabBook** at the end of the book.

Reducing Friction
1. Stack **two or three heavy books** on a table. Use one finger to push the books across the table.

REVIEW FOR TEST-READINESS

Section Review includes a comprehensive assessment of the section's **Objectives**.

Chapter Review checks students' understanding of all of the chapter **Objectives** with vocabulary, multiple-choice, short answer, **Critical Thinking**, and **Interpreting Graphics** questions.

Standardized Test Preparation gives students skill practice in reading, math, and interpreting graphics to help them succeed on the **End-of-Grade Test**.

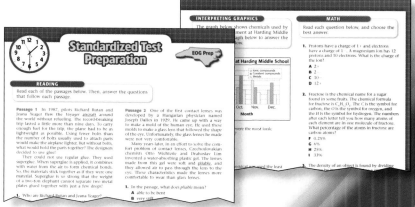

A Teacher Edition that is functional and easy-to-use

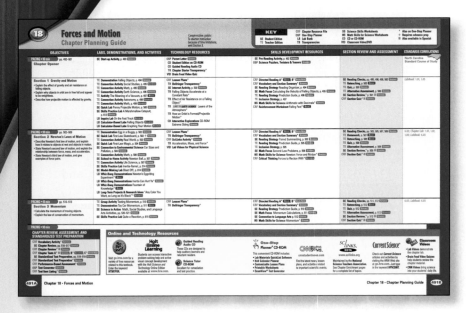

The **Chapter Organizer** is an easy-to-follow visual planning guide that provides the support you need to plan your lessons.

You'll be glad to know that we've included a convenient time-saving guide suggesting how to use the wealth of program resources. The **Chapter Organizer:**

- integrates all labs, technology, and print resources.
- is organized according to time requirements.
- includes section correlations to the **North Carolina Standard Course of Study.**
- rates activities by ability level to help you select those that are appropriate for your class.

Chapter Resources and Worksheets are shown as reduced pages to make choosing appropriate worksheets easy. Available resources and worksheets are grouped by

- Visual Resources
- Meeting Individual Needs
- Review and Assessment
- Applications and Extensions

Chapter Enrichment provides additional information for each section in the chapter, including interesting facts that spark student interest. Also included is a selection of **SciLinks** for more information about the topics listed.

The **Lesson Cycle** provides a structure for the teaching strategies included in the Teacher's wrap. **Focus** uses objectives to focus student attention on the upcoming content; **Motivate** includes activities and discussions to get students excited about learning; **Teach** includes **Teaching** and **Reading Strategies;** and **Close** provides additional assessment including **Alternative Assessment.** Correlations to the **North Carolina Standard Course of Study** are found at the beginnning of each chapter.

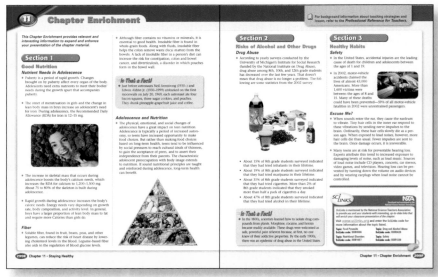

ACTIVITIES AND DEMONSTRATIONS FOR EVERY LEARNING LEVEL

Activities in the teacher's wrap are labeled by ability level—**Basic, General,** and **Advanced**—helping you choose appropriate activities for each student.

- **Basic** activities are designed to be accessible to all students.
- **General** activities are appropriate for most students and require more critical-thinking skills than Basic activities.
- **Advanced** activities are more challenging than General activities and can be used to extend learning.

Learning styles—**Interpersonal, Intrapersonal, Auditory, Kinesthetic, Logical, Visual,** and **Verbal**—are addressed throughout so you can adapt material to different ways of learning. In addition, some labels identify the activities that help with **Co-op Learning** and **English Language Learners.**

Bellringer activities begin each section with an activity designed to get students thinking. **Bellringers** are also available on transparency.

Bellringer

Have students describe their position in the classroom using a reference point and a set of reference directions. For example, a student might say, "I sit three desks behind Ahmed's desk," or "I sit 2 m east of the vent hood and 10 m north of the emergency shower."

Activity, Group Activity, Connection Activity, Demonstrations, and **Homework** provide more quick activities that you can integrate into your lesson.

ACTIVITY ——— **GENERAL**

Bridge Building Have students work in groups to build a bridge using toothpicks and glue. The bridge should span a 15 cm gap and be wide enough to hold a toy car. Students should identify the forces acting on their bridge. (An alternate and less time consuming activity would be to have students build a house of cards that can support a 500 g mass.) **LS Kinesthetic**

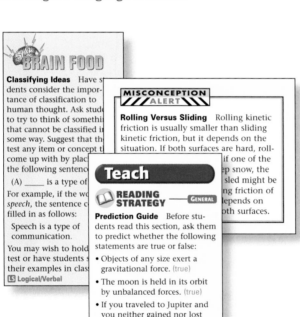

BRAIN FOOD

Classifying Ideas Have students consider the importance of classification to human thought. Ask students to try to think of something that cannot be classified in some way. Suggest that they test any item or concept they come up with by placing the following sentence:

(A) _____ is a type of For example, if the word speech, the sentence could filled in as follows:

Speech is a type of communication.

You may wish to hold test or have students their examples in class **LS Logical/Verbal**

MISCONCEPTION ALERT

Rolling Versus Sliding Rolling kinetic friction is usually smaller than sliding kinetic friction, but it depends on the situation. If both surfaces are hard, roll- if one of the sled might be ng friction of epends on th surfaces.

Teach

READING STRATEGY **GENERAL**

Prediction Guide Before students read this section, ask them to predict whether the following statements are true or false:

- Objects of any size exert a gravitational force. (true)
- The moon is held in its orbit by unbalanced forces. (true)
- If you traveled to Jupiter and you neither gained nor lost mass, your weight on Jupiter would be much greater than your weight on Earth. (true)

LS Verbal

TEACHING TIPS AND ENGAGING FEATURES KEEP STUDENTS INTERESTED AND INVOLVED.

- Reading and Teaching Strategies
- Misconception Alert
- Cultural Awareness
- Scientists at Odds
- Weird Science
- Brain Food
- Connections to other disciplines and sciences
- Science Humor
- Is That a Fact!

INCLUSION STRATEGIES MAKE MATERIAL ACCESSIBLE TO ALL.

Written by professionals in the field of special needs education, **Inclusion Strategies** address many different learning exceptionalities in the classroom.

- Hearing Impaired
- Visually Impaired
- Developmentally Delayed
- Attention Deficit Disorder
- Behavior Control Issues
- Gifted and Talented

INCLUSION Strategies

- *Gifted and Talented*
- *Behavior Control Issues*

Students may benefit from expanding on a topic. Ask these students to make a list of 30 items in the classroom, 15 of which would work as thermal conductors and 15 that would work as thermal insulators. English Language Learners

LS Logical

Complete assessment every step of the way

Holt Science & Technology North Carolina provides many ways to accurately measure students' mastery of content.

CUSTOM ASSESSMENT WITH THE ONE-STOP PLANNER CD-ROM WITH TEST GENERATOR

With Holt's *One-Stop Planner CD-ROM* create, revise, and edit quizzes, section and chapter reviews, and chapter tests. Thousands of questions, organized by chapter and correlated to the **North Carolina Standard Course of Study,** allow you to customize tests for your classroom. **Performance-Based Assessment** is also included.

SECTION ASSESSMENT

Reading Check is found at least once on each two-page spread. Students are encouraged to check their understanding of content by answering these questions found throughout the chapter and comparing their answers to the answer key in the **Appendix.**

Section Review provides a summary of the section and a comprehensive assessment of students' understanding of section **Objectives. Math, Interpreting Graphics,** and **Critical Thinking** questions are included.

Section Quiz in the *Teacher Edition* and the *Chapter Resource Files* provides additional questions to check students' understanding.

Alternative Assessment gives you different evaluation options, such as expository writing and concept mapping, to ensure a thorough assessment.

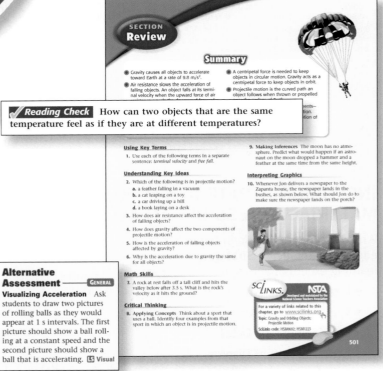

CHAPTER ASSESSMENT

Chapter Review checks students' understanding of all of the section **Objectives** with vocabulary, multiple-choice, short-answer, critical-thinking, and interpreting graphics questions. Question types are similar to those found on **Chapter Tests**, making this an excellent resource for pretest practice.

- **Assignment Guide** in the *Teacher Edition* lets you see which review questions correlate with a specific section's content.

- **Study Guide** provides blackline masters of the **Section** and **Chapter Reviews** to help students prepare for testing.

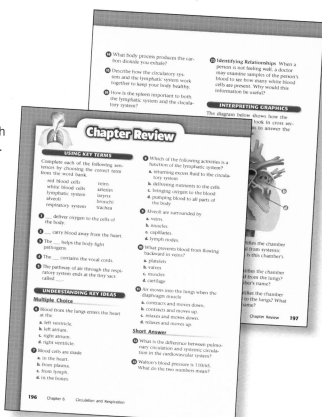

Standardized Test Preparation helps students prepare for the **End-of-Grade Test** with skill practice in reading, math, and interpreting graphics. There are two full pages of test preparation in the *Student Edition* and blackline masters in the *Chapter Resource Files.*

Test Doctor in the *Teacher Edition* helps you diagnose why a student answered a **Standardized Test Preparation** question incorrectly.

Chapter Resource Files include **Performance-Based Assessment** plus three levels of **Chapter Tests** to meet the needs of your classroom—Special Needs, General, and Advanced. In addition, a **Test Item Listing** correlated to the **North Carolina Standard Course of Study** is available so you can quickly see all of the available test items located on the *One-Stop Planner CD-ROM.*

Assessment Checklists & Rubrics provide guidelines for evaluating your students' progress. You can create a customized checklist for each class to help you gather daily scores and determine grades.

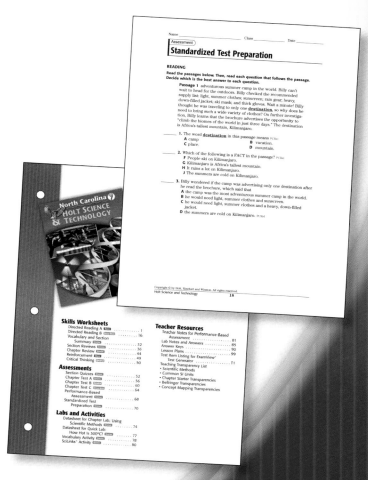

Resources to make teaching easier

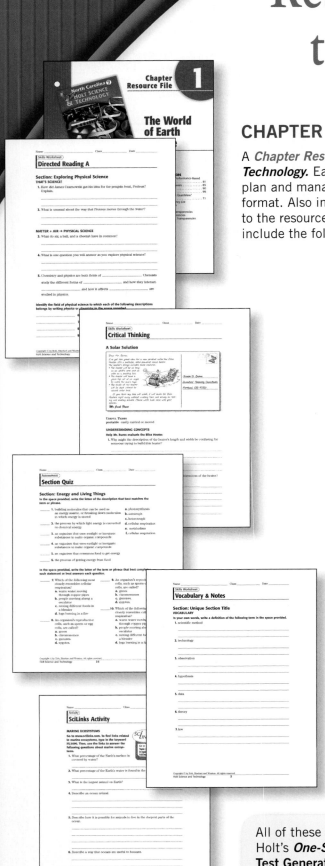

CHAPTER RESOURCE FILES

A *Chapter Resource File* is provided for each chapter of **Holt Science & Technology.** Each *Chapter Resource File* provides everything you need to plan and manage your lessons for the chapter in a convenient, time-saving format. Also included is a **Program Resource Introduction File,** your guide to the resources in each *Chapter Resource File. Chapter Resource Files* include the following:

Skills Worksheets
- Directed Reading A: Basic
- Directed Reading B: Special Needs
- Vocabulary and Section Summary
- Section Reviews
- Chapter Review
- Reinforcement
- Critical Thinking

Assessments
- Section Quizzes
- Chapter Test A: General
- Chapter Test B: Advanced
- Chapter Test C: Special Needs
- Performance-Based Assessment
- Standardized Test Preparation

Labs and Activities
- Datasheet for Chapter Lab
- Datasheets for Quick Labs
- Datasheets for LabBook Labs
- Vocabulary Activity
- SciLinks Activity

Teacher Resources
- Teacher Notes for Performance-Based Assessment
- Lab Notes and Answers
- Answer Keys
- Lesson Plans (correlated to the **North Carolina Standard Course of Study**)
- Test Item Listing for ExamView® Test Generator (correlated to the **North Carolina Standard Course of Study**)

All of these additional resources can also be found in one place on Holt's *One-Stop Planner CD-ROM.* Also included on this CD-ROM is a **Test Generator** that allows you to customize your quizzes and tests.

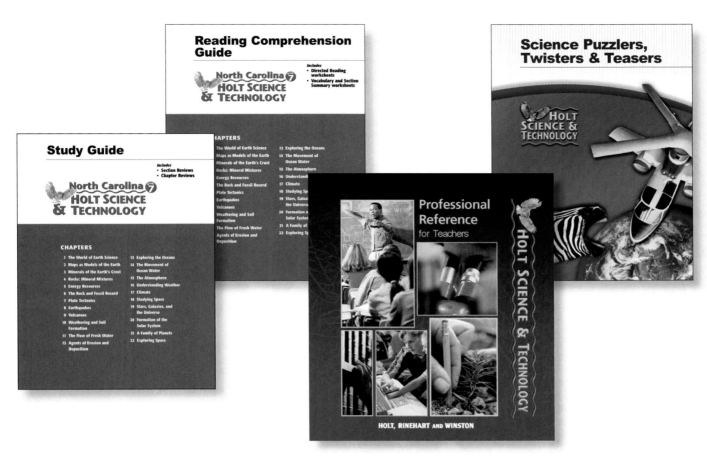

Study Guide contains **Section** and **Chapter Review Worksheets.** Answers are contained in the corresponding *Chapter Resource File.*

Reading Comprehension Guide includes **Directed Reading Worksheets** and **Vocabulary** and **Section Summary** worksheets to improve students' understanding of the text.

Program Teaching Resources includes a variety of resources for additional skill development—Science Puzzlers, Twisters & Teasers; Science Skills Worksheets; Math Skills for Science; Science Fair Guide; Assessment Checklists & Rubrics.

Professional Reference for Teachers provides current information about issues in science education today. In professional articles, you can learn more about the National Education Standards, block scheduling, classroom management, and more.

Holt Science Posters includes seven colorful posters.

Holt Anthology of Science Fiction sparks your students' imaginations.

Holt Science Skills Workshop: Reading in the Content Area contains exercises that target key reading skills using excerpts from Holt's science textbooks.

Teaching Transparencies includes 300 full-color transparencies that visually reinforce important science concepts.

Additional Transparencies includes Bellringer, Chapter Starter, and Concept Mapping Transparencies.

SPANISH RESOURCES BRING HOLT SCIENCE & TECHNOLOGY TO ENGLISH-LANGUAGE LEARNERS.

These translations open the door to students who are frequently locked out.

- Spanish glossary in the English *Student Edition*
- **Study Guide** in Spanish
- **Assessments** in Spanish

Technology that expands your teaching options

One-Stop Planner CD-ROM®
with Test Generator

Holt Science & Technology North Carolina provides the correct combination of integrated technology resources—including CD-ROMs, videotapes, and DVD products—to make teaching more effective, efficient, and creative.

Planning and managing lessons has never been easier than with this convenient, all-in-one CD-ROM that includes the following time-saving features:

Printable:

- Teaching Resources
- Transparency Masters
- Special Needs Resources

Customizable:

- **Lesson Plans:** traditional and block-scheduling lesson plans correlated to the **North Carolina Standard Course of Study** in several word-processing formats
- **Holt Calendar Planner:** a tool that allows you to manage your time and resources by the day, week, month, or year
- **PowerPoint® Resources:** graphic organizers and key concepts for each section that teachers can use to develop their own customized lectures

Powerful:

- **ExamView® Test Generator:** test items organized by chapter, plus thousands of editable questions correlated to the **North Carolina Standard Course of Study,** so you can put together your own tests and quizzes
- **Lab Materials QuickList Software:** a tool to easily create a customizable list of lab materials you need
- **Holt PuzzlePro:** an easy way to create crossword puzzles and word searches that make learning vocabulary fun
- **Interactive** *Teacher Edition:* the entire teacher text, with links to related Teaching Resources; planning has never been easier

North Carolina 7
HOLT SCIENCE & TECHNOLOGY

One-Stop Planner®
with Test Generator
CD-ROM for Macintosh® and Windows®

Printable
Teaching Resources
Special Needs Resources

Customizable
Lesson Plans
Holt Calendar Planner
PowerPoint® Presentations

Video
At the Click of a mouse!

Powerful
Test Generator
Lab Materials QuickList
Holt PuzzlePro
Interactive Teacher Edition

CD-ROM RESOURCES

Guided Reading Audio CD Program provides a direct reading of each chapter. This program helps struggling readers and English-language learners better understand the text.

Interactive Explorations CD-ROM turns a computer into a virtual laboratory where students help solve a selection of real-world problems.

Science Tutor CD-ROM serves as a personal tutor to help students practice what they learn. Immediate feedback is provided.

Student Edition on CD-ROM provides students with the entire textbook on a CD-ROM so that they have less to carry home.

Visual Concepts CD-ROM provides you with graphics, animations, and movie clips that demonstrate key chapter concepts. Visual Concepts work well as a student tutor or a teacher-presentation tool.

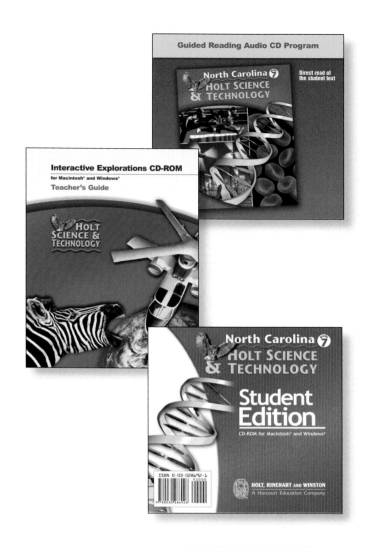

VIDEO RESOURCES

Lab Videos (on videotape and DVD) make it easier for you to integrate more experiments into your lessons without the preparation time and costs of a traditional laboratory setup.

Brain Food Video Quizzes (on videotape and DVD) are game-show style quizzes that assess students' progress and motivate students to study.

HRW Earth Science Videotape takes your students on a geology "field trip" with full-motion video.

CNN Presents Science in the News: Video Library allows your students to see the impact of science in their everyday lives with the following videos: Scientists in Action, Multicultural Connections, Science, Technology & Society, and Eye on the Environment. This program includes a **Teacher's Guide** and **Critical-Thinking Worksheets.**

Online resources available anytime, anywhere!

ENHANCED ONLINE EDITIONS ARE PORTABLE, EXPANDABLE, AND INTERACTIVE, AND YET WEIGH NOTHING AT ALL.

Enhanced Online Editions of **Holt Science & Technology** engage students in ways that were never before possible. You'll find the following:

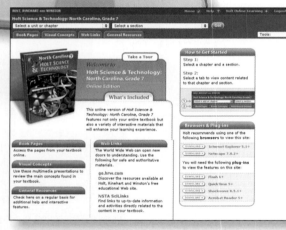

- Entire *Student Edition* online
- Web links
- **Visual Concepts** for student study or teacher presentation
- General tools, such as a glossary
- **Classroom Manager** and **One-Stop Planner** to create a lesson and manage resources.

This web service, developed and maintained by the National Science Teachers Association, contains a large collection of prescreened links that include current information and activities directly related to chapter topics.

- Prescreening saves you valuable time searching for relevant and up-to-date Web sites.
- Sites are reviewed by science-content experts and educators.
- **Internet Connect** boxes within each chapter offer opportunities to enrich, enhance, and extend learning.
- Each topic leads to many links.

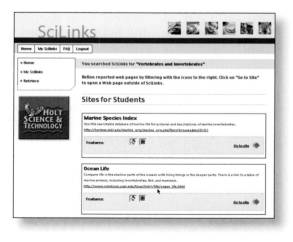

Current Science®

Current Science is a science magazine with articles that speak directly to middle school students and relate to students' lives. A collection of articles and activities have been placed online and are correlated to the text.

CNN student News™

cnnstudentnews.com

cnnstudentsnews.com is the ultimate news and information Web site for both teachers and students. The site includes news as it happens, classroom resources, activities, and lesson plans.

go.hrw.com enriches student learning with activities and resources keyed to the chapters in the textbook.

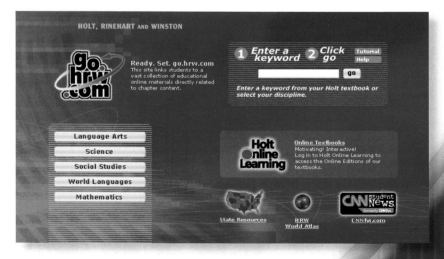

A complete lab program that makes learning meaningful

Using Scientific Methods
Inquiry Lab

Roly-Poly Races

Have you ever watched a bug run? Did you wonder why it was running? The bug you saw running was probably reacting to a stimulus. In other words, something happened to make the bug run! One characteristic of living things is that they respond to stimuli. In this activity, you will study the movement of roly-polies. Roly-polies are also called *pill bugs.* But they are not really bugs; they are land-dwelling animals called *isopods.* Isopods live in dark, moist areas under rocks or wood. You will provide stimuli to determine how fast your isopod can move and what affects its speed and direction. Remember that isopods are living things and must be treated gently and respectfully.

Ask a Question

1 Ask a question such as, "Which stimuli cause pill bugs to run?"

Form a Hypothesis

2 Using your question as a guide, form a hypothesis. For example, you could form the following hypothesis: "Light, sound, and touch stimulate pill bugs to run."

Test the Hypothesis

3 Choose a partner, and decide together how you will run your roly-poly race. Discuss some gentle ways to stimulate your isopods to move. Choose five or six things that might cause movement, such as a gentle nudge or a change in temperature, sound, or light. Check your choices with your teacher.

4 Make a data table similar to the table below. Label the columns with the stimuli that you've chosen. Label the rows "Isopod 1," "Isopod 2," "Isopod 3," and "Isopod 4."

Isopod Responses			
	Stimulus 1	Stimulus 2	Stimulus 3
Isopod 1			
Isopod 2			
Isopod 3			
Isopod 4			

OBJECTIVES

Observe responses to stimuli.

Analyze responses to stimuli.

MATERIALS

- chalk (1 stick)
- container, plastic, small, with lid
- gloves, protective
- isopod (4)
- potato, raw (1 small slice)
- ruler, metric
- soil (8 oz)
- stopwatch

SAFETY

5 Place a layer of soil that is 1 cm or 2 cm deep in a small plastic container. Add a small slice of potato and a piece of chalk. Your isopods will eat these items.

6 Place four isopods in your container. Observe them for a minute or two before you perform your tests. Record your observations.

7 Decide which stimulus you want to test first. Carefully arrange the isopods at the "starting line." The starting line can be an imaginary line at one end of the container.

8 Gently stimulate each isopod at the same time and in the same way. In your data table, record the isopods' responses to the stimulus. Be sure to record the distance that each isopod travels. Don't forget to time the race.

9 Repeat steps 7–8 for each stimulus. Be sure to wait at least 2 min between trials.

Analyze the Results

1 Describing Events Describe the way that isopods move. Do their legs move together?

2 Analyzing Results Did your isopods move before or between the trials? Did the movement seem to have a purpose, or were the isopods responding to a stimulus? Explain.

Draw Conclusions

3 Interpreting Information Did any of the stimuli make the isopods move faster or go farther? Explain.

Applying Your Data

Like isopods and all other living things, humans react to stimuli. Describe three stimuli that might cause humans to run.

Holt Science & Technology North Carolina provides a strong and flexible lab program that meets lab science requirements, regardless of lab equipment limits or time restrictions.

Chapter Labs—**Inquiry Labs, Skills Practice Labs,** and **Model Making Labs**— include clear procedures, demonstrate scientific concepts, and help develop students' understanding of scientific methods. All labs have been classroom-tested and reviewed for reliability, safety, and efficiency. Labs are rated in the *Teacher Edition,* making it easy for you to select labs that are appropriate for your classroom.

Lab Videos (on videotape and DVD) demonstrate the **Chapter Labs,** making it easy for you to integrate more experiments into your lessons without the preparation time and costs of a traditional laboratory setup. **Lab Videos** can also provide reinforcement and reteaching opportunities for students.

LabBook provides additional experiments at the end of the *Student Edition,* giving you even more full-length labs to choose from.

Datasheets for all **Quick Labs, Chapter Labs,** and **LabBook Labs** are available in the *Chapter Resource Files.*

T16

START-UP ACTIVITY

Making Rain

Do you have the power to make rain? Yes!—on a small scale. In this activity, you will cause water to change state in the same way that rain is formed. This process is one way that water is reused on Earth.

Start-Up Activity is an engaging activity at the beginning of the chapter that motivates students to learn.

Quick Lab

Heat Exchange

1. Fill a **film canister** with **hot water.** Insert the

Quick Lab is easy to execute and requires minimal time and materials—great for an in-class activity, teacher demonstration, or group presentation.

School to Home

How You Measure Matters

Measure the length and width of a desk or table, but do not use a ruler. Pick

School-to-Home Activity provides an opportunity for parents or guardians to get involved with student learning. These activities require little or no equipment and do not require safety precautions.

Internet Activity

For another activity related to this chapter, go to **go.hrw.com** and type in the keyword **HP5WPSW.**

Internet Activity sends students online for a variety of projects, such as creating scientist biographies and writing science articles.

Language Arts Activity

WRITING SKILL Write your own short story about a mysterious to the reade but do not the story. Be

Social Studies Activity

WRITING SKILL Research a location where there is forest fires. forests or pa about the iss of the debat

Math Activity

In space flight, astronauts experience changes in gravity that affect their bodies in several ways. Because of gravity, a person who has a mass of 50 kg weighs 110 pounds on Earth. But on the

Cross-Disciplinary Activity gives students the opportunity to see how science relates to social studies, language arts, or mathematics.

Motivate

Demonstration — GENERAL

Ball-and-Ring Heat Expansion

Obtain a metal ball-and-ring set. Heat the ball for a minute or

You can also integrate additional activities from the *Teacher Edition* into your lessons— **Activity, Group Activity, Connection Activity, Demonstration,** and **Homework.**

Lab options for every need

Holt Science & Technology North Carolina provides a variety of additional meaningful activities that are cost effective and fun. A variety of ancillary materials complement and complete your presentations.

Calculator-Based Labs integrate calculator use into science labs, providing a link to help students develop mathematics skills. **20 labs in all!**

Whiz-Bang Demonstrations include compelling demonstrations that students will enjoy—proving that learning science can be fun, as well as meaningful. **65 labs in all!**

Labs You Can Eat spark student interest, while explaining important scientific concepts. **25 labs in all!**

Inquiry Labs introduce students to the world of science inquiry and foster the skills necessary to develop hands-on science literacy. **23 labs in all!**

EcoLabs & Field Activities provide students with ideas for exploring the world of science outside the classroom. **23 labs in all!**

Long-Term Projects and Research Ideas help students think about science as a long-term process. Students are encouraged to study topics they find intriguing and to construct their own types of investigation. **2 for every chapter!**

Materials ordering made easy

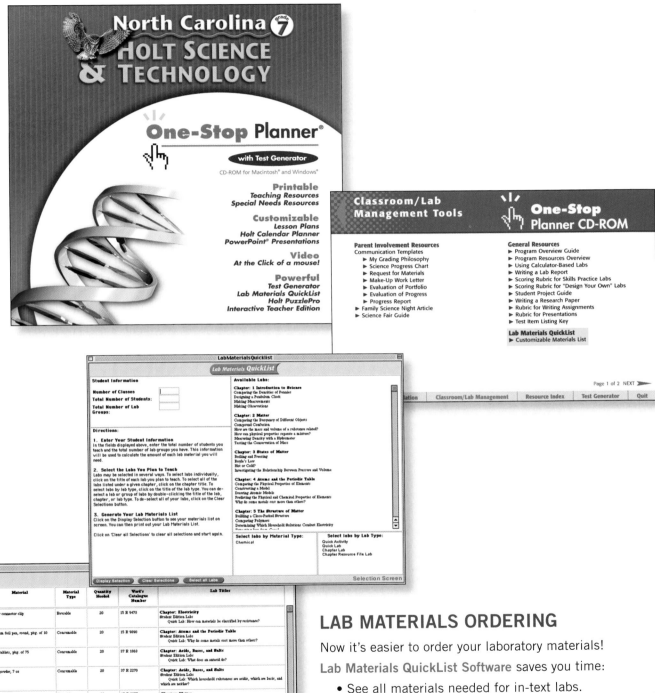

LAB MATERIALS ORDERING

Now it's easier to order your laboratory materials!

Lab Materials QuickList Software saves you time:

- See all materials needed for in-text labs.
- Create a customized list of materials.
- Quickly create a list of the items you need.
- Find everything conveniently located on the *One-Stop Planner CD-ROM.*

Meeting Individual Needs

Students have a wide range of abilities and learning exceptionalities. These pages show you how *Holt Science & Technology* provides resources and strategies to help you tailor your instruction to engage every student in your classroom. Furthermore, activities in the *Teacher Edition* are labeled with one or more learning styles designed to engage a variety of skills and strengths in every student.

- **LS Visual** activities emphasize learning through pictures, colors, and shapes.
- **LS Verbal** activities emphasize learning through words.
- **LS Logical** activities emphasize learning through patterns, reason, or numbers.
- **LS Kinesthetic** activities emphasize learning through physical activity and touch.
- **LS Auditory** activities emphasize learning through sound.
- **LS Interpersonal** activities emphasize learning through interactions with others.
- **LS Intrapersonal** activities emphasize learning through independent work and reflection.

Learning exceptionality	Inclusion Strategies and Activities	
Learning Disabilities and Slow Learners Students who have dyslexia or dysgraphia, students reading below grade level, students having difficulty understanding abstract or complex concepts, and slow learners	• Inclusion Strategies labeled **Learning Disabled** • Activities and Alternative Assessments labeled **Basic** • **Reteaching** activities	• Activities labeled **Visual, Kinesthetic,** or **Auditory** • Hands-on activities or projects • Oral presentations instead of written tests or assignments
Developmental Delays Students who are functioning far below grade level because of mental retardation, autism, or brain injury; goals are to learn or retain basic concepts	• Inclusion Strategies labeled **Developmentally Delayed** • Activities and Alternative Assessments labeled **Basic**	• **Reteaching** activities • Project-based activities
Attention Deficit Disorders Students experiencing difficulty completing a task that has multiple steps, difficulty handling long assignments, or difficulty concentrating without sensory input from physical activity	• Inclusion Strategies labeled **Attention Deficit Disorder** • Activities and Alternative Assessments labeled **Basic** • **Reteaching** activities • Activities labeled **Co-op Learning**	• Activities labeled **Visual, Kinesthetic,** or **Auditory** • Concepts broken into small chunks • Oral presentations instead of written tests or assignments
English as a Second Language Students learning English	• Activities labeled **English-Language Learners** • Activities labeled **Basic**	• **Reteaching** activities • Activities labeled **Visual**
Gifted and Talented Students who are performing above grade level and demonstrate aptitude in crosscurricular assignments	• Inclusion Strategies labeled **Gifted and Talented** • Activities and Alternative Assessments labeled **Advanced**	• **Connection** activities • Activities that involve multiple tasks, a strong degree of independence, and student initiative
Hearing Impairments Students who are deaf or who have difficulty hearing	• Inclusion Strategies labeled **Hearing Impaired** • Activities labeled **Visual**	• Activities labeled **Co-op Learning** • Assessments that use written presentations
Visual Impairments Students who are blind or who have difficulty seeing	• Inclusion strategies labeled **Visually Impaired** • Activities labeled **Auditory**	• Activities labeled **Co-op Learning** • Assessments that use oral presentations
Behavior Control Issues Students learning to manage their behavior	• Inclusion Strategies labeled **Behavior Control Issues** • Activities labeled **Basic**	• Assignments that actively involve students and help students develop confidence and improved behaviors

GENERAL INCLUSION STRATEGIES

The following strategies can help you modify instruction to help students who struggle with common classroom difficulties.

A student experiencing difficulty with...	May benefit if you...	
Beginning assignments	• Assign work in small amounts • Have the student use cooperative or paired learning • Provide varied and interesting activities	• Allow choice in assignments or projects • Reinforce participation • Seat the student closer to you
Following directions	• Gain the student's attention before giving directions • Break up the task into small steps • Give written directions rather than oral directions • Use short, simple phrases	• Stand near the student when you are giving directions • Have the student repeat directions to you • Prepare the student for changes in activity • Give visual cues by posting general routines • Reinforce improvement in or approximation of following directions
Keeping track of assignments	• Have the student use folders for assignments • Have the student use assignment notebooks	• Have the student keep a checklist of assignments and highlight assignments when they are turned in
Reading the textbook	• Provide outlines of the textbook content • Reduce the length of required reading • Allow extra time for reading • Have the students read aloud in small groups	• Have the student use peer or mentor readers • Have the student use books on tape or CD • Discuss the content of the textbook in class after reading
Staying on task	• Reduce distracting elements in the classroom • Provide a task-completion checklist • Seat the student near you	• Provide alternative ways to complete assignments, such as oral projects taped with a buddy
Behavioral or social skills	• Model the appropriate behaviors • Establish class rules, and reiterate them often • Reinforce positive behavior • Assign a mentor as a positive role model to the student • Contract with the student for expected behaviors • Reinforce the desired behaviors or any steps toward improvement	• Separate the student from any peer who stimulates the inappropriate behavior • Provide a "cooling off" period before talking with the student • Address academic/instructional problems that may contribute to disruptive behaviors • Include parents in the problem-solving process through conferences, home visits, and frequent communication
Attendance	• Recognize and reinforce attendance by giving incentives or verbal praise • Emphasize the importance of attendance by letting the student know that he or she was missed when he or she was absent	• Encourage the student's desire to be in school by planning activities that are likely to be enjoyable, giving the student a preferred responsibility to be performed in class, and involving the student in extracurricular activities • Schedule problem-solving meeting with parents, faculty, or both
Test-taking skills	• Prepare the student for testing by teaching ways to study in pairs, such as using flashcards, practice tests, and study guides, and by promoting adequate sleep, nourishment, and exercise • Decrease visual distraction by improving the visual design of the test through use of larger type, spacing, consistent layout, and shorter sentences	• During testing, allow the student to respond orally on tape or to respond using a computer; to use notes; to take breaks; to take the test in another location; to work without time constraints; or to take the test in several short sessions

Reading features that foster understanding

Holt Science & Technology North Carolina makes instruction accessible to all students—advanced learners, students having difficulty mastering content, and those needing more practice or hands-on experiences.

Every page begins with a new head, making the text easy to navigate and more accessible.

Each section begins with a **Reading Warm-up** that lists objectives and terms covered in the section. This feature helps students focus on the content being presented and understand what they read.

Reading Strategy helps students better understand what they read. Strategies provided include the following: **Reading Organizer, Prediction Guide, Discussion, Paired Summarizing, Brainstorming,** and **Mnemonics.**

Key Terms are highlighted in yellow and defined in the margin, helping students increase their science vocabulary.

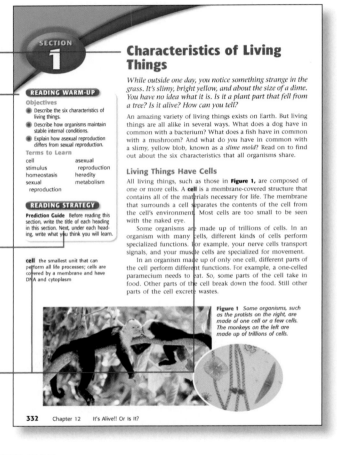

SECTION 1

Characteristics of Living Things

While outside one day, you notice something strange in the grass. It's slimy, bright yellow, and about the size of a dime. You have no idea what it is. Is it a plant part that fell from a tree? Is it alive? How can you tell?

An amazing variety of living things exists on Earth. But living things are all alike in several ways. What does a dog have in common with a bacterium? What does a fish have in common with a mushroom? And what do *you* have in common with a slimy, yellow blob, known as a *slime mold*? Read on to find out about the six characteristics that all organisms share.

READING WARM-UP

Objectives
- Describe the six characteristics of living things.
- Describe how organisms maintain stable internal conditions.
- Explain how asexual reproduction differs from sexual reproduction.

Terms to Learn

cell	asexual
stimulus	reproduction
homeostasis	heredity
sexual	metabolism
reproduction	

READING STRATEGY

Prediction Guide Before reading this section, write the title of each heading in this section. Next, under each heading, write what you think you will learn.

Living Things Have Cells

All living things, such as those in **Figure 1,** are composed of one or more cells. A **cell** is a membrane-covered structure that contains all of the materials necessary for life. The membrane that surrounds a cell separates the contents of the cell from the cell's environment. Most cells are too small to be seen with the naked eye.

Some organisms are made up of trillions of cells. In an organism with many cells, different kinds of cells perform specialized functions. For example, your nerve cells transport signals, and your muscle cells are specialized for movement.

In an organism made up of only one cell, different parts of the cell perform different functions. For example, a one-celled paramecium needs to eat. So, some parts of the cell take in food. Other parts of the cell break down the food. Still other parts of the cell excrete wastes.

cell the smallest unit that can perform all life processes; cells are covered by a membrane and have DNA and cytoplasm

Figure 1 *Some organisms, such as the protists on the right, are made of one cell or a few cells. The monkeys on the left are made up of trillions of cells.*

PRE-READING ACTIVITY

Graphic Organizer

Spider Map Before you read the chapter, create the graphic organizer entitled "Spider Map" described in the **Study Skills** section of the Appendix. Label the circle "Motion." Create a leg for each law of motion, a leg for gravity, and a leg for momentum. As you read the chapter, fill in the map with details about how motion is related to the law...

READING STRATEGY

Reading Organizer As you read this section, create an outline of the section. Use the headings from the section in your outline.

READ FOR UNDERSTANDING

Each chapter provides suggestions to help your students read for understanding.

- **Pre-Reading Activity** provides **FoldNotes** or **Graphic Organizer** activities to help students organize information presented in the chapter. Students are encouraged to take notes and then categorize what they read. In addition, the **Appendix** provides complete instruction on how to create and use the reading strategies suggested in pre-reading activities.

- **Reading Check** provides students with opportunities to check their comprehension as they read. Answers are included in the **Appendix.**

- Additional **Reading Strategies** in the *Teacher Edition* emphasize key concepts in order to guide reading and ensure comprehension.

- **Standardized Test Preparation** enables students to test their comprehension skills by reading a passage and answering a series of questions in a standardized test format. Practice is included at the end of each chapter and a blackline master of the test is located in the *Chapter Resource Files.*

ADDITIONAL RESOURCES HELP STUDENTS DEVELOP READING COMPREHENSION SKILLS.

Reading Comprehension Guide includes **Directed Reading Worksheets** and **Vocabulary** and **Section Summary Worksheets** that make reading an active process.

- **Directed Reading Worksheets** guide students through each section and focus their attention on key elements. Available in two levels: Basic and Special Needs.

- **Vocabulary** and **Section Summary** worksheets help students review vocabulary words and provide a bulleted list of main topics from each section.

Reinforcement Worksheets, found in the *Chapter Resource Files,* make reviewing and reinforcing chapter content easy.

Guided Reading Audio CD Program, a direct reading of the student text, is helpful to students who benefit from different learning modalities.

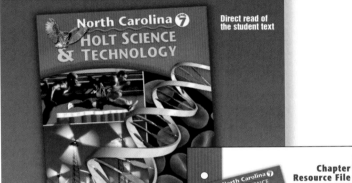

HOLT SCIENCE SKILLS WORKSHOP: READING IN THE CONTENT AREA

Target the reading skills specific to the comprehension of science texts with these activities and exercises. Students learn to analyze text structures, recognize patterns, and organize information in ways that help them construct meaning.

T23

Linking science to other disciplines

Science does not occur in a vacuum. It is an integral part of the human quest to understand the world. Connection features help students become more aware of the interconnectedness of their school studies and prepare them for standardized testing.

Science in Action features provide short articles designed to spark students' interest in science topics. Cross-Disciplinary activities including social studies, language arts, and math activities are also included for each article. Students can extend their learning by visiting **go.hrw.com.**

Connection to Language Arts links science with various language arts skills.

Holt Anthology of Science Fiction connects science to literature with interesting and relevant stories.

Writing Skills icon occurs in any activity that requires students to practice their writing skills.

Connection to Social Studies links science to social studies, presenting students with opportunities to see how science relates to history, geography, and wider society concerns.

Connection to Science links various sciences to explain phenomena in the natural world. This feature provides students with opportunities to recognize and explore important links to sciences such as environmental science, geology, physics, and oceanography.

CONNECTION TO Language Arts

WRITING SKILL **Gravity Story**
Suppose you had a device that could increase or decrease the gravitational force of small sections of Earth. In your **science journal,** write a short story describing what you might do with the device, what you would expect to see, and what effect the device would have on the weight of objects.

WRITING SKILL

CONNECTION TO Astronomy

Light Speed Light waves from stars and galaxies travel great distances that are best expressed in light-[...] distance a ray of light can travel in one ye[...] waves from these stars have traveled billi[...] reaching Earth. Do the following calculati[...] **nal:** If light travels at a speed of 300,000[...] a light-minute? (Hint: There are 60 s in a[...]

CONNECTION TO Social Studies

Navigation GPS is a complex navigation system[...] Before GPS was devel[...] travelers and explorers[...] other techniques, such[...] compasses and stars, t[...] their way. Research an[...] form of navigation, and[...] a poster that summari[...] you learn.

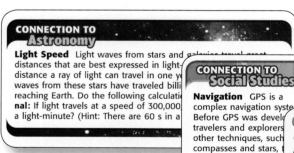

CONNECTION ACTIVITY Earth Science — GENERAL

Ancient Mountains Provide a large wall map of the world, and provide map pins o[...] tacks in three colors. Have students locate the following mountain ranges on a map. Have students place pins on the map for each range to match the eras when each range was formed. Use the following list for reference:

CONNECTION to Math — GENERAL

Energy Loss There are 12,000 units of the sun's energy available to grass, which occupies the base of an energy pyramid. Grass stores this 10% of available energy in its tissues. This energy becomes available to the next consumer, a prairie dog. In turn, the prairie dog, a consumer of grass, stores 10% of the energy that was stored in the grass. A coyote, a consumer of prairie dogs, stores 10% of the energy that was stored in the prairie dog. Calculate the units of food energy stored in the grass, the prairie dog, and the

ADDITIONAL MATH CONNECTIONS

Math Practice provides practice in simple mathematical computations. Students can hone math skills by using the exercises provided in this feature.

MATH PRACTICE

Calculating Charge

Calculating the charge of an ion is the same as adding integers (positive or negative whole numbers and 0) that have opposite signs. You write the number of protons as a positive integer and the number of electrons as a negative integer. Then, you add the integers. Calculate

Math Focus feature links mathematics directly to the science being presented. Problems are solved to show students the natural links between these two disciplines. Following the solved problem, students are presented with an application that checks their understanding.

MATH FOCUS

Momentum Calculations   What is the momentum of an ostrich with a mass of 120 kg that runs with a velocity of 16 m/s north?

Step 1: Write the equation for momentum.

$$p = m \times v$$

Step 2: Replace m and v with the values given in the problem, and solve.

$$p = 120 \text{ kg} \times 16 \text{ m/s north}$$

$$p = 19,200 \text{ kg} \bullet \text{m/s north}$$

Math Activity in **Science in Action** provides additional integrated exposure to mathematics problems.

Math ACTIVITY

Suppose that each dolphin in the Navy's program is trained for 5 years and each trained dolphin works for 25 years. If 10 dolphins began training each year for 10 years, how many would be working at the end of those 10 years? How many would still be in training?

Math Skills

8. Find the average speed of a person who swims 105 m in 70 s.

9. What is the average acceleration of a subway train that speeds up from 9.6 m/s to 12 m/s in 0.8 s on a straight section of track?

Math Skills problem is presented in most Section Reviews, providing additional math practice.

Standardized Test Preparation tests students' math abilities with questions in a standardized test format. Practice is included at the end of each chapter, and a blackline master is located in the *Chapter Resource Files*.

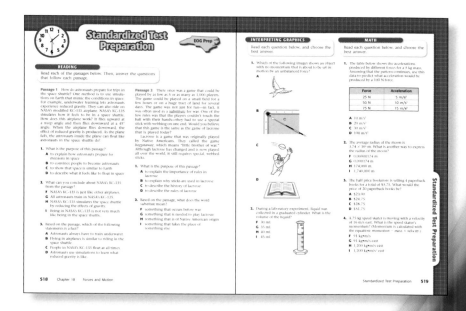

Math Refresher, found in the **Appendix,** reviews basic math skills such as averages, ratios, percentages, and more.

Math Skills for Science helps students develop and apply basic math skills to scientific problems.

Science and Math Skills Worksheets

The **Holt Science & Technology** program helps you meet the needs of a wide variety of students, regardless of their skill level. The following pages provide examples of the worksheets available to improve your students' science and math skills whether they already have a strong science and math background or are weak in these areas. Samples of assessment checklists and rubrics are also provided.

In addition to the skills worksheets represented here, **Holt Science & Technology** provides a variety of worksheets that are correlated directly with each chapter of the program. Representations of these worksheets are found at the beginning of each chapter in this *Teacher Edition*.

Many worksheets are also available on the Holt Web site. The address is **go.hrw.com**.

Science Skills Worksheets: Thinking Skills

BEING FLEXIBLE

USING YOUR SENSES

THINKING OBJECTIVELY

UNDERSTANDING BIAS
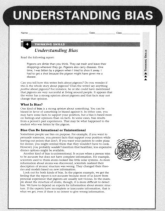

USING LOGIC
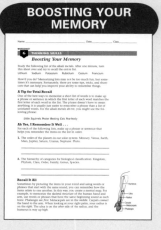

BOOSTING YOUR MEMORY

IMPROVING YOUR STUDY HABITS

READING A SCIENCE TEXTBOOK

Science Skills Worksheets: Experimenting Skills

SAFETY RULES!

DOING A LAB WRITE-UP

UNDERSTANDING VARIABLES

WORKING WITH HYPOTHESES

DESIGNING AN EXPERIMENT

USING THE INTERNATIONAL SYSTEM OF UNITS (SI)

MEASURING

Science Skills Worksheets: Researching Skills

CHOOSING YOUR TOPIC
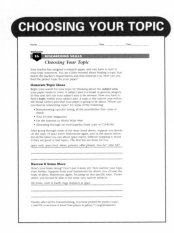

ORGANIZING YOUR RESEARCH

FINDING USEFUL SOURCES

RESEARCHING ON THE WEB

Science Skills Worksheets: Researching Skills (continued)

IDENTIFYING BIAS

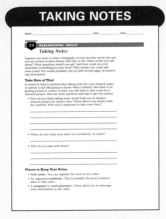

TAKING NOTES

Science Skills Worksheets: Communicating Skills

SCIENCE WRITING

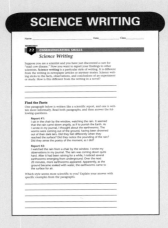

SCIENCE DRAWING

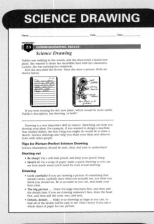

USING MODELS TO COMMUNICATE

INTRODUCTION TO GRAPHS

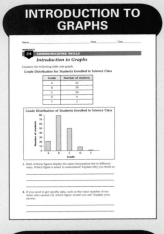

GRASPING GRAPHING

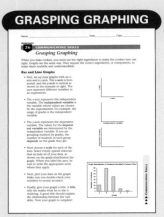

INTERPRETING YOUR DATA

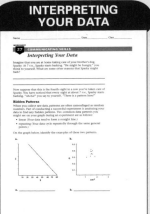

RECOGNIZING BIAS IN GRAPHS

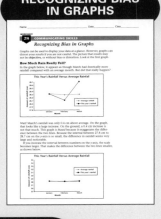

MAKING DATA MEANINGFUL

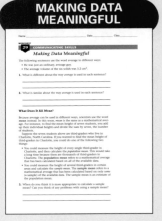

HINTS FOR ORAL PRESENTATIONS

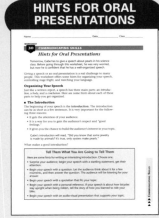

Math Skills for Science

ADDITION AND SUBTRACTION

WORKSHEET 1 — MATH SKILLS
Addition Review

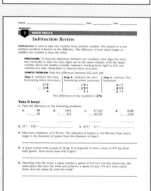

WORKSHEET 2 — MATH SKILLS
Subtraction Review

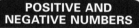

MULTIPLICATION

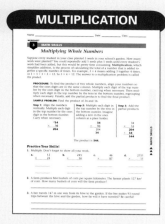

WORKSHEET 3 — MATH SKILLS
Multiplying Whole Numbers

WORKSHEET 4 — MATH SKILLS
A Shortcut for Multiplying Large Numbers

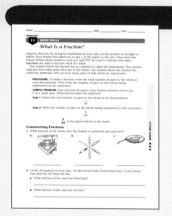

DIVISION

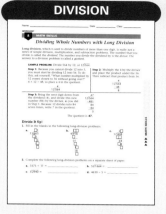

WORKSHEET 5 — MATH SKILLS
Dividing Whole Numbers with Long Division

WORKSHEET 6 — MATH SKILLS
Checking Division with Multiplication

AVERAGES

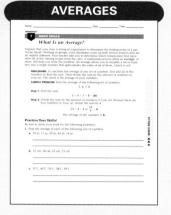

WORKSHEET 7 — MATH SKILLS
What Is an Average?

WORKSHEET 8 — MATH SKILLS
Average, Mode, and Median

POSITIVE AND NEGATIVE NUMBERS

WORKSHEET 9 — MATH SKILLS
Comparing Integers on a Number Line

WORKSHEET 10 — MATH SKILLS
Arithmetic with Positive and Negative Numbers

FRACTIONS

WORKSHEET 11 — MATH SKILLS
What Is a Fraction?

WORKSHEET 12 — MATH SKILLS
Reducing Fractions to Lowest Terms

WORKSHEET 13 — MATH SKILLS
Improper Fractions and Mixed Numbers

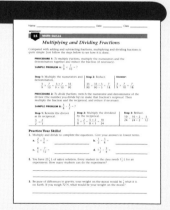

WORKSHEET 14 — MATH SKILLS
Adding and Subtracting Fractions

WORKSHEET 15 — MATH SKILLS
Multiplying and Dividing Fractions

Math Skills for Science (continued)

RATIOS AND PROPORTIONS

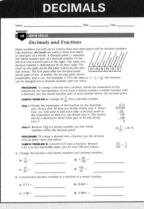

DECIMALS

PERCENTAGES

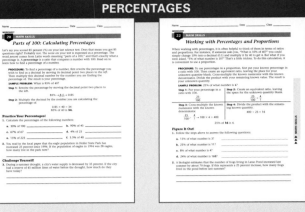

POWERS OF 10

SCIENTIFIC NOTATION

SI MEASUREMENT AND CONVERSION

Math Skills for Science (continued)

GEOMETRY

THE UNIT FACTOR AND DIMENSIONAL ANALYSIS

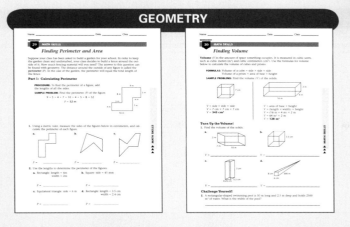

MATH IN SCIENCE: INTEGRATED SCIENCE

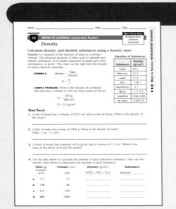

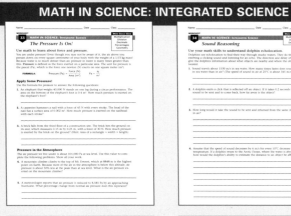

Math Skills for Science (continued)

MATH IN SCIENCE: LIFE SCIENCE

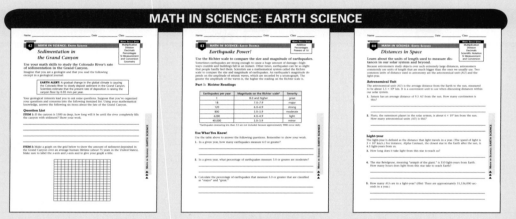

MATH IN SCIENCE: EARTH SCIENCE

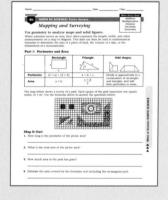

Math Skills for Science (continued)

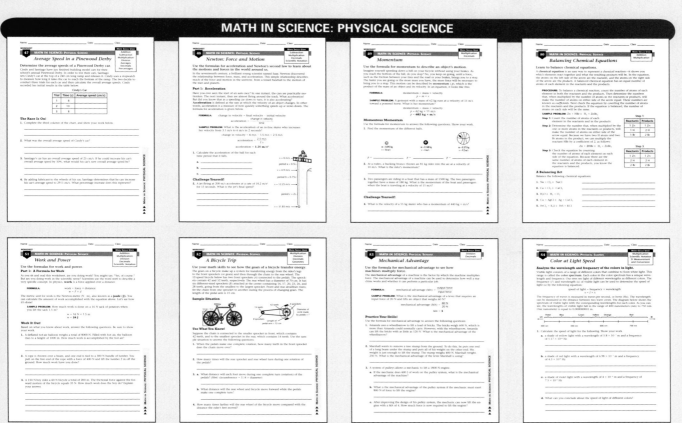

MATH IN SCIENCE: PHYSICAL SCIENCE

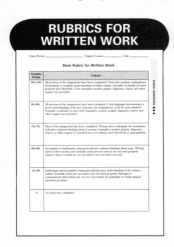

Assessment Checklist & Rubrics

The following is just a sample of over 50 checklists and rubrics contained in this booklet.

RUBRICS FOR WRITTEN WORK

RUBRIC FOR EXPERIMENTS

TEACHER EVALUATION OF COOPERATIVE LEARNING

TEACHER EVALUATION OF STUDENT PROGRESS

Pacing and Compression Guide

Pacing and Compression Guide

Pacing Each **Chapter Planning Guide** breaks down the chapter into instructional blocks. Each instructional block consists of sections and labs that you can cover in 45 or 90 minutes. The **Chapter Planning Guide** also lists activities, demonstrations, and resources that are available to accompany each section.

20 Work and Machines
Chapter Planning Guide

Compression guide: To shorten instruction because of time limitations, omit Section 3.

OBJECTIVES	LABS, DEMONSTRATIONS, AND ACTIVITIES	TECHNOLOGY RESOURCES
PACING • 90 min pp. 550–557 **Chapter Opener**	SE **Start-up Activity**, p. 551 GENERAL	OSP **Parent Letter** GENERAL CD **Student Edition on CD-ROM** CD **Guided Reading Audio CD** TR **Chapter Starter Transparency*** VID **Brain Food Video Quiz**
Section 1 Work and Power • Determine when work is being done on an object. • Calculate the amount of work done on an object. • Explain the difference between work and power.	TE **Activity** Work in Sports, p. 552 GENERAL TE **Activity** Work Done on a Spring Scale, p. 554 GENERAL SE **Quick Lab** Get to Work!, p. 555 ◆ GENERAL CRF **Datasheet for Quick Lab*** SE **Skills Practice Lab** A Powerful Workout, p. 572 GENERAL CRF **Datasheet for Chapter Lab*** LB **Inquiry Lab** Get an Arm and an Egg Up* ADVANCED SE **Science in Action** Math, Social Studies, and Language Arts Activities, pp. 578–579 GENERAL	CRF **Lesson Plans*** TR **Bellringer Transparency*** TR Work or Not Work?* TR Force Times Distance* TR *LINK TO LIFE SCIENCE* A Pair of Muscles in the Arm* CRF **SciLinks Activity*** GENERAL VID **Lab Videos for Physical Science**
PACING • 45 min pp. 558–563 **Section 2 What Is a Machine?** • Explain how a machine makes work easier. • Describe and give examples of the force-distance trade-off that occurs when a machine is used. • Calculate mechanical advantage. • Explain why machines are not 100% efficient.	TE **Connection Activity** Home Economics, p. 558 GENERAL TE **Activity** Machines as Solutions to Problems, p. 560 ADVANCED TE **Connection Activity** Graphing, p. 560 GENERAL TE **Connection Activity** Life Science, p. 561 GENERAL TE **Connection Activity** History, p. 561 GENERAL SE **School-to-Home Activity** Useful Friction, p. 562 GENERAL LB **Whiz-Bang Demonstrations** Pull-Ease, Please!* BASIC LB **Whiz-Bang Demonstrations** A Clever Lever* BASIC	CRF **Lesson Plans*** TR **Bellringer Transparency*** TR Input Force and Distance* TR Machines Change the Size and/or Direction of a Force* SE **Internet Activity**, p. 560 GENERAL
PACING • 45 min pp. 564–571 **Section 3 Types of Machines** • Identify and give examples of the six types of simple machines. • Analyze the mechanical advantage provided by each simple machine. • Identify the simple machines that make up a compound machine.	TE **Activity** Loads on a First-Class Level, p. 564 GENERAL TE **Activity** Classifying Tools, p. 565 GENERAL TE **Connection Activity** Real World, p. 566 GENERAL TE **Activity** Wheels and Axles, p. 567 BASIC TE **Activity** Gears, p. 567 ADVANCED TE **Activity** Zippers, p. 569 GENERAL TE **Activity** Screws, p. 569 BASIC TE **Connection Activity** Math, p. 569 GENERAL SE **School-to-Home Activity** Everyday Machines, p. 570 GENERAL SE **Skills Practice Lab** Inclined to Move, p. 618 GENERAL SE **Skills Practice Lab** Wheeling and Dealing, p. 619 ADVANCED SE **Inquiry Lab** Building Machines, p. 621 BASIC LB **Long-Term Projects & Research Ideas** To Complicate Things* ADVANCED CRF **Datasheet for LabBook***	CRF **Lesson Plans*** TR **Bellringer Transparency***

PACING • 90 min

CHAPTER REVIEW, ASSESSMENT, AND STANDARDIZED TEST PREPARATION

CRF **Vocabulary Activity*** GENERAL
SE **Chapter Review**, pp. 574–575 GENERAL
CRF **Chapter Review*** ■ GENERAL
CRF **Chapter Tests A*** ■ GENERAL, **B*** ADVANCED, **C*** SPECIAL NEEDS
SE **Standardized Test Preparation**, pp. 576–577 GENERAL
CRF **Standardized Test Preparation*** GENERAL
CRF **Performance-Based Assessment*** GENERAL
OSP **Test Generator** GENERAL
CRF **Test Item Listing*** GENERAL

Online and Technology Resources

Visit **go.hrw.com** for a variety of free resources related to this textbook. Enter the keyword **HT5R7WRK**.

Holt Online Learning

Students can access interactive problem-solving help and active visual concept development with the *Holt Science and Technology* Online Edition available at **www.hrw.com**.

Guided Reading Audio CD

These CDs are designed to help auditory learners and reluctant readers.

Science Tutor CD-ROM

Excellent for remediation and test practice.

549A Chapter 20 • Work and Machines

Assessment
Each chapter includes enough chapter assessment material to fill two 45-minute periods.

T34

Compression In many cases, a chapter contains more material than you will have time to teach. The Compression Guide in each **Chapter Planning Guide** suggests sections or labs you can omit if you are short on time. The sections or labs that can be omitted often contain advanced material. You may wish to also consider using the material suggested for omission as extension material for advanced students.

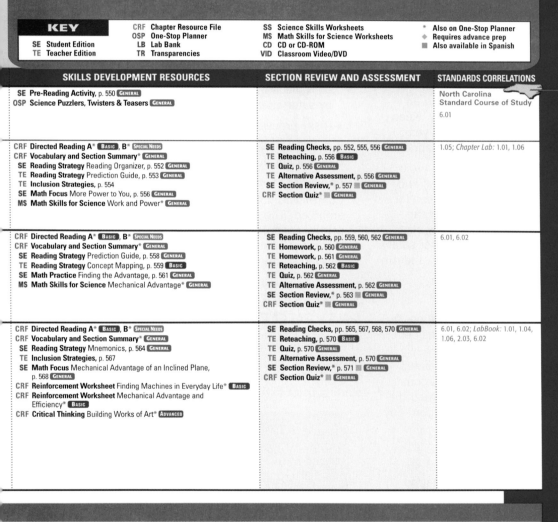

KEY		
SE Student Edition	**CRF** Chapter Resource File	**SS** Science Skills Worksheets
TE Teacher Edition	**OSP** One-Stop Planner	**MS** Math Skills for Science Worksheets
	LB Lab Bank	**CD** CD or CD-ROM
	TR Transparencies	**VID** Classroom Video/DVD

* Also on One-Stop Planner
♦ Requires advance prep
■ Also available in Spanish

SKILLS DEVELOPMENT RESOURCES	SECTION REVIEW AND ASSESSMENT	STANDARDS CORRELATIONS
SE Pre-Reading Activity, p. 550 GENERAL **OSP** Science Puzzlers, Twisters & Teasers GENERAL		North Carolina Standard Course of Study 6.01
CRF Directed Reading A* BASIC, B* SPECIAL NEEDS **CRF** Vocabulary and Section Summary* GENERAL **SE** Reading Strategy Reading Organizer, p. 552 GENERAL **TE** Reading Strategy Prediction Guide, p. 553 GENERAL **TE** Inclusion Strategies, p. 554 **SE** Math Focus More Power to You, p. 556 GENERAL **MS** Math Skills for Science Work and Power* GENERAL	**SE** Reading Checks, pp. 552, 555, 556 GENERAL **TE** Reteaching, p. 556 BASIC **TE** Quiz, p. 556 GENERAL **TE** Alternative Assessment, p. 556 GENERAL **SE** Section Review,* p. 557 GENERAL **CRF** Section Quiz* ■ GENERAL	1.05; *Chapter Lab:* 1.01, 1.06
CRF Directed Reading A* BASIC, B* SPECIAL NEEDS **CRF** Vocabulary and Section Summary* GENERAL **SE** Reading Strategy Prediction Guide, p. 558 GENERAL **TE** Reading Strategy Concept Mapping, p. 559 BASIC **SE** Math Practice Finding the Advantage, p. 561 GENERAL **MS** Math Skills for Science Mechanical Advantage* GENERAL	**SE** Reading Checks, pp. 559, 560, 562 GENERAL **TE** Homework, p. 560 GENERAL **TE** Homework, p. 561 GENERAL **TE** Reteaching, p. 562 BASIC **TE** Quiz, p. 562 GENERAL **TE** Alternative Assessment, p. 562 GENERAL **SE** Section Review,* p. 563 GENERAL **CRF** Section Quiz* ■ GENERAL	6.01, 6.02
CRF Directed Reading A* BASIC, B* SPECIAL NEEDS **CRF** Vocabulary and Section Summary* GENERAL **SE** Reading Strategy Mnemonics, p. 564 GENERAL **TE** Inclusion Strategies, p. 567 **SE** Math Focus Mechanical Advantage of an Inclined Plane, p. 568 GENERAL **CRF** Reinforcement Worksheet Finding Machines in Everyday Life* BASIC **CRF** Reinforcement Worksheet Mechanical Advantage and Efficiency* BASIC **CRF** Critical Thinking Building Works of Art* ADVANCED	**SE** Reading Checks, pp. 565, 567, 568, 570 GENERAL **TE** Reteaching, p. 570 BASIC **TE** Quiz, p. 570 GENERAL **TE** Alternative Assessment, p. 570 GENERAL **SE** Section Review,* p. 571 ■ GENERAL **CRF** Section Quiz* ■ GENERAL	6.01, 6.02; *LabBook:* 1.01, 1.04, 1.06, 2.03, 6.02

Correlations
Each section includes correlations to the **North Carolina Standard Course of Study** so you can easily see where standards are covered.

One-Stop Planner® CD-ROM
This convenient CD-ROM includes:
• Lab Materials QuickList Software
• Holt Calendar Planner
• Customizable Lesson Plans
• Printable Worksheets
• ExamView® Test Generator

CNN student News
cnnstudentnews.com
Find the latest news, lesson plans, and activities related to important scientific events.

SCiLINKS. NSTA
www.scilinks.org
Maintained by the **National Science Teachers Association.** See Chapter Enrichment pages for a complete list of topics.

Current Science®
Check out *Current Science* articles and activities by visiting the HRW Web site at **go.hrw.com.** Just type in the keyword **HP5CS08T.**

Classroom Videos
• Lab Videos demonstrate the chapter lab.
• Brain Food Video Quizzes help students review the chapter material.
• CNN Videos bring science into your students' daily life.

Safety in your laboratory

RISK ASSESSMENT

MAKING YOUR LABORATORY A SAFE PLACE TO WORK AND LEARN

Concern for safety must begin before any activity in the classroom and before students enter the lab. A careful review of the facilities should be a basic part of preparation for each school term. You should investigate the physical environment, identify any safety risks, and inspect your work areas for compliance with safety regulations.

The review of the lab should be thorough, and all safety issues must be addressed immediately. Keep a file of your review, and add to the list each year. This will allow you to continue to raise the standard of safety in your lab and classroom.

Many classroom experiments, demonstrations, and other activities are classics that have been used for years. This familiarity may lead to a comfort that can obscure inherent safety concerns. Review all experiments, demonstrations, and activities for safety concerns before presenting them to the class. Identify and eliminate potential safety hazards.

1. Identify the Risks

Before introducing any activity, demonstration, or experiment to the class, analyze it and consider what could possibly go wrong. Carefully review the list of materials to make sure they are safe. Inspect the equipment in your lab or classroom to make sure it is in good working order. Read the procedures to make sure they are safe. Record any hazards or concerns you identify.

2. Evaluate the Risks

Minimize the risks you identified in the last step without sacrificing learning. Remember that no activity you perform in the lab or classroom is worth risking injury. Thus, extremely hazardous activities, or those that violate your school's policies, must be eliminated. For activities that present smaller risks, analyze each risk carefully to determine its likelihood. If the pedagogical value of the activity does not outweigh the risks, the activity must be eliminated.

3. Select Controls to Address Risks

Even low-risk activities require controls to eliminate or minimize the risks. Make sure that in devising controls you do not substitute an equally or more hazardous alternative. Some control methods include the following:

- Explicit verbal and written warnings may be added or posted.
- Equipment may be rebuilt or relocated, parts may be replaced, or equipment be replaced entirely by safer alternatives.
- Risky procedures may be eliminated.
- Activities may be changed from student activities to teacher demonstrations.

4. Implement and Review Selected Controls

Controls do not help if they are forgotten or not enforced. The implementation and review of controls should be as systematic and thorough as the initial analysis of safety concerns in the lab and laboratory activities.

SOME SAFETY RISKS AND PREVENTATIVE CONTROLS

The following list describes several possible safety hazards and controls that can be implemented to resolve them. This list is not complete, but it can be used as a starting point to identify hazards in your laboratory.

Identified risk	Preventative control
Facilities and Equipment	
Lab tables are in disrepair, room is poorly lighted and ventilated, faucets and electrical outlets do not work or are difficult to use because of their location.	Work surfaces should be level and stable. There should be adequate lighting and ventilation. Water supplies, drains, and electrical outlets should be in good working order. Any equipment in a dangerous location should not be used; it should be relocated or rendered inoperable.
Wiring, plumbing, and air circulation systems do not work or do not meet current specifications.	Specifications should be kept on file. Conduct a periodic review of all equipment, and document compliance. Damaged fixtures must be labeled as such and must be repaired as soon as possible.
Eyewash fountains and safety showers are present, but no one knows anything about their specifications.	Ensure that eyewash fountains and safety showers meet the requirements of the ANSI standard (Z358.1).
Eyewash fountains are checked and cleaned once at the beginning of each school year. No records are kept of routine checks and maintenance on the safety showers and eyewash fountains.	Flush eyewash fountains for 5 min. every month to remove any bacteria or other organisms from pipes. Test safety showers (measure flow in gallons per min.) and eyewash fountains every 6 months and keep records of the test results.
Labs are conducted in multipurpose rooms, and equipment from other courses remains accessible.	Only the items necessary for a given activity should be available to students. All equipment should be locked away when not in use.
Students are permitted to enter or work in the lab without teacher supervision.	Lock all laboratory rooms whenever a teacher is not present. Supervising teachers must be trained in lab safety and emergency procedures.
Safety equipment and emergency procedures	
Fire and other emergency drills are infrequent, and no records or measurements are made of the results of the drills.	Always carry out critical reviews of fire or other emergency drills. Be sure that plans include alternate routes. Don't wait until an emergency to find the flaws in your plans.
Emergency evacuation plans do not include instructions for securing the lab in the event of an evacuation during a lab activity.	Plan actions in case of emergency: establish what devices should be turned off, which escape route to use, and where to meet outside the building.
Fire extinguishers are in out-of-the-way locations, not on the escape route.	Place fire extinguishers near escape routes so that they will be of use during an emergency.
Fire extinguishers are not maintained. Teachers are not trained to use them.	Document regular maintenance of fire extinguishers. Train supervisory personnel in the proper use of extinguishers. Instruct students not to use an extinguisher but to call for a teacher.

Identified risk	Preventative control
Safety equipment and emergency procedures, *continued*	
Teachers in labs and neighboring classrooms are not trained in CPR or first aid.	Teachers should receive training. The American Red Cross and other groups offer training. Certifications should be kept current with frequent refresher courses.
Teachers are not aware of their legal responsibilities in case of an injury or accident.	Review your faculty handbook for your responsibilities regarding safety in the classroom and laboratory. Contact the legal counsel for your school district to find out the extent of their support and any rules, regulations, or procedures you must follow.
Emergency procedures are not posted. Emergency numbers are kept only at the switchboard or main office. Instructions are given verbally only at the beginning of the year.	Emergency procedures should be posted at all exits and near all safety equipment. Emergency numbers should be posted at all phones, and a script should be provided for the caller to use. Emergency procedures must be reviewed periodically, and students should be reminded of them at the beginning of each activity.
Spills are handled on a case-by-case basis and are cleaned up with whatever materials happen to be on hand.	Have the appropriate equipment and materials available for cleaning up; replace them before expiration dates. Make sure students know to alert you to spilled chemicals, blood, and broken glass.
Work habits and environment	
Safety wear is only used for activities involving chemicals or hot plates.	Aprons and goggles should be worn in the lab at all times. Long hair, loose clothing, and loose jewelry should be secured.
There is no dress code established for the laboratory; students are allowed to wear sandals or open-toed shoes.	Open-toed shoes should never be worn in the laboratory. Do not allow any footwear in the lab that does not cover feet completely.
Students are required to wear safety gear, but teachers and visitors are not.	Always wear safety gear in the lab. Keep extra equipment on hand for visitors.
Safety is emphasized at the beginning of the term but is not mentioned later in the year.	Safety must be the first priority in all lab work. Students should be warned of risks and instructed in emergency procedures for each activity.
There is no assessment of students' knowledge and attitudes regarding safety.	Conduct frequent safety quizzes. Only students with perfect scores should be allowed to work in the lab.
You work alone during your preparation period to organize the day's labs.	Never work alone in a science laboratory or a storage area.
Safety inspections are conducted irregularly and are not documented. Teachers and administrators are unaware of what documentation will be necessary in case of a lawsuit.	Safety reviews should be frequent and regular. All reviews should be documented, and improvements must be implemented immediately. Contact legal counsel for your district to make sure your procedures will protect you in case of a lawsuit.

Identified risk	Preventative control
Purchasing, storing, and using chemicals	
The storeroom is too crowded, so you decide to keep some equipment on the lab benches.	Do not store reagents or equipment on lab benches and keep shelves organized. Never place reactive chemicals (in bottles, beakers, flasks, wash bottles, etc.) near the edges of a lab bench.
You prepare solutions from concentrated stock to save money.	Reduce risks by ordering diluted instead of concentrated substances.
You purchase plenty of chemicals to be sure that you won't run out or to save money.	Purchase chemicals in class-size quantities. Do not purchase or have on hand more than one year's supply of each chemical.
You don't generally read labels on chemicals when preparing solutions for a lab because you already know about a chemical.	Read each label to be sure it states the hazards and describes the precautions and first aid procedures (when appropriate) that apply to the contents in case someone else has to deal with that chemical in an emergency.
You never read the Material Safety Data Sheets (MSDSs) that come with your chemicals.	Always read the Material Safety Data Sheet (MSDS) for a chemical before using it and follow the precautions described. File and organize MSDSs for all chemicals where they can be found easily in case of an emergency.
The main stockroom contains chemicals that haven't been used for years.	Do not leave bottles of chemicals unused on the shelves of the lab for more than one week or unused in the main stockroom for more than one year. Dispose of or use up any leftover chemicals.
No extra precautions are taken when flammable liquids are dispensed from their containers.	When transferring flammable liquids from bulk containers, ground the container, and before transferring to a smaller metal container, ground both containers.
Students are told to put their broken glass and solid chemical wastes in the trash can.	Have separate containers for trash, for broken glass, and for different categories of hazardous chemical wastes.
You store chemicals alphabetically instead of by hazard class. Chemicals are stored without consideration of possible emergencies (fire, earthquake, flood, etc.), which could compound the hazard.	Use MSDSs to determine which chemicals are incompatible. Store chemicals by the hazard class indicated on the MSDS. Store chemicals that are incompatible with common fire-fighting media like water (such as alkali metals) or carbon dioxide (such as alkali and alkaline-earth metals) under conditions that eliminate the possibility of a reaction with water or carbon dioxide if it is necessary to fight a fire in the storage area.
Corrosives are kept above eye level, out of reach from anyone who is not authorized to be in the storeroom.	Always store corrosive chemicals on shelves below eye level. Remember, fumes from many corrosives can destroy metal cabinets and shelving.
Chemicals are kept on the stockroom floor on the days that they will be used so that they are easy to find.	Never store chemicals or other materials on floors or in the aisles of the laboratory or storeroom, even for a few minutes.

Safety symbols and safety guidelines for students

EYE PROTECTION

- Wear safety goggles, and know where the eyewash station is located and how to use it.
- Avoid swinging objects, which can cause serious injury.
- Avoid directly looking at a light source, as this may cause permanent eye damage.

HAND SAFETY

- Wear latex or nitrile gloves to protect yourself from chemicals in the lab.
- Use a hot mitt to handle resistors, light sources, and other equipment that may be hot. Allow equipment to cool before handling it and storing it.

CLOTHING PROTECTION

- Wear a laboratory apron to protect your clothing.
- Tie back long hair, secure loose clothing, and remove loose jewelry to prevent their getting caught in moving parts or coming in contact with chemicals.

HEATING SAFETY

- When using a Bunsen burner or a hot plate, always wear safety goggles and a laboratory apron to protect your eyes and clothing. Tie back long hair, secure loose clothing, and remove loose jewelry.
- Never leave a hot plate unattended while it is turned on.
- If your clothing catches on fire, walk to the emergency lab shower, and use the shower to put out the fire.
- Wire coils may heat up rapidly during experiments. If heating occurs, open the switch immediately, and handle the equipment with a hot mitt.
- Allow all equipment to cool before storing it.

CHEMICAL SAFETY

- Do not eat or drink anything in the lab. Never taste chemicals.
- If a chemical gets on your skin or clothing or in your eyes, rinse it immediately with lukewarm water, and alert your teacher.
- If a chemical is spilled, tell your teacher, but do not clean it up yourself unless your teacher says it is OK to do so.

ELECTRICAL SAFETY

- Never close a circuit until it has been approved by your teacher. Never rewire or adjust any element of a closed circuit.
- Never work with electricity near water; be sure the floor and all work surfaces are dry.
- If the pointer of any kind of meter moves off the scale, open the circuit immediately by opening the switch.
- Light bulbs or wires that are conducting electricity can become very hot.
- Do not work with any batteries, electrical devices, or magnets other than those provided by your teacher.

ANIMAL SAFETY

- Handle animals only as directed by your teacher.
- Always treat animals carefully and with respect.
- Wash your hands thoroughly after handling any animal.

PLANT SAFETY

- Wash your hands thoroughly after handling any part of a plant.

SHARP/POINTED OBJECTS

- Use knives and other sharp instruments with extreme care.
- Do not cut an object while holding it in your hands. Instead, place it on a suitable work surface for cutting.

Detailed Correlation of

North Carolina 7
HOLT SCIENCE & TECHNOLOGY

to the North Carolina
Standard Course of Study and
Grade Level Competencies
for Science, Grade 7

Strands: The Nature of Science, Science as Inquiry, Science and Technology, Science
in Personal and Social Perspectives Strands provide the context for content goals.

COMPETENCY GOAL 1:

**The learner will design and conduct investigations to demonstrate an understanding
of scientific inquiry.**

Objective		Page Correlation
1.01	Identify and create questions and hypotheses that can be answered through scientific investigations.	SE 5, 7, 28, 216, 217, 244, 292, 293, 342, 343, 394, 395, 514, 572, 594, 602, 603, 611, 613, 617, 618, 619
1.02	Develop appropriate experimental procedures for: • Given questions. • Student generated questions.	SE 66, 67, 102, 216, 217, 268, 269, 342, 343, 394, 395, 515, 584, 587, 588, 594, 602, 603, 609
1.03	Apply safety procedures in the laboratory and in field studies: • Recognize potential hazards. • Safely manipulate materials and equipment. • Conduct appropriate procedures.	SE 28, 102, 194, 195, 216, 217, 244, 342, 343, 474, 484, 485, 584, 587, 588, 591, 594, 596, 597, 602, 603, 609, 610, 611
1.04	Analyze variables in scientific investigations: • Identify dependent and independent. • Use of a Control. • Manipulate. • Describe relationships between. • Define operationally.	SE 194, 195, 216, 217, 244, 320, 620
1.05	Analyze evidence to: • Explain observations. • Make inferences and predictions. • Develop the relationship between evidence and explanation.	SE 166, 167, 216, 217, 244, 342, 343, 471, 474, 485, 514, 515, 543, 555, 594, 596, 597, 602, 603, 613
1.06	Use mathematics to gather, organize, and present quantitative data resulting from scientific investigations: • Measurement. • Analysis of data. • Graphing. • Prediction models.	SE 102, 136, 372, 452, 542, 543, 572, 573, 587, 590, 591, 605, 610, 618, 619, 620

1.07	Prepare models and/or computer simulations to: • Test hypotheses. • Evaluate how data fit.	**SE** 268, 269, 424, 446
1.08	Use oral and written language to: • Communicate findings. • Defend conclusions of scientific investigations.	**SE** 102, 136, 194, 195, 216, 217, 244, 264, 320, 394, 395, 584, 587, 588, 590, 591, 594, 596, 597, 601
1.09	Use technologies and information systems to: • Research. • Gather and analyze data. • Visualize data. • Disseminate findings to others.	**SE** 21, 78, 131, 236, 268, 269, 440, 601
1.10	Analyze and evaluate information from a scientifically literate viewpoint by reading, hearing, and/or viewing: • Scientific text. • Articles. • Events in the popular press.	**SE** 21, 601

COMPETENCY GOAL 2:

The learner will demonstrate an understanding of technological design.

Objective		Page Correlation
2.01	Explore evidence that "technology" has many definitions: • Artifact or hardware. • Methodology or technique. • System of production. • Social-technical system.	**SE** 7, 64, 250, 251, 490
2.02	Use information systems to: • Identify scientific needs, human needs, or problems that are subject to technological solution. • Locate resources to obtain and test ideas.	**SE** 7, 64, 250, 251, 591
2.03	Evaluate technological designs for: • Application of scientific principles. • Risks and benefits. • Constraints of design. • Consistent testing protocols.	**SE** 64, 65, 72, 591, 621

| 2.04 | Apply tenets of technological design to make informed consumer decisions about:
• Products.
• Processes.
• Systems. | SE 64, 65, 250 |

COMPETENCY GOAL 3:

The learner will conduct investigations and utilize appropriate technologies and information systems to build an understanding of the atmosphere.

Objective		Page Correlation
3.01	Explain the composition, properties and structure of the atmosphere: • Mixture of gases. • Stratified layers. • Each layer has distinct properties. • As altitude increases, air pressure decreases. • Equilibrium.	SE 40, 41, 42, 43, 44, 45
3.02	Describe properties that can be observed and measured to predict air quality: • Particulate matter. • Ozone.	SE 57, 59, 63
3.03	Conclude that the good health of environments and organisms requires: • The monitoring of air quality. • Taking steps to maintain healthy air quality. • Stewardship.	SE 62, 63, 64, 65
3.04	Evaluate how humans impact air quality including: • Air quality standards. • Point and non-point sources of air pollution in North Carolina. • Financial and economic trade-offs. • Local air quality issues.	SE 56, 57, 58, 59, 60, 61, 62, 63

3.05	Examine evidence that atmospheric properties can be studied to predict atmospheric conditions and weather hazards: • Humidity. • Temperature. • Wind speed and direction. • Air pressure. • Precipitation. • Tornados. • Hurricanes. • Floods. • Storms.	SE 77, 78, 79, 88, 89, 90, 91, 92, 93, 94, 95, 96, 97, 98, 99, 100, 101, 109
3.06	Assess the use of technology in studying atmospheric phenomena and weather hazards: • Satellites. • Weather maps. • Predicting. • Recording. • Communicating information about conditions.	SE 94, 98, 99, 100, 101, 109

COMPETENCY GOAL 4:

The learner will conduct investigations, use models, simulations, and appropriate technologies and information systems to build an understanding of the complementary nature of the human body system.

Objective	Page Correlation
4.01	Analyze how human body systems interact to provide for the needs of the human organism: • Musculoskeletal. • Cardiovascular. • Endocrine and • Nervous. • Digestive and Circulatory. • Excretory. • Reproductive. • Respiratory. • Immune. • Nervous system.	SE 154, 155, 156, 157, 158, 159, 160, 161, 176, 177, 178, 179, 180, 181, 182, 183, 184, 185, 186, 187, 188, 189, 190, 191, 192, 193, 205, 212, 226, 228, 229, 234, 235, 240, 241, 242, 243, 258, 259, 260, 261, 284, 285, 286, 287, 288, 289, 290, 291

4.02	Describe how systems within the human body are defined by the functions it performs.	SE 152, 153, 154, 158, 162, 176, 177, 178, 179, 180, 181, 182, 183, 184, 185, 186, 187, 188, 189, 190, 191, 192, 193, 204, 212, 226, 240, 258, 259, 260, 261, 284, 285, 286, 287, 288, 289, 290, 291
4.03	Explain how the structure of an organ is adapted to perform specific functions within one or more systems: • Liver. • Heart. • Lung. • Brain. • Stomach. • Kidney.	SE 176, 177, 178, 179, 180, 181, 190, 191, 192, 193, 207, 209, 213, 230, 231, 241
4.04	Evaluate how systems in the human body help regulate the internal environment.	SE 148, 149, 176, 177, 178, 179, 180, 181, 182, 183, 184, 185, 186, 187, 188, 189, 190, 191, 192, 193, 204, 215, 229, 235, 240, 241, 242, 243, 284, 285, 286, 287, 288, 289, 290, 291, 333
4.05	Analyze how an imbalance in homeostasis may result from a disruption in any human system.	SE 149
4.06	Describe growth and development of the human organism.	SE 262, 263, 264, 265, 266, 267
4.07	Explain the effects of environmental influences on human embryo development and human health including: • Smoking. • Alcohol. • Drugs. • Diet.	SE 262, 263, 264, 265, 266, 267
4.08	Explain how understanding human body systems can help make informed decisions regarding health.	SE 308, 309, 310, 311, 312, 313, 314, 315, 316, 317, 318, 319

COMPETENCY GOAL 5:

The learner will conduct investigations and utilize appropriate technologies and information systems to build an understanding of heredity and genetics.

Objective		Page Correlation
5.01	Explain the significance of genes to inherited characteristics: • Genes are the units of information. • Parents transmit genes to their offspring. • Some medical conditions and diseases are genetic.	SE 254, 255, 256, 257, 410, 421, 422, 438, 442, 443
5.02	Explain the significance of reproduction: • Sorting and recombination of parents' genetic material. • Potential variation among offspring.	SE 254, 255, 256, 257, 403, 416, 417
5.03	Identify examples and patterns of human genetic traits: • Dominant and recessive. • Incomplete dominance.	SE 407, 414
5.04	Analyze the role of probability in the study of heredity: • Role of each parent in transfer of genetic traits. • Analysis of pedigrees.	SE 412, 422, 424, 425, 607
5.05	Summarize the genetic transmittance of disease.	SE 421, 422, 423, 431, 443
5.06	Evaluate evidence that human characteristics are a product of: • Inheritance. • Environmental factors. • Lifestyle choices.	SE 415, 431

COMPETENCY GOAL 6:

The learner will conduct investigations, use models, simulations, and appropriate technologies and information systems to build an understanding of motion and forces.

Objective		Page Correlation
6.01	Demonstrate ways that simple machines can change force.	SE 551, 559, 560, 561, 564, 565, 566, 567, 569, 575, 577
6.02	Analyze simple machines for mechanical advantage and efficiency.	SE 561, 562, 563, 567, 568, 569, 570, 571, 574, 575, 577, 619, 620
6.03	Evaluate motion in terms of Newton's Laws: • The force of friction retards motion. • For every action there is an equal and opposite reaction. • The greater the force, the greater the change in motion. • An object's motion is the result of the combined effect of all forces acting on the object. • A moving object that is not subjected to a force will continue to move at a constant speed in a straight line. • An object at rest will remain at rest.	SE 465, 466, 467, 470, 471, 472, 473, 502, 503, 504, 505, 506, 507, 508, 509, 513, 530, 531, 614, 615, 616
6.04	Analyze that an object's motion is always judged relative to some other object or point.	SE 458
6.05	Describe and measure quantities that characterize moving objects and their interactions within a system: • Time. • Distance. • Mass. • Force. • Velocity. • Center of mass. • Acceleration.	SE 459, 460, 461, 462, 480, 481, 484, 485, 486, 487
6.06	Investigate and analyze the real world interactions of balanced and unbalanced forces: • Sports and recreation. • Transportation. • The human body.	SE 467, 468, 469

North Carolina

grade 7

HOLT SCIENCE
& TECHNOLOGY

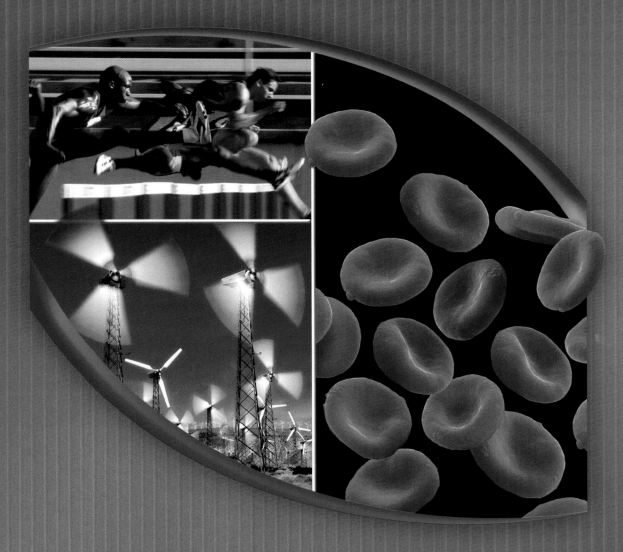

HOLT, RINEHART AND WINSTON

A Harcourt Education Company

Orlando • **Austin** • New York • San Diego • Toronto • London

Acknowledgments

Contributing Authors

Katy Z. Allen
Science Writer
Wayland, Massachusetts

Linda Ruth Berg, Ph.D.
Adjunct Professor
Natural Sciences
St. Petersburg College
St. Petersburg, Florida

Barbara Christopher
Science Writer and Editor
Austin, Texas

Leila Dumas
Former Physics Teacher
Austin, Texas

Jennie Dusheck
Science Writer
Santa Cruz, California

Kathleen Kaska
*Former Life and Earth Science
Teacher and Science
Department Chair*

William G. Lamb, Ph.D.
*Winningstad Chair in the
Physical Sciences*
Oregon Episcopal School
Portland, Oregon

Robert J. Sager, M.S., J.D., L.G.
*Coordinator and Professor of
Earth Science*
Pierce College
Lakewood, Washington

Mark F. Taylor, Ph.D.
Associate Professor of Biology
Biology Department
Baylor University
Waco, Texas

North Carolina Teacher Consultants

Pamela B. Heath
*Director of Middle Grades
Education*
Lenoir County Public
Schools
Kinston, North Carolina

James Thomas Heldreth III
Science Teacher
Eastern Guilford Middle
School
Gibsonville, North Carolina

Brian Herndon
Instructional Specialist
Gaston County Schools
Gastonia, North Carolina

Dorothea Holley
Teacher
Southwest Middle School
Charlotte, North Carolina

Larry Hollis
*Earth and Environmental
Science Teacher*
Southwest Middle School
Charlotte, North Carolina

Beverly Lyons
*Science Teacher and
Department Chair*
Hanes Middle School
Winston-Salem, North
Carolina

Donna Roberts
Science Teacher
Concord Middle School
Concord, North Carolina

Patricia Sherron-Underwood
*K–8 Math and Science
Curriculum Specialist*
Curriculum and Instruction
Department
Randolph County School
District
Asheboro, North Carolina

Carolyn Woolsey
Science Teacher
Southwest Middle School
Charlotte, North Carolina

Inclusion Specialists

Karen Clay
*Inclusion Specialist
Consultant*
Boston, Massachusetts

Ellen McPeek Glisan
Special Needs Consultant
San Antonio, Texas

Safety Reviewer

Jack Gerlovich, Ph.D.
Associate Professor
School of Education
Drake University
Des Moines, Iowa

Academic Reviewers

David M. Armstrong, Ph.D.
Professor
Ecology and Evolutionary
Biology
University of Colorado
Boulder, Colorado

John Brockhaus, Ph.D.
*Professor of Geospatial
Information Science and
Director of Geospatial
Information Science
Program*
Department of Geography
and Environmental
Engineering
United States Military
Academy
West Point, New York

Howard L. Brooks, Ph.D.
*Professor of Physics and
Astronomy*
Department of Physics
and Astronomy
DePauw University
Greencastle, Indiana

Joe W. Crim, Ph.D.
*Professor and Head of
Cellular Biology*
Department of Cellular
Biology
University of Georgia
Athens, Georgia

William E. Dunscombe
Chairman
Biology Department
Union County College
Cranford, New Jersey

Acknowledgments

continued on page 691

Requests for permission to make copies of any part of the work should be mailed to the following address: Permissions Department, Holt, Rinehart and Winston, 10801 N. MoPac Expressway, Building 3, Austin, Texas 78759.

ONE-STOP PLANNER is a trademark licensed to Holt, Rinehart and Winston, registered in the United States of America and/or other jurisdictions.

CNN is a registered trademark and **CNN STUDENT NEWS** is a trademark of Cable News Network LP, LLLP, an AOL Time Warner Company.

Current Science is a registered trademark of Weekly Reader Corporation.

The **SciLinks** trademark and service are owned and provided by the National Science Teachers Association. All rights reserved.

Printed in the United States of America

ISBN 0-03-023147-7

1 2 3 4 5 6 7 048 08 07 06 05 04

Contents in Brief

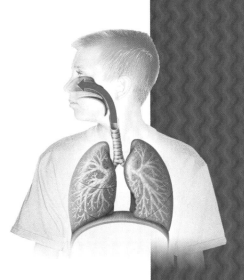

Contents

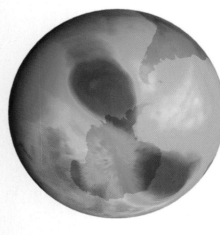

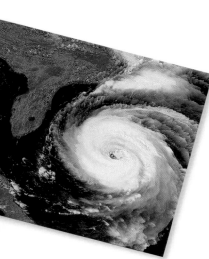

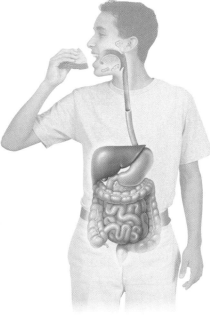

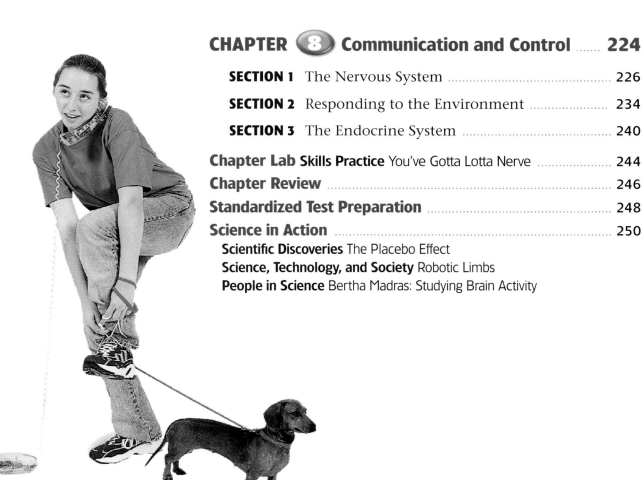

Contents   **vii**

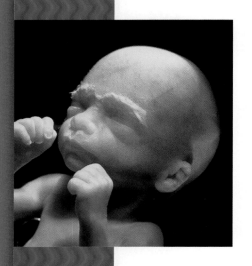

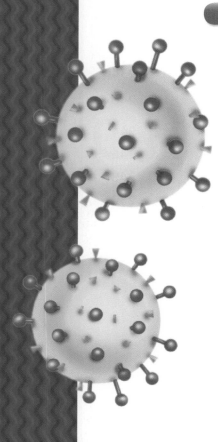

Contents **ix**

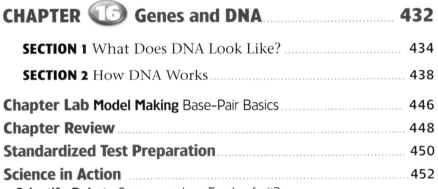

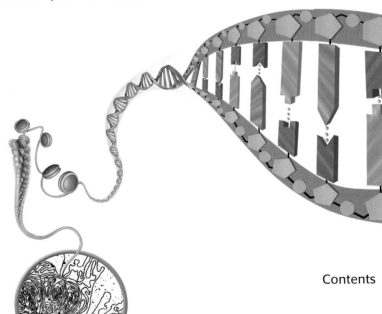

Contents   **xi**

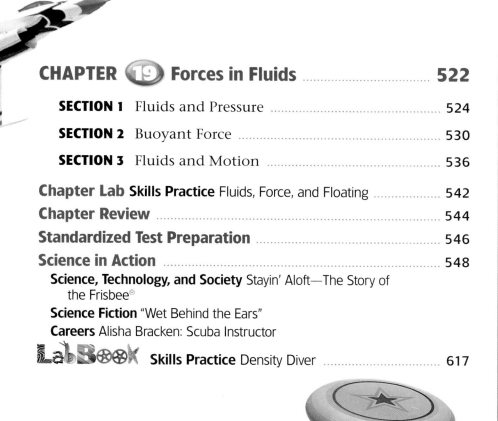

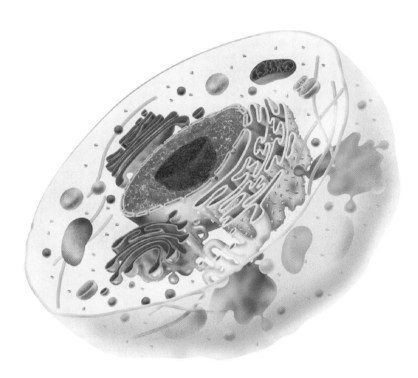

Chapter Labs and LabBook

The more labs, the better!

Take a minute to browse the variety of exciting **labs** in this textbook. Labs appear within the chapters and in a special LabBook in the back of the textbook. All labs are designed to help you experience science firsthand. But please don't forget to be safe. Read the Safety First! section before starting any of the labs.

Contents   **xvii**

Start your engines with an activity!

Get motivated to learn by doing the two activities at the beginning of each chapter. The **Pre-Reading Activity** helps you organize information as you read the chapter. The **Start-up Activity** helps you gain scientific understanding of the topic through hands-on experience.

PRE-READING ACTIVITY

FOLDNOTES

Graphic Organizer

START-UP ACTIVITY

READING STRATEGY

Remembering what you read doesn't have to be hard!

A **Reading Strategy** at the beginning of every section provides tips to help you remember and/or organize the information covered in the section.

Contents   **xix**

Quick Lab

School to Home

Science brings you closer together!

Bring science into your home by doing **School-to-Home Activities** with a parent or another adult in your household.

INTERNET ACTIVITY

MATH PRACTICE

MATH FOCUS

Science and math go hand in hand.

The **Math Focus** and **Math Practice** items show you many ways that math applies directly to science and vice versa.

Connection to...

One subject leads to another.

You may not realize it at first, but different subjects are related to each other in many ways. Each **Connection** explores a topic from the viewpoint of another discipline. In this way, all of the subjects you learn about in school merge to improve your understanding of the world around you.

Science in Action

Science moves beyond the classroom!

Read **Science in Action** articles to learn more about science in the real world. These articles will give you an idea of how interesting, strange, helpful, and action-packed science is. At the end of each chapter, you will find three short articles. And if your thirst is still not quenched, go to **go.hrw.com** for in-depth coverage.

How to Use Your Textbook

Your Roadmap for Success with Holt Science and Technology

Reading Warm-Up

A Reading Warm-Up at the beginning of every section provides you with the section's objectives and key terms. The objectives tell you what you'll need to know after you finish reading the section.

Key terms are listed for each section. Learn the definitions of these terms because you will most likely be tested on them. Each key term is highlighted in the text and is defined at point of use and in the margin. You can also use the glossary to locate definitions quickly.

STUDY TIP Reread the objectives and the definitions to the key terms when studying for a test to be sure you know the material.

Get Organized

A Reading Strategy at the beginning of every section provides tips to help you organize and remember the information covered in the section. Keep a science notebook so that you are ready to take notes when your teacher reviews the material in class. Keep your assignments in this notebook so that you can review them when studying for the chapter test.

SECTION 1

Introduction to Body Systems

Imagine jumping into a lake. At first, your body feels very cold. You may even shiver. But eventually you get used to the cold water. How does this happen?

Your body gets used to cold water because of homeostasis (HOH mee OH STAY sis). **Homeostasis** is the maintenance of a stable internal environment in the body. When you jump into a cold lake, homeostasis helps your body stay warm.

READING WARM-UP

Objectives
- Describe homeostasis and what happens when it is disrupted.
- Describe how tissues, organs, and organ systems are related.
- List 12 organ systems.
- Identify how organ systems work together to maintain homeostasis.

Terms to Learn
homeostasis
tissue
organ

READING STRATEGY

Reading Organizer As you read this section, make a concept map by using the terms above.

homeostasis the maintenance of a constant internal state in a changing environment

Staying in Balance

The environment around you is always changing. Your body has to adjust to these conditions. For example, generally, on a hot day, your body is able to react to maintain your body temperature and avoid overheating. As shown in **Figure 1**, all living organisms have to maintain homeostasis.

Maintaining homeostasis is not easy. Your body needs nutrients and oxygen. Your body needs wastes removed. And your body needs to defend itself against disease. A single cell cannot do all of these jobs for the entire body. Fortunately, your body has many kinds of cells. Some cells remove wastes. Other cells carry oxygen or defend your body against disease. Together, these cells help your internal environment stay stable.

Figure 1 *These penguins have adaptations that help them maintain homeostasis in the cold environment in which they live.*

148 Chapter 5 Body Organization and Structure

Be Resourceful—Use the Web

SCILINKS®

Internet Connect boxes in your textbook take you to resources that you can use for science projects, reports, and research papers. Go to scilinks.org, and type in the SciLinks code to get information on a topic.

go.hrw.com

Visit go.hrw.com Find worksheets, **Current Science®** magazine articles online, and other materials that go with your textbook at **go.hrw.com.** Click on the textbook icon and the table of contents to see all of the resources for each chapter.

Falling Out of Balance

Sometimes, your body cannot maintain homeostasis. For example, if you don't eat the right foods, your cells may not get the nutrients they need. Maybe your body systems can't fight off a disease caused by bacteria or viruses. So, homeostasis is disrupted. What happens when homeostasis is disrupted? Cells may be damaged or may die. When this happens, you can become sick, as shown in **Figure 2**. Sometimes, people die when homeostasis is disrupted.

Figure 2 When homeostasis is disrupted, a person can become sick.

Temperature Regulation

When you are hot, your body gives off heat. You also sweat. When sweat evaporates from your skin, your body is cooled. Sweating is a process that helps your body maintain homeostasis. Sometimes, the body cannot cool down. This happens when cells do not get what they need, such as water for sweat. If the body gets too hot, cells may be damaged.

The body also has ways to keep you warm on cold days. When you are cold, you shiver, which helps you stay warm. Sometimes, the body cannot stay warm. Body temperature falls below normal in a condition called *hypothermia*.

Moving Materials

Your cells need nutrients for life processes. If nutrients are not delivered, the cells cannot complete their life processes. So, the cells will die. These life processes often make wastes, which must be removed from cells. Many wastes are toxic. If a cell cannot get rid of them, the wastes will damage the cell.

Reading Check Explain the importance of moving materials into and out of cells. *(See the Appendix for answers to Reading Checks.)*

Nervous System Your nervous system receives and sends electrical messages throughout your body.

Digestive System Your digestive system breaks down the food you eat into nutrients that your body can absorb.

Lymphatic System The lymphatic system returns leaked fluids to blood vessels and helps defend against disease.

Endocrine System Your glands send out chemical messages, which control body functions.

SECTION Review

Summary

- Homeostasis is the maintenance of a stable internal environment.
- A group of cells that work together is a tissue. Tissues form organs. Organs that work together form organ systems.
- There are 12 major organ systems in the human body.
- Organ systems work together to help the body maintain homeostasis.

Using Key Terms

1. In your own words, write a definition for the term *homeostasis*.

Understanding Key Ideas

2. Which of the following statements describes how tissues, organs, and organ systems are related?
   a. Organs form tissues, which form organ systems.
   b. Organ systems form organs, which form tissues.
   c. Tissues form organs, which form organ systems.
   d. None of the above

3. List the 12 organ systems.

Math Skills

4. The human skeleton has 206 bones. The human skull has 22 bones. What percentage of human bones are skull bones?

Critical Thinking

5. **Applying Concepts** The circulatory system delivers nutrients to cells in the body. What might happen to homeostasis if this system were disrupted? Explain your answer.

6. **Predicting Consequences** Predict what might happen if the human body did not have specialized cells, tissues, organs, and organ systems to maintain homeostasis.

Developed and maintained by the National Science Teachers Association

For a variety of links related to this chapter, go to www.scilinks.org

Topic: Tissues and Organs; Body Systems
SciLinks code: HSM1530; HSM0184

153

Use the Illustrations and Photos

Art shows complex ideas and processes. Learn to analyze the art so that you better understand the material you read in the text.

Tables and graphs display important information in an organized way to help you see relationships.

A picture is worth a thousand words. Look at the photographs to see relevant examples of science concepts that you are reading about.

Answer the Section Reviews

Section Reviews test your knowledge of the main points of the section. Critical Thinking items challenge you to think about the material in greater depth and to find connections that you infer from the text.

STUDY TIP When you can't answer a question, reread the section. The answer is usually there.

Do Your Homework

Your teacher may assign worksheets to help you understand and remember the material in the chapter.

STUDY TIP Don't try to answer the questions without reading the text and reviewing your class notes. A little preparation up front will make your homework assignments a lot easier. Answering the items in the Chapter Review will help prepare you for the chapter test.

Holt Online Learning

Visit Holt Online Learning

If your teacher gives you a special password to log onto the Holt Online Learning site, you'll find your complete textbook on the Web. In addition, you'll find some great learning tools and practice quizzes. You'll be able to see how well you know the material from your textbook.

CNN Student News™

Visit CNN Student News

You'll find up-to-date events in science at cnnstudentnews.com.

SAFETY FIRST!

Exploring, inventing, and investigating are essential to the study of science. However, these activities can also be dangerous. To make sure that your experiments and explorations are safe, you must be aware of a variety of safety guidelines. You have probably heard of the saying, "It is better to be safe than sorry." This is particularly true in a science classroom where experiments and explorations are being performed. Being uninformed and careless can result in serious injuries. Don't take chances with your own safety or with anyone else's.

The following pages describe important guidelines for staying safe in the science classroom. Your teacher may also have safety guidelines and tips that are specific to your classroom and laboratory. Take the time to be safe.

Safety Rules!

Start Out Right

Always get your teacher's permission before attempting any laboratory exploration. Read the procedures carefully, and pay particular attention to safety information and caution statements. If you are unsure about what a safety symbol means, look it up or ask your teacher. You cannot be too careful when it comes to safety. If an accident does occur, inform your teacher immediately regardless of how minor you think the accident is.

If you are instructed to note the odor of a substance, wave the fumes toward your nose with your hand. Never put your nose close to the source.

Safety Symbols

All of the experiments and investigations in this book and their related worksheets include important safety symbols to alert you to particular safety concerns. Become familiar with these symbols so that when you see them, you will know what they mean and what to do. It is important that you read this entire safety section to learn about specific dangers in the laboratory.

Eye protection

Clothing protection

Hand safety

Heating safety

Electric safety

Chemical safety

Animal safety

Sharp object

Plant safety

Eye Safety

Wear safety goggles when working around chemicals, acids, bases, or any type of flame or heating device. Wear safety goggles any time there is even the slightest chance that harm could come to your eyes. If any substance gets into your eyes, notify your teacher immediately and flush your eyes with running water for at least 15 minutes. Treat any unknown chemical as if it were a dangerous chemical. Never look directly into the sun. Doing so could cause permanent blindness.

Avoid wearing contact lenses in a laboratory situation. Even if you are wearing safety goggles, chemicals can get between the contact lenses and your eyes. If your doctor requires that you wear contact lenses instead of glasses, wear eye-cup safety goggles in the lab.

Safety Equipment

Know the locations of the nearest fire alarms and any other safety equipment, such as fire blankets and eyewash fountains, as identified by your teacher, and know the procedures for using the equipment.

Neatness

Keep your work area free of all unnecessary books and papers. Tie back long hair, and secure loose sleeves or other loose articles of clothing, such as ties and bows. Remove dangling jewelry. Don't wear open-toed shoes or sandals in the laboratory. Never eat, drink, or apply cosmetics in a laboratory setting. Food, drink, and cosmetics can easily become contaminated with dangerous materials.

Certain hair products (such as aerosol hair spray) are flammable and should not be worn while working near an open flame. Avoid wearing hair spray or hair gel on lab days.

Sharp/Pointed Objects

Use knives and other sharp instruments with extreme care. Never cut objects while holding them in your hands. Place objects on a suitable work surface for cutting.

Be extra careful when using any glassware. When adding a heavy object to a graduated cylinder, tilt the cylinder so that the object slides slowly to the bottom.

Chemicals

Wear safety goggles when handling any potentially dangerous chemicals, acids, or bases. If a chemical is unknown, handle it as you would a dangerous chemical. Wear an apron and protective gloves when you work with acids or bases or whenever you are told to do so. If a spill gets on your skin or clothing, rinse it off immediately with water for at least 5 minutes while calling to your teacher.

Never mix chemicals unless your teacher tells you to do so. Never taste, touch, or smell chemicals unless you are specifically directed to do so. Before working with a flammable liquid or gas, check for the presence of any source of flame, spark, or heat.

Heat

Wear safety goggles when using a heating device or a flame. Whenever possible, use an electric hot plate as a heat source instead of using an open flame. When heating materials in a test tube, always angle the test tube away from yourself and others. To avoid burns, wear heat-resistant gloves whenever instructed to do so.

Electricity

Be careful with electrical cords. When using a microscope with a lamp, do not place the cord where it could trip someone. Do not let cords hang over a table edge in a way that could cause equipment to fall if the cord is accidentally pulled. Do not use equipment with damaged cords. Be sure that your hands are dry and that the electrical equipment is in the "off" position before plugging it in. Turn off and unplug electrical equipment when you are finished.

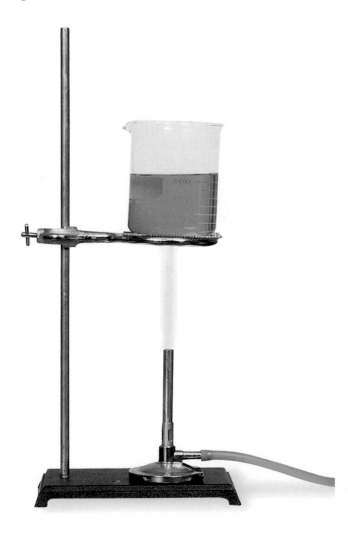

Animal Safety

Always obtain your teacher's permission before bringing any animal into the school building. Handle animals only as your teacher directs. Always treat animals carefully and respectfully. Wash your hands thoroughly after handling any animal.

Plant Safety

Do not eat any part of a plant or plant seed used in the laboratory. Wash your hands thoroughly after handling any part of a plant. When in nature, do not pick any wild plants unless your teacher instructs you to do so.

Glassware

Examine all glassware before use. Be sure that glassware is clean and free of chips and cracks. Report damaged glassware to your teacher. Glass containers used for heating should be made of heat-resistant glass.

Science in Our World
Chapter Planning Guide

Compression guide:
To shorten instruction because of time limitations, omit Section 1.

OBJECTIVES	LABS, DEMONSTRATIONS, AND ACTIVITIES	TECHNOLOGY RESOURCES
PACING • 90 min pp. 2–9 **Chapter Opener**	**SE** Start-up Activity, p. 3 ◆ GENERAL	**OSP** Parent Letter GENERAL **CD** Student Edition on CD-ROM **CD** Guided Reading Audio CD **TR** Chapter Starter Transparency* **VID** Brain Food Video Quiz
Section 1 Asking About Life • Describe three methods of investigation. • Identify benefits of science in the world around you. • Describe five jobs that use science.	**TE** Group Activity Scientists in Your Town, p. 4 ◆ GENERAL **TE** Group Activity Wildlife Safari, p. 7 ◆ GENERAL **TE** Demonstration Spreading Disease, p. 6 **TE** Connection Activity Environmental Science, p. 8 ◆ BASIC **LB** Long-Term Projects & Research Ideas The Length of a Fethel* ADVANCED	**CRF** Lesson Plans* **TR** Bellringer Transparency* **TE** Internet Activity p. 5 GENERAL
PACING • 90 min pp. 10–17 **Section 2 Scientific Methods** • Explain why scientists use scientific methods. • Determine the appropriate design of a controlled experiment. • Use information in tables and graphs to analyze experimental results. • Explain how scientific knowledge can change.	**TE** Activity Now You See It, p. 10 ◆ GENERAL **TE** Connection Activity Social Studies, p. 11 GENERAL **TE** Demonstration Frog Call, p. 12 ◆ GENERAL **TE** Activity Test a Hypothesis, p. 12 ADVANCED **TE** Activity Roots of Words, p. 13 BASIC **TE** Activity Writing Predictions, p. 13 GENERAL **TE** Connection Activity Math, p. 16 BASIC **SE** Skills Practice Lab Does It All Add Up?, p. 28 ◆ GENERAL **LB** Whiz-Bang Demonstrations Air Ball* ◆ GENERAL **LB** Whiz-Bang Demonstrations Getting to the Point* ◆ GENERAL	**CRF** Lesson Plans* **TR** Bellringer Transparency* **TR** Scientific Methods* **VID** Lab Videos for Life Science
PACING • 45 min pp. 18–21 **Section 3 Scientific Models** • Give examples of three types of models. • Identify the benefits and limitations of models. • Compare the ways that scientists use hypotheses, theories, and laws.	**TE** Group Activity Classifying, p. 19 ◆ GENERAL **SE** Model-Making Lab A Window to a Hidden World, p. 761 ◆ GENERAL **CRF** Datasheet for LabBook* **LB** Inquiry Lab One Side or Two?* ◆ GENERAL **SE** Science in Action Math, Social Studies, and Language Arts Activities, pp. 34–35 GENERAL	**CRF** Lesson Plans* **TR** Bellringer Transparency*
PACING • 45 min pp. 22–27 **Section 4 Tools, Measurement, and Safety** • Collect, record, and analyze information by using various tools. • Explain the importance of the International System of Units. • Calculate area and density. • Identify lab safety symbols, and demonstrate safe practices during lab investigations.	**TE** Demonstration Tools of the Trade, p. 22 ◆ GENERAL **SE** Quick Lab No Rules Allowed, p. 23 **TE** Connection Activity International System of Units, p. 23 ◆ GENERAL **TE** Group Activity X Rays, p. 23 GENERAL **SE** Math Focus Significant Figures, p. 24 GENERAL **TE** Demonstration Displacement, p. 25 ◆ BASIC **SE** Connection to Social Studies Archimedes, p. 26 ◆ GENERAL	**CRF** Lesson Plans* **TR** Bellringer Transparency* **TR** Compound Light Microscope* **TR** Common SI Units and Conversions* **TR** *LINK TO PHYSICAL SCIENCE* Three Temperature Scales* **CRF** SciLinks Activity* GENERAL **CD** Interactive Explorations CD-ROM Something's Fishy! GENERAL

PACING • 90 min

CHAPTER REVIEW, ASSESSMENT, AND STANDARDIZED TEST PREPARATION

CRF Vocabulary Activity* GENERAL
SE Chapter Review, pp. 30–31 GENERAL
CRF Chapter Review* ■ GENERAL
CRF Chapter Tests A* ■ GENERAL, B* ADVANCED, C* SPECIAL NEEDS
SE Standardized Test Preparation, pp. 32–33 GENERAL
CRF Standardized Test Preparation* GENERAL
CRF Performance-Based Assessment* GENERAL
OSP Test Generator GENERAL
CRF Test Item Listing* GENERAL

Online and Technology Resources

Visit **go.hrw.com** for a variety of free resources related to this textbook. Enter the keyword **HT5D7SW7**.

Holt Online Learning

Students can access interactive problem-solving help and active visual concept development with the *Holt Science and Technology* Online Edition available at **www.hrw.com**.

Guided Reading Audio CD

These CDs are designed to help auditory learners and reluctant readers.

Science Tutor CD-ROM

Excellent for remediation and test practice.

SKILLS DEVELOPMENT RESOURCES

SECTION REVIEW AND ASSESSMENT

STANDARDS CORRELATIONS

SE Pre-Reading Activity, p. 2 **GENERAL**
OSP Science Puzzlers, Twisters & Teasers **GENERAL**
SS Science Skills Reading a Science Textbook* **ADVANCED**

North Carolina
Standard Course of Study

CRF Directed Reading A* **BASIC**, **B*** **SPECIAL NEEDS**
CRF Vocabulary and Section Summary* **GENERAL**
SE Reading Strategy Reading Organizer, p. 4 **GENERAL**
TE Reading Strategy Reading Organizer, p. 5 **GENERAL**
SE Connection to Biology Technology and Aging, p. 7 **GENERAL**
TE Inclusion Strategies, p. 8

SE Reading Checks, pp. 4, 7, 9 **GENERAL**
TE Homework, p. 7 **ADVANCED**
TE Reteaching, p. 8 **BASIC**
TE Quiz, p. 8 **GENERAL**
TE Alternative Assessment, p. 8 **GENERAL**
SE Section Review,* p. 9 ■ **GENERAL**
CRF Section Quiz* ■ **GENERAL**

1.01

CRF Directed Reading A* **BASIC**, **B*** **SPECIAL NEEDS**
CRF Vocabulary and Section Summary* **GENERAL**
SE Reading Strategy Reading Organizer, p. 10 **GENERAL**
TE Reading Strategy Mnemonics, p. 11 **BASIC**
SE Connection to Environmental Science Minnesota's Deformed Frogs, p. 12 **GENERAL**
SE Connection to Language Arts "Leading Doctors Say…", p. 13 **GENERAL**
SE Math Practice Averages, p. 16 **GENERAL**
MS Math Skills for Science What Is an Average? **GENERAL**
CRF Reinforcement Worksheet The Mystery of the Bubbling Top* **BASIC**
CRF Critical Thinking The Case of the Bulge* **ADVANCED**

SE Reading Checks, pp. 10, 12, 14, 16 **GENERAL**
TE Homework, p. 13 **GENERAL**
TE Reteaching, p. 16 **BASIC**
TE Quiz, p. 16 **GENERAL**
TE Alternative Assessment, p. 16 **ADVANCED**
SE Section Review,* p. 17 ■ **GENERAL**
CRF Section Quiz* ■ **GENERAL**

1.01, 2.01, 2.02

CRF Directed Reading A* **BASIC**, **B*** **SPECIAL NEEDS**
CRF Vocabulary and Section Summary* **GENERAL**
SE Reading Strategy Reading Organizer, p. 18 **GENERAL**
SE Connection to Environmental Science Samples, p. 19 **GENERAL**
TE Reading Strategy Paired Reading, p. 19 **BASIC**
SE Connection to Chemistry Model Cocaine in the Brain, p. 21 **GENERAL**
SS Science Skills Study Habits **GENERAL**
MS Math Skills for Science Arithmetic with Decimals* **GENERAL**

SE Reading Checks, pp. 19, 20 **GENERAL**
TE Reteaching, p. 20 **BASIC**
TE Quiz, p. 20 **GENERAL**
TE Homework, p. 20 **ADVANCED**
TE Alternative Assessment, p. 20 **GENERAL**
SE Section Review,* p. 21 ■ **GENERAL**
CRF Section Quiz* ■ **GENERAL**

1.09, 1.10

CRF Directed Reading A* **BASIC**, **B*** **SPECIAL NEEDS**
CRF Vocabulary and Section Summary* **GENERAL**
SE Reading Strategy Reading Organizer, p. 22 **GENERAL**
TE Inclusion Strategies, p. 23 ◆
MS Math Skills for Science A Formula for SI Catch-up* **GENERAL**
MS Math Skills for Science What Is SI?* **GENERAL**
MS Math Skills for Science Finding Perimeter and Area* **GENERAL**
MS Math Skills for Science Finding Volume* **GENERAL**
SS Science Skills Safety Rules! **GENERAL**

SE Reading Checks, pp. 22, 25, 27 **GENERAL**
TE Reteaching, p. 26 **BASIC**
TE Quiz, p. 26 **GENERAL**
TE Alternative Assessment, p. 26 **BASIC**
TE Homework, p. 24 **BASIC**
SE Section Review,* p. 27 ■ **GENERAL**
CRF Section Quiz* ■ **GENERAL**

One-Stop Planner® CD-ROM

This convenient CD-ROM includes:
• Lab Materials QuickList Software
• Holt Calendar Planner
• Customizable Lesson Plans
• Printable Worksheets
• ExamView® Test Generator

cnnstudentnews.com

Find the latest news, lesson plans, and activities related to important scientific events.

www.scilinks.org

Maintained by the **National Science Teachers Association.** See Chapter Enrichment pages for a complete list of topics.

Current Science®

Check out **Current Science** articles and activities by visiting the HRW Web site at **go.hrw.com.** Just type in the keyword **HL5CS01T.**

Classroom Videos

• **Lab Videos** demonstrate the chapter lab.
• **Brain Food Video Quizzes** help students review the chapter material.
• **CNN Videos** bring science into your students' daily life.

Visual Resources

CHAPTER STARTER TRANSPARENCY

Imagine . . .

You are walking through a field with some classmates. Suddenly you notice that there are frogs hopping around all over the place! You and your classmates start catching the frogs with a net. As you lift the first frog from the net, you notice something. Its legs seem to be broken. You look at your friend's frog. It seems to be injured, too. You look at another. A frog with no eyes? Wait a minute! These frogs aren't injured. They're deformed! What are these, aliens from outer space?

Believe it or not, this really happened to a group of students from Le Sueur, Minnesota, during a visit to a wildlife refuge. About half of the frogs they collected were deformed. The students and their teacher were stunned by what they found. What could have caused these deformities? Was it just some weird natural phenomenon, or were the frogs exposed to some sort of chemical? The students gathered more information on the frogs and alerted local scientists. Students and scientists from all over the country are now working together to solve the mystery of the freaky frogs.

The students, like almost all scientists, began their research by noticing something about the natural world and then asking questions about what they observed. In this chapter, you will learn how questions fuel the study of science and how scientists go about finding answers to those questions.

BELLRINGER TRANSPARENCIES

Section: Asking About Life
Have you ever wondered how homing pigeons find their way home? Do you know why the dinosaurs went extinct? Write five questions about the natural world that you hope to have answered in this class.

Record your questions in your **science journal.**

Section: Scientific Methods
Which do you think is more important: imagination or knowledge? Can one exist without the other?

Reflect on this in your **science journal.** You may want to think of some famous scientists to write about in your answer. Then share your answer with the class and have a debate.

TEACHING TRANSPARENCIES

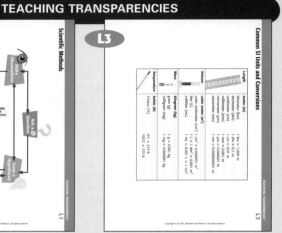

L1 — Scientific Methods

L3 — Common SI Units and Conversions

TEACHING TRANSPARENCIES

P39 — Three Temperature Scales

LINK TO PHYSICAL SCIENCE

Chapter: Heat and Heat Technology

CONCEPT MAPPING TRANSPARENCY

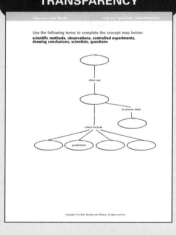

Use the following terms to complete the concept map below: scientific methods, observations, controlled experiments, drawing conclusions, scientists, questions

Planning Resources

LESSON PLANS

Lesson Plan SAMPLE

Section: Waves

Pacing
Regular Schedule: with lab(s):2 days   without lab(s)2 days
Block Schedule: with lab(s): 1 1/2 days   without lab(s)1 day

Objectives
1. Relate the seven properties of life to a living organism.
2. Describe seven themes that can help you to organize what you learn about biology.
3. Identify the tiny structures that make up all living organisms.
4. Differentiate between reproduction and heredity and between metabolism and homeostasis.

National Science Education Standards Covered
LSInter6:Cells have particular structures that underlie their functions.
LSMat1:Most cell functions involve chemical reactions.
LSBeh1:Cells store and use information to guide their functions.
UCP1:Cell functions are regulated.
SI1: Cells can differentiate and form complete multicellular organisms.
PS1: Species evolve over time.
ESS1: The great diversity of organisms is the result of more than 3.5 billion years of evolution.
ESS2: Natural selection and its evolutionary consequences provide a scientific explanation for the fossil record of ancient life forms as well as for the striking molecular similarities observed among the diverse species of living organisms.
ST1: The millions of different species of plants, animals, and microorganisms that live on Earth today are related by descent from common ancestors.
ST2: The energy for life primarily comes from the sun.
SPSP1: The complexity and organization of organisms accommodates the need for obtaining, transforming, transporting, releasing, and eliminating the matter and energy used to sustain the organism.
SPSP6: As matter and energy flows through different levels of organization of living systems—cells, organs, communities—and between living systems and the physical environment, chemical elements are recombined in different ways.
HNS1: Organisms have behavioral responses to internal changes and to external stimuli.

PARENT LETTER

SAMPLE

Dear Parent,

Your son's or daughter's science class will soon begin exploring the chapter entitled "The World of Physical Science." In this chapter, students will learn about how the scientific method applies to the world of physical science and the role of physical science in the world. By the end of the chapter, students should demonstrate a clear understanding of the chapter's main ideas and be able to discuss the following topics:

1. physical science as the study of energy and matter (Section 1)
2. the role of physical science in the world around them (Section 1)
3. careers that rely on physical science (Section 1)
4. the steps used in the scientific method (Section 2)
5. examples of technology (Section 2)
6. how the scientific method is used to answer questions and solve problems (Section 2)
7. how our knowledge of science changes over time (Section 2)
8. how models represent real objects or systems (Section 3)
9. examples of different ways models are used in science (Section 3)
10. the importance of the International System of Units (Section 4)
11. the appropriate units to use for particular measurements (Section 4)
12. how area and density are derived quantities (Section 4)

Questions to Ask Along the Way

You can help your son or daughter learn about these topics by asking interesting questions such as the following:

• What are some surprising careers that use physical science?
• What is a characteristic of a good hypothesis?
• When is it a good idea to use a model?
• Why do Americans measure things in terms of inches and yards instead of centimeters and meters ?

TEST ITEM LISTING

TEST ITEM LISTING
The World of Science SAMPLE

MULTIPLE CHOICE

1. A limitation of models is that
   a. they are large enough to see.
   b. they do not act exactly like the things that they model.
   c. they are smaller than the things that they model.
   d. they model unfamiliar things.
   Answer: B   Difficulty: 1   Section: 1   Objective: 2

2. The length 10 m is equal to
   a. 100 cm.   c. 10,000 mm.
   b. 1,000 cm.   d. Both (b) and (c)
   Answer: A   Difficulty: 1   Section: 3   Objective: 2

3. To be valid, a hypothesis must be
   a. testable.   c. made into a law.
   b. supported by evidence.   d. Both (a) and (b)
   Answer: B   Difficulty: 1   Section: 3   Objective: 2

4. The statement "Sheila has a stain on her shirt" is an example of a(n)
   a. law.   c. observation.
   b. hypothesis.   d. prediction.
   Answer: B   Difficulty: 1   Section: 3

5. A hypothesis is often developed out of
   a. observations.   c. laws.
   b. experiments.   d. Both (a) and (b)
   Answer: B   Difficulty: 1   Section: 3   Objective: 2

6. How many milliliters are in 3.5 kL?
   a. 3,500 mL   c. 3,500, 000 mL
   b. 0.0035 mL.   d. 35,000 mL.
   Answer: B   Difficulty: 1   Section: 3   Objective: 2

7. A map of Seattle is an example of a
   a. law.   c. model.
   b. theory.   d. unit.
   Answer: B   Difficulty: 1   Section: 3   Objective: 2

8. A lab has the safety icons shown below. These icons mean that you should wear
   a. only safety goggles.   c. safety goggles and a lab apron.
   b. only a lab apron.   d. safety goggles, a lab apron, and gloves.
   Answer: B   Difficulty: 1   Section: 3   Objective: 2

9. The law of conservation of mass says the m of mass before a chemical change is
   a. more than the total mass after the change.
   b. less than the total mass after the change.
   c. the same as the total mass after the change.
   d. not the same as the total mass after the change.
   Answer: B   Difficulty: 1   Section: 3   Objective: 2

10. In which of the following areas might you find a geochemist at work?
    a. studying the chemistry of rocks   c. studying forestry
    b. studying forestry   d. studying the atmosphere
    Answer: B   Difficulty: 1   Section: 3   Objective: 2

One-Stop Planner® CD-ROM

This CD-ROM includes all of the resources shown here and the following time-saving tools:

• *Lab Materials QuickList Software*

• *Customizable lesson plans*

• *Holt Calendar Planner*

• *The powerful ExamView® Test Generator*

Meeting Individual Needs

DIRECTED READING A
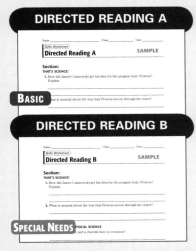

Skills Worksheet
Directed Reading A SAMPLE

Section:
THAT'S SCIENCE!
1. How did James Czarnowski get his idea for the penguin boat, Proteus? Explain.

What is unusual about the way that Proteus moves through the water?

BASIC

DIRECTED READING B

Name ___ Class ___ Date ___
Skills Worksheet
Directed Reading B SAMPLE

Section:
THAT'S SCIENCE!
1. How did James Czarnowski get his idea for the penguin boat, Proteus? Explain.

2. What is unusual about the way that Proteus moves through the water?

SPECIAL NEEDS PHYSICAL SCIENCE
and a cheetah have in common?

VOCABULARY ACTIVITY
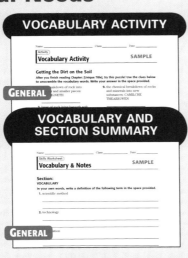

Activity
Vocabulary Activity SAMPLE

Getting the Dirt on the Soil
After you finish reading Chapter: [Unique Title], try this puzzle! Use the clues below to unscramble the vocabulary words. Write your answer in the space provided.

GENERAL

VOCABULARY AND SECTION SUMMARY

Skills Worksheet
Vocabulary & Notes SAMPLE

Section:
VOCABULARY
In your own words, write a definition of the following term in the space provided.
1. scientific method

2. technology

GENERAL

REINFORCEMENT
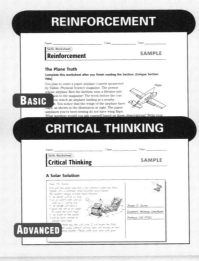

Skills Worksheet
Reinforcement SAMPLE

The Plane Truth
Complete this worksheet after you finish reading the Section: [Unique Section Title]

BASIC

CRITICAL THINKING

Skills Worksheet
Critical Thinking SAMPLE

A Solar Solution

ADVANCED

SCILINKS ACTIVITY

Activity
SciLinks Activity SAMPLE

MARINE ECOSYSTEMS
Go to www.scilinks.com. To find links related to marine ecosystems, type in the keyword HL5490. Then, use the links to answer the questions about marine ecosystems.

GENERAL

SCIENCE PUZZLERS, TWISTERS & TEASERS

CHAPTER
1 SCIENCE PUZZLERS, TWISTERS & TEASERS
The World of Life Science

Listening In
1. Figure out what step in the scientific method the scientists are practicing. Write the name of the step in the blank.
 a. "Wow! I can't believe how green the grass is over there. Why isn't it brown like on our side of the mountain?"

 b. "All right, Nan, flip that switch and cross your fingers."

GENERAL

Labs and Activities

LONG-TERM PROJECTS & RESEARCH IDEAS

PROJECT
1 STUDENT WORKSHEET DESIGN YOUR OWN
The Length of a Fethel

Measure for Measure
1. Sharing scientific discoveries in the ancient world would probably have been a lot harder than it is now.

Long-Term Project Ideas
2. What if your system of measurement was based on the volume of a goldfish, the mass of a kernel of corn, and the length of a videocassette?

ADVANCED

WHIZ-BANG DEMONSTRATIONS
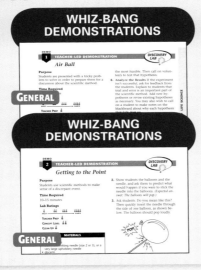

DEMO
1 TEACHER-LED DEMONSTRATION DISCOVERY LAB
Air Ball

Purpose
Students are presented with a tricky problem to solve in order to prepare them for a discussion about the scientific method.

Time Required

GENERAL

WHIZ-BANG DEMONSTRATIONS

DEMO
2 TEACHER-LED DEMONSTRATION DISCOVERY LAB
Getting to the Point

Purpose
Students use scientific methods to make sense of a discrepant event.

Time Required
10–15 minutes

GENERAL MATERIALS

INQUIRY LABS

LAB
1 STUDENT WORKSHEET DISCOVERY LAB
One Side or Two?

How many sides does a piece of paper have? The answer seems obvious enough: two, a front side and a back side.

METHOD Ask a Question
How many sides does a piece of paper have?

The Line Stops Here
1. Cut a 75-cm strip of adding-machine tape. Bring the two ends of the strip together, but give one end half a twist.
2. Tape the two ends together to form a Möbius strip, as shown.

Make a Prediction
3. How many sides do you think the strip has?

Conduct an Experiment
4. At a dot near the middle of the strip. Starting from the dot, draw a line down the length of the strip until you reach a boundary.

Analyze the Results
5. Where did the line end? How much of the Möbius strip has a line drawn on it?

Draw Conclusions
6. How many sides does a Möbius strip have? How do you know?

GENERAL

DATASHEETS FOR QUICK LABS

TEACHER RESOURCE PAGE
Quick Lab DATASHEET FOR QUICK LAB
Reaction to Stress SAMPLE

Background
The graph below illustrates changes that occur in the membrane potential of a neuron during an action potential. Use the graph to answer the following questions. Refer to Figure 3 as needed.

DATASHEETS FOR CHAPTER LABS

TEACHER RESOURCE PAGE
Skills Practice Lab DATASHEET FOR CHAPTER LAB
Using Scientific Methods SAMPLE

Teacher's Notes
TIME REQUIRED
One 45-minute class period.

DATASHEETS FOR LABBOOK

TEACHER RESOURCE PAGE
Skills Practice Lab DATASHEET FOR LABBOOK LAB
Does It All Add Up? SAMPLE

Teacher's Notes
TIME REQUIRED
One 45-minute class period.

Review and Assessments

SECTION QUIZ
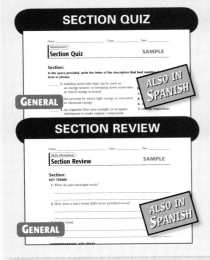

Assessment
Section Quiz SAMPLE

Section:
In the space provided, write the letter of the description that best matches the term or phrase.
1. building molecules that can be used as an energy source or breaking down molecules in which energy is stored
2. the process by which light energy is converted to chemical energy
3. an organism that uses sunlight or inorganic substances to make organic compounds

a.
b.
c.
d.
e.
f. cellular respiration

GENERAL

SECTION REVIEW

Skills Worksheet
Section Review SAMPLE

Section:
KEY TERMS
1. What do paleontologists study?

2. How does a trace fossil differ from petrified wood?

fossil.

GENERAL ALSO IN SPANISH
UNDERSTANDING KEY IDEAS

CHAPTER REVIEW
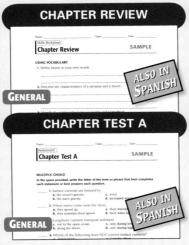

Skills Worksheet
Chapter Review SAMPLE

USING VOCABULARY
1. Define biome in your own words.

2. Describe the characteristics of a savanna and a desert.

GENERAL ALSO IN SPANISH

CHAPTER TEST A

Name ___ Class ___ Date ___
Assessment
Chapter Test A SAMPLE

MULTIPLE CHOICE
In the space provided, write the letter of the term or phrase that best completes each statement or best answers each question.
1. Surface currents are formed by
 a. the moon's gravity.   c. wind.
 b. the sun's gravity.   d. increased water density.
When waves come near the shore,
 a. they speed up.   c. their wavelength increases.
 b. they maintain their speed.   d. their wave height increases.
Longshore currents transport sediment
 a. out to the open ocean.   c. only during low tide.
 b. along the shore.   d. only during high tide.
4. Which of the following does NOT control surface currents?

GENERAL ALSO IN SPANISH

CHAPTER TEST B
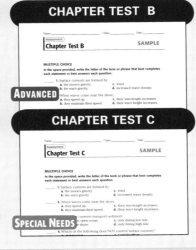

Assessment
Chapter Test B SAMPLE

MULTIPLE CHOICE
In the space provided, write the letter of the term or phrase that best completes each statement or best answers each question.
1. Surface currents are formed by
 a. the moon's gravity.   c. wind.
 b. the sun's gravity.   d. increased water density.
When waves come near the shore,
 a. they speed up.   c. their wavelength increases.
 b. they maintain their speed.   d. their wave height increases.

ADVANCED

CHAPTER TEST C

Assessment
Chapter Test C SAMPLE

MULTIPLE CHOICE
In the space provided, write the letter of the term or phrase that best completes each statement or best answers each question.
1. Surface currents are formed by
 a. the moon's gravity.   c. wind.
 b. the sun's gravity.   d. increased water density.
When waves come near the shore,
 a. they speed up.   c. their wavelength increases.
 b. they maintain their speed.   d. their wave height increases.
Longshore currents transport sediment
 a. out to the open ocean.   c. only during low tide.
 b. along the shore.   d. only during high tide.
4. Which of the following does NOT control surface currents?

SPECIAL NEEDS

STANDARDIZED TEST PREPARATION
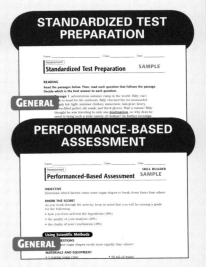

Assessment
Standardized Test Preparation SAMPLE

READING
Read the passages below. Then, read each question that follows the passage. Decide which is the best answer to each question.

Passage 1 adventurous nature camp in the world. Billy can't wait to head for the outdoors.

GENERAL

PERFORMANCE-BASED ASSESSMENT

Name ___ Class ___ Date ___ SKILL BUILDER
Assessment
Performanced-Based Assessment SAMPLE

OBJECTIVE
Determine which factors cause some sugar shapes to break down faster than others.

KNOW THE SCORE!
As you work through the activity, keep in mind that you will be earning a grade for the following:
• how you form and test the hypothesis (30%)
• the quality of your analysis (30%)
• the clarity of your conclusions (30%)

Using Scientific Methods
QUESTIONS
sugar shapes erode more rapidly than others?
MATERIALS AND EQUIPMENT
1 regular sugar cube   • 90 mL of water

GENERAL

This Chapter Enrichment provides relevant and interesting information to expand and enhance your presentation of the chapter material.

Section 1

Science and Scientists

Deformed Frogs

- The discovery of deformed frogs by Minnesota middle school students in 1995 sparked much attention around the country. Since that summer, reports of amphibian deformations have poured into agencies from many parts of the continent.

- The reported deformities include extra limbs, malformed or missing limbs, and facial malformations. Deformities have been documented in 44 states and involve nearly 60 species. In some local populations, up to 60% of the amphibians exhibit deformities.

Dr. Pepperberg's Studies on Parrots

- Parrots, or psittacids, are rarely mentioned during discussions of animal intelligence, but recent studies indicate that they are intelligent animals. Dr. Irene Pepperberg, while an associate professor at the University of Arizona's Department of Ecology and  Evolutionary Biology, demonstrated that African gray parrots can process information and make decisions.

- Pepperberg has studied Alex, an African gray parrot, for more than 20 years. Pepperberg says that she has used a variety of techniques to establish a form of interspecies communication with Alex. "The existence of such behavior," she says, "demonstrates that at least one avian species is capable of interactive, referential communication."

- Alex can count and identify more than 35 objects, including paper, a key, wood, and grain; can recognize seven colors; can identify five shapes; and can combine names to identify, request, refuse, and categorize more than 100 objects. Alex even learned to boss around lab assistants to modify his environment.

Is That a Fact!

- In this century, the Siberian, or Amur, tiger has survived wars, revolutions, and deforestation in eastern Asia. Its numbers in the wild were below 100 in the 1940s, but conservation efforts have brought numbers to around 400. There are now more than 4,500 km² of protected areas for these tigers in Russia. About 500 additional Siberian tigers live in captivity.

Section 2

Scientific Methods

Vanishing Amphibians

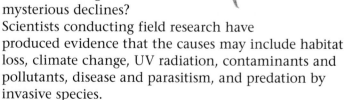

- Scientists are perplexed by steady declines in the world's amphibian populations since the mid-1980s. What is causing these mysterious declines? Scientists conducting field research have produced evidence that the causes may include habitat loss, climate change, UV radiation, contaminants and pollutants, disease and parasitism, and predation by invasive species.

- Alarmingly, declines are not simply occurring in places where human impacts are obvious; some of the most dramatic declines are happening in wilderness areas and parks. In the United States, declines are particularly serious in California, the Rocky Mountains, the Southwest, and Puerto Rico. Worldwide, areas of concern include Australia and Central America.

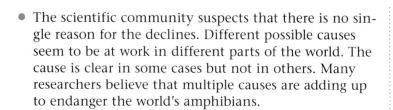
- The scientific community suspects that there is no single reason for the declines. Different possible causes seem to be at work in different parts of the world. The cause is clear in some cases but not in others. Many researchers believe that multiple causes are adding up to endanger the world's amphibians.

Is That a Fact!

◆ The continental United States is home to at least 230 amphibian species.

Section 3

Scientific Models

Modeling Dinosaurs

- In 1995, the unearthing of a rare fossil *Parasaurolophus* skull prompted a unique form of computer-based modeling. Scientists hypothesized that the cavity-filled crest atop the skull might have been used to produce a low-frequency sound that could vary in pitch. In 1997, scientists in New Mexico used computed tomography scans and powerful computers to simulate the sounds that the crest could have produced. The same techniques may be used in other engineering applications, such as predicting the strength of structural materials.

A Model Birthday

- In 1953, scientists James Watson and Francis Crick assembled the first accurate model of a DNA molecule. Their discovery of DNA's structure was celebrated as one of the key scientific achievements of the 20th century. Fifty years later, the anniversary of this event was marked by a variety of commemorative events. Art historian Martin Kemp dubbed the double helix "the Mona Lisa of modern science."

Section 4

Tools, Measurement, and Safety

Masses of Precious Gems

- The carat is a unit of mass used only for expressing the mass of precious gems. The masses of diamonds, rubies, emeralds, sapphires, aquamarines, zircons, spinels, opals, and pearls are expressed carats. The carat is equal to 4 grains. The grain is also a unit of mass, but its definition differs from country to country. For example, an English grain is approximately 64.8 g, but a French grain is approximately 53.1 g. Because this difference could cause confusion and disputes among jewelers and their customers, the metric carat was defined in 1907 as exactly 0.200 g.

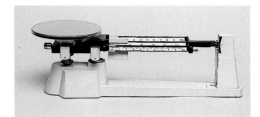

Is That a Fact!

◆ Very few countries have not officially adopted the International System of Units (SI). Among these countries are the United States, Bangladesh, and Liberia. Other countries either use the SI or are in the process of making the transition.

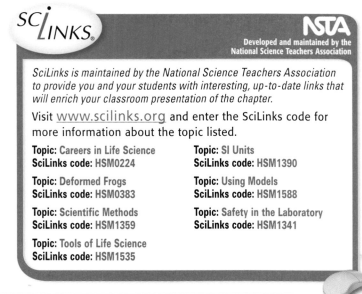

SCiLINKS®

NSTA
Developed and maintained by the National Science Teachers Association

SciLinks is maintained by the National Science Teachers Association to provide you and your students with interesting, up-to-date links that will enrich your classroom presentation of the chapter.

Visit www.scilinks.org and enter the SciLinks code for more information about the topic listed.

Topic: Careers in Life Science
SciLinks code: HSM0224

Topic: Deformed Frogs
SciLinks code: HSM0383

Topic: Scientific Methods
SciLinks code: HSM1359

Topic: Tools of Life Science
SciLinks code: HSM1535

Topic: SI Units
SciLinks code: HSM1390

Topic: Using Models
SciLinks code: HSM1588

Topic: Safety in the Laboratory
SciLinks code: HSM1341

Overview

Tell students that this chapter will introduce them to the world of science around them—the world of plants and animals, volcanoes and earthquakes, television and cell phones. Students will see that science is about asking questions and using scientific methods to find answers and build knowledge. Science is also about using models and tools to investigate questions and share answers.

Assessing Prior Knowledge

Students should be familiar with the following topics:

- measurement
- basic arithmetic

Identifying Misconceptions

Students may have limited ideas about what "science" is. Even after significant amounts of direct instruction, students often maintain misconceptions, such as the idea that science is just facts to be memorized. Also, students may have prior conceptions that science is boring or hard or that it involves conducting elaborate experiments in a lab. As you begin this chapter, query students about their conceptions of science. Help students recognize that science is a body of knowledge that may change over time.

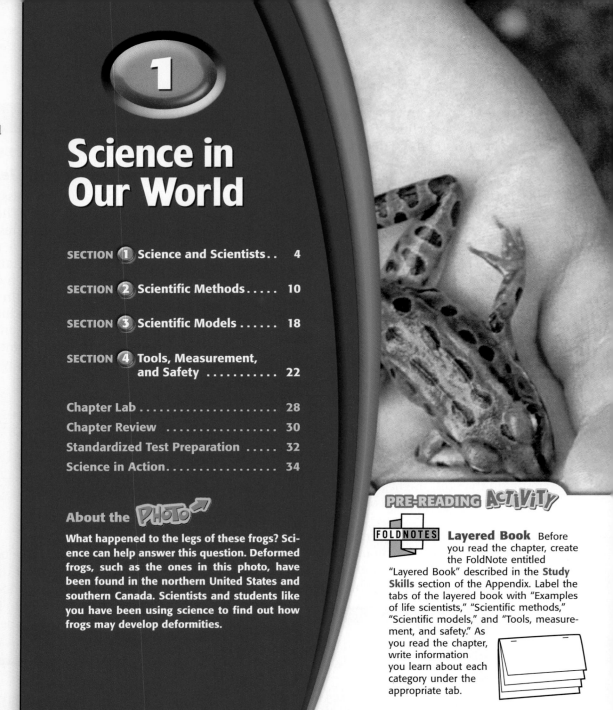

Science in Our World

About the PHOTO

What happened to the legs of these frogs? Science can help answer this question. Deformed frogs, such as the ones in this photo, have been found in the northern United States and southern Canada. Scientists and students like you have been using science to find out how frogs may develop deformities.

PRE-READING ACTIVITY

FOLDNOTES **Layered Book** Before you read the chapter, create the FoldNote entitled "Layered Book" described in the **Study Skills** section of the Appendix. Label the tabs of the layered book with "Examples of life scientists," "Scientific methods," "Scientific models," and "Tools, measurement, and safety." As you read the chapter, write information you learn about each category under the appropriate tab.

Standards Correlations

North Carolina Standard Course of Study

1.01 Identify and create questions and hypotheses that can be answered through scientific investigations. (Chapter Opener, Section 1, Chapter Lab)

1.03 Apply safety procedures in the laboratory and in field studies, recognize potential hazards, safely manipulate materials and equipment, [and] conduct appropriate procedures. (Chapter Lab)

1.09 Use technologies and information systems to: Research, gather and analyze data, visualize data, [and] disseminate findings to others. (Section 3)

1.10 Analyze and evaluate information from a scientifically literate viewpoint by reading, hearing, and/or viewing: Scientific text, articles, [and] events in the popular press. (Section 3)

2.01 Explore evidence that "technology" has many definitions: artifact or hardware, methodology or technique, system of production, [and] social-technical system. (Section 1)

2.02 Use information systems to: Identify scientific needs, human needs, or problems that are subject to technological solution, [and] locate resources to obtain and test ideas. (Section 1)

- can, coffee, 1/2–1 lb size, empty
- objects, various, small (such as rocks, nuts, washers, pencils, silverware, small toys, dried fruit, crumpled paper, or paper clips)
- sock, sport, long

Safety Caution: Cover any sharp edges around the rim of the coffee cans with tape. Be sure that the objects placed in the cans are safe to handle. Students should wear safety gloves.

Teacher's Notes: You must prepare this activity ahead of time. Fill the cans with four or five small objects. Try to choose some common and some uncommon objects that would require more than one of the senses to identify. To assemble each setup, cut the toe out of a sport sock, stretch the open toe around the open end of the coffee can, and use duct tape to secure the sock to the can.

Answers
1. Students may guess wrong based on assumptions made from the first thing they notice (such as the sound or shape of the object).
2. Students are likely to make observations using hearing, touch (including sensing weight), and perhaps smell but not sight or taste.

START-UP ACTIVITY
A Little Bit of Science
In this activity, you'll find out that you can learn about the unknown without having to see it.

Procedure
1. Your teacher will give you a **coffee can** to which a **sock** has been attached. Do not look into the can.
2. Reach through the opening in the sock. You will feel **several objects** inside the can.
3. Record observations you make about the objects by feeling them, shaking the can, and so on.
4. What do you think is in the can? List your guesses. State some reasons for your guesses.
5. Pour the contents of the can onto your desk. Compare your list with what was in the can.

Analysis
1. Did you guess the contents of the can correctly? What might have caused you to guess wrongly?
2. What observations did you make about each of the objects while they were in the can? Which of your senses did you use?

Chapter Starter Transparency
Use this transparency to help students begin thinking about the world of life science and using scientific methods.

CHAPTER RESOURCES
Technology

 **Transparencies**
- Chapter Starter Transparency

 Student Edition on CD-ROM

 Guided Reading Audio CD

Classroom Videos
- Brain Food Video Quiz

Workbooks

 Science Puzzlers, Twisters & Teasers
- The World of Life Science **GENERAL**

Focus

Overview

This section defines science and explains that science often starts with a question. Students learn that scientists use several types of investigations to find answers to their questions. Students also learn about some ways that science affects their lives and about some jobs that use science.

 Bellringer

Have students write five questions about the natural world. (Sample answers: How do homing pigeons find their way home? Why do volcanoes erupt? Why doesn't dry ice melt?)

Ask several students to share their questions with the class.

Motivate

Group ACTIVITY — GENERAL

Scientists in Your Town
Organize the class into groups. Have the groups brainstorm about what types of people in the community use science in their jobs. Have each group choose a scientist to interview by phone or e-mail. Encourage students to consider a variety of professions. Invite a person who uses science to visit the class. **LS Verbal**

READING WARM-UP

Objectives
- Describe three methods of investigation.
- Identify benefits of science in the world around you.
- Describe five jobs that use science.

Terms to Learn
science

READING STRATEGY

Prediction Guide Before reading this section, write the title of each heading in this section. Next, under each heading, write what you think you will learn.

science the knowledge obtained by observing natural events and conditions in order to discover facts and formulate laws or principles that can be verified or tested

Science and Scientists

You are enjoying a picnic on a summer day. Crumbs from your sandwich fall to the ground, and ants carry the crumbs away. You wonder, Why do ants show up at picnics?

Congratulations! You just took one of the first steps of being a scientist. How did you do it? You observed the world around you. Then, you asked a question about your observations. And asking a question is part of what science is all about.

Start with a Question

The world around you is full of amazing things. Single-celled algae float unseen in ponds. Volcanoes erupt with explosive force. Mars may have had water in the past. And 40-ton whales glide through the oceans. These things or others, such as those shown in **Figure 1,** may lead you to ask a question. A question is the beginning of science. **Science** is the knowledge obtained by observing the natural world in order to discover facts and to formulate laws and principles that can be verified or tested.

✓ Reading Check What is science? (*See the Appendix for answers to Reading Checks.*)

In Your Own Neighborhood

Take a look around your home, school, and neighborhood. Often, you take things that you use or see every day for granted. But one day you might look at something in a new way. That's when a question hits you! The student in **Figure 1** didn't have to look very far to realize that he had some questions to ask.

The World and Beyond

You don't have to stop at questions about things in your neighborhood. Ask questions about atoms or galaxies, pandas and bamboo, or earthquakes. A variety of plants and animals live in a variety of places. And each place has a unique combination of rocks, soil, and water.

You can even ask questions about places other than those on Earth. Look outward to the moon, the sun, and the planets in our solar system. Beyond that, you have the rest of the universe! There are enough questions to keep scientists busy for a long time.

Figure 1 *Part of science is asking questions about the world around you.*

CHAPTER RESOURCES

Chapter Resource File
- Lesson Plan
- Directed Reading A **BASIC**
- Directed Reading B **SPECIAL NEEDS**

Technology
- Transparencies
  - Bellringer

Workbooks
- Science Skills
  - Reading a Science Textbook **GENERAL**

Answer to Reading Check

Science is the knowledge obtained by observing natural events and conditions in order to discover facts and formulate laws or principles that can be verified or tested.

Investigation: The Search for Answers

After you ask a question, it's time to look for an answer. But how do you start your investigation? Several methods may be used.

Research

You can find answers to some of your questions by doing research, as **Figure 2** shows. You can ask someone who knows a lot about the subject of your question. You can find information in textbooks, encyclopedias, and magazines. You can search on the Internet. You might read a report of an experiment that someone did. But be sure to think about the sources of your information. Use information only from reliable sources.

Observation

You can also find answers to questions by making careful observations. For example, if you want to know how spiders spin their webs, look for a web. When you find one, return to observe the spider as it spins. But be careful in making observations. Sometimes, what people expect to observe affects what they do observe. For example, most plants need light to grow. Does that mean that all plants need bright sunlight? Do some plants prefer shade? Some people might "observe" that bright light is the only answer. To test an observation, you may have to do an experiment.

Experimentation

You might answer the question about light and shade by doing a simple experiment, such as the one shown in **Figure 3.** Your research and your observations can help you plan your experiment. What should you do if your experiment needs something that is hard to get? For example, what do you do if you want to know whether a certain plant grows in space? Don't give up! Try to find results from someone else's experiment!

Figure 2 A library is a good place to begin your search for answers.

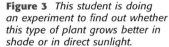
Ask a Question

The next time you're outside, look carefully around you. Think of a science-related question that you would like to answer. Write the question in your **science journal.** Discuss with a parent which methods of investigation would be most likely to help you answer your question.

Figure 3 This student is doing an experiment to find out whether this type of plant grows better in shade or in direct sunlight.

Essay — GENERAL

For an internet activity related to this chapter, have students go to **go.hrw.com** and type in the keyword **HL5LIVW.**

SCIENCE HUMOR

Q: What's the difference between a friendly dog and a marine biologist?

A: One's a tail wagger; the other's a whale tagger!

Spreading Disease Before class, make a phenolphthalein solution (dissolve 2 g in 100 mL of 95% ethanol, then add 100 mL of water) and a sodium hydroxide solution (dissolve 20 g in 1 L of water). Prepare a test tube and a plastic eyedropper for each student. Fill one of the test tubes halfway with sodium hydroxide solution and all the rest halfway with water. Have students wear safety goggles, a lab apron, and protective gloves for this activity. Tell students that one classmate is "infected." Have students exchange 10 drops of the liquid in their test tube with four different partners. Place one drop of phenolphthalein in each test tube. Anyone whose liquid turns pink is now "infected."

Disposal Information: Add 0.1 M HCl until the pH is between 5 and 9; pour down the drain. **LS** Intrapersonal

Using the Figure — GENERAL

Recycling Have students measure the mass of an empty aluminum soft-drink can. (The mass of one can should be close to 14.7 g.) Have students estimate the number of cans the class uses in 30 days. Finally, have students calculate the amount of each resource shown in **Figure 5** that would be saved by recycling these cans. (Sample answer: If each of 25 students uses 60 cans in 30 days, the resources saved are 0.0864 metric tons of chemical products, 302.4 kWh of energy, and 0.0864 metric tons of ore.) **LS** Logical

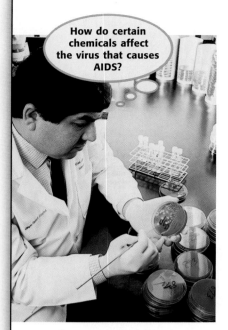

How do certain chemicals affect the virus that causes AIDS?

Figure 4 *Abdul Lakhani studies AIDS to find a cure for the disease.*

Why Ask Questions?

Although scientists cannot answer every question immediately, they do find some interesting answers. Do any of the answers really matter? Absolutely! As you study science, you will see how science affects you and society around you.

Fighting Diseases

Polio is a disease that can cause paralysis by affecting the brain and nerves. Do you know anyone who has had polio? You probably don't. But in 1952, polio infected 58,000 Americans. Fortunately, vaccines developed in 1955 and 1956 have eliminated polio in the United States. In fact, the virus that causes polio has been wiped out in most of the world.

Today, scientists are searching for cures for diseases such as mad cow disease, tuberculosis, and acquired immune deficiency syndrome (AIDS). The scientist in **Figure 4** is learning more about AIDS, which kills millions of people every year.

Saving Resources

Science also helps answer the question, How can we make resources last longer? Recycling is one answer. Think about the last time that you recycled an aluminum can. By recycling that can, you saved more than just the aluminum, as **Figure 5** shows. Using science, people have developed more-efficient methods and better equipment for recycling aluminum, paper, steel, glass, and even some plastics. In this way, science helps make resources last longer.

Figure 5 **Resources Saved Through Recycling**

  Compared with producing aluminum from its ore, recycling 1 metric ton (1.1 tons) of aluminum:

 produces 95% less air pollution

 saves 4 metric tons (4.4 tons) of ore

 produces 4 metric tons (4.4 tons) fewer chemical products

 uses 14,000 kWh less energy

produces 97% less water pollution

Fighting Disease Shisaburo Kitasato, born in 1852, was a Japanese scientist who was one of the first to discover the bacteria that cause tetanus, diphtheria, and bubonic plague. Kitasato developed a procedure to grow pure tetanus bacteria. This procedure enabled him to develop treatments for tetanus infections and led him to discover techniques and materials that he would later use to fight diphtheria and the plague.

In an attempt to help endangered animals, researchers at the Texas A&M Reproductive Sciences Laboratory in College Station, Texas, have begun Project Noah's Ark. This project collects the eggs, sperm, embryos, and DNA of endangered animals and stores them in liquid nitrogen.

Answering Society's Questions

Sometimes, society faces a question that does not seem to have an immediate answer. For example, at one time, the question of how to reduce air pollution did not have any obvious, reasonable answers. The millions of people who depended on their cars could not just stop driving. As the problem of air pollution became more important to people, scientists developed different technologies to address it For example, one source of air pollution is exhaust from cars. Through science, people have developed cleaner-burning gasoline. People have even developed new ways to clean up exhaust before it leaves the tailpipe of a car!

✓ Reading Check How can society influence the types of technologies that are developed?

Scientists All Around You

Believe it or not, scientists work in many different places. If you think about it, any person who asks questions and looks for answers could be called a scientist! Keep reading to learn about just a few people who use science in their jobs.

Zoologist

A *zoologist* (zoh AHL uh jist) is a person who studies the lives of animals. Dale Miquelle, shown in **Figure 6,** is part of a team of Russian and American zoologists studying the Siberian tiger. The tigers have almost become extinct after being hunted and losing their homes. By learning about the tigers' living space and food needs, zoologists hope to make a plan that will help the tigers survive better in the wild.

Figure 6 *To learn how much land a Siberian tiger covers, Dale Miquelle tracks a tiger that is wearing a radio-transmitting collar.*

Science Involves Processes Ask students how the processes of asking questions, doing research, making observations, and doing experiments work together to increase scientific knowledge. You may need to remind students of the definition of *science*. **LS Logical**

Quiz — GENERAL

1. What are three ways that a scientist can investigate a question? (research, observation, and experimentation)

2. Why is science important to you and the world around you? (Science helps save lives, resources, and the environment.)

3. What do you think is the most important technological development in the last 10 years? Explain why you think so. (Answers may vary. The key is how the student connects the technological development to a need in society.)

Alternative Assessment — BASIC

Animal Aid Have students research what is being done to preserve animal habitats in their area. Have students also find out what they can do to promote animal preservation. Students can determine what types of scientists are involved in preservation efforts. Have students make a poster or do a presentation to show what they learned. **LS Verbal**

Figure 7 *This geochemist may work outdoors when collecting rock samples from the field. Then, he may work indoors as he analyzes the samples in his laboratory.*

Geochemist

Some scientists work outdoors most of the time. Other scientists spend much of their time in the laboratory. A geochemist (JEE oh KEM ist), such as the one shown in **Figure 7,** may work in both places. A *geochemist* is a person who specializes in the chemistry of rocks, minerals, and soil.

Geochemists determine the economic value of these materials. They also try to find out what the environment was like when these materials formed and what has happened to the materials since they first formed.

Mechanic

Do you have a machine that needs repairs? Call a mechanic, such as Gene Webb in **Figure 8.** Mechanics work on everything from cars to the space shuttle. Mechanics use science to solve problems. Mechanics must find answers to questions about why a machine is not working. Then, they must find a way to make it work. Mechanics also think of ways to improve the machine, to make it work faster or more efficiently.

Figure 8 *A mechanic can help keep a car's engine running smoothly.*

Oceanographer

An *oceanographer* studies the ocean. Some oceanographers study waves and ocean currents. Others study plants and animals that live in the ocean. Still others study the ocean floor, including how it forms.

While studying the ocean floor, oceanographers discovered black smokers. Black smokers are cracks where hot water (around 300°C!) from beneath Earth's surface comes up. These vents in the ocean floor are home to some strange animals, including red-tipped tube worms and blind white crabs.

INCLUSION Strategies

• Gifted and Talented

Ask students to extend their understanding of polio and other diseases by researching these questions:

• How does polio affect the body?

• When was polio common?

• Why did people stop getting polio?

• What other diseases used to be more serious threats than they are now?

LS Logical

CONNECTION ACTIVITY

Language Arts — BASIC

"The Tyger" Have students read William Blake's poem "The Tyger," and read the poem aloud to the class. Ask students what the author of the poem thinks about tigers and what comes to students' minds when they read the poem. Have students write a poem about their favorite animal. **LS Verbal**

Volcanologist

If black smokers aren't hot enough for you, perhaps you would like to become a volcanologist (VAHL kuh NAHL uh jist). A *volcanologist* studies one of Earth's most interesting processes—volcanoes. The volcanologist shown in **Figure 9** is photographing lava flowing from Mt. Etna, a volcano in Italy. Mt. Etna's lava may reach temperatures of 1,050°C. By learning more about volcanoes, volcanologists hope to get better at predicting when a volcano will erupt. Being able to predict eruptions would help save lives.

 Reading Check What does a volcanologist do?

Figure 9 *Volcanologists gain a better understanding of the inside of the Earth by studying the makeup of lava.*

SECTION Review

Summary

- Science is a process of gathering knowledge about the natural world by making observations and asking questions.
- Science begins by asking a question.
- Even if science cannot answer the question right away, the answers that scientists find may be very important.
- A question may lead to a scientific investigation, including research, observations, and experimentation.
- Science can help save lives, fight diseases, save resources, and protect the environment.
- A variety of people may become scientists for a variety of reasons.

Using Key Terms

1. In your own words, write a definition for the term *science*.

Understanding Key Ideas

2. A zoologist might study any of the following EXCEPT
   a. shellfish living in ponds.
   b. the reason that mole rats live in large groups underground.
   c. environmental threats to sea turtles.
   d. rocks and minerals in the Painted Desert.

3. Describe five careers that use science.

4. How are observation and experimentation different?

5. How may what people expect to observe affect what they do observe? How can people avoid this problem?

Math Skills

6. Students in a science class collected 50 frogs from a pond. They found that 15 of the frogs had serious deformities. What percentage of the frogs had deformities?

Critical Thinking

7. **Making Inferences** An ad for deluxe garbage bags says that the bags are 30% stronger than regular garbage bags. Describe how science can help you find out if this claim is true.

8. **Identifying Relationships** Make a list of three things that you consider to be a problem in society. Give an example of how new technology might solve these problems.

9. **Applying Concepts** Look at Figure 9. Write five questions about what you see. Describe how science might help you answer your questions. Share your questions with your classmates.

SCI**LINKS**.

NSTA

Developed and maintained by the National Science Teachers Association

For a variety of links related to this chapter, go to www.scilinks.org

Topic: Careers in Science
SciLinks code: HSM0244

Answer to Reading Check

A volcanologist studies volcanoes and their products, such as lava and gases.

Answers to Section Review

1. Science is the knowledge gathered by observing the real world, asking questions, and testing ideas.

2. d

3. Answers may vary and may include descriptions of a zoologist, a mechanic, an oceanographer, a geochemist, or a volcanologist.

4. An observation is a fact or event that you see, note, and record. An experiment is a process for discovering something that you don't know.

5. Sample answer: If a person strongly supports a particular hypothesis, he or she may see only the evidence that supports that hypothesis. For example, if a person believes strongly that a meteor caused dinosaurs to become extinct, the person might overlook evidence that one or more diseases played a part in the extinction of dinosaurs. Scientists can avoid this problem by keeping an open mind and letting the evidence lead to conclusions rather than making a conclusion and then looking for evidence to support it.

6. $15 \div 50 \times 100 = 30\%$ of the frogs were deformed

7. Sample answer: An experiment could test which garbage bag is stronger and how much stronger it is. Then, the test results could be compared with the claim in the ad.

8. Sample answer: inefficient cars: new power sources, such as hydrogen cells; cancer: new medicines and other therapies; drug use among children: high-tech ways to capture dealers and medicines to prevent drug addiction.

9. Answers may vary. Accept all reasonable responses. Students' questions and answers should relate to Figure 9.

SECTION

2

Focus

Overview

This section introduces scientific methods used by scientists through a case study of an actual investigation of deformed frogs. The section also demonstrates the development of testable hypotheses and the importance of sharing information among scientists.

Bellringer

Ask students to write a brief response to this question:

"Which is more important, imagination or knowledge?"

Have students share their responses and then debate this question. Raise the point that many important scientists were known for their original thinking and sometimes faced resistance to their new ideas.

Motivate

ACTIVITY ———— GENERAL

Now You See It As an exercise in observation, display a collection of assorted shapes on the overhead projector. Allow the students to look at the shapes for 15 seconds. Turn the projector off, and have the students spend 5 minutes describing or drawing as many of the shapes as they can in their **science journal.** Visual/Intrapersonal

READING WARM-UP

Objectives

● Explain why scientists use scientific methods.

● Determine the appropriate design of a controlled experiment.

● Use information in tables and graphs to analyze experimental results.

● Explain how scientific knowledge can change.

Terms to Learn

scientific methods
hypothesis
controlled experiment
variable

READING STRATEGY

Reading Organizer As you read this section, make a flowchart of the possible steps in scientific methods.

scientific methods a series of steps followed to solve problems

Scientific Methods

Imagine that your class is on a field trip to a wildlife refuge. You discover several deformed frogs. You wonder what could be causing the frogs' deformities.

A group of students from Le Sueur, Minnesota, actually made this discovery! By making observations and asking questions about the observations, the students used scientific methods.

What Are Scientific Methods?

When scientists observe the natural world, they often think of a question or problem. But scientists don't just guess at answers. They use scientific methods. **Scientific methods** are the ways in which scientists follow steps to answer questions and solve problems. The steps used for all investigations are the same. But the order in which the steps are followed may vary, as shown in **Figure 1.** Scientists may use all of the steps or just some of the steps during an investigation. They may even repeat some of the steps. The order depends on what works best to answer the question. No matter where scientists work or what questions they try to answer, all scientists have two things in common. They are curious about the natural world, and they use similar methods to investigate it.

✔ **Reading Check** What are scientific methods? (*See the Appendix for answers to Reading Checks.*)

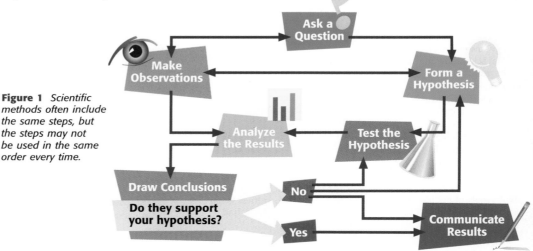

Figure 1 *Scientific methods often include the same steps, but the steps may not be used in the same order every time.*

CHAPTER RESOURCES

Chapter Resource File

• Lesson Plan
• Directed Reading A **BASIC**
• Directed Reading B **SPECIAL NEEDS**

Technology

Transparencies
• Bellringer
• Scientific Methods

Answer to Reading Check

a series of steps used by scientists to solve problems

Figure 7 UV Light Experiment

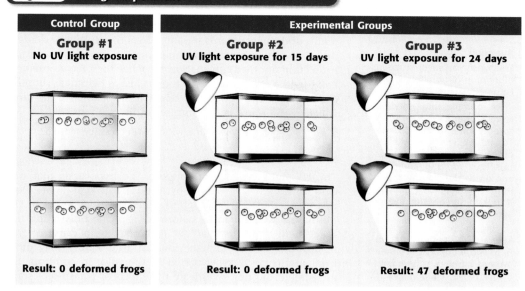

Control Group

Group #1
No UV light exposure

Result: 0 deformed frogs

Experimental Groups

Group #2
UV light exposure for 15 days

Result: 0 deformed frogs

Group #3
UV light exposure for 24 days

Result: 47 deformed frogs

Collecting Data

Figure 7 shows the experimental setup to test Hypothesis 3. As **Table 1** shows, there are 100 eggs in each group. Scientists always try to test many individuals. They want to be sure that differences between control and experimental groups are caused by the variable and not by differences between individuals. The larger the groups are, the smaller the effect of a difference between individual frogs will be. The larger the groups are, the more likely it is that the variable is responsible for any changes and the more accurate the data collected are likely to be.

Scientists test a result by repeating the experiment. If an experiment gives the same results each time, scientists are more certain about the variable's effect on the outcome. Scientists keep clear, accurate, honest records of their data so that other scientists can repeat the experiment and verify the results.

Analyze the Results

After scientists finish their tests, they must organize their data and analyze the results. Scientists may organize data in a table or a graph. The data collected from the UV light experiment are shown in the bar graph in **Figure 8**. Analyzing the results helps scientists explain and focus on the effect of the variable. For example, the graph shows that the length of UV exposure has an effect on the development of frog deformities.

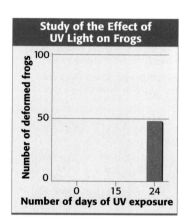

Study of the Effect of UV Light on Frogs

Number of deformed frogs

Number of days of UV exposure

Figure 8 *This graph shows that 24 days of UV exposure had an effect on frog deformities, while less exposure had no effect.*

CONNECTION to Real Life ———— GENERAL

Frog Investigations In August 1995, students from the Minnesota New Country School in Le Sueur, Minnesota, noticed deformed frogs while on a field trip to a nearby wetland area. The school notified local authorities, fueling a wave of public attention and scientific investigations. The UV light experiment described in this section is an actual example. Have students use the Internet to find other studies on frog deformities. **LS** Intrapersonal/Logical

Answer to Math Practice

$[(8 + 8 + 5) \div 3] = [21 \div 3] = 7$
The average is 7 days.
$[(6 + 5 + 4) \div 3] = [15 \div 3] = 5$
The average is 5 days.

Answer to Reading Check

because the scientist has learned something

Reteaching ——— BASIC

Experimental Setup Have students propose other experiments that scientists could use to test the effect of UV light on frogs. Discuss how such an experiment might be set up. **LS** Logical/Verbal

Quiz ——— GENERAL

1. Why is it important to have a control group when doing an experiment? (Data from the experimental groups are compared with data from the control group to see the effect caused by changes to the variable.)

2. Why should a hypothesis be testable? (If a hypothesis is not testable, there is no way to support it or to show it to be wrong.)

Alternative Assessment ——— ADVANCED

Using Scientific Methods Have students use scientific methods to answer a simple, everyday question. The students should set up experiments, keep careful records, and then summarize their results and present them to the class. **LS** Logical/Intrapersonal

MATH PRACTICE

Averages

Finding the average, or mean, of a group of numbers is a common way to analyze data.

For example, three seeds were kept at 25°C and sprouted in 8, 8, and 5 days. To find the average number of days that it took the seeds to sprout, add 8, 8, and 5 and divide the sum by 3, the number of subjects (seeds). It took these seeds an average of 7 days to sprout.

Suppose three seeds were kept at 30°C and sprouted in 6, 5, and 4 days. What's the average number of days that it took these seeds to sprout?

Figure 9 This student scientist is communicating the results of his investigation at a science fair.

Draw Conclusions

After scientists have analyzed the data from several experiments, they can draw conclusions. They decide whether the results of the experiments support a hypothesis. When scientists find that a hypothesis is not supported by the tests, they must try to find another explanation for what they have observed. Proving that a hypothesis is wrong is just as helpful as supporting it. Why? Either way, the scientist has learned something, which is the purpose of using scientific methods.

Reading Check How can a wrong hypothesis be helpful?

Is It the Answer?

The UV light experiment supports the hypothesis that frog deformities can be caused by exposure to UV light. Does this mean that UV light definitely caused frogs living in the Minnesota wetland to be deformed? No, the only thing this experiment shows is that UV light may be a cause of frog deformities. Results of tests done in a laboratory may differ from results of tests performed in the wild. In addition, the experiment did not investigate the effects of parasites or some other substance on the frogs. In fact, many scientists now think that more than one factor could be causing the deformities.

Sometimes, similar investigations or experiments give different results. For example, another research team may have had results that did not support the UV light hypothesis. In such a case, scientists must work together to decide if the differences in the results are scientifically significant. Often, making that decision takes more experiments and more evidence.

Communicate Results

Scientists form a global community. After scientists complete their investigations, they communicate their results to other scientists. The student in **Figure 9** is explaining the results of a science project.

Scientists regularly share their results for several reasons. First, other scientists may then repeat the experiments to see if they get the same results. Second, the information can be considered by other scientists with similar interests. The scientists can then compare hypotheses and form consistent explanations. New data may strengthen existing hypotheses or show that the hypotheses need to be altered. There are many paths from observations and questions to communicating results.

CONNECTION ACTIVITY
Math ——— BASIC

Averages Remind students how to calculate the average (or *mean*) of a group of numbers by using the following formula:

$$average = \\ sum\ of\ all\ data\ points \div \\ total\ number\ of\ data\ points$$

Emphasize that averages are often used to summarize or look for trends in data. Have students answer the following questions:

1. Four students ran a 100 m race in the following times: 15 s, 19 s, 21 s, and 25 s. What was the average time? ($[15 + 19 + 21 + 25] \div 4 = 20$ s)

2. Three children were picking berries. One picked 51 berries, the second picked 64 berries, and the third picked 68 berries. What was the average number of berries picked? ($[51 + 64 + 68] \div 3 = 61$ berries)

LS Logical   English Language Learners

SECTION Review

Summary

- Scientific methods are the ways in which scientists follow steps to answer questions and solve problems.

- Any information you gather through your senses is an observation. Observations often lead to the formation of questions and hypotheses.

- A hypothesis is a possible explanation or answer to a question. A well-formed hypothesis is testable by experiment.

- A controlled experiment tests only one factor at a time and consists of a control group and one or more experimental groups.

- After testing a hypothesis, scientists analyze the results and draw conclusions about whether the hypothesis is supported.

- Communicating results allows others to check the results, add to their knowledge, and design new experiments.

Using Key Terms

1. Use the following terms in the same sentence: *hypothesis*, *controlled experiment*, and *variable*.

Understanding Key Ideas

2. The steps of scientific methods
   a. are exactly the same in every investigation.
   b. must be used in the same order every time.
   c. are not used in the same order every time.
   d. always end with a conclusion.

3. What is the appropriate design of a controlled experiment?

4. What causes scientific knowledge to change?

Math Skills

5. Calculate the average of the following values: 4, 5, 6, 6, and 9.

Critical Thinking

6. **Analyzing Methods** Why was UV light chosen to be the variable in the frog experiment?

7. **Analyzing Processes** Why are there many ways to follow the steps of scientific methods?

8. **Making Inferences** Why might two scientists working on the same problem draw different conclusions?

9. **Making Inferences** Why do scientists use scientific methods?

Interpreting Graphics

10. The table below shows how long it takes for bacteria to double. Plot the information on a graph. Put temperature on the *x*-axis and the time to double on the *y*-axis. Do not graph values for which there is no growth. At what temperature do the bacteria multiply the fastest?

Temperature (°C)	Time to double (min)
10	130
20	60
25	40
30	29
37	17
40	19
45	32
50	no growth

11. What would happen if you changed the scale of the graph by using values of 0 to 300 minutes on the *y*-axis? How might that change affect your interpretation of the data?

SCiLINKS.

NSTA
Developed and maintained by the National Science Teachers Association

For a variety of links related to this chapter, go to www.scilinks.org

Topic: Scientific Methods; Deformed Frogs
SciLinks code: HSM1359; HSM0383

5. $[(4 + 5 + 6 + 6 + 9) \div 5] = [30 \div 5] = 6$

6. Sample answer: Because the scientists were trying to test the hypothesis that UV light causes deformities, UV light was the factor that needed to be varied—the variable.

7. Sample answer: because sometimes scientists need to go back and change a step and sometimes not every step is important to an investigation

8. Sample answer: They may have tested different variables, and other factors in the control and experimental groups may have differed.

9. Sample answer: Scientists use scientific methods because one or more of the steps are used in every experiment, which helps ensure that experimental results are accurate.

10. See sample graph below. The temperature at which bacteria multiply most quickly is 37°C.

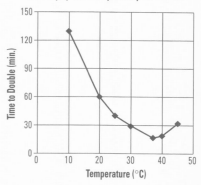

11. Data on the graph would not change, but the shape of the curve would change, which might cause errors.

Answers to Section Review

1. Sample answer: One way to test a hypothesis is to conduct a controlled experiment that tests only one variable.

2. c

3. A controlled experiment is properly designed if it tests only one factor at a time and it consists of a control group and one or more experimental groups.

4. Scientific knowledge changes because scientists conduct experiments to test new hypotheses. Their results build upon existing knowledge.

CHAPTER RESOURCES

Chapter Resource File

- Section Quiz **GENERAL**
- Section Review **GENERAL**
- Vocabulary and Section Summary **GENERAL**
- Reinforcement Worksheet **BASIC**
- Critical Thinking **ADVANCED**

Workbooks

Math Skills for Science
- What Is an Average? **BASIC**

SECTION

3

Focus

Overview

This section discusses the role of models in science and defines three types of models. Students learn that models are important tools despite their limitations. Students learn about theories and laws and the differences between theories and laws.

🎧 Bellringer

Ask students to write answers to the following questions:

• What is a model?

• Name several types of models.

• What models have you used?

LS Verbal

Motivate

Discussion ——— GENERAL

Toys as Models Show students a variety of toys. Ask students how toys are similar to and different from objects that the toys represent. Ask students whether the toys are limited as models, and whether any limitations of toys are good or bad. Introduce the idea of scale models. (The toys are similar to the objects that they represent, but toys are usually smaller. A limitation of toys is that they do not act like the objects represented. The limitations may be good or bad—a teddy bear won't hurt you, but you can't drive a toy car to the store.) **LS** Verbal

---

READING WARM-UP

Objectives

● Give examples of three types of models.

● Identify the benefits and limitations of models.

● Compare the ways that scientists use hypotheses, theories, and laws.

Terms to Learn

model
theory
law

READING STRATEGY

Reading Organizer As you read this section, create an outline of the section. Use the headings from the section in your outline.

model a pattern, plan, representation, or description designed to show the structure or workings of an object, system, or concept

---

Scientific Models

How can you see the parts of a cell? Unless you had superhuman eyesight, you couldn't see inside most cells without using a microscope.

What would you do if you didn't have a microscope? Looking at a model of a cell would help! A model of a cell can help you understand what the parts of a cell look like.

Types of Scientific Models

A **model** is a representation of an object or system. Scientific models are used to help explain how something works or to describe the structure of something. A model may be used to predict future events. However, models have limitations. A model is never exactly like the real thing. If it were, it would not be a model. Three major kinds of scientific models are physical, mathematical, and conceptual models.

Physical Models

A model volcano and a miniature steam engine are examples of physical models. Some physical models, such as a model of a cell, look like the thing that they model. But a limitation of the model of a cell is that the model is not alive and doesn't act exactly like a cell. Other physical models, such as the model of a skyscraper in **Figure 1,** look and act at least somewhat like the thing that they model. Scientists often use the model that is simplest to use but that still serves their purpose.

Figure 1 *The model of the skyscraper doesn't act like the real building in every way, which is both a benefit and a limitation of the model.*

CHAPTER RESOURCES

Chapter Resource File

 • Lesson Plan
• Directed Reading A BASIC
• Directed Reading B SPECIAL NEEDS

Technology

🖴 **Transparencies**
• Bellringer

Workbooks

 Math Skills for Science
• Using Proportions and Cross-Multiplication GENERAL
• Punnett Square Popcorn GENERAL

Is That a Fact!

Small Cells, Large Cells All animals are made of cells, and most animal cells are only 10 to 20 μm long—too small to see with the naked eye. However, some cells may be seen easily without the aid of a microscope. The yolk of an ostrich egg is the largest single cell. An ostrich egg can be 25 cm in diameter!

Figure 2 Mathematical Model: A Punnett Square

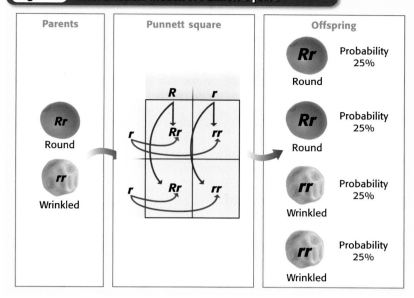

Parents	Punnett square	Offspring

Rr Round
rr Wrinkled

Rr Probability 25% Round
Rr Probability 25% Round
rr Probability 25% Wrinkled
rr Probability 25% Wrinkled

Mathematical Models

A mathematical model may be made up of numbers, equations, and other forms of data. Some mathematical models are simple and can be used easily. The Punnett square shown in **Figure 2** helps scientists study the passing of traits from parents to offspring. Using this model, scientists can predict how often certain traits will appear in the offspring of certain parents.

Computers are useful for creating and manipulating mathematical models. They make fewer mistakes and can keep track of more variables than a person can. But a computer model can also be incorrect in many ways. The more complex a model is, the more carefully scientists must build and test the model.

✓ Reading Check What type of model is a Punnett square? (*See the Appendix for answers to Reading Checks.*)

Conceptual Models

The third type of model is the conceptual model. Some conceptual models are systems of ideas. Others compare unfamiliar things with familiar things to help explain unfamiliar ideas. The idea that the solar system formed from a spinning disk of gas is a conceptual model. Scientists also use conceptual models to classify behaviors of animals. Scientists can then predict how an animal might respond to a certain action based on behaviors that have already been observed.

CONNECTION TO Environmental Science

Samples Scientists studying deformed frogs in Minnesota wanted to know at what stage in the frogs' development the deformities happened. So, the scientists collected a large sample of frogs in all stages of development.

The larger a sample is, the more accurately it represents the whole population. If, for example, a sample of frogs is too small, one unusual frog may make the results of the study inaccurate. If the sample has too many old frogs or too many tadpoles, the sample is unrepresentative of the whole population. Give an example of an unrepresentative sample. Make a poster describing how that sample might make the experimental results inaccurate.

Figure 3 *This computer-generated model doesn't just look like a dinosaur. It may also open and close its jaws in much the same way that a dinosaur does.*

theory an explanation that ties together many hypotheses and observations

law a summary of many experimental results and observations; a law tells how things work

Benefits of Models

Models often represent things that are small, large, or complicated. Models can also represent things that do not exist. For example, **Figure 3** is a model of one type of dinosaur. Dinosaurs died out millions of years ago. Some popular movies about dinosaurs have used computer models like this one because dinosaurs are extinct. But the movies would not be as realistic if they did not have the scientific models.

A model can be a kind of hypothesis, and scientists can test a model. To build a model of an organism, even an extinct one, scientists gather information from fossils and other observations. Then, scientists can test whether the model fits their ideas about how an organism moved or what it ate.

Limits of Models

Models are useful, but they are not perfect. For example, the model in **Figure 3** gives scientists an idea of how the dinosaur looked. But to find out how strong the dinosaur's jaws were, scientists might build a physical model that has pressure sensors in the jaw. That model would provide data about bite strength. Scientists may use different models to represent the same thing, such as the dinosaur's jaw. But the kind of model and the model's complexity depend on the model's purpose.

Even a model jaw that has pressure sensors is not perfect. Scientists can compare the dinosaur bite with the bite of a crocodile. Next, scientists use their model to conduct tests. Scientists might then estimate how hard the dinosaur could bite. But without a live dinosaur, the result is still a hypothesis.

Building Scientific Knowledge

Sometimes, scientists draw different conclusions from the same data. Other times, new results show that old conclusions are wrong. Scientists are always asking new questions or looking at old questions from a different angle. As scientists find new answers, scientific knowledge continues to grow and change.

Scientific Theories

For every hypothesis, more than one prediction can be made. Each time another prediction is proven true, the hypothesis gains more support. Over time, scientists tie together everything that they have learned. An explanation that ties together many related observations, facts, and tested hypotheses is called a **theory.** Theories are conceptual models that help organize scientific thinking. Theories are used to explain observations and to predict what might happen in the future.

✓ *Reading Check* How do scientists use theories?

Scientific Laws

What happens when a theory and its models correctly predict the results of many experiments? A scientific law may be formed. In science, a **law** is a summary of many experimental results and observations. A scientific law is a statement of what *will* happen in a specific situation. A law tells you how things work.

Scientific laws are at work around you every day. For example, the law of gravity states that objects will always fall toward the center of Earth. And inside your cells, many laws of chemistry are at work to keep you alive.

Scientific Change

New scientific ideas may take time to be accepted as facts, scientific theories, or scientific laws. Scientists should be open to new ideas but should always test new ideas by using scientific methods. If new evidence challenges an accepted idea, scientists must reexamine the old evidence and reevaluate the old idea. In this way, the process of building scientific knowledge never ends.

CONNECTION TO Chemistry

Model Cocaine in the Brain
Analyze and evaluate information from a scientifically literate viewpoint by reading scientific texts, magazine articles, and newspaper articles about how drugs, such as cocaine, affect brain chemistry. Create a model to show what you have learned. Use your model to describe possible treatments for drug addiction.

ACTIVITY

SECTION Review

Summary

- Models represent objects or systems. Often, they use familiar things to represent unfamiliar things. Three main types of models are physical, mathematical, and conceptual models. Models have limitations but are useful and can be changed based on new evidence.
- Scientific knowledge is built as scientists form and revise scientific hypotheses, models, theories, and laws.

Using Key Terms

In each of the following sentences, replace the incorrect term with the correct term from the word bank.

theory   law   hypothesis

1. A conclusion is an explanation that matches many hypotheses but may still change.

2. A model tells you exactly what to expect in certain situations.

Understanding Key Ideas

3. A limitation of models is that
   a. they are large enough to see.
   b. they do not act exactly like the things that they model.
   c. they are smaller than the things that they model.
   d. they model unfamiliar things.

4. What type of model would you use to test the hypothesis that global warming is causing polar icecaps to melt? Explain.

Math Skills

5. If Jerry is 2.1 m tall, how tall is a scale model of Jerry that is 10% of his size?

Critical Thinking

6. **Applying Concepts** You want to make a model of an extinct plant. What are two kinds of models that you might use? Describe the advantages and disadvantages of each type of model.

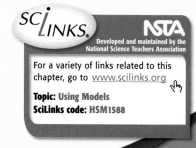

SCiLINKS.

NSTA
Developed and maintained by the National Science Teachers Association

For a variety of links related to this chapter, go to www.scilinks.org

Topic: Using Models
SciLinks code: HSM1588

Answer to Connection to Chemistry
Students will find information in a variety of sources, such as newspapers, weekly magazines, science periodicals, and the Internet. Students should evaluate and compare the information that they find in the popular press and the information that they find in scientific journals and on university Web sites. Most students will probably make a model of a neuron or a neural synapse and include neurotransmitters. Students' models may include computer models, physical models, or posters.

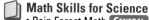

CHAPTER RESOURCES

Chapter Resource File
- Section Quiz GENERAL
- Section Review GENERAL
- Vocabulary and Section Summary GENERAL

Workbooks

Math Skills for Science
- Rain Forest Math GENERAL
- Scale of Organisms GENERAL

Science Skills
- Using Models to Communicate GENERAL
- Introduction to Graphs GENERAL

Answers to Section Review

1. A theory is an explanation that matches many hypotheses but may still change.

2. A law tells you exactly what to expect in certain situations.

3. b

4. Sample answer: I would use a computer to create a mathematical model that uses climate data and predicts what may happen under a certain set of conditions, such as an increase in the global temperature.

5. 10% of 2.1 m = 0.21 m, or 21 cm

6. The model plant could be a physical model. The advantages of a physical model include that the model could be as large or as small as needed (including life-sized) and could be moved about as needed. Disadvantages include that the model is not alive and could not grow as a real plant grows. The model plant could also be a conceptual model (perhaps developed by using a computer). The advantages of this model include that the computer could make the plant "grow" as a real plant might grow and would allow scientists to change the model slightly to see the impact of a small change. The disadvantages of this model include that the model is not alive and cannot be put out into the rain to see if it can withstand a high wind.

SECTION
4

Focus

Overview

This section describes several tools that scientists use to gather information. Students also learn about the International System of Units (SI). Students learn the units and tools associated with quantities such as mass and volume. Finally, students learn about lab safety and safety symbols.

⊙ Bellringer

Have students write an answer to the following question:

> Why do you think scientists use tools such as graduated cylinders and stopwatches?

Ask students to share their answers with the class, and briefly discuss their responses. **LS** Logical

Motivate

Demonstration —— GENERAL

Tools of the Trade Demonstrate the use and care of a graduated cylinder and a balance to the class. **LS** Visual/Verbal

---

READING WARM-UP

Objectives

● Collect, record, and analyze information by using various tools.
● Explain the importance of the International System of Units.
● Calculate area and density.
● Identify lab safety symbols, and demonstrate safe practices during lab investigations.

Terms to Learn

meter	volume
area	temperature
mass	density

READING STRATEGY

Reading Organizer As you read this section, make a concept map by using the terms above.

Tools, Measurement, and Safety

Would you use a hammer to tighten a bolt on a bicycle? No, you wouldn't. You need the right tools to fix a bike.

Scientists use a variety of tools in their experiments. A tool is anything that helps you do a task.

Tools for Measuring

You might remember that one way to collect data is to take measurements. To get the best measurements, you need the proper tools. Stopwatches, metersticks, and balances are tools that you can use to make measurements. Thermometers, spring scales, and graduated cylinders are also helpful tools. Some of the uses of these tools are shown in **Figure 1.**

✓ **Reading Check** Name six tools used for taking measurements. (*See the Appendix for answers to Reading Checks.*)

Tools for Analyzing

After you collect data, you need to analyze them. Perhaps you need to find the average of your data. Calculators are handy tools to help you do calculations quickly. Or you might show your data in a graph or a figure. A computer that has the correct software can help you make neat, colorful figures. Of course, even a pencil and graph paper are tools that you can use to graph your data.

Figure 1   Measurement Tools

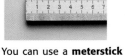

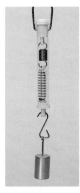

You can use a **graduated cylinder** to measure volume.

You can use a **thermometer** to measure temperature.

You can use a **meterstick** to measure length.

You can use a **balance** to measure mass.

You can use a **stopwatch** to measure time.

You can use a **spring scale** to measure force.

CHAPTER RESOURCES

Chapter Resource File

● **Lesson Plan**
● **Directed Reading A** BASIC
● **Directed Reading B** SPECIAL NEEDS

Technology

Transparencies
● Bellringer
● Common SI Units

Workbooks

Math Skills for Science
● Creating Exponents GENERAL

Answer to Reading Check

stopwatch, graduated cylinder, meterstick, spring scale, balance, and thermometer

---

Units of Measurement

The ability to make accurate and reliable measurements is an important skill in science. Many systems of measurement are used throughout the world. At one time in England, the standard for an inch was three grains of barley placed end to end. Other modern standardized units were originally based on parts of the body, such as the foot. Such systems were not very reliable. Their units were based on objects that had different sizes.

The International System of Units

In the late 1700s, the French Academy of Sciences began to form a global measurement system now known as the *International System of Units,* or SI. Today, most scientists and almost all countries use this system. One advantage of using SI measurements is that doing so helps scientists share and compare their observations and results.

Another advantage of SI units is that all units are based on the number 10, which makes conversions from one unit to another easy. The table in **Table 1** contains commonly used SI units for length, volume, mass, and temperature.

No Rulers Allowed
1. Measure the width of your desk, but don't use a ruler.
2. Select another object to use as your unit of measurement.
3. Compare your measurement with those of your classmates.
4. Explain why it is important to use standard units of measurement.

Table 1 Common SI Units and Conversions

Length	meter (m)	
	kilometer (km)	1 km = 1,000 m
	decimeter (dm)	1 dm = 0.1 m
	centimeter (cm)	1 cm = 0.01 m
	millimeter (mm)	1 mm = 0.001 m
	micrometer (μm)	1 μm = 0.000001 m
	nanometer (nm)	1 nm = 0.000000001 m
Volume	cubic meter (m³)	
	cubic centimeter (cm³)	1 cm³ = 0.000001 m³
	liter (L)	1 L = 1 dm³ = 0.001 m³
	milliliter (mL)	1 mL = 0.001 L = 1 cm³
Mass	kilogram (kg)	
	gram (g)	1 g = 0.001 kg
	milligram (mg)	1 mg = 0.000001 kg
Temperature	Kelvin (K)	0°C = 273 K
	Celsius (°C)	100°C = 373 K

Science Bloopers

Just a Second The second is the SI unit for time. The second was originally defined as $\frac{1}{86,400}$ of a mean solar day. Later, astronomers discovered that a day is not a constant interval of time: the gravitational attraction of the moon slows Earth's rotation, so each day is about 40 ns longer than the previous day! Now, the definition of a *second* is based on the movement of an electron between energy levels in a cesium atom.

Cultural Awareness
ADVANCED

It All Adds Up! Devices that assist in calculations have been around for a long time. A variety of cultures have used many variations of the computer, including the "pebble computer" and the abacus. Have students research and prepare presentations about some of these early "computers," including how they work. **English Language Learners**
LS Verbal

Research — GENERAL

The SI in the United States The United States is the only industrialized nation in the world that does not officially use the SI. Talk about some of the reasons the country has had such a hard time changing systems. Then, ask students to research the history of the English system and the SI. Suggest that they also investigate English measurements, such as the furlong and the stone. **LS Verbal/Logical**

Answers to MathFocus

1. 125.5 km × 8.225 km = 1,032 km²

Teacher's Note: There are several rules for determining significant digits and for using significant digits in calculations. One rule is given in the activity. Another rule is that in the addition and subtraction of numbers, the result can be no more certain than the least certain number in the calculation.

CONNECTION to Physical Science — GENERAL

How Hot? Although students may be most familiar with the Fahrenheit scale, remind them that they will be using the Celsius scale in their science class. Use the teaching transparency "Three Temperature Scales" to demonstrate the importance of paying attention to the units in which a temperature is given. **LS Logical/Visual**

Figure 2 *This scientist is using a metric ruler to measure a lizard's length. The unit chosen to describe an object, such as this lizard, depends on the size of the object being measured.*

meter the basic unit of length in the SI (symbol, m)

area a measure of the size of a surface or a region

Measurement

Scientists report measured quantities in a way that shows the precision of the measurement. To do so, they use significant figures. *Significant figures* are the digits in a measurement that are known with certainty. The MathFocus below will help you understand significant figures and will teach you how to use the correct number of digits. Now that you have a standardized system of units for measuring things, you can use the system to measure length, area, mass, volume, and temperature.

Length

How long is a lizard? Well, a **meter** (m) is the basic SI unit of length. However, a scientist, such as the one in **Figure 2,** would use centimeters (cm) to describe a small lizard's length. If you divide 1 m into 100 parts, each part equals 1 cm. So, 1 cm is one-hundredth of a meter. Even though 1 cm seems small, some things are even smaller. Scientists describe the length of very small objects in micrometers (μm) or nanometers (nm). To see these small objects, scientists use powerful microscopes.

Area

How much paper would you need to cover the top of your desk? To answer this question, you must find the area of the desk. **Area** is a measure of the size of the surface of an object. To calculate the area of a square or a rectangle, measure the length and width. Then, use the following equation:

$$area = length \times width$$

Units for area are square units, such as square meters (m²), square centimeters (cm²), and square kilometers (km²).

Significant Figures Calculate the area of a carpet that is 3.145 m long (four significant figures) and 5.75 m (three significant figures) wide. (Hint: In multiplication and division problems, the answer cannot have more significant figures than the measurement that has the smallest number of significant figures does.)

Step 1: Write the equation for area.

$$area = length \times width$$

Step 2: Replace *length* and *width* with the measurements given, and solve.

$$area = 3.125 \text{ m} \times 5.75 \text{ m} = 18.08375 \text{ m}^2$$

Step 3: Round the answer to get the correct number of significant figures. Here, the correct number of significant figures is three, because the value with the smallest number of significant figures has three significant figures.

$$area = 18.1 \text{ m}^2$$

Now Its Your Turn

1. Use a calculator to perform the following calculation: 125.5 km × 8.225 km. Write the answer with the correct number of significant figures.

CHAPTER RESOURCES

Technology

 Transparencies
- **LINK TO PHYSICAL SCIENCE** Three Temperature Scales

Workbooks

 Math Skills for Science
- What Is SI? GENERAL
- A Formula for SI Catch-Up GENERAL
- Finding Perimeter and Area GENERAL
- Finding Volume GENERAL

Science Skills
- Recognizing Bias in Graphs GENERAL
- Interpreting Your Data GENERAL

Is That a Fact!

Why Is SI the Abbreviation for the International System of Units? The International System of Units is abbreviated *SI* because it stands for *Système International d'Unités,* which is French.

Figure 3 *Adding the rock changes the water level from 70 mL to 80 mL. So, the rock displaces 10 mL of water. Because 1 mL = 1 cm³, the volume of the rock is 10 cm³.*

Mass

How large a rock can a rushing stream move? The answer depends on the energy of the stream and the mass of the rock. **Mass** is a measure of the amount of matter in an object. The kilogram (kg) is the basic unit for mass in the SI. Kilograms are used to describe the mass of a large rock. Grams are used to measure the mass of smaller objects. One thousand grams equals 1 kg. For example, a medium-sized apple has a mass of about 100 g. Masses of very large objects are given in metric tons. A metric ton equals 1,000 kg.

✓ Reading Check What is the basic SI unit for mass?

Volume

Think about moving some magnets to a laboratory. How many magnets will fit into a box? The answer depends on the volume of the box and the volume of each magnet. **Volume** is a measure of the size of a body in three-dimensional space. In this case, you need the volumes of the box and of the magnets.

The volume of a liquid is often given in liters (L). Liters are based on the meter. A cubic meter (1 m³) is equal to 1,000 L. So, 1,000 L will fit into a box measuring 1 m on each side. A milliliter (mL) will fit into a box measuring 1 cm on each side. So, 1 mL = 1 cm³. Graduated cylinders are used to measure the volume of liquids.

The volume of a large, solid object is given in cubic meters (m³). The volumes of smaller objects can be given in cubic centimeters (cm³) or cubic millimeters (mm³). The volume of a box can be calculated by multiplying the object's length, width, and height. The volume of an irregularly shaped object can be found by measuring the volume of liquid that the object displaces. You can see how this works in **Figure 3.**

mass a measure of the amount of matter in an object

volume a measure of the size of a body or region in three-dimensional space

---

SI Estimation Display or name various objects one at a time. For each object, call on a different student to estimate some dimension or characteristic of the object in SI units. Have another student verify the measurement. [LS] Visual/Logical

Quiz ——— GENERAL

1. What are the SI units for length, mass, and temperature? (the meter, the kilogram, and the kelvin or degree Celsius)

2. What is the area of a piece of cake whose sides measure 9.4 cm and 9.0 cm? (9.4 cm × 9.0 cm = 84.6 cm²)

3. How could you find the volume of an irregularly shaped pebble? (by using a graduated cylinder to measure the amount of water displaced by the pebble)

4. What is density? (the ratio of the mass of a substance to the volume of a substance)

Answer to Connection to Social Studies

Students should find many discoveries from which to choose. Archimedes studied pulleys and levers, hydrostatics (the study of liquids at rest, especially in relation to storage tanks, dams, bulkheads, and hydraulic machinery), and parabolas and ellipses. He invented integral calculus, the Archimedes screw, Archimedes' claw, and perhaps the catapult.

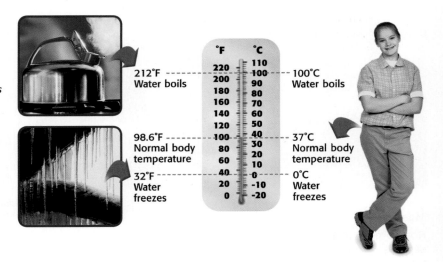

Figure 4 *This thermometer shows the relationship between degrees Fahrenheit and degrees Celsius.*

°F   °C
212°F   220   110   100°C
Water boils 200 100 Water boils
         180   90
         160   80
         140   70
         120   60
98.6°F   100   50   37°C
Normal body 80   40   Normal body
temperature 60   30   temperature
             40   20
32°F   40   0   0°C
Water   20   -10   Water
freezes 0   -20   freezes

temperature the measure of how hot (or cold) something is

density the ratio of the mass of a substance to the volume of the substance

CONNECTION TO
Social Studies

Archimedes (287 BCE–212 BCE) Archimedes was a Greek mathematician. He was probably the greatest mathematician and scientist that classical Greek civilization produced and is considered to be one of the greatest mathematicians of all time. Archimedes was very interested in putting his theoretical discoveries to practical use. Use the library or Internet to research Archimedes. Make a poster that illustrates one of his scientific or mathematical discoveries.

Temperature

How hot is melted iron? To answer this question, a scientist would measure the temperature of the liquid metal. **Temperature** is a measure of how hot or cold something is. You probably use degrees Fahrenheit (°F) to describe temperature. Scientists commonly use degrees Celsius (°C), although the kelvin (K) is the official SI base unit for temperature. You will use degrees Celsius in this book. The thermometer in **Figure 4** compares the Fahrenheit and Celsius scales.

Density

If you measure the mass and volume of an object, you have the measurements that you need to find the density of the object. **Density** is the amount of matter in a given volume. You cannot measure density directly. But after you have measured the mass and the volume, you can use the following equation to calculate density:

$$density = \frac{mass}{volume}$$

Density is the ratio of mass to volume, so units often used for density are grams per milliliter (g/mL) and grams per cubic centimeter (g/cm³). Density may be difficult to understand. Think of a table-tennis ball and a golf ball. They have similar volumes. But a golf ball has more mass than a table-tennis ball does. So the golf ball has a greater density.

MISCONCEPTION
ALERT

Mass Confusion Students may confuse density with mass or weight. Ask students the following question: "Which has more mass: 1 kg of feathers or 1 kg of lead?" If students answer that lead has more mass, remind them that the kilogram is a unit for mass, so the masses are the same. Density is mass in a given volume. Feathers are much less dense than lead is, so the volume of 1 kg of feathers is much larger than that of 1 kg of lead.

CONNECTION ACTiViTY
Art ——— BASIC

Draw It Have students create an illustrated dictionary of vocabulary terms that were used in this section. Some terms, such as *density* and *temperature,* may be challenging. Students can share their dictionaries with the rest of the class. [LS] Visual/Logical

Safety Rules!

Science is exciting and fun, but it can also be dangerous. Don't take any chances! Always follow your teacher's instructions. Don't take shortcuts—even when you think there is no danger. Before starting an experiment, get your teacher's permission. Read the lab procedures carefully. Pay special attention to safety information and caution statements. **Figure 5** shows the safety symbols used in this book. Get to know these symbols and their meanings. Do so by reading the safety information in the front of this book. **This is important!** If you are still unsure about what a safety symbol means, ask your teacher.

Reading Check Why are safety symbols important?

Figure 5 Safety Symbols

 Eye Protection

 Clothing Protection

 Hand Safety

Heating Safety

 Electric Safety

Sharp Object

Chemical Safety

Animal Safety

Plant Safety

SECTION Review

Summary

- Scientists use a variety of tools to measure and analyze the world around them.

- The International System of Units (SI) is a simple, reliable, and uniform system of measurement that is used by most scientists.

- The basic units of measurement in the SI are the meter (for length), the kilogram (for mass), and the Kelvin (for temperature).

- Before starting any science activity or science lab, review the safety symbols and the safety rules for that activity or lab. Don't take chances with your health and safety.

Using Key Terms

Complete each of the following sentences by choosing the correct term from the word bank.

mass	area
volume	temperature

1. A measure of the size of a surface or a region is called ___.

2. Scientists use kilograms when measuring an object's ___.

3. The ___ of a liquid is usually described in liters.

Understanding Key Ideas

4. SI units are
   a. based on standardized measurements of body parts.
   b. almost always based on the number 10.
   c. used to measure only length.
   d. used only in France.

5. What is temperature?

6. If you wanted to measure the mass of a fly, which SI unit would be most appropriate?

Math Skills

7. What is the area of a soccer field that is 110 m long and 85 m wide?

8. What is the density of silver if a 6 cm³ piece of silver has a mass of 63 g?

Critical Thinking

9. **Applying Concepts** Some people are thinking about sending humans to the moon and then to the planet Mars. Why is it important for scientists around the world to use the International System of Units as they make these plans?

10. **Making Inferences** Give an example of something that can happen if you do not follow safety rules.

11. **Applying Concepts** What tool would you use to measure the mass of the air in a basketball?

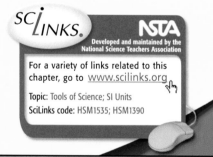

SCILINKS

NSTA
Developed and maintained by the National Science Teachers Association

For a variety of links related to this chapter, go to www.scilinks.org

Topic: Tools of Science; SI Units
SciLinks code: HSM1535; HSM1390

Answer to Reading Check

Safety symbols alert you to particular safety concerns or specific dangers in a lab.

CHAPTER RESOURCES

Chapter Resource File

- **Section Quiz** GENERAL
- **Section Review** GENERAL
- **Vocabulary and Section Summary** GENERAL
- **SciLinks Activity** GENERAL
- **Datasheet for Quick Lab**

Technology

- **Interactive Explorations CD-ROM**
  - **Something's Fishy** GENERAL

Workbooks

- **Science Skills**
  - **Safety Rules!** GENERAL

Alternative Assessment ——— GENERAL

Writing **More on Density** Because dense materials, such as rock, tend to sink, sometimes we forget that huge, seaworthy ships are made of very dense materials, such as steel. Ships have even been made of concrete. Have students conduct research on the Internet on any of the following topics:

- why ships float
- what materials have been used in the history of ship building
- how ships are designed
- how ships are constructed
- concrete-canoe competitions (held at many universities)

Students should report their findings in a short paper.

LS Verbal/Logical

Answers to Section Review

1. area
2. mass
3. volume
4. b
5. Temperature is a measure of how hot or cold something is.
6. the gram or the milligram
7. 110 m × 85 m = 9,350 m²
8. 63 g ÷ 6 cm³ = 10.5 g/cm³
9. Sample answer: The importance of the SI can be seen in space travel. If one person is using one system of measurements and another person is using a different system, one person might forget to indicate that he or she is using a different system. As a result, the spaceship could go way off course or could be traveling too fast to land safely.
10. Sample answer: You could get hurt by an unknown chemical.
11. The tool for measuring mass, even the mass of air, is a balance.

Does It All Add Up?

Teacher's Notes

Time Required

One 45-minute class period

Lab Ratings

EASY ————→ HARD

Teacher Prep 🧪🧪
Student Set-Up 🧪
Concept Level 🧪🧪
Clean Up 🧪

MATERIALS

The materials listed on the student page are enough for a group of 2–3 students. Prepare a jug of plain water labeled "Liquid A" and a jug of either isopropyl alcohol (2-propanol, $CH_3CH(OH)CH_3$) or denatured ethyl alcohol (95% ethanol, CH_3CH_2OH) labeled "Liquid B." Safety thermometers are recommended.

Safety Caution

Remind students to review all safety cautions and icons before beginning this lab activity. Caution students to handle thermometers with care and to treat all unknown chemicals as dangerous. Alcohol is flammable and poisonous. Students should wear goggles and aprons at all times. A fire extinguisher and fire blanket should be nearby. Know how to use them. The room should be well ventilated, and students should be familiar with evacuation procedures.

Kevin McCurdy
Elmwood Junior High School
Rogers, Arkansas

Does It All Add Up?

Your math teacher won't tell you this, but did you know that sometimes 2 + 2 does not appear to equal 4?! In this experiment, you will use scientific methods to predict, measure, and observe the mixing of two unknown liquids. You will learn that a scientist does not set out to prove a hypothesis but to test it and that sometimes the results just don't seem to add up!

Make Observations

1 Put on your safety goggles, gloves, and lab apron. Examine the beakers of liquids A and B provided by your teacher. Write down as many observations as you can about each liquid. **Caution:** Do not taste, touch, or smell the liquids.

2 Pour exactly 25 mL of liquid A from the beaker into each of two 50 mL graduated cylinders. Combine these samples in one of the graduated cylinders. Record the final volume. Pour the liquid back into the beaker of liquid A. Rinse the graduated cylinders. Repeat this step for liquid B.

Form a Hypothesis

3 Based on your observations and on prior experience, formulate a testable hypothesis that states what you expect the volume to be when you combine 25 mL of liquid A with 25 mL of liquid B.

4 Make a prediction based on your hypothesis. Use an if-then format. Explain the basis for your prediction.

OBJECTIVES

Apply scientific methods to predict, measure, and observe the mixing of two unknown liquids.

MATERIALS

- beakers, 100 mL (2)
- Celsius thermometer
- glass-labeling marker
- graduated cylinders, 50 mL (3)
- liquid A, 75 mL
- liquid B, 75 mL
- protective gloves

SAFETY

CHAPTER RESOURCES

Chapter Resource File

- **Datasheet for Chapter Lab**
- **Lab Notes and Answers**

Technology

Classroom Videos
- Lab Video

Data Table

	Contents of cylinder A	Contents of cylinder B	Mixing results: predictions	Mixing results: observations
Volume				
Appearance		DO NOT WRITE IN BOOK		
Temperature				

Test the Hypothesis

5 Make a data table like the one above.

6 Mark one graduated cylinder "A." Carefully pour exactly 25 mL of liquid A into this cylinder. In your data table, record its volume, appearance, and temperature.

7 Mark another graduated cylinder "B." Carefully pour exactly 25 mL of liquid B into this cylinder. Record its volume, appearance, and temperature in your data table.

8 Mark the empty third cylinder "A + B."

9 In the "Mixing results: predictions" column in your table, record the prediction you made earlier. Each classmate may have made a different prediction.

10 Carefully pour the contents of both cylinders into the third graduated cylinder.

11 Observe and record the total volume, appearance, and temperature in the "Mixing results: observations" column of your table.

Analyze the Results

1 **Analyzing Data** Discuss your predictions as a class. How many different predictions were there? Which predictions were supported by testing? Did any measurements surprise you?

Draw Conclusions

2 **Drawing Conclusions** Was your hypothesis supported or disproven? Either way, explain your thinking. Describe everything that you think you learned from this experiment.

3 **Analyzing Methods** Explain the value of incorrect predictions.

CHAPTER RESOURCES

Workbooks

Whiz-Bang Demonstrations
- Air Ball GENERAL
- Getting to the Point GENERAL

Inquiry Labs
- One Side or Two? GENERAL

Long-Term Projects & Research Ideas
- The Length of a Fethel ADVANCED

Disposal Informations

Set out a disposal container. Have students pour their water-alcohol mix and any alcohol they have left over into the container at the end of the procedure. Make sure the pH is between 5 and 9, dilute it with 10 times as much water, and pour it down the drain.

Lab Notes

Do not reveal the identity of the liquids until the end of the lab! In this lab, students will likely be surprised to discover that 25 mL of liquid A (water) plus 25 mL of liquid B (an alcohol) do not make 50 mL of the mixture. Spaces between molecules of alcohol become filled with water molecules, resulting in a lower total volume. The water-alcohol mixture will be cloudy and bubbly for a brief time after mixing and may emit some heat. Have students record observations until the mixture becomes clear and then make their final measurements and observations.

Try the following demonstration in order to model the mixing of water and alcohol molecules for your students. Mix 25 mL of marbles with 25 mL of round BB-gun pellets. The BBs will settle between the marbles, and the result will be a total volume less than 50 mL.

Analyze the Results

Note: All answers in this lab are based on student observations and may vary.

1. Students may make some unusual predictions. You may want to lead them into questions about volume. Encourage them to think of many ways to observe and characterize the two liquids. Avoid giving away the explanation too quickly.

Draw Conclusions

2. Check that students are clear about whether or not their hypothesis was supported and in what ways their observations supported or disproved their hypothesis.

3. Incorrect predictions can lead to new questions and a new understanding of the way things work.

Chapter Review

Assignment Guide

Section	Questions
1	13
2	2, 4, 7–8, 14, 19–22
3	3, 6, 15–17
4	5, 9–12, 18, 23–25
1 and 2	1

ANSWERS

Using Key Terms

1. Sample answer: You can use scientific methods to study science.

2. Sample answer: A variable is the only factor that should change during a controlled experiment.

3. Sample answer: A theory is an explanation for a broad range of observations and hypotheses. A hypothesis is an explanation for a specific set of observations and can be tested.

4. Sample answer: A controlled experiment tests one factor at a time by comparing a control group with an experimental group. A variable is a factor that changes in an experiment.

5. Sample answer: Area is a measure of a flat surface. Volume is a measure of space or size in three dimensions.

6. Sample answer: A physical model, such as a car, is a physical representation of an object, a real automobile. A conceptual model is a system of ideas. It may compare an idea with something familiar.

USING KEY TERMS

1. Use the following terms in the same sentence: *science* and *scientific methods*.

2. Use the following terms in the same sentence: *controlled experiment* and *variable*.

For each pair of terms, explain how the meanings of the terms differ.

3. *theory* and *hypothesis*

4. *controlled experiment* and *variable*

5. *area* and *volume*

6. *physical model* and *conceptual model*

UNDERSTANDING KEY IDEAS

Multiple Choice

7. The steps of scientific methods
   a. must all be used in every scientific investigation.
   b. must always be used in the same order.
   c. often start with a question.
   d. always result in the development of a theory.

8. In a controlled experiment,
   a. a control group is compared with one or more experimental groups.
   b. there are at least two variables.
   c. all factors should be different.
   d. a variable is not needed.

9. Which of the following tools is best for measuring 100 mL of water?
   a. 10 mL graduated cylinder
   b. 150 mL graduated cylinder
   c. 250 mL beaker
   d. 500 mL beaker

10. Which of the following is NOT an SI unit?
    a. meter
    b. foot
    c. liter
    d. kilogram

11. A pencil is 14 cm long. How many millimeters long is it?
    a. 1.4 mm
    b. 140 mm
    c. 1,400 mm
    d. 1,400,000 mm

12. The directions for a lab include the safety icons shown below. These icons mean that

   a. you should be careful.
   b. you are going into the laboratory.
   c. you should wash your hands first.
   d. you should wear safety goggles, a lab apron, and gloves during the lab.

Short Answer

13. List three ways that science is beneficial to living things.

14. Why do hypotheses need to be testable?

Understanding Key Ideas

7. c
8. a
9. b
10. b
11. b
12. d

13. Sample answer: Science can be used to find cures for diseases, to create new power sources, and to predict earthquakes.

14. Hypotheses need to be testable in order to be useful. If no information can be gathered to either support or disprove a hypothesis, the hypothesis is merely an idea that cannot be built upon scientifically.

15. Sample answer: A scientist studying animals might use a radio collar to track the animal's location, a computer database program to record data, and a computer mapping program to draw maps.

15 Give an example of how a scientist might use computers and technology.

16 List three types of models, and give an example of each.

17 What are some advantages and limitations of models?

18 Which SI units can be used to describe the volume of an object? Which SI units can be used to describe the mass of an object?

19 In a controlled experiment, why should there be several individuals in the control group and in each of the experimental groups?

CRITICAL THINKING

20 **Concept Mapping** Use the following terms to create a concept map: *observations, predictions, questions, controlled experiments, variable,* and *hypothesis.*

21 **Making Inferences** Investigations often begin with observation. What limits the observations that scientists can make?

22 **Forming Hypotheses** A scientist who studies mice makes the following observation: on the day the mice are fed vitamins with their meals, they perform better in mazes. What hypothesis would you form to explain this phenomenon? Write a testable prediction based on your hypothesis.

INTERPRETING GRAPHICS

The pictures below show how an egg can be measured by using a beaker and water. Use the pictures below to answer the questions that follow.

Before: 125 mL   After: 200 mL

23 What kind of measurement is being taken?

a. area

b. length

c. mass

d. volume

24 Which of the following is an accurate measurement of the egg in the picture?

a. 75 cm³

b. 125 cm³

c. 125 mL

d. 200 mL

25 Make a double line graph using the data in the table below.

Number of Frogs		
Date	Normal	Deformed
1995	25	0
1996	21	0
1997	19	1
1998	20	2
1999	17	3
2000	20	5

18. The SI units used to describe volume are liters (L), units based on the liter, and units based on the cubic meter. The SI units used to describe the mass of an object are kilograms (kg) and other units based on the gram.

19. The more individuals there are in the groups, the more confident scientists can be that differences between the groups were caused by the variable and not by natural differences between individual organisms.

Critical Thinking

20. 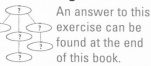 An answer to this exercise can be found at the end of this book.

21. Sample answer: Observations are limited by human senses or by technology. Things that cannot be observed may exist.

22. Sample answer: Vitamins help the mice remember the maze. A testable prediction might be "I predict that if I give some mice vitamins before they run the maze and I do not give vitamins to other mice before they run the maze, the mice who get the vitamins will perform better on the maze.

Interpreting Graphics

23. d

24. a
(200 mL − 125 mL = 75 mL = 75 cm³)

25. See the graph below.

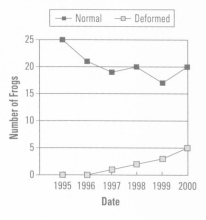

16. Sample answer: Physical models include toys and a model of a cell or a human body. Mathematical models include a Punnett square and equations to calculate physical forces. Conceptual models include theories about how the solar system formed or how life evolved on Earth.

17. Sample answer: advantages of models: they are easier to see and manipulate than the real thing might be, and they can simplify concepts; limitations: models do not behave exactly like the real thing, so they may not accurately predict results

Standardized Test Preparation

EOG Prep

READING

Passage 1

1. C
2. F
3. C

 TEST DOCTOR

Question 2: Answering this question correctly requires the reader to pick up context clues from the sentence and yet not overgeneralize the contents of the entire passage. In the first sentence in which the word *naturalist* is used, the person is strongly associated with both animals and plants, supporting answer F. The second use of the word *naturalist* is associated with the word *theory* (answer H), but a specific theory is named, so the association is not strong.

READING

Read each of the passages below. Then, answer the questions that follow the passage.

Passage 1 Zoology is the study of animals. Zoology dates back more than 2,300 years, to ancient Greece. There, the philosopher Aristotle observed and theorized about animal behavior. About 200 years later, Galen, a Greek physician, began dissecting and experimenting with animals. However, there were few advances in zoology until the 1700s and 1800s. During this period, the Swedish <u>naturalist</u> Carolus Linnaeus developed a classification system for plants and animals, and British naturalist Charles Darwin published his theory of evolution by natural selection.

1. According to the passage, when did major advances in Zoology begin?
   - **A** About 2,300 years ago
   - **B** About 2,100 years ago
   - **C** During the 1700s and 1800s
   - **D** Only during recent history

2. Which of the following is a possible meaning of the word *naturalist,* as used in the passage?
   - **F** a scientist who studies plants and animals
   - **G** a scientist who studies animals
   - **H** a scientist who studies theory
   - **I** a scientist who studies animal behavior

3. Which of the following is the **best** title for this passage?
   - **A** Greek Zoology
   - **B** Modern Zoology
   - **C** The Origins of Zoology
   - **D** Zoology in the 1700s and 1800s

Passage 2 When looking for answers to a problem, scientists build on existing knowledge. For example, scientists have wondered if there is some relationship between Earth's core and Earth's magnetic field. To form a hypothesis, scientists started with what they knew: Earth has a dense, solid inner core and a molten outer core. Scientists then created a computer <u>model</u> to simulate how Earth's magnetic field might be generated.

They tried different things with their model until the model produced a magnetic field that matched that of the real Earth. The model predicted that Earth's inner core spins in the same direction as the rest of the Earth, but the inner core spins slightly faster than Earth's surface. If the hypothesis is correct, it might explain how Earth's magnetic field is produced. Although scientists cannot reach the Earth's core to examine it directly, they can test whether other observations match what is predicted by their hypothesis.

1. What does the word *model* refer to in this passage?
   - **A** a giant plastic globe
   - **B** a representation of the Earth created on a computer
   - **C** a computer terminal
   - **D** a technology used to drill into the Earth's core

2. Which of the following is the **best** summary of the passage?
   - **F** Scientists can use models to help them answer difficult and complex questions.
   - **G** Scientists have discovered the source of Earth's magnetic field.
   - **H** The spinning of Earth's molten inner core causes Earth's magnetic field.
   - **I** Scientists make a model of a problem and then ask questions about the problem.

Passage 2

1. B
2. F

 **TEST DOCTOR**

Question 2: Answer F is correct. The question requires the reader to choose the statement that best encompasses all of the ideas presented in the passage. Answers G and H state information that was presented in the passage, but in these cases the information was supporting detail and not the focus of the passage. Answer I is sounds a little like the passage but is actually just the opposite of the steps described in the passage. For this type of question, suggest that students look for the answer that best tells the "story" of the passage.

The table below shows the plans for an experiment in which bees will be observed visiting flowers. Use the table to answer the questions that follow.

Bee Experiment				
Group	Type of bee	Time of day	Type of plant	Flower color
#1	Honey-bee	9:00 A.M.– 10:00 A.M.	Portland rose	red
#2	Honey-bee	9:00 A.M.– 10:00 A.M.	Portland rose	yellow
#3	Honey-bee	9:00 A.M.– 10:00 A.M.	Portland rose	white
#4	Honey-bee	9:00 A.M.– 10:00 A.M.	Portland rose	pink

1. Which factor is the variable in this experiment?
  A the type of bee
  B the time of day
  C the type of plant
  D the color of the flowers

2. Which of the following hypotheses could be tested by this experiment?
  F Honeybees prefer to visit rose plants.
  G Honeybees prefer to visit red flowers.
  H Honeybees prefer to visit flowers in the morning.
  I Honey bees prefer to visit Portland rose flowers between 9 and 10 A.M.

3. Which of the following is the **best** reason why the Portland rose plant is included in all of the groups to be studied?
  A The type of plant is a control factor; any type of flowering plant could be used as long as all plants were of the same type.
  B The experiment will test whether bees prefer the Portland rose over other flowers.
  C An experiment should always have more than one variable.
  D The Portland rose is a very common plant.

Read each question below, and choose the best answer.

1. A survey of students was conducted to find out how many people were in each student's family. The replies from five students were as follows: 3, 3, 4, 4, and 6. What was the average family size?
  A 3
  B 3.5
  C 4
  D 5

2. In the survey above, if one more student were surveyed, which reply would make the average lower?
  F 3
  G 4
  H 5
  I 6

3. If an object that is 5 μm long were magnified by 1,000, how long would that object then appear?
  A 5 μm
  B 5 mm
  C 1,000 μm
  D 5,000 mm

4. How many meters are in 50 km?
  F 50 m
  G 500 m
  H 5,000 m
  I 50,000 m

5. What is the area of a square whose sides measure 4 m each?
  A 16 m
  B 16 m²
  C 32 m
  D 32 m²

Standardized Test Preparation

Chapter Resource File

• **Standardized Test Preparation** GENERAL

Workbooks

North Carolina Standardized Test Preparation
• Provides practice for the EOG test.

State Resources

For specific resources for your state, visit **go.hrw.com** and type in the keyword **HSMSTR**.

1. D
2. G
3. A

TEST DOCTOR

Question 1: This question requires students to understand the meaning of the term *variable* for a scientific experiment. The variable should be the one factor that varies in the experiment. The table indicates that the type of bee (answer A), the time of day (answer B), and the type of plant (answer C) were the same for all groups and thus could not be the variable.

1. C
2. F
3. B
4. I
5. B

TEST DOCTOR

Question 2: To answer this question, the student could recalculate the average for each of the possible values. There is also a shortcut: because the average is already 4, the only value that would lower the average would be one that is less than 4. Regardless of the method, remind students to check their answer by recalculating with their chosen value to ensure that their answer meets the requirements.

Question 3: This question merely requires knowledge of the standard prefixes used in SI. The symbol *μ* represents the prefix *micro-* and indicates 1/1,000,000th; the symbol *m* represents the prefix *milli-* and indicates 1/1,000th. Thus, 1 μm is 1/1,000th of 1 mm and 5 μm × 1,000 = 5 mm. Many standardized tests provide a table of SI units and conversions for reference during the test.

Scientific Debate

Background

There are three main ingredients of a fire: oxygen, heat, and fuel. Firefighters call this the *fire triangle*, and their goal is to eliminate at least one ingredient. Two groups of firefighters are sent into a forest fire: *hotshots* and *smokejumpers*. Hotshots build a *firebreak* in order to stop the spread of the fire. They clear an area of land of anything that could become fuel for the fire, such as trees, bushes, and grass. The smokejumpers jump from airplanes into remote places to fight small blazes or to start *backfires* in order to eliminate fuel from an oncoming fire.

Science Fiction

ACTIVITY ——————— **GENERAL**

Further Reading If students liked this story, recommend other stories by Edward D. Hoch, such as the following:

- *The Monkey's Clue*
- *The Stolen Sapphire*
- *The Night, My Friend: Stories of Crime & Suspense*

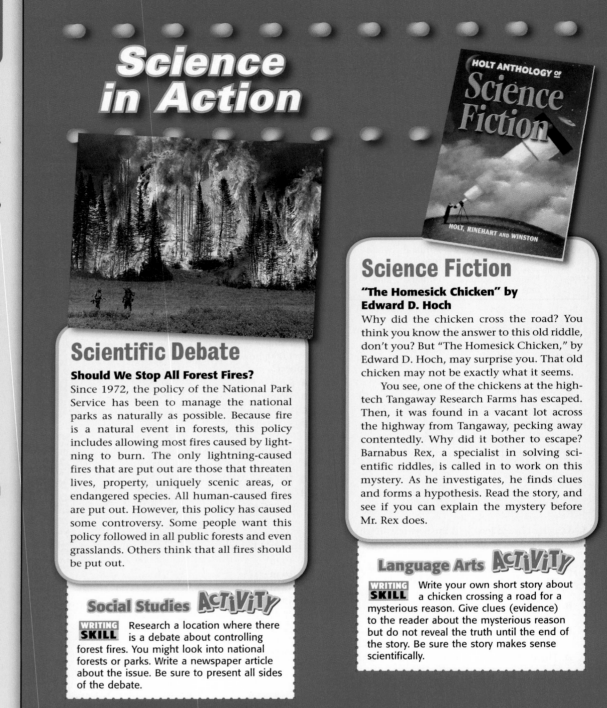

Science in Action

HOLT ANTHOLOGY OF
Science Fiction

HOLT, RINEHART AND WINSTON

Scientific Debate

Should We Stop All Forest Fires?

Since 1972, the policy of the National Park Service has been to manage the national parks as naturally as possible. Because fire is a natural event in forests, this policy includes allowing most fires caused by lightning to burn. The only lightning-caused fires that are put out are those that threaten lives, property, uniquely scenic areas, or endangered species. All human-caused fires are put out. However, this policy has caused some controversy. Some people want this policy followed in all public forests and even grasslands. Others think that all fires should be put out.

Social Studies ACTIVITY

WRITING SKILL Research a location where there is a debate about controlling forest fires. You might look into national forests or parks. Write a newspaper article about the issue. Be sure to present all sides of the debate.

Science Fiction

"The Homesick Chicken" by Edward D. Hoch

Why did the chicken cross the road? You think you know the answer to this old riddle, don't you? But "The Homesick Chicken," by Edward D. Hoch, may surprise you. That old chicken may not be exactly what it seems.

You see, one of the chickens at the high-tech Tangaway Research Farms has escaped. Then, it was found in a vacant lot across the highway from Tangaway, pecking away contentedly. Why did it bother to escape? Barnabus Rex, a specialist in solving scientific riddles, is called in to work on this mystery. As he investigates, he finds clues and forms a hypothesis. Read the story, and see if you can explain the mystery before Mr. Rex does.

Language Arts ACTIVITY

WRITING SKILL Write your own short story about a chicken crossing a road for a mysterious reason. Give clues (evidence) to the reader about the mysterious reason but do not reveal the truth until the end of the story. Be sure the story makes sense scientifically.

Answer to Social Studies Activity

Student articles should reflect objective, journalistic style and present more than one perspective on the issue. Encourage students to research areas that are close to where they live.

Answer to Language Arts Activity

Student stories should include logical clues and have a logical ending. Encourage students to read each other's stories and give each other feedback on the use of scientific reasoning in the story.

People in Science

Matthew Henson

Arctic Explorer Matthew Henson was born in Maryland in 1866. His parents were freeborn sharecroppers. When Henson was a young boy, his parents died. He then went to look for work as a cabin boy on a ship. Several years later, Henson had traveled around the world and had become educated in the areas of geography, history, and mathematics. In 1898, Henson met U.S. Naval Lieutenant Robert E. Peary. Peary was the leader of Arctic expeditions between 1886 and 1909.

Peary asked Henson to accompany him as a navigator on several trips, including trips to Central America and Greenland. One of Peary's passions was to be the first person to reach the North Pole. It was Henson's vast knowledge of mathematics and carpentry that made Peary's trek to the North Pole possible. In 1909, Henson was the first person to reach the North Pole. Part of Henson's job as navigator was to drive ahead of the party and blaze the first trail. As a result, he often arrived ahead of everyone else. On April 6, 1909, Henson reached the approximate North Pole 45 minutes ahead of Peary. Upon his arrival, he exclaimed, "I think I'm the first man to sit on top of the world!"

Math Activity

On the last leg of their journey, Henson and Peary traveled 664.5 km in 16 days! On average, how far did Henson and Peary travel each day?

To learn more about these Science in Action topics, visit go.hrw.com and type in the keyword **HZ5SW7F**.

Check out Current Science® articles related to this chapter by visiting go.hrw.com. Just type in the keyword HZ5CS01.

Answer to Math Activity
664.5 km ÷ 16 days = 41.53 km/day.

People in Science

Background

Apart from enduring subfreezing temperatures, sudden snowstorms, and slow starvation, Peary's team had to deal with the unique conditions of ice sheets that cover the Arctic Ocean. Movements of water currents under the ice cause constant changes on its surface. These changes include "pressure ridges," or small, steep mountains of ice that well up on the surface, and "leads," or open lanes of water caused from drifts or rents in the ice. Twice, Henson saved Peary's life by pulling him out of the freezing water of a suddenly formed lead.

Activity ———— GENERAL

The Explorers Club has been an international meeting place for explorers and scientists since 1904. Some of the most famous and influential field researchers in the world have been invited to join its ranks. Have students research past members of this organization. Then, have them plot on a map all the places these members have explored or discovered. (Students will find that some of the famous members of the Explorers Club include Tenzing Norgay and Sir Edmund Hillary, the first people to climb Mount Everest, Theodore Roosevelt, 26th President and founding member, Roald Amundsen, the first to reach the South Pole and sail the Northwest Passage, Herbert Hoover, 34th President, and Richard Byrd, the first aviator to fly over the Antarctic.)

LS Logical

UNIT

1

TIMELINE

The Atmosphere, Weather, and Climate

In this unit, you will learn about Earth's atmosphere, including how it affects conditions on the Earth's surface. The constantly changing weather is always a good topic for conversation, but forecasting the weather is not an easy task. Climate, on the other hand, is much more predictable. This timeline shows some of the events that have occurred as scientists have tried to better understand Earth's atmosphere, weather, and climate.

1281

A sudden typhoon destroys a fleet of Mongolian ships about to reach Japan. This "divine wind," or *kamikaze* in Japanese, saves the country from invasion and conquest.

1778

Carl Scheele concludes that air is mostly made of nitrogen and oxygen.

1838

John James Audubon publishes *The Birds of America.*

1974

Chlorofluorocarbons (CFCs) are recognized as harmful to the ozone layer.

1982

Weather information becomes available 24 hours a day, 7 days a week, on commercial TV.

1655

Saturn's rings are recognized as such. Galileo Galilei had seen them in 1610, but his telescope was not strong enough to show that they were rings.

1718

Gabriel Fahrenheit builds the first mercury thermometer.

1749

Benjamin Franklin explains how updrafts of air are caused by the sun's heating of the local atmosphere.

1920

Serbian scientist Milutin Milankovitch determines that over tens of thousands of years, changes in the Earth's motion through space have profound effects on climate.

1945

The first atmospheric test of an atomic bomb takes place near Alamogordo, New Mexico.

1985

Scientists discover an ozone hole over Antarctica.

1986

The world's worst nuclear accident takes place at Chernobyl, Ukraine, and spreads radiation through the atmosphere as far as the western United States.

1999

The first nonstop balloon trip around the world is successfully completed when Brian Jones and Bertrand Piccard land in Egypt.

2003

A record 393 tornadoes are observed in the United States during one week in May.

The path of radioactive material released from Chernobyl

The Breitling Orbiter 3 lands in Egypt on March 21, 1999.

The Atmosphere
Chapter Planning Guide

Compression guide:
To shorten instruction because of time limitations, omit the Chapter Lab.

OBJECTIVES	LABS, DEMONSTRATIONS, AND ACTIVITIES	TECHNOLOGY RESOURCES
PACING • 90 min pp. 38–45 **Chapter Opener**	**SE** Start-up Activity, p. 39 ◆ GENERAL **TR** Chapter Starter Transparency* **VID** Brain Food Video Quiz	**OSP** Parent Letter GENERAL **CD** Student Edition on CD-ROM **CD** Guided Reading Audio CD
Section 1 Characteristics of the Atmosphere • Describe the composition of Earth's atmosphere. • Explain why air pressure changes with altitude. • Explain how air temperature changes with atmospheric composition. • Describe the layers of the atmosphere.	**SE** Connection to Physics Air-Pressure Experiment, p. 41 GENERAL **TE** Group Activity It's a Gas!, p. 41 ◆ ADVANCED **SE** Skills Practice Lab Under Pressure! p. 66 ◆ GENERAL **CRF** Datasheet for Chapter Lab* **LB** Whiz-Bang Demonstrations Blue Sky* ◆ ADVANCED	**CRF** Lesson Plans* **TR** Bellringer Transparency* **TR** Layers of the Atmosphere* **TR** LINK TO LIFE SCIENCE The Connection Between Photosynthesis and Respiration* **VID** Lab Videos for Earth Science
PACING • 90 min pp. 46–49 **Section 2 Atmospheric Heating** • Describe what happens to solar energy that reaches Earth. • Summarize the processes of radiation, conduction, and convection. • Explain the relationship between the greenhouse effect and global warming.	**TE** Connection to Environmental Science, p. 47 ◆ GENERAL **TE** Group Activity Model Greenhouses, p. 48 ◆ BASIC **LB** Inquiry Labs Boiling Over!* GENERAL **LB** EcoLabs & Field Activities That Greenhouse Effect!* ◆ GENERAL **LB** Calculator-Based Lab The Greenhouse Effect* ADVANCED **LB** Calculator-Based Lab Heating of Land and Water* ◆ ADVANCED	**CRF** Lesson Plans* **TR** Bellringer Transparency* **TR** Scattering, Absorption, and Reflection* **TR** Radiation, Conduction, and Convection* **TR** The Greenhouse Effect*
PACING • 45 min pp. 50–55 **Section 3 Global Winds and Local Winds** • Explain the relationship between air pressure and wind direction. • Describe global wind patterns. • Explain the causes of local wind patterns.	**TE** Demonstration Air Movement, p. 50 GENERAL **TE** Activity Coriolis Effect, p. 52 ◆ BASIC **SE** Connection to Social Studies Local Breezes, p. 55 GENERAL **SE** Skills Practice Lab Go Fly a Bike!, p. 582 GENERAL **CRF** Datasheet for LabBook* **SE** Science in Action Math, Social Studies, and Language Arts, pp. 72–73 GENERAL	**CRF** Lesson Plans* **TR** Bellringer Transparency* **TR** Pressure Belts* **TR** The Coriolis Effect* **TR** Global Winds* **TR** Sea and Land Breezes*
PACING • 45 min pp. 56–61 **Section 4 Air Pollution** • Compare primary and secondary air pollutants. • Identify point-sources and nonpoint-sources of air pollution in North Carolina. • Identify sources of human-caused air pollution. • Describe how acid precipitation affects the environment.	**SE** Connection to Biology Cleaning the Air with Plants, p. 58 GENERAL **TE** Connection Activity Real World, p. 58 GENERAL **SE** Quick Lab Testing for Particulates, p. 59 GENERAL **TE** Demonstration Acid Rain, p. 59 BASIC **SE** Quick Lab Neutralizing Acid Precipitation, p. 60 GENERAL **LB** Long-Term Projects & Research Ideas A Breath of Fresh Ether?* ADVANCED	**CRF** Lesson Plans* **TR** Bellringer Transparency* **TR** The Formation of Smog* **TR** Sources of Indoor Air Pollution* **CD** Interactive Explorations CD-ROM Moose Malady GENERAL
PACING • 45 min pp. 62–65 **Section 5 Maintaining Air Quality** • List three effects of air pollution on the human body. • Describe how air quality is monitored and measured. • Describe how air quality is communicated to the public. • Identify ways to reduce air pollution.	**TE** Connection Activity Health, p. 62 GENERAL **SE** Connection to Environmental Science The Ozone Hole, p. 63 GENERAL **TE** Activity Air Quaity Index, p. 63 GENERAL **TE** Demonstration Guest Speaker, p. 63 GENERAL **TE** Internet Activity, p. 64 GENERAL	**CRF** Lesson Plans* **TR** Bellringer Transparency* **CRF** SciLinks Activity* GENERAL

PACING • 90 min

CHAPTER REVIEW, ASSESSMENT, AND STANDARDIZED TEST PREPARATION

CRF Vocabulary Activity* GENERAL
SE Chapter Review, pp. 68–69 GENERAL
CRF Chapter Review* ▮▮ GENERAL
CRF Chapter Tests A* ▮▮ GENERAL, B* ADVANCED, C* SPECIAL NEEDS
SE Standardized Test Preparation, pp. 70–71 GENERAL
CRF Standardized Test Preparation* GENERAL
CRF Performance-Based Assessment* GENERAL
OSP Test Generator GENERAL
CRF Test Item Listing* GENERAL

Online and Technology Resources

Visit **go.hrw.com** for a variety of free resources related to this textbook. Enter the keyword **HT5R7TAM**.

Holt Online Learning

Students can access interactive problem-solving help and active visual concept development with the *Holt Science and Technology* Online Edition available at **www.hrw.com**.

Guided Reading Audio CD

These CDs are designed to help auditory learners and reluctant readers.

Science Tutor CD-ROM

Excellent for remediation and test practice.

SKILLS DEVELOPMENT RESOURCES	SECTION REVIEW AND ASSESSMENT	STANDARDS CORRELATIONS
SE Pre-Reading Activity, p. 38 `GENERAL` **OSP** Science Puzzlers, Twisters & Teasers `GENERAL`		North Carolina Standard Course of Study
CRF Directed Reading A* `BASIC`, B* `SPECIAL NEEDS` **CRF** Vocabulary and Section Summary* `GENERAL` **SE** Reading Strategy Mnemonics, p. 40 `GENERAL` **TE** Reading Strategy Reading Organizer, p. 41 `BASIC` **SE** Math Practice Modeling the Atmosphere, p. 42 `GENERAL` **TE** Inclusion Strategies, p. 43 **CRF** Reinforcement Worksheet Earth's Amazing Atmosphere* `BASIC`	**SE** Reading Checks, pp. 40, 42, 44 `GENERAL` **TE** Reteaching, p. 44 `BASIC` **TE** Quiz, p. 44 `GENERAL` **TE** Alternative Assessment, p. 44 `GENERAL` **SE** Section Review,* p. 45 ■ `GENERAL` **CRF** Section Quiz* ■ `GENERAL`	3.01, *Chapter Lab:* 1.02
CRF Directed Reading A* `BASIC`, B* `SPECIAL NEEDS` **CRF** Vocabulary and Section Summary* `GENERAL` **SE** Reading Strategy Reading Organizer, p. 46 `GENERAL` **TE** Inclusion Strategies, p. 47 ◆	**SE** Reading Checks, pp. 47, 49 `GENERAL` **TE** Reteaching, p. 48 `BASIC` **TE** Quiz, p. 48 `GENERAL` **TE** Alternative Assessment, p. 48 `GENERAL` **SE** Section Review,* p. 49 ■ `GENERAL` **CRF** Section Quiz* ■ `GENERAL`	
CRF Directed Reading A* `BASIC`, B* `SPECIAL NEEDS` **CRF** Vocabulary and Section Summary* `GENERAL` **SE** Reading Strategy Prediction Guide, p. 50 `GENERAL`	**SE** Reading Checks, pp. 51, 52, 55 `GENERAL` **TE** Homework, p. 52 `GENERAL` **TE** Reteaching, p. 54 `BASIC` **TE** Quiz, p. 54 `GENERAL` **TE** Alternative Assessment, p. 54 ◆ `GENERAL` **SE** Section Review,* p. 55 ■ `GENERAL` **CRF** Section Quiz* ■ `GENERAL`	*Science in Action:* 2.03
CRF Directed Reading A* `BASIC`, B* `SPECIAL NEEDS` **CRF** Vocabulary and Section Summary* `GENERAL` **SE** Reading Strategy Reading Organizer, p. 56 `GENERAL` **CRF** Critical Thinking The Extraordinary GBG5K* `ADVANCED`	**SE** Reading Checks, pp. 56, 59, 60 `GENERAL` **TE** Reteaching, p. 60 `BASIC` **TE** Quiz, p. 60 `GENERAL` **TE** Alternative Assessment, p. 60 `BASIC` **SE** Section Review,* p. 61 ■ `GENERAL` **CRF** Section Quiz* ■ `GENERAL`	3.02, 3.04
CRF Directed Reading A* `BASIC`, B* `SPECIAL NEEDS` **CRF** Vocabulary and Section Summary* `GENERAL` **SE** Reading Strategy Reading Organizer, p. 62 `GENERAL`	**SE** Reading Checks, pp. 62, 65 `GENERAL` **TE** Reteaching, p. 64 `BASIC` **TE** Quiz, p. 64 `GENERAL` **TE** Alternative Assessment, p. 64 `BASIC` **SE** Section Review,* p. 65 ■ `GENERAL` **CRF** Section Quiz* ■ `GENERAL`	2.01, 2.02, 2.03 204, 3.03, 3.04

One-Stop Planner® CD-ROM

This convenient CD-ROM includes:
- **Lab Materials QuickList Software**
- **Holt Calendar Planner**
- **Customizable Lesson Plans**
- **Printable Worksheets**
- **ExamView® Test Generator**

cnnstudentnews.com

Find the latest news, lesson plans, and activities related to important scientific events.

www.scilinks.org

Maintained by the **National Science Teachers Association**. See Chapter Enrichment pages for a complete list of topics.

Check out *Current Science* articles and activities by visiting the HRW Web site at **go.hrw.com.** Just type in the keyword **HZ5CS15T.**

Classroom Videos

- **Lab Videos** demonstrate the chapter lab.
- **Brain Food Video Quizzes** help students review the chapter material.
- **CNN Videos** bring science into your students' daily life.

Visual Resources

CHAPTER STARTER TRANSPARENCY

This Really Happened!

On August 17, 1998, Steve Fossett was well on his way to making the first around-the-world balloon flight. It was his fourth attempt, and after 10 days and 22,910 km, he had already traveled two-thirds of the way. At the time, this was farther than any other balloonist had traveled in history. But something happened in the dark morning hours that ended Fossett's flight and nearly cost him his life.

While floating over the Pacific Ocean at 8,839 m above sea level, Fossett noticed a row of thunderstorms below. Suddenly his balloon, the *Solo Spirit*, hit an unexpected air disturbance and was sucked downward at a rate of more than 420 km/h. Knowing he was in danger, Fossett climbed out of his bubble hatch

and cut loose the heavy tanks of fuel and oxygen to slow the balloon's fall. He then prepared himself for the crash.

When Fossett regained consciousness, his capsule was upside down, half full of water, and on fire. With a satellite radio beacon to give his location and a small life boat, Fossett scrambled out of the capsule to await his rescue.

Fossett experienced firsthand how unpredictable our atmosphere can be. He was fortunate to have survived. The atmosphere can be unpredictable and dangerous, but it also provides us with gases needed for our survival on Earth. In this chapter you will learn how the Earth's atmosphere affects you and how you affect it.

BELLRINGER TRANSPARENCIES

Section: Characteristics of the Atmosphere
List the ways that the atmosphere is different from outer space.

Write your list in your **science journal.**

Section: Atmospheric Heating
How is food heated in an oven? How is food heated on a range top?

Record your response in your **science journal.**

TEACHING TRANSPARENCIES

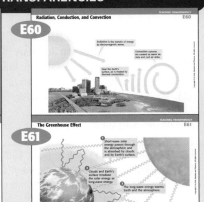

E58 — Layers of the Atmosphere

E59 — Scattering, Absorption, and Reflection

E60 — Radiation, Conduction, and Convection

E61 — The Greenhouse Effect

TEACHING TRANSPARENCIES

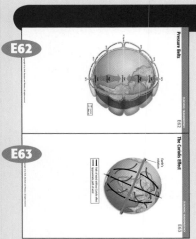

E62 — Pressure Belts

E63 — The Coriolis Effect

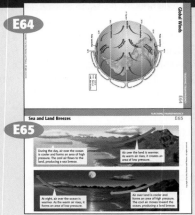

E64 — Global Winds

E65 — Sea and Land Breezes

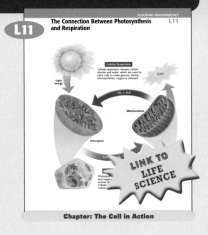

L11 — **The Connection Between Photosynthesis and Respiration**

Chapter: The Cell in Action

CONCEPT MAPPING TRANSPARENCY

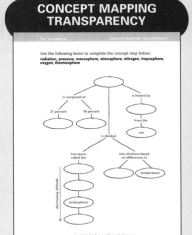

Use the following terms to complete the concept map below:
radiation, pressure, mesosphere, atmosphere, nitrogen, troposphere, oxygen, thermosphere

Planning Resources

LESSON PLANS

Lesson Plan SAMPLE

Section: Waves

Pacing
Regular Schedule: with lab(s)2 days without lab(s)2 days
Block Schedule: with lab(s) 1 1/2 days without lab(s)1 day

Objectives
1. Relate the seven properties of life to a living organism.
2. Describe seven themes that can help you to organize what you learn about biology.
3. Identify the tiny structures that make up all living organisms.
4. Differentiate between reproduction and heredity and between metabolism and homeostasis.

National Science Education Standards Covered
LSInter6:Cells have particular structures that underlie their functions.
LSMat1:Most cell functions involve chemical reactions.
LSBeh1:Cells store and use information to guide their functions.
UCP1:Cell functions are regulated.
SI1: Cells can differentiate and form complete multicellular organisms.
PS1: Species evolve over time.
ESS1: The great diversity of organisms is the result of more than 3.5 billion years of evolution.
ESS2: Natural selection and its evolutionary consequences provide a scientific explanation for the fossil record of ancient life forms as well as for the striking molecular similarities observed among the diverse species of living organisms.
ST1: The millions of different species of plants, animals, and microorganisms that live on Earth today are related by descent from common ancestors.
ST2: The energy for life primarily comes from the sun.
SPSP1: The complexity and organization of organisms accommodates the need for obtaining, transforming, transporting, releasing, and eliminating the matter and energy used to sustain the organism.
SPSP6: As matter and energy flows through different levels of organization of living systems—cells, organs, communities—and between living systems and the physical environment, chemical elements are recombined in different ways.
HNS1: Organisms have behavioral responses to internal changes and to external stimuli.

PARENT LETTER

SAMPLE

Dear Parent,

Your son's or daughter's science class will soon begin exploring the chapter entitled "The World of Physical Science." In this chapter, students will learn about how the scientific method applies to the world of physical science and the role of physical science in the world. By the end of the chapter, students should demonstrate a clear understanding of the chapter's main ideas and be able to discuss the following topics:

1. physical science as the study of energy and matter (Section 1)
2. the role of physical science in the world around them (Section 1)
3. careers that rely on physical science (Section 1)
4. the steps used in the scientific method (Section 2)
5. examples of technology (Section 2)
6. how the scientific method is used to answer questions and solve problems (Section 2)
7. how your knowledge of science changes over time (Section 2)
8. how models represent real objects or systems (Section 3)
9. examples of different ways models are used in science (Section 3)
10. the importance of the International System of Units (Section 4)
11. the appropriate units to use for particular measurements (Section 4)
12. how area and density are derived quantities (Section 4)

Questions to Ask Along the Way

You can help your son or daughter learn about these topics by asking interesting questions such as the following:

• What are some surprising careers that use physical science?
• What is a characteristic of a good hypothesis?
• When is it a good idea to use a model?
• Why do Americans measure things in terms of inches and yards instead of centimeters and meters?

TEST ITEM LISTING

TEST ITEM LISTING
The World of Earth Science SAMPLE

MULTIPLE CHOICE

1. A limitation of models is that
   a. they are large enough to see.
   b. they do not act exactly like the things that they model.
   c. they are smaller than the things that they model.
   d. they model unfamiliar things.
   Answer: B Difficulty: 1 Section: 3 Objective: 2

2. The length 10 m is equal to
   a. 100 cm. c. 10,000 mm.
   b. 1,000 cm. d. Both (b) and (c)
   Answer: D Difficulty: 1 Section: 3 Objective: 2

3. To be valid, a hypothesis must be
   a. testable. c. made into a law.
   b. supported by evidence. d. Both (a) and (b)
   Answer: B Difficulty: 1 Section: 3 Objective: 2

4. The statement "Sheila has a stain on her shirt" is an example of a(n)
   a. law. c. observation.
   b. hypothesis. d. prediction.
   Answer: S Difficulty: 1 Section: 3 Objective: 2 1

5. A hypothesis is often developed out of
   a. observations. c. laws.
   b. experiments. d. Both (a) and (b)
   Answer: B Difficulty: 1 Section: 3 Objective: 2

6. How many milliliters are in 3.5 kL?
   a. 3,500 mL. c. 3,500, 000 mL.
   b. 0.0035 mL. d. 35,000 mL.
   Answer: C Difficulty: 1 Section: 3 Objective: 2

7. A map of Seattle is an example of a
   a. law. c. model.
   b. theory. d. unit.
   Answer: C Difficulty: 1 Section: 3 Objective: 2

8. A lab has the safety icons shown below. These icons mean that you should wear
   a. only safety goggles. c. safety goggles and a lab apron.
   b. only a lab apron. d. safety goggles, a lab apron, and gloves.
   Answer: D Difficulty: 1 Section: 3 Objective: 2

9. The law of conservation of mass says the the al mass before a chemical change is
   a. more than the total mass after the change.
   b. less than the total mass after the change.
   c. the same as the total mass after the change.
   d. not the same as the total mass after the change.
   Answer: C Difficulty: 1 Section: 3 Objective: 2

10. In which of the following areas might you find a geochemist at work?
    a. studying the chemistry of rocks. c. studying fishes
    b. studying forestry d. studying the chemistry
    Answer: B Difficulty: 1 Section: 3 Objective: 2

 One-Stop Planner® CD-ROM

This CD-ROM includes all of the resources shown here and the following time-saving tools:

• *Lab Materials QuickList Software*
• *Customizable lesson plans*
• *Holt Calendar Planner*
• *The powerful ExamView® Test Generator*

Meeting Individual Needs

DIRECTED READING A

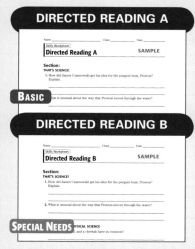

Skills Worksheet
Directed Reading A   SAMPLE

Section:
THAT'S SCIENCE!
1. How did James Czarnowski get his idea for the penguin boat, Proteus? Explain.

What is unusual about the way that Proteus moves through the water?

BASIC

DIRECTED READING B

Skills Worksheet
Directed Reading B   SAMPLE

Section:
THAT'S SCIENCE!
1. How did James Czarnowski get his idea for the penguin boat, Proteus? Explain.

2. What is unusual about the way that Proteus moves through the water?

SPECIAL NEEDS   PHYSICAL SCIENCE

VOCABULARY ACTIVITY

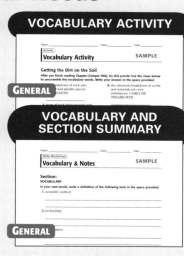

Activity
Vocabulary Activity   SAMPLE

Getting the Dirt on the Soil
After you finish reading Chapter: [Unique Title], try this puzzle! Use the clues below to unscramble the vocabulary words. Write your answer in the space provided.

9. the chemical breakdown of rocks and minerals into new substances: CAMILCHE THEARIGWEN

GENERAL

VOCABULARY AND SECTION SUMMARY

Skills Worksheet
Vocabulary & Notes   SAMPLE

Section:
VOCABULARY
In your own words, write a definition of the following term in the space provided.
1. scientific method

2. technology

GENERAL

REINFORCEMENT

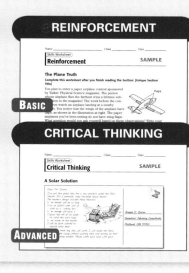

Skills Worksheet
Reinforcement   SAMPLE

The Plane Truth
Complete this worksheet after you finish reading the Section: [Unique Section Title]

You plan to enter a paper airplane contest sponsored by Talkin' Physical Science magazine. The person whose airplane flies the farthest wins a lifetime subscription to the magazine! The week before the contest, you watch an airplane landing at a nearby airport. You notice that the wings of the airplane have flaps, as shown in the illustration at right. The paper airplanes you've been testing do not have these flaps. What question would you ask yourself based on these observations? Write your

Flaps

BASIC

CRITICAL THINKING

Skills Worksheet
Critical Thinking   SAMPLE

A Solar Solution

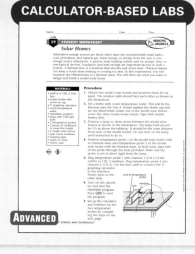

ADVANCED

SCILINKS ACTIVITY

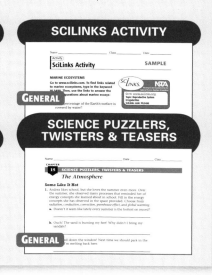

Activity
SciLinks Activity   SAMPLE

MARINE ECOSYSTEMS
Go to www.scilinks.com. To find links related to marine ecosystems, type in the keyword HL5400. Then, use the questions to answer the questions about marine ecosystems.

percentage of the Earth's surface is covered by water?

GENERAL

SCIENCE PUZZLERS, TWISTERS & TEASERS

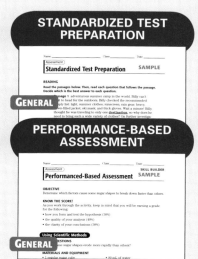

CHAPTER
15   SCIENCE PUZZLERS, TWISTERS & TEASERS
The Atmosphere

Some Like It Hot
1. Andrea likes school, but she loves the summer even more. Over the summer, she observed many processes that reminded her of energy concepts she learned about in school. Fill in the energy concepts she has observed in the space provided. Choose from radiation, conduction, convection, greenhouse effect, and global warming.
a. Doesn't it seem like late every summer is the hottest on record?

b. Ouch! The sand is burning my feet! Why didn't I bring my sandals?

GENERAL

Labs and Activities

ECOLABS & FIELD ACTIVITIES

Name _____ Date _____
FIELD ACTIVITY
14   STUDENT WORKSHEET   MAKING MODELS
That Greenhouse Effect!

Welcome to another round of *That Greenhouse Effect!*—the game show on which the contestants not only predict outcomes but also use their keen intellect while working against the clock. I am your host Blaise Hafet. Today, contestants are up to investigate the results of the greenhouse effect. First let's introduce our contestants.

Professor Luke Whaem, who will determine whether the light surfaces or the air above dark surfaces is cooler. At venus land station is Ms. Sylvia Aguapiler, two-time medalist in swimming. Mr. Phil Ruetort, a landscape architect, is at the wet-soil-versus-dry-soil station. Mr. Ed Bloomi, a local

GENERAL

LONG-TERM PROJECTS & RESEARCH IDEAS

Name _____ Date _____ Class _____
PROJECT
43   STUDENT WORKSHEET   DESIGN YOUR OWN
A Breath of Fresh Ether?

Not long ago, most people believed the Earth's atmosphere was part of a substance that filled all space—even beyond the moon and the planets of our solar system. The substance was called ether. In 1887, physicists A. A. Michelson and E. W. Morley conducted an experiment that produced astonishing results and finally showed that this kind of ether did not exist.

INTERNET
KEYWORDS
Michelson-Morley
Albert Einstein

A Brilliant Failure
The Michelson-Morley experiment has been called the most brilliant failure in scientific history. What was the experiment? How did the test conclude that other did not exist? How were the results of the experiment explained at the time? How did Albert Einstein later explain the results? Write a newspaper story about the experiment as if you were reporting it as it happened.

Other Research Ideas
1. How did sailors cross the ocean before engines? Early ex-

ADVANCED

WHIZ-BANG DEMONSTRATIONS

DEMO
27   TEACHER-LED DEMONSTRATION   DISCOVERY LAB
Blue Sky

Purpose
Students investigate why the midday sky is blue and why sunsets are red.

Time Required
10–15 minutes

Lab Ratings
TEACHER PREP
CONCEPT LEVEL
CLEAN UP

MATERIALS
• empty aquarium
• tap water
• flashlight or slide projector
• powdered milk or powdered coffee creamer
• blank white card

Advance Preparation
Prepare a solution as follows to simulate the atmosphere.
• Fill the aquarium with water, and shine a beam of light into the water so that the beam is parallel to the length of the aquarium.
• Stir a small amount of powdered milk or powdered coffee creamer into the water. As you do so, the beam of light will become more noticeable.
• Continue to add powder until the beam is clearly visible from across the room. Do not add too much powder! Remove the beam of light.

Before performing this demonstration for the class, you may wish to turn out the lights and allow time for everyone's eyes to adjust to the darkness.

HELPFUL HINT
If students have difficulty seeing the colors, try dimming the lights in the classroom further or using a narrower beam of light. One way to produce a narrow beam is to use a hole punch to create a hole in an unexposed black slide or an index card cut to the size of a slide. Then place the slide or index card in a slide projector and focus the projector to obtain a sharp, narrow beam.

What to Do
1. Ask students to offer an explanation of why the sky is often blue at midday and orange-red at sunset. (*Accept all reasonable responses.*) Tell them that you will now perform a demonstration to help them determine the answer.
2. Shine the beam of light through the tank from one end of the aquarium. Encourage a few students at a time to walk around the tank and observe the beam from different positions.
3. Ask a volunteer to hold up a white card at the other end of the tank in the path of the beam. This will allow students to observe the color of the light as it leaves the water.
4. After students have made their initial observations, add more powder to the water. Students should observe that the colors along the beam change from blue-white to yellow-orange.
5. Offer students a chance to revise their previous explanations based on what they have just observed.

continued…

ADVANCED

CALCULATOR-BASED LABS

LAB
19   STUDENT WORKSHEET   MAKING MODELS
Solar Homes

Alternative energy sources are those other than the nonrenewable fossil fuels—coal, petroleum, and natural gas. Solar energy, or energy from the sun, is one energy source alternative. A passive solar heating system uses no pumps, fans, or mechanical devices. Insulation and heat storage are important factors in such a system. A thermal mass is a material that absorbs and stores heat. Thermal masses can keep a home from heating or cooling too fast. In this experiment, you will examine the effectiveness of a thermal mass. You will then use what you learn to design and build a model solar home.

MATERIALS
• LabPro or CBL 2 interface
• empty bottle with screw-on cap
• TI graphing calculator
• room-temperature water
• DataMate program
• lamp with 100-watt bulb
• 2 temperature probes
• 2 pieces of cardboard to cover the model
• 2 model solar homes
• solar home windows
• masking tape
• watch or clock
• metric ruler

Procedure
1. Obtain two model solar homes and position them 20 cm apart. The window sides should face each other as shown in the illustration.
2. Fill a bottle with room-temperature water. This will be the thermal mass for Part A. Firmly tighten the bottle cap and lay the filled bottle inside one of the model solar homes. Leave the other model home empty. Tape both model homes shut.
3. Position a lamp to shine down between the model solar homes as shown in the illustration. The lamp bulb should be 10 cm above the tabletop. It should be the same distance from each of the model homes. Do not turn on the lamp until instructed to do so.
4. Position temperature probe 1 in the model solar home with no thermal mass and temperature probe 2 in the model solar home with the thermal mass. In both cases, pass half of the probe through the hole provided. Make sure the probe is not in direct light from the lamp.
5. Plug temperature probe 1 into channel 1 (CH 1) of the LabPro or CBL 2 interface. Plug temperature probe 2 into channel 2 (CH 2). Use the link cable to connect the TI graphing calculator to the interface. Firmly press in the cable ends.
6. Turn on the calculator and start the DataMate program. Press to start the program.
7. Set up the calculator and interface for the two temperature probes by completing the steps on the next page.

ADVANCED

DATASHEETS FOR QUICKLABS

TEACHER RESOURCE PAGE
Quick Lab
Reaction to Stress   DATASHEET FOR QUICK LAB   SAMPLE

Background
The graph below illustrates changes that occur in the membrane potential of a neuron during an action potential. Use the graph to answer the following questions. Refer to Figure 3 as needed.

DATASHEETS FOR CHAPTER LABS

TEACHER RESOURCE PAGE
Skills Practice Lab
Using Scientific Methods   DATASHEET FOR CHAPTER LAB   SAMPLE

Teacher's Notes
TIME REQUIRED
One 45-minute class period.

DATASHEETS FOR LABBOOK

TEACHER RESOURCE PAGE
Skills Practice Lab
Does It All Add Up?   DATASHEET FOR LABBOOK LAB   SAMPLE

Teacher's Notes
TIME REQUIRED
One 45-minute class period.

Review and Assessments

SECTION QUIZ

Assessment
Section Quiz   SAMPLE

Section:
In the space provided, write the letter of the description that best matches the term or phrase.
_____ 1. building molecules that can be used as an energy source, or breaking down molecules in which energy is stored
_____ the process by which light energy is converted to chemical energy
_____ an organism that uses inorganic substances to make organic compounds

ALSO IN SPANISH

GENERAL

SECTION REVIEW

Skills Worksheet
Section Review   SAMPLE

Section:
KEY TERMS
1. What do paleontologists study?

2. How does a trace fossil differ from petrified wood?

fossil

ALSO IN SPANISH

GENERAL
UNDERSTANDING KEY IDEAS

CHAPTER REVIEW

Skills Worksheet
Chapter Review   SAMPLE

USING VOCABULARY
1. Define biome in your own words.

2. Describe the characteristics of a savanna and a desert.

ALSO IN SPANISH

GENERAL

CHAPTER TEST A

Assessment
Chapter Test A   SAMPLE

MULTIPLE CHOICE
In the space provided, write the letter of the term or phrase that best completes each statement or best answers each question.
_____ 1. Surface currents are formed by
   a. the moon's gravity.   **c.** wind.
   b. the sun's gravity.   **d.** increased water density.
_____ 2. When waves come near the shore,
   a. they speed up.   **c.** their wavelength increases.
   b. they maintain their speed.   **d.** their wave height increases.

ALSO IN SPANISH

GENERAL

CHAPTER TEST B

Assessment
Chapter Test B   SAMPLE

MULTIPLE CHOICE
In the space provided, write the letter of the term or phrase that best completes each statement or best answers each question.
_____ 1. Surface currents are formed by
   a. the moon's gravity.   **c.** wind.
   b. the sun's gravity.   **d.** increased water density.
_____ 2. When waves come near the shore,
   a. they speed up.   **c.** their wavelength increases.
   b. they maintain their speed.   **d.** their wave height increases.

ADVANCED

CHAPTER TEST C

Assessment
Chapter Test C   SAMPLE

MULTIPLE CHOICE
In the space provided, write the letter of the term or phrase that best completes each statement or best answers each question.
_____ 1. Surface currents are formed by
   a. the moon's gravity.   **c.** wind.
   b. the sun's gravity.   **d.** increased water density.
_____ 2. When waves come near the shore,
   a. they speed up.   **c.** their wavelength increases.
   b. they maintain their speed.   **d.** their wave height increases.
currents transport sediment
   a. out to the open ocean.   c. only during low tide.
   b. only during high
4. Which of the following does NOT control surface currents?

SPECIAL NEEDS

STANDARDIZED TEST PREPARATION

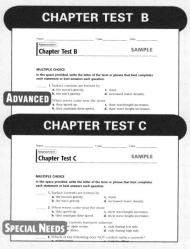

Assessment
Standardized Test Preparation   SAMPLE

READING
Read the passages below. Then, read each question that follows the passage. Decide which is the best answer to each question.

Passage 1 I adventurous summer camp in the world. Billy can't to head for the outdoors. Billy checked the recommended supply list: light, summer clothes, sunscreen, rain gear, heavy, non-filled jacket, ski mask, and thick gloves. Wait a minute! Billy thought he was traveling to only one *destination*, so why does he need to bring such a wide variety of clothes? On further consideration

GENERAL

PERFORMANCE-BASED ASSESSMENT

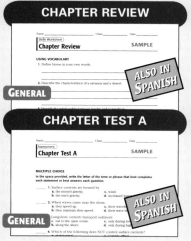

Assessment
Performanced-Based Assessment   SKILL BUILDER   SAMPLE

OBJECTIVE
Determine which factors cause some sugar shapes to break down faster than others.

KNOW THE SCORE!
As you work through the activity, keep in mind that you will be earning a grade for the following:
• how you form and test the hypothesis (30%)
• the quality of your analysis (30%)
• the clarity of your conclusions (30%)

Using Scientific Methods
QUESTIONS
some sugar shapes erode more rapidly than others?

MATERIALS AND EQUIPMENT
• 1 regular sugar cube   • 30 mL of water

GENERAL

This Chapter Enrichment provides relevant and interesting information to expand and enhance your presentation of the chapter material.

Section 1

Characteristics of the Atmosphere

Take a Deep Breath!

- Near the Earth's surface, the atmosphere consists of 78.08% nitrogen, 20.95% oxygen, 0.93% argon, 0.03% carbon dioxide, and traces of water vapor. Scientists theorize that about 95% of the oxygen present in today's atmosphere formed as a byproduct of photosynthesis.

Is That a Fact!

- ◆ The Earth's troposphere contains almost 90% of the atmosphere's total mass. In the troposphere, temperature decreases at an average rate of 6.4°C/km as altitude increases.

Section 2

Atmospheric Heating

Specific Heat

- Water has a very high *specific heat,* which means that a great deal of thermal energy is needed to increase the temperature of water. Thus, water heats and cools very slowly. Rock, on the other hand, has a very low specific heat, so it heats and cools more quickly. For this reason, areas of high pressure (anticyclones) form over bodies of water, and areas of low pressure (cyclones) form over landmasses during the summer months. During the winter months, cyclones tend to form over bodies of water, and anticyclones tend to form over landmasses.

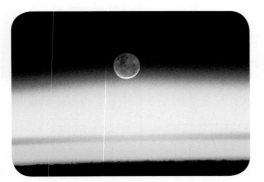

Is That a Fact!

- ◆ The summer monsoon in Asia is caused because central Asia heats up more quickly than the Indian Ocean. As the air above central Asia warms, it rises, creating an area of low pressure that draws moisture-laden air toward central Asia. When this moist air encounters the Himalayas, it cools quickly and releases its moisture in the form of torrential rains.

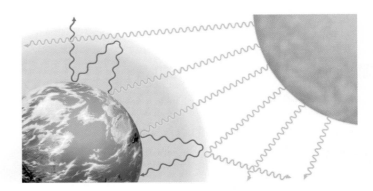

Global Warming—An Idea Before Its Time!

- Since the 1970s, global warming has been a topic of concern. However, a global warming model was proposed as early as 1896 by a Swedish physicist and chemist named Svante Arrhenius. Arrhenius theorized that the carbon dioxide released from burning coal would increase the intensity of Earth's greenhouse effect and lead to global warming. In 1954, it was first suggested that deforestation increases the amount of CO_2 in the atmosphere. Since then, numerous scientific studies have examined the effects of carbon dioxide on the temperature of Earth's atmosphere.

Section 3

Global Winds and Local Winds

Gustave Coriolis

- Gustave Gaspard Coriolis was a French mathematician and engineer who lived and worked in Paris from 1792 to 1843. His most well-known contribution to science is a paper published in 1835 that introduces the Coriolis effect. In "On the Equations of Relative Motion of Systems of Bodies," Coriolis argued that an inertial force (the Coriolis force) acts on a rotating object at a right angle to the object's motion. We now know that the "Coriolis force" is an apparent force.

- The rotation of the Earth causes matter in motion to appear to be deflected from its path. The Coriolis effect influences the general direction of global winds and open-ocean circulation, as well as the rotational movements of weather systems, such as cyclones and anticyclones.

Is That a Fact!

- When airplanes fly north or south, pilots have to make corrections to counteract the Coriolis effect.

Jet Streaks

- Jet streaks are winds within jet streams that flow faster than the adjacent winds. Jet streaks influence storm formation and precipitation associated with storms. Rising jet streaks and the low-pressure area that forms beneath them present favorable conditions for storms to form. Sinking jet streaks inhibit storm formation and precipitation.

Section 4

Air Pollution

Indoor Air Quality in U.S. Schools

- According to the U.S. Environmental Protection Agency, 20% of the U.S. population are students in the nation's 115,000 elementary schools, middle schools, and high schools. Half of these schools suffer from problems related to poor indoor air quality. Because of the amount of time students spend in schools and the susceptibility of children to air pollutants, students are at greater risk from poor indoor air quality at these facilities.

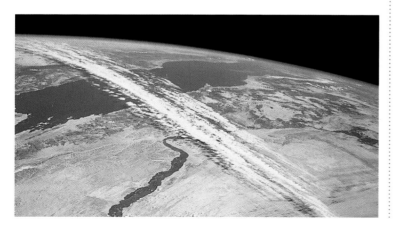

Section 5

Maintaining Air Quality

Global Distillation

- Scientists have found high levels of airborne contaminants in the breast milk of Inuit women in Greenland and Arctic Canada. Researchers think that the contaminants arrived in these remote areas by a process called *global distillation*. In this process, contaminants are redistributed around the globe by atmospheric currents. Contaminants tend to concentrate in polar areas for the same reason that water vapor condenses on cold glass: gaseous substances tend to condense at colder temperatures.

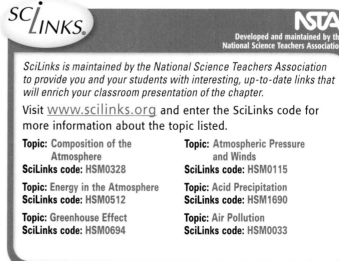

SciLinks is maintained by the National Science Teachers Association to provide you and your students with interesting, up-to-date links that will enrich your classroom presentation of the chapter.

Visit www.scilinks.org and enter the SciLinks code for more information about the topic listed.

Topic: Composition of the Atmosphere
SciLinks code: HSM0328

Topic: Atmospheric Pressure and Winds
SciLinks code: HSM0115

Topic: Energy in the Atmosphere
SciLinks code: HSM0512

Topic: Acid Precipitation
SciLinks code: HSM1690

Topic: Greenhouse Effect
SciLinks code: HSM0694

Topic: Air Pollution
SciLinks code: HSM0033

Overview

Tell students that this chapter will help them learn about the atmosphere. They will study the circulation of energy in the atmosphere and the greenhouse effect. They will also learn about global winds, air quality, and air pollution.

Assessing Prior Knowledge

Students should be familiar with the following topics:

- changes of state
- radiation, conduction, and convection

Identifying Misconceptions

Because air cannot be seen, students may assume that the atmosphere has no mass and is therefore not subject to the physical laws that affect matter. Point out that air, like water, is a fluid. A *fluid* is any material that can flow and that takes the shape of its container. Students may find it easier to visualize wind if they think of air flowing like water. For example, the Coriolis effect affects the ocean currents as well as the global winds. Similarly, the convection of gases in the atmosphere is similar to the convection of bodies of water in the ocean. Be sure to explain that all fluids move according to specific laws of fluid dynamics.

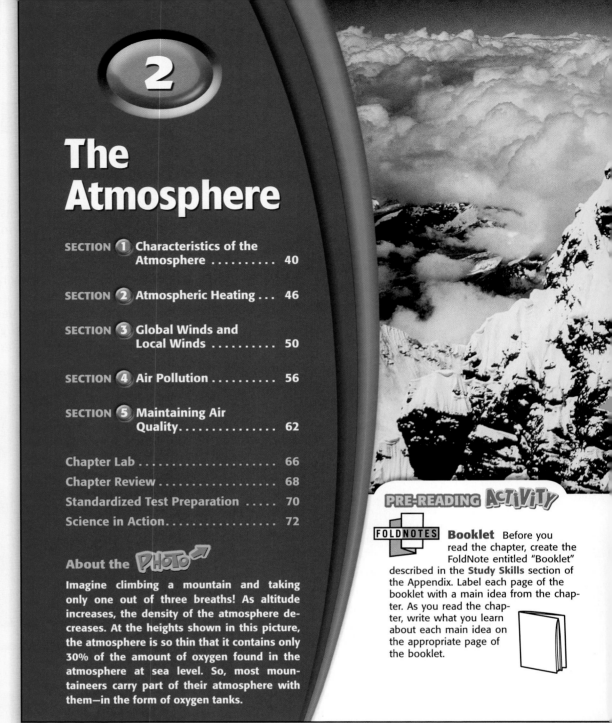

2
The Atmosphere

About the PHOTO

Imagine climbing a mountain and taking only one out of three breaths! As altitude increases, the density of the atmosphere decreases. At the heights shown in this picture, the atmosphere is so thin that it contains only 30% of the amount of oxygen found in the atmosphere at sea level. So, most mountaineers carry part of their atmosphere with them—in the form of oxygen tanks.

PRE-READING ACTIVITY

FOLDNOTES **Booklet** Before you read the chapter, create the FoldNote entitled "Booklet" described in the **Study Skills** section of the Appendix. Label each page of the booklet with a main idea from the chapter. As you read the chapter, write what you learn about each main idea on the appropriate page of the booklet.

Standards Correlations

North Carolina Standard Course of Study

1.02 (partial) Develop appropriate experimental procedures for: . . . Student generated questions . . . (Chapter Lab)

2.01 Explore evidence that "technology" has many definitions: Artifact or hardware, Methodology or technique, System of production, [and] Social-technical system. (Section 5)

2.02 (partial) Use information systems to: Identify scientific needs, human needs, or problems that are subject to technological solution . . . (Section 5)

2.03 (partial) Evaluate technological designs for: . . . Application of scientific principles . . . [and] Risks and benefits . . . (Science in Action and Section 5)

2.04 (partial) Apply tenets of technological design to make informed consumer decisions about: . . . Products . . . (Section 5)

3.01 Explain the composition, properties and structure of the atmosphere: Mixture of gases, Stratified layers, Each layer has distinct properties, As altitude increases, air pressure decreases, [and] Equilibrium. (Section 1)

START-UP ACTIVITY

MATERIALS

FOR THE CLASS
- balloon, large (2)
- meterstick
- notebook
- pencil
- pushpins (3)
- safety goggles

Teacher's Note: This activity may work best as a demonstration. You may find it easier to balance the meterstick yourself, or to create a stand on which to balance the meterstick.

Answers

1. Answers may vary. Students should note that the meterstick became unbalanced when the balloon was popped. The reason for this change is that the popped balloon contained air, which has mass.

2. Sample answer: Yes, air has mass. Because air has mass, it is subject to the gravitational attraction of the Earth. The atmosphere is held around the Earth by gravity.

START-UP ACTIVITY

Does Air Have Mass?

In this activity, you will compare an inflated balloon with a deflated balloon to find out if air has mass.

Procedure

1. In a **notebook,** answer the following questions: Does air have mass? Will an inflated balloon weigh more than a deflated balloon?

2. Inflate **two large balloons,** and tie the balloons closed. Attach each balloon to opposite ends of a **meterstick** using identical **pushpins.** Balance the meterstick on a **pencil** held by a volunteer. Check that the meterstick is perfectly balanced.

3. Predict what will happen when you pop one balloon. Record your predictions.

4. Put on **safety goggles,** and carefully pop one of the balloons with a **pushpin.**

5. Record your observations.

Analysis

1. Explain your observations. Was your prediction correct?

2. Based on your results, does air have mass? If air has mass, is the atmosphere affected by Earth's gravity? Explain your answers.

3.02 Describe properties that can be observed and measured to predict air quality: Particulate matter, [and] Ozone. (Section 4)

3.03 Conclude that the good health of environments and organisms requires: The monitoring of air quality, Taking steps to maintain healthy air quality, [and] Stewardship. (Section 5)

3.04 Evaluate how humans impact air quality including: Air quality standards, Point and non-point sources of air pollution in North Carolina, Financial and economic trade-offs, [and] Local air quality issues. (Sections 4 and 5)

Chapter Starter Transparency
Use this transparency to help students begin thinking about the atmosphere.

CHAPTER RESOURCES

Technology

Transparencies
- Chapter Starter Transparency

READING SKILLS

Student Edition on CD-ROM

Guided Reading Audio CD

Classroom Videos
- Brain Food Video Quiz

Workbooks

Science Puzzlers, Twisters & Teasers
- The Atmosphere GENERAL

Overview

This section defines the atmosphere and explains its basic characteristics. It describes the atmosphere's composition and explains how pressure and temperature are related to altitude. The section also discusses the four layers of the Earth's atmosphere.

 Bellringer

Have students list the ways that the atmosphere is different from outer space. Tell students that a little more than a century ago, many scientists believed that the Earth's atmosphere blended with a hypothetical substance called *ether* that filled the entire universe. In 1887, the physicist A. A. Michelson demonstrated that the universe is not filled with ether.

Motivate

Identifying Preconceptions — GENERAL

Atmospheric Composition
Before students read the section, ask them these questions:

• What is the most common gas in the atmosphere? (nitrogen)

• Does air contain anything other than gases? (solids, such as dust, and liquids, such as water)

LS Logical

READING WARM-UP

Objectives

● Describe the composition of Earth's atmosphere.

● Explain why air pressure changes with altitude.

● Explain how air temperature changes with atmospheric composition.

● Describe the layers of the atmosphere.

Terms to Learn

atmosphere   stratosphere
air pressure   mesosphere
troposphere   thermosphere

READING STRATEGY

Mnemonics As you read this section, create a mnemonic device to help you remember the layers of the Earth's atmosphere.

Characteristics of the Atmosphere

If you were lost in the desert, you could survive for a few days without food and water. But you wouldn't last more than five minutes without the atmosphere.

The **atmosphere** is a mixture of gases that surrounds Earth. In addition to containing the oxygen you need to breathe, the atmosphere protects you from the sun's damaging rays. The atmosphere is always changing. Every breath you take, every tree that is planted, and every vehicle you ride in affects the atmosphere's composition.

The Composition of the Atmosphere

As you can see in **Figure 1,** the atmosphere is made up mostly of nitrogen gas. The oxygen you breathe makes up a little more than 20% of the atmosphere. In addition to containing nitrogen and oxygen, the atmosphere contains small particles, such as dust, volcanic ash, sea salt, dirt, and smoke. The next time you turn off the lights at night, shine a flashlight, and you will see some of these tiny particles floating in the air.

Water is also found in the atmosphere. Liquid water (water droplets) and solid water (snow and ice crystals) are found in clouds. But most water in the atmosphere exists as an invisible gas called *water vapor*. When atmospheric conditions change, water vapor can change into solid or liquid water, and rain or snow might fall from the sky.

✓ **Reading Check** Describe the three physical states of water in the atmosphere. (*See the Appendix for answers to Reading Checks.*)

Figure 1 Composition of the Atmosphere

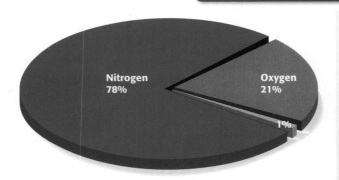

Nitrogen, the most common atmospheric gas, is released when dead plants and dead animals break down and when volcanoes erupt.

Nitrogen 78%

Oxygen 21%

1%

Oxygen, the second most common atmospheric gas, is made by phytoplankton and plants.

The remaining 1% of the atmosphere is made up of argon, carbon dioxide, water vapor, and other gases.

CHAPTER RESOURCES

Chapter Resource File

• **Lesson Plan**
• **Directed Reading A** BASIC
• **Directed Reading B** SPECIAL NEEDS

Technology

Transparencies
• Bellringer
• *LINK TO* **LIFE SCIENCE** The Connection Between Photosynthesis and Respiration

---

Answer to Reading Check

Water can be liquid (rain), solid (snow or ice), or gas (water vapor).

Atmospheric Pressure and Temperature

You may be surprised to learn that you carry a 700 km column of air every day. Although air is not heavy, at sea level, a square inch of surface area is under almost 15 lb of air.

As Altitude Increases, Air Pressure Decreases

The atmosphere is held around the Earth by gravity. Gravity acts to move gas molecules in the atmosphere toward Earth's center. The force of gravity is balanced by air pressure. **Air pressure** is the measure of the force with which air molecules push on a surface. Air pressure is strongest at the Earth's surface because more air is above you. As you move farther away from the Earth's surface, fewer gas molecules are above you. So, as altitude (distance from sea level) increases, air pressure decreases. Think of the forces of air pressure and gravity as a human pyramid, as shown in **Figure 2.** The people at the bottom of the pyramid can feel all the weight of the people on top. The people at the bottom push up to balance the weight of the people above them. In a similar way, air pressure and gravity exist near a state of balance or equilibrium.

Atmospheric Composition Affects Air Temperature

Air temperature also changes as altitude increases. The temperature differences result mainly from the way solar energy is absorbed as it moves through the atmosphere. Some parts of the atmosphere are warmer because they contain a high percentage of gases that absorb solar energy. Other parts of the atmosphere contain less of these gases and are cooler.

Lower pressure

Higher pressure

Figure 2 *As in a human pyramid, air pressure increases closer to the Earth's surface.*

atmosphere a mixture of gases that surrounds a planet or moon

air pressure the measure of the force with which air molecules push on a surface

MISCONCEPTION ALERT

Water Vapor Is a Gas Make sure students realize that water vapor is an invisible gas. The steam they observe coming out of a pot of boiling water is composed of water droplets that form as water vapor cools and condenses on particles in the air. Similarly, clouds appear in the sky when the air cools enough for water vapor to condense and form liquid droplets.

WEIRD SCIENCE

An experiment in 1664 demonstrated the force exerted by air pressure. Most of the air was removed from a hollow sphere whose halves had been sealed together with an airtight gasket. Sixteen horses were needed to pull the metal hemispheres apart!

Teach, continued

Using the Figure — BASIC

Atmospheric Layers Have students refer to **Figure 3** to answer these questions:

• Which layer of the atmosphere is closest to Earth? (the troposphere)

• How does temperature change within the stratosphere? (For the first few kilometers, the temperature remains fairly constant. Then, the temperature begins rising steeply and levels off again toward the top of the layer.)

• Which atmospheric layer has the greatest range of temperatures? (the thermosphere)

Students may notice that the iridescent cloud in the thermosphere is an aurora and that the white layer near the top of the stratosphere represents the ozone layer. The space shuttles orbit at an altitude of about 300 km. **LS** Visual

Answer to Reading Check

The troposphere is the layer of turning or change. The stratosphere is the layer in which gases are layered and do not mix vertically. The mesosphere is the middle layer. The thermosphere is the layer in which temperatures are highest.

Modeling the Atmosphere
In teams, use a metric ruler to create an illustrated scale model of the atmosphere similar to the one shown on this page. Assume that the atmosphere is about 700 km high. If you reduced the height of the atmosphere by a factor of 100,000, your scale model would be 7 m long, and the troposphere would be 16 cm long. Think of a creative way to display your model. You could use sidewalk chalk, stakes and string, poster board, or other materials approved by your teacher. Do some research to add interesting information about each layer.

Figure 3 *The layers of the atmosphere are defined by changes in temperature.*

Layers of the Atmosphere

Based on temperature changes, the Earth's atmosphere is divided into four layers, as shown in **Figure 3.** These layers are the *troposphere, stratosphere, mesosphere,* and *thermosphere.* Although these words might sound complicated, the name of each layer gives you clues about its features.

For example, *-sphere* means "ball," which suggests that each layer of the atmosphere surrounds the Earth like a hollow ball. *Tropo-* means "turning" or "change," and the troposphere is the layer where gases turn and mix. *Strato-* means "layer," and the stratosphere is the sphere where gases are layered and do not mix very much. *Meso-* means "middle," and the mesosphere is the middle layer. Finally, *thermo-* means "heat," and the thermosphere is the sphere where temperatures are highest.

✓ Reading Check What does the name of each atmospheric layer mean?

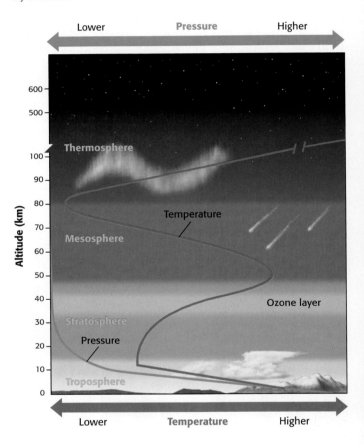

CHAPTER RESOURCES

Technology

 Transparencies
• Layers of the Atmosphere

Is That a Fact!

The oxygen in the Earth's current atmosphere is produced primarily by phytoplankton (tiny, drifting sea plants) and land plants that release oxygen during photosynthesis.

The Troposphere: The Layer in Which We Live

The lowest layer of the atmosphere, which lies next to the Earth's surface, is called the **troposphere.** The troposphere is also the densest atmospheric layer. It contains almost 90% of the atmosphere's total mass! Almost all of the Earth's carbon dioxide, water vapor, clouds, air pollution, weather, and life-forms are in the troposphere. As shown in **Figure 4,** temperatures vary greatly in the troposphere. Differences in air temperature and density cause gases in the troposphere to mix continuously.

The Stratosphere: Home of the Ozone Layer

The atmospheric layer above the troposphere is called the **stratosphere. Figure 5** shows the boundary between the stratosphere and the troposphere. Gases in the stratosphere are layered and do not mix as much as gases in the troposphere. The air is also very thin in the stratosphere and contains little moisture. The lower stratosphere is extremely cold. Its temperature averages –60°C. But temperature rises as altitude increases in the stratosphere. This rise happens because ozone in the stratosphere absorbs ultraviolet radiation from the sun, which warms the air. Almost all of the ozone in the stratosphere is contained in the ozone layer. The *ozone layer* protects life on Earth by absorbing harmful ultraviolet radiation.

The Mesosphere: The Middle Layer

Above the stratosphere is the mesosphere. The **mesosphere** is the middle layer of the atmosphere. It is also the coldest layer. As in the troposphere, the temperature decreases as altitude increases in the mesosphere. Temperatures can be as low as –93°C at the top of the mesosphere.

Figure 4 *As altitude increases in the troposphere, temperature decreases. Snow remains all year on this mountaintop.*

troposphere the lowest layer of the atmosphere, in which temperature decreases at a constant rate as altitude increases

stratosphere the layer of the atmosphere that is above the troposphere and in which temperature increases as altitude increases

mesosphere the layer of the atmosphere between the stratosphere and the thermosphere and in which temperature decreases as altitude increases

Figure 5 *This photograph of Earth's atmosphere was taken from space. The troposphere is the yellow layer; the stratosphere is the white layer.*

Reteaching ———— BASIC

Describing the Atmosphere

On the board, make a table entitled "The Atmosphere." Include the following headings:

"Layer," "Altitude range," "Temperature range," and "Other features."

Have volunteers contribute information for each section of the table. **English Language Learners**

LS Verbal

Quiz ———— GENERAL

1. List the layers of the atmosphere, starting with the one closest to Earth. (troposphere, stratosphere, mesosphere, thermosphere)

2. Explain how density affects the transfer of thermal energy in the air. (The less dense the air is, the less effective it is at transferring thermal energy. Particles must collide with one another to transfer energy. Particles that are farther apart are less likely to collide with other particles.)

Alternative Assessment ———— GENERAL

Writing **Poetry** Have each student write a poem that creatively yet accurately describes each layer of Earth's atmosphere. Allow time for volunteers to read their poem aloud or to display the poem for others to read on their own.

LS Intrapersonal

thermosphere the uppermost layer of the atmosphere, in which temperature increases as altitude increases

The Thermosphere: The Edge of the Atmosphere

The uppermost atmospheric layer is called the **thermosphere.** In the thermosphere, temperature again increases with altitude. Atoms of nitrogen and oxygen absorb high-energy solar radiation and release thermal energy, which causes temperatures in the thermosphere to be 1,000°C or higher.

When you think of an area that has high temperatures, you probably think of a place that is very hot. Although the thermosphere has very high temperatures, it does not feel hot. Temperature is different from heat. Temperature is a measure of the average energy of particles in motion. The high temperature of the thermosphere means that particles in that layer are moving very fast. Heat, however, is the transfer of thermal energy between objects of different temperatures. Particles must touch one another to transfer thermal energy. The space between particles in the thermosphere is so great that particles do not transfer much energy. In other words, the density of the thermosphere is so low that particles do not often collide and transfer energy. **Figure 6** shows how air density affects the heating of the troposphere and the thermosphere.

Reading Check Why doesn't the thermosphere feel hot?

Figure 6 Temperature in the Troposphere and the Thermosphere

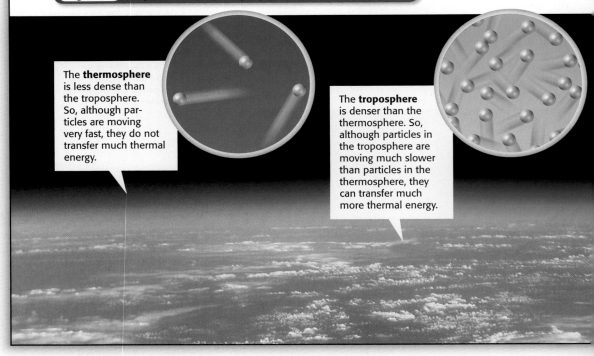

The **thermosphere** is less dense than the troposphere. So, although particles are moving very fast, they do not transfer much thermal energy.

The **troposphere** is denser than the thermosphere. So, although particles in the troposphere are moving much slower than particles in the thermosphere, they can transfer much more thermal energy.

Answer to Reading Check

The thermosphere does not feel hot because air molecules are spaced far apart and cannot collide to transfer much thermal energy.

CONNECTION to Physical Science ———— BASIC

Thermal Energy Have students imagine a sink full of hot water. Ask them to pretend that they have removed a cup of the hot water from the sink. Students should agree that both volumes of water have the same temperature at this point. Explain that the sink has more thermal energy than the cup because the sink contains more water (and therefore more particles in motion) than the cup. Ask students to help you come up with other examples to explain these ideas.

The Ionosphere: Home of the Auroras

In the upper mesosphere and the lower thermosphere, nitrogen and oxygen atoms absorb harmful solar energy. As a result, the thermosphere's temperature rises, and gas particles become electrically charged. Electrically charged particles are called *ions*. Therefore, this part of the thermosphere is called the *ionosphere*. As shown in **Figure 7,** in polar regions these ions radiate energy as shimmering lights called *auroras*. The ionosphere also reflects AM radio waves. When conditions are right, an AM radio wave can travel around the world by reflecting off the ionosphere. These radio signals bounce off the ionosphere and are sent back to Earth.

Figure 7 *Charged particles in the ionosphere cause auroras, or northern and southern lights.*

SECTION Review

Summary

- Nitrogen and oxygen make up most of Earth's atmosphere.
- Air pressure decreases as altitude increases.
- The composition of atmospheric layers affects their temperature.
- The troposphere is the lowest atmospheric layer. It is the layer in which we live.
- The stratosphere contains the ozone layer, which protects us from harmful UV radiation.
- The mesosphere is the coldest atmospheric layer.
- The thermosphere is the uppermost layer of the atmosphere.

Using Key Terms

1. Use each of the following terms in a separate sentence: *air pressure, atmosphere, troposphere, stratosphere, mesosphere,* and *thermosphere.*

Understanding Key Ideas

2. Why does the temperature of different layers of the atmosphere vary?
   a. because air temperature increases as altitude increases
   b. because the amount of energy radiated from the sun varies
   c. because of interference by humans
   d. because of the composition of gases in each layer

3. Why does air pressure decrease as altitude increases?

4. How can the thermosphere have high temperatures but not feel hot?

5. What determines the temperature of atmospheric layers?

6. What two gases make up most of the atmosphere?

Math Skills

7. If an average cloud has a density of 0.5 g/m³ and has a volume of 1,000,000,000 m³, what is the weight of an average cloud?

Critical Thinking

8. **Applying Concepts** Apply what you know about the relationship between altitude and air pressure to explain why rescue helicopters have a difficult time flying at altitudes above 6,000 m.

9. **Making Inferences** If the upper atmosphere is very thin, why do space vehicles heat up as they enter the atmosphere?

10. **Making Inferences** Explain why gases such as helium can escape Earth's atmosphere.

For a variety of links related to this chapter, go to www.scilinks.org

Topic: Composition of the Atmosphere
SciLinks code: HSM0328

Cultural Awareness GENERAL

CHAPTER RESOURCES

Chapter Resource File

- Section Quiz GENERAL
- Section Review GENERAL
- Vocabulary and Section Summary GENERAL
- Reinforcement Worksheet BASIC

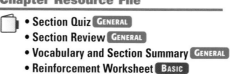

Answers to Section Review

1. Sample answer: Air pressure is caused by gravity pulling air molecules in the atmosphere toward the Earth. The atmosphere is a mixture of gases that surrounds the Earth. The troposphere is the layer where most weather occurs. The stratosphere is where the ozone layer is located. The mesosphere is the middle atmospheric layer. The thermosphere is the atmospheric layer with the highest temperatures.

2. d

3. Air pressure decreases as altitude increases because the atmosphere is less dense at higher altitudes.

4. Temperatures in the thermosphere are high because particles are moving quickly in the thermosphere. The thermosphere does not feel hot because it is not very dense, so particles cannot collide to transfer much thermal energy.

5. The temperature of atmospheric layers varies because of the way solar energy is absorbed by different gases.

6. nitrogen and oxygen

7. 0.5 g/m³ × 1,000,000,000 m³ = 500,000,000 g, or 500,000 kg

8. Answers may vary. Students should recognize that air density is lower at higher altitudes. Helicopters need air to provide lift. At altitudes higher than 6,000 m, air density is so low that it is difficult for helicopters to fly.

9. Answers may vary. Space vehicles reenter the atmosphere at a very high rate of speed. Although the atmosphere is not very dense at the altitude that space vehicles reenter, the vehicles are traveling fast enough to compress air in front of them. This layer of air transfers thermal energy to the spacecraft's exterior.

10. Answers may vary. Helium does not have enough mass to be held by the Earth's gravitational attraction.

Focus

Overview

This section discusses how the atmosphere is heated by energy from the sun. Thermal energy is transferred by radiation, thermal conduction, and convection. The section concludes with a discussion of the greenhouse effect and global warming.

 Bellringer

Ask students to explain how food is heated in an oven. (The heating coil heats the air in the oven by radiation and thermal conduction. The hot air circulates by convection and heats the food and its container. The hot container heats the food by thermal conduction.)

Motivate

ACTiViTY ———— BASIC

Popcorn Make some popcorn the "old-fashioned" way—use a hot plate or stove top, a pan with a lid, oil, and popcorn kernels. Have volunteers explain how the processes of convection, conduction, and radiation are involved. Explain that a kernel pops when the water stored inside changes to water vapor and expands suddenly. Share the treat with students if time allows. **LS** Kinesthetic

---

READING WARM-UP

Objectives

● Describe what happens to solar energy that reaches Earth.

● Summarize the processes of radiation, conduction, and convection.

● Explain the relationship between the greenhouse effect and global warming.

Terms to Learn

radiation
thermal conduction
convection
global warming
greenhouse effect

READING STRATEGY

Reading Organizer As you read this section, make a table comparing radiation, conduction, and convection.

Atmospheric Heating

You are lying in a park. Your eyes are closed, and you feel the warmth of the sun on your face. You may have done this before, but have you ever stopped to think that it takes a little more than eight minutes for the energy that warms your face to travel from a star that is 149,000,000 km away?

Energy in the Atmosphere

In the scenario above, your face was warmed by energy from the sun. Earth and its atmosphere are also warmed by energy from the sun. In this section, you will find out what happens to solar energy as it enters the atmosphere.

Radiation: Energy Transfer by Waves

The Earth receives energy from the sun by radiation. **Radiation** is the transfer of energy as electromagnetic waves. Although the sun radiates a huge amount of energy, Earth receives only about two-billionths of this energy. But this small fraction of energy is enough to drive the weather cycle and make Earth habitable. **Figure 1** shows what happens to solar energy once it enters the atmosphere.

Figure 1 *Energy from the sun is absorbed by the atmosphere, land, and water and is changed into thermal energy.*

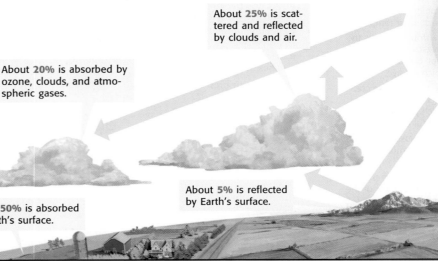

About **25%** is scattered and reflected by clouds and air.

About **20%** is absorbed by ozone, clouds, and atmospheric gases.

About **5%** is reflected by Earth's surface.

About **50%** is absorbed by Earth's surface.

CHAPTER RESOURCES

Chapter Resource File

 • **Lesson Plan**
 • **Directed Reading A** BASIC
 • **Directed Reading B** SPECIAL NEEDS

Technology

 Transparencies
 • Bellringer
 • Scattering, Absorption, and Reflection
 • Radiation, Conduction, and Convection

MISCONCEPTION ///ALERT\\\

Thermal Conduction Point out that compared with radiation and convection, thermal conduction plays a relatively minor role in heating the atmosphere. Only the thin layer of air that comes in contact with the Earth's surface is heated by thermal conduction. However, thermal energy that is absorbed and reradiated by the land and oceans play a major role in heating the atmosphere.

Conduction: Energy Transfer by Contact

If you have ever touched something hot, you have experienced the process of conduction. **Thermal conduction** is the transfer of thermal energy through a material. Thermal energy is always transferred from warm to cold areas. When air molecules come into direct contact with the warm surface of Earth, thermal energy is transferred to the atmosphere.

Convection: Energy Transfer by Circulation

If you have ever watched a pot of water boil, you have observed convection. **Convection** is the transfer of thermal energy by the circulation or movement of a liquid or gas. Most thermal energy in the atmosphere is transferred by convection. For example, as air is heated, it becomes less dense and rises. Cool air is denser, so it sinks. As the cool air sinks, it pushes the warm air up. The cool air is eventually heated by the Earth's surface and begins to rise again. This cycle of warm air rising and cool air sinking causes a circular movement of air, called a *convection current,* as shown in **Figure 2.**

✓ **Reading Check** How do differences in air density cause convection currents? (*See the Appendix for answers to Reading Checks.*)

radiation the transfer of energy as electromagnetic waves

thermal conduction the transfer of energy as heat through a material

convection the transfer of thermal energy by the circulation or movement of a liquid or gas

Figure 2 *The processes of radiation, thermal conduction, and convection heat Earth and its atmosphere.*

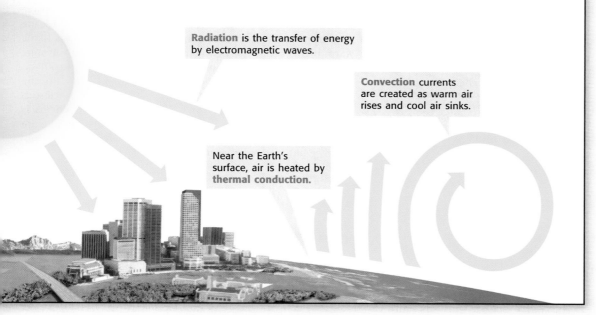

Radiation is the transfer of energy by electromagnetic waves.

Convection currents are created as warm air rises and cool air sinks.

Near the Earth's surface, air is heated by **thermal conduction.**

INCLUSION Strategies

- **Developmentally Delayed**
- **Hearing Impaired**

This activity will demonstrate how different colors absorb different amounts of solar energy. Obtain two 2 L soda bottles. Paint one bottle white and the other bottle black. Place the open end of a small, prestretched balloon on the mouth of both bottles. Make sure the balloons form an airtight seal.

Organize students into pairs, and ask them to observe the bottles. If possible, pass the bottles around. Ask students to predict what will happen when the bottles are placed in bright sunlight. Ask students to write their predictions in their **science journal.** Now, place both bottles in bright sunlight. Within a few minutes, the students will notice that the balloon on the black bottle starts to expand. The balloon of the white bottle remains limp. Have student pairs record their observations. **English Language Learners**

LS Logical

Answer to Reading Check

Cold air is more dense than warm air, so cold air sinks and warm air rises. This produces convection currents.

CONNECTION ACTIVITY

Environmental Science — GENERAL

The Heat Island Effect Cities that have few green spaces and a lot of asphalt can have temperatures 10°C higher than surrounding rural areas do. This phenomenon is called the *heat island effect.* The heat island effect occurs because concrete buildings and asphalt absorb solar radiation and reradiate thermal energy, which elevates temperatures and increases the production of smog. The effect is worse in urban areas that have little surface water and few trees because the evaporation of water and plant transpiration cool the air. To counteract the heat island effect, cities have begun to preserve green spaces and plant trees. Some cities are beginning to use construction materials that have a higher reflectivity, such as white rooftops and concrete streets. Have groups of students create a model city in a large box or aquarium. Using two light bulbs and a thermometer, students should test strategies to reduce the heat island effect. **LS** Logical

Reteaching — BASIC

Greenhouse Review Reproduce **Figure 3** on the board, and ask student volunteers to explain how the greenhouse effect works. **LS** Visual/Verbal

Quiz — GENERAL

1. A metal spoon left in a bowl of hot soup feels hot. Which process—radiation, thermal conduction, or convection—is mainly responsible for heating the spoon? (thermal conduction)

2. What is a convection current? (the circular movement of warm and cool particles in a liquid or gas)

3. How does a greenhouse stay warm? (Sunlight passes through the glass. Objects in the structure absorb some of the radiant energy. In turn, the objects radiate this energy as thermal energy. The glass prevents the thermal energy from escaping, which warms the greenhouse.)

Alternative Assessment — GENERAL

Writing Have students write a two-paragraph essay that explains the concepts in this section. The essay should contain the following terms: *radiation, thermal conduction, convection, greenhouse gas, greenhouse effect, global warming,* and *radiation balance.* Student volunteers can read their essays to the class. **LS** Verbal

---

Figure 3 The Greenhouse Effect

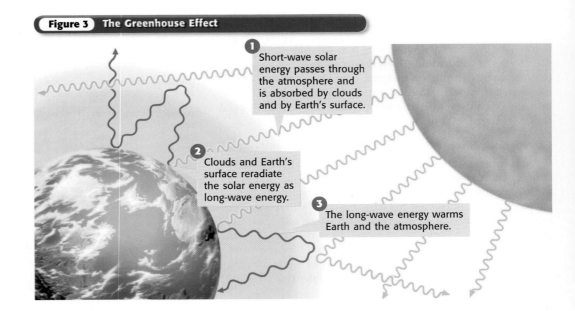

1. Short-wave solar energy passes through the atmosphere and is absorbed by clouds and by Earth's surface.

2. Clouds and Earth's surface reradiate the solar energy as long-wave energy.

3. The long-wave energy warms Earth and the atmosphere.

greenhouse effect the warming of the surface and lower atmosphere of Earth that occurs when water vapor, carbon dioxide, and other gases absorb and reradiate thermal energy

The Greenhouse Effect and Life on Earth

As you have learned, about 70% of the radiation that enters Earth's atmosphere is absorbed by clouds and by the Earth's surface. This energy is converted into thermal energy that warms the planet. In other words, short-wave visible light is absorbed and reradiated into the atmosphere as long-wave thermal energy. So, why doesn't this thermal energy escape back into space? Most of it does, but the atmosphere is like a warm blanket that traps enough energy to make Earth livable. This process, shown in **Figure 3,** is called the greenhouse effect. The **greenhouse effect** is the process by which gases in the atmosphere, such as water vapor and carbon dioxide, absorb thermal energy and radiate it back to Earth. This process is called the greenhouse effect because the gases function like the glass walls and roof of a greenhouse, which allow solar energy to enter but prevent thermal energy from escaping.

The Radiation Balance: Energy In, Energy Out

For Earth to remain livable, the amount of energy received from the sun and the amount of energy returned to space must be approximately equal. Solar energy that is absorbed by the Earth and its atmosphere is eventually reradiated into space as thermal energy. Every day, the Earth receives more energy from the sun. The balance between incoming energy and outgoing energy is known as the *radiation balance.*

Group ACTIVITY — BASIC

Model Greenhouses Have students work in groups to make model greenhouses by placing a thermometer inside a jar and anchoring the thermometer with modeling clay. Next, have students seal each jar with a lid. Have each group put its model in a different sunny spot. Students should observe and record changes in temperature every day for 1 week. Students can compare the temperatures recorded with the temperatures in a control jar that lacks a lid. Help students infer that solar energy enters a greenhouse and is converted to thermal energy and that the glass prevents most of the thermal energy from escaping. **LS** Kinesthetic

English Language Learners

Greenhouse Gases and Global Warming

Many scientists have become concerned about data that show that average global temperatures have increased in the past 100 years. Such an increase in average global temperatures is called **global warming**. Some scientists have hypothesized that an increase of greenhouse gases in the atmosphere may be the cause of this warming trend. Greenhouse gases are gases that absorb thermal energy in the atmosphere.

Human activity, such as the burning of fossil fuels and deforestation, may be increasing levels of greenhouse gases, such as carbon dioxide, in the atmosphere. If this hypothesis is correct, increasing levels of greenhouse gases may cause average global temperatures to continue to rise. If global warming continues, global climate patterns could be disrupted. Plants and animals that are adapted to live in specific climates would be affected. However, climate models are extremely complex, and scientists continue to debate whether the global warming trend is the result of an increase in greenhouse gases.

global warming a gradual increase in average global temperature

✔️ **Reading Check** What is a greenhouse gas?

SECTION Review

Summary

● Energy from the sun is transferred through the atmosphere by radiation, thermal conduction, and convection.

● Radiation is energy transfer by electromagnetic waves. Thermal conduction is energy transfer by direct contact. Convection is energy transfer by circulation.

● The greenhouse effect is Earth's natural heating process. Increasing levels of greenhouse gases could cause global warming.

Using Key Terms

1. Use each of the following terms in a separate sentence: *thermal conduction, radiation, convection, greenhouse effect,* and *global warming.*

Understanding Key Ideas

2. Which of the following is the best example of thermal conduction?
   a. a light bulb warming a lampshade
   b. an egg cooking in a frying pan
   c. water boiling in a pot
   d. gases circulating in the atmosphere

3. Describe three ways that energy is transferred in the atmosphere.

4. What is the difference between the greenhouse effect and global warming?

5. What is the radiation balance?

Math Skills

6. Find the average of the following temperatures: 73.2°F, 71.1°F, 54.6°F, 65.5°F, 78.2°F, 81.9°F, and 82.1°F.

Critical Thinking

7. **Identifying Relationships** How does the process of convection rely on radiation?

8. **Applying Concepts** Describe global warming in terms of the radiation balance.

For a variety of links related to this chapter, go to www.scilinks.org

Topic: Energy in the Atmosphere
SciLinks code: HSM0512

Answer to Reading Check

A greenhouse gas is a gas that absorbs thermal energy in the atmosphere.

CHAPTER RESOURCES

Chapter Resource File
- Section Quiz GENERAL
- Section Review GENERAL
- Vocabulary and Section Summary GENERAL

Technology
- Transparencies
  • The Greenhouse Effect

SECTION
3

Focus

Overview

This section explains what wind is and describes how differences in atmospheric pressure cause air to move. Students will also learn about global and local winds.

 Bellringer

Have students write a poem about moving air. The poem should include an explanation of why air moves.

Motivate

Demonstration — GENERAL

Air Movement Create an area of high pressure by filling a plastic container with ice. Create an area of low pressure by heating a hot plate. Place the container of ice and the hot plate approximately 30 cm from each other. Make sure the container of ice is slightly higher than the hot plate. Light a splint or long match, and let it burn for a few seconds. Extinguish the splint or match over the ice, and place the smoking end close to the ice. Ask students to observe the movement of the smoke. The smoke should move from the ice to the hot plate (from an area of high pressure to an area of low pressure). **LS Visual**

READING WARM-UP

Objectives

- Explain the relationship between air pressure and wind direction.
- Describe global wind patterns.
- Explain the causes of local wind patterns.

Terms to Learn

wind	westerlies
Coriolis effect	trade winds
polar easterlies	jet stream

READING STRATEGY

Prediction Guide Before reading this section, write the title of each heading in this section. Next, under each heading, write what you think you will learn.

wind the movement of air caused by differences in air pressure

Global Winds and Local Winds

If you open the valve on a bicycle tube, the air rushes out. Why? The air inside the tube is at a higher pressure than the air is outside the tube. In effect, letting air out of the tube created a wind.

Why Air Moves

The movement of air caused by differences in air pressure is called **wind.** The greater the pressure difference, the faster the wind moves. The devastation shown in **Figure 1** was caused by winds that resulted from extreme differences in air pressure.

Air Rises at the Equator and Sinks at the Poles

Differences in air pressure are generally caused by the unequal heating of the Earth. The equator receives more direct solar energy than other latitudes, so air at the equator is warmer and less dense than the surrounding air. Warm, less dense air rises and creates an area of low pressure. This warm, rising air flows toward the poles. At the poles, the air is colder and denser than the surrounding air, so it sinks. As the cold air sinks, it creates areas of high pressure around the poles. This cold polar air then flows toward the equator.

Figure 1 *In 1992, Hurricane Andrew became the most destructive hurricane in U.S. history. The winds from the hurricane reached 264 km/h.*

CHAPTER RESOURCES

Chapter Resource File

- **Lesson Plan**
- **Directed Reading A** BASIC
- **Directed Reading B** SPECIAL NEEDS

Technology

Transparencies
- Bellringer
- Pressure Belts

Cultural Awareness GENERAL

Animals and Air Pressure Changes in atmospheric pressure are often said to affect fish. Egyptian fishers notice that mullet move with the wind to prevent getting stuck in muddy water. According to Caribbean lore, a container of shark oil will grow cloudy when a hurricane is imminent. Have students find out about other organisms that might indicate changes in air pressure and other atmospheric phenomena. **LS Intrapersonal**

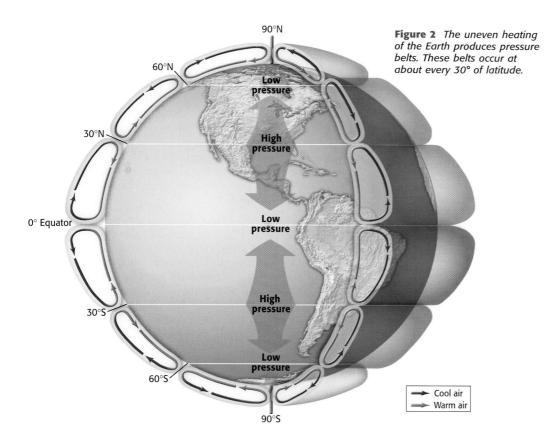

90°N

60°N

Low
pressure

30°N

High
pressure

0° Equator

Low
pressure

High
pressure

30°S

Low
pressure

60°S

90°S

→ Cool air
→ Warm air

Figure 2 *The uneven heating of the Earth produces pressure belts. These belts occur at about every 30° of latitude.*

MISCONCEPTION ALERT

What Causes Wind? Make sure students understand that air circulates because of temperature differences that cause pressure differences in the atmosphere. The sun heats the Earth, which heats the air above it by radiation and conduction. This warm air is less dense than the colder air above it, so the warm air rises, while the cold, denser air sinks. Air is colder near the poles because less solar energy reaches the ground at the poles than at the equator. Because air is warmer and less dense at the equator, air tends to rise and circulate toward the poles.

Answer to Reading Check

Sinking air causes areas of high pressure because sinking air presses down on the air beneath it.

Pressure Belts Are Found Every 30°

You may imagine that wind moves in one huge, circular pattern from the poles to the equator. In fact, air travels in many large, circular patterns called *convection cells.* Convection cells are separated by *pressure belts,* bands of high pressure and low pressure found about every 30° of latitude, as shown in **Figure 2.** As warm air rises over the equator and moves toward the poles, the air begins to cool. At about 30° north and 30° south latitude, some of the cool air begins to sink. Cool, sinking air causes high pressure belts near 30° north and 30° south latitude. This cool air flows back to the equator, where it warms and rises again. At the poles, cold air sinks and moves toward the equator. Air warms as it moves away from the poles. Around 60° north and 60° south latitude, the warmer air rises, which creates a low pressure belt. This air flows back to the poles.

Reading Check Why does sinking air cause areas of high pressure? (*See the Appendix for answers to Reading Checks.*)

CONNECTION to
Physical Science ———— **ADVANCED**

Katabatic Winds A katabatic wind is the movement of air due to the influence of gravity. This flow can range from a gentle breeze to gale-force winds. The world's strongest katabatic winds occur in Antarctica because there is plenty of cold air and the highest spot is near the center of the continent. Because the continent is basically cone shaped, winds radiate from the South Pole, accelerating like a car rolling down a hill. Cold, dense air rushes down mountainsides, tumbles across the ice sheets, and spills out over the ocean. The winds can blow for months, and they sometimes reach speeds as fast as 320 km/h! Use dry ice and a mountain made of modeling clay to demonstrate this phenomenon. **LS** Kinesthetic

Coriolis Effect Try the following activity to help students who have problems understanding the Coriolis effect. You will need a globe, some flour, an eyedropper, red food coloring, and water. Mix a few drops of food coloring with water, and fill the eyedropper with the solution. Dust the globe thoroughly with flour. If the flour doesn't stick, mist the globe lightly with water, and sprinkle the flour over the globe. Enlist a volunteer to slowly spin the globe counterclockwise to simulate Earth's rotation. Have another volunteer slowly drop water from the dropper at the top of the globe, at the North Pole. Students will observe that the water is deflected westward in the Northern Hemisphere.

LS Kinesthetic   English Language Learners

Answer to Reading Check

the westerlies

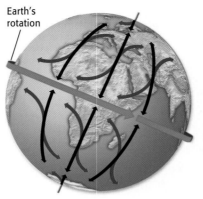

Earth's rotation

➡ Path of wind without Coriolis effect
➡ Approximate path of wind

Figure 3 *The Coriolis effect in the Northern Hemisphere causes winds traveling north to appear to curve to the east and winds traveling south to appear to curve to the west.*

Coriolis effect the apparent curving of the path of a moving object from an otherwise straight path due to the Earth's rotation

polar easterlies prevailing winds that blow from east to west between 60° and 90° latitude in both hemispheres

westerlies prevailing winds that blow from west to east between 30° and 60° latitude in both hemispheres

trade winds prevailing winds that blow east to west from 30° latitude to the equator in both hemispheres

The Coriolis Effect

As you have learned, pressure differences cause air to move between the equator and the poles. But try spinning a globe and using a piece of chalk to trace a straight line from the equator to the North Pole. The chalk line curves because the globe was spinning. Like the chalk line, winds do not travel directly north or south, because the Earth is rotating. The apparent curving of the path of winds and ocean currents due to the Earth's rotation is called the **Coriolis effect.** Because of the Coriolis effect in the Northern Hemisphere, winds traveling north curve to the east, and winds traveling south curve to the west, as shown in **Figure 3.**

Global Winds

The combination of convection cells found at every 30° of latitude and the Coriolis effect produces patterns of air circulation called *global winds.* **Figure 4** shows the major global wind systems: polar easterlies, westerlies, and trade winds. Winds such as easterlies and westerlies are named for the direction from which they blow.

Polar Easterlies

The wind belts that extend from the poles to 60° latitude in both hemispheres are called the **polar easterlies.** The polar easterlies are formed as cold, sinking air moves from the poles toward 60° north and 60° south latitude. In the Northern Hemisphere, polar easterlies can carry cold arctic air over the United States, producing snow and freezing weather.

Westerlies

The wind belts found between 30° and 60° latitude in both hemispheres are called the **westerlies.** The westerlies flow toward the poles from west to east. The westerlies can carry moist air over the United States, producing rain and snow.

Trade Winds

In both hemispheres, the winds that blow from 30° latitude almost to the equator are called **trade winds.** The Coriolis effect causes the trade winds to curve to the west in both hemispheres. Early traders used the trade winds to sail from Europe to the Americas. As a result, the winds became known as "trade winds."

✓ Reading Check If the trade winds carried traders from Europe to the Americas, what wind system carried traders back to Europe?

Homework ━━━━ GENERAL

The Coriolis Effect Many people often assume that the Coriolis effect affects the direction that water drains from sink basins or toilet bowls. Challenge students to devise an experiment to test this assumption. Students should record their data and present their data to the class. If time allows, graph the class results, and discuss any trends that appear.

LS Intrapersonal

CHAPTER RESOURCES
Technology

 Transparencies
• The Coriolis Effect
• Global Winds

The Doldrums

The trade winds of the Northern and Southern Hemispheres meet in an area around the equator called the *doldrums*. In the doldrums, there is very little wind because the warm, rising air creates an area of low pressure. The name *doldrums* means "dull" or "sluggish."

The Horse Latitudes

At about 30° north and 30° south latitude, sinking air creates an area of high pressure. The winds at these locations are weak. These areas are called the *horse latitudes*. According to legend, this name was given to these areas when sailing ships carried horses from Europe to the Americas. When the ships were stuck in this windless area, horses were sometimes thrown overboard to save drinking water for the sailors. Most of the world's deserts are located in the horse latitudes because the sinking air is very dry.

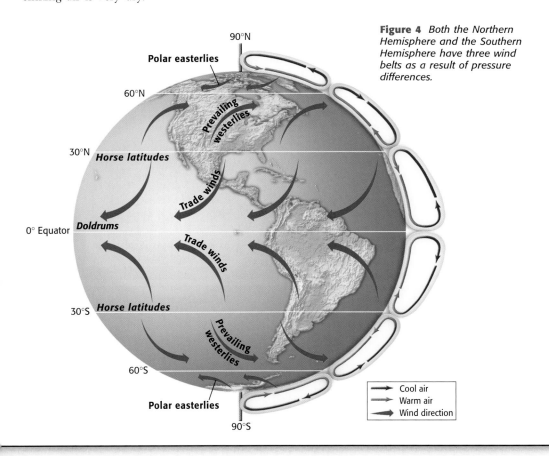

Figure 4 *Both the Northern Hemisphere and the Southern Hemisphere have three wind belts as a result of pressure differences.*

Using the Figure—BASIC

Wind Systems Have students use **Figure 4** to answer the following questions:

• Where are the trade winds? (The trade winds blow from 30° north and south latitudes to the equator.)

• Describe the motion of the trade winds in the Southern Hemisphere. (They move from the southeast to the northwest.)

• How do the westerlies flow in the Northern Hemisphere? (The westerlies flow from the southwest to the northeast.)

LS Logical

MISCONCEPTION ALERT

The Coriolis "Force" The Coriolis effect is not a force. When an object appears to be deflected from its path, it is not the object that is deflected but the Earth that has moved. Because the Earth is rotating, the Earth moves out from under the object that is passing over the surface. The change of the Earth's position gives the path traveled by the object the appearance of being curved. However, the Coriolis "force" can be used in mathematical equations to predict the movement of objects.

Science Bloopers

The Coriolis Effect During a World War I naval engagement off the Falkland Islands, British gunners were astonished to see that their artillery shells were landing 100 yd to the left of German ships. The gunners had made corrections for the Coriolis effect at 50° north latitude, not 50° south of the equator. Consequently, their shells fell at a distance from the target equal to twice the Coriolis deflection!

Is That a Fact!

Because the air descending over the horse latitudes has lost most of its moisture, the land around these latitudes receives very little precipitation. In fact, the Earth's largest deserts are in these areas.

Concept Mapping Have students create a concept map using the vocabulary and concepts in this section. **LS Visual**

Quiz ——————— GENERAL

1. How does air temperature over landmasses and adjacent bodies of water change between day and night? (During the day, the air is cooler over water. At night, the air is cooler over land.)

2. List two kinds of breezes that result from local topography. (mountain and valley breezes)

Alternative Assessment ——— GENERAL

Modeling Sea and Land Breezes
Give each group two baking pans—one filled with sand and the other filled with ice. Groups should carefully warm the sand in an oven until the sand is very warm. Have the groups place the pans side by side. Then, they should fold a cardboard wind screen in three places so that it surrounds both pans. As they hold a burning splint at the boundary between the pans, students should see smoke travel toward the hot sand in the same way that the wind blows toward the beach during the daytime. Ask them to explain their observations and try to simulate a land breeze. (They could simulate a land breeze by letting the sand cool and replacing the ice with warm water.) **LS Kinesthetic**

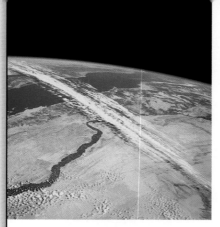

Figure 5 *The jet stream forms this band of clouds as it flows above the Earth.*

jet stream a narrow belt of strong winds that blow in the upper troposphere

Jet Streams: Atmospheric Conveyor Belts

The flight from Seattle to Boston can be 30 minutes faster than the flight from Boston to Seattle. Why? Pilots take advantage of a jet stream similar to the one shown in **Figure 5.** The **jet streams** are narrow belts of high-speed winds that blow in the upper troposphere and lower stratosphere. These winds can reach maximum speeds of 400 km/h. Unlike other global winds, the jet streams do not follow regular paths around the Earth. Knowing the path of a jet stream is important not only to pilots but also to meteorologists. Because jet streams affect the movement of storms, meteorologists can track a storm if they know the location of a jet stream.

Local Winds

Local winds generally move short distances and can blow from any direction. Local geographic features, such as a shoreline or a mountain, can produce temperature differences that cause local winds. For example, the formation of sea and land breezes is shown in **Figure 6.** During the day, the land heats up faster than the water, so the air above the land becomes warmer than the air above the ocean. The warm land air rises, and the cold ocean air flows in to replace it. At night, the land cools faster than water, so the wind blows toward the ocean.

Figure 6   Sea and Land Breezes

During the day, air over the ocean is cooler and forms an area of high pressure. The cool air flows to the land, producing a sea breeze.

Air over the land is warmer. As warm air rises, it creates an area of low pressure.

At night, air over the ocean is warmer. As the warm air rises, it forms an area of low pressure.

Air over land is cooler and forms an area of high pressure. The cool air moves toward the ocean, producing a land breeze.

CONNECTION to Life Science ——— GENERAL

High-Altitude Highway Migrating birds use jet streams and local winds as aerial highways to reach their destinations. Insects and spiders also take advantage of wind currents. Glider plane pilots have reported seeing air so thick with spiders that it looked like snow, and ships 800 km out at sea have been deluged with spiders falling from the sky! Dangling from the end of long, silk streamers, spiders ride updrafts until they reach a wind current. They occasionally reach altitudes of 4 km. There they can travel for weeks, rolling in their streamers and dropping from the sky after covering up to 300 km. Students might enjoy finding radar entomology Internet sites for people who track traveling insects.

Mountain Breezes and Valley Breezes

Mountain and valley breezes are other examples of local winds caused by an area's geography. Campers in mountainous areas may feel a warm afternoon quickly change into a cold night soon after the sun sets. During the day, the sun warms the air along the mountain slopes. This warm air rises up the mountain slopes, creating a valley breeze. At nightfall, the air along the mountain slopes cools. This cool air moves down the slopes into the valley, producing a mountain breeze.

Reading Check Why does the wind tend to blow down from mountains at night?

CONNECTION TO Social Studies

Local Breezes The chinook, the shamal, the sirocco, and the Santa Ana are all local winds. Find out about an interesting local wind, and create a poster-board display that shows how the wind forms and how it affects human cultures.

ACTIVITY

SECTION Review

Summary

- Winds blow from areas of high pressure to areas of low pressure.
- Pressure belts are found approximately every 30° of latitude.
- The Coriolis effect causes wind to appear to curve as it moves across the Earth's surface.
- Global winds include the polar easterlies, the westerlies, and the trade winds.
- Local winds include sea and land breezes and mountain and valley breezes.

Using Key Terms

1. In your own words, write a definition for each of the following terms: *wind, Coriolis effect, jet stream, polar easterlies, westerlies,* and *trade winds.*

Understanding Key Ideas

2. Why does warm air rise and cold air sink?
   a. because warm air is less dense than cold air
   b. because warm air is denser than cold air
   c. because cold air is less dense than warm air
   d. because warm air has less pressure than cold air does

3. What are pressure belts?

4. What causes winds?

5. How does the Coriolis effect affect wind movement?

6. How are sea and land breezes similar to mountain and valley breezes?

7. Would there be winds if the Earth's surface were the same temperature everywhere? Explain your answer.

Math Skills

8. Flying an airplane at 500 km/h, a pilot plans to reach her destination in 5 h. But she finds a jet stream moving 250 km/h in the direction she is traveling. If she gets a boost from the jet stream for 2 h, how long will the flight last?

Critical Thinking

9. **Making Inferences** In the Northern Hemisphere, why do westerlies flow from the west but trade winds flow from the east?

10. **Applying Concepts** Imagine you are near an ocean in the daytime. You want to go to the ocean, but you don't know how to get there. How might a local wind help you find the ocean?

SCI LINKS.

NSTA
Developed and maintained by the National Science Teachers Association

For a variety of links related to this chapter, go to www.scilinks.org

Topic: Atmospheric Pressure and Winds
SciLinks code: HSM0115

Answers to Section Review

1. Sample answer: Wind is the movement of air from areas of high pressure to areas of low pressure. The Coriolis effect is the apparent deflection of a moving object due to Earth's rotation. Jet streams are high altitude belts of strong winds. Polar easterlies are global winds that blow from the poles toward 60° north and 60° south latitude. Westerlies are global winds that blow between 30° and 60° latitude in both hemispheres. Trade winds are global winds that blow between 30° latitude and the equator in both hemispheres.

CHAPTER RESOURCES

Chapter Resource File
- Section Quiz GENERAL
- Section Review GENERAL
- Vocabulary and Section Summary GENERAL

Technology
- Transparencies
  - Sea and Land Breezes

2. a

3. Pressure belts are bands of high and low pressure that are found about every 30° of latitude.

4. Winds are caused by the unequal heating of the Earth's surface, which causes pressure differences.

5. The Coriolis effect causes winds to appear to be deflected to the east or west depending on the direction that the winds are traveling in each hemisphere. Because of the Coriolis effect, winds in the Northern Hemisphere appear to curve to the right, and winds in the Southern Hemisphere appear to curve to the left.

6. Both types of breezes result from pressure differences caused by unequal heating of materials.

7. Because unequal heating of the Earth's surface causes winds, there would probably not be winds near Earth's surface if Earth's surface were the same temperature everywhere.

8. 500 km/h × 5 h = 2,500 km
(500 km/h + 250 km/h) × 2 h = 1,500 km
2,500 km − 1,500 km = 1,000 km
1,000 km ÷ 500 km = 2 h
2 h + 2 h = 4 h

9. Both winds are affected by the Coriolis effect. In the Northern Hemisphere, the westerlies travel in a northerly direction. They appear to be deflected to the northeast by the Coriolis effect. In contrast, in the Northern Hemisphere, the trade winds blow in a southerly direction, so they appear to be deflected to the southwest.

10. During the day, a sea breeze is caused by cooler air over the water moving toward the land. Walking toward the sea breeze would lead you to the ocean.

Answer to Reading Check

At night, the air along the mountain slopes cools. This cool air moves down the slopes into the valley and produces a mountain breeze.

Focus

Overview

This section discusses the causes and effects of air pollution. Students learn the difference between primary and secondary pollutants and learn examples of point and nonpoint-source pollutants of North Carolina. Finally, students learn about the causes and effects of acid precipitation.

Bellringer

Write the following quotation on the board. "I thought I saw a blue jay this morning. But the smog was so bad that it turned out to be a cardinal holding its breath."—Michael J. Cohen. Tell students that sometimes humor gets people's attention about a serious issue more readily than any other method. Divide the class into small groups, and tell them to use humor, as Cohen did, to complete the following sentence: "You know the air is polluted when . . ." Have each group share their sentence with the class.

Answer to Reading Check

Sample answer: smoke, dust, and sea salt

READING WARM-UP

Objectives

● Compare primary and secondary air pollutants.

● Identify point-sources and nonpoint-sources of air pollution in North Carolina.

● Identify sources of human-caused air pollution.

● Describe how acid precipitation affects the environment.

Terms to Learn

air pollution
acid precipitation

READING STRATEGY

Reading Organizer As you read this section, make a table that identifies major sources of air pollution and the effects of each.

air pollution the contamination of the atmosphere by the introduction of pollutants from human and natural sources

---

Air Pollution

In December 1952, one of London's dreaded "pea souper" fogs settled on the city. But this was no ordinary fog—it was thick with coal smoke and air pollution. It burned people's lungs, and the sky grew so dark that people could not see their hands in front of their faces. When the fog lifted four days later, thousands of people were dead!

London's killer fog shocked the world and caused major changes in England's air-pollution laws. People began to think that air pollution was not simply a part of urban life that had to be endured. Air pollution had to be reduced. Although this event is an extreme example, air pollution is common in many parts of the world. However, nations are taking major steps to reduce air pollution. But what is air pollution? **Air pollution** is the contamination of the atmosphere by the introduction of pollutants from human and natural sources. Air pollutants are classified according to their source as either primary pollutants or secondary pollutants.

Primary Pollutants

Pollutants that are put directly into the air by human or natural activity are *primary pollutants*. Primary pollutants from natural sources include dust, sea salt, volcanic gases and ash, smoke from forest fires, and pollen. Primary pollutants from human sources include carbon monoxide, dust, smoke, and chemicals from paint and other substances. In urban areas, vehicle exhaust is a common source of primary pollutants. Examples of primary pollutants are shown in **Figure 1.**

✓ **Reading Check** List three primary pollutants from natural sources. (*See the Appendix for answers to Reading Checks.*)

Figure 1 **Examples of Primary Pollutants**

Industrial emissions

Vehicle exhaust

Volcanic ash

CHAPTER RESOURCES

Chapter Resource File

• Lesson Plan
• Directed Reading A BASIC
• Directed Reading B SPECIAL NEEDS

Technology

Transparencies
• Bellringer
• The Formation of Smog

Is That a Fact!

In 1999, North Carolina was ranked 11th in human population and second in hog population. In fact, with 10 million hogs, the state has more pigs than it has people. Hog waste emits ammonia, which is considered an air pollutant. After the ammonia is emitted, it can fall back to Earth in rain. Excess ammonia can overload coastal estuaries with nutrients, which can cause problems for fish and the organisms that depend on the fish for food.

Secondary Pollutants

Pollutants that form when primary pollutants react with other primary pollutants or with naturally occurring substances are *secondary pollutants*. Ozone and smog are examples of secondary pollutants. Ozone is formed when sunlight reacts with vehicle exhaust and air. You may have heard of "Ozone Action Day" warnings in your community. When such a warning is issued, people are discouraged from outdoor physical activity because ozone can damage their lungs. In the stratosphere, ozone forms a protective layer that absorbs harmful radiation from the sun. Near the Earth's surface, however, ozone is a dangerous pollutant that negatively affects the health of organisms. **Figure 2** shows how smog is formed.

Point and Nonpoint-Source Pollutants

All sources of pollutants can be classified as either point-source pollutants or non-point source pollutants. *Point-source pollutants* are pollutants that are released from a single source. Examples of point-source pollutants in North Carolina are smoke from burning brush, chemical wastes and gases from agricultural industries as shown in **Figure 3,** and particulate matter. Particulate matter is any small particle of dust, dirt, or soot in the air. *Nonpoint-source pollutants* are pollutants that come from many different sources and are often difficult to identify. Examples of nonpoint-source pollutants in North Carolina include ozone and haze. Ozone forms when emissions from industries and motor vehicles react with air and sunlight. Haze forms when emissions from power plants react with air.

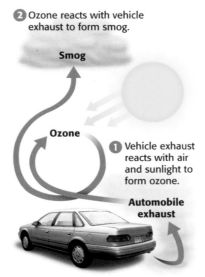

❷ Ozone reacts with vehicle exhaust to form smog.

Smog

Ozone

❶ Vehicle exhaust reacts with air and sunlight to form ozone.

Automobile exhaust

Figure 2 *Smog forms when sunlight reacts with ozone and vehicle exhaust.*

Figure 3 *Chemicals such as methane from animal waste, are considered point-source pollutants.*

Motivate

Identifying Preconceptions — GENERAL

Indoor Air Pollution Explain that the air inside buildings can be polluted by a variety of sources. Ask students to list possible sources of indoor air pollution. If students have difficulty coming up with examples, tell them that air pollution is often invisible. Chalk dust, cooking oils, carpets, insulation, tobacco smoke, paints, glues, copier machines, space heaters, gas appliances, and fireplaces are just a few sources of indoor air pollution. **LS** Verbal

Teach

Group ACTIVITY — GENERAL

Point and Nonpoint-source Pollution In small groups, have students research the point and nonpoint-sources of air pollution in their county. They should consider transportation, industry, agriculture, and electricity production. Where is the pollution coming from? What are the primary air pollutants? How does their county compare with other counties in the state? How does North Carolina compare with the rest of the country? Have the groups report their findings on a large poster. **LS** Interpersonal/Visual

Answer to Connection to Biology Activity

Plants that are effective at removing indoor air pollutants include: philodendrons, spider plants, golden pothos, gerbera daisies, chrysanthemums, corn plant, peace lily, and English ivy.

ACTIVITY — BASIC

Classifying Pollutants List the following pollutants on the board: smog, house dust, acid rain, pollen, soot, ground-level ozone, volcanic ash, and acid rain. Beside the list, make a two-column table with the following column headings: "Primary pollutants" and "Secondary pollutants." Help students classify each pollutant as either a primary pollutant (house dust, pollen, volcanic ash, and soot) or a secondary pollutant (ground-level ozone, smog, and acid rain).
LS Verbal

CONNECTION TO Biology

Cleaning the Air with Plants Did you know that common houseplants can help fight indoor air pollution? Some houseplants are so effective at removing air pollutants that NASA might use them as part of the life-support system in future space stations. Back on Earth, you can use plants to clean the air in your school or home. Research the top 10 air-cleaning houseplants, and find out if you can grow any of them in your classroom or home.
ACTIVITY

Figure 4 *There are many sources of indoor air pollution. Indoor air pollution can be difficult to detect because it is often invisible.*

Sources of Human-Caused Air Pollution

Human-caused air pollution comes from a variety of sources. A major source of air pollution today is transportation. Cars contribute about 10% to 20% of the human-caused air pollution in the United States. Vehicle exhaust contains nitrogen oxide, which contributes to smog formation and acid precipitation. However, pollution controls and cleaner gasoline have greatly reduced air pollution from vehicles.

Industrial Air Pollution

Many industrial plants and electric power plants burn fossil fuels, such as coal, to produce energy. Burning some types of coal without pollution controls can release large amounts of air pollutants. Some industries also produce chemicals that can pollute the air. Oil refineries, chemical manufacturing plants, dry-cleaning businesses, furniture refinishers, and auto body shops are all potential sources of air pollution.

Indoor Air Pollution

Sometimes, the air inside a building can be more polluted than the air outside. Some sources of indoor air pollution are shown in **Figure 4.** *Ventilation,* or the mixing of indoor air with outdoor air, can reduce indoor air pollution. Another way to reduce indoor air pollution is to limit the use of chemical solvents and cleaners.

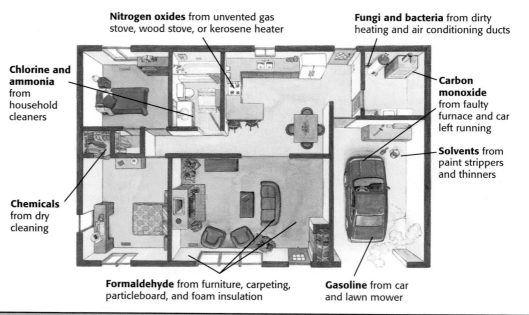

Nitrogen oxides from unvented gas stove, wood stove, or kerosene heater

Fungi and bacteria from dirty heating and air conditioning ducts

Chlorine and ammonia from household cleaners

Carbon monoxide from faulty furnace and car left running

Solvents from paint strippers and thinners

Chemicals from dry cleaning

Formaldehyde from furniture, carpeting, particleboard, and foam insulation

Gasoline from car and lawn mower

CHAPTER RESOURCES

Technology

Transparencies
• Sources of Indoor Air Pollution

CONNECTION to Physical Science — GENERAL

Incomplete Combustion Explain that much of human-caused air pollution results from incomplete combustion. *Combustion,* another word for "burning," is the process by which substances combine with oxygen rapidly to produce thermal energy. Byproducts are produced when a substance does not burn completely, as in an automobile engine. Some of these byproducts, such as carbon monoxide, are harmful to living things.

Acid Precipitation

When fossil fuels are burned, they can release sulfur dioxide and nitrogen oxide into the atmosphere. When these pollutants combine with water in the atmosphere, they form sulfuric acid and nitric acid. Precipitation such as rain, sleet, or snow that contains these acids from air pollution is called **acid precipitation.** Precipitation is naturally acidic, but sulfuric acid and nitric acid can make it so acidic that it can negatively affect the environment. In most areas of the world, pollution controls have helped reduce acid precipitation.

Acid Precipitation and Plants

Plant communities have adapted over long periods of time to the natural acidity of the soil in which they grow. Acid precipitation can cause the acidity of soil to increase. This process, called *acidification*, changes the balance of a soil's chemistry in several ways. When the acidity of soil increases, some nutrients are broken down. Nutrients that plants need for growth get washed away by acidic rainwater. Increased acidity also releases aluminum and other toxic metals from the soil. Some of these toxic metals are absorbed by the roots of plants.

Reading Check How does acid precipitation affect plants?

The Effects of Acid Precipitation on Forests

Forest ecology is complex. Scientists are still trying to fully understand the long-term effects of acid precipitation on groups of plants and their habitats. In some areas of the world, however, acid precipitation has damaged large areas of forest. The effects of acid precipitation are most noticeable in Eastern Europe, as shown in **Figure 5.** Forests in the northeastern United States and in eastern Canada have also been affected by acid precipitation.

acid precipitation rain, sleet, or snow that contains a high concentration of acids

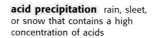

Testing for Particulates

1. Particulates are pollutants such as dust that are extremely small. In this lab, you will measure the amount of particulates in the air. Begin by covering **ten 5 in. × 7 in. index cards** with a thin coat of **petroleum jelly.**

2. Hang the cards in various locations inside and outside your school.

3. One day later, use a **magnifying lens** to count the number of particles on the cards. Which location had the fewest number of particulates? Which location had the highest number of particulates? Hypothesize why.

Figure 5 *This forest in Poland was damaged by acid precipitation.*

Activity — GENERAL

Rain Catcher Install a rain-catching device outside the school where it can be easily accessed. After each rain, have students collect the water sample for testing. Using a pH meter (or litmus paper if a pH meter is unavailable), find the pH of each sample. The pH of pure water is 7, and the pH of average rainwater should be about 5.5. How does the pH of the students' sample compare? Instruct students to keep a record of their findings in their **science journal.** **LS Logical**

Answer to Reading Check

Answers may vary. Acid precipitation may decrease the soil nutrients that are available to plants.

Pollution Terms Have students use each of the following terms in a sentence that correctly conveys the meaning of the term: *vehicle exhaust, secondary pollutants, smog, acid precipitation, industrial pollutants, ozone, primary pollutants,* and *air pollution.* **LS** Visual

Quiz —————— GENERAL

1. Classify each of the following pollutants as either a primary or secondary air pollutant: smog, tobacco smoke, chalk dust, and acid rain. (Sample answer: Tobacco smoke and chalk dust are primary pollutants. Smog and acid rain are secondary pollutants.)

2. What is acid precipitation? (Acid precipitation is rain, sleet, or snow that contains a high concentration of acids.)

Alternative Assessment —— BASIC

Critical Reading Have students find an article about air pollution in a popular periodical or newspaper. Students should photocopy the article on 11 × 17 paper. Then, ask students to critique the article's strengths and weaknesses and write comments in the margin of the paper. **LS** Verbal

Figure 6 *Acid shock, which is a rapid change in a body of water's acidity, can prevent fish from absorbing oxygen and nutrients. Acid shock can cause populations of fish to die.*

Acid Precipitation and Aquatic Ecosystems

Aquatic organisms have adapted to live in water that has a particular range of acidity. If acid precipitation increases the acidity of a lake or stream, aquatic plants, fish, and other aquatic organisms living in the lake or stream may die.

The effects of acid precipitation are worst in the spring, when the acidic snow that built up in the winter melts and acidic water flows into lakes and rivers. A rapid change in a body of water's acidity is called *acid shock.* Acid shock can cause large numbers of fish in a population to die, as shown in **Figure 6.** Acid shock can affect how fish absorb oxygen and nutrients. To reduce the effects of acid precipitation on aquatic ecosystems, some communities add powdered limestone (calcium carbonate) to acidified lakes in the spring. Limestone neutralizes acids in the lakes. Unfortunately, limestone cannot prevent all acid damage to lakes.

✓ **Reading Check** Why is powdered limestone added to lakes in the spring instead of the fall?

Acid Precipitation and Humans

Acid precipitation can also affect humans. An increase in soil acidity can cause toxic metals, such as aluminum and mercury, to be released from the soil. These toxic metals can find their way into crops, water, fish, and then eventually into the human body. Studies have also shown that acid precipitation may harm the respiratory health of children.

Neutralizing Acid Precipitation

1. Pour 1/2 tbsp of **vinegar** into one cup of **distilled water,** and stir the mixture well. Check the pH of the mixture by using pH paper. The pH should be about 4.

2. Crush one stick of **blackboard chalk** into powder. Pour the powder into the vinegar and water mixture. Check the pH of the mixture.

3. Did the vinegar and water mixture become more or less acidic after the powdered chalk was poured in?

Answer to Reading Check

Powdered limestone is used to counteract the effects of acidic snowmelt from snow that accumulated during the winter.

Answers to Quick Lab

3. The mixture will become less acidic; as the acidic vinegar dissolves the basic limestone, the solution will become more basic.

International Cooperation

Controlling acid precipitation is complicated. Pollutants that are released in one area may later fall to the ground as acid precipitation in an area hundreds of kilometers away. Sometimes, pollution from one country results in acid precipitation in another country. For example, almost half of the acid precipitation that falls in southeastern Canada results from pollution produced in the United States. In the spirit of cooperation, the governments of Canada and the United States signed the Canada-U.S. Air Quality Agreement in 1991. Both countries agreed to reduce acidic emissions that flowed across the Canada-U.S. boundary. More of these international agreements may be necessary to control acid precipitation.

CONNECTION TO
Chemistry

Acidity of Precipitation
Acidity is measured by using a pH scale, the units of which range from 1 to 14. Solutions that have a pH of less than 7 are acidic. Research recorded pH levels of acid rain in your area. Then, compare these pH levels with the pH levels of other common acids, such as lemon juice and acetic acid.

SECTION Review

Summary

- Primary pollutants are pollutants that are put directly into the air by human or natural activity. Secondary pollutants form when primary pollutants react with other primary pollutants or with naturally occurring substances.

- Point-source pollutants in North Carolina are smoke, outdoor odors, and particulate matter. Nonpoint-source pollutants in North Carolina are ozone and haze.

- Transportation, industry, and natural sources are the main sources of air pollution.

- Acid precipitation can have harmful effects on plants, animals, and humans.

Using Key Terms

The statements below are false. For each statement, replace the underlined term to make a true statement.

1. <u>Air pollution</u> is a sudden change in the acidity of a stream or lake.

2. <u>Smog</u> is rain, sleet, or snow that has a high concentration of acid.

Understanding Key Ideas

3. Which of the following is a primary pollutant?
   a. ozone
   b. smog
   c. vehicle exhaust
   d. rain

4. List the main point-source pollutants and nonpoint-source pollutants in North Carolina.

Critical Thinking

5. **Expressing Opinions** How do you think that nations should resolve air-pollution problems that cross national boundaries?

Interpreting Graphics

Use the map to answer the questions below.

6. Which areas have the most acidic precipitation?

7. Boston is a larger city than Buffalo is, but the precipitation measured in Buffalo is more acidic than the precipitation in Boston. Explain why.

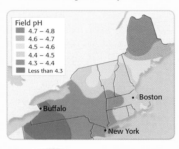

Field pH
- 4.7 – 4.8
- 4.6 – 4.7
- 4.5 – 4.6
- 4.4 – 4.5
- 4.3 – 4.4
- Less than 4.3

• Buffalo   • Boston
        • New York

SCLINKS
NSTA
Developed and maintained by the
National Science Teachers Association

For a variety of links related to this chapter, go to www.scilinks.org
Topic: Acid Precipitation
SciLinks code: HSM1690

CHAPTER RESOURCES

Chapter Resource File

- Section Quiz **GENERAL**
- Section Review **GENERAL**
- Vocabulary and Section Summary **GENERAL**
- Critical Thinking **ADVANCED**
- Datasheet for Quick Lab
- Datasheet for Quick Lab

Technology

 Interactive Explorations CD-ROM
- Moose Malady **GENERAL**

Focus

Overview

This section discusses the effects of air pollution on the human body. It also describes how air quality is monitored, measured, and communicated to the public. Finally, the section describes ways to reduce air pollution.

 Bellringer

Bring a filter mask to class. Have each student make a list of three situations in which one might wear such a mask. (working with dust, microbes, or paint)

Motivate

CONNECTION ACTIVITY
Health ———— GENERAL

Respiratory Diseases Have students find out about respiratory diseases that can be aggravated by air pollution, such as asthma. Have students compile their findings into tables that list the diseases, the diseases' symptoms, the ways that the diseases are treated, the age groups most commonly afflicted by the diseases, and the relationship between the diseases and the air pollutants. **LS** Logical

Answer to Reading Check

Sample answer: coughing, headaches, and irritation to the eyes

---

READING WARM-UP

Objectives
- List three effects of air pollution on the human body.
- Describe how air quality is monitored and measured.
- Describe how air quality is communicated to the public.
- Identify ways to reduce air pollution.

READING STRATEGY

Reading Organizer As you read this section, create an outline of the section. Use the headings from the section in your outline.

Maintaining Air Quality

Have you ever seen or heard a weather forecaster report the day's air quality? Have you ever had to stay indoors because the air outside was unhealthy?

The air quality in your area affects your health and your everyday life. It's important to learn about the air quality in your area and to know the short-term and long-term effects of air pollution on your health.

Air Pollution and Human Health

Daily exposure to small amounts of air pollution can cause serious health problems. Children, elderly people, and people who have asthma, allergies, lung problems, and heart problems are especially vulnerable to the effects of air pollution.

Short-Term and Long-Term Effects

Many of the effects of air pollution on the human body are short-term effects and are immediately noticeable. Coughing, headaches, irritation to the eyes, nose, and throat, and an increase in asthma-related problems are only a few short-term effects. One good way to avoid experiencing any short-term effects of air pollution is staying indoors on days when the air quality is poor in your area. People who cannot stay indoors because of their jobs, such as the police officer in **Figure 1,** can wear masks and other gear to protect themselves from air pollution.

Long-term effects of air pollution, such as lung cancer and heart disease, may not be noticed until many years after an individual has been exposed to pollutants.

 Reading Check List three short-term effects of air pollution on human health. (*See the Appendix for answers to Reading Checks.*)

Figure 1 *This police officer wears a mask to protect him from harmful pollutants as he directs traffic in Bangkok, Thailand.*

WEIRD SCIENCE

Ice core samples from Greenland show that there was large-scale lead pollution in the atmosphere more than 2,000 years ago. The lead can be traced to Roman silver mines in southern Spain. The smelting of silver ore released large amounts of lead into the atmosphere.

CHAPTER RESOURCES

Chapter Resource File
- Lesson Plan
- Directed Reading A **BASIC**
- Directed Reading B **SPECIAL NEEDS**

Technology
- Transparencies
  - Bellringer

Monitoring Air Quality

In 1970, the United States Congress passed the Clean Air Act. The Clean Air Act is a law that gives the Environmental Protection Agency (EPA) the authority to regulate the amount of air pollutants that can be released from any source, such as cars and factories.

Air Quality Standards

The EPA sets air quality standards for each state to follow. There are specific standards regarding levels of pollutants, such as carbon monoxide, lead, and ozone. These standards restrict how much of each pollutant can be released. The EPA works to improve air quality in areas where the air quality is poor and to prevent air pollution in areas where the air quality is healthy. There are two types of standards—primary and secondary. Primary standards protect against the effects of air pollution on human health and secondary standards protect against the effects of air pollution on crops, vegetation, and buildings. If air quality worsens, the EPA can set stricter standards. The Clean Air Act was strengthened in 1990.

Air Quality Index

The EPA and local governments are responsible for setting and enforcing air quality standards, as well as for reporting the air quality to the public. The Air Quality Index (AQI), shown in **Table 1,** is used to provide the public with daily air quality information. The AQI measures the air quality of an area with a value from 0 to 500. The AQI is determined after air pollution monitors record the concentrations of the major pollutants in an area. The higher the AQI, the higher the level of air pollution, and the higher the health risk. Once the AQI value is determined for a certain area, a level of health concern and color is also given.

Table 1 Air Quality Index

Air Quality Index (AQI) Values	Levels of Health Concern	Colors
0 to 50	Good	Green
51 to 100	Moderate	Yellow
101 to 150	Unhealthy for sensitive groups	Orange
151 to 200	Unhealthy	Red
201 to 300	Very Unhealthy	Purple
301 to 500	Hazardous	Maroon

CONNECTION TO Environmental Science

WRITING SKILL **The Ozone Hole** In 1985, scientists reported an alarming discovery about the Earth's protective ozone layer. Over the Antarctic regions, the ozone layer was thinning. Chemicals called *CFCs* were causing ozone to break down into oxygen, which does not block the sun's harmful ultraviolet (UV) rays. The thinning of the ozone layer creates an ozone hole, which allows more UV radiation to reach the Earth's surface. UV radiation is dangerous to organisms because it damages genes and can cause skin cancer. Using the Internet or library resources research the current state of the ozone layer. Also, find out if *CFCs* are still being used today.

Teach

ACTIVITY —— GENERAL

Air Quality Index (AQI) Have students keep track of the Air Quality Index (AQI) for their city or region over several weeks, or for the school year. Have students look for trends. For example, have students answer the following questions: "Does the air quality vary during different times of the year? At different temperatures? Different days of the week? Can you explain these differences? Do students with asthma notice a difference on "yellow" or "orange" days?" Students can find data from past years on the Internet. **LS Logical**

Demonstration —— GENERAL

Guest Speaker Have a guest from the North Carolina Department of Environment and Natural Resources (NCDENR) come to your school to teach about energy conservation and pollution control. Ask the speaker to present ways that students can make a difference, directly or indirectly, in the quality of the air they breathe. If a representative from the NCDENR is not available, consider contacting your local power company.

Homework —— ADVANCED

Radon Radon is a naturally occurring gas that results from the decay of uranium, particularly in igneous rocks such as granite. Have students use the Internet to research the health problems associated with radon. Have students assess the potential for significant radon concentrations in your community and write a short informative essay based on their findings. **LS Intrapersonal**

CONNECTION ACTIVITY Real World —— GENERAL

Local Air Pollution and Weather Air quality varies greatly from place to place. Even in one location, air quality can change seasonally or from day to day. Have students research the air quality where they live. Ask students to consider the following questions: "What are the sources of air pollution where you live? What weather conditions lead to the worst and best air quality in your area?" **LS Interpersonal**

Figure 2 *This power plant is leading the way in clean-coal technology. The plant turns coal into a gas before it is burned, so fewer pollutants are released.*

Reducing Air Pollution

Much progress has been made in reducing air pollution. The Clean Air Act, stricter air quality standards, advancements in technology, and lifestyle changes all help reduce air pollution.

Controlling Air Pollution from Industry

The Clean Air Act requires many industries to use pollution-control devices such as scrubbers. A *scrubber* is a device that is used to remove some pollutants before they are released by smokestacks. Scrubbers in coal-burning power plants remove particles such as ash from the smoke. Other industrial plants, such as the power plant shown in **Figure 2,** focus on burning fuel more efficiently so that fewer pollutants are released.

Figure 3 *Many states require cars to get emissions tests. Regulating the amount of emissions that vehicles release helps reduce air pollution.*

Reducing Motor Vehicle Emissions

A large percentage of air pollution in the United States comes from the vehicles we drive. To reduce air pollution from vehicles, the EPA requires car makers to meet a certain standard for vehicle exhaust. Devices such as catalytic converters remove many pollutants from exhaust and help cars meet this standard. To make sure that cars continue to meet this standard, some states require vehicles to pass an emissions inspection, as shown in **Figure 3.**

Cleaner fuels and more-efficient engines have also helped reduce air pollution from vehicles. Car makers are also designing cars that run on fuels other than gasoline. Some of these cars run on hydrogen or natural gas. Hybrid cars, which are becoming more common, use gasoline and electric power to reduce emissions.

INTERNET ACTIVITY
Short Story — GENERAL

For an internet activity related to this chapter, have students go to **go.hrw.com** and type in the keyword **HZ5ATMW.**

Ways To Reduce Air Pollution

People can make choices that can help reduce air pollution. For example, you can reduce air pollution by carpooling, using public transportation, walking, or biking to your destination, as shown in **Figure 4**. Planning ahead to combine trips or errands instead of making multiple trips also helps reduce pollution. Keeping cars and other gas-powered machines in good condition helps reduce the amount of fuel the engine consumes, and therefore reduces the amount of emissions the engine releases.

Conserving electricity also helps reduce air pollution. Turning off lights and other electrical appliances when they are not in use can reduce the amount of air pollution that is created when electricity is generated. You can also learn more about reducing air pollution by talking to your state environmental agency or by joining a group that is working to reduce air pollution in your area.

✔ Reading Check Describe one way that you can help reduce air pollution.

Figure 4 *In Copenhagen, Denmark, companies loan free bicycles in exchange for publicity. The program helps reduce air pollution and auto traffic.*

SECTION Review

Summary

- Coughing, headaches, and an increase in asthma-related problems are three effects of air pollution on the human body.
- The EPA and local governments set and enforce air quality standards, and inform the public about air quality.
- Air pollution can be reduced by legislation, such as the Clean Air Act; by technology, such as scrubbers; and by changes in lifestyle.

Understanding Key Ideas

1. Which of the following is a long-term effect of air pollution on the human body?
   a. irritation to the eyes
   b. lung cancer
   c. headaches
   d. coughing

2. Describe the Clean Air Act. When was the Clean Air Act passed by Congress?

3. Explain how the EPA ensures that areas maintain healthy air quality.

4. What do the EPA's primary and secondary air quality standards protect?

5. Describe three effects of air pollution on human health.

6. How can industries help reduce the air pollution they release?

7. What is the Air Quality Index?

Critical Thinking

8. **Identifying Relationships** How can advancements in technology help reduce motor vehicle emissions?

9. **Applying Concepts** List three ways that your community can reduce air pollution. How can you raise awareness in your community about how to reduce air pollution?

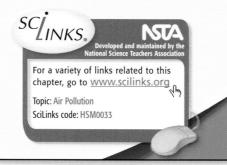

SCi LINKS **NSTA**
Developed and maintained by the National Science Teachers Association

For a variety of links related to this chapter, go to www.scilinks.org

Topic: Air Pollution
SciLinks code: HSM0033

CHAPTER RESOURCES

Chapter Resource File

- Section Quiz **GENERAL**
- Section Review **GENERAL**
- Vocabulary & Notes **GENERAL**
- SciLinks Worksheet **GENERAL**

Under Pressure!

Teacher's Notes

Time Required
One 45-minute class period plus 15 minutes each day for 3 or 4 days

Lab Ratings

EASY —————————→ HARD

Teacher Prep 🧪🧪
Student Set-Up 🧪🧪🧪🧪
Concept Level 🧪🧪
Clean Up 🧪🧪

MATERIALS
The materials listed on the student page are enough for a group of 2–4 students.

Safety Caution
Remind students to review all safety cautions and icons before beginning this lab activity.

Preparation Notes
A week before the activity, have students bring in large coffee cans. Jars can substitute for coffee cans in this experiment. For more-accurate results, make sure students place their barometers in a shaded area. As students work on this lab in class, have them collect newspaper clippings of daily weather reports.

Under Pressure!

Imagine that you are planning a picnic with your friends, so you look in the newspaper for the weather forecast. The temperature this afternoon should be in the low 80s. This temperature sounds quite comfortable! But you notice that the newspaper's forecast also includes the barometer reading. What's a barometer? And what does the reading tell you? In this activity, you will build your own barometer and will discover what this tool can tell you.

OBJECTIVES

Predict how changes in air pressure affect a barometer.

Build a barometer to test your hypothesis.

MATERIALS

- balloon
- can, coffee, large, empty, 10 cm in diameter
- card, index
- scissors
- straw, drinking
- tape, masking, or rubber band

SAFETY

Ask a Question

1 How can I use a barometer to detect changes in air pressure?

Form a Hypothesis

2 Write a few sentences that answer the question above.

Test the Hypothesis

3 Stretch the balloon a few times. Then, blow up the balloon, and let the air out. This step will make your barometer more sensitive to changes in atmospheric pressure.

4 Cut off the open end of the balloon. Next, stretch the balloon over the open end of the coffee can. Then, attach the balloon to the can with masking tape or a rubber band.

Terry J. Rakes
Elmwood Jr. High
Rogers, Arkansas

CHAPTER RESOURCES

Chapter Resource File
- • Datasheet for Chapter Lab
- • Lab Notes and Answers

Technology
 Classroom Videos
  • Lab Video

 LabBook

 • Go Fly a Bike!

5 Cut one end of the straw at an angle to make a pointer.

6 Place the straw on the stretched balloon so that the pointer is directed away from the center of the balloon. Five centimeters of the end of the straw should hang over the edge of the can. Tape the straw to the balloon as shown in the illustration at right.

7 Tape the index card to the side of the can as shown in the illustration at right. Congratulations! You have just made a barometer!

8 Now, use your barometer to collect and record information about air pressure. Place the barometer outside for 3 or 4 days. On each day, mark on the index card where the tip of the straw points.

Analyze the Results

1 **Explaining Events** What atmospheric factors affect how your barometer works? Explain your answer.

2 **Recognizing Patterns** What does it mean when the straw moves up?

3 **Recognizing Patterns** What does it mean when the straw moves down?

Draw Conclusions

4 **Applying Conclusions** Compare your results with the barometric pressures listed in your local newspaper. What kind of weather is associated with high pressure? What kind of weather is associated with low pressure?

5 **Evaluating Results** Does the barometer you built support your hypothesis? Explain your answer.

Applying Your Data

Now, you can use your barometer to measure the actual air pressure! Get the weather section from your local newspaper for the same 3 or 4 days that you were testing your barometer. Find the barometer reading in the newspaper for each day, and record the reading beside that day's mark on your index card. Use these markings on your card to create a scale with marks at regular intervals. Transfer this scale to a new card and attach it to your barometer.

Analyze the Results

1. A change in air pressure will affect how the barometer works. Temperature changes may also affect the barometer.

2. An upward movement of the straw indicates that the atmospheric pressure is increasing. Air pressure is pushing on the balloon, which causes the pointer to rise.

3. A downward movement of the straw indicates that the atmospheric pressure is decreasing. Less air pressure causes the pointer to dip downward.

Draw Conclusions

4. Clear, dry days are associated with high pressure. Cloudy, rainy, or humid days are associated with low pressure. A sudden drop in air pressure usually indicates that a storm is on the way.

5. Answers will vary depending on the hypothesis. Students should explain how their barometer was affected by atmospheric pressure and why the experiment supported or disproved their hypothesis.

Applying Your Data

Make sure students are aware that barometric pressure changes throughout the day. Students should try to get recorded pressures for the same time of day that they were testing their barometer. Some Internet sites provide weather reports that are updated hourly. Be sure to tell students that their barometric measurements will be approximate.

Chapter Review

Assignment Guide

Section	Questions
1	2, 6, 7–9, 11, 16–18, 24
2	3, 4, 10, 12, 13, 25, 27
3	5, 28, 29
4	14, 19–21, 26
5	15, 22, 23
1 and 3	1

ANSWERS

Using Key Terms

1. Sample answer: Air pressure is the measure of the force with which air molecules are pushing on a surface. Wind is the movement of air caused by differences in air pressure.

2. Sample answer: The troposphere is the lowest layer of the Earth's atmosphere. The thermosphere is the uppermost layer of the Earth's atmosphere.

3. Sample answer: The greenhouse effect is the Earth's natural heating process, by which gases in the atmosphere absorb and reradiate thermal energy. Global warming is a rise in average global temperature.

4. Sample answer: Convection is the transfer of thermal energy by the circulation of a liquid or gas. Thermal conduction is the transfer of thermal energy through a material.

USING KEY TERMS

For each pair of terms, explain how the meanings of the terms differ.

1. *air pressure* and *wind*

2. *troposphere* and *thermosphere*

3. *greenhouse effect* and *global warming*

4. *convection* and *thermal conduction*

5. *global wind* and *local wind*

6. *stratosphere* and *mesosphere*

UNDERSTANDING KEY IDEAS

Multiple Choice

7. What is the most abundant gas in the atmosphere?
   a. oxygen
   b. hydrogen
   c. nitrogen
   d. carbon dioxide

8. A major source of oxygen for the Earth's atmosphere is
   a. sea water.
   b. the sun.
   c. plants.
   d. animals.

9. The bottom layer of the atmosphere, where almost all weather occurs, is the
   a. stratosphere.
   b. troposphere.
   c. thermosphere.
   d. mesosphere.

10. What percentage of the solar energy that reaches the outer atmosphere is absorbed at the Earth's surface?
    a. 20%   c. 50%
    b. 30%   d. 70%

11. The ozone layer is located in the
    a. stratosphere.
    b. troposphere.
    c. thermosphere.
    d. mesosphere.

12. By which method does most thermal energy in the atmosphere circulate?
    a. conduction   c. advection
    b. convection   d. radiation

13. The balance between incoming energy and outgoing energy is called
    a. the convection balance.
    b. the conduction balance.
    c. the greenhouse effect.
    d. the radiation balance.

14. Which of the following pollutants is NOT a primary pollutant?
    a. car exhaust
    b. acid precipitation
    c. smoke from a factory
    d. fumes from burning plastic

15. The Clean Air Act
    a. controls the amount of air pollutants that can be released from many sources.
    b. requires cars to run on fuels other than gasoline.
    c. requires many industries to use scrubbers.
    d. Both (a) and (c)

5. Sample answer: A global wind is a large-scale pattern of air circulation in the atmosphere. A local wind generally flows short distances and can blow from any direction.

6. Sample answer: The stratosphere is the atmospheric layer above the troposphere, where temperature rises with altitude. The mesosphere is between the stratosphere and thermosphere, where temperature decreases with increasing altitude.

Understanding Key Ideas

7. c	12. b
8. c	13. d
9. b	14. b
10. c	15. d
11. a	

Short Answer

16 Why does the atmosphere become less dense as altitude increases?

17 Explain why air rises when it is heated.

18 What is the main cause of temperature changes in the atmosphere?

19 What are secondary pollutants, and how do they form? Give an example of a secondary pollutant.

20 Give one example of a point-source pollutant and one example of a nonpoint-source pollutant in North Carolina.

21 Describe two sources of human-caused air pollution and describe what can be done to reduce the air pollution each creates.

22 What do the primary and secondary air quality standards protect?

23 How is air quality information communicated to the public? Why is this information important to the public?

CRITICAL THINKING

24 Concept Mapping Use the following terms to create a concept map: *mesosphere, stratosphere, layers, temperature, troposphere,* and *atmosphere.*

25 Identifying Relationships What is the relationship between the greenhouse effect and global warming?

26 Applying Concepts How does acid precipitation affect plants, animals, and humans? What can be done to reduce acid precipitation?

27 Making Inferences The atmosphere of Venus has a very high level of carbon dioxide. How might this fact influence the greenhouse effect on Venus?

INTERPRETING GRAPHICS

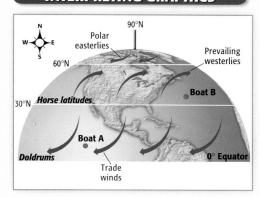

Use the diagram above to answer the questions that follow. When answering the questions that follow, assume that ocean currents do not affect the path of the boats.

28 If Boat A traveled to 50°N, from which direction would the prevailing winds blow?

29 If Boat B sailed with the prevailing westerlies in the Northern Hemisphere, in which direction would the boat be traveling?

---

19. Secondary pollutants form when primary pollutants react with other primary pollutants or with other naturally occurring substances. Acid rain is an example of a secondary pollutant.

20. A point-source pollutant in North Carolina is smoke from burning brush. A nonpoint-source pollutant in North Carolina is ozone.

21. Two sources of human-caused air pollution are industrial plants and motor vehicles. Industrial plants can reduce air pollution by using scrubbers. Walking or biking to your destination can help reduce emissions from motor vehicles.

22. Primary standards protect against the effects of air pollution on human health. Secondary standards protect against the effects of air pollution on crops, vegetation, and buildings.

23. Air quality information is communicated to the public through the Air Quality Index. This information is important because it states whether the air quality in an area is healthy or unhealthy.

Critical Thinking

24. An answer to this exercise can be found at the end of this book.

25. Global warming is a gradual rise in Earth's average temperature. It is possibly caused by an increase in the greenhouse effect.

26. Acid precipitation can decrease soil nutrients available to plants and can cause acid shock to occur in aquatic ecosystems. It can also cause respiratory problems in children. Pollution controls and international agreements can help reduce acid precipitation.

27. The greater concentration of carbon dioxide in Venus's atmosphere causes the greenhouse effect to be more extreme on Venus than on Earth.

Interpreting Graphics

28. east

29. northeast

---

16. As altitude increases, there are fewer gas molecules. Gravity pulls most of the atmosphere's gas molecules close to the Earth's surface, which makes the lower layers more dense than the upper layers.

17. Air rises as it is heated because it becomes less dense.

18. The temperature differences in the atmosphere result mainly from the way solar energy is absorbed. Some layers are warmer because they contain gases that absorb solar energy.

Teacher's Note

To provide practice under more realistic testing conditions, give students 20 minutes to answer all of the questions in this Standardized Test Preparation.

MISCONCEPTION ///ALERT

Answers to the standardized test preparation can help you identify student misconceptions and misunderstandings.

Passage 1

1. D

2. F

✚ TEST DOCTOR

Question 2: All of the answer options may appear similar. Remind students that they must read the passage carefully to discover the correct answer choice.

READING

Read each of the passages below. Then, answer the questions that follow each passage.

Passage 1 An important part of the EPA's Acid Rain Program is the allowance trading system, which is designed to reduce sulfur dioxide emissions. In this system, 1 ton of sulfur dioxide (SO_2) emission is equivalent to one <u>allowance</u>. A limited number of allowances are allocated for each year. Companies purchase the allowances from the EPA and are allowed to produce as many tons of SO_2 as they have allowances for the year. Companies can buy, sell, or trade allowances, but if they exceed their allowances, they must pay a fine. The system allows a company to determine the most cost-effective ways to comply with the Clean Air Act. A company can reduce emissions by using technology that conserves energy, using renewable energy sources, or updating its pollution-control devices and using low-sulfur fuels.

1. According to the passage, which of the following methods can a company use to reduce emissions?

A preserving wildlife habitat

B lobbying Congress

C using high-sulfur fuels

D using technology that conserves energy

2. In the passage, what does *allowance* mean?

F an allotment for a pollutant

G an allocation of money for reducing pollution

H an alleviation of pollution

I an allegation of pollution

Passage 2 The chinook, or "snow eater," is a dry wind that blows down the eastern side of the Rocky Mountains from New Mexico to Alaska. Arapaho Indians gave the chinook its name because of its ability to melt large amounts of snow very quickly. Chinooks form when moist air is forced over a mountain range. The air cools as it rises. As the air cools, it releases moisture by raining or snowing. As the dry air flows over the mountaintop, it compresses and heats the air below. The warm, dry wind that results is worthy of the name "snow eater" because it melts a half meter of snow in a few hours! The temperature change caused when a chinook rushes down a mountainside can also be dramatic. In 1943 in Spearfish, South Dakota, the temperature at 7:30 in the morning was –4°F. But two minutes later, a chinook caused the temperature to soar 49° to 45°F.

1. Which of the following descriptions best explains why the chinook is called "the snow eater"?

A The chinook is so cold that it prevents the formation of snow in the atmosphere.

B The chinook is so warm that it prevents the formation of snow in the atmosphere.

C The chinook is a warm wind that has high humidity.

D The chinook is a warm wind that has low humidity.

2. According to the passage, at what time did the temperature reach 45°F in Spearfish, South Dakota?

F 7:30 P.M.

G 7:32 P.M.

H 7:30 A.M.

I 7:32 A.M.

Passage 2

1. D

2. I

✚ TEST DOCTOR

Question 2: Students may see the time *7:30* in the text and conclude that H is the answer to Question 2. Remind students to read the passage thoroughly. The most obvious answer is not always the correct choice.

Use the illustration below to answer the questions that follow.

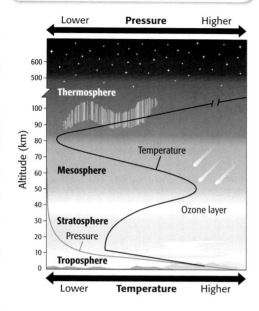

1. Which of the following statements describes how temperature changes in the mesosphere?

A Temperature increases as altitude increases.

B Temperature decreases as altitude increases.

C Temperature decreases as pressure increases.

D Temperature does not change as pressure increases.

2. In which layers does temperature decrease as pressure decreases?

F the troposphere and the mesosphere

G the troposphere and the stratosphere

H the ozone layer and the troposphere

I the ozone layer and the thermosphere

3. A research balloon took measurements at 23 km, 35 km, 52 km, 73 km, 86 km, 92 km, 101 km, and 110 km. Which measurements were taken in the mesosphere?

A measurements at 23 km and 35 km

B measurements at 52 km and 73 km

C measurements at 86 km and 92 km

D measurements at 101 km and 110 km

Read each question below, and choose the best answer.

1. An airplane is flying at a speed of 500 km/h when it encounters a jet stream moving in the same direction at 150 km/h. If the plane flies with the jet stream, how much farther will the plane travel in 1.5 h?

A 950 km

B 525 km

C 225 km

D 150 km

2. Today's wind speed was measured at 18 km/h. What was the wind speed in meters per hour?

F 1.8 m/h

G 180 m/h

H 1,800 m/h

I 18,000 m/h

3. Rockport received 24.1 cm of rain on Monday, 12.5 cm of rain on Tuesday, and 5.8 cm of rain on Thursday. The rest of the week, it did not rain. How much rain did Rockport receive during the week?

A 18.3 cm

B 36.6 cm

C 42.4 cm

D 45.7 cm

4. A weather station recorded the following temperatures during a 5 h period: 15°C, 18°C, 13°C, 15°C, and 20°C. What was the average temperature during this period?

F 14.2°C

G 15.2°C

H 16.2°C

I 20.2°C

5. The temperature in Waterford, Virginia, increased 1.3°C every hour for 5 h. If the temperature in the morning was −4°C, what was the temperature 4 h later?

A 2.5°C

B 2.3°C

C 1.3°C

D 1.2°C

Standardized Test Preparation

1. B

2. F

3. B

TEST DOCTOR

Question 1: This is a complex graphic that may appear intimidating to students at first. The illustration synthesizes three types of data: altitude, temperature, and pressure. To help students answer this question, have them analyze each statement and eliminate the incorrect statements until they are left with the correct choice.

1. C

2. I

3. C

4. H

5. D

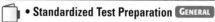
TEST DOCTOR

Question 4: Students may choose answer choice I if they divide the total temperature by 4 instead of 5. Remind students to always double-check the number of numbers that they are asked to average. If scrap paper is available during the test, it is a good strategy to write down all of the numbers given in a test question before solving a problem.

CHAPTER RESOURCES

Chapter Resource File

 • Standardized Test Preparation **GENERAL**

Workbooks

North Carolina Standardized Test Preparation
• Provides practice for the EOG test.

State Resources

 For specific resources for your state, visit **go.hrw.com** and type in the keyword **HSMSTR**.

Science, Technology, and Society

ACTIVITY ————— BASIC

The HyperSoar jet looks like a giant paper airplane. This design makes the jet more aerodynamic, so it is able to glide for long distances. Organize students into small groups, and have them design and test paper airplanes for gliding ability. Have a contest, and give a prize for the best glider.

Weird Science

ACTIVITY ————— GENERAL

Students can learn a lot about NEXRAD radar and animal migrations by visiting the Clemson University Radar Ornithology Web Site. The Web Site has NEXRAD images of bird, bat, and insect migrations. Images of bat migrations are especially interesting. When bats leave their roosts in the evening, they usually fly in a spiral pattern. This pattern is shown as a crescent shape in the radar images. Insects are indicated by a dotted pattern that is similar to the pattern that birds make but insects have a lower reflectivity because they are less dense.

Science in Action

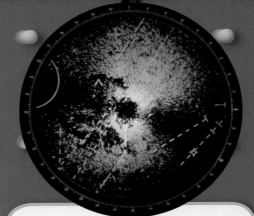

Science, Technology, and Society

The HyperSoar Jet

Imagine traveling from Chicago to Tokyo in 72 minutes. If the HyperSoar jet becomes a reality, you may be able to travel to the other side of the world in less time than it takes to watch a movie! To accomplish this amazing feat, the jet would "skip" across the upper stratosphere. To begin skipping, the jet would climb above the stratosphere, turn off its engines, and glide for about 60 km. Then, gravity would pull the jet down to where the air is denser. The denser air would cause the jet to soar upward. In this way, the jet would skip across a layer of dense air until it was ready to land. Each 2-minute skip would cover about 450 km, and the HyperSoar would be able to fly at Mach 10—a speed of 3 km/s!

Math ACTIVITY

A trip on the HyperSoar from Chicago to Tokyo would require about 18 "skips." Each skip is 450 km. If the trip is 10,123 km, how many kilometers will the jet travel when it is not skipping?

Weird Science

Radar Zoology

"For tonight's forecast, expect a light shower of mayflies. A wave of warblers will approach from the south. Tomorrow will be cloudy, and a band of free-tailed bats will move to the south in the early evening." Such a forecast may not make the evening news, but it is a familiar scenario for radar zoologists. Radar zoologists use a type of radar called *NEXRAD* to track migrating birds, bands of bats, and swarms of insects. NEXRAD tracks animals in the atmosphere in the same way that it tracks storms. The system sends out a microwave signal. If the signal hits an object, some of the energy reflects back to a receiver. NEXRAD has been especially useful to scientists who study bird migration. Birds tend to migrate at night, when the atmosphere is more stable, so until now, nighttime bird migration has been difficult to observe. NEXRAD has also helped identify important bird migration routes and critical stopovers. For example, scientists have discovered that many birds migrate over the Gulf of Mexico instead of around it.

Social Studies ACTIVITY

Geography plays an important role in bird migration. Many birds ride the "thermals" produced by mountain ranges. Find out what thermals are, and create a map of bird migration routes over North America.

Answer to Math Activity
10,123 km − (18 skips × 450 km) = 2023 km

Answer to Social Studies Activity
Thermals are strong updrafts created by rising columns of warm air. When warm air encounters a mountain or ridge, it may rise sharply upward. Birds take advantage of thermals to conserve energy. Maps of bird migration routes are available on the Internet. The four major migratory routes in North America are the Central Flyway, the Mississippi Flyway, the Atlantic Flyway, and the Pacific Flyway.

Ellen Paneok

Bush Pilot For Ellen Paneok, understanding weather patterns is a matter of life and death. As a bush pilot, she flies mail, supplies, and people to remote villages in Alaska that can be reached only by plane. Bad weather is one of the most serious challenges Paneok faces. "It's beautiful up here," she says, "but it can also be harsh." One dangerous situation is landing a plane in mountainous regions. "On top of a mountain you can't tell which way the wind is blowing," Paneok says. In this case, she flies in a rectangular pattern to determine the wind direction. Landing a plane on the frozen Arctic Ocean is also dangerous. In white-out conditions, the horizon can't be seen because the sky and the ground are the same color. "It's like flying in a milk bottle full of milk," Paneok says. In these conditions, she fills black plastic garbage bags and drops them from the plane to help guide her landing.

Paneok had to overcome many challenges to become a pilot. As a child, she lived in seven foster homes before being placed in an all-girls' home at the age of 14. In the girls' home, she read a magazine about careers in aviation and decided then and there that she wanted to become a pilot. At first, she faced a lot of opposition from people telling her that she wouldn't be able to become a pilot. Now, she encourages young people to pursue their goals. "If you decide you want to go for it, go for it. There may be obstacles in your way, but you've just got to find a way to go over them, get around them, or dig under them," she says.

Ellen Paneok is shown at right with two of her Inupiat passengers.

Language Arts ACTIVITY

Beryl Markham lived an exciting life as a bush pilot delivering mail and supplies to remote areas of Africa. Read about her life or the life of Bessie Coleman, one of the most famous African American women in the history of flying.

To learn more about these Science in Action topics, visit **go.hrw.com** and type in the keyword **HZ5ATMF**.

Current Science

Check out Current Science® articles related to this chapter by visiting **go.hrw.com**. Just type in the keyword **HZ5CS15**.

SCIENCE HUMOR

Ellen Paneok has had many exciting adventures during her years of flying in Alaska. When the weather turns bad, she sometimes has to spend the night in small villages where the only available bed is in the jail house. Once, she had to chase two polar bears off the runway before she could land. After she landed, Paneok was starting to unload the plane when she realized that she didn't know exactly where the polar bears had gone. "You've never seen anyone unload a thousand pounds off an airplane so fast," she laughs.

Careers

Background

Ellen Paneok is a native Alaskan Eskimo who has been flying for 26 years. She says that the biggest personal reward of working as a bush pilot is the opportunity to interact with the people in the bush, many of whom are her relatives or close friends. In addition to working as a commercial pilot, Paneok serves as a board member of an air museum. In this role, she flies antique airplanes at air shows and other exhibitions. She has also written several magazine articles and creates and sells Indian art. She has illustrated a book and is also interested in photography.

Answer to Language Arts Activity

Beryl Markham's autobiography *West with the Night* is often found on high school reading lists. Advanced students may enjoy reading about her life.

Understanding Weather
Chapter Planning Guide

OBJECTIVES	LABS, DEMONSTRATIONS, AND ACTIVITIES	TECHNOLOGY RESOURCES
PACING • 90 min pp. 74–83 **Chapter Opener**	**SE** Start-up Activity, p. 75 ◆ `GENERAL`	**OSP** Parent Letter `GENERAL` **CD** Student Edition on CD-ROM **CD** Guided Reading Audio CD **TR** Chapter Starter Transparency* **VID** Brain Food Video Quiz
Section 1 Water in the Air • Explain how water moves through the water cycle. • Describe how relative humidity is affected by temperature and levels of water vapor. • Describe the relationship between dew point and condensation. • List three types of cloud forms. • Identify four kinds of precipitation.	**TE** Group Activity Air Molecules, p. 76 `GENERAL` **TE** Demonstration Water in Air, p. 77 ◆ `BASIC` **TE** Activity Sentence Completion, p. 78 `GENERAL` **SE** Quick Lab Out of Thin Air, p. 79 `GENERAL` **SE** Connection to Language Arts Cloud Clues, p. 80 `GENERAL` **TE** Activity Naming Clouds, p. 81 `BASIC` **TE** Connection Activity Language Arts, p. 81 `GENERAL` **SE** Inquiry Lab Boiling Over!, p. 102 ◆ `GENERAL` **SE** Skills Practice Lab Let It Snow!, p. 587 `GENERAL` **LB** Whiz-Bang Demonstrations It's Raining Again* ◆ `GENERAL` **LB** Calculator-Based Lab Relative Humidity* ◆ `GENERAL`	**CRF** Lesson Plans* **TR** Bellringer Transparency* **TR** The Water Cycle* **TR** Cloud Types Based on Form and Altitude* **SE** Internet Activity, p. 78 `GENERAL` **CRF** SciLinks Activity `GENERAL` **VID** Lab Videos for Earth Science
PACING • 45 min pp. 84–89 **Section 2 Air Masses and Fronts** • Identify the four kinds of air masses that influence weather in the United States. • Describe the four major types of fronts. • Explain how fronts cause weather changes. • Explain how cyclones and anticyclones affect the weather.	**TE** Demonstration Density, p. 85 ◆ `GENERAL` **TE** Activity Using Maps, p. 87 `BASIC` **LB** Whiz-Bang Demonstrations When Air Bags Collide* ◆ `GENERAL` **LB** Long-Term Projects & Research Ideas A Storm on the Horizon* `ADVANCED` **SE** Science in Action Math, Social Studies, and Language Arts Activities, pp. 108–109	**CRF** Lesson Plans* **TR** Bellringer Transparency* **TR** Cold and Warm Fronts* **TR** Occluded and Stationary Fronts*
PACING • 45 min pp. 90–97 **Section 3 Severe Weather** • Describe how lightning forms. • Describe the formation of thunderstorms, tornadoes, and hurricanes. • Describe the characteristics of thunderstorms, tornadoes, and hurricanes. • Explain how to stay safe during severe weather.	**TE** Demonstration Modeling Thunder, p. 90 ◆ `GENERAL` **TE** Connection Activity Math, p. 91 `GENERAL` **TE** Connection Activity Real World, p. 92 `GENERAL` **TE** Activity Weather and Energy, p. 94 `GENERAL` **TE** Group Activity Hurricane Newscast, p. 94 `GENERAL` **SE** School-to-Home Activity Natural Disaster Plan, p. 95 `GENERAL` **TE** Connection Activity Meteorology, p. 95 `ADVANCED` **LB** Inquiry Labs When Disaster Strikes* `BASIC`	**CRF** Lesson Plans* **TR** Bellringer Transparency* **CRF** SciLinks Activity* `GENERAL` **TR** *LINK TO PHYSICAL SCIENCE* How Lightning Forms
PACING • 45 min pp. 98–101 **Section 4 Forecasting the Weather** • Describe the different types of instruments used to take weather measurements. • Explain how radar and weather satellites help meteorologists forecast the weather. • Explain how to interpret a weather map.	**TE** Demonstration Air Pressure and Barometers, p. 98 ◆ `GENERAL` **TE** Connection Activity Real World, p. 99 `GENERAL` **TE** Connection Activity Math, p. 100 `GENERAL` **SE** Skills Practice Lab Watching the Weather, p. 584 `GENERAL` **SE** Model-Making Lab Gone With the Wind, p. 588 ◆ `GENERAL` **LB** EcoLabs & Field Activities Rain Maker or Rain Faker?* ◆ `ADVANCED`	**CRF** Lesson Plans* **TR** Bellringer Transparency*

PACING • 90 min

CHAPTER REVIEW, ASSESSMENT, AND STANDARDIZED TEST PREPARATION

CRF Vocabulary Activity* `GENERAL`
SE Chapter Review, pp. 104–105 `GENERAL`
CRF Chapter Review* ■ `GENERAL`
CRF Chapter Tests A* ■ `GENERAL`, B* `ADVANCED`, C* `SPECIAL NEEDS`
SE Standardized Test Preparation, pp. 106–107 `GENERAL`
CRF Standardized Test Preparation* `GENERAL`
CRF Performance-Based Assessment* `GENERAL`
OSP Test Generator `GENERAL`
CRF Test Item Listing* `GENERAL`

Online and Technology Resources

Visit **go.hrw.com** for a variety of free resources related to this textbook. Enter the keyword **HT5R7WEA**.

Holt Online Learning

Students can access interactive problem-solving help and active visual concept development with the *Holt Science and Technology* Online Edition available at **www.hrw.com**.

Guided Reading Audio CD

These CDs are designed to help auditory learners and reluctant readers.

Science Tutor CD-ROM

Excellent for remediation and test practice.

SKILLS DEVELOPMENT RESOURCES	SECTION REVIEW AND ASSESSMENT	STANDARDS CORRELATIONS
SE Pre-Reading Activity, p. 74 `GENERAL` **OSP** Science Puzzlers, Twisters & Teasers* `GENERAL`		North Carolina Standard Course of Study
CRF Directed Reading A* `BASIC`, B* `SPECIAL NEEDS` **CRF** Vocabulary and Section Summary* `GENERAL` **SE** Reading Strategy Paired Summarizing, p. 76 `GENERAL` **SE** Math Practice Relative Humidity, p. 77 `GENERAL` **TE** Inclusion Strategies, p. 78 ◆ **TE** Reading Strategy Sequencing, p. 80 `GENERAL`	**SE** Reading Checks, pp. 76, 78, 79, 81 `GENERAL` **TE** Homework, p. 80 `BASIC` **TE** Reteaching, p. 82 `BASIC` **TE** Quiz, p. 82 `GENERAL` **TE** Alternative Assessment, p. 82 `ADVANCED` **TE** Homework, p. 82 `ADVANCED` **SE** Section Review,* p. 83 ■ `GENERAL` **CRF** Section Quiz* ■ `GENERAL`	3.05; *Chapter Lab:* 1.02, 1.03, 1.06, 1.08; *LabBook:* 1.02, 1.03, 1.06, 1.08
CRF Directed Reading A* `BASIC`, B* `SPECIAL NEEDS` **CRF** Vocabulary and Section Summary* `GENERAL` **SE** Reading Strategy Reading Organizer, p. 84 `GENERAL`	**SE** Reading Checks, pp. 85, 87, 89 `GENERAL` **TE** Homework, p. 84 `GENERAL` **TE** Reteaching, p. 88 `BASIC` **TE** Quiz, p. 88 `GENERAL` **TE** Alternative Assessment, p. 88 `GENERAL` **SE** Section Review,* p. 89 ■ `GENERAL` **CRF** Section Quiz* ■ `GENERAL`	3.05
CRF Directed Reading A* `BASIC`, B* `SPECIAL NEEDS` **CRF** Vocabulary and Section Summary* `GENERAL` **SE** Reading Strategy Reading Organizer, p. 90 `GENERAL` **TE** Inclusion Strategies, p. 92 ◆ **CRF** Reinforcement Worksheet Precipitation Situations* `BASIC`	**SE** Reading Checks, pp. 91, 93, 94 `GENERAL` **TE** Homework, p. 93 `ADVANCED` **TE** Reteaching, p. 96 `BASIC` **TE** Quiz, p. 96 `GENERAL` **TE** Alternative Assessment, p. 96 `GENERAL` **SE** Section Review,* p. 97 ■ `GENERAL` **CRF** Section Quiz* ■ `GENERAL`	3.05
CRF Directed Reading A* `BASIC`, B* `SPECIAL NEEDS` **CRF** Vocabulary and Section Summary* `GENERAL` **SE** Reading Strategy Reading Organizer, p. 98 `GENERAL` **MS** Math Skills for Science Using Temperature Scales* `GENERAL` **CRF** Critical Thinking Commanding the Sky* `ADVANCED`	**SE** Reading Checks, p. 98 `GENERAL` **TE** Reteaching, p. 100 `BASIC` **TE** Quiz, p. 100 `GENERAL` **TE** Alternative Assessment, p. 100 `GENERAL` **SE** Section Review,* p. 101 ■ `GENERAL` **CRF** Section Quiz* ■ `GENERAL`	3.05, 3.06; *LabBook:* 1.02, 1.03, 1.06, 1.08

One-Stop Planner® CD-ROM

This convenient CD-ROM includes:
- Lab Materials QuickList Software
- Holt Calendar Planner
- Customizable Lesson Plans
- Printable Worksheets
- ExamView® Test Generator

cnnstudentnews.com

Find the latest news, lesson plans, and activities related to important scientific events.

NSTA

www.scilinks.org

Maintained by the **National Science Teachers Association.** See Chapter Enrichment pages for a complete list of topics.

Current Science®

Check out *Current Science* articles and activities by visiting the HRW Web site at **go.hrw.com.** Just type in the keyword **HZ5CS16T.**

Classroom Videos
- **Lab Videos** demonstrate the chapter lab.
- **Brain Food Video Quizzes** help students review the chapter material.
- **CNN Videos** bring science into your students' daily life.

Visual Resources

CHAPTER STARTER TRANSPARENCY

Understanding Weather · CHAPTER STARTER

Would You Believe . . . ?

In May of 1997, a springtime tornado wreaked havoc on Jarrell, Texas. The Jarrell tornado was one of the rarest and most powerful tornadoes, with winds estimated at more than 410 km/h. The twister peeled the asphalt from paved roads, stripped fields of corn bare, and destroyed an entire neighborhood.

North America experiences more tornadoes than any other continent—averaging about 700 per year. Most of these tornadoes hit an area in the central United States called Tornado Alley. Tornado Alley covers most of the Great Plains, extending from Texas across Oklahoma, Kansas, southern Nebraska, Iowa, and South Dakota. But what causes these tornadoes, and why is the Great Plains so vulnerable?

In the spring and early summer, cold, dry air from the North Pole clashes with warm, moist air from the Tropics. This clash forces the warm air to rise and become unstable. When there is a large contrast between the two clashing air masses, the chances that a tornado will form are increased.

Tornado Alley experiences more tornadoes than any other area because its flatness and location on the Earth's surface make it possible for warm and cold air masses to collide with one another.

In this chapter you will learn about what causes weather, the different types of air masses, and how weather can suddenly turn violent.

BELLRINGER TRANSPARENCIES

Understanding Weather · BELLRINGER TRANSPARENCY

Section: Water in the Air
Observe two glasses of water. One filled with ice water, and one filled with warm water. Why do water droplets form on the outside of the cold glass? Where do the water beads come from? Why don't the water beads form on the warm glass? Have you seen this happen before on other containers? On your soda can? On a coffee cup or a soup bowl?

Write your answers in your **science journal**.

Section: Air Masses and Fronts
How would you describe the air you are breathing right now? Is it warm or cool? Humid or dry? Is it stale, sweet, or salty? The air you are breathing right now was hundreds of miles away yesterday. Do you know how or why air moves from one place to another?

Write your response in your **science journal**.

TEACHING TRANSPARENCIES

E68 — The Water Cycle

E69 — Cloud Types Based on Form and Altitude

TEACHING TRANSPARENCIES

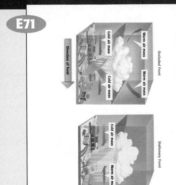

E70 — Cold and Warm Fronts

E71 — Occluded and Stationary Fronts

P69 — How Lightning Forms

LINK TO PHYSICAL SCIENCE

Chapter: Introduction to Electricity

CONCEPT MAPPING TRANSPARENCY

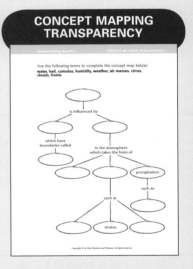

Understanding Weather · CONCEPT MAPPING TRANSPARENCY

Use the following terms to complete the concept map below: water, hail, cumulus, humidity, weather, air masses, cirrus, clouds, fronts

Planning Resources

LESSON PLANS

Lesson Plan — SAMPLE

Section: Waves

Pacing
Regular Schedule: with lab(s):2 days · without lab(s):2 days
Block Schedule: with lab(s): 1 1/2 days · without lab(s):1 day

Objectives
1. Relate the seven properties of life to a living organism.
2. Describe seven themes that can help you to organize what you learn about biology.
3. Identify the tiny structures that make up living organisms.
4. Differentiate between reproduction and heredity and between metabolism and homeostasis.

National Science Education Standards Covered
LSInter6: Cells have particular structures that underlie their functions.
LSMat1: Most cell functions involve chemical reactions.
LSBeh1: Cells store and use information to guide their functions.
UCP1: Cell functions are regulated.
SI1: Cells can differentiate and form complete multicellular organisms.
PS1: Species evolve over time.
ESS1: The great diversity of organisms is the result of more than 3.5 billion years of evolution.
ESS2: Natural selection and its evolutionary consequences provide a scientific explanation for the fossil record of ancient life forms as well as for the striking molecular similarities observed among the diverse species of living organisms.
ST1: The millions of different species of plants, animals, and microorganisms that live on Earth today are related by descent from common ancestors.
ST2: The energy for life primarily comes from the sun.
SPSP1: The complexity and organization of organisms accommodate the need for obtaining, transforming, transporting, releasing, and eliminating the matter and energy used to sustain the organism.
SPSP6: As matter and energy flows through different levels of organization of living systems—cells, organs, communities—and between living systems and the physical environment, chemical elements are recombined in different ways.
HNS1: Organisms have behavioral responses to internal changes and to external stimuli.

PARENT LETTER

SAMPLE

Dear Parent,

Your son's or daughter's science class will soon begin exploring the chapter entitled "The World of Physical Science." In this chapter, students will learn about how the scientific method applies to the world of physical science and the role of physical science in the world. By the end of the chapter, students should demonstrate a clear understanding of the chapter's main ideas and be able to discuss the following topics:

1. physical science as the study of energy and matter (Section 1)
2. the role of physical science in the world around them (Section 1)
3. careers that rely on physical science (Section 1)
4. the steps used in the scientific method (Section 2)
5. examples of technology (Section 2)
6. how the scientific method is used to answer questions and solve problems (Section 2)
7. how our knowledge of science changes over time (Section 2)
8. how models represent real objects or systems (Section 3)
9. examples of different ways models are used in science (Section 3)
10. the importance of the International System of Units (Section 4)
11. the appropriate units to use for particular measurements (Section 4)
12. how area and density are derived quantities (Section 4)

Questions to Ask Along the Way

You can help your son or daughter learn about these topics by asking interesting questions such as the following:

• What are some surprising careers that use physical science?
• What is a characteristic of a good hypothesis?
• When is it a good idea to use a model?
• Why do Americans measure things in terms of inches and yards instead of centimeters and meters?

TEST ITEM LISTING

TEST ITEM LISTING
The World of Earth Science — SAMPLE

MULTIPLE CHOICE

1. A limitation of models is that
a. they are large enough to see.
b. they do not act exactly like the things that they model.
c. they are smaller than the things that they model.
d. they model unfamiliar things.
Answer: B   Difficulty: 1   Section: 3   Objective: 2

2. The length 10 m is equal to
a. 100 cm.   c. 10,000 mm.
b. 1,000 cm.   d. Both (b) and (c)
Answer: B   Difficulty: 1   Section: 3   Objective: 2

3. To be valid, a hypothesis must be
a. testable.   c. made into a law.
b. supported by evidence.   d. Both (a) and (b)
Answer: D   Difficulty: 1   Section: 2   Objective: 2   1

4. The statement "Sheila has a stain on her shirt" is an example of a(n)
a. law.   c. observation.
b. hypothesis.   d. prediction.
Answer: B   Difficulty: 1   Section: 3   Objective: 2

5. A hypothesis is often developed out of
a. observations.   c. laws.
b. experiments.   d. Both (a) and (b)
Answer: B   Difficulty: 1   Section: 2   Objective: 2

6. How many milliliters are in 3.5 kL?
a. 3,500 mL   c. 3,500, 000 mL
b. 0.0035 mL   d. 35,000 mL
Answer: B   Difficulty: 1   Section: 3   Objective: 2

7. A map of Seattle is an example of a
a. law.   c. model.
b. theory.   d. unit.
Answer: B   Difficulty: 1   Section: 3   Objective: 2

8. A lab has the safety icons shown below. These icons mean that you should wear
a. only safety goggles.   c. safety goggles and a lab apron.
b. only a lab apron.   d. safety goggles, a lab apron, and gloves.
Answer: B   Difficulty: 1   Section: 3   Objective: 2

9. The law of conservation of mass says the total mass before a chemical change is
a. more than the total mass after the change.
b. less than the total mass after the change.
c. the same as the total mass after the change.
d. not the same as the total mass after the change.
Answer: B   Difficulty: 1   Section: 3   Objective: 2

10. In which of the following areas would you find a geochemist at work?
a. studying the chemistry of rocks   c. studying biology
b. studying forestry   d. studying the atmosphere
Answer: B   Difficulty: 1   Section: 3   Objective: 2

One-Stop Planner® CD-ROM

This CD-ROM includes all of the resources shown here and the following time-saving tools:

• *Lab Materials QuickList Software*
• *Customizable lesson plans*
• *Holt Calendar Planner*
• *The powerful ExamView® Test Generator*

Meeting Individual Needs

DIRECTED READING A
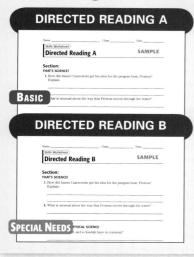
BASIC

DIRECTED READING B
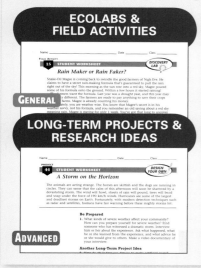
SPECIAL NEEDS

VOCABULARY ACTIVITY
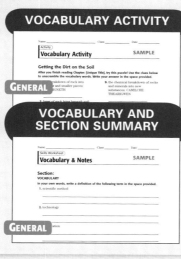
GENERAL

VOCABULARY AND SECTION SUMMARY
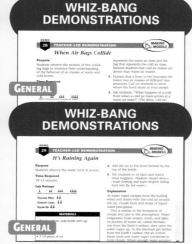
GENERAL

REINFORCEMENT
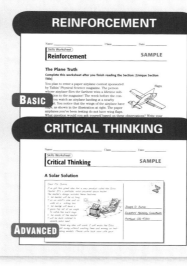
BASIC

CRITICAL THINKING
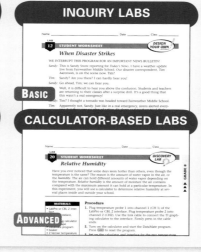
ADVANCED

SCILINKS ACTIVITY

GENERAL

SCIENCE PUZZLERS, TWISTERS & TEASERS
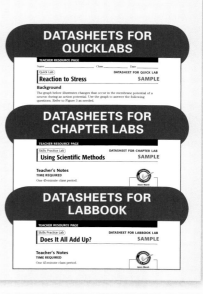
GENERAL

Labs and Activities

ECOLABS & FIELD ACTIVITIES
GENERAL

LONG-TERM PROJECTS & RESEARCH IDEAS

ADVANCED

WHIZ-BANG DEMONSTRATIONS
GENERAL

WHIZ-BANG DEMONSTRATIONS
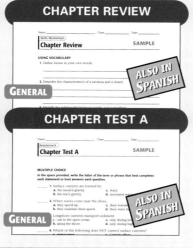
GENERAL

INQUIRY LABS
BASIC

CALCULATOR-BASED LABS
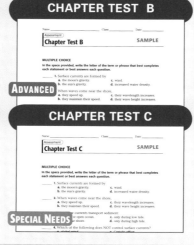
ADVANCED

DATASHEETS FOR QUICKLABS

DATASHEETS FOR CHAPTER LABS

DATASHEETS FOR LABBOOK
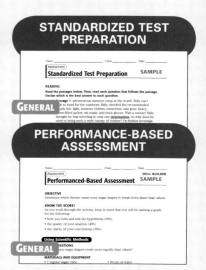

Review and Assessments

SECTION QUIZ
GENERAL — ALSO IN SPANISH

SECTION REVIEW
GENERAL — ALSO IN SPANISH

CHAPTER REVIEW
GENERAL — ALSO IN SPANISH

CHAPTER TEST A
GENERAL — ALSO IN SPANISH

CHAPTER TEST B
ADVANCED

CHAPTER TEST C
SPECIAL NEEDS

STANDARDIZED TEST PREPARATION
GENERAL

PERFORMANCE-BASED ASSESSMENT
GENERAL

This Chapter Enrichment provides relevant and interesting information to expand and enhance your presentation of the chapter material.

Section 1

Water in the Air

Earth's Water Cycle

- The atmosphere contains only about 0.001% of the total volume of water on the planet (about 1.46×10^9 km³).
- The rate at which water evaporates into Earth's atmosphere is about 5.1×10^{17} L per year.
- About 78% of all precipitation falls over Earth's oceans. Of the 22% that falls on land, about 65% returns to the air by evaporation.

Clouds

- Clouds may be composed of water droplets, ice crystals, or a combination of the two. For example, cirrus clouds are made of only ice crystals; stratus clouds are made of only water droplets; and altostratus clouds are mixtures of ice and liquid water. Cumulonimbus clouds, which produce snowflakes and hail, consist of water droplets near the bottom of the clouds and ice crystals in the upper parts of the clouds.

Is That a Fact!

- The largest hailstone ever recorded fell on Coffeyville, Kansas, on September 3, 1970. The hailstone was the size of a softball and weighed 0.75 kg.

Precipitation

- Due to differences in condensation rates within the cloud, not all of the millions of droplets of water that make up a cloud are the same size. Larger drops collide and merge with smaller drops to form raindrops.

Section 2

Air Masses and Fronts

Fronts

- As a warm front approaches, the first clouds to appear in the sky are the high clouds: cirrus, cirrostratus, and cirrocumulus. As the warm front moves closer, medium-height clouds, then low clouds appear. As the warm front arrives, the temperature and air pressure drop. In the Northern Hemisphere, winds generally blow from the northeast. Nimbostratus clouds bring drizzly precipitation, which may fall within 24 hours of the first cloud sighting.

- When a cold front enters an area, cumulonimbus clouds can produce thunderstorms, heavy rain, or snow along the front. After the cold front passes through an area, winds change direction and barometric pressure rises. Behind the cold front, temperatures usually fall, which brings cool, clear weather to the area.

Section 3

Severe Weather

Tornadoes

- Meteorologists rate tornado intensity using the Fujita Tornado Intensity Scale. An F0 tornado is a relatively weak storm that may damage chimneys, tree branches, and billboard signs. An F1 tornado is a moderate storm that can peel the surfaces off roofs, overturn mobile homes, and push moving cars off roads. F2 and F3 tornadoes cause considerable to severe damage by tearing roofs off houses, overturning railroad cars, and uprooting mature trees. An F4 tornado is a devastating storm that levels houses and other buildings and tosses cars into the air. The most severe tornado is an F5 tornado, which can lift houses off their foundations and carry them great distances. An F5 tornado can also carry cars over 100 m and strip the bark off trees.

Hurricanes

- On the Saffir-Simpson Scale, hurricanes fall into five categories. Category 1 hurricanes have sustained winds between 74 and 95 km/h and usually cause relatively minimal damage. Category 2 hurricanes cause moderate damage with winds ranging between 96 and 110 km/h. Category 3 hurricanes cause extensive damage with winds that blow between 111 and 130 km/h. Category 4 hurricanes have sustained winds between 131 and 155 km/h. Category 5 hurricanes, like Hurricane Andrew, which struck Florida in 1992, have sustained winds of more than 155 km/h. Category 5 hurricanes are classified as catastrophic storms.

Is That a Fact!
- ◆ A hurricane is called a *willy-willy* in Australia, a *taino* in Haiti, a *baguio* in the Philippines, and a *cordonazo* in western Mexico.

Section 4

Forecasting the Weather
Weather-Prediction Methods

- One of the simplest methods of weather prediction, the *persistence method,* assumes that the atmospheric conditions at the time of a weather forecast will not change in the near future. This method is fairly accurate in areas where weather patterns change very slowly, such as in southern California, where summer weather typically changes very little from day to day. Other methods are described below.

- The *trends method* involves determining high- and low-pressure areas, gauging the velocity of weather fronts, and locating areas of clouds and precipitation. A forecaster then uses these data to predict where these weather phenomena will be in the future. This method of weather prediction works well only when weather systems maintain constant velocities for a long period of time.

- The *climatology method* involves averaging weather data that have accumulated over many years to make a forecast. This method is accurate when weather patterns are similar to those expected for a given time of year.

- The *numerical weather-prediction (NWP)* method uses complex computer programs to generate models of probable air temperature, barometric pressure, wind velocity, and precipitation. A meteorologist then analyzes how he or she thinks the features predicted by the computer will interact to produce the day's weather. Despite its flaws, the NWP method is one of the most reliable methods available.

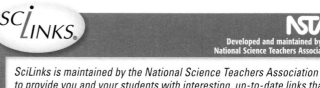

SCiLINKS.

NSTA
Developed and maintained by the
National Science Teachers Association

SciLinks is maintained by the National Science Teachers Association to provide you and your students with interesting, up-to-date links that will enrich your classroom presentation of the chapter.

Visit www.scilinks.org and enter the SciLinks code for more information about the topic listed.

Topic: The Water Cycle
SciLinks code: HSM1626

Topic: Severe Weather
SciLinks code: HSM1383

Topic: Air Masses and Fronts
SciLinks code: HSM0032

Topic: Forecasting the Weather
SciLinks code: HSM0606

Overview

This chapter introduces some fundamental principles of meteorology and weather forecasting. Students learn about relative humidity, clouds, air masses and fronts, severe weather, and weather forecasting.

Assessing Prior Knowledge

Students should be familiar with the following topics:

• the water cycle
• characteristics of the atmosphere

Identifying Misconceptions

Students may think that weather forecasting is extremely complicated. Point out that the science of meteorology relies on a few simple concepts, such as relative humidity, simple gas laws, and the movement of air masses. The tools needed to forecast weather are inexpensive and easy to use. If students become familiar with these tools and concepts, they will understand the basic science of meteorology. As you teach this chapter, work as a class every day to forecast the next day's weather. Review the predictions at the beginning of each class. Forecasts should improve as students learn more about weather.

3

Understanding Weather

About the PHOTO

Flamingos in the bathroom? This may look like someone's idea of a practical joke, but in fact, it's a practical idea! These flamingos reside at the Miami-Metro Zoo in Florida. They were put in the bathroom for protection against the incredibly dangerous winds of Hurricane Floyd in September of 1999.

PRE-READING ACTIVITY

FOLDNOTES **Four-Corner Fold**
Before you read the chapter, create the FoldNote entitled "Four-Corner Fold" described in the **Study Skills** section of the Appendix. Label the flaps of the four-corner fold with "Water in the air," "Air masses and fronts," "Severe weather," and "Forecasting the weather." Write what you know about each topic under the appropriate flap. As you read the chapter, add other information that you learn.

Standards Correlations

North Carolina Standard Course of Study

1.02 Develop appropriate experimental procedures for: Given questions, [and] Student generated questions. (Chapter Lab and LabBook)

1.03 (partial) Apply safety procedures in the laboratory . . . : Recognize potential hazards, Manipulate materials and equipment, [and] Conduct appropriate procedures. (Chapter Lab and LabBook)

1.06 Use mathematics to gather, organize, and present quantitative data resulting from scientific

investigations: Measurement, [and] Analysis of data . . . (Chapter Lab and LabBook)

1.08 Use oral and written language to: Communicate findings, [and] Defend conclusions of scientific investigations. (Chapter Lab and LabBook)

3.05 Examine evidence that atmospheric properties can be studied to predict atmospheric conditions and weather hazards: Humidity, Temperature, Wind speed and direction, Air pressure, Precipitation, Tornado Hurricanes, Floods, [and] Storms. (Sections 1, 2, 3, and 4 and Science in Action)

FOR EACH GROUP
- beaker (2)
- container, clear plastic
- cooking oil (500 mL)
- water (500 mL)

Teacher's Notes: Students should be able to distinguish the oil from the water when the two liquids are poured together. If not, try the experiment again using water with food coloring.

Answers

1. The oil rises to the top and sits on the surface of the water.

2. Answers may vary.

3. Sample answer: The warm air mass would be pushed up by the cold air mass.

START-UP ACTIVITY

Meeting of the Masses

In this activity, you will model what happens when two air masses that have different temperature characteristics meet.

Procedure

1. Pour **500 mL of water** into a **beaker.** Pour **500 mL of cooking oil** into a **second beaker.** The water represents a dense cold air mass. The cooking oil represents a less dense warm air mass.

2. Predict what would happen to the two liquids if you tried to mix them.

3. Pour the contents of both beakers into a **clear, plastic, rectangular container** at the same time from opposite ends of the container.

4. Observe the interaction of the oil and water.

Analysis

1. What happens when the liquids meet?

2. Does the prediction that you made in step 2 of the Procedure match your results?

3. Using your results, hypothesize what would happen if a cold air mass met a warm air mass.

3.06 Assess the use of technology in studying atmospheric phenomena and weather hazards: Satellites, Weather maps, Predicting, Recording, [and] Communicating information about conditions. (Section 4 and Science in Action)

Chapter Starter Transparency
Use this transparency to help students begin thinking about the types of conditions that produce tornadoes.

CHAPTER RESOURCES

Technology

Transparencies
- Chapter Starter Transparency   READING SKILLS

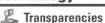 **Student Edition on CD-ROM**

 **Guided Reading Audio CD**

 Classroom Videos
- Brain Food Video Quiz

Workbooks

Science Puzzlers, Twisters & Teasers
- Understanding Weather   GENERAL

Focus

Overview

This section discusses the water cycle, relative humidity, types of clouds, and forms of precipitation.

 Bellringer

Place a glass of ice water and a glass of warm water on your desk. Ask students: "Why do water drops form on the cold glass? Where does the water come from? Why are there no water drops on the warm glass?"

Motivate

Group ACTIVITY — GENERAL

Air Molecules Divide the class in half. Half of the students will pretend to be air molecules; half will pretend to be water molecules. Ask the "air molecules" to stand four feet apart in a square grid. Then, have the "water molecules" stand between the air molecules without touching anyone. Tell students that they are modeling a warm air mass. Cool the air mass by moving the air molecules closer together so that eventually they are holding hands. As the temperature drops, the water molecules will be expelled as "precipitation." Finally, ask the air molecules to stand with their shoulders touching to show how a cold air mass expels the water molecules. Kinesthetic

---

Water in the Air

What will the weather be this weekend? Depending on what you have planned, knowing the answer to this question could be important. A picnic in the rain can be a mess!

Have you ever wondered what weather is? **Weather** is the condition of the atmosphere at a certain time and place. The condition of the atmosphere is affected by the amount of water in the air. So, to understand weather, you need to understand how water cycles through Earth's atmosphere.

The Water Cycle

Water in liquid, solid, and gaseous states is constantly being recycled through the water cycle. The *water cycle* is the continuous movement of water from sources on Earth's surface—such as lakes, oceans, and plants—into the air, onto and over land, into the ground, and back to the surface. The movement of water through the water cycle is shown in **Figure 1.**

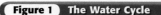 **Reading Check** What is the water cycle? (*See the Appendix for answers to Reading Checks.*)

READING WARM-UP

Objectives
- Explain how water moves through the water cycle.
- Describe how relative humidity is affected by temperature and levels of water vapor.
- Describe the relationship between dew point and condensation.
- List three types of cloud forms.
- Identify four kinds of precipitation.

Terms to Learn

weather	cloud
humidity	precipitation
relative humidity	
condensation	

READING STRATEGY

Paired Summarizing Read this section silently. In pairs, take turns summarizing the material. Stop to discuss ideas that seem confusing.

Figure 1 The Water Cycle

Condensation occurs when water vapor cools and changes from a gas to a liquid. Clouds form by this process.

Evaporation occurs when liquid water changes into water vapor, which is a gas.

Precipitation occurs when rain, snow, sleet, or hail falls from the clouds onto Earth's surface.

Runoff is water, usually from precipitation, that flows across land and collects in rivers, streams, and eventually the ocean.

CHAPTER RESOURCES

Chapter Resource File
- **Lesson Plan**
- **Directed Reading A** BASIC
- **Directed Reading B** SPECIAL NEEDS

Technology

Transparencies
- Bellringer
- The Water Cycle

Answer to Reading Check

The water cycle is the continuous movement of water from Earth's oceans and rivers into the atmosphere, into the ground, and back into the oceans and rivers.

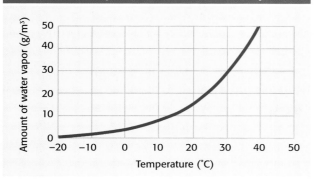

Amount of Water Vapor Air Can Hold at Various Temperatures

Figure 2 *This graph shows that as air gets warmer, the amount of water vapor that the air can hold increases.*

Humidity

As water evaporates from lakes, oceans, and plants, it becomes *water vapor,* or moisture in the air. Water vapor is invisible. The amount of water vapor in the air is called **humidity.** As water evaporates and becomes water vapor, the humidity of the air increases. The air's ability to hold water vapor changes as the temperature of the air changes. **Figure 2** shows that as the temperature of the air increases, the air's ability to hold water vapor also increases.

Relative Humidity

One way to express humidity is through relative humidity. **Relative humidity** is the amount of water vapor in the air compared with the maximum amount of water vapor that the air can hold at a certain temperature. So, relative humidity is given as a percentage. When air holds all of the water that it can at a given temperature, it is said to be *saturated.* Saturated air has a relative humidity of 100%. But how do you find the relative humidity of air that is not saturated? If you know the maximum amount of water vapor that air can hold at a given temperature and the actual amount of water vapor in the air, you can calculate the relative humidity.

Suppose that 1 m³ of air at a certain temperature can hold 24 g of water vapor. However, you know that the air actually contains 18 g of water vapor. You can calculate the relative humidity by using the following formula:

$$\frac{actual\ water\ vapor\ content\ (g/m^3)}{saturation\ water\ vapor\ content\ (g/m^3)} \times 100 = relative\ humidity\ (\%)$$

$$\frac{18\ g/m^3}{24\ g/m^3} = 75\%$$

weather the short-term state of the atmosphere, including temperature, humidity, precipitation, wind, and visibility

humidity the amount of water vapor in the air

relative humidity the ratio of the amount of water vapor in the air to the maximum amount of water vapor the air can hold at a set temperature

Relative Humidity

Assume that 1 m³ of air at 25°C contains 11 g of water vapor. At this temperature, the air can hold 24 g/m³ of water vapor. Calculate the relative humidity of the air.

CONNECTION to Life Science — ADVANCED

Hair Hygrometer When the air is humid, hair becomes frizzy. Hair is made of a protein called *keratin.* Each hair fiber has a scaly outer cuticle, which you can feel by running your fingers up and down a single hair. The scales allow moisture to enter the inner part of the hair fiber. When the air is humid, hair absorbs moisture and becomes longer and frizzy. Hair dries out and becomes shorter when the air is dry. Because humidity can cause hair length to change by as much as 2.5%, a device called a *hair hygrometer* can very accurately measure changes in humidity. Have students design and build their own hair hygrometers. Plans for making a hair hygrometer are available on the Internet. Note: This project will not work on very short hair. **LS Kinesthetic**

ACTIVITY — GENERAL

Sentence Completion After students have read this page, have them complete the following sentences:

• If the humidity is low, a _____ amount of water will evaporate from a wet-bulb thermometer and the _____ between the wet-bulb reading and the dry-bulb reading of the psychrometer will be high. (large, temperature difference)

• If the dry bulb reads 10°C, and the difference between the thermometers is 8°C, the relative humidity is _____. (15%)

LS Verbal

Cultural Awareness — GENERAL

Hopi Rainmakers Have students research the rainmakers in Hopi Indian culture. Students might find out about *Leenangkatsina,* whose flute brings rain; *Qaleetaqa,* who carries lightning and a bull-roarer to bring rain; and *Si'o Sa'lakwmana* or *Pawtiwa,* both of whom bring rain and mist to villages. **LS Interpersonal**

Answer to Reading Check

A psychrometer is used to measure relative humidity.

INTERNET ACTIVITY

For another activity related to this chapter, go to **go.hrw.com** and type in the keyword **HZ5WEAW**.

Factors Affecting Relative Humidity

Two factors that affect relative humidity are amount of water vapor and temperature. At constant temperature and pressure, as the amount of water vapor in air changes, the relative humidity changes. The more water vapor there is in the air, the higher the relative humidity is. If the amount of water vapor in the air stays the same but the temperature changes, the relative humidity changes. The relative humidity decreases as the temperature rises and increases as the temperature drops.

Measuring Relative Humidity

A *psychrometer* (sie KRAHM uht uhr) is an instrument that is used to measure relative humidity. A psychrometer consists of two thermometers, one of which is a wet-bulb thermometer. The bulb of a wet-bulb thermometer is covered with a damp cloth. The other thermometer is a dry-bulb thermometer.

The difference in temperature readings between the thermometers indicates the amount of water vapor in the air. The larger the difference between the two readings is, the less water vapor the air contains and thus the lower the humidity is. **Figure 3** shows how to use a table of differences between wet-bulb and dry-bulb readings to determine relative humidity.

✓ Reading Check What tool is used to measure relative humidity?

Figure 3 Determining Relative Humidity

Find the relative humidity by locating the column head that is equal to the difference between the wet-bulb and dry-bulb readings. Then, locate the row head that equals the temperature reading on the dry-bulb thermometer. The value that lies where the column and row intersect equals the relative humidity. You can see a psychrometer below.

	Relative Humidity (%)							
Dry-bulb reading (°C)	Difference between wet-bulb reading and dry-bulb reading (°C)							
	1	2	3	4	5	6	7	8
0	81	64	46	29	13			
2	84	68	52	37	22	7		
4	85	71	57	43	29	16		
6	86	73	60	48	35	24	11	
8	87	75	63	51	40	29	19	8
10	88	77	66	55	44	34	24	15
12	89	78	68	58	48	39	29	21
14	90	79	70	60	51	42	34	26
16	90	81	71	63	54	46	38	30
18	91	82	73	65	57	49	41	34
20	91	83	74	66	59	51	44	37

INCLUSION Strategies

• **Learning Disabled** • **Attention Deficit Disorder**
Have student groups make a pyschrometer. Give each group two identical thermometers, gauze, tape, water, a rubber band, and an 8 1/2 in. × 11 in. piece of cardboard. Ask each group to wrap the gauze around the bulb of a thermometer and attach it firmly with the rubber band. Next, have students wet the gauze. Then, have students place the thermometers side by side with the bulbs hanging over the edge of a desk. Students should tape the thermometers securely to the desk. Have students use the cardboard to carefully fan the thermometers until the temperature of the wet-bulb thermometer stops decreasing. Have students subtract the wet-bulb temperature from the dry-bulb temperature and record the difference. Then, have students determine the relative humidity of the air in the classroom using **Figure 3**. **LS Kinesthetic**

How a Wet-Bulb Thermometer Works

A wet-bulb thermometer works differently than a dry-bulb thermometer, which measures only air temperature. As air passes over the wet-bulb thermometer, the water in the cloth evaporates. As the water evaporates, the cloth cools. If the humidity is low, the water will evaporate more quickly and the temperature reading on the wet-bulb thermometer will drop. If the humidity is high, only a small amount of water will evaporate from the cloth of the wet-bulb thermometer and the change in temperature will be small.

Reading Check **Explain how a wet-bulb thermometer works.**

Condensation

You have probably seen water droplets form on the outside of a glass of ice water, as shown in **Figure 4.** Where did those water drops come from? The water came from the surrounding air, and droplets formed as a result of condensation. **Condensation** is the process by which a gas, such as water vapor, becomes a liquid. Before condensation can occur, the air must be saturated, which means that the air must have a relative humidity of 100%. Condensation occurs when saturated air cools.

Dew Point

Air can become saturated when water vapor is added to the air through evaporation. Air can also become saturated when it cools to its dew point. The *dew point* is the temperature at which a gas condenses into a liquid. At its dew point, air is saturated. The ice in the glass of water causes the air surrounding the glass to cool to its dew point.

Before water vapor can condense, though, it must have a surface to condense on. In the case of the glass of ice water, water vapor condenses on the outside of the glass.

Figure 4 *Condensation occurred when the air next to the glass cooled to its dew point.*

condensation the change of state from a gas to a liquid

Out of Thin Air

1. Pour **room-temperature water** into a **plastic container,** such as a drinking cup, until the water level is near the top of the cup.
2. Observe the outside of the container, and record your observations.
3. Add **one or two ice cubes** to the container of water.
4. Watch the outside of the container for any changes.
5. What happened to the outside of the container?
6. What is the liquid on the container?
7. Where did the liquid come from? Explain your answer.

Discussion ——— GENERAL

What Dew You Think Have students decide if the following statements are true or false:

- Condensation is the process in which a liquid changes to a gas. (false)
- Dew point is the temperature to which air must cool before it becomes saturated. (true)
- The dew you observe on grass forms on hot, cloudy, windless nights. (false)

LS Verbal

Answer to Reading Check

The bulb of a wet-bulb thermometer is covered with moistened material. The bulb cools as water evaporates from the material. If the air is dry, more water will evaporate from the material, and the temperature recorded by the thermometer will be low. If the air is humid, less water will evaporate from the material, and the temperature recorded by the thermometer will be higher.

Answers to Quick Lab

5. Liquid droplets formed on the outside of the container.
6. The liquid is water.
7. The air next to the cup cooled to below its dew point, and water vapor condensed on the cup.

Sequencing After students read this page, have them arrange the following steps in a logical order:

- Water vapor condenses on smoke, dust, salt, and other small particles suspended in the air. (4)
- The relative humidity of the air increases. (2)
- Warm air rises and cools. (1)
- Air eventually becomes saturated. (3)
- Millions of tiny drops of liquid water collect to form a cloud. (5)

LS Logical

Debate ——— ADVANCED

Cloud Seeding Meteorologists sometimes use a technique known as *cloud seeding* to try to cause or increase precipitation. Have groups of students research this technique and write a position paper about it. After students have gathered their information, have small groups debate the pros and cons of artificially stimulating precipitation. **LS** Verbal

Figure 5 Three Forms of Clouds

Cumulus clouds look like piles of cotton balls.

Stratus clouds are not as tall as cumulus clouds, but they cover more area.

Cirrus clouds are made of ice crystals.

cloud a collection of small water droplets or ice crystals suspended in the air, which forms when the air is cooled and condensation occurs

CONNECTION TO Language Arts

Cloud Clues Did you know that the name of a cloud actually describes the characteristics of the cloud? For example, the word *cumulus* comes from the Latin word meaning "heap." A cumulus cloud is a puffy, white cloud, which could be described as a "heap" of clouds. Use a dictionary or the Internet to find the word origins of the names of the other cloud types you learn about in this section.

Clouds

Have you ever wondered what clouds are and how they form? A **cloud** is a collection of millions of tiny water droplets or ice crystals. Clouds form as warm air rises and cools. As the rising air cools, it becomes saturated. When the air is saturated, the water vapor changes to a liquid or a solid, depending on the air temperature. At temperatures above freezing, water vapor condenses on small particles in the air and forms tiny water droplets. At temperatures below freezing, water vapor changes to a solid to form ice crystals. Clouds are classified by form, as shown in **Figure 5,** and by altitude.

Cumulus Clouds

Puffy, white clouds that tend to have flat bottoms are called *cumulus clouds* (KYOO myoo luhs KLOWDZ). Cumulus clouds form when warm air rises. These clouds generally indicate fair weather. However, when these clouds get larger, they produce thunderstorms. Thunderstorms come from a kind of cumulus cloud called a *cumulonimbus cloud* (KYOO myoo loh NIM buhs KLOWD). Clouds that have names that include *-nimbus* or *nimbo-* are likely to produce precipitation.

Stratus Clouds

Clouds called *stratus clouds* (STRAYT uhs KLOWDZ) are clouds that form in layers. Stratus clouds cover large areas of the sky and often block out the sun. These clouds can be caused by a gentle lifting of a large body of air into the atmosphere. *Nimbostratus clouds* (NIM boh STRAYT uhs KLOWDZ) are dark stratus clouds that usually produce light to heavy, continuous rain. *Fog* is a stratus cloud that has formed near the ground.

Homework ——— BASIC

Cloud Models On a poster board, have students use cotton balls to make models of different types of clouds at different altitudes. Students should create labels to describe the clouds and the types of weather with which they are associated.

English Language Learners

LS Visual/Intrapersonal

MISCONCEPTION ALERT

Contrails What appears to be white smoke from an airplane's engine is not smoke at all. Condensation trails, or contrails, form as the combustion of the aircraft's fuel forms water vapor which condenses and freezes along the airplane's exhaust tail. A thick contrail that will not dissipate is a sign that a frontal system is approaching.

Cirrus Clouds

As you can see in **Figure 5,** *cirrus clouds* (SIR uhs KLOWDZ) are thin, feathery, white clouds found at high altitudes. Cirrus clouds form when the wind is strong. If they get thicker, cirrus clouds indicate that a change in the weather is coming.

Clouds and Altitude

Clouds are also classified by the altitude at which they form. **Figure 6** shows two altitude groups used to describe clouds and the altitudes at which they form in the middle latitudes. The prefix *cirro-* is used to describe clouds that form at high altitudes. For example, a cumulus cloud that forms high in the atmosphere is called a *cirrocumulus cloud.* The prefix *alto-* describes clouds that form at middle altitudes. Clouds that form at low altitudes do not have a specific prefix to describe them.

Reading Check At what altitude does an altostratus cloud form?

Figure 6 **Cloud Types Based on Form and Altitude**

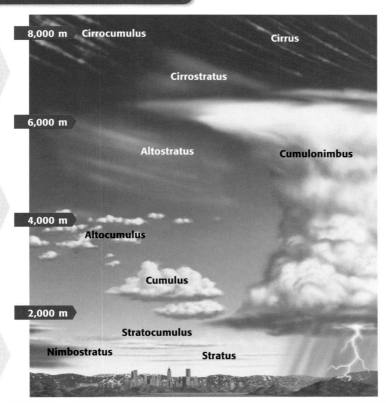

High Clouds Because of the cold temperatures at high altitude, high clouds are made up of ice crystals. The prefix *cirro-* is used to describe high clouds.

Middle Clouds Middle clouds can be made up of both water drops and ice crystals. The prefix *alto-* is used to describe middle clouds.

Low Clouds Low clouds are made up of water drops. There is no specific prefix used to describe low clouds.

8,000 m — Cirrocumulus — Cirrus

Cirrostratus

6,000 m

Altostratus — Cumulonimbus

4,000 m

Altocumulus

Cumulus

2,000 m

Stratocumulus

Nimbostratus — Stratus

Answer to Reading Check
Altostratus clouds form at middle altitudes.

CHAPTER RESOURCES

Technology

Transparencies
• Cloud Types Based on Form and Altitude

Figure 7 *Snowflakes are six-sided ice crystals that can be several millimeters to several centimeters in size.*

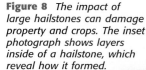
precipitation any form of water that falls to the Earth's surface from the clouds

Precipitation

When water from the air returns to Earth's surface, it returns as precipitation. **Precipitation** is water, in solid or liquid form, that falls from the air to Earth. There are four major forms of precipitation—rain, snow, sleet, and hail.

Rain

The most common form of precipitation is *rain*. A cloud produces rain when the water drops in the cloud become large enough to fall. A water drop in a cloud begins as a droplet that is smaller than the period at the end of this sentence. Before such a water drop falls as rain, it must become about 100 times its original size.

Sleet and Snow

Sleet forms when rain falls through a layer of freezing air. The rain freezes in the air, which produces falling ice. *Snow* forms when temperatures are so cold that water vapor changes directly to a solid. Snow can fall as single ice crystals or can join to form snowflakes, as shown in **Figure 7.**

Hail

Balls or lumps of ice that fall from clouds are called *hail*. Hail forms in cumulonimbus clouds. When updrafts of air in the clouds carry raindrops high in the clouds, the raindrops freeze and hail forms. As hail falls, water drops coat it. Another updraft of air can send the hail up again. Here, the water drops collected on the hail freeze to form another layer of ice on the hail. This process can happen many times. Eventually, the hail becomes too heavy to be carried by the updrafts and so falls to Earth's surface, as shown in **Figure 8.**

Figure 8 *The impact of large hailstones can damage property and crops. The inset photograph shows layers inside of a hailstone, which reveal how it formed.*

SECTION Review

Summary

- Weather is the condition of the atmosphere at a certain time and place. Weather is affected by the amount of water vapor in the air.
- The water cycle describes the movement of water above, on, and below Earth's surface.
- Humidity describes the amount of water vapor in the air. Relative humidity is a way to express humidity.

- When the temperature of the air cools to its dew point, the air has reached saturation and condensation occurs.
- Clouds form as air cools to its dew point. Clouds are classified by form and by the altitude at which they form.
- Precipitation occurs when the water vapor that condenses in the atmosphere falls back to Earth in solid or liquid form.

Using Key Terms

1. In your own words, write a definition for each of the following terms: *relative humidity, condensation, cloud,* and *precipitation*.

Understanding Key Ideas

2. Which of the following clouds is most likely to produce light to heavy, continuous rain?
   a. cumulus cloud
   b. cumulonimbus cloud
   c. nimbostratus cloud
   d. cirrus cloud

3. How is relative humidity affected by the amount of water vapor in the air?

4. What does a relative humidity of 75% mean?

5. Describe the path of water through the water cycle.

6. What are four types of precipitation?

Critical Thinking

7. **Applying Concepts** Why are some clouds formed from water droplets, while others are made up of ice crystals?

8. **Applying Concepts** How can rain and hail fall from the same cumulonimbus cloud?

9. **Identifying Relationships** What happens to relative humidity as the air temperature drops below the dew point?

Interpreting Graphics

Use the image below to answer the questions that follow.

10. What type of cloud is shown in the image?

11. How is this type of cloud formed?

12. What type of weather can you expect when you see this type of cloud? Explain.

For a variety of links related to this chapter, go to www.scilinks.org

Topic: The Water Cycle
SciLinks code: HSM1626

CONNECTION to Physical Science—GENERAL

Water Molecules Explain that a water molecule has a positive end and a negative end. Opposite charges attract, so the positive end of one water molecule attracts the negative end of another. This attraction helps explain why small water droplets that collide are able to form relatively large raindrops.

CHAPTER RESOURCES

Chapter Resource File
- Section Quiz GENERAL
- Section Review GENERAL
- Vocabulary and Section Summary GENERAL
- Datasheet for Quick Lab

Answers to Section Review

1. Sample answer: Relative humidity is the amount of water vapor the air contains compared with the maximum amount it can hold at a given temperature. Condensation is a process that occurs when air reaches its saturation point. A cloud is a mass of air that contains millions of condensed water droplets. Precipitation is solid or liquid water that falls from a cloud.

2. c

3. If the amount of water vapor in the air increases, the relative humidity also increases.

4. The air contains 75% of the maximum amount of water it can hold at a given temperature.

5. Sample answer: Water evaporates from the Earth's surface and rises into the atmosphere. The air cools as it rises. As the air cools, water condenses and falls as precipitation. The precipitation falls to the Earth.

6. rain, snow, sleet, and hail

7. Sample answer: Clouds that form at high altitudes are usually colder than clouds that form at lower altitudes. The cold, high-altitude clouds can be composed of ice crystals.

8. Sample answer: Cumulonimbus clouds can be very tall. Rain can form at the bottom of the cloud, and hail can form near the top of the cloud.

9. As the air temperature drops below the dew point, relative humidity increases to the saturation point, and condensation occurs.

10. a cumulus cloud

11. Cumulus clouds form when warm, moist air rises.

12. Sample answer: Cumulus clouds usually indicate fair weather. However, when cumulus clouds grow large, they can become cumulonimbus clouds, which often produce thunderstorms.

Focus

Overview

In this section, students learn about air masses and the ways that they affect weather in the United States. Students also learn about fronts—the boundaries between air masses.

Bellringer

Ask students to write down as many different qualities of air as possible. (Students might note that air can be humid or dry, can be hot or cold, or can have high pressure or low pressure.) Tell students that the air they are breathing now was hundreds of miles away yesterday. Ask them to think about what caused that air to move. Explain that air masses tend to flow from areas of high pressure to areas of low pressure, just as the air inside a balloon escapes when the balloon is punctured.

Motivate

Discussion ——— GENERAL

Air Masses and You Have students use **Figure 1** to determine which type of air mass is mainly responsible for the weather in your area. Have students describe the general temperatures and humidity typical of your area. Have students compare their results with information in this section. LS Visual

---

CHAPTER RESOURCES

Chapter Resource File

• Lesson Plan
• Directed Reading A BASIC
• Directed Reading B SPECIAL NEEDS

Technology

Transparencies
• Bellringer

Air Masses and Fronts

Have you ever wondered how the weather can change so quickly? For example, the weather may be warm and sunny in the morning and cold and rainy by afternoon.

READING WARM-UP

Objectives

● Identify the four kinds of air masses that influence weather in the United States.

● Describe the four major types of fronts.

● Explain how fronts cause weather changes.

● Explain how cyclones and anticyclones affect the weather.

Terms to Learn

air mass   cyclone
front   anticyclone

READING STRATEGY

Reading Organizer As you read this section, make a table comparing cold, warm, occluded, and stationary fronts.

Changes in weather are caused by the movement and interaction of air masses. An **air mass** is a large body of air where temperature and moisture content are similar throughout. In this section, you will learn about air masses and their effect on weather.

Air Masses

Air masses are characterized by their moisture content and temperature. The moisture content and temperature of an air mass are determined by the area over which the air mass forms. These areas are called *source regions*. An example of a source region is the Gulf of Mexico. An air mass that forms over the Gulf of Mexico is warm and wet because this area is warm and has a lot of water that evaporates. There are many types of air masses, each of which is associated with a particular source region. The characteristics of these air masses are represented on maps by a two-letter symbol, as shown in **Figure 1.** The first letter indicates the moisture content that is characteristic of the air mass. The second letter represents the temperature that is characteristic of the air mass.

| Figure 1 | Air Masses That Affect Weather in North America |

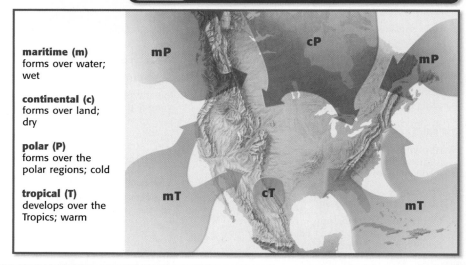

maritime (m)
forms over water; wet

continental (c)
forms over land; dry

polar (P)
forms over the polar regions; cold

tropical (T)
develops over the Tropics; warm

Homework ——— GENERAL

Researching Weather Lore Have students research weather lore at the library or on the Internet to find out if the stories have a scientific basis. For example, students could research the saying, "Red sky at night, sailors delight; red sky at morning, sailors take warning." LS Intrapersonal/Logical

---

Figure 2 *Cold air masses that form over the North Atlantic Ocean can bring severe weather, such as blizzards, in the winter.*

Cold Air Masses

Most of the cold winter weather in the United States is influenced by three polar air masses. A continental polar (cP) air mass forms over northern Canada, which brings extremely cold winter weather to the United States. In the summer, a cP air mass generally brings cool, dry weather.

A maritime polar (mP) air mass that forms over the North Pacific Ocean is cool and very wet. This air mass brings rain and snow to the Pacific Coast in the winter and cool, foggy weather in the summer.

A maritime polar air mass that forms over the North Atlantic Ocean brings cool, cloudy weather and precipitation to New England in the winter, as shown in **Figure 2.** In the summer, the air mass brings cool weather and fog.

Warm Air Masses

Four warm air masses influence the weather in the United States. A maritime tropical (mT) air mass that develops over warm areas in the Pacific Ocean is milder than the maritime polar air mass that forms over the Pacific Ocean.

Other maritime tropical air masses develop over the warm waters of the Gulf of Mexico and the Atlantic Ocean. These air masses move north across the East Coast and into the Midwest. In the summer, they bring hot and humid weather, hurricanes, and thunderstorms, as shown in **Figure 3.** In the winter, they bring mild, often cloudy weather.

A continental tropical (cT) air mass forms over the deserts of northern Mexico and the southwestern United States. This air mass moves northward and brings clear, dry, and hot weather in the summer.

✓ Reading Check What type of air mass contributes to the hot and humid summer weather in the midwestern United States? (*See the Appendix for answers to Reading Checks.*)

air mass a large body of air where temperature and moisture content are constant throughout

Figure 3 *Warm air masses that develop over the Gulf of Mexico bring thunderstorms in the summer.*

Local Weather Local weather patterns are heavily influenced by air masses, which tend to bring predictable weather. All cultures have names for familiar weather patterns. For example, in Tunisia, Africa, weather forecasters often predict "hot and *chili*" conditions. This forecast may not make sense to people elsewhere, but to a Tunisian, *chili* refers to a hot wind blowing from the North African desert. Similarly, in parts of the eastern United States, people refer to the hot, dry, and relatively windless weeks of August as the "dog days" of summer. Have interested students research the names and characteristics of typical weather patterns in other countries. LS **Interpersonal**

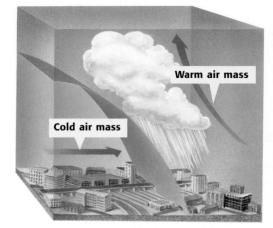

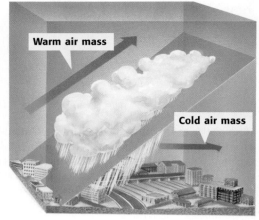

Figure 4 Fronts That Affect Weather in North America

Cold Front

Warm air mass

Cold air mass

Direction of front

Warm Front

Warm air mass

Cold air mass

Direction of front

front the boundary between air masses of different densities and usually different temperatures

Fronts

Air masses that form from different areas often do not mix. The reason is that the air masses have different densities. For example, warm air is less dense than cold air. So, when two types of air masses meet, warm air generally rises. The area in which two types of air masses meet is called a **front.** The four kinds of fronts—cold fronts, warm fronts, occluded fronts, and stationary fronts—are shown in **Figure 4.** Fronts are associated with weather in the middle latitudes.

Cold Front

A cold front forms where cold air moves under warm air, which is less dense, and pushes the warm air up. Cold fronts can move quickly and bring thunderstorms, heavy rain, or snow. Cooler weather usually follows a cold front because the air mass behind the cold front is cooler and drier than the air mass that it is replacing.

Warm Front

A warm front forms where warm air moves over cold, denser air. In a warm front, the warm air gradually replaces the cold air. Warm fronts generally bring drizzly rain and are followed by clear and warm weather.

CONNECTION to History GENERAL

WWI and Meteorology During World War I, European nations stopped broadcasting weather reports, fearing that they would be used by advancing enemy troops. This left nonaligned countries such as Norway to develop their own meteorology program. Norwegian meteorologists responded by forming the famous Bergen School, which greatly advanced the field of meteorology. They discovered that air masses formed from source regions and found that these masses traveled with the winds. Influenced by the war, the meteorologists described air masses using military terms. They imagined Europe as a battleground where different air masses fought like armies trying to advance on each other. The boundary between the air masses, where the "battle" occurs, was called the *front*.

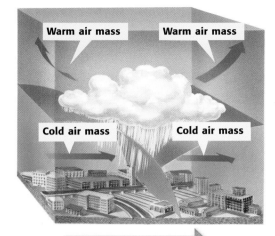

Occluded Front

Warm air mass · Warm air mass

Cold air mass · Cold air mass

Direction of front

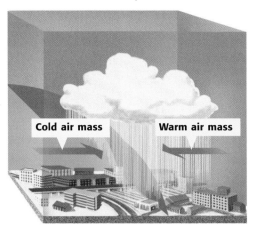

Stationary Front

Cold air mass · Warm air mass

Occluded Front

An occluded front forms when a warm air mass is caught between two colder air masses. The coldest air mass moves under and pushes up the warm air mass. The coldest air mass then moves forward until it meets a cold air mass that is warmer and less dense. The colder of these two air masses moves under and pushes up the warmer air mass. Sometimes, though, the two colder air masses mix. An occluded front has cool temperatures and large amounts of rain and snow.

✔ Reading Check What type of weather would you expect an occluded front to produce?

Stationary Front

A stationary front forms when a cold air mass meets a warm air mass. In this case, however, both air masses do not have enough force to lift the warm air mass over the cold air mass. So, the two air masses remain separated. This may happen because there is not enough wind to keep the air masses pushing against each other. A stationary front often brings many days of cloudy, wet weather.

CONNECTION to Physical Science— GENERAL

Specific Heat Water has a very high *specific heat*, which means that a great deal of thermal energy is needed to increase the temperature of water. Thus, water heats and cools very slowly. Rock, on the other hand, has a very low specific heat, so it heats rather quickly. For this reason, areas of high pressure (anticyclones) form over bodies of water, and areas of low pressure (cyclones) form over landmasses during the summer months. Because water tends to retain heat and rock tends to lose heat quickly, cyclones tend to form over bodies of water and anticyclones tend to form over landmasses during the winter months.

ACTIVITY ——— BASIC

Using Maps Have students collect the daily weather maps from a newspaper for 1 week. Have students locate the high and low pressure systems on the map and track the movement of these systems. Ask students to analyze the types of weather that are associated with the pressure systems. At the end of the week, ask students to predict the weather for their area for the next week according to the position and movement of the high- and low-pressure systems.
LS Visual

Close

Reteaching ───── BASIC

Section Outline Have students copy the section headings and then create an outline that includes at least two points for each heading. Students can use their outline as a study guide.

LS Visual/Verbal

Quiz ───── GENERAL

1. What type of weather is associated with a continental polar air mass in the summer? (cool and dry)

2. What is the area called over which an air mass forms? (source region)

3. Explain how a cold front develops. (A cold front develops when a cold air mass moves under a warm air mass, which forces the warmer air upward.)

4. What kind of weather is associated with a stationary front? (The weather will probably be cloudy and rainy as long as the front lies over an area. After the front passes, the weather will usually clear up.)

Alternative Assessment ───── GENERAL

United States Air Masses Have students list five places in the United States that they have visited or would like to visit and the air masses that affect the weather in those places.

LS Intrapersonal

Figure 5 *This satellite image shows a cyclone system forming.*

cyclone an area in the atmosphere that has lower pressure than the surrounding areas and has winds that spiral toward the center

anticyclone the rotation of air around a high-pressure center in the direction opposite to Earth's rotation

Air Pressure and Weather

You may have heard a weather reporter on TV or radio talking about areas of low pressure and high pressure. These areas of different pressure affect the weather.

Cyclones

Areas that have lower pressure than the surrounding areas do are called **cyclones.** Cyclones are areas where air masses come together, or converge, and rise. **Figure 5** shows a satellite image of the formation of a cyclone system.

Anticyclones

Areas that have high pressure are called **anticyclones.** Anticyclones are areas where air moves apart, or diverges, and sinks. The sinking air is denser than the surrounding air, and the pressure is higher. Cooler, denser air moves out of the center of these high-pressure areas toward areas of lower pressure. **Figure 6** shows how wind can spiral out of an anticyclone and into a cyclone.

Figure 6 *As the colder, denser air spirals out of the anticyclone, it moves towards areas of low pressure, which sometimes forms a cyclone.*

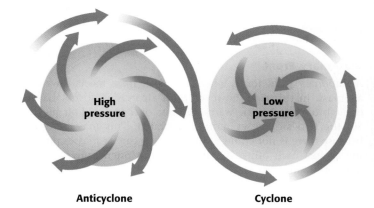

High pressure

Low pressure

Anticyclone

Cyclone

CONNECTION to Life Science ───── GENERAL

Aching Joints and Air Pressure Why do people complain of aching joints before a thunderstorm? A study found that nearly 75% of arthritis sufferers felt more pain in their joints when air pressure was falling. Although this effect has been thoroughly documented, there is no definitive evidence of why it occurs.

Cyclones, Anticyclones, and Weather

You have learned what cyclones and anticyclones are. So, now you might be wondering how do cyclones and anticyclones affect the weather? As the air in the center of a cyclone rises, it cools and forms clouds and rain. The rising air in a cyclone causes stormy weather. In an anticyclone, the air sinks. As the air sinks, it gets warmer and absorbs moisture. The sinking air in an anticyclone brings dry, clear weather. By keeping track of cyclones and anticyclones, meteorologists can predict the weather.

Reading Check Describe the different types of weather that a cyclone and an anticyclone can produce.

CONNECTION TO Astronomy

Storms on Jupiter Cyclones and anticyclones occur on Jupiter, too! Generally, cyclones on Jupiter appear as dark ovals, and anticyclones appear as bright ovals. Jupiter's Great Red Spot is an anticyclone that has existed for centuries. Research the existence of cyclones and anticyclones on other bodies in our solar system.

SECTION Review

Summary

- Air masses are characterized by moisture content and temperature.
- A front occurs where two air masses meet.
- Four major types of fronts are cold, warm, occluded, and stationary fronts.
- Differences in air pressure cause cyclones, which bring stormy weather, and anticyclones, which bring dry, clear weather.

Using Key Terms

For each pair of terms, explain how the meanings of the terms differ.

1. *front* and *air mass*

2. *cyclone* and *anticyclone*

Understanding Key Ideas

3. What kind of front forms when a cold air mass displaces a warm air mass?
   a. a cold front
   b. a warm front
   c. an occluded front
   d. a stationary front

4. What are the major air masses that influence the weather in the United States?

5. What is one source region of a maritime polar air mass?

6. What are the characteristics of an air mass whose two-letter symbol is cP?

7. What are the four major types of fronts?

8. How do fronts cause weather changes?

9. How do cyclones and anticyclones affect the weather?

Math Skills

10. A cold front is moving toward the town of La Porte at 35 km/h. The front is 200 km away from La Porte. How long will it take the front to get to La Porte?

Critical Thinking

11. **Applying Concepts** How do air masses that form over the land and ocean affect weather in the United States?

12. **Identifying Relationships** Why does the Pacific Coast have cool, wet winters and warm, dry summers? Explain.

13. **Applying Concepts** Which air masses influence the weather where you live? Explain.

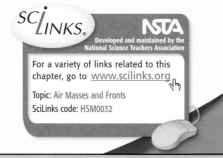

For a variety of links related to this chapter, go to www.scilinks.org

Topic: Air Masses and Fronts
SciLinks code: HSM0032

Answer to Reading Check

An anticyclone can produce dry, clear weather.

CHAPTER RESOURCES

Chapter Resource File
- Section Quiz **GENERAL**
- Section Review **GENERAL**
- Vocabulary and Section Summary **GENERAL**

Focus

Overview

In this section, students will learn about severe weather. The section explores thunderstorms, tornadoes, and hurricanes. Students learn about the causes of severe weather and about severe weather safety.

 Bellringer

Have students write a one-paragraph description of a thunderstorm. Ask them to describe the weather conditions immediately before, during, and after a thunderstorm. Ask students to describe how the storm affects each of their senses.

Motivate

Demonstration — GENERAL

Modeling Thunder Inflate a balloon with air, and tie it closed. Explain that thunder occurs when lightning superheats air, which causes the gases to expand rapidly. The air in the balloon is under pressure, so it will also expand rapidly if the pressure is suddenly released. The rapid expansion of air causes vibrations that we hear as sound. Hold up a pin or needle, pause, and pop the balloon with a flourish.

LS Kinesthetic

READING WARM-UP

Objectives

● Describe how lightning forms.
● Describe the formation of thunderstorms, tornadoes, and hurricanes.
● Describe the characteristics of thunderstorms, tornadoes, and hurricanes.
● Explain how to stay safe during severe weather.

Terms to Learn

thunderstorm   tornado
lightning   hurricane
thunder

READING STRATEGY

Reading Organizer As you read this section, create an outline of the section. Use the headings from the section in your outline.

thunderstorm a usually brief, heavy storm that consists of rain, strong winds, lightning, and thunder

Severe Weather

CRAAAACK! BOOM! What made that noise? You didn't expect it, and it sure made you jump.

A big boom of thunder has probably surprised you at one time or another. And the thunder was probably followed by a thunderstorm. A thunderstorm is an example of severe weather. *Severe weather* is weather that can cause property damage and sometimes death.

Thunderstorms

Thunderstorms can be very loud and powerful. **Thunderstorms,** such as the one shown in **Figure 1,** are small, intense weather systems that produce strong winds, heavy rain, lightning, and thunder. Thunderstorms can occur along cold fronts. But thunderstorms can develop in other places, too. There are only two atmospheric conditions required to produce thunderstorms: warm and moist air near Earth's surface and an unstable atmosphere. The atmosphere is unstable when the surrounding air is colder than the rising air mass. The air mass will continue to rise as long as the surrounding air is colder than the air mass.

When the rising warm air reaches its dew point, the water vapor in the air condenses and forms cumulus clouds. If the atmosphere is extremely unstable, the warm air will continue to rise, which causes the cloud to grow into a dark, cumulonimbus cloud. Cumulonimbus clouds can reach heights of more than 15 km.

Figure 1 *A typical thunderstorm, such as this one over Dallas, Texas, generates an enormous amount of electrical energy.*

CHAPTER RESOURCES

Chapter Resource File

 • **Lesson Plan**
     • **Directed Reading A** BASIC
     • **Directed Reading B** SPECIAL NEEDS

Technology

 Transparencies
     • Bellringer
     • *LINK TO PHYSICAL SCIENCE* How Lightning Forms

MISCONCEPTION ///ALERT\\\

"The Same Place Twice" Inform students that the old saying, "Lightning never strikes twice in the same place," is not true. Lightning has struck the same place, and even the same person, more than once. Ray Sullivan, a retired national park ranger, has been hit seven times by lightning. Luckily, he has survived the strikes.

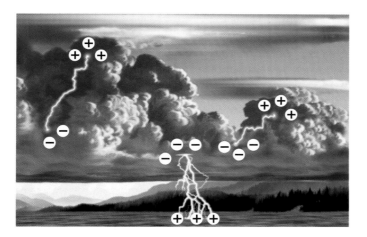

Figure 2 *The upper part of a cloud usually carries a positive electric charge, while the lower part of the cloud carries mainly negative charges.*

Lightning

Thunderstorms are very active electrically. **Lightning** is an electric discharge that occurs between a positively charged area and a negatively charged area, as shown in **Figure 2**. Lightning can happen between two clouds, between Earth and a cloud, or even between two parts of the same cloud. Have you ever touched someone after scuffing your feet on the carpet and received a mild shock? If so, you have experienced how lightning forms. While you walk around, friction between the floor and your shoes builds up an electric charge in your body. When you touch someone else, the charge is released.

When lightning strikes, energy is released. This energy is transferred to the air and causes the air to expand rapidly and send out sound waves. **Thunder** is the sound that results from the rapid expansion of air along the lightning strike.

Severe Thunderstorms

Severe thunderstorms can produce one or more of the following conditions: high winds, hail, flash floods, and tornadoes. Hailstorms damage crops, dent the metal on cars, and break windows. Flash flooding that results from heavy rains causes millions of dollars in property damage annually. And every year, flash flooding is a leading cause of weather-related deaths.

Lightning, as shown in **Figure 3,** happens during all thunderstorms and is very powerful. Lightning is responsible for starting thousands of forest fires each year and for killing or injuring hundreds of people a year in the United States.

✓ **Reading Check** What is a severe thunderstorm? (*See the Appendix for answers to Reading Checks.*)

lightning an electric discharge that takes place between two oppositely charged surfaces, such as between a cloud and the ground, between two clouds, or between two parts of the same cloud

thunder the sound caused by the rapid expansion of air along an electrical strike

Figure 3 *Lightning often strikes the tallest object in an area, such as the Eiffel Tower in Paris, France.*

Answer to Reading Check
A severe thunderstorm is a thunderstorm that produces high winds, hail, flash floods, or tornadoes.

• Hearing Impaired
• Attention Deficit Disorder
• Developmentally Delayed

Students will make a model of a tornado in a plastic bottle. Organize students into groups of three or four students. Give each group a clear, plastic 2 L soda bottle, water, salt, a teaspoon, liquid detergent and food coloring. Ask each group to fill the bottle with water up to 1 in. from the top and then add 1 tsp of salt. Next, have students cover the bottle and shake it until the salt has dissolved. Add a drop of liquid detergent and a drop of food coloring. Tell students to cover the bottle tightly, and move the bottle in a swirling motion. Ask students to record what they observe in their **science journal.**

LS Kinesthetic

CONNECTION ACTIVITY
Real World ——— GENERAL

Lightning Safety Students may be surprised to learn that, on average, lightning kills more people in the United States than tornadoes or hurricanes do. Discuss lightning safety tips with students, and have students create a poster showing what to do during a thunderstorm.

LS Visual/Verbal

---

tornado a destructive, rotating column of air that has very high wind speeds, is visible as a funnel-shaped cloud, and touches the ground

Tornadoes

Tornadoes happen in only 1% of all thunderstorms. A **tornado** is a small, spinning column of air that has high wind speeds and low central pressure and that touches the ground. A tornado starts out as a funnel cloud that pokes through the bottom of a cumulonimbus cloud and hangs in the air. The funnel cloud becomes a tornado when it makes contact with Earth's surface. **Figure 4** shows how a tornado forms.

> **Figure 4** **How a Tornado Forms**

❶ Wind moving in two directions causes a layer of air in the middle to begin to spin like a roll of toilet paper.

❷ The spinning column of air is turned to a vertical position by strong updrafts of air in the cumulonimbus cloud. The updrafts of air also begin to spin.

❸ The spinning column of air moves to the bottom of the cumulonimbus cloud and forms a funnel cloud.

❹ The funnel cloud becomes a tornado when it touches the ground.

⚡ BRAIN FOOD

Tornado Formation Most tornadoes develop from thunderstorms at the leading edge of a cold front. Ask students to think about why this is so. (The cool air wedges under the warm air, which may result in wind moving in opposite directions. This movement may cause a layer of air to spin. Rapidly rising warm air can turn the spinning layer into a vertical funnel.) **LS** Verbal

⚛ WEIRD SCIENCE

People have reported seeing "naked" chickens after tornadoes strike rural areas. A likely explanation is that tornadoes cause chickens to shed their feathers, or molt. Chickens often molt when attacked. As the chickens molt, the strong tornadic winds blow their feathers off.

Figure 5 *The tornado that hit Kissimmee, Florida, in 1998 had wind speeds of up to 416 km/h.*

Twists of Terror

About 75% of the world's tornadoes occur in the United States. Most of these tornadoes happen in the spring and early summer when cold, dry air from Canada meets warm, moist air from the Tropics. The size of a tornado's path of destruction is usually about 8 km long and 10 to 60 m wide. Although most tornadoes last only a few minutes, they can cause a lot of damage. Their ability to cause damage is due to their strong spinning winds. The average tornado has wind speeds between 120 and 180 km/h, but rarer, more violent tornadoes can have spinning winds of up to 500 km/h. The winds of tornadoes have been known to uproot trees and destroy buildings, as shown in **Figure 5.** Tornadoes are capable of picking up heavy objects, such as mobile homes and cars, and hurling them through the air.

Hurricanes

A large, rotating tropical weather system that has wind speeds of at least 120 km/h is called a **hurricane,** shown in **Figure 6.** Hurricanes are the most powerful storms on Earth. Hurricanes have different names in different parts of the world. In the western Pacific Ocean, hurricanes are called *typhoons*. Hurricanes that form over the Indian Ocean are called *cyclones*.

Most hurricanes form in the areas between 5° and 20° north latitude and between 5° and 20° south latitude over warm, tropical oceans. At higher latitudes, the water is too cold for hurricanes to form. Hurricanes vary in size from 160 to 1,500 km in diameter and can travel for thousands of kilometers.

✓ Reading Check What are some other names for hurricanes?

hurricane a severe storm that develops over tropical oceans and whose strong winds of more than 120 km/h spiral in toward the intensely low-pressure storm center

Figure 6 *This photograph of Hurricane Fran was taken from space.*

Answer to Reading Check

Hurricanes are also called *typhoons* or *cyclones.*

CONNECTION to History — GENERAL

Hurricanes and American History Hurricanes played a significant role in early American history. In 1609, a fleet of ships with settlers from England who were bound for Virginia was blown off course by a hurricane. Some of the ships landed in Bermuda instead, and the settlers started the first European colony there. Stories of the storm and the shipwrecks may have inspired William Shakespeare to write *The Tempest.*

Homework — ADVANCED

PORTFOLIO **Disaster Plan** Have students find out how to protect themselves during a thunderstorm, tornado, or hurricane. Using their findings, students should draw up a disaster plan for severe weather. The plan should include general information as well as things that might be specific to their family, such as what to do with the family pet(s), how to assist a person who uses a wheelchair or walker, and so on. Suggest that students review the plan with their family. **LS** Intrapersonal

Writing **Weather and Energy**
Tell students that creating severe weather takes a lot of energy. Have them research the relationship between energy and storm formation. For example, as a warm air mass rises, energy from water condensation helps fuel hurricanes. The energy released by a typical hurricane in 1 day is equal to detonating four hundred 20-megaton hydrogen bombs. Challenge students to research these concepts in books, magazines, and the Internet and to compile their findings into a short report. **LS Intrapersonal**

Hurricane Newscast Have students work in groups to learn about a hurricane of their choosing. Have students find out where the storm formed, what path it followed, what damage it did, and how people recovered from the damage. Ask students to focus on the people involved in the hurricane, from the meteorologists to relief workers. Have groups present the information they gathered as a series of simulated newscasts. **LS Auditory/ Interpersonal** Co-op Learning

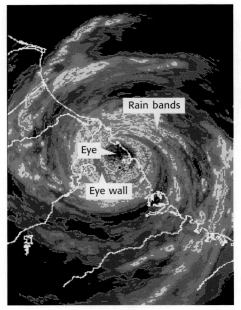

Figure 7 *The photo above gives you a bird's-eye view of a hurricane.*

How a Hurricane Forms

A hurricane begins as a group of thunderstorms moving over tropical ocean waters. Winds traveling in two different directions meet and cause the storm to spin. Because of the Coriolis effect, the storm turns counterclockwise in the Northern Hemisphere and clockwise in the Southern Hemisphere.

A hurricane gets its energy from the condensation of water vapor. Once formed, the hurricane is fueled through contact with the warm ocean water. Moisture is added to the warm air by evaporation from the ocean. As the warm, moist air rises, the water vapor condenses and releases large amounts of energy. The hurricane continues to grow as long as it is over its source of warm, moist air. When the hurricane moves into colder waters or over land, it begins to die because it has lost its source of energy. **Figure 7** and **Figure 8** show two views of a hurricane.

✓ **Reading Check** Where do hurricanes get their energy?

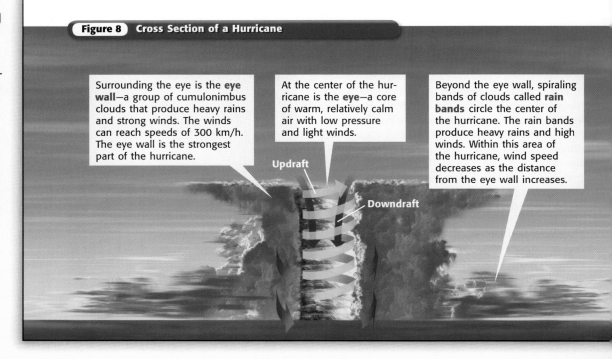

Figure 8 **Cross Section of a Hurricane**

Surrounding the eye is the **eye wall**—a group of cumulonimbus clouds that produce heavy rains and strong winds. The winds can reach speeds of 300 km/h. The eye wall is the strongest part of the hurricane.

At the center of the hurricane is the **eye**—a core of warm, relatively calm air with low pressure and light winds.

Beyond the eye wall, spiraling bands of clouds called **rain bands** circle the center of the hurricane. The rain bands produce heavy rains and high winds. Within this area of the hurricane, wind speed decreases as the distance from the eye wall increases.

Updraft

Downdraft

Answer to Reading Check
Hurricanes get their energy from the condensation of water vapor.

Damage Caused by Hurricanes

Hurricanes can cause a lot of damage when they move near or onto land. Wind speeds of most hurricanes range from 120 to 150 km/h. Some can reach speeds as high as 300 km/h. Hurricane winds can knock down trees and telephone poles and can damage and destroy buildings and homes.

While high winds cause a great deal of damage, most hurricane damage is caused by flooding associated with heavy rains and storm surges. A *storm surge* is a wall of water that builds up over the ocean because of the strong winds and low atmospheric pressure. The wall of water gets bigger as it nears the shore, and it reaches its greatest height when it crashes onto the shore. Depending on the hurricane's strength, a storm surge can be 1 to 8 m high and 65 to 160 km long. Flooding causes tremendous damage to property and lives when a storm surge moves onto shore, as shown in **Figure 9.**

Severe Weather Safety

Severe weather can be very dangerous, so it is important to keep yourself safe. One way to stay safe is to turn on the radio or TV during a storm. Your local radio and TV stations will let you know if a storm has gotten worse.

Thunderstorm Safety

Lightning is one of the most dangerous parts of a thunderstorm. Lightning is attracted to tall objects. If you are outside, stay away from trees, which can get struck down. If you are in the open, crouch down. Otherwise, you will be the tallest object in the area! Stay away from bodies of water. If lightning hits water while you are in it, you could be hurt or could even die.

Figure 9 *A hurricane's storm surge can cause severe damage to homes near the shoreline.*

Natural Disaster Plan

WRITING SKILL Every family should have a plan to deal with weather emergencies. With a parent, discuss what your family should do in the event of severe weather. Together, write up a plan for your family to follow in case of a natural disaster. Also, make a disaster supply kit that includes enough food and water to last several days.

Hurricane Tracking Meteorologists know where to look for hurricanes. Most hurricanes originate in an area called the *doldrums*, a narrow zone near the equator, and move in a curved path like a parabola. People have been tracking hurricanes for more than 50 years. New instruments, such as radar and geosynchronous weather satellites, allow meteorologists to track building pressure systems and make predictions about the path a tropical storm or a hurricane may take. U.S. military aircraft have even been used for informational reconnaissance, flying into hurricanes to measure wind velocities and direction, pressure, thermal structure, and the location of the eye. The ability to identify potential storm threats allows communities in the path of a hurricane time to prepare for the storm or to evacuate to safety. The National Hurricane Center monitors and stores information on hurricanes. Have students track a hurricane and write an autobiography of a hurricane from its birth to its death.
LS Verbal

MISCONCEPTION ALERT

Tropical Storm or Hurricane? Students may be confused by the terms *tropical storm* and *hurricane*. The difference between a hurricane and a tropical storm is wind speed. To qualify as a tropical storm, wind speed must be at least 63 km/h but no greater than 119 km/h. If wind speed is greater than 119 km/h, the storm is considered to be a hurricane.

Close

Reteaching ———— BASIC
Comparing Severe Weather
Have students work in pairs or small groups to design a poster that compares and contrasts thunderstorms, tornadoes, and hurricanes. Then, have the groups display their posters around the classroom. **LS** Visual

Quiz ———— GENERAL
1. What is the relationship between lightning and thunder? (Lightning is an electric discharge that forms between clouds or between a cloud and the ground. The air around the lightning bolt expands rapidly to produce sound waves that we call *thunder*.)

2. Explain why tornadoes often destroy buildings in their paths. (A tornado's strong winds often destroy buildings in the tornado's path.)

3. Why do hurricanes not form over land? (A hurricane gets its energy from the evaporation of enormous volumes of water in warm, moist air. These volumes of water are not present over landmasses.)

Alternative Assessment ———— GENERAL
Concept Mapping Have students make a severe-weather concept map. Tell them that their map should illustrate how thunderstorms, tornadoes, and hurricanes form and what their characteristics are. **LS** Visual

Figure 10 *During a tornado warning, it is best to protect yourself by crouching against a wall and covering the back of your head and neck with your hands or a book.*

Figure 11 *These store owners are boarding up their windows to protect the windows from strong winds during a hurricane.*

Tornado Safety

Weather forecasters use watches and warnings to let people know about tornadoes. A *watch* is a weather alert that lets people know that a tornado may happen. A *warning* is a weather alert that lets people know that a tornado has been spotted.

If there is a tornado warning for your area, find shelter quickly. The best place to go is a basement or cellar. Or you can go to a windowless room in the center of the building, such as a bathroom, closet, or hallway, as **Figure 10** shows. If you are outside, lie down in a large, open field or a deep ditch.

Flood Safety

An area can get so much rain that it begins to flood. So, like tornadoes, floods have watches and warnings. However, little warning can usually be given. A flash flood is a flood that rises and falls very suddenly. The best thing to do during a flood is to find a high place to wait out the flood. You should always stay out of floodwaters. Even shallow water can be dangerous if it is moving fast.

Hurricane Safety

If a hurricane is in your area, your local TV or radio station will keep you updated on its condition. People living on the shore may be asked to evacuate the area. If you live in an area where hurricanes strike, your family should have a disaster supply kit that includes enough water and food to last several days. To protect the windows in your home, you should cover them with plywood, as shown in **Figure 11**. Most important, you must stay indoors during the storm.

Science Bloopers

Native Meteorologists The Seminole Indians of Florida have used their own observations of nature to successfully predict severe weather. In one instance, their observations of plants and animals indicated that a hurricane was approaching. Although the weather bureau predicted the storm would miss the area, the Seminoles evacuated—and were spared the storm's destruction. In another instance, meteorologists were so sure of their predictions of a hurricane approaching that heavy equipment was moved away from the endangered area so that it would be available later to help relief efforts. The Seminoles thought otherwise and remained in the area. The hurricane never reached Florida.

Summary

- Thunderstorms are intense weather systems that produce strong winds, heavy rain, lightning, and thunder.
- Lightning is a large electric discharge that occurs between two oppositely charged surfaces. Lightning releases a great deal of energy and can be very dangerous.
- Tornadoes are small, rotating columns of air that touch the ground and can cause severe damage.

- A hurricane is a large, rotating tropical weather system. Hurricanes cause strong winds and can cause severe property damage.
- In the event of severe weather, it is important to stay safe. Listening to your local TV or radio station for updates and remaining indoors and away from windows are good rules to follow.

Using Key Terms

Complete each of the following sentences by choosing the correct term from the word bank.

hurricane	storm surge
tornado	lightning

1. Thunderstorms are very active electrically and often cause ___.

2. A ___ forms when a funnel cloud pokes through the bottom of a cumulonimbus cloud and makes contact with the ground.

Understanding Key Ideas

3. The safest thing to do if you are caught outdoors during a tornado is to
   a. stay near buildings and roads.
   b. head for an open area.
   c. seek shelter near a large tree.
   d. None of the above

4. Describe how tornadoes form.

5. At what latitudes do hurricanes usually form?

6. What is lightning? What happens when lightning strikes?

Critical Thinking

7. **Applying Concepts** What items do you think you would need in a disaster kit? Explain.

8. **Identifying Relationships** What happens to a hurricane as it moves over land? Explain.

Interpreting Graphics

Use the diagram below to answer the questions that follow.

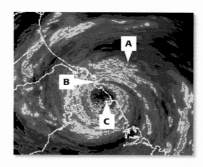

9. Describe what is happening at point C.

10. What is point B?

11. What kind of weather can you expect at point A?

SCiLINKS.

NSTA

Developed and maintained by the
National Science Teachers Association

For a variety of links related to this chapter, go to www.scilinks.org

Topic: Severe Weather
SciLinks code: HSM1383

Answers to Section Review

1. lightning
2. tornado
3. b
4. A tornado develops when wind traveling in two different directions causes the air in the middle to rotate. The rotating column of air is turned upright by updrafts that begin spinning with it. The rotating air works its way down to the bottom of the cloud and forms a funnel cloud. When the funnel cloud touches the ground, it is called a *tornado*.
5. Most hurricanes form between 5° and 20° latitude in both hemispheres.
6. Lightning is a large electric discharge that occurs between two oppositely charged surfaces. When lightning strikes, the air expands rapidly, causing thunder.
7. Answers may vary.
8. When a hurricane moves over land, it begins to lose energy because there is less warm, moist air over land.
9. Point C is the eye of the hurricane, which is an area of warm, relatively calm air with low pressure and light winds.
10. Point B is the eye wall. It is composed of a group of cumulonimbus clouds that produce very strong winds.
11. Point A is in the rain band. In the rain band, winds can be strong and rain can be heavy.

CHAPTER RESOURCES

Chapter Resource File

- Section Quiz **GENERAL**
- Section Review **GENERAL**
- Vocabulary and Section Summary **GENERAL**
- Reinforcement Worksheet **BASIC**
- SciLinks Activity **GENERAL**

Focus

Overview

This section introduces instruments used to forecast and report the weather, such as thermometers, barometers, weather balloons, and radar. Students will also learn how meteorologists use weather maps to depict the data they gather.

 Bellringer

Pose this question to students: "If you did not have the benefit of the weather forecast on the news, radio, or television, how would you forecast the weather?" (Answers will vary. Possible answers include observing the sky and noticing the direction and intensity of the winds.)

Motivate

Demonstration — GENERAL

Air Pressure and Barometers
Low pressure usually indicates stormy weather, and high pressure usually indicates clear weather. If possible, show students a barometer, and tell them that barometers are still widely used in weather forecasting. Show students how to read a barometer and how to use the movable pointer to track if air pressure is increasing or decreasing.

English Language Learners

LS Visual

READING WARM-UP

Objectives

● Describe the different types of instruments used to take weather measurements.

● Explain how radar and weather satellites help meteorologists forecast the weather.

● Explain how to interpret a weather map.

Terms to Learn

thermometer
barometer
anemometer

READING STRATEGY

Reading Organizer As you read this section, make a table comparing the different instruments used to collect weather data.

Figure 1 *Weather balloons carry radio transmitters that send measurements to stations on the ground.*

CHAPTER RESOURCES

Chapter Resource File

• Lesson Plan
• Directed Reading A **BASIC**
• Directed Reading B **SPECIAL NEEDS**

Technology

Transparencies
• Bellringer

Forecasting the Weather

You watch the weather forecast on the evening news. The news is good—there's no rain in sight. But how can the weather forecasters tell that it won't rain?

Weather affects how you dress and how you plan your day, so it is important to get accurate weather forecasts. But where do weather reporters get their information? And how do they predict the weather? A *weather forecast* is a prediction of weather conditions over the next 3 to 5 days. A *meteorologist* is a person who observes and collects data on atmospheric conditions to make weather predictions. In this section, you will learn how weather data are collected and shown.

Weather-Forecasting Technology

To accurately forecast the weather, meteorologists need to measure various atmospheric conditions, such as air pressure, humidity, precipitation, temperature, wind speed, and wind direction. Meteorologists use special instruments to collect data on weather conditions both near and far above Earth's surface.

High in the Sky

Weather balloons carry electronic equipment that can measure weather conditions as high as 30 km above Earth's surface. Weather balloons, such as the one in **Figure 1,** carry equipment that measures temperature, air pressure, and relative humidity. By tracking the balloons, meteorologists can also measure wind speed and direction.

✓ Reading Check How do meteorologists gather data on atmospheric conditions above Earth's surface? (*See the Appendix for answers to Reading Check.*)

Answer to Reading Check

Meteorologists use weather balloons to collect atmospheric data above Earth's surface.

Windsock

Figure 2 Meteorologists use these tools to collect atmospheric data.

Thermometer

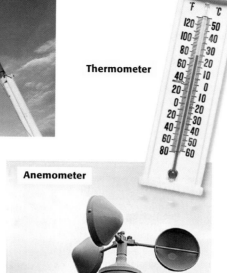

Anemometer

Measuring Air Temperature and Pressure

A tool used to measure air temperature is called a **thermometer.** Most thermometers use a liquid sealed in a narrow glass tube, as shown in **Figure 2.** When air temperature increases, the liquid expands and moves up the glass tube. As air temperature decreases, the liquid shrinks and moves down the tube.

A **barometer** is an instrument used to measure air pressure. A mercurial barometer consists of a glass tube that is sealed at one end and placed in a container full of mercury. As the air pressure pushes on the mercury inside the container, the mercury moves up the glass tube. The greater the air pressure is, the higher the mercury will rise.

Measuring Wind Direction

Wind direction can be measured by using a windsock or a wind vane. A windsock, shown in **Figure 2,** is a cone-shaped cloth bag open at both ends. The wind enters through the wide end and leaves through the narrow end. Therefore, the wide end points into the wind. A wind vane is shaped like an arrow with a large tail and is attached to a pole. As the wind pushes the tail of the wind vane, the wind vane spins on the pole until the arrow points into the wind.

Measuring Wind Speed

An instrument used to measure wind speed is called an **anemometer.** An anemometer, as shown in **Figure 2,** consists of three or four cups connected by spokes to a pole. The wind pushes on the hollow sides of the cups and causes the cups to rotate on the pole. The motion sends a weak electric current that is measured and displayed on a dial.

thermometer an instrument that measures and indicates temperature

barometer an instrument that measures atmospheric pressure

anemometer an instrument used to measure wind speed

CONNECTION to
Life Science ——— GENERAL

Feeling the Pressure Although airplane cabins are pressurized, passengers still feel the pressure change as the plane climbs and descends. Middle ear barotrauma is an earache caused by a difference in pressure between the air and a person's middle ear. The eustachian tube, a passageway between the middle ear and the throat, fails to open wide enough to equalize the pressure. Chewing gum, yawning, or swallowing often alleviates the condition.

MISCONCEPTION
///ALERT

High Noon and Midnight Students may think that the lowest and highest temperatures occur in the middle of the night and in the middle of the day. Actually, the lowest temperatures usually occur around sunrise because the Earth's surface has radiated thermal energy all night. The highest temperatures usually occur in the late afternoon.

Teach

CONNECTION ACTIVITY
Real World ——— GENERAL

Weather Watchers Before sophisticated weather forecasts, people learned to carefully observe the world around them for evidence of changing weather. These clues can be found everywhere. Have groups of students research and test these and other observations.

- Birds fly higher when fair weather is coming. (They fly high to avoid the increased air resistance of a high pressure air mass.)
- Heavy dew condenses early in fair night air. If there is little or no dew, the chance for rain is good.
- Halos form around the sun or moon as light shines through ice particles in the clouds of an advancing rainstorm.
- As a pre-rain low pressure front moves in, odors trapped in objects by high pressure air masses are suddenly released.
- Ants travel in lines when rain is coming and scatter when the weather is clear.
- Robins sing high in fair weather and sing low if rain is approaching.
- Flying insects swarm before a rain; they bite the most when the air is moist.
- Clouds lower as a low pressure system approaches. This signals that a storm is coming.
- Swallows and bats fly lowest when air pressure decreases before a storm. Their sensitive ears are more comfortable when these animals are flying close to the ground (where air pressure is highest).

LS Intrapersonal Co-op Learning

Figure 3 *Using Doppler radar, meteorologists can predict a tornado up to 20 minutes before it touches the ground.*

Radar and Satellites

Radar is used to find the location, movement, and amount of precipitation. It can also detect what form of precipitation a weather system is carrying. You might have seen a kind of radar called *Doppler radar* used in a local TV weather report. **Figure 3** shows how Doppler radar is used to track precipitation. *Weather satellites* that orbit Earth provide the images of weather systems that you see on TV weather reports. Satellites can track storms and measure wind speeds, humidity, and temperatures at different altitudes.

Weather Maps

In the United States, the National Weather Service (NWS) and the National Oceanic and Atmospheric Administration (NOAA) collect and analyze weather data. The NWS produces weather maps based on information gathered from about 1,000 weather stations across the United States. On these maps, each station is represented by a station model. A *station model* is a small circle that shows the location of the weather station. As shown in **Figure 4,** surrounding the small circle is a set of symbols and numbers, which represent the weather data.

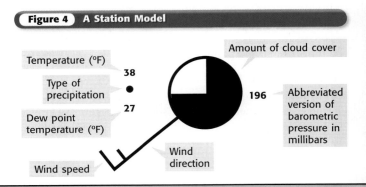

Figure 4 A Station Model

Temperature (°F) — 38
Type of precipitation
Dew point temperature (°F) — 27
Wind speed
Wind direction
Amount of cloud cover
196 — Abbreviated version of barometric pressure in millibars

Reading a Weather Map

Weather maps that you see on TV include lines called *isobars*. Isobars are lines that connect points of equal air pressure. Isobars that form closed circles represent areas of high or low pressure. These areas are usually marked on a map with a capital *H* or *L*. Fronts are also labeled on weather maps, as you can see on the weather map in **Figure 5**.

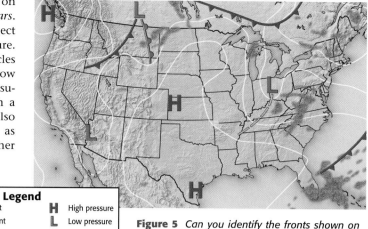

Legend

Cold front		**H**	High pressure
Warm front		**L**	Low pressure
Low pressure trough			Rain
Isobar			Fog

Figure 5 *Can you identify the fronts shown on the weather map?*

SECTION Review

Summary

- Meteorologists use several instruments, such as weather balloons, thermometers, barometers, anemometers, windsocks, weather vanes, radar, and weather satellites, to forecast the weather.
- Station models show the weather conditions at various points across the United States.
- Weather maps show areas of high and low pressure as well as the location of fronts.

Using Key Terms

1. In your own words, write a definition for each of the following terms: *thermometer, barometer,* and *anemometer.*

Understanding Key Ideas

2. Which of the following instruments measures air pressure?
   a. thermometer
   b. barometer
   c. anemometer
   d. windsock

3. How does radar help meteorologists forecast the weather?

4. What does a station model represent?

Math Skills

5. If it is 75°F outside, what is the temperature in degrees Celsius? (Hint: °F = (°C × 9/5) + 32)

Critical Thinking

6. **Applying Concepts** Why would a meteorologist compare a new weather map with one that is 24 h old?

7. **Making Inferences** In the United States, why is weather data gathered from a large number of station models?

8. **Making Inferences** How might several station models from different regions plotted on a map help a meteorologist?

SCILINKS.

NSTA
Developed and maintained by the National Science Teachers Association

For a variety of links related to this chapter, go to www.scilinks.org

Topic: Forecasting the Weather
SciLinks code: HSM0606

CHAPTER RESOURCES

Chapter Resource File

- Section Quiz `GENERAL`
- Section Review `GENERAL`
- Vocabulary and Section Summary `GENERAL`
- Critical Thinking `ADVANCED`

Workbooks

- Math Skills for Science
  - Using Temperature Scales `GENERAL`

Boiling Over!

Teacher's Notes

Time Required
One 45-minute class period

Lab Ratings

EASY ——————————— HARD

Teacher Prep 🧪
Student Set-Up 🧪🧪🧪
Concept Level 🧪🧪
Clean Up 🧪🧪

MATERIALS
The materials listed on the student page are enough for a group of 3–4 students.

Safety Caution
Remind students to review all safety cautions and icons before beginning this lab activity.

Preparation Notes
Begin the activity by leading a discussion of how thermometers work. Have students observe a regular thermometer. Ask students what parts make a thermometer work. (the bulb, a tube, and air in the tube)

Using Scientific Methods
Inquiry Lab

Boiling Over!

Safety Industries, Inc., would like to produce and sell thermometers that are safer than mercury thermometers. The company would like your team of inventors to design a thermometer that uses water instead of mercury. The company will offer a contract to the team that creates the best design of a water thermometer. Good luck!

OBJECTIVES

Construct a device that uses water to measure temperature.

Calibrate the new device by using a mercury thermometer.

MATERIALS

- bottle, plastic
- can, aluminum soda
- card, index, 3 in. × 5 in.
- clay, modeling (1 lb)
- container, yogurt, with lid
- cup, plastic-foam, large (2)
- film canister
- food coloring, red (1 bottle)
- funnel, plastic or paper cone
- gloves, heat-resistant
- hot plate
- ice, cube (5 or 6)
- pan, aluminum pie
- pitcher
- plastic tubing, 5 mm diameter, 30 cm long
- ruler, metric
- straw, plastic, inflexible, clear (1)
- tape, transparent (1 roll)
- thermometer, Celsius
- water, tap

SAFETY

Ask a Question

1 What causes the liquid in a thermometer to rise? How can I use this information to make a thermometer?

Form a Hypothesis

2 Brainstorm with a classmate to design a thermometer that uses only water to measure temperature. Sketch your design. Write a one-sentence hypothesis that describes how your thermometer will work.

Test the Hypothesis

3 Following your design, build a thermometer by using only materials from the materials list. Like a mercury thermometer, your thermometer needs a bulb and a tube. However, the liquid in your thermometer will be water.

4 To test your design, place the aluminum pie pan on a hot plate. Use the pitcher to carefully pour water into the pan until the pan is half full. Turn on the hot plate, and heat the water.

5 Put on your safety goggles and heat-resistant gloves, and carefully place the "bulb" of your thermometer in the hot water. Observe the water level in the tube. Does the water level rise?

6 If the water level does not rise, change your design as necessary and repeat steps 3–5. When the water level in your thermometer does rise, sketch the design of this thermometer as your final design.

7 After you decide on your final design, you must calibrate your thermometer by using a laboratory thermometer. Tape an index card to your thermometer's tube so that the part of the tube that sticks out from the "bulb" of your thermometer touches the card.

Daniel Bugenhagen
Yutan Jr.–Sr. High
Yutan, Nebraska

CHAPTER RESOURCES

Chapter Resource File

- Datasheet for Chapter Lab
- Lab Notes and Answers

Technology

📀 **Classroom Videos**
  - Lab Video

LabBook

- Watching the Weather
- Let It Snow!
- Gone with the Wind

8. Place the plastic funnel or the cone-shaped paper funnel into a plastic-foam cup. Carefully pour hot water from the pie pan into the funnel. Be sure that no water splashes or spills.

9. Place your thermometer and a laboratory thermometer in the hot water. As your thermometer's water level rises, mark the level on the index card. At the same time, observe and record the temperature of the laboratory thermometer, and write this value beside your mark on the card.

10. Repeat steps 8–9 using warm tap water.

11. Repeat steps 8–9 using ice water.

12. Draw evenly spaced scale markings between your temperature markings on the index card. Write the temperatures that correspond to the scale marks on the index card.

Analyze the Results

1 Analyzing Results How well does your thermometer measure temperature?

Draw Conclusions

2 Drawing Conclusions Compare your thermometer design with other students' designs. How would you change your design to make your thermometer measure temperature better?

3 Applying Conclusions Take a class vote to see which design should be used by Safety Industries. Why was this thermometer design chosen? How did it differ from other designs in the class?

Lab Notes

A water thermometer has a receptacle containing water and air and a tube protruding from the receptacle. A trick to getting the water thermometer to work well is to allow a lot of air in the "bulb" because air expands more than water. As the air heats, it expands and pushes the water upward in the tube. One way to build such a thermometer is to put a straw in a soda can and seal the opening of the can with modeling clay so that water can escape only by moving upward, out of the straw. It is important that students' thermometers are tightly sealed. A sample design is shown below.

Analyze the Results

1. Answers may vary. Accept all reasonable responses.

Draw Conclusions

2. Answers may vary. Accept all reasonable responses.

3. Accept all reasonable responses.

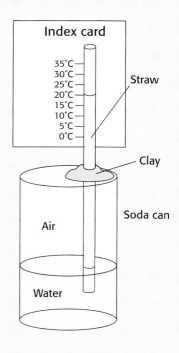

Chapter Review

Assignment Guide

SECTION	QUESTIONS
1	1, 2, 7–12, 17, 21, 29–32
2	3, 4, 13–14, 18, 19
3	5, 15, 20, 22–28
4	6, 16
2 and 3	24
2 and 4	33, 34

ANSWERS

Using Key Terms

1. Relative humidity is the amount of water vapor the air contains relative to the maximum amount it can hold at a given temperature. Dew point is the temperature to which air must cool to be saturated.

2. Condensation is the change of state from a gas to a liquid. Precipitation is water that falls from the atmosphere to the Earth.

3. An air mass is a large body of air that has the same moisture and temperature throughout. A front is the boundary between two different air masses.

4. Lightning is a large electric discharge that occurs between two oppositely charged surfaces. Thunder is the sound that results from the rapid expansion of air along a lightning strike.

USING KEY TERMS

For each pair of terms, explain how the meanings of the terms differ.

1. *relative humidity* and *dew point*

2. *condensation* and *precipitation*

3. *air mass* and *front*

4. *lightning* and *thunder*

5. *tornado* and *hurricane*

6. *barometer* and *anemometer*

UNDERSTANDING KEY IDEAS

Multiple Choice

7. The process in which water changes from a liquid to gas is called
   a. precipitation.
   b. condensation.
   c. evaporation.
   d. water vapor.

8. What is the relative humidity of air at its dew point?
   a. 0%   c. 75%
   b. 50%   d. 100%

9. Which of the following is NOT a type of condensation?
   a. fog   c. snow
   b. cloud   d. dew

10. High clouds made of ice crystals are called ___ clouds.
    a. stratus   c. nimbostratus
    b. cumulus   d. cirrus

11. Large thunderhead clouds that produce precipitation are called ___ clouds.
    a. nimbostratus   c. cumulus
    b. cumulonimbus   d. stratus

12. Strong updrafts within a thunderhead can produce
    a. snow.   c. sleet.
    b. rain.   d. hail.

13. A maritime tropical air mass contains
    a. warm, wet air.   c. warm, dry air.
    b. cold, moist air. d. cold, dry air.

14. A front that forms when a warm air mass is trapped between cold air masses and is forced to rise is a(n)
    a. stationary front. c. occluded front.
    b. warm front.   d. cold front.

15. A severe storm that forms as a rapidly rotating funnel cloud is called a
    a. hurricane.   c. typhoon.
    b. tornado.   d. thunderstorm.

16. The lines connecting points of equal air pressure on a weather map are called
    a. contour lines.   c. isobars.
    b. highs.   d. lows.

Short Answer

17. Explain the relationship between condensation and dew point.

5. A tornado is a small, rotating column of air with high wind speed that touches the ground. A hurricane is a large, rotating tropical weather system with wind speeds equal to or greater than 119 km/h.

6. A barometer is an instrument used to measure air pressure. An anemometer is an instrument used to measure wind speed.

Understanding Key Ideas

7. c   12. d
8. d   13. a
9. c   14. c
10. d   15. b
11. b   16. c

17. Air must cool to a temperature below its dew point before condensation can occur.

18. Stationary fronts generally bring many days of cloudy, wet weather.

19. An air mass that forms over the Gulf of Mexico is warm and wet.

18 Describe the conditions along a stationary front.

19 What are the characteristics of an air mass that forms over the Gulf of Mexico?

20 Explain how a hurricane develops.

21 Describe the water cycle, and explain how it affects weather.

22 List the major similarities and differences between hurricanes and tornadoes.

23 Explain how a tornado forms.

24 Describe an interaction between weather and ocean systems.

25 What is a station model? What types of information do station models provide?

26 What type of technology is used to locate and measure the amount of precipitation in an area?

27 List two ways to keep yourself informed during severe weather.

28 Explain why staying away from flood-water is important even when the water is shallow.

CRITICAL THINKING

29 **Concept Mapping** Use the following terms to create a concept map: *evaporation, relative humidity, water vapor, dew, psychrometer, clouds,* and *fog*.

30 **Making Inferences** If both the air temperature and the amount of water vapor in the air change, is it possible for the relative humidity to stay the same? Explain.

31 **Applying Concepts** What can you assume about the amount of water vapor in the air if there is no difference between the wet- and dry-bulb readings of a psychrometer?

32 **Identifying Relationships** Explain why the concept of relative humidity is important to understanding weather.

INTERPRETING GRAPHICS

Use the weather map below to answer the questions that follow.

33 Where are thunderstorms most likely to occur? Explain your answer.

34 What are the weather conditions in Tulsa, Oklahoma? Explain your answer.

---

20. A hurricane begins as a group of thunderstorms moving over tropical ocean waters. Winds traveling in two different directions collide, which causes the storm to rotate over an area of low pressure. The hurricane is fueled by the condensation of water vapor.

21. The water cycle is the continuous movement of water from the Earth's surface, to the air, and back to the surface. Weather is affected by evaporation, condensation, and precipitation of water in the air.

CHAPTER RESOURCES

Chapter Resource File

- **Chapter Review** GENERAL
- **Chapter Test A** GENERAL
- **Chapter Test B** ADVANCED
- **Chapter Test C** SPECIAL NEEDS
- **Vocabulary Activity** GENERAL

Workbooks

Study Guide
- Assessment resources are also available in Spanish.

---

22. Sample answer: Both begin as a result of thunderstorms and are centered around low pressure. Hurricanes occur over water, and tornadoes generally occur over land.

23. Cold, dry air meets warm, moist air and starts to spin. Updrafts of air turn the spinning column vertical. The column moves to the bottom of the cloud and becomes a funnel cloud. A funnel cloud becomes a tornado when it touches the ground.

24. Sample answer: Evaporating ocean water fuels hurricanes in tropical regions.

25. Sample answer: A station model represents the location of a weather station and shows temperature, precipitation, wind direction, and other data.

26. Radar is used to find the location, movement, and amount of precipitation.

27. Sample answer: Turn the TV and radio to local stations for weather information.

28. Sample answer: Even shallow water can be dangerous if it is moving quickly.

Critical Thinking

29. An answer to this exercise can be found at the end of this book.

30. Sample answer: If air temperature rises, then the air can hold more water. If vapor content in the air also increases, then relative humidity could stay the same.

31. Sample answer: It can be assumed that the relative humidity is 100% because no water evaporated.

32. Sample answer: Precipitation can occur only when the air is saturated, which is when the relative humidity is 100%.

Interpreting Graphics

33. Thunderstorms are most likely to occur in Chicago because a cold front is approaching.

34. Tulsa is experiencing a stationary front and is probably receiving drizzly precipitation.

Standardized Test Preparation

Teacher's Note

To provide practice under more realistic testing conditions, give students 20 minutes to answer all of the questions in this Standardized Test Preparation.

MISCONCEPTION ALERT

Answers to the standardized test preparation can help you identify student misconceptions and misunderstandings.

READING

Passage 1

1. B
2. H
3. D

TEST DOCTOR

Question 3: Students may think that all the answer choices could be correct. It is true that violent tornadoes can destroy paved roads, damage crops, and damage homes. However, the question asks for a characteristic of violent storms. Answers A, B, and C list things a tornado can do, which are actions, not characteristics. The only answer that describes a characteristic of violent tornadoes is answer D.

READING

Read each of the passages below. Then, answer the questions that follow each passage.

Passage 1 In May 1997, a springtime tornado <u>wreaked</u> havoc on Jarrell, Texas. The Jarrell tornado was a powerful tornado, whose wind speeds were estimated at more than 410 km/h. The winds of the twister were so strong that they peeled the asphalt from paved roads, stripped fields of corn bare, and destroyed an entire neighborhood. Some tornadoes, such as the one that struck the town of Jarrell, are classified as violent tornadoes. Only 2% of the tornadoes that occur in the United States are categorized as violent tornadoes. Despite the fact that these types of tornadoes do not occur often, 70% of all tornado-related deaths are a result of violent tornadoes.

1. In the passage, what does the word *wreaked* mean?
   - **A** smelled
   - **B** caused
   - **C** prevented
   - **D** removed

2. Which of the following can be concluded from the passage?
   - **F** Tornadoes often hit Jarrell, Texas.
   - **G** Most tornadoes fall into the violent category.
   - **H** The tornado that hit Jarrell was a rare type of tornado.
   - **I** Tornadoes always happen during the spring.

3. Which of the following **best** describes a characteristic of violent tornadoes?
   - **A** Violent tornadoes destroy paved roads.
   - **B** Violent tornadoes damage crops.
   - **C** Violent tornadoes damage homes.
   - **D** Violent tornadoes have extremely strong winds.

Passage 2 Water evaporates into the air from Earth's surface. This water returns to Earth's surface as <u>precipitation</u>. Precipitation is water, in solid or liquid form, that falls from the air to Earth. The four major types of precipitation are rain, snow, sleet, and hail. The most common form of precipitation is rain.

A cloud produces rain when the cloud's water drops become large enough to fall. A raindrop begins as a water droplet that is smaller than the period at the end of this sentence. Before a water drop falls as rain, it must become about 100 times this beginning size. Water drops get larger by joining with other water drops. When the water drops become too heavy, they fall as precipitation.

1. In this passage, what does *precipitation* mean?
   - **A** acceleration
   - **B** haste
   - **C** water that falls from the atmosphere to Earth
   - **D** separating a substance from a solution as a solid

2. What is the main idea of the second paragraph?
   - **F** Rain occurs when the water droplets in clouds become large enough to fall.
   - **G** Raindrops are very small at first.
   - **H** Water droplets join with other water droplets to become larger.
   - **I** Rain is a form of precipitation.

3. According to the passage, which step happens last in the formation of precipitation?
   - **A** Water droplets join.
   - **B** Water droplets fall to the ground.
   - **C** Water droplets become heavy.
   - **D** Water evaporates into the air.

Passage 2

1. C
2. F
3. B

TEST DOCTOR

Question 1: Both answers C and D are correct definitions for the word "precipitation." However, in this paragraph precipitation is defined as water returning to Earth's surface, so only answer C is correct.

Use each diagram below to answer the question that follows each diagram.

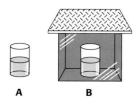

A   **B**

1. During an experiment, the setup shown in the diagram above is maintained for 72 h. Which of the following is the most likely outcome?

   A Beaker A will hold less water than beaker B will.

   B The amount of water in beaker A and beaker B will stay the same.

   C The amount of water in beaker A and beaker B will change by about the same amount.

   D Beaker B will hold less water than beaker A will.

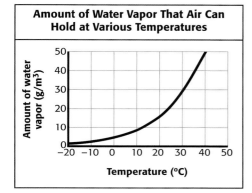

Amount of Water Vapor That Air Can Hold at Various Temperatures

2. Look at the line graph above. Which statement is consistent with the line graph?

   F The ability of air to hold moisture increases as temperature increases.

   G The ability of air to hold moisture decreases as temperature increases.

   H The ability of air to hold moisture decreases and then increases as temperature increases.

   I The ability of air to hold moisture stays the same regardless of temperature.

Read each question below, and choose the best answer.

1. The speed of light is 3.00×10^8 m/s. What is another way to express this measure?

   A 3,000,000,000 m/s

   B 300,000,000 m/s

   C 3,000,000 m/s

   D 300,000 m/s

2. A hurricane is moving 122 km/h. How long will it take to hit the coast, which is 549 km away?

   F 4.2 h

   G 4.5 h

   H 4.8 h

   I 5.2 h

3. A front is moving 15 km/h in an easterly direction. At that rate, how far will the front travel in 12 h?

   A 0.8 km

   B 1.25 km

   C 27 km

   D 180 km

4. On average, 2 out of every 100 tornadoes are classified as violent tornadoes. If there are 400 tornadoes in 1 year, which is the best prediction of the number of tornadoes that will be classified as violent tornadoes during that year?

   F 2

   G 4

   H 8

   I 16

5. The air temperature in the morning was 27°C. During the day, a front moved into the region and caused the temperature to drop to 18°C. By how many degrees did the temperature drop?

   A 1°C

   B 9°C

   C 11°C

   D 19°C

Standardized Test Preparation

1. A
2. F

✚ TEST DOCTOR

Question 2: Some students may have difficulty interpreting graphs. To help students understand trends in graphs, have them choose two places on the curved line in the graph. It is best if students choose points that are easy to evaluate, such as points where grid lines cross. On this graph, students could choose the points where $x = 10$, $y = 10$ and $x = 30$, $y = 30$. Then, ask students to notice that when one number increased, the other also increased.

1. B
2. G
3. D
4. H
5. B

✚ TEST DOCTOR

Question 4: This question asks students to evaluate a ratio. Students may have difficulty deciding which numbers should go together when comparing the ratio. Tell students to look for the words *out of* as a clue about which numbers are part of the same fraction in a ratio. In this case, "2 out of every 100 tornadoes" would indicate a fraction of 2/100. Then, the question can be interpreted as "How many tornadoes out of 400 are violent?" This interpretation produces a fraction of $x/400$.

CHAPTER RESOURCES

Chapter Resource File

 • Standardized Test Preparation **GENERAL**

Workbooks

 North Carolina Standardized Test Preparation
• Provides practice for the EOG test.

State Resources

 For specific resources for your state, visit **go.hrw.com** and type in the keyword **HSMSTR**.

Science Fiction

Background

Ray Bradbury is one of the world's most celebrated writers. He was born in the small town of Waukegan, Illinois, in 1920. He and his family moved several times and eventually ended up in Los Angeles. There he began a writing career that has spanned more than 60 years!

Bradbury has earned top honors in the field of literature, including the World Fantasy Award for lifetime work and the Grand Master Award from Science Fiction Writers of America. An unusual honor came when an astronaut named a crater on the moon Dandelion Crater after Ray Bradbury's novel *Dandelion Wine*.

Weird Science

CONNECTION ACTIVITY
History —————— BASIC

Have students research a list of traditional weather signs. Once a class list is compiled, begin keeping a weather log. Students should record observations, make a prediction, and then check their predictions the following day.

Science in Action

Science Fiction

"All Summer in a Day" by Ray Bradbury

It is raining, just as it has been for seven long years. For the people who live on Venus, constant rain is a fact of life. But today is a special day—a day when the rain stops and the sun shines. This day comes once every seven years. At school, the students have been looking forward to this day for weeks. But Margot longs to see the sun even more than the others do. The reason for her longing makes the other kids jealous, and jealous kids can be cruel. What happens to Margot? Find out by reading Ray Bradbury's "All Summer in a Day" in the *Holt Anthology of Science Fiction*.

Language Arts ACTIVITY

WRITING SKILL What would living in a place where it rained all day and every day for seven years be like? Write a short story describing what your life would be like if you lived in such a place. In your story, describe what you and your friends would do for fun after school.

Weird Science

Can Animals Forecast the Weather?

Before ways of making sophisticated weather forecasts were developed, people observed animals and insects for evidence of changing weather. By observing the behavior of certain animals and insects, you, too, can detect changing weather! For example, did you know that birds fly higher when fair weather is coming? And a robin's song is high pitched in fair weather and low pitched as rain approaches. Ants travel in lines when rain is coming and scatter when the weather is clear. You can tell how hot the weather is by listening for the chirping of crickets—crickets chirp faster as the temperature rises!

Math ACTIVITY

To estimate the outdoor temperature in degrees Fahrenheit, count the number of times that a cricket chirps in 15 s and add 37. If you count 40 chirps in 15 s, what is the estimated temperature?

Answer to Language Arts Activity
Answers may vary. Accept any reasonable answer.

Answer to Math Activity
40 chirps + 37 = 77°F

Careers

Cristy Mitchell

Meteorologist Predicting floods, observing a tornado develop inside a storm, watching the growth of a hurricane, and issuing flood warnings are all in a day's work for Cristy Mitchell. As a meteorologist for the National Weather Service, Mitchell spends each working day observing the powerful forces of nature. When asked what made her job interesting, Mitchell replied, "There's nothing like the adrenaline rush you get when you see a tornado coming!"

Perhaps the most familiar field of meteorology is weather forecasting. However, meteorology is also used in air-pollution control, weather control, agricultural planning, and even criminal and civil investigations. Meteorologists also study trends in Earth's climate.

Meteorologists such as Mitchell use high-tech tools—computers and satellites—to collect data. By analyzing such data, Mitchell is able to forecast the weather.

Social Studies ACTIVITY

An almanac is a type of calendar that contains various information, including weather forecasts and astronomical data, for every day of the year. Many people used almanacs before meteorologists started to forecast the weather on TV. Use an almanac from the library to find out what the weather was on the day that you were born.

go.hrw.com
To learn more about these Science in Action topics, visit go.hrw.com and type in the keyword **HZ5WEAF**.

Current Science
Check out Current Science® articles related to this chapter by visiting go.hrw.com. Just type in the keyword **HZ5CS16**.

Answer to Social Studies Activity
Answers may vary. Accept any well-supported answer.

Climate
Chapter Planning Guide

Compression guide:
To shorten instruction because of time limitations, omit Section 2.

OBJECTIVES	LABS, DEMONSTRATIONS, AND ACTIVITIES	TECHNOLOGY RESOURCES
PACING • 90 min pp. 110–119 **Chapter Opener**	SE **Start-up Activity**, p. 111 GENERAL	OSP **Parent Letter** GENERAL CD **Student Edition on CD-ROM** CD **Guided Reading Audio CD** TR **Chapter Starter Transparency*** VID **Brain Food Video Quiz**
Section 1 What is Climate? • Explain the difference between weather and climate. • Identify five factors that determine climates. • Identify the three climate zones of the world.	TE **Connection Activity** Math, p. 113 GENERAL TE **Activity** Modeling the Earth and Sun, p. 114 ◆ BASIC SE **Quick Lab** A Cool Breeze, p. 115 GENERAL CRF **Datasheet for Quick Lab*** TE **Connection Activity** Geography, p. 115 ADVANCED SE **School-to-Home Activity** Using a Map, p. 116 GENERAL SE **Skills Practice Lab** Biome Business, p. 136 GENERAL CRF **Datasheet for Chapter Lab*** SE **Skills Practice Lab** For the Birds, p. 591 GENERAL CRF **Datasheet for LabBook*** LB **Whiz-Bang Demonstrations** How Humid Is It?* GENERAL	CRF **Lesson Plans*** TR **Bellringer Transparency*** TR **The Seasons*** TR **The Circulation of Warm and Cold Air*** TR **The Earth's Land Biomes*** VID **Lab Videos for Earth Science**
PACING • 45 min pp. 120–123 **Section 2 The Tropics** • Locate and describe the tropical zone. • Describe the biomes found in the tropical zone.	TE **Activity** Country Profile, p. 120 GENERAL TE **Connection Activity** Life Science, p. 121 GENERAL SE **Science in Action** Math, Social Studies, and Language Arts Activities, pp. 142–143 GENERAL	CRF **Lesson Plans*** TR **Bellringer Transparency*** TR **LINK TO LIFE SCIENCE** Gas Exchange in Leaves* CRF **SciLinks Activity*** GENERAL
PACING • 45 min pp. 124–129 **Section 3 Temperate and Polar Zones** • Locate and describe the temperate zone and the polar zone. • Describe the different biomes found in the temperate zone and the polar zone. • Explain what a microclimate is.	TE **Activity** Camp Climate, p. 124 GENERAL TE **Demonstration** Mock Permafrost, p. 127 ◆ GENERAL SE **School-to-Home Activity** Your Biome, p. 128 GENERAL LB **Calculator-Based Labs** What Causes the Seasons?* ◆ ADVANCED SE **Connection to Physics** Hot Roofs!, p. 129 ◆ GENERAL	CRF **Lesson Plans*** TR **Bellringer Transparency***
PACING • 45 min pp. 130–135 **Section 4 Changes in Climate** • Describe how the Earth's climate has changed over time. • Summarize four different theories that attempt to explain why the Earth's climate has changed. • Explain the greenhouse effect and its role in global warming.	TE **Demonstration** The Greenhouse Effect, p. 130 ◆ GENERAL TE **Activity** Ancient Climates, p. 131 ADVANCED TE **Activity** Volcanic Eruptions, p. 132 GENERAL TE **Connection Activity** Real World, p. 133 ADVANCED SE **School-to-Home Activity** Reducing Pollution, p. 135 GENERAL LB **Long-Term Projects & Research Ideas** Sun-Starved in Fairbanks* ADVANCED	SE **Internet Activity**, p. 131 GENERAL CRF **Lesson Plans*** TR **Bellringer Transparency*** TR **The Milankovitch Theory***

PACING • 90 min

CHAPTER REVIEW, ASSESSMENT, AND STANDARDIZED TEST PREPARATION

CRF **Vocabulary Activity*** ■ GENERAL
SE **Chapter Review**, pp. 138–139 GENERAL
CRF **Chapter Review*** ■ GENERAL
CRF **Chapter Tests A*** ■ GENERAL, **B*** ADVANCED, **C*** SPECIAL NEEDS
SE **Standardized Test Preparation**, pp. 140–141 GENERAL
CRF **Standardized Test Preparation*** GENERAL
CRF **Performance-Based Assessment*** GENERAL
OSP **Test Generator** GENERAL
CRF **Test Item Listing*** GENERAL

Online and Technology Resources

Visit **go.hrw.com** for a variety of free resources related to this textbook. Enter the keyword **HT5R7CLM**.

 Holt Online Learning

Students can access interactive problem-solving help and active visual concept development with the *Holt Science and Technology* Online Edition available at **www.hrw.com**.

 Guided Reading Audio CD

These CDs are designed to help auditory learners and reluctant readers.

 Science Tutor CD-ROM

Excellent for remediation and test practice.

SKILLS DEVELOPMENT RESOURCES	SECTION REVIEW AND ASSESSMENT	STANDARDS CORRELATIONS
SE Pre-Reading Activity, p. 110 `GENERAL` **OSP Science Puzzlers, Twisters & Teasers** `GENERAL`		North Carolina Standard Course of Study
CRF Directed Reading A* `BASIC`, **B*** `SPECIAL NEEDS` **CRF Vocabulary and Section Summary*** `GENERAL` **SE Reading Strategy** Discussion, p. 112 `GENERAL` **TE Inclusion Strategies**, p. 116 ◆	**SE Reading Checks**, pp. 112, 114, 116, 117, 118 `GENERAL` **TE Homework**, p. 117 **TE Reteaching**, p. 118 `BASIC` **TE Quiz**, p. 118 `GENERAL` **TE Alternative Assessment**, p. 118 `GENERAL` **SE Section Review,*** p. 119 ■ `GENERAL` **CRF Section Quiz*** ■ `GENERAL`	*Chapter Lab:* 1.06, 1.08; *LabBook:* 1.03, 1.06, 1.08, 2.02, 2.03
CRF Directed Reading A* `BASIC`, **B*** `SPECIAL NEEDS` **CRF Vocabulary and Section Summary*** `GENERAL` **SE Reading Strategy** Reading Organizer, p. 120 `GENERAL` **SE Connection to Social Studies** Living in the Tropics, p. 121 `GENERAL` **SE Connection to Biology** Animal and Plant Adaptations, p. 122 `GENERAL` **MS Math Skills for Science** Rain-Forest Math* `GENERAL` **SS Science Skills** Finding Useful Sources* `GENERAL`	**SE Reading Checks**, pp. 120, 123 `GENERAL` **TE Reteaching**, p. 122 `BASIC` **TE Quiz**, p. 122 `GENERAL` **TE Alternative Assessment**, p. 122 `GENERAL` **SE Section Review,*** p. 123 ■ `GENERAL` **CRF Section Quiz*** ■ `GENERAL`	
CRF Directed Reading A* `BASIC`, **B*** `SPECIAL NEEDS` **CRF Vocabulary and Section Summary*** `GENERAL` **SE Reading Strategy** Reading Organizer, p. 124 `GENERAL` **TE Inclusion Strategies**, p. 126 **CRF Reinforcement Worksheet** A Tale of Three Climates* `BASIC`	**SE Reading Checks**, pp. 124, 126, 129 `GENERAL` **TE Homework**, p. 127 `ADVANCED` **TE Reteaching**, p. 128 `BASIC` **TE Quiz**, p. 128 `GENERAL` **TE Alternative Assessment**, p. 128 `GENERAL` **SE Section Review,*** p. 129 ■ `GENERAL` **CRF Section Quiz*** ■ `GENERAL`	
CRF Directed Reading A* `BASIC`, **B*** `SPECIAL NEEDS` **CRF Vocabulary and Section Summary*** `GENERAL` **SE Reading Strategy** Paired Summarizing, p. 130 `GENERAL` **SE Connection to Astronomy** Sunspots, p. 133 `GENERAL` **SE Math Practice** The Ride to School, p. 134 `GENERAL` **CRF Critical Thinking** Cyberspace Heats Up* `ADVANCED` **SS Science Skills** Understanding Bias* `GENERAL`	**SE Reading Checks**, pp. 131, 132, 135 `GENERAL` **TE Reteaching**, p. 134 `BASIC` **TE Quiz**, p. 134 `GENERAL` **TE Alternative Assessment**, p. 134 `GENERAL` **SE Section Review,*** p. 135 ■ `GENERAL` **CRF Section Quiz*** ■ `GENERAL`	

One-Stop Planner® CD-ROM

This convenient CD-ROM includes:
- Lab Materials QuickList Software
- Holt Calendar Planner
- Customizable Lesson Plans
- Printable Worksheets
- ExamView® Test Generator

cnnstudentnews.com

Find the latest news, lesson plans, and activities related to important scientific events.

www.scilinks.org

Maintained by the **National Science Teachers Association**. See Chapter Enrichment pages for a complete list of topics.

Current Science®

Check out **Current Science** articles and activities by visiting the HRW Web site at go.hrw.com. Just type in the keyword **HZ5CS17T**.

Classroom Videos

- **Lab Videos** demonstrate the chapter lab.
- **Brain Food Video Quizzes** help students review the chapter material.
- **CNN Videos** bring science into your students' daily life.

Visual Resources

CHAPTER STARTER TRANSPARENCY

BELLRINGER TRANSPARENCIES

TEACHING TRANSPARENCIES

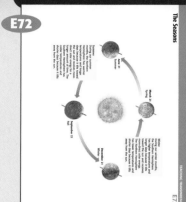
E72

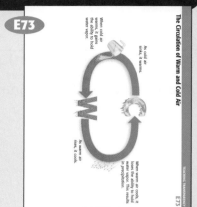
E73

TEACHING TRANSPARENCIES

E74

E75

L47

CONCEPT MAPPING TRANSPARENCY

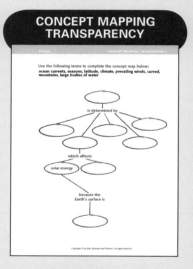

Planning Resources

LESSON PLANS

PARENT LETTER

TEST ITEM LISTING

One-Stop Planner® CD-ROM

This CD-ROM includes all of the resources shown here and the following time-saving tools:

- *Lab Materials QuickList Software*
- *Customizable lesson plans*
- *Holt Calendar Planner*
- *The powerful ExamView® Test Generator*

Meeting Individual Needs

DIRECTED READING A
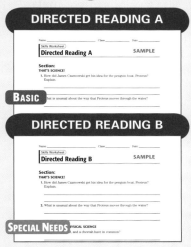

BASIC

DIRECTED READING B

SPECIAL NEEDS

VOCABULARY ACTIVITY
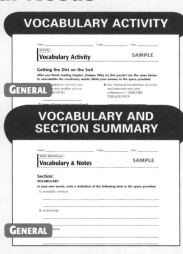

GENERAL

VOCABULARY AND SECTION SUMMARY

GENERAL

REINFORCEMENT

BASIC

CRITICAL THINKING

ADVANCED

SCILINKS ACTIVITY
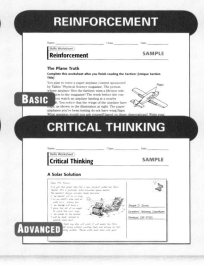

GENERAL

SCIENCE PUZZLERS, TWISTERS & TEASERS

Climate

GENERAL

Labs and Activities

LONG-TERM PROJECTS & RESEARCH IDEAS

Sun-Starved in Fairbanks

ADVANCED

WHIZ-BANG DEMONSTRATIONS
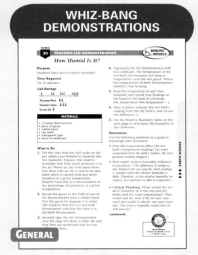

How Humid Is It?

GENERAL

CALCULATOR-BASED LABS
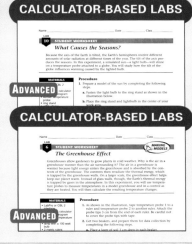

What Causes the Seasons?

ADVANCED

CALCULATOR-BASED LABS

The Greenhouse Effect

ADVANCED

DATASHEETS FOR QUICKLABS

Reaction to Stress

DATASHEETS FOR CHAPTER LABS

Using Scientific Methods

DATASHEETS FOR LABBOOK

Does It All Add Up?

Review and Assessments

SECTION QUIZ

GENERAL — ALSO IN SPANISH

SECTION REVIEW

GENERAL — ALSO IN SPANISH

CHAPTER REVIEW
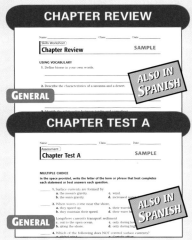

GENERAL — ALSO IN SPANISH

CHAPTER TEST A

GENERAL — ALSO IN SPANISH

CHAPTER TEST B
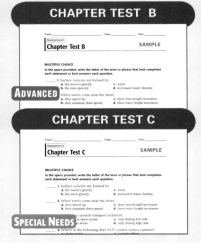

ADVANCED

CHAPTER TEST C

SPECIAL NEEDS

STANDARDIZED TEST PREPARATION
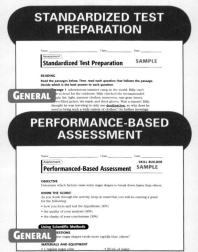

GENERAL

PERFORMANCE-BASED ASSESSMENT

Performance-Based Assessment

GENERAL

This Chapter Enrichment provides relevant and interesting information to expand and enhance your presentation of the chapter material.

Section 1

What Is Climate?
Climatology

- The study of climate can be traced back to Greek scientists of the sixth century BCE. In fact, the word *climate* comes from the Greek word *klíma,* meaning "an inclination" of the sun's rays. Climatology can be divided into three branches—global climatology, regional climatology, and physical climatology. Global climatology investigates the general circulation of wind and water currents around the Earth. Regional climatology studies the characteristic weather patterns and related phenomena of a particular region. Physical climatology analyzes statistics concerning climatic factors such as temperature, moisture, wind, and air pressure.

Global Winds

- Global winds are patterns of air circulation that travel across the Earth. These winds include the trade winds, the prevailing westerlies, and the polar easterlies.

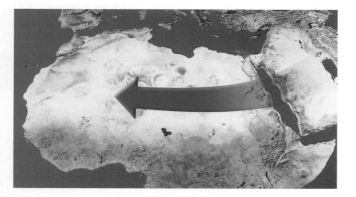

- In both hemispheres, the trade winds blow from 30° latitude to the equator. The Coriolis effect makes the trade winds curve to the right in the Northern Hemisphere, moving northeast to southwest. In the Southern Hemisphere, the trade winds curve to the left and move from southeast to northwest.

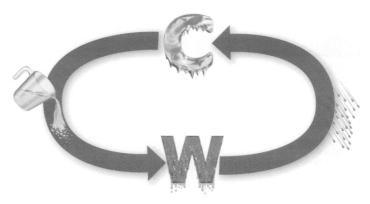

- The prevailing westerlies are found in both the Northern and Southern Hemispheres between 30° and 60° latitude. In the Northern Hemisphere, the westerlies blow from the southwest to the northeast. In the Southern Hemisphere, they blow from the northwest to the southeast.

- The polar easterlies extend from the poles to 60° latitude in both hemispheres. The polar easterlies blow from the northeast to the southwest in the Northern Hemisphere. In the Southern Hemisphere, these winds blow from the southeast to the northwest.

Section 2

The Tropics
Climate Classification

- Because climate is a complicated and somewhat abstract concept, more than 100 classification models have been devised, which vary according to the data on which the classifications are based. For instance, there have been attempts to classify climates according to factors such as soil formation, rock weathering, and even effects on human comfort!

- In 1966, Werner Terjung, an American geographer, developed a physiological climate classification. This system categorized climates according to their effects on people's comfort levels. The system focused on four factors that might affect human comfort—temperature, relative humidity, wind speed, and solar radiation.

Section 3

Temperate and Polar Zones
The Köppen System

- The most widely used climate classification system is the Köppen system. This system, named for Wladimir Köppen, the German botanist and climatologist who developed it, uses vegetation regions and average weather statistics to classify local climates. Each vegetation region is characterized by the natural vegetation that is predominant there. Critics have found fault with the Köppen system because it considers only average monthly temperatures and precipitation, ignoring other factors, such as winds, cloud cover, and daily temperature extremes.

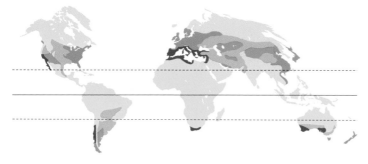

Section 4

Changes in Climate
Pangaea

- In 1620, the British philosopher Francis Bacon noted that Africa and South America looked as if they could fit together like puzzle pieces. But it was not until the early 20th century that the German meteorologist Alfred Wegener proposed a theory that all the continents were once one landmass. Wegener's hypothesis was supported by the existence of similar plant and animal fossils on different continents. Although his theory was initially ridiculed, Wegener was vindicated after World War II when sea-floor spreading and a mechanism for continental drift were discovered.

Pangaea

Is That a Fact!

◆ *Pangaea*, the name Wegener gave to the supercontinent, is Greek for "all Earth."

The Greenhouse Effect

- Gases such as water vapor, carbon dioxide and methane are known as greenhouse gases because they absorb and reradiate thermal energy in Earth's atmosphere. Greenhouse gases are necessary for life on Earth because they keep Earth's average temperature at 15°C. Without them, Earth would be frozen; the average temperature would be about –18°C.

Is That a Fact!

◆ Burning 1 gal of gasoline can produce 9 kg of carbon dioxide.

Developed and maintained by the
National Science Teachers Association

SciLinks is maintained by the National Science Teachers Association to provide you and your students with interesting, up-to-date links that will enrich your classroom presentation of the chapter.

Visit www.scilinks.org and enter the SciLinks code for more information about the topic listed.

Topic: What Is Climate?
SciLinks code: HSM1659

Topic: Modeling Earth's Climate
SciLinks code: HSM0976

Topic: Climates of the World
SciLinks code: HSM0302

Topic: Changes in Climate
SciLinks code: HSM0252

Overview

Tell students that this chapter describes different climates around the world and the factors that influence climate. This chapter also explains how climate can change over time.

Assessing Prior Knowledge

Students should be familiar with the following topics:
- weather patterns
- latitudes of the Earth

Identifying Misconceptions

Students may think that the Earth is farther away from the sun during winter and closer to the sun in the summer. Point out that the seasons are caused by the Earth's tilt, not by the distance between the Earth and the sun. Students may also think that the only factor that influences climate is a location's distance from the equator. Explain that this chapter will introduce many factors that influence climate.

4

Climate

About the PHOTO

Would you like to hang out on this ice with the penguins? You probably would not. You would be shivering, and your teeth would be chattering. However, these penguins feel comfortable. They have thick feathers and lots of body fat to keep them warm. Like other animals, penguins have adapted to their climate, which allows them to live comfortably in that climate. So, you will never see one of these penguins living comfortably on a hot, sunny beach in Florida!

PRE-READING ACTIVITY

FOLDNOTES **Pyramid** Before you read the chapter, create the FoldNote entitled "Pyramid" described in the **Study Skills** section of the Appendix. Label the sides of the pyramid with "Tropical climate," "Temperate climate," and "Polar climate." As you read the chapter, define each climate zone, and write characteristics of each climate zone on the appropriate pyramid side.

Standards Correlations

North Carolina Standard Course of Study

1.03 (partial) Apply safety procedures in the laboratory . . . : Recognize potential hazards, Manipulate materials and equipment, [and] Conduct appropriate procedures. (LabBook)

1.06 (partial) Use mathematics to gather, organize, and present quantitative data resulting from scientific investigations: Measurement, Analysis of data, [and] Graphing. . . . (Chapter Lab and LabBook)

1.08 Use oral and written language to: Communicate findings, [and] Defend conclusions of scientific investigations. (Chapter Lab, LabBook)

2.02 Use information systems to: Identify scientific needs, human needs, or problems that are subject to technological solution, [and] Locate resources to obtain and test ideas. (LabBook)

2.03 (partial) Evaluate technological designs for: Application of scientific principles, Risks and benefits, [and] Constraints of design. . . (LabBook)

FOR EACH GROUP
- adhesive putty
- globe
- lamp
- thermometers (2)

Safety Caution: Remind students to review all safety cautions and icons before beginning this lab activity. Students should not touch the lamp's bulb while it is on or immediately after it has been turned off.

Teacher's Notes: If you have time, encourage students to repeat the experiment, positioning one thermometer at the equator and one at the South Pole. Have students compare their results.

Answers

1. yes; The final temperature at the globe's North Pole was cooler than the final temperature at the globe's equator.

2. The temperature readings at the North Pole and the equator are different because the globe's equator received more direct energy from the lamp than the globe's North Pole received.

START-UP ACTIVITY

What's Your Angle?

Try this activity to see how the angle of the sun's solar rays influences temperatures on Earth.

Procedure

1. Place a **lamp** 30 cm from a **globe.**

2. Point the lamp so that the light shines directly on the globe's equator.

3. Using **adhesive putty,** attach a **thermometer** to the globe's equator in a vertical position. Attach **another thermometer** to the globe's North Pole so that the tip points toward the lamp.

4. Record the temperature reading of each thermometer.

5. Turn on the lamp, and let the light shine on the globe for 3 minutes.

6. After 3 minutes, turn off the lamp and record the temperature reading of each thermometer again.

Analysis

1. Was there a difference between the final temperature at the globe's North Pole and the final temperature at the globe's equator? If so, what was it?

2. Explain why the temperature readings at the North Pole and the equator may be different.

Chapter Starter Transparency
Use this transparency to help students begin thinking about the relationship between elevation and climate.

CHAPTER RESOURCES

Technology

Transparencies
- Chapter Starter Transparency

 READING SKILLS

Student Edition on CD-ROM

Guided Reading Audio CD

Classroom Videos
- Brain Food Video Quiz

Workbooks

Science Puzzlers, Twisters & Teasers
- Climate **GENERAL**

Focus

Overview

In this section, students will learn the difference between weather and climate. They will examine how latitude, prevailing winds, geography, and ocean currents affect an area's climate. Finally, students will learn about the three major climate zones of the world.

 Bellringer

Have students imagine that they have entered a contest for a free trip to a place that has a perfect climate. To win, they must describe their idea of a perfect climate in 25 words or less.

Motivate

Discussion ——— GENERAL

Latitude and Climate Ask students to find locations on a United States or world map where they would like to visit. Write the locations and their latitudinal positions on the board. Review with students that latitude is the distance north or south from the equator, expressed in degrees. Ask students to help you list some observations about the climate in each location. Make sure students notice the relationship between latitude and climate. **LS** Verbal

---

READING WARM-UP

Objectives
- Explain the difference between weather and climate.
- Identify five factors that determine climates.
- Identify the three climate zones of the world.

Terms to Learn

weather   elevation
climate   surface current
latitude   biome
prevailing winds

READING STRATEGY

Discussion Read this section silently. Write down questions that you have about this section. Discuss your questions in a small group.

What Is Climate?

Suppose you receive a call from a friend who is coming to visit you tomorrow. To decide what clothing to bring, he asks about the current weather in your area.

You step outside to see if rain clouds are in the sky and to check the temperature. But what would you do if your friend asked you about the climate in your area? What is the difference between weather and climate?

Climate Vs. Weather

The main difference between weather and climate is the length of time over which both are measured. **Weather** is the condition of the atmosphere at a particular time. Weather conditions vary from day to day and include temperature, humidity, precipitation, wind, and visibility. **Climate,** on the other hand, is the average weather condition in an area over a long period of time. Climate is mostly determined by two factors—temperature and precipitation. Different parts of the world can have different climates, as shown in **Figure 1.** But why are climates so different? The answer is complicated. It includes factors in addition to temperature and precipitation, such as latitude, wind patterns, mountains, large bodies of water, and ocean currents.

✓ **Reading Check** How is climate different from weather? (*See the Appendix for answers to Reading Checks.*)

Figure 1 *How does the climate in northern Africa differ from the climate where you live?*

CHAPTER RESOURCES

Chapter Resource File

- Lesson Plan
- Directed Reading A **BASIC**
- Directed Reading B **SPECIAL NEEDS**

Technology

- **Transparencies**
  - Bellringer

Answer to Reading Check

Climate is the average weather condition in an area over a long period of time. Weather is the condition of the atmosphere at a particular time.

Latitude

Think of the last time you looked at a globe. Do you recall the thin, horizontal lines that circle the globe? Those lines are called lines of latitude. **Latitude** is the distance north or south, measured in degrees, from the equator. In general, the temperature of an area depends on its latitude. The higher the latitude is, the colder the climate tends to be. One of the coldest places on Earth, the North Pole, is 90° north of the equator. However, the equator, at latitude 0°, is usually hot.

As shown in **Figure 2,** if you were to take a trip to different latitudes in the United States, you would experience different climates. For example, the climate in Washington, D.C., which is at a higher latitude, is different from the climate in Texas.

Solar Energy and Latitude

Solar energy, which is energy from the sun, heats the Earth. The amount of direct solar energy a particular area receives is determined by latitude. **Figure 3** shows how the curve of the Earth affects the amount of direct solar energy at different latitudes. Notice that the sun's rays hit the equator directly, at almost a 90° angle. At this angle, a small area of the Earth's surface receives more direct solar energy than at a lesser angle. As a result, that area has high temperatures. However, the sun's rays strike the poles at a lesser angle than they do the equator. At this angle, the same amount of direct solar energy that hits the area at the equator is spread over a larger area at the poles. The result is lower temperatures at the poles.

Figure 2 *Winter in south Texas (top) is different from winter in Washington D.C. (bottom).*

weather the short-term state of the atmosphere, including temperature, humidity, precipitation, wind, and visibility

climate the average weather condition in an area over a long period of time

latitude the distance north or south from the equator; expressed in degrees

Figure 3 The sun's rays strike the Earth's surface at different angles because the surface is curved.

Sun's rays

Equator

Teach

CONNECTION ACTIVITY
Math———————— GENERAL

Circumference of the Earth
Each degree or line of latitude is approximately 111 km apart, and 180 lines of latitude circle the Earth. Have students calculate the circumference of the Earth from pole to pole.

(111 km × 180 lines = 19,980 km from North Pole to South Pole, then multiply by 2 to get 39,960 km—the total distance around the Earth)
LS Logical

Cultural Awareness   GENERAL

Charles Edward Anderson
Charles Edward Anderson was the first African American to receive a doctorate in meteorology. Anderson began his career in meteorology during World War II. He was a captain in the United States Air Force and served as a weather officer for the Tuskegee Airmen Regiment. He earned his doctorate in 1960 from the Massachusetts Institute of Technology. His work focused on cloud physics, the forecasting of severe storms, and weather on other planets.

Cultural Awareness   GENERAL

Weather Folklore Weather and climate have inspired a great number of rhymes, greetings, sayings, and other folklore. Here is one example you may have heard: "Red skies at night, sailors delight. Red skies in morning, sailors take warning." In the hot, wet climate of Venezuela, indigenous people sometimes greet each other by saying, "How have the mosquitoes used you?" Russia's cold climate inspired the saying, "There's no bad weather, only bad clothing." Invite students to interview friends and relatives or research weather and climate folklore in another country. Have students share their findings with the class. **LS** Interpersonal

Modeling the Earth and Sun

Ask two volunteers to act as the Earth and the sun. Give the "sun" a flashlight and the "Earth" a globe with a half-meridian mounting. Turn off the lights, and have the volunteers sit on the floor. Ask the "sun" to shine the flashlight on the globe, and ask the "Earth" to slowly spin the globe counter-clockwise. Have the class notice which parts of the globe are most exposed to the light. Next, have the "Earth" slowly make a complete revolution around the "sun" while rotating the globe at the same time. Make sure that the volunteer always keeps the axis of the globe oriented in the same direction. Stop the "Earth" at each season so that students can observe the flashlight's rays on the two hemispheres. If necessary, repeat this activity with other volunteers.

LS Kinesthetic/Visual **Co-op Learning**

Seasons and Latitude

In most places in the United States, the year consists of four seasons. But there are places in the world that do not have such seasonal changes. For example, areas near the equator have approximately the same temperatures and same amount of daylight year-round. Seasons happen because the Earth is tilted on its axis at a 23.5° angle. This tilt affects how much solar energy an area receives as Earth moves around the sun. **Figure 4** shows how latitude and the tilt of the Earth determine the seasons and the length of the day in a particular area.

✓ **Reading Check** Why is there less seasonal change near the equator?

Figure 4 The Seasons

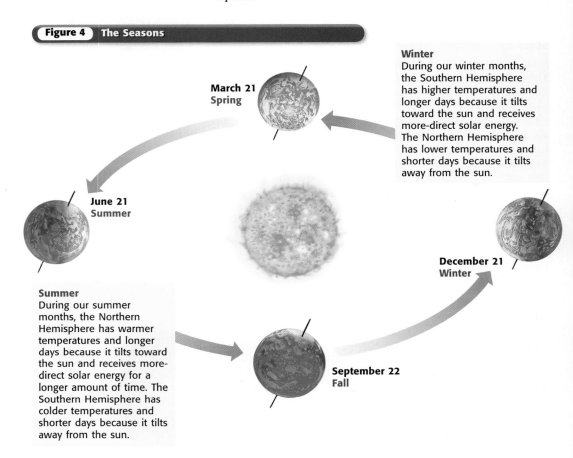

March 21 Spring

June 21 Summer

Winter
During our winter months, the Southern Hemisphere has higher temperatures and longer days because it tilts toward the sun and receives more-direct solar energy. The Northern Hemisphere has lower temperatures and shorter days because it tilts away from the sun.

December 21 Winter

Summer
During our summer months, the Northern Hemisphere has warmer temperatures and longer days because it tilts toward the sun and receives more-direct solar energy for a longer amount of time. The Southern Hemisphere has colder temperatures and shorter days because it tilts away from the sun.

September 22 Fall

Answer to Reading Check

Locations near the equator have less seasonal variation because the tilt of the Earth does not change the amount of energy these locations receive from the sun.

CHAPTER RESOURCES
Technology
Transparencies   • The Seasons   • The Circulation of Warm and Cold Air

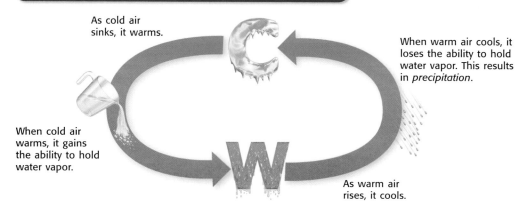

Figure 5 The Circulation of Warm Air and Cold Air

As cold air sinks, it warms.

When warm air cools, it loses the ability to hold water vapor. This results in *precipitation*.

When cold air warms, it gains the ability to hold water vapor.

As warm air rises, it cools.

Prevailing Winds

Winds that blow mainly from one direction are **prevailing winds**. Before you learn how the prevailing winds affect climate, take a look at **Figure 5** to learn about some of the basic properties of air.

Prevailing winds affect the amount of precipitation that a region receives. If the prevailing winds form from warm air, they may carry moisture. If the prevailing winds form from cold air, they will probably be dry.

The amount of moisture in prevailing winds is also affected by whether the winds blow across land or across a large body of water. Winds that travel across large bodies of water absorb moisture. Winds that travel across land tend to be dry. Even if a region borders the ocean, the area might be dry. **Figure 6** shows an example of how dry prevailing winds can cause the land to be dry though the land is near an ocean.

prevailing winds winds that blow mainly from one direction during a given period

Quick Lab

A Cool Breeze

1. Hold a **thermometer** next to the top edge of a **cup** of **water** containing two **ice cubes.** Record the temperature next to the cup.

2. Have your lab partner fan the surface of the cup with a **paper fan.** Record the temperature again. Has the temperature changed? Why or why not?

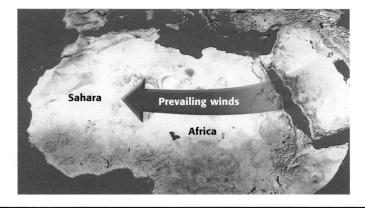

Sahara

Prevailing winds

Africa

Figure 6 The Sahara Desert, in northern Africa, is extremely dry because of the dry prevailing winds that blow across the continent.

Quick Lab

MATERIALS

FOR EACH GROUP
• cup
• ice cubes (2)
• paper fan
• thermometer
• water

Answers

2. Sample answer: yes; The temperature dropped after we fanned the surface of the cup. The air traveling across the cup's surface was cooled by the ice, thereby changing the air temperature.

CONNECTION ACTIVITY
Geography ——— ADVANCED

Writing **Monsoons** Monsoons are recurrent global weather patterns that dramatically affect the populations, economies, and environments of South Asia. The wet summer monsoon usually begins mid-June, when temperatures rise sharply in Asia's interior and cause the air above the land to warm and rise. This movement creates a low pressure area that draws warm, moist air inland from the Indian and Pacific Oceans. This moisture-laden air cools as it moves across the continent, causing heavy rains, thunderstorms, and flooding to occur. The heaviest rains occur where this air mass meets the foothills of the Himalayas. During the winter, the interior of Asia cools rapidly. This cool, dense air creates an immense high-pressure center, which forces cool, dry air to flow outward toward the oceans. As the air mass travels, it warms and becomes even drier. Warm, dry winters result. Encourage students to write a report about the effect of monsoons on South Asia. **LS Intrapersonal**

Teach, continued

Answer to School-to-Home Activity

Mountain ranges in the United States are the Sierra Nevada, the Rocky Mountains, and the Appalachian Mountains; yes; Climate varies from one side of the mountain range to the other, so one side is densely vegetated and the other side is much drier and less vegetated. The prevailing winds blow from the side with the most vegetation.

Using the Figure — BASIC

Wet Winds Remind students that winds traveling across large bodies of water, such as the ocean, absorb moisture. Have students study **Figure 7.** The inset photographs were taken in California's Sierra Nevada mountain range. Ask students to examine the photographs closely and describe as many details as possible. Then ask students to consider which side of the mountain is likely to be closer to a large body of water. (the left side) **English Language Learners**
LS Visual

Answer to Reading Check

The atmosphere becomes less dense and loses its ability to absorb and hold thermal energy at higher elevations.

SCHOOL to HOME

Using a Map
With your parent, use a physical map to locate the mountain ranges in the United States. Does climate vary from one side of a mountain range to the other? If so, what does this tell you about the climatic conditions on either side of the mountain? From what direction are the prevailing winds blowing?

ACTIVITY

Mountains

Mountains can influence an area's climate by affecting both temperature and precipitation. Kilimanjaro is the tallest mountain in Africa. It has snow-covered peaks year-round, even though it is only about 3° (320 km) south of the equator. Temperatures on Kilimanjaro and in other mountainous areas are affected by elevation. **Elevation** is the height of surface landforms above sea level. As the elevation increases, the ability of air to transfer energy from the ground to the atmosphere decreases. Therefore, as elevation increases, temperature decreases.

Mountains also affect the climate of nearby areas by influencing the distribution of precipitation. **Figure 7** shows how the climates on two sides of a mountain can be very different.

Reading Check Why does the atmosphere become cooler at higher elevations?

Figure 7 *Mountains block the prevailing winds and affect the climate on the other side.*

The Wet Side
Mountains force air to rise. The air cools as it rises, releasing moisture as snow or rain. The land on the windward side of the mountain is usually green and lush because the wind releases its moisture.

The Dry Side
After dry air crosses the mountain, the air begins to sink. As the air sinks, it is warmed and absorbs moisture. The dry conditions created by the sinking, warm air usually produce a desert. This side of the mountain is in a *rain shadow.*

INCLUSION Strategies

• *Developmentally Delayed* • *Hearing Impaired*
• *Learning Disabled*

Organize students into small groups. Give each group a clear plastic rectangular pan, a paper cup, hot water, and cold water. Have students poke 10 holes into the sides of the paper cup and tape the cup to the corner of the pan. Fill the pan two-thirds full with cold water. Have students put three drops of food coloring into the hot water and pour it into the paper cup. Have students record and explain their observations. (Students will observe the colored water diffuse through the holes in the cup. The hot water will not mix very much with the cold water. Most of the hot water will "float" on top. Explain that hot and cold air move in similar ways as hot and cold water do.) **LS Kinesthetic** **English Language Learners**

Large Bodies of Water

Large bodies of water can influence an area's climate. Water absorbs and releases heat slower than land does. Because of this quality, water helps to moderate the temperatures of the land around it. So, sudden or extreme temperature changes rarely take place on land near large bodies of water. For example, the state of Michigan, which is surrounded by the Great Lakes, has more-moderate temperatures than other places at the same latitude. The lakes also increase the moisture content of the air, which leads to heavy snowfall in the winter. This "lake effect" can cause 350 inches of snow to drop in one year!

Ocean Currents

The circulation of ocean surface currents has a large effect on an area's climate. **Surface currents** are streamlike movements of water that occur at or near the surface of the ocean. **Figure 8** shows the pattern of the major ocean surface currents.

As surface currents move, they carry warm or cool water to different locations. The surface temperature of the water affects the temperature of the air above it. Warm currents heat the surrounding air and cause warmer temperatures. Cool currents cool the surrounding air and cause cooler temperatures. The Gulf Stream current carries warm water northward off the east coast of North America and past Iceland. Iceland is an island country located just below the Arctic Circle. The warm water from the Gulf Stream heats the surrounding air and creates warmer temperatures in southern Iceland. Iceland experiences milder temperatures than Greenland, its neighboring island. Greenland's climate is cooler because Greenland is not influenced by the Gulf Stream.

✔ **Reading Check** Why does Iceland experience milder temperatures than Greenland?

elevation the height of an object above sea level

surface current a horizontal movement of ocean water that is caused by wind and that occurs at or near the ocean's surface

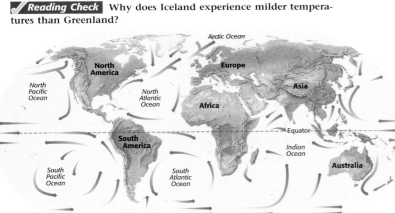

Figure 8 *The red arrows represent the movement of warm surface currents. The blue arrows represent the movement of cold surface currents.*

Homework ——— **ADVANCED**

Using Maps Have students look at a map and find cities that are at about the same latitude in a single continent. For example, Guadalajara and Tampico, in Mexico, are at about the same latitude, as are San Francisco, California, and Wichita, Kansas. Students should research the annual rainfall and temperature for each city. They can create a bar graph showing the differences in rainfall for each city, and students should attempt to explain the patterns they notice by identifying physical features on the map. If their data contradict what they have learned in this section, ask them to suggest explanations. **LS Visual**

Answer to Reading Check

The Gulf Stream current carries warm water past Iceland, which heats the air and causes milder temperatures.

Is That a Fact!

Large lakes, such as the Great Lakes, in the United States and Canada, and Lake Victoria, in Africa, affect local climates. This phenomenon, called the *lake effect,* helps keep the surrounding land cooler in the summer and warmer in the winter.

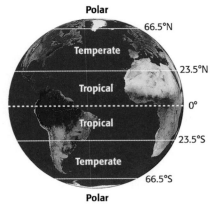

Figure 9 *The three major climate zones are determined by latitude.*

biome a large region characterized by a specific type of climate and certain types of plant and animal communities

Climates of the World

Have you seen any polar bears in your neighborhood lately? You probably have not. That's because polar bears live only in very cold arctic regions. Why are the animals in one part of the world so different from the animals in other parts? One of the differences has to do with climate. Plants and animals that have adapted to one climate may not be able to live in another climate. For example, frogs would not be able to survive at the North Pole.

Climate Zones

The Earth's three major climate zones—tropical, temperate, and polar—are shown in **Figure 9.** Each zone has a temperature range that relates to its latitude. However, in each of these zones, there are several types of climates because of differences in the geography and the amount of precipitation. Because of the various climates in each zone, there are different biomes in each zone. A **biome** is a large region characterized by a specific type of climate and certain types of plant and animal communities. **Figure 10** shows the distribution of the Earth's land biomes. In which biome do you live?

✓ **Reading Check** What factors distinguish one biome from another biome?

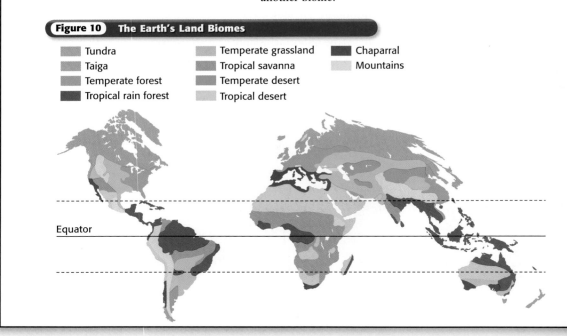

Figure 10 **The Earth's Land Biomes**

- Tundra
- Taiga
- Temperate forest
- Tropical rain forest
- Temperate grassland
- Tropical savanna
- Temperate desert
- Tropical desert
- Chaparral
- Mountains

Equator

Answer to Reading Check
Each biome has a different climate and different plant and animal communities.

SECTION Review

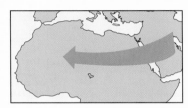

Summary

- Weather is the condition of the atmosphere at a particular time. This condition includes temperature, humidity, precipitation, wind, and visibility.
- Climate is the average weather condition in an area over a long period of time.
- The higher the latitude, the cooler the climate.
- Prevailing winds affect the climate of an area by the amount of moisture they carry.

- Mountains influence an area's climate by affecting both temperature and precipitation.
- Large bodies of water and ocean currents influence the climate of an area by affecting the temperature of the air over the water.
- The three climate zones of the world are the tropical zone, the temperate zone, and the polar zone.

Using Key Terms

1. In your own words, write a definition for each of the following terms: *weather, climate, latitude, prevailing winds, elevation, surface currents,* and *biome*.

Understanding Key Ideas

2. Which of the following affects climate by causing the air to rise?
   a. mountains
   b. ocean currents
   c. large bodies of water
   d. latitude

3. What is the difference between weather and climate?

4. List five factors that determine climates.

5. Explain why there is a difference in climate between areas at 0° latitude and areas at 45° latitude.

6. List the three climate zones of the world.

Critical Thinking

7. **Analyzing Relationships** How would seasons be different if the Earth did not tilt on its axis?

8. **Applying Concepts** During what months does Australia have summer? Explain.

Interpreting Graphics

Use the map below to answer the questions that follow.

9. Would you expect the area that the arrow points to to be moist or dry? Explain your answer.

10. Describe how the climate of the same area would change if the prevailing winds traveled from the opposite direction. Explain how you came to this conclusion.

SCI LINKS®

NSTA

Developed and maintained by the National Science Teachers Association

For a variety of links related to this chapter, go to www.scilinks.org

Topic: What Is Climate?
SciLinks code: HSM1659

CHAPTER RESOURCES

Chapter Resource File
- Section Quiz GENERAL
- Section Review GENERAL
- Vocabulary and Section Summary GENERAL
- Datasheet for Quick Lab

Technology

Transparencies
- The Earth's Land Biomes

Answers to Section Review

1. Sample answer: Weather is the condition of the atmosphere at a certain time. Climate is the average weather in an area over a long period of time. Latitude is the distance in degrees north or south of the equator. Prevailing winds are winds that blow mainly in one direction. Elevation is the height of surface landforms above sea level. Surface currents are streamlike movements of water that occur at or near the surface of the ocean. A biome is a large region characterized by a specific type of climate and certain types of plants and animals.

2. a

3. Weather is the condition of the atmosphere at a particular time. Climate is the average weather of a given area.

4. latitude, prevailing winds, mountains, large bodies of water, and ocean currents

5. Areas at different latitudes receive different amounts of solar energy because the Earth's surface is curved, and because the Earth is tilted on its axis.

6. tropical zone, temperate zone, and polar zone

7. If the Earth were not tilted on its axis, there would be no seasons.

8. Australia has summer during December, January, February, and March. This is because Australia is in the Earth's Southern Hemisphere, and the Southern Hemisphere is tilted away from the sun during these months.

9. dry

10. Accept all reasonable answers. If the prevailing winds blew from the Atlantic ocean, the area would have a wet climate with plenty of precipitation.

Focus

Overview

In this section, students learn the location and the characteristics of the tropical climate zone and the different biomes that are found in this climate.

Bellringer

Ask students to describe the differences between a deer and a camel. Where would they find these animals? Ask students to think about how climate influences the animals that live in certain areas.

Motivate

ACTIVITY ———— GENERAL

Writing **Country Profile** Have each student choose a country in the tropics to focus on for this section. Students should record the area's latitude and geographic characteristics. Tell students to find pictures from magazines or the Internet of the people, plants, and animals that live in the country. Then have students use the pictures to create a poster of the country they chose. Students should include information on average monthly rainfall and temperature. **LS** Visual

---

READING WARM-UP

Objectives
- Locate and describe the tropical zone.
- Describe the biomes found in the tropical zone.

Terms to Learn
tropical zone

READING STRATEGY

Reading Organizer As you read this section, make a table comparing *tropical rain forests, tropical savannas,* and *tropical deserts.*

The Tropics

Where in the world do you think you could find a flying dragon gliding above you from one treetop to the next?

Don't worry. This flying dragon, or tree lizard, is only about 20 cm long, and it eats only insects. With winglike skin flaps, the flying dragon can glide from one treetop to the next. But, you won't find this kind of animal in the United States. These flying dragons live in Southeast Asia, which is in the tropical zone.

The Tropical Zone

The region that surrounds the equator and that extends from about 23.5° north latitude to 23.5° south latitude is called the **tropical zone.** The tropical zone is also known as the Tropics. Latitudes in the tropical zone receive the most solar radiation. Temperatures are therefore usually hot, except at high elevations.

Within the tropical zone, there are three major types of biomes—tropical rain forest, tropical desert, and tropical savanna. These three biomes have high temperatures. But they differ in the amount of precipitation, soil characteristics, vegetation, and kinds of animals. **Figure 1** shows the distribution of these biomes.

✔ *Reading Check* At what latitudes would you find the tropical zone? (*See the Appendix for answers to Reading Checks.*)

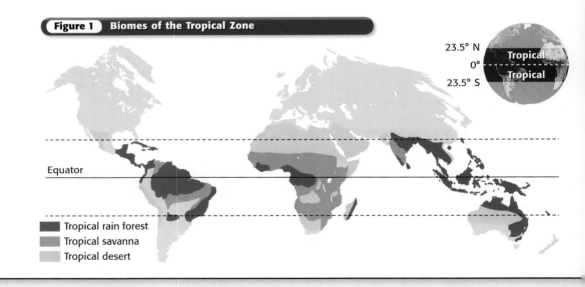

Figure 1 Biomes of the Tropical Zone

23.5° N
0°
23.5° S
Tropical
Tropical

Equator

■ Tropical rain forest
■ Tropical savanna
■ Tropical desert

CHAPTER RESOURCES

Chapter Resource File
- Lesson Plan
- Directed Reading A **BASIC**
- Directed Reading B **SPECIAL NEEDS**

Technology
- Transparencies
  - Bellringer
  - **LINK TO LIFE SCIENCE** Gas Exchange in Leaves

Workbooks
- Math Skills for Science
  - Rainforest Math **GENERAL**

Answer to Reading Check
You would find the tropical zone from 23.5° north latitude to 23.5° south latitude.

Tropical Rain Forest

- Average Temperature Range 25°C to 28°C (77°F to 82°F)
- Average Yearly Precipitation 200 cm or more
- Soil Characteristics thin and nutrient poor

Tropical Rain Forests

Tropical rain forests are always warm and wet. Because they are located near the equator, they receive strong sunlight year-round. So, there is little difference between seasons in tropical rain forests.

Tropical rain forests contain the greatest number of animal and plant species of any biome. Animals found in tropical rain forests include monkeys, parrots, tree frogs, tigers, and leopards. Plants found in tropical rain forests include mahogany, vines, ferns, and bamboo. But in spite of the lush vegetation, shown in **Figure 2,** the soil in rain forests is poor. The rapid decay of plants and animals returns nutrients to the soil. But these nutrients are quickly absorbed and used by the plants. The nutrients that are not immediately used by the plants are washed away by the heavy rains. The soil is left thin and nutrient poor.

Figure 2 *In tropical rain forests, many of the trees form above-ground roots that provide extra support for the trees in the thin, nutrient-poor soil.*

tropical zone the region that surrounds the equator and that extends from about 23.5° north latitude to 23.5° south latitude

CONNECTION TO Social Studies

WRITING SKILL **Living in the Tropics** The tropical climate is very hot and humid. People who live in the Tropics have had to adapt to feel comfortable in that climate. For example, in the country of Samoa, some people live in homes that have no walls, which are called *fales*. Fales have only a roof, which provides shade. The openness of the home allows cool breezes to flow through the home. Research other countries in the Tropics. See how the climate influences the way the people live in those countries. Then, in your **science journal,** describe how the people's lifestyle helps them adapt to the climate.

WEIRD SCIENCE

In addition to having land biomes, Earth has marine biomes. However, marine biomes are less influenced by latitude than they are by water depth. Some of the animals that inhabit the deeper biomes have very interesting adaptations. For example, the anglerfish, which lives in total darkness uses a luminescent "lure" that trails from the fish's jaw and attracts prey within reach of its enormous, sharp teeth.

Concept Mapping Have students create a concept map that shows how each of the three biomes in the tropical zone is influenced by precipitation and temperature. **LS** Visual

Quiz ── GENERAL

1. What are three biomes in the tropical zone? (tropical rain forest, tropical savannas, and tropical deserts)

2. What do all tropical biomes have in common? (They are all between 23.5° north latitude and 23.5° south latitude.)

Alternative Assessment ── GENERAL

PORTFOLIO **Building a Biome** Tell students that they are going to create an imaginary biome. Tell them to write the characteristics of their biome on a sheet of paper. Students should include the biome's annual precipitation, average temperature, topography, and latitude. When students have finished creating their imaginary biomes, ask them to write down the types of organisms that they think would inhabit their biomes. If students want, they can make drawings of some of the imaginary organisms. Invite students to share their work with the class. **LS** Intrapersonal

Tropical Savanna

- Average Temperature Range 27°C to 32°C (80°F to 90°F)
- Average Yearly Precipitation 100 cm
- Soil Characteristics generally nutrient poor

Figure 3 *The grass of a tropical savanna can be as tall as 5 m.*

Tropical Savannas

Tropical savannas, or grasslands, are composed of tall grasses and a few scattered trees. The climate is usually very warm. Tropical savannas have a dry season that lasts four to eight months and that is followed by short periods of rain. Savanna soils are generally nutrient poor. However, grass fires, which are common during the dry season, leave the soils nutrient enriched. An African savanna is shown in **Figure 3.**

Many plants have adapted to fire and use it to promote development. For example, some species need fire to break open their seeds' outer skin. Only after this skin is broken can each seed grow. For other species, heat from the fire triggers the plants to drop their seeds into the newly enriched soil.

Animals that live in tropical savannas include giraffes, lions, crocodiles, and elephants. Plants include tall grasses, trees, and thorny shrubs.

CONNECTION TO Biology

WRITING SKILL **Animal and Plant Adaptations** Animals and plants adapt to the climate in which they live. These adaptations cause certain animals and plants to be unique to particular biomes. For example, the camel, which is unique to the desert, has adapted to going for long periods of time without water. Research other animals or plants that live in the Tropics. Then, in your **science journal,** describe the characteristics that help them survive in the Tropics.

Is That a Fact!

The world's largest desert, the Sahara, covers more than 9 million square kilometers—about the size of the United States. In contrast, the largest desert in the United States is the Mojave Desert. It covers 38,900 km², which is nearly twice the size of New Jersey.

CONNECTION to Real World ── GENERAL

Desertification Deserts are expanding at an accelerating rate. In the last 100 years, the estimated area of land occupied by deserts rose from 9.4% to 23.3%. Many factors have contributed to this phenomenon, including climatic shifts, overgrazing, and overuse of the land through inefficient agricultural practices. As a class, find out what is being done to stop desertification in western Africa and other areas of the world.

Tropical Deserts

A desert is an area that receives less than 25 cm of rainfall per year. Because of this low yearly rainfall, deserts are the driest places on Earth. Desert plants, such as those shown in **Figure 4,** are adapted to survive in places that have little water. Animals such as rats, lizards, snakes, and scorpions have also adapted to survive in these deserts.

There are two kinds of deserts—hot deserts and cold deserts. Hot deserts are caused by cool, sinking air masses. Many hot deserts, such as the Sahara, in Africa, are tropical deserts. Daily temperatures in tropical deserts often vary from very hot daytime temperatures (50°C) to cool nighttime temperatures (20°C). Because of the dryness of deserts, the soil is poor in organic matter, which is needed for plants to grow.

✔ Reading Check What animals would you find in a tropical desert?

Tropical Desert
- **Average Temperature Range 16°C to 50°C (61°F to 120°F)**
- **Average Yearly Precipitation 0–25 cm**
- **Soil Characteristics poor in organic matter**

Figure 4 *Plants such as succulents have fleshy stems and leaves to store water.*

Answers to Section Review

1. Sample answer: The tropical zone is the climate region that surrounds the equator and that extends from about 23.5° north latitude to 23.5° south latitude.
2. b
3. thin and nutrient poor
4. Some savanna plant species need fire to break open their seeds' outer skin in order to grow. Also, for other plant species, the heat from the fire triggers the plant to drop its seeds into the newly enriched soil.
5. 27°C + 28°C + 29°C + 29°C = 113°C
   113°C ÷ 4 = 28.25°C
6. Sample answer: Tropical biomes differ in the amount of precipitation they receive, the average temperature range, soil characteristics, vegetation, and kinds of animals.
7. Sample answer: A plant in a tropical rain forest would have to adapt to an environment that received a large amount of rain that would leach nutrients from the soil. A plant in a tropical desert would have to adapt to a very hot, dry environment.
8. tropical desert

SECTION Review

Summary

- The tropical zone is located around the equator, between 23.5° north and 23.5° south latitude.
- Temperatures are usually hot in the tropical zone.
- Tropical rain forests are warm and wet. They have the greatest number of plant and animal species of any biome.
- Tropical savannas are grasslands that have a dry season.
- Tropical deserts are hot and receive little rain.

Using Key Terms

1. In your own words, write a definition for the term *tropical zone*.

Understanding Key Ideas

2. Which of the following tropical biomes has less than 50 cm of precipitation a year?
   a. rain forest   c. grassland
   b. desert   d. savanna
3. What are the soil characteristics of a tropical rain forest?
4. In what ways have savanna vegetation adapted to fire?

Math Skills

5. Suppose that in a tropical savanna, the temperature was recorded every hour for 4 h. The recorded temperatures were 27°C, 28°C, 29°C, and 29°C. Calculate the average temperature for this 4 h period.

Critical Thinking

6. **Analyzing Relationships** How do the tropical biomes differ?
7. **Making Inferences** How would you expect the adaptations of a plant in a tropical rain forest to differ from the adaptations of a tropical desert plant? Explain.
8. **Analyzing Data** An area has a temperature range of 30°C to 40°C and received 10 cm of rain this year. What biome is this area in?

SCLINKS®

NSTA
Developed and maintained by the National Science Teachers Association

For a variety of links related to this chapter, go to www.scilinks.org

Topic: Climates of the World
SciLinks code: HSM0302

Answer to Reading Check

Answers may vary. Sample answer: rats, lizards, snakes, and scorpions

CHAPTER RESOURCES

Chapter Resource File
- Section Quiz **GENERAL**
- Section Review **GENERAL**
- Vocabulary and Section Summary **GENERAL**
- Reinforcement Worksheet **BASIC**
- SciLinks Activity **GENERAL**

SECTION
3

Focus

Overview

In this section, students will learn the location and the characteristics of the temperate climate zone and the polar climate zone. They will also learn about microclimates and about different biomes that are found in these climate zones.

 Bellringer

Tell students that they are taking a trip to the North Pole. In order to pack, they need to know what the climate is like. Have students write a description of what they would expect the climate to be like at the North Pole.

Motivate

Group ACTiViTY — GENERAL

Camp Climate Have groups write a brochure for a summer camp in a temperate biome of their choice. Suggest that they include information about the environment that will entice people to come and helpful tips about how to prepare for the area's climate.

LS Visual **Co-op Learning**

READING WARM-UP

Objectives

- Locate and describe the temperate zone and the polar zone.
- Describe the different biomes found in the temperate zone and the polar zone.
- Explain what a microclimate is.

Terms to Learn

temperate zone
polar zone
microclimate

READING STRATEGY

Reading Organizer As you read this section, create an outline of the section. Use the headings from the section in your outline.

Temperate and Polar Zones

Which season is your favorite? Do you like the change of colors in the fall, the flowers in the spring, or do you prefer the hot days of summer?

If you live in the continental United States, chances are you live in a biome that experiences seasonal change. Seasonal change is one characteristic of the temperate zone. Most of the continental United States is in the temperate zone, which is the climate zone between the Tropics and the polar zone.

The Temperate Zone

The climate zone between the Tropics and the polar zone is the **temperate zone.** Latitudes in the temperate zone receive less solar energy than latitudes in the Tropics do. Because of this, temperatures in the temperate zone tend to be lower than in the Tropics. Some biomes in the temperate zone have a mild change of seasons. Other biomes in the country can experience freezing temperatures in the winter and very hot temperatures in the summer. The temperate zone consists of the following four biomes—temperate forest, temperate grassland, chaparral, and temperate desert. Although these biomes have four distinct seasons, the biomes differ in temperature and precipitation and have different plants and animals. **Figure 1** shows the distribution of the biomes found in the temperate zone.

✓ Reading Check Where is the temperate zone? (*See the Appendix for answers to Reading Checks.*)

Figure 1 Biomes of the Temperate Zone

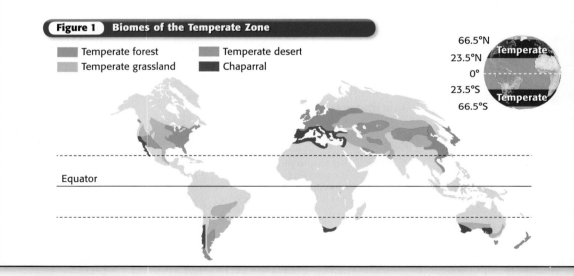

- Temperate forest
- Temperate grassland
- Temperate desert
- Chaparral

CHAPTER RESOURCES

Chapter Resource File

- **Lesson Plan**
- **Directed Reading A** BASIC
- **Directed Reading B** SPECIAL NEEDS

Technology

 Transparencies
- Bellringer

Answer to Reading Check

The temperate zone is located between the Tropics and the polar zone.

Temperate Forest
- **Average Temperature Range**
  0°C to 28°C (32°F to 82°F)
- **Average Yearly Precipitation**
  76 to 250 cm
- **Soil Characteristics**
  very fertile, organically rich

Temperate Forests

The temperate forest biomes tend to have high amounts of rainfall and seasonal temperature differences. Summers are often warm, and winters are often cold. Animals such as deer, bears, and foxes live in temperate forests. **Figure 2** shows deciduous trees in a temperate forest. *Deciduous* describes trees that lose their leaves at the end of the growing season. The soils in deciduous forests are usually fertile because of the high organic content from decaying leaves that drop every winter. Another type of tree found in the temperate forest is the evergreen. *Evergreens* are trees that keep their leaves year-round.

Temperate Grasslands

Temperate grasslands, such as those shown in **Figure 3,** are regions that receive too little rainfall for trees to grow. This biome has warm summers and cold winters. Examples of animals that are found in temperate grasslands include bison in North America and kangaroo in Australia. Grasses are the most common kind of plant found in this biome. Because grasslands have the most-fertile soils of all biomes, much of the grassland has been plowed to make room for croplands.

Figure 3 *At one time, the world's grasslands covered about 42% of Earth's total land surface. Today, they occupy only about 12% of the Earth's total land surface.*

Figure 2 *Deciduous trees have leaves that change color and drop when temperatures become cold.*

temperate zone the climate zone between the Tropics and the polar zone

Temperate Grassland
- **Average Temperature Range**
  –6°C to 26°C (21°F to 78°F)
- **Average Yearly Precipitation**
  38 to 76 cm
- **Soil Characteristics**
  most-fertile soils of all biomes

CONNECTION to Social Studies — GENERAL

Harvesting Fog Chile's arid northern desert land is one of the driest places on Earth. It receives so little rainfall that the yearly average is listed as "immeasurable." Surprisingly, people live there. They get drinking water by harvesting the fog. The village of Chungungo has built 75 fog-catching nets that supply 11,000 L of clean water per day. The nets, which look like giant volleyball nets, are positioned in the hills above the town. As the mountain fog passes through the nets, beads of water collect and are channeled to a pipeline that supplies the village with water. Scientists believe that this technology could be used in 30 other countries to supply safe and inexpensive water for drinking and agriculture.

Answer to Reading Check

Temperate deserts are cold at night because low humidity and cloudless skies allow energy to escape.

Chaparral

- **Average Temperature Range** 11°C to 26°C (51°F to 78°F)
- **Average Yearly Precipitation** 48 to 56 cm
- **Soil Characteristics** rocky, nutrient-poor soils

Figure 4 Some plant species found in chaparral require fire to reproduce.

Figure 5 The Great Basin Desert is in the rain shadow of the Sierra Nevada.

Chaparrals

Chaparral regions, as shown in **Figure 4,** have cool, wet winters and hot, dry summers. Animals, such as coyotes and mountain lions live in chaparrals. The vegetation is mainly evergreen shrubs. These shrubs are short, woody plants with thick, waxy leaves. The waxy leaves are adaptations that help prevent water loss in dry conditions. These shrubs grow in rocky, nutrient-poor soil. Like tropical-savanna vegetation, chaparral vegetation has adapted to fire. In fact, some plants, such as chamise, can grow back from their roots after a fire.

Temperate Deserts

The temperate desert biomes, like the one shown in **Figure 5,** tend to be cold deserts. Like all deserts, cold deserts receive less than 25 cm of precipitation yearly. Examples of animals that live in temperate deserts are lizards, snakes, bats, and toads. And the types of plants found in temperate deserts include cacti, shrubs, and thorny trees.

Temperate deserts can be very hot in the daytime. But, unlike hot deserts, they are often very cold at night. This large change in temperature between day and night is caused by low humidity and cloudless skies. These conditions allow for a large amount of energy to heat the Earth's surface during the day. However, these same characteristics allow the energy to escape at night. This causes temperatures to drop. You probably rarely think of snow and deserts together. But temperate deserts often receive light snow during the winter.

Reading Check Why are temperate deserts cold at night?

Temperate Desert

- **Average Temperature Range** 1°C to 50°C (34°F to 120°F)
- **Average Yearly Precipitation** 0 to 25 cm
- **Soil Characteristics** poor in organic matter

INCLUSION Strategies

- **Behavior Control Issues**
- **Gifted and Talented**
- **Visually Impaired**

Organize students into small groups. Assign each group two biomes to categorize. Groups will need their textbook, additional resource books such as an encyclopedia, two large sheets of paper, various magazines to cut pictures from, and glue. For each biome, ask each group to record on paper the definition, a description with a picture, typical plants or animals that live in the biome, one or two locations of the biome, and something unique about this biome. For extra credit, ask students to hypothesize how geography may affect the climate of the locations they chose. Have groups share with the rest of the class what they documented. **LS Visual/Kinesthetic**

Figure 6   Biomes of the Polar Zone

Equator

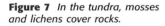
Tundra
Taiga

66.5°N
0°
66.5°S
Polar
Polar

The Polar Zone

The climate zone located at the North or South Pole and its surrounding area is called the **polar zone.** Polar climates have the coldest average temperatures of all the climate zones. Temperatures in the winter stay below freezing. The temperatures during the summer remain cool. **Figure 6** shows the distribution of the biomes found in the polar zone.

polar zone the North or South Pole and its surrounding area

Tundra

The tundra biome, as shown in **Figure 7,** has long, cold winters with almost 24 hours of night. It also has short, cool summers with almost 24 hours of daylight. In the summer, only the top meter of soil thaws. Underneath the thawed soil lies a permanently frozen layer of soil, called *permafrost.* This frozen layer prevents the water in the thawed soil from draining. Because of the poor drainage, the upper soil layer is muddy. This muddy layer of soil makes a great breeding ground for insects, such as mosquitoes. Many birds migrate to the tundra during the summer to feed on the insects. Other animals that live in the tundra are caribou, reindeer, and polar bears. Plants in this biome include mosses and lichens.

Figure 7 *In the tundra, mosses and lichens cover rocks.*

Tundra

- **Average Temperature Range**
  −27°C to 5°C (−17°F to 41°F)
- **Average Yearly Precipitation**
  0 to 25 cm
- **Soil Characteristics**
  frozen

Demonstration — GENERAL

Mock Permafrost   Prepare for the demonstration by punching five holes in the bottom of two coffee cans and filling each can one-third full with potting soil. Slowly add water to one can until it begins to drain through the bottom. The soil should be moist but not saturated. Allow the excess water to drain, and pack the soil firmly. Place that can in a freezer for 6 to 8 hours. Bring the two cans to class, and have students gather at a sink. Hold the can with the unfrozen soil over the sink, and slowly pour a glass of water onto the soil. Repeat with the frozen can. Discuss with students why muddy or "marshy" areas form in the frozen soil and why the soil did not drain. **LS** Visual

Homework — ADVANCED

Graphing   Have students construct a bar graph that compares the average yearly precipitation ranges for the six biomes discussed in this section. Have students use their graph to determine which biomes receive the most rain, which biomes receive the least rain, and which biome has the widest variation in annual precipitation. Suggest that students obtain yearly precipitation records for their local region and compare these records with the information in their graph. Students may also be able to construct their graph on a computer or graphing calculator. **LS** Visual/Logical

---

MISCONCEPTION ALERT

Tundra   Students may think that the tundra is a relatively small and barren portion of the world. Actually, one-tenth of the Earth's land is tundra, and about 600 species of plants are native to the biome. Ninety-nine percent of those plants are perennials—the growing season is too short for annuals, which need time to produce flowers and seeds.

WEIRD SCIENCE

Lichens are organisms that thrive in the polar zone. Some lichens in the Arctic have been determined to be 4,500 years old. To protect themselves from the cold, some lichens live 2 cm inside rocks! Despite their ability to survive in extremely harsh arctic conditions, most lichens have an extremely low tolerance for sulfur dioxide in air pollution. As a result, they are usually not found in industrialized areas.

Close

Reteaching — **BASIC**

Temperate Versus Polar Ask students to take out two pieces of paper. On one piece of paper, have students write "temperate zone." On the other piece of paper, have students write "polar zone." Have students write all the characteristics of each climate zone on its respective paper. Then have students share what they wrote with the class. Compile a class list on the board. **LS** Logical

Quiz — **GENERAL**

1. Can a climate zone contain more than one biome?
(A climate zone may contain several different biomes.)

2. What is a microclimate?
(a small area that has unique climate characteristics)

Alternative Assessment — **GENERAL**

Climate Zone Organizers Help students learn the characteristics of each of the nine biomes by having them make a graphic organizer for each climate zone. Have students match the appropriate biomes with each climate zone. Each graphic organizer should contain information about the biomes' temperature, precipitation, soil, plants, and animals. Students can also include magazine photographs that show plants and animals that inhabit each biome. **LS** Visual *English Language Learners*

Taiga

- Average Temperature Range −10°C to 15°C (14°F to 59°F)
- Average Yearly Precipitation 40 to 61 cm
- Soil Characteristics acidic

Figure 8 *The taiga, such as this one in Washington, have mostly evergreens for trees.*

microclimate the climate of a small area

SCHOOL to HOME

WRITING SKILL **Your Biome** With your parents, explore the biome in the area where you live. What kinds of animals and plants live in your area? Write a one-page paper that describes the biome and why the biome of your area has its particular climate.

ACTIVITY

Taiga (Northern Coniferous Forest)

Just south of the tundra lies the taiga biome. The taiga, as shown in **Figure 8,** has long, cold winters and short, warm summers. Animals commonly found here are moose, bears, and rabbits. The majority of the trees are evergreen needle-leaved trees called *conifers,* such as pine, spruce, and fir trees. The needles and flexible branches allow these trees to shed heavy snow before they can be damaged. Conifer needles are made of acidic substances. When the needles die and fall to the soil, they make the soil acidic. Most plants cannot grow in acidic soil. Because of the acidic soil, the forest floor is bare except for some mosses and lichens.

Microclimates

The climate and the biome of a particular place can also be influenced by local conditions. **Microclimate** is the climate of a small area. The alpine biome is a cold biome found on mountains all around the world. The alpine biome can even be found on mountains in the Tropics! How is this possible? The high elevation affects the area's climate and therefore its biome. As the elevation increases, the air's ability to transfer heat from the ground to the atmosphere by conduction decreases, which causes temperatures to decrease. In winter, the temperatures are below freezing. In summer, average temperatures range from 10°C to 15°C. Plants and animals have had to develop special adaptations to live in this severe climate.

Answer to School-to-Home Activity
Answers may vary. Students should recognize different plants and animals found in their area. Encourage students to use field guides and the Web sites of local parks to identify plants and animals. Students should also be able to describe the climate of their biome and explain why their biome has this particular climate, based on latitude, prevailing winds, mountains, bodies of water, and ocean currents.

Cities

Cities are also microclimates. In a city, temperatures can be 1°C to 2°C warmer than the surrounding rural areas. Have you ever walked barefoot on a black asphalt street on a hot summer day? Doing so burns your feet because buildings and pavement made of dark materials absorb solar radiation instead of reflecting it. There is also less vegetation in a city to take in the sun's rays. This absorption and re-radiation of heat by buildings and pavement heats the surrounding air. In turn, the temperatures rise.

✓ Reading Check Why do cities have higher temperatures than the surrounding rural areas?

CONNECTION TO Physics

Hot Roofs! Scientists studied roofs on a sunny day when the air temperature was 13°C. They recorded roof temperatures ranging from 18°C to 61°C depending on color and material of the roof. Place thermometers on outside objects that are made of different types of materials and that are different colors. Please stay off the roof! Is there a difference in temperatures? **ACTIVITY**

SECTION Review

Summary

● The temperate zone is located between the Tropics and the polar zone. It has moderate temperatures.

● Temperate forests, temperate grasslands, and temperate deserts are biomes in the temperate zone.

● The polar zone includes the North or South Pole and its surrounding area. The polar zone has the coldest temperatures.

● The tundra and the taiga are biomes within the polar zone.

Using Key Terms

1. In your own words, write a definition for the term *microclimate*.

Complete each of the following sentences by choosing the correct term from the word bank.

    temperate zone   polar zone
    microclimate

2. The coldest temperatures are found in the ___.

3. The ___ has moderate temperatures.

Understanding Key Ideas

4. Which of the following biomes has the driest climate?
   a. temperate forests
   b. temperate grasslands
   c. chaparrals
   d. temperate deserts

5. Explain why the temperate zone has lower temperatures than the Tropics.

6. Describe how the latitude of the polar zone affects the climate in that area.

7. Explain why the tundra can sometimes experience 24 hours of daylight or 24 hours of night.

8. How do conifers make the soil they grow in too acidic for other plants to grow?

Math Skills

9. Texas has an area of about 700,000 square kilometers. Grasslands compose about 20% of this area. About how many square kilometers of grassland are there in Texas?

Critical Thinking

10. **Identifying Relationships** Which biome would be more suitable for growing crops, temperate forest or taiga? Explain.

11. **Making Inferences** Describe the types of animals and vegetation you might find in the Alpine biome.

SCILINKS **NSTA**
Developed and maintained by the National Science Teachers Association

For a variety of links related to this chapter, go to www.scilinks.org

Topic: Modeling Earth's Climate
SciLinks code: HSM0976

Answer to Reading Check

Cities have higher temperatures than the surrounding rural areas because buildings and pavement absorb solar radiation instead of reflecting it.

CHAPTER RESOURCES

Chapter Resource File

- Section Quiz **GENERAL**
- Section Review **GENERAL**
- Vocabulary and Section Summary **GENERAL**
- Reinforcement Worksheet **BASIC**

Workbooks

Science Skills
- Finding Useful Sources **GENERAL**

Answers to Section Review

1. Sample answer: A microclimate is the climate of a small area.

2. polar zone

3. temperate zone

4. d

5. The temperate zone has lower temperatures than the Tropics because it is located at a higher latitude.

6. Because the polar zone is at a higher latitude than the other climate zones, it receives less direct solar energy and therefore has lower temperatures.

7. The Earth is tilted so that during the summer, high latitudes are pointed toward the sun. Therefore, polar regions receive 24 hours of daylight each day. In the winter, the Earth is tilted so that high latitudes are pointed away from the sun. Therefore, polar regions experience 24 hours of night each day.

8. The needles of conifers are acidic. When the needles fall to the ground, they make the soil acidic, which makes it difficult for many other plants to grow.

9. 700,000 km² × 0.20 = 140,000 km²

10. Sample answer: A temperate forest would be better for growing crops than the taiga because the soil in the forest is very fertile and organically rich. The taiga would be a difficult place to grow crops because the soil is acidic from the conifer needles.

11. Students should choose plants and animals that are adapted to very cold climates in the mountains. Sample answer: mountain goat, snow leopard, moss

Focus

Overview

In this section, students will learn how the Earth's climate has changed in the past. Students will learn about different causes of climate change. Students will also learn about the greenhouse effect and its role in global warming.

Bellringer

Have students imagine that the climate of the area where they live has changed, so it is now warmer than it used to be. Have students write down five different ways they think the area would be affected by warmer temperatures.

Motivate

Demonstration —— GENERAL

The Greenhouse Effect Tell students that the glass windows in a greenhouse are similar to the Earth's atmosphere. The glass allows radiant energy to enter but prevents thermal energy from escaping. Have students place a thermometer in a plastic bag on a sunny windowsill. Place another thermometer next to the plastic bag. After 30 minutes, have a student read the two thermometers and compare the difference in temperature. **English Language Learners**

 Kinesthetic

READING WARM-UP

Objectives

- Describe how the Earth's climate has changed over time.
- Summarize four different theories that attempt to explain why the Earth's climate has changed.
- Explain the greenhouse effect and its role in global warming.

Terms to Learn

ice age
global warming
greenhouse effect

READING STRATEGY

Paired Summarizing Read this section silently. In pairs, take turns summarizing the material. Stop to discuss ideas that seem confusing.

ice age a long period of climate cooling during which ice sheets cover large areas of Earth's surface; also known as a glacial period

---

Changes in Climate

As you have probably noticed, the weather changes from day to day. Sometimes, the weather can change several times in one day! But have you ever noticed the climate change?

On Saturday, your morning baseball game was canceled because of rain, but by that afternoon the sun was shining. Now, think about the climate where you live. You probably haven't noticed a change in climate, because climates change slowly. What causes climatic change? Studies indicate that human activity may cause climatic change. However, natural factors also can influence changes in the climate.

Ice Ages

The geologic record indicates that the Earth's climate has been much colder than it is today. In fact, much of the Earth was covered by sheets of ice during certain periods. An **ice age** is a period during which ice collects in high latitudes and moves toward lower latitudes. Scientists have found evidence of many major ice ages throughout the Earth's geologic history. The most recent ice age began about 2 million years ago.

Glacial Periods

During an ice age, there are periods of cold and periods of warmth. These periods are called glacial and interglacial periods. During *glacial periods,* the enormous sheets of ice advance. As they advance, they get bigger and cover a larger area, as shown in **Figure 1.** Because a large amount of water is frozen during glacial periods, the sea level drops.

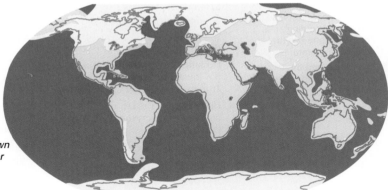

Figure 1 *During glacial periods, ice sheets (as shown in light blue), cover a larger portion of the Earth.*

CHAPTER RESOURCES

Chapter Resource File

- Lesson Plan
- Directed Reading A **BASIC**
- Directed Reading B **SPECIAL NEEDS**

Technology

Transparencies
- Bellringer
- The Milankovitch Theory

Interglacial Periods

Warmer times that happen between glacial periods are called *interglacial periods*. During an interglacial period, the ice begins to melt and the sea level rises again. The last interglacial period began 10,000 years ago and is still happening. Why do these periods occur? Will the Earth have another glacial period in the future? These questions have been debated by scientists for the past 200 years.

Motions of the Earth

There are many theories about the causes of ice ages. Each theory tries to explain the gradual cooling that begins an ice age. This cooling leads to the development of large ice sheets that periodically cover large areas of the Earth's surface.

The *Milankovitch theory* explains why an ice age isn't just one long cold spell. Instead, the ice age alternates between cold and warm periods. Milutin Milankovitch, a Yugoslavian scientist, proposed that changes in the Earth's orbit and in the tilt of the Earth's axis cause ice ages. His theory is shown in **Figure 2.** In a 100,000 year period, the Earth's orbit changes from elliptical to circular. This changes the Earth's distance from the sun. In turn, it changes the temperature on Earth. Changes in the tilt of the Earth also influence the climate. The more the Earth is tilted, the closer the poles are to the sun.

✓ Reading Check What are the two things Milankovitch says causes ice ages? (*See the Appendix for answers to Reading Checks.*)

INTERNET ACTIVITY

For another activity related to this chapter, go to **go.hrw.com** and type in the keyword **HZ5CLMW.**

Figure 2 **The Milankovitch Theory**

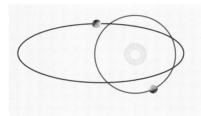 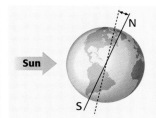 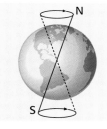

① Over a period of 100,000 years, the Earth's orbit slowly changes from a more circular shape to a more elliptical shape and back again. When Earth's orbit is elliptical, Earth receives more energy from the sun. When its orbit is more circular, Earth receives less energy from the sun.

② Over a period of 41,000 years, the tilt of the Earth's axis varies between 22.2° and 24.5°. When the tilt is at 24.5°, the poles receive more solar energy.

③ The Earth's axis traces a complete circle every 26,000 years. The circular motion of the Earth's axis determines the time of year that the Earth is closest to the sun.

MISCONCEPTION ALERT

Ice Ages and Glacial Periods Students may be confused about the difference between an ice age and a glacial period. An ice age is the gradual cooling of the planet over thousands of years. During this time, glaciers repeatedly spread outward from the Earth's poles toward the equator. Ice ages are characterized by glacial periods (when glaciers spread) and interglacial periods (when glaciers retreat). Glacial periods can happen rather quickly—often in less than 30 years. Ice cores indicate that sudden glaciation periods could be caused by changes in major ocean currents or by volcanic eruptions. Currently, we are in an interglacial period of an ice age.

Volcanic Eruptions
Have students research and write a short report on a large volcanic eruption. Reports should include where the volcano is located, what damage the eruption caused, and what the eruption's long-term effects were. **LS** Intrapersonal

CONNECTION to
Geology ———— GENERAL

Climate Change Due to Plate Tectonics Tectonic activity will continue to rearrange the Earth's continents in the future. Europe and North America will continue to spread apart, allowing greater circulation between the Arctic and Atlantic Oceans. At the same time, Antarctica will move away from the South Pole. Ask students to imagine that they have been transported 50 million years into the future. How is the Earth different in terms of the events just described? Have students create a story or comic about the Earth of the distant future. (Sample answer: Earth will be much warmer. The sea level will be higher because ocean currents will reach both polar regions, warming them. Antarctica will no longer be an icebound continent. Additionally, the continents will be rearranged, and some of today's prominent geographic features, such as the Rocky Mountains, will be significantly eroded.)
LS Intrapersonal/Visual

Figure 3 *Much of Pangaea—the part that is now Africa, South America, India, Antarctica, Australia, and Saudi Arabia—was covered by continental ice sheets.*

Plate Tectonics

The Earth's climate is further influenced by plate tectonics and continental drift. One theory proposes that ice ages happen when the continents are positioned closer to the polar regions. About 250 million years ago, all the continents were connected near the South Pole in one giant landmass called *Pangaea,* as shown in **Figure 3.** During this time, ice covered a large area of the Earth's surface. As Pangaea broke apart, the continents moved toward the equator, and the ice age ended. During the last ice age, many large landmasses were positioned in the polar zones. Antarctica, northern North America, Europe, and Asia were covered by large sheets of ice.

Volcanic Eruptions

Many natural factors can affect global climate. Catastrophic events, such as volcanic eruptions, can influence climate. Volcanic eruptions send large amounts of dust, ash, and smoke into the atmosphere. Once in the atmosphere, the dust, smoke, and ash particles act as a shield. This shield blocks the sun's rays, which causes the Earth to cool. **Figure 4** shows how dust particles from a volcanic eruption block the sun.

✓ *Reading Check* How can volcanoes change the climate?

Figure 4 **Volcanic Dust in the Atmosphere**

Volcanic eruptions, such as the 1980 eruption of Mount St. Helens, as shown at right, produce dust that reflects sunlight.

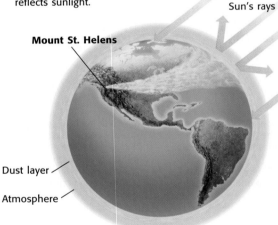

Sun's rays

Mount St. Helens

Dust layer

Atmosphere

Answer to Reading Check
Dust, ash, and smoke from volcanic eruptions block the sun's rays, which causes the Earth to cool.

Figure 5 *Some scientists believe that a 10 km chunk of rock smashed into the Earth 65 million years ago, which caused the climatic change that resulted in the extinction of dinosaurs.*

Asteroid Impact

Imagine a rock the size of a car flying in from outer space and crashing in your neighborhood. This rock, like the one shown in **Figure 5,** is called an asteroid. An *asteroid* is a small, rocky object that orbits the sun. Sometimes, asteroids enter our atmosphere and crash into the Earth. What would happen if an asteroid 1 km wide, which is more than half a mile long, hit the Earth? Scientists believe that if an asteroid this big hit the Earth, it could change the climate of the entire world.

When a large piece of rock slams into the Earth, it causes debris to shoot into the atmosphere. *Debris* is dust and smaller rocks. This debris can block some of the sunlight and thermal energy. This would lower average temperatures, which would change the climate. Plants wouldn't get the sunlight they needed to grow, and animals would find surviving difficult. Scientists believe such an event is what caused dinosaurs to become extinct 65 million years ago when a 10 km asteroid slammed into the Earth and changed the Earth's climate.

The Sun's Cycle

Some changes in the climate can be linked to changes in the sun. You might think that the sun always stays the same. However, the sun follows an 11-year cycle. During this cycle, the sun changes from a solar maximum to a solar minimum. During a solar minimum, the sun produces a low percentage of high-energy radiation. But when the sun is at its solar maximum, it produces a large percentage of high-energy radiation. This increase in high-energy radiation warms the winds in the atmosphere. This change in turn affects climate patterns around the world.

CONNECTION TO Astronomy

Sunspots Sunspots are dark areas on the sun's surface. The number of sunspots changes with the sun's cycle. When the cycle is at a solar maximum, there are many sunspots. When the cycle is at a solar minimum, there are fewer sunspots. If the number of sunspots was low in 1997, in what year will the next low point in the cycle happen?

CONNECTION to Language Arts — GENERAL

Roots of Words Have students look up the Latin and Greek roots of key terms and note the common roots. For example, the Spanish equivalent of *atmosphere* is *atmosfera,* derived from the Greek root *atmos* (vapor) and the Latin *sphaira* (sphere or ball). Provide English language learners with translations of the key terms in this section, or have them consult the Spanish glossary. **LS Intrapersonal** — English Language Learners

Answer to Connection to Astronomy

The sun has an 11-year cycle. If the solar minimum occurred in 1997, the next solar minimum would be in 2008.

CONNECTION ACTIVITY Real World — ADVANCED

Reducing CO₂ Emissions
Fossil fuels, which release carbon dioxide into the air, are often used to heat water. So, washing clothes in cold water instead of hot water can reduce the amount of carbon dioxide released into the atmosphere. For example, a household that uses cold water to do two loads of laundry a week releases about 225 kg *less* carbon dioxide into the atmosphere each year. Have students calculate what the annual reduction in released carbon dioxide would be if the family of every student in the class used cold water for two loads of laundry a week. **LS Logical**

Cultural Awareness GENERAL

Ancient Chinese Meteorology
Predicting climatic changes is difficult because weather data have been accurately recorded for less than 200 years. However, the meteorological records of the Chinese date back to 1216 BCE. While these records do not indicate temperature, they do record rainfall, sleet, snow, humidity, and wind direction. The records also include comments on unusually warm or cool temperatures. Have interested students research the reasons for collecting the data and find out how the data are used today.

Reteaching — BASIC

Changing Climate Ask students to describe the climate in their area. Then review the factors that might affect the climate. Have students describe how each factor would affect the climate in their area.

LS Intrapersonal

Quiz — GENERAL

1. Why does the sea level fall during glacial periods? (because much of Earth's water is frozen during a glacial period)

2. How might a major volcanic eruption have brought about an ice age? (Dust, smoke, and ash from a volcanic eruption entered the atmosphere and acted as a shield, blocking out many of the sun's rays and causing the Earth to cool.)

3. How might global warming affect coastal areas? (The warmer temperatures could cause polar icecaps to melt, which would raise the sea level and cause flooding in coastal areas.)

Alternative Assessment — GENERAL

PORTFOLIO **Climate Collage** Have students make a collage about global cooling or warming. They can include images of how they think the Earth would appear and descriptions of the likely causes of climate change. English Language Learners

LS Visual

MATH PRACTICE

The Ride to School

1. The round-trip distance from your home to school is 20 km.
2. You traveled from home to school and from school to home 23 times in a month.
3. The vehicle in which you took your trips travels 30 km/gal.
4. If burning 1 gal of gasoline produces 9 kg of carbon dioxide, how much carbon dioxide did the vehicle release during the month?

global warming a gradual increase in the average global temperature

greenhouse effect the warming of the surface and lower atmosphere of Earth that occurs when carbon dioxide, water vapor, and other gases in the air absorb and trap thermal energy

Global Warming

A gradual increase in the average global temperature that is due to a higher concentration of gases, such as carbon dioxide in the atmosphere, is called **global warming.** To understand how global warming works, you must first learn about the greenhouse effect.

Greenhouse Effect

The Earth's natural heating process, in which gases in the atmosphere trap thermal energy, is called the **greenhouse effect.** The car in **Figure 6** shows how the greenhouse effect works. The car's windows stop most of the thermal energy from escaping, and the inside of the car gets hot. On Earth, instead of glass stopping the thermal energy, atmospheric gases absorb the thermal energy. When this happens, the thermal energy stays in the atmosphere and keeps the Earth warm. Many scientists believe that the rise in global temperatures is due to an increase of carbon dioxide, an atmospheric gas. Most evidence shows that the increase in carbon dioxide is caused by the burning of fossil fuels.

Another factor that may add to global warming is the clearing of forests. In many countries, forests are being burned to clear land for farming. Burning of the forests releases more carbon dioxide. Because plants use carbon dioxide to make food, destroying the trees decreases a natural way of removing carbon dioxide from the atmosphere.

Figure 6 *Sunlight streams into the car through the clear, glass windows. The seats absorb the radiant energy and change it into thermal energy. The energy is then trapped in the car.*

Answer to Math Practice

10 km × 2 = 20 km/day

20 km/day × 23 trips = 460 km/mo

460 km ÷ 30 km/gal = 15.3 kg CO_2

Answer to School-to-Home Activity

Sample answer: The city could pass legislation that requires all vehicle emissions to be below a certain standard. The city could provide incentives for car pooling. The city could also improve the public transportation system and create more public transportation routes.

Consequences of Global Warming

Many scientists think that if the global temperature continues to rise, the ice caps will melt and cause flooding. Melted ice-caps would raise the sea level and flood low-lying areas, such as the coasts.

Areas that receive little rainfall, such as deserts, might receive even less because of increased evaporation. Desert animals and plants would find surviving harder. Warmer and drier climates could harm crops in the Midwest of the United States. But farther north, such as in Canada, weather conditions for farming could improve.

Reading Check How would warmer temperatures affect deserts?

Reducing Pollution
Your city just received a warning from the Environmental Protection Agency for exceeding the automobile fuel emissions standards. Discuss with your parent ways that the city can reduce the amount of automobile emissions.

SECTION Review

Summary

- The Earth's climate experiences glacial and interglacial periods.
- The Milankovitch theory states that the Earth's climate changes as its orbit and the tilt of its axis change.
- Climate changes can be caused by volcanic eruptions, asteroid impact, the sun's cycle, and by global warming.
- Excess carbon dioxide is believed to contribute to global warming.

Using Key Terms

1. Use the following term in a sentence: *ice age*.

2. In your own words, write a definition for each of the following terms: *global warming* and *greenhouse effect*.

Understanding Key Ideas

3. Describe the possible causes of an ice age.

4. Which of the following can cause a change in the climate due to dust particles?
   a. volcanic eruptions
   b. plate tectonics
   c. solar cycles
   d. ice ages

5. How has the Earth's climate changed over time?

6. What might have caused the Earth's climate to change?

7. Which period of an ice age are we in currently? Explain.

8. Explain how the greenhouse effect warms the Earth.

Math Skills

9. After a volcanic eruption, the average temperature in a region dropped from 30° to 18°C. By how many degrees Celsius did the temperature drop?

Critical Thinking

10. **Analyzing Relationships** How will the warming of the Earth affect agriculture in different parts of the world? Explain.

11. **Predicting Consequences** How would deforestation (the cutting of trees) affect global warming?

For a variety of links related to this chapter, go to www.scilinks.org

Topic: Changes in Climate
SciLinks code: HSM0252

Answer to Reading Check

The deserts would receive even less rainfall, making it harder for plants and animals in the desert to survive.

CHAPTER RESOURCES

Chapter Resource File
- Section Quiz GENERAL
- Section Review GENERAL
- Vocabulary and Section Summary GENERAL
- Critical Thinking ADVANCED

Workbooks

Science Skills
- Understanding Bias GENERAL

Answers to Section Review

1. Sample answer: Milankovitch theorized that ice ages were caused by changes in the Earth's orbit and changes in the tilt of the Earth's axis.

2. Sample answer: Global warming is the gradual increase in the average global temperature due to a higher concentration of greenhouse gases in the atmosphere. The greenhouse effect is the warming of the surface and lower atmosphere of the Earth that occurs when carbon dioxide, water vapor, and other gases in the air absorb and trap thermal energy.

3. Ice ages could be caused by changes in the Earth's orbit, in the tilt of the Earth's axis, by plate tectonics, volcanic eruptions, or asteroid impacts.

4. a

5. The Earth has experienced periods of cold and warm temperatures called glacial and interglacial periods.

6. The Earth's climate may have changed because of the change in the Earth's orbit, a change in the tilt of the Earth's axis, plate tectonics, volcanic eruptions, impact from a large asteroid, the sun's cycle, and global warming.

7. We are in an interglacial period. Ice sheets are melting instead of advancing.

8. The greenhouse effect occurs when gases in the atmosphere trap thermal energy and warm the Earth.

9. $30°C - 18°C = 12°C$

10. Sample answer: Global warming might improve farming at higher latitudes. Closer to the equator, an increase in evaporation and less rainfall might make growing crops difficult.

11. Answers may vary. Sample answer: Trees store carbon, so deforestation could cause carbon dioxide levels in the air to increase, which might increase global warming.

Biome Business

Teacher's Notes

Time Required
One 45-minute class period

Lab Ratings

EASY ———————————→ HARD

Teacher Prep 🧪
Student Set-Up 🧪
Concept Level 🧪🧪
Clean Up 🧪

MATERIALS
Note that student groups will need a general map to identify their biome location.

Preparation Notes
Remind students not to use seasonal terms such as *spring* and *fall* because some of the biomes in the Southern Hemisphere may experience seasons that are opposite from the seasons of the Northern Hemisphere.

Skills Practice Lab

OBJECTIVES

Interpret data in a climatograph.

Identify the biome for each climatograph.

■ Tundra
■ Taiga
■ Temperate forest
■ Tropical rain forest
■ Temperate grassland
■ Tropical savanna
■ Temperate desert
■ Tropical desert
■ Chaparral
■ Mountains

Biome Business

You have just been hired as an assistant to a world-famous botanist. You have been provided with climatographs for three biomes. A *climatograph* is a graph that shows the monthly temperature and precipitation of an area in a year.

You can use the information provided in the three graphs to determine what type of climate each biome has. Next to the climatograph for each biome is an unlabeled map of the biome. Using the maps and the information provided in the graphs, you must figure out what the environment is like in each biome. You can find the exact location of each biome by tracing the map of the biome and matching it to the map at the bottom of the page.

Procedure

1 Look at each climatograph. The shaded areas show the average precipitation for the biome. The red line shows the average temperature.

2 Use the climatographs to determine the climate patterns for each biome. Compare the map of each biome with the map below to find the exact location of each biome.

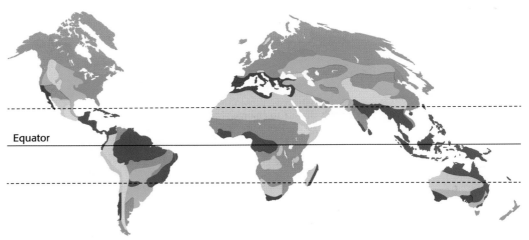

Equator

CHAPTER RESOURCES

Chapter Resource File
📁 • Datasheet for Chapter Lab
• Lab Notes and Answers

Technology
💿 **Classroom Videos**
• Lab Video

LabBook

• Global Impact
• For the Birds

David Sparks
Redwater Jr. High
Redwater, Texas

Analyze Results

1 **Analyzing Data** Describe the precipitation patterns of each biome by answering the following questions:

a. In which month does the biome receive the most precipitation?

b. Do you think that the biome is dry, or do you think that it is wet from frequent rains?

2 **Analyzing Data** Describe the temperature patterns of each biome by answering the following questions:

a. In the biome, which months are warmest?

b. Does the biome seem to have temperature cycles, like seasons, or is the temperature almost always the same?

c. Do you think that the biome is warm or cold? Explain.

Biome A

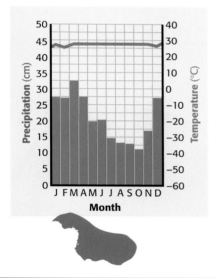

Month

Draw Conclusions

3 **Drawing Conclusions** Name each biome.

4 **Applying Conclusions** Where is each biome located?

Biome B

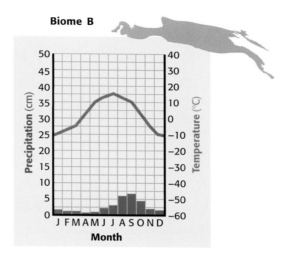

Month

Biome C

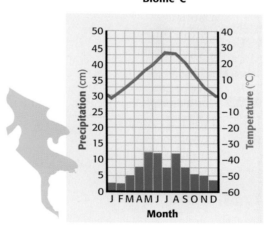

Month

Analyze the Results

1.a. In Biome A, the rain is heaviest in March. In Biome B, the rain is heaviest in September. In Biome C, the rain is heaviest in May.

b. Biome A is very wet. Biomes B and C are relatively dry, but some months are rainier than others.

2.a. Biome A has a relatively constant temperature throughout the year. Biomes B and C experience their warmest months from June to August.

b. Biome A has a constant temperature throughout the year. Biomes B and C experience temperature cycles.

c. Biome A is warm, and the temperature is high year-round. Biome B has a cooler climate, and the climatograph shows cooler temperatures year-round. Biome C has a moderate climate in the early and late months of the year, but the temperature is quite hot in the middle months of the year.

Draw Conclusions

3. Biome A is a tropical rain forest. Biome B is a taiga. Biome C is a temperate grassland.

4. Biome A is located on the western coast of Africa, near the equator. Biome B is located in northern Asia. Biome C is located in the midwestern United States.

CHAPTER RESOURCES

Workbooks

Whiz-Bang Demonstrations
• How Humid Is it? **GENERAL**

Long-Term Projects & Research Ideas
• Sun-Starved in Fairbanks **ADVANCED**

Calculator-Based Labs
• The Greenhouse Effect **ADVANCED**
• What Causes the Seasons? **ADVANCED**

Assignment Guide

SECTION	QUESTIONS
1	1, 6, 9, 12, 13, 18–20, 24–26
2	7
3	2, 8, 14, 15, 23
4	10, 16, 21,
1 and 2	3
1 and 4	4, 5, 17
2 and 3	11, 22

ANSWERS

Using Key Terms

1. Sample answer: A biome is one large region characterized by a specific type of climate, and the tropical zone is an even larger region, consisting of several biomes.

2. Sample answer: Weather is the condition of the atmosphere at a particular time, and climate is the average weather condition of an area.

3. Sample answer: The temperate zone is between the Tropics and the polar zone. The polar zone includes the North and South Poles and their surrounding areas.

4. global warming

5. microclimate

Understanding Key Ideas

6. d   9. c
7. a   10. c
8. b   11. b

USING KEY TERMS

For each pair of terms, explain how the meanings of the terms differ.

1 *biome* and *tropical zone*

2 *weather* and *climate*

3 *temperate zone* and *polar zone*

Complete each of the following sentences by choosing the correct term from the word bank.

biome   microclimate
ice age   global warming

4 One factor that could add to ___ is an increase in pollution.

5 A city is an example of a(n) ___.

UNDERSTANDING KEY IDEAS

Multiple Choice

6 Which of the following is a factor that affects climate?
   a. prevailing winds
   b. latitude
   c. ocean currents
   d. All of the above

7 The biome that has a temperature range of 28°C to 32°C and an average yearly precipitation of 100 cm is the
   a. tropical savanna.
   b. tropical desert.
   c. tropical rain forest.
   d. None of the above

8 Which of the following biomes is NOT found in the temperate zone?
   a. temperate forest
   b. taiga
   c. chaparral
   d. temperate grassland

9 In which of the following is the tilt of the Earth's axis considered to have an effect on climate?
   a. global warming
   b. the sun's cycle
   c. the Milankovitch theory
   d. asteroid impact

10 Which of the following substances contributes to the greenhouse effect?
   a. smoke
   b. smog
   c. carbon dioxide
   d. All of the above

11 In which of the following climate zones is the soil most fertile?
   a. the tropical climate zone
   b. the temperate climate zone
   c. the polar climate zone
   d. None of the above

---

12. Higher latitudes receive less solar radiation because the sun's rays strike the Earth's surface at a less direct angle. This spreads the same amount of solar energy over a larger area, resulting in lower temperatures.

13. The amount of precipitation an area receives can depend on whether the region's prevailing winds form from a warm air mass or from a cold air mass. If the winds form from a warm air mass, they will probably carry moisture. If the winds form from a cold air mass, they will probably be dry. Precipitation is more likely to occur when the prevailing winds are warm and moist.

14. Answers may vary. Sample answer: Alpine biomes on tropical mountains are examples of a microclimate. Less dense air at higher elevations retains less thermal energy and less precipitation than air at lower elevations.

15. The tundras and deserts receive very little precipitation.

16. Carbon dioxide is a greenhouse gas. Deforestation decreases the amount of trees, which naturally recycle carbon dioxide in the atmosphere. If the trees are burned, carbon dioxide will be released into the atmosphere, and global warming will increase.

Short Answer

12 Why do higher latitudes receive less solar radiation than lower latitudes do?

13 How does wind influence precipitation patterns?

14 Give an example of a microclimate. What causes the unique temperature and precipitation characteristics of this area?

15 How are tundras and deserts similar?

16 How does deforestation influence global warming?

CRITICAL THINKING

17 **Concept Mapping** Use the following terms to create a concept map: *global warming, deforestation, changes in climate, greenhouse effect, ice ages,* and *the Milankovitch theory.*

18 **Analyzing Processes** Explain how ocean surface currents cause milder climates.

19 **Identifying Relationships** Describe how the tilt of the Earth's axis affects seasonal changes in different latitudes.

20 **Evaluating Conclusions** Explain why the climate on the eastern side of the Rocky Mountains differs drastically from the climate on the western side.

21 **Applying Concepts** What are some steps you and your family can take to reduce the amount of carbon dioxide that is released into the atmosphere?

22 **Applying Concepts** If you wanted to live in a warm, dry area, which biome would you choose to live in?

23 **Evaluating Data** Explain why the vegetation in areas that have a tundra climate is sparse even though these areas receive precipitation that is adequate to support life.

INTERPRETING GRAPHICS

Use the diagram below to answer the questions that follow.

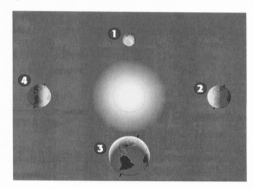

24 At what position—1, 2, 3, or 4—is it spring in the Southern Hemisphere?

25 At what position does the South Pole receive almost 24 hours of daylight?

26 Explain what is happening in each climate zone in both the Northern and Southern Hemispheres at position 4.

---

19. Sample answer: Due to the Earth's tilt, higher latitudes in the Northern Hemisphere receive more solar energy in June, July, and August, causing summer during that period. Because the Southern Hemisphere is tilted away from the sun during these months, higher latitudes in that hemisphere receive less direct solar energy, which causes winter.

20. Sample answer: The climate differs on each side of the Rocky Mountains because the mountains affect the distribution of precipitation. The western side receives more precipitation because, as the warm air is forced to rise, it releases precipitation. As the dry air crosses the mountain, it sinks, warming and absorbing moisture. Therefore, the eastern side is much warmer and drier.

21. Sample answer: conserve electricity, use public transportation, and plant trees

22. tropical savanna or tropical desert

23. Tundra soil is frozen for most of the year. In the summer, only the top meter thaws. The frozen soil underneath prevents the water from properly draining, which makes it difficult for some vegetation to grow.

Interpreting Graphics

24. 3

25. 2

26. In the tropical zone, temperatures are warm. The temperate zone in the Northern Hemisphere is experiencing summer. The temperate zone in the Southern Hemisphere is experiencing winter. The polar zone in the Northern Hemisphere is experiencing almost 24 hours of daylight. The polar zone in the Southern Hemisphere is experiencing almost 24 hours of night.

Critical Thinking

17. An answer to this exercise can be found at the end of this book.

18. Sample answer: Warm surface currents heat the surrounding air. A warm surface current might bring warmer temperatures to an area of land at a higher latitude that might normally be colder.

CHAPTER RESOURCES

Chapter Resource File

- Chapter Review **GENERAL**
- Chapter Test A **GENERAL**
- Chapter Test B **ADVANCED**
- Chapter Test C **SPECIAL NEEDS**
- Vocabulary Activity **GENERAL**

Workbooks

Study Guide
- Assessment resources are also available in Spanish.

Standardized Test Preparation

Teacher's Note

To provide practice under more realistic testing conditions, give students 20 minutes to answer all of the questions in this Standardized Test Preparation.

MISCONCEPTION ALERT

Answers to the standardized test preparation can help you identify student misconceptions and misunderstandings.

READING

Passage 1

1. C
2. G
3. C

TEST DOCTOR

Question 1: Some students may think the word *decipher* means "to question" or to "calculate" because students may relate these words to how scientists use computers to determine why climate changes, which is discussed in the passage.

Question 3: This fact is mentioned in the sentence: "For example, 6,000 years ago today's desert in North Africa was grassland and shallow lakes." If students chose A, they may not have realized that the climate of North Africa has changed.

Passage 2

1. C
2. F
3. A

READING

Read each of the passages below. Then, answer the questions that follow each passage.

Passage 1 Earth's climate has gone through many changes. For example, 6,000 years ago today's desert in North Africa was grassland and shallow lakes. Hippopotamuses, crocodiles, and early Stone Age people shared the shallow lakes that covered the area. For many years, scientists have known that Earth's climate has changed. What they didn't know was why it changed. Today, scientists can use supercomputers and complex computer programs to help them find the answer. Now, scientists may be able to <u>decipher</u> why North Africa's lakes and grasslands became a desert. And that information may be useful for predicting future heat waves and ice ages.

1. In this passage, what does *decipher* mean?
   - **A** to question
   - **B** to cover up
   - **C** to explain
   - **D** to calculate

2. According to the passage, which of the following statements is true?
   - **F** Scientists did not know that Earth's climate has changed.
   - **G** Scientists have known that Earth's climate has changed.
   - **H** Scientists have known why Earth's climate has changed.
   - **I** Scientists know that North Africa was always desert.

3. Which of the following is a fact in the passage?
   - **A** North African desert areas never had lakes.
   - **B** North American desert areas never had lakes.
   - **C** North African desert areas had shallow lakes.
   - **D** North Africa is covered with shallow lakes.

Passage 2 El Niño, which is Spanish for "the child," is the name of a weather event that occurs in the Pacific Ocean. Every 2 to 12 years, the interaction between the ocean surface and atmospheric winds creates El Niño. This event influences weather patterns in many regions of the world. For example, in Indonesia and Malaysia, El Niño meant <u>drought</u> and forest fires in 1998. Thousands of people in these countries suffered respiratory ailments caused by breathing the smoke from these fires. Heavy rains in San Francisco created extremely high mold-spore counts. These spores caused problems for people who have allergies. In San Francisco, the spore count in February is usually between 0 and 100. In 1998, the count was often higher than 8,000.

1. In this passage, what does *drought* mean?
   - **A** windy weather
   - **B** stormy weather
   - **C** long period of dry weather
   - **D** rainy weather

2. What can you infer about mold spores from reading the passage?
   - **F** Some people in San Francisco are allergic to mold spores.
   - **G** Mold spores are only in San Francisco.
   - **H** A higher mold-spore count helps people with allergies.
   - **I** The mold-spore count was low in 1998.

3. According to the passage, which of the following statements is true?
   - **A** El Niño causes droughts in Indonesia and Malaysia.
   - **B** El Niño occurs every year.
   - **C** El Niño causes fires in San Francisco.
   - **D** El Niño last occurred in 1998.

TEST DOCTOR

Question 1: If students chose B, they may think that *drought* means "stormy weather" because heavy rains were mentioned in the passage. However, droughts are long periods of dry weather.

The chart below shows types of organisms in an unknown biome. Use the chart below to answer the questions that follow.

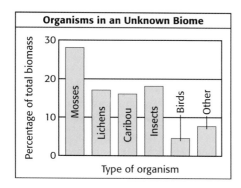

Organisms in an Unknown Biome

1. *Biomass* is a term that means "the total mass of all living things in a certain area." The graph above shows the relative percentages of the total biomass for different plants and animals in a given area. What type of biome does the graph represent?
   A rain forest
   B chaparral
   C tundra
   D taiga

2. Approximately what percentage of biomass is made up of caribou?
   F 28%
   G 25%
   H 16%
   I 5%

3. Approximately what percentage of biomass is made up of lichens and mosses?
   A 45%
   B 35%
   C 25%
   D 16%

Read each question below, and choose the best answer.

1. In a certain area of the savanna that is 12 km long and 5 km wide, there are 180 giraffes. How many giraffes are there per square kilometer in this area?
   A 12
   B 6
   C 4
   D 3

2. If the air temperature near the shore of a lake measures 24°C and the temperature increases by 0.055°C every 10 m traveled away from the lake, what would the air temperature 1 km from the lake be?
   F 5°C
   G 25°C
   H 29.5°C
   I 35°C

3. In a temperate desert, the temperature dropped from 50°C at noon to 37°C by nightfall. By how many degrees Celsius did the noon temperature drop?
   A 13°C
   B 20°C
   C 26°C
   D 50°C

4. Earth is tilted on its axis at a 23.5° angle. What is the measure of the angle that is complementary to a 23.5° angle?
   F 66.5°
   G 67.5°
   H 156.5°
   I 336.5°

5. After a volcanic eruption, the average temperature in a region dropped from 30°C to 18°C. By what percentage did the temperature drop?
   A 30%
   B 25%
   C 40%
   D 15%

Standardized Test Preparation

1. C
2. H
3. A

 **TEST DOCTOR**

Question 3: Letter A is the total percentage of biomass for lichens and mosses. If students chose D, they chose the percentage of biomass only for lichens.

1. D
2. H
3. C
4. H
5. C

TEST DOCTOR

Question 2: If students chose B, they probably did not convert 1 km to meters before calculating how much the temperature increased.

Question 4: If students chose I, they subtracted 23.5° from 360°. Students should subtract 23.5° from 180° to get the supplementary angle, which is H, 156.5°.

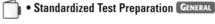

CHAPTER RESOURCES

Chapter Resource File

• Standardized Test Preparation GENERAL

Workbooks

North Carolina Standardized Test Preparation
• Provides practice for the EOG test.

State Resources

For specific resources for your state, visit **go.hrw.com** and type in the keyword **HSMSTR**.

Scientific Debate

Debate — GENERAL

Organize the class into two teams. Have each team research global warming. After their research is complete, have each team prepare a position paper which states and supports their stance on the issues central to global warming. Using their position papers, have the teams engage in a debate about global warming. **LS Interpersonal**

Science, Technology, and Society

ACTIVITY — GENERAL

Have students design a model of an ice core. Have students fill a plastic foam cup one-third full with water. Place the cup of water in the freezer overnight. Add about 2 cm of water to the cup of frozen water. Then sprinkle ashes into the water to simulate the debris released from a volcanic eruption. Have the students put the cup in the freezer overnight again. Students may continue to add layers to their ice core to simulate conditions such as acid rain. Make sure students record each layer and mark the layer on the plastic foam cup. When the cup is filled, have students carefully remove the ice from the cup and analyze their findings. **LS Kinesthetic**

Science in Action

Scientific Debate

Global Warming

Many scientists believe that pollution from burning fossil fuels is causing temperatures on Earth to rise. Higher average temperatures can cause significant changes in climate. These changes may make survival difficult for animals and plants that have adapted to a biome.

However, other scientists believe that there isn't enough evidence to prove that global warming exists. They argue that any increase in temperatures around the world can be caused by a number of factors other than pollution, such as the sun's cycle.

Language Arts ACTIVITY

WRITING SKILL Read articles that present a variety of viewpoints on global warming. Then, write your own article supporting your viewpoint on global warming.

Science, Technology, and Society

Ice Cores

How do scientists know what Earth's climate was like thousands of years ago? Scientists learn about Earth's past climates by studying ice cores. An ice core is collected by drilling a tube of ice from glaciers and polar ice sheets. Layers in the ice core contain substances that landed in the snow during a particular year or season, such as dust from desert storms, ash from volcanic eruptions, and carbon dioxide from pollution. By studying the layers of the ice cores, scientists can learn what factors influenced the past climates.

Math ACTIVITY

An area has an average yearly rainfall of 20 cm. In 1,000 years, if the average yearly rainfall decreases by 6%, what would the new average yearly rainfall be?

Answer to Language Arts Activity
Students should supply articles with a variety of viewpoints on global warming.

Answer to Math Activity
20 cm × 0.06 = 1.2 cm
20 cm − 1.2 cm = 18.8 cm

People in Science

Mercedes Pascual

Climate Change and Disease Mercedes Pascual is a theoretical ecologist at the University of Michigan. Pascual has been able to help the people of Bangladesh save lives by using information about climate changes to predict outbreaks of the disease cholera. Cholera can be a deadly disease that people usually contract by drinking contaminated water. Pascual knew that in Bangladesh, outbreaks of cholera peak every 3.7 years. She noticed that this period matches the frequency of the El Niño Southern Oscillations, which is a weather event that occurs in the Pacific Ocean. El Niño affects weather patterns in many regions of the world, including Bangladesh. El Niño increases the temperatures of the sea off the coast of Bangladesh. Pascual found that increased sea temperatures lead to higher numbers of the bacteria that cause cholera. In turn, more people contract cholera. But because of the research conducted by Pascual and other scientists, the people of Bangladesh can better predict and prepare for outbreaks of cholera.

Social Studies ACTIVITY

WRITING SKILL Research the effects of El Niño. Write a report describing El Niño and its affect on a country other than Bangladesh.

go.hrw.com
To learn more about these Science in Action topics, visit go.hrw.com and type in the keyword HZ5CLMF.

Current Science
Check out Current Science® articles related to this chapter by visiting go.hrw.com. Just type in the keyword HZ5CS17.

People in Science

Teaching Strategy · GENERAL

Tell students that cholera is caused by a bacterium that infects the intestines and causes diarrhea and vomiting. If the infection is severe, death may result from dehydration. Encourage students to find out more about cholera, the areas where it is most prevalent, and the ways that it can be controlled. **LS Intrapersonal**

Answer to Social Studies Activity

Many areas of the world are affected by El Niño. For example, El Niño causes droughts in Southeast Asia. Students may also find that El Niño affects the rate of other diseases such as dengue fever and malaria.

Human Body Systems

Like a finely tuned machine, your body is made up of many systems that work together. Your lungs take in oxygen. Your brain reacts to things you see, hear, and smell and sends signals through your nervous system that cause you to react to those things. Your digestive system converts the food you eat into energy that the cells of your body can use. And those are just a few things that your body can do!

In this unit, you will study the systems of your body. You'll discover how the parts of your body work together.

Around 3000 BCE

Ancient Egyptian doctors are the first to study the human body scientifically.

1824

Jean Louis Prevost and Jean Batiste Dumas prove that sperm is essential for fertilization.

1766

Albrecht von Haller determines that nerves control muscle movement and that all nerves are connected to the spinal cord or to the brain.

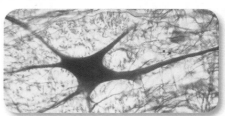

1940

During World War II in Italy, Rita Levi-Montalcini is forced to leave her work at a medical school laboratory because she is Jewish. She sets up a laboratory in her bedroom and studies the development of the nervous system.

Around 500 BCE

Indian surgeon Susrata performs operations to remove cataracts.

1492

Christopher Columbus lands in the West Indies.

1543

Andreas Vesalius publishes the first complete description of the structure of the human body.

1616

William Harvey discovers that blood circulates and that the heart acts as a pump.

1893

Daniel Hale Williams, an African American surgeon, becomes the first person to repair a tear in the pericardium, the sac around the heart.

1922

Frederick Banting, Charles Best, and John McLeod discover insulin.

1930

Karl Landsteiner receives a Nobel Prize for his discovery of the four human blood types.

1982

Dr. William DeVries implants an artificial heart in Barney Clark.

1998

The first sucessful hand transplant is performed in France.

2001

Drs. Laman A. Gray, Jr. and Robert D. Dowling at Jewish Hospital in Louisville, Kentucky, implant the first self-contained mechanical human heart.

Compression guide:
To shorten instruction because of time limitations, omit Section 1.

OBJECTIVES	LABS, DEMONSTRATIONS, AND ACTIVITIES	TECHNOLOGY RESOURCES
PACING • 90 min pp. 146–153 **Chapter Opener**	**SE** Start-up Activity, p. 147 `GENERAL`	**OSP** Parent Letter `GENERAL` **CD** Student Edition on CD-ROM **CD** Guided Reading Audio CD **TR** Chapter Starter Transparency* **VID** Brain Food Video Quiz
Section 1 Introduction to Body Systems • Describe homeostasis and what happens when it is disrupted. • Describe how tissues, organs, and organ systems are related. • List 12 organ systems. • Identify how organ systems work together to maintain homeostasis.	**TE** Group Activity Homeostasis Analogies, p. 149 `BASIC` **TE** Connection Activity History, p. 151 `ADVANCED`	**CRF** Lesson Plans* **TR** Bellringer Transparency* **TR** Organ Systems* **CRF** SciLinks Activity* `GENERAL`
PACING • 45 min pp. 154–157 **Section 2 The Skeletal System** • Identify the major organs of the skeletal system. • Describe four functions of bones. • Describe three joints. • List three injuries and two diseases that affect bones and joints.	**TE** Activity Locating Bones, p. 154 `GENERAL` **SE** Quick Lab Pickled Bones, p. 155 ◆ `GENERAL` **CRF** Datasheet for Quick Lab* **TE** Demonstration Bone Dissection, p. 155 ◆ `BASIC`	**CRF** Lesson Plans* **TR** Bellringer Transparency* **TR** The Skeleton* **TR** *LINK TO PHYSICAL SCIENCE* Machines Change the Size and/or Direction of a Force*
PACING • 45 min pp. 158–161 **Section 3 The Muscular System** • List three kinds of muscle tissue. • Describe how skeletal muscles move bones. • Compare aerobic exercise with resistance exercise. • Describe two muscular system injuries.	**TE** Group Activity Poster Project, p. 158 `GENERAL` **SE** School-to-Home Activity Power in Pairs, p. 159 `GENERAL` **TE** Demonstration Muscle Contraction, p. 159 `BASIC` **SE** Connection to Chemistry Muscle Function, p. 160 `GENERAL` **SE** Inquiry Lab Muscles at Work, p. 594 ◆ `GENERAL` **CRF** Datasheet for LabBook* **LB** Inquiry Labs On a Wing and a Layer* ◆ `GENERAL`	**CRF** Lesson Plans* **TR** Bellringer Transparency* **TR** A Pair of Muscles in the Arm*
PACING • 90 min pp. 162–165 **Section 4 The Integumentary System** • List four functions of skin. • Describe the two layers of skin. • Describe the structure and function of hair and nails. • Describe two kinds of damage that can affect skin.	**TE** Activity Measuring Temperature, p. 163 ◆ `GENERAL` **TE** Connection Activity Real World, p. 164 `GENERAL` **SE** Skills Practice Lab Seeing Is Believing, p. 166 `GENERAL` **CRF** Datasheet for Chapter Lab* **SE** Science in Action Math, Social Studies, and Language Arts Activities, pp. 172–173 `GENERAL` **LB** Long-Term Projects & Research Ideas Mapping the Human Body* `ADVANCED`	**CRF** Lesson Plans* **TR** Bellringer Transparency* **TR** Structures of the Skin* **VID** Lab Videos for Life Science **TE** Internet Activity, p. 163 `GENERAL`

PACING • 90 min

CHAPTER REVIEW, ASSESSMENT, AND STANDARDIZED TEST PREPARATION

CRF Vocabulary Activity* `GENERAL`
SE Chapter Review, pp. 168–169 `GENERAL`
CRF Chapter Review* ■ `GENERAL`
CRF Chapter Tests A* ■ `GENERAL`, B* `ADVANCED`, C* `SPECIAL NEEDS`
SE Standardized Test Preparation, pp. 170–171 `GENERAL`
CRF Standardized Test Preparation* `GENERAL`
CRF Performance-Based Assessment* `GENERAL`
OSP Test Generator `GENERAL`
CRF Test Item Listing* `GENERAL`

Online and Technology Resources

Visit **go.hrw.com** for a variety of free resources related to this textbook. Enter the keyword **HT5R7BD1**.

Students can access interactive problem-solving help and active visual concept development with the *Holt Science and Technology* Online Edition available at **www.hrw.com**.

 Guided Reading Audio CD

These CDs are designed to help auditory learners and reluctant readers.

 Science Tutor CD-ROM

Excellent for remediation and test practice.

SKILLS DEVELOPMENT RESOURCES	SECTION REVIEW AND ASSESSMENT	STANDARDS CORRELATIONS
SE Pre-Reading Activity, p. 146 GENERAL **OSP** Science Puzzlers, Twisters & Teasers GENERAL		North Carolina Standard Course of Study
CRF Directed Reading A* BASIC, B* SPECIAL NEEDS **CRF** Vocabulary and Section Summary* GENERAL **SE** Reading Strategy Reading Organizer, p. 148 GENERAL **SE** Connection to Chemistry Adapting After Surgery, p. 149 GENERAL **TE** Reading Strategy Prediction Guide, p. 150 BASIC **TE** Inclusion Strategies, p. 151	**SE** Reading Checks, pp. 149, 150, 151, 152 GENERAL **TE** Reteaching, p. 152 BASIC **TE** Quiz, p. 152 GENERAL **TE** Alternative Assessment, p. 152 GENERAL **SE** Section Review,* p. 153 ■ GENERAL **CRF** Section Quiz* ■ GENERAL	4.02, 4.04, 4.05
CRF Directed Reading A* BASIC, B* SPECIAL NEEDS **CRF** Vocabulary and Section Summary* GENERAL **SE** Reading Strategy Reading Organizer, p. 154 GENERAL **SE** Connection to Environmental Science Bones from the Ocean, p. 156 GENERAL **MS** Math Skills for Science Mechanical Advantage* GENERAL **CRF** Reinforcement Worksheet The Hipbone's Connected to the… BASIC **CRF** Critical Thinking The Tissue Engineering Debate* ADVANCED	**SE** Reading Checks, pp. 155, 156 GENERAL **TE** Reteaching, p. 156 BASIC **TE** Quiz, p. 156 GENERAL **SE** Section Review,* p. 157 ■ GENERAL **TE** Alternative Assessment, p. 157 GENERAL **CRF** Section Quiz* ■ GENERAL	4.01, 4.02
CRF Directed Reading A* BASIC, B* SPECIAL NEEDS **CRF** Vocabulary and Section Summary* GENERAL **SE** Reading Strategy Discussion, p. 158 GENERAL **SE** Math Practice Runner's Time, p. 161 GENERAL **MS** Math Skills for Science The Unit Factor and Dimensional Analysis* GENERAL **CRF** Reinforcement Worksheet Muscle Map* BASIC	**SE** Reading Checks, pp. 159, 161 GENERAL **TE** Reteaching, p. 160 BASIC **TE** Quiz, p. 160 GENERAL **TE** Alternative Assessment, p. 160 GENERAL **TE** Homework, p. 160 ADVANCED **SE** Section Review,* p. 161 ■ GENERAL **CRF** Section Quiz* ■ GENERAL	4.01, 4.02; *LabBook:* 1.01, 1.02, 1.03, 1.05, 1.08
CRF Directed Reading A* BASIC, B* SPECIAL NEEDS **CRF** Vocabulary and Section Summary* GENERAL **SE** Reading Strategy Paired Summarizing, p. 162 GENERAL **TE** Inclusion Strategies, p. 163 **SE** Connection to Social Studies Using Hair, p. 164 GENERAL	**SE** Reading Checks, pp. 163, 164 GENERAL **TE** Reteaching, p. 164 BASIC **TE** Quiz, p. 164 GENERAL **TE** Alternative Assessment, p. 164 ADVANCED **SE** Section Review,* p. 165 ■ GENERAL **CRF** Section Quiz* ■ GENERAL	4.02; *Chapter Lab:* 1.05

One-Stop Planner® CD-ROM

This convenient CD-ROM includes:
- **Lab Materials QuickList Software**
- **Holt Calendar Planner**
- **Customizable Lesson Plans**
- **Printable Worksheets**
- **ExamView® Test Generator**

cnnstudentnews.com

Find the latest news, lesson plans, and activities related to important scientific events.

www.scilinks.org

Maintained by the **National Science Teachers Association.** See Chapter Enrichment pages for a complete list of topics.

Current Science®

Check out *Current Science* articles and activities by visiting the HRW Web site at **go.hrw.com.** Just type in the keyword **HL5CS22T.**

Classroom Videos

- **Lab Videos** demonstrate the chapter lab.
- **Brain Food Video Quizzes** help students review the chapter material.
- **CNN Videos** bring science into your students' daily life.

Visual Resources

CHAPTER STARTER TRANSPARENCY

This Really Happened!

BELLRINGER TRANSPARENCIES

Section: Introduction to Body Systems
Match the body system in the first column with the correct function in the second column:

1. respiratory system
2. muscular system
3. digestive system
4. circulatory system
5. endocrine system

a. regulates body functions
b. breaks down food
c. pumps blood
d. absorbs oxygen
e. moves bones

Record your answers in your **science journal**.

Section: The Skeletal System
Brainstorm some problems you would have if you lacked bones. Do you know any kinds of animals that don't have bones? Do you know of any animals that wear their "skeletons" on the outside of their bodies?

Record your answers in your **science journal**.

TEACHING TRANSPARENCIES

L78 — Organ Systems

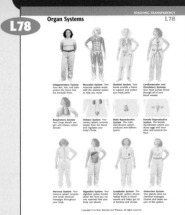

L79 — The Skeleton

TEACHING TRANSPARENCIES

L80 — A Pair of Muscles in the Arm

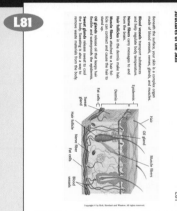

L81 — Structures of the Skin

P31 — Machines Change the Size and/or Direction of a Force

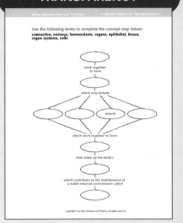

LINK TO PHYSICAL SCIENCE

Chapter: Work, Machines, and Energy

CONCEPT MAPPING TRANSPARENCY

Use the following terms to complete the concept map below:
connective, nervous, homeostasis, organs, epithelial, tissue, organ systems, cells

Planning Resources

LESSON PLANS

Lesson Plan — SAMPLE

Section: Waves

Pacing
Regular Schedule: with lab(s):2 days   without lab(s)1 days
Block Schedule: with lab(s):1 1/2 days   without lab(s)1 day

Objectives
1. Relate the seven properties of life to a living organism.
2. Describe seven themes that can help you to organize what you learn about biology.
3. Identify the tiny structures that make up all living organisms.
4. Differentiate between reproduction and heredity and between metabolism and homeostasis.

National Science Education Standards Covered
LSInter6:Cells have particular structures that underlie their functions.
LSMat1:Most cell functions involve chemical reactions.
LSBeh1:Cells store and use information to guide their functions.
UCP1:Cell functions are regulated.
SE1: Cells can differentiate and form complete multicellular organisms.
PS1: Species evolve over time.
ESS1: The great diversity of life is the result of more than 3.5 billion years of evolution.
ESS2: Natural selection and its evolutionary consequences provide a scientific explanation for the fossil record of ancient life forms as well as for the striking molecular similarities observed among the diverse species of living organisms.
ST1: The millions of different species of plants, animals, and microorganisms that live on Earth today are related by descent from common ancestors.
ST2: The energy for life primarily comes from the sun.
SPSP1: The complexity and organization of organisms accommodate the need for obtaining, transforming, transporting, releasing, and eliminating the matter and energy used to sustain the organism.
SPSP6: As matter and energy flows through different levels of organization of living systems—cells, organs, communities—and between living systems and the physical environment, chemical elements are recombined in different ways.
HNS1: Organisms have behavioral responses to internal changes and to external stimuli.

PARENT LETTER

SAMPLE

Dear Parent,

Your son's or daughter's science class will soon begin exploring the chapter entitled "The World of Physical Science." In this chapter, students will learn about how the scientific method applies to the world of physical science and the role of physical science in the world. By the end of the chapter, students should demonstrate a clear understanding of the chapter's main ideas and be able to discuss the following topics:

1. physical science as the study of energy and matter (Section 1)
2. the role of physical science in the world around them (Section 1)
3. careers that rely on physical science (Section 1)
4. the steps used in the scientific method (Section 2)
5. examples of technology (Section 2)
6. how the scientific method is used to answer questions and solve problems (Section 2)
7. how our knowledge of science changes over time (Section 2)
8. how models represent real objects or systems (Section 3)
9. examples of different ways models are used in science (Section 3)
10. the importance of the International System of Units (Section 4)
11. the appropriate units to use for particular measurements (Section 4)
12. how area and density are derived quantities (Section 4)

Questions to Ask Along the Way

You can help your son or daughter learn about these topics by asking interesting questions such as the following:

• What are some surprising careers that use physical science?
• What is a characteristic of a good hypothesis?
• When is it a good idea to use a model?
• Why do Americans measure things in terms of inches and yards instead of centimeters and meters?

TEST ITEM LISTING

TEST ITEM LISTING
The World of Science   SAMPLE

MULTIPLE CHOICE

1. A limitation of models is that
   a. they are large enough to see.
   b. they do not act exactly like the things that they model.
   c. they are smaller than the things that they model.
   d. they model unfamiliar things.
   Answer: B   Difficulty: 1   Section: 3   Objective: 2

2. The length 10 m is equal to
   a. 100 cm.   c. 10,000 mm.
   b. 1,000 cm.   d. Both (b) and (c)
   Answer: B   Difficulty: 1   Section: 3   Objective: 2

3. To be valid, a hypothesis must be
   a. testable.   c. made into a law.
   b. supported by evidence.   d. Both (a) and (b)
   Answer: B   Difficulty: 1   Section: 2   Objective: 2   1

4. The statement "Sheila has a stain on her shirt" is an example of a(n)
   a. law.   c. observation.
   b. hypothesis.   d. prediction.
   Answer: B   Difficulty: 1   Section: 3   Objective: 2

5. A hypothesis is often developed out of
   a. observations.   c. laws.
   b. experiments.   d. Both (a) and (b)
   Answer: B   Difficulty: 1   Section: 2   Objective: 2

6. How many milliliters are in 3.5 kL?
   a. 3,500 mL.   c. 3,500, 000 mL.
   b. 0.0035 mL.   d. 35,000 mL.
   Answer: B   Difficulty: 1   Section: 3   Objective: 2

7. A map of Seattle is an example of a
   a. law.   c. model.
   b. theory.   d. unit.
   Answer: B   Difficulty: 1   Section: 3   Objective: 2

8. A lab has the safety icons shown below. These icons mean that you should wear
   a. only safety goggles.   c. safety goggles and a lab apron.
   b. only a lab apron.   d. safety goggles, a lab apron, and gloves.
   Answer: B   Difficulty: 1   Section: 1   Objective: 2

9. The law of conservation of mass says that the tot al mass before a chemical change is
   a. more than the total mass after the change.
   b. less than the total mass after the change.
   c. the same as the total mass after the change.
   d. not the same as the total mass after the change.
   Answer: B   Difficulty: 1   Section: 3   Objective: 2

10. In which of the following areas might you find a geochemist at work?
    a. studying the chemistry of rocks   c. studying fishes
    b. studying kinetics   d. studying the atmosphere
    Answer: B   Difficulty: 1   Section: 3   Objective: 2

One-Stop Planner® CD-ROM

This CD-ROM includes all of the resources shown here and the following time-saving tools:

• **Lab Materials QuickList Software**
• **Customizable lesson plans**
• **Holt Calendar Planner**
• **The powerful ExamView® Test Generator**

For a preview of available worksheets covering math and science skills, see pages T26–T33. All of these resources are also on the One-Stop Planner®.

Meeting Individual Needs

DIRECTED READING A

Name _____ Class _____ Date _____
Skills Worksheet
Directed Reading A   SAMPLE

Section:
THAT'S SCIENCE!
1. How did James Czarnowski get his idea for the penguin boat, Proteus? Explain.

___ that is unusual about the way that Proteus moves through the water?

BASIC

DIRECTED READING B

Name _____ Class _____ Date _____
Skills Worksheet
Directed Reading B   SAMPLE

Section:
THAT'S SCIENCE!
1. How did James Czarnowski get his idea for the penguin boat, Proteus? Explain.

2. What is unusual about the way that Proteus moves through the water?

SPECIAL NEEDS PHYSICAL SCIENCE
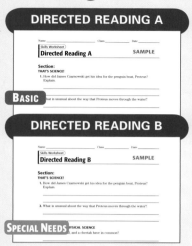

VOCABULARY ACTIVITY

Name _____ Class _____ Date _____
Activity
Vocabulary Activity   SAMPLE

Getting the Dirt on the Soil
After you finish reading the vocabulary words. Write your answer in the space provided.

___ breakdown of rock into ___ and smaller pieces
___ GNETH

9. the chemical breakdown of rocks and minerals into new substances CAMILCHE THEAIRGWEN

GENERAL
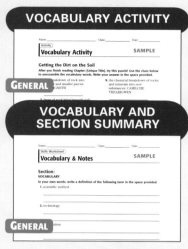

VOCABULARY AND SECTION SUMMARY

Name _____ Class _____ Date _____
Skills Worksheet
Vocabulary & Notes   SAMPLE

Section:
VOCABULARY
In your own words, write a definition of the following term in the space provided.

1. scientific method

2. technology

GENERAL

REINFORCEMENT

Name _____ Class _____ Date _____
Skills Worksheet
Reinforcement   SAMPLE

The Plane Truth
Complete this worksheet after you finish reading the Section: [Unique Section Title]

You plan to enter a paper airplane contest sponsored by Talkin' Physical Science magazine. The person whose airplane flies the farthest wins a lifetime subscription to the magazine! The week before the contest you watch an airplane landing at a nearby ___. You notice that the wings of the airplane have ___, as shown in the illustration at right. The paper airplanes you've been testing do not have wing flaps. What question would you ask yourself based on these observations? Write your question in the space below.

BASIC
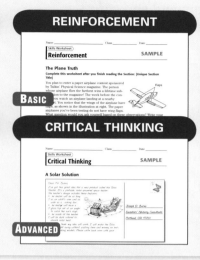

CRITICAL THINKING

Name _____ Class _____ Date _____
Skills Worksheet
Critical Thinking   SAMPLE

A Solar Solution

ADVANCED
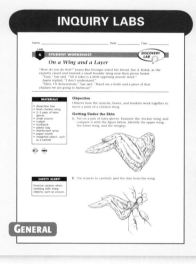

SCILINKS ACTIVITY

Name _____ Class _____ Date _____
Activity
SciLinks Activity   SAMPLE

MARINE ECOSYSTEMS
Go to www.scilinks.com. To find links related to marine ecosystems, type in the keyword HL5450. Then, use the links to answer the questions about marine ecosys-

___ percentage of the Earth's surface is covered by water?

GENERAL
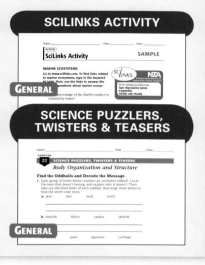

SCIENCE PUZZLERS, TWISTERS & TEASERS

Name _____ Date _____ Class _____
CHAPTER
22 **SCIENCE PUZZLERS, TWISTERS & TEASERS**
Body Organization and Structure

Find the Oddballs and Decode the Message
1. Each group of terms below contains an unrelated oddball. Circle the term that doesn't belong, and explain why it doesn't. Then take out the third letter of each oddball. Rearrange those letters to find the secret code word.
   a. skin   hair   nails   teeth

   b. smooth   flexor   cardiac   skeletal

   ___ joint   ligament   cartilage

GENERAL

Labs and Activities

LONG-TERM PROJECTS & RESEARCH IDEAS

Name _____ Date _____ Class _____
PROJECT
22 **STUDENT WORKSHEET**   DESIGN YOUR OWN
Mapping the Human Body

How would you make a three-dimensional map of every centimeter of a human body? The scientists working on the National Library of Medicine's *Visible Human Project* figured out an incredible way to do it. The project has produced accurate computer-generated images of two human beings—the *Visible Human Male* and the *Visible Human Female*.

INTERNET KEYWORDS
Visible Human Project
Visible Human Male
Visible Human Female

The Visible Human Project
1. Use the Internet or library resources to find out more about how these models of the human body were created. How will these models be used? Write a science article about the Visible Human Project.

Other Research Ideas
2. Did you know that some amputees feel sensations in their amputated limbs? Research *ghost limb syndrome* or *phantom limb syndrome*, a common condition among amputees. What are the symptoms of this condition? What do doctors and researchers think are the causes of this condition? How can phantom limb syndrome be treated? Present your findings to the class.
3. Did you know that octopuses have three hearts? Why are some organs, such as your kidneys and lungs, duplicated, while others, such as your heart, brain, and liver, are not? Compare human anatomy with the anatomy of two animals that aren't mammals. Make a poster display to illustrate your findings.

Long-Term Projects
4. Surgery once required the use of large incisions and large scalpels, but a type of surgery called arthroscopic surgery uses very small incisions and surgical tools that are only 3–4 mm across? Find out more about arthroscopic surgery. What types of injuries is it used for? How effective is it? Interview some people who have had this type of surgery, and write an article about their experiences.
5. Have you ever noticed that some athletes get injured more than others, even though they participate in the same sport? Interview a doctor or other health professional who treats sports-related injuries. Ask about problems that can be avoided by healthy habits and fitness training. Create a pamphlet that outlines some common injuries and ways to prevent them.

ADVANCED
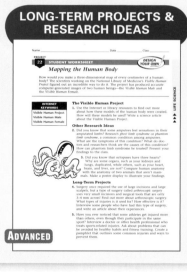

INQUIRY LABS

Name _____ Date _____ Class _____
LAB
6 **STUDENT WORKSHEET**   DISCOVERY LAB
On a Wing and a Layer

"How do you do that?" Juana Bea Stronger asked her friend, Sue A. Robik, as the expertly raised and lowered a small boulder lying near their picnic basket.
"Easy," Sue said. "All it takes is a little opposing muscle work."
"Here, I'll demonstrate," Sue said. "Hand me a knife and a piece of that chicken we are going to barbecue?"

MATERIALS
- dissection tray
- fresh chicken wing
- 2–3 pairs of latex gloves
- small scissors
- scalpel
- toothpick
- plastic bag
- disinfectant spray
- paper towels
- weighted object, such as a barbell

Objective
Observe how the muscles, bones, and tendons work together to move a joint of a chicken wing.

Getting Under the Skin
1. Put on a pair of latex gloves. Examine the chicken wing, and compare it with the figure below. Identify the upper wing, the lower wing, and the wingtip.

SAFETY ALERT!
Exercise caution when working with sharp objects, such as scissors.

2. Use scissors to carefully peel the skin from the wing.

GENERAL

DATASHEETS FOR QUICK LABS

TEACHER RESOURCE PAGE
Name _____ Class _____ Date _____
Quick Lab   DATASHEET FOR QUICK LAB
Reaction to Stress   SAMPLE

Background
The graph below illustrates changes that occur in the membrane potential of a neuron during an action potential. Use the graph to answer the following questions. Refer to Figure 3 as needed.

DATASHEETS FOR CHAPTER LABS

TEACHER RESOURCE PAGE
Name _____ Class _____ Date _____
Skills Practice Lab   DATASHEET FOR CHAPTER LAB
Using Scientific Methods   SAMPLE

Teacher's Notes
TIME REQUIRED

DATASHEETS FOR LABBOOK

TEACHER RESOURCE PAGE
Name _____ Class _____ Date _____
Skills Practice Lab   DATASHEET FOR LABBOOK LAB
Does It All Add Up?   SAMPLE

Teacher's Notes
TIME REQUIRED
One 45-minute class period.

Review and Assessments

SECTION QUIZ

Name _____ Class _____ Date _____
Assessment
Section Quiz   SAMPLE

Section:
In the space provided, write the letter of the description that best matches the term or phrase.

___ 1. building molecules that can be used as an energy source or breaking down molecules in which energy is stored
___ ___ the process by which light energy is converted to chemical energy
___ 3. an organism that uses sunlight or inorganic substances to make organic compounds

ALSO IN SPANISH

GENERAL

SECTION REVIEW

Name _____ Class _____ Date _____
Skills Worksheet
Section Review   SAMPLE

Section:
KEY TERMS
1. What do paleontologists study?

2. How does a trace fossil differ from petrified wood?

___ fossil.

UNDERSTANDING KEY IDEAS

ALSO IN SPANISH

GENERAL

CHAPTER REVIEW

Name _____ Class _____ Date _____
Skills Worksheet
Chapter Review   SAMPLE

USING VOCABULARY
1. Define biome in your own words.

2. Describe the characteristics of a savanna and a desert.

___ the relationship between taxis and symbol?

ALSO IN SPANISH

GENERAL
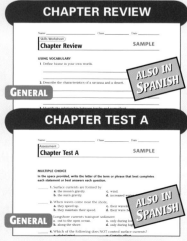

CHAPTER TEST A

Name _____ Class _____ Date _____
Assessment
Chapter Test A   SAMPLE

MULTIPLE CHOICE
In the space provided, write the letter of the term or phrase that best completes each statement or best answers each question.

___ 1. Surface currents are formed by
   a. the moon's gravity.   c. wind.
   b. the sun's gravity.   d. increased water density.
___ 2. When waves come near the shore,
   a. they speed up.   c. their wavelength increases.
   b. they maintain their speed.   d. their wave height increases.

ALSO IN SPANISH

GENERAL
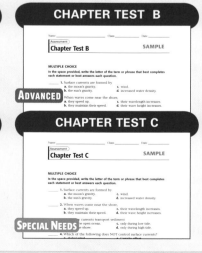

CHAPTER TEST B

Name _____ Class _____ Date _____
Assessment
Chapter Test B   SAMPLE

MULTIPLE CHOICE
In the space provided, write the letter of the term or phrase that best completes each statement or best answers each question.

___ 1. Surface currents are formed by
   a. the moon's gravity.   c. wind.
   b. the sun's gravity.   d. increased water density.
___ 2. When waves come near the shore,
   a. they speed up.   c. their wavelength increases.
   b. they maintain their speed.   d. their wave height increases.

ADVANCED

CHAPTER TEST C

Name _____ Class _____ Date _____
Assessment
Chapter Test C   SAMPLE

MULTIPLE CHOICE
In the space provided, write the letter of the term or phrase that best completes each statement or best answers each question.

___ 1. Surface currents are formed by
   a. the moon's gravity.   c. wind.
   b. the sun's gravity.   d. increased water density.
___ 2. When waves come near the shore,
   a. they speed up.   c. their wavelength increases.
   b. they maintain their speed.   d. their wave height increases.
___ 3. Longshore currents transport sediment
   a. out to the open ocean.   c. only during low tide.
   b. along the shore.   d. only during high tide.
___ 4. Which of the following does NOT control surface currents?

SPECIAL NEEDS

STANDARDIZED TEST PREPARATION

Name _____ Class _____ Date _____
Assessment
Standardized Test Preparation   SAMPLE

READING
Read the passages below. Then, read each question that follows the passage. Decide which is the best answer to each question.

Passage 1 adventures summer camp in the world. Billy can't ___ to head for the outdoors. Billy checked the recommended gear list: light, summer clothes; sunscreen; rain gear; heavy, two-billed jacket; ski mask; and thick gloves. Wait a minute? Billy thought he was traveling to only one **destination**, so why does he need to bring such a wide variety of clothes? On further investiga-

GENERAL

PERFORMANCE-BASED ASSESSMENT

Name _____ Class _____ Date _____
Assessment
Performanced-Based Assessment   SKILL BUILDER SAMPLE

OBJECTIVE
Determine which factors cause some sugar shapes to break down faster than others.

KNOW THE SCORE!
As you work through the activity, keep in mind that you will be earning a grade for the following:
- how you form and test the hypothesis (30%)
- the quality of your analysis (40%)
- the clarity of your conclusions (30%)

Using Scientific Methods
QUESTIONS
___ sugar shapes erode more rapidly than others?

MATERIALS AND EQUIPMENT
- 1 regular sugar cube
- 90 mL of water

GENERAL
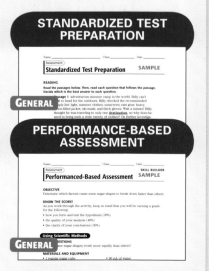

This Chapter Enrichment provides relevant and interesting information to expand and enhance your presentation of the chapter material.

Section 1

Introduction to Body Systems

Tissues

- Tissues differ from each other in terms of the shape and size of cells, the amount and kind of material between the cells, and the special functions the tissues perform to maintain proper functioning of the body.

- Connective tissue is the most abundant tissue in the body. It displays the most variety in form and type. All connective tissue, however, can be classified into one of four types: dense connective tissue (cartilage and bone), loose connective tissue (found beneath the skin and around nerves, blood vessels, and organs), liquid connective tissue (blood and lymph), and adipose tissue (where the body stores energy as droplets of fat).

- Although bone is considerably harder than other body tissues, it accounts for only about 14% of a person's total body weight.

Section 2

The Skeletal System

The Human Skeleton

- The skeleton provides support for soft tissue. Also, it regulates body minerals and produces both red and white blood cells. There are typically 206 bones in the adult human body, but extra bones, particularly those in the hands and feet, can increase that number. The number of bones in children varies with age.

- The skeleton forms from more than 800 centers of ossification. All of the bony elements are generally not completely united to form an adult skeleton until a person reaches his or her mid-20s.

- The skeletons of male and female humans are slightly different. The most pronounced differences are in the pelvis. A female's pelvis is adapted for childbearing and thus has a larger pelvic inlet. Women who are malnourished during childhood typically do not develop the wider pelvis, which can make natural childbirth dangerous or even fatal for them.

- An individual's age can be determined by looking at the skeleton alone. A younger individual's dentition and bone fusion patterns indicate his or her age. In adults, age determination is more difficult because one must rely solely on signs of skeletal deterioration.

Bones

- Each bone is surrounded by a strong fibrous covering called a *periosteum*. Articular surfaces are covered in cartilage.

- Bones are made of three types of cells: osteoblasts, osteocytes, and osteoclasts. Osteoblasts are bone-producing cells. Osteocytes are bone-maintaining cells. Osteoclasts are bone-destroying cells.

- For its weight, bone is 5 times stronger than steel.

Joints

- Doctors typically classify joints by structure rather than movement. The three types of joint structures are called *fibrous*, *cartilaginous*, and *synovial*. Fibrous joints (such as those in the skull) are immovable joints in which a fibrous tissue or a hyaline cartilage connects the bones. Cartilaginous joints (such as those in the rib cage) are slightly moveable joints in which cartilage connects the bones. Synovial joints (such as the knee) are freely moving joints in which synovial membranes cover the cartilage and ligaments connecting the bone.

Section 3

The Muscular System

Skeletal Muscles

- There are more than 600 skeletal muscles in the human body. They are often organized into the following groups: muscles of the head and the neck, muscles of the trunk, muscles of the upper limbs, and muscles of the lower limbs.

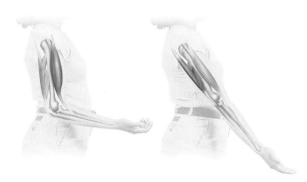

Types of Muscle Cells

- When observed through a microscope, the three types of muscles are clearly identifiable. Cells of smooth muscles have a long, tapered shape; no clearly defined striations; and a large central nucleus. Skeletal muscle cells are long and tapered and characterized by distinct light- and dark-colored bands. Each cell has multiple nuclei because several skeletal muscle cells merge, and the cell membranes become indistinct. The cells of cardiac muscle have one or more nuclei and have an irregular, branched shape.

Section 4

The Integumentary System

Skin

- One square inch of skin can hold as many as 650 sweat glands, 20 blood vessels, and more than 1,000 nerve endings.

- Each person has a unique series of ridges and indentations called *fingerprints* on the tips of his or her fingers. No two people have the same fingerprints. Fingerprints help the fingers to grip slippery surfaces. Each person also has unique patterns on the tips of his or her toes.

Is That a Fact!

- More than three-fourths of the dust in some homes is made up of dead skin cells!

Hair and Nails

- Only mammals have true hair. All mammals have hair somewhere on their bodies.

- The body's most visible signs of aging occur in the integumentary system. Skin becomes thin, dry, wrinkled, and less supple. Dark-colored age spots may develop. Hair turns gray or white and may begin to fall out. Hair follicles decrease in number. Sweat glands become less active, so older people are less tolerant to extremely hot weather.

- Hair that is kept short grows an average of 2 cm per month. Growth slows to about 1 cm per month when hair reaches about 30 cm long. Fingernails grow about 2 cm each year. The fastest-growing nail is on the middle finger. Fingernails grow three to four times more quickly than toenails do.

SciLINKS

Developed and maintained by the
National Science Teachers Association

SciLinks is maintained by the National Science Teachers Association to provide you and your students with interesting, up-to-date links that will enrich your classroom presentation of the chapter.

Visit www.scilinks.org and enter the SciLinks code for more information about the topic listed.

Topic: Tissues and Organs
SciLinks code: HSM1530

Topic: Muscular System
SciLinks code: HSM1008

Topic: Body Systems
SciLinks code: HSM0184

Topic: Integumentary System
SciLinks code: HSM0803

Topic: Skeletal System
SciLinks code: HSM1399

Overview

Tell students that this chapter will help them learn about human body systems. In particular, the chapter will introduce students to the skeletal, muscular, and integumentary systems.

Assessing Prior Knowledge

Students should be familiar with the following topics:

• cells

• body organization

Identifying Misconceptions

As students learn the material in this chapter, some of them may be confused about the concept of homeostasis. Students should understand that homeostasis is a state in which the internal environment of the human body is stable. Help students understand that because the external environment is always changing, the human body must adjust to these changes to maintain homeostasis within the body. Students should also understand that all cells in the body play a role in homeostasis, but because there are many kinds of cells, no single cell has to do all of the jobs necessary for homeostasis.

Body Organization and Structure

About the PHOTO

Lance Armstrong has won the Tour de France several times. These victories are especially remarkable because he was diagnosed with cancer in 1996. But with medicine and hard work, he grew strong enough to win one of the toughest events in all of sports.

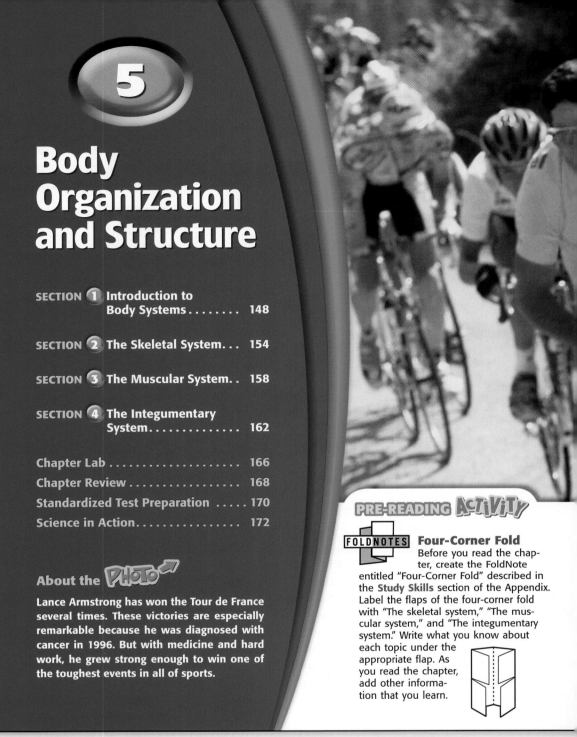

PRE-READING ACTIVITY

FOLDNOTES **Four-Corner Fold**
Before you read the chapter, create the FoldNote entitled "Four-Corner Fold" described in the **Study Skills** section of the Appendix. Label the flaps of the four-corner fold with "The skeletal system," "The muscular system," and "The integumentary system." Write what you know about each topic under the appropriate flap. As you read the chapter, add other information that you learn.

Standards Correlations

North Carolina Standard Course of Study

1.01 Identify and create questions and hypotheses that can be answered through scientific investigations. (LabBook)

1.02 (partial) Develop appropriate experimental procedures for: . . . Student generated questions. (LabBook)

1.03 Apply safety procedures in the laboratory and in field studies, Recognize potential hazards, Safely manipulate materials and equipment, [and] Conduct appropriate procedures. (LabBook)

1.05 Analyze evidence to: Explain observations, Make inferences and predictions, [and] Develop the relationship between evidence and explanation. (Chapter Lab and LabBook)

1.08 Use oral and written language to: Communicate findings, [and] Defend conclusions of scientific investigations. (LabBook)

4.01 (partial) Analyze how human body systems interact to provide for the needs of the human organism: Muscular-skeletal. (Sections 2 and 3)

Safety Caution: Students should clean up the water that results from the melting ice, especially if it drips onto the floor.

Answers

1. Answers may vary, but students should feel discomfort that is intense enough to make them want to drop the ice.

2. Answers may vary. Students' hands will return to normal at varying rates, but most students should answer that it took a few minutes.

3. Students should recognize that the integumentary, circulatory, and cardiovascular systems played roles in returning their hands to normal. Point out that the redness reflects an increased blood supply to the cold area. By bringing warmth to the hand, the blood helps to restore the hand to normal.

4. Answers may vary, but students should recognize that the nervous system detected the discomfort and sent signals to other body systems to respond. Some students may note that they jerked away from the discomfort.

START-UP ACTIVITY

Too Cold for Comfort

Your nervous system sends you messages about your body. For example, if someone steps on your toe, your nervous system sends you a message. The pain you feel is a message that tells you to move your toe to safety. Try this exercise to watch your nervous system in action.

Procedure

1. Hold **a few pieces of ice** in one hand. Allow the melting water to drip into a **dish.** Hold the ice until the cold is uncomfortable. Then, release the ice into the dish.

2. Compare the hand that held the ice with your other hand. Describe the changes you see.

Analysis

1. What message did you receive from your nervous system while you held the ice?

2. How quickly did the cold hand return to normal?

3. What organ systems do you think helped restore your hand to normal?

4. Think of a time when your nervous system sent you a message, such as an uncomfortable feeling of heat, cold, or pain. How did your body react?

4.02 Describe how systems within the human body are defined by the functions it performs. (Sections 1, 2, 3, and 4)

4.04 Evaluate how systems in the human body help regulate the internal environment. (Section 1)

4.05 Analyze how an imbalance in homeostasis may result from a disruption in any human system. (Section 1)

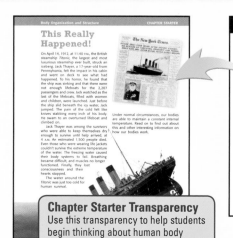

This Really Happened!

On April 14, 1912, at 11:40 P.M., the British steamship *Titanic*, the largest and most luxurious steamship ever built, struck an iceberg. Jack Thayer, a 17-year-old from Pennsylvania, felt the impact in his cabin and went on deck to see what had happened. To his horror, he found that the ship was sinking and that there were not enough lifeboats for the 2,207 passengers and crew. Jack watched as the last of the lifeboats, filled with women and children, were launched. Just before the ship slid beneath the icy water, Jack jumped. The pain of the cold felt like knives stabbing every inch of his body. He swam to an overturned lifeboat and climbed on.

Jack Thayer was among the survivors who were able to keep themselves dry enough to survive until help arrived, at 4 A.M. An estimated 1,500 people died. Even those who were wearing life jackets couldn't survive the extreme temperature of the water. The freezing water caused their body systems to fail. Breathing became difficult, and muscles no longer functioned. Finally, they lost consciousness and their hearts stopped.

The water around the *Titanic* was just too cold for human survival.

Under normal circumstances, our bodies are able to maintain a constant internal temperature. Read on to find out about this and other interesting information on how our bodies work.

Chapter Starter Transparency
Use this transparency to help students begin thinking about human body systems.

CHAPTER RESOURCES

Technology

 Transparencies
• Chapter Starter Transparency **READING SKILLS**

 Student Edition on CD-ROM

 Guided Reading Audio CD

 Classroom Videos
• Brain Food Video Quiz

Workbooks

Science Puzzlers, Twisters & Teasers
• Body Organization and Structure **GENERAL**

SECTION

1

Focus

Overview

This section describes homeostasis and introduces the basic organization of the human body. Students will learn about the four major tissues of the body and that the body's organs are arranged by function into 12 organ systems.

Bellringer

Write the names of the following organ systems on the board or an overhead projector: *respiratory system, muscular system, digestive system, cardiovascular system,* and *endocrine system.* Then, write the following functions: *to pump blood, to enable movement, to send out chemical messages, to absorb oxygen,* and *to break down food.* Ask students to match each organ system with its correct function. (The respiratory system absorbs oxygen. The muscular system enables movement. The digestive system breaks down food. The cardiovascular system pumps blood. The endocrine system sends out chemical messages.)

READING WARM-UP

Objectives

- Describe homeostasis and what happens when it is disrupted.
- Describe how tissues, organs, and organ systems are related.
- List 12 organ systems.
- Identify how organ systems work together to maintain homeostasis.

Terms to Learn

homeostasis
tissue
organ

READING STRATEGY

Reading Organizer As you read this section, make a concept map by using the terms above.

homeostasis the maintenance of a constant internal state in a changing environment

Introduction to Body Systems

Imagine jumping into a lake. At first, your body feels very cold. You may even shiver. But eventually you get used to the cold water. How does this happen?

Your body gets used to cold water because of homeostasis (HOH mee OH STAY sis). **Homeostasis** is the maintenance of a stable internal environment in the body. When you jump into a cold lake, homeostasis helps your body stay warm.

Staying in Balance

The environment around you is always changing. Your body has to adjust to these conditions. For example, generally, on a hot day, your body is able to react to maintain your body temperature and avoid overheating. As shown in **Figure 1,** all living organisms have to maintain homeostasis.

Maintaining homeostasis is not easy. Your body needs nutrients and oxygen. Your body needs wastes removed. And your body needs to defend itself against disease. A single cell cannot do all of these jobs for the entire body. Fortunately, your body has many kinds of cells. Some cells remove wastes. Other cells carry oxygen or defend your body against disease. Together, these cells help your internal environment stay stable.

Figure 1 *These penguins have adaptations that help them maintain homeostasis in the cold environment in which they live.*

CHAPTER RESOURCES

Chapter Resource File

- **Lesson Plan**
- **Directed Reading A** BASIC
- **Directed Reading B** SPECIAL NEEDS

Technology

Transparencies
- Bellringer

Falling Out of Balance

Sometimes, your body cannot maintain homeostasis. For example, if you don't eat the right foods, your cells may not get the nutrients they need. Maybe your body systems can't fight off a disease caused by bacteria or viruses. So, homeostasis is disrupted. What happens when homeostasis is disrupted? Cells may be damaged or may die. When this happens, you can become sick, as shown in **Figure 2.** Sometimes, people die when homeostasis is disrupted.

Temperature Regulation

When you are hot, your body gives off heat. You also sweat. When sweat evaporates from your skin, your body is cooled. Sweating is a process that helps your body maintain homeostasis. Sometimes, the body cannot cool down. This happens when cells do not get what they need, such as water for sweat. If the body gets too hot, cells may be damaged.

The body also has ways to keep you warm on cold days. When you are cold, you shiver, which helps you stay warm. Sometimes, the body cannot stay warm. Body temperature falls below normal in a condition called *hypothermia.*

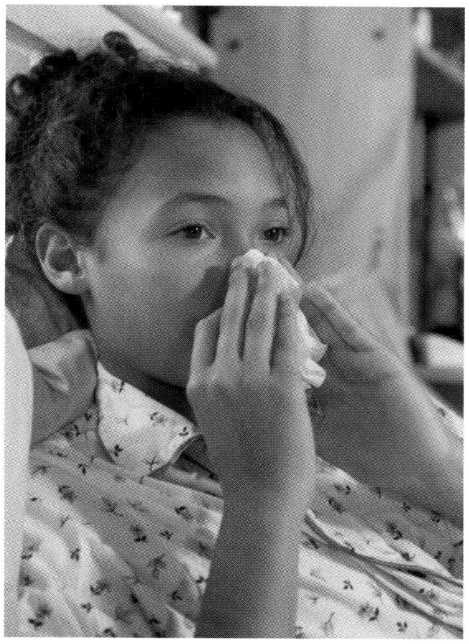

Figure 2 *When homeostasis is disrupted, a person can become sick.*

Moving Materials

Your cells need nutrients for life processes. If nutrients are not delivered, the cells cannot complete their life processes. So, the cells will die. These life processes often make wastes, which must be removed from cells. Many wastes are toxic. If a cell cannot get rid of them, the wastes will damage the cell.

Reading Check Explain the importance of moving materials into and out of cells. (*See the Appendix for answers to Reading Checks.*)

CONNECTION TO Chemistry

WRITING SKILL **Adapting After Surgery** People can survive the removal of some parts of the body. For example, doctors may remove a patient's gall bladder, spleen, or large intestine because of disease or injury. However, the patient's body must make adjustments to maintain a stable internal environment. Examine how the body adjusts to the loss of a body part due to disease or injury. Identify how the body changes in order to maintain a stable internal environment. In your **science journal,** write a newspaper article about your findings.

Is That a Fact!

The Pompeii worm, *Alvinella pompejana,* can survive a temperature difference of 60°C between its head and its tail! Scientists theorize that a coating of furry bacteria living on the worm's back allows the worm to endure such extreme temperature differences.

Answer to Reading Check

Cells need nutrients moved into the cells and wastes moved out of the cell in order to maintain homeostasis.

Motivate

Discussion ——— GENERAL

Homeostasis Before students read this section, ask them to relate what they know about how different animals adjust to outside temperatures. (Most students will likely relate how ectotherms and endotherms adjust body temperature.) Ask students how the idea of homeostasis fits into what they know about animals and temperature regulation. (Students should recognize that temperature regulation is a function of homeostasis.) **LS** Logical/Verbal

Teach

Group ACTIVITY — BASIC

Homeostasis Analogies Have students work in small groups. Ask students to make posters that use analogies to explain homeostasis. Encourage students to draw images and write explanations on their posters. For example, a poster could show a hot room and a thermostat that cools the room down to represent temperature regulation. Or, the poster could show a dumpster and a garbage truck to represent the removal of wastes from cells. Have students share their posters with the class. **LS** Visual/Logical

Answer to Connection to Chemistry

Answers may vary depending on the body part examined. Sample answer: The large intestine plays a role in water absorption. When it is removed, the body must adjust to ensure cells get enough water. Often, the small intestine takes on some of the roles of the large intestine.

READING STRATEGY — BASIC

Prediction Guide Before students read the pages that describe the body's tissues and organs, ask whether each of the following statements is true or false.

- Homeostasis is the body's ability to maintain a stable internal environment. (true)
- The human body has four main types of tissues. (true)
- An organ is a group of tissues that work together. (true)

LS Verbal

Debate — ADVANCED

Transplant Ethics Thousands of people in the United States are waiting for organ transplants. The average cost of an organ transplant is $120,000. Encourage students to research and debate the ethical issues surrounding transplants. The following are suggested topics:

- Should transplants happen at all?
- Who should get a transplant?
- Should a child receive a transplant before an older person does?

LS Logical/Interpersonal

Body Organization

As you may know, your body is made up of billions of cells. A cell is the basic unit of all living things. You have many kinds of cells. For example, you have muscle cells and nerve cells.

Cells Form Tissues

Various kinds of cells make up the parts of the body. These cells work together in much the same way that players on a soccer team do. Just as each person on a soccer team has a role during a game, each cell in your body has a job in maintaining homeostasis. For example, muscle cells are cells that can contract, or become shorter. They allow movement. Nerve cells receive and transmit electrical impulses, or messages.

A group of similar cells working together forms a **tissue.** Your body has four main kinds of tissue. The four kinds of tissue are shown in **Figure 3.** Each kind of tissue is made up of its own kind of cells. For example, muscle cells make up muscle tissue, and nerve cells make up nervous tissue.

Each kind of tissue may have variations based on the specific function of the tissue. For example, both bone and blood are kinds of connective tissue. However, the tissues differ. The connective tissue of bones supports the body and protects organs, so it is a solid. The connective tissue of blood moves throughout the body, so it is a liquid.

tissue a group of similar cells that perform a common function

✓ Reading Check How are cells and tissues related?

Figure 3 **Four Kinds of Tissue**

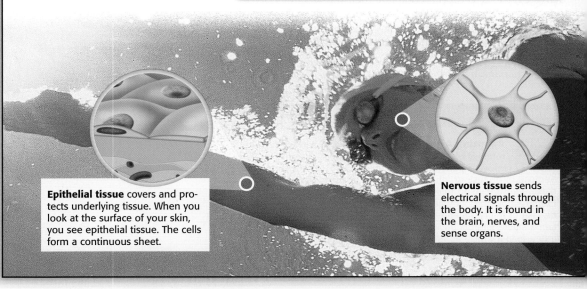

Epithelial tissue covers and protects underlying tissue. When you look at the surface of your skin, you see epithelial tissue. The cells form a continuous sheet.

Nervous tissue sends electrical signals through the body. It is found in the brain, nerves, and sense organs.

Answer to Reading Check
A group of similar cells that work together form tissues.

CONNECTION to Art — ADVANCED

Leonardo da Vinci Leonardo da Vinci studied the human body in detail. He believed that every structure had a specific function. He drew many sketches of the body from different points of view. Have interested students examine da Vinci's paintings and drawings and compare them to modern medical images of the human body. **LS** Visual

Figure 4 — Organization of the Stomach

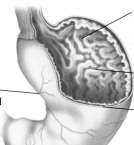

The stomach is an organ. The four kinds of tissue work together so that the stomach can carry out digestion.

Nervous tissue in the stomach partly controls the production of acids that aid in the digestion of food. Nervous tissue signals when the stomach is full.

Epithelial tissue lines the stomach.

Blood and another **connective tissue** called *collagen* are found in the wall of the stomach.

Layers of **muscle tissue** break up and mix stomach contents.

Tissues Form Organs

One kind of tissue alone cannot do all of the things that several kinds of tissue working together can do. Two or more tissues working together form an **organ.** Your stomach, shown in **Figure 4,** uses all four kinds of tissue to carry out digestion.

organ a collection of tissues that carry out a specialized function of the body

Organs Form Systems

Your stomach does a lot to help you digest your food. But the stomach doesn't do it all. Your stomach works with other organs, such as the small and large intestines, to digest your food. Organs that work together make up an *organ system*.

✓ Reading Check How is the stomach part of an organ system?

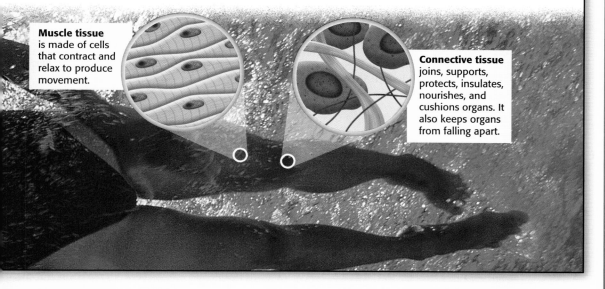

Muscle tissue is made of cells that contract and relax to produce movement.

Connective tissue joins, supports, protects, insulates, nourishes, and cushions organs. It also keeps organs from falling apart.

Answer to Reading Check
The stomach works with other organs, such as the small and large intestines, to digest food.

Organizing Information To help students understand and identify the 12 major organ systems of the body, have them make a table with the following headings: "Name of organ system," "Function(s)," and "Main organs." Have students use the table to review the information presented on these pages.
LS Logical

Quiz — GENERAL

Ask students whether each of the following statements is true or false. Have students correct false statements.

1. Homeostasis is the maintenance of a stable internal environment. (true)

2. Epithelial tissue sends electrical signals throughout the body. (false; Nervous tissue sends electrical signals throughout the body and epithelial tissue covers and protects underlying tissue.)

3. Blood is a type of connective tissue. (true)

Alternative Assessment — GENERAL

Writing **Organ Systems** In their **science journal,** have students describe three of the organ systems introduced in this section. Have them describe the functions and primary organs of each system and include drawings of each system. **LS Verbal**

Working Together

Organ systems work together to maintain homeostasis. Your body has 12 major organ systems, as shown in **Figure 5.** The circulatory and cardiovascular systems are shown together. The cardiovascular system includes your heart and blood vessels. Additionally, these organs are part of the circulatory system, which also includes blood. Together, these two systems deliver the materials your cells need to survive. This is just one example of how organ systems work together to keep you healthy.

✔ **Reading Check** Give an example of how organ systems work together in the body.

Figure 5 Organ Systems

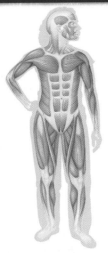

Integumentary System Your skin protects you from disease and regulates body temperature.

Muscular System Your muscular system works with the skeletal system to help you move.

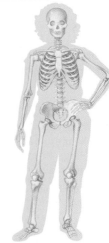

Skeletal System Your bones provide a frame to support and protect your body parts.

Cardiovascular and Circulatory Systems Your heart pumps blood through all of your blood vessels.

Respiratory System Your lungs absorb oxygen and release carbon dioxide.

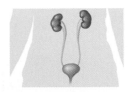

Urinary System Your urinary system removes wastes from the blood and regulates your body's fluids.

Male Reproductive System The male reproductive system produces and delivers sperm.

Female Reproductive System The female reproductive system produces eggs and nourishes and protects the fetus.

Answer to Reading Check

Sample answer: The cardiovascular system includes the heart and blood vessels. These organs are also part of the circulatory system, which includes blood. Together, these systems deliver the materials cells need to survive.

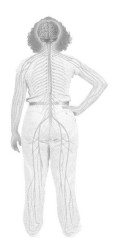

Nervous System Your nervous system receives and sends electrical messages throughout your body.

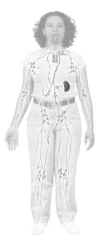

Digestive System Your digestive system breaks down the food you eat into nutrients that your body can absorb.

Lymphatic System The lymphatic system returns leaked fluids to blood vessels and helps defend against disease.

Endocrine System Your glands send out chemical messages, which control body functions.

SECTION Review

Summary

- Homeostasis is the maintenance of a stable internal environment.
- A group of cells that work together is a tissue. Tissues form organs. Organs that work together form organ systems.
- There are 12 major organ systems in the human body.
- Organ systems work together to help the body maintain homeostasis.

Using Key Terms

1. In your own words, write a definition for the term *homeostasis*.

Understanding Key Ideas

2. Which of the following statements describes how tissues, organs, and organ systems are related?
   a. Organs form tissues, which form organ systems.
   b. Organ systems form organs, which form tissues.
   c. Tissues form organs, which form organ systems.
   d. None of the above

3. List the 12 organ systems.

Math Skills

4. The human skeleton has 206 bones. The human skull has 22 bones. What percentage of human bones are skull bones?

Critical Thinking

5. **Applying Concepts** The circulatory system delivers nutrients to cells in the body. What might happen to homeostasis if this system were disrupted? Explain your answer.

6. **Predicting Consequences** Predict what might happen if the human body did not have specialized cells, tissues, organs, and organ systems to maintain homeostasis.

SCILINKS.

NSTA
Developed and maintained by the National Science Teachers Association

For a variety of links related to this chapter, go to www.scilinks.org

Topic: Tissues and Organs; Body Systems
SciLinks code: HSM1530; HSM0184

CHAPTER RESOURCES

Chapter Resource File

- Section Quiz GENERAL
- Section Review GENERAL
- Vocabulary and Section Summary GENERAL
- SciLinks Activity GENERAL

Technology

 Transparencies
- Organ Systems

Focus

Overview

This section introduces the skeletal system and describes the functions of bones. The section also illustrates the internal structure of bones and three joints.

Bellringer

Have students brainstorm problems that they would have if they lacked bones. (Students should understand that they would have no defined structure, mineral storage, organ protection, blood cells, or mobility.)

Motivate

ACTiViTY ——— GENERAL

Locating Bones Review with students that the skeletal system supports the body and protects delicate body parts. Encourage students to press the skin in various parts of their body to feel their bones. Ask students to describe any parts of their body where they cannot feel their bones. (Answers may vary but should include the abdomen, nose, and ears.) As you point to various parts of the body, ask students what organs the bones protect. (Sample answers: The skull protects the brain. The ribs protect the heart and lungs.) **Kinesthetic/Visual**

The Skeletal System

When you hear the word skeleton, *you may think of the remains of something that has died. But your skeleton is not dead. It is very much alive.*

You may think your bones are dry and brittle. But they are alive and active. Bones, cartilage, and the connective tissue that holds bones together make up your **skeletal system.**

Bones

The average adult human skeleton has 206 bones. Bones help support and protect parts of your body. They work with your muscles so you can move. Bones also help your body maintain homeostasis by storing minerals and making blood cells. **Figure 1** shows the functions of your skeleton.

READING WARM-UP

Objectives
● Identify the major organs of the skeletal system.
● Describe four functions of bones.
● Describe three joints.
● List three injuries and two diseases that affect bones and joints.

Terms to Learn
skeletal system
joint

READING STRATEGY

Reading Organizer As you read this section, create an outline of the section. Use the headings from the section in your outline.

skeletal system the organ system whose primary function is to support and protect the body and to allow the body to move

Figure 1 The Skeleton

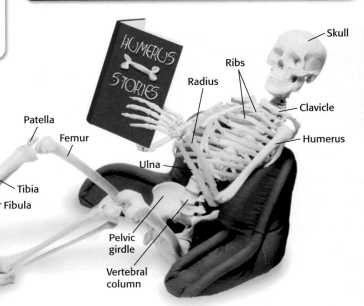

Skull
Ribs
Radius
Clavicle
Humerus
Ulna
Patella
Femur
Tibia
Fibula
Pelvic girdle
Vertebral column

Protection Your heart and lungs are protected by ribs, your spinal cord is protected by vertebrae, and your brain is protected by the skull.

Storage Bones store minerals that help your nerves and muscles function properly. Long bones store fat that can be used for energy.

Movement Skeletal muscles pull on bones to produce movement. Without bones, you would not be able to sit, stand, walk, or run.

Blood Cell Formation Some of your bones are filled with a special material that makes blood cells. This material is called *marrow*.

CHAPTER RESOURCES

Chapter Resource File
- **Lesson Plan**
- **Directed Reading A** BASIC
- **Directed Reading B** SPECIAL NEEDS

Technology
- **Transparencies**
  - Bellringer
  - The Skeleton

SCIENCE HUMOR

Q: Why didn't the skeleton cross the road?

A: It didn't have the guts.

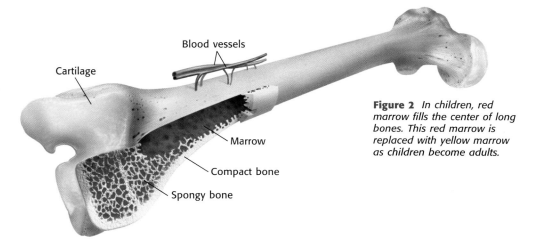

Blood vessels

Cartilage

Marrow

Compact bone

Spongy bone

Figure 2 *In children, red marrow fills the center of long bones. This red marrow is replaced with yellow marrow as children become adults.*

Bone Structure

A bone may seem lifeless. But a bone is a living organ made of several different tissues. Bone is made of connective tissue and minerals. These minerals are deposited by living cells called *osteoblasts* (AHS tee oh BLASTS).

If you look inside a bone, you will notice two kinds of bone tissue. If the bone tissue does not have any visible open spaces, it is called *compact bone*. Compact bone is rigid and dense. Tiny canals within compact bone contain small blood vessels. Bone tissue that has many open spaces is called *spongy bone*. Spongy bone provides most of the strength and support for a bone.

Bones contain a soft tissue called *marrow*. There are two types of marrow. Red marrow produces both red and white blood cells. Yellow marrow, found in the central cavity of long bones, stores fat. **Figure 2** shows a cross section of a long bone, the femur.

Bone Growth

Did you know that most of your skeleton used to be soft and rubbery? Most bones start out as a flexible tissue called *cartilage*. When you were born, you didn't have much true bone. But as you grew, most of the cartilage was replaced by bone. During childhood, most bones still have growth plates of cartilage. These growth plates provide a place for bones to continue to grow.

Feel the end of your nose. Or bend the top of your ear. These areas are two places where cartilage is never replaced by bone. These areas stay flexible.

 **Reading Check** How do bones grow? (*See the Appendix for answers to Reading Checks.*)

Pickled Bones

1. Place a **clean chicken bone** in a **jar of vinegar.**
2. After 1 week, remove the bone and rinse it with **water.**
3. Describe the changes that you can see or feel.
4. How has the bone's strength changed?
5. What did the vinegar remove?

Answer to Reading Check

Sample answer: As people grow, most of the cartilage that they start out with is replaced with bone.

Teach

Demonstration —— BASIC

Bone Dissection Ask a local butcher to cut a long bone from a pig, a cow, or a sheep in half lengthwise to expose the bone's internal structure. If a bone is not available from a butcher, obtain a preserved long bone from a biological supply house. Point out to students the differences in structure and location of spongy bone and compact bone. Also point out any cartilage that might remain on the bone. Ask students what makes the bone relatively lightweight for its size. (Students should infer that the air spaces in the spongy bone make the bone relatively lightweight for its size.) **English Language Learners** **LS Logical/Visual**

Quick Lab

MATERIALS

FOR EACH GROUP
• chicken bone, clean
• jar of vinegar

Safety Caution: Remind students to review all safety cautions and icons before beginning this lab activity.

Answers

3. Sample answer: The bone becomes more flexible.
4. Sample answer: The bone has become weaker. Because it is no longer rigid, it will not be able to provide the support and protection it once did.
5. Sample answer: The hard minerals in the leg bone dissolved in the vinegar.

Discussion — GENERAL

Joints After students read about the different kinds of joints, ask them the following questions.

• What kind of joint do you use when you bend your knee? (hinge joint)

• What kind of joint moves when you swing your arm back and forth? (ball-and-socket joint) Name another location in your body where this type of joint is located. (hip)

LS Verbal

Close

Reteaching — BASIC

Skeletal System Have students work in pairs to review the functions of the skeletal system. Students should stop each other if a concept is confusing or if they need clarification.

LS Interpersonal

Quiz — GENERAL

1. What is the difference between compact bone and spongy bone? (Sample answer: Compact bone has no visible, open spaces. Spongy bone has many visible spaces.)

2. Where in the body are ball-and-socket joints found? (hip and shoulder) Where are hinge joints? (knee) Where are gliding joints? (wrist and ankle)

Figure 3 Three Joints

Gliding Joint
Gliding joints allow bones in the hand and wrist to glide over one another and give some flexibility to the area.

Ball-and-Socket Joint
As a video-game joystick lets you move your character all around, the shoulder lets your arm move freely in all directions.

Hinge Joint
As a hinge allows a door to open and close, the knee enables you to flex and extend your lower leg.

joint a place where two or more bones meet

Joints

A place where two or more bones meet is called a **joint.** Your joints allow your body to move when your muscles contract. Some joints, such as fixed joints, allow little or no movement. Many of the joints in the skull are fixed joints. Other joints, such as your shoulder, allow a lot of movement. Joints can be classified based on how the bones in a joint move. For example, your shoulder is a ball-and-socket joint. Three joints are shown in **Figure 3.**

Joints are held together by *ligaments* (LIG uh muhnts). Ligaments are strong elastic bands of connective tissue. They connect the bones in a joint. Also, cartilage covers the ends of many bones. Cartilage helps cushion the area in a joint where bones meet.

✓ **Reading Check** Describe the basic structure of joints.

CONNECTION TO Environmental Science

WRITING SKILL **Bones from the Ocean** Sometimes, a bone or joint may become so damaged that it needs to be repaired or replaced with surgery. Often, replacement parts are made from a metal, such as titanium. However, some scientists have discovered that coral skeletons from coral reefs in the ocean can be used to replace human bone. Research bone surgery. Identify why doctors use metals such as titanium. Then, identify the advantages that coral may offer. Write a report discussing your findings.

Answer to Reading Check
Sample answer: Joints are held together by ligaments. Cartilage cushions the area in a joint where bones meet.

Answer to Connection to Environmental Science
Answers may vary. Students should understand that titanium is a relatively nonreactive metal, so it is used for bone replacement. Students should also demonstrate an understanding that coral easily binds to existing bone. You may want to ask students to examine the impact of coral bone replacement on the environment.

Skeletal System Injuries and Diseases

Sometimes, parts of the skeletal system are injured. As shown in **Figure 4,** bones may be fractured, or broken. Joints can also be injured. A dislocated joint is a joint in which one or more bones have been moved out of place. Another joint injury, called a *sprain*, happens if a ligament is stretched too far or torn.

There are also diseases of the skeletal system. *Osteoporosis* (AHS tee OH puh ROH sis) is a disease that causes bones to become less dense. Bones become weak and break more easily. Age and poor eating habits can make it more likely for people to develop osteoporosis. Other bone diseases affect the marrow or make bones soft. A disease that affects the joints is called *arthritis* (ahr THRIET is). Arthritis is painful. Joints may swell or stiffen. As they get older, some people are more likely to have some types of arthritis.

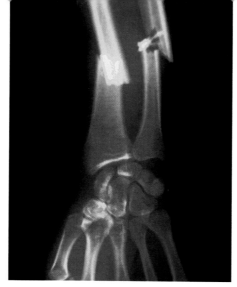

Figure 4 *This X ray shows that the two bones of the forearm have been fractured, or broken.*

Answers to Section Review

1. Sample answer: The skeletal system includes bones, cartilage, and connective tissue, and it provides support to the body.

2. c

3. Sample answer: Bones protect organs. Bones store materials that help nerves and muscles function properly. Along with skeletal muscles, bones make it possible to move. Finally, marrow in bones produces blood cells.

4. gliding joints, hinge joints, and ball-and-socket joints

5. Sample answer: Osteoporosis is a disease that causes bones to become less dense. Bones become weak and break more easily. Arthritis is a painful joint disease that causes joints to swell or stiffen.

6. 14 days (6 weeks $\times$ 7 days/week = 42 days; 42 days $\times$ 1/3 = 14 days)

7. Sample answer: Children are still growing, so they need more blood cells as their bodies get bigger. After children become adults, they don't need as many new blood cells, so long bones store fat instead.

8. Sample answer: Growth plates are places where bones continue to grow. If children did not have growth plates, their bones would not continue to grow.

SECTION Review

Summary

- The skeletal system includes bones, cartilage, and the connective tissue that connects bones.
- Bones protect the body, store minerals, allow movement, and make blood cells.
- Joints are places where two or more bones meet.
- Skeletal system injuries include fractures, dislocations, and sprains. Skeletal system diseases include osteoporosis and arthritis.

Using Key Terms

1. In your own words, write a definition for the term *skeletal system.*

Understanding Key Ideas

2. Which of the following is NOT an organ of the skeletal system?
   a. bone
   b. cartilage
   c. muscle
   d. None of the above

3. Describe four functions of bones.

4. What are three joints?

5. Describe two diseases that affect the skeletal system.

Math Skills

6. A broken bone usually heals in about six weeks. A mild sprain takes one-third as long to heal. In days, about how long does it take a mild sprain to heal?

Critical Thinking

7. **Identifying Relationships** Red bone marrow produces blood cells. Children have red bone marrow in their long bones, while adults have yellow bone marrow, which stores fat. Why might adults and children have different kinds of marrow?

8. **Predicting Consequences** What might happen if children's bones didn't have growth plates of cartilage?

Developed and maintained by the National Science Teachers Association

For a variety of links related to this chapter, go to www.scilinks.org

Topic: Skeletal System
SciLinks code: HSM1399

CONNECTION to Physical Science — GENERAL

Levers Students may be surprised to learn that their arms and legs are machines. Human limbs are levers, and levers are the simplest kind of machine. Levers allow people to apply, increase, and change the direction of force. Use the teaching transparency titled "Machines Change the Size and/or Direction of a Force" to illustrate this point. **LS** Visual

Focus

Overview

This section introduces students to the major parts of the muscular system and describes three types of muscle. This section also describes movement, aerobic exercise, and resistance exercise. The section discusses muscular system injuries and ways to prevent them.

🔊 Bellringer

On the board or an overhead projector, write the following: "List at least five parts of your body that you use to drink a glass of water." (Sample answer: fingers, hands, arm, lips, and tongue) Remind students that all of the parts that they use, including the eyes that they use to see the glass, are controlled by muscles.

Motivate

Group **ACTIVITY** — GENERAL

Poster Project Have students create a poster illustrating the three types of muscle. Students should include information about where the muscle is found, what it looks like, and whether it is involuntary or voluntary. Have students present their posters to the class.

LS Verbal/Visual

READING WARM-UP

Objectives
- List three kinds of muscle tissue.
- Describe how skeletal muscles move bones.
- Compare aerobic exercise with resistance exercise.
- Describe two muscular system injuries.

Terms to Learn

muscular system

READING STRATEGY

Discussion Read this section silently. Write down questions that you have about this section. Discuss your questions in a small group.

The Muscular System

Have you ever tried to sit still, without moving any muscles at all, for one minute? It's impossible! Somewhere in your body, muscles are always working.

You use muscles when you eat and breathe. Muscles, along with your skeleton, hold you upright and let you move. If all of your muscles rested at once, you would collapse. The **muscular system** is made up of the muscles that let you move.

Kinds of Muscle

Figure 1 shows the three kinds of muscle in your body. *Smooth muscle* is found in the digestive tract and in the walls of blood vessels. *Cardiac muscle* is found only in your heart. *Skeletal muscle* is attached to your bones for movement. Skeletal muscle also helps protect your inner organs.

Muscle action can be voluntary or involuntary. Muscle action that is under your control is *voluntary*. Muscle action that is not under your control is *involuntary*. Smooth muscle and cardiac muscle are involuntary muscles. Skeletal muscles can be both voluntary and involuntary muscles. For example, you can blink your eyes anytime you want to. But your eyes will also blink automatically.

Figure 1   **Three Kinds of Muscle**

Skeletal muscle enables bones to move.

Smooth muscle moves food through the digestive system.

Cardiac muscle pumps blood around the body.

CHAPTER RESOURCES

Chapter Resource File

- **Lesson Plan**
- **Directed Reading A** BASIC
- **Directed Reading B** SPECIAL NEEDS

Technology

Transparencies
- Bellringer
- A Pair of Muscles in the Arm

Is That a Fact!

Horses can sleep standing up. Their legs can support their weight on their bones without the use of muscles. When horses fall asleep and their muscles relax, their leg bones lock in place underneath them and hold them upright for the duration of their nap.

Figure 2 A Pair of Muscles in the Arm

Skeletal muscles, such as the biceps and triceps muscles, work in pairs. When the biceps muscle contracts, the arm bends. When the triceps muscle contracts, the arm straightens.

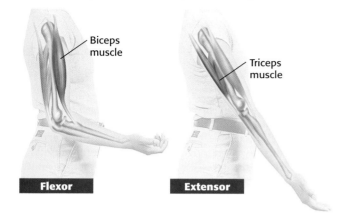

Biceps muscle

Triceps muscle

Flexor

Extensor

Movement

Skeletal muscles can make hundreds of movements. You can see many of these movements by watching a dancer, a swimmer, or even someone smiling or frowning. When you want to move, signals travel from your brain to your skeletal muscle cells. The muscle cells then contract, or get shorter.

Muscles Attach to Bones

Strands of tough connective tissue connect your skeletal muscles to your bones. These strands are called *tendons*. When a muscle that connects two bones gets shorter, the bones are pulled closer to each other. For example, tendons attach the biceps muscle to a bone in your shoulder and to a bone in your forearm. When the biceps muscle contracts, your forearm bends toward your shoulder.

Muscles Work in Pairs

Your skeletal muscles often work in pairs. Usually, one muscle in the pair bends part of the body. The other muscle straightens part of the body. A muscle that bends part of your body is called a *flexor* (FLEKS uhr). A muscle that straightens part of your body is an *extensor* (ek STEN suhr). As shown in **Figure 2,** the biceps muscle of the arm is a flexor. The triceps muscle of the arm is an extensor.

Reading Check Describe how muscles work in pairs. (*See the Appendix for answers to Reading Checks.*)

muscular system the organ system whose primary function is movement and flexibility

SCHOOL to HOME

Power in Pairs

Ask a parent to sit in a chair and place a hand palm up under the edge of a table. Tell your parent to apply gentle upward pressure. Feel the front and back of your parent's upper arm. Next, ask your parent to push down on top of the table. Feel your parent's arm again. What did you notice about the muscles in your parent's arm when he or she was pressing up? pushing down?

ACTIVITY

Answer to Reading Check

Sample answer: One muscle, the flexor, bends part of the body. Another muscle, the extensor, straightens part of the body.

Answer to School-to-Home Activity

Sample answer: While my parent pushes down, the muscles in the back of my parent's arm contract, and while my parent pushes up, the muscles in the front of the arm contract.

Teach

Demonstration ─── BASIC

Muscle Contraction Ask a student to stand in a doorway with his or her arms and hands relaxed and palms turned inward. Ask the student to raise his or her hands against the door frame (backs of the hands on the frame) and press steadily against the frame for about 30 to 40 seconds. Then, ask the student to relax and step away from the door. Have the rest of the class observe what happens to the student's arms. (The student's arms should rise slowly without obvious effort by the student.) Explain that the student's arms rise because the muscles that were pushing against the door frame are still shortened, or contracted. **English Language Learners**

LS Kinesthetic/Visual

CONNECTION to Real World ─── ADVANCED

Polio In the early 1900s, tens of thousands of people, mostly children, were stricken with polio, a viral disease that paralyzes muscles. Often, polio would leave its victims unable to walk or move. An Australian nurse, Sister Elizabeth Kenny, treated patients by using flexible hot wraps and exercise instead of immobilizing casts. Using her treatments, patients avoided paralysis. Largely because Kenny had no formal medical education, the doctors and hospital administrators of the time fought against her practices. Eventually, her successes became well known, and her contributions began the field of physical therapy. Have students research Kenny's story and the opposition that she faced. Have them give a report to the class. **LS Verbal**

Exercise Ask students to demonstrate different resistance and aerobic exercises. Then, ask students to explain the benefits of each exercise. Make sure students have warmed up before their demonstrations.

LS Kinesthetic

Quiz ——————————— GENERAL

1. What is the difference between voluntary muscle action and involuntary muscle action? (Sample answer: Voluntary muscle action is action that you can control. Involuntary muscle action is not under your control.)

2. What kind of muscle bends part of your body? (flexor) What kind of muscle straightens part of your body? (extensor)

3. What are the risks of using anabolic steroids? (Anabolic steroids can damage the heart, liver, and kidneys and can cause high blood pressure. They can cause bones to stop growing.)

Alternative Assessment ——— GENERAL

Crossword Puzzle Have students work in groups of four. Have groups make crossword puzzles using the vocabulary terms and other important terms in this section. Have groups exchange puzzles with each other.

LS Verbal   English Language Learners

Figure 3 *This girl is strengthening her heart and improving her endurance by doing aerobic exercise. This boy is doing resistance exercise to build strong muscles.*

Use It or Lose It

What happens when someone wears a cast for a broken arm? Skeletal muscles around the broken bone become smaller and weaker. The muscles weaken because they are not exercised. Exercised muscles are stronger and larger. Strong muscles can help other organs, too. For example, contracting muscles squeeze blood vessels. This action increases blood flow without needing more work from the heart.

Certain exercises can give muscles more strength and endurance. More endurance lets muscles work longer without getting tired. Two kinds of exercise can increase muscle strength and endurance. They are resistance exercise and aerobic exercise. You can see an example of each kind in **Figure 3.**

Resistance Exercise

Resistance exercise is a great way to strengthen skeletal muscles. During resistance exercise, people work against the resistance, or weight, of an object. Some resistance exercises, such as curl-ups, use your own weight for resistance.

Aerobic Exercise

Steady, moderately intense activity is called *aerobic exercise.* Jogging, cycling, skating, swimming, and walking are aerobic exercises. This kind of exercise can increase muscle strength. However, aerobic exercise mostly strengthens the heart and increases endurance.

CONNECTION TO Chemistry

Muscle Function Body chemistry is very important for healthy muscle function. Spasms or cramps happen if too much sweating, poor diet, or illness causes a chemical imbalance in muscles. Identify three chemicals that the body needs for muscles to work properly. Make a poster explaining how people can make sure that they have enough of each chemical.

ACTIVITY

Homework ——————— ADVANCED

Injuries For one month, have students read the sports section in a local newspaper or look for articles in sports magazines about injuries sustained by athletes. Ask students to identify and count the types of injuries, such as sprains and strains. Have students compile their information on bar graphs in which they record the kinds of injuries on the *x*-axis and the number of injuries on the *y*-axis.

LS Logical

Answer to Connection to Chemistry

Students should discuss the importance of minerals, such as magnesium, calcium, potassium, or sodium, to muscle function. Students should identify important dietary sources of these minerals.

Muscle Injury

Any exercise program should be started slowly. Starting slowly means you are less likely to get hurt. You should also warm up for exercise. A *strain* is an injury in which a muscle or tendon is overstretched or torn. Strains often happen because a muscle has not been warmed up. Strains also happen when muscles are worked too hard.

People who exercise too much can hurt their tendons. The body can't repair an injured tendon before the next exercise session. So, the tendon becomes inflamed. This condition is called *tendinitis*. Often, a long rest is needed for the injured tendon to heal.

Some people try to make their muscles stronger by taking drugs. These drugs are called *anabolic steroids* (A nuh BAH lik STER OIDZ). They can cause long-term health problems. Anabolic steroids can damage the heart, liver, and kidneys. They can also cause high blood pressure. If taken before the skeleton is mature, anabolic steroids can cause bones to stop growing.

 Reading Check What are the risks of using anabolic steroids?

MATH PRACTICE

Runner's Time

Jan has decided to enter a 5 km road race. She now runs 5 km in 30 min. She would like to decrease her time by 15% before the race. What will her time be when she reaches her goal?

SECTION Review

Summary

- The three kinds of muscle tissue are smooth muscle, cardiac muscle, and skeletal muscle.
- Skeletal muscles work in pairs. Skeletal muscles contract to move bones.
- Resistance exercise improves muscle strength. Aerobic exercise improves heart strength and muscle endurance.
- Strains are injuries that affect muscles and tendons. Tendinitis affects tendons.

Using Key Terms

1. In your own words, write a definition for the term *muscular system*.

Understanding Key Ideas

2. Muscles
   a. work in pairs.
   b. move bones by relaxing.
   c. get smaller when exercised.
   d. All of the above

3. Describe three kinds of muscle.

4. List two kinds of exercise. Give an example of each.

5. Describe two muscular system injuries.

Math Skills

6. If Trey can do one curl-up every 2.5 s, about how long will it take him to do 35 curl-ups?

Critical Thinking

7. **Applying Concepts** Describe some of the muscle action needed to pick up a book. Include flexors and extensors in your description.

8. **Predicting Consequences** If aerobic exercise improves heart strength, what likely happens to heart rate as the heart gets stronger? Explain your answer.

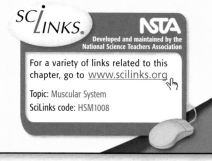

SCiLINKS

NSTA
Developed and maintained by the National Science Teachers Association

For a variety of links related to this chapter, go to www.scilinks.org

Topic: Muscular System
SciLinks code: HSM1008

Answer to Reading Check

Sample answer: Anabolic steroids can damage the heart, liver, and kidneys. They can also cause high blood pressure. Anabolic steroids can cause bones to stop growing.

CHAPTER RESOURCES

Chapter Resource File

- Section Quiz GENERAL
- Section Review GENERAL
- Vocabulary and Section Summary GENERAL
- Reinforcement Worksheet BASIC

Workbooks

Math Skills for Science
- The Unit Factor and Dimensional Analysis GENERAL

Answer to Math Practice

25 min, 30 s (30 min × 0.85 = 25.5 min)

Answers to Section Review

1. Sample answer: The muscular system is the group of muscles that allow people to move.

2. a

3. Sample answer: Smooth muscle is found in the digestive tract and in the walls of blood vessels. Cardiac muscle is found only in the heart. Skeletal muscle is attached to bones for movement.

4. Sample answer: Curl-ups are a resistance exercise. Jogging is an aerobic exercise.

5. Sample answer: A strain is an injury in which a muscle or tendon is overstretched or torn. Tendinitis is a condition in which a tendon becomes inflamed when the body doesn't have enough time to repair the tendon between exercise sessions.

6. 87.5 s (35 curl-ups × 2.5 curl-ups/s = 87.5 s)

7. Sample answer: An extensor in the back of my arm straightens out my arm as I reach for the book. Flexors in my hand let me close my fingers on the book, and a flexor in my arm bends my arm as I pick up the book.

8. Sample answer: As the heart gets stronger, the heart likely will pump more blood with each beat. The heart will not need to work as hard to pump the same amount of blood. So, heart rate will likely decrease.

Focus

Overview

This section introduces students to the major functions of the integumentary system and describes the major parts of skin and their functions. Students will also learn about common skin injuries.

 ### Bellringer

Write the following questions on the board or an overhead projector: "When do you see dogs panting?" (Sample answer: on hot days or after they have run) "Why do you think dogs pant?" (Sample answer: Dogs don't sweat the way humans do. Dogs pant to regulate their body temperature.)

Motivate

Discussion ——— GENERAL

Homeostasis Relay the following story to students: "More than 200 years ago, Dr. Charles Blagden tested how mammals regulate body temperature. He spent 45 min in a room with an uncooked steak. The temperature in the room measured 126°C (260°F)." Ask students what they think happened to Dr. Blagden and the steak. (Dr. Blagden emerged from the room unharmed, but the steak was cooking! Living people and mammals can regulate their body temperature.)
LS Logical

READING WARM-UP

Objectives
- List four functions of skin.
- Describe the two layers of skin.
- Describe the structure and function of hair and nails.
- Describe two kinds of damage that can affect skin.

Terms to Learn
integumentary system
epidermis
dermis

READING STRATEGY

Paired Summarizing Read this section silently. In pairs, take turns summarizing the material. Stop to discuss ideas that seem confusing.

integumentary system the organ system that forms a protective covering on the outside of the body

The Integumentary System

What part of your body has to be partly dead to keep you alive? Here are some clues: It comes in many colors, it is the largest organ in the body, and it is showing right now!

Did you guess your skin? If you did, you guessed correctly. Your skin, hair, and nails make up your **integumentary system** (in TEG yoo MEN tuhr ee SIS tuhm). The integumentary system covers your body and helps you maintain homeostasis.

Functions of Skin

Why do you need skin? Here are four good reasons:

- Skin protects you by keeping water in your body and foreign particles out of your body.
- Skin keeps you in touch with the outside world. Nerve endings in your skin let you feel things around you.
- Skin helps regulate your body temperature. Small organs in the skin called *sweat glands* make sweat. Sweat is a salty liquid that flows to the surface of the skin. As sweat evaporates, the skin cools.
- Skin helps get rid of wastes. Several kinds of waste chemicals can be removed in sweat.

As shown in **Figure 1,** skin comes in many colors. Skin color is determined by a chemical called *melanin*. If a lot of melanin is present, skin is very dark. If little melanin is present, skin is very light. Melanin absorbs ultraviolet light from the sun. So, melanin reduces damage that can lead to skin cancer. However, all skin, even dark skin, is vulnerable to cancer. Skin should be protected from sunlight whenever possible.

Figure 1 *Variety in skin color is caused by the pigment melanin. The amount of melanin varies from person to person.*

CHAPTER RESOURCES

Chapter Resource File

- **Lesson Plan**
- **Directed Reading A** BASIC
- **Directed Reading B** SPECIAL NEEDS

Technology

Transparencies
- Bellringer
- Structures of the Skin

Is That a Fact!

In an average adult, the skin has a surface area of about 2 m² and has a mass of about 4 kg. The skin on the human body varies in thickness from about 5 mm on the soles of the feet to about 0.5 mm on the eyelids.

Figure 2 Structures of the Skin

Beneath the surface, your skin is a complex organ made of blood vessels, nerves, glands, and muscles.

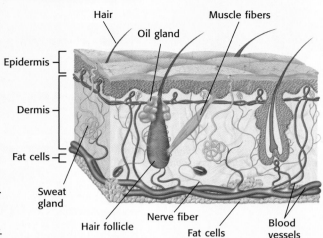

Hair
Oil gland
Muscle fibers
Epidermis
Dermis
Fat cells
Sweat gland
Hair follicle
Nerve fiber
Fat cells
Blood vessels

Blood vessels transport substances and help regulate body temperature.

Nerve fibers carry messages to and from the brain.

Hair follicles in the dermis make hair.

Muscle fibers attached to a hair follicle can contract and cause the hair to stand up.

Oil glands release oil that keeps hair flexible and waterproofs the epidermis.

Sweat glands release sweat to cool the body. Sweating is also a way to remove waste materials from the body.

Layers of Skin

Skin is the largest organ of your body. In fact, the skin of an adult covers an area of about 2 m²! However, there is more to skin than meets the eye. Skin has two main layers: the epidermis (EP uh DUHR mis) and the dermis. The **epidermis** is the outermost layer of skin. You see the epidermis when you look at your skin. The thicker layer of skin that lies beneath the epidermis is the **dermis.**

Epidermis

The epidermis is made of epithelial tissue. Even though the epidermis has many layers of cells, it is as thick as only two sheets of paper over most of the body. It is thicker on the palms of your hands and on the soles of your feet. Most cells in the epidermis are dead. These cells are filled with a protein called *keratin*. Keratin helps make the skin tough.

Dermis

The dermis lies beneath the epidermis. The dermis has many fibers made of a protein called *collagen*. These fibers provide strength. They also let skin bend without tearing. The dermis contains many small structures, as shown in **Figure 2.**

Reading Check Describe the dermis. How does it differ from the epidermis? (*See the Appendix for answers to Reading Checks.*)

epidermis the surface layer of cells on a plant or animal

dermis the layer of skin below the epidermis

Your epidermis is showing!

Answer to Reading Check

The dermis is the layer of skin that lies beneath the epidermis. It is composed of a protein called *collagen*, while the epidermis contains keratin.

INCLUSION Strategies

• **Learning Disabled**
• **Developmentally Delayed**
• **Hearing Impaired**

Students can often better retain information if they create a visual image. Have students work in groups of four. Give each group a sheet of poster board. Have students divide the poster board into four sections and draw memory clues to help them remember the four functions of the skin. **LS Visual**

ACTIVITY — GENERAL

MATERIALS

FOR EACH GROUP
• clock or watch
• cotton balls
• fan
• thermometers, Celsius (2)
• water at room temperature

Measuring Temperature Have students work in groups of four students. Have students wrap the bulb of each thermometer with a cotton ball and then wet one of the cotton balls. Have students record the beginning temperature of each thermometer and then hold both thermometers in front of a fan. Students should record the temperature of each thermometer every minute for 5 min. Ask students: "How do the temperatures of the thermometers differ?" (Sample answer: The thermometer with the wet cotton has a lower temperature.) "Why?" (Sample answer: Evaporation lowers the temperature.) "How does this process relate to what happens when you sweat?" (Sample answer: As sweat evaporates from the body, the skin becomes cooler.) **LS Kinesthetic**

INTERNET ACTIVITY Brochure — GENERAL

For an internet activity related to this chapter, have students go to **go.hrw.com** and type in the keyword **HL5BD1W.**

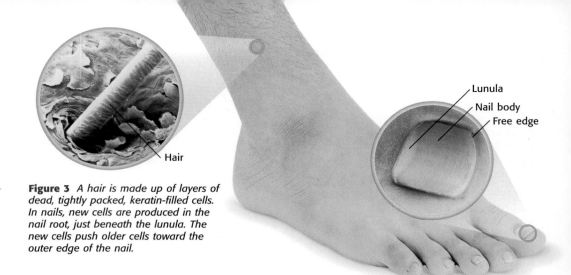

Figure 3 *A hair is made up of layers of dead, tightly packed, keratin-filled cells. In nails, new cells are produced in the nail root, just beneath the lunula. The new cells push older cells toward the outer edge of the nail.*

Labels: Lunula, Nail body, Free edge, Hair

Reteaching — BASIC

Hair and Nails Ask students to relate the functions of hair and nails. Then, ask students to describe how hair and nails form. **LS Verbal**

Quiz — GENERAL

1. What are four functions of skin? (to keep moisture in and foreign particles out, to provide information about the outside world, to help regulate body temperature, and to remove wastes)

2. Describe the two layers of skin. (The epidermis is the outer-most layer of skin and contains epithelial tissue and mostly dead cells. The dermis lies beneath the epidermis and contains collagen.)

Alternative Assessment — ADVANCED

PORTFOLIO **Skin Art** Have students make a colorful drawing of a cross section of skin. Have students make their drawings from memory and label and describe the function of blood vessels, nerve fibers, muscle fibers, hair follicles, oil glands, and sweat glands. **LS Visual**

CONNECTION TO Social Studies

WRITING SKILL **Using Hair** Many traditional cultures use animal hair to make products, such as rugs and blankets. Identify a culture that uses animal hair. In your **science journal,** write a report describing how the culture uses animal hair.

Hair and Nails

Hair and nails are important parts of the integumentary system. Like skin, hair and nails are made of living and dead cells. **Figure 3** shows hair and nails.

A hair forms at the bottom of a tiny sac called a *hair follicle.* The hair grows as new cells are added at the hair follicle. Older cells get pushed upward. The only living cells in a hair are in the hair follicle. Like skin, hair gets its color from melanin.

Hair helps protect skin from ultraviolet light. Hair also keeps particles, such as dust and insects, out of your eyes and nose. In most mammals, hair helps regulate body temperature. A tiny muscle attached to the hair follicle contracts. If the follicle contains a hair, the hair stands up. The lifted hairs work like a sweater. They trap warm air around the body.

A nail grows from living cells in the *nail root* at the base of the nail. As new cells form, the nail grows longer. Nails protect the tips of your fingers and toes. So, your fingers and toes can be soft and sensitive for a keen sense of touch.

Reading Check Describe how nails grow.

Skin Injuries

Skin is often damaged. Fortunately, your skin can repair itself, as shown in **Figure 4.** Some damage to skin is very serious. Damage to the genetic material in skin cells can cause skin cancer. Skin may also be affected by hormones that cause oil glands in skin to make too much oil. This oil combines with dead skin cells and bacteria to clog hair follicles. The result is acne. Proper cleansing can help but often cannot prevent this problem.

CONNECTION Real World ACTiViTY — GENERAL

PORTFOLIO **Protection from the Sun** Skin cancer is the most common kind of cancer. Hundreds of thousands of new cases of skin cancer are reported each year. Ask interested students to research ways people can prevent skin cancer. Have students create informative brochures about their findings. **LS Verbal/Visual**

Answer to Reading Check

Sample answer: A nail grows from living cells in the nail root at the base of the nail. As new cells form, the nail grows longer.

Figure 4 How Skin Heals

① A blood clot forms over a cut to stop bleeding and to keep bacteria from entering the wound. Bacteria-fighting cells then come to the area to kill bacteria.

② Damaged cells are replaced through cell division. Eventually, all that is left on the surface is a scar.

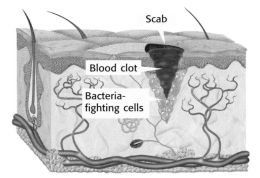

Scab

Blood clot

Bacteria-fighting cells

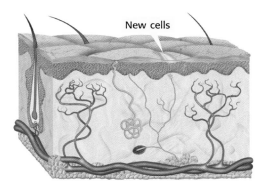

New cells

SECTION Review

Summary

- Skin keeps water in the body, keeps foreign particles out of the body, lets people feel things around them, regulates temperature, and removes wastes.

- The two layers of skin are the epidermis and the dermis.

- Hair grows from hair follicles. Nails grow from nail roots.

- Skin may develop skin cancer. Acne may develop if skin produces too much oil.

Using Key Terms

1. In your own words, write a definition for each of the following terms: *integumentary system*, *epidermis*, and *dermis*.

Understanding Key Ideas

2. Which of the following is NOT a function of skin?
   a. to regulate body temperature
   b. to keep water in the body
   c. to move your body
   d. to get rid of wastes

3. Describe the two layers of skin.

4. How do hair and nails develop?

5. Describe how a cut heals.

Math Skills

6. On average, hair grows 0.3 mm per day. How many millimeters does hair grow in 30 days? in a year?

Critical Thinking

7. **Making Inferences** Why do you feel pain when you pull on your hair or nails, but not when you cut them?

8. **Analyzing Ideas** The epidermis on the palms of your hands and on the soles of your feet is thicker than it is anywhere else on your body. Why might this skin need to be thicker?

SCiLINKS®

NSTA
Developed and maintained by the National Science Teachers Association

For a variety of links related to this chapter, go to www.scilinks.org

Topic: Integumentary System
SciLinks code: HSM0803

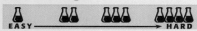

Seeing Is Believing

Teacher's Notes

Time Required

One 45-minute class period and 5 to 10 minutes every other day for 2 weeks

Lab Ratings

EASY ———————————— HARD

Teacher Prep 🜂
Student Set-Up 🜂
Concept Level 🜂
Clean Up 🜂

MATERIALS

The materials listed on the student page are enough for 1–2 students. This lab may be done with several different types of marking methods. The fingernail is very hard and is not very porous. Marking the nail permanently is a challenge. A permanent marker, such as a laundry-marking pen, may need to be refreshed only once a day. Fingernail polish may be an acceptable alternative. Acrylic paint may also be used.

Safety Caution

Remind students to review all safety cautions and icons before beginning this lab activity.

Skills Practice Lab

OBJECTIVES

Measure nail growth over time.
Draw a graph of nail growth.

MATERIALS

- graph paper (optional)
- metric ruler
- permanent marker

SAFETY

Seeing Is Believing

Like your hair and skin, fingernails are part of your body's integumentary system. Nails, shown in the figure below, are a modification of the outer layer of the skin. Nails grow from the nail bed and will grow continuously throughout your life. In this activity, you will measure the rate at which fingernails grow.

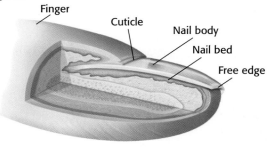

Finger
Cuticle
Nail body
Nail bed
Free edge

Procedure

1. Use a permanent marker to mark the center of the nail bed on your right index finger, as shown in the figure below. **Caution:** Do not get ink on your clothing.

Mark
Base of nail

2. Measure from the mark to the base of your nail. Record the measurement, and label the measurement "Day 1."

3. Repeat steps 1 and 2 for your left index finger.

4. Let your fingernails grow for 2 days. Normal daily activity will not wash away the mark completely, but you may need to freshen the mark.

5. Measure the distance from the mark on your nail to the base of your nail. Record this distance, and label the measurement "Day 3."

Kathy LaRoe
East Valley Middle School
East Helena, Montana

CHAPTER RESOURCES

Chapter Resource File

- **Datasheet for Chapter Lab**
- **Lab Notes and Answers**

Technology

Classroom Videos
- Lab Video

LabBook

- Muscles at Work

6 Continue measuring and recording the growth of your nails every other day for 2 weeks. Refresh the mark as necessary. You may continue to file or trim your nails as usual throughout the course of the lab.

7 After you have completed your measurements, use them to create a graph similar to the graph below.

Fingernail Growth

Analyze the Results

1 **Describing Events** Did the nail on one hand grow faster than the nail on the other hand?

2 **Examining Data** Did your nails grow at a constant rate, or did your nails grow more quickly at certain times?

Draw Conclusions

3 **Making Predictions** If one nail grew more quickly than the other nail, what might explain the difference in growth?

4 **Analyzing Graphs** Compare your graph with the graphs of your classmates. Do you notice any differences in the graphs based on gender or physical characteristics, such as height? If so, describe the difference.

Applying Your Data

Do additional research to find out how nails are important to you. Also, identify how nails can be used to indicate a person's health or nutrition. Based on what you learn, describe how your nail growth indicates your health or nutrition.

CHAPTER RESOURCES

Workbooks

Inquiry Labs
• On a Wing and a Layer **GENERAL**

Long-Term Projects & Research Ideas
• Mapping the Human Body **ADVANCED**

Applying Your Data
Students should discover that the appearance of a nail can reflect the health of an individual. Abnormalities in color, such as white, yellow, or red nail beds, can indicate serious problems such as liver, lung, and heart diseases. Other problems indicated by nail appearance are bacterial or fungal infections of the nails and poor nutrition.

Lab Notes

Few topics are as important to students as gaining knowledge and understanding of their own body. As they develop, students can't help but observe how they are changing physically. In this lab, students witness the growth of their own fingernails.

Tell students that the graphed data shown in this lab are only an example and will not be the same as their own data.

Analyze the Results

1. Answers may vary. Many students may note that rates of growth vary.

2. Answers may vary. Some students will answer that their nails did not grow at a constant rate.

Draw Conclusions

3. The nails of the dominant hand grow faster than those of the other hand. Damage to the nail root can affect how quickly a nail grows. Also, circulation to the area affects growth. If one hand receives poor circulation, the nail will grow at a slower rate.

4. Some students may note differences in nail growth. While these differences likely are not related to height, they are related to nutrition. Someone who does not have enough of certain minerals, such as calcium and magnesium, in his or her diet will have slower nail growth. Nail growth is also affected by age, time of year, and gender. Nail growth slows as people get older. Nails grow faster in the summer than they do in the winter. Often, men's nails grow faster than women's nails do.

Chapter Review

Assignment Guide

SECTION	QUESTIONS
1	2, 5, 7, 13, 17
2	1, 6, 12, 14, 18, 20–21
3	8, 10–11, 15
4	3–4, 9, 16, 19, 23–27
2 and 3	22

ANSWERS

Using Key Terms

1. joint
2. Homeostasis
3. epidermis
4. integumentary system
5. organ
6. skeletal system

Understanding Key Ideas

7. c
8. c
9. a
10. d
11. Sample answer: Muscles are connected to bones by tendons. When a muscle that connects two bones contracts, the bones are pulled closer together. Muscles often work in pairs.
12. Sample answer: The skeletal system includes the bones, cartilage, and connective tissue whose primary function is to support the body. The skeletal system protects organs, stores minerals, allows movement, and produces blood cells.

USING KEY TERMS

Complete each of the following sentences by choosing the correct term from the word bank.

homeostasis
joint
tissue
epidermis
integumentary system

organ
skeletal system
muscular system
dermis

1. A(n) ___ is a place where two or more bones meet.

2. ___ is the maintenance of a stable internal environment.

3. The outermost layer of skin is the ___.

4. The organ system that includes skin, hair, and nails is the ___.

5. A(n) ___ is made up of two or more tissues working together.

6. The ___ supports and protects the body, stores minerals, and allows movement.

UNDERSTANDING KEY IDEAS

Multiple Choice

7. Which of the following lists shows the way in which the body is organized?
   a. cells, organs, organ systems, tissues
   b. tissues, cells, organs, organ systems
   c. cells, tissues, organs, organ systems
   d. cells, tissues, organ systems, organs

8. Which muscle tissue can be both voluntary and involuntary?
   a. smooth muscle
   b. cardiac muscle
   c. skeletal muscle
   d. All of the above

9. The integumentary system
   a. helps regulate body temperature.
   b. helps the body move.
   c. stores minerals.
   d. None of the above

10. Muscles
    a. work in pairs.
    b. can be voluntary or involuntary.
    c. become stronger if exercised.
    d. All of the above

Short Answer

11. How do muscles move bones?

12. Describe the skeletal system, and list four functions of bones.

13. Give an example of how organ systems work together.

14. List three injuries and two diseases that affect the skeletal system.

13. Sample answer: The circulatory and cardiovascular systems work closely together to maintain homeostasis. The cardiovascular system includes the heart and blood vessels. These structures are also part of the circulatory system, which includes blood. These two systems work together to deliver the materials that cells need to survive.

14. fractures, dislocations, sprains, osteoporosis, and arthritis

15 Compare aerobic exercise and resistance exercise.

16 What are two kinds of damage that may affect skin?

CRITICAL THINKING

17 Concept Mapping Use the following terms to create a concept map: *tissues, muscle tissue, connective tissue, cells, organ systems, organs, epithelial tissue,* and *nervous tissue.*

18 Making Comparisons Compare the shapes of the bones of the human skull with the shapes of the bones of the human leg. How do the shapes differ? Why are the shapes important?

19 Making Inferences Compare your elbows and fingertips in terms of the texture and sensitivity of the skin on these parts of your body. Why might the skin on these body parts differ?

20 Making Inferences Imagine that you are building a robot. Your robot will have a skeleton similar to a human skeleton. If the robot needs to be able to move a limb in all directions, what kind of joint would be needed? Explain your answer.

21 Analyzing Ideas Human bones are dense and are often filled with marrow. But many bones of birds are hollow. Why might birds have hollow bones?

22 Identifying Relationships Why might some muscles fail to work properly if a bone is broken?

INTERPRETING GRAPHICS

Use the cross section of skin below to answer the questions that follow.

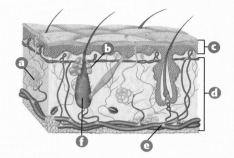

23 What is d called? What substance is most abundant in this layer?

24 What is the name and function of a?

25 What is the name and function of b?

26 Which letter corresponds to the part of the skin that is made up of epithelial tissue that contains dead cells?

27 Which letter corresponds to the part of the skin from which hair grows? What is this part called?

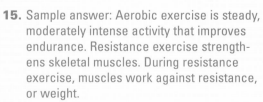

15. Sample answer: Aerobic exercise is steady, moderately intense activity that improves endurance. Resistance exercise strengthens skeletal muscles. During resistance exercise, muscles work against resistance, or weight.

16. Sample answer: Damage to genetic material in skin cells can cause skin cancer. If oil glands in skin produce too much oil, hair follicles may be clogged, which causes acne.

Critical Thinking

17. An answer to this exercise can be found at the end of the book.

18. Sample answer: Leg bones are long and skinny, while skull bones are thin and wide. Many skull bones are curved. Leg bones enable walking and standing, while skull bones are designed to protect the brain.

19. Sample answer: The skin on the elbows is thin, loose, and sometimes rough. The skin on the fingertips is thicker, but more sensitive to touch. The skin on elbows allows elbows to bend because it is loose and can stretch. The skin on the fingers is important for the sense of touch.

20. Sample answer: The robot would need a ball-and-socket joint. A ball-and-socket joint allows movement in all directions.

21. Sample answer: Dense bones that are filled with marrow weigh more than hollow bones. Because most birds fly, they need lighter bones. So, birds' bones are hollow.

22. Sample answer: If a bone is broken, flexors or extensors likely will not work properly. These muscles will not be able to pull on a bone in the way that they do when a bone is not broken. Also, if the area where the muscle attaches is damaged, the ability of the muscle to pull on the bone may be affected.

Interpreting Graphics

23. dermis; collagen

24. Sample answer: Sweat glands release sweat to cool the body.

25. Sample answer: Oil glands release oil to keep hair flexible and to waterproof the epidermis.

26. c

27. f; hair follicle

Standardized Test Preparation

Teacher's Note

To provide practice under more realistic testing conditions, give students 20 minutes to answer all of the questions in this Standardized Test Preparation.

MISCONCEPTION ALERT

Answers to the standardized test preparation can help you identify student misconceptions and misunderstandings.

READING

Passage 1

1. C
2. F
3. B

TEST DOCTOR

Question 2: Some students may answer that a skin graft is skin made of plastic because plastic bandages are discussed in the passage. Some students may think that a skin graft is damaged skin that has been removed, but it is undamaged skin that has been removed to replace damaged skin. Finally, some students may think that a skin graft is burned skin because burns are mentioned in the passage.

Standardized Test Preparation

READING

Read the passages below. Then, answer the questions that follow each passage.

Passage 1 Sometimes, doctors perform a <u>skin graft</u> to transfer some of a person's healthy skin to an area where skin has been damaged. Doctors perform skin grafts because skin is often the best "bandage" for a wound. Like cloth or plastic bandages, skin protects the wound. Skin allows the wound to breathe. Unlike cloth or plastic bandages, skin can regenerate itself as it covers a wound. But sometimes a person's skin is so severely damaged (by burns, for example) that the person doesn't have enough skin to spare.

1. Based on the passage, what can skin do that manufactured bandages can't do?
   - **A** Skin can protect a wound.
   - **B** Skin can stop more skin from being damaged.
   - **C** Skin can regenerate itself.
   - **D** Skin can prevent burns.

2. In the passage, what does the term *skin graft* most likely mean?
   - **F** a piece of skin transplanted from one part of the body to another
   - **G** a piece of skin made of plastic
   - **H** a piece of damaged skin that has been removed from the body
   - **I** burned skin

3. Based on the passage, why might a severe burn victim not receive a skin graft?
   - **A** Manufactured bandages are better.
   - **B** He or she doesn't have enough healthy skin.
   - **C** There isn't enough damaged skin to repair.
   - **D** Skin is the best bandage for a wound.

Passage 2 Making sure that your body maintains homeostasis is not an easy task. The task is difficult because your internal environment is always changing. Your body must do many different jobs to maintain homeostasis. Each cell in your body has a specific job in maintaining homeostasis. Your cells are organized into groups. A group of similar cells working together forms a tissue. Your body has four main kinds of tissue—epithelial tissue, connective tissue, muscle tissue, and nervous tissue. These tissues work together to form organs, which help maintain homeostasis.

1. Based on the passage, which of the following statements about tissues is true?
   - **A** Tissues do not help maintain homeostasis.
   - **B** Tissues form organ systems.
   - **C** Tissues are changing because the body's internal environment is always changing.
   - **D** There are four kinds of tissue.

2. According to the passage, which of the following statements about homeostasis is true?
   - **F** It is easy for the body to maintain homeostasis.
   - **G** The body must do different jobs to maintain homeostasis.
   - **H** Your internal environment rarely changes.
   - **I** Organs and organ systems do not help maintain homeostasis.

3. Which of the following statements about cells is false?
   - **A** Cells are organized into different groups.
   - **B** Cells form tissues.
   - **C** Cells work together.
   - **D** Cells don't maintain homeostasis.

Passage 2

1. D
2. G
3. D

TEST DOCTOR

Question 1: Some students may answer that tissues do not help maintain homeostasis. However, because all cells in the body have a role in homeostasis, so do tissues. Some students may answer that tissues form organ systems, but tissues form organs. Some students may answer that tissues are always changing, but this is not mentioned in the passage.

The line graph below shows hair growth over time. Use the graph to answer the questions that follow.

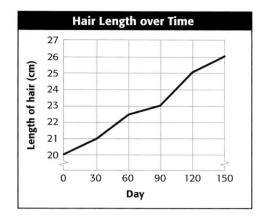

Hair Length over Time

1. How long was the hair on day 60?
   A 20.0 cm
   B 21.0 cm
   C 22.5 cm
   D 23.0 cm

2. On which day was hair length 23 cm?
   F day 60
   G day 90
   H day 120
   I day 150

3. From day 0 to day 150, what is the average amount that hair grows every 30 days?
   A 0.5 cm
   B 1.2 cm
   C 1.5 cm
   D 2.0 cm

4. Based on the average amount of hair growth per 30-day period, how long would it take the hair to grow another 3.6 cm?
   F 30 days
   G 60 days
   H 90 days
   I 120 days

MATH

Read each question below, and choose the best answer.

1. About 40% of a person's mass is muscle tissue. If Max has a mass of 40 kg, about how much muscle tissue does he have?
   A 16 kg
   B 20 kg
   C 24 kg
   D 30 kg

2. When running, an adult inhales about 72 L of air per minute. That amount is 12 times the amount that an adult needs while resting. How much air does an adult inhale while resting?
   F 6 L/min
   G 12 L/min
   H 60 L/min
   I 64 L/min

3. Maggie likes to do bench presses, a resistance exercise. She bench presses 10 kg. If Maggie added 2 kg every 2 weeks, how long would it take her to reach 20 kg?
   A 4 weeks
   B 5 weeks
   C 10 weeks
   D 12 weeks

4. A box of 25 bandages costs $4.00. A roll of tape costs $1.50. Troy needs 125 bandages and 3 rolls of tape for a first-aid kit. Which of the following equations shows the cost of first-aid supplies, x?
   F $x = (125 \times 4.00) + (3 \times 1.50)$
   G $x = (25 \times 4.00) + (3 \times 1.50)$
   H $x = [(25 \times 4.00) \div 125] + (3 \times 1.50)$
   I $x = [(125 \div 25) \times 4.00] + (3 \times 1.50)$

5. Stephen wants to run a 10 K race. Right now, he can run 5 K. What is the percentage increase from 5 K to 10 K?
   A 50%
   B 100%
   C 200%
   D 500%

Standardized Test Preparation

1. C
2. G
3. B
4. H

 TEST DOCTOR

Question 3: Students can calculate average hair growth by examining the total hair growth (6 cm) and the number of 30-day periods (5). In calculating the average growth, students should find that hair grows about 1.2 cm every 30 days (6 cm ÷ 5 = 1.2 cm). If students round their answers, they may incorrectly answer 1.0 cm or 1.5 cm.

MATH

1. A
2. F
3. C
4. I
5. B

TEST DOCTOR

Question 2: Students may answer 12 L because the number 12 is introduced in the question. Students may answer 60 L if they subtract 12 from 72 L. Students may answer 64 L if they assume that people need 12% less air rather than 12 times less air.

Question 5: To find percentage increase, students must find the difference between 10 K and 5 K, divide it by 5 K, and multiply by 100. If students divide 5 K by 10 K, they will get the incorrect answer of 50%. If they divide 10 K by 5 K, they will get the incorrect answer of 200%. Finding the difference between 10 K and 5 K and multiplying the answer by 100 without dividing first will yield the incorrect answer of 500%.

CHAPTER RESOURCES

Chapter Resource File
- Standardized Test Preparation GENERAL

Workbooks
North Carolina Standardized Test Preparation
- Provides practice for the EOG test.

State Resources
For specific resources for your state, visit **go.hrw.com** and type in the keyword **HSMSTR.**

Weird Science

Background

The way that a wound heals when engineered skin is used is far better than the way that a wound heals when engineered skin is not used—more scar tissue forms. Scar tissue is weaker and more brittle than the skin that the scar tissue replaces. Scar tissue does not stretch and grow, which is a particularly difficult problem for children suffering from burns. Engineered skin also helps reduce the disfigurement associated with scarring. One significant limitation of the engineered skin is that when it is new, it lacks sweat glands. Patients who have large skin grafts need to be cautious about overexercising and exposure to the sun.

Science, Technology, and Society

ACTiViTY————GENERAL

Have students model having a prosthetic hand by using a clothespin to pick up papers, hold a pencil to write their name, and tie their shoes. Have them discuss how it feels, and have them try to imagine what having an artificial hand would be like. Then, ask students to brainstorm ways that they might improve their "prosthetic hand" (the clothespin).

Science in Action

Weird Science

Engineered Skin

Your skin is your first line of defense against the outside world. Your skin keeps you safe from dehydration and infection, helps regulate body temperature, and helps remove some wastes. But what happens if a large portion of skin is damaged? Skin may not be able to function properly. For someone who has a serious burn, a doctor often uses skin from an undamaged part of the person's body to repair the damaged skin. But some burn victims don't have enough undamaged skin to spare. Doctors have discovered ways to engineer skin that can be used in place of human skin.

Math ACTiViTY

A doctor repaired 0.35 m² of an adult patient's skin with engineered skin. If an adult has about 2 m² of skin, what percentage of the patient's skin was repaired?

Science, Technology, and Society

Beating the Odds

Sometimes, people are born without limbs or lose limbs in accidents. Many of these people have prostheses (prahs THEE SEEZ), or human-made replacements for the body parts. Until recently, many of these prostheses made it more difficult for many people to participate in physical activities, such as sports. But new designs have led to lighter, more comfortable prostheses that move the way that a human limb does. These new designs have allowed athletes with physical disabilities to compete at higher levels.

Social Studies ACTiViTY

Research the use of prostheses throughout history. Create a timeline showing major advances in prosthesis use and design.

Answer to Math Activity
17.5% (0.35 m² ÷ 2 m² × 100 = 17.5%)

Answer to Social Studies Activity
Students' timelines should display an understanding of how modern technology has improved prosthesis design. Timelines should include the use of wooden prostheses, expand into the use of metal and the development of plastics and other synthetics in prosthesis construction, and discuss modern ergonomic designs.

Careers

Zahra Beheshti

Physical Therapist A physical therapist is a licensed professional who helps people recover from injuries by using hands-on treatment instead of medicines. Dr. Zahra Beheshti is a physical therapist at the Princeton Physical Therapy Center in New Jersey. She often helps athletes who suffer from sports injuries.

After an injury, a person may go through a process called *rehabilitation* to regain the use of the injured body part. The most common mistake made by athletes is that they play sports before completely recovering from injuries. Dr. Beheshti explains, "Going back to their usual pre-injury routine could result in another injury."

Dr. Beheshti also teaches patients about preventing future sports injuries. "Most injuries happen when an individual engages in strenuous activities without a proper warm-up or cool-down period." Being a physical therapist is rewarding work. Dr. Beheshti says, "I get a lot of satisfaction when treating patients and see them regain their function and independence and return to their normal life."

Language Arts ACTiViTy

WRITING SKILL Interview a physical therapist who works in or near your community. Write a newspaper article about your interview.

To learn more about these Science in Action topics, visit go.hrw.com and type in the keyword HL5BD1F.

Current Science

Check out Current Science® articles related to this chapter by visiting go.hrw.com. Just type in the keyword HL5CS22.

6 # Circulation and Respiration
Chapter Planning Guide

Compression guide:
To shorten instruction because of time limitations, omit the Chapter Lab.

OBJECTIVES	LABS, DEMONSTRATIONS, AND ACTIVITIES	TECHNOLOGY RESOURCES
PACING • 90 min pp. 174–181 **Chapter Opener**	**SE** Start-up Activity, p. 175 GENERAL	**OSP** Parent Letter GENERAL **CD** Student Edition on CD-ROM **CD** Guided Reading Audio CD **TR** Chapter Starter Transparency* **VID** Brain Food Video Quiz
Section 1 The Cardiovascular System • List four main parts of the cardiovascular system, and describe their functions. • Describe the two types of circulation of blood in the body. • List four cardiovascular problems.	**TE** Connection Activity Math, p. 177 GENERAL **TE** Activity Viewing Blood Vessels, p. 178 ◆ GENERAL **TE** Group Activity Circulate!, p. 179 ◆ GENERAL **LB** Whiz-Bang Demonstrations Get the Beat* ◆ BASIC	**CRF** Lesson Plans* **TR** Bellringer Transparency* **TR** The Flow of Blood Through the Heart* **TR** The Flow of Blood Through the Body* **TE** Internet Activity, p. 181 GENERAL
PACING • 45 min pp. 182–185 **Section 2** Blood • Identify the four main components of blood. • Describe three functions of blood. • Explain how blood pressure is measured. • Explain what the ABO blood types are and why they are important.	**TE** Activity Making a Model of Blood, p. 183 ◆ BASIC **SE** Science in Action Math, Social Studies, and Language Arts Activities, pp. 200–201 GENERAL **LB** Calculator-Based Labs A Hot Hand* ◆ ADVANCED	**CRF** Lesson Plans* **TR** Bellringer Transparency*
PACING • 45 min pp. 186–189 **Section 3** The Lymphatic System • Describe the relationship between the lymphatic system and the circulatory system. • Identify six parts of the lymphatic system, and describe their functions.	**SE** Connection to Social Studies Vent Your Spleen, p. 188 GENERAL	**CRF** Lesson Plans* **TR** Bellringer Transparency* **CRF** SciLinks Activity* GENERAL
PACING • 90 min pp. 190–193 **Section 4** The Respiratory System • Describe the parts of the respiratory system and their functions. • Explain how breathing happens. • Discuss the relationship between the respiratory system and the cardiovascular system. • Identify two respiratory disorders.	**TE** Activity Deep Breathing, p. 190 GENERAL **TE** Activity Investigating Speech, p. 191 GENERAL **SE** Connection to Chemistry Oxygen and Blood, p. 192 GENERAL **SE** Quick Lab Why Do People Snore?, p. 193 GENERAL **SE** Skills Practice Labs Carbon Dioxide Breath, p. 194 ◆ GENERAL **SE** Model-Making Labs Build a Lung, p. 595 ◆ GENERAL **LB** Whiz-Bang Demonstrations Take a Deep Breath* ◆ GENERAL **LB** EcoLabs & Field Activities There's Something in the Air* ◆ GENERAL **LB** Long-Term Projects & Research Ideas Getting to the Heart* ◆ ADVANCED	**CRF** Lesson Plans* **TR** Bellringer Transparency* **TR** The Role of Blood in Respiration* **TR** *LINK TO PHYSICAL SCIENCE* Exhaling, Pressure, and Fluid Flow* **VID** Lab Videos for Life Science

PACING • 90 min

CHAPTER REVIEW, ASSESSMENT, AND STANDARDIZED TEST PREPARATION

CRF Vocabulary Activity* GENERAL
SE Chapter Review, pp. 196–197 GENERAL
CRF Chapter Review* ■ GENERAL
CRF Chapter Tests A* GENERAL, B* ADVANCED, C* SPECIAL NEEDS
SE Standardized Test Preparation, pp. 198–199 GENERAL
CRF Standardized Test Preparation* GENERAL
CRF Performance-Based Assessment* GENERAL
OSP Test Generator GENERAL
CRF Test Item Listing* GENERAL

Online and Technology Resources

Visit **go.hrw.com** for a variety of free resources related to this textbook. Enter the keyword **HT5R7BD2**.

Holt Online Learning

Students can access interactive problem-solving help and active visual concept development with the *Holt Science and Technology* Online Edition available at **www.hrw.com**.

Guided Reading Audio CD

These CDs are designed to help auditory learners and reluctant readers.

Science Tutor CD-ROM

Excellent for remediation and test practice.

KEY

		CRF	Chapter Resource File	SS	Science Skills Worksheets	*	Also on One-Stop Planner
		OSP	One-Stop Planner	MS	Math Skills for Science Worksheets	◆	Requires advance prep
SE	Student Edition	LB	Lab Bank	CD	CD or CD-ROM	■	Also available in Spanish
TE	Teacher Edition	TR	Transparencies	VID	Classroom Video/DVD		

SKILLS DEVELOPMENT RESOURCES	SECTION REVIEW AND ASSESSMENT	STANDARDS CORRELATIONS
SE **Pre-Reading Activity,** p. 174 `GENERAL` OSP **Science Puzzlers, Twisters & Teasers** `GENERAL`		North Carolina Standard Course of Study
CRF **Directed Reading A*** `BASIC`, **B*** `SPECIAL NEEDS` CRF **Vocabulary and Section Summary*** `GENERAL` SE **Reading Strategy** Paired Summarizing, p. 176 `GENERAL` TE **Reading Strategy** Mnemonics, p. 178 `GENERAL` SE **Math Practice** The Beat Goes On, p. 180 `GENERAL` MS **Math Skills for Science** Multiplying Whole Numbers* `BASIC` CRF **Reinforcement Worksheet** Matchmaker, Matchmaker* `GENERAL` CRF **Reinforcement Worksheet** Colors of the Heart* `BASIC` CRF **Critical Thinking** Doctor for a Day* `ADVANCED`	SE **Reading Checks,** pp. 176, 178, 180 `GENERAL` TE **Homework,** p. 177 `GENERAL` TE **Homework,** p. 177 `GENERAL` TE **Reteaching,** p. 180 `BASIC` TE **Quiz,** p. 180 `GENERAL` TE **Alternative Assessment,** p. 180 `GENERAL` SE **Section Review,*** p. 181 ■ `GENERAL` CRF **Section Quiz*** ■ `GENERAL`	4.01, 4.02, 4.03, 4.04
CRF **Directed Reading A*** `BASIC`, **B*** `SPECIAL NEEDS` CRF **Vocabulary and Section Summary*** `GENERAL` SE **Reading Strategy** Reading Organizer, p. 182 `GENERAL` TE **Discussion** Blood, p. 182 `GENERAL` TE **Reading Strategy** Asking Questions, p. 183 `GENERAL` TE **Inclusion Strategies,** p. 184	SE **Reading Checks,** pp. 182, 183, 184, 185 `GENERAL` TE **Reteaching,** p. 184 `BASIC` TE **Quiz,** p. 184 `GENERAL` TE **Alternative Assessment,** p. 184 `GENERAL` SE **Section Review,*** p. 185 ■ `GENERAL` CRF **Section Quiz*** ■ `GENERAL`	4.01, 4.02, 4.04
CRF **Directed Reading A*** `BASIC`, **B*** `SPECIAL NEEDS` CRF **Vocabulary and Section Summary*** `GENERAL` SE **Reading Strategy** Prediction Guide, p. 186 `GENERAL` TE **Research** Lymphatic System and Disease, p. 187 `ADVANCED` TE **Reading Strategy** Paired Summarizing, p. 187 `GENERAL`	SE **Reading Checks,** pp. 186–188 `GENERAL` TE **Reteaching,** p. 188 `BASIC` TE **Quiz,** p. 188 `GENERAL` TE **Alternative Assessment,** p. 188 `ADVANCED` SE **Section Review,*** p. 189 ■ `GENERAL` CRF **Section Quiz*** ■ `GENERAL`	4.01, 4.02, 4.04
CRF **Directed Reading A*** `BASIC`, **B*** `SPECIAL NEEDS` CRF **Vocabulary and Section Summary*** `GENERAL` SE **Reading Strategy** Reading Organizer, p. 190 `GENERAL` TE **Inclusion Strategies,** p. 191	SE **Reading Checks,** pp. 191, 192 `GENERAL` TE **Reteaching,** p. 192 `BASIC` TE **Quiz,** p. 192 `GENERAL` TE **Alternative Assessment,** p. 192 `ADVANCED` SE **Section Review,*** p. 193 ■ `GENERAL` CRF **Section Quiz*** ■ `GENERAL`	4.01, 4.02, 4.03, 4.04; *Chapter Lab:* 1.03, 1.04, 1.08

One-Stop Planner® CD-ROM

This convenient CD-ROM includes:
- Lab Materials QuickList Software
- Holt Calendar Planner
- Customizable Lesson Plans
- Printable Worksheets
- ExamView® Test Generator

cnnstudentnews.com

Find the latest news, lesson plans, and activities related to important scientific events.

SCILINKS.® NSTA

www.scilinks.org

Maintained by the **National Science Teachers Association.** See Chapter Enrichment pages for a complete list of topics.

Check out *Current Science* articles and activities by visiting the HRW Web site at **go.hrw.com.** Just type in the keyword **HL5CS23T.**

Classroom Videos

- **Lab Videos** demonstrate the chapter lab.
- **Brain Food Video Quizzes** help students review the chapter material.
- **CNN Videos** bring science into your students' daily life.

Visual Resources

CHAPTER STARTER TRANSPARENCY

This Really Happened!

The human heart is normally a very dependable organ. It may beat more than 100,000 times per day for a person's entire life. During this time it pumps millions of liters of blood through the body. When there is a serious problem with the heart, it is life threatening. In the past, heart failure resulted in immediate death. But in 1969, Dr. Denton Cooley, of the Texas Heart Institute, kept a patient alive for 5 days after the patient's heart failed. How did he do it? He used an artificial heart that he designed himself.

The design of artificial hearts has improved considerably since Dr. Cooley's first model. The electric artificial heart shown above right is one of the more recent test models. Its mass is about 680 g—only a little heavier than a real human heart. Newer test models are even smaller and lighter. These artificial hearts have special sensors and micro-processors that regulate the beat and respond to changes in blood pressure.

Currently, there is no artificial heart that can permanently replace the human heart. The human heart is a sophisticated organ that serves the cardiovascular system, one of the body's pathways for circulating fluids. In this chapter you will also read about the lymphatic system and the respiratory system and how all of these systems are related.

BELLRINGER TRANSPARENCIES

Section: The Cardiovascular System
In 2 to 3 minutes, list as many song titles and lyrics as you can that contain the word *heart*. What ideas are associated with the heart? Why do you think the heart is part of so many songs?

Write your answers in your **science journal**.

Section: Blood
What does blood do? List as many functions of blood as you can think of in your **science journal**. Think about the following phrase: "Blood is thicker than water." Have you ever heard someone use this phrase? What do you think it means?

TEACHING TRANSPARENCIES

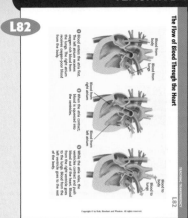

The Flow of Blood Through the Heart

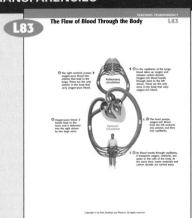

The Flow of Blood Through the Body

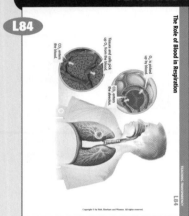

The Role of Blood in Respiration

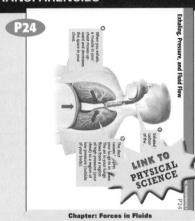

Exhaling, Pressure, and Fluid Flow

LINK TO PHYSICAL SCIENCE

Chapter: Forces in Fluids

CONCEPT MAPPING TRANSPARENCY

Use the following terms to complete the concept map below: arteries, cardiovascular system, bronchi, alveoli, capillaries, respiratory system, cellular respiration, blood

Planning Resources

LESSON PLANS

Lesson Plan SAMPLE

Section: Waves

Pacing
Regular Schedule: with lab(s):2 days without lab(s)2 days
Block Schedule: with lab(s): 1 1/2 days without lab(s)1 day

Objectives
1. Relate the seven properties of life to a living organism.
2. Describe seven themes that can help you to organize what you learn about biology.
3. Identify the tiny structures that make up all living organisms.
4. Differentiate between reproduction and heredity and between metabolism and homeostasis.

National Science Education Standards Covered
LSInter6:Cells have particular structures that underlie their functions.
LSMat1:Most cell functions involve chemical reactions.
LSBeh1:Cells store and use information to guide their functions.
UCP1:Cell functions are regulated.
SI1: Cells can differentiate and form complete multicellular organisms.
PS1: Species evolve over time.
ESS1: The great diversity of organisms is the result of more than 3.5 billion years of evolution.
ESS2: Natural selection and its evolutionary consequences provide a scientific explanation for the fossil record of ancient life forms as well as for the striking molecular similarities observed among the diverse species of living organisms.
ST1: The millions of different species of plants, animals, and microorganisms that live on Earth today are related by descent from common ancestors.
ST2: The energy for life primarily comes from the sun.
SPSP1: The complexity and organization of organisms accommodates the need for obtaining, transforming, transporting, releasing, and eliminating the matter and energy used to sustain the organisms.
SPSP6: As matter and energy flows through different levels of organization of living systems—cells, organs, communities—and between living systems and the physical environment, chemical elements are recombined in different ways.
HNS1: Organisms have behavioral responses to internal changes and to external stimuli.

PARENT LETTER

SAMPLE

Dear Parent,

Your son's or daughter's science class will soon begin exploring the chapter entitled "The World of Physical Science." In this chapter, students will learn about how the scientific method applies to the world of physical science and how the scientific method applies to the world around them. By the end of this chapter, students should demonstrate a clear understanding of the chapter's main ideas and be able to discuss the following topics:

1. physical science as the study of energy and matter (Section 1)
2. the role of physical science in the world around them (Section 1)
3. careers that rely on physical science (Section 1)
4. the steps used in the scientific method (Section 2)
5. examples of technology (Section 2)
6. how the scientific method is used to answer questions and solve problems (Section 2)
7. how our knowledge of science changes over time (Section 2)
8. how models represent real objects or systems (Section 3)
9. examples of different ways models are used in science (Section 3)
10. the importance of the International System of Units (Section 4)
11. the appropriate units to use for particular measurements (Section 4)
12. how area and density are derived quantities (Section 4)

Questions to Ask Along the Way

You can help your son or daughter learn about these topics by asking interesting questions such as the following:

• What are some surprising careers that use physical science?
• What is a characteristic of a good hypothesis?
• When is it a good idea to use a model?
• Why do Americans measure things in terms of inches and yards instead of centimeters and meters?

TEST ITEM LISTING

TEST ITEM LISTING
The World of Science SAMPLE

MULTIPLE CHOICE

1. A limitation of models is that
   a. they are large enough to see.
   b. they do not act exactly like the things that they model.
   c. they are smaller than the things that they model.
   d. they model unfamiliar things.
   Answer: B   Difficulty: 1   Section: 3   Objective: 2

2. The length 10 m is equal to
   a. 100 cm.   c. 10,000 mm.
   b. 1,000 cm.   d. Both (b) and (c)
   Answer: B   Difficulty: 1   Section: 3   Objective: 2

3. To be valid, a hypothesis must be
   a. testable   c. made into a law.
   b. supported by evidence   d. Both (a) and (b)
   Answer: B   Difficulty: 1   Section: 2   Objective: 2 1

4. The statement "Sheila has a stain on her shirt" is an example of a(n)
   a. law.   c. observation.
   b. hypothesis.   d. prediction.
   Answer: B   Difficulty: 1   Section: 3   Objective: 2

5. A hypothesis is often developed out of
   a. observations   c. laws.
   b. experiments   d. Both (a) and (b)
   Answer: B   Difficulty: 1   Section: 2   Objective: 2

6. How many milliliters are in 3.5 kL?
   a. 3,500 mL.   c. 3,500, 000 mL.
   b. 0.0035 mL.   d. 35,000 mL.
   Answer: B   Difficulty: 1   Section: 3   Objective: 2

7. A map of Seattle is an example of a
   a. law   c. model
   b. theory.   d. unit.
   Answer: B   Difficulty: 1   Section: 3   Objective: 2

8. A lab has the safety icons shown below. These icons mean that you should wear
   a. only safety goggles.   c. safety goggles and a lab apron.
   b. only a lab apron.   d. safety goggles, a lab apron, and gloves.
   Answer: B   Difficulty: 1   Section: 3   Objective: 2

9. The law of conservation of mass says the tot al mass before a chemical change is
   a. more than the total mass after the change
   b. less than the total mass after the change
   c. the same as the total mass after the change
   d. not the same as the total mass after the change
   Answer: B   Difficulty: 1   Section: 3   Objective: 2

10. Which of the following areas might you find a geochemist at work?
    a. studying the chemistry of rocks.   c. studying fishes
    b. studying forestry   d. studying the atmosphere
    Answer: B   Difficulty: 1   Section: 3   Objective: 2

One-Stop Planner® CD-ROM

This CD-ROM includes all of the resources shown here and the following time-saving tools:

• **Lab Materials QuickList Software**
• **Customizable lesson plans**
• **Holt Calendar Planner**
• **The powerful ExamView® Test Generator**

Meeting Individual Needs

DIRECTED READING A

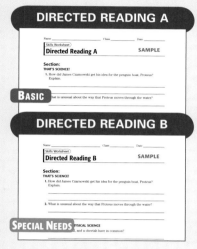

BASIC

DIRECTED READING B

SPECIAL NEEDS

VOCABULARY ACTIVITY

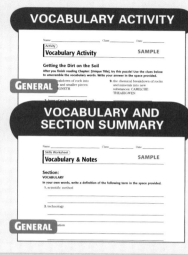

GENERAL

VOCABULARY AND SECTION SUMMARY

GENERAL

REINFORCEMENT

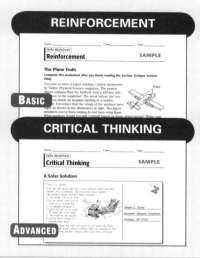

BASIC

CRITICAL THINKING

ADVANCED

SCILINKS ACTIVITY

GENERAL

SCIENCE PUZZLERS, TWISTERS & TEASERS

GENERAL

Labs and Activities

ECOLABS & FIELD ACTIVITIES

GENERAL

WHIZ-BANG DEMONSTRATIONS

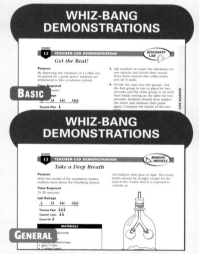

BASIC

WHIZ-BANG DEMONSTRATIONS

GENERAL

LONG-TERM PROJECTS & RESEARCH IDEAS

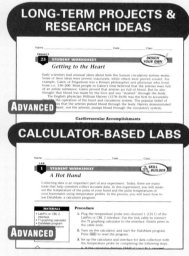

ADVANCED

CALCULATOR-BASED LABS

ADVANCED

DATASHEETS FOR QUICK LABS

DATASHEETS FOR CHAPTER LABS

DATASHEETS FOR LABBOOK

Review and Assessments

SECTION QUIZ

ALSO IN SPANISH

GENERAL

SECTION REVIEW

GENERAL

ALSO IN SPANISH

CHAPTER REVIEW

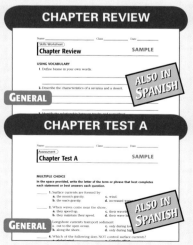

ALSO IN SPANISH

GENERAL

CHAPTER TEST A

GENERAL

ALSO IN SPANISH

CHAPTER TEST B

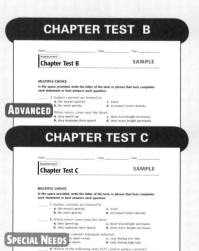

ADVANCED

CHAPTER TEST C

SPECIAL NEEDS

STANDARDIZED TEST PREPARATION

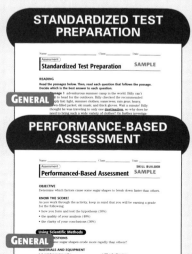

GENERAL

PERFORMANCE-BASED ASSESSMENT

GENERAL

This Chapter Enrichment provides relevant and interesting information to expand and enhance your presentation of the chapter material.

Section 1

The Cardiovascular System
The Flow of Blood

- William Harvey (1578–1657) is credited with being the first European to discover the circulation of the blood through the body.

- Based on his dissections of animals, Harvey rightly concluded that the heart was a muscle that served to pump blood through the body. Harvey correctly maintained that arteries carry blood away from the heart and veins carry blood toward the heart. His views, for which many other physicians ridiculed him, contradicted conventional wisdom and theories of the famous physician Galen (129–c. 201 CE).

Atherosclerosis

- Atherosclerosis is a disease of the arteries in which the inside layer of the arterial walls thickens with plaque. Plaque forms in areas where the inner arterial wall has been damaged. As the walls of an artery thicken, the diameter of the vessel narrows, which impedes blood flow.

- Cigarette smoking, high blood pressure, obesity, inactivity, high cholesterol level, and a family history of heart disease are risk factors for atherosclerosis.

Hypertension

- Like people who have atherosclerosis, people afflicted with hypertension may not exhibit symptoms of the disease for years. In fact, hypertension is often called "the silent killer." Although blood pressure varies within a wide range across the population, a person whose resting blood pressure is consistently at the high end of that range is said to have hypertension.

- Smoking, obesity, stress, excessive consumption of alcohol, and diabetes mellitus exacerbate high blood pressure.

Stroke

- A stroke occurs when the brain is damaged because of an interruption in the blood flow or the leakage of blood from the blood vessels. Atherosclerosis and hypertension are some of the causes of strokes.

Heart Attack

- A heart attack occurs when part of the heart muscle dies because of blood and oxygen deprivation. About 1 million people in the United States have a heart attack each year.

Section 2

Blood
Blood Types and Rh Factor

- Human blood has four ABO types (A, B, AB, and O), which are determined by surface antigens on red blood cells (RBCs). Blood is also either Rh+ or Rh−. If RBCs have an Rh antigen (a protein on the surface of the cells), the blood is Rh+. If an Rh antigen is not present, the blood is Rh−. People have one of the following blood types: A+, A−, B+, B−, AB+, AB−, O+, or O−.

- People make antibodies against the antigens that their RBCs do not have. People who have Rh− blood (no Rh antigens) make antibodies against the Rh antigen only after being exposed to Rh+ blood. For example, people who have type B− blood make A antibodies that attack any blood cell that has an A antigen. They may also make Rh antibodies that will attack any blood cell that has an Rh antigen on it. So, people who have type B− blood who have been exposed to Rh+ blood cannot be given A+, A−, B+, AB+, or AB− blood.

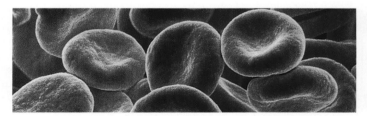

- Type O− blood can be given to anyone because its RBCs do not have any A, B, or Rh antigens that a recipient's antibodies could attack. For this reason, a type O− person is said to be a universal donor. Type AB+ people are called *universal recipients*; they can be given any type of blood because they do not make any antibodies against A, B, or Rh antigens.

Section 3

The Lymphatic System

Lymphocytes

- Lymphocytes are white blood cells that specialize in fighting pathogens. The two main kinds of lymphocytes are B cells and T cells.

- About 10 % of lymphocytes are B cells. When confronted with foreign antigens, B cells produce antibodies that destroy the antigens. This process is called *humoral immunity.*

- About 90 % of lymphocytes are T cells, which form in the bones and mature in the thymus. Cells called *killer T cells* locate and attack cells on whose surface are foreign antigens. This type of immunity is called *cell-mediated immunity.*

- HIV infects and destroys lymphocytes called *helper T cells.* When a person's helper T cell count falls below 200 cells per cubic millimeter of blood, the person is diagnosed with AIDS.

Is That a Fact!

- ◆ The tonsils reach their largest size when a person is about seven years old. Then, the tonsils begin to shrink.

Section 4

The Respiratory System

Control of Breathing

- Unless a person consciously holds his or her breath or changes the rate of his or her breathing, breathing is controlled automatically by breathing control centers in the base of the brain (in the medulla oblongata and in the pons).

- Hiccups are a result of a sudden, jerky contraction of the diaphragm. When a person eats too much food, the full stomach may irritate the diaphragm muscle and cause the muscle to contract jerkily. However, other causes of hiccups are unknown.

Is That a Fact!

- ◆ Each day, about 2,000 adolescents in the United States become regular daily smokers each day. The habit will eventually kill one-third of these children.

- ◆ Children who have asthma are particularly at risk from their parents' second-hand smoke. Each year, second-hand smoke increases the number of asthma attacks and the severity of the symptoms in 200,000 to 1 million children who have asthma.

Smoking

- Tobacco smoking has been implicated in more than 90% of lung cancers among men. Among people who do not smoke, 3,000 cases of lung cancer are linked to second-hand cigarette smoke each year.

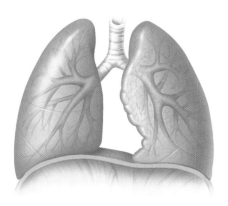

Developed and maintained by the National Science Teachers Association

SciLinks is maintained by the National Science Teachers Association to provide you and your students with interesting, up-to-date links that will enrich your classroom presentation of the chapter.

Visit www.scilinks.org and enter the SciLinks code for more information about the topic listed.

Topic: The Cardiovascular System
SciLinks code: HSM0221

Topic: The Lymphatic System
SciLinks code: HSM0891

Topic: Cardiovascular Problems
SciLinks code: HSM0220

Topic: The Immune System
SciLinks code: HSM0786

Topic: Blood
SciLinks code: HSM0175

Topic: The Respiratory System
SciLinks code: HSM1307

Topic: Blood Donations
SciLinks code: HSM0178

Topic: Respiratory Disorders
SciLinks code: HSM1306

Overview

Tell students that this chapter will help them learn about their cardiovascular, lymphatic, and respiratory systems. The chapter has a separate section about blood and a clear description of the way that the cardiovascular system and blood make up the circulatory system.

Assessing Prior Knowledge

Students should be familiar with the following topics:

- the basic life processes
- cells

Identifying Misconceptions

As students learn the material in this chapter, some of them may be confused about the difference between cells and molecules. When asked to draw a molecule, many students will draw something that resembles a cell. Instruction should describe the relationship between molecules and cells. Also, many students may think that proteins and molecules are bigger than cells. The concepts of the cell and the molecule are important when studying the way that blood transports materials to cells and the way that gases are exchanged in the lungs. Use a Venn diagram to help clarify the relationship between atoms, molecules and cells.

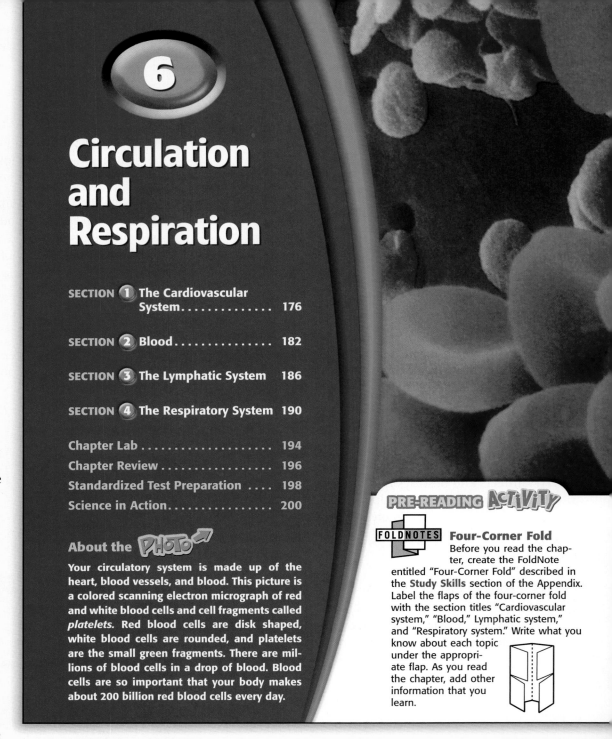

6

Circulation and Respiration

About the PHOTO

Your circulatory system is made up of the heart, blood vessels, and blood. This picture is a colored scanning electron micrograph of red and white blood cells and cell fragments called *platelets*. Red blood cells are disk shaped, white blood cells are rounded, and platelets are the small green fragments. There are millions of blood cells in a drop of blood. Blood cells are so important that your body makes about 200 billion red blood cells every day.

PRE-READING ACTIVITY

FOLDNOTES **Four-Corner Fold**
Before you read the chapter, create the FoldNote entitled "Four-Corner Fold" described in the **Study Skills** section of the Appendix. Label the flaps of the four-corner fold with the section titles "Cardiovascular system," "Blood," "Lymphatic system," and "Respiratory system." Write what you know about each topic under the appropriate flap. As you read the chapter, add other information that you learn.

Standards Correlations

North Carolina Standard Course of Study

1.03 Apply safety procedures in the laboratory and in field studies: Recognize potential hazards, Safely manipulate materials and equipment, [and] Conduct appropriate procedures. (Chapter Lab)

1.04 (partial) Analyze variables in scientific investigations: . . . Manipulate [and] Describe relationships between . . . (Chapter Lab)

1.08 Use oral and written language to: Communicate findings [and] Defend conclusions of scientific investigations. (Chapter Lab)

4.01 (partial) Analyze how human body systems interact to provide for the needs of the human organism: . . . Cardiovascular, Digestive and Circulatory, [and] Respiratory . . . (Sections 1, 2, 3, and 4)

4.02 Describe how systems within the human body are defined by the functions it performs. (Sections 1, 2, 3, and 4)

4.03 (partial) Explain how the structure of an organ is adapted to perform specific functions within one or more systems: . . . Heart [and] Lung . . . (Sections 1 and 4)

4.04 Evaluate how systems in the human body help regulate the internal environment. (Sections 1, 2, 3, and 4)

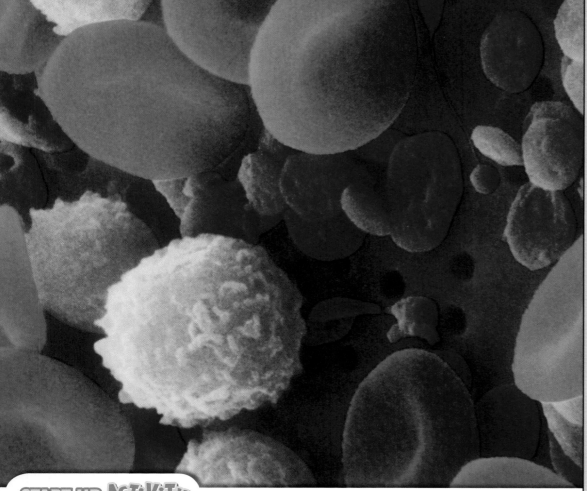

Safety Caution: Have students bring in a signed permission slip for this activity. Any students who have a health problem that may be worsened by exercise should be excused from the exercise portion of this activity. Instruct students who feel pain or become dizzy or tired to stop exercising immediately. Some students may feel embarrassed to exercise in front of their peers. You may want to invite a few volunteers to perform the exercise portion instead of having all of the students exercise.

Answers

1. Students should notice that their heart rate goes up when they are exercising. Explanations may vary, but students should understand that during exercise an increase in circulation rate is needed to ensure delivery of sufficient oxygen and fuel to the body.

2. Sample answer: An increased heart rate increases the rate of blood flow and delivers red blood cells to the body more quickly.

3. Sample answer: When I stop exercising, my body no longer needs extra oxygen and fuel, so my heart rate returns to normal after a period of rest.

START-UP ACTIVITY

Exercise Your Heart

How does your heart respond to exercise? You can see this reaction by measuring your pulse.

Procedure

1. Take your pulse while remaining still. (Take your pulse by placing your fingers on the inside of your wrist just below your thumb.)

2. Using a **watch with a second hand,** count the number of heart beats in 15 s. Then, multiply this number by 4 to calculate the number of beats in 1 minute.

3. Do some moderate physical activity, such as jumping jacks or jogging in place, for 30 s.

4. Stop and calculate your heart rate again.
   Caution: Do not perform this exercise if you have difficulty breathing, if you have high blood pressure or asthma, or if you get dizzy easily.

5. Rest for 5 min.

6. Take your pulse again.

Analysis

1. How did exercise affect your heart rate? Why do you think this happened?

2. How does your heart rate affect the rate at which red blood cells travel throughout your body?

3. Did your heart rate return to normal (or almost normal) after you rested? Why or why not?

This Really Happened!

The human heart is normally a very dependable organ. It may beat more than 100,000 times per day for a person's entire life. During this time it pumps millions of liters of blood through the body. When there is a serious problem with the heart, it is life threatening.

In the past, heart failure resulted in immediate death. But in 1969, Dr. Denton Cooley, of the Texas Heart Institute, kept a patient alive for 5 days after the patient's heart failed. How did he do it? He used an artificial heart that he designed himself.

The design of artificial hearts has shown above right is one of the more recent test models. Its mass is about 680 g—only a little heavier than a real human heart. Newer test models are even smaller and lighter. These artificial hearts have special sensors and microprocessors that regulate the beat and respond to changes in blood pressure.

Currently, there is no artificial heart that can permanently replace the human heart. The human heart is a sophisticated organ that serves the cardiovascular system, one of the body's pathways for circulating fluids. In this chapter you will also read about the lymphatic system and

Chapter Starter Transparency
Use this transparency to help students begin thinking about their circulatory system and its functions.

CHAPTER RESOURCES

Technology

 Transparencies
• Chapter Starter Transparency

READING SKILLS

 Student Edition on CD-ROM

Guided Reading Audio CD

Classroom Videos
• Brain Food Video Quiz

Workbooks

 Science Puzzlers, Twisters & Teasers
• Circulation and Respiration **GENERAL**

Focus

Overview

This section introduces the structures and functions of the cardiovascular and circulatory systems. Students study the three types of blood vessels, trace the path of blood in the body, and learn about blood types.

 **Bellringer**

Ask students to list as many song titles, phrases, and slogans that contain the word *heart* as they can in two to three minutes. Ask for examples, and list the examples on the board. Ask for reasons that the word *heart* is the focus of so many songs and slogans.

Motivate

Discussion ——— GENERAL

Cardiovascular System Ask students to describe or diagram the flow of blood through their body. Remind students that their body is made up of trillions of cells. Ask students how they think that oxygen and nutrients get to each cell. Give a general description of the roles of the heart and the blood vessels, and discuss how sturdy these structures must be to work for a lifetime. **LS** Verbal/Logical

---

The Cardiovascular System

When you hear the word heart, *what do you think of first? Many people think of romance. Some people think of courage. But the heart is much more than a symbol of love or bravery. Your heart is an amazing pump.*

The heart is an organ that is part of your circulatory system. The *circulatory system* includes your heart; your blood; your veins, capillaries, and arteries; and your lymphatic system.

Your Cardiovascular System

Your heart creates pressure every time it beats. This pressure moves blood to every cell in your body through your cardiovascular system (KAR dee OH VAS kyoo luhr SIS tuhm). The **cardiovascular system** consists of the heart and the three types of blood vessels that carry blood throughout your body. The word *cardio* means "heart," and *vascular* means "blood vessel." The blood vessels—arteries, capillaries, and veins—carry blood pumped by the heart. **Figure 1** shows the major arteries and veins.

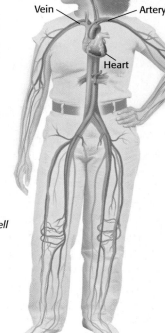

Vein — Artery

Heart

✓ *Reading Check* What are the four main parts of the cardiovascular system? (*See the Appendix for answers to Reading Checks.*)

Figure 1 *The cardiovascular system carries blood to every cell in your body.*

READING WARM-UP

Objectives
● List four main parts of the cardiovascular system, and describe their functions.
● Describe the two types of circulation of blood in the body.
● List four cardiovascular problems.

Terms to Learn
cardiovascular   pulmonary
  system   circulation
artery   systemic
capillary   circulation
vein

READING STRATEGY

Paired Summarizing Read this section silently. In pairs, take turns summarizing the material. Stop to discuss ideas that seem confusing.

cardiovascular system a collection of organs that transport blood throughout the body

---

CHAPTER RESOURCES

Chapter Resource File

- Lesson Plan
- Directed Reading A BASIC
- Directed Reading B SPECIAL NEEDS

Technology

Transparencies
- Bellringer
- The Flow of Blood Through the Heart

Workbooks

Math Skills for Science
- The Unit Factor and Dimensional Analysis

Answer to Reading Check

The four main parts of the cardiovascular system are the heart and the arteries, capillaries, and veins.

The Heart

Your *heart* is an organ made mostly of cardiac muscle tissue. It is about the size of your fist and is almost in the center of your chest cavity. Like hearts of all mammals, your heart has a left side and a right side that are separated by a thick wall. The right side of the heart pumps oxygen-poor blood to the lungs. The left side pumps oxygen-rich blood to the body. As you can see in **Figure 2,** each side has an upper chamber and a lower chamber. Each upper chamber is called an *atrium* (plural, *atria*). Each lower chamber is called a *ventricle.*

Flaplike structures called *valves* are located between the atria and ventricles and in places where large arteries are attached to the heart. As blood moves through the heart, these valves close to prevent blood from going backward. The "lub-dub, lub-dub" sound of a beating heart is caused by the valves closing. **Figure 3** shows the flow of blood through the heart.

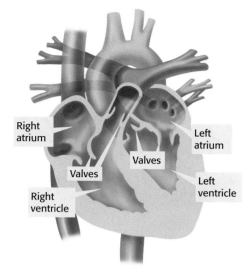

Right atrium

Left atrium

Valves

Valves

Right ventricle

Left ventricle

Figure 2 *The heart pumps blood through blood vessels. The vessels carrying oxygen-rich blood are shown in red. The vessels carrying oxygen-poor blood are shown in blue.*

Figure 3 The Flow of Blood Through the Heart

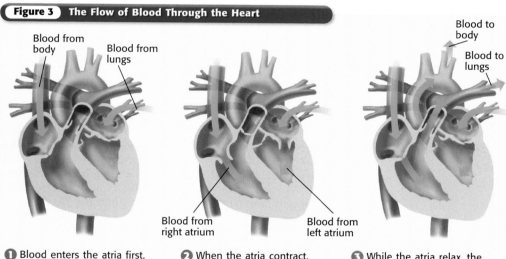

Blood from body

Blood from lungs

Blood from right atrium

Blood from left atrium

Blood to body

Blood to lungs

❶ Blood enters the atria first. The left atrium receives oxygen-rich blood from the lungs. The right atrium receives oxygen-poor blood from the body.

❷ When the atria contract, blood is squeezed into the ventricles.

❸ While the atria relax, the ventricles contract and push blood out of the heart. Blood from the right ventricle goes to the lungs. Blood from the left ventricle goes to the rest of the body.

Homework ——— GENERAL

Poster Project Have students make a poster showing a diagram of the heart. Remind students to label each chamber of the heart properly and to use arrows to indicate the flow of blood. Students can also include diagrams of the lungs and of the rest of the body to show how blood flows to and from the heart. **LS** Visual

Teach

CONNECTION ACTIVITY
Math ——— GENERAL

The Pump in Your Chest Your heart beats about 100,800 times per day. With every beat, about 70 mL of blood is pumped out of your heart. In 1 h, how many liters of blood does your heart pump out? (294 L)

About how many liters of blood does your heart pump out in a day? (7,056 L) Help students visualize this amount by showing them a liter of water. **LS** Logical/ Visual

Homework ——— GENERAL

Making Models Have students make a model of the human heart that shows the path of blood through the heart. Models can be drawings or three-dimensional constructions. Have students present their completed models to the class. Provide yarn or a pen light so that students can demonstrate to the class the flow of blood through their model heart. English Language Learners
LS Visual

CONNECTION to
Chemistry ——— ADVANCED

Pacemaker Contraction of the heart is started by a structure called the *sinoatrial node,* a small cluster of cells embedded in the upper wall of the right atrium. Have students research the sinoatrial node (and the atrioventricular node, which stimulates the ventricles to contract) and make a model or a poster showing how these special cells control the heartbeat.

(Students should find that the heartbeat is not triggered by the nervous system, that the atria contract almost simultaneously, and that the contraction spreads to the ventricles but that there is a short delay during which the atria empty blood into the ventricles.)

Mnemonics Challenge students to create mnemonic devices to help them recall the flow of blood in the body. For example, arteries carry blood away from the heart, and both *artery* and *away* begin with the letter *a*.
LS Verbal

CONNECTION to Real World —— BASIC

Blood Vessels Have students rank blood vessels in order from thickest vessel wall to thinnest vessel wall. Have students explain why wall thicknesses vary. (arteries—blood is under pressure; veins—blood is not under as much pressure as in arteries, but walls do not need to be as thin as capillaries; capillaries—their walls are thinnest because the walls must allow for gas, nutrient, and waste exchange with cells) **English Language Learners**
LS Logical

ACTIVITY —— GENERAL

Viewing Blood Vessels Set up microscope stations that have prepared slides of an artery and a vein. Have students view the slides and match them with the descriptions of arteries and veins in the textbook. Have students sketch what they see under the microscope and write descriptive words beside each sketch. **English Language Learners**
LS Visual

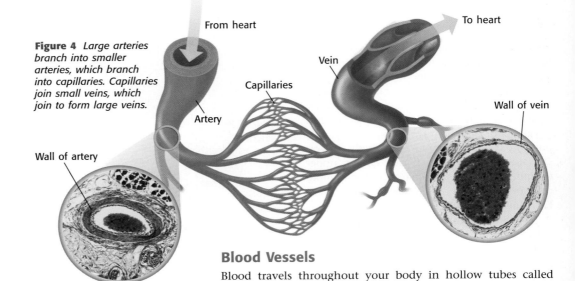

Figure 4 *Large arteries branch into smaller arteries, which branch into capillaries. Capillaries join small veins, which join to form large veins.*

From heart
To heart
Vein
Capillaries
Artery
Wall of vein
Wall of artery

artery a blood vessel that carries blood away from the heart to the body's organs

capillary a tiny blood vessel that allows an exchange between blood and cells in other tissue

vein in biology, a vessel that carries blood to the heart

Blood Vessels

Blood travels throughout your body in hollow tubes called *blood vessels*. The three types of blood vessels—arteries, capillaries, and veins—are shown in **Figure 4**.

Arteries

A blood vessel that carries blood away from the heart is an **artery**. Arteries have thick walls, which contain a layer of smooth muscle. Each heartbeat pumps blood into your arteries at high pressure. This pressure is your *blood pressure*. Artery walls stretch and are usually strong enough to stand the pressure. Your *pulse* is caused by the rhythmic change in your blood pressure.

Capillaries

Nutrients, oxygen, and other substances must leave blood and get to your body's cells. Carbon dioxide and other wastes leave body cells and are carried away by blood. A **capillary** is a tiny blood vessel that allows these exchanges between body cells and blood. These exchanges can take place because capillary walls are only one cell thick. Capillaries are so narrow that blood cells must pass through them in single file. No cell in the body is more than three or four cells away from a capillary.

Veins

After leaving capillaries, blood enters veins. A **vein** is a blood vessel that carries blood back to the heart. As blood travels through veins, valves in the veins keep the blood from flowing backward. When skeletal muscles contract, they squeeze nearby veins and help push blood toward the heart.

✓ Reading Check Describe the three types of blood vessels.

WEIRD SCIENCE

Babies that have certain congenital heart defects are blue at birth. The condition, called *cyanosis*, can be caused by low levels of oxygen in the blood. Oxygen-poor blood may be a result of defects in the heart. These defects cause oxygen-poor blood to be pumped to the body before it is pumped to the lungs. These defects can be repaired surgically.

Answer to Reading Check

Arteries have thick, stretchy walls and carry blood away from the heart. Capillaries are tiny blood vessels that allow the exchange of oxygen, carbon dioxide, and nutrients between cells and blood. Veins are blood vessels that carry blood back to the heart.

Two Types of Circulation

Where does blood get the oxygen to deliver to your body? From your lungs! Your heart pumps blood to the lungs. In the lungs, carbon dioxide leaves the blood and oxygen enters the blood. The oxygen-rich blood then flows back to the heart. This circulation of blood between your heart and lungs is called **pulmonary circulation** (PUL muh NER ee SUHR kyoo LAY shuhn).

The oxygen-rich blood returning to the heart from the lungs is then pumped to the rest of the body. The circulation of blood between the heart and the rest of the body is called **systemic circulation** (sis TEM ik SUHR kyoo LAY shuhn). Both types of circulation are shown in **Figure 5**.

pulmonary circulation the flow of blood from the heart to the lungs and back to the heart through the pulmonary arteries, capillaries, and veins

systemic circulation the flow of blood from the heart to all parts of the body and back to the heart

---

Figure 5 **The Flow of Blood Through the Body**

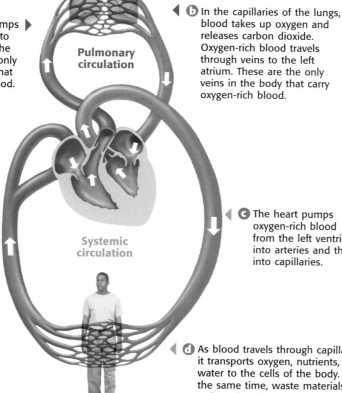
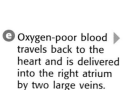

ⓐ The right ventricle pumps oxygen-poor blood into arteries that lead to the lungs. These are the only arteries in the body that carry oxygen-poor blood.

ⓑ In the capillaries of the lungs, blood takes up oxygen and releases carbon dioxide. Oxygen-rich blood travels through veins to the left atrium. These are the only veins in the body that carry oxygen-rich blood.

Pulmonary circulation

ⓔ Oxygen-poor blood travels back to the heart and is delivered into the right atrium by two large veins.

Systemic circulation

ⓒ The heart pumps oxygen-rich blood from the left ventricle into arteries and then into capillaries.

ⓓ As blood travels through capillaries, it transports oxygen, nutrients, and water to the cells of the body. At the same time, waste materials and carbon dioxide are carried away.

MISCONCEPTION ALERT

Pulmonary Circulation Students may think that blood from the heart enters one lung and leaves from the other. However, each lung is serviced by its own vessels that carry blood to and from the heart.

CHAPTER RESOURCES

Technology

Transparencies
• The Flow of Blood Through the Body

MATERIALS

FOR EACH CLASS
• balloon, blue, inflated (or blue paper disk) (5)
• balloon, red, inflated (or red paper disk) (5)
• diagram, "The Flow of Blood Through the Body"
• station, marked by (cardboard boxes, flags, or other markers) (8)

Circulate! Organize the class into five teams for a relay race. The race should proceed as follows:

1. Students begin in the left ventricle carrying a red balloon, which represents an oxygenated blood cell.

2. They travel through the aorta.

3. After passing through the aorta, students carry oxygenated blood to the muscles and exchange the red balloon for a blue one.

4. From the muscles, students carry blood loaded with CO_2 to the right atrium.

5. From the right atrium, students travel into the right ventricle.

6. Students travel through the pulmonary artery.

7. From the pulmonary artery, students travel into the lungs, where they exchange their CO_2 for oxygen (they exchange blue balloons for red ones).

8. Carrying oxygenated blood (red balloons), students enter the left atrium and are ready to begin again or hand off their balloons.

Walk one student at a time through the pathway; then, have the teams send students through in a relay race. **LS** **Kinesthetic/Interpersonal** **Co-op Learning** **English Language Learners**

Reteaching   BASIC

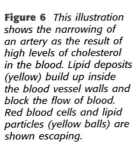

Owner's Guide Have students make an owner's guide for their cardiovascular system. The guide should include a description of the various components of the system as well as information about the care and maintenance of the system. Encourage students to include a diagram or flowchart to illustrate their guide. **LS Verbal**

Quiz   GENERAL

Ask students whether each of the statements below is true or false. Have students correct false statements.

1. High blood pressure makes arteries stronger. (false)

2. Capillaries and veins have the same function. (false)

3. A major cause of heart disease is atherosclerosis. (true)

4. Arteries carry blood to the body and to the lungs. (true)

Alternative Assessment   GENERAL

Spider Map Have students make a spider map using the key terms in this chapter. Have them label the circle "Cardiovascular system," and have them make a leg for each of the other key terms. **LS Logical**

MATH PRACTICE

The Beat Goes On

A person's heart averages about 70 beats per minute.

1. Calculate how many times a heart beats in a day.

2. If a person lives for 75 years, how many times will his or her heart beat?

3. If an athlete's heart beats 50 times a minute, how many fewer times than an average heart will his or her heart beat in 30 days?

Cardiovascular Problems

More than just your heart and blood vessels are at risk if you have cardiovascular problems. Your whole body may be harmed. Cardiovascular problems can be caused by smoking, high levels of cholesterol in the blood, stress, physical inactivity, or heredity. Eating a healthy diet and getting plenty of exercise can reduce the risk of having cardiovascular problems.

Atherosclerosis

Heart diseases are the leading cause of death in the United States. A major cause of heart diseases is a cardiovascular disease called *atherosclerosis* (ATH uhr OH skluh ROH sis). Atherosclerosis happens when cholesterol (kuh LES tuhr AWL) builds up inside of blood vessels. This cholesterol buildup causes the blood vessels to become narrower and less elastic. **Figure 6** shows how clogged the pathway through a blood vessel can become. When an artery that supplies blood to the heart becomes blocked, the person may have a heart attack.

✓ **Reading Check** Why is atherosclerosis dangerous?

High Blood Pressure

Atherosclerosis may be caused by hypertension. *Hypertension* is abnormally high blood pressure. The higher the blood pressure, the greater the risk of a heart attack, heart failure, kidney disease, and stroke. A *stroke* is when a blood vessel in the brain becomes clogged or ruptures. As a result, that part of the brain receives no oxygen. Without oxygen, brain cells die.

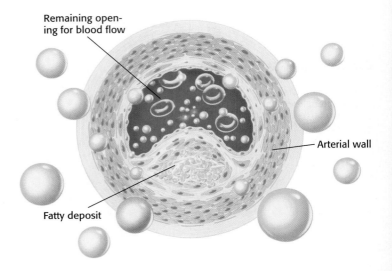

Remaining opening for blood flow

Arterial wall

Fatty deposit

Figure 6 *This illustration shows the narrowing of an artery as the result of high levels of cholesterol in the blood. Lipid deposits (yellow) build up inside the blood vessel walls and block the flow of blood. Red blood cells and lipid particles (yellow balls) are shown escaping.*

CHAPTER RESOURCES

Workbooks

📖 **Math Skills for Science**
- Multiplying Whole Numbers **BASIC**
- Counting the Zeros **GENERAL**
- Creating Exponents **GENERAL**
- Multiplying and Dividing in Scientific Notation **ADVANCED**

Heart Attacks and Heart Failure

Two cardiovascular problems are heart attacks and heart failure. A *heart attack* happens when heart muscle cells die and part of the heart muscle is damaged. As shown in **Figure 7**, arteries that deliver oxygen to the heart may be blocked. Without oxygen, heart muscle cells die quickly. When enough heart muscle cells die, the heart may stop.

Heart failure is different. *Heart failure* happens when the heart cannot pump enough blood to meet the body's needs. Organs, such as the brain, lungs, and kidneys, may be damaged by lack of oxygen or nutrients, or by the buildup of fluids or wastes.

Figure 7 Heart Attack

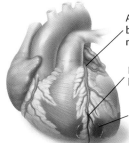

Artery delivering blood to heart muscle

Location of blocked artery

Area of heart damaged by lack of oxygen to heart muscle

SECTION Review

Summary

- The cardiovascular system is made up of the heart and three types of blood vessels.
- The three types of blood vessels are arteries, veins, and capillaries.
- Oxygen-poor blood flows from the heart through the lungs, where it picks up oxygen.
- Oxygen-rich blood flows from the heart to the rest of the body.
- Cardiovascular problems include atherosclerosis, hypertension, heart attacks, and strokes.

Using Key Terms

For each pair of terms, explain how the meanings of the terms differ.

1. *artery* and *vein*
2. *systemic circulation* and *pulmonary circulation*

Understanding Key Ideas

3. Which of the following is true of blood in the pulmonary veins?
   a. The blood is going to the body.
   b. The blood is oxygen poor.
   c. The blood is going to the lungs.
   d. The blood is oxygen rich.

4. What are the four parts of the cardiovascular system? Describe the functions of each part.

5. What is the difference between a heart attack and heart failure?

Math Skills

6. An adult male's heart pumps about 2.8 million liters of blood a year. If his heart beats 70 times a minute, how much blood does his heart pump with each beat?

Critical Thinking

7. **Identifying Relationships** How is the heart's structure related to its function?

8. **Making Inferences** One of aspirin's effects is that it prevents platelets from being too "sticky." Why might doctors prescribe aspirin for patients who have had a heart attack?

9. **Analyzing Ideas** Veins and arteries are everywhere in your body. When a pulse is taken, it is usually taken at an artery in the neck or wrist. Explain why.

10. **Making Comparisons** Why is the structure of arteries different from the structure of capillaries?

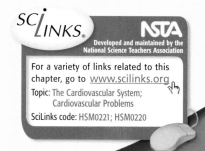

SCILINKS®

NSTA
Developed and maintained by the National Science Teachers Association

For a variety of links related to this chapter, go to www.scilinks.org
Topic: The Cardiovascular System; Cardiovascular Problems
SciLinks code: HSM0221; HSM0220

INTERNET ACTIVITY
Short Story ———— GENERAL

For an Internet activity related to this chapter, have students go to **go.hrw.com** and type in the keyword **HL5BD2W**.

CHAPTER RESOURCES

Chapter Resource File

- Section Quiz **GENERAL**
- Section Review **GENERAL**
- Vocabulary and Section Summary **GENERAL**
- Reinforcement Worksheet **BASIC**
- Critical Thinking **ADVANCED**

Answers to Section Review

1. Arteries have stretchy, thick walls and carry blood away from the heart. Veins have valves and carry blood toward the heart.

2. Blood travels to and from the lungs in pulmonary circulation. Blood travels to and from the body in systemic circulation.

3. d

4. Sample answer: heart: to pump blood to lungs and to all parts of the body; arteries: to carry blood from the heart to the lungs and to all parts of the body; capillaries: to allow the exchange of gases, nutrients, and wastes between cells and blood; veins: to carry blood back to the heart

5. Sample answer: A heart attack happens when heart muscle cells get insufficient oxygen and die, which may cause the heart to stop beating. Heart failure is when the heart cannot pump enough blood to meet the needs of the body.

6. about 76 mL per beat

7. Sample answer: The heart is made mostly of muscle tissue. This muscle pumps the blood through the body. Valves, located between the atria and the ventricles and located where arteries are attached to the heart, stop blood from flowing in the wrong direction.

8. Sample answer: A doctor might prescribe aspirin to keep platelets from sticking together and blocking an artery or vein, especially one in the heart. Such a blockage might cause another heart attack.

9. The wrist and the neck are two places where a large artery is close to the surface of the skin and the pulse can be felt.

10. Arteries and capillaries have different functions: arteries carry blood under pressure away from the heart, and capillaries allow the exchange of gases, nutrients and wastes in cells.

Focus

Overview

In this section, students learn about blood, the parts of blood, and blood types.

🔊 Bellringer

Ask students to list three things that they know about blood, such as the parts of blood, the places where blood cells form, the function of blood in the body, and the way in which blood is donated.

Motivate

Discussion ———— GENERAL

Blood Have students describe a time when their skin was cut and describe what their blood looked like. List the words that students use to describe their blood. Based on students' experiences with blood and bleeding, lead a discussion about the structure and functions of blood. Have students read these pages and compare their descriptions of blood with the one in the textbook. Ask students the following questions: "Can you see individual blood cells when you bleed?" (no) "Why or why not?" (They are too small.) "How are red blood cells important to other cells in the body?" (They have hemoglobin, which helps red blood cells carry oxygen to other cells in the body.) **LS Verbal**

READING WARM-UP

Objectives

- Identify the four main components of blood.
- Describe three functions of blood.
- Explain how blood pressure is measured.
- Explain what the ABO blood types are and why they are important.

Terms to Learn

blood
blood pressure

READING STRATEGY

Reading Organizer As you read this section, create an outline of the section. Use the headings from the section in your outline.

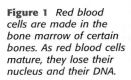

blood the fluid that carries gases, nutrients, and wastes through the body and that is made up of plasma, red blood cells, platelets, and white blood cells

---

Blood

Blood is part of the circulatory system. It travels through miles and miles of blood vessels to reach every cell in your body. So, you must have a lot of blood, right?

Well, actually, an adult human body has about 5 L of blood. Your body probably has a little less than that. All the blood in your body would not fill two 3 L soda bottles.

What Is Blood?

Your *circulatory system* is made up of your heart, your blood vessels, and blood. **Blood** is a connective tissue made up of plasma, red blood cells, platelets, and white blood cells. Blood carries oxygen and nutrients to all parts of your body.

✓ **Reading Check** What are the four main components of blood? *(See the Appendix for answers to Reading Checks.)*

Plasma

The fluid part of the blood is called plasma (PLAZ muh). *Plasma* is a mixture of water, minerals, nutrients, sugars, proteins, and other substances. Red blood cells, white blood cells, and platelets are found in plasma.

Red Blood Cells

Most blood cells are *red blood cells,* or RBCs. RBCs, such as the ones shown in **Figure 1,** take oxygen to every cell in your body. Cells need oxygen to carry out their functions. Each RBC has hemoglobin (HEE moh GLOH bin). *Hemoglobin* is an oxygen-carrying protein. Hemoglobin clings to the oxygen you inhale. RBCs can then transport oxygen throughout the body. Hemoglobin also gives RBCs their red color.

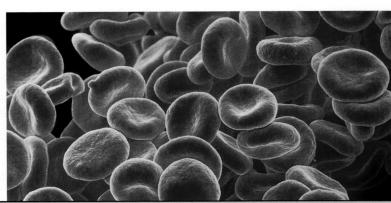

Figure 1 *Red blood cells are made in the bone marrow of certain bones. As red blood cells mature, they lose their nucleus and their DNA.*

CHAPTER RESOURCES

Chapter Resource File

- **Lesson Plan**
- **Directed Reading A** BASIC
- **Directed Reading B** SPECIAL NEEDS

Technology

Transparencies
- Bellringer

Answer to Reading Check

plasma, red blood cells, white blood cells, and platelets

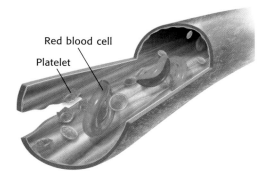

Red blood cell

Platelet

Fibers

Figure 2 *Platelets release chemicals in damaged vessels and cause fibers to form. The fibers make a "net" that traps blood cells and stops bleeding.*

Platelets

Drifting among the blood cells are tiny particles called platelets. *Platelets* are pieces of larger cells found in bone marrow. These larger cells remain in the bone marrow, but fragments are pinched off and enter the bloodstream as platelets. Platelets last for only 5 to 10 days, but they are an important part of blood. When you cut or scrape your skin, you bleed because blood vessels have been opened. As soon as bleeding starts, platelets begin to clump together in the damaged area. They form a plug that helps reduce blood loss, as shown in **Figure 2.** Platelets also release chemicals that react with proteins in plasma. The reaction causes tiny fibers to form. The fibers help create a blood clot.

White Blood Cells

Sometimes *pathogens* (PATH uh juhnz)—bacteria, viruses, and other microscopic particles that can make you sick—enter your body. When they do, they often meet *white blood cells,* or WBCs. WBCs, shown in **Figure 3,** help keep you healthy by destroying pathogens. WBCs also help clean wounds.

WBCs fight pathogens in several ways. Some WBCs squeeze out of blood vessels and move around in tissues, searching for pathogens. When they find a pathogen, they destroy it. Other WBCs release antibodies. *Antibodies* are chemicals that identify or destroy pathogens. WBCs also keep you healthy by destroying body cells that have died or been damaged. Most WBCs are made in bone marrow. Some WBCs mature in the lymphatic system.

✔ Reading Check Why are WBCs important to your health?

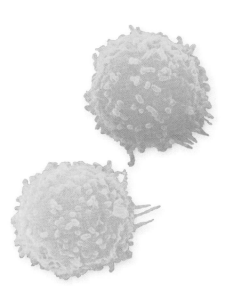

Figure 3 *White blood cells defend the body against pathogens. These white blood cells have been colored yellow to make their shape easier to see.*

Answer to Reading Check
White blood cells identify and attack pathogens that may make you sick.

Close

Reteaching ———— BASIC

Blood Types The subject of blood types may be confusing. Review the material in **Figure 4** to reinforce the material presented in the text. Help students compare the shapes of the antigens on each red blood cell with the shapes of the antibodies that bind to the antigens. **LS** Verbal

Quiz ———— GENERAL

1. Which antibodies will a person who has type AB blood produce? (none)

2. Can a person who has type O blood receive blood from a person who has type AB blood? Why or why not? (No, the type O blood will have antibodies that attack the A and B antigens in the AB blood.)

3. In your own words, define the term *transfusion*. (A transfusion occurs when a person is given an injection of blood to replace blood that has been lost.)

Alternative Assessment ———— GENERAL

Blood Groups Have students write a report about Karl Landsteiner (1868–1943), a Nobel Prize-winning scientist. (Landsteiner discovered that some mixtures of blood are compatible and others are not and that he could divide the population into different groups based on how blood from one group of people reacted with blood from another group.) **LS** Verbal

---

blood pressure the force that blood exerts on the walls of the arteries

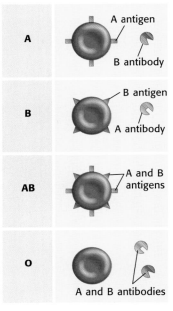

Figure 4 *This figure shows which antigens and antibodies may be present in each blood type.*

Body Temperature Regulation

Your blood does more than supply your cells with oxygen and nutrients. It also helps regulate your body temperature. When your brain senses that your body temperature is rising, it signals blood vessels in your skin to enlarge. As the vessels enlarge, heat from your blood is transferred to your skin. This transfer helps lower your temperature. When your brain senses that your temperature is normal, it instructs your blood vessels to return to their normal size.

Blood Pressure

Every time your heart beats, it pushes blood out of the heart and into your arteries. The force exerted by blood on the inside walls of arteries is called **blood pressure.**

Blood pressure is expressed in millimeters of mercury (mm Hg). For example, a blood pressure of 110 mm Hg means the pressure on the artery walls can push a narrow column of mercury to a height of 110 mm.

Blood pressure is usually given as two numbers, such as 110/70 mm Hg. Systolic (sis TAHL ik) pressure is the first number. *Systolic pressure* is the pressure inside large arteries when the ventricles contract. The surge of blood causes the arteries to bulge and produce a pulse. The second number, *diastolic* (DIE uh STAHL ik) *pressure,* is the pressure inside arteries when the ventricles relax. For adults, a blood pressure of 120/80 mm Hg or below is considered healthy. High blood pressure can cause heart or kidney damage.

✔ *Reading Check* **What is the difference between systolic pressure and diastolic pressure?**

Blood Types

Every person has one of four blood types: A, B, AB, or O. Your blood type refers to the type of chemicals you have on the surface of your RBCs. These surface chemicals are called *antigens* (AN tuh juhnz). Type A blood has A antigens; type B has B antigens; and type AB has both A and B antigens. Type O blood has neither the A nor the B antigen.

The different blood types have different antigens on their RBCs. They may also have different antibodies in the plasma. These antibodies react to antigens of other blood types as if the antigens were pathogens. As shown in **Figure 4,** type A blood has antibodies that react to type B blood. If a person with type A blood receives type B blood, the type B antibodies attach themselves to the type B RBCs. These RBCs begin to clump together, and the clumps may block blood vessels. A reaction to the wrong blood type may be fatal.

INCLUSION Strategies

• Learning Disabled   • Developmentally Delayed
Some students may have difficulty remembering a variety of details, such as the functions of different types of blood cells. Help students develop hints or clues, such as mnemonic or visual clues, that will help them remember the main jobs of red and white blood cells.

(Examples of clues include <u>RE</u>d = <u>RE</u>spiration and <u>Wh</u>ite = <u>WI</u>pe out problems.)
LS Verbal

Answer to Reading Check
Systolic pressure is the pressure inside arteries when the ventricles contract. Diastolic pressure is the pressure inside the arteries when the ventricles are relaxed.

Blood Types and Transfusions

Sometimes, a person must be given a blood transfusion. A *transfusion* is the injection of blood or blood components into a person to replace blood that has been lost because of surgery or an injury. **Figure 5** shows bags of blood that may be given in a transfusion. The blood type is clearly marked. Because the ABO blood types have different antigen-antibody reactions, a person receiving blood cannot receive blood from just anyone. **Table 1** shows blood transfusion possibilities.

Table 1 Blood Transfusion Possibilities		
Type	**Can receive**	**Can donate to**
A	A, O	A, AB
B	B, O	B, AB
AB	all	AB only
O	O	all

Reading Check People with type O blood are sometimes called universal donors. Why might this be true?

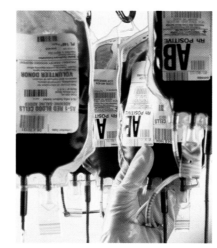
Figure 5 The blood type must be clearly labeled on blood stored for transfusions.

SECTION Review

Summary

- Blood's four main components are plasma, red blood cells, platelets, and white blood cells.
- Blood carries oxygen and nutrients to cells, helps protect against disease, and helps regulate body temperature.
- Blood pressure is the force blood exerts on the inside walls of arteries.
- Every person has one of four ABO blood types.
- Mixing blood types may be fatal.

Using Key Terms

1. Use each of the following terms in a separate sentence: *blood* and *blood pressure*.

Understanding Key Ideas

2. A person with type B blood can donate blood to people with which type(s) of blood?
   a. B, AB
   b. A, AB
   c. AB only
   d. All types

3. List the four main components of blood and tell what each component does.

4. Why is it important for a doctor to know a patient's blood type?

Math Skills

5. A person has a systolic pressure of 174 mm Hg. What percentage of normal (120 mm Hg) is this?

Critical Thinking

6. **Identifying Relationships** How does the body use blood and blood vessels to help maintain proper body temperature?

7. **Predicting Consequences** Some blood conditions and diseases affect the ability of red blood cells to deliver oxygen to cells of the body. Predict what might happen to a person with a disease of that type.

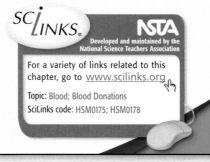

SCILINKS®

NSTA
Developed and maintained by the
National Science Teachers Association

For a variety of links related to this chapter, go to www.scilinks.org

Topic: Blood; Blood Donations
SciLinks code: HSM0175; HSM0178

Focus

Overview

This section introduces students to the lymphatic system. Students will also learn about the relationship between blood and lymph.

Bellringer

Ask students, "Do you know people who have had their tonsils out? What are tonsils? What is their function? Where are they located in the body?" Have students write the answers to these questions in their **science journal.** Tell students that if they are not sure of the answers to make an educated guess at them: (Tonsils are small masses of lymphatic tissue at the back of the tongue and in the throat. Their function is to trap pathogens that might otherwise get into the body and cause disease.)

Motivate

Discussion —— GENERAL

Swollen Glands Ask students if a doctor has ever felt their neck or under their jaw when they were sick. Ask them if they know what the doctor was checking. Encourage students who have had this experience to share it with the class. Then, invite students to explore the purpose of this type of examination.

 Verbal   English Language Learners

READING WARM-UP

Objectives
● Describe the relationship between the lymphatic system and the circulatory system.
● Identify six parts of the lymphatic system, and describe their functions.

Terms to Learn

lymphatic system	thymus
lymph	spleen
lymph node	tonsils

READING STRATEGY

Prediction Guide Before reading this section, write the title of each heading in this section. Next, under each heading, write what you think you will learn.

lymphatic system a collection of organs whose primary function is to collect extracellular fluid and return it to the blood

lymph the fluid that is collected by the lymphatic vessels and nodes

---

The Lymphatic System

Every time your heart pumps, a little fluid is forced out of the thin walls of the capillaries. Some of this fluid collects in the spaces around your cells. What happens to this fluid?

Most of the fluid is reabsorbed through the capillaries into your blood. But some is not. Your body has a second circulatory system called the lymphatic (lim FAT ik) system.

The **lymphatic system** is the group of organs and tissues that collect the excess fluid and return it to your blood. The lymphatic system also helps your body fight pathogens.

Vessels of the Lymphatic System

The fluid collected by the lymphatic system is carried through vessels. The smallest vessels of the lymphatic system are *lymph capillaries*. Lymph capillaries absorb some of the fluid and particles from between the cells. These particles are too large to enter blood capillaries. Some of these particles are dead cells or pathogens. The fluid and particles absorbed into lymph capillaries are called **lymph.**

As shown in **Figure 1,** lymph capillaries carry lymph into larger vessels called *lymphatic vessels*. Skeletal muscles squeeze these vessels to force lymph through the lymphatic system. Valves inside lymphatic vessels stop backflow. Lymph drains into the large neck veins of the cardiovascular system.

Reading Check How is the lymphatic system related to the cardiovascular system? (*See the Appendix for answers to Reading Checks.*)

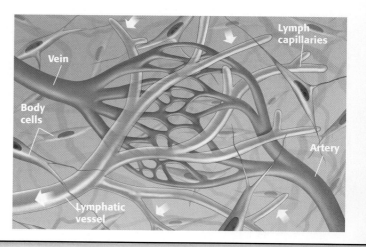

Figure 1 *The white arrows show the movement of lymph into lymph capillaries and through lymphatic vessels.*

CHAPTER RESOURCES

Chapter Resource File

- Lesson Plan
- Directed Reading A BASIC
- Directed Reading B SPECIAL NEEDS

Technology

Transparencies
- Bellringer

Answer to Reading Check

The lymphatic system is a secondary circulatory system in the body. The lymphatic system collects fluid and particles from between the cells and returns them to the cardiovascular system.

Other Parts of the Lymphatic System

In addition to vessels and capillaries, several organs and tissues are part of the lymphatic system. These organs and tissues are shown in **Figure 2**. Bone marrow plays an important role in your lymphatic system. The other parts of the lymphatic system are the lymph nodes, the thymus gland, the spleen, and the tonsils.

Bone Marrow

Bones—part of your skeletal system—are very important to your lymphatic system. *Bone marrow* is the soft tissue inside of bones. Bone marrow is where most red and white blood cells, including lymphocytes (LIM foh SIETS), are produced. *Lymphocytes* are a type of white blood cell that helps your body fight pathogens.

Lymph Nodes

As lymph travels through lymphatic vessels, it passes through lymph nodes. **Lymph nodes** are small, bean-shaped masses of tissue that remove pathogens and dead cells from the lymph. Lymph nodes are concentrated in the armpits, neck, and groin.

Lymph nodes contain lymphocytes. Some lymphocytes—called *killer T cells*—surround and destroy pathogens. Other lymphocytes—called *B cells*—produce antibodies that attach to pathogens. These marked pathogens clump together and are then destroyed by other cells.

When bacteria or other pathogens cause an infection, WBCs may multiply greatly. The lymph nodes fill with WBCs that are fighting the infection. As a result, some lymph nodes may become swollen and painful. Your doctor may feel these swollen lymph nodes to see if you have an infection. In fact, if your lymph nodes are swollen and sore, you or your parent can feel them, too. Swollen lymph nodes are sometimes an early clue that you have an infection.

Thymus

T cells develop from immature lymphocytes produced in the bone marrow. Before these cells are ready to fight infections, they develop further in the thymus. The **thymus** is the gland that produces T cells that are ready to fight infection. The thymus is located behind the breastbone, just above the heart. Mature lymphocytes from the thymus travel through the lymphatic system to other areas of your body.

lymph node an organ that filters lymph and that is found along the lymphatic vessels

thymus the main gland of the lymphatic system; it produces mature T lymphocytes

Figure 2 The Lymphatic System

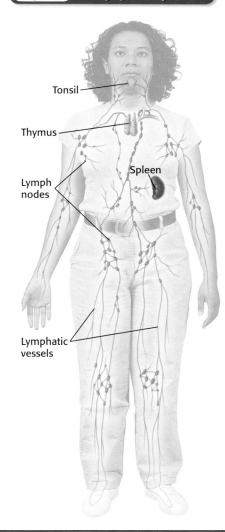

Tonsil

Thymus

Spleen

Lymph nodes

Lymphatic vessels

SCIENTISTS AT ODDS

First to Publish? The Danish physician Thomas Bartholin (1616–1680) is often credited with being the first person to describe the lymphatic system. His Swedish contemporary Olof Rudbeck (1630–1702), known as Rudbeck the Elder, also studied the lymphatic system and published his own description of the lymphatic system. For several years, Bartholin and Rudbeck engaged in a bitter dispute over who deserved the credit for discovering lymph glands and the lymphatic system.

Reteaching — BASIC

Planning a Brochure Ask students to outline and plan a brochure or pamphlet explaining the lymphatic system. Students do not have to make the brochure; they must only plan it. The brochure or pamphlet should be similar to one that you might find in a doctor's office. **LS** Verbal

Quiz — GENERAL

1. What is one function of the tonsils? (The tonsils contain white blood cells, which help fight pathogens.)

2. How is the lymphatic system a circulatory system? (The lymphatic system collects fluid that is not reabsorbed by the capillaries and returns it to the bloodstream.)

Alternative Assessment — ADVANCED

Model of Lymphatic System Have students make a life-sized model of the lymphatic system. Provide students with butcher paper, dried beans, glue, and markers. Then, have students use their model to demonstrate the way that the lymphatic system and the cardiovascular system interact. **LS** Visual/Kinesthetic

English Language Learners

spleen the largest lymphatic organ in the body

CONNECTION TO Social Studies

WRITING SKILL **Vent Your Spleen** Why do we say that someone is "venting his spleen"? What does it mean? Conduct library or Internet research about this phrase. Write a report on what you have learned.

Spleen

Your spleen is the largest lymphatic organ. The **spleen** stores and produces lymphocytes. It is a purplish organ about the size of your fist. Your spleen is soft and spongy. It is located in the upper left side of your abdomen. As blood flows through the spleen, lymphocytes attack or mark pathogens in the blood. If pathogens cause an infection, the spleen may also release lymphocytes into the bloodstream.

In addition to being part of the lymphatic system, the spleen produces, monitors, stores, and destroys blood cells. When red blood cells (RBCs) are squeezed through the spleen's capillaries, the older and more fragile cells burst. These damaged RBCs are then taken apart by some of the cells in the spleen. Some parts of these RBCs may be reused. For this reason, you can think of the spleen as the red-blood-cell recycling center.

The spleen has two important functions. The *white pulp,* shown in **Figure 3**, is part of the lymphatic system. It helps to fight infections. The *red pulp,* also shown in **Figure 3,** removes unwanted material, such as defective red blood cells, from the blood. However, it is possible to lead a healthy life without your spleen. If the spleen is damaged or removed, other organs in the body take over many of its functions.

Reading Check What are two important functions of the spleen?

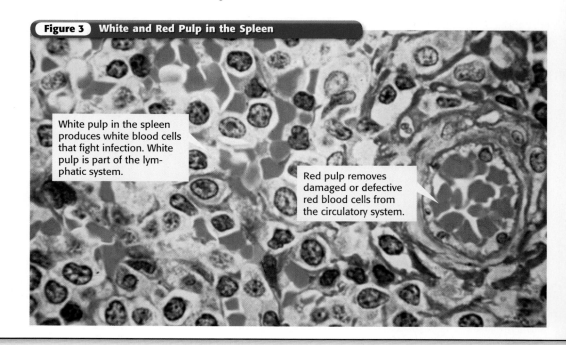

Figure 3 **White and Red Pulp in the Spleen**

White pulp in the spleen produces white blood cells that fight infection. White pulp is part of the lymphatic system.

Red pulp removes damaged or defective red blood cells from the circulatory system.

Answer to Reading Check

The white pulp of the spleen is part of the lymphatic system. It helps fight infections by storing and producing lymphocytes. The red pulp of the spleen removes unwanted material, such as defective red blood cells, from the circulatory system.

Tonsils

The lymphatic system includes your tonsils. **Tonsils** are lymphatic tissue in the nasal cavity and at the back of the mouth on either side of the tongue. Each tonsil is about the size of a large olive.

Tonsils help defend the body against infection. Lymphocytes in the tonsils trap pathogens that enter the throat. Sometimes, tonsils become infected and are red, swollen, and very sore. Severely infected tonsils may be covered with patches of white, infected tissue. Sore, swollen tonsils, such as those in **Figure 4,** make swallowing difficult.

Sometimes, a doctor will suggest surgery to remove the tonsils. In the past, this surgery was frequently done in childhood. It is less common today. Surgery is now done only if a child has frequent, severe tonsil infections or if a child's tonsils are so enlarged that breathing is difficult.

tonsils small, rounded masses of lymphatic tissue located in the pharynx and in the passage from the mouth to the pharynx

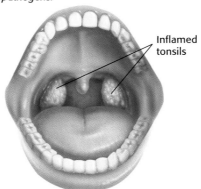

Figure 4 *Tonsils help protect your throat and lungs from infection by trapping pathogens.*

Inflamed tonsils

SECTION Review

Summary

- The lymphatic system collects fluid from between the cells and returns it to the blood.
- The lymphatic system contains cells that help the body fight disease.
- The lymphatic system consists of lymphatic vessels, lymph, and tissues and organs throughout the body.
- The thymus, spleen, and tonsils contain lymphocytes that help fight pathogens.

Using Key Terms

1. Use each of the following terms in a separate sentence: *lymph nodes, spleen,* and *tonsils.*

Understanding Key Ideas

2. Lymph
   - **a.** is the same as blood.
   - **b.** is fluid in the cells.
   - **c.** drains into your muscles.
   - **d.** is fluid collected by lymphatic vessels.

3. Name six parts of the lymphatic system. Tell what each part does.

4. How are your cardiovascular and lymphatic systems related?

Math Skills

5. One cubic millimeter of blood contains 5 million RBCs and 10,000 WBCs. How many times more RBCs are there than WBCs?

Critical Thinking

6. **Expressing Opinions** Some people have frequent, severe tonsil infections. These infections can be treated with medicine, and the infections usually go away after a few days. Do you think removing tonsils in such a case is a good idea? Explain.

7. **Analyzing Ideas** Why is it important that lymphatic tissue is spread throughout the body?

SCILINKS.

NSTA
Developed and maintained by the
National Science Teachers Association

For a variety of links related to this chapter, go to www.scilinks.org

Topic: The Lymphatic System
SciLinks code: HSM0891

Answers to Section Review

1. Sample answer: Sometimes, when you are sick, your lymph nodes get swollen. Your spleen is an organ that is part of the circulatory system and the lymphatic system. Tonsils are lymphatic tissue at the back of your throat.

2. d

3. lymph vessels and capillaries, bone marrow, lymph nodes, thymus, spleen, and tonsils; lymph vessels and capillaries: they carry lymph from the body to the cardiovascular system; bone marrow: it is the tissue in which white blood cells are produced; lymph nodes: they remove pathogens and dead cells from lymph; thymus: it is the gland in which killer T cells mature; spleen: it produces and stores lymphocytes; tonsils: they trap pathogens

4. The lymphatic system collects particles and excess fluid from around your cells and returns them to the bloodstream, which is part of your cardiovascular system. The two systems work together to help the body fight pathogens: both lymph and blood carry white blood cells around the body to fight pathogens.

5. There are 500 times as many RBCs as WBCs.

6. Answers may vary as students offer their opinions. The most important part of the answer is the reasoning and the way in which the ideas that lead to the opinion are supported.

7. Sample answer: It is important for lymphatic tissue to be spread throughout the body so that fluid and particles from around every cell can be removed and pathogens in any part of the body can be identified and attacked.

Overview

This section introduces students to the respiratory system. Students will learn about the flow of air in the respiratory system and about the way that the respiratory and the circulatory systems are related.

 **Bellringer**

Ask students, "Are breathing and respiration the same thing?" (No, breathing is only one part of respiration. Respiration also includes cellular respiration.)

Motivate

ACTIVITY ——————— GENERAL

Deep Breathing Have students place their hands on either side of their rib cage and breathe deeply several times. Then, ask students to describe what they felt while they breathed in and out. (Students should feel their rib cage moving up and expanding during inhalation and moving down and returning to its initial size during exhalation.)

LS Kinesthetic   English Language Learners

 READING WARM-UP

Objectives

● Describe the parts of the respiratory system and their functions.

● Explain how breathing happens.

● Discuss the relationship between the respiratory system and the cardiovascular system.

● Identify two respiratory disorders.

Terms to Learn

respiration   trachea
respiratory system   bronchus
pharynx   alveoli
larynx

 READING STRATEGY

Reading Organizer As you read this section, make a flowchart of the steps of the process of respiration.

respiration the exchange of oxygen and carbon dioxide between living cells and their environment; includes breathing and cellular respiration

respiratory system a collection of organs whose primary function is to take in oxygen and expel carbon dioxide

---

The Respiratory System

Breathing—you do it all the time. You're doing it right now. You hardly ever think about it, though, unless you suddenly can't breathe.

Then, it becomes very clear that you have to breathe in order to live. But why is breathing important? Your body needs oxygen in order to get energy from the foods you eat. Breathing makes this process possible.

Respiration and the Respiratory System

The words *breathing* and *respiration* are often used to mean the same thing. However, breathing is only one part of respiration. **Respiration** is the process by which a body gets and uses oxygen and releases carbon dioxide and water. Respiration is divided into two parts. The first part is breathing, which involves inhaling and exhaling. The second part is cellular respiration, which involves chemical reactions that release energy from food.

Breathing is made possible by your respiratory system. The **respiratory system** is the group of organs that take in oxygen and get rid of carbon dioxide. The nose, throat, lungs, and passageways that lead to the lungs make up the respiratory system. **Figure 1** shows the parts of the respiratory system.

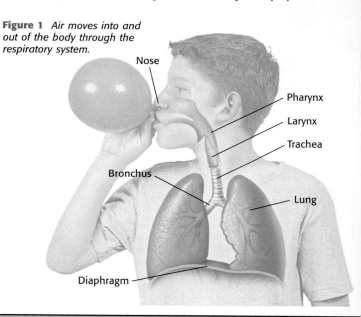

Figure 1 *Air moves into and out of the body through the respiratory system.*

Nose
Pharynx
Larynx
Trachea
Bronchus
Lung
Diaphragm

CHAPTER RESOURCES

Chapter Resource File

📁 • Lesson Plan
   • Directed Reading A **BASIC**
   • Directed Reading B **SPECIAL NEEDS**

Technology

🗄 **Transparencies**
   • Bellringer
   • The Role of Blood in Respiration

Cultural Awareness GENERAL

Adapting to High Altitudes Newcomers to Peruvian villages in the Andes Mountains may get headaches, feel nauseated, and be short of breath. Why? The newcomer is suffering from a lack of oxygen. Villagers don't have these problems; they have adapted to the elevation. Over time, villagers develop lungs that are larger than those of a newcomer. Villagers also have more red blood cells than newcomers have.

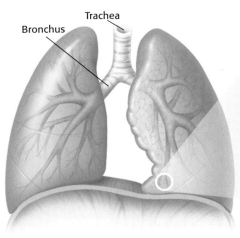

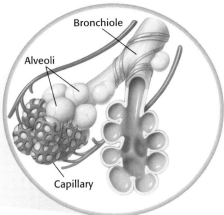

Figure 2 *Inside your lungs, the bronchi branch into bronchioles. The bronchioles lead to tiny sacs called alveoli.*

Nose, Pharynx, and Larynx

Your *nose* is the main passageway into and out of the respiratory system. Air can be breathed in through and out of the nose. Air can also enter and leave through the mouth.

From the nose, air flows into the **pharynx** (FAR ingks), or throat. Food and drink also travel through the pharynx on the way to the stomach. The pharynx branches into two tubes. One tube, the *esophagus,* leads to the stomach. The other tube is the larynx (LAR ingks). The larynx leads to the lungs.

The **larynx** is the part of the throat that contains the vocal cords. The *vocal cords* are a pair of elastic bands that stretch across the larynx. Muscles connected to the larynx control how much the vocal cords are stretched. When air flows between the vocal cords, the cords vibrate. These vibrations make sound.

Trachea

The larynx guards the entrance to a large tube called the **trachea** (TRAY kee uh), or windpipe. Your body has two large, spongelike lungs. The trachea, shown in **Figure 2,** is the passageway for air traveling from the larynx to the lungs.

Bronchi and Alveoli

The trachea splits into two branches called **bronchi** (BRAHNG kie) (singular, *bronchus*). One bronchus connects to each lung. Each bronchus branches into smaller tubes that are called *bronchioles* (BRAHNG kee OHLZ). In the lungs, each bronchiole branches to form tiny sacs that are called **alveoli** (al VEE uh LIE) (singular, *alveolus*). The alveoli provide a large amount of surface area.

Reading Check Describe how the lung's structure relates to its function. (*See the Appendix for answers to Reading Checks.*)

pharynx the passage from the mouth to the larynx and esophagus

larynx the area of the throat that contains the vocal cords and produces vocal sounds

trachea the tube that connects the larynx to the lungs

bronchus one of the two tubes that connect the lungs with the trachea

alveoli any of the tiny air sacs of the lungs where oxygen and carbon dioxide are exchanged

Teach

ACTIVITY ————— GENERAL

Investigating Speech   Ask students to place their hands lightly on their neck near the larynx and to say, "ah." Have students keep their hands in place and alternate between blowing as they would blow out candles on a birthday cake and saying "ah." Then, ask students the following questions:

• What happened when you said "ah"? (The neck vibrated.)

• What happened when you blew without saying anything? (The neck stopped vibrating, but air still rushed out of the mouth.)

• What caused the sound and the vibrations when you said "ah"? (Air rushing past the vocal cord muscles in the larynx caused the muscles to vibrate. This vibration caused the sound.)

Point out that speech is made up of sounds that are voiced and sounds that are not voiced. If students are unconvinced, have them say "sssssssss" (the snake sound) while touching their neck near the larynx. Then, have them say "zzzzz" (buzz like a bee) while touching their neck. Students should find that their neck vibrates when they pronounce "z," which is voiced, but does not vibrate when they pronounce "s," which is not voiced.   **English Language Learners**

LS Verbal

Answer to Reading Check

Sample answer: In the lungs, each bronchiole branches to form thousands of alveoli. These small sacs allow for the exchange of oxygen and carbon dioxide. The alveoli provide a large amount of surface area, which allows gases to be exchanged efficiently.

Close

Reteaching — BASIC

Section Outline Have students make an outline of this section by using the chapter title, subheads, and key terms as topics. Help them fill in their outline to make a useful study tool.
LS Logical

Quiz — GENERAL

Ask students whether each of the statements below is true or false. Have students correct false statements.

1. SARS is caused by air pollution. (false)

2. There are two main bronchi —one for each lung— in the human body. (true)

3. The lungs are made of muscle tissue. (false)

Alternative Assessment — ADVANCED

Lung Models Have students make models of healthy lungs and lungs damaged by smoking. Photographs of healthy lungs and damaged lungs can be found in literature from the American Lung Association and the American Cancer Society and in various science and health textbooks.
LS Visual/Kinesthetic English Language Learners

Answer to Connection to Chemistry

Because there is less oxygen in the air at high altitudes, it is difficult for the body to get the oxygen needed.

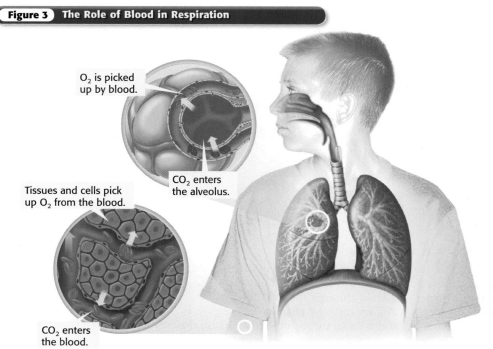

Figure 3 The Role of Blood in Respiration

O₂ is picked up by blood.

CO₂ enters the alveolus.

Tissues and cells pick up O₂ from the blood.

CO₂ enters the blood.

Breathing

When you breathe, air is sucked into or forced out of your lungs. However, your lungs have no muscles of their own. Instead, breathing is done by the diaphragm (DIE uh FRAM) and rib muscles. The *diaphragm* is a dome-shaped muscle beneath the lungs. When you inhale, the diaphragm contracts and moves down. The chest cavity's volume increases. At the same time, some of your rib muscles contract and lift your rib cage. As a result, your chest cavity gets bigger and a vacuum is created. Air is sucked in. Exhaling is this process in reverse.

Breathing and Cellular Respiration

In *cellular respiration,* oxygen is used by cells to release energy stored in molecules of glucose. Where does the oxygen come from? When you inhale, you take in oxygen. This oxygen diffuses into red blood cells and is carried to tissue cells. The oxygen then diffuses out of the red blood cells and into each cell. Cells use the oxygen to release chemical energy. During the process, carbon dioxide (CO_2) and water are produced. Carbon dioxide is exhaled from the lungs. **Figure 3** shows how breathing and blood circulation are related.

✓ **Reading Check** What is cellular respiration?

CONNECTION TO Chemistry

Oxygen and Blood When people who live at low elevations travel up into the mountains, they may find themselves breathing heavily even when they are not exerting themselves. Why might this happen?

Answer to Reading Check

Cellular respiration is the process inside a cell in which oxygen is used to release energy stored in molecules of glucose. During the process, carbon dioxide (CO_2) and water are released.

CONNECTION to Physical Science — GENERAL

Air Pressure and Breathing Lead a discussion about the ways in which the body creates changes in air pressure to make breathing possible. The teaching transparency "Exhaling, Pressure, and Fluid Flow" is a helpful illustration of the process of breathing. **LS Visual/Logical**

Respiratory Disorders

Millions of people suffer from respiratory disorders. Respiratory disorders include asthma, emphysema, and severe acute respiratory syndrome (SARS). Asthma causes the bronchioles to narrow. A person who has asthma has difficulty breathing. An asthma attack may be triggered by irritants such as dust or pollen. SARS is caused by a virus. A person who has SARS may have a fever and difficulty breathing. Emphysema happens when the alveoli have been damaged. People who have emphysema have trouble getting the oxygen they need. **Figure 4** shows a lung damaged by emphysema.

Figure 4 *The photo on the left shows a healthy lung. The photo on the right shows the lung of a person who had emphysema.*

Why Do People Snore?

1. Get a **15 cm² sheet of wax paper.**
2. Hum your favorite song.
3. Then, take the wax paper and press it against your lips. Hum the song again.
4. How was your humming different when wax paper was pressed to your mouth?
5. Use your observations to guess what might cause snoring.

SECTION Review

Summary

- Air travels to the lungs through the nose or mouth, pharynx, larynx, trachea, and bronchi.
- In the lungs, the bronchi branch into bronchioles, which branch into alveoli.
- Breathing involves lungs, muscles in the rib cage, and the diaphragm.
- Oxygen enters the blood through the alveoli in the lungs. Carbon dioxide leaves the blood and is exhaled.
- Respiratory disorders include asthma, SARS, and emphysema.

Using Key Terms

For each pair of terms, explain how the meanings of the terms differ.

1. *pharynx* and *larynx*

Understanding Key Ideas

2. Which of the following are respiratory disorders?
   a. SARS, alveoli, and asthma
   b. alveoli, emphysema, and SARS
   c. larynx, asthma, and SARS
   d. SARS, emphysema, and asthma
3. Explain how breathing happens.
4. Describe how your cardiovascular and respiratory systems work together.

Math Skills

5. Total lung capacity (TLC) is about 6 L. A person can exhale about 3.6 L. What percentage of TLC cannot be exhaled?

Critical Thinking

6. **Interpreting Statistics** About 6.3 million children in the United States have asthma. About 4 million of them had an asthma attack last year. What do these statistics tell you about the relationship between asthma and asthma attacks?

7. **Identifying Relationships** If a respiratory disorder causes lungs to fill with fluid, how might this affect a person's health?

For a variety of links related to this chapter, go to www.scilinks.org

Topic: The Respiratory System; Respiratory Disorders

SciLinks code: HSM1307; HSM1306

Is That a Fact!

The lungs contain about 300 million alveoli. The alveoli provide a tremendous surface area for gas exchange. In fact, because of this large capacity for gas exchange, a person can breathe easily with only one lung.

CHAPTER RESOURCES

Chapter Resource File

- Section Quiz `GENERAL`
- Section Review `GENERAL`
- Vocabulary and Section Summary `GENERAL`
- Datasheet for Quick Lab

Technology

Transparencies
- **LINK TO PHYSICAL SCIENCE** Exhaling, Pressure, and Fluid Flow

---

MATERIALS

FOR EACH GROUP
- wax paper, 15 cm² sheet

Answers

4. A strong vibrating sound was made when the paper was pressed against the lips.
5. Sample answer: Most snoring happens when soft tissues in the mouth block a person's airway and vibrate.

Answers to Section Review

1. The pharynx is the passage from the mouth to the larynx and esophagus, while the larynx is the part of the throat that contains the vocal cords.
2. d
3. When you breathe, air is sucked into or forced out of your lungs. A muscle called the *diaphragm* contracts and increases chest-cavity volume, which creates a vacuum. The vaccum pulls air in through the nose or mouth. Then, the air travels through the pharynx, larynx, trachea, and bronchi to reach the lungs.
4. The respiratory system brings in oxygen and expels carbon dioxide, and the cardiovascular system transports those gases to and from the lungs.
5. 6 L − 3.6 L = 2.4 L unexhaled
   2.4 L ÷ 6 L = 0.40, or 40% of TLC cannot be exhaled
6. Sample answer: These statistics tell us that last year not every child who had asthma had an asthma attack.
7. Sample answer: The alveoli in the lungs are made for the exhange of gases, not liquids. Fluids in the lungs would prevent a person from getting all of the oxygen needed to maintain regular activity. The person might feel weak or tired. Also, the person could not get rid of the carbon dioxide from the cells, which might cause a problem, too.

Skills Practice Lab

Carbon Dioxide Breath

Teacher's Notes

Time Required
One 45-minute class period

Lab Ratings

EASY ———————————— HARD

Teacher Prep 🔬🔬
Student Set-Up 🔬🔬
Concept Level 🔬🔬
Clean Up 🔬🔬

MATERIALS
You may wish to substitute brom-thymol blue indicator solution for the phenol red indicator. The bromthymol blue will turn green in the presence of CO_2. Clear plastic cups (6 oz or 8 oz) may be used instead of 150 mL flasks if glassware is in short supply or if you have concerns about breakage.

Safety Caution
Remind students to review all safety cautions and icons before beginning this lab activity.

Lab Notes
Tell students that carbon dioxide is in the air in the classroom. They may need to cover their indicator solution to delay the reaction with the air. Tell them not to leave the indicator solution sitting exposed for several minutes before it is used.

Skills Practice Lab

OBJECTIVES

Detect the presence of carbon dioxide in your breath.

Compare the data for carbon dioxide in your breath with the data from your classmates.

MATERIALS

- calculator (optional)
- clock with a second hand, or a stopwatch
- Erlenmeyer flask, 150 mL
- eyedropper
- gloves, protective
- graduated cylinder, 150 mL
- paper towels
- phenol red indicator solution
- plastic drinking straw
- water, 100 mL

SAFETY

Carbon Dioxide Breath

Carbon dioxide is important to both plants and animals. Plants take in carbon dioxide during photosynthesis and give off oxygen as a byproduct of the process. Animals—including you—take in oxygen during respiration and give off carbon dioxide as a byproduct of the process.

Procedure

1. Put on your gloves, safety goggles, and apron.

2. Use the graduated cylinder to pour 100 mL of water into a 150 mL flask.

3. Using an eyedropper, carefully place four drops of phenol red indicator solution into the water. The water should turn orange.

4. Place a plastic drinking straw into the solution of phenol red and water. Drape a paper towel over the flask to prevent splashing.

5. Carefully blow through the straw into the solution. **Caution:** Do not inhale through the straw. Do not drink the solution, and do not share a straw with anyone.

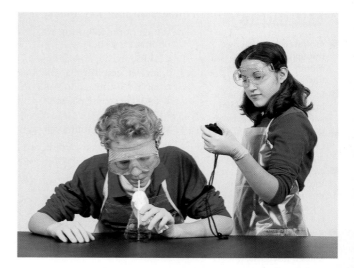

Yvonne Brannum
Hine Junior High School
Washington, D.C.

CHAPTER RESOURCES

Chapter Resource File
- **Datasheet for Chapter Lab**
- **Lab Notes and Answers**

Technology
Classroom Videos
- Lab Video

LabBook
- Build a Lung

6. Your lab partner should begin keeping time as soon as you start to blow through the straw. Have your lab partner time how long the solution takes to change color. Record the time.

Analyze the Results

1. **Describing Events** Describe what happens to the indicator solution.

2. **Examining Data** Compare your data with those of your classmates. What was the longest length of time it took to see a color change? What was the shortest? How do you account for the difference?

3. **Constructing Graphs** Make a bar graph that compares your data with the data of your classmates.

Draw Conclusions

4. **Interpreting Information** Do you think that there is a relationship between the length of time the solution takes to change color and the person's physical characteristics, such as which gender the tester is or whether the tester has an athletic build? Explain your answer.

5. **Making Predictions** Predict how exercise might affect the results of your experiment. For example, would you predict that the level of carbon dioxide in the breath of someone who was exercising would be higher or lower than the carbon dioxide level in the breath of someone who was sitting quietly? Would you predict that the level of carbon dioxide in the breath would affect the timing of any color change in the phenol solution?

Applying Your Data

Do jumping jacks or sit-ups for 3 minutes, and then repeat the experiment. Did the phenol solution still change color? Did your exercising change the timing? Describe and explain any change.

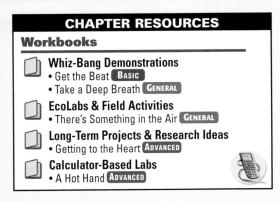

CHAPTER RESOURCES

Workbooks

Whiz-Bang Demonstrations
- Get the Beat BASIC
- Take a Deep Breath GENERAL

EcoLabs & Field Activities
- There's Something in the Air GENERAL

Long-Term Projects & Research Ideas
- Getting to the Heart ADVANCED

Calculator-Based Labs
- A Hot Hand ADVANCED

Chapter Review

Assignment Guide

Section	Questions
1	2, 6, 8, 10, 24–26
2	1, 7, 13, 21–22
3	3, 8, 16, 23
4	4–5, 9, 11–12, 14, 18, 20
1, 2, and 3	15, 19
1, 2, and 4	17

ANSWERS

Using Key Terms

1. Red blood cells
2. Arteries
3. lymphatic system
4. larynx
5. alveoli

Understanding Key Ideas

6. b
7. d
8. a
9. c
10. b
11. a
12. Pulmonary circulation carries blood to the lungs and back to the heart. Systemic circulation carries blood from the heart to the rest of the body and then returns the blood to the heart.
13. The first number, systolic pressure, is pressure in arteries when ventricles contract. The second number, diastolic pressure, is pressure in arteries when ventricles relax.

USING KEY TERMS

Complete each of the following sentences by choosing the correct term from the word bank.

red blood cells veins
white blood cells arteries
lymphatic system larynx
alveoli bronchi
respiratory system trachea

1 ___ deliver oxygen to the cells of the body.

2 ___ carry blood away from the heart.

3 The ___ helps the body fight pathogens.

4 The ___ contains the vocal cords.

5 The pathway of air through the respiratory system ends at the tiny sacs called ___.

UNDERSTANDING KEY IDEAS

Multiple Choice

6 Blood from the lungs enters the heart at the
   a. left ventricle.
   b. left atrium.
   c. right atrium.
   d. right ventricle.

7 Blood cells are made
   a. in the heart.
   b. from plasma.
   c. from lymph.
   d. in the bones.

8 Which of the following activities is a function of the lymphatic system?
   a. returning excess fluid to the circulatory system
   b. delivering nutrients to the cells
   c. bringing oxygen to the blood
   d. pumping blood to all parts of the body

9 Alveoli are surrounded by
   a. veins.
   b. muscles.
   c. capillaries.
   d. lymph nodes.

10 What prevents blood from flowing backward in veins?
   a. platelets
   b. valves
   c. muscles
   d. cartilage

11 Air moves into the lungs when the diaphragm muscle
   a. contracts and moves down.
   b. contracts and moves up.
   c. relaxes and moves down.
   d. relaxes and moves up.

Short Answer

12 What is the difference between pulmonary circulation and systemic circulation in the cardiovascular system?

13 Walton's blood pressure is 110/65. What do the two numbers mean?

14 What body process produces the carbon dioxide you exhale?

15 Describe how the circulatory system and the lymphatic system work together to keep your body healthy.

16 How is the spleen important to both the lymphatic system and the circulatory system?

17 Briefly describe the path that oxygen follows in your respiratory system and your circulatory system.

CRITICAL THINKING

18 **Concept Mapping** Use the following terms to create a concept map: *blood, oxygen, alveoli, capillaries,* and *carbon dioxide.*

19 **Making Comparisons** Compare and contrast the functions of the circulatory system and the lymphatic system.

20 **Identifying Relationships** Why do you think there are hairs in your nose?

21 **Applying Concepts** After a person donates blood, the blood is stored in one-pint bags until it is needed for a transfusion. A healthy person has about 5 million RBCs in each cubic millimeter (1 mm³) of blood.
  a. How many RBCs are in 1 mL of blood? (One milliliter is equal to 1 cm³ and to 1,000 mm³.)
  b. How many RBCs are there in 1 pt? (One pint is equal to 473 mL.)

22 **Predicting Consequences** What would happen if all of the red blood cells in your blood disappeared?

23 **Identifying Relationships** When a person is not feeling well, a doctor may examine samples of the person's blood to see how many white blood cells are present. Why would this information be useful?

INTERPRETING GRAPHICS

The diagram below shows how the human heart would look in cross section. Use the diagram to answer the questions that follow.

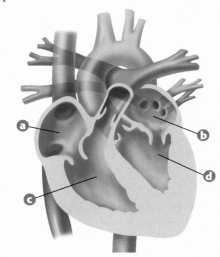

24 Which letter identifies the chamber that receives blood from systemic circulation? What is this chamber's name?

25 Which letter identifies the chamber that receives blood from the lungs? What is this chamber's name?

26 Which letter identifies the chamber that pumps blood to the lungs? What is this chamber's name?

16. The spleen is important to the circulatory system because it removes old or damaged red blood cells. It is important to the lymphatic system because it stores white blood cells, which help fight disease.

17. Oxygen comes into the body through the nose or mouth, travels to the lungs, and enters the alveoli. In the alveoli, oxygen moves through the capillary walls and enters the blood. The circulatory system carries the blood from the lungs to the heart, which pumps the blood to all parts of the body. Oxygen is carried by red blood cells to every body cell.

Critical Thinking

18. An answer to this exercise can be found at the end of the book.

19. Sample answer: The circulatory system and the lymphatic system use fluids to carry substances to and from all parts of the body. The circulatory system delivers oxygen and nutrients to the cells and removes wastes from the cells. The lymphatic system helps fight disease and infection.

20. The hairs catch dust and other foreign particles, which helps keep your lungs clean.

21. a. 5 billion (5,000,000,000) cells
  b. 2.365 trillion (2,365,000,000,000) cells

22. Sample answer: In a short time, I would probably die because my body could not get the oxygen it needs.

23. The immune system produces white blood cells to fight pathogens. A high white blood cell count tells the doctor that the person may have an infection.

Interpreting Graphics

24. a, the right atrium

25. b, the left atrium

26. c, the right ventricle

---

14. Carbon dioxide is a product of cellular respiration, which occurs in the body's cells.

15. Sample answer: The circulatory system delivers oxygen, nutrients, and white blood cells to all parts of the body. The lymphatic system returns excess fluid from between the cells to the circulatory system.

CHAPTER RESOURCES

Chapter Resource File

  • Chapter Review **GENERAL**
  • Chapter Test A **GENERAL**
  • Chapter Test B **ADVANCED**
  • Chapter Test C **SPECIAL NEEDS**
  • Vocabulary Activity **GENERAL**

Workbooks

 Study Guide
  • Assessment resources are also available in Spanish.

Teacher's Note

To provide practice under more realistic testing conditions, give students 20 minutes to answer all of the questions in this Standardized Test Preparation.

MISCONCEPTION ALERT

Answers to the standardized test preparation can help you identify student misconceptions and misunderstandings.

READING

Passage 1

1. C
2. I
3. C

TEST DOCTOR

Question 2: Students may select the incorrect answers F or H because the passage is about sneezing and mentions heredity. Students may select incorrect answer G because they may recall that some plants show phototropism, or a response to light.

READING

Read each of the passages below. Then, answer the questions that follow each passage.

Passage 1 For some reason, about one in five people sneeze when they step from a dimly lit area into a brightly lit area. In fact, some may sneeze a dozen times or more! Fortunately, the sneezing usually stops relatively quickly. This sneeze reaction is called a <u>photic</u> sneeze reflex (FOHT ik SNEEZ REE fleks). No one knows for certain why it happens. A few years ago, some geneticists studied the photic sneeze reflex. They named it the *ACHOO syndrome*. Scientists know that the ACHOO syndrome runs in families. So, the photic sneeze may be hereditary and can be passed from parent to child. Sometimes, even the number of times in a row that each person sneezes is the same throughout a family.

1. According to the passage, the ACHOO syndrome is most likely to be which of the following?
   A contagious
   B photosynthetic
   C hereditary
   D allergic

2. In the passage, what does *photic* mean?
   F having to do with sneezing
   G having to do with plants
   H having to do with genetics
   I having to do with light

3. Which of the following statements is one clue that the photic sneeze reflex can be passed from parent to child?
   A The reflex is triggered by bright light.
   B Sneezing usually stops after a few sneezes.
   C Family members even sneeze the same number of times.
   D Scientists do not know what causes the ACHOO syndrome.

Passage 2 The two main functions of blood are transporting nutrients and oxygen from the lungs to cells and carrying carbon dioxide and other waste materials away from cells to the lungs or other organs. Blood also transfers body heat to the body surface and plays a role in defending the body against disease. The respiratory system transports gases to and from blood. The respiratory system and blood work together to carry out external respiration and internal respiration. <u>External respiration</u> is the exchange of gases between the atmosphere and blood. Internal respiration is the exchange of gases between blood and the cells of the body.

1. In the passage, what does *external respiration* mean?
   A the exchange of gases outdoors
   B the inhalation of gases as you breathe in
   C the exchange of gases between blood and the atmosphere
   D the exhalation of gases as you breathe out

2. Which of the following statements is a fact in the passage?
   F The respiratory system transports oxygen to all the cells of the body.
   G The respiratory system is part of the circulatory system.
   H Blood is a kind of cardiac tissue.
   I Blood transports oxygen to cells.

3. According to the passage, what are two of the roles blood plays in the human body?
   A transferring body heat and defending against disease
   B defending against disease and transporting gases to the circulatory system
   C transporting carbon dioxide to body cells and transferring body heat
   D external respiration and atmosphere

Passage 2

1. C
2. I
3. A

TEST DOCTOR

Question 3: Students may select incorrect answers B or C if they do not read the passage carefully. Blood does not transport gases to the circulatory system (answer B) or transport carbon dioxide to the body cells (answer C). Students may select incorrect answer D if they do not see that the question asks for two roles.

Use the graph below to answer the questions that follow.

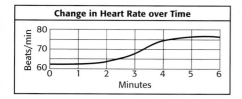

Change in Heart Rate over Time

1. What is the most likely explanation for the change seen after the two-minute mark?

A The person started exercising.

B The person fell asleep.

C The person inhaled.

D The person sat down.

2. How much faster is the heart beating during minute 5 than during minute 2?

F 10 beats per minute more

G 12 beats per minute more

H 15 beats per minute more

I 17 beats per minute more

3. About how many minutes did it take for this person's heart rate to go from 65 beats per minute to 75 beats per minute?

A 0.7 minute

B 1.0 minute

C 1.7 minutes

D 4.0 minutes

4. After how many minutes does this person's heart rate return to its resting rate?

F 1.0 minute

G 2.0 minutes

H 5.0 minutes

I There is not enough information to determine the answer.

MATH

Read each question below, and choose the best answer.

1. If Jim's heart beats 73 times every minute, Jen's heart beats 68 times every minute, and Leigh's heart beats 81 times every minute, what is the average heart rate for these 3 people?

A 73 beats per minute

B 74 beats per minute

C 141 beats per minute

D 222 beats per minute

2. The Griffith family has 4 dogs. Each of the dogs eats between 0.9 kg and 1.3 kg of food every day. Which is a reasonable estimate of the total amount of food all 4 dogs eat every day?

F 1 kg of food

G 3 kg of food

H 4 kg of food

I 8 kg of food

3. Assume that the average person's resting heart rate is 70 beats per minute. The resting heart rate of a particular person is 10 beats per minute more than the average person's. If a person with the higher heart rate lives 75 years, about how many more times will his or her heart beat than the average person's heart in that time?

A 3,942

B 394,200

C 3,942,000

D 394,200,000

4. At rest, the cells of the human body use about 250 mL of oxygen per minute. At that rate, how much oxygen would the cells of the human body use every 24 hours?

F about 36 L

G about 360 L

H about 36,000 L

I about 360,000 L

Standardized Test Preparation

1. A

2. G

3. C

4. I

 **TEST DOCTOR**

Question 2: Students may select any of the incorrect answers if they do not look closely at the graph. The heart rate increases from about 64 beats per minute to 76 beats per minute.

Question 4: Students may select answer F, G, or H by guessing because they think that they should be able to find on the graph the point at which the heart rate returns to normal. However, the heart rate does not return to normal during the time period shown on the graph.

MATH

1. B

2. H

3. D

4. G

 **TEST DOCTOR**

Question 3: Students may select any of the incorrect answers because they have not kept track of the proper number of decimal places in this two-step problem.

Question 4: Students may select incorrect answer I if they forget to convert milliliters to liters in their final answer.

CHAPTER RESOURCES

Chapter Resource File

 • Standardized Test Preparation **GENERAL**

Workbooks

 North Carolina Standardized Test Preparation
• Provides practice for the EOG test.

State Resources

 For specific resources for your state, visit **go.hrw.com** and type in the keyword **HSMSTR**.

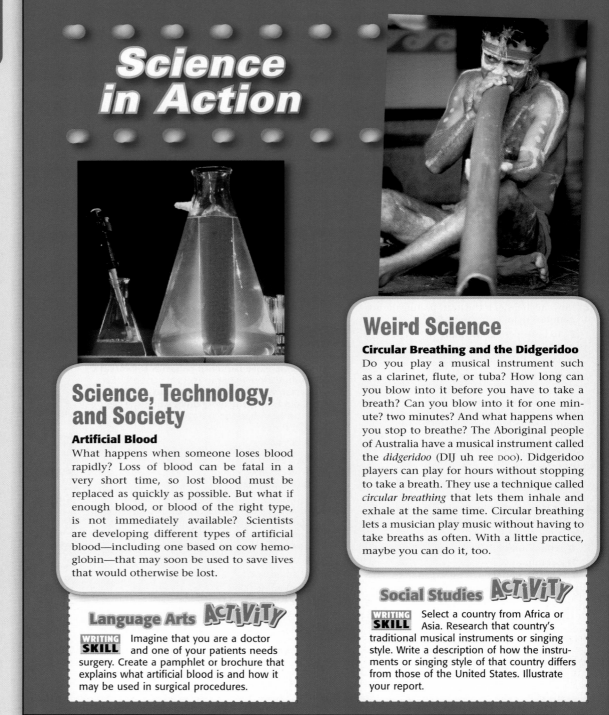

Science in Action

Science, Technology, and Society

Background

Because of the dangers associated with giving someone blood of the wrong type, people have searched for safe blood substitutes for hundreds of years. At one time, even wine was proposed as a substitute! Four substances are in advanced clinical trials in the United States. PolyHeme and Hemolink are derived from modified human hemoglobin. Hemopure is made from modified bovine hemoglobin. Oxygent is entirely synthetic and is made from an emulsion of perfluorocarbon molecules.

Weird Science

Background

Drawings of men playing an instrument that appears to be a didjeridu appear in caves in Australia. Evidence indicates that the didjeridu has been in Australia for about 1,000 years. Aboriginals, though, trace the history of the instrument back to the "Dreamtime," the very beginning of their people. The first reference by Westerners comes from a man named T. B. Wilson in 1835. Wilson described an aboriginal man playing an instrument that was made of bamboo and was about 1 m long.

Science, Technology, and Society

Artificial Blood

What happens when someone loses blood rapidly? Loss of blood can be fatal in a very short time, so lost blood must be replaced as quickly as possible. But what if enough blood, or blood of the right type, is not immediately available? Scientists are developing different types of artificial blood—including one based on cow hemoglobin—that may soon be used to save lives that would otherwise be lost.

Language Arts ACTIVITY

WRITING SKILL Imagine that you are a doctor and one of your patients needs surgery. Create a pamphlet or brochure that explains what artificial blood is and how it may be used in surgical procedures.

Weird Science

Circular Breathing and the Didgeridoo

Do you play a musical instrument such as a clarinet, flute, or tuba? How long can you blow into it before you have to take a breath? Can you blow into it for one minute? two minutes? And what happens when you stop to breathe? The Aboriginal people of Australia have a musical instrument called the *didgeridoo* (DIJ uh ree DOO). Didgeridoo players can play for hours without stopping to take a breath. They use a technique called *circular breathing* that lets them inhale and exhale at the same time. Circular breathing lets a musician play music without having to take breaths as often. With a little practice, maybe you can do it, too.

Social Studies ACTIVITY

WRITING SKILL Select a country from Africa or Asia. Research that country's traditional musical instruments or singing style. Write a description of how the instruments or singing style of that country differs from those of the United States. Illustrate your report.

Answer to Language Arts Activity

Students' brochures should be attractive, well illustrated, and informative. Brochures should explain which type of artificial blood the patient may receive and whether the patient or the doctor (or student) recommends the type of artificial blood to be used.

Answer to Social Studies Activity

Students' reports will vary depending on the country or region, the instrument, and the musical or singing style that the students have selected. Reports should be clear, interesting, and informative. Students should provide sources and references for their report, and their report should include illustrations that enhance the report.

Anthony Roberts, Jr.

Leader in Training Anthony Roberts, Jr., has asthma. When he was in the 5th grade, his school counselor told him about a summer camp—The Boggy Creek Gang Camp—that was just being built. His counselor said that the camp was designed to serve kids who have asthma or other disabilities and diseases, such as AIDS, cancer, diabetes, epilepsy, hemophilia, heart disease, kidney disease, rheumatic diseases, and sickle cell anemia. Kids, in other words, who might otherwise never go to summer camp. Anthony jumped at the chance to go. Now, Anthony is too old to be a camper, and he is too young to be a regular counselor. But he can be a *Leader in Training* (LIT). Some camps have LIT programs that help young people make the transition from camper to counselor.

For Anthony, the chance to be an LIT fit perfectly with his love of camping and with his desire to work with kids with disabilities. Anthony remembers the fun he had and wants to help other kids have the same summer fun he did.

Math Activity

Research how many children under 17 years of age in the United States have asthma. Make a bar graph that shows how the number of children who have asthma has changed since 1981. What does this graph tell you about rates of asthma among children in the United States?

To learn more about these Science in Action topics, visit **go.hrw.com** and type in the keyword **HL5BD2F.**

Current Science

Check out Current Science® articles related to this chapter by visiting go.hrw.com. Just type in the keyword **HL5CS23.**

People in Science
Teaching Strategy—GENERAL

If appropriate for your class, begin by talking in a general way about summer vacation: what students like to do, how they spend their time, whether they go to summer camp (day camp or residence camp), and whether they know of anyone (no names) who has asthma or another disability that might make summer camp activities difficult. Then, discuss the Boggy Creek Gang Camp and Anthony Roberts, Jr., and his role as a leader in training. Your class may be interested to know that the Boggy Creek Gang Camp is one of the Hole in the Wall camps started by actor Paul Newman. The Hole in the Wall Gang was the outlaw gang of which Butch Cassidy was a member. Newman portrayed Cassidy in the 1969 film *Butch Cassidy and the Sundance Kid.*

Answers to Math Activity

Students should find that asthma rates for children under 17 have increased from 3.2% in 1981 to 5.7% in 2001. Students should be able to update the figures each year as more-current data is published. Bar graphs should reflect the growth in the rate from the 1980s to the present. As an extension, students can research the costs associated with asthma in children or can research the ways in which asthma rates differ between races.

The Digestive and Urinary Systems
Chapter Planning Guide

Compression guide:
To shorten instruction because of time limitations, omit the Chapter Lab.

OBJECTIVES	LABS, DEMONSTRATIONS, AND ACTIVITIES	TECHNOLOGY RESOURCES
PACING • 90 min pp. 202–211 **Chapter Opener**	SE **Start-up Activity,** p. 203 ◆ GENERAL	OSP **Parent Letter** GENERAL CD **Student Edition on CD-ROM** CD **Guided Reading Audio CD** TR **Chapter Starter Transparency*** VID **Brain Food Video Quiz**
Section 1 The Digestive System • Compare mechanical digestion with chemical digestion. • Describe the parts and functions of the digestive system.	SE **Quick Lab** Break It Up!, p. 205 ◆ GENERAL CRF **Datasheet for Quick Lab*** TE **Demonstration** Measuring Saliva, p. 205 BASIC TE **Demonstration** Peristalsis, p. 207 ◆ GENERAL TE **Connection Activity** Chemistry, p. 208 ◆ GENERAL TE **Activity** Examining Tissue, p. 208 ◆ ADVANCED SE **School-to-Home Activity** Bile Model, p. 209 GENERAL TE **Activity** Digestive Tract, p. 209 BASIC SE **Connection to Environmental Science** Waste Away, p. 210 GENERAL SE **Skills Practice Lab** As the Stomach Churns, p. 216 ◆ GENERAL CRF **Datasheet for Chapter Lab*** SE **Skills Practice Lab** Enzymes in Action, p. 596 ◆ GENERAL CRF **Datasheet for LabBook*** LB **Whiz-Bang Demonstrations** Liver Let Live* ◆ GENERAL	CRF **Lesson Plans*** TR **Bellringer Transparency*** TR **The Digestive System*** TR **The Role of Enzymes in Protein Digestion*** TR **The Stomach; The Small Intestine and Villi*** TR **LINK TO EARTH SCIENCE** Mohs' Hardness Scale*** CRF **SciLinks Activity*** GENERAL TE **Internet Activity,** p. 209 GENERAL VID **Lab Videos for Life Science**
PACING • 45 min pp. 212–215 **Section 2 The Urinary System** • Describe the parts and functions of the urinary system. • Explain how the kidneys filter blood. • Describe three disorders of the urinary system.	TE **Activity** Defining Terms, p. 213 BASIC TE **Demonstration** Kidney Structure, p. 213 ◆ GENERAL SE **Science in Action** Math, Social Studies, and Language Arts Activities, pp. 222–223 GENERAL LB **Long-Term Projects & Research Ideas** Copying the Kidney* ADVANCED	CRF **Lesson Plans*** TR **Bellringer Transparency*** TR **How the Kidneys Filter Blood***

PACING • 90 min

CHAPTER REVIEW, ASSESSMENT, AND STANDARDIZED TEST PREPARATION

CRF **Vocabulary Activity*** GENERAL
SE **Chapter Review,** pp. 218–219 GENERAL
CRF **Chapter Review*** ■ GENERAL
CRF **Chapter Tests A*** ■ GENERAL, **B*** ADVANCED, **C*** SPECIAL NEEDS
SE **Standardized Test Preparation,** pp. 220–221 GENERAL
CRF **Standardized Test Preparation*** GENERAL
CRF **Performance-Based Assessment*** GENERAL
OSP **Test Generator** GENERAL
CRF **Test Item Listing*** GENERAL

Online and Technology Resources

Visit **go.hrw.com** for a variety of free resources related to this textbook. Enter the keyword **HT5R7BD3**.

 Holt Online Learning

Students can access interactive problem-solving help and active visual concept development with the *Holt Science and Technology* Online Edition available at **www.hrw.com**.

 Guided Reading Audio CD

These CDs are designed to help auditory learners and reluctant readers.

 Science Tutor CD-ROM

Excellent for remediation and test practice.

SKILLS DEVELOPMENT RESOURCES	SECTION REVIEW AND ASSESSMENT	STANDARDS CORRELATIONS
SE **Pre-Reading Activity,** p. 202 `GENERAL` OSP **Science Puzzlers, Twisters & Teasers** `GENERAL`		North Carolina Standard Course of Study
CRF **Directed Reading A*** `BASIC`**, B*** `SPECIAL NEEDS` CRF **Vocabulary and Section Summary*** `GENERAL` SE **Reading Strategy** Prediction Guide, p. 204 `GENERAL` TE **Reading Strategy** Activity, p. 206 `BASIC` SE **Math Practice** Tooth Truth, p. 207 `GENERAL` TE **Inclusion Strategies,** p. 207 SE **Connection to Social Studies** Parasites, p. 208 `GENERAL` TE **Connection to Math** Liver Regeneration, p. 209 `GENERAL` CRF **Critical Thinking** Frankenstein's Food* `ADVANCED`	SE **Reading Checks,** pp. 205, 207, 209, 210 `GENERAL` TE **Homework,** p. 205 `GENERAL` TE **Homework,** p. 209 `GENERAL` TE **Reteaching,** p. 210 `BASIC` TE **Quiz,** p. 210 `GENERAL` TE **Alternative Assessment,** p. 210 `ADVANCED` SE **Section Review,*** p. 211 ■ `GENERAL` CRF **Section Quiz*** ■ `GENERAL`	4.01, 4.02, 4.03, 4.04; *Chapter Lab:* 1.01, 1.02, 1.03, 1.04, 1.05, 1.08; *LabBook:* 1.03, 1.05, 1.08
CRF **Directed Reading A*** `BASIC`**, B*** `SPECIAL NEEDS` CRF **Vocabulary and Section Summary*** `GENERAL` SE **Reading Strategy** Reading Organizer, p. 212 `GENERAL` SE **Connection to Language Arts** Beverage Ban, p. 214 `GENERAL` TE **Inclusion Strategies,** p. 214 CRF **Reinforcement Worksheet** Annie Apple's Amazing Adventure* `BASIC`	SE **Reading Checks,** pp. 213, 214 `GENERAL` TE **Reteaching,** p. 214 `BASIC` TE **Quiz,** p. 214 `GENERAL` TE **Alternative Assessment,** p. 214 `GENERAL` SE **Section Review,*** p. 215 ■ `GENERAL` CRF **Section Quiz*** ■ `GENERAL`	4.01, 4.02, 4.03, 4.04

One-Stop Planner® CD-ROM

This convenient CD-ROM includes:
- Lab Materials QuickList Software
- Holt Calendar Planner
- Customizable Lesson Plans
- Printable Worksheets
- ExamView® Test Generator

cnnstudentnews.com

Find the latest news, lesson plans, and activities related to important scientific events.

NSTA

www.scilinks.org

Maintained by the **National Science Teachers Association.** See Chapter Enrichment pages for a complete list of topics.

Current Science®

Check out *Current Science* articles and activities by visiting the HRW Web site at **go.hrw.com.** Just type in the keyword **HL4CS24T.**

Classroom Videos

- **Lab Videos** demonstrate the chapter lab.
- **Brain Food Video Quizzes** help students review the chapter material.
- **CNN Videos** bring science into your students' daily life.

Visual Resources

CHAPTER STARTER TRANSPARENCY

This Really Happened!

In 1822, a Canadian fur trader named Alexis St. Martin accidentally shot himself in his left side. An army surgeon named Dr. William Beaumont was able to save St. Martin's life, but the wound never completely healed. A hole approximately 6 cm in diameter remained open in his side, leading through skin and muscle right into his stomach.

Dr. Beaumont seized the opportunity to perform some amazing experiments. To find out what happens to food in the stomach, Dr. Beaumont tied different kinds of food onto strings and inserted them into the opening. He watched the

stomach squeeze and relax as it digested the bits of food. When he removed the food, he could see that it had changed. He also found that food changed when he placed it in a test tube with juices from St. Martin's stomach. Beaumont was able to determine that the stomach's juices, not just its squeezing action, were responsible for turning the food to mush.

What began as an unfortunate accident for Alexis St. Martin ended up helping Dr. Beaumont answer many important questions about how food is digested. Read on to find out about the digestive system.

BELLRINGER TRANSPARENCIES

Section: The Digestive System

How does your circulatory system get the nutrients that it carries to your cells? Describe as best you can the process that turns food into nutrients that cells can use.

Write your answers in your **science journal.**

Section: The Urinary System

Your blood must be cleaned regularly. Without looking in your textbook, guess how the body cleans the blood. Think about what organs might be used to clean your blood. Do you know what medical procedure you must undergo if your body is no longer able to clean its own blood?

Write your answers in your **science journal,** and then check your answer against the textbook.

TEACHING TRANSPARENCIES

L85 The Digestive System

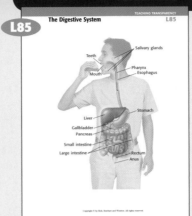

L86 The Role of Enzymes in Protein Digestion

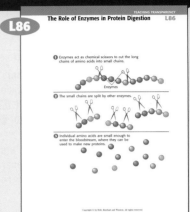

TEACHING TRANSPARENCIES

L87 The Stomach

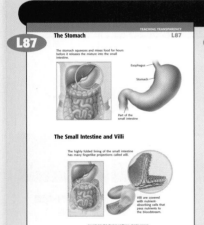

The Small Intestine and Villi

L88 How the Kidneys Filter Blood

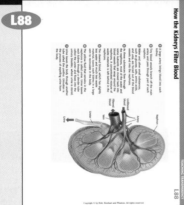

E6 Mohs Hardness Scale

LINK TO EARTH SCIENCE

Chapter: Minerals of the Earth's Crust

CONCEPT MAPPING TRANSPARENCY

Use the following terms to complete the concept map below: **food, digestive system, mechanical digestion, chemical digestion, proteins, enzymes, nutrients**

Planning Resources

LESSON PLANS

Lesson Plan SAMPLE

Section: Waves

Pacing
Regular Schedule: with lab(s):2 days   without lab(s):2 days
Block Schedule: with lab(s):1 1/2 days   without lab(s):1 day

Objectives
1. Relate the seven properties of life to a living organism.
2. Describe seven themes that can help you to organize what you learn about biology.
3. Identify the tiny structures that make up all living organisms.
4. Differentiate between reproduction and heredity and between metabolism and homeostasis.

National Science Education Standards Covered
LS1Inter6:Cells have particular structures that underlie their functions.
LS Mat1: Most cell functions involve chemical reactions.
LS1Beh1:Cells store and use information to guide their functions.
UCP1:Cell functions are regulated.
SI1: Cells can differentiate and from complete multicellular organisms.
PS1: Species evolve over time.
ESS1: The great diversity of organisms is the result of more than 3.5 billion years of evolution.
ESS2: Natural selection and its evolutionary consequences provide a scientific explanation for the fossil record of ancient life forms as well as for the striking molecular similarities observed among the diverse species of living organisms.
ST1: The millions of different species of plants, animals, and microorganisms that live on Earth today are related by descent from common ancestors.
ST2: The energy for life primarily comes from the sun.
SPSP1: The complexity and organization of organisms accommodates the need for obtaining, transforming, transporting, releasing, and eliminating the matter and energy used to sustain the organism.
SPSP6: As matter and energy flows through different levels of organization of living systems—cells, organs, communities—and between living systems and the physical environment, chemical elements are recombined in different ways.
HNS1: Organisms have behavioral responses to internal changes and to external stimuli.

PARENT LETTER

Dear Parent,

Your son's or daughter's science class will soon begin exploring the chapter entitled "The World of Physical Science." In this chapter, students will learn about how the scientific method applies to the world of physical science and the role of physical science in the world. By the end of the chapter, students should demonstrate a clear understanding of the chapter's main ideas and be able to discuss the following topics:

1. physical science as the study of energy and matter (Section 1)
2. the role of physical science in the world around them (Section 1)
3. careers that rely on physical science (Section 1)
4. the steps used in the scientific method (Section 2)
5. examples of technology (Section 2)
6. how the scientific method is used to answer questions and solve problems (Section 2)
7. how our knowledge of physical science changes over time (Section 2)
8. how models represent real objects or systems (Section 3)
9. examples of different ways models are used in science (Section 3)
10. the importance of the International System of Units (Section 4)
11. the appropriate units to use for particular measurements (Section 4)
12. how area and density are derived quantities (Section 4)

Questions to Ask Along the Way

You can help your son or daughter learn about these topics by asking interesting questions such as the following:

* What are some surprising careers that use physical science?
* What is a characteristic of a good hypothesis?
* When is it a good idea to use a model?
* Why do Americans measure things in terms of inches and yards instead of centimeters and meters?

TEST ITEM LISTING

TEST ITEM LISTING
The World of Science SAMPLE

MULTIPLE CHOICE

1. A limitation of models is that
a. they are large enough to see.
b. they do not act exactly like the things that they model.
c. they are smaller than the things that they model.
d. they model unfamiliar things.
Answer: B   Difficulty: 1   Section: 3   Objective: 2

2. The length 10 m is equal to
a. 100 cm.   c. 10,000 mm.
b. 1,000 cm.   d. Both (b) and (c)
Answer: D   Difficulty: 1   Section: 3   Objective: 2

3. To be valid, a hypothesis must be
a. testable.   c. made into a law.
b. supported by evidence.   d. Both (a) and (b)
Answer: B   Difficulty: 1   Section: 1   Objective: 2

4. The statement "Sheila has a stain on her shirt" is an example of a(n)
a. law.   c. observation.
b. hypothesis.   d. prediction.
Answer: B   Difficulty: 1   Section: 2   Objective: 2

5. A hypothesis is often developed out of
a. observations.   c. laws.
b. experiments.   d. Both (a) and (b)
Answer: D   Difficulty: 1   Section: 2   Objective: 2

6. How many milliliters are in 3.5 kL?
a. 3,500 mL.   c. 3,500, 000 mL.
b. 0.0035 mL.   d. 35,000 mL.
Answer: B   Difficulty: 1   Section: 3   Objective: 2

7. A map of Seattle is an example of a
a. law.   c. model.
b. theory.   d. unit.
Answer: B   Difficulty: 1   Section: 3   Objective: 2

8. A lab has the safety icons shown below. These icons mean that you should wear
a. only safety goggles.   c. safety goggles and a lab apron.
b. only a lab apron.   d. safety goggles, a lab apron, and gloves.
Answer: B   Difficulty: 1   Section: 1   Objective: 2

9. The law of conservation of mass says the lot of mass before a chemical change is
a. more than the total mass after the change.
b. less than the total mass after the change.
c. the same as the total mass after the change.
d. not the same as the total mass after the change.
Answer: B   Difficulty: 1   Section: 1   Objective: 2

10. In which of the following areas would you find a geochemist at work?
a. studying the chemistry of rocks   c. studying fishes
b. studying forestry   d. studying the atmosphere
Answer: B   Difficulty: 1   Section: 3   Objective: 2

One-Stop Planner® CD-ROM

This CD-ROM includes all of the resources shown here and the following time-saving tools:

* *Lab Materials QuickList Software*
* *Customizable lesson plans*
* *Holt Calendar Planner*
* *The powerful ExamView® Test Generator*

Meeting Individual Needs

DIRECTED READING A

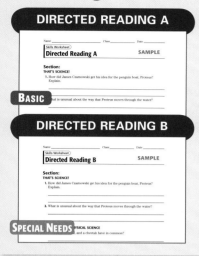

BASIC

DIRECTED READING B

SPECIAL NEEDS

VOCABULARY ACTIVITY

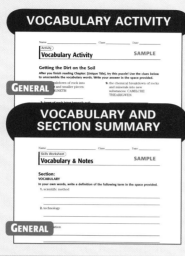

GENERAL

VOCABULARY AND SECTION SUMMARY

GENERAL

REINFORCEMENT

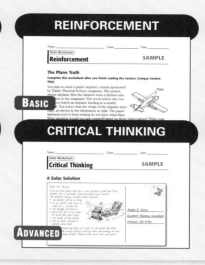

BASIC

CRITICAL THINKING

ADVANCED

SCILINKS ACTIVITY

GENERAL

SCIENCE PUZZLERS, TWISTERS & TEASERS

GENERAL

Labs and Activities

LONG-TERM PROJECTS & RESEARCH IDEAS

ADVANCED

WHIZ-BANG DEMONSTRATIONS

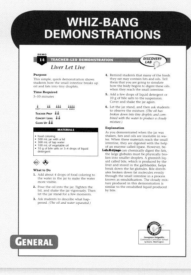

GENERAL

DATASHEETS FOR QUICK LABS

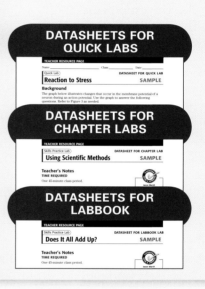

DATASHEETS FOR CHAPTER LABS

DATASHEETS FOR LABBOOK

Review and Assessments

SECTION QUIZ

GENERAL

SECTION REVIEW

GENERAL

CHAPTER REVIEW

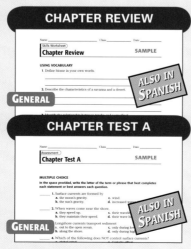

GENERAL

CHAPTER TEST A

GENERAL

CHAPTER TEST B

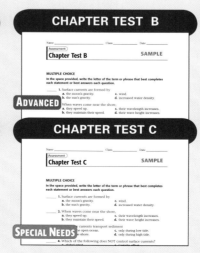

ADVANCED

CHAPTER TEST C

SPECIAL NEEDS

STANDARDIZED TEST PREPARATION

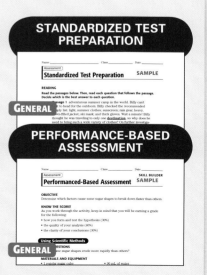

GENERAL

PERFORMANCE-BASED ASSESSMENT

GENERAL

This Chapter Enrichment provides relevant and interesting information to expand and enhance your presentation of the chapter material.

Section 1

The Digestive System
Parts of the System

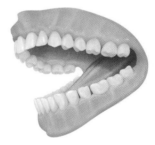

- The digestive system is composed of two sets of organs: those that make up the digestive tract and those that are called *accessory organs*. The digestive tract is a continuous tube consisting of the mouth, including the teeth and the tongue, the pharynx, the esophagus, the stomach, the small intestine, the large intestine, rectum, and anus.

- The accessory digestive organs include the salivary glands, the gallbladder, the liver, and the pancreas.

Is That a Fact!
- The digestive tract in a cadaver is about 9 m long. However, because of muscle tone, the digestive tract of a living person is considerably shorter.

The Stomach
- In short people, the stomach is found high in the abdomen and runs horizontally. In tall people, the stomach tends to run vertically, forming a **J** shape.

Is That a Fact!
- It takes from about four to eight seconds for food to pass from the top of the throat to the stomach.
- It takes less than two seconds for liquids to pass from the top of the throat to the stomach.

The Intestines
- The small intestine is the longest portion of the digestive tract. It is about 6 m long and 2.5 cm in diameter.
- Unlike the small intestine, the large intestine does not have villi and does not secrete digestive enzymes.

The Appendix
- The appendix is an offshoot of the large intestine and is 5 to 10 cm long. Like the tonsils, the appendix contains a large amount of lymphoid tissue.

- Occasionally, doctors begin an appendectomy on patients misdiagnosed with appendicitis. Instead of having appendicitis, however, the patients have had holes in the lining of their intestines made by parasitic worms. The incidence of intestinal parasitic worms is increasing as eating raw fish, such as sushi and sashimi, becomes more popular.

Food Poisoning
- Food poisoning is characterized by nausea, vomiting, abdominal cramps, and diarrhea. The two most common culprits are the bacteria *Salmonella* and *Shigella*.

- *Salmonella* is typically spread by poorly cooked meat and feces-contaminated hands. *Salmonella* infects the microvilli in the intestinal lining, causing blisters. If *Salmonella* poisoning is not treated promptly, the bacteria may spread throughout the body.

- *Shigella* is commonly found among people who have visited developing countries. It is spread via food, feces, fingers, flies, and contaminated public bodies of water, such as swimming pools.

Eating Disorders
- Anorexia nervosa and bulimia nervosa are two common eating disorders that are characterized by an obsessive fear of gaining weight. Often, underlying psychological factors initiate these disorders.

- Anorexia nervosa is an eating disorder characterized by self-induced starvation. People with this condition refuse to eat and often exercise obsessively. Although the disorder can affect anyone, adolescent girls and young women are commonly afflicted. Boys, especially those involved in weight-conscious sports such as wrestling, can also suffer from anorexia nervosa.

- Bulimia nervosa is a binge-purge syndrome in which those afflicted binge on enormous amounts of food and then force themselves to vomit or use laxatives to eliminate the food. The binge-purge cycle may be repeated several times per day or only a couple of times per week.

- Although bulimics generally maintain a normal body weight and appear to be healthy, they are not healthy. They tend to have swollen salivary glands, pancreatitis, and liver and kidney problems. In addition, they are at risk of heart failure and stomach rupture, both of which can result in death. Excessive vomiting damages the esophagus and the stomach and wears away tooth enamel.

- Treatment for eating disorders may include diet control, often by means of hospitalization, behavior modification, nutrition education, and use of antidepressants.

Section 2

The Urinary System

Filtering Wastes

- The urinary system functions primarily to maintain the correct balance of salts and water and to remove metabolic, nitrogen-containing wastes, such as urea, from the body in the form of urine.

- The digestive system, the circulatory system, and the respiratory system also excrete wastes. The digestive system excretes food wastes in the form of feces. The circulatory and respiratory systems work together to rid the body of carbon dioxide.

- The yellow color of urine comes from the yellow pigment urochrome.

The Kidneys

- The kidneys are surrounded and kept in their proper place in the body by fat. People who become too thin risk damage to the kidneys and other related urinary problems. As much as 1,200 mL of blood passes through the nephrons each minute.

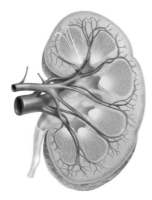

Is That a Fact!

- ◆ Urinary bladders of average size can contain as much as 1 L of urine!

- ◆ The kidneys require up to one-fourth of the body's oxygen supply to carry out their functions.

- ◆ The kidneys filter about 180 L of fluid from the blood each day. About 99% of this fluid is returned to the bloodstream. The other 1% leaves the body in the form of urine.

- ◆ A person who donates a kidney can maintain normal kidney functions. The remaining kidney enlarges and carries out the functions previously performed by two kidneys.

The Urinary Bladder

- Like the stomach, the size of the bladder varies with the amount of its contents. The bladder can hold 300 mL of urine without increasing its internal pressure significantly. At 500 mL of urine, the bladder is fairly full and may be 12.5 cm in length.

SciLINKS

NSTA
Developed and maintained by the
National Science Teachers Association

SciLinks is maintained by the National Science Teachers Association to provide you and your students with interesting, up-to-date links that will enrich your classroom presentation of the chapter.

Visit www.scilinks.org and enter the SciLinks code for more information about the topic listed.

Topic: The Digestive System
SciLinks code: HSM0409

Topic: Urinary System Ailments
SciLinks code: HSM1584

**Topic: Problems in the
        Digestive System**
SciLinks code: HSM1218

Topic: Tapeworms
SciLinks code: HSM1492

Topic: The Urinary System
SciLinks code: HSM1583

Overview

In this chapter, students will learn about the digestive and urinary systems of the human body. Students will learn how the digestive system breaks down food into building blocks the body can use and how the digestive and urinary systems eliminate wastes from the body.

Assessing Prior Knowledge

Students should be familiar with the following topics:

- cellular structure and function
- body organization

Identifying Misconceptions

Students may have misconceptions regarding the digestive and urinary systems. Many people commonly refer only to the stomach when discussing eating and digestion. So, some students may not know other organs are also part of the digestive system. Students may also mistakenly think that all digestion is mechanical. Though mechanical digestion is important, chemical digestion reduces food into subunits the body can use.

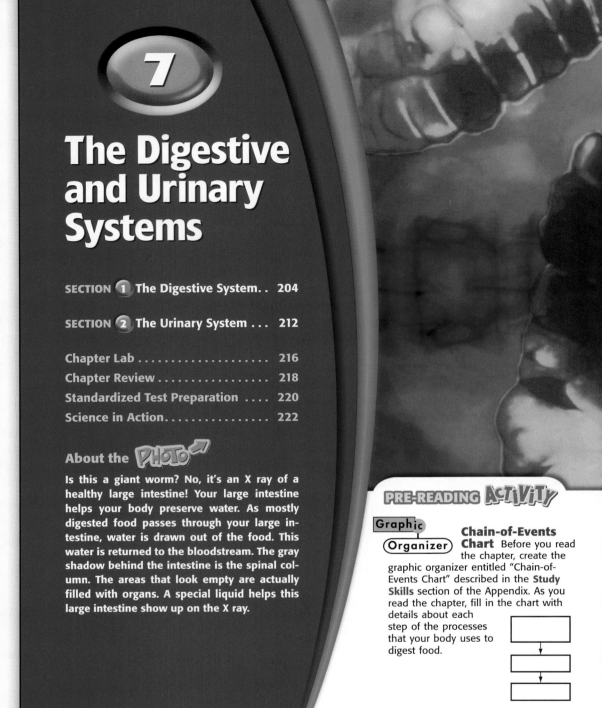

The Digestive and Urinary Systems

About the PHOTO

Is this a giant worm? No, it's an X ray of a healthy large intestine! Your large intestine helps your body preserve water. As mostly digested food passes through your large intestine, water is drawn out of the food. This water is returned to the bloodstream. The gray shadow behind the intestine is the spinal column. The areas that look empty are actually filled with organs. A special liquid helps this large intestine show up on the X ray.

PRE-READING ACTIVITY

Graphic Organizer

Chain-of-Events Chart Before you read the chapter, create the graphic organizer entitled "Chain-of-Events Chart" described in the **Study Skills** section of the Appendix. As you read the chapter, fill in the chart with details about each step of the processes that your body uses to digest food.

Standards Correlations

North Carolina Standard Course of Study

1.01 Identify and create questions and hypotheses that can be answered through scientific investigations. (Chapter Lab)

1.02 Develop appropriate experimental procedures for: Given questions [and] Student generated questions. (Chapter Lab)

1.03 Apply safety procedures in the laboratory and in field studies, Recognize potential hazards, Safely manipulate materials and equipment, [and] Conduct appropriate procedures. (Chapter Lab and LabBook)

1.04 Analyze variables in scientific investigations: Identify dependent and independent, Use of a Control, Manipulate, Describe relationships between, [and] Define operationally. (Chapter Lab)

1.05 Analyze evidence to: Explain observations, Make inferences and predictions, [and] Develop the relationship between evidence and explanation. (Chapter Lab and LabBook)

1.08 Use oral and written language to: Communicate findings [and] Defend conclusions of scientific investigations. (Chapter Lab and LabBook)

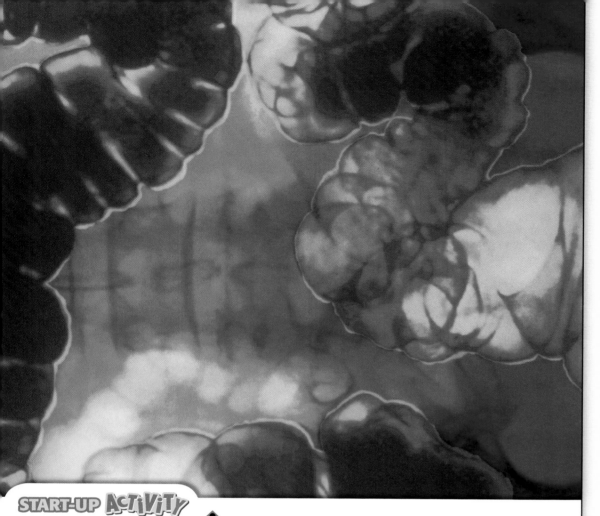

MATERIALS

FOR EACH STUDENT
- bag, plastic, sealable
- flour, 200 mL
- vegetable oil, 100 mL
- water, 100 mL

Safety Caution: Tell students not to ingest any of the materials used in this investigation. Using strong bags or doubling the bags works best. Have paper towels on hand, and clean up any spills immediately. Spilled liquids are a slipping hazard.

Answers

1. Sample answer: Before I squeezed the bag, the contents were well dispersed. Once I began squeezing the bag, the oil was mixed into the flour mixture.

2. Sample answer: The stomach is a muscular, baglike organ that is involved in the physical and chemical digestion of food. By squeezing the bag, I am modeling the muscular contractions of the stomach. (Note: This activity does not model the chemical digestion that occurs in the stomach.)

3. Sample answer: This is a good model of how the stomach works. Squeezing the bag helps show how the stomach mechanically mashes food. But the model does not have acids and enzymes that also help a real stomach break down food.

START-UP ACTiViTY

Changing Foods

The stomach breaks down food by, in part, squeezing the food. You can model the action of the stomach in the following activity.

Procedure

1. Add **200 mL of flour** and **100 mL of water** to a **resealable plastic bag.**

2. Mix **100 mL of vegetable oil** with the flour and water.

3. Seal the plastic bag.

4. Shake the bag until the flour, water, and oil are well mixed.

5. Remove as much air from the bag as you can, and reseal the bag carefully.

6. Knead the bag carefully with your hands for 5 min. Be careful to keep the bag sealed.

Analysis

1. Describe the mixture before and after you kneaded the bag.

2. How might the changes you saw in the mixture relate to how your stomach digests food?

3. Do you think this activity is a good model of how your stomach works? Explain your answer.

4.01 (partial) Analyze how human body systems interact to provide for the needs of the human organism: . . . Digestive and Circulatory, [and] Excretory . . . (Sections 1 and 2)

4.02 Describe how systems within the human body are defined by the functions it performs. (Sections 1 and 2)

4.03 (partial) Explain how the structure of an organ is adapted to perform specific functions within one or more systems: Liver, . . . Stomach, [and] Kidney. (Sections 1 and 2)

4.04 Evaluate how systems in the human body help regulate the internal environment. (Sections 1 and 2)

This Really Happened!

In 1822, a Canadian fur trader named Alexis St. Martin accidentally shot himself in his left side. An army surgeon named Dr. William Beaumont was able to save St. Martin's life, but the wound never completely healed. A hole approximately 6 cm in diameter remained open in his side, leading through skin and muscle right into his stomach.

Dr. Beaumont seized the opportunity stomach squeeze and relax as it digested the bits of food. When he removed the food, he could see that it had changed. He also found that food changed when he placed it in a test tube with juices from St. Martin's stomach. Beaumont was able to determine that the stomach's juices, not just its squeezing action, were responsible for turning the food to mush.

What began as an unfortunate acci-

Chapter Starter Transparency
Use this transparency to help students begin thinking about how the human body digests food.

CHAPTER RESOURCES

Technology

 Transparencies
- Chapter Starter Transparency

READING SKILLS

Student Edition on CD-ROM

Guided Reading Audio CD

Classroom Videos
- Brain Food Video Quiz

Workbooks

 Science Puzzlers, Twisters & Teasers
- The Digestive and Urinary Systems **GENERAL**

Focus

Overview

This section introduces the structures and functions of the digestive system. Students will compare mechanical digestion with chemical digestion and will learn to trace the path of food through the digestive system.

Bellringer

Ask students to answer the following questions:

• How does your circulatory system obtain the nutrients that it brings to your cells? (from the digestive system)

• Describe as best you can the process that turns food into nutrients that cells can use. (Sample answer: Food is broken down into smaller pieces by chewing and by the muscles of the digestive system. Chemicals in the digestive system then break these smaller pieces into nutrients that cells can use.)

READING WARM-UP

Objectives

● Compare mechanical digestion with chemical digestion.

● Describe the parts and functions of the digestive system.

Terms to Learn

digestive system
esophagus
stomach
pancreas
small intestine
liver
gallbladder
large intestine

READING STRATEGY

Prediction Guide Before reading this section, write the title of each heading in this section. Next, under each heading, write what you think you will learn.

digestive system the organs that break down food so that it can be used by the body

The Digestive System

It's your last class before lunch, and you're starving! Finally, the bell rings, and you get to eat!

You feel hungry because your brain receives signals that your cells need energy to maintain homeostasis. Eating is just the beginning. Your body must change food into substances that your cells can use. Your **digestive system,** shown in **Figure 1,** is a group of organs that work together to break down food so that it can be used by the body.

Digestive System at a Glance

The most obvious part of your digestive system is a series of tubelike organs called the *digestive tract*. Food passes through the digestive tract. The digestive tract includes your mouth, pharynx, esophagus, stomach, small intestine, large intestine, rectum, and anus. The liver, gallbladder, pancreas, and salivary glands are also part of the digestive system. But food does not pass through these organs.

 **Figure 1** The Digestive System

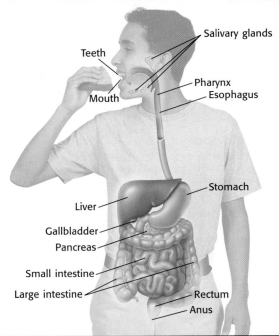

Salivary glands
Teeth
Pharynx
Mouth
Esophagus
Liver
Stomach
Gallbladder
Pancreas
Small intestine
Large intestine
Rectum
Anus

CHAPTER RESOURCES

Chapter Resource File

• **Lesson Plan**
• **Directed Reading A** BASIC
• **Directed Reading B** SPECIAL NEEDS

Technology

Transparencies
• Bellringer
• The Role of Enzymes in Protein Digestion

Cultural Awareness   GENERAL

World Diets Have students research the diets of people in countries such as Japan, India, Israel, Egypt, Mexico, and Russia. Encourage students to discover strategies that people in these countries use to obtain a nutritious diet, and have students compare the diets of people in each country with the diets of people in the United States. You may also want to have students compare the diets based on fat or cholesterol intake. **Verbal/Logical**

Breaking Down Food

The digestive system works with the circulatory system, which includes the heart, blood vessels, and blood, to deliver the materials cells need to function. Digestion is the process of breaking down food into a form that can pass from the digestive tract into the bloodstream. There are two types of digestion. The breaking, crushing, and mashing of food is called *mechanical digestion*. In *chemical digestion*, large molecules are broken down into nutrients. Nutrients are substances that the body needs for energy and for growth, maintenance, and repair.

Three major types of nutrients—carbohydrates, proteins, and fats—make up most of the food you eat. Substances called *enzymes* break some nutrients into smaller particles that the body can use. For example, proteins are chains of smaller molecules called *amino acids*. Proteins are too large to be absorbed into the bloodstream. So, enzymes cut up the chain of amino acids. The amino acids are small enough to pass into the bloodstream. This process is shown in **Figure 2**.

Reading Check How do the digestive and circulatory systems work together? (*See the Appendix for answers to Reading Checks.*)

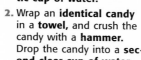
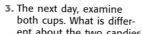

Break It Up!

1. Drop **one piece of hard candy** into a **clear plastic cup of water.**
2. Wrap an **identical candy** in a **towel**, and crush the candy with a **hammer.** Drop the candy into a **second clear cup of water.**
3. The next day, examine both cups. What is different about the two candies?
4. What type of digestion is represented by breaking the hard candy?
5. How does chewing your food help the process of digestion?

Figure 2   The Role of Enzymes in Protein Digestion

❶ Enzymes act as chemical scissors to cut the long chains of amino acids into small chains.

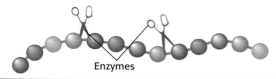

Enzymes

❷ The small chains are split by other enzymes.

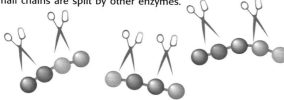

❸ Individual amino acids are small enough to enter the bloodstream, where they can be used to make new proteins.

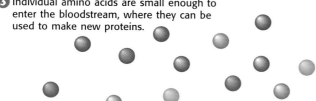

Motivate

Demonstration — GENERAL

Measuring Saliva Show students a 2 L beaker or other transparent container. Pour 1.2 L (2.6 pt) of water into the container, and explain that this amount of water represents the amount of saliva an average person produces in one day. Ask students to discuss what roles saliva might play in the body, specifically in the process of digestion. (Answers might include lubricating the mouth and related organs, moistening food, and breaking down molecules into nutrients that cells can use.) **LS** Logical/Visual

Teach

MATERIALS

FOR EACH STUDENT
• hammer
• hard candy, 2 identical pieces
• towel
• water, in 2 identical clear plastic cups

Safety Caution: Tell students not to ingest or taste any of the materials, including the candy, in this Quick Lab. Students should wear safety goggles while crushing the candy. Students should strike hammers away from their face and hands.

Answers

3. The crushed candy dissolved in the water. The whole candy did not dissolve as much.
4. Chewing, one form of mechanical digestion, is represented by breaking the candy.
5. Chewing breaks the large chunks of food into smaller pieces. Greater surface area is then available for enzymes to digest the food.

Homework — GENERAL

Kinds of Digestion Ask students to indicate which of the following activities represent mechanical digestion and which represent chemical digestion: The teeth cut and grind food, the stomach churns food, enzymes in saliva break down carbohydrates in food, and enzymes break down proteins in food. (mechanical—the teeth cutting and grinding food, the stomach churning food; chemical—enzymes in saliva breaking down carbohydrates in food, enzymes breaking down proteins in food) **LS** Logical

Answer to Reading Check

The digestive system works with the circulatory system to deliver the materials cells need to function. The digestive system breaks down food into a form that can be carried by the circulatory system.

✏️ *Writing* **Activity** Before students read the text on these pages, have them read the headings aloud. Then ask students to formulate one question that they expect the text under each heading to answer. Have students write their questions down. Possible questions include the following:

• "What happens in the mouth?"

• "Why is chewing important?"

• "What makes the stomach's environment harsh?"

LS **Verbal**

CONNECTION to Earth Science — GENERAL

Enamel Tooth enamel is made primarily of carbonated calcium hydroxyapatite. Fluoride compounds, taken internally while the teeth are growing, strengthen the enamel by forming the enamel out of fluoroapatite, an apatite material more acid resistant than natural enamel. Applying fluoride to the outside of teeth after the teeth have formed can also help strengthen the enamel by changing the natural hydroxyapatite in the tooth to fluoroapatite. Use the teaching transparency "Mohs' Hardness Scale" to illustrate that in geology, apatite is in the middle of the hardness scale for minerals. LS **Visual**

Digestion Begins in the Mouth

Chewing is important for two reasons. First, chewing creates small, slippery pieces of food that are easier to swallow than big, dry pieces are. Second, small pieces of food are easier to digest.

Teeth

Teeth are very important organs for mechanical digestion. With the help of strong jaw muscles, teeth break and grind food. The outermost layer of a tooth, the *enamel*, is the hardest material in the body. Enamel protects nerves and softer material inside the tooth. **Figure 3** shows a cross section of a tooth.

Have you ever noticed that your teeth have different shapes? Look at **Figure 4** to locate the different kinds of teeth. The molars are well suited for grinding food. The *premolars* are perfect for mashing food. The sharp teeth at the front of your mouth, the *incisors* and *canines,* are for shredding food.

Saliva

As you chew, the food mixes with a liquid called *saliva*. Saliva is made in salivary glands located in the mouth. Saliva contains an enzyme that begins the chemical digestion of carbohydrates. Saliva changes complex carbohydrates into simple sugars.

Leaving the Mouth

Once the food has been reduced to a soft mush, the tongue pushes it into the throat, which leads to a long, straight tube called the **esophagus** (i SAHF uh guhs). The esophagus squeezes the mass of food with rhythmic muscle contractions called *peristalsis* (PER uh STAL sis). Peristalsis forces the food into the stomach.

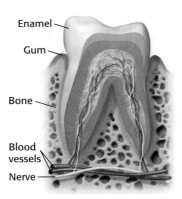

Figure 3 *A tooth, such as this molar, is made of many kinds of tissue.*

Labels: Enamel, Gum, Bone, Blood vessels, Nerve

esophagus a long, straight tube that connects the pharynx to the stomach

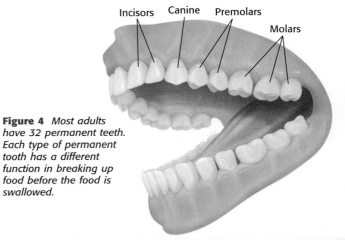

Figure 4 *Most adults have 32 permanent teeth. Each type of permanent tooth has a different function in breaking up food before the food is swallowed.*

Labels: Incisors, Canine, Premolars, Molars

MISCONCEPTION ⚠ ALERT

Teeth and Bones Students may mistakenly assume that teeth are made of bone. Point out that although enamel and dentin are similar to bone in appearance and calcium content, they are not bone. Bone contains blood vessels, but enamel and dentin do not.

Figure 5 · The Stomach

The stomach squeezes and mixes food for hours before it releases the mixture into the small intestine.

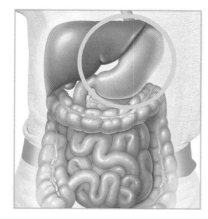

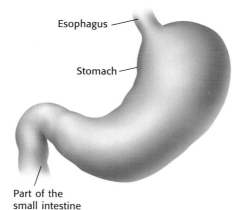

Esophagus

Stomach

Part of the small intestine

The Harsh Environment of the Stomach

The **stomach** is a muscular, saclike, digestive organ attached to the lower end of the esophagus. The stomach is shown in **Figure 5**. The stomach continues the mechanical digestion of your meal by squeezing the food with muscular contractions. While this squeezing is taking place, tiny glands in the stomach produce enzymes and acid. The enzymes and acid work together to break food into nutrients. Stomach acid also kills most bacteria that you might swallow with your food. After a few hours of combined mechanical and chemical digestion, your peanut butter and jelly sandwich has been reduced to a soupy mixture called *chyme* (KIEM).

Reading Check How is the structure of the stomach related to its function?

Leaving the Stomach

The stomach slowly releases the chyme into the small intestine through a small ring of muscle that works like a valve. This valve keeps food in the stomach until the food has been thoroughly mixed with digestive fluids. Each time the valve opens and closes, it lets a small amount of chyme into the small intestine. Because the stomach releases chyme slowly, the intestine has more time to mix the chyme with fluids from the liver and pancreas. These fluids help digest food and stop the harsh acids in chyme from hurting the small intestine.

stomach the saclike, digestive organ between the esophagus and the small intestine that breaks down food into a liquid by the action of muscles, enzymes, and acids

Tooth Truth

Young children get a first set of 20 teeth called *baby teeth*. These teeth usually fall out and are replaced by 32 permanent teeth. How many more permanent teeth than baby teeth does a person have? What is the ratio of baby teeth to permanent teeth? Be sure to express the ratio in its most reduced form.

Demonstration — GENERAL

Peristalsis Help students visualize the process of peristalsis by performing the following demonstration. Fill a 75 cm section of rubber tubing with water, and have an assistant pinch and hold both ends of the tubing shut. Wrap your fists around the tubing near one of the assistant's hands, and slowly "walk" your hands to the other end of the tubing, being careful to squeeze the water from the starting end to the other end of the tubing. When your hands reach the other end of the tubing, point the end into a basin or bucket away from all students, and have the assistant release his or her grip on that end. Water should stream out of the tubing. Point out that this is what the esophagus does when it squeezes food into the stomach. **LS Kinesthetic/Visual** English Language Learners

Answer to Reading Check

The stomach is a muscular, saclike organ with tiny glands that release enzymes and acids. This structure helps the stomach break down food mechanically and chemically.

Cultural Awareness — GENERAL

Lactose Intolerance Many adults of African and Asian descent have some form of lactose intolerance. They lack the enzyme lactase, which is needed to digest the sugar lactose in dairy products. Lactose intolerance is generally less common in people of European descent.

Answer to Math Practice

People have 12 more teeth as adults than they do as young children. The ratio of baby teeth to adult teeth is 20:32, which reduces to 5:8.

INCLUSION Strategies

• *Hearing Impaired*   • *Visually Impaired*
• *Developmentally Delayed*

Some students struggle with abstract concepts. Models that students can see and touch help make these ideas clearer. A model can help students understand how a long length of intestines fits within a small area in the human body. Organize the class into teams of three or four students. Have each team simulate intestinal folds using the following model:

1. Cut each of the three sheets of 8 1/2 × 11 paper into 8 strips (total of 24 strips per team).

2. Tape the 24 strips end to end.

3. Repeatedly bend the long strip into irregular lengths so that the folded paper also fits into about a 3 2/3 in. square. English Language Learners
LS Visual

Changes As food is digested, it undergoes both physical and chemical changes. Ask students to categorize the following activities as either physical changes or chemical changes:

• chewing food (physical change)

• enzymes in saliva breaking down carbohydrates (chemical change)

• squeezing and churning food in the stomach (physical change)

• breaking down food with pancreatic juice (chemical change)

LS Logical

ACTIVITY ——————— ADVANCED

Examining Tissue Provide students with a compound light microscope and prepared slides of several different digestive organs. You might want to include cross sections of tissue from the stomach, the small intestine, the liver, and the pancreas. Review the proper use of microscopes before allowing students to operate them, and make sure that students do not work with broken or cracked slides. Have students observe the specimens, compare the different cross sections, and make sketches. **LS** Visual

pancreas the organ that lies behind the stomach and that makes digestive enzymes and hormones that regulate sugar levels

small intestine the organ between the stomach and the large intestine where most of the breakdown of food happens and most of the nutrients from food are absorbed

CONNECTION TO Social Studies

WRITING SKILL **Parasites** Intestinal parasites are organisms, such as roundworms and hookworms, that infect people and live in their digestive tract. Worldwide, intestinal parasites infect more than 1 billion people. Some parasites can be deadly. Research intestinal parasites in a library or on the Internet. Then, write a report on a parasite, including how it spreads, what problems it causes, how many people have it, and what can be done to stop it.

The Pancreas and Small Intestine

Most chemical digestion takes place after food leaves the stomach. Proteins, carbohydrates, and fats in the chyme are digested by the small intestine and fluids from the pancreas.

The Pancreas

When the chyme leaves the stomach, the chyme is very acidic. The pancreas makes fluids that protect the small intestine from the acid. The **pancreas** is an oval organ located between the stomach and small intestine. The chyme never enters the pancreas. Instead, the pancreatic fluid flows into the small intestine. This fluid contains enzymes that chemically digest chyme and contains bicarbonate, which neutralizes the acid in chyme. The pancreas also functions as a part of the endocrine system by making hormones that regulate blood sugar.

The Small Intestine

The **small intestine** is a muscular tube that is about 2.5 cm in diameter. Other than having a small diameter, it is really not that small. In fact, if you stretched the small intestine out, it would be longer than you are tall—about 6 m! If you flattened out the surface of the small intestine, it would be larger than a tennis court! How is this possible? The inside wall of the small intestine is covered with fingerlike projections called *villi*, shown in **Figure 6.** The surface area of the small intestine is very large because of the villi. The villi are covered with tiny, nutrient-absorbing cells. Once the nutrients are absorbed, they enter the bloodstream.

Figure 6 The Small Intestine and Villi

The highly folded lining of the small intestine has many fingerlike projections called *villi*.

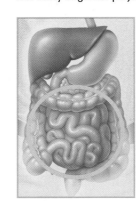
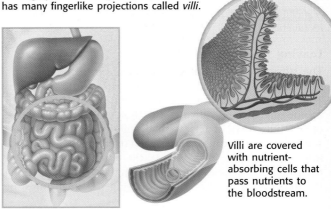

Villi are covered with nutrient-absorbing cells that pass nutrients to the bloodstream.

Answer to Connection to Social Studies

Sample answer: The World Health Organization reports that the intestinal parasite *Ascaris lumbricoides* (a kind of roundworm) kills 60,000 people every year. Symptoms include abdominal pain, intestinal blockage, and vomiting. The disease can be treated with medicines. Roundworms are spread by poor sanitary practices, such as using untreated human waste as fertilizer. Improved sanitary practices help control the spread of roundworms.

SCIENCE HUMOR

A man walks into a doctor's office with a stalk of celery in one ear and a carrot in the other. The man says, "Doc, I'm just not feeling well these days." The doctor replies, "I think that's because you haven't been eating right."

Figure 7   The Liver and the Gallbladder

Food does not move through the liver, gallbladder, and pancreas even though these organs are linked to the small intestine.

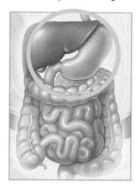
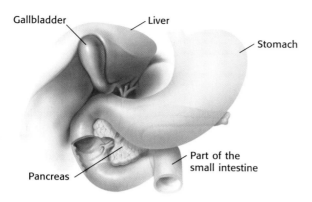

Gallbladder
Liver
Stomach
Part of the small intestine
Pancreas

The Liver and Gallbladder

The **liver** is a large, reddish brown organ that helps with digestion. A human liver can be as large as a football. Your liver is located toward your right side, slightly higher than your stomach, as shown in **Figure 7.** The liver helps with digestion in the following ways:

- It makes bile to break up fat.
- It stores nutrients.
- It breaks down toxins.

liver the largest organ in the body; it makes bile, stores and filters blood, and stores excess sugars as glycogen

gallbladder a sac-shaped organ that stores bile produced by the liver

Breaking Up Fat

Although bile is made by the liver, bile is temporarily stored in a small, saclike organ called the **gallbladder,** shown in **Figure 7.** Bile is squeezed from the gallbladder into the small intestine, where the bile breaks large fat droplets into very small droplets. This mechanical process allows more fat molecules to be exposed to digestive enzymes.

✓ **Reading Check**   How does bile help digest fat?

Storing Nutrients and Protecting the Body

After nutrients are broken down, they are absorbed into the bloodstream and carried through the body. Nutrients that are not needed right away are stored in the liver. The liver then releases the stored nutrients into the bloodstream as needed. The liver also captures and detoxifies many chemicals in the body. For instance, the liver produces enzymes that break down alcohol and many other drugs.

SCHOOL to HOME

Bile Model

You can model the way bile breaks down fat and oil. With a parent, put a small amount of water in a small jar. Then, add a few drops of vegetable oil to the water. Notice that the two liquids separate. Next, add a few drops of liquid dishwashing soap to the water, tighten the lid securely onto the jar, and shake the jar. What happened to the three liquids in the jar? Finally, make a model of the liver and investigate how its structure and functions are related.

Answer to School-to-Home Activity

Sample answer: Before the dishwashing soap was added, the liquids separated. After the soap was added and the jar was shaken, the oil and water mixed. Students should discover many things about the liver. For example, they should learn that the liver is the largest internal organ, has two major blood vessels, has multiple ducts, and has many different types of cells. Some of these cells store fats and vitamins. Some students may state that the liver receives blood both from the heart and intestines. Students should relate structural facts with the functions of the liver.

ACTIVITY — BASIC

Digestive Tract Help students remember the route that food takes through the digestive tract by providing them with additional practice. Begin by showing students a model or illustration of the digestive tract. Then have students take turns naming and identifying, in order, the organs through which food travels through the digestive tract. (The proper sequence is as follows: mouth, pharynx, esophagus, stomach, small intestine, and large intestine.)
LS Logical/Visual

Homework — GENERAL

Concept Mapping List the following terms on the board:

digestive system, mouth, stomach, liver, pancreas, gallbladder, teeth, salivary glands, saliva, digestive tract, esophagus, throat, tongue, small intestine

Then have students copy the terms onto a piece of paper and construct a concept map using these terms and linking words between them. **LS** Logical

Answer to Reading Check

Bile breaks large fat droplets into very small droplets. This process allows more fat molecules to be exposed to digestive enzymes.

CONNECTION to Math — GENERAL

Liver Regeneration Tell students that as much as 75% of a person's liver can be removed or impaired before the liver stops functioning. Ask students to calculate how much of a 1 kg liver must remain for it to function. ($25\% \times 1{,}000$ g $=250$ g or 0.25 kg)
LS Logical

Creating Graphs Provide students with the following average lengths of the digestive organs:

esophagus—25 cm, stomach—25 cm, small intestine—6 m, large intestine—1.5 m

Then have students prepare a bar graph to compare the average lengths of each digestive organ listed. English Language Learners

LS Logical

Quiz — **GENERAL**

Ask students whether each of the statements below is true or false.

1. Digestion begins when food reaches the stomach. (false)

2. Breaking, crushing, and mashing food is an example of chemical digestion. (false)

3. Saliva contains enzymes, which begin the chemical digestion of food. (true)

4. The esophagus connects the mouth with the small intestine directly. (false)

Alternative Assessment — **ADVANCED**

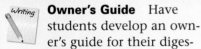

Writing **Owner's Guide** Have students develop an owner's guide for their digestive system. The guide should include information about the structures of the digestive system and a diagram of the location of these body structures.

LS Verbal

---

large intestine the wider and shorter portion of the intestine that removes water from mostly digested food and that turns the waste into semisolid feces, or stool

CONNECTION TO Environmental Science

Waste Away Feces and other human wastes contain microorganisms and other substances that can contaminate drinking water. Every time you flush a toilet, the water and wastes go through the sewer to a wastewater treatment plant. At the wastewater treatment plant, the disease-causing microorganisms are removed, and the clean water is released back to rivers, lakes, and streams. Find out where the wastewater treatment plants are in your area. Report to your class where their wastewater goes. **ACTIVITY**

Figure 8 *The large intestine is the final organ of digestion.*

The End of the Line

Material that can't be absorbed into the blood is pushed into the large intestine. The **large intestine** is the organ of the digestive system that stores, compacts, and then eliminates indigestible material from the body. The large intestine, shown in **Figure 8,** has a larger diameter than the small intestine. The large intestine is about 1.5 m long, and has a diameter of about 7.5 cm.

In the Large Intestine

Undigested material enters the large intestine as a soupy mixture. The large intestine absorbs most of the water in the mixture and changes the liquid into semisolid waste materials called *feces,* or *stool.*

Whole grains, fruits, and vegetables contain a carbohydrate, called *cellulose,* that humans cannot digest. We commonly refer to this material as *fiber.* Fiber keeps the stool soft and keeps material moving through the large intestine.

✔ **Reading Check** How does eating fiber help digestion?

Leaving the Body

The *rectum* is the last part of the large intestine. The rectum stores feces until they can be expelled. Feces pass to the outside of the body through an opening called the *anus.* It has taken each of your meals about 24 hours to make this journey through your digestive system.

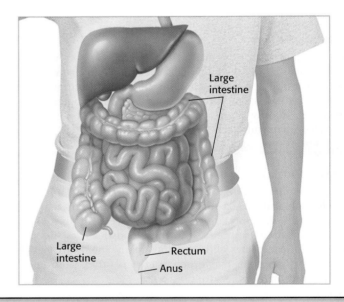

Large intestine

Large intestine

Rectum

Anus

Is That a Fact!

Scientists once thought that only stress and heredity caused peptic ulcers. But in 1982, Australian scientists Robin Warren and Barry Marshall discovered a species of bacterium that was common to many ulcer patients. By infecting himself with the bacterium, succumbing to peptic ulcers, and then curing himself with antibiotics, Dr. Marshall proved that this species of bacterium was responsible for some ulcers.

Answer to Reading Check
Fiber keeps the stool soft and keeps material moving through the large intestine.

SECTION Review

Summary

- Your digestive system is a group of organs that work together to digest food so that the nutrients from food can be used by the body.
- The breaking and mashing of food is called *mechanical digestion*. Chemical digestion is the process that breaks large food molecules into simpler molecules.
- The stomach mixes food with acid and enzymes that break down nutrients. The mixture is called *chyme*.

- In the small intestine, pancreatic fluid and bile are mixed with chyme.
- From the small intestine, nutrients enter the bloodstream and are circulated to the body's cells.
- The liver makes bile, stores nutrients, and breaks down toxins.
- The large intestine absorbs water, changing liquid waste into semisolid stool, or feces.

Using Key Terms

1. Use each of the following terms in a separate sentence: *digestive system, large intestine,* and *small intestine.*

Understanding Key Ideas

2. Which of the following is NOT a function of the liver?
   a. to secrete bile   **c.** to detoxify chemicals
   b. to store nutrients   **d.** to compact wastes

3. What is the difference between mechanical digestion and chemical digestion?

4. What happens to the food that you eat when it gets to your stomach?

5. Describe the role of the liver, gallbladder, and pancreas in digestion.

6. Put the following steps of digestion in order.
   a. Food is chewed by the teeth in the mouth.
   b. Water is absorbed by the large intestine.
   c. Food is reduced to chyme in the stomach.
   d. Food moves down the esophagus.
   e. Nutrients are absorbed by the small intestine.
   f. The pancreas releases enzymes.

Critical Thinking

7. **Evaluating Conclusions** Explain the following statement: "Digestion begins in the mouth."

8. **Identifying Relationships** How would the inability to make saliva affect digestion?

Interpreting Graphics

9. Label and describe the function of each of the organs in the diagram below.

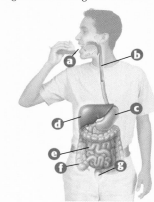

Developed and maintained by the National Science Teachers Association

For a variety of links related to this chapter, go to www.scilinks.org

Topic: The Digestive System
SciLinks code: HSM0409

CHAPTER RESOURCES

Chapter Resource File

- Section Quiz **GENERAL**
- Section Review **GENERAL**
- Vocabulary and Section Summary **GENERAL**
- Critical Thinking **ADVANCED**
- SciLinks Activity **GENERAL**
- Datasheet for Quick Lab

Answers to Section Review

1. Sample answer: The digestive system breaks down food so that cells can use the nutrients. The large intestine reabsorbs water from digested food. The small intestine absorbs nutrients from digested food.

2. d

3. Mechanical digestion usually involves the crushing and mashing of whole bites of food. Mechanical digestion prepares the food for chemical digestion, which is the process of changing large molecules of food into smaller molecules that can be absorbed into the bloodstream.

4. The contractions of the stomach break food into smaller pieces. Chemical digestion by enzymes, water, and acids breaks bonds in the food molecules.

5. The liver stores nutrients and makes bile, which is used in the digestion of fat. Bile is stored in a small, baglike organ called the gallbladder. The pancreas makes pancreatic juice, which contains enzymes for digesting chyme and contains bicarbonate for neutralizing the acid in chyme.

6. a, d, c, f, e, b

7. Mechanical and chemical digestion begin in the mouth. As you chew, you are physically breaking down food. Saliva contains an enzyme that begins the chemical digestion of carbohydrates.

8. Sample answer: Without saliva, swallowing would be more difficult and the chemical digestion of carbohydrates would not begin until the food reached the stomach.

9. Sample answer: a: The mouth and teeth chew food, beginning mechanical digestion. b: The esophagus squeezes food into the stomach. c: The stomach kneads food and adds acids and enzymes. d: The liver creates bile, which helps break down fat. e: The small intestine absorbs nutrients. f: The large intestine compacts wastes. g: The rectum passes food from the body.

Focus

Overview

This section introduces the structures and the functions of the urinary system. Students will learn how the kidneys filter blood. Students will also learn about some major problems of the urinary system and their causes.

 Bellringer

Tell students that the blood must be cleaned regularly. Then ask students to speculate, without looking in the textbook, how the body cleans blood. Once students have written a description of the cleaning process, allow them to check their answers in their textbook.

Motivate

Discussion —— GENERAL

Mongolian Gerbils Tell students that Mongolian gerbils are desert animals that never drink. Ask students how they think Mongolian gerbils obtain water. (They get water from the foods they eat.) Ask students how they think the gerbils have adapted to their habitat. (These animals have adapted to use water very efficiently, losing little or none from their lungs, skin, and urine.)

LS Verbal/Logical

The Urinary System

As blood travels through the tissues, it picks up waste produced by the body's cells. Your blood is like a train that comes to town to drop off supplies and take away garbage. If the waste is not removed, your body can actually be poisoned.

Excretion is the process of removing waste products from the body. Three of your body systems have a role in excretion. Your integumentary system releases waste products and water when you sweat. Your respiratory system releases carbon dioxide and water when you exhale. Finally, the **urinary system** contains the organs that remove waste products from your blood.

Cleaning the Blood

As your body performs the chemical activities that keep you alive, waste products, such as carbon dioxide and ammonia, are made. Your body has to get rid of these waste products to stay healthy. The urinary system, shown in **Figure 1**, removes these waste products from the blood.

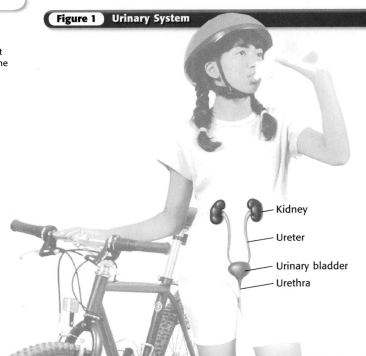

Figure 1 Urinary System

- Kidney
- Ureter
- Urinary bladder
- Urethra

SCIENCE HUMOR

Q: What does the kidney say when it plays baseball with the other urinary organs?

A: Bladder up!

The Kidneys as Filters

The **kidneys** are a pair of organs that constantly clean the blood. Your kidneys filter about 2,000 L of blood each day. Your body holds only 5.6 L of blood, so your blood cycles through your kidneys about 350 times per day!

Inside each kidney, shown in **Figure 2,** are more than 1 million nephrons. **Nephrons** are microscopic filters in the kidney that remove wastes from the blood. Nephrons remove many harmful substances. One of the most important substances removed by nephrons is urea (yoo REE uh), which contains nitrogen and is formed when cells use protein for energy.

✔ Reading Check How are nephrons related to the function of kidneys? (*See the Appendix for answers to Reading Checks.*)

kidney one of the pair of organs that filter water and wastes from the blood and that excrete products as urine

nephron the unit in the kidney that filters blood

Figure 2 — How the Kidneys Filter Blood

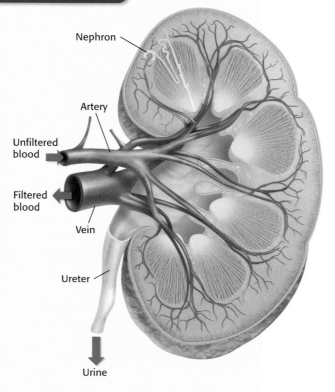

① A large artery brings blood into each kidney.

② Tiny blood vessels branch off the main artery and pass through part of each nephron.

③ Water and other small substances, such as glucose, salts, amino acids, and urea, are forced out of the blood vessels and into the nephrons.

④ As these substances flow through the nephrons, most of the water and some nutrients are moved back into blood vessels that wrap around the nephrons. A concentrated mixture of waste materials is left behind in the nephrons.

⑤ The cleaned blood, which has slightly less water and much less waste material, leaves each kidney in a large vein to recirculate in the body.

⑥ The yellow fluid that remains in the nephrons is called *urine.* Urine leaves each kidney through a slender tube called the *ureter* and flows into the *urinary bladder,* where urine is stored.

⑦ Urine leaves the body through another tube called the *urethra. Urination* is the process of expelling urine from the body.

Labels: Nephron, Artery, Unfiltered blood, Filtered blood, Vein, Ureter, Urine

---

MISCONCEPTION ALERT

Water in Foods Students may think that they get water only from the water that they drink. But many foods, such as fruits and vegetables, supply some of the water that people need to carry on life processes.

Answer to Reading Check

The function of kidneys is to filter blood. Nephrons are microscopic filters inside the kidney that make this possible.

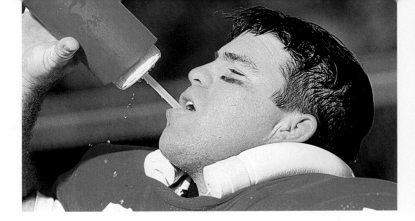

Close

Figure 3 *Drinking water when you exercise helps replace the water you lose when you sweat.*

Water In, Water Out

You drink water every day. You lose water every day in sweat and urine. You need to get rid of as much water as you drink. If you don't, your body will swell up. So, how does your body keep the water levels in balance? The balance of fluids is controlled by chemical messengers in the body called *hormones*.

Sweat and Thirst

When you are too warm, as the boy in **Figure 3** is, you lose a lot of water in the form of sweat. The evaporation of water from your skin cools you down. As the water content of the blood drops, the salivary glands produce less saliva. This is one of the reasons you feel thirsty.

Antidiuretic Hormone

When you get thirsty, other parts of your body react to the water shortage, too. A hormone called *antidiuretic hormone* (AN tee DIE yoo RET ik HAWR mohn), or ADH, is released. ADH signals the kidneys to take water from the nephrons. The nephrons return the water to the bloodstream. Thus, the kidneys make less urine. When your blood has too much water, small amounts of ADH are released. The kidneys react by allowing more water to stay in the nephrons and leave the body as urine.

Diuretics

Some beverages contain caffeine, which is a *diuretic* (DIE yoo RET ik). Diuretics cause the kidneys to make more urine, which decreases the amount of water in the blood. When you drink a beverage that contains water and caffeine, the caffeine increases fluid loss. So, your body gets to use less of the water from the caffeinated beverage than from a glass of water.

✔ **Reading Check** What are diuretics?

Urinary System Problems

The urinary system regulates body fluids and removes wastes from the blood. Any problems with water regulation can become dangerous for your body and disrupt homeostasis. Some common urinary system problems are described below.

- **Bacterial Infections** Bacteria can get into the bladder and ureters through the urethra and cause painful infections. Infections should be treated early, before they spread to the kidneys. Infections in the kidneys can permanently damage the nephrons.

- **Kidney Stones** Sometimes, salts and other wastes collect inside the kidneys and form kidney stones like the one in **Figure 4.** Some kidney stones interfere with urine flow and cause pain. Most kidney stones pass naturally from the body, but sometimes they must be removed by a doctor.

- **Kidney Disease** Damage to nephrons can prevent normal kidney functioning and can lead to kidney disease. If a person's kidneys do not function properly, a kidney machine can be used to filter waste from the blood.

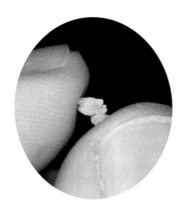

Figure 4 *This kidney stone had to be removed from a patient's urinary system.*

SECTION Review

Summary

- The urinary system removes liquid waste as urine. The filtering structures in the kidney are called *nephrons.*

- Most of the water in the blood is returned to the bloodstream. Urine passes through the ureter, into the bladder, and out of the body through the urethra.

- Disorders of the urinary system include infections, kidney stones, and kidney disease.

Using Key Terms

1. In your own words, write a definition for the term *urinary system.*

Understanding Key Ideas

2. Which event happens first?
   - **a.** Water is absorbed into blood.
   - **b.** A large artery brings blood into the kidney.
   - **c.** Water enters the nephrons.
   - **d.** The nephron separates water from wastes.

3. How do kidneys filter blood?

4. Describe three disorders of the urinary system.

Math Skills

5. A study has shown that 75% of teenage boys drink 34 oz of soda per day. How many 12 oz cans of soda would a boy drink in a week if he drank 34 oz per day?

Critical Thinking

6. **Applying Concepts** Which of the following contains more water: the blood going into the kidney or the blood leaving it?

7. **Predicting Consequences** When people have one kidney removed, their other kidney can often keep their blood clean. But the remaining kidney often changes. Predict how the remaining kidney may change to do the work of two kidneys.

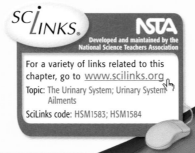

For a variety of links related to this chapter, go to www.scilinks.org

Topic: The Urinary System; Urinary System Ailments

SciLinks code: HSM1583; HSM1584

CHAPTER RESOURCES

Chapter Resource File

- Section Quiz GENERAL
- Section Review GENERAL
- Vocabulary and Section Summary GENERAL
- Reinforcement Worksheet BASIC

As the Stomach Churns

Teacher's Notes

Time Required

One 45-minute class period and another 15 minutes after 24 hours

Lab Ratings

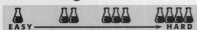

EASY ——————→ HARD

Teacher Prep 🧪🧪
Student Set-Up 🧪🧪
Concept Level 🧪🧪
Clean Up 🧪🧪

MATERIALS

The materials listed on the student page are enough for one student or a group of 2–4 students. The two tenderizers should be available at the grocery store. You will need to examine the different brands of powdered or liquid tenderizers. You may substitute fresh papaya or pineapple juices if they are available, if both types of the other tenderizers cannot be found.

As the Stomach Churns

The stomach, as you know, performs not only mechanical digestion but also chemical digestion. As the stomach churns, which moves the food particles around, the digestive fluids—acid and enzymes—are added to begin protein digestion.

Commercially prepared meat tenderizers contain enzymes from plants that break down, or digest, proteins. Two types of meat tenderizer are commonly available at grocery stores. One type of tenderizer contains an enzyme called *papain,* from papaya. Another type of tenderizer contains an enzyme called *bromelain,* from pineapple. In this lab, you will test the effects of these two types of meat tenderizers on beef stew meat.

OBJECTIVES

Demonstrate chemical digestion in the stomach.

Investigate three forms of chemical digestion.

MATERIALS

- beef stew meat, 1 cm cubes (3)
- eyedropper
- gloves, protective
- graduated cylinder, 25 mL
- hydrochloric acid, very dilute, 0.1 M
- measuring spoon, 1/4 tsp
- meat tenderizer, commercially prepared, containing bromelain
- meat tenderizer, commercially prepared, containing papain
- tape, masking
- test tubes (4)
- test-tube marker
- test-tube rack
- water

SAFETY

Ask a Question

❶ Determine which question you will answer through your experiment. That question may be one of the following: Which meat tenderizer will work faster? Which one will make the meat more tender? Will the meat tenderizers change the color of the meat or water? What might these color changes, if any, indicate?

Form a Hypothesis

❷ Form a hypothesis from the question you formed in step 1. **Caution:** Do not taste any of the materials in this activity.

Test the Hypothesis

❸ Identify all variables and controls present in your experiment. In your notebook, make a data table that includes these variables and controls. Use this data table to record your observations and results.

❹ Label one test tube with the name of one tenderizer, and label the other test tube with the name of the other tenderizer. Label the third test tube "Control." What will the test tube labeled "Control" contain?

Safety Caution

Remind students to review all safety cautions and icons before beginning this lab activity. Caution students that HCl is a chemical they should handle very carefully. You may choose to dispense the HCl yourself. Tell students that if any HCl comes in contact with their skin, they should wash the area with plenty of water immediately and they should notify you as they wash. Tell students not to taste any materials used in this or any lab.

CHAPTER RESOURCES

Chapter Resource File
📁 • Datasheet for Chapter Lab
• Lab Notes and Answers

Technology
📹 **Classroom Videos**
• Lab Video

LabBook
• Enzymes in Action

⑤ Pour 20 mL of water into each test tube.

⑥ Use the eyedropper to add four drops of very dilute hydrochloric acid to each test tube. **Caution:** Hydrochloric acid can burn your skin. If any acid touches your skin, rinse the area with running water and tell your teacher immediately.

⑦ Use the measuring spoon to add 1/4 tsp of each meat tenderizer to its corresponding test tube.

⑧ Add one cube of beef to each test tube.

⑨ Record your observations for each test tube immediately, after 5 min, after 15 min, after 30 min, and after 24 h.

Analyze the Results

❶ **Describing Events** Did you immediately notice any differences in the beef in the three test tubes? At what time interval did you notice a significant difference in the appearance of the beef in the test tubes? Explain the differences.

❷ **Examining Data** Did one meat tenderizer perform better than the other? Explain how you determined which performed better.

Draw Conclusions

❸ **Evaluating Results** Was your hypothesis supported? Explain your answer.

❹ **Applying Conclusions** Many animals that sting have venom composed of proteins. Explain how applying meat tenderizer to the wound helps relieve the pain of such a sting.

CHAPTER RESOURCES
Workbooks

 Whiz-Bang Demonstrations
• Liver Let Live GENERAL

 Long-Term Projects & Research Ideas
• Copying the Kidney ADVANCED

Yvonne Brannum
Hine Junior High School
Washington, D.C.

Test the Hypothesis
4. The "Control" tube will contain everything that goes into the other tubes except the meat tenderizer.

Analyze the Results
1. There should be very little difference in the three test tubes at first. Differences will be mild until after 24 hours, when a significant difference will be noticed between the "Control" tube and the experimental tubes.

2. Both tenderizers should work in a similar way. If one tenderizer is noted to be more efficient, students should be able to describe how they tested the stew meat to demonstrate the difference.

Draw Conclusions
3. Answers will vary, but students should be able to explain how their hypothesis was supported or how their experimental results did not support their hypothesis. Students should also identify dependent and independent variables in their evaluations and compare the results for the independent variables, the two types of meat tenderizers, to the results for the control.

4. Students may conclude that certain digestive enzymes break down proteins. Breaking down the protein in venom often makes the venom less harmful and less painful. Explain to students that using meat tenderizer on an insect bite is only first aid and is not intended to substitute for medical attention. Emphasize that snakebites require immediate medical attention.

Chapter Review

Assignment Guide

SECTION	QUESTIONS
1	1–2, 5–6, 8, 10–17, 19–26
2	3–4, 7, 9, 18

ANSWERS

Using Key Terms

1. pancreas
2. stomach
3. kidney
4. urinary system
5. digestive system
6. large intestine

Understanding Key Ideas

7. c
8. d
9. c
10. d
11. b
12. a
13. d
14. c
15. a

USING KEY TERMS

Complete each of the following sentences by choosing the correct term from the word bank.

pancreas	digestive system
large intestine	stomach
kidney	small intestine
nephron	urinary system

1 The ____ secretes juices into the small intestine.

2 The saclike organ at the end of the esophagus is called the ____.

3 The ____ is an organ that contains millions of nephrons.

4 A group of organs that removes waste from the blood and excretes it from the body is called the ____.

5 The ____ is a group of organs that work together to break down food.

6 Indigestible material is formed into feces in the ____.

UNDERSTANDING KEY IDEAS

Multiple Choice

7 The hormone that signals the kidneys to make less urine is
- **a.** urea.
- **b.** caffeine.
- **c.** ADH.
- **d.** ATP.

8 Which of the following organs aids digestion by producing bile?
- **a.** stomach
- **b.** pancreas
- **c.** small intestine
- **d.** liver

9 The part of the kidney that filters the blood is the
- **a.** artery.
- **b.** ureter.
- **c.** nephron.
- **d.** urethra.

10 The fingerlike projections that line the small intestine are called
- **a.** emulsifiers.
- **b.** fats.
- **c.** amino acids.
- **d.** villi.

11 Which of the following is NOT part of the digestive tract?
- **a.** mouth
- **b.** kidney
- **c.** stomach
- **d.** rectum

12 The soupy mixture of food, enzymes, and acids in the stomach is called
- **a.** chyme.
- **b.** villi.
- **c.** urea.
- **d.** vitamins.

13 The stomach helps with
- **a.** storing food.
- **b.** chemical digestion.
- **c.** physical digestion.
- **d.** All of the above

14 The gall bladder stores
- **a.** food.
- **b.** urine.
- **c.** bile.
- **d.** villi.

15 The esophagus connects the
- **a.** pharynx to the stomach.
- **b.** stomach to the small intestine.
- **c.** kidneys to the nephrons.
- **d.** stomach to the large intestine.

Short Answer

16 Why is it important for the pancreas to release bicarbonate into the small intestine?

17 How does the structure of the small intestine help the small intestine absorb nutrients?

18 What is a kidney stone?

CRITICAL THINKING

19 **Concept Mapping** Use the following terms to create a concept map: *teeth, stomach, digestion, bile, saliva, mechanical digestion, gallbladder,* and *chemical digestion.*

20 **Predicting Consequences** How would digestion be affected if the liver were damaged?

21 **Analyzing Processes** When you put a piece of carbohydrate-rich food, such as bread, a potato, or a cracker, into your mouth, the food tastes bland. But if this food sits on your tongue for a while, the food will begin to taste sweet. What digestive process causes this change in taste?

22 **Making Comparisons** The recycling process for one kind of plastic begins with breaking the plastic into small pieces. Next, chemicals are used to break the small pieces of plastic down to its building blocks. Then, those building blocks are used to make new plastic. How is this process both like and unlike human digestion?

INTERPRETING GRAPHICS

The bar graph below shows how long the average meal spends in each portion of your digestive tract. Use the graph below to answer the questions that follow.

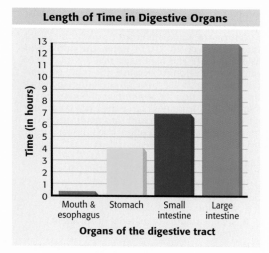

Length of Time in Digestive Organs

Time (in hours) vs. Organs of the digestive tract

23 In which part of your digestive tract does the food spend the longest amount of time?

24 On average, how much longer does food stay in the small intestine than in the stomach?

25 Which organ mixes food with special substances to make chyme? Approximately how long does food remain in this organ?

26 Bile breaks large fat droplets into very small droplets. How long is the food in your body before it comes into contact with bile?

CHAPTER RESOURCES

Chapter Resource File

- Chapter Review **GENERAL**
- Chapter Test A **GENERAL**
- Chapter Test B **ADVANCED**
- Chapter Test C **SPECIAL NEEDS**
- Vocabulary Activity **GENERAL**

Workbooks

Study Guide
- Assessment resources are also available in Spanish.

16. Bicarbonate neutralizes the acidic chyme coming in from the stomach. By neutralizing the acid, the bicarbonate protects the lining of the small intestine.

17. The long length, folds, and villi increase the surface area that comes into contact with the food that is being digested in the small intestine, allowing more nutrients to be absorbed.

18. a stone made of salts and the wastes that sometimes collect in the kidney

Critical Thinking

19. 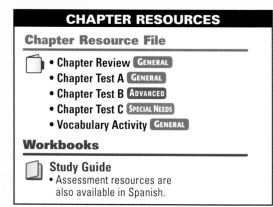 An answer to this exercise can be found at the end of this book.

20. Sample answer: Digestion would be poor. The liver makes bile, which aids in the digestion of fats. If the liver were damaged, it might not make bile, and so the body could not digest fats well.

21. Sample answer: Saliva causes chemical digestion of the carbohydrate-rich food, breaking it down into simple sugars, which taste sweet.

22. Sample answer: The process of breaking down the plastic mechanically and chemically so that its building blocks can be reused is similar to the way the body digests food. But the recycling process does not result in the growth or repair of a living organism, so recycling is different from digestion.

Interpreting Graphics

23. in the large intestine

24. 3 hours

25. The stomach mixes food with enzymes and acid to make a soupy mixture called chyme. Food stays in the stomach for approximately 4 hours.

26. just over 4 hours

Standardized Test Preparation

Teacher's Note

To provide practice under more realistic testing conditions, give students 20 minutes to answer all of the questions in this Standardized Test Preparation.

MISCONCEPTION ALERT

Answers to the standardized test preparation can help you identify student misconceptions and misunderstandings.

READING

Passage 1

1. D
2. F

✚ TEST DOCTOR

Question 1: Students may not understand that solutions have higher concentrations when the amount of dissolved material is the same in less liquid. Students may think the reverse is true: increasing the amount of liquid increases the concentration.

Question 2: Only answer F contains information contained in the passage. Though the other answers may be true, they are not facts from the passage.

READING

Read the passage below. Then, read each question that follows the passage. Decide which is the best answer to each question.

Passage 1 When you lose water, your blood becomes <u>more concentrated</u>. Think about how you make a powdered drink, such as lemonade. If you use the same amount of powder in 1 L of water as you do in 2 L of water, the drinks will taste different. The lemonade made with 1 L of water will be stronger because it is more concentrated. Losing water through sweating increases the concentration of sodium and potassium in your blood. The kidneys force the extra potassium out of the blood stream and into nephrons. From the nephrons, the potassium is eliminated from the body in urine.

1. The words *more concentrated* in this passage refer to
   - **A** the same amount of water with different amounts of material dissolved in it.
   - **B** small amounts of material dissolved in small amounts of water.
   - **C** large amounts of material dissolved in large amounts of water.
   - **D** a given amount of material dissolved in a smaller amount of water.

2. Which of the following statements is a fact from the passage?
   - **F** Blood contains both potassium and sodium.
   - **G** Losing too much sodium is dangerous.
   - **H** Potassium and sodium can be replaced by drinking an exercise drink.
   - **I** Tears contain sodium.

Passage 2 Three major types of nutrients—<u>carbohydrates</u>, proteins, and fats—make up most of the food you eat. Chemical substances called *enzymes* break these nutrients into smaller particles for the body to use. For example, proteins, which are chains of smaller molecules called *amino acids,* are too large to be absorbed into the bloodstream. So, enzymes cut the chain of amino acids. These amino acids are small enough to pass into the bloodstream to be used by the body.

1. According to the passage, what is a carbohydrate?
   - **A** an enzyme
   - **B** a substance made of amino acids
   - **C** a nutrient
   - **D** the only substance in a healthy diet

2. Which of the following statements is a fact from the passage?
   - **F** Carbohydrates, fats, and proteins are three major types of nutrients.
   - **G** Proteins are made of fats and carbohydrates.
   - **H** Some enzymes create chains of proteins.
   - **I** Fats are difficult to digest.

3. Which of the following can be inferred from the passage?
   - **A** To be useful to the body, nutrients must be small enough to enter the bloodstream.
   - **B** Carbohydrates are made of amino acids.
   - **C** Amino acids are made of proteins.
   - **D** Without enough protein, the body cannot grow.

Passage 2

1. C
2. F
3. A

✚ TEST DOCTOR

Question 3: In the passage, students are told that proteins need to be broken down because they are too large to be absorbed into the bloodstream. So, students may infer that, to be useful, nutrients have to be small enough to enter the bloodstream.

Use the figure below to answer the questions that follow.

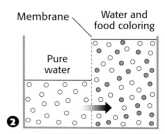

Membrane
Pure water | Water and food coloring

❶

Membrane | Water and food coloring
Pure water

❷

1. The container is divided by a membrane. What can you conclude from the diagram?

A Water molecules can pass through the membrane.

B Food-coloring molecules can pass through the membrane.

C Both water molecules and food-coloring molecules can pass through the membrane.

D Neither water molecules nor food-coloring molecules can pass through the membrane.

2. If the membrane has holes that separate molecules by size,

F food-coloring molecules are larger than water molecules.

G water molecules are larger than food-coloring molecules.

H water molecules and food-coloring molecules are the same size.

I the holes are smaller than both water molecules and food-coloring molecules.

3. The concentration of food-coloring molecules in the columns labeled "Water and food coloring"

A is greater in 2 than in 1.

B is greater in 1 than in 2.

C is the same in 1 and 2.

D cannot change.

MATH

Read each question below, and choose the best answer.

1. Cora is 1.5 m tall. Cora's small intestine is 6 m long. How many times longer is Cora's small intestine than her height?

A 3 times longer

B 4 times longer

C 5 times longer

D 6 times longer

2. During a water-balance study that was performed for one day, a woman drank 1,500 mL of water. The food she ate contained 750 mL of water, and her body produced 250 mL of water internally during normal body processes. She lost 900 mL of water in sweat, 1,500 mL in urine, and 100 mL in feces. Overall, how much water did she gain or lose during the day?

F She gained 1,500 mL of water.

G She lost 900 mL of water.

H She gained as much water as she lost.

I She lost twice as much water as she gained.

3. There are 6 blue marbles, 2 red marbles, and 4 green marbles in a bag. If someone selects 1 marble at random from the bag, what is the probability that the marble will be blue?

A 1/5

B 1/4

C 1/3

D 1/2

Standardized Test Preparation

1. A
2. F
3. B

 **TEST DOCTOR**

Question 1: Students interpreting the graphic may not understand that the arrow indicates that water molecules pass from one side of the membrane to the other. Students also may not realize that some membranes have holes small enough to separate molecules.

Question 3: Students may not realize that as water passes through the membrane, the water is diluting the food coloring. Increasing the number of water molecules without increasing the number of food-coloring molecules decreases the concentration of food-coloring.

MATH

1. B
2. H
3. D

TEST DOCTOR

Question 2: Students struggling with this type of question may benefit from practicing organizing information. This type of gain-and-loss question is best answered by setting up a table with gains in one column and losses in another. After adding up all the gains and losses separately, students can subtract the sum of the losses column from the sum of the gains column. This final number is the net loss or gain. A positive answer represents a gain; a negative answer represents a loss.

CHAPTER RESOURCES

Chapter Resource File

• Standardized Test Preparation **GENERAL**

Workbooks

North Carolina Standardized Test Preparation
• Provides practice for the EOG test.

State Resources

For specific resources for your state, visit **go.hrw.com** and type in the keyword **HSMSTR**.

Weird Science

Background

In many parts of the world, dangerous parasitic infections are common health problems. For example, onchocerciasis, or river blindness, is a parasitic disease spread by flies. Worldwide, almost 18 million people suffer from this disease. And dracunculiasis, or Guinea worm disease, is a painful parasitic illness caused by a long, thin worm that infests many tissues and ulcerates the skin as the worm leaves the body.

Science, Technology, and Society

Teaching Strategy — GENERAL

Invite students to brainstorm the ways that doctors diagnose diseases. List their ideas on the board. Have students identify diseases with each diagnostic method. Then have students read the feature and compare this method of diagnosis with the others on their list. Have them discuss the advantages and disadvantages of the pill camera and other diagnostic tools with which they are familiar. **LS** Verbal

Science in Action

Weird Science

Tapeworms

What if you found out that you had a constant mealtime companion who didn't want just a bite but wanted it all? And what if that companion never asked for your permission? This mealtime companion might be a tapeworm. Tapeworms are invertebrate flatworms. These flatworms are parasites. A parasite is an organism that obtains its food by living in or on another organism. A tapeworm doesn't have a digestive tract of its own. Instead, a tapeworm absorbs the nutrients digested by the host. Some tape worms can grow to be over 10 m long. Cooking beef, pork, and fish properly can help prevent people from getting tapeworms. People or animals who get tapeworms can be treated with medicines.

Social Studies ACTIVITY

WRITING SKILL The World Health Organization and the Pan American Health Organization have made fighting intestinal parasites in children a high priority. Conduct library or Internet research on Worm Busters, which is a program for fighting parasites. Write a brief report of your findings.

Science, Technology, and Society

Pill Cameras

Open wide and say "Ahhhh." When you have a problem with your mouth or teeth, doctors can examine you pretty easily. But when people have problems that are further down their digestive tract, examination becomes more difficult. So, some doctors have recently created a tiny, disposable camera that patients can swallow. As the camera travels down the digestive tract, the camera takes pictures and sends them to a tiny recorder that patients wear on their belt. The camera takes about 57,000 images during its trip. Later, doctors can review the pictures and see the pictures of the patient's entire digestive tract.

Math ACTIVITY

If a pill camera takes 57,000 images while it travels through the digestive system and takes about two pictures per second, how many hours is the camera in the body?

Answer to Social Studies Activity

Sample answer: The Worm Busters program helps eliminate parasites in Latin America. The program provides medicine to millions of children who suffer from intestinal parasites.

Answer to Math Activity

57,000 images at 2 images per second means the camera is in the body for 28,500 seconds, or 475 minutes, or almost 8 hours.

Christy Krames

Medical Illustrator Christy Krames is a medical illustrator. For 19 years, she has created detailed illustrations of the inner workings of the human body. Medical illustrations allow doctors and surgeons to share concepts, theories, and techniques with colleagues and allow students to learn about the human body.

Medical illustrators often draw tiny structures or body processes that would be difficult or impossible to photograph. For example, a photograph of a small intestine can show the entire organ. But a medical illustrator can add to the photograph an enlarged drawing of the tiny villi inside the intestine. Adding details helps to better explain how small parts of organs work together so that the organs can function.

Medical illustration requires knowledge of both art and science. So, Christy Krames studied both art and medicine in college. Often, Krames must do research before she draws a subject. Her research may include reading books, observing surgical procedures, or even dissecting a pig's heart. This research results in accurate and educational drawings of the inner body.

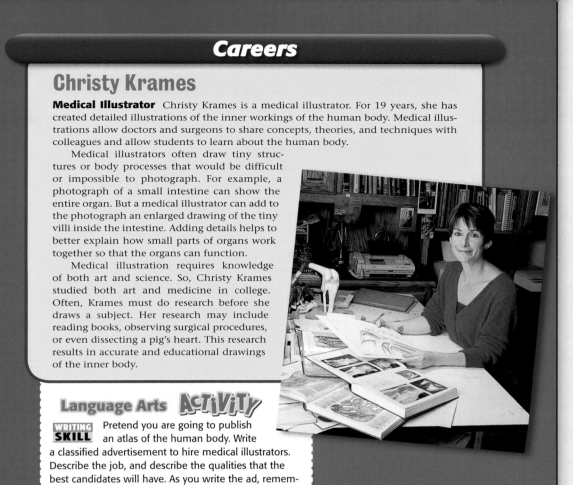

Language Arts ACTIVITY

WRITING SKILL Pretend you are going to publish an atlas of the human body. Write a classified advertisement to hire medical illustrators. Describe the job, and describe the qualities that the best candidates will have. As you write the ad, remember you are trying to persuade the best illustrators to contact you.

go.hrw.com
To learn more about these Science in Action topics, visit go.hrw.com and type in the keyword **HL5BD3F.**

Current Science
Check out Current Science® articles related to this chapter by visiting go.hrw.com. Just type in the keyword **HL5CS24.**

Communication and Control
Chapter Planning Guide

Compression guide:
To shorten instruction because of time limitations, omit Section 2.

OBJECTIVES	LABS, DEMONSTRATIONS, AND ACTIVITIES	TECHNOLOGY RESOURCES
PACING • 90 min pp. 224–233 **Chapter Opener**	**SE** Start-up Activity, p. 235 `GENERAL`	**OSP** Parent Letter `GENERAL` **CD** Student Edition on CD-ROM **CD** Guided Reading Audio CD **TR** Chapter Starter Transparency* **VID** Brain Food Video Quiz
Section 1 The Nervous System • Describe the relationship between the central nervous system and the peripheral nervous system. • Compare the somatic nervous system with the autonomic nervous system. • List one function of each part of the brain.	**TE** Activity Nerve Cells and Other Cells, p. 227 `ADVANCED` **TE** Group Activity Simulating Neuronal Impulses, p. 228 `BASIC` **TE** Group Activity Model the PNS, p. 229 `ADVANCED` **TE** Group Activity Reteaching the Brain, p. 230 `BASIC` **TE** Connection Activity Language Arts, p. 231 `GENERAL` **TE** Connection Activity Real World, p. 231 `GENERAL` **SE** Quick Lab Building a Neuron, p. 232◆ `GENERAL` **CRF** Datasheet for Quick Lab*	**CRF** Lesson Plans* **TR** Bellringer Transparency* **TR** A Typical Neuron* **TR** What Is a Nerve?* **TR** Regions of the Brain* **TR** The Spinal Cord* **CRF** SciLinks Activity* `GENERAL`
PACING • 90 min pp. 234–239 **Section 2 Responding to the Environment** • List five sensations that are detected by receptors in the skin. • Describe how a feedback mechanism works. • Describe how light relates to sight. • Describe how the senses of hearing, taste, and smell work.	**TE** Group Activity Losing Your Senses, p. 234 `GENERAL` **TE** Activity "Ol' Three Eyes," p. 235 `BASIC` **TE** Activity Do You Hear Colors?, p. 235 `ADVANCED` **TE** Activity Pupil Action, p. 236 ◆ `GENERAL` **SE** Quick Lab Where's the Dot?, p. 237 `GENERAL` **CRF** Datasheet for Quick Lab* **SE** Connection to Physics, p. 238 `GENERAL` **SE** Skills Practice Lab You've Gotta Lotta Nerve, p. 244 ◆ `GENERAL` **CRF** Datasheet for Chapter Lab* **LB** Whiz-Bang Demonstrations Now You See It, Now You Don't* ◆ `GENERAL` **LB** Labs You Can Eat A Salty Sweet Experiment* ◆ `GENERAL`	**CRF** Lesson Plans* **TR** Bellringer Transparency* **TR** *LINK TO PHYSICAL SCIENCE* Measuring Wavelengths; Measuring Frequency* **SE** Internet Activity, p. 236 `GENERAL` **VID** Lab Videos for Life Science
PACING • 45 min pp. 240–243 **Section 3 The Endocrine System** • Explain why the endocrine system is important to the body. • Identify five glands of the endocrine system, and describe what their hormones do. • Describe how feedback mechanisms stop and start hormone release. • Name two hormone imbalances.	**SE** Connection to Language Arts Working Together, p. 241 `GENERAL` **LB** Long-Term Projects & Research Ideas Man Versus Machine* ◆ `ADVANCED` **SE** Science in Action Math, Social Studies, and Language Arts Activities, pp. 250–251 `GENERAL`	**CRF** Lesson Plans* **TR** Bellringer Transparency*

PACING • 90 min

CHAPTER REVIEW, ASSESSMENT, AND STANDARDIZED TEST PREPARATION

CRF Vocabulary Activity* `GENERAL`
SE Chapter Review, pp. 246–247 `GENERAL`
CRF Chapter Review* ■ `GENERAL`
CRF Chapter Tests A* ■ `GENERAL`, B* `ADVANCED`, C* `SPECIAL NEEDS`
SE Standardized Test Preparation, pp. 248–249 `GENERAL`
CRF Standardized Test Preparation* `GENERAL`
CRF Performance-Based Assessment* `GENERAL`
OSP Test Generator `GENERAL`
CRF Test Item Listing* `GENERAL`

Online and Technology Resources

Visit **go.hrw.com** for a variety of free resources related to this textbook. Enter the keyword **HT5R7BD4.**

Holt Online Learning

Students can access interactive problem-solving help and active visual concept development with the *Holt Science and Technology* Online Edition available at **www.hrw.com.**

Guided Reading Audio CD

These CDs are designed to help auditory learners and reluctant readers.

Science Tutor CD-ROM

Excellent for remediation and test practice.

KEY		CRF Chapter Resource File	SS Science Skills Worksheets	* Also on One-Stop Planner
		OSP One-Stop Planner	MS Math Skills for Science Worksheets	◆ Requires advance prep
SE	Student Edition	LB Lab Bank	CD CD or CD-ROM	■ Also available in Spanish
TE	Teacher Edition	TR Transparencies	VID Classroom Video/DVD	

SKILLS DEVELOPMENT RESOURCES	SECTION REVIEW AND ASSESSMENT	STANDARDS CORRELATIONS
SE Pre-Reading Activity, p. 234 (GENERAL) **OSP** Science Puzzlers, Twisters & Teasers (GENERAL)		North Carolina Standard Course of Study
CRF Directed Reading A* (BASIC), B* (SPECIAL NEEDS) **CRF** Vocabulary and Section Summary* (GENERAL) **SE** Reading Strategy Discussion, p. 226 (GENERAL) **SE** Math Practice Time to Travel, p. 227 (GENERAL) **TE** Reading Strategy Formulating Questions, p. 227 (BASIC) **TE** Inclusion Strategies, p. 227 **SE** Connection to Chemistry Keeping Your Balance, p. 229 (GENERAL) **TE** Reading Strategy Prediction Guide, p. 230 (GENERAL) **CRF** Reinforcement Worksheet This System is Just "Two" Nervous!* (BASIC)	**SE** Reading Checks, pp. 226, 227, 228, 229, 230, 231, 232 (GENERAL) **TE** Homework, p. 230 (GENERAL) **TE** Homework, p. 231 (BASIC) **TE** Reteaching, p. 232 (BASIC) **TE** Quiz, p. 232 (GENERAL) **TE** Alternative Assessment, p. 232 (GENERAL) **SE** Section Review,* p. 233 ■ (GENERAL) **CRF** Section Quiz* ■ (GENERAL)	4.01, 4.02, 4.03, 4.04
CRF Directed Reading A* (BASIC), B* (SPECIAL NEEDS) **CRF** Vocabulary and Section Summary* (GENERAL) **SE** Reading Strategy Reading Organizer, p. 234 (GENERAL) **MS** Math Skills for Science Multiplying and Dividing in Scientific Notation* (ADVANCED) **CRF** Reinforcement Worksheet The Eyes Have It* (BASIC) **CRF** Critical Thinking There's a Microchip in My Eye!* (ADVANCED)	**SE** Reading Checks, pp. 234, 235, 236, 237, 238 (GENERAL) **TE** Homework, p. 235 (ADVANCED) **TE** Reteaching, p. 238 (BASIC) **TE** Quiz, p. 238 (GENERAL) **TE** Alternative Assessment, p. 238 (GENERAL) **SE** Section Review,* p. 239 ■ (GENERAL) **CRF** Section Quiz* ■ (GENERAL)	4.01, 4.04, *Chapter Lab:* 1.01, 1.03, 1.04, 1.05, 1.08
CRF Directed Reading A* (BASIC), B* (SPECIAL NEEDS) **CRF** Vocabulary and Section Summary* (GENERAL) **SE** Reading Strategy Discussion, p. 240 (GENERAL) **TE** Inclusion Strategies, p. 242 **CRF** Reinforcement Worksheet Every Gland Lends a Hand* (BASIC)	**SE** Reading Checks, pp. 241, 242 (GENERAL) **TE** Reteaching, p. 242 (BASIC) **TE** Quiz, p. 242 (GENERAL) **TE** Alternative Assessment, p. 242 (GENERAL) **SE** Section Review,* p. 243 ■ (GENERAL) **TE** Homework, p. 243 (GENERAL) **CRF** Section Quiz* ■ (GENERAL)	4.01, 4.02, 4.03, 4.04

One-Stop Planner® CD-ROM

This convenient CD-ROM includes:
- Lab Materials QuickList Software
- Holt Calendar Planner
- Customizable Lesson Plans
- Printable Worksheets
- ExamView® Test Generator

cnnstudentnews.com

Find the latest news, lesson plans, and activities related to important scientific events.

www.scilinks.org

Maintained by the **National Science Teachers Association**. See Chapter Enrichment pages for a complete list of topics.

Check out *Current Science* articles and activities by visiting the HRW Web site at **go.hrw.com.** Just type in the keyword **HL5CS25T.**

Classroom Videos

- **Lab Videos** demonstrate the chapter lab.
- **Brain Food Video Quizzes** help students review the chapter material.
- **CNN Videos** bring science into your students' daily life.

Visual Resources

CHAPTER STARTER TRANSPARENCY

BELLRINGER TRANSPARENCIES

TEACHING TRANSPARENCIES
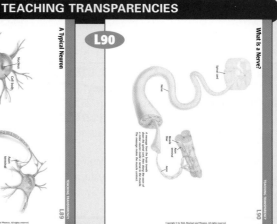

TEACHING TRANSPARENCIES
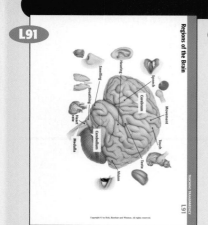
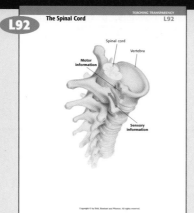
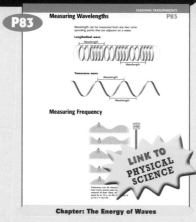

CONCEPT MAPPING TRANSPARENCY
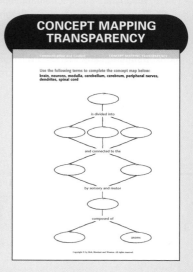

Planning Resources

LESSON PLANS

PARENT LETTER

TEST ITEM LISTING

One-Stop Planner® CD-ROM

This CD-ROM includes all of the resources shown here and the following time-saving tools:

- *Lab Materials QuickList Software*
- *Customizable lesson plans*
- *Holt Calendar Planner*
- *The powerful ExamView® Test Generator*

Meeting Individual Needs

DIRECTED READING A
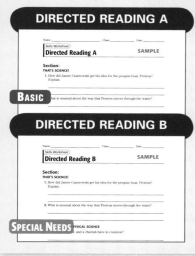
BASIC

DIRECTED READING B
SPECIAL NEEDS

VOCABULARY ACTIVITY
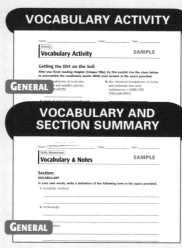
GENERAL

VOCABULARY AND SECTION SUMMARY
GENERAL

REINFORCEMENT
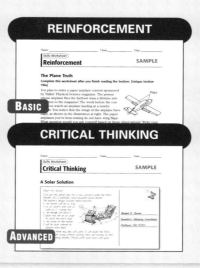
BASIC

CRITICAL THINKING
ADVANCED

SCILINKS ACTIVITY

GENERAL

SCIENCE PUZZLERS, TWISTERS & TEASERS
GENERAL

Labs and Activities

LONG-TERM PROJECTS & RESEARCH IDEAS
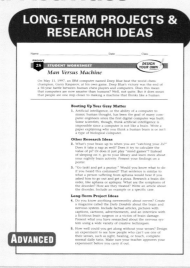
ADVANCED

WHIZ-BANG DEMONSTRATIONS
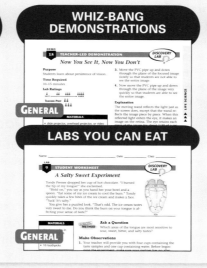
GENERAL

LABS YOU CAN EAT
GENERAL

DATASHEETS FOR QUICK LABS

DATASHEETS FOR CHAPTER LABS

DATASHEETS FOR LABBOOK

Review and Assessments

SECTION QUIZ

GENERAL

SECTION REVIEW
GENERAL

CHAPTER REVIEW
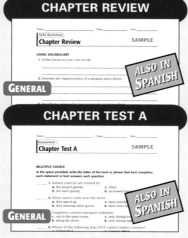
GENERAL

CHAPTER TEST A
GENERAL

CHAPTER TEST B
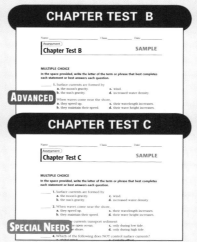
ADVANCED

CHAPTER TEST C
SPECIAL NEEDS

STANDARDIZED TEST PREPARATION
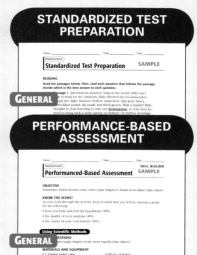
GENERAL

PERFORMANCE-BASED ASSESSMENT
GENERAL

This Chapter Enrichment provides relevant and interesting information to expand and enhance your presentation of the chapter material.

Section 1

The Nervous System

The Brain

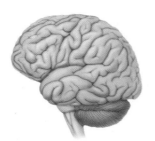

- The cerebral cortex is the main part of the exterior surface of the brain. The surface area of the brain is about 1,500 cm² to 2,000 cm², or about the size of 1 to 2 pages of a newspaper. To fit within the skull, the cortex is folded, forming *gyri* (folds) and *sulci* (grooves). Several large sulci divide the cortex into lobes: the frontal lobe, parietal lobe, occipital lobe, and temporal lobe. Each lobe has a different function.

- Computerized scanning techniques allow physicians to observe the brain in action and to detect brain abnormalities. Scanning techniques include CAT scanning, MRI scanning, radionucleotide scanning, ultrasound scanning, and PET scanning.

Is That a Fact!

◆ The cerebral cortex makes up more than 80% of the total human brain mass.

The Spinal Cord

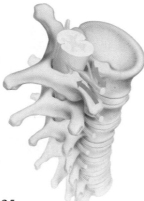

- Like the brain, the spinal cord contains both gray matter and white matter. The center of the spinal cord is made up of neuron cell bodies and is called *gray matter.* The outer layer of the spinal cord is made up of axons that traverse the spinal cord. This outer part of the spinal cord is called *white matter.*

- The spinal cord is protected by 25 bones, including the vertebrae and the sacrum. These bones are connected by joints and are separated by cartilaginous disks.

Section 2

Responding to the Environment

Hearing Loss

- There are two principal kinds of deafness: conductive deafness and sensorineural deafness.

- Conductive deafness results when transmission of sound from the outer ear to the inner ear fails. It may occur as a result of earwax buildup or damage to the middle ear.

- Sensorineural deafness results when sounds reach the inner ear but are not transmitted to the brain because of damaged inner ear structures or damaged nerves that carry information from the ear to the brain.

Is That a Fact!

◆ Sensorineural deafness occurs in 1 out of every 1,000 babies.

The Eye Doctor

- A variety of healthcare professionals have qualifications to treat different aspects of eye disorders and to correct vision problems.

- Ophthalmologists are physicians who specialize in the eyes. An ophthalmologist can examine eyes, prescribe corrective lenses, treat eye disorders, and perform eye surgery.

- An optometrist can examine and test eyes and can prescribe corrective lenses in the form of glasses or contact lenses.

- An optician may only fit and adjust glasses and contact lenses.

Is That a Fact!

◆ Using contact lenses to correct poor vision was first recorded in 1508 by Leonardo da Vinci (1452–1519).

◆ The first contact lens was made of glass. It covered the entire frontal surface of the eyeball. This first contact lens was made by Adolf Fick in 1887.

The Sense of Taste

- The water and enzymes in saliva break down the food and drink that we consume into small molecules and ions. After passing through pores in the taste buds, these molecules and ions stimulate small nerve endings, which send messages to the brain. These messages form our sense of taste.

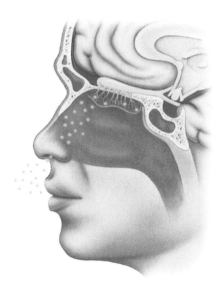

- People often lose their sense of taste when they lose their sense of smell. This loss occurs when olfactory bulbs are damaged or when the person has a stuffy nose. It is rare for a person to maintain the sense of smell and to lose the sense of taste.

Section 3

The Endocrine System

Exocrine and Endocrine Glands

- There are two main types of glands in the body: exocrine glands and endocrine glands. Exocrine glands, such as sweat glands and salivary glands, secrete substances through ducts to a local area.

- Unlike exocrine glands, endocrine glands secrete substances directly into the bloodstream (no ducts are involved). The substances secreted by endocrine glands—called hormones—are carried by the bloodstream to all parts of the body. A hormone may affect just a few cells or may have an effect on several organs or tissues.

The Pituitary Gland

- The pituitary gland is often called the *master gland* because its secretions regulate several other endocrine glands.

- About 10% of brain tumors affect the pituitary gland. Although usually benign, these tumors can have a great effect on the body because they can affect the production of the pituitary hormones.

- Because of the pituitary gland's location in the brain, enlargement of the gland can cause vision disorders by creating pressure on the optic nerve.

Diabetes

- The term *diabetes* refers to more than one disorder. The three kinds of diabetes include *diabetes insipidus* (a rare condition) and two types of *diabetes mellitus* (called *type 1* and *type 2 diabetes*). Type 1 diabetes requires regular injections of insulin. Type 2 diabetes can often be controlled by changes in diet and plenty of exercise, although insulin injections may be necessary.

Is That a Fact!

- ◆ Approximately one in every 400 to 500 children and adolescents in the United States has type 1 diabetes.

- ◆ About 16.9 million people age 20 years or older have diabetes. Of these 16.9 million people, 90% to 95% have type 2 diabetes.

SCiLINKS

NSTA
Developed and maintained by the National Science Teachers Association

SciLinks is maintained by the National Science Teachers Association to provide you and your students with interesting, up-to-date links that will enrich your classroom presentation of the chapter.

Visit www.scilinks.org and enter the SciLinks code for more information about the topic listed.

Topic: Nervous System
SciLinks code: HSM1023

Topic: Sensory Receptors
SciLinks code: HSM1379

Topic: The Senses
SciLinks code: HSM1378

Topic: Hormones
SciLinks code: HSM0758

Topic: The Eye
SciLinks code: HSM0560

Topic: Endocrine System
SciLinks code: HSM0504

Overview

In this chapter, students will learn how the body receives, processes, and responds to information. The chapter describes the nervous system and how senses respond to stimuli. The chapter also describes how the endocrine system is part of the body's communication and control system.

Assessing Prior Knowledge

Students should be familiar with the following topics:

- cells and the activities of cells
- sensory interactions with the environment
- body structure and organization

Identifying Misconceptions

Some students may be confused about the different levels of the nervous system. A large diagram or other visual aid may help you teach this chapter by showing the central and peripheral nervous systems and the parts of the peripheral nervous system. Also, many students associate a stimulus with its source (i.e., light comes from the bulb) and do not understand that some stimuli travel as energy from one place to another. As a result, students may have difficulty understanding how light and vision are related.

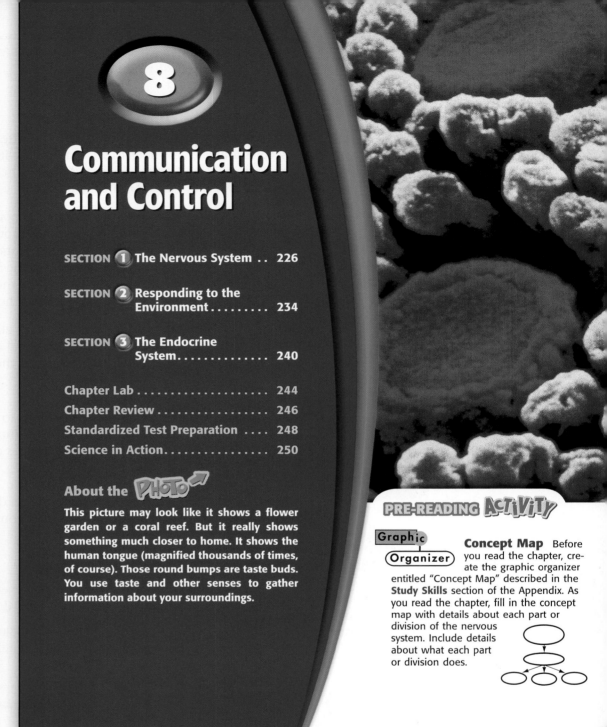

8

Communication and Control

About the PHOTO

This picture may look like it shows a flower garden or a coral reef. But it really shows something much closer to home. It shows the human tongue (magnified thousands of times, of course). Those round bumps are taste buds. You use taste and other senses to gather information about your surroundings.

PRE-READING ACTIVITY

Graphic Organizer

Concept Map Before you read the chapter, create the graphic organizer entitled "Concept Map" described in the **Study Skills** section of the Appendix. As you read the chapter, fill in the concept map with details about each part or division of the nervous system. Include details about what each part or division does.

Standards Correlations

North Carolina Standard Course of Study

1.01 Identify and create questions and hypotheses that can be answered through scientific investigations. (Chapter Lab)

1.03 Apply safety procedures in the laboratory and in field studies, recognize potential hazards, safely manipulate materials and equipment, [and] conduct appropriate procedures. (Chapter Lab)

1.04 Analyze variables in scientific investigations: Identify dependent and independent, use of a control, manipulate, describe relationships between, [and] define operationally. (Chapter Lab)

1.05 Analyze evidence to: Explain observations, make inferences and predictions, [and] develop the relationship between evidence and explanation. (Chapter Lab)

1.08 Use oral and written language to: Communicate findings, [and] Defend conclusions of scientific investigations. (Chapter Lab)

2.01 (partial) Explore evidence that "technology" has many definitions: . . . hardware, methodology or technique, . . . [and] social-technical system. (Science in Action)

2.04 Apply tenets of technological design to make informed consumer decisions about: Products, Processes, [and] Systems. (Science in Action)

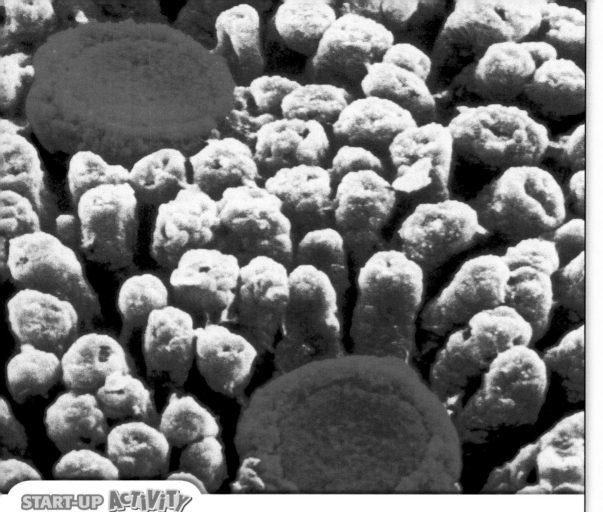

Safety Caution: Remind students to handle the meterstick carefully and to keep it away from their face and far away from the faces and eyes of their classmates.

Teacher's Notes: Allow students to have a practice trial. Instruct students to look only at the ruler and not at their partner. Point out that looking at their partner could distort the results of the investigation because the partner might give a clue about when he or she will drop the meterstick.

Answers
1. Sample answer: I am right handed, and I use each hand differently. Each hand has different abilities.

2. Sample answer: One person might respond more quickly than another depending on how rested a person is, how well a person can concentrate on the activity, and how strong a person's hands are.

START-UP ACTIVITY

Act Fast!
If you want to catch an object, your brain sends a message to the muscles in your arm. In this exercise, you will see how long sending that message takes.

Procedure
1. Sit in a **chair** with one arm in a "handshake" position. Your partner should stand facing you, holding a **meterstick** vertically. The stick should be positioned so that it will fall between your thumb and fingers.

2. Tell your partner to let go of the meterstick without warning you. Catch the stick between your thumb and fingers. Your partner should catch the meterstick if it tips over.

3. Record the number of centimeters that the stick dropped before you caught it. That distance represents your reaction time.

4. Repeat steps 1–3 three times. Calculate the average distance.

5. Repeat steps 1–4 with your other hand.

6. Trade places with your partner, and repeat steps 1–5.

Analysis
1. Compare the reaction times of your own hands. Why might one hand react more quickly than the other?

2. Compare your results with your partner's. Why might one person react more quickly than another?

4.01 (partial) Analyze how human body systems interact to provide for the needs of the human organism: . . . endocrine and nervous, . . . [and] nervous system. (Sections 1, 2, and 3)

4.02 Describe how systems within the human body are defined by the functions it performs. (Sections 1 and 3)

4.03 (partial) Explain how the structure of an organ is adapted to perform specific functions within one or more systems: . . . brain. (Sections 1 and 3)

4.04 Evaluate how systems in the human body help regulate the internal environment. (Sections 1, 2, and 3)

Chapter Starter Transparency
Use this transparency to help students begin thinking about their nervous system and their environment.

CHAPTER RESOURCES
Technology

Transparencies
• Chapter Starter Transparency

Student Edition on CD-ROM

Guided Reading Audio CD

Classroom Videos
• Brain Food Video Quiz

Workbooks

Science Puzzlers, Twisters & Teasers
• Communication and Control GENERAL

Focus

Overview

This section introduces the structures and functions of the nervous system. Students will learn the differences between the central nervous system and the peripheral nervous system, and will learn about the parts of the peripheral nervous system.

 Bellringer

Have students list as many different functions of the brain as they can. Have students predict how the brain coordinates all the different activities.

Motivate

Discussion ———— GENERAL

Reacting to Stimuli Ask students to describe a time when they reacted quickly to something. Have them describe not only what happened but also how quickly they were able to react and what they were thinking about as they reacted. Sample experiences include jerking a hand away from a hot object, quickly catching a falling object, and extending one's hand out to brace for a fall. Based on students' experiences, lead a discussion about how quickly the nervous system is able to respond to a stimulus.

LS Intrapersonal

READING WARM-UP

Objectives

- Describe the relationship between the central nervous system and the peripheral nervous system.
- Compare the somatic nervous system with the autonomic nervous system.
- List one function of each part of the brain.

Terms to Learn

central nervous system
peripheral nervous system
neuron
nerve
brain

READING STRATEGY

Discussion Read this section silently. Write down questions that you have about this section. Discuss your questions in a small group.

---

central nervous system (CNS) the brain and the spinal cord

peripheral nervous system (PNS) all of the parts of the nervous system except for the brain and the spinal cord

---

The Nervous System

Which of the following activities do NOT involve your nervous system: eating, playing a musical instrument, reading a book, running, or sleeping?

This is a trick question. All of these activities involve your nervous system. In fact, your nervous system controls almost everything you do.

Two Systems Within a System

The nervous system acts as the body's central command post. Its has two basic functions. First, it gathers and interprets information. This information comes from inside your body and from the world outside your body. Then, the nervous system responds to that information as needed.

The nervous system has two parts: the central nervous system and the peripheral (puh RIF uhr uhl) nervous system. The **central nervous system** (CNS) is your brain and spinal cord. The CNS processes and responds to all messages coming from the peripheral nervous system. The **peripheral nervous system** (PNS) is all of the parts of the nervous system except for the brain and the spinal cord. The PNS connects all parts of the body to the CNS. The PNS uses specialized structures, called *nerves*, to carry information between your body and your CNS. **Figure 1** shows the major divisions of the nervous system.

✓ **Reading Check** Explain the difference between the CNS and the PNS. (*See the Appendix for answers to Reading Checks.*)

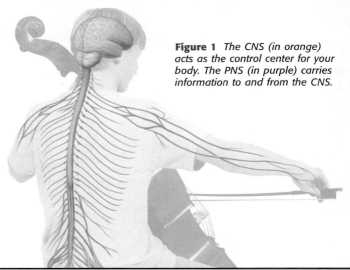

Figure 1 *The CNS (in orange) acts as the control center for your body. The PNS (in purple) carries information to and from the CNS.*

CHAPTER RESOURCES

Chapter Resource File

- **Lesson Plan**
- **Directed Reading A** BASIC
- **Directed Reading B** SPECIAL NEEDS

Technology

Transparencies
- Bellringer
- A Typical Neuron

Answer to Reading Check

The CNS is the brain and the spinal cord. The PNS is all of the parts of the nervous system except the brain and the spinal cord.

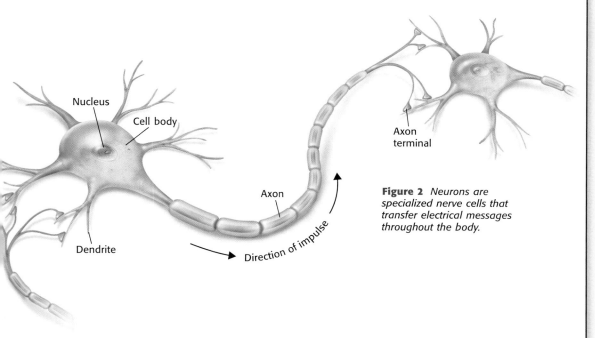

Nucleus

Cell body

Axon terminal

Dendrite

Axon

Direction of impulse

Figure 2 *Neurons are specialized nerve cells that transfer electrical messages throughout the body.*

The Peripheral Nervous System

Messages about your environment travel through the nervous system along neurons. A **neuron** (NOO RAHN) is a nerve cell that is specialized to transfer messages in the form of fast-moving electrical energy. These electrical messages are called *impulses*. Impulses may travel as fast as 150 m/s or as slow as 0.2 m/s. **Figure 2** shows a typical neuron transferring an impulse.

Neuron Structure

In many ways, a neuron is similar to other cells. A neuron has a large region in its center called the *cell body*. The cell body has a nucleus and cell organelles. But neurons also have special structures called dendrites and axons. *Dendrites* are usually short, branched extensions of the cell. Neurons receive information from other cells through their dendrites. A neuron may have many dendrites, which allows it to receive impulses from thousands of other cells.

Impulses are carried away from the cell body by axons. *Axons* are elongated extensions of a neuron. They can be very short or quite long. Some long axons extend almost 1 m from your lower back to your toes. The end of an axon often has branches that allow information to pass to other cells. The tip of each branch is called an *axon terminal*.

✓ Reading Check In your own words, describe a neuron.

neuron a nerve cell that is specialized to receive and conduct electrical impulses

Time to Travel

To calculate how long an impulse takes to travel a certain distance, you can use the following equation:

$$time = \frac{distance}{speed}$$

If an impulse travels 100 m/s, about how long would it take an impulse to travel 10 m?

Is That a Fact!

Male canaries sing a new song every year. Male canaries replace old brain cells related to song production with new neurons each spring. In the spring, the brain-cell clusters associated with vocalization grow larger. So males compose their new melodies and females learn to recognize the males by their new songs. In the fall, when the birds stop singing, the brain clusters shrink.

Answer to Reading Check

A neuron is a cell that has a cell body and a nucleus. A neuron also has dendrites that receive signals from other neurons and axons that send signals to other neurons.

Group ACTIVITY — BASIC

Simulating Neuronal Impulses

Ask students to form a circle and hold hands. Explain that each person in the circle represents a neuron. Every left hand represents a dendrite, every body represents a cell body, and every right hand represents an axon. Join the circle, and initiate a nerve impulse by gently squeezing the hand of the student to your right. Instruct students to pass the nerve impulse to the person to their right by gently squeezing his or her hand. Once students understand the mechanics of the activity, have them call out *dendrite, cell body,* and *axon* as the impulse is passed along the circle.
 Kinesthetic/ Interpersonal   English Language Learners

Discussion — GENERAL

Following an Impulse
Ask students to imagine that an electrical impulse is sent from the brain along neurons, similar to the one shown in **Figure 2,** and along a nerve, as shown in **Figure 3.** Discuss with students the path of the impulse from the brain, along the neuron to the spinal cord, and then along the nerve to the muscle. Draw a diagram on the board. Then, ask students to predict what will happen in the muscle next. (The muscle will move and send a message back to the brain to tell the brain of its new position.)
Visual/Verbal

---

nerve a collection of nerve fibers (axons) through which impulses travel between the central nervous system and other parts of the body

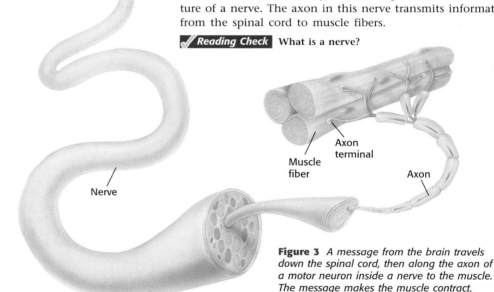

Spinal cord

Nerve

Muscle fiber

Axon terminal

Axon

Figure 3 *A message from the brain travels down the spinal cord, then along the axon of a motor neuron inside a nerve to the muscle. The message makes the muscle contract.*

CHAPTER RESOURCES

Technology

📦 **Transparencies**
• What Is a Nerve?

Information Collection

Remember that neurons are a type of nerve cell that carries impulses. Some neurons are *sensory neurons*. These neurons gather information about what is happening in and around your body. They have specialized nerve endings called *receptors*. Receptors detect changes inside and outside the body. For example, receptors in your eyes detect light. Sensory neurons then send this information to the CNS for processing.

Delivering Orders

Neurons that send impulses from the brain and spinal cord to other systems are called *motor neurons*. When muscles get impulses from motor neurons, they respond by contracting. For example, motor neurons cause muscles around your eyes to contract when you are in bright light. These muscles make you squint. Squinting lets less light enter the eyes. Motor neurons also send messages to your glands, such as sweat glands. These messages tell sweat glands to start or stop making sweat.

Nerves

The central nervous system is connected to the rest of your body by nerves. A **nerve** is a collection of axons bundled together with blood vessels and connective tissue. Nerves are everywhere in your body. Most nerves have axons of both sensory neurons and motor neurons. Axons are parts of nerves, but nerves are more than just axons. **Figure 3** shows the structure of a nerve. The axon in this nerve transmits information from the spinal cord to muscle fibers.

✓ *Reading Check* What is a nerve?

Answer to Reading Check

A nerve is a collection of nerve fibers, or axons, bundled together with blood vessels, through which impulses travel between the central nervous system and other parts of the body.

Somatic and Autonomic Nervous Systems

Remember, the PNS connects your CNS to the rest of your body. And the PNS has two main parts—the sensory part (sensory neurons) and the motor part (motor neurons). You know that sensory nerves collect information from your senses and send that information to the CNS. You also know that motor nerves carry out the CNS's responses to that sensory information. To carry those responses, the motor part of the PNS has two kinds of nerves: somatic nerves and autonomic nerves.

Somatic Nervous System

Most of the neurons that are part of the *somatic nervous system* are under your conscious control. These are the neurons that stimulate skeletal muscles. They control voluntary movements, such as writing, talking, smiling, or jumping.

Autonomic Nervous System

Autonomic nerves do not need your conscious control. These neurons are part of the autonomic nervous system. The *autonomic nervous system* controls body functions that you don't think about, such as digestion and heart rate (the number of times your heart beats per minute).

The main job of the autonomic nervous system is to keep all the body's functions in balance. Depending on the situation, the autonomic nervous system can speed up or slow down these functions. The autonomic nervous system has two divisions: the *sympathetic division* and the *parasympathetic division*. These two divisions work together to keep your internal environment stable. This is called *homeostasis*. Some of these functions are shown in **Table 1**.

Reading Check Describe three functions of the PNS.

Table 1 Effects of the Autonomic Nervous System on the Body

Organ	Effect of sympathetic division	Effect of parasympathetic division
Eyes	pupils dilate (grow larger; makes it easier to see objects)	pupils constrict (vision normal)
Heart	heart rate increases (increases blood flow)	heart rate slows (blood flow slows)
Lungs	bronchioles dilate (grow larger; increases oxygen in blood)	bronchioles constrict
Blood vessels	blood vessels dilate (increases blood flow except to digestion)	little or no effect
Intestines	digestion slows (reduces blood flow to stomach and intestines)	digestion returns to normal

📖 READING STRATEGY — GENERAL

Prediction Guide Before students read about the central nervous system, ask them whether the following statements are true or false.

1. The brain is the body's largest organ. (false)

2. The largest part of the brain is the cerebrum. (true)

3. The medulla is responsible for speech and balance. (false)

4. The spinal cord is about as big around as your thumb. (true)

Have students evaluate their answers after they have read this section. **LS** Verbal

Group ACTiViTY — BASIC

Reteaching the Brain If students have difficulty distinguishing the structures of the brain, have them make a life-size model of the brain. Organize the class into groups of two or three. Give each group modeling clay of different colors. Each group should have enough clay to make a life-size model of the brain. Instruct students to make labels for the parts of the brain. They should include the cerebrum, cerebellum, medulla, and the top of the spinal cord. Also, have students label the hemispheres. Allow students to use their models as you finish teaching about the brain. **LS** Kinesthetic — English Language Learners

brain the mass of nerve tissue that is the main control center of the nervous system

The Central Nervous System

The central nervous system receives information from the sensory neurons. Then it responds by sending messages to the body through motor neurons in the PNS.

The Control Center

The largest organ in the nervous system is the brain. The **brain** is the main control center of the nervous system. Many processes that the brain controls happen automatically. These processes are called *involuntary*. For example, you couldn't stop digesting food even if you tried. On the other hand, some actions controlled by your brain are *voluntary*. When you want to move your arm, your brain sends signals along motor neurons to muscles in your arm. Then, the muscles contract, and your arm moves. The brain has three main parts—the cerebrum (suh REE bruhm), the cerebellum (SER uh BEL uhm), and the medulla (mi DUHL uh). Each part has its own job.

✔️ **Reading Check** What is the difference between a voluntary action and an involuntary action?

The Cerebrum

The largest part of your brain is called the *cerebrum*. It looks like a mushroom cap. This dome-shaped area is where you think and where most memories are stored. It controls voluntary movements and allows you to sense touch, light, sound, odors, taste, pain, heat, and cold.

The cerebrum has two halves, called *hemispheres*. The left hemisphere directs the right side of the body, and the right hemisphere directs the left side of the body. **Figure 4** shows some of the activities that each hemisphere controls. However, most brain activities use both hemispheres.

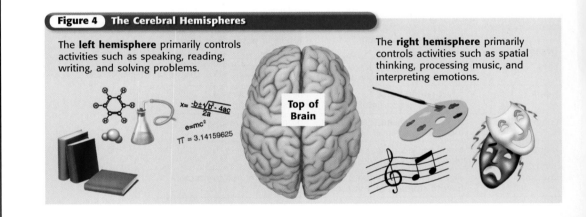

Figure 4 **The Cerebral Hemispheres**

The **left hemisphere** primarily controls activities such as speaking, reading, writing, and solving problems.

The **right hemisphere** primarily controls activities such as spatial thinking, processing music, and interpreting emotions.

Top of Brain

Homework — GENERAL

✏️ *Writing* **Dream Research** Dreaming, sleepwalking, and daydreaming are all phenomena of the brain. Have students research one of these topics and give group presentations to the class. They may use posters, signs, songs, skits, oral reports, and other techniques for their presentations. **LS** Verbal/Visual

Answer to Reading Check

A voluntary action is an action over which you have conscious control. Voluntary activities include throwing a ball, playing a video game, talking to your friends, taking a bite of food, and raising your hand to answer a question in class. An involuntary action is an action that happens automatically. It is an action or process over which you have no conscious control.

The Cerebellum

The second-largest part of your brain is the *cerebellum*. It lies beneath the back of the cerebrum. The cerebellum processes sensory information from your body, such as from skeletal muscles and joints. This allows the brain to keep track of your body's position. If you begin to lose your balance, the cerebellum sends impulses telling different skeletal muscles to contract. Those muscles shift a person's weight and keep a person, such as the girl in **Figure 5,** from losing her balance.

The Medulla

The *medulla* is the part of the brain that connects to your spinal cord. The medulla is about 3 cm long, and you can't live without it. It controls involuntary processes in other body systems, such as the circulatory system (blood pressure and heart rate) and the respiratory system (involuntary breathing).

Your medulla constantly receives sensory impulses from receptors in your blood vessels. It uses this information to regulate your blood pressure. If your blood pressure gets too low, the medulla sends out impulses that tell blood vessels to tighten up. As a result, blood pressure rises. The medulla also sends impulses to the heart to make the heart beat faster or slower. **Figure 6** shows the location of the parts of the brain and some of the functions of each part.

Reading Check Explain why the medulla is important.

Figure 5 *Your cerebellum causes skeletal muscles to make adjustments so that you will stay upright.*

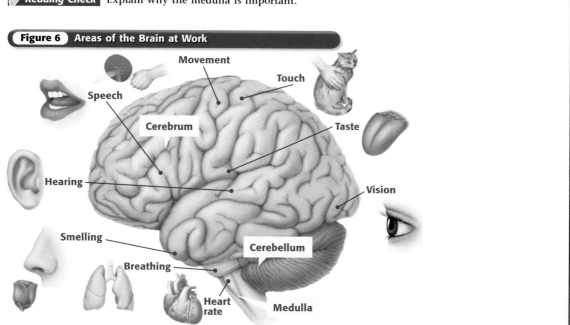
Figure 6 | **Areas of the Brain at Work**

Movement · Touch · Speech · Cerebrum · Taste · Hearing · Vision · Smelling · Cerebellum · Breathing · Heart rate · Medulla

Is That a Fact!

Synapses form in a human baby's brain at the rate of 3 billion a second. At 8 months old, a baby's brain has about 1,000 trillion connections. After that, the number begins to decline. Half the connections die by the time the child reaches age 10, leaving about 500 trillion connections.

CHAPTER RESOURCES

Technology

Transparencies
• Regions of the Brain

Homework ___ BASIC

Concept Mapping List the following terms on the board:

brain, hemispheres, cerebrum, cerebellum, medulla, spinal cord, central nervous system, peripheral nervous system, sensory neurons, and *motor neurons*.

Discuss each term with students. Then, for homework, have students use the terms to construct a concept map. **LS Verbal**

CONNECTION ACTIVITY
Language Arts ___ GENERAL

Writing **Thanks for the Memories** Long-term memory enables us to recall events that happened to us long ago. These memories can be triggered by a stimulus, such as a song or a smell, or they can be deliberately recalled. Recalling memories helps us to refresh them and makes them last a lifetime. Ask students to write down their earliest memory, their happiest recollection, or their most embarrassing moment. Interested students may share their favorites. **LS Verbal**

Answer to Reading Check

The medulla is important because it controls your heart rate, blood pressure, and ordinary breathing.

CONNECTION ACTIVITY
Real World ___ GENERAL

Writing **Fainting** Students have probably seen people faint in movies or television shows. Fainting and other forms of unconsciousness, except sleeping, are usually the result of some problem in the brain. Have students research fainting and write a short explanation about what causes fainting. (Fainting is often caused by suddenly low blood pressure and insufficient blood flow to the cerebrum.) **LS Verbal**

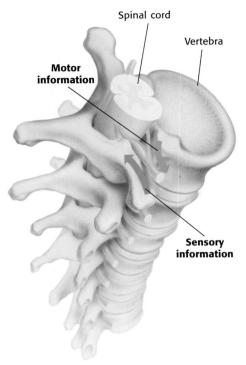

Figure 7 *The spinal cord carries information to and from the brain. Vertebrae protect the spinal cord.*

Labels: Spinal cord, Vertebra, Motor information, Sensory information

The Spinal Cord

Your spinal cord, which is part of your central nervous system, is about as big around as your thumb. The spinal cord is made of neurons and bundles of axons that pass impulses to and from the brain. As shown in **Figure 7,** the spinal cord is surrounded by protective bones called *vertebrae* (VUHR tuh BRAY).

The nerve fibers in your spinal cord allow your brain to communicate with your peripheral nervous system. Sensory neurons in your skin and muscles send impulses along their axons to your spinal cord. The spinal cord carries impulses to your brain. The brain interprets these impulses as pain, temperature, or other sensations. The brain then responds to the situation. Impulses moving from the brain down the spinal cord are relayed to motor neurons. Motor neurons carry the impulses along their axons to muscles and glands all over your body.

✓ *Reading Check* **Describe the path of an impulse from the skin to the brain and the path of the response.**

Spinal Cord Injury

A spinal cord injury may block all information to and from the brain. Sensory information coming from below the injury may not get to the brain. For example, a spinal cord injury may block all sensory impulses from the feet and legs. People with such an injury would not be able to sense pain, touch, or temperature with their feet. And motor commands from the brain to the injured area may not reach the peripheral nerves. So, the person would not be able to move his or her legs.

Each year, thousands of people are paralyzed by spinal cord injuries. Many of these injuries happen in car accidents and could be avoided by wearing a seat belt. Among young people, spinal cord injuries are sometimes related to sports or other activities. These injuries might be prevented by wearing proper safety equipment.

Building a Neuron

1. Your teacher will provide at least four different colors of **modeling clay.** Build a model of a neuron by using different-colored clay for the various parts of the neuron.

2. Use **tape** to attach your model neuron to a **piece of plain white paper.**

3. On the paper, label each part of the neuron. Draw an arrow from the label to the part.

4. Using a **colored pencil, marker,** or **crayon,** draw arrows showing the path of an impulse traveling in your neuron. Tell whether the impulse is a sensory impulse or a motor impulse. Then, describe what will happen when the impulse reaches its destination.

SECTION Review

Summary

- The central nervous system (CNS) includes the brain and the spinal cord.
- The peripheral nervous system (PNS) is all the parts of the nervous system except the brain and spinal cord.
- The peripheral nervous system has nerves made up of axons of neurons.
- Sensory neurons have receptors that detect information about the body and its environment. Motor neurons carry messages from the brain and spinal cord to other parts of the body.

- The PNS has two types of motor nerves—somatic nerves and autonomic nerves.
- The cerebrum is the largest part of the brain and controls thinking, sensing, and voluntary movement.
- The cerebellum is the part of the brain that keeps track of the body's position and helps maintain balance.
- The medulla controls involuntary processes, such as heart rate, blood pressure, body temperature, and breathing.

Using Key Terms

1. In your own words, write a definition for each of the following terms: *neuron* and *nerve*.

2. Use the following terms in the same sentence: *brain* and *peripheral nervous system*.

Understanding Key Ideas

3. Someone touches your shoulder and you turn around. Which sequence do your impulses follow?
   a. motor neuron, sensory neuron, CNS response
   b. motor neuron, CNS response, sensory neuron
   c. sensory neuron, motor neuron, CNS response
   d. sensory neuron, CNS response, motor neuron

4. Describe one function of each part of the brain.

5. Compare the somatic nervous system with the autonomic nervous system.

6. Explain how a severe injury to the spinal cord can affect other parts of the body.

Critical Thinking

7. **Applying Concepts** Some medications slow a person's nervous system. These drugs are often labeled "May cause drowsiness." Explain why a person needs to know about this side effect.

8. **Making Inferences** Explain how the structure of your brain is adapted to perform specific functions within one or more systems.

Interpreting Graphics

Use the figure below to answer the questions that follow.

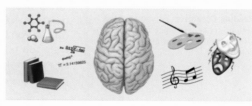

9. Which hemisphere of the brain recognizes and processes words, numbers, and letters? faces, places, and objects?

10. For a person whose left hemisphere is primarily in control, would it be easier to learn to play a new computer game by reading the rules and following instructions or by watching a friend play and imitating his actions?

Developed and maintained by the National Science Teachers Association

For a variety of links related to this chapter, go to www.scilinks.org

Topic: Nervous System
SciLinks code: HSM1023

Answers to Section Review

1. Sample answer: A neuron is a special nerve cell that can receive and conduct electrical impulses. A nerve is a bundle of axons and other tissues connecting the CNS and PNS.

2. Sample answer: The peripheral nervous system consists of nerves that connect all parts of your body to your brain and spinal cord.

3. d

4. Sample answer: The cerebrum controls speech and touch. The cerebellum receives sensory input and helps you balance. The medulla controls involuntary processes such as heart rate and blood pressure.

CHAPTER RESOURCES

Chapter Resource File

- • Section Quiz GENERAL
- • Section Review GENERAL
- • Vocabulary and Section Summary GENERAL
- • Reinforcement Worksheet BASIC
- • SciLinks Activity GENERAL
- • Datasheet for Quick Lab

Technology

Transparencies
- • The Spinal Cord

5. Sample answer: The somatic nervous system controls actions that are under conscious control, such as singing or shaking hands. The autonomic nervous system controls body processes and functions that are not under your conscious control, such as pupil dilation and digestion.

6. Sample answer: A spinal injury may damage nerves in the spinal cord that send or receive messages between the brain and the body. Damage to the nerves may stop those messages and keep the person from either receiving sensory inputs or making any movements that would be controlled by the damaged nerves.

7. Sample answer: A drug that causes drowsiness may affect the way that impulses travel in neurons. Affecting the impulses may increase the time it takes a message to get to the brain or the time it takes a message to get from the brain to muscles. It is important to be aware of this side effect so that activities that require a fast reaction time, such as driving, can be avoided.

8. Sample answer: The brain consists of neurons that send messages to and receive messages from every body system. The brain is also organized into structures, such as the cerebrum or the medulla. The cerebrum is further structured so that each side controls different activities, such as problem solving on the left and processing music on the right. The medulla controls involuntary functions in more than one body system, such as the respiratory and circulatory systems.

9. left; right

10. Sample answer: It would be easier to learn the new game by reading the rules and following the instructions.

Focus

Overview

This section describe how the body responds to its environment. It introduces the five senses: touch, sight, hearing, taste, and smell. Students will learn about the receptor cells that are unique to each sense.

🔔 Bellringer

Ask students to list the five senses and draw an organ associated with each sense as well as an object detected by each sense. For example, students may draw an ear and a bell to represent the sense of hearing.

Motivate

Losing Your Senses

Organize the class into groups of three or four students, and assign each group a sense. Each group should imagine what it would be like to live without that sense. Allow students 10 to 15 minutes to develop a skit or example of life without the assigned sense. **LS** Intrapersonal/
Kinesthetic
Co-op Learning   English Language
                        Learners

READING WARM-UP

Objectives
- List four sensations that are detected by receptors in the skin.
- Describe how a feedback mechanism works.
- Describe how light relates to sight.
- Describe how the senses of hearing, taste, and smell work.

Terms to Learn
integumentary system
reflex
feedback mechanism
retina
cochlea

READING STRATEGY

Reading Organizer As you read this section, create an outline of the section. Use the headings from the section in your outline.

integumentary system the organ system that forms a protective covering on the outside of the body

---

Responding to the Environment

You feel a tap on your shoulder. Who tapped you? You turn to look, hoping to see a friend. Your senses are on the job!

The tap produces impulses in sensory receptors on your shoulder. These impulses travel to your brain. Once the impulses reach your brain, they create an awareness called a *sensation*. In this case, the sensation is of your shoulder being touched. But you still do not know who tapped you. So, you turn around. The sensory receptors in your eyes send impulses to your brain. Now, your brain recognizes your best friend.

Sense of Touch

Touch is what you feel when sensory receptors in the skin are stimulated. It is the sensation you feel when you shake hands or feel a breeze. As shown in **Figure 1,** skin has different kinds of receptors. Each kind of receptor responds mainly to one kind of stimulus. For example, *thermoreceptors* respond to temperature change. Each kind of receptor produces a specific sensation of touch, such as pressure, temperature, pain, or vibration. Skin is part of the integumentary (in TEG yoo MEN tuhr ee) system. The **integumentary system** protects the body from damage. It includes hair, skin, and nails.

✔ **Reading Check** List four sensations that your skin can detect. (*See the Appendix for answers to Reading Checks.*)

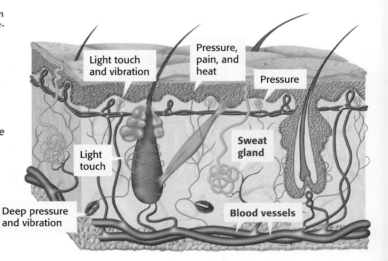

Figure 1 *Each type of receptor in your skin has its own structure and function.*

CHAPTER RESOURCES

Chapter Resource File

📁 • **Lesson Plan**
   • **Directed Reading A** **BASIC**
   • **Directed Reading B** **SPECIAL NEEDS**

Technology

💾 **Transparencies**
   • Bellringer

Workbooks

📘 **Study Guide**
   • Multilplying and Dividing in Scientific Notation **GENERAL**

Answer to Reading Check
Skin can detect pressure, temperature, pain, and vibration.

Responding to Sensory Messages

Think about how all your body systems interact to provide for everything that you need. For example, when you step on something sharp, as the man in **Figure 2** did, pain receptors in the skin on your foot or toe send impulses to your spinal cord. Almost immediately, a message to move your foot travels back to the muscles in your leg and foot. Without thinking, you quickly lift your foot. This immediate, involuntary action is called a **reflex.** Your brain isn't telling your leg to move. In fact, by the time the message reaches your brain, your leg and foot have already moved. If you had to wait for your brain to act, you toes might be seriously hurt!

reflex an involuntary and almost immediate movement in response to a stimulus

feedback mechanism a cycle of events in which information from one step controls or affects a previous step

Reading Check Why are reflexes important?

Feedback Mechanisms

Most of the time, the brain processes information from skin receptors. For example, on a hot day, heat receptors in your skin detect an increase in your temperature. The receptors send impulses to the brain. Your brain responds by sending messages to sweat glands to make sweat. As sweat evaporates, it cools your body. Your brain also signals blood vessels in your skin to dilate (open wider). Blood flow increases. Thermal energy from blood in your skin moves to the air around you. This also cools your body. As your body cools, it sends messages to your brain. The brain responds by signalling sweat glands and blood vessels to reduce their activity.

This cooling process is one of your body's feedback mechanisms. A **feedback mechanism** is a cycle of events in which information from one step controls or affects a previous step. The temperature-regulating feedback mechanism helps keep your body temperature within safe limits. This cooling mechanism works like a thermostat on an air conditioner. Once a room reaches the right temperature, the thermostat sends a message to the air conditioner to stop blowing cold air.

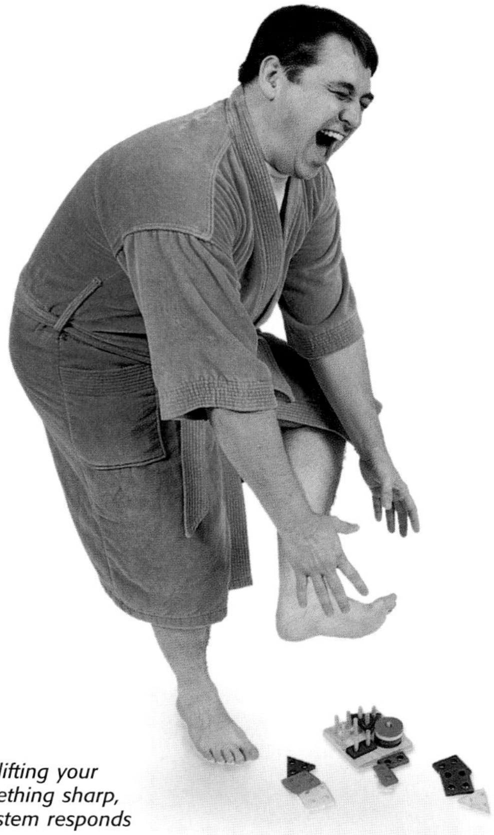

Figure 2 *A reflex, such as lifting your foot when you step on something sharp, is one way your nervous system responds to your environment.*

Teach

Homework — ADVANCED

Other Reflexes Have students use the Internet or the library to research different reflexes the body has. They are probably familiar with the knee-jerk reflex, but they may not be aware of reflexes associated with eye blinks and loud noises. Have students create a visual or other presentation to show what they have learned. LS Visual

English Language Learners

CONNECTION to Environmental Science — ADVANCED

Writing **Climate and Feedback** Scientists have learned that there are feedback mechanisms in the environment. Changes in the environment can produce positive or negative feedback that affects Earth's climate. Have students research feedback mechanisms and the environment and write a report explaining how the feedback mechanisms may affect humans. LS Verbal

ACTIVITY — BASIC

Writing **"Ol' Three Eyes"** *Tuatara* are an ancient species of reptile. Their closest relatives became extinct 65 million years ago. One unusual feature of tuatara is that they have three eyes. The third eye is really a light-sensitive gland. Have students research tuatara and write a report on these unusual "living fossils." Encourage students to illustrate their reports. LS Verbal

ACTIVITY — ADVANCED

Writing **Do You Hear Colors?** About one out of every 25,000 people has *synesthesia*. These people experience a blend of senses. For example, one person sees blue when a particular note is played on a piano. Another person gets a very bitter taste in his mouth when he makes hamburger patties with his hands. Have students conduct Internet or library research and write a report on synesthesia and how it affects people who have it. LS Verbal

Answer to Reading Check

Reflexes are important because they can protect you from injury.

Writing **Pupil Action** Ask students to write a paragraph that explains what happens to their eyes and vision when they first leave a dark movie theater on a sunny day. Students should discuss the change from dim to bright light and its effects on the pupils as well as on their ability to see. **LS** Verbal

Discussion ——— GENERAL

Eye Strain For us to see objects within a distance of 6 m, the muscles in the eye must work constantly to focus. Long periods of focusing on very near objects, such as a book, can tire the eye muscles and cause eyestrain. Ask students to suggest ways to avoid straining the eye muscles during these activities. (Answers may include taking breaks from the activity once an hour and looking up and allowing the eyes to relax occasionally.) **LS** Logical

Answer to Reading Check

Light strikes cells on the retina and triggers impulses in those cells. The impulses are carried to the brain, which interprets the impulses as images that you "see."

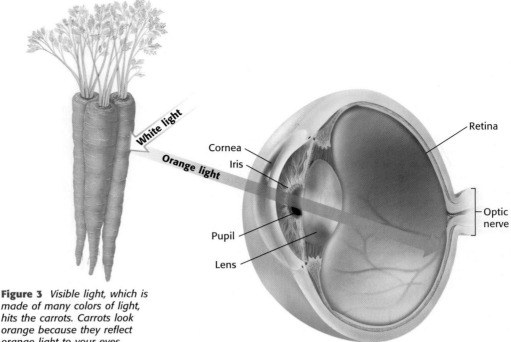

Figure 3 *Visible light, which is made of many colors of light, hits the carrots. Carrots look orange because they reflect orange light to your eyes.*

retina the light-sensitive inner layer of the eye; it receives images formed by the lens and transmits them through the optic nerve to the brain

INTERNET ACTIVITY

For another activity related to this chapter, go to **go.hrw.com** and type in the keyword **HL5BD4W.**

Sense of Sight

Sight is the sense that allows you to see the size, shape, motion, and color of objects around you. You see an object when it sends or reflects visible light toward your eyes. Your eyes detect this light, which enables your brain to form visual images.

Your eyes are complex sensory organs, as you can see in **Figure 3.** The front of the eye is covered by a clear membrane called the *cornea.* The cornea protects the eye but allows light to enter. Light from an object enters the front of your eye through an opening called the *pupil.* The light then travels through the lens to the back of the eye. There, the light strikes the **retina,** a layer of light-sensitive cells.

The retina is packed with photoreceptors. A *photoreceptor* is a special neuron that changes light into electrical impulses. The retina has two kinds of photoreceptors: rods and cones. Rods are very sensitive to dim light. They are important for night vision. Impulses from rods are interpreted as black-and-white images. Cones are very sensitive to bright light. Impulses from cones allow you to see fine details and colors.

Impulses from the rods and cones travel along axons. The impulses leave the back of each eye through an optic nerve. The optic nerve carries the impulses to your brain, where the impulses are interpreted as the images that you see.

✓ **Reading Check** Describe how light and sight are related.

MISCONCEPTION
////ALERT

Colorblindness Students may think that people who are colorblind see in black and white. People who are colorblind can usually perceive colors, but certain colors may appear very similar to one another. This similarity is caused by a lack of at least one of the three cones in the eye. Many people do not know that they are colorblind because they have learned to distinguish other differences in their perception of colors.

Reacting to Light

Your pupil looks like a black dot in the center of your eye. In fact, it is an opening that lets light enter the eye. The pupil is surrounded by the *iris,* a ring of muscle. The iris controls the amount of light that enters the eye and gives the eye its color. In bright light, the iris contracts, which makes the pupil smaller. A smaller pupil reduces the amount of light entering the eye and passing onto the retina. In dim light, the iris opens the pupil and lets in more light.

Reading Check How does your iris react to bright light?

Focusing the Light

Light travels in straight lines until it passes through the cornea and the lens. The *lens* is an oval-shaped piece of clear, curved material behind the iris. Muscles in the eye change the shape of the lens in order to focus light onto the retina. When you look at objects close to the eye, the lens becomes more curved. When you look at objects far away, the lens gets flatter.

Figure 4 shows some common vision problems. In some eyes, the lens focuses the light in front of the retina, which results in nearsightedness. If the lens focuses the light just behind the retina, the result is farsightedness. Glasses, contact lenses, or surgery can usually correct these vision problems.

Where's the Dot?

1. Hold your **book** at arm's length, and close your right eye. Focus your left eye on the black dot below.

   ●

2. Slowly move the book toward your face until the white dot disappears. You may need to try a few times to get this result. The white dot doesn't always disappear for every person.
3. Describe your observations.
4. Use the library or the Internet to research the optic nerve and to find out why the white dot disappears.

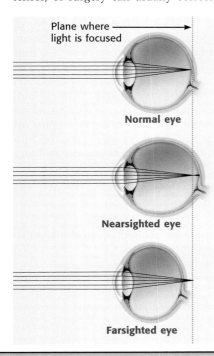

Plane where light is focused

Normal eye

Nearsighted eye

Farsighted eye

Figure 4 *A concave lens bends light rays outward to correct nearsightedness. A convex lens bends light rays inward to correct farsightedness.*

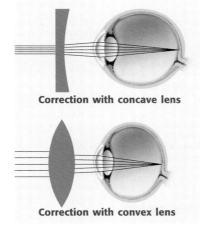

Correction with concave lens

Correction with convex lens

Is That a Fact!

Young people often hold a book close to their face when reading, while adults hold a book farther away. The closest point on which a person can focus, called the *near point of vision,* changes with age. A typical child can focus on an object about 10 cm from his or her eyes (objects closer than the near point of vision can be seen but appear fuzzy). The change in the near point of vision is caused by the lens's decreasing elasticity over time.

Model of a Sense Organ Have students choose one sense organ and make a model showing how that organ interacts with the brain. Allow students to choose from an assortment of materials for their model. Ask students to explain their model to the class. **LS Kinesthetic** English Language Learners

Quiz — GENERAL

Ask students whether each of the statements below is true or false. Have students correct false statements.

1. Rods help you see color and detail in bright light. (false; "cones" is correct)

2. Cones provide a colorful view of the world. (true)

3. Your brain combines signals from the senses of smell and hearing to give you a sensation of flavor. (false; "smell and taste" is correct)

Alternative Assessment — GENERAL

Making Sense of It Have students write and illustrate a brochure that explains each of the senses. The brochure should be written for somone who does not know much about science. **LS Verbal/Visual** English Language Learners

Answer to Reading Check

Neurons in the cochlea convert waves into electrical impulses that the brain interprets as sound.

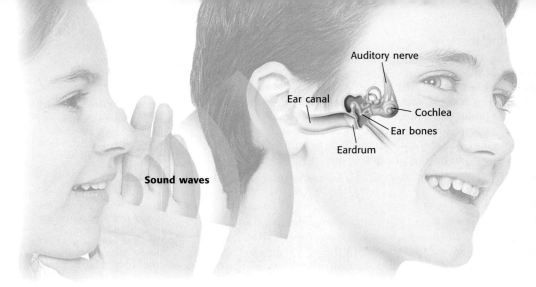

Figure 5 *A sound wave travels into the outer ear. It is converted into bone vibrations in the middle ear, then into liquid vibrations in the inner ear, and finally, into nerve impulses that travel to the brain.*

cochlea a coiled tube that is found in the inner ear and that is essential to hearing

CONNECTION TO Physics

WRITING SKILL **Elephant Talk** Sound is produced by vibrating objects. Some sounds, called *infrasonic sounds*, are too low for human ears to detect. Research how elephants use infrasonic sounds to communicate with each other, and write a report about what you learn.

Sense of Hearing

Sound is produced when something, such as a drum, vibrates. Vibrations push on nearby air particles, which push on other air particles. The vibrations create waves of sound energy. Hearing is the sense that allows you to experience sound energy.

Ears are organs specialized for hearing. Each ear has an outer, middle, and inner portion, as shown in **Figure 5.** Sound waves reaching the outer ear are funneled into the middle ear. There, the waves make the eardrum vibrate. The eardrum is a thin membrane separating the outer ear from the middle ear. The vibrating eardrum makes tiny bones in the middle ear vibrate. One of these bones vibrates against the **cochlea** (KAHK lee uh), a fluid-filled organ of the inner ear. Inside the cochlea, vibrations make waves just like the waves you make by tapping on a glass of water. Neurons in the cochlea change the waves into electrical impulses. These impulses travel along the auditory nerve to the area of the brain that interprets sound.

✓ **Reading Check** Why is the cochlea important to hearing?

Sense of Taste

Taste is the sense that allows you to detect chemicals and distinguish flavors. Your tongue is covered with tiny bumps called *papillae* (puh PIL ee). Most papillae contain taste buds. Taste buds contain clusters of *taste cells,* the receptors for taste. Taste cells respond to dissolved food molecules. Taste cells react to four basic tastes: sweetness, sourness, saltiness, and bitterness. When the brain combines information from all of the taste buds, you taste a "combination" flavor.

CONNECTION to Physical Science — ADVANCED

Owls Hunt by Hearing Students are probably familiar with the idea that owls see well in the dark. Students may not know that some owls actually hunt by listening for mice tunneling under the snow. Have students research the many adaptations that help owls hear well. Students can present their findings on a poster or by making a model of an owl's head that shows how an owl uses its hearing to hunt. **LS Verbal**

WEIRD SCIENCE

Some spicy foods, such as chile peppers, contain a chemical compound called *capsaicin*. Capsaicin triggers the pain receptors in the mouth. These receptors react to capsaicin exactly as they would to heat. This is why spicy foods, such as jalapeño peppers, feel like they are burning your mouth. In fact, no damage from heat actually happens—the burning is all in your mind!

Sense of Smell

As you can see in **Figure 6,** receptors for smell are located on *olfactory cells* in the upper part of your nasal cavity. An olfactory cell is a nerve cell that responds to chemical molecules in the air. You smell something when the receptors react to molecules that have been inhaled. The molecules dissolve in the moist lining of the nasal cavity and trigger an impulse. Olfactory cells send those impulses to the brain, which interprets the impulses as odors.

Taste buds and olfactory cells both detect dissolved molecules. Your brain combines information from both senses to give you sensations of flavor.

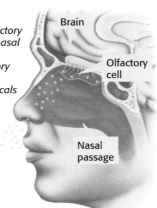

Figure 6 *Olfactory cells line the nasal cavity. These cells are sensory receptors that react to chemicals in the air.*

Brain

Olfactory cell

Nasal passage

SECTION Review

Summary

- Touch allows you to respond to temperature, pressure, pain, and vibration on the skin.
- Reflexes and feedback mechanisms help you respond to your environment.
- Sight allows you to respond to light energy.
- Hearing allows you to respond to sound energy.
- Taste allows you to distinguish flavors.
- Smell allows you to perceive different odors.

Using Key Terms

1. In your own words, write a definition for each of the following terms: *reflex* and *feedback mechanism.*

2. Use each of the following terms in a separate sentence: *retina* and *cochlea.*

Understanding Key Ideas

3. Three sensations that receptors in the skin detect are
   a. light, smell, and sound.
   b. touch, pain, and odors.
   c. temperature, pressure, and pain.
   d. pressure, sound, and touch.

4. Explain how light and sight are related.

5. Describe how your senses of hearing, taste, and smell work.

6. Explain why you might have trouble seeing bright colors at a candlelit dinner.

7. How is your sense of taste similar to your sense of smell, and how do these senses work together?

8. Describe how the feedback mechanism that regulates body temperature works.

Math Skills

9. Suppose a nerve impulse must travel 0.90 m from your toe to your central nervous system. If the impulse travels at 150 m/s, calculate how long it will take the impulse to arrive. If the impulse travels at 0.2 m/s, how long will it take the impulse to arrive?

Critical Thinking

10. **Making Inferences** Why is it important for the human body to have reflexes?

11. **Applying Concepts** Rods help you detect objects and shapes in dim light. Explain why it is important for human eyes to have both rods and cones.

SCLINKS

NSTA
Developed and maintained by the
National Science Teachers Association

For a variety of links related to this chapter, go to www.scilinks.org

Topic: The Senses; The Eye
SciLinks code: HSM1378; HSM0560

Answers to Section Review

1. Sample answer: A reflex is an unconscious, immediate response to a stimulus. A feedback mechanism is a series of steps in which one step affects a previous step.

2. Sample answer: The retina converts light to electrical impulses. The cochlea converts sound to electrical impulses.

3. c

4. Sample answer: Light enters the eye and strikes the retina. Cells in the retina are triggered by light and produce electrical impulses that are sent to the brain, where they are interpreted as images you see.

5. Sample answer: The ear converts sound waves into electrical impulses. The brain interprets these impulses as sounds. Taste buds in the papillae respond to four basic tastes (sweetness, bitterness, sourness, and saltiness) and send messages to the brain, which produces a "flavor." Smell receptors on olfactory cells respond to chemicals in the air and send impulses to the brain, which interprets them as odors.

6. Sample answer: Cones in the retina, which produce impulses that are interpreted as colors, do not work as well in dim light.

7. Sample answer: Receptors for smell detect chemicals in air. Receptors for taste detect chemicals in your mouth. The chemicals trigger impulses that the brain interprets as smells or tastes. The brain combines information from the mouth and the nose to give you a sensation of flavor.

8. Sample answer: The brain receives information about body temperature. If body temperature is too high or too low, the brain tells the body to take steps to correct its temperature. The brain receives information about the adjustments. When body temperature is correct, the brain tells the body to stop what it was doing to raise or lower the temperature.

9. 0.90 m ÷ 150 m/s = 0.006 s; 0.90 m ÷ 0.2 m/s = 4.5 s

10. Sample answer: Reflexes are important becaus they protect us by acting faster than the body would act if the brain had to process information and send a message.

11. In bright light, cones trigger impulses that are interpreted as images that provide information about color, shape, and motion. At night, rods allow you to detect something in the dark, even if you can't tell much about its color or shape. Together, cones and rods give you information about your environment.

CHAPTER RESOURCES

Chapter Resource File

- Section Quiz **GENERAL**
- Section Review **GENERAL**
- Vocabulary and Section Summary **GENERAL**
- Reinforcement Worksheet **BASIC**
- Critical Thinking **ADVANCED**
- Datasheet for Quick Lab

SECTION
3

Focus

Overview

In this section, students will learn about the endocrine system and how endocrine glands control the body's slower, long-term processes via hormones. They will also learn the location and function of specific endocrine glands.

 Bellringer

Write the following on the board:

Unscramble the following words, and write them on a piece of paper:

nalgd	(gland)
meornoh	(hormone)
noclotr	(control)

Motivate

Discussion ——— GENERAL

Endocrine System Ask students to think of a time when they were suddenly frightened. Discuss with students how their pulse rate and breathing rate were different before and after being scared. (Both rates should be elevated during and after the scare.) Tell students that the endocrine system and the autonomic nervous system, acting together, are responsible for the changes that occurred in their pulse rate and breathing rate. **LS** Verbal

---

READING WARM-UP

Objectives

- Explain why the endocrine system is important to the body.
- Identify five glands of the endocrine system, and describe what their hormones do.
- Describe how feedback mechanisms stop and start hormone release.
- Name two hormone imbalances.

Terms to Learn

endocrine system
gland
hormone

READING STRATEGY

Discussion Read this section silently. Write down questions that you have about this section. Discuss your questions in a small group.

endocrine system a collection of glands and groups of cells that secrete hormones that regulate growth, development, and homeostasis

gland a group of cells that make special chemicals for the body

---

The Endocrine System

Have you ever heard of an epinephrine (EP uh NEPH rin) rush? You might have had one without realizing it. Exciting situations, such as riding a roller coaster or watching a scary movie, can cause your body to release epinephrine.

Epinephrine is a chemical messenger produced by the adrenal glands. Adrenal glands are part of a second body-control system, the endocrine system.

Glands and Hormones

The **endocrine system** is a collection of glands and groups of cells that secrete hormones. A **gland** is a group of cells that make special chemical messengers for your body. These chemical messengers are called hormones. A **hormone** is a chemical messenger made in one cell or tissue that causes a change in another cell or tissue in another part of the body. Endocrine system hormones regulate growth, development, and homeostasis. Hormones flow through the bloodstream to all parts of the body. Thus, an endocrine gland near your brain can control an organ—or many organs—somewhere else in your body.

In the situation shown in **Figure 1,** the adrenal glands release the hormone *epinephrine*. Epinephrine increases your heartbeat and breathing rate. This response is called the "fight-or-flight" response. When you are frightened, angry, or excited, the "fight-or-flight" response prepares you to fight the danger or to run from it.

Figure 1 *When you have to move quickly to avoid danger, your adrenal glands make more blood-glucose available for energy.*

CHAPTER RESOURCES

Chapter Resource File

- **Lesson Plan**
- **Directed Reading A** BASIC
- **Directed Reading B** SPECIAL NEEDS

Technology

Transparencies
- Bellringer

Is That a Fact!

Epinephrine occurs naturally in the human body, but it is also administered as a drug by doctors. It can be injected into the heart to help revive a person who has suffered a heart attack. Epinephrine is also sometimes used to dilate the bronchioles in the lungs of people who have asthma or who have severe allergic reactions, such as reactions to bee stings.

More Endocrine Glands

Your body has several other endocrine glands. Some of these glands have many functions. For example, your pituitary gland stimulates skeletal growth and helps the thyroid gland work properly. It also regulates the amount of water in the blood. And the pituitary gland stimulates the birth process in women.

Your thyroid gland is very important during infancy and childhood. Thyroid hormones control the secretion of growth hormones for normal body growth. Thyroid hormones also control the development of the central nervous system. And they control your metabolism. *Metabolism* is the sum of all the chemical processes that take place in an organism.

Your thymus gland is important to your immune system. Cells called *killer T cells* grow and mature in the thymus gland. These T cells help destroy or neutralize cells or substances that invade your body. The names and some of the functions of endocrine glands are shown in **Figure 2.**

✔ *Reading Check* Name two endocrine glands, and explain why they are important to your body. *(See the Appendix for answers to Reading Checks.)*

hormone a substance that is made in one cell or tissue and that causes a change in another cell or tissue in a different part of the body

CONNECTION TO Language Arts

WRITING SKILL **Working Together** Write a report analyzing how your nervous system and your endocrine system work together to provide for your needs. Especially, evaluate how these two systems work together to help regulate your internal environment. Illustrate your report.

Figure 2 Endocrine Glands and Their Functions

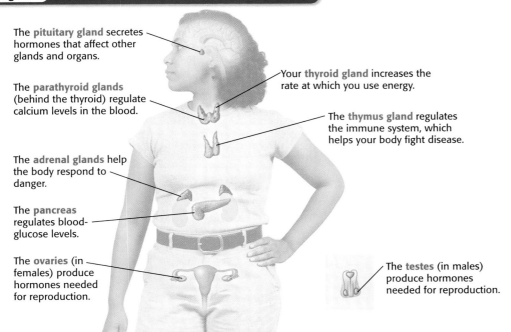

The **pituitary gland** secretes hormones that affect other glands and organs.

The **parathyroid glands** (behind the thyroid) regulate calcium levels in the blood.

The **adrenal glands** help the body respond to danger.

The **pancreas** regulates blood-glucose levels.

The **ovaries** (in females) produce hormones needed for reproduction.

Your **thyroid gland** increases the rate at which you use energy.

The **thymus gland** regulates the immune system, which helps your body fight disease.

The **testes** (in males) produce hormones needed for reproduction.

Is That a Fact!

Since the mid-1980s research at Rutgers University shows that some potent hormones produced in the last trimester of pregnancy prepare and motivate mothers to care for their young. The most important of these hormones is oxytocin. Oxytocin causes the uterus to contract, so oxytocin is in the mother's brain at the time the mother meets her newborn. Some scientists believe oxytocin helps the mother to bond with her new baby.

Fight-or-Flight Have students, working in pairs, tell each other about a time when they were frightened and to describe the physical responses they had. Make a list of all responses. Discuss with students how one hormone causes many of these changes. Ask students, "What is the purpose of all these changes?" (They all get the body ready to fight or run from danger.)
LS Interpersonal/Intrapersonal

Quiz ——— GENERAL

Ask students whether each of the statements below is true or false. Have students correct false statements.

1. Hormones are chemicals secreted into the bloodstream. (true)

2. All endocrine glands come in pairs. (false; Some endocrine glands, such as the pituitary, are not paired.)

3. Hormones are regulated by feedback mechanisms. (true)

Alternative Assessment ——— GENERAL

 Writing **New Hormone** Have students write a story about a new hormone that controls a function, such as the ability to tell jokes, not discussed in this lesson. Students should describe a feedback control of this hormone. LS Verbal

Controlling the Endocrine Glands

Do you remember the feedback mechanisms at work in the nervous system? Endocrine glands control similar feedback mechanisms. For example, the pancreas has specialized cells that make two different hormones, *insulin* and *glucagon*. As shown in **Figure 3,** these two hormones control the level of glucose in the blood. Insulin lowers blood-glucose levels by telling the liver to convert glucose into glycogen and to store glycogen for future use. Glucagon has the opposite effect. It tells the liver to convert glycogen into glucose and to release the glucose into the blood.

✓ **Reading Check** What does insulin do?

Figure 3 Blood-Glucose Feedback Control

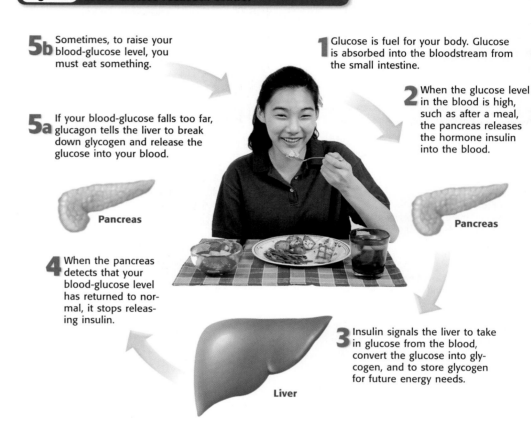

5b Sometimes, to raise your blood-glucose level, you must eat something.

5a If your blood-glucose falls too far, glucagon tells the liver to break down glycogen and release the glucose into your blood.

Pancreas

4 When the pancreas detects that your blood-glucose level has returned to normal, it stops releasing insulin.

1 Glucose is fuel for your body. Glucose is absorbed into the bloodstream from the small intestine.

2 When the glucose level in the blood is high, such as after a meal, the pancreas releases the hormone insulin into the blood.

Pancreas

3 Insulin signals the liver to take in glucose from the blood, convert the glucose into glycogen, and to store glycogen for future energy needs.

Liver

INCLUSION Strategies

• *Gifted and Talented* • *Hearing Impaired*
Some students benefit from exploring topics in greater depths. Ask students to divide a large piece of poster board in half. On one half, have them show a healthy pancreas with healthy insulin production and usage. On the other half, have them show a pancreas that could belong to a person with *diabetes mellitus.* English Language Learners
LS Visual

Answer to Reading Check
Insulin helps regulate the amount of glucose in the blood.

Hormone Imbalances

Occasionally, an endocrine gland makes too much or not enough of a hormone. For example, when a person's blood-glucose level rises, the pancreas secretes insulin. Insulin sends a message to the liver to convert glucose into glycogen. The liver stores glycogen for future use. But a person whose body does not use insulin properly or whose pancreas does not make enough insulin has a condition called *diabetes mellitus* (DIE uh BEET EEZ muh LIET uhs). A person who has diabetes may need daily injections of insulin to keep his or her blood-glucose levels within safe limits. Some patients, such as the woman in **Figure 4,** receive their insulin automatically from a small machine worn next to the body.

Another hormone imbalance is when a child's pituitary gland doesn't make enough growth hormone. As a result, the child's growth is stunted. Fortunately, if the problem is detected early, a doctor can prescribe growth hormone and monitor the child's growth. If the pituitary makes too much growth hormone, a child may grow taller than expected.

Figure 4 *This woman has diabetes and receives insulin from a device that monitors her blood-glucose level.*

Using Key Terms

1. Use the following terms in the same sentence: *endocrine system, glands,* and *hormone.*

Understanding Key Ideas

2. Identify five endocrine glands, and explain why their hormones are important to your body.

3. Hormone imbalances may cause
   a. feedback and insulin.
   b. diabetes and stunted growth.
   c. thyroid and pituitary.
   d. glucose and glycogen.

4. How do feedback mechanisms control hormone production?

Math Skills

5. One's bedtime blood-glucose level is normally 140 mg/dL. Ty's blood-glucose level is 189 mg/dL at bedtime. What percentage above 140 mg/dL is Ty's level?

Critical Thinking

6. **Making Inferences** Glucose is a source of energy. Epinephrine quickly increases the blood-glucose level. Why is epinephrine important in times of stress?

7. **Applying Concepts** The hormone glucagon is released when glucose levels fall below normal. Explain how the hormones glucagon and insulin work together to control blood-glucose levels.

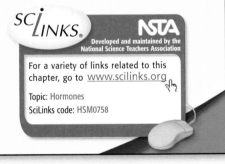

For a variety of links related to this chapter, go to www.scilinks.org

Topic: Hormones
SciLinks code: HSM0758

Homework — **GENERAL**

Researching Steroids Tell students that hormones are used as medicines to treat endocrine disorders. However, other hormones, such as anabolic steroids, are abused to increase athletic prowess. Have students research the effects and dangers of abusing anabolic steroids. Have them write a brief report or prepare an oral presentation to share their findings. **Verbal**

CHAPTER RESOURCES

Chapter Resource File

- Section Quiz **GENERAL**
- Section Review **GENERAL**
- Vocabulary and Section Summary **GENERAL**
- Reinforcement Worksheet **BASIC**

Skills Practice Lab

You've Gotta Lotta Nerve

You've Gotta Lotta Nerve

Teacher's Notes

Time Required

One 45-minute class period

Lab Ratings

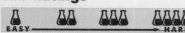

EASY ————————→ HARD

Teacher Prep 🧪
Student Set-Up 🧪
Concept Level 🧪🧪
Clean Up 🧪

MATERIALS

The materials listed on the student page are enough for a group of 3 students. If more appropriate for your class, substitute fine point ball point pens for the dissecting pins.

Safety Caution

Remind students to review all safety cautions and icons before beginning this lab activity. Remind students to be safe and gentle with each other in this exercise and to respect the sensitivity and comfort of their peers. Tell students that they will not be testing for pain. The protective cover on the sharp end of the dissecting pin must remain in place at all times.

OBJECTIVES

Locate areas on the skin that respond to certain stimuli.

Determine which areas on the skin are more sensitive to certain kinds of stimuli.

MATERIALS

- dissecting pin with a small piece of cork or a small rubber stopper covering the sharp end
- eyedropper, plastic
- paper, graphing
- pens or markers, washable, fine point
- ruler, metric
- tap water, hot
- water, very cold

SAFETY

Your skin has thousands of nerve receptors that detect sensations, such as temperature, pain, and pressure. Your brain is designed to filter out or ignore most of the input it receives from these skin receptors. If the brain did not filter input, simply wearing clothes would trigger so many responses that you couldn't function.

Some areas of the skin, such as the back of your hand, are more sensitive than others. In this activity, you will map the skin receptors for heat, cold, and pressure on the back of your hand.

Procedure

1. Form a group of three. One of you will volunteer the back of your hand for testing, one will do the testing, and the third will record the results.

2. Use a fine-point, washable marker or pen and a metric ruler to mark a 3 cm × 3 cm square on the back of one person's hand. Draw a grid within the area. Space the lines approximately 0.5 cm apart. You will have 36 squares in the grid when you are finished, as shown in the photograph below.

3. Mark off three 3 cm × 3 cm areas on a piece of graph paper. Make a grid in each area exactly as you did on the back of your partner's hand. Label one grid "Cold," another grid "Hot," and the third grid "Pressure."

Lab Notes

This activity works best if the student whose hand is being tested looks away or is loosely blindfolded while his or her hand is being tested. Often, students will say they feel something when they think they should feel something. Students should be given the choice of being blindfolded or looking away.

CHAPTER RESOURCES

Chapter Resource File
- Datasheet for Chapter Lab
- Lab Notes and Answers

Technology
- Classroom Videos
  - Lab Video

4 Use the eyedropper to apply one small droplet of cold water on each square in the grid on your partner's hand. Your partner should turn away while being tested. On your graph paper, mark an X on the "Cold" grid to show where your partner felt the cold droplet. Carefully blot the water off your partner's hand after several drops.

5 Repeat the test using hot-water droplets. The hot water should not be hot enough to hurt your partner. Mark an X on the "Hot" grid to indicate where your partner felt the hot droplet.

6 Repeat the test by using the head (not the point!) of the pin. Touch the skin to detect pressure receptors. Use a very light touch. On the graph paper, mark an X on the "Pressure" grid to indicate where your partner felt the pressure.

Analyze the Results

1 Organizing Data Count the number of Xs in each grid. How many heat receptor responses are there per 3 cm²? How many cold receptor responses are there? How many pressure receptor responses are there?

2 Explaining Events Do you have areas on the back of your hand where the receptors overlap? Explain your answer.

3 Recognizing Patterns How do you think the results of this experiment would be similar or different if you mapped an area of your forearm? of the back of your neck? of the palm of your hand?

Draw Conclusions

4 Interpreting Information Prepare a written report that includes a description of your investigation and a discussion of your answers to items 1–3. What conclusions can you draw from your results?

> #### Applying Your Data
> Use the library or the Internet to research what happens if a receptor is continuously stimulated. Does the kind of receptor make a difference? Does the intensity or strength of the stimulus make a difference? Explain your answers.

CLASSROOM TESTED & APPROVED

Christopher Wood
Western Rockingham Middle School
Madison, North Carolina

Disposal Information
Provide receptacles for used dissecting pins and eyedroppers. Be sure students know the location of the receptacles and deposit their sharp items in the designated containers. Dispose of sharp items properly to eliminate the risk of injury.

Analyze the Results

1. Answers may vary. Some groups will have more receptors in each category than others.

2. Students may notice that receptors in the same square on the grid can sense heat, cold, and pressure. Students may explain this reaction by noting that they have different kinds of receptors in the same spot. Students may also explain this by noting that the same receptor responds to more than one stimulus. Some students may interpret hot and cold as variations of a single sensation—temperature. They may also determine that the blunt head of the pin might have been cold and that they felt its temperature instead of the pressure.

3. Answers may vary. Different areas of the body are more sensitive than others.

Draw Conclusions

4. Answers may vary. Students should provide logical, well-reasoned conclusions that are supported by the details and results of the experiment. Students should discuss the answers to items 1–3.

Applying Your Data

Students will find that responses to a constant stimulus differ depending on the type and intensity of the stimulus. A person may become insensitive to an odor or even mild pain over time. Intense, sudden, or continued stimuli, such as heat, pain, or noise, may do much damage to a person over time.

Assignment Guide

SECTION	QUESTIONS
1	1–2, 6, 10–11, 13, 15, 18, 22
2	4, 7, 8, 16, 19–21
3	3, 5, 9, 12, 14, 17, 23–26

ANSWERS

Using Key Terms

1. central nervous system
2. retina
3. hormone
4. reflex
5. insulin
6. neuron

Understanding Key Ideas

7. c
8. a
9. d
10. a
11. d
12. d
13. Sample answer: The main difference is that the somatic nervous system controls voluntary movements and activities, and the autonomic nervous system controls body functions that you do not need to think about. Both systems are important because together they keep your body active and alive. You are able to do all of your voluntary activities while your body functions are controlled by the autonomic nervous system.

USING KEY TERMS

Complete each of the following sentences by choosing the correct term from the word bank.

insulin   axon
hormone   nerve
retina   central nervous
neuron   system
reflex

1 The two parts of your _____ are your brain and spinal cord.

2 Sensory receptors in the _____ detect light.

3 Epinephrine is a(n) _____ that triggers the fight-or-flight response.

4 A(n) _____ is an involuntary and almost immediate movement in response to a stimulus.

5 One hormone that helps to regulate blood-glucose levels is _____ .

6 A(n) _____ is a specialized cell that receives and conducts electrical impulses.

UNDERSTANDING KEY IDEAS

Multiple Choice

7 Which of the following has receptors for smelling?

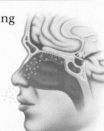

  a. cochlea cells
  b. thermoreceptors
  c. olfactory cells
  d. optic nerve

8 Which of the following allow you to see the world in color?

  a. cones
  b. rods
  c. lenses
  d. retinas

9 Which of the following glands makes insulin?

  a. adrenal gland
  b. pituitary gland
  c. thyroid gland
  d. pancreas

10 The peripheral nervous system does NOT include

  a. the spinal cord.
  b. axons.
  c. sensory receptors.
  d. motor neurons.

11 Which part of the brain regulates blood pressure?

  a. right cerebral hemisphere
  b. left cerebral hemisphere
  c. cerebellum
  d. medulla

12 The process in which the endocrine system, the digestive system, and the circulatory system control the level of blood glucose is an example of

  a. a reflex.
  b. an endocrine gland.
  c. the fight-or-flight response.
  d. a feedback mechanism.

14. Sample answer: The endocrine system is important because it produces chemical messengers called *hormones* that regulate body processes such as growth, fluid balance, and development.

15. Sample answer: The PNS receives stimuli from inside and outside the body and sends messages to the CNS. The CNS processes the messages and sends responses. The PNS carries the responses to the part of the body that will respond to a stimulus.

Short Answer

13 What is the difference between the somatic nervous system and the autonomic nervous system? Why are both systems important to the body?

14 Why is the endocrine system important to your body?

15 What is the relationship between the CNS and the PNS?

16 What is the function of the bones in the middle ear?

17 Describe two interactions between the endocrine system and the body that happen when a person is frightened.

CRITICAL THINKING

18 **Concept Mapping** Use the following terms to create a concept map: *nervous system, spinal cord, medulla, peripheral nervous system, brain, cerebrum, central nervous system,* and *cerebellum.*

19 **Making Comparisons** Compare a feedback mechanism with a reflex.

20 **Analyzing Ideas** Why is it important to have a lens that can change shape inside the eye?

21 **Applying Concepts** Why is it important that reflexes happen without thinking about them?

22 **Predicting Consequences** What would happen if your autonomic nervous system stopped working?

23 **Making Comparisons** How are the nervous system and the endocrine system similar? How are they different?

INTERPRETING GRAPHICS

Use the diagram below to answer the questions that follow.

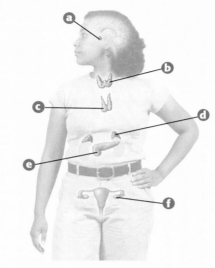

24 Which letter identifies the gland that regulates blood-glucose level?

25 Which letter identifies the gland that releases a hormone that stimulates the birth process?

26 Which letter identifies the gland that helps the body fight disease?

 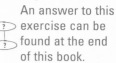
CHAPTER RESOURCES

Chapter Resource File

 • Chapter Review GENERAL
• Chapter Test A GENERAL
• Chapter Test B ADVANCED
• Chapter Test C SPECIAL NEEDS
• Vocabulary Activity GENERAL

Workbooks

 Study Guide
• Assessment resources are also available in Spanish.

Standardized Test Preparation

Teacher's Note

To provide practice under more realistic testing conditions, give students 20 minutes to answer all of the questions in this Standardized Test Preparation.

MISCONCEPTION ALERT

Answers to the standardized test preparation can help you identify student misconceptions and misunderstandings.

READING

Passage 1

1. B
2. H
3. D

TEST DOCTOR

Question 1: The correct answer, B, is not explicitly stated in the passage. Students must read the passage to find out that a synapse is the gap between an axon and another cell. Students may select answer A if they confuse the neurotransmitters with the gap across which neurotransmitters work.

Question 3: Students may select incorrect answers A or C if they are not clear about what a synapse is. A synapse is not part of a cell; a synapse is a space between nerve cells. Impulses cannot just a synapse; they are transmitted by neurotransmitters.

READING

Read each of the passages below. Then, answer the questions that follow each passage.

Passage 1 The axon terminals of neurons usually do not touch the other cells. There is a small gap between an axon terminal and another cell. This space where a neuron meets another cell is called a *synapse*. When a nerve impulse arrives at an axon terminal, the impulse cannot cross the gap. Instead, the impulse triggers the release of chemicals called *neurotransmitters*. These neurotransmitters cross the synapse between the axon terminal and the cell. When neurotransmitters reach the next cell, they signal the cell to react in a certain way. There are many kinds of neurotransmitters. Some neurotransmitters tell cells to start an action. Other neurotransmitters tell cells to stop an action.

1. What is the space between a neuron terminal and a receiving cell called?
   A a neurotransmitter
   B a synapse
   C an axon
   D a nerve

2. Why are neurotransmitters necessary?
   F They tell muscle cells to contract or relax.
   G They create a gap that axons must cross.
   H They carry messages across the synapse.
   I They release chemical signals called *impulses*.

3. Which of the following statements is a fact in the passage?
   A A synapse is an extension of a nerve cell.
   B The space between an axon terminal and another cell is filled with neurons.
   C Nerve impulses jump from an axon to another cell.
   D There are many kinds of neurotransmitters.

Passage 2 Hormones are chemical messengers released by cells that <u>regulate</u> other cells in the body. Hormones regulate many body processes. Hormones control growth, direct the production and use of energy, keep body temperature within normal limits, and direct responses to stimuli outside the body. Hormones carry chemical messages that tell cells to change their activities. For example, one hormone tells the heart to beat faster. Another hormone tells certain cells to make proteins and stimulates bone and muscle growth. Each hormone communicates with specific cells. Each hormone is like a key that opens only one kind of lock. A hormone's message can be received only by cells that have the right kind of lock. Hormones control many important body functions, so their messages must be delivered properly.

1. According to the passage, which of the following statements about hormones is true?
   A Hormones tell cells to change their activities.
   B Hormones are electrical messengers.
   C Hormones are like locks.
   D Hormones are not important to your body.

2. What does the word *regulate* mean?
   F to control or direct
   G to beat faster
   H to raise your temperature
   I to reverse

3. According to the passage, what are two ways that one particular hormone affects the body?
   A controls your temperature and heart rate
   B responds to stimuli and makes proteins
   C stimulates bone growth and makes proteins
   D coordinates energy production and use and decreases temperature

---

Passage 2

1. A
2. F
3. C

TEST DOCTOR

Question 2: This question asks students to determine the meaning of the word *regulate* from the context of the passage. Students may select incorrect answers G, H, or I if they confuse a specific type of command or regulation with the more general definition of the word.

Question 3: Students may select incorrect answers A, B, or D if they read only the general list of hormone effects. Only one sentence in the passage refers to a particular hormone that has two effects, so the correct answer is C.

The diagram below shows a typical neuron. Use the diagram below to answer the questions that follow.

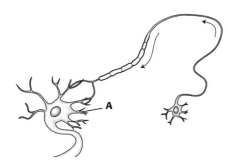

1. What does A represent?

   A a cell body   **C** a dendrite
   B an axon   **D** an axon terminal

2. Which of the following represents the path that an impulse in a neuron travels?

   F dendrite, cell body, axon, axon terminal
   G axon, axon terminal, cell body, dendrite
   H dendrite, nucleus, cell body, axon
   I nucleus, cell body, nucleus, axon

3. To where is an impulse that reaches an axon terminal transmitted?

   A another axon terminal
   B the brain
   C a reflex
   D dendrites of another neuron

4. What does having many dendrites allow a neuron to do?

   F to be locked into place in the body
   G to receive impulses from many other cells
   H to send impulses to surrounding cells
   I to get necessary nutrition

5. Which of the following statements about an axon is true?

   A An axon is part of a gland.
   B An axon connects the cell body to the axon terminal.
   C An axon detects sights and sounds.
   D An axon carries chemical messages.

MATH

Read each question below, and choose the best answer.

1. Sound travels about 335 m/s. How many kilometers would a sound travel in 1 min? (One kilometer is equal to 1,000 meters.)

   A 335,000 km
   B 20,100 km
   C 20.1 km
   D 0.335 km

2. Some axons send one impulse every 2.5 milliseconds. How many impulses could one of these axons send every second? (One second is equal to 1,000 milliseconds.)

   F 4 impulses
   G 40 impulses
   H 400 impulses
   I 4,000 impulses

3. The table below shows the results of Miguel's blood-glucose tests. Miguel ate lunch at 12:00 noon. His blood glucose was measured every hour after that time. What was the average hourly decrease in blood-glucose level?

Blood Glucose	
Time tested	Blood-glucose level (mg/1,000 mL)
1:00 P.M.	178
2:00 P.M.	112
3:00 P.M.	100
4:00 P.M.	89

   A approximately 160 mg/1,000 mL
   B approximately 120 mg/1,000 mL
   C approximately 30 mg/1,000 mL
   D approximately 22 mg/1,000 mL

4. Your brain has about 1 billion neurons. How is 1 billion expressed in scientific notation?

   F 1×10^3
   G 1×10^6
   H 1×10^9
   I 1×10^{12}

Standardized Test Preparation

1. C
2. F
3. D
4. G
5. B

✚ TEST DOCTOR

Question 3: Answer D is correct because when an impulse reaches an axon terminal, it is carried across the synapse by neurotransmitters to the dendrites of another neuron. Students may select incorrect answer A if they forget the difference between a dendrite and an axon terminal.

Question 5: Answer B is correct because an axon is the part of the nerve cell that runs from the nerve cell body and ends in an axon terminal. Students may select incorrect answer D if they confuse the chemical messages carried across a synapse by neurotransmitters with the electrical impulses carried by axons.

MATH

1. C
2. H
3. C
4. H

✚ TEST DOCTOR

Question 1: Students may select incorrect answers A or D if they simply multiply or divide 335 by 1,000. They will have neglected to include the factor of 60 s/min. Students may select incorrect answer B if they forget to convert meters to kilometers.

Question 4: Students may select incorrect answers F, G, or I if they count the wrong number of decimal places when figuring the exponent.

CHAPTER RESOURCES

Chapter Resource File

📁 • Standardized Test Preparation **GENERAL**

Workbooks

📘 **North Carolina Standardized Test Preparation**
• Provides practice for the EOG test.

State Resources

🗺️ For specific resources for your state, visit **go.hrw.com** and type in the keyword **HSMSTR**.

Scientific Discoveries

Discussion ——— GENERAL

Encourage a class discussion on the placebo effect by asking students the following questions:

- Do you think other therapies, such as acupuncture, homeopathy, or chiropractic care could act as placebos? (Answers may vary.)

- Do you think it would ever be ethical for a doctor to give a patient a placebo? (Answers may vary.)

- Do you think a person could become addicted to a placebo? (Answers may vary.)

Science, Technology, and Society

Discussion ——— GENERAL

If a disabled person could be hooked up to a computer, then so could anyone. Discuss the possibilities of having computers directly connected to the human brain. Ask students the following questions: What are some things that computers can do that humans can't? (Answers may vary.) What are some of the possibilities for memory, information retrieval, and new sorts of senses? (Answers may vary.) What can humans do that computers can't? (Answers may vary.)

Science in Action

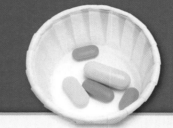

Scientific Discoveries

The Placebo Effect

A placebo (pluh SEE boh) is an inactive substance, such as a sugar pill, used in experimental drug trials. Some of the people who are test subjects are given a placebo as if it were the drug being tested. Usually, neither the doctor conducting the trial nor the test subjects know whether a person is taking a placebo or the test drug. In theory, any change in a subject's condition should be the result of the test drug. But for many years, scientists have known about the *placebo effect,* the effect of feeling better after taking the placebo pill. What makes someone who takes the placebo feel better? By studying brain activity, scientists are beginning to understand the placebo effect.

Science, Technology, and Society

Robotic Limbs

Cyborgs, or people that are part human and part robot, have been part of science fiction for many years and usually have super-human strength and X-ray vision. Meanwhile there are ordinary people on Earth who have lost the use of their arms and legs and could use some robot power. However, until recently, they have had to settle for clumsy mechanical limbs that were not a very good substitute for a real arm or hand. Today, thanks to advances in technology, scientists are developing artificial limbs—and eyes and ears—that can be wired directly into the nervous system and can be controlled by the brain. In the near future, artificial limbs and some artificial organs will be much more like the real thing.

Social Studies

Research the differences and similarities between ancient Chinese medical practices and traditional Western medical treatment. Both types of treatment rely in part on a patient's mental and emotional response to treatment. How might the placebo effect be part of both medical traditions? Create a poster showing the results of your research.

Language Arts ACTIVITY

WRITING SKILL At the library or on the Internet, find examples of optical or visual illusions. Research how the brain processes visual information and how the brain "sees" and interprets these illusions. Write a report about why the brain seems to be fooled by visual tricks. How can understanding the brain's response to illusions help scientists create artificial vision?

Answer to Social Studies Activity

Students' posters may include a variety of ancient medical practices, including acupuncture, acupressure, and herbal medicines. The student should indicate that, in addition to the physical effect of the treatment, any medical treatment always includes a mental or emotional component that may be strengthened or weakened by the treatment being employed.

Answer to Language Arts Activity

Current brain research is still trying to find the answers to why the brain is fooled by optical or visual illusions. Students may find information in a variety of places, including science magazines such as *Scientific American* and a number of Internet Web sites.

People in Science

Bertha Madras

Studying Brain Activity The brain is an amazing organ. Sometimes, though, drugs or disease keep the brain from working properly. Bertha Madras is a biochemist who studies drug addiction. Dr. Madras studies brain activity to see how substances, such as cocaine, target cells or areas in the brain. Using a variety of brain scanning techniques, Dr. Madras can observe a brain on drugs. She can see how a drug affects the normal activity of the brain. During her research, Dr. Madras realized that some of her results could be applied to Parkinson's disease and to attention deficit hyperactivity disorder (ADHD) in adults. Her research has led to new treatments for both problems.

Math ACTIVITY

Using a search engine on a computer connected to the Internet, search the Internet for "reaction time experiment." Go to one of the Web sites and take the response-time experiment. Record the time that it took you to respond. Repeat the test nine more times, and record your response time for each trial. Then, make a line graph or a bar graph of your response times. Did your response times change? In what way did they change?

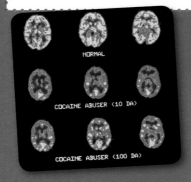

NORMAL

COCAINE ABUSER (10 DA)

COCAINE ABUSER (100 DA)

go.hrw.com

To learn more about these Science in Action topics, visit go.hrw.com and type in the keyword **HL5BD4F**.

Current Science

Check out Current Science® articles related to this chapter by visiting go.hrw.com. Just type in the keyword **HL5CS25**.

People in Science

Background

Bertha Madras, Ph.D., is a Professor of Psychobiology in the Department of Psychiatry at Harvard Medical School. She also serves as Chair of the Division of Neurochemistry at the New England Regional Primate Research Center (part of Harvard Medical School).

Madras has published more than 100 articles and served on a number of committees dedicated to brain and drug research. Madras also volunteers her time as a science teacher and regularly speaks to groups about the impact of drugs on the brain. To help people understand how drugs affect the brain, Madras has developed an exhibit and a CD-ROM called "Changing Your Mind: Drugs in the Brain."

Answer to Math Activity

Students will find several response-time experiments on the Internet. Students may find that their response times improved as they repeated the experiment, perhaps indicating that they were improving their ability to anticipate the cue and to respond to it. Other students may find that their response times declined as they played, indicating that their brains and muscles had become fatigued. Students' graphs should indicate what kind of experiment they took and should reflect their response times.

Reproduction and Development
Chapter Planning Guide

Compression guide:
To shorten instruction because of time limitations, omit the Chapter Lab.

OBJECTIVES	LABS, DEMONSTRATIONS, AND ACTIVITIES	TECHNOLOGY RESOURCES
PACING • 90 min pp. 252–257 **Chapter Opener**	SE **Start-up Activity,** p. 253 ◆ GENERAL	OSP **Parent Letter** GENERAL CD **Student Edition on CD-ROM** CD **Guided Reading Audio CD** TR **Chapter Starter Transparency*** VID **Brain Food Video Quiz**
Section 1 Animal Reproduction • Distinguish between asexual and sexual reproduction. • Explain the difference between external and internal fertilization. • Identify the three different types of mammalian reproduction.	TE **Activity** Asexual or Sexual Reproduction?, p. 255 BASIC TE **Demonstration** The Amazing Egg, p. 255 ◆ GENERAL TE **Connection Activity** Chemistry, p. 255 ADVANCED SE **Science in Action** Math, Social Studies, and Language Arts Activities, pp. 274–275 ◆ GENERAL	CRF **Lesson Plans*** TR **Bellringer Transparency*** TE **Internet Activity,** p. 257 GENERAL
PACING • 45 min pp. 258–261 **Section 2 Human Reproduction** • Identify the structures and functions of the male and female reproductive systems. • Describe two reproductive system problems.	TE **Connection Activity** Language Arts, p. 259 GENERAL SE **School-to-Home Activity** Twins and More, p. 260 GENERAL TE **Group Activity** Reproductive System Cancer, p. 260 GENERAL SE **Connection to Social Studies** Understanding STDs, p. 261 GENERAL TE **Connection Activity** Language Arts, p. 260 ADVANCED	CRF **Lesson Plans*** TR **Bellringer Transparency*** TR **The Male Reproductive System*** TR **The Female Reproductive System***
PACING • 90 min pp. 262–267 **Section 3 Growth and Development** • Summarize the processes of fertilization and implantation. • Describe the development of the embryo and the fetus. • Identify the stages of human development from birth to death.	SE **School-to-Home Activity** Growing Up, p. 263 GENERAL TE **Activity** Making Models, p. 263 ◆ GENERAL SE **Connection to Social Studies** Nourishing the Fetus, p. 264 GENERAL TE **Connection Activity** Language Arts, p. 265 GENERAL TE **Connection Activity** Earth Science, p. 265 GENERAL SE **Quick Lab** Life Grows On, p. 266 GENERAL CRF **Datasheet for Quick Lab*** SE **Skills Practice Lab** It's a Comfy, Safe World!, p. 268 ◆ GENERAL CRF **Datasheet for Chapter Lab*** SE **Skills Practice Lab** My, How You've Grown!, p. 598 ◆ GENERAL CRF **Datasheet for LabBook*** LB **Long-Term Projects & Research Ideas** Get a Whiff of This!* ◆ ADVANCED	CRF **Lesson Plans*** TR **Bellringer Transparency*** TR Stages of Human Development* TR **LINK TO PHYSICAL SCIENCE** How Sonar Works* CRF **SciLinks Activity*** GENERAL VID **Lab Videos for Life Science**

PACING • 90 min

CHAPTER REVIEW, ASSESSMENT, AND STANDARDIZED TEST PREPARATION

CRF **Vocabulary Activity*** GENERAL
SE **Chapter Review,** pp. 270–271 GENERAL
CRF **Chapter Review*** ▪ GENERAL
CRF **Chapter Tests A*** ▪ GENERAL, **B*** ADVANCED, **C*** SPECIAL NEEDS
SE **Standardized Test Preparation,** pp. 272–273 GENERAL
CRF **Standardized Test Preparation*** GENERAL
CRF **Performance-Based Assessment*** GENERAL
OSP **Test Generator** GENERAL
CRF **Test Item Listing*** GENERAL

Online and Technology Resources

Visit **go.hrw.com** for a variety of free resources related to this textbook. Enter the keyword **HT5R7BD5**.

Students can access interactive problem-solving help and active visual concept development with the *Holt Science and Technology* Online Edition available at **www.hrw.com**.

 Guided Reading Audio CD

These CDs are designed to help auditory learners and reluctant readers.

 Science Tutor CD-ROM

Excellent for remediation and test practice.

SKILLS DEVELOPMENT RESOURCES	SECTION REVIEW AND ASSESSMENT	STANDARDS CORRELATIONS
SE Pre-Reading Activity, p. 252 GENERAL **OSP** Science Puzzlers, Twisters & Teasers GENERAL		North Carolina Standard Course of Study
CRF Directed Reading A* BASIC, B* SPECIAL NEEDS **CRF** Vocabulary and Section Summary* GENERAL **SE** Reading Strategy Prediction Guide, p. 254 GENERAL **SE** Connection to Language Arts Nature or Nurture, p. 255 GENERAL **TE** Inclusion Strategies, p. 256 GENERAL **SS** Science Skills Organizing Your Research BASIC	**TE** Homework, p. 254 GENERAL **SE** Reading Checks, pp. 255, 256, 257 GENERAL **TE** Reteaching, p. 256 BASIC **TE** Quiz, p. 256 GENERAL **TE** Alternative Assessment, p. 256 GENERAL **TE** Homework, p. 256 GENERAL **SE** Section Review,* p. 257 ■ GENERAL **CRF** Section Quiz* ■ GENERAL	5.01, 5.02
CRF Directed Reading A* BASIC, B* SPECIAL NEEDS **CRF** Vocabulary and Section Summary* GENERAL **SE** Reading Strategy Reading Organizer, p. 258 GENERAL **SE** Math Practice Counting Eggs, p. 259 GENERAL **TE** Reading Strategy Activity, p. 259 GENERAL **MS** Math Skills for Science Multiplying Whole Numbers* GENERAL **MS** Math Skills for Science Dividing Whole Numbers with Long Division* GENERAL **MS** Math Skills for Science Parts of 100: Calculating Percentages* GENERAL	**SE** Reading Checks, pp. 258, 260 GENERAL **TE** Reteaching, p. 260 BASIC **TE** Quiz, p. 260 GENERAL **TE** Alternative Assessment, p. 260 GENERAL **SE** Section Review,* p. 261 ■ GENERAL **CRF** Section Quiz* ■ GENERAL	4.01, 4.02
CRF Directed Reading A* BASIC, B* SPECIAL NEEDS **CRF** Vocabulary and Section Summary* GENERAL **SE** Reading Strategy Discussion, p. 262 GENERAL **TE** Reading Strategy Answering Questions, p. 263 GENERAL **TE** Inclusion Strategies, p. 263 GENERAL **TE** Connection to Math Factor of Increase, p. 264 GENERAL **CRF** Reinforcement Worksheet The Beginning of a Life* GENERAL **CRF** Critical Thinking One to Grow On!* ADVANCED	**SE** Reading Checks, pp. 262, 263, 264, 266 GENERAL **TE** Reteaching, p. 266 BASIC **TE** Quiz, p. 266 GENERAL **TE** Alternative Assessment, p. 266 ADVANCED **SE** Section Review,* p. 267 ■ GENERAL **CRF** Section Quiz* ■ GENERAL	1.08, 4.06, 4.07; *Chapter Lab:* 1.02, 1.07, 1.09

One-Stop Planner® CD-ROM

This convenient CD-ROM includes:
- **Lab Materials QuickList Software**
- **Holt Calendar Planner**
- **Customizable Lesson Plans**
- **Printable Worksheets**
- **ExamView® Test Generator**

cnnstudentnews.com

Find the latest news, lesson plans, and activities related to important scientific events.

www.scilinks.org

Maintained by the **National Science Teachers Association.** See Chapter Enrichment pages for a complete list of topics.

Check out **Current Science** articles and activities by visiting the HRW Web site at **go.hrw.com.** Just type in the keyword **HL5CS26T.**

Classroom Videos

- **Lab Videos** demonstrate the chapter lab.
- **Brain Food Video Quizzes** help students review the chapter material.
- **CNN Videos** bring science into your students' daily life.

Visual Resources

CHAPTER STARTER TRANSPARENCY

Strange but True!

BELLRINGER TRANSPARENCIES

Section: Animal Reproduction
Do you know how birds, ants, humans, and sea stars reproduce? Write down any differences that you are aware of in how these animals reproduce. Also write down any differences that you know of in how these animals raise their young.

Write your answers in your **science journal.**

Section: Human Reproduction
You may have heard of *cloning* in recent news stories. Do you know what cloning is? If so, write out a definition for cloning. Would cloning be considered asexual or sexual reproduction? Do you think that cloning human beings could be considered as a kind of reproduction? Why or why not? Do you know of any organisms that naturally reproduce by cloning? If so, write out a few examples of these animals.

Record your answers in your **science journal.**

TEACHING TRANSPARENCIES

L93 — The Male Reproductive System

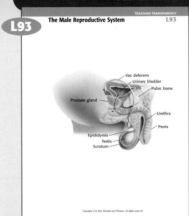

L94 — The Female Reproductive System

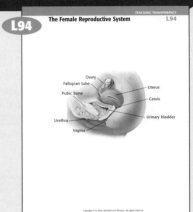

TEACHING TRANSPARENCIES

L95 — Stages of Human Development

P90 — How Sonar Works

A fish finder sends ultrasonic waves down into the water. The time it takes for the echo to return helps determine the location of the fish.

LINK TO PHYSICAL SCIENCE

Chapter: The Nature of Sound

CONCEPT MAPPING TRANSPARENCY

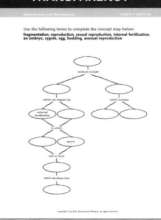

Use the following terms to complete the concept map below:
fragmentation, reproduction, sexual reproduction, internal fertilization, an embryo, zygote, egg, budding, asexual reproduction

Planning Resources

LESSON PLANS

Lesson Plan SAMPLE

Section: Waves

Pacing
Regular Schedule: with lab(s):2 days without lab(s):2 days
Block Schedule: with lab(s) 1 1/2 days without lab(s):1 day

Objectives
1. Relate the seven properties of life to a living organism.
2. Describe seven themes that can help you to organize what you learn about biology.
3. Identify the tiny structures that make up all living organisms.
4. Differentiate between reproduction and heredity and between metabolism and homeostasis.

National Science Education Standards Covered
LSInter6:Cells have particular structures that underlie their functions.
LSMat1:Most cell functions involve chemical reactions.
LSBeh1:Cells store and use information to guide their functions.
UCP1:Cell functions are regulated.
SI1: Cells can differentiate and form complete multicellular organisms.
PS1: Species evolve over time.
ESS1: The great diversity of organisms is the result of more than 3.5 billion years of evolution.
ESS2: Natural selection and its evolutionary consequences provide a scientific explanation for the fossil record of ancient life forms as well as for the striking molecular similarities observed among the diverse species of living organisms.
ST1: The millions of different species of plants, animals, and microorganisms that live on Earth today are related by descent from common ancestors.
ST2: The energy for life primarily comes from the sun.
SPSP1: The complexity and organization of organisms accommodates the need for obtaining, transforming, transporting, releasing, and eliminating the matter and energy used to sustain the organism.
SPSP6: As matter and energy flows through different levels of organization of living systems—cells, organs, communities—and between living systems and the physical environment, chemical elements are recombined in different ways.
HNS1: Organisms have behavioral responses to internal changes and to external stimuli.

PARENT LETTER

SAMPLE

Dear Parent,

Your son's or daughter's science class will soon begin exploring the chapter entitled "The World of Physical Science." In this chapter, students will learn about how the scientific method applies to the world of physical science and the role of physical science in the world. By the end of the chapter, students should demonstrate a clear understanding of the chapter's main ideas and be able to discuss the following topics:

1. physical science as the study of energy and matter (Section 1)
2. the role of physical science in the world around them (Section 1)
3. careers that rely on physical science (Section 1)
4. the steps used in the scientific method (Section 2)
5. examples of technology (Section 2)
6. how the scientific method is used to answer questions and solve problems (Section 2)
7. how our knowledge of science changes over time (Section 2)
8. how models represent real objects or systems (Section 3)
9. examples of different ways models are used in science (Section 3)
10. the importance of the International System of Units (Section 4)
11. the appropriate units to use for particular measurements (Section 4)
12. how area and density are derived quantities (Section 4)

Questions to Ask Along the Way

You can help your son or daughter learn about these topics by asking interesting questions such as the following:

• What are some surprising careers that use physical science?
• What is a characteristic of a good hypothesis?
• When is it a good idea to use a model?
• Why do Americans measure things in terms of inches and yards instead of centimeters and meters ?

TEST ITEM LISTING

TEST ITEM LISTING
The World of Science SAMPLE

MULTIPLE CHOICE

1. A limitation of models is that
   a. they are large enough to see.
   b. they do not act exactly like the things that they model.
   c. they are smaller than the things that they model.
   d. they model unfamiliar things.
   Answer: B   Difficulty: 1   Section: 3   Objective: 2

2. The length 10 m is equal to
   a. 100 cm.   c. 10,000 mm.
   b. 1,000 cm.   d. Both (b) and (c)
   Answer: B   Difficulty: 1   Section: 3   Objective: 2

3. To be valid, a hypothesis must be
   a. testable.   c. made into a law.
   b. supported by evidence.   d. Both (a) and (b)
   Answer: B   Difficulty: 1   Section: 3   Objective: 2

4. The statement "Stella has a stain on her shirt" is an example of a(n)
   a. law.   c. observation.
   b. hypothesis.   d. prediction.
   Answer: B   Difficulty: 1   Section: 3   Objective: 2

5. A hypothesis is often developed out of
   a. observations.   c. laws.
   b. experiments.   d. Both (a) and (b)
   Answer: B   Difficulty: 1   Section: 3   Objective: 2

6. How many milliliters are in 3.5 kL?
   a. 3,500 mL   c. 3,500, 000 mL
   b. 0.035 mL   d. 35,000 mL
   Answer: B   Difficulty: 1   Section: 3   Objective: 2

7. A map of Seattle is an example of a
   a. law.   c. model.
   b. theory.   d. unit.
   Answer: B   Difficulty: 1   Section: 3   Objective: 2

8. Jab has the safety icons shown below. These icons mean that you should wear
   a. only safety goggles.   c. safety goggles and a lab apron.
   b. only a lab apron.   d. safety goggles, a lab apron, and gloves.
   Answer: B   Difficulty: 1   Section: 3   Objective: 2

9. The law of conservation of mass says the tot al mass before a chemical change is
   a. more than the total mass after the change.
   b. less than the total mass after the change.
   c. the same as the total mass after the change.
   d. not the same as the total mass after the change.
   Answer: B   Difficulty: 1   Section: 3   Objective: 2

10. In which of the following areas might you find a geochemist at work?
   a. studying the chemistry of rocks   c. studying the atmosphere
   b. studying forestry   d. studying the atmosphere
   Answer: B   Difficulty: 1   Section: 3   Objective: 2

One-Stop Planner® CD-ROM

This CD-ROM includes all of the resources shown here and the following time-saving tools:

• *Lab Materials QuickList Software*

• *Customizable lesson plans*

• *Holt Calendar Planner*

• *The powerful ExamView® Test Generator*

Meeting Individual Needs

DIRECTED READING A
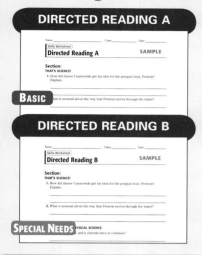
BASIC

DIRECTED READING B

SPECIAL NEEDS

VOCABULARY ACTIVITY

GENERAL

VOCABULARY AND SECTION SUMMARY

GENERAL

REINFORCEMENT
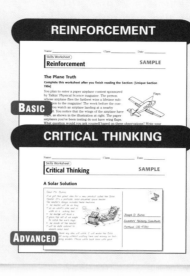
BASIC

CRITICAL THINKING

ADVANCED

SCILINKS ACTIVITY

GENERAL

SCIENCE PUZZLERS, TWISTERS & TEASERS
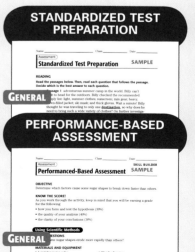
GENERAL

Labs and Activities

LONG-TERM PROJECTS & RESEARCH IDEAS
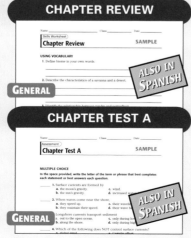
ADVANCED

DATASHEETS FOR QUICK LABS

DATASHEETS FOR CHAPTER LABS

DATASHEETS FOR LABBOOK
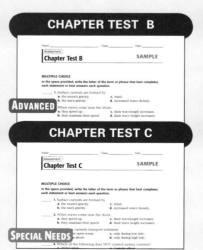

Review and Assessments

SECTION QUIZ
GENERAL — ALSO IN SPANISH

SECTION REVIEW
GENERAL — ALSO IN SPANISH

CHAPTER REVIEW
GENERAL — ALSO IN SPANISH

CHAPTER TEST A
GENERAL — ALSO IN SPANISH

CHAPTER TEST B
ADVANCED

CHAPTER TEST C
SPECIAL NEEDS

STANDARDIZED TEST PREPARATION
GENERAL

PERFORMANCE-BASED ASSESSMENT
GENERAL

This Chapter Enrichment provides relevant and interesting information to expand and enhance your presentation of the chapter material.

Section 1

Animal Reproduction

Asexual Reproduction

- The most common forms of asexual reproduction are binary fission, budding, and fragmentation. Binary fission is used mainly by bacteria.

- A major advantage of asexual reproduction is that it does not require a mate. Asexual reproduction also allows animals to produce many offspring in a short period of time. Many animals that do not move around, such as sea sponges, reproduce asexually.

Sexual Reproduction

- Because sexual reproduction brings together genetic material from two parents, there is greater variation among animals that reproduce sexually versus those that reproduce asexually.

Fertilization

- In external fertilization, eggs can be fertilized without physical contact between the parents. Instead, chemical signals coordinate the fertilization process, ensuring that the parents release their sex cells at the appropriate time.

- Internal fertilization requires a more sophisticated reproductive system, including organs for delivering and storing sperm. Fertilized eggs can develop externally, as with birds, or internally, as with placental mammals. Internally protected embryos are more likely to survive, but placental females do not usually produce as many offspring as do egg-laying females.

Is That a Fact!

- ◆ Some animal species that reproduce sexually don't have separate sexes. Instead, every individual contains male and female sexual characteristics. This situation is known as *hermaphrodism*. Hermaphrodites, such as earthworms, usually exchange sex cells with one another. Some hermaphrodites can reproduce by themselves as well.

Section 2

Human Reproduction

The Male Reproductive System

- Male reproductive functions mainly concern sperm production. The head of a sperm contains DNA, and the tail region contains mitochondria. The mitochondria are "engines" for the sperm, providing the sperm's tail with the energy to whip back and forth.

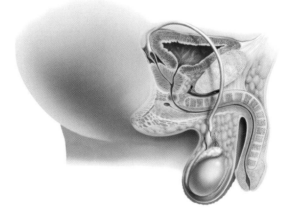

- The process of maturation of sperm from germ cells to spermatozoa takes about 74 days. Even then, they cannot yet penetrate an ovum. First they must "ripen" in the epididymis, a process that takes about 10 days. Though the maturation process is lengthy, once sperm are fully mature, they can remain viable for about 6 weeks.

Is That a Fact!

- ◆ If the seminiferous tubules—the bundle of tubes that makes up each testicle—were joined together and extended, they would be more than 200 m long!

The Female Reproductive System

- The ovaries are the primary female reproductive organs. About the size of large almonds, the ovaries are located on either side of the uterus, each anchored by an ovarian ligament. These tiny organs secrete the hormones largely responsible for development during puberty. They are also responsible for releasing eggs.

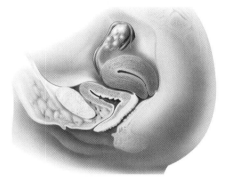

- Every menstrual cycle, several ova begin to ripen. In most cases, however, only one egg reaches maturity at a time. This mature, ripened ovum, encased in a Graafian follicle, travels to the surface of the ovary, where it remains until midcycle, when ovulation occurs. Then, the Graafian follicle, distended with fluid, ruptures, sending the egg into the abdominal cavity. The fallopian tube then captures the ovum, and the ovum begins its descent to the uterus.

Sexually Transmitted Diseases

- Chlamydia is the most prevalent bacterial sexually transmitted disease (STD) in North America. Caused by an organism called *Chlamydia trachomatis,* its symptoms include a frequent desire to urinate, pain with urination, and penile or vaginal discharge. In women, there are often few symptoms in the early stages. Troublesome as the symptoms are, the consequences are worse: chlamydia is a major cause of infertility. If left untreated, it can cause *pelvic inflammatory disease* and, in women, the subsequent inability to conceive. In men, infection that reaches the testes results in infertility.

- Also known as *salpingitis,* pelvic inflammatory disease (PID) is an infection of the fallopian tubes, uterus, and cervix. While a number of bacteria can cause PID, the usual culprits are chlamydia and gonorrhea. Although these infections can be completely cured with antibiotics, PID often leaves the fallopian tubes—the conduits between the ovaries and the uterus—scarred, making conception difficult or impossible. Other potential consequences of PID include ectopic pregnancy, peritonitis, and death.

Section 3

Growth and Development

Sex Determination

- One pair of human chromosomes determines the sex of a baby. There are two types of these sex chromosomes: X and Y. Because the egg contains only the X chromosome, the gender of the baby is determined by the father's sperm, which may contain either an X or a Y chromosome. If a sperm containing an X chromosome joins with an egg, the baby will be a girl. If a sperm containing a Y chromosome fertilizes the egg, the baby will be a boy.

Fetal Development

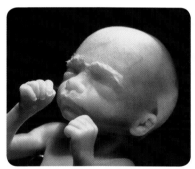

- The development of a baby from a single cell progresses at an astounding rate. Early in development, the embryo resembles a tiny tadpole, with a rounded body and tail. About 4 weeks after fertilization (the 6th week of pregnancy), however, limb buds—with knee and elbow joints evident—form, and facial features are recognizable. By the ninth week, nerves and muscles have developed enough that the fetus can move independently. By 12 weeks, the fetus is about 7.6 cm long and has a mass of about 28 g.

SciLINKS.

Developed and maintained by the National Science Teachers Association

SciLinks is maintained by the National Science Teachers Association to provide you and your students with interesting, up-to-date links that will enrich your classroom presentation of the chapter.

Visit www.scilinks.org and enter the SciLinks code for more information about the topic listed.

Topic: Animal Reproduction
SciLinks code: HSM0075

Topic: Before Birth
SciLinks code: HSM0140

Topic: Reproduction
SciLinks code: HSM1293

Topic: Growth and Development
SciLinks code: HSM0700

Topic: Reproductive System Irregularities and Disorders
SciLinks code: HSM1298

Overview

Tell students that this chapter will help them learn about how animals, including people, reproduce. The chapter describes asexual and sexual reproduction in animals. The chapter also describes human reproduction and development.

Assessing Prior Knowledge

Students should be familiar with the following topics:

• cells and cellular activities

• mammals

• human body organization and structure

Identifying Misconceptions

Students may have some confusion about forms of reproduction that do not involve "mating," such as asexual reproduction or external fertilization. Students may also be confused that offspring inherit traits from both parents equally. Girls may believe they get more of their traits from their mother, and boys may believe they share more with their father. Students may or may not be familiar with the words *gene* and *chromosome*. Very few students have a good grasp of the chemical basis for inheritance.

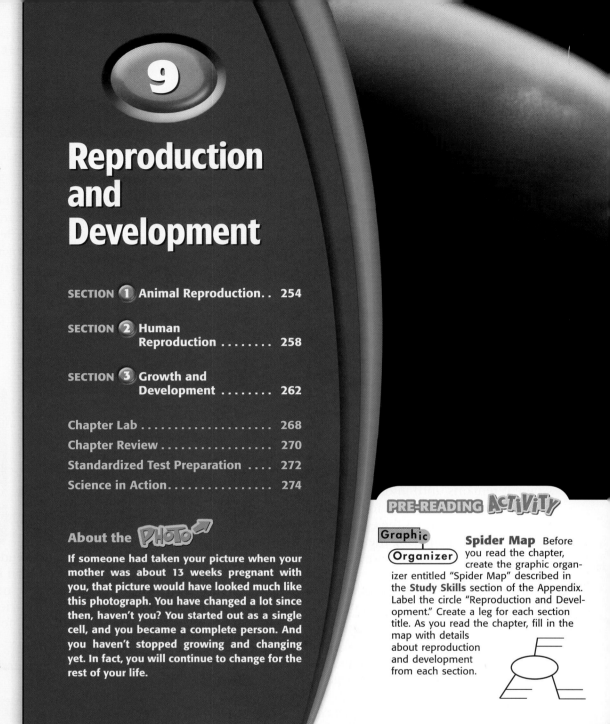

Reproduction and Development

About the PHOTO

If someone had taken your picture when your mother was about 13 weeks pregnant with you, that picture would have looked much like this photograph. You have changed a lot since then, haven't you? You started out as a single cell, and you became a complete person. And you haven't stopped growing and changing yet. In fact, you will continue to change for the rest of your life.

PRE-READING ACTIVITY

Graphic Organizer

Spider Map Before you read the chapter, create the graphic organizer entitled "Spider Map" described in the **Study Skills** section of the Appendix. Label the circle "Reproduction and Development." Create a leg for each section title. As you read the chapter, fill in the map with details about reproduction and development from each section.

Standards Correlations

North Carolina Standard Course of Study

1.02 (partial) Develop appropriate experimental procedures for: Given questions . . . (Chapter Lab)

1.07 (partial) Prepare models and/or computer simulations to: Test hypotheses . . . (Chapter Lab)

1.08 (partial) Use oral and written language to: Communicate findings . . . (Section 3)

1.09 Use technologies and information systems to: Research [and] Gather and analyze data. (Chapter Lab)

4.01 (partial) Analyze how human body systems interact to provide for the needs of the human organism: . . . Reproductive . . . (Section 2)

4.02 Describe how systems within the human body are defined by the functions it performs. (Section 2)

4.06 Describe growth and development of the human organism. (Section 3)

4.07 Explain the effects of environmental influences on human embryo development and human health including: Smoking, Alcohol, Drugs, [and] Diet. (Section 3)

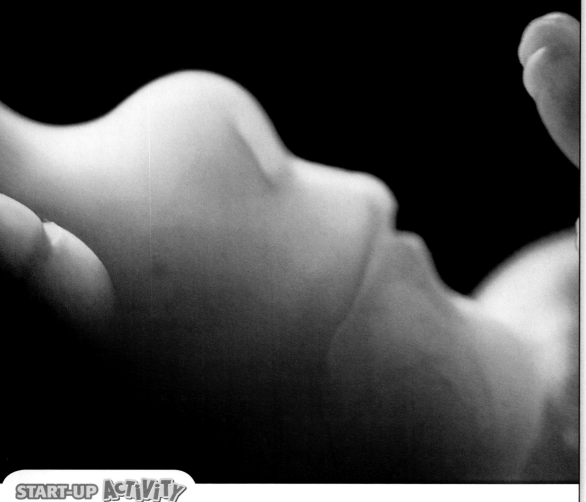

Teacher's Notes: Instructions for taking measurements (demonstrate these techniques for your students): Measure head height by standing next to the board with one ear against it. On the board, mark the top of the head and the bottom of the chin. Measure the distance between the marks. Find the total body height by measuring the distance from the top-of-the-head mark to the ground. Leg length should be measured from the hip where the leg bends when you sit down. Hold a meterstick parallel to the floor at your hips. Have someone then use the tape measure to measure the distance from the meterstick to the floor. Prior to class, write the measurements of at least three adults, such as yourself and two other teachers, on the board.

Answer

1. The student's head height will probably be a greater proportion of his or her overall height than the adults' head height. The student's leg length should be about 50% of his or her overall height, which should match the leg-length proportion of adults.

START-UP ACTIVITY

How Grows It?

As you read this paragraph, you are slowly aging. Your body is growing into the body of an adult. But does your body have the same proportions that an adult's body has? Complete this activity to find out.

Procedure

1. Have a classmate use a **tape measure** and **meterstick** to measure your total height, head height, and leg length. Your teacher will tell you how to take these measurements.

2. Use the following equations to calculate your head height–to–total body height proportion and your leg length–to–total body height proportion.

$$\frac{\text{head}}{\text{proportion}} = \frac{\text{head height}}{\text{body height}} \times 100$$

$$\frac{\text{leg}}{\text{proportion}} = \frac{\text{leg length}}{\text{body height}} \times 100$$

3. Your teacher will give you the head, body, and leg measurements of three adults. Calculate the head-body and leg-body proportions of each of the three adults. Record all of the measurements and calculations.

Analysis

1. Compare your proportions with the proportions of the three adults.

5.01 (partial) Explain the significance of genes to inherited characteristics: Genes are the units of information [and] Parents transmit genes to their offspring . . . (Section 1)

5.02 Explain the significance of reproduction: Sorting and recombination of parents' genetic material . . . (Section 1)

Strange but True!

A tiny animal is resting peacefully in a warm, dark space. Suddenly it finds itself driven out into the cold and light. The chilly temperature is almost unbearable for its hairless body. The glaring light is disorienting to its blurry vision. Driven by instinct, the animal starts crawling up and up to the promise of warmth and security. If it slips and falls to the ground, it will die. Almost 30 minutes pass before it reaches its destination—a pouch in its mother's abdomen. Inside the pouch, it finds a nipple that will supply milk for several months as the animal grows and develops.

Can you guess what animal has just been born? That's right, a baby kangaroo, called a joey. Joeys are born in a very early stage of development. They continue to develop inside their mother's pouch until they are able to eat solid food such as grasses and other plants.

Like all living things, kangaroos eventually grow old and die. They must reproduce to pass on their genetic heritage. There are many ways of reproducing, as you will discover in this chapter. But reproduction is only part of the story. Development, or the way organisms grow, is also an important part of the cycle of life.

Chapter Starter Transparency
Use this transparency to help students begin thinking about reproduction and human growth and development.

CHAPTER RESOURCES

Technology

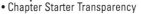
Transparencies
• Chapter Starter Transparency

READING SKILLS

Student Edition on CD-ROM

Guided Reading Audio CD

Classroom Videos
• Brain Food Video Quiz

Workbooks

Science Puzzlers, Twisters & Teasers
• Reproduction and Development GENERAL

Focus

Overview

In this section, students learn about asexual and sexual reproduction. Students also learn about internal and external fertilization. Finally, students learn about differences in mammalian reproduction.

🔊 Bellringer

Write the following list on the board:

a. bird   **c.** ants

b. human   **d.** sea stars

Ask students to write a paragraph explaining how they think reproduction differs between these four animals.

Motivate

Discussion ——— GENERAL

Reproduction If appropriate for your students, lead a discussion and ask students to think about the similarities and differences between the ways animals, such as the ones listed above, reproduce. Birds and ants lay eggs, but humans and sea stars don't. Females and males mate to reproduce in humans, ants, and birds, but not in sea stars. Help them understand that the end result of reproduction is the same for all animal species, but the means differ widely.
LS Verbal

READING WARM-UP

Objectives

- Distinguish between asexual and sexual reproduction.
- Explain the difference between external and internal fertilization.
- Identify the three different types of mammalian reproduction.

Terms to Learn

asexual reproduction
sexual reproduction
egg
sperm
external fertilization
internal fertilization

READING STRATEGY

Prediction Guide Before reading this section, write the title of each heading in this section. Next, under each heading, write what you think you will learn.

asexual reproduction reproduction that does not involve the union of sex cells and in which a single parent produces offspring that are genetically identical to the parent

---

Animal Reproduction

The life span of some living things is short compared with ours. For example, a fruit fly lives only about 40 days. Other organisms live much longer than we do. Some bristlecone pine trees, for example, are nearly 5,000 years old.

But all living things eventually die. If a species is to survive, its members must reproduce.

Asexual Reproduction

Some animals, particularly simpler ones, reproduce asexually. In **asexual reproduction,** a single parent has offspring that are genetically identical to the parent.

One kind of asexual reproduction is called budding. *Budding* happens when a part of the parent organism pinches off and forms a new organism. The new organism separates from the parent and lives independently. The hydra, shown in **Figure 1,** reproduces by budding. The new hydra is genetically identical to its parent.

Fragmentation is a second kind of asexual reproduction. In *fragmentation,* parts of an organism break off and then develop into a new individual that is identical to the original one. Certain organisms, such as flatworms called *planaria,* reproduce by fragmentation. A third type of asexual reproduction, similar to fragmentation, is *regeneration.* When an organism capable of regeneration, such as the sea star in **Figure 2,** loses a body part, that part may develop into an entirely new organism.

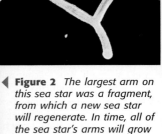

Figure 1 *The hydra bud will separate from its parent. Buds from other organisms, such as certain corals, remain attached to the parent.*

Figure 2 *The largest arm on this sea star was a fragment, from which a new sea star will regenerate. In time, all of the sea star's arms will grow to the same size.*

CHAPTER RESOURCES

Chapter Resource File

- 📘 • Lesson Plan
  - • Directed Reading A **BASIC**
  - • Directed Reading B **SPECIAL NEEDS**

Technology

- 💾 **Transparencies**
  - • Bellringer

Workbooks

- 📙 **Science Skills**
  - • Organizing Your Research **BASIC**

Homework ——— GENERAL

Making Tables Ask students to make a table in their **science journal.** In one column, they will list 10 mammals. In the next column, they will indicate how each mammal produces young. From the information in this section, students should be able to indicate whether the animal is a monotreme, a marsupial, or a placental. Students should fill in the table to the best of their knowledge, research the correct answers, and put them in an additional column. **LS** Logical

---

Sexual Reproduction

Most animals reproduce sexually. In **sexual reproduction,** offspring are formed when genetic information from more than one parent combines. Sexual reproduction in animals usually requires two parents—a male and a female. The female parent produces sex cells called **eggs.** The male parent produces sex cells called **sperm.** When an egg's nucleus and a sperm's nucleus join, a fertilized egg, called a *zygote* (ZIE GOHT), is created. This joining of an egg and sperm is known as *fertilization.*

Human cells—except eggs and sperm and mature red blood cells—contain 46 chromosomes. Eggs and sperm are formed by a process called *meiosis.* In humans, meiosis is the division of one cell that has 46 chromosomes into four cells that have 23 chromosomes each. When an egg and a sperm join to form a zygote, the original number of 46 chromosomes is restored.

Genetic information is found in *genes.* Genes are located on *chromosomes* (KROH muh SOHMZ) made of the cell's DNA. During fertilization, the egg and sperm each contribute chromosomes to the zygote. The combination of genes from the two parents results in a zygote that grows into a unique individual. **Figure 3** shows how genes mix through three generations.

✔ **Reading Check** What is sexual reproduction? (*See the Appendix for answers to Reading Checks.*)

sexual reproduction reproduction in which sex cells from two parents unite to produce offspring that share traits from both parents

egg a sex cell produced by a female

sperm the male sex cell

Figure 3 Inheriting Genes

Eggs and sperm contain chromosomes. You inherit chromosomes— and the genes on them—from both of your parents. Your parents each inherited chromosomes from their parents.

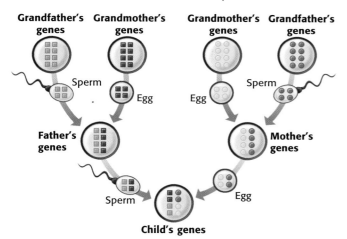

Grandfather's genes — Grandmother's genes — Grandmother's genes — Grandfather's genes — Sperm — Egg — Egg — Sperm — Father's genes — Mother's genes — Sperm — Egg — Child's genes

CONNECTION TO Language Arts

WRITING SKILL **Nature or Nurture?** Scientists debate whether genetics or upbringing is more important in shaping people. Use the Internet or library to research the issue of "nature versus nurture." Find information about identical twins who were raised apart. When you finish your research, write a persuasive essay supporting one side of the debate. Include evidence to support your argument.

ACTIVITY — **BASIC**

Asexual or Sexual Reproduction? Help students differentiate between sexual and asexual reproduction by having them make a poster that includes all the pertinent information. Students should use a different primary color for sexual and asexual reproduction and include artwork depicting the cells involved. The diagrams should state whether or not the resulting offspring are genetically identical to their parent(s). English Language Learners **LS Visual**

CONNECTION ACTIVITY Chemistry — **ADVANCED**

PORTFOLIO Encourage interested students to use the library or the Internet to research the role that incubation temperature plays in the reproductive process of some reptile and amphibian species. Have students draw diagrams or make a poster illustrating the effect of temperature on reproduction and development. Give students time to present their findings to the class. **LS Visual**

Teach

Demonstration — **GENERAL**
The Amazing Egg Bird eggs are fertilized internally but develop externally, which requires good packaging. The egg shell gives the developing embryo a stable, safe environment. Using an ordinary chicken egg, demonstrate that the shape of the egg keeps it from rolling away from the mother. Next, wrap your hand around the egg. Demonstrate that the shape of the egg is protective against squeezing pressure from the outside. Tell students that the egg is shaped to withstand the pressures of passing through the chicken and of incubation. It is designed to be easy to break from within so that even a young chick can peck its way out. English Language Learners **LS Visual**

Answer to Reading Check
Sexual reproduction is reproduction in which the sex cells (egg and sperm) of two parents unite to form a new individual.

Answer to Connection to Language Arts
Opinions may vary. Make sure students have provided information to support their answers. Sources of information may include journals such as *Scientific American* and reputable studies of twins.

Answer to Reading Check

External fertilization is when sex cells unite outside of the female's body. Internal fertilization is when sex cells unite inside the female's body.

Reteaching ——— BASIC

Outline Discuss with students how to make an outline of this section. Ask students to volunteer to share their outline to reteach the class. **LS** Logical

Quiz ——— GENERAL

1. How do the offspring created by asexual reproduction differ from those created by sexual reproduction? (Offspring from asexual reproduction are genetically identical to the parent. Offspring from sexual reproduction have genetic material from two parents and are genetically different from their parents.)

2. Why does external fertilization usually take place in moist environments? (External fertilization usually takes place in moist environments so that the delicate zygotes do not dry out.)

Alternative Assessment ——— GENERAL

Concept Mapping Have students create a concept map using the new terms in this section and the section title. **LS** Verbal

Figure 4 *Some fish, such as these clownfish, fertilize their eggs externally. The eggs are the orange mass on the rock.*

external fertilization the union of sex cells outside the bodies of the parents

internal fertilization fertilization of an egg by sperm that occurs inside the body of a female

Figure 5 *This zebra has just been born, but he is already able to stand. Within an hour, he will be able to run.*

Internal and External Fertilization

Fertilization can happen either outside or inside the female's body. When the sperm fertilizes the eggs outside the female's body, the process is called **external fertilization.** External fertilization must take place in a moist environment so that the delicate zygotes won't dry out. Some fishes, such as those in **Figure 4,** reproduce by external fertilization.

Many amphibians, such as frogs, use external fertilization. For example, the female frog releases her eggs. At the same time, the male frog releases his sperm over the eggs to fertilize them. Frogs usually leave the zygotes to develop on their own. In about two weeks, the fertilized eggs hatch into tadpoles.

Internal Fertilization

When the egg and sperm join inside the female's body, the process is called **internal fertilization**. Internal fertilization allows the female animal to protect the developing egg inside her body. Reptiles, birds, mammals, and some fishes reproduce by internal fertilization. Many animals that use internal fertilization can lay fertilized eggs. Female chickens, for example, usually lay one or two eggs after internal fertilization has taken place.

In most mammals, one or more fertilized eggs develop inside the mother's body. Many mammals give birth to young that are well developed. Young zebras, such as the one in **Figure 5,** can stand up and nurse almost immediately after birth.

✓ **Reading Check** What is the difference between external and internal fertilization?

Homework ——— GENERAL

Writing **Montremes** Encourage students to research an egg-laying mammal. Then, have them write and illustrate a short story about how the egg develops into a new individual. **LS** Verbal

INCLUSION Strategies

- *Behavior Control Issues*   - *Visually Impaired*
- *Attention Deficit Disorder*

Organize the students into teams of two or three. Have each team find an animal that has a pouch for its babies. Ask the teams to create a presentation giving what the name of the animal is, where the animal lives, how the baby gets into the pouch, and how long the baby stays in the pouch. Make sure no animal choices are repeated. **LS** Verbal

Mammals

All mammals reproduce sexually. All mammals nurture their young with milk. And all mammals reproduce in one of the following three ways:

- **Monotreme** *Monotremes* (MAHN oh TREEMZ) are mammals that lay eggs. After the eggs are incubated and hatch, the young are nourished by milk that oozes from pores on the mother's belly. Echidnas and platypuses are monotremes.

- **Marsupial** Mammals that give birth to partially developed live young, such as the kangaroo in **Figure 6,** are *marsupials* (mahr SOO pee uhlz). Most marsupials have pouches where their young continue to develop after birth. Opossums, koalas, wombats, and Tasmanian devils are marsupials.

- **Placental Mammal** There are more than 4,000 species of placental mammals, including armadillos, humans, and bats. Placental mammals are nourished inside their mother's body before birth. Newborn placental mammals are more developed than newborn monotremes or marsupials are.

✓ Reading Check Name two ways that all mammals are alike.

Figure 6 *The red kangaroo is a marsupial. A young kangaroo, such as this one in its mother's pouch, is called a joey.*

SECTION Review

Summary

- In asexual reproduction, a single parent produces offspring that are genetically identical to the parent.
- In sexual reproduction, an egg from one parent combines with a sperm from the other parent.
- Fertilization can be external or internal.
- All mammals reproduce sexually and nurture their young with milk.

Using Key Terms

For each pair of terms, explain how the meanings of the terms differ.

1. *internal fertilization* and *external fertilization*

2. *asexual reproduction* and *sexual reproduction*

Understanding Key Ideas

3. In humans, each egg and each sperm contain
   a. 23 chromosomes.
   b. 46 chromosomes.
   c. 69 chromosomes.
   d. 529 chromosomes.

4. List three types of asexual reproduction.

5. How do monotremes differ from marsupials?

6. Describe the process of meiosis.

7. Are humans placental mammals, monotremes, or marsupials? Explain.

Math Skills

8. Some bristlecone pine needles last 40 years. If a tree lives for 3,920 years, how many sets of needles might it grow?

Critical Thinking

9. **Making Inferences** Why is reproduction as important to a bristlecone pine as it is to a fruit fly?

10. **Applying Concepts** Describe one advantage of internal fertilization over external fertilization.

SCI LINKS® NSTA
Developed and maintained by the National Science Teachers Association

For a variety of links related to this chapter, go to www.scilinks.org
Topic: Reproduction
SciLinks code: HSM1293

INTERNET ACTIVITY
Sequence Board — GENERAL

For an internet activity related to this chapter, have students go to **go.hrw.com** and type in the keyword **HL5BD5W.**

CHAPTER RESOURCES

Chapter Resource File

- Section Quiz GENERAL
- Section Review GENERAL
- Vocabulary and Section Summary GENERAL
- Reinforcement Worksheet BASIC

Focus

Overview

In this section, students learn about the male and female reproductive systems. Students also learn about multiple births and some problems of the reproductive system.

Bellringer

Have students write answers to these questions: Do you think that cloning human beings could be considered reproduction? Why or why not? What kind of reproduction is it?

Motivate

Discussion ——— GENERAL

Bird and Human Ask students to compare reproduction in birds with reproduction in humans. (Both birds and humans fertilize their eggs internally. Birds lay eggs and protect them. Birds keep the eggs warm while obtaining food for themselves. Human mothers carry a baby inside their body, so the baby is always protected. After eggs hatch or the baby is born, parents protect and care for the baby. Humans take care of their offspring for much longer than birds care for theirs.) **LS** Verbal

Answer to Reading Check

testes, epididymis, vas deferens, urethra, penis

READING WARM-UP

Objectives

● Identify the structures and functions of the male and female reproductive systems.

● Describe two reproductive system problems.

Terms to Learn

testes   uterus
penis   vagina
ovary

READING STRATEGY

Reading Organizer As you read this section, create an outline of the section. Use the headings from the section in your outline.

testes the primary male reproductive organs, which produce sperm and testosterone (singular, *testis*)

penis the male organ that transfers sperm to a female and that carries urine out of the body

---

Human Reproduction

About nine months after a human sperm and egg combine, a mother gives birth to her baby. But how do humans make eggs and sperm?

The Male Reproductive System

The male reproductive system, shown in **Figure 1,** produces sperm and delivers it to the female reproductive system. The **testes** (singular, *testis*) are a pair of organs that make sperm and testosterone (tes TAHS tuhr OHN). Testosterone is the main male sex hormone. It helps regulate the production of sperm and the development of male characteristics.

As sperm leave a testis, they are stored in a tube called an *epididymis* (EP uh DID i mis). Sperm mature in the epididymis. Another tube, called a *vas deferens* (vas DEF uh RENZ), passes from the epididymis into the body and through the *prostate gland*. The prostate gland surrounds the neck of the bladder. As sperm move through the vas deferens, they mix with fluids from several glands, including the prostate gland. This mixture of sperm and fluids is called *semen*.

To leave the body, semen passes through the vas deferens into the *urethra* (yoo REE thruh). The urethra is the tube that runs through the penis. The **penis** is the external organ that transfers semen into the female's body.

✓ Reading Check Describe the path that sperm take from the testes to the penis. (*See the Appendix for answers to Reading Checks.*)

Figure 1 The Male Reproductive System

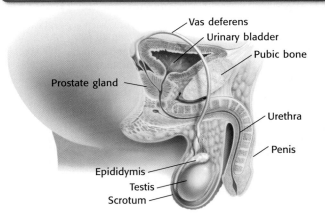

CHAPTER RESOURCES

Chapter Resource File

- **Lesson Plan**
- **Directed Reading A** BASIC
- **Directed Reading B** SPECIAL NEEDS

Technology

Transparencies
- Bellringer
- The Male Reproductive System

Is That a Fact!

Mumps, a common childhood disease, poses a risk to males who contract it during puberty or adulthood. When mumps occurs after childhood, it can cause inflammation of the testes, known as *acute orchitis,* which, in rare cases, can result in sterility.

Figure 2 | The Female Reproductive System

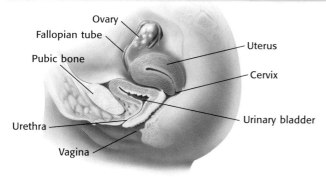

Ovary
Fallopian tube
Pubic bone
Uterus
Cervix
Urinary bladder
Urethra
Vagina

The Female Reproductive System

The female reproductive system, shown in **Figure 2,** produces eggs, nurtures fertilized eggs (zygotes), and gives birth. The two **ovaries** are the organs that make eggs. Ovaries also release estrogen (ES truh juhn) and progesterone (proh JES tuhr OHN), the main female sex hormones. These hormones regulate the release of eggs and development of female characteristics.

The Egg's Journey

During *ovulation* (AHV yoo LAY shuhn), an egg is released from an ovary and passes into a *fallopian* (fuh LOH pee uhn) *tube.* A fallopian tube leads from each ovary to the uterus. The egg passes through the fallopian tube into the uterus. Fertilization usually happens in the fallopian tube. If the egg is fertilized, the resulting zygote enters the uterus. The zygote may become embedded in the thickened lining of the uterus. The **uterus** is the organ in which a zygote develops into a baby.

When a baby is born, he or she passes from the uterus through the vagina and emerges outside the body. The **vagina** is the canal between the outside of the body and the uterus.

Menstrual Cycle

From puberty through her late 40s or early 50s, a woman's reproductive system goes through monthly changes. These changes prepare the body for pregnancy and are called the *menstrual cycle* (MEN struhl SIE kuhl). The first day of *menstruation* (MEN STRAY shuhn), the monthly discharge of blood and tissue from the uterus, is counted as the first day of the cycle. Menstruation lasts about 5 days. When menstruation ends, the lining of the uterus thickens. Ovulation occurs on about the 14th day of the cycle. If the egg is not fertilized within a few days, menstruation begins and flushes the egg away. The cycle—which usually takes about 28 days—starts again.

ovary in the female reproductive system of animals, an organ that produces eggs

uterus in female mammals, the hollow, muscular organ in which a fertilized egg is embedded and in which the embryo and fetus develop

vagina the female reproductive organ that connects the outside of the body to the uterus

MATH PRACTICE

Counting Eggs

1. The average woman ovulates each month from about age 12 to about age 50. How many mature eggs could she produce from age 18 to age 50?

2. A female's ovaries typically contain 2 million immature eggs. If she ovulates regularly from age 12 to age 50, what percentage of her eggs will mature?

CONNECTION ACTIVITY
Language Arts — GENERAL

Word Origins The words *male* and *female* actually originate from two unrelated Latin words. *Female* comes from *femella,* meaning "girl," while *male* comes from *masculus,* meaning "male." Have students select the names of any five parts of the male and female reproductive systems. Then, have students find the origins of those terms and write a brief history of each one.
LS Verbal

CHAPTER RESOURCES

Technology

Transparencies
• The Female Reproductive System

Workbooks

Math Skills for Science
• Multiplying Whole Numbers GENERAL
• Dividing Whole Numbers with Long Division GENERAL
• Parts of 100: Calculating Percentages GENERAL

Teach

📖 READING STRATEGY —— GENERAL

Activity Draw students' attention to **Figures 1** and **2.** Have them write the new terms in their **science journal,** leaving a few lines between each term. As students read the section, have them fill in definitions that explain the new terms in their own words. LS Verbal

Discussion —— GENERAL

Multiple Births A Russian woman in the 18th century gave birth to 69 children, with 67 living to reach adulthood. Ask students: "If this woman began ovulation at age 12 and stopped ovulating at age 50, and pregnancy lasts 9 months, how could she have had so many children?" Write the following answer on the board to demonstrate how it is possible that she had 69 children: She had 27 pregnancies, all of them producing 2 or more children. She had 16 pairs of twins, 7 sets of triplets, 4 sets of quadruplets.
$(16 \times 2) + (7 \times 3) + (4 \times 4) = 69$
LS Logical

Answers to Math Practice

1. $50\ y - 12\ y = 38\ y$
   $38\ y \times 12$ eggs/year $= 456$ eggs
   She can produce about 456 mature eggs in her lifetime.

2. 456 mature eggs/2,000,000 possible eggs $= 0.000228 \times 100 = 0.0228\%$ of her eggs may possibly mature.

Reteaching — BASIC

Puzzle Making Organize the class into small groups. Challenge each group to create a crossword puzzle using the Terms to Learn and italicized terms from the section. Have each group write appropriate clues and construct a puzzle. Then, have groups exchange puzzles. Allow time for students to solve the puzzles. **LS** Logical/Interpersonal

Quiz — GENERAL

1. What purpose does the epididymis serve? (the site where sperm mature and are stored before sperm leave the testes)

2. What is menstruation? (the monthly discharge of blood and tissue from the uterus)

Alternative Assessment — GENERAL

Tracing the Path If appropriate for your class, ask students to make diagrams that illustrate the path an egg or sperm must travel before fertilization. Have them label anatomical structures and indicate, with arrows, the direction in which the sex cell travels. **LS** Visual

English Language Learners

Figure 3 *Identical twins have genes that are exactly the same. Many identical twins who are raised apart have similar personalities and interests.*

SCHOOL to HOME

Twins and More

With a parent, discuss some challenges that are created by the birth of twins, triplets, quadruplets, or other multiples. Include financial, mental, emotional, and physical challenges.

Create a poster that shows these challenges and ways to meet them.

If twins or other multiples are in your family, discuss how the individuals differ and how they are alike.

ACTIVITY

Multiple Births

Have you ever seen identical twins? Sometimes, they are so similar that even their parents have trouble telling them apart. The boys in **Figure 3** are identical twins. Fraternal twins, the other type of twins, are more common than identical twins are. Fraternal twins can look very different from each other. In every 1,000 births, there are about 30 sets of twins. About one-third of all twin births are identical twins.

Twins are the most common multiple births. But humans sometimes have triplets (3 babies). In the United States, there are about two sets of triplets in every 1,000 births. Humans also have quadruplets (4 babies), quintuplets (5 babies), and more. These types of multiple births are rare. Births of quintuplets or more happen only once in about 53,000 births.

✔ **Reading Check** What is the frequency of twin births?

Reproductive System Problems

In most cases, the reproductive system functions flawlessly. But like any body system, the reproductive system sometimes has problems. These problems include disease and infertility.

STDs

Chlamydia, herpes, and hepatitis B are common sexually transmitted diseases. A *sexually transmitted disease,* or STD, is a disease that can pass from a person who is infected with the STD to an uninfected person during sexual contact. STDs are also called *sexually transmitted infections,* or STIs. These diseases affect many people each year, as shown in **Table 1.**

An STD you may have heard of is *acquired immune deficiency syndrome* (AIDS). AIDS is caused by *human immunodeficiency virus* (HIV). But you may not have heard of the STD *hepatitis B,* a liver disease also caused by a virus. This virus is spread in several ways, including sexual contact. In the United States, about 140,000 new cases of hepatitis B happen each year.

Table 1 The Spread of STDs in the United States	
STD	**Approximate number of new cases each year**
Chlamydia	3 to 10 million
Genital HPV (human papillomavirus)	5.5 million
Genital herpes	1 million
Gonorrhea	650,000
Syphilis	70,000
HIV/AIDS	40,000 to 50,000

CONNECTION ACTIVITY
Language Arts — ADVANCED

Writing **Fertility Drugs and Multiple Births** Have students conduct Internet or library research and write a report on how fertility drugs may have affected the number and frequency of multiple births in the last 15 years. **LS** Verbal

Group ACTIVITY — GENERAL

Reproductive System Cancer Have students work in small groups to research breast, testicular, ovarian, prostate, or cervical cancer. Students should focus on the incidence of the disease, its risk factors, and the importance of early detection. Have students use the information they gather to design and create a public service brochure—complete with artwork—designed to educate the public about the disease. Allow students time to present and discuss their brochures in class. **LS** Visual

Cancer

Sometimes, cancer happens in reproductive organs. *Cancer* is a disease in which cells grow at an uncontrolled rate. Cancer cells start out as normal cells. Then, something triggers uncontrolled cell growth. Different kinds of cancer have different triggers.

In men, the two most common reproductive system cancers are cancer of the testes and cancer of the prostate gland. In women, the two most common reproductive system cancers are breast cancer and cancer of the cervix. The *cervix* is the lower part, or neck, of the uterus. The cervix opens to the vagina.

Infertility

In the United States, about 15% of married couples have difficulty producing offspring. Many of these couples are *infertile,* or unable to have children. Men may be infertile if they do not produce enough healthy sperm. Women may be infertile if they do not ovulate normally.

Sexually transmitted diseases, such as gonorrhea and chlamydia, can lead to infertility in women. STD-related infertility occurs in men, but not as commonly as it does in women.

CONNECTION TO Social Studies

Understanding STDs Select one of the STDs in **Table 1.** Make a poster or brochure that identifies the cause of the disease, describes its symptoms, explains how it affects the body, and tells how it can be treated. Include a bar graph that shows the number of cases in different age groups.

ACTIVITY

SECTION Review

Summary

- The male reproductive system produces sperm and delivers it to the female reproductive system.

- The female reproductive system produces eggs, nurtures zygotes, and gives birth.

- Humans usually have one child per birth, but multiple births, such as those of twins or triplets, are possible.

- Human reproduction can be affected by cancer, infertility, and disease.

Using Key Terms

1. Use the following terms in the same sentence: *uterus* and *vagina*.

Understanding Key Ideas

2. Describe two problems of the reproductive system.

3. Identify the structures and functions of the male and female reproductive systems.

4. Identical twins happen once in 250 births. How many pairs of these twins might be at a school with 2,750 students?

   a. 1
   b. 11
   c. 22
   d. 250

Math Skills

5. In one country, 7 out of 1,000 infants die before their first birthday. Convert this figure to a percentage. Is your answer greater than or less than 1%?

Critical Thinking

6. **Making Inferences** What is the purpose of the menstrual cycle?

7. **Applying Concepts** Twins can happen when a zygote splits in two or when two eggs are fertilized. How can these two ways of twin formation explain how identical twins differ from fraternal twins?

8. **Predicting Consequences** How might cancer of the testes affect a man's ability to make sperm?

SCLINKS®

NSTA
Developed and maintained by the National Science Teachers Association

For a variety of links related to this chapter, go to www.scilinks.org
Topic: Reproduction System Irregularities or Disorders
SciLinks code: HSM1298

CHAPTER RESOURCES

Chapter Resource File

- Section Quiz **GENERAL**
- Section Review **GENERAL**
- Vocabulary and Section Summary **GENERAL**

Answers to Section Review

1. Sample answer: A woman's vagina is the canal that connects the uterus to the outside world.

2. One reproductive system problem is infertility. Infertility is when a man or a woman is unable to have children. Sexually transmitted diseases (STDs) are a second reproductive system problem. STDs can infect the reproductive system and may cause infertility.

3. testes (males): make sperm and produce testosterone (helps regulate sperm production and the development of male characteristics); penis (males): the external male organ that transfers semen into the female's body; ovaries (females): organs that make eggs and release estrogen and progesterone (which regulate the release of eggs and the development of female characteristics); uterus (females): the organ in which the fertilized egg develops; vagina (females): the canal that connects the uterus to the outside world, through which a baby passes when it is born

4. b

5. 7/1,000 = 0.007; Then, convert to a percentage by moving the decimal point two places to the right: 0.7%; This is less than 1%.

6. The menstrual cycle is the series of changes through which a female's reproductive system goes in order to prepare the female for pregnancy. The cycle usually takes about 28 days.

7. When a single fertilized egg splits in two, each cell contains identical genes. If each cell develops into a separate baby, they will be identical twins. When two separate eggs are fertilized, their genes are different. This results in fraternal twins.

8. Sample answer: Cancer is uncontrolled cell growth. In the testes, this uncontrolled growth could destroy cells and damage the production of sperm and the production of testosterone.

Focus

Overview

In this section, students learn about fertilization and implantation. Students are also introduced to the different stages of growth of a fetus in utero, culminating in the birth of a baby. Finally, students learn about stages of human development, from birth through adulthood.

🔊 Bellringer

Write the following on the board:

Name the stages of physical development you have passed through thus far in your life.

Have students list the stages in their **science journal.** Remind students that their growth and development began while they were still in the uterus. (Students may list stages such as the following: crawling, walking, talking, growing taller, and puberty.)

Motivate

Discussion —— GENERAL

Life Stages Ask students to list as many characteristics of each of the following as they can: infancy, childhood, adolescence, and adulthood. Tell students that while there are individual differences, all people go through these stages. Logical

---

READING WARM-UP

Objectives

- Summarize the processes of fertilization and implantation.
- Describe the development of the embryo and the fetus.
- Identify the stages of human development from birth to death.

Terms to Learn

embryo
placenta
umbilical cord
fetus

READING STRATEGY

Discussion Read this section silently. Write down questions that you have about this section. Discuss your questions in a small group.

---

embryo a developing human, from fertilization through the first 8 weeks of development (the 10th week of pregnancy)

placenta the partly fetal and partly maternal organ by which materials are exchanged between fetus and mother

---

CHAPTER RESOURCES

Chapter Resource File

- **Lesson Plan**
- **Directed Reading A** BASIC
- **Directed Reading B** SPECIAL NEEDS

Technology

🗃 **Transparencies**
- Bellringer

Growth and Development

Every one of us started out as a single cell. How did that cell become a person made of trillions of cells?

A single cell divides many times and develops into a baby. But the development of a baby from a single cell is only the first stage of human development. Think about how you will change between now and when you become a grandparent!

From Fertilization to Embryo

Ordinarily, the process of human development starts when a man deposits millions of sperm into a woman's vagina. A few hundred sperm make it through the uterus into a fallopian tube. There, a few sperm cover the egg. Usually, only one sperm gets through the outer coating of the egg. When this happens, it triggers a response—a membrane forms around the egg to keep other sperm from entering. When the sperm's nucleus joins with the nucleus of the egg, the egg becomes fertilized.

The fertilized egg (zygote) travels down the fallopian tube toward the uterus. This journey takes 5 to 6 days. During the trip, the zygote undergoes cell division many times. Eleven to 12 days after fertilization, the zygote has become a tiny ball of cells called an **embryo.** The embryo implants itself in the uterus. *Implantation* happens when the zygote embeds itself in the thick, nutrient-rich lining of the uterus. Fertilization and implantation are outlined in **Figure 1.**

✓ **Reading Check** Describe the process of fertilization and implantation. (*See the Appendix for answers to Reading Checks.*)

Figure 1 **Fertilization and Implantation**

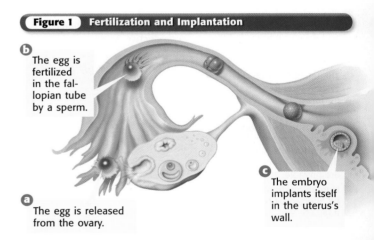

ⓑ The egg is fertilized in the fallopian tube by a sperm.

ⓒ The embryo implants itself in the uterus's wall.

ⓐ The egg is released from the ovary.

Answer to Reading Check

Fertilization happens when the nucleus of a sperm unites with the nucleus of an egg. Implantation happens after the fertilized egg travels down the fallopian tube to the uterus and embeds itself in the wall of the uterus.

From Embryo to Fetus

After implantation, the placenta (pluh SEN tuh) begins to grow. The **placenta** is a special two-way exchange organ. It has a network of blood vessels that provides the embryo with oxygen and nutrients from the mother's blood. Wastes produced by the embryo are removed in the placenta. They are carried by the mother's blood so that her body can excrete them. The embryo's blood and the mother's blood flow very near each other in the placenta, but they normally do not mix.

Reading Check Why is the placenta important?

Weeks 1 and 2

Doctors commonly count the time of a woman's pregnancy as starting from the first day of her last menstrual period. Even though fertilization has not yet taken place, that day is a convenient date from which to start counting. A normal pregnancy lasts about 280 days, or 40 weeks, from that day.

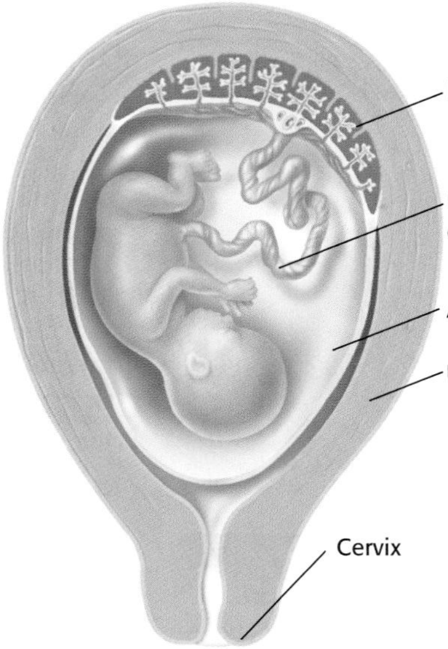

Figure 2 *The placenta, amnion, and umbilical cord are the life support system for the fetus. This fetus is about 20 to 22 weeks old.*

Weeks 3 and 4

Fertilization takes place at about the end of week 2. In week 3, after fertilization, the zygote moves to the uterus. As the zygote travels, it divides many times. It becomes a ball of cells that implants itself in the wall of the uterus. The zygote is now called an *embryo*. At the end of week 4, implantation is complete and the woman is pregnant. The embryo's blood cells begin to form. At this point, the embryo is about 0.2 mm long.

umbilical cord the structure that connects the fetus to the placenta

Weeks 5 to 8

Weeks 5 to 8 of pregnancy are weeks 3 to 6 of embryonic development. In this stage, the embryo becomes surrounded by a thin membrane called the *amnion* (AM nee AHN). The amnion is filled with amniotic fluid and protects the growing embryo from bumps and injury. During week 5, the umbilical cord forms. The **umbilical cord** (uhm BIL i kuhl KAWRD) is a cord that connects the embryo to the placenta. **Figure 2** shows the umbilical cord, amnion, and placenta.

In this stage, the heart, brain, other organs, and blood vessels start to form. They grow quickly. In weeks 5 and 6, eyes and ears take shape. The spinal cord begins to develop. In week 6, tiny limb buds appear. These buds will become arms and legs. In week 8, muscles start developing. Nerves grow into the shoulders and upper arms. Fingers and toes start to form. The embryo, now about 16 mm long, can swallow and blink.

SCHOOL to HOME

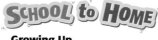

Growing Up

With a parent, discuss the physical and mental changes that you went through between your birth and your first day of school. Make a poster illustrating those changes.

ACTIVITY

Teach

ACTIVITY — GENERAL

Making Models Students may have difficulty understanding how the placenta functions. To help them understand, have groups of students make a clay model of the diagram in **Figure 2.** Encourage groups to learn more about the placenta in order to add more detail to their diagram. English Language Learners
LS Kinesthetic

Answer to Reading Check

The placenta is important because it provides the embryo with oxygen and nutrients from the mother's blood. Wastes from the embryo also travel to the placenta, where they are carried to the mother so the mother can excrete them.

READING STRATEGY — GENERAL

Answering Questions Ask students to write down the following question and fill in the correct answers as they read the section: At what stage of development does each of the following events take place? The fetus is felt kicking (weeks 15–16), the brain and spinal cord begin to form (weeks 5–6), and the fetus practices breathing by moving its lungs up and down (weeks 25–26). **LS Verbal**

INCLUSION Strategies

- *Behavior Control Issues* • *Visually Impaired*
- *Attention Deficit Disorder*

Divide the class into six teams. Give each team several pages of newspapers and an empty plastic grocery bag. Choose a "stuffer" in each group. Make sure students with behavior control issues are "stuffers." Assign each team one of the pregnancy months three through nine. Have teams research the actual size of the baby during their assigned month, and have them stuff their bags to simulate the baby's size. Have teams line their "babies" up in order. Add the following to the lineup for months one through three:

- small pebble or piece of rice (month 1)
- small rock or a peanut (month 2)
- grocery bag that has a very small filled area about 2 inches in diameter and whose unneeded ends are cut off (month 3)

LS Kinesthetic

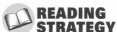

BRAIN FOOD

Writing **Seahorses** Seahorses are one of very few kinds of organisms in which the male carries the fertilized eggs. Ask students to research the reproductive and parenting behaviors of seahorses. Have them make a poster showing their findings. (After courtship, the female deposits eggs into the pouch of her male mate. The male then fertilizes the eggs and carries them until they develop. After a gestation period of between 10 and 60 days, depending on the species, tiny, fully formed sea horses emerge from an opening in the pouch.)

Answer to Reading Check

The embryo is now called a *fetus;* the fetus's face begins to look more human and it can swallow, the fetus grows rapidly (it triples in size), and the fetus begins to make movements that the mother can feel.

Answer to Connection to Social Studies

Taking drugs, drinking alcohol, and smoking can lead to low birth weights, birth defects, and miscarriages. Student reports may discuss fetal alcohol syndrome (FAS) or what happens when a child is addicted to a drug at birth.

---

fetus a developing human from seven or eight weeks after fertilization until birth

CONNECTION TO Social Studies

WRITING SKILL **Nourishing the Fetus** The fetus gets its only nutrition from the food that its mother eats. To ensure the health of the fetus, the mother needs to eat healthy foods and take special vitamins. A mother can hurt her fetus's health by taking drugs, drinking alcohol, or smoking. Research the potential consequences of taking drugs, drinking alcohol, or smoking while pregnant. In your **science journal,** write a report about what you learn.

Weeks 9 to 16

At week 9, the fetus may begin to make tiny movements. After week 10, the embryo is called a **fetus** (FEET uhs). In about week 13, the fetus's face begins to look more human. During this stage, fetal muscles grow stronger. As a result, the fetus can make a fist and begins to move. The fetus grows rapidly during this stage. It doubles, and then triples, its size within a month. For example, in week 10, the fetus is about 36 mm long. A little later, at week 16, the fetus is about 108 mm to 116 mm long. Use **Figure 3** to follow some of the changes that take place in the fetus as it develops.

✔ **Reading Check** Describe three changes the fetus undergoes during weeks 9 to 16.

Weeks 17 to 24

By week 17, the fetus can make faces. Usually, in week 18, the fetus starts to make movements that the mother can feel. By week 18, the fetus can hear sounds through the mother's uterus. It may even jump at loud noises. By week 23, the fetus's movements may be quite vigorous! If the fetus were born after week 24, it might survive. But babies born at 24 weeks require a lot of help. In weeks 17 to 24, the fetus grows to between 25 cm and 30 cm in length.

Weeks 25 to 36

At about 25 or 26 weeks, the fetus's lungs are well developed but not fully mature. The fetus still gets oxygen from its mother through the placenta. The fetus will not take its first breath of air until it is born. By the 32nd week, the fetus's eyes can open and close. Studies of fetal heart rate and brain activity show that fetuses respond to light. Some scientists have observed brain activity and eye movements in sleeping fetuses that resemble those activities in sleeping children or adults. These scientists think that a sleeping fetus may dream. After 36 weeks, the fetus is almost ready to be born.

Birth

At 37 to 38 weeks, the fetus is fully developed. A full-term pregnancy usually lasts about 40 weeks. Typically, as birth begins, the mother's uterus begins a series of muscular contractions called *labor.* Usually, these contractions push the fetus through the mother's vagina, and the baby is born. The newborn is still connected to the placenta by its umbilical cord, which is tied and cut. All that will remain of the point where the umbilical cord was attached is the baby's navel. Soon, the mother expels the placenta, and labor is complete.

CONNECTION to Math ——— GENERAL

Factor of Increase Have students calculate the factor of increase in a fetus's body length from the 8th week, when it is about 2.5 cm long, to the 5th month, when it is about 25 cm long, to birth, when it is about 50 cm long. (2.5 cm to 25 cm is an increase by a factor of 10, 25 cm to 50 cm is an increase by a factor of 2, and 2.5 cm to 50 cm is an increase by a factor of 20) **LS Logical**

Is That a Fact!

Between conception and birth, the developing fetus increases in size from a single cell to 6 trillion cells! After birth, infants and children continue to grow rapidly. For example, girls attain three-quarters of their adult height by the age of 7 1/2. Boys attain three-quarters of their adult height by the age of 9.

Figure 3 Pregnancy Timeline

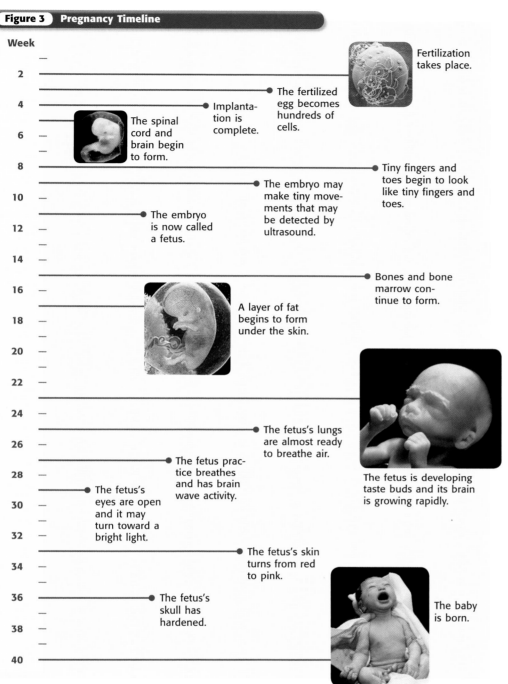

Week

2 — Fertilization takes place.

4 — The fertilized egg becomes hundreds of cells.

Implantation is complete.

The spinal cord and brain begin to form.

6 —

8 — Tiny fingers and toes begin to look like tiny fingers and toes.

The embryo may make tiny movements that may be detected by ultrasound.

10 —

The embryo is now called a fetus.

12 —

14 —

16 — Bones and bone marrow continue to form.

18 — A layer of fat begins to form under the skin.

20 —

22 —

24 —

26 — The fetus's lungs are almost ready to breathe air.

The fetus practice breathes and has brain wave activity.

28 —

The fetus's eyes are open and it may turn toward a bright light.

The fetus is developing taste buds and its brain is growing rapidly.

30 —

32 —

The fetus's skin turns from red to pink.

34 —

36 — The fetus's skull has hardened.

The baby is born.

38 —

40 —

From Birth to Adulthood
Have students work in pairs to design, create, and illustrate a pamphlet or brochure that briefly describes human growth and development from birth to old age.
LS Interpersonal

Quiz — GENERAL

1. What is implantation? (It is the process by which an embryo embeds itself in the uterus.)

2. What functions does the placenta serve? (It is a two-way exchange organ that allows oxygen and nutrients to travel to the fetus from the mother and allows wastes to travel from the fetus to the mother.)

Alternative Assessment — ADVANCED

Life as a Fetus Ask students to imagine that they have not yet been born. Have them write first-person stories describing their time in utero. Encourage creativity, but direct students to include the stages of development they went through as a fetus. Allow time for students to share their stories with the class.

Figure 4 Stages of Human Development

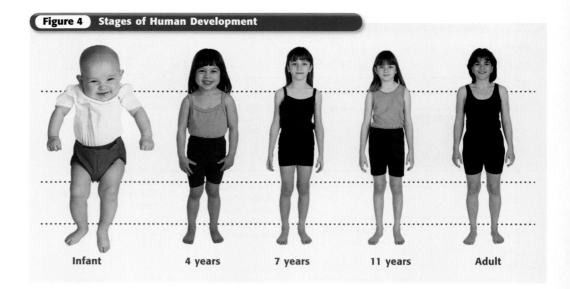

Infant   4 years   7 years   11 years   Adult

Life Grows On
Use **Figure 4** to complete this activity.

1. Use a **ruler** to measure the infant's head height. Then, measure the infant's entire height, including the head.

2. Calculate the ratio of the infant's head height to the infant's total height.

3. Repeat these measurements and calculations for the other stages.

4. Does a baby's head grow faster or slower than the rest of the body? Why do you think this is so?

From Birth to Death

After birth, the human body goes through several stages of development. Some of those stages are shown in **Figure 4.**

Infancy and Childhood

Generally, infancy is the stage from birth to age 2. During infancy, you grew quickly and your baby teeth appeared. As your nervous system developed, you became more coordinated and started to walk.

Childhood—another period of fast growth—lasts from age 2 to puberty. Your baby teeth were replaced by permanent teeth. And your muscles became more coordinated, which allowed you to ride a bicycle, jump rope, and do other activities.

Adolescence

The stage from puberty to adulthood is adolescence. During puberty, a person's reproductive system becomes mature. In most boys, puberty takes place between the ages of 11 and 16. During this time, the young male's body becomes more muscular, his voice becomes deeper, and body and facial hair appear. In most girls, puberty takes place between the ages of 9 and 14. During puberty in females, the amount of fat in the hips and thighs increases, the breasts enlarge, body hair appears, and menstruation begins.

✓ **Reading Check** Name an important change that takes place during adolescence.

Answer to Reading Check
A person's reproductive system becomes mature.

MATERIALS

FOR EACH STUDENT
• calculator, if available
• ruler

Answers
Slower; Newborns have large heads to hold the large brains that enable them to learn quickly. In infancy, their bodies begin to catch up in size.

Adulthood

From about age 20 to age 40, you will be a young adult. You will be at the peak of your physical development. Beginning around age 30, changes associated with aging begin. These changes are gradual and different for everyone. Some early signs of aging include loss of flexibility in muscles, deterioration of eyesight, increase in body fat, and some loss of hair.

The aging process continues in middle age (between 40 and 65 years old). During this time, hair may turn gray, athletic abilities will decline, and skin may wrinkle. A person who is more than 65 years old is considered an older adult. Although the aging process continues, many older adults lead very active lives, as is shown in **Figure 5.**

Figure 5 *Older adults can still enjoy activities that they enjoyed when they were younger.*

SECTION Review

Summary

- Fertilization occurs when a sperm from the male joins with an egg from the female.
- The embryo and fetus undergo many changes between implantation and birth.
- The first stage of human development lasts from fertilization to birth.
- After birth, a human goes through four more stages of growth and development.

Using Key Terms

1. In your own words, write a definition for the term *umbilical cord.*

2. Use the following terms in the same sentence: *embryo* and *fetus.*

Understanding Key Ideas

3. After birth, the two periods of most rapid growth are
   a. infancy and adolescence.
   b. childhood and adulthood.
   c. infancy and childhood.
   d. adolescence and adulthood.

4. After birth, which stage of human development is the longest?
   a. infancy
   b. childhood
   c. adolescence
   d. adulthood

5. Describe the development of the embryo and the fetus.

6. What is the function of the placenta?

7. Summarize the processes of fertilization and implantation.

8. What are five stages of human development?

Math Skills

9. Suppose a person is 80 years old and that puberty took place when he or she was 12 years old.
   a. Calculate the percentage of the person's life that he or she spent in each of the four stages of development that follow birth.
   b. Make a bar graph showing the percentage for each stage.

Critical Thinking

10. **Applying Concepts** Why does the egg's covering change after a sperm has entered the egg?

11. **Analyzing Ideas** Do you think any one stage of development is more important than other stages? Explain your answer.

Developed and maintained by the National Science Teachers Association

For a variety of links related to this chapter, go to www.scilinks.org
Topic: Before Birth; Growth and Development
SciLinks code: HSM0140; HSM0700

Answers to Section Review

1. The umbilical cord is a cord that forms during the 5th week of pregnancy and connects the embryo or fetus to the placenta.

2. An embryo is less developed than a fetus.

3. c

4. d

CHAPTER RESOURCES

Chapter Resource File

- Section Quiz GENERAL
- Section Review GENERAL
- Vocabulary and Section Summary GENERAL
- Reinforcement Worksheet BASIC
- Critical Thinking ADVANCED
- SciLinks Activity GENERAL

Technology

Transparencies
- The Stages of Human Development

---

5. Sample answer: An embryo begins as a single fertilized egg cell, then develops into a ball of cells that embeds itself in the wall of the uterus. Soon, the amnion, placenta, and umbilical cord form to protect and nourish the embryo. The embryo develops and, after week 10, it is called a fetus. By week 12, all the major organ systems have begun to form and grow. By week 16, the fetus is moving strongly enough for the mother to feel the movements. From week 12 to week 40, all body systems continue to grow and strengthen. At week 40 or so, the fetus is ready to be born.

6. The placenta is the organ that allows oxygen and nutrients to get from the mother's blood to the fetus and allows wastes from the fetus to get to the mother's blood.

7. Fertilization happens when a sperm's nucleus unites with an egg's nucleus to form a zygote or embryo. Implantation takes place when an embryo embeds itself in the wall of the uterus.

8. fertilization to birth; infancy, childhood, adolescence, and adulthood

9. a. • infancy: 2 y/80 y = 0.025, or 2.5%
   • childhood (10 years, from age 2 to age 12): 10 y/80 y = 12.5%
   • adolescence (age 12 to age 20): 8 y/80 y = 10%
   • adulthood (age 20 to age 80): 60 y/80 y = 75%
   b. Length of bars on bar graph should reflect percentages shown above.

10. The membrane keeps other sperm from entering the egg and uniting with the nucleus. This is important because it helps maintain the characteristic chromosome number.

11. Sample answer: Adolescence is the most important stage because that is when humans reach sexual maturity. Without sexual maturity, the species could not survive.

It's a Comfy, Safe World!

Teacher's Notes

Time Required
Two 45-minute class periods

Lab Ratings

Teacher Prep 🧪🧪
Student Set-Up 🧪
Concept Level 🧪
Clean Up 🧪🧪🧪

MATERIALS

This lab may require some large plastic bags, a meterstick, and various other materials depending on the students' designs. Soft-boiled eggs will simplify the cleanup. Students may wear gloves.

Safety Caution

Remind students to review all safety cautions and icons before beginning this lab activity. Students should wash their hands after handling the eggs.

Lab Notes

Students will be dropping their models, so this lab should be done over a large plastic sheet. You may want to do this lab outside because it is may be quite messy. Students can modify their models in any way they feel will improve the protection.

It's a Comfy, Safe World!

Before birth, baby birds live inside a hard, protective shell until the baby has used up all the food supply. Most mammal babies develop within their mother's uterus, in which they are surrounded by fluid and connected to a placenta, before they are born. Before human babies are born, they lead a comfy life. By the seventh month, they lie around sucking their thumb, blinking their eyes, and perhaps even dreaming.

Ask a Question

❶ Inside which structure is a developing organism better protected from bumps and blows: the uterus of a placental mammal or the egg of a bird?

Form a Hypothesis

❷ A placental mammal's uterus protects a developing organism from bumps and blows better than a bird's egg does.

Test the Hypothesis

❸ Brainstorm several ideas about how you will construct and test your model of a mammalian uterus. Then, use the materials provided by your teacher to build your model. A peeled, soft-boiled egg will represent the fetus inside your model uterus.

❹ Make a data table similar to **Table 1** below. Test your model, examine the egg for damage, and record your results.

OBJECTIVES

Construct a model of a human uterus protecting a fetus.

Compare the protection that a bird's egg gives a developing baby bird with the protection that a human uterus gives a fetus.

MATERIALS

- computer (optional)
- cotton, soft fabric, or other soft materials
- eggs, soft-boiled and in the shell (2 to 4)
- eggs, soft-boiled and peeled (3 or 4)
- gloves, protective
- mineral oil, cooking oil, syrup, or other thick liquid
- plastic bags, sealable
- water

SAFETY

Table 1 First Model Test	
Original model	**Modified model**
DO NOT WRITE IN BOOK	

❺ Modify your model as necessary; test this modified model using another peeled, soft-boiled egg; and record your results.

Randy Christian
Stovall Junior High School
Houston, Texas

CHAPTER RESOURCES

Chapter Resource File

- **Datasheet for Chapter Lab**
- **Lab Notes and Answers**

Technology

Classroom Videos
- Lab Video

LabBook

- My, How You've Grown!

6 When you are satisfied with the design of your model, obtain another peeled, soft-boiled egg and an egg in the shell. The egg in the shell represents the baby bird inside the egg.

7 Make a data table similar to **Table 2** below. Test your new eggs, examine them for damage, and record your results in your data table.

Table 2	Final Model Test
	Test Results
Model	DO NOT WRITE IN BOOK
Egg in shell	

Analyze the Results

1 **Explaining Events** Explain any differences in the test results for the model and the egg in a shell.

2 **Analyzing Results** What modification to your model was the most effective in protecting the fetus?

Draw Conclusions

3 **Evaluating Data** Review your hypothesis. Did your data support your hypothesis? Why or why not?

4 **Evaluating Models** What modifications to your model might make it more like a uterus?

Applying Your Data

Use the Internet or the library to find information about the development of monotremes, such as the echidna or the platypus, and marsupials, such as the koala or the kangaroo. Then, using what you have learned in this lab, compare the development of placental mammals with that of marsupials and monotremes.

Analyze the Results

1. Answers may vary, but an egg inside a viscous liquid in a plastic bag, wrapped in soft cotton and placed inside another bag, should not be damaged when dropped from a height of 1 m. An egg protected only by a shell should break. In general, the more protected the fetus or egg, the more resistant to damage it is and the less damage it will suffer when dropped from a height of 1 m.

2. Answers may vary according to students' modifications. Most students will observe that the more soft wrapping and/or viscous fluid protecting the egg, the better the egg survived the drop from 1 m.

Draw Conclusions

3. Students' answers may vary depending on their hypothesis and the data collected. Accept all reasonable answers.

4. Students' answers may vary depending on their model and the data collected. Accept all reasonable answers.

Applying Your Data

Students should recognize that all mammals have internal fertilization of eggs. Students should include the ideas that monotreme mammals lay eggs with leathery shells and, after the eggs hatch, nurture their young with milk that oozes from pores in the mother's skin. Marsupial mammals give birth to live young that are very underdeveloped; the young move to a pouch and continue their development in the pouch. Placental mammals also give birth to live young, but their young are more developed than those of marsupial mammals. Even so, placental mammals may have to care for their young for several years.

Assignment Guide

Section	Questions
1	1, 3, 6, 10, 18–19, 21
2	2, 4–5, 7–8, 11, 12, 13 16–17, 20, 21
3	9, 12, 14–15
2 and 3	22–25

ANSWERS

Using Key Terms

1. Internal fertilization means that the eggs are fertilized inside the female's body. External fertilization is when the eggs are fertilized outside the female's body.

2. Testes are male organs that produce sperm. Ovaries are female organs that produce eggs.

3. Asexual reproduction is when a single parent has off-spring that are genetically identical to the parent. Sexual reproduction happens when sex cells from two parents unite.

4. Fertilization happens when the nucleus of a sperm unites with the nucleus of an egg. Implantation is when the embryo embeds itself in the wall of the uterus.

5. The umbilical cord links the fetus with the placenta. The placenta is the organ that helps the fetus get oxygen and nutrients and get rid of wastes.

USING KEY TERMS

For each pair of terms, explain how the meanings of the terms differ.

1 *internal fertilization* and *external fertilization*

2 *testes* and *ovaries*

3 *asexual reproduction* and *sexual reproduction*

4 *fertilization* and *implantation*

5 *umbilical cord* and *placenta*

UNDERSTANDING KEY IDEAS

Multiple Choice

6 The sea star reproduces asexually by
   a. fragmentation.
   b. budding.
   c. external fertilization.
   d. internal fertilization.

7 Which list shows in order sperm's path through the male reproductive system?
   a. testes, epididymis, urethra, vas deferens
   b. epididymis, urethra, testes, vas deferens
   c. testes, vas deferens, epididymis, urethra
   d. testes, epididymis, vas deferens, urethra

8 Identical twins are the result of
   a. a fertilized egg splitting in two.
   b. two separate eggs being fertilized.
   c. budding in the uterus.
   d. external fertilization.

9 If the onset of menstruation is counted as the first day of the menstrual cycle, on what day of the cycle does ovulation typically occur?
   a. 2nd day
   b. 5th day
   c. 14th day
   d. 28th day

10 How do monotremes differ from placental mammals?
   a. Monotremes are not mammals.
   b. Monotremes have hair.
   c. Monotremes nurture their young with milk.
   d. Monotremes lay eggs.

11 All of the following are sexually transmitted diseases EXCEPT
   a. chlamydia.
   b. AIDS.
   c. infertility.
   d. genital herpes.

12 Where do fertilization and implantation, respectively, take place?
   a. uterus, fallopian tube
   b. fallopian tube, vagina
   c. uterus, vagina
   d. fallopian tube, uterus

Short Answer

13 Which human reproductive organs produce sperm? produce eggs?

14 Explain how the fetus gets oxygen and nutrients and how it gets rid of waste.

15 What are four stages of human life following birth?

Understanding Key Ideas

6. a
7. d
8. a
9. c
10. d
11. c
12. d
13. The testes produce sperm, and the ovaries produce eggs.
14. The placenta is a specialized organ that allows the fetus to get oxygen and get rid of wastes.

15. infancy, childhood, adolescence, adulthood

16. Sample answer: Infertility is a problem because it may prevent people from having babies. STDs are a problem because they can damage a person's reproductive system, and they may also cause infertility. Cancer is a problem because it can damage a person's reproductive system.

17. Drawings should resemble the images in Section 2, Figure 1, The Male Reproductive System, and Figure 2, The Female Reproductive System.

16 Name three problems that can affect the human reproductive system, and explain why each is a problem.

17 Draw a diagram showing the structures of the male and female reproductive systems. Label each structure, and explain how each structure contributes to fertilization and implantation.

CRITICAL THINKING

18 **Concept Mapping** Use the following terms to create a concept map: *asexual reproduction, budding, external fertilization, fragmentation, reproduction, internal fertilization,* and *sexual reproduction.*

19 **Identifying Relationships** The environment in which organisms live may change over time. For example, a wet, swampy area may gradually become a grassy area with a small pond. Explain how sexual reproduction may give species that live in a changing environment a survival advantage.

20 **Applying Concepts** What is the function of the uterus? How is this function related to the menstrual cycle?

21 **Making Inferences** In most human body cells, the 46 chromosomes are duplicated during cell division so that each new cell receives 46 chromosomes. Cells that make eggs and sperm also split and duplicate their 46 chromosomes. But then, in the process of meiosis, the two cells split again to form four cells (egg or sperm) that each have 23 chromosomes. Why is meiosis important to human reproduction and to the human species?

INTERPRETING GRAPHICS

The following graph illustrates the cycles of the female hormone estrogen and the male hormone testosterone. The blue line shows the estrogen level in a female over 28 days. The red line shows the testosterone level in a male over the same amount of time. Use the graph below to answer the questions that follow.

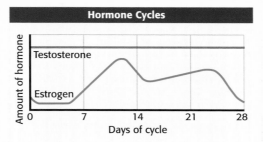

Hormone Cycles

Testosterone

Estrogen

Amount of hormone

Days of cycle
0   7   14   21   28

22 What is the major difference between the levels of the two hormones over the 28 days?

23 What cycle do you think estrogen affects?

24 Why might the level of testosterone stay the same?

25 Do you think that the above estrogen cycle would change in a pregnant woman? Explain your answer.

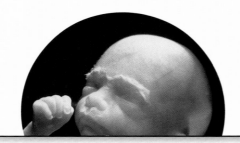

CHAPTER RESOURCES

Chapter Resource File

- Chapter Review GENERAL
- Chapter Test A GENERAL
- Chapter Test B ADVANCED
- Chapter Test C SPECIAL NEEDS
- Vocabulary Activity GENERAL

Workbooks

Study Guide
- Assessment resources are also available in Spanish.

Critical Thinking

18. An answer to this exercise can be found at the end of this book.

19. Sample answer: Sexual reproduction produces offspring that have genetic information from two different parents. Some of that information may enable the offspring to do better in a changing environment than other members of the species. As a result, there is a greater chance that the beneficial information will be passed on to the next generation.

20. The uterus, an organ in the female reproductive system, is where an embryo develops into a fetus. Every month, it builds up tissue that can help nourish a developing embryo. If no embryo implants, the tissue will discharge in menstruation.

21. Meiosis ensures that the characteristic human chromosome number remains the same. Because sex cells from two separate parents combine to form a zygote, each sex cell needs only half the 46 chromosomes that all other human body cells have. Meiosis also ensures that offspring will have a mix of genetic information.

Interpreting Graphics

22. Estrogen levels fluctuate, but testosterone stays at the same level throughout the month.

23. Estrogen affects the menstrual cycle.

24. Testosterone levels stay the same because men continually produce sperm and do not prepare for a possible pregnancy.

25. Sample answer: Yes, I think it might change because estrogen affects the menstrual cycle. During pregnancy, the menstrual cycle stops, so the level of estrogen will level off until the pregnancy is over.

Teacher's Note

To provide practice under more realistic testing conditions, give students 20 minutes to answer all of the questions in this Standardized Test Preparation.

MISCONCEPTION ALERT

Answers to the standardized test preparation can help you identify student misconceptions and misunderstandings.

READING

Passage 1

1. B
2. H
3. C

TEST DOCTOR

Question 2: This fact is mentioned in the following sentences: "Normal human body temperature is about 37°C. Normal sperm production and development cannot take place at that high temperature." Students may not put the two sentences together to extract the fact. Some students may choose answer I because they have mistakenly read "37°F" for the correct "37°C."

Question 3: Students may skip over the word "tubes" in the question and answer the more general question "Where are sperm made?" by choosing answer A.

READING

Read each of the passages below. Then, answer the questions that follow each passage.

Passage 1 The male reproductive system is made up of internal and external organs. The external organs of this system are the penis and the scrotum. The scrotum is a skin-covered sac that hangs outside the body. Normal human body temperature is about 37°C. Normal sperm production and development cannot take place at that temperature. Normal sperm production and development takes place at lower temperatures. That is why the testes rest in the scrotum, outside the body. The scrotum is about 2°C cooler than the body. Inside each testis are masses of tightly coiled tubes, called *seminiferous tubules,* in which sperm are produced when conditions are right.

1. In this passage, what does the word *external* mean?
   - **A** not part of the body
   - **B** outside the body
   - **C** inside the body
   - **D** lasting a long time

2. Which of the following statements is a fact according to the passage?
   - **F** The temperature in the scrotum is higher than body temperature.
   - **G** Testes are internal organs of the male reproductive system.
   - **H** Normal sperm production cannot take place at normal body temperature.
   - **I** Normal human body temperature is about 37°F.

3. What are the tubes in which sperm are made called?
   - **A** testes
   - **B** scrotum
   - **C** seminiferous tubules
   - **D** external organs

Passage 2 In a normal pregnancy, the fertilized egg travels to the uterus and implants itself in the uterus's wall. But, in about 7 out of 1,000 pregnancies in the United States, a woman has an ectopic pregnancy. The term *ectopic* is from two Greek words meaning "out of place." In an ectopic pregnancy, the fertilized egg implants itself in an ovary, a fallopian tube, or another area of the female reproductive system that is not the lining of the uterus. Because the zygote cannot develop properly outside of the uterus, an ectopic pregnancy can be very dangerous for both the mother and zygote. As the zygote grows, it causes the mother pain and bleeding. For example, an ectopic pregnancy in a fallopian tube can rupture the tube and cause abdominal bleeding. If an ectopic pregnancy is not treated quickly enough, the mother may die.

1. In the passage, what does the term *ectopic pregnancy* probably mean?
   - **A** a pregnancy that takes place at the wrong time
   - **B** a type of pregnancy that happens about 7 out of 100 times in the United States
   - **C** a type of pregnancy caused by a problem with a fallopian tube
   - **D** a pregnancy in which the zygote implants itself in the wrong place

2. Which of the following statements is a fact according to the passage?
   - **F** Ectopic pregnancies take place in about 7% of all pregnancies.
   - **G** The ectopic pregnancy rate in the United States is less than 1%.
   - **H** Ectopic pregnancies take place in the uterus.
   - **I** An ectopic pregnancy is harmless.

Passage 2

1. D
2. G

TEST DOCTOR

Question 2: The passage states that ectopic pregnancies happen in about 7 out of 1,000 pregnancies, which is 0.7%. The correct answer is therefore answer G. Students may read "7 out of 1000" as "7 out of 100," and would pick incorrect answer F.

Use the diagrams below to answer the questions that follow.

A.
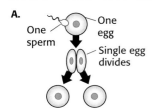
One sperm — One egg — Single egg divides

B. Two sperm
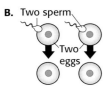
Two eggs

1. Which diagram of cell division would produce identical twins: A or B?

A diagram B, because each egg is fertilized by a separate sperm cell

B both diagram A and diagram B, because twins result in both cases

C diagram A, because a single fertilized egg separates into two halves

D diagram B, because two eggs are released by an ovary

2. Which of the following could describe fraternal twins?

F both boys

G both girls

H one girl and one boy

I any of these combinations

3. Which diagram of cell division could explain triplets, two of whom are identical and one of whom is fraternal?

A diagram A

B diagram B

C either diagram A or diagram B

D neither diagram A or diagram B

Read each question below, and choose the best answer.

1. Identify the group that contains equivalent fractions, decimals, and percents.

A 7/10, 0.7, 7%

B 1/2, 0.5, 50%

C 3/8, 0.38, 38%

D 3/100, 0.3, 33%

2. A geologist was exploring a cave. She spent 2.7 h exploring on Saturday and twice as many hours exploring on Sunday. Which equation could be used to find n, the total number of hours the geologist spent exploring the cave on those 2 days?

F $n = 2 \div 2.7$

G $n = 2.7 + (2 \times 2.7)$

H $n = 2.7 + 2.7 + 2$

I $n = 2 \times 2.7$

3. Which of the following story problems can be solved by the equation below?

$$(60 + 70 + 68 + 80 + x) \div 5 = 70$$

A The heights of four buildings in South Braintree are 60 ft, 70 ft, 68 ft, and 80 ft. Find x, the average height of the buildings.

B The weights of four dogs Jason is raising are 60 lb, 70 lb, 68 lb, and 80 lb. Find x, the sum of the weights of the four dogs.

C Kayla's first four handmade bracelets sold for $60, $70, $68, and $80. Find x, the amount for which Kayla needs to sell her fifth bracelet to have an average selling price of $70.

D The times it took Taylor to complete each of four 100 m practice swims were 60 s, 70 s, 68 s, and 80 s. Find x, the average time it took Taylor to complete his practice swims.

Standardized Test Preparation

1. C

2. I

3. D

TEST DOCTOR

Question 1: Students may select answer B because twins do result in both cases. However, identical twins happen only when a single fertilized egg splits in two.

Question 2: Students may think that fraternal twins, even if they are not identical, must still be of the same sex. The correct answer is I; fraternal twins may be two boys, two girls, or one of each, because fraternal twins develop from two separate fertilized eggs, not from the splitting of one egg.

1. B

2. G

3. C

TEST DOCTOR

Question 2: Students often have trouble converting a word problem into a number statement. Students may select answer H or I because those answers are similar to the correct answer. Students who have problems writing number statements often overlook an important clue in the word problem, and their statement is incomplete.

Question 3: This is another word problem, but it is a little more complex than question 2. Students must realize that the average has already been calculated and that what they are seeking is the quantity that gives the average. Answer C is the only answer in which the average is given; the other three answers ask to solve for the average.

CHAPTER RESOURCES

Chapter Resource File

• Standardized Test Preparation GENERAL

Workbooks

North Carolina Standardized Test Preparation
• Provides practice for the EOG test.

State Resources

For specific resources for your state, visit **go.hrw.com** and type in the keyword **HSMSTR**.

Science in Action

Science, Technology, and Society

Discussion ——— ADVANCED

Lead students in a discussion about the implications of fetal-surgery technology for treating fetal disorders. What sorts of disorders might be successfully treated? (anatomical disorders and discrete tumors) What types of disorders would be more difficult to treat? (genetic disorders and disorders affecting the entire fetus)

Scientific Discoveries

Background

The word *laser* is actually an abbreviation for **l**ight **a**mplification by **s**timulated **e**mission of **r**adiation. Lasers can pump energy into a solid, liquid, gas, or semiconductor to produce a beam. Carbon dioxide and helium-neon are common gas lasers. Ruby is a common solid-state laser. Each medium produces a laser with a different wavelength. Semiconductor (or diode) lasers emit a wavelength of 630 nm. They are so weak that they can be used as pointers. Carbon dioxide lasers, emitting a wavelength of 10,600 nm, are so strong that they can cut through steel!

Doctors operated on a fetus, whose hand is visible in this photo, to correct spina bifida.

Science, Technology, and Society

Fetal Surgery

Sometimes, a developing fetus has a serious medical problem. In many cases, surgery after birth can correct the problem. But some problems can be treated while the fetus is still in the uterus. For example, fetal surgery may be used to correct spina bifida (part of the spinal cord is exposed because the backbone doesn't form properly). Doctors now can fix several types of problems before a baby is born.

Social Studies ACTIVITY

WRITING SKILL Research the causes of spina bifida. Write a brochure telling expectant mothers what precautions they can take to prevent spina bifida.

Scientific Discoveries

Lasers and Acne

Many people think that acne affects only teenagers, but acne can strike at any age. Some acne is mild, but some is severe. Now, for some severe cases of acne, lasers may provide relief. That's right—lasers can be used to treat acne! Surgeons who specialize in the health and diseases of the skin use laser light to treat the skin disease known as *acne*.

In addition, laser treatments may stimulate the skin cells that produce collagen. Collagen is a protein found in connective tissue. Increased production of collagen in the skin improves the skin's texture and helps smooth out acne scars.

Language Arts ACTIVITY

WRITING SKILL Write a story about how severe acne affects a teen's life. Tell what happens when a doctor refers the teen to a specialist for laser treatment and how the successful treatment changes the teen's life.

Answer to Social Studies Activity

Spina bifida (a Latin term meaning *split spine*) is a group of congenital birth defects that affect the development of the central nervous system—the brain and the spinal cord—and nerve tissues. Spina bifida occurs about 10 to 20 times per 1,000 births. With severe spina bifida, a person's legs and feet are paralyzed. There are often problems with bowel and bladder control. The long-term effects of spina bifida depend on the type and severity of the defect. Up to 75% of the cases of spina bifida could be prevented if the mother takes folic acid daily before pregnancy and during the first trimester.

Answer to Language Arts Activity

Students' stories may reflect the emotional, social, and psychological impact that severe acne can have and the positive effects laser treatments may have for the acne sufferer. Improved self-confidence, a better self-image, and more-successful social interactions may be some of the benefits.

Careers

Reva Curry

Diagnostic Medical Sonographer Sounds are everywhere in our world. But only some of those sounds—such as your favorite music playing on the stereo or the dog barking next door—are sounds that we can hear. There are sound waves whose frequency is too high for us to hear. These high-pitched sounds are called *ultrasound*. Some animals, such as bats, use ultrasound to hunt and to avoid midair collisions.

Humans use ultrasound, too. Ultrasound machines can peer inside the human body to look at hearts, blood vessels, and fetuses. Diagnostic medical sonographers are people who use sonography equipment to diagnose medical problems and to follow the growth and development of a fetus before it is born. One of the leading professionals in the field of diagnostic medical sonography is Dr. Reva Curry. Dr. Curry spent many years as a sonographer. Her primary job was to use high-tech instruments to create ultrasound images of parts of the body and interpret the results for other medical professionals. Today, Dr. Curry works with students as the dean of a community college.

Math ACTIVITY

At 20°C, the speed of sound in water is 1,482 m/s and in steel is 5,200 m/s. How long would it take a sound to travel 815.1 m in water? In that same length of time, how far would a sound travel in a steel beam?

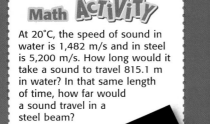

go.hrw.com

To learn more about these Science in Action topics, visit go.hrw.com and type in the keyword **HL5BD5F**.

Current Science

Check out Current Science® articles related to this chapter by visiting go.hrw.com. Just type in the keyword **HL5CS26**.

Careers

Discussion ——— GENERAL

Generate interest in diagnostic medical sonography by inviting a diagnostic medical sonographer from a local hospital or clinic. Before the visit, discuss with the class Dr. Curry's story and any experiences the students may have had with sonography or other diagnostic imaging techniques. Have students prepare questions for the guest speaker prior to the visit. Your guest may show a video of the procedure itself and interpret some actual sonograms. The students should have the opportunity for an open discussion with the practitioner and thereby get first-hand knowledge about the profession.

Answers to Math Activity

1. 0.55 s

2. 2,860 m

Human Health

In many ways, living in the 21st century is good for your health. Many deadly diseases that plagued our ancestors now have cures. Some diseases, such as smallpox, have been wiped out entirely. And others can be prevented by vaccines and other methods. Many researchers, including the people on this timeline, have worked to understand diseases and to find cures.

But people still get sick, and many diseases have no cure. In this unit, you will learn how your body protects itself and fights illness. You will also learn about ways to keep yourself healthy so that your body can operate in top form.

1403

The first quarantine is imposed in Venice, Italy, to stop the spread of the plague, or Black Death.

1717

Lady Mary Wortley Montague introduces a smallpox vaccine in England.

1854

Nurse Florence Nightingale introduces hygienic standards into military hospitals during the Crimean War.

1895

X rays are discovered by Wilhelm Roentgen.

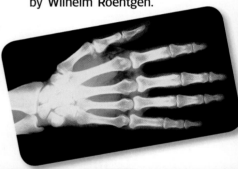

1953

Cigarette smoking is linked to lung cancer.

1816
R. T. Laënnec invents the stethoscope.

1853
Charles Gerhardt synthesizes aspirin for the first time.

1900
Walter Reed discovers that yellow fever is carried by mosquitoes.

1906
Upton Sinclair writes *The Jungle*, which describes unsanitary conditions in the Chicago stockyards and leads to the creation of the Pure Food and Drug Act.

1921
A tuberculosis vaccine is produced.

1979
Smallpox is eradicated.

1997
Researchers discover that high doses of alcohol in early pregnancy switch off a gene that controls brain, heart, limb, and skull development in the fetus.

2003
More than 8,000 people are infected with severe acute respiratory syndrome (SARS), which is caused by a newly discovered virus.

Compression guide:
To shorten instruction because of time limitations, omit the LabBook Lab.

OBJECTIVES	LABS, DEMONSTRATIONS, AND ACTIVITIES	TECHNOLOGY RESOURCES
PACING • 90 min pp. 278–283 **Chapter Opener**	SE **Start-up Activity**, p. 279 `GENERAL`	OSP **Parent Letter** `GENERAL` CD **Student Edition on CD-ROM** CD **Guided Reading Audio CD** TR **Chapter Starter Transparency*** VID **Brain Food Video Quiz**
Section 1 Disease • Explain the difference between infectious diseases and noninfectious diseases. • Identify five ways that you might come into contact with a pathogen. • Discuss four methods that have helped reduce the spread of disease.	SE **Connection to Social Studies** Disease and History, p. 281 `GENERAL` TE **Activity** Using Microscopes, p. 281 `BASIC` SE **School-to-Home Activity** Label Check, p. 282 `GENERAL` TE **Connection to Physical Science** Pasteurization, p. 282 SE **Skills Practice Lab** Passing the Cold, p. 292 ◆ `GENERAL` CRF **Datasheet for Chapter Lab*** SE **Science In Action** Math, Social Studies and Language Arts Activites, pp. 298–299	CRF **Lesson Plans*** TR **Bellringer Transparency*** TR **LINK TO PHYSICAL SCIENCE** Thermal Energy in Water*** VID **Lab Videos for Life Science**
PACING • 45 min pp. 284–291 **Section 2 Your Body's Defenses** • Describe how your body keeps out pathogens. • Explain how the immune system fights infections. • Describe four challenges to the immune system.	TE **Activity** Reactions to Illness, p. 284 `GENERAL` SE **Quick Lab** Only Skin Deep, p. 285 `GENERAL` CRF **Datasheet for Quick Lab*** TE **Activity** Follow the Path, p. 286 `BASIC` TE **Group Activity** Immunity Skit, p. 287 `ADVANCED` SE **Connection to Chemistry** Bent out of Shape, p. 288 `GENERAL` TE **Connection Activity** Real World, p. 288 `GENERAL` TE **Activity** Concept Mapping, p. 290 `GENERAL` SE **Model-Making Lab** Antibodies to the Rescue, p. 599 `GENERAL` CRF **Datasheet for LabBook*** LB **Long-Term Projects & Research Ideas** A Chuckle a Day Keeps the Doctor Away* `ADVANCED`	CRF **Lesson Plans*** TR **Bellringer Transparency*** TR **An Antibody's Shape Fits an Antigen*** TR **Immune Response: A*** TR **Immune Response: B*** SE **Internet Activity**, p. 286 `GENERAL` CRF **SciLinks Activity*** `GENERAL`

PACING • 90 min

CHAPTER REVIEW, ASSESSMENT, AND STANDARDIZED TEST PREPARATION

CRF **Vocabulary Activity*** `GENERAL`
SE **Chapter Review**, pp. 294–295 `GENERAL`
CRF **Chapter Review*** ■ `GENERAL`
CRF **Chapter Tests A*** ■ `GENERAL`, **B*** `ADVANCED`, **C*** `SPECIAL NEEDS`
SE **Standardized Test Preparation**, pp. 296–297 `GENERAL`
CRF **Standardized Test Preparation*** `GENERAL`
CRF **Performance-Based Assessment*** `GENERAL`
OSP **Test Generator** `GENERAL`
CRF **Test Item Listing*** `GENERAL`

Online and Technology Resources

Visit **go.hrw.com** for a variety of free resources related to this textbook. Enter the keyword **HT5R7BD6.**

 Holt Online Learning

Students can access interactive problem-solving help and active visual concept development with the *Holt Science and Technology* Online Edition available at **www.hrw.com.**

 Guided Reading Audio CD

These CDs are designed to help auditory learners and reluctant readers.

 Science Tutor CD-ROM

Excellent for remediation and test practice.

SKILLS DEVELOPMENT RESOURCES	SECTION REVIEW AND ASSESSMENT	STANDARDS CORRELATIONS
SE Pre-Reading Activity, p. 278 `GENERAL` **OSP** Science Puzzlers, Twisters & Teasers* `GENERAL`		North Carolina Standard Course of Study
CRF Directed Reading A* `BASIC`, B* `SPECIAL NEEDS` **CRF** Vocabulary and Section Summary* `GENERAL` **SE** Reading Strategy Paired Summarizing, p. 280 `GENERAL` **TE** Inclusion Strategies, p. 281 **SE** Math Practice Epidemic!, p. 283 `GENERAL` **CRF** Critical Thinking Vaccine for Super Bug Found!* `ADVANCED`	**SE** Reading Checks, pp. 281, 283 `GENERAL` **TE** Reteaching, p. 282 `BASIC` **TE** Quiz, p. 282 `GENERAL` **TE** Alternative Assessment, p. 282 `GENERAL` **SE** Section Review,* p. 283 ■ `GENERAL` **CRF** Section Quiz* ■ `GENERAL`	*Chapter Lab:* 1.01
CRF Directed Reading A* `BASIC`, B* `SPECIAL NEEDS` **CRF** Vocabulary and Section Summary* `GENERAL` **SE** Reading Strategy Reading Organizer, p. 284 `GENERAL` **TE** Inclusion Strategies, p. 288 **CRF** Reinforcement Worksheet Immunity Teamwork* `GENERAL`	**SE** Reading Checks, pp. 285, 286, 289, 290 `GENERAL` **TE** Homework, p. 289 `GENERAL` **TE** Reteaching, p. 290 `BASIC` **TE** Quiz, p. 290 `GENERAL` **TE** Alternative Assessment, p. 290 `ADVANCED` **SE** Section Review,* p. 291 ■ `GENERAL` **CRF** Section Quiz* ■ `GENERAL`	4.01, 4.02, 4.04

One-Stop Planner® CD-ROM

This convenient CD-ROM includes:
• Lab Materials QuickList Software
• Holt Calendar Planner
• Customizable Lesson Plans
• Printable Worksheets
• ExamView® Test Generator

cnnstudentnews.com

Find the latest news, lesson plans, and activities related to important scientific events.

NSTA

www.scilinks.org

Maintained by the **National Science Teachers Association.** See Chapter Enrichment pages for a complete list of topics.

Check out *Current Science* articles and activities by visiting the HRW Web site at **go.hrw.com.** Just type in the keyword **HL5CS27T.**

Classroom Videos

• **Lab Videos** demonstrate the chapter lab.
• **Brain Food Video Quizzes** help students review the chapter material.
• **CNN Videos** bring science into your students' daily life.

Visual Resources

CHAPTER STARTER TRANSPARENCY

BELLRINGER TRANSPARENCIES

TEACHING TRANSPARENCIES

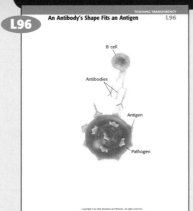

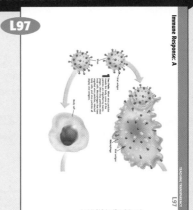

TEACHING TRANSPARENCIES

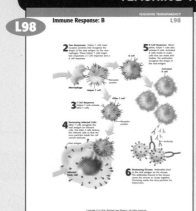

CONCEPT MAPPING TRANSPARENCY

Planning Resources

LESSON PLANS

PARENT LETTER

TEST ITEM LISTING

One-Stop Planner® CD-ROM

This CD-ROM includes all of the resources shown here and the following time-saving tools:

- *Lab Materials QuickList Software*
- *Customizable lesson plans*
- *Holt Calendar Planner*
- *The powerful ExamView® Test Generator*

Meeting Individual Needs

DIRECTED READING A
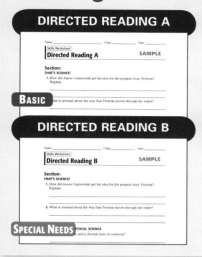

BASIC

DIRECTED READING B
SPECIAL NEEDS

VOCABULARY ACTIVITY
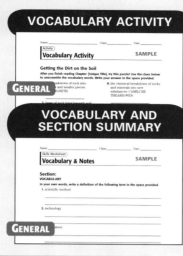

GENERAL

VOCABULARY AND SECTION SUMMARY
GENERAL

REINFORCEMENT

BASIC

CRITICAL THINKING
ADVANCED

SCILINKS ACTIVITY
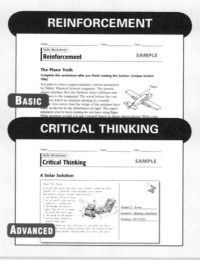

GENERAL

SCIENCE PUZZLERS, TWISTERS & TEASERS
GENERAL

Labs and Activities

LONG-TERM PROJECTS & RESEARCH IDEAS

ADVANCED

DATASHEETS FOR QUICK LABS

DATASHEETS FOR CHAPTER LABS

DATASHEETS FOR LABBOOK

Review and Assessments

SECTION QUIZ

GENERAL

SECTION REVIEW
GENERAL

CHAPTER REVIEW
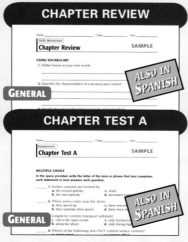

GENERAL

CHAPTER TEST A
GENERAL

CHAPTER TEST B
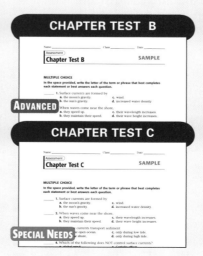

ADVANCED

CHAPTER TEST C
SPECIAL NEEDS

STANDARDIZED TEST PREPARATION
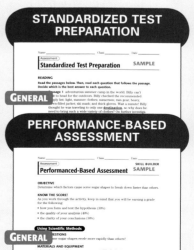

GENERAL

PERFORMANCE-BASED ASSESSMENT
GENERAL

Chapter 10 • Chapter Resources   277D

This Chapter Enrichment provides relevant and interesting information to expand and enhance your presentation of the chapter material.

Section 1

Disease

Pathogens and the Diseases That They Cause

- Pathogens are agents that cause disease. Pathogens can be living or nonliving. Living pathogens include bacteria, protists, fungi, worms, and insects. Nonliving pathogens include viruses, viroids, and prions.

- Bacterial diseases include bubonic plague, cholera, dental caries, Lyme disease, pneumonia, and typhoid fever.

- Viral diseases include colds, influenza, chickenpox, measles, rubella, mumps, smallpox, infectious hepatitis, polio, and AIDS.

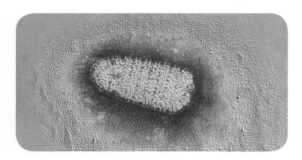

- Protists cause malaria, Chagas' disease, toxoplasmosis, and giardiasis. Common fungal diseases include ringworm, athlete's foot, vaginal yeast infections, jock itch, and histoplasmosis.

Is That a Fact!

- ◆ Bacteria were the first organisms to inhabit Earth. They are thought to have been the only organisms on Earth for about 1 billion years.

- ◆ All other life-forms are thought to have evolved from ancestral forms of bacteria.

- ◆ Some species of bacteria can reproduce every 20 min. Given unlimited resources, one bacterium could produce 1 million kilograms of bacteria in a day!

Emerging Viruses

- The news is full of instances in which new viruses have suddenly begun to infect people. Examples include HIV, which became common in the 1980s, hantavirus, which caused an outbreak in 1993, new strains of Ebola, which were announced in the 1990s, and a corona virus causing SARS, which became common in 2003. Such viruses are called *emerging viruses*.

- Emerging viruses can evolve or mutate from an existing virus that was not infectious. They can also spread from one species to another. Another way that a virus can suddenly emerge is through globalization. When people build roads through a previously isolated area or travel to new places, viruses can spread.

Types of Vaccines

- Vaccines are generally harmless forms of a pathogen or parts of a pathogen that are introduced into the body to help the immune system develop antibodies against the pathogen should the disease-causing form enter the body in the future.

- There are several ways that vaccines are prepared today. One way to make a vaccine is to inactivate the viruses or to kill the bacteria that cause the disease. Another way is to use a similar strain of pathogen or an attenuated or weakened version of the pathogen. The latter kind of vaccine is sometimes called a *live attenuated vaccine*.

Section 2

Your Body's Defenses

The Body's Defenses Against Pathogens

- The body has two main kinds of defenses against disease—specific and nonspecific defenses.

- The body's so-called first and second lines of defense are its nonspecific defense mechanisms. The first line of defense consists of the skin, the mucous membranes, and the secretions of the mucous membranes. Oil, sweat, tears, mucus, and saliva wash pathogens away and contain enzymes that digest the cell walls of microbes.

- The body's second line of defense includes white blood cells that ingest or destroy foreign agents detected in the body. The second line of defense also includes proteins that help cells avoid infection by foreign agents. Antimicrobial proteins include complement proteins and interferons. Also part of the body's second line of defense is its inflammatory response, which occurs in response to cuts or other incisions through the skin.

Fever

- A fever occurs when the body's temperature rises above 98.6°F (37°C) when measured orally.

- Fevers, which commonly accompany infectious diseases, help the body thwart invading pathogens. However, fevers may also accompany noninfectious conditions, such as dehydration and heart attack.

Is That a Fact!

◆ A very high fever can cause a coma, seizures, or brain damage.

AIDS

- AIDS is the final stage in an HIV infection. Upon infection, the viruses first multiply quickly and are quickly fought off by immune system cells. Some viruses remain in the body and replicate slowly over time. Immune system cells continue the fight, sometimes for many years. HIV attacks helper T cells, and when the number of helper T cells falls below a certain level, a person is said to have AIDS.

- HIV is spread through the exchange of blood and other body fluids. It is not spread through casual contact.

- There is no cure for AIDS at this time. There are only drug regimens that may prolong the life of some patients.

- The best way to avoid contracting AIDS is to avoid the behaviors known to put one at risk for acquiring HIV. These behaviors include sharing needles and engaging in unprotected sexual contact.

Allergic Reactions

- The first time a person is exposed to an allergen, such as pollen, he or she usually shows no allergic response. As when a vaccine is administered, the body produces antibodies against the allergen. Thus prepared, the body develops the allergic response upon subsequent exposures to the allergen.

Is That a Fact!

◆ Allergic responses may be a defense mechanism left over from the body's defenses against parasitic worms. This hypothesis comes from the observation that the body's method of combating parasitic worms is very similar to the allergic response seen in hay fever and asthma.

SCI**LINKS**

NSTA
Developed and maintained by the
National Science Teachers Association

SciLinks is maintained by the National Science Teachers Association to provide you and your students with interesting, up-to-date links that will enrich your classroom presentation of the chapter.

Visit www.scilinks.org and enter the SciLinks code for more information about the topic listed.

opic: **What Causes Diseases?**
SciLinks code: **HSM1653**

Topic: **Allergies**
SciLinks code: **HSM0048**

Topic: **Pathogens**
SciLinks code: **HSM1118**

Topic: **Cancer and HIV**
SciLinks code: **HSM0208**

Topic: **Body Defenses**
SciLinks code: **HSM0181**

Overview

Tell students that this chapter will help them learn about diseases, including how infectious diseases are spread, how the body defends against diseases, and what problems can arise with the immune system.

Assessing Prior Knowledge

Students should be familiar with the following topics:

• bacteria and viruses

• body systems

Identifying Misconceptions

As students learn the material in this chapter, some of them may be confused about how diseases are spread. For example, warnings to bundle up during cold weather may lead students to think that cold weather causes infectious disease. Help them understand that pathogens cause infectious disease. Furthermore, some students may think that all microorganisms are harmful. Emphasize that although some microorganisms can cause disease, life as we know it would be impossible without microbes.

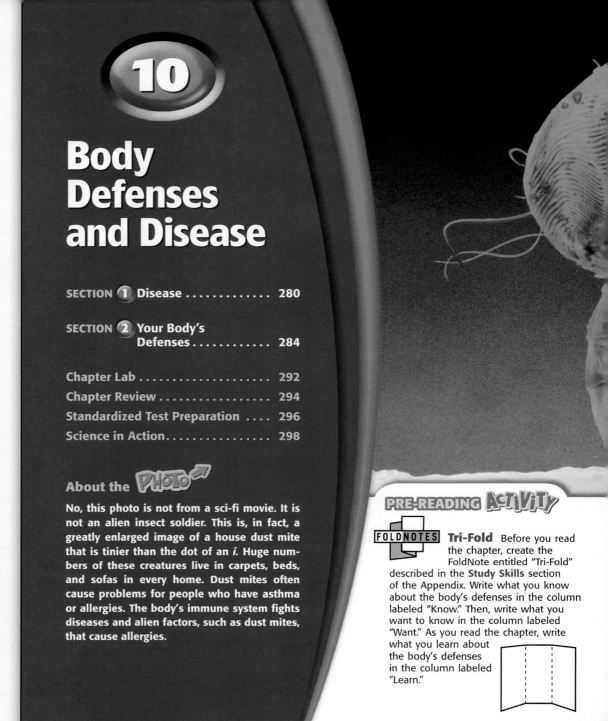

10

Body Defenses and Disease

About the PHOTO

No, this photo is not from a sci-fi movie. It is not an alien insect soldier. This is, in fact, a greatly enlarged image of a house dust mite that is tinier than the dot of an *i*. Huge numbers of these creatures live in carpets, beds, and sofas in every home. Dust mites often cause problems for people who have asthma or allergies. The body's immune system fights diseases and alien factors, such as dust mites, that cause allergies.

PRE-READING ACTIVITY

FOLDNOTES **Tri-Fold** Before you read the chapter, create the FoldNote entitled "Tri-Fold" described in the **Study Skills** section of the Appendix. Write what you know about the body's defenses in the column labeled "Know." Then, write what you want to know in the column labeled "Want." As you read the chapter, write what you learn about the body's defenses in the column labeled "Learn."

Standards Correlations

North Carolina Standard Course of Study

1.01 Identify and create questions and hypotheses that can be answered through scientific investigations. (Chapter Lab)

4.01 (partial) Analyze how human body systems interact to provide for the needs of the human organism: . . . Immune . . . (Section 2)

4.02 Describe how systems within the human body are defined by the functions it performs. (Section 2)

4.04 Evaluate how systems in the human body help regulate the internal environment. (Section 2)

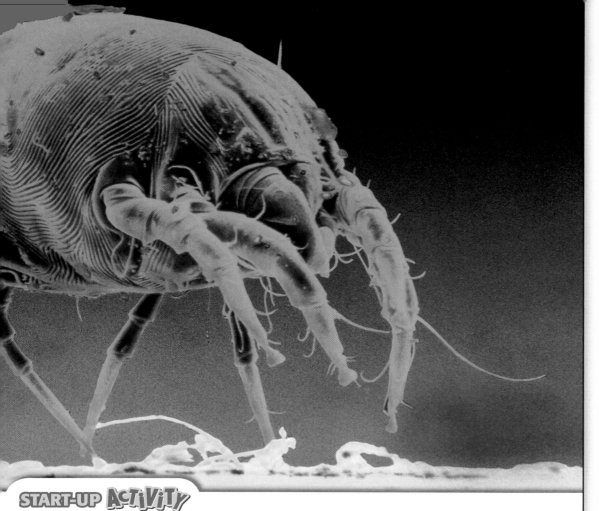

START-UP ACTIVITY

MATERIALS

FOR EACH GROUP
- agar, nutrient
- gloves, protective
- marbles (2)
- Petri dishes (2)
- soap
- tape, transparent
- water, warm

Safety Caution: Remind students to review all safety cautions and icons before beginning this lab activity. Tell students not to open the Petri dishes once they are sealed. Treat all growth in the Petri dishes as pathogenic, and dispose of the dishes as you would any other biohazard.

Teacher's Notes: Keep the lids on the Petri dishes except when rolling the marble on the agar. Doing so will help keep outside contamination to a minimum. In step 6, it might be helpful to use an incubator set at 37°C.

Answers

1. Descriptions may vary. The Petri dish labeled "Unwashed" should have the most bacterial growth.

2. Sample answer: It is important to wash my hands to help decrease the number of microorganisms I put in my mouth.

START-UP ACTIVITY

Invisible Invaders

In this activity, you will see tiny organisms grow.

Procedure

1. Obtain **two Petri dishes containing nutrient agar.** Label them "Washed" and "Unwashed."

2. Rub **two marbles** between the palms of your hands. Observe the appearance of the marbles.

3. Roll one marble in the Petri dish labeled "Unwashed."

4. Put on a pair of **disposable gloves.** Wash the other marble with **soap** and **warm water** for 4 min.

5. Roll the washed marble in the Petri dish labeled "Washed."

6. Secure the lids of the Petri dishes with **transparent tape.** Place the dishes in a warm, dark place. Do not open the Petri dishes after they are sealed.

7. Record changes in the Petri dishes for 1 week.

Analysis

1. How did the washed and unwashed marbles compare? How did the Petri dishes differ after several days?

2. Why is it important to wash your hands before eating?

Chapter Starter Transparency
Use this transparency to help students begin thinking about the way that vaccines help defend the body.

CHAPTER RESOURCES

Technology

 Transparencies
- Chapter Starter Transparency   **READING SKILLS**

Student Edition CD-ROM

Guided Reading Audio CD

 Classroom Videos
- Brain Food Video Quiz

Workbooks

 Science Puzzlers, Twisters & Teasers
- Body Defenses and Disease **GENERAL**

Overview

This section introduces the difference between noninfectious diseases and infectious diseases. Students will learn how they can come into contact with pathogens and how cleanliness, pasteurization, vaccines, and antibiotics can help reduce the spread of pathogens.

Bellringer

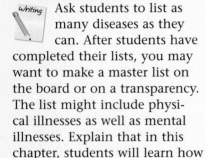

Writing Ask students to list as many diseases as they can. After students have completed their lists, you may want to make a master list on the board or on a transparency. The list might include physical illnesses as well as mental illnesses. Explain that in this chapter, students will learn how pathogens cause illnesses and how illnesses can be prevented.

Objectives

- Explain the difference between infectious diseases and noninfectious diseases.
- Identify five ways that you might come into contact with a pathogen.
- Discuss four methods that have helped reduce the spread of disease.

Terms to Learn

noninfectious disease
infectious disease
pathogen
immunity

READING STRATEGY

Paired Summarizing Read this section silently. In pairs, take turns summarizing the material. Stop to discuss ideas that seem confusing.

noninfectious disease a disease that cannot spread from one individual to another

infectious disease a disease that is caused by a pathogen and that can be spread from one individual to another

pathogen a virus, microorganism, or other organism that causes disease

Disease

You've probably heard it before: "Cover your mouth when you sneeze!" "Wash your hands!" "Don't put that in your mouth!"

What is all the fuss about? When people say these things to you, they are concerned about the spread of disease.

Causes of Disease

When you have a *disease,* your normal body functions are disrupted. Some diseases, such as most cancers and heart disease, are not spread from one person to another. They are called **noninfectious diseases.**

Noninfectious diseases can be caused by a variety of factors. For example, a genetic disorder causes the disease hemophilia (HEE moh FIL ee uh), in which a person's blood does not clot properly. Smoking, lack of physical activity, and a high-fat diet can greatly increase a person's chances of getting certain noninfectious diseases. Avoiding harmful habits may help you avoid noninfectious diseases.

A disease that can be passed from one living thing to another is an **infectious disease.** Infectious diseases are caused by agents called **pathogens.** Viruses and some bacteria, fungi, protists, and worms may all cause diseases. **Figure 1** shows some enlarged images of common pathogens.

Figure 1 **Pathogens**

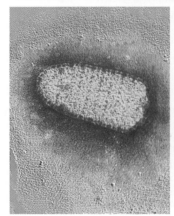
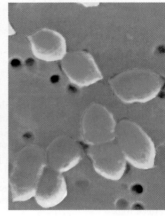

▲ This virus causes rabies. ▲ *Streptococcus* bacteria can cause strep throat.

Pathways to Pathogens

There are many ways pathogens can be passed from one person to another. Being aware of them can help you stay healthy.

Air

Some pathogens travel through the air. For example, a single sneeze, such as the one shown in **Figure 2,** releases thousands of tiny droplets of moisture that can carry pathogens.

Contaminated Objects

You may already know that if you drink from a glass that an infected person has just used, you could become infected with a pathogen. A person who is sick may leave bacteria or viruses on many other objects, too. For example, contaminated doorknobs, keyboards, combs, and towels can pass pathogens.

Person to Person

Some pathogens are spread by direct person-to-person contact. You can become infected with some illnesses by kissing, shaking hands, or touching the sores of an infected person.

Animals

Some pathogens are carried by animals. For example, humans can get a fungus called *ringworm* from handling an infected dog or cat. Also, ticks may carry bacteria that cause Lyme disease or Rocky Mountain spotted fever.

Food and Water

Drinking water in the United States is generally safe. But water lines can break, or treatment plants can become flooded. These problems may allow microorganisms to enter the public water supply. Bacteria growing in foods and beverages can cause illness, too. For example, meat, fish, and eggs that are not cooked enough can still contain dangerous bacteria or parasites. Even leaving food out at room temperature can give bacteria such as salmonella the chance to grow and produce toxins in the food. Refrigerating foods can slow the growth of many of these pathogens. Because bacteria grow in food, washing all used cooking surfaces and tools is also important.

✔ Reading Check Why must you cook meat and eggs thoroughly? (*See the Appendix for answers to Reading Checks.*)

Figure 2 *A sneeze can force thousands of pathogen-carrying droplets out of your body at up to 160 km/h.*

CONNECTION TO Social Studies

Disease and History Many diseases have shaped history. For example, yellow fever, which is caused by a virus that is spread by mosquitoes, was one of the obstacles in building the Panama Canal. Only after people learned how to prevent the spread of the yellow fever virus could the canal be completed.

Use information from Internet and library research to create a poster describing how one infectious disease affected history.

Most products that require pasteurization also require refrigeration because once the products are opened, they are vulnerable to getting bacteria in them. Refrigeration helps slow the growth of the bacteria.

Reteaching ——— BASIC

Reviewing Pathways Have students make a chart titled "How to Stay Healthy." In one column, they can list the ways that pathogens are encountered. In a second column, students can list ways to prevent becoming infected. **LS** Logical

Quiz ——— GENERAL

Ask students whether the following statements are true or false.

1. All diseases are caused by pathogens. (false)

2. You can become infected with some pathogens by shaking hands with an infected person. (true)

3. Pasteurization uses very cold temperatures to kill bacteria. (false)

Alternative Assessment ——— GENERAL

Pamphlet Have students develop a disease-prevention pamphlet. Encourage students to include illustrations. **LS** Verbal

SCHOOL to HOME

Label Check

At home or in a local store, find a product that has been pasteurized. In your **science journal,** write down other safety information you find on the label, including the product's refrigeration needs. Why do you think most products that require pasteurization also require refrigeration?

ACTIVITY

immunity the ability to resist or to recover from an infectious disease

Figure 3 Today, pasteurization is used to kill pathogens in many different types of food, including dairy products, shellfish, and juices.

Putting Pathogens in Their Place

Until the twentieth century, surgery patients often died of bacterial infections. But doctors learned that simple cleanliness could help prevent the spread of some diseases. Today, hospitals and clinics use a variety of technologies to prevent the spread of pathogens. For example, ultraviolet radiation, boiling water, and chemicals are used to kill pathogens in health facilities.

Pasteurization

During the mid-1800s, Louis Pasteur, a French scientist, discovered that microorganisms caused wine to spoil. The uninvited microorganisms were bacteria. Pasteur devised a method of using heat to kill most of the bacteria in the wine. This method is called *pasteurization* (PAS tuhr i ZAY shuhn), and it is still used today. The milk that the girl in **Figure 3** is drinking has been pasteurized.

Vaccines and Immunity

In the late 1700s, no one knew what a pathogen was. During this time, Edward Jenner studied a disease called *smallpox*. He observed that people who had been infected with cowpox seemed to have protection against smallpox. These people had a resistance to the disease. The ability to resist or recover from an infectious disease is called **immunity.** Jenner's work led to the first modern vaccine. A *vaccine* is a substance that helps your body develop immunity to a disease.

Today, vaccines are used all over the world to prevent many serious diseases. Modern vaccines contain pathogens that are killed or specially treated so that they can't make you very sick. The vaccine is enough like the pathogen to allow your body to develop a defense against the disease.

CONNECTION to Physical Science— GENERAL

Pasteurization Pasteurization is the process of killing harmful bacteria by using thermal energy. Milk is pasteurized in one of two ways: by heating it to 63°C for 30 min or by heating it to 72°C for 16 s. The organisms that can survive pasteurization will eventually spoil the milk, but they are generally not harmful to people.

Boiling the milk would kill even more of the bacteria —not just the harmful ones—but would also change the milk. Use the teaching transparency titled "Thermal Energy in Water" to illustrate how increasing the temperature of a substance increases the substance's thermal energy. **LS** Visual

Antibiotics

Have you ever had strep throat? If so, you have had a bacterial infection. Bacterial infections can be a serious threat to your health. Fortunately, doctors can usually treat these kinds of infections with antibiotics. An *antibiotic* is a substance that can kill bacteria or slow the growth of bacteria. Antibiotics may also be used to treat infections caused by other microorganisms, such as fungi. You may take an antibiotic when you are sick. Always take antibiotics according to your doctor's instructions to ensure that all the pathogens are killed.

Viruses, such as those that cause colds, are not affected by antibiotics. Antibiotics can kill only living things, and viruses are not alive. The only way to destroy viruses in your body is to locate and kill the cells they have invaded.

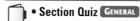 **Reading Check** Frank caught a bad cold just before the opening night of a school play. He visited his doctor and asked her to prescribe antibiotics for his cold. The doctor politely refused and advised Frank to stay home and get plenty of rest. Why do you think the doctor refused to give Frank antibiotics?

Epidemic!
You catch a cold and return to your school while sick. Your friends don't have immunity to your cold. On the first day, you expose five friends to your cold. The next day, each of those friends passes the virus to five more people. If this pattern continues for 5 more days, how many people will be exposed to the virus?

SECTION Review

Summary

- Noninfectious diseases cannot be spread from one person to another.
- Infectious diseases are caused by pathogens that are passed from one living thing to another.
- Pathogens can travel through the air or can be spread by contact with other people, contaminated objects, animals, food, or water.
- Cleanliness, pasteurization, vaccines, and antibiotics help control the spread of pathogens.

Using Key Terms

1. In your own words, write a definition for each of the following terms: *infectious disease, noninfectious disease,* and *immunity.*

Understanding Key Ideas

2. Vaccines contain
   a. treated pathogens.
   b. heat.
   c. antibiotics.
   d. pasteurization.

3. List five ways that you might come into contact with a pathogen.

4. Name four ways to help keep safe from pathogens.

Math Skills

5. If 10 people with the virus each expose 25 more people to the virus, how many people will be exposed to the virus?

Critical Thinking

6. **Identifying Relationships** Why might the risk of infectious disease be high in a community that has no water treatment facility?

7. **Analyzing Methods** Explain what might happen if a doctor did not wear gloves when treating patients.

8. **Applying Concepts** Why do vaccines for diseases in animals help prevent some illnesses in people?

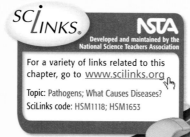

For a variety of links related to this chapter, go to www.scilinks.org

Topic: Pathogens; What Causes Diseases?
SciLinks code: HSM1118; HSM1653

Answer to Reading Check

Frank's doctor did not prescribe antibiotics because Frank had a cold. Colds are caused by viruses. Antibiotics cannot stop viruses.

CHAPTER RESOURCES

Chapter Resource File

- Section Quiz GENERAL
- Section Review GENERAL
- Vocabulary and Section Summary GENERAL
- Reinforcement Worksheet BASIC

Technology

Transparencies
- LINK TO PHYSICAL SCIENCE Thermal Energy in Water

Answers to Math Practice

1st day: five people exposed
2nd day: 25 (5^2) people exposed
7th day: 78,125 (5^7) people exposed

Answers to Section Review

1. Sample answer: An infectious disease is an illness caused by a pathogen. A noninfectious disease is an illness that is not caused by a pathogen. Immunity is the ability to resist or recover from an infectious disease.

2. a

3. Answers may vary but may include being sneezed on by an infected person, touching an infected person, having sexual contact with an infected person, eating infected food, or breathing in the pathogen.

4. Sample answer: keeping clean, pasteurization, vaccines, and antibiotics

5. $10 \times 25 = 250$

6. Sample answer: Without water treatment, a community's water supply can easily become infected with pathogens. These pathogens can be ingested or can contaminate objects washed in the water.

7. Sample answer: A doctor who does not wear gloves might spread an infectious disease from one patient to another.

8. Sample answer: Some animal diseases, such as rabies, can also infect people. Preventing the spread of these diseases in animals makes the diseases less likely to be spread to humans.

Focus

Overview

In this section, students will learn how the skin keeps pathogens out of the body and how the immune system works. Students will also learn about allergies and other immune system problems.

🔊 Bellringer

Have students make a list of the ways that pathogens might enter the body. (Examples include through the mouth, ears, nose, and cuts in the skin. Pathogens can travel in the water, in the air, and in food.)

Motivate

ACTIVITY ——————— GENERAL

Reactions to Illness Ask students to think of a time when they were ill. Have students list the ways in which their body reacted to the illness. (Answers might include having a fever, chills, a runny nose, a sore throat, a rash, and throbbing pain.) Encourage students to share their lists with a partner. Then, have students skim this lesson and try to link their body's reactions with the reactions of the immune system to pathogenic invasions.

 Interpersonal

READING WARM-UP

Objectives
- Describe how your body keeps out pathogens.
- Explain how the immune system fights infections.
- Describe four challenges to the immune system.

Terms to Learn

immune system
macrophage
T cell
B cell
antibody

memory B cell
allergy
autoimmune disease
cancer

READING STRATEGY

Reading Organizer As you read this section, make a flowchart of the steps of how your body responds to a virus.

Your Body's Defenses

Bacteria and viruses can be in the air, in the water, and on all the surfaces around you.

Your body must constantly protect itself against pathogens that are trying to invade it. But how does your body do that? Luckily, your body has its own built-in defense system.

First Lines of Defense

For a pathogen to harm you, it must attack a part of your body. Usually, though, very few of the pathogens around you make it past your first lines of defense.

Many organisms that try to enter your eyes or mouth are destroyed by special enzymes. Pathogens that enter your nose are washed down the back of your throat by mucus. The mucus carries the pathogens to your stomach, where most are quickly digested.

Your skin is made of many layers of flat cells. The outermost layers are dead. As a result, many pathogens that land on your skin have difficulty finding a live cell to infect. As **Figure 1** shows, the dead skin cells are constantly dropping off your body as new skin cells grow from beneath. As the dead skin cells flake off, they carry away viruses, bacteria, and other microorganisms. In addition, glands secrete oil onto your skin's surface. The oil contains chemicals that kill many pathogens.

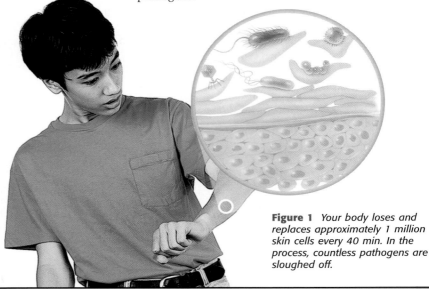

Figure 1 *Your body loses and replaces approximately 1 million skin cells every 40 min. In the process, countless pathogens are sloughed off.*

CHAPTER RESOURCES

Chapter Resource File

- **Lesson Plan**
- **Directed Reading A** BASIC
- **Directed Reading B** SPECIAL NEEDS

Technology

Transparencies
- Bellringer
- An Antibody's Shape Fits an Antigen

WEIRD SCIENCE

Earwax is one of the body's defenses against foreign invaders. Wax collects dirt, bacteria, fungi, and other foreign matter that could cause an ear infection.

Failure of First Lines

Sometimes, skin is cut or punctured and pathogens can enter the body. The body acts quickly to keep out as many pathogens as possible. Blood flow to the injured area increases. Cell parts in the blood called *platelets* help seal the open wound so that no more pathogens can enter.

The increased blood flow also brings cells that belong to the **immune system,** the body system that fights pathogens. The immune system is not localized in any one place in your body. It is not controlled by any one organ, such as the brain. Instead, it is a team of individual cells, tissues, and organs that work together to keep you safe from invading pathogens.

Cells of the Immune System

The immune system consists mainly of three kinds of cells. One kind is the macrophage (MAK roh FAYJ). **Macrophages** engulf and digest many microorganisms or viruses that enter your body. If only a few microorganisms or viruses have entered a wound, the macrophages can easily stop them.

The other two main kinds of immune-system cells are T cells and B cells. **T cells** coordinate the immune system and attack many infected cells. **B cells** are immune-system cells that make antibodies. **Antibodies** are proteins that attach to specific antigens. *Antigens* are substances that stimulate an immune response. Your body is capable of making billions of different antibodies. Each antibody usually attaches to only one kind of antigen, as illustrated in **Figure 2.**

Reading Check How do macrophages help fight disease? (*See the Appendix for answers to Reading Checks.*)

Only Skin Deep

1. Cut an **apple** in half.
2. Place **plastic wrap** over each half. The plastic wrap will act as skin.
3. Use **scissors** to cut the plastic wrap on one of the apple halves, and then use an **eyedropper** to drip **food coloring** on each apple half. The food coloring represents pathogens coming into contact with your body.
4. What happened to each apple half?
5. How is the plastic wrap similar to skin?
6. How is the plastic wrap different from skin?

immune system the cells and tissues that recognize and attack foreign substances in the body

macrophage an immune system cell that engulfs pathogens and other materials

T cell an immune system cell that coordinates the immune system and attacks many infected cells

B cell a white blood cell that makes antibodies

antibody a protein made by B cells that binds to a specific antigen

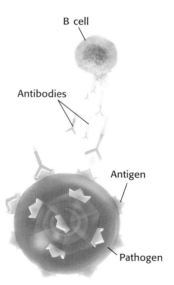

Figure 2 *An antibody's shape is very specialized. It matches an antigen like a key fits a lock.*

ADVANCED

Disease and Conquest In the 16th century, Hernando Cortes and the Spanish conquistadors overwhelmed and conquered the flourishing cultures of what is now Mexico. One reason the Europeans were able to overtake the Native Americans so quickly is that the Europeans incidentally brought with them diseases such as smallpox. These diseases were new to the populations in the Americas, and they devastated entire nations. In the span of just two generations, an estimated 12,000,000 to 25,000,000 Native Americans died as a result of European diseases. Have interested students research and report on the role that disease played when the Europeans settled in North and South America. **LS** Verbal

Teach

Quick Lab

MATERIALS

FOR EACH STUDENT
• apple (cut in half)
• eyedropper
• food coloring
• plastic wrap
• scissors

Safety Caution: Tell students to cut in a direction away from their face and hands. Students should not ingest the apple or the food coloring after the activity. Food coloring can stain hands and clothes.

Teacher's Note: You may want to provide gloves and smocks for this activity. Dark food coloring, such as blue, green, and red, works best in this activity. Yellow does not show up as well as the darker colors. Instruct students to limit themselves to three drops of food coloring per apple half.

Answers

4. The apple half with the uncut wrap was not affected by the food coloring. The apple half with the cut wrap was dyed by the food coloring that seeped through the slits.

5. Sample answer: The plastic wrap is similar to skin because it keeps foreign substances out and protects the soft tissue underneath it.

6. Sample answer: The plastic wrap is different from skin because it cannot heal the wound or swell to help close the wound.

Answer to Reading Check

Macrophages engulf, or eat, any microorganisms or viruses that enter your body.

Follow the Path Have students trace the proper sequence of the pictures across these two pages. Point out that each picture has its own caption that begins with a bold heading. Then, have students outline the information on these two pages by listing the bold headings in order on a sheet of paper. Have pairs of students compare their outlines.

LS Visual English Language Learners

Using the Figure — GENERAL

Identifying Cells As students look at the pictures on these pages, point out that the pictures are numbered. After students have studied the sequence of events portrayed in the pictures, have them point to each kind of white blood cell shown in the pictures on these two pages as you call out the names of the cells: *helper T cell, killer T cell, B cell,* and *macrophage.* Then, ask students to describe the role of each kind of white blood cell.

LS Visual English Language Learners

INTERNET ACTIVITY

For another activity related to this chapter, go to **go.hrw.com** and type in the keyword **HL5BD6W.**

Responding to a Virus

If virus particles enter your body, some of the particles may pass into body cells and begin to replicate. Other virus particles will be engulfed and broken up by macrophages. This is just the beginning of the immune response. The process your immune system uses to fight an invading virus is summarized in the figure below.

✓ **Reading Check** What are two things that can happen to virus particles when they enter the body?

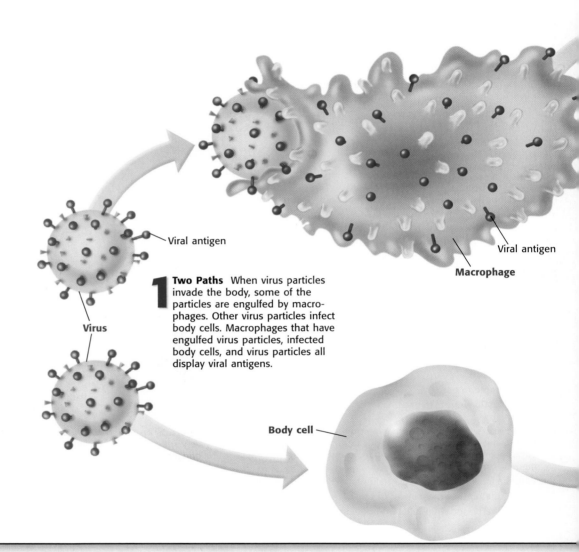

Viral antigen

Virus

Viral antigen

Macrophage

1 Two Paths When virus particles invade the body, some of the particles are engulfed by macrophages. Other virus particles infect body cells. Macrophages that have engulfed virus particles, infected body cells, and virus particles all display viral antigens.

Body cell

CHAPTER RESOURCES

Technology

🗄 **Transparencies**
• Immune Response: A
• Immune Response: B

Answer to Reading Check

If a virus particle enters the body, it may pass into body cells and begin to replicate. Or it may be engulfed and broken up by macrophages.

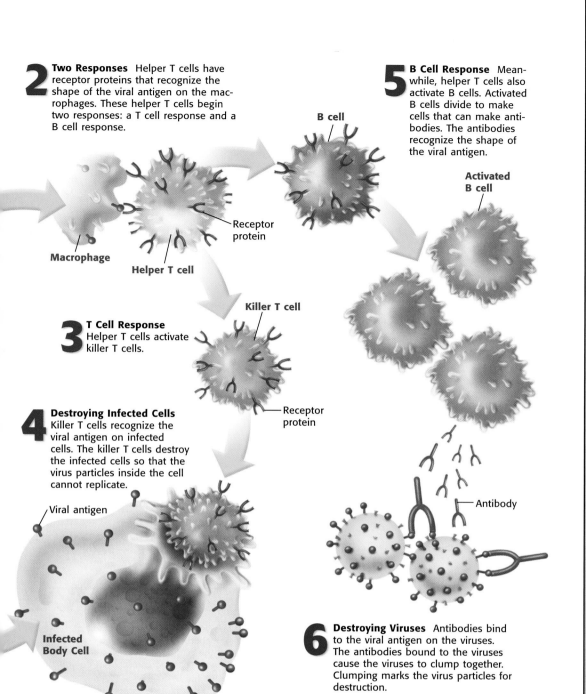

2 **Two Responses** Helper T cells have receptor proteins that recognize the shape of the viral antigen on the macrophages. These helper T cells begin two responses: a T cell response and a B cell response.

B cell

Receptor protein

Macrophage

Helper T cell

Killer T cell

3 **T Cell Response** Helper T cells activate killer T cells.

Receptor protein

4 **Destroying Infected Cells** Killer T cells recognize the viral antigen on infected cells. The killer T cells destroy the infected cells so that the virus particles inside the cell cannot replicate.

Viral antigen

Infected Body Cell

5 **B Cell Response** Meanwhile, helper T cells also activate B cells. Activated B cells divide to make cells that can make antibodies. The antibodies recognize the shape of the viral antigen.

Activated B cell

Antibody

6 **Destroying Viruses** Antibodies bind to the viral antigen on the viruses. The antibodies bound to the viruses cause the viruses to clump together. Clumping marks the virus particles for destruction.

WEIRD SCIENCE

In some cases, a pregnant woman may form antibodies against the blood of the baby she is carrying. The situation is likely to occur when the mother's blood is Rh-negative, meaning it lacks the Rh antigen, and the baby's blood is Rh-positive, meaning it carries the Rh antigen. The mother's immune system recognizes the Rh antigen as foreign and begins to attack the baby's blood cells.

Is That a Fact!

In 1918, a strain of flu viruses called the *Spanish flu* killed at least 20 million people. That number is more than the number of people killed in combat in World War I.

Treating Allergies An allergy is usually treated in two ways once the allergen is identified. An allergist may try to desensitize a patient to the allergen by administering small, periodic doses of the allergen. In addition, an allergist may prescribe drugs to minimize the body's reactions to the allergen. Have interested students contact an allergist and conduct an interview about his or her work. **LS** Interpersonal/Verbal

Research ———— **GENERAL**

Immune Disorders Have students find an article or news report about one of the immune disorders discussed in this lesson. Have students work in small groups to prepare a written or oral report that summarizes one of the articles and links the article it to the concepts presented in this chapter. **LS** Inerpersonal/Verbal

Answer to Connection to Chemistry

As the egg white cooks, the proteins change shape. The change in shape causes the proteins to form a solid mass.

Figure 3 *You may not feel well when you have a fever. But a fever is one way that your body fights infections.*

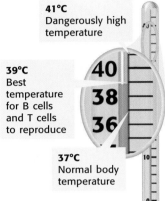

41°C
Dangerously high temperature

39°C
Best temperature for B cells and T cells to reproduce

40
38
36

37°C
Normal body temperature

Figure 4 *A slight fever helps immune cells reproduce. But a fever of more than a few degrees can become dangerous.*

memory B cell a B cell that responds to an antigen more strongly when the body is reinfected with an antigen than it does during its first encounter with the antigen

Fevers

The man in **Figure 3** is sick and has a fever. What is a fever? When macrophages activate the helper T cells, they send a chemical signal that tells your brain to turn up the thermostat. In a few minutes, your body's temperature can rise several degrees. A moderate fever of one or two degrees actually helps you get well faster because it slows the growth of some pathogens. As shown in **Figure 4,** a fever also helps B cells and T cells multiply faster.

Memory Cells

Your immune system can respond to a second encounter faster than it can respond the first time. B cells must have had previous contact with a pathogen before they can make the correct antibodies. During the first encounter with a new pathogen, specialized B cells make antibodies that are effective against that particular invader. This process takes about 2 weeks, which is far too long to prevent an infection. Therefore, the first time you are infected, you usually get sick.

A few of the B cells become memory B cells. **Memory B cells** are cells in your immune system that "remember" how to make an antibody for a particular pathogen. If the pathogen shows up again, the memory B cells produce B cells that make enough antibodies in just 3 or 4 days to protect you.

CONNECTION TO Chemistry

Bent out of Shape When you have a fever, the heat of the fever changes the shape of viral or bacterial proteins, slowing or preventing the reproduction of the pathogen. With an adult present, observe how an egg white changes as it cooks. What do you think happens to the protein in the egg white as it cooks?

ACTiViTY

INCLUSION Strategies

• *Learning Disabled*
• *Attention Deficit Disorder*

Many students have trouble differentiating between allergies and autoimmune diseases. Help students by repeating that autoimmune diseases happen when the body mistakenly attacks its own tissues, and that allergies happen when the immune system mistakenly attacks harmless substances that enter the body. Then, use the following drill:

Which of the following are allergic reactions and which are autoimmune responses?

• sneezing at pollen (allergic reaction)
• the immune system attacking a nerve cell (autoimmune response)
• the immune system attacking the body cells that make insulin (autoimmune response)
• the immune system attacking the proteins in peanut butter (allergic reaction)
LS Verbal

Challenges to the Immune System

The immune system is a very effective body-defense system, but it is not perfect. The immune system is unable to deal with some diseases. There are also conditions in which the immune system does not work properly.

Allergies

Sometimes, the immune system overreacts to antigens that are not dangerous to the body. This inappropriate reaction is called an **allergy.** Allergies may be caused by many things, including certain foods and medicines. Many people have allergic reactions to pollen, shown in **Figure 5.** Symptoms of allergic reactions range from a runny nose and itchy eyes to more serious conditions, such as asthma.

Doctors are not sure why the immune system overreacts in some people. Scientists think allergies might be useful because the mucus draining from your nose carries away pollen, dust, and microorganisms.

Autoimmune Diseases

A disease in which the immune system attacks the body's own cells is called an **autoimmune disease.** In an autoimmune disease, immune-system cells mistake body cells for pathogens. One autoimmune disease is rheumatoid arthritis (ROO muh TOYD ahr THRIET IS), in which the immune system attacks the joints. A common location for rheumatoid arthritis is the joints of the hands, as shown in **Figure 6.** Other autoimmune diseases include type 1 diabetes, multiple sclerosis, and lupus.

✓ Reading Check Name four autoimmune diseases.

allergy a reaction to a harmless or common substance by the body's immune system

autoimmune disease a disease in which the immune system attacks the organism's own cells

Figure 5 Pollen is one substance that can cause allergic reactions.

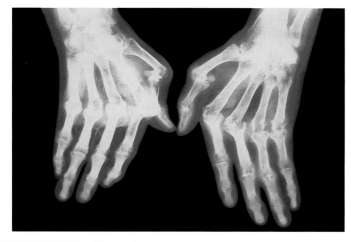

Figure 6 In rheumatoid arthritis, immune-system cells cause joint-tissue swelling, which can lead to joint deformities.

Answer to Reading Check
rheumatoid arthritis, diabetes, multiple sclerosis, and lupus

Close

Reteaching — BASIC

Reviewing HIV You can use the figures from this section that illustrate an immune response to help students understand how HIV hurts the immune system. HIV infects and destroys helper T cells. Have students cover and hide the helper T cell illustrated in the figure. Then, ask students how destroying helper T cells would affect the immune response. (Students should be able to see that both the B cell and T cell responses to infection would be stopped if the helper T cells were eliminated.) **LS** Visual/Auditory

Quiz — GENERAL

Ask students whether the following statements are true or false.

1. Antibodies are specific to certain pathogens. (true)

2. An allergy is caused by the immune system attacking the cells of the body. (false)

3. People with AIDS have too many killer T cells. These cells begin to attack the body's cells, and AIDS is the result. (false)

Alternative Assessment — ADVANCED

Writing Have students choose one of the disorders discussed in this section and prepare a report or a presentation about it. Encourage students to discuss the immune response and the cells of the immune system. **LS** Verbal

| Figure 7 | Immune Cells Fighting Cancer |

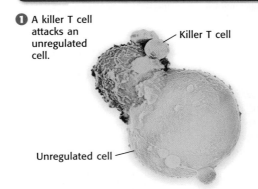

❶ A killer T cell attacks an unregulated cell.

Killer T cell

Unregulated cell

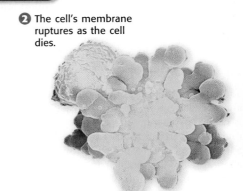

❷ The cell's membrane ruptures as the cell dies.

cancer a disease in which the cells begin dividing at an uncontrolled rate and become invasive

Cancer

Healthy cells divide at a carefully regulated rate. Occasionally, a cell doesn't respond to the body's regulation and begins dividing at an uncontrolled rate. As can be seen in **Figure 7,** killer T cells destroy this type of cell. Sometimes, the immune system cannot control the division of these cells. **Cancer** is the condition in which cells divide at an uncontrolled rate.

Many cancers will invade nearby tissues. They can also enter the cardiovascular system or lymphatic system. Cancers can then be transported to other places in the body. Cancers disrupt the normal activities of the organs they have invaded, sometimes leading to death. Today, though, there are many treatments for cancer. Surgery, radiation, and certain drugs can be used to remove or kill cancer cells or slow their division.

AIDS

The human immunodeficiency virus (HIV) causes acquired immune deficiency syndrome (AIDS). Most viruses infect cells in the nose, mouth, lungs, or intestines, but HIV is different. HIV infects the immune system itself, using helper T cells as factories to produce more viruses. You can see HIV particles in **Figure 8.** The helper T cells are destroyed in the process. Remember that the helper T cells put the B cells and killer T cells to work.

People with AIDS have very few helper T cells, so nothing activates the B cells and killer T cells. Therefore, the immune system cannot attack HIV or any other pathogen. People with AIDS don't usually die of AIDS itself. They die of other diseases that they are unable to fight off.

Figure 8 *The blue particles on this helper T cell are human immunodeficiency viruses. They replicated inside the T cell.*

✓ **Reading Check** What virus causes AIDS?

ACTiViTy — GENERAL

Writing **Concept Mapping** Have students define the new terms presented in this chapter and then use the terms in a concept map. Have students use the chapter title as the first concept in their map. **LS** Visual/Logical

Answer to Reading Check

HIV causes AIDS.

Summary

- Macrophages engulf pathogens, display antigens on their surface, and activate helper T cells. The helper T cells put the killer T cells and B cells to work.
- Killer T cells kill infected cells. B cells make antibodies.
- Fever helps speed immune-cell growth and slow pathogen growth.
- Memory B cells remember how to make an antibody for a pathogen that the body has previously fought.

- An allergy is the overreaction of the immune system to a harmless antigen.
- Autoimmune diseases are responses in which the immune system attacks healthy tissue.
- Cancer cells are cells that undergo uncontrolled division.
- AIDS is a disease that results when the human immunodeficiency virus kills helper T cells.

Using Key Terms

For each pair of terms, explain how the meanings of the terms differ.

1. *B cell* and *T cell*

2. *autoimmune disease* and *allergy*

Understanding Key Ideas

3. Your body's first line of defense against pathogens includes
   a. skin.
   b. macrophages.
   c. T cells.
   d. B cells.

4. List three ways your body defends itself against pathogens.

5. Name three different cells in the immune system, and describe how they respond to pathogens.

6. Describe four challenges to the immune system.

7. What characterizes a cancer cell?

Critical Thinking

8. **Identifying Relationships** Can your body make antibodies for pathogens that you have never been in contact with? Why or why not?

9. **Applying Concepts** If you had chickenpox at age 7, what might prevent you from getting chickenpox again at age 8?

Interpreting Graphics

10. Look at the graph below. Over time, people with AIDS become very sick and are unable to fight off infection. Use the information in the graph below to explain why this occurs.

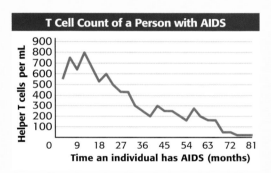

T Cell Count of a Person with AIDS

Helper T cells per mL: 900, 800, 700, 600, 500, 400, 300, 200, 100

Time an individual has AIDS (months): 0, 9, 18, 27, 36, 45, 54, 63, 72, 81

SCILINKS.

NSTA
Developed and maintained by the National Science Teachers Association

For a variety of links related to this chapter, go to www.scilinks.org

Topic: Body Defenses; Allergies
SciLinks code: HSM0181; HSM0048

CHAPTER RESOURCES

Chapter Resource File

- Section Quiz GENERAL
- Section Review GENERAL
- Vocabulary and Section Summary GENERAL
- SciLinks Activity GENERAL
- Datasheet for Quick Lab

Answers to Section Review

1. Sample answer: B cells pathogens by making antibodies. T cells fight pathogens by coordinating responses and killing infected cells directly.

2. Sample answer: In an autoimmune disease, the immune system attacks the body's tissues. In an allergy, the immune system overreacts to antigens that are not part of the body.

3. a

4. Sample answer: Skin keeps most pathogens out. Chemical defenses are in your eyes, stomach, and mouth. If you have a cut in your skin, blood platelets help close the wound so that more microorganisms cannot enter. Microorganisms that do enter encounter immune system cells.

5. Sample answer: a macrophage engulfs pathogens and stick antigens on their outer membranes, helper T cells activate killer T cells and B cells, and killer T cells kill any body cell infected with pathogens.

6. allergy, the body has an inappropriate reaction to a harmless antigen; autoimmune disease: the immune system reacts to body tissues; cancer: cells of the body divide uncontrollably; AIDS: HIV reduces the number of helper T cells, so the body cannot mount a defense against pathogens

7. A cell becomes cancerous when it starts dividing at an uncontrolled rate.

8. Sample answer: No, the body makes antibodies against specific pathogens. If a pathogen has never been met, the immune system would not have had any reason to make an antibody against it.

9. Sample answer: memory B cells

10. Sample answer: People who have AIDS become less able to fight infections because their helper T cell count decreases over time.

Passing the Cold

Teacher's Notes

Time Required
One 45-minute class period

Lab Ratings

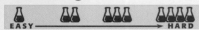

EASY ———————→ HARD

Teacher Prep 🧪🧪
Student Set-Up 🧪🧪
Concept Level 🧪🧪
Clean Up 🧪🧪

MATERIALS

Prepare a phenolphthalein indicator solution ahead of time. Dilute the indicator solution in water. Add 10 mL of the indicator to 40 mL of water. This solution is enough for one student. Mix a 1.5 % NaOH solution. Mix 15 g NaOH with 1 L of water. All but one student will receive 50 mL of this solution.

Safety Caution: Remind students that although they are working with a very low concentration of an alkaline solution, they should work safely with all materials. All spills should be cleaned up immediately. Skin exposed to solutions should be washed immediately with plenty of running water. Remind students that they must never mix unknown solutions without teacher supervision and approval.

OBJECTIVES

Investigate how diseases spread.

Analyze data about how diseases spread.

MATERIALS

- beaker or a cup, 200 mL
- eyedropper
- gloves, protective
- solution, unknown, 50 mL

SAFETY

Passing the Cold

There are more than 100 viruses that cause the symptoms of the common cold. Any of the viruses can be passed from person to person—through the air or through direct contact. In this activity, you will track the progress of an outbreak in your class.

Ask a Question

1 With other members of your group, form a question about the spread of disease. For example "How are cold viruses passed from person to person?" or "How can the progress of an outbreak be modeled?"

Form a Hypothesis

2 Form a hypothesis based on the question you asked.

Test the Hypothesis

3 Obtain an empty cup or beaker, an eyedropper, and 50 mL of one of the solutions from your teacher. Only one student will have the "cold virus" solution. You will see a change in your solution when you have become "infected."

4 Your teacher will divide the class into two equal groups. If there is an extra student, that person will record data on the board. Otherwise, the teacher will act as the recorder.

5 The two groups should form straight lines, facing each other.

6 Each time your teacher says the word *mix,* fill your eyedropper with your solution, and place 10 drops of your solution in the beaker of the person in the line opposite you without touching your eyedropper to the other liquid.

7 Gently stir the liquid in your cup with your eyedropper. Do not put your eyedropper in anyone else's solution.

8 If your solution changes color, raise your hand so that the recorder can record the number of students who have been "infected."

9 Your teacher will instruct one line to move one person to the right. Then, the person at the end of the line without a partner should go to the other end of the line.

Edith McAlanis
Socorro Middle School
El Paso, Texas

CHAPTER RESOURCES

Chapter Resource File

- 📁 • **Datasheet for Chapter Lab**
  - • **Lab Notes and Answers**

Technology

- 📹 **Classroom Videos**
  - • Lab Video

- • Antibodies to the Rescue

Results of Experiment			
Trial	Number of infected people	Total number of people	Percentage of infected people
1			
2			
3			
4			
5			
6			
7			
8			
9			
10			

DO NOT WRITE IN BOOK

10 Repeat steps 5–9 nine more times for a total of 10 trials.

11 Return to your desk, and create a data table in your notebook similar to the table above. The column with the title "Total number of people" will remain the same in every row. Enter the data from the board into your data table.

12 Find the percentage of infected people for the last column by dividing the number of infected people by the total number of people and multiplying by 100 in each line.

Analyze the Results

1 **Describing Events** Did you become infected? If so, during which trial did you become infected?

2 **Examining Data** Did everyone eventually become infected? If so, how many trials were necessary to infect everyone?

Draw Conclusions

3 **Interpreting Information** Explain at least one reason why this simulation may underestimate the number of people who might have been infected in real life.

4 **Applying Conclusions** Use your results to make a line graph showing the change in the infection percentage per trial.

Applying Your Data

Do research in the library or on the Internet to find out some of the factors that contribute to the spread of a cold virus. What is the best and easiest way to reduce your chances of catching a cold? Explain your answer.

CHAPTER RESOURCES

Workbooks

Long-Term Projects & Research Ideas
• A Chuckle a Day Keeps the Doctor Away **ADVANCED**

Applying Your Data

Colds are usually spread by close contact with a person who is infected. Colds may be more prevalent in the winter because people tend to stay indoors, where they are in closer contact with each other. The cold virus is carried on the microdroplets in a cough or sneeze and by unwashed hands. The best and easiest way to reduce the chances of catching a cold is to avoid crowded places, wash one's hands thoroughly and frequently when people in close proximity have colds, and avoid touching one's face near one's eyes. Eating a healthy diet and getting plenty of rest and exercise will help a person stay in good general health.

Preparation Notes

Phenolphthalein is a base indicator and will turn pink in the presence of NaOH. One student (or two, if your class is large) will be given 50 mL of the indicator. This student will represent the original "infected" individual. (It is more fun if no one knows who the original infected student is at first.) All other students will be given the NaOH solution.

Prepare a results chart similar to the student table on the board. You will need to record results while the students are performing the experiment.

When you switch the students between trials, the student on the end will need to move to the other end of the line so that all students will have a new partner for each trial. In case of an odd number of students, you will need to participate, or you may use one student volunteer to record results on the board.

Analyze the Results

1.–2. If there are 10 students (two rows of 5 students facing each other), it will take six trials for everyone to become infected.

Draw Conclusions

3. In real life, colds are spread by more than one means. Coughing, sneezing, and touching with unwashed hands are ways to spread a cold. More than one person in a classroom may have a cold.

4. The line graphs should accurately reflect student data.

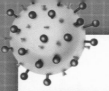

Assignment Guide

SECTION	QUESTIONS
1	1, 7–9, 15, 19
2	2–6, 10–14, 16–18, 20–21

ANSWERS

Using Key Terms

1. infectious disease
2. pathogen
3. T cells
4. antibody
5. allergy
6. Cancer

Understanding Key Ideas

7. b
8. d
9. c
10. d
11. d
12. d
13. Sample answer: When a macrophage engulfs a pathogen, it places pieces of the pathogen called *antigens* on its outer membrane. The antigens attract helper T cells.
14. Helper T cells activate B cells and killer T cells.
15. from animals and from the air

USING KEY TERMS

Complete each of the following sentences by choosing the correct term from the word bank.

antibody	cancer
infectious disease	B cell
noninfectious disease	T cell
pathogen	allergy

1 A(n) _____ is caused by a pathogen.

2 Antibiotics can be used to kill a(n) _____.

3 Macrophages attract helper _____.

4 A(n) _____ binds to an antigen.

5 An immune-system overreaction to a harmless substance is a(n) _____.

6 _____ is the unregulated growth of cells.

UNDERSTANDING KEY IDEAS

Multiple Choice

7 Pathogens are
   a. all viruses and microorganisms.
   b. viruses and microorganisms that cause disease.
   c. noninfectious organisms.
   d. all bacteria that live in water.

8 Which of the following is an infectious disease?
   a. allergies
   b. rheumatoid arthritis
   c. asthma
   d. a common cold

9 The skin keeps pathogens out by
   a. staying warm enough to kill pathogens.
   b. releasing killer T cells onto the surface.
   c. shedding dead cells and secreting oils.
   d. All of the above

10 Memory B cells
   a. kill pathogens.
   b. activate killer T cells.
   c. activate killer B cells.
   d. produce B cells that make antibodies.

11 A fever
   a. slows pathogen growth.
   b. helps B cells multiply faster.
   c. helps T cells multiply faster.
   d. All of the above

12 Macrophages
   a. make antibodies.
   b. release helper T cells.
   c. live in the gut.
   d. engulf pathogens.

Short Answer

13 Explain how macrophages start an immune response.

14 Describe the role of helper T cells in responding to an infection.

15 Name two ways that you come into contact with pathogens.

CRITICAL THINKING

16 **Concept Mapping** Use the following terms to create a concept map: *macrophages, helper T cells, B cells, antibodies, antigens, killer T cells,* and *memory B cells.*

17 **Identifying Relationships** Why does the disappearance of helper T cells in AIDS patients damage the immune system?

18 **Predicting Consequences** Many people take fever-reducing drugs as soon as their temperature exceeds 37°C. Why might it not be a good idea to reduce a fever immediately with drugs?

19 **Evaluating Data** The risk of dying from a whooping cough vaccine is about one in 1 million. In contrast, the risk of dying from whooping cough is about one in 500. Discuss the pros and cons of this vaccination.

INTERPRETING GRAPHICS

The graph below compares the concentration of antibodies in the blood the first time you are exposed to a pathogen with the concentration of antibodies the next time you are exposed to the pathogen. Use the graph below to answer the questions that follow.

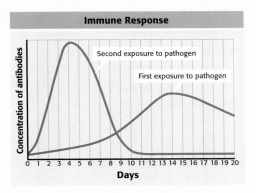

Immune Response

Second exposure to pathogen

First exposure to pathogen

Concentration of antibodies

Days

20 Are there more antibodies present during the first week of the first exposure or the first week of the second exposure? Why do you think this is so?

21 What is the difference in recovery time between the first exposure and second exposure? Why?

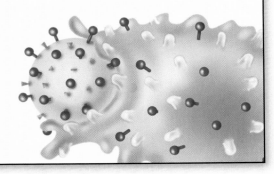

CHAPTER RESOURCES

Chapter Resource File

- Chapter Review **GENERAL**
- Chapter Test A **GENERAL**
- Chapter Test B **ADVANCED**
- Chapter Test C **SPECIAL NEEDS**
- Vocabulary Activity **GENERAL**

Workbooks

Study Guide
- Assessment resources are also available in Spanish.

Teacher's Note

To provide practice under more realistic testing conditions, give students 20 minutes to answer all of the questions in this Standardized Test Preparation.

MISCONCEPTION ///ALERT\\\

Answers to the standardized test preparation can help you identify student misconceptions and misunderstandings.

READING

Passage 1

1. A
2. G
3. D

✚ TEST DOCTOR

Question 2: Students may mistakenly select answer H, but the passage does not state that all bacteria mutate. Tell students to be wary of answers that use the words *always* or *never*. Answers framed in absolute terms may be overstating ideas from the passage. Although the word *outside* is not used explicitly in this passage, the passage does use the word *surround*. To surround a cell, the membrane would have to be located outside the cell.

READING

Read each of the passages below. Then, answer the questions that follow each passage.

Passage 1 Bacteria are becoming resistant to many human-made antibiotics, which means that the drugs no longer affect the bacteria. Scientists now face the challenge of developing new antibiotics that can overcome the resistant strains of bacteria.

Antibiotics from animals are different from some human-made antibiotics. These antibiotics bore holes through the membranes that surround bacterial cells, causing the cells to disintegrate and die. Bacterial membranes don't <u>mutate</u> often, so they are less likely to become resistant to the animal antibiotics.

1. In this passage, what does *mutate* mean?
   A to change
   B to grow
   C to form
   D to degrade

2. Based on the passage, which of the following statements is a fact?
   F Bacterial membranes are on the inside of the bacterial cell.
   G Bacterial membranes are on the outside of the bacterial cell.
   H All strains of bacteria mutate.
   I Bacterial membranes never change.

3. Based on the passage, which of the following sentences is false?
   A Antibiotics from animals are different from human-made antibiotics.
   B Antibiotics from animals bore holes in bacterial membranes.
   C Bacterial membranes don't change very often.
   D Bacteria rarely develop resistance to human-made antibiotics.

Passage 2 Drinking water in the United States is generally safe, but water lines can break, or treatment plants can become flooded, allowing microorganisms to enter the public water supply. Bacteria in foods and beverages can cause illness, too. Refrigerating foods can slow the growth of many of these <u>pathogens</u>, but meat, fish, and eggs that are not cooked enough can still contain dangerous bacteria or parasites. Leaving food out at room temperature can give bacteria such as *salmonella* time to grow and produce toxins in the food. For these reasons, it is important to wash all used cooking tools.

1. Which of the following statements can you infer from this passage?
   A Treatment plants help keep drinking water safe.
   B Treatment plants never become flooded.
   C Eliminating treatment plants would help keep water safe.
   D New treatment plants are better than old ones.

2. Which of the following statements can you infer from the passage?
   F Bacteria that live in food produce more toxins than molds produce.
   G Cooking food thoroughly kills bacteria living in the food.
   H Some bacteria are helpful to humans.
   I Illnesses caused by bacteria living in food are seldom serious.

3. According to this passage, what do pathogens cause?
   A disease
   B flooding
   C water-line breaks
   D water supplies

Passage 2

1. A
2. G
3. A

✚ TEST DOCTOR

Question 1: Students may mistakenly select answer D, which is a probable answer. But the passage does not distinguish between the effectiveness of new and old plants. Although the passage does not state explicitly that water treatment plants help keep drinking water safe, the first sentence does imply that microorganisms can endanger public health when treatment plants stop working.

INTERPRETING GRAPHICS

The graph below shows the reported number of people living with HIV/AIDS. Use the graph to answer the questions that follow.

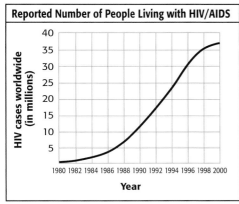

Reported Number of People Living with HIV/AIDS

Source: Joint United Nations Program on HIV/AIDS

1. When did the number of people living with HIV/AIDS reach 5 million?
- **A** 1985
- **B** 1986
- **C** 1987
- **D** 1988

2. When did the number of people living with HIV/AIDS reach 30 million?
- **F** 1996
- **G** 1997
- **H** 1998
- **I** 1999

3. When was the rate of increase of people with HIV/AIDS the **greatest**?
- **A** from 1980 to 1982
- **B** from 1984 to 1986
- **C** from 1988 to 1990
- **D** from 1998 to 2000

4. What percentage of the people who are infected with HIV do not yet have AIDS?
- **F** 10%
- **G** 24%
- **H** 75%
- **I** There is not enough information to determine the answer.

5. If the virus continued to spread as the graph indicates, in the year 2002, about how many people would be infected with HIV?
- **A** 30 million
- **B** 35 million
- **C** 39 million
- **D** 60 million

6. Which part of the graph indicates the rate of infection?
- **F** *x*-axis
- **G** *y*-axis
- **H** slope of the line being graphed
- **I** number of years in the sample

MATH

Read each question below, and choose the best answer.

1. Suppose you have 50,000 flu viruses on your fingers and you rub your eyes. Only 20,000 viruses enter your eyes, 10,000 dissolve in chemicals, and 10,000 are washed down into your nose. Of those, you sneeze out 2,000. How many viruses are left to wash down the back of your throat and possibly start an infection?
- **A** 50,000
- **B** 10,000
- **C** 8,000
- **D** 5,000

2. In which of the following lists are the numbers in order from smallest to greatest?
- **F** 0.027, 0.072, 0.270, 0.720
- **G** 0.270, 0.072, 0.720, 0.270
- **H** 0.072, 0.027, 0.270, 0.720
- **I** 0.720, 0.270, 0.072, 0.027

Standardized Test Preparation

 TEST DOCTOR

 **TEST DOCTOR**

CHAPTER RESOURCES

Chapter Resource File

 • Standardized Test Preparation `GENERAL`

Workbooks

 North Carolina Standardized Test Preparation
• Provides practice for the EOG test.

State Resources

 For specific resources for your state, visit **go.hrw.com** and type in the keyword **HSMSTR**.

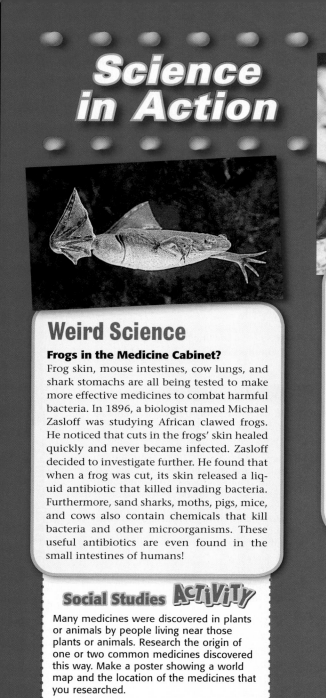

Science in Action

Weird Science

Background

Modern scientific study of antibiotics began in the 1800s. Louis Pasteur discovered that bacteria spread infectious diseases, and Robert Koch developed methods for isolating and growing different kinds of bacteria. A breakthrough in treating bacterial diseases came in the early 1900s, when Alexander Fleming discovered penicillin, an antibiotic formed from mold. Streptomycin, a fungal antibiotic, was discovered by Selman A. Waksman in 1943. Doctors now use antibiotics to treat diseases such as strep throat, bacterial meningitis, and tuberculosis.

Scientific Discoveries

Background

The number of people who are allergic to peanuts has increased significantly in recent years, and scientists are not sure why. There has been speculation about the connection between infant creams containing peanut oil and the development of peanut allergies, but nothing has been proven yet. A child is more likely to have a peanut allergy if one of his or her parents is also allergic. Most people who have a peanut allergy also have asthma.

Weird Science

Frogs in the Medicine Cabinet?

Frog skin, mouse intestines, cow lungs, and shark stomachs are all being tested to make more effective medicines to combat harmful bacteria. In 1896, a biologist named Michael Zasloff was studying African clawed frogs. He noticed that cuts in the frogs' skin healed quickly and never became infected. Zasloff decided to investigate further. He found that when a frog was cut, its skin released a liquid antibiotic that killed invading bacteria. Furthermore, sand sharks, moths, pigs, mice, and cows also contain chemicals that kill bacteria and other microorganisms. These useful antibiotics are even found in the small intestines of humans!

Social Studies ACTIVITY

Many medicines were discovered in plants or animals by people living near those plants or animals. Research the origin of one or two common medicines discovered this way. Make a poster showing a world map and the location of the medicines that you researched.

Scientific Discoveries

Medicine for Peanut Allergies

Scientists estimate that 1.5 million people in the United States suffer from peanut allergies. Every year 50 to 100 people in the United States die from an allergic reaction to peanuts. Peanuts and peanut oil are used to make many foods. People who have a peanut allergy sometimes mistakenly eat these foods and suffer severe reactions. A new drug has been discovered to help people control severe reactions. The drug is called TNX-901. The drug is actually an antibody that binds to the antibodies that the body makes during the allergic reaction to the peanuts. By binding these antibodies, the drug controls the allergic response.

Math ACTIVITY

During the testing of the new drug, 84 people were given four injections over the course of 4 months. One-fourth of the people participating received injections of a control that had no medicine in it. The rest of the people participating received different doses of the drug. How many people received the control? How many people received medicine? How many shots containing medicine were administered during the 4-month test?

Answer to Social Studies Activity

Answers may vary but may discuss the origins of the drugs aspirin and digitalis.

Answer to Math Activity

Twenty-one people received a control, and 63 people received medicine. Two hundred fifty-two shots containing medicine were administered.

Terrel Shepherd III

Nurse Terrel Shepherd III is a registered nurse (RN) at Texas Children's Hospital in Houston, Texas. RNs have many responsibilities. These responsibilities include giving patients their medications, assessing patients' health, and establishing intravenous access. Nurses also serve as a go-between for the patient and the doctor. Although most nurses work in hospitals or clinics, some nurses work for corporations. Pediatric nurses such as Shepherd work specifically with infants, children, and adolescents. The field of nursing offers a wide variety of job opportunities including home-care nurses, traveling nurses, and flight nurses. The hospital alone has many areas of expertise for nurses, including geriatrics (working with the elderly), intensive care, administration, and surgery. Traditionally, nursing has been considered to be a woman's career. However, since nursing began as a profession, men and women have practiced nursing. A career in nursing is possible for anyone who does well in science, enjoys people, and wants to make a difference in people's lives.

Language Arts ACTiViTY

WRITING SKILL Create a brochure that persuades people to consider a career in nursing. Describe nursing as a career, the benefits of becoming a nurse, and the education needed to be a nurse. Illustrate the brochure with pictures of nurses from the Internet or from magazines.

To learn more about these Science in Action topics, visit go.hrw.com and type in the keyword **HL5BD6F**.

Current Science

Check out Current Science® articles related to this chapter by visiting go.hrw.com. **Just type in the keyword HL5CS27.**

Staying Healthy
Chapter Planning Guide

Compression guide:
To shorten instruction because of time limitations, omit Section 3.

OBJECTIVES	LABS, DEMONSTRATIONS, AND ACTIVITIES	TECHNOLOGY RESOURCES
PACING • 90 min pp. 300–307 **Chapter Opener**	SE **Start-up Activity**, p. 301 `GENERAL`	OSP **Parent Letter** `GENERAL` CD **Student Edition on CD-ROM** CD **Guided Reading Audio CD** TR **Chapter Starter Transparency*** VID **Brain Food Video Quiz**
Section 1 Good Nutrition • Identify the six groups of nutrients and explain their importance to good health. • Describe the Food Guide Pyramid. • Understand how to read Nutrition Facts labels. • Explain the dangers of various nutritional disorders.	TE **Activity** Nutrient Table, p. 303 `GENERAL` TE **Connection Activity** Math, p. 303 `ADVANCED` SE **Quick Lab** Brown Bag Test, p. 305 ◆ `GENERAL` CRF **Datasheet for Quick Lab*** TE **Activity** Food Guide Pyramid, p. 305 `BASIC` SE **Inquiry Lab** To Diet or Not to Diet, p. 601 `GENERAL` CRF **Datasheet for LabBook*** LB **Labs You Can Eat** Snack Attack* ◆ `GENERAL` LB **Long-Term Projects & Research Ideas** Breakfast, Lunch, and Dinner of Champions* `ADVANCED`	CRF **Lesson Plans*** TR **Bellringer Transparency*** TR *LINK TO PHYSICAL SCIENCE* Covalent Bonds in a Water Molecule* TR **The Food Guide Pyramid*** TR **Nutrition Facts Label*** CRF **SciLinks Activity*** `GENERAL`
PACING • 45 min pp. 308–313 **Section 2 Risks of Alcohol and Other Drugs** • Describe the difference between psychological and physical dependence. • Explain the hazards of tobacco, alcohol, and illegal drugs. • Distinguish between positive and negative uses of drugs.	TE **Activity** Poster Project, p. 308 `GENERAL` TE **Connection Activity** Real World, p. 311 `ADVANCED` SE **School-to-Home Activity** Good Reasons, p. 312 `GENERAL`	CRF **Lesson Plans*** TR **Bellringer Transparency***
PACING • 90 min pp. 314–319 **Section 3 Healthy Habits** • Describe three important aspects of good hygiene. • Explain why exercise and sleep are important to good health. • Describe methods of handling stress. • List three ways to stay safe at home, on the road, and outdoors. • Plan what you would do in the case of an accident.	TE **Activity** Don't Kick These Habits!, p. 314 `GENERAL` TE **Connection Activity** Real World, p. 316 `GENERAL` TE **Group Activity** Poster Project, p. 317 `GENERAL` SE **Skills Practice Lab** Keep It Clean, p. 320 ◆ `GENERAL` CRF **Datasheet for Chapter Lab*** LB **Inquiry Labs** Consumer Challenge* `GENERAL` LB **Calculator-Based Labs** Counting Calories* `ADVANCED`	CRF **Lesson Plans*** TR **Bellringer Transparency*** SE **Internet Activity**, p. 316 `GENERAL` VID **Lab Videos for Life Science**

PACING • 90 min

CHAPTER REVIEW, ASSESSMENT, AND STANDARDIZED TEST PREPARATION

CRF **Vocabulary Activity*** `GENERAL`
SE **Chapter Review**, pp. 322–323 `GENERAL`
CRF **Chapter Review*** ■ `GENERAL`
CRF **Chapter Tests A*** ■ `GENERAL`, **B*** `ADVANCED`, **C*** `SPECIAL NEEDS`
SE **Standardized Test Preparation**, pp. 324–325 `GENERAL`
CRF **Standardized Test Preparation*** `GENERAL`
CRF **Performance-Based Assessment*** `GENERAL`
OSP **Test Generator** `GENERAL`
CRF **Test Item Listing*** `GENERAL`

Online and Technology Resources

Visit **go.hrw.com** for a variety of free resources related to this textbook. Enter the keyword **HT5R7BD7.**

Students can access interactive problem-solving help and active visual concept development with the *Holt Science and Technology* Online Edition available at **www.hrw.com.**

 Guided Reading Audio CD

These CDs are designed to help auditory learners and reluctant readers.

Science Tutor CD-ROM

Excellent for remediation and test practice.

SKILLS DEVELOPMENT RESOURCES	SECTION REVIEW AND ASSESSMENT	STANDARDS CORRELATIONS
SE Pre-Reading Activity, p. 300 GENERAL **OSP Science Puzzlers, Twisters & Teasers** GENERAL		North Carolina Standard Course of Study
CRF Directed Reading A* BASIC **, B*** SPECIAL NEEDS **CRF Vocabulary and Section Summary*** GENERAL **SE Reading Strategy** Reading Organizer, p. 302 GENERAL **SE Connection to Oceanography** Nutritious Seaweed, p. 304 GENERAL **SE Math Practice** What Percentage?, p. 306 GENERAL **CRF Critical Thinking** A Daily Routine* ADVANCED **CRF Reinforcement Worksheet** To Eat or Not to Eat…* BASIC	**SE Reading Checks,** pp. 303, 305, 306 GENERAL **TE Homework,** p. 304 GENERAL **TE Reteaching,** p. 306 BASIC **TE Quiz,** p. 306 GENERAL **TE Alternative Assessment,** p. 306 GENERAL **SE Section Review,*** p. 307 ■ GENERAL **CRF Section Quiz*** ■ GENERAL	LabBook: 1.08, 1.09, 1.10
CRF Directed Reading A* BASIC **, B*** SPECIAL NEEDS **CRF Vocabulary and Section Summary*** GENERAL **SE Reading Strategy** Reading Organizer, p. 308 GENERAL **TE Inclusion Strategies,** p. 310	**SE Reading Checks,** pp. 309, 311, 312 GENERAL **TE Homework,** p. 309 GENERAL **TE Homework,** p. 310 GENERAL **TE Reteaching,** p. 312 BASIC **TE Quiz,** p. 312 GENERAL **TE Alternative Assessment,** p. 312 GENERAL **TE Homework,** p. 312 GENERAL **SE Section Review,*** p. 313 ■ GENERAL **CRF Section Quiz*** ■ GENERAL	4.08
CRF Directed Reading A* BASIC **, B*** SPECIAL NEEDS **CRF Vocabulary and Section Summary*** GENERAL **SE Reading Strategy** Prediction Guide, p. 314 GENERAL **SE Connection to Language Arts** Dreamy Poetry, p. 315 GENERAL **TE Reading Strategy** Prediction Guide, p. 315 GENERAL **TE Inclusion Strategies,** p. 318	**SE Reading Checks,** pp. 315, 317, 319 GENERAL **TE Homework,** p. 316 GENERAL **TE Homework,** p. 317 GENERAL **TE Reteaching,** p. 318 BASIC **TE Quiz,** p. 318 GENERAL **TE Alternative Assessment,** p. 318 ADVANCED **SE Section Review,*** p. 319 ■ GENERAL **CRF Section Quiz*** ■ GENERAL	4.08; Chapter Lab: 1.04, 1.08

One-Stop Planner® CD-ROM

This convenient CD-ROM includes:
- Lab Materials QuickList Software
- Holt Calendar Planner
- Customizable Lesson Plans
- Printable Worksheets
- ExamView® Test Generator

cnnstudentnews.com

Find the latest news, lesson plans, and activities related to important scientific events.

www.scilinks.org

Maintained by the **National Science Teachers Association.** See Chapter Enrichment pages for a complete list of topics.

Check out **Current Science** articles and activities by visiting the HRW Web site at **go.hrw.com.** Just type in the keyword **HL5CS28T.**

Classroom Videos

- **Lab Videos** demonstrate the chapter lab.
- **Brain Food Video Quizzes** help students review the chapter material.
- **CNN Videos** bring science into your students' daily life.

Visual Resources

CHAPTER STARTER TRANSPARENCY

Imagine . . .

You are part of a nationwide survey of more than 6,000 teenagers. Scientists from the Centers for Disease Control and Prevention are concerned about teen health. They think that certain behaviors put too many teenagers at risk for cancer, heart disease, and other illnesses. The researchers ask you about five health habits: Do you smoke cigarettes? Do you exercise regularly? Do you eat plenty of fruits and vegetables? Do you eat a lot of high-fat foods, such as hamburgers, fried foods, and junk foods? Do you sometimes drink alcohol?

This survey of people aged 12 to 17 was actually taken, and 20 percent of those surveyed smoke cigarettes. In addition, 36 percent get little exercise, 85 percent do not eat enough fruits and vegetables, 34 percent eat too many high-fat foods, and 16 percent sometimes drink large amounts of alcohol. Over half of the teenagers (63 percent) engage in two or more of these health risk behaviors.

Where do you fit into this national survey? Are your habits healthy or risky? This chapter will give you plenty of information about keeping yourself healthy and increasing your chances of having a long, active life.

BELLRINGER TRANSPARENCIES

Section: Good Nutrition
Match the terms in the first column with the descriptions in the second column.
1. nutrients
2. Calories
3. carbohydrates
4. proteins
5. unsaturated fats
6. minerals

a. units of energy
b. found in vegetable oils
c. necessary for life processes
d. include calcium
e. build the body
f. main source of energy

Write your answers in your **science journal.**

Section: Risks of Alcohol and Other Drugs
Do you think that drugs are good or bad for you? What are some dangerous drugs, and what makes them dangerous? Are there ever any positive uses for dangerous drugs? Are there any dangers involved with using "good" drugs, such as antibiotics or other medicines?

Explain your thoughts in your **science journal.**

TEACHING TRANSPARENCIES

L99

The Food Guide Pyramid

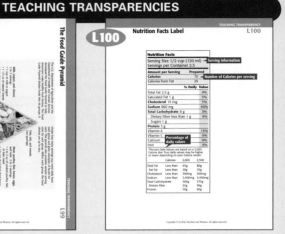

L100

Nutrition Facts Label

TEACHING TRANSPARENCIES

P54

Covalent Bonds in a Water Molecule

The oxygen atom shares one of its electrons with each of the two hydrogen atoms. Each hydrogen atom shares its 1 electron with the oxygen atom. Each hydrogen atom now has an outer level filled with 2 electrons.

This drawing of a diagram for water shows only the outermost level of electrons for each atom. But you still see how the atoms share electrons.

LINK TO PHYSICAL SCIENCE

Chapter: Chemical Bonding

CONCEPT MAPPING TRANSPARENCY

Use the following terms to complete the concept map below:
narcotics, minerals, saturated fat, nicotine, tobacco, vitamins

Planning Resources

LESSON PLANS

SAMPLE

Lesson Plan

Section: Waves

Pacing
Regular Schedule: with lab(s):2 days   without lab(s):2 days
Block Schedule: with lab(s): 1 1/2 days without lab(s):1 day

Objectives
1. Relate the seven properties of life to a living organism.
2. Describe seven themes that can help you to organize what you learn about biology.
3. Identify the tiny structures that make up all living organisms.
4. Differentiate between reproduction and heredity and between metabolism and homeostasis.

National Science Education Standards Covered
LSInter4:Cells have particular structures that underlie their functions.
LSMat1: Most cell functions involve chemical reactions.
LSBeh1:Cells store and use information to guide their functions.
UCP1:Cell functions are regulated.
SI1: Cells can differentiate and form complete multicellular organisms.
PS1: Species evolve over time.
ESS1: The great diversity of organisms is the result of more than 3.5 billion years of evolution.
ESS2: Natural selection and its evolutionary consequences provide a scientific explanation for the fossil record of ancient life forms as well as for the striking molecular similarities observed among the diverse species of living organisms.
ST1: The millions of different species of plants, animals, and microorganisms that live on Earth today are related by descent from common ancestors.
ST2: The energy for life primarily comes from the sun.
SPSP1: The complexity and organization of organisms accommodates the need for obtaining, transforming, transporting, releasing, and eliminating the matter and energy used to sustain the organism.
SPSP6: As matter and energy flows through different levels of organization of living systems—cells, organs, communities—and between living systems and the physical environment, chemical elements are recombined in different ways.
HNS1: Organisms have behavioral responses to internal changes and to external stimuli.

PARENT LETTER

SAMPLE

Dear Parent,

Your son's or daughter's science class will soon begin exploring the chapter entitled "The World of Physical Science." In this chapter, students will learn about how the scientific method applies to the world of physical science and the role of physical science in the world. By the end of the chapter, students should demonstrate a clear understanding of the chapter's main ideas and be able to discuss the following topics:

1. physical science is the study of energy and matter (Section 1)
2. the role of physical science in the world around them (Section 1)
3. careers that rely on physical science (Section 1)
4. the steps used in the scientific method (Section 2)
5. examples of technology (Section 2)
6. how the scientific method is used to answer questions and solve problems (Section 2)
7. how our knowledge of science changes over time (Section 2)
8. how models represent real objects or systems (Section 3)
9. examples of different ways models are used in science (Section 3)
10. the importance of the International System of Units (Section 4)
11. the appropriate units to use for particular measurements (Section 4)
12. how area and density are derived quantities (Section 4)

Questions to Ask Along the Way

You can help your son or daughter learn about these topics by asking interesting questions such as the following:

* What are some surprising careers that use physical science?
* What is a characteristic of a good hypothesis?
* When is it a good idea to use a model?
* Why do Americans measure things in terms of inches and yards instead of centimeters and meters ?

TEST ITEM LISTING

TEST ITEM LISTING
The World of Science   **SAMPLE**

MULTIPLE CHOICE

1. A limitation of models is that
   a. they are large enough to see.
   b. they do not act exactly like the things that they model.
   c. they are smaller than the things that they model.
   d. they model unfamiliar things.
   Answer: B   Difficulty: 1   Section: 3   Objective: 2

2. The length 10 m is equal to
   a. 100 cm.   c. 10,000 mm.
   b. 1,000 cm.   d. Both (b) and (c)
   Answer: B   Difficulty: 1   Section: 2   Objective: 2

3. To be valid, a hypothesis must be
   a. testable.   c. made into a law.
   b. supported by evidence   d. Both (a) and (b)
   Answer: B   Difficulty: 1   Section: 2   Objective: 1

4. The statement "Sheila has a stain on her shirt" is an example of a(n)
   a. law.   c. observation.
   b. hypothesis.   d. prediction.
   Answer: B   Difficulty: 1   Section: 3   Objective: 2

5. A hypothesis is often developed out of
   a. observations.   c. laws.
   b. experiments.   d. Both (a) and (b)
   Answer: B   Difficulty: 1   Section: 2   Objective: 2

6. How many milliliters are in 3.5 kL?
   a. 3,500 mL   c. 3,500, 000 mL
   b. 0.0035 mL.   d. 35,000 mL.
   Answer: B   Difficulty: 1   Section: 3   Objective: 2

7. A map of Seattle is an example of a
   a. law.   c. model.
   b. theory.   d. unit.
   Answer: B   Difficulty: 1   Section: 3   Objective: 2

8. A lab has the safety icons shown below. These icons mean that you should wear
   a. only safety goggles.   c. safety goggles and a lab apron.
   b. only a lab apron.   d. safety goggles, a lab apron, and gloves
   Answer: B   Difficulty: 1   Section: 1   Objective: 2

9. The law of conservation of mass says the lot al mass before a chemical change is
   a. more than the total mass after the change.
   b. less than the total mass after the change.
   c. the same as the total mass after the change.
   d. not the same as the total mass after the change.
   Answer: B   Difficulty: 1   Section: 2   Objective: 2

10. To which of the following areas might you find a geochemist at work?
    a. studying the chemistry of rocks   c. studying lakes
    b. studying forestry   d. studying the atmosphere
    Answer: B   Difficulty: 1   Section: 3   Objective: 2

One-Stop Planner® CD-ROM

This CD-ROM includes all of the resources shown here and the following time-saving tools:

* **Lab Materials QuickList Software**
* **Customizable lesson plans**
* **Holt Calendar Planner**
* **The powerful ExamView® Test Generator**

Meeting Individual Needs

DIRECTED READING A

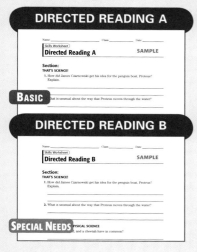

Name ___ Class ___ Date ___

Skills Worksheet
Directed Reading A SAMPLE

Section:
THAT'S SCIENCE!

1. How did James Czarnowski get his idea for the penguin boat, Proteus? Explain.

___ What is unusual about the way that Proteus moves through the water?

BASIC

DIRECTED READING B

Name ___ Class ___ Date ___

Skills Worksheet
Directed Reading B SAMPLE

Section:
THAT'S SCIENCE!

1. How did James Czarnowski get his idea for the penguin boat, Proteus? Explain.

2. What is unusual about the way that Proteus moves through the water?

SPECIAL NEEDS ___ PHYSICAL SCIENCE

VOCABULARY ACTIVITY

Activity
Vocabulary Activity SAMPLE

Getting the Dirt on the Soil

After you finish reading Chapter [Unique Title], try this puzzle! Use the clues below to unscramble the vocabulary words. Write your answer in the space provided.

___ breakdown of rock into ___ and smaller pieces: GNETH
9. the chemical breakdown of rocks and minerals into new substances: CAMLCHE THEARIGWEN

___ of rock lying beneath soil

GENERAL

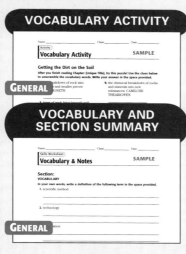

VOCABULARY AND SECTION SUMMARY

Skills Worksheet
Vocabulary & Notes SAMPLE

Section:
VOCABULARY

In your own words, write a definition of the following term in the space provided.

1. scientific method

2. technology

GENERAL

REINFORCEMENT

Skills Worksheet
Reinforcement SAMPLE

The Plane Truth

Complete this worksheet after you finish reading the Section: [Unique Section Title]

You plan to enter a paper airplane contest sponsored by Talkin' Physical Science magazine. The person whose airplane flies the farthest wins a lifetime subscription to the magazine! The week before the contest, you watch an airplane landing at a nearby airport. You notice that the wings of the airplane have flaps, as shown in the illustration at right. The paper airplanes you've been trying to do not have wing flaps. What question would you ask yourself based on these observations? Write your...

BASIC

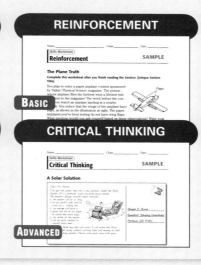
Flaps

CRITICAL THINKING

Skills Worksheet
Critical Thinking SAMPLE

A Solar Solution

Dear Mr. Dunne,

ADVANCED

SCILINKS ACTIVITY

Activity
SciLinks Activity SAMPLE

MARINE ECOSYSTEMS
Go to www.scilinks.org. To find links related to marine ecosystems, type in the keyword HL5450. Then, use the links to answer the questions about marine ecosys-...

___ percentage of the Earth's surface is covered by water?

GENERAL

SCIENCE PUZZLERS, TWISTERS & TEASERS

CHAPTER 28 SCIENCE PUZZLERS, TWISTERS & TEASERS
Staying Healthy

Mixed-up Inside

1. Each of these puzzles contains two scrambled terms from the chapter. In each case, one of the things can be found in the other. The terms can consist of up to three words. Fill in the blanks with the correct terms.

___ is in ___   ___ are in ___

GENERAL

Labs and Activities

LONG-TERM PROJECTS & RESEARCH IDEAS

PROJECT 28 STUDENT WORKSHEET DESIGN YOUR OWN
Breakfast, Lunch, and Dinner of Champions

As you wait for the signal, you can feel the butterflies in your stomach. Your heart is racing, the crowd is starting to go wild. Before you take another breath, the starting shot is fired, and you take off on your bicycle.

Being able to compete as an athlete takes a lot of discipline and training, as well as mental and physical endurance—that's not all. The food you put into your body affects how you feel and how much energy you have. If you were a professional athlete, you probably would need to follow a specific diet to give yourself maximum energy.

INTERNET KEYWORD
fluoridation

Eating for the Gold

1. How does an athlete get the energy he or she needs? Find out how much energy we use for our body processes, such as breathing. Research the additional energy it takes to play a particular sport and the number of hours per day a professional athlete usually trains for that sport. Then research various foods and people's diet for an athlete in training. Keep in mind that a professional athlete may have different nutrient requirements than a less-active person has. Make a video detailing the best foods and diet for an athlete in training.

2. What does your drinking water have in common with toothpaste? Fluoride! Fluoride is added to drinking water to help protect your teeth from cavities. There is still a controversy surrounding this practice. Why is fluoride added to drinking water? How much fluoride is added? Why do some people think fluoride should not be added to drinking water? What evidence supports adding or not adding fluoride? What do you think? Write a position paper supporting your view.

3. SURGEON GENERAL'S WARNING: "Smoking Causes Lung Cancer, Heart Disease, Emphysema, and May Complicate Pregnancy." Cigarette manufacturers are required by law to print warning labels, such as the one above, on all cigarette packages and advertisements. Why did the Surgeon General require these warnings on cigarettes? What evidence is there that smoking causes health problems? Research the history of cigarette warning labels and the trend toward limiting the places where smoking is allowed. Write an essay about the history of smoking in the United States.

ADVANCED

LABS YOU CAN EAT

LAB 10 TEACHER'S PREPARATORY GUIDE SKILL BUILDER
Snack Attack

Purpose
Students test a variety of snack foods for their relative fat content.

Time Required
One and a half 45-minute class periods

Lab Ratings
TEACHER PREP ▲▲▲
STUDENT SET-UP ▲▲▲▲
CONCEPT LEVEL ▲▲▲
CLEAN UP ▲▲

Advance Preparation
Gather six low-fat and regular samples of various snack food items, such as cheese, potato chips, candy bars, and cookies. Finely crush each of the items. Place 2 g of each sample in a small cup for each group. Peel and finely chop samples of avocado and apple, and then mash the samples or use a food processor if one is available. Place 2 g of each of these samples in a small cup for each group. Bring the packages from the various snack items to class so students can read the nutritional labels. Or you may wish to bring a photocopy of each label for each group.

You may wish to put the food samples for the class in a central location to make it easier for students to collect their samples.

Safety Information
Students should be careful when using the scissors.

Teaching Strategies
The serving size for each item will vary. Because the actual fat content varies depending on the serving size, it is easier for students to compare percentages of fat for portions of the same weight.

When performing the experiment, it may be easier for students to see the size of the fat stain by holding the test panel up to the light. The stained paper will be translucent, and the students will be able to mark where the light passes through. When trying to determine why the stains may have shrunk, students might think that the fat evaporated. You may need to encourage them to correctly relate the shrinking stains to water evaporation.

The fat content for an avocado is 16 percent, while an apple has no appreciable fat content. Because the diameter of the fat in the food samples, students should be able to calculate the fat content for the avocado and the apple.

Evaluation Strategies
For help evaluating this lab, see the Rubric for Performance Assessment on the *Assessment Checklist & Rubric*. This rubric is also available in the One-Stop Planner CD-ROM.

46 HOLT SCIENCE AND TECHNOLOGY

GENERAL

INQUIRY LABS

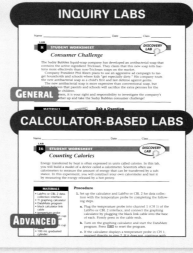

LAB 8 STUDENT WORKSHEET DISCOVERY LAB
Consumer Challenge

The Sudsy Bubbles liquid-soap company has developed an antibacterial soap that contains the active ingredient Triclosan. They claim that this new soap kills bacteria more effectively than non-Triclosan soaps on the market.

Company President Phil Kleen plans to use an aggressive ad campaign to target households and schools where kids "get especially dirty." His company touts the new antibacterial soap as a child's first and last defense against germs. The new antibacterial soap is more expensive than conventional soap, but Phil believes that parents and schools will sacrifice the extra pennies for the health of the children.

However, it is your right and responsibility to investigate the company's claims. Gather up and take the Sudsy Bubbles consumer challenge!

MATERIALS Ask a Question

GENERAL

CALCULATOR-BASED LABS

LAB 16 STUDENT WORKSHEET DISCOVERY LAB
Counting Calories

Energy transferred by heat is often expressed in units called calories. In this lab, you will build a model of a device called a calorimeter. Scientists often use calorimeters to measure the amount of energy that can be transferred by a substance. In this experiment, you will construct your own calorimeter and test it by measuring the energy released by a hot penny.

MATERIALS
- LabPro or CBL 2 data-collection interface
- TI graphing calculator
- DataMate program
- black calculator link cable
- temperature probe
- penny
- tongs
- 100 mL graduated cylinder

Procedure
1. Set up the calculator and LabPro or CBL 2 for data collection with the temperature probe by completing the following steps.
   a. Plug the temperature probe into channel 1 (CH 1) of the LabPro or CBL 2 interface, and connect the graphing calculator by plugging the black link cable into the base of each. Firmly press in the cable ends.
   b. Turn on the graphing calculator and start the DataMate program. Press ↖ to reset the program.
   c. If the calculator displays a temperature probe in CH 1, proceed directly to step 2. If it does not, continue with...

ADVANCED

DATASHEETS FOR QUICK LABS

TEACHER RESOURCE PAGE

Quick Lab DATASHEET FOR QUICK LAB
Reaction to Stress SAMPLE

Background
The graph below illustrates changes that occur in the membrane potential of a neuron during an action potential. Use the graph to answer the following questions. Refer to Figure 3 as needed.

DATASHEETS FOR CHAPTER LABS

TEACHER RESOURCE PAGE

Skills Practice Lab DATASHEET FOR CHAPTER LAB
Using Scientific Methods SAMPLE

Teacher's Notes
TIME REQUIRED
One 45-minute class period.

DATASHEETS FOR LABBOOK

TEACHER RESOURCE PAGE

Skills Practice Lab DATASHEET FOR LABBOOK LAB
Does It All Add Up? SAMPLE

Teacher's Notes
TIME REQUIRED
One 45-minute class period.

Review and Assessments

SECTION QUIZ

Name ___ Class ___ Date ___

Assessment
Section Quiz SAMPLE

Section:
In the space provided, write the letter of the description that best matches the term or phrase.

___ 1. building molecules that can be used as an energy source or breaking down molecules in which energy is stored
___ the process by which light energy is converted to chemical energy
___ an organism that uses sunlight or inorganic substances to make organic compounds

a. cellular respiration

GENERAL

ALSO IN SPANISH

SECTION REVIEW

Skills Worksheet
Section Review SAMPLE

Section:
KEY TERMS

1. What do paleontologist study?

2. How does a trace fossil differ from petrified wood?

___ fossil.

GENERAL

ALSO IN SPANISH

CHAPTER REVIEW

Skills Worksheet
Chapter Review SAMPLE

USING VOCABULARY

1. Define biome in your own words.

2. Describe the characteristics of a savanna and a desert.

___ Identify the relationship between the two and explain...

GENERAL

ALSO IN SPANISH

CHAPTER TEST A

Assessment
Chapter Test A SAMPLE

MULTIPLE CHOICE
In the space provided, write the letter of the term or phrase that best completes each statement or best answers each question.

___ 1. Surface currents are formed by
   a. the moon's gravity.   c. wind.
   b. the sun's gravity.   d. increased water density.
___ 2. When waves come near the shore,
   a. they speed up.   c. their wavelength increases.
   b. they maintain their speed. d. their wave height increases.
Longshore currents transport sediment
   a. out to the open ocean.   c. only during low...
   b. along the shore.   d. only during high tide.
___ 4. Which of the following does NOT control surface currents?

GENERAL

ALSO IN SPANISH

CHAPTER TEST B

Assessment
Chapter Test B SAMPLE

MULTIPLE CHOICE
In the space provided, write the letter of the term or phrase that best completes each statement or best answers each question.

___ 1. Surface currents are formed by
   a. the moon's gravity.   c. wind.
   b. the sun's gravity.   d. increased water density.
When waves come near the shore,
   a. they speed up.   c. their wavelength increases.
   b. they maintain their speed. d. their wave height increases.

ADVANCED

CHAPTER TEST C

Assessment
Chapter Test C SAMPLE

MULTIPLE CHOICE
In the space provided, write the letter of the term or phrase that best completes each statement or best answers each question.

___ 1. Surface currents are formed by
   a. the moon's gravity.   c. wind.
   b. the sun's gravity.   d. increased water density.
___ 2. When waves come near the shore,
   a. they speed up.   c. their wavelength increases.
   b. they maintain their speed. d. their wave height increases.
___ currents transport sediment
   a. open ocean.   c. only during low tide.
   b. ...   d. only during high tide.
___ 4. Which of the following does NOT control surface currents?

SPECIAL NEEDS

STANDARDIZED TEST PREPARATION

Assessment
Standardized Test Preparation SAMPLE

READING
Read the passages below. Then, read each question that follows the passage. Decide which is the best answer to each question.

Passage 1 I adventurous summer camp in the world. Billy can't wait to head for the outdoors. Billy checked the recommended packing list: light, summer clothes, raincover, rain gear, heavy, ___ fleece jacket, ski mask, and thick gloves. Wait a minute! Billy thought he was traveling to only one destination, so why does he need to bring such a wide variety of clothes? On further investiga-...

GENERAL

PERFORMANCE-BASED ASSESSMENT

Assessment SKILL BUILDER
Performanced-Based Assessment SAMPLE

OBJECTIVE
Determine which factors cause some sugar shapes to break down faster than others

KNOW THE SCORE!
As you work through this activity, keep in mind that you will be earning a grade for the following:
• how you form and test the hypothesis (30%)
• the clarity of your analysis (40%)
• the clarity of your conclusions (30%)

Using Scientific Methods

___ STIONS ___ sugar shapes erode more rapidly than others?

MATERIALS AND EQUIPMENT
• 1 regular sugar cube   • 90 mL of water

GENERAL

This Chapter Enrichment provides relevant and interesting information to expand and enhance your presentation of the chapter material.

Section 1

Good Nutrition

Nutrient Needs in Adolescence

- Puberty is a period of rapid growth. Changes brought on by puberty affect every organ of the body. Adolescents need extra nutrients to meet their bodies' needs during the growth spurt that accompanies puberty.

- The onset of menstruation in girls and the change in lean body mass in boys increase an adolescent's need for iron. During adolescence, the Recommended Daily Allowance (RDA) for iron is 12–15 mg.

- The increase in skeletal mass that occurs during adolescence boosts the body's calcium needs, which increases the RDA for calcium to 1,200–1,500 mg. About 75 to 80% of the skeleton is built during adolescence.

- Rapid growth during adolescence increases the body's caloric needs. Energy needs vary depending on growth rate, body composition, and activity level. In general, boys have a larger proportion of lean body mass to fat and require more Calories than girls do.

Fiber

- Soluble fiber, found in fruit, beans, peas, and other legumes, can reduce the risk of heart disease by lowering cholesterol levels in the blood. Legume-based fiber also aids in the regulation of blood glucose levels.

- Although fiber contains no vitamins or minerals, it is essential to good health. Insoluble fiber is found in whole-grain foods. Along with fluids, insoluble fiber helps the colon remove waste (fecal matter) from the bowels. A lack of insoluble fiber in a person's diet can increase the risk for constipation, colon and bowel cancer, and diverticulosis, a disorder in which pouches form in the bowel wall.

Is That a Fact!

- ◆ Just before astronauts Neil Armstrong (1930–) and Edwin Aldrin Jr. (1930–1999) embarked on the first moonwalk on July 20, 1969, each astronaut ate four bacon squares, three sugar cookies, and peaches. They drank pineapple-grapefruit juice and coffee.

Adolescence and Nutrition

- The physical, emotional, and social changes of adolescence have a great impact on teen nutrition. Adolescence is typically a period of increased autonomy, so teens have increased opportunity to make food choices. But rather than making food choices based on long-term health, teens tend to be influenced by social pressures to reach cultural ideals of thinness, to gain the acceptance of peers, and to assert their independence from their parents. The characteristic adolescent preoccupation with body image extends to nutrition. If sound nutritional principles are taught and reinforced during adolescence, long-term health can benefit.

Section 2

Risks of Alcohol and Other Drugs
Drug Abuse

● According to yearly surveys conducted by the University of Michigan's Institute for Social Research (funded by the National Institute on Drug Abuse), drug abuse among 8th, 10th, and 12th grade students has decreased over the last few years. That doesn't mean that drug abuse is no longer a problem. The following are some statistics from the 2002 survey:

- About 15% of 8th grade students surveyed indicated that they had tried inhalants in their lifetime.
- About 19% of 8th grade students surveyed indicated that they had tried marijuana in their lifetime.
- About 31% of 8th grade students surveyed indicated that they had tried cigarettes. More than 2% of 8th grade students indicated that they smoked more than half a pack of cigarettes a day.
- About 47% of 8th grade students surveyed indicated that they had tried alcohol in their lifetime.

Is That a Fact!

◆ In the 1800s, scientists learned how to isolate drug compounds from plants. Morphine, cocaine, and heroin became readily available. These drugs were welcomed as safe, powerful pain relievers because, at first, no one knew of their addictive properties. By the early 1900s, there was an epidemic of drug abuse in the United States.

Section 3

Healthy Habits
Safety

● In the United States, accidental injuries are the leading cause of death for children and adolescents between the ages of 1 and 19.

● In 2002, motor-vehicle accidents claimed the lives of almost 43,000 Americans. More than 1,600 victims were between the ages of 8 and 15. Many of these deaths could have been prevented—59% of all motor-vehicle fatalities in 2002 were unrestrained passengers.

Excuse Me?

● When sounds enter the ear, they cause the eardrum to vibrate. Tiny hair cells in the inner ear respond to these vibrations by sending nerve impulses to the brain. Ordinarily, these hair cells slowly die as a person ages. When exposed to loud noises, however, more hair cells die than usual. Fewer impulses are sent to the brain. Once damage occurs, it is irreversible.

● Many teens are at risk for preventable hearing loss. Experts attribute this trend to increased exposure to damaging levels of noise, such as loud music. Sources of loud noise include CD players, concerts, car stereos, video games, and television. Hearing loss can be prevented by turning down the volume on audio devices and by wearing earplugs when loud noise cannot be controlled.

SCiLINKS

NSTA
Developed and maintained by the National Science Teachers Association

SciLinks is maintained by the National Science Teachers Association to provide you and your students with interesting, up-to-date links that will enrich your classroom presentation of the chapter.

Visit www.scilinks.org and enter the SciLinks code for more information about the topic listed.

Topic: Food Pyramids
SciLinks code: HSM0598

Topic: Nutritional Disorders
SciLinks code: HSM1057

Topic: Drug and Alcohol Abuse
SciLinks code: HSM0428

Topic: Safety
SciLinks code: HSM1339

Overview

Tell students that this chapter will help them learn about good nutrition, the risks of drugs, and how they can take care of themselves to stay healthy.

Assessing Prior Knowledge

Students should be familiar with the following topics:

• body systems

• disease

Identifying Misconceptions

As students learn the material in this chapter, some of them may express misconceptions about drugs. Some students may not recognize that drugs, such as caffeine (found in many sodas, teas, and coffee) or herbal additives (including chamomile, ginseng, and echinacea), are found in some of the foods they eat. You may also want to point out that many of the products that claim to make people think more clearly, control weight, and increase energy contain drugs. Some students may have misconceptions about alcohol, including the belief that alcohol is not a drug, that beer and wine are safer than liquor, and that alcohol is not addictive.

11

Staying Healthy

About the PHOTO

What do you see in this photo? Sure, you can see five students facing the camera, but what else does the picture tell you? The bright eyes, happy smiles, and shiny hair show radiant health. Having a clear mind and a long, active life depend on having a healthy body. Keeping your body healthy depends on eating well; avoiding drugs, cigarettes, and alcohol; and staying safe.

PRE-READING ACTIVITY

FOLDNOTES **Booklet** Before you read the chapter, create the FoldNote entitled "Booklet" described in the **Study Skills** section of the Appendix. Label each page of the booklet with a main idea from the chapter. As you read the chapter, write what you learn about each main idea on the appropriate page of the booklet.

Standards Correlations

North Carolina Standard Course of Study

1.04 (partial) Analyze variables in scientific investigations: . . . Use of a Control [and] Manipulate . . . (Chapter Lab)

1.08 Use oral and written language to: Communicate findings [and] Defend conclusions of scientific investigations. (Chapter Lab and LabBook)

1.09 Use technologies and information systems to: Research, Gather and analyze data, Visualize data, [and] Disseminate findings to others. (LabBook)

1.10 Analyze and evaluate information from a scientifically literate viewpoint by reading, hearing, and/or viewing: Scientific text, Articles, Events in the popular press. (LabBook)

4.08 Explain how understanding human body systems can help make informed decisions regarding health. (Sections 2 and 3)

START-UP ACTiViTy

MATERIALS

FOR EACH GROUP
• paper
• pen or pencil
• questionnaire

Teacher's Notes: To ensure privacy, you may want to have students complete their questionnaires at home. Many students will be uncomfortable sharing personal information.

Answers

1. Answers may vary.
2. Answers may vary. Students should recognize that the first four items on the questionnaire are considered good habits, and the fifth item is considered a bad habit.

START-UP ACTiViTy

Conduct a Survey

How healthy are the habits of your classmates? Find out for yourself.

Procedure

1. Copy and answer yes or no to each of the five questions at right. Do not put your name on the survey.

Analysis

1. As a class, record the data from the completed surveys in a chart. For each question, calculate the percentage of your class that answered yes.
2. What good and bad habits do your classmates have?

① Do you exercise at least three times a week?

② Do you wear a seat belt every time you ride in a car?

③ Do you eat five or more servings of fruits and vegetables every day?

④ Do you use sunscreen to protect your skin when you are outdoors?

⑤ Do you eat a lot of high-fat foods?

Imagine . . .

You are part of a nationwide survey of more than 6,000 teenagers. Scientists from the Centers for Disease Control and Prevention are concerned about teen health. They think that certain behaviors put too many teenagers at risk for cancer, heart disease, and other illnesses. The researchers ask you about five health habits: Do you ever smoke cigarettes? Do you ever smoke cigarettes? Do those surveyed smoke cigarettes. In addition, 36 percent get little exercise, 85 percent do not eat enough fruits and vegetables, 34 percent eat too many high-fat foods, and 16 percent sometimes drink large amounts of alcohol. Over half of the teenagers (63 percent) engage in two or more of these health-risk behaviors.

Chapter Starter Transparency
Use this transparency to help students begin thinking about health and good nutrition.

CHAPTER RESOURCES

Technology

 **Transparencies**
• Chapter Starter Transparency

READING
SKILLS

 Student Edition on CD-ROM

Guided Reading Audio CD

Classroom Videos
• Brain Food Video Quiz

Workbooks

 Science Puzzlers, Twisters & Teasers
• Staying Healthy GENERAL

Good Nutrition

Does the saying "You are what you eat" mean that you are pizza? No, but substances in pizza help build your body.

Protein in the cheese may become part of your hair. Carbohydrates in the crust can give you energy for your next race.

Focus

Overview

In this section, students will learn about the six essential nutrients and why these nutrients are important for good health. Dietary guidelines and the food pyramid are used to illustrate the principles of sound nutrition, and students will learn how to use these tools. Finally, students will learn about nutritional disorders.

 Bellringer

Post the following lists on the board or an overhead projector:

Column A

1. nutrients
2. Calories
3. carbohydrates
4. proteins
5. unsaturated fats
6. minerals

Column B

a. units of energy
b. found in vegetable oils
c. necessary for life processes
d. include calcium
e. build the body
f. main source of energy

Challenge students to match the terms in column A with the descriptions in column B.
(1. c; 2. a; 3. f; 4. e; 5. b; 6. d)

READING WARM-UP

Objectives

- Identify the six groups of nutrients, and explain their importance to good health.
- Describe the Food Guide Pyramid.
- Understand how to read Nutrition Facts labels.
- Explain the dangers of various nutritional disorders.

Terms to Learn

nutrient   mineral
carbohydrate   vitamin
protein   malnutrition
fat

READING STRATEGY

Reading Organizer As you read this section, create an outline of the section. Use the headings from the section in your outline.

nutrient a substance in food that provides energy or helps form body tissues and that is necessary for life and growth

carbohydrate a class of energy-giving nutrients that includes sugars, starches, and fiber

Nutrients

Are you more likely to have potato chips or broccoli for a snack? If you eat many foods that are high in fat, such as potato chips, your food choices probably are not as healthy as they could be. Broccoli is a healthier food than potato chips. But eating only broccoli, as the person in **Figure 1** is doing, does not give you a balanced diet.

To stay healthy, you need to take in **nutrients,** or substances that provide the materials needed for life processes. Nutrients are grouped into six classes: *carbohydrates, proteins, fats, water, vitamins,* and *minerals.* Carbohydrates, proteins, and fats provide energy for the body in units called *Calories* (Cal).

Carbohydrates

Carbohydrates are your body's main source of energy. A **carbohydrate** is a chemical composed of simple sugars. There are two types of carbohydrates: simple and complex. *Simple carbohydrates* are sugars. They are easily digested and give you quick energy. *Complex carbohydrates* are made up of many sugar molecules linked together. They are digested slowly and give you long-lasting energy. Some complex carbohydrates are good sources of fiber. Fiber is a part of a healthy diet and is found in whole-grain foods, such as brown rice and whole-wheat bread. Many fruits and vegetables also contain fiber.

Figure 1 *Eating only one food, even a healthy food, will not give you all the substances your body needs.*

CHAPTER RESOURCES

Chapter Resource File

- **Lesson Plan**
- **Directed Reading A** BASIC
- **Directed Reading B** SPECIAL NEEDS

Technology

Transparencies
- Bellringer
- *LINK TO PHYSICAL SCIENCE* Covalent Bonds in a Water Molecule

CONNECTION to
Physical Science ———— GENERAL

Water Molecules Water is a very simple molecule that is made up of one oxygen atom and two hydrogen atoms. Water is vital to all living organisms. Remind students that water makes up nearly 70% of the human body. Illustrate the water molecule using the teaching transparency titled "Covalent Bonds in a Water Molecule."
LS Visual

Protein

Proteins are found in body fluids, muscle, bone, and skin. **Proteins** are nutrients used to build and repair your body. Your body makes the proteins it needs, but it must have the necessary building blocks, called *amino acids*. Your digestive system breaks down protein into individual amino acids that are then used to make new proteins. Some foods, such as poultry, fish, milk, and eggs, provide all of the amino acids your body needs. Foods that contain all of these essential amino acids are called *complete proteins. Incomplete proteins* contain only some of the essential amino acids. Most plant foods contain incomplete protein, but eating a variety of plant foods will provide all of the amino acids your body needs.

✔ **Reading Check** What is an incomplete protein? (*See the Appendix for answers to Reading Checks.*)

Figure 2 *This sample meal provides many of the nutrients a growing teenager needs.*

Fats

Another class of nutrients that is important to a healthy meal, such as the meal shown in **Figure 2,** is fat. **Fats** are energy-storage nutrients. Fats are needed to store and transport vitamins, produce hormones, keep skin healthy, and provide insulation. Fats also provide more energy than either proteins or carbohydrates. There are two types of fats: saturated and unsaturated. *Saturated fats* are found in meat, dairy products, coconut oil, and palm oil. Saturated fats raise blood cholesterol levels. Although *cholesterol* is a fat-like substance found naturally in the body, high levels can increase the risk of heart disease. *Unsaturated fats* and foods high in fiber may help reduce blood cholesterol levels. Your body cannot make unsaturated fats. They must come from vegetable oils and fish in your diet. The body needs both kinds of fats.

protein a molecule that is made up of amino acids and that is needed to build and repair body structures and to regulate processes in the body

fat an energy-storage nutrient that helps the body store some vitamins

Water

You cannot survive for more than a few days without water. Your body is about 70% water. Water is in every cell of your body. The main functions of water are to transport substances, regulate body temperature, and provide lubrication. Some scientists think you should drink at least eight glasses of water a day. When you exercise you need more water, as shown in **Figure 3.** You also get water from other liquids you drink and the foods you eat. Fresh fruits and vegetables, juices, soups, and milk are good sources of water.

Figure 3 *When you exercise, you need to drink more water.*

Answer to Reading Check

An incomplete protein does not contain all of the essential amino acids.

Is That a Fact!

Frozen vegetables are often just as nutritious as fresh vegetables are.

Writing **Diets** Have students examine a popular diet trend. Then, have students evaluate the diet in terms of its ability to meet the body's nutrient and energy needs. If a diet does not meet the body's needs, encourage students to identify changes to the diet that will make the diet healthful. Have students write reports about their findings. **LS** Verbal

Homework ——— GENERAL

Essential Vitamins Have students research the physical effects of vitamin deficiencies for at least three essential vitamins. Ask students to create informative brochures about their findings. **LS** Verbal

BRAIN FOOD

Vitamins Point out that many vitamin manufacturers promote their products by claiming that their vitamins are "natural" or "organic," rather than synthetic (manufactured). These vitamins are almost always more expensive than their synthetic counterparts. Point out that most experts agree that organic and synthetic vitamins are identical in both structure and function.

mineral a class of nutrients that are chemical elements that are needed for certain body processes

vitamin a class of nutrients that contain carbon and that are needed in small amounts to maintain health and allow growth

Table 1	Some Essential Vitamins	
Vitamin	**What it does**	**Where you get it**
A	keeps skin and eyes healthy; builds strong bones and teeth	yellow and orange fruits and vegetables, leafy greens, meats, and milk
B (various forms)	helps body use carbohydrates; helps blood, nerves, and heart function	meats, whole grains, beans, peas, nuts, and seafood
C	strengthens tissues; helps the body absorb iron, fight disease	citrus fruits, leafy greens, broccoli, peppers, and cabbage
D	builds strong bones and teeth; helps the body use calcium and phosphorus	sunlight, enriched milk, eggs, and fish
E	protects red blood cells from destruction; keeps skin healthy	oils, fats, eggs, whole grains, wheat germ, liver, and leafy greens
K	assists with blood clotting	leafy greens, tomatoes, and potatoes

Minerals

If you eat a balanced diet, you should get all of the vitamins and minerals you need. **Minerals** are elements that are essential for good health. You need six minerals in large amounts: calcium, chloride, magnesium, phosphorus, potassium, and sodium. There are at least 12 minerals that are required in very small amounts. These include fluorine, iodine, iron, and zinc. Calcium is necessary for strong bones and teeth. Magnesium and sodium help the body use proteins. Potassium is needed to regulate your heartbeat and produce muscle movement, and iron is necessary for red blood cell production.

Vitamins

Vitamins are another class of nutrients. **Vitamins** are compounds that control many body functions. Only vitamin D can be made by the body, so you have to get most vitamins from food. **Table 1** provides information about six essential vitamins.

CONNECTION TO Oceanography

Nutritious Seaweed Kelp, a type of seaweed, is a good source of iodine. This nutritious food is grown on special farms off the coasts of China and Japan. What other nutritious foods come from the sea?

Answer to Connection to Oceanography

Sample answer: Other nutritious seafoods include fish and shellfish.

WEIRD SCIENCE

You are what you eat, and sometimes, you can even look like it! Eating a lot of carrots can give skin a yellowish color, a harmless condition. Tomatoes can give skin a reddish color. In 1960, a doctor examined a patient whose skin was orange. It turned out that the patient was eating a lot of carrots and tomatoes. The two colors mixed, and *voilà*, the patient had orange skin!

Eating for Good Health

Now you have learned which nutrients you need for good health. But how can you be sure to get all the important nutrients in the right amounts? To begin, keep in mind that most teenage girls need about 2,200 Cal per day, and most boys need about 2,800 Cal. Because different foods contain different nutrients, *where* you get your Calories is as important as *how many* you get. The Food Guide Pyramid, shown in **Figure 4,** can help you make good food choices.

Reading Check Using the Food Guide Pyramid below, design a healthy lunch that includes one food from each food group.

Quick Lab

Brown Bag Test

1. Cut a **brown paper bag** into squares.
2. Gather a variety of **foods.** Place a piece of each food on a different square and leave overnight.
3. What do you see when you remove the food?
4. Which food had the most oil? Which food had the least?

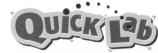

Figure 4 The Food Guide Pyramid

The U.S. Department of Agriculture and the Department of Health and Human Services developed the Food Guide Pyramid to help Americans make healthy food choices. The Food Guide Pyramid divides foods into six groups. It shows how many servings you need daily from each group and gives examples of foods for each. This pyramid also provides sample serving sizes for each group. Within each group, the food choices are up to you.

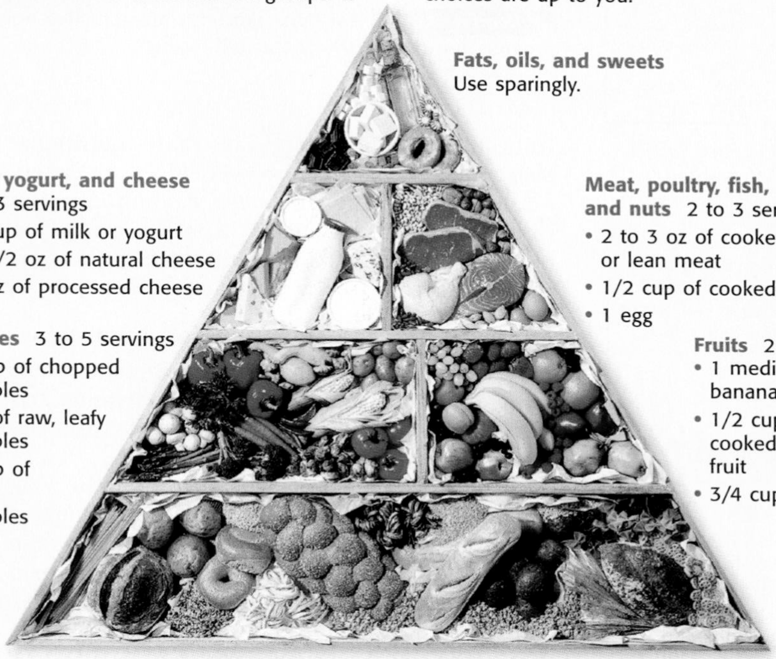

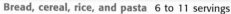

Fats, oils, and sweets Use sparingly.

Milk, yogurt, and cheese 2 to 3 servings
- 1 cup of milk or yogurt
- 1 1/2 oz of natural cheese
- 2 oz of processed cheese

Meat, poultry, fish, beans, eggs, and nuts 2 to 3 servings
- 2 to 3 oz of cooked poultry, fish, or lean meat
- 1/2 cup of cooked dried beans
- 1 egg

Vegetables 3 to 5 servings
- 1/2 cup of chopped vegetables
- 1 cup of raw, leafy vegetables
- 3/4 cup of cooked vegetables

Fruits 2 to 4 servings
- 1 medium apple, banana, or orange
- 1/2 cup of chopped, cooked, or canned fruit
- 3/4 cup of fruit juice

Bread, cereal, rice, and pasta 6 to 11 servings
- 1 slice of bread
- 1 oz of ready-to-eat cereal
- 1/2 cup of rice or pasta
- 1/2 cup of cooked cereal

Quick Lab

MATERIALS

FOR EACH GROUP
- bag, paper, brown
- foods (5–10 different kinds)

Answers

3. Students should see oil spots after the food is removed. Foods which lack oils will likely not leave spots.
4. Answers may vary. The food with the highest fat content will likely leave the largest amount of oil behind.

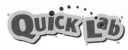

Activity — BASIC

Food Guide Pyramid Have students keep track of the food that they eat during a single day. Then, have students determine how many servings from each of the food groups they consumed. Have students determine the percentage of recommended servings these numbers represent. For example, two glasses of milk and a grilled cheese sandwich represent 100% of the recommended daily dairy servings. One apple is 25–50% of the recommended daily fruit servings. Encourage students to identify how they could change their diet to make it more healthful. **LS Logical**

Debate — ADVANCED

Changing the Pyramid Many nutrition experts think that the Food Guide Pyramid should be updated to reflect new discoveries about healthy eating habits. Ask students to research the proposed revisions to the Food Guide Pyramid. Then, have students debate whether the Food Guide Pyramid should be changed. **LS Verbal/Logical**

Answer to Reading Check

Sample answer: a peanut butter sandwich, a glass of milk, and fresh fruit and vegetable slices

CHAPTER RESOURCES

Technology

Transparencies
- The Food Guide Pyramid

Memory Game Ask students to create a memory game about the six essential nutrients. Give students 12 index cards. On six of the cards, students should list each nutrient. On the other six cards, they should list the role each nutrient plays in the body. Ask students to turn over the cards, scramble them, and turn over cards individually to match each with the appropriate nutrient or function. **LS** Kinesthetic/Verbal

1. What are the six essential nutrients? (carbohydrates, proteins, fats, water, vitamins, and minerals)

2. What are the effects of obesity? (Sample answer: Obesity increases the risk of high blood pressure, heart disease, and diabetes. Some obese people may suffer from malnutrition.)

Concept Mapping Have students create a concept map using the new terms from the section and any additional words that are necessary. Have students begin their concept map with the phrase "Good nutrition." **LS** Logical

Nutrition Facts	
Serving Size 1/2 cup (120 ml) ◀ **Serving information**	
Servings per Container 2.5	

Amount per Serving	Prepared
Calories	70 ◀ **Number of Calories per serving**
Calories from Fat	25

	% Daily Value
Total Fat 2.5 g	4%
Saturated Fat 1 g	5%
Cholesterol 15 mg	5%
Sodium 960 mg	40%
Total Carbohydrate 8 g	3%
Dietary Fiber less than 1 g	4%
Sugars 1 g	
Protein 3 g	
Vitamin A	15%
Vitamin C	0%
Calcium ◀ **Percentage of daily values**	0%
Iron	4%

*Percent Daily Values are based on a 2,000 Calorie diet. Your daily values may be higher or lower depending on your Calorie needs:

		Calories	2,000	2,500
Total Fat	Less than		65g	80g
Sat Fat	Less than		20g	25g
Cholesterol	Less than		300mg	300mg
Sodium	Less than		2,400mg	2,400mg
Total Carbohydrate			300g	375g
Dietary Fiber			25g	30g
Protein			50g	60g

Figure 5 *Nutrition Facts labels provide a lot of information.*

malnutrition a disorder of nutrition that results when a person does not consume enough of each of the nutrients that are needed by the human body

What Percentage?

Use the Nutrition Facts label above to answer the following question. The recommended daily value of fat is 72 g for teenage girls and 90 g for teenage boys. What percentage of the daily recommended fat value is provided in one cup of soup?

Reading Food Labels

Packaged foods must have Nutrition Facts labels. **Figure 5** shows a Nutrition Facts label for chicken noodle soup. Nutrition Facts labels show what amount of each nutrient is in one serving of the food. You can tell whether a food is high or low in a nutrient by looking at its daily value. Reading food labels can help you make healthy eating choices. The percentage of daily values shown is based on a diet that consists of 2,000 Cal per day. Most teenagers need more than 2,000 Cal per day. The number of Calories needed depends on factors such as height, weight, age, and level of activity. Playing sports and exercising use up Calories that need to be replaced for you to grow.

✔ Reading Check For what nutrients does chicken noodle soup provide more than 10% of the daily value?

Nutritional Disorders

Unhealthy eating habits can cause nutritional disorders. **Malnutrition** occurs when someone does not eat enough of the nutrients needed by the body. Malnutrition can result from eating too few or too many Calories or not taking in enough of the right nutrients. Malnutrition affects how one looks and how quickly one's body can repair damage and fight illness.

Anorexia Nervosa and Bulimia Nervosa

Anorexia nervosa (AN uh REKS ee uh nuhr VOH suh) is an eating disorder characterized by self-starvation and an intense fear of gaining weight. Anorexia nervosa can lead to severe malnutrition.

Bulimia nervosa (boo LEE mee uh nuhr VOH suh) is a disorder characterized by binge eating followed by induced vomiting. Sometimes, people suffering from bulimia nervosa use laxatives or diuretics to rid their bodies of food and water. Bulimia nervosa can damage teeth and the digestive system and can lead to kidney and heart failure.

Both anorexia and bulimia can cause weak bones, low blood pressure, and heart problems. These eating disorders can be fatal if not treated. If you are worried that you or someone you know may have an eating disorder, talk to an adult.

Math Practice

3.5% for girls (2.5 g ÷ 72 g × 100 = 3.5%)
2.8% for boys (2.5 g ÷ 90 g × 100 = 2.8%)

Answer to Reading Check

One serving of chicken noodle soup provides more than 10% of the daily recommended allowance of vitamin A and sodium.

Obesity

Eating too much food that is high in fat and low in other nutrients, such as junk food and fast food, can lead to malnutrition. *Obesity* (oh BEE suh tee) is having an extremely high percentage of body fat. People suffering from obesity may not be eating a variety of foods that provide them with the correct balance of essential nutrients. Having an inactive lifestyle can also contribute to obesity.

Obesity increases the risk of high blood pressure, heart disease, and diabetes. Eating a more balanced diet and exercising regularly can help reduce obesity. Obesity may also be caused by other factors. Scientists are studying the links between obesity and heredity.

SECTION Review

Summary

- A healthy diet has a balance of carbohydrates, proteins, fats, water, vitamins, and minerals.
- The Food Guide Pyramid is a good guide for healthy eating.
- Nutrition Facts labels provide information needed to plan a healthy diet.
- Anorexia nervosa and bulimia nervosa cause malnutrition and damage to many body systems.
- Obesity can lead to heart disease and diabetes.

Using Key Terms

1. In your own words, write a definition for each of the following terms: *nutrient, mineral,* and *vitamin.*

Understanding Key Ideas

2. Malnutrition can be caused by
   a. obesity.
   b. bulimia nervosa.
   c. anorexia nervosa.
   d. All of the above

3. What information is found on a Nutrition Facts label?

4. Give an example of a carbohydrate, a protein, and a fat.

5. If vitamins and minerals do not supply energy, why are they important to a healthy diet?

6. How do anorexia nervosa and bulimia nervosa differ?

7. How can someone who is obese suffer from malnutrition?

Math Skills

8. If you eat 2,500 Cal per day and 20% are from fat, 30% are from protein, and 50% are from carbohydrates, how many Calories of each nutrient do you eat?

Critical Thinking

9. **Applying Concepts** Name some of the nutrients that can be found in a glass of milk.

10. **Identifying Relationships** Explain how eating a variety of foods can help ensure good nutrition.

11. **Predicting Consequences** How would your growth be affected if your diet consistently lacked important nutrients?

12. **Applying Concepts** Explain how you can use the Nutrition Facts label to choose food that is high in calcium.

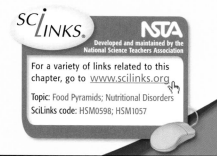

SCI**LINKS**

NSTA
Developed and maintained by the
National Science Teachers Association

For a variety of links related to this chapter, go to www.scilinks.org

Topic: Food Pyramids; Nutritional Disorders
SciLinks code: HSM0598; HSM1057

Answers to Section Review

1. Sample answer: A nutrient is a substance that your body needs to keep working. A mineral is nutrient that your body needs for certain body processes. A vitamin is a nutrient that controls many body functions and must be obtained from food.

2. d

3. Sample answer: A Nutrition Facts label shows how much of each nutrient is in a single serving of a packaged food.

4. Sample answer: Bread is a carbohydrate, oil is a fat, and fish contains protein.

CHAPTER RESOURCES

Chapter Resource File

- Section Quiz **GENERAL**
- Section Review **GENERAL**
- Vocabulary and Section Summary **GENERAL**
- Reinforcement Worksheet **BASIC**
- Critical Thinking **ADVANCED**
- SciLinks Activity **GENERAL**
- Datasheet for Quick Lab

Technology

Transparencies
- Nutrition Facts Label

5. Sample answer: Vitamins and minerals help control body functions, such as heartbeat and muscle movement, and they help build body parts, such as bones and blood cells.

6. Sample answer: Anorexia nervosa is an eating disorder in which a person starves himself or herself. Bulimia nervosa is an eating disorder in which a person eats and then induces vomiting.

7. Sample answer: A person who is obese can suffer from malnutrition because his or her diet may be high in fat, and he or she does not get enough of the other essential nutrients.

8. 500 Cal from fat (2,500 Cal × 0.2 = 500 Cal), 750 Cal from protein (2,500 Cal × 0.3 = 750 Cal), 1,250 Cal from carbohydrates (2,500 Cal × 0.5 = 1,250 Cal)

9. Accept all reasonable answers. All six types of nutrients can be found in milk.

10. Sample answer: Because different foods contain different nutrients, eating a variety of foods can help people get a variety of nutrients. Many of these nutrients are needed for good nutrition.

11. Sample answer: If your diet lacked Calories, your body would not have the energy to grow. If your diet lacked minerals, such as calcium, your body would not have the building blocks needed to remain healthy and grow.

12. Sample answer: The Nutrition Facts label lists the percentage of daily value for calcium found in a single serving of food. Reading the labels of foods helps people make sure that they eat foods high in calcium.

Risks of Alcohol and Other Drugs

You see them in movies and on television and read about them in magazines. But what are drugs?

You are exposed to information, and misinformation, about drugs every day. So, how can you make the best decisions?

What Is a Drug?

Any chemical substance that causes a physical or psychological change is called a **drug.** Drugs come in many forms, as shown in **Figure 1.** Some drugs enter the body through the skin. Other drugs are swallowed, inhaled, or injected. Drugs are classified by their effects. *Analgesics* (AN'l JEE ziks) relieve pain. *Antibiotics* (AN tie bie AHT iks) fight bacterial infections, and *antihistamines* (AN tie HIS tuh MEENZ) control cold and allergy symptoms. *Stimulants* speed up the central nervous system, and *depressants* slow it down. When used correctly, legal drugs can help your body heal. When used illegally or improperly, however, drugs can do great harm.

Dependence and Addiction

The body can develop *tolerance* to a drug. Tolerance means that larger and larger doses of the drug are needed to get the same effect. The body can also form a *physical dependence* or need for a drug. If the body doesn't receive a drug that it is physically dependent on, withdrawal symptoms occur. Withdrawal symptoms include nausea, vomiting, pain, and tremors.

Addiction is the loss of control of drug-taking behavior. Once addicted, a person finds it very hard to stop taking a drug. Sometimes, the need for a drug is not due only to physical dependence. Some people also form *psychological dependence* on a drug, which means that they feel powerful cravings for the drug.

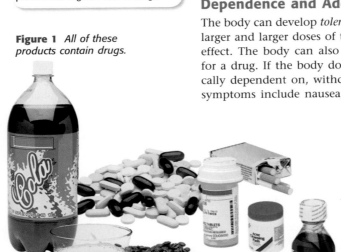

Figure 1 *All of these products contain drugs.*

 SCIENCE

Humans may not be the only organisms that use drugs. Chimpanzees have been observed swallowing the leaves of a plant that is known to be effective against infections and parasites. Muriqui monkeys of Brazil may be able to control their fertility with certain plants, and howler monkeys may even select the sex of their offspring by eating different plants.

Types of Drugs

There are many kinds of drugs. Some drugs are made from plants, and some are made in a lab. You can buy some drugs at the grocery store, while others can be prescribed only by a doctor. Some drugs are illegal to buy, sell, or possess.

Herbal Medicines

Information about herbal medicines has been handed down for centuries, and some herbs contain chemicals with important healing properties. The tea in **Figure 2** contains chamomile and is made from a plant. Chamomile has chemicals in it that can help you sleep. However, herbs are drugs and should be used carefully. The Federal Drug Administration does not regulate herbal medicines or teas and cannot guarantee their safety.

Over-the-Counter and Prescription Drugs

Over-the-counter drugs can be bought without a prescription. A prescription is written by a doctor and describes the drug, directions for use, and the amount of the drug to be taken.

Many over-the-counter and prescription drugs are powerful healing agents. However, some drugs also produce unwanted side effects. *Side effects* are uncomfortable symptoms, such as nausea, headaches, drowsiness, or more serious problems.

Whether purchased with or without a prescription, all drugs must be used with care. Information on proper use can be found on the label. **Figure 3** shows some general drug safety tips.

✔ **Reading Check** What is the difference between an over-the-counter drug and a prescription drug? (*See the Appendix for answers to Reading Checks.*)

drug any substance that causes a change in a person's physical or psychological state

addiction a dependence on a substance, such as alcohol or another drug

Figure 2 *Some herbs can be purchased in health-food stores. Medicinal herbs should always be used with care.*

Figure 3	**Drug Safety Tips**

- Never take another person's prescription medicine.
- Read the label before each use. Always follow the instructions on the label and those provided by your doctor or pharmacist.
- Do not take more or less medication than prescribed.
- Consult a doctor if you have any side effects.
- Throw away leftover and out-of-date medicines.

Answer to Reading Check

Over-the-counter drugs can be bought without a prescription. Prescription drugs can be bought only with a prescription from a doctor or other medical professional.

• *Behavior Control Issues*
• *Hearing Impaired*
• *Learning Disabled*

Students often benefit from small-group work. Have students work in groups of four. Have them create information webs with large circles in the center and small circles surrounding the large circles. Tell students to write each of the following phrases inside a large circle: "Problems caused by cigarettes" and "Smokeless tobacco hazards." Tell students to add six small circles to the cigarette web and three small circles to the smokeless tobacco web and to write a risk in each of the small circles. **LS** Visual

Discussion ——— GENERAL

Advertising Alcohol Tell students that beer, liquor, and wine companies in the United States spend billions of dollars annually on advertising and promotion. Display for students a selection of advertisements for beer, liquor, or wine taken from magazines. Encourage students to identify advertising tactics that might attract youth. (Students might note that the ads often show groups of young, beautiful, and active people in outdoor settings. These ads imply that people cannot have fun without alcohol.) **LS** Verbal

---

Figure 4 **Effects of Smoking**

▼ Healthy lung tissue of a nonsmoker   ▼ Damaged lung tissue of a smoker

nicotine a toxic, addictive chemical that is found in tobacco and that is one of the major contributors to the harmful effects of smoking

alcoholism a disorder in which a person repeatedly drinks alcoholic beverages in an amount that interferes with the person's health and activities

Figure 5 *This car was in an accident involving a drunk driver.*

Tobacco

Cigarettes are addictive, and smoking has serious health effects. **Nicotine** (NIK uh TEEN) is a chemical in tobacco that increases heart rate and blood pressure and is extremely addictive. Smokers experience a decrease in physical endurance. **Figure 4** shows the effects of smoking on the cilia of your lungs. Cilia clean the air you breathe and prevent debris from entering your lungs. Smoking increases the chances of lung cancer, and it has been linked to other cancers, emphysema, chronic bronchitis, and heart disease. Experts estimate that there are more than 430,000 deaths related to smoking each year in the United States. Secondhand smoke also poses significant health risks.

Like cigarettes, smokeless, or chewing, tobacco is addictive and can cause health problems. Nicotine is absorbed through the lining of the mouth. Smokeless tobacco increases the risk of several cancers, including mouth and throat cancer. It also causes gum disease and yellowing of the teeth.

Alcohol

It is illegal in most of the United States for people under the age of 21 to use alcohol. Alcohol slows down the central nervous system and can cause memory loss. Excessive use of alcohol can damage the liver, pancreas, brain, nerves, and cardiovascular system. In very large quantities, alcohol can cause death. Alcohol is a factor in more than half of all suicides, murders, and accidental deaths. **Figure 5** shows the results of one alcohol-related accident. Alcohol also affects decision making and can lead you to take unhealthy risks.

People can suffer from **alcoholism,** which means that they are physically and psychologically dependent on alcohol. Alcoholism is considered a disease, and genetic factors are thought to influence the development of alcoholism in some people.

Is That a Fact!

About 90% of first-time cigarette smokers will become addicted to cigarettes. Fewer than half of these people are able to quit smoking, which puts their health at great risk. About 90% of people who get lung cancer are smokers or former smokers. Cigarette smokers are also at greater risk of getting cancers of the larynx, lip, esophagus, bladder, pancreas, and kidneys.

Homework ——— GENERAL

Avoiding Alcohol Tell students that counteradvertising is an effective technique for deterring alcohol abuse. Have students work in small groups to create a magazine advertisement against alcohol abuse. Consider hanging the advertisements in the classroom or around the school. **LS** Verbal

Figure 6 *Smoking marijuana can make your health and dreams go up in smoke.*

Marijuana

Marijuana is an illegal drug that comes from the Indian hemp plant. Marijuana affects different people in different ways. It may increase anxiety or cause feelings of paranoia. Marijuana slows reaction time, impairs thinking, and causes a loss of coordination. Regular use of marijuana can affect many areas of your life, as described in **Figure 6.**

Cocaine

Cocaine and its more purified form, crack, are made from the coca plant. Both drugs are illegal and highly addictive. Users can become addicted to them in a very short time. Cocaine can produce feelings of intense excitement followed by anxiety and depression. Both drugs increase heart rate and blood pressure and can cause heart attacks, even among first-time users.

✓ Reading Check What are two dangers to users of cocaine?

Narcotics and Designer Drugs

Drugs made from the opium plant are called **narcotics.** Some narcotics are used to treat severe pain. Narcotics are illegal unless prescribed by a doctor. Some narcotics are never legal. For example, heroin is one of the most addictive narcotics and is always illegal. Heroin is usually injected, and users often share needles. Therefore, heroin users have a high risk of becoming infected with diseases such as hepatitis and AIDS. Heroin users can also die of an overdose of the drug.

Other illegal drugs include inhalants, barbiturates (bahr BICH uhr itz), amphetamines (am FET uh MEENZ), and *designer drugs.* Designer drugs are made by making small changes to existing drugs. Ecstasy, or "X," is a designer drug that causes feelings of well-being. Over time, the drug causes lesions (LEE zhuhnz), or holes, in a user's brain, as shown in **Figure 7.** Ecstasy users are also more likely to develop depression.

narcotic a drug that is derived from opium and that relieves pain and induces sleep

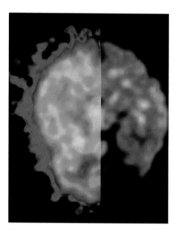

Figure 7 *The brain scan on the left shows a healthy brain. The scan on the right is from a teenager who has regularly used Ecstasy.*

Answer to Reading Check
First-time use of cocaine can cause a heart attack or can cause a person to become addicted.

Reteaching — BASIC

Reviewing Drugs Ask students to briefly describe the drugs discussed in the section. Have students identify effects that these drugs can have on the body.
LS Verbal

Quiz — GENERAL

1. What is drug abuse? (Sample answer: Drug abuse is the improper or illegal use of drugs.)

2. What is nicotine? (Nicotine is the drug in tobacco that increases heart rate and blood pressure and is extremely addictive.)

3. What are designer drugs? Give an example. (Sample answer: Designer drugs are drugs made by making small changes to existing drugs. Ecstasy is a designer drug.)

Alternative Assessment — GENERAL

Making Tables Have students prepare tables describing alcohol, tobacco, marijuana, cocaine, LSD, and heroin. Have students define each and describe the effects of the drug on the body. In addition, have students indicate whether the drug is legal and whether it is addictive.
LS Logical/Verbal

Figure 8 *Drug abuse can leave you depressed and feeling alone.*

Figure 9 Drug Myths

Myth **"It's only alcohol, not drugs."**

Reality Alcohol is a mood-altering and mind-altering drug. It affects the central nervous system and is addictive.

Myth **"I won't get hooked on one or two cigarettes a day."**

Reality Addiction is not related to the amount of a drug used. Some people become addicted after using a drug once or twice.

Myth **"I can quit any time I want."**

Reality Addicts may quit and return to drug usage many times. Their inability to stay drug-free shows how powerful the addiction is.

Good Reasons

WRITING SKILL Discuss with your parent the possible effects of drug abuse on your family. Then, write yourself a letter giving reasons why you should stay drug-free. Put your letter in a safe place. If you ever find yourself thinking about using drugs, take out your letter and read it.

ACTiViTY

Hallucinogens

Hallucinogens (huh LOO si nuh juhnz) distort the senses and cause mood changes. Users have hallucinations, which means that they see and hear things that are not real. LSD and PCP are powerful, illegal hallucinogens. Sniffing glue or solvents can also cause hallucinations and serious brain damage.

Drug Abuse

A drug user takes a drug to prevent or improve a medical condition. The drug user obtains the drug legally and uses the drug properly. A drug abuser does not take a drug to relieve a medical condition. An abuser may take drugs for the temporary good feelings they produce, to escape from problems, or to belong to a group. The drug is often obtained illegally, and it is often taken without knowledge of the drug's dangers.

Reading Check What is the difference between drug use and drug abuse?

How Drug Abuse Starts

Nicotine, alcohol, and marijuana are sometimes called *gateway drugs* because they are often the first drugs a person abuses. The abuse of other, more dangerous drugs may follow the abuse of gateway drugs. Peer pressure is often the reason that young people begin to use drugs. Teenagers may drink, smoke, or try marijuana to make friends or avoid being teased. Because drug abusers often stand out, it can sometimes be hard to see that many teenagers do not abuse drugs.

Many teenagers begin using illegal drugs to feel part of a group, but drug abuse has many serious consequences. Drug abuse can lead to problems with friends, family, school, and handling money. These problems often lead to depression and social isolation, as shown in **Figure 8.**

Many people who start using drugs do not recognize the dangers. Misinformation about drugs is everywhere. Several common drug myths are discussed in **Figure 9.**

Homework — GENERAL

Writing **Drug Report** Have students write a short paper about one of the following drugs: alcohol, marijuana, cocaine, LSD, PCP, ecstasy, or heroin. Ask students to describe the type of drug, common names for the drug, what the drug is made from, the effects of the drug, the penalty for possession of the drug, and what help is available to those who are addicted to the drug. **LS** Verbal

Answer to Reading Check

Drug use is the proper use of a legal drug. Drug abuse is either the use of an illegal drug or the improper use of a legal drug.

Getting Off Drugs

People who abuse drugs undergo emotional and physical changes. Teenagers who had few problems often begin to have problems with school, family, and money when they start to use drugs.

The first step to quitting drugs is to admit to abusing drugs and to decide to stop. It is important for the addicted person to get the proper medical treatment. There are drug treatment centers, like the one shown in **Figure 10**, available to help. Getting off drugs can be extremely difficult. Withdrawal symptoms are often painful, and powerful cravings for a drug can continue long after a person quits. But people who stop abusing drugs lead happier and healthier lives.

Figure 10 *Drug treatment centers help people get off drugs and back on track to healthier, happier lives.*

SECTION Review

Summary

- Physical dependence causes withdrawal symptoms when a person stops using a drug. Psychological dependence causes powerful cravings.
- There are many types of drugs, including over-the-counter, prescription, and herbal medicines.
- Tobacco contains the highly addictive chemical nicotine.
- Abuse of alcohol can lead to alcoholism.
- Illegal drugs include marijuana, cocaine, hallucinogens, designer drugs, and many narcotics.
- Getting off drugs requires proper medical treatment.

Using Key Terms

1. In your own words, write a definition for the terms *drug, addiction,* and *narcotic.*

Understanding Key Ideas

2. Which of the following products does NOT contain a drug?
   a. cola
   b. fruit juice
   c. herbal tea
   d. cough syrup

3. Describe the difference between physical and psychological dependence.

4. What is the difference between drug use and drug abuse?

5. How does addiction occur, and what are two consequences of drug addiction?

6. Name two different kinds of illegal drugs, and give examples of each.

Math Skills

7. If 2,200 people between the ages of 16 and 20 die every year in alcohol-related car crashes, how many die every day?

Critical Thinking

8. **Analyzing Relationships** How are nicotine, alcohol, heroin, and cocaine similar? How are they different?

9. **Analyzing Ideas** What are two ways that a person who abuses drugs can get in trouble with the law?

10. **Predicting Consequences** How can drug abuse damage family relationships?

11. **Making Inferences** Driving a car while under the influence of drugs can put others in danger. Describe another situation in which one person's drug abuse could put other people in danger.

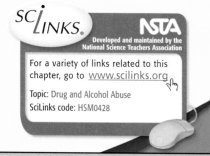

SCI LINKS
Developed and maintained by the National Science Teachers Association

For a variety of links related to this chapter, go to www.scilinks.org

Topic: Drug and Alcohol Abuse
SciLinks code: HSM0428

Answers to Section Review

1. Sample answer: A drug is any substance that changes a person's physical or emotional state. Addiction happens when someone becomes dependent on a drug. A narcotic is a drug that is derived from opium and that is used to treat pain.

2. b

CHAPTER RESOURCES

Chapter Resource File

- Section Quiz GENERAL
- Section Review GENERAL
- Vocabulary and Section Summary GENERAL

3. Sample answer: When someone forms a physical dependence, he or she suffers from withdrawal symptoms if he or she stops using a drug. Someone who has a psychological dependence on a drug feels powerful cravings for the drug.

4. Sample answer: Drug use is the legal and proper use of a drug to prevent or improve a medical condition. Drug abuse is the improper and illegal use of drugs, often for the feelings the drugs produce, to escape from problems, and to fit in.

5. Sample answer: Addiction is the loss of control of drug-taking behavior. Addiction can cause problems at school, at home, and with money.

6. Sample answer: Narcotics include opium and heroin. LSD and PCP are hallucinogens.

7. 6 people/day
   (2,200 people ÷ 365 days = 6 people/day)

8. Sample answer: Nicotine, alcohol, heroin, and cocaine are all addictive. Nicotine and alcohol are legal for many people, but cocaine and heroin are illegal.

9. Sample answers: A person who abuses drugs can get in trouble with the law because many drugs are illegal. Also drug abuse can cause money troubles, which might lead someone to steal. Some people may drink and drive, which is illegal even if a person is old enough to legally drink alcohol.

10. Sample answer: Drug abuse can cause stress in a family because drug abuse causes failing grades and depression.

11. Sample answer: People who abuse drugs often make bad decisions. For example, a drug abuser may try to go swimming in dangerous water. A person who tried to help a drug abuser who makes a bad decision could be hurt.

Focus

Overview

In this section, students will learn how hygiene, exercise, rest, and stress management can enhance their well-being. Students will learn how stress affects the body. Finally, students will learn how injuries can be prevented.

🔔 Bellringer

Tell students the following information: "In the 1800s and earlier, people who sustained simple cuts on their skin often ended up with serious infections. That rarely happens now." Then, ask students to explain why infections are less common now than they once were. (Sample answer: People now understand the importance of washing wounds with soap to keep them clean. People also have antiseptics and antibiotics today.)

Motivate

ACTIVITY ——————— GENERAL

Don't Kick These Habits! Ask students to list some of their daily hygienic habits. (Sample answers: washing hands, bathing, brushing teeth, washing dishes, and using clean utensils to eat)
LS Verbal

READING WARM-UP

Objectives
- Describe three important aspects of good hygiene.
- Explain why exercise and sleep are important to good health.
- Describe methods of handling stress.
- List three ways to stay safe at home, on the road, and outdoors.
- Plan what you would do in the case of an accident.

Terms to Learn
hygiene
aerobic exercise
stress

READING STRATEGY

Prediction Guide Before reading this section, write the title of each heading in this section. Next, under each heading, write what you think you will learn.

hygiene the science of health and ways to preserve health

Figure 1 *A slumped posture strains your lower back.*

Healthy Habits

Do you like playing sports or acting in plays? How does your health affect your favorite activities?

Whatever you do, the better your health is, the better you can perform. Keeping yourself healthy is a daily responsibility.

Taking Care of Your Body

The science of preserving and protecting your health is known as **hygiene.** It sounds simple, but washing your hands is the best way to prevent the spread of disease and infection. You should always wash your hands after using the bathroom and before and after handling food. Taking care of your skin, hair, and teeth is important for good hygiene. Good hygiene includes regularly using sunscreen, shampooing your hair, and brushing and flossing your teeth daily.

Good Posture

Posture is also important to health. Good posture helps you look and feel your best. Bad posture strains your muscles and ligaments and makes breathing difficult. To have good posture, imagine a vertical line passing through your ear, shoulder, hip, knee, and ankle when you stand, as shown in **Figure 1.** When working at a desk, you should maintain good posture by pulling your chair forward and planting your feet firmly on the floor.

When you have good posture, your ear, shoulder, hip, knee, and ankle are in a straight line.

Bad posture strains your muscles and ligaments and can make breathing difficult.

CHAPTER RESOURCES

Chapter Resource File

- Lesson Plan
- Directed Reading A **BASIC**
- Directed Reading B **SPECIAL NEEDS**

Technology

- **Transparencies**
  - Bellringer

CONNECTION to
Earth Science ——— ADVANCED

Fossil Hygiene Tell students that they may use fossils as part of their daily hygienic habits. Many toothpastes contain diatomaceous earth, which consists of fossilized diatoms—protist producers with silica shells. The silica in diatomaceous earth polishes the surface of teeth. Ask interested students to research how diatomaceous earth formed and other uses for it. Have students make a poster about their findings. **LS** Visual

Exercise

Aerobic exercise at least three times a week is essential to good health. **Aerobic exercise** is vigorous, constant exercise of the whole body for 20 minutes or more. Walking, running, swimming, and biking are all examples of aerobic exercise. **Figure 2** shows another popular aerobic exercise—basketball.

Aerobic exercise increases the heart rate. As a result, more oxygen is taken in and distributed throughout the body. Over time, aerobic exercise strengthens the heart, lungs, and bones. It burns Calories, helps your body conserve some nutrients, and aids digestion. It also gives you more energy and stamina. Aerobic exercise protects your physical and mental health.

✔ **Reading Check** What are two benefits of regular exercise? (*See the Appendix for answers to Reading Checks.*)

Figure 2 *Aerobic exercise can be fun if you choose an activity you enjoy.*

Sleep

Believe it or not, teenagers actually need more sleep than younger children. Do you ever fall asleep in class, like the girl in **Figure 3,** or feel tired in the middle of the afternoon? If so, you may not be getting enough sleep. Scientists say that teenagers need about 9.5 hours of sleep each night.

At night, the body goes through several cycles of progressively deeper sleep, with periods of lighter sleep in between. If you do not sleep long enough, you will not enter the deepest, most restful period of sleep.

aerobic exercise physical exercise intended to increase the activity of the heart and lungs to promote the body's use of oxygen

Figure 3 *If you fall asleep easily during the day, you are probably not getting enough sleep.*

CONNECTION TO Language Arts

Dreamy Poetry

You are not wrong, who deem
That my days have been a dream;
Yet if hope has flown away
In a night, or in a day,
In a vision, or in none,
Is it therefore the less gone?
All that we see or seem
Is but a dream within a dream.

(Edgar Allan Poe,
"A Dream Within a Dream")

What do you think Poe means by "a dream within a dream?" Why do you think there are many poems written about dreams or sleep?

WEIRD SCIENCE

Regular, intense exercise decreases body fat. For female athletes who participate in intense exercise frequently, this loss of body fat can restrict the release of estrogen. When this occurs in prepubescent athletes, it delays the onset of puberty. Menstruation is delayed, and the period of bone growth is sometimes extended.

Answer to Connection to Language Arts

Sample answer: "A dream within a dream" could refer to the sense that everything people feel is based on events that have already happened. There are many poems written about dreams because dreams are often strange and can cause strong emotions.

Discussion ———— GENERAL

Happy Stress Point out to students that although many people think that the term *stress* refers only to the emotional and physical response to negative events, many positive situations also cause stress. Encourage students to identify "happy" events that can create stress. (Sample answers: a new job, the addition of a sibling, and moving to a new house) Point out that stress, whatever its source, produces a physiological reaction that is designed to prepare the body for difficult situations. **LS** Logical/Verbal

CONNECTION ACTIVITY
Real World ———— GENERAL

Writing **Sleep Disorders**
Scientists who study people's sleep patterns have learned that about 33% of the general population suffers from a sleep disorder. Ask interested students to research some of these sleep disorders. Students should identify the disorder, characteristics of the disorder, symptoms of the disorder, and ways in which the disorder is treated. Ask students to write a newspaper article about their findings. **LS** Verbal

Figure 4 *Can you identify all of the things in this picture that could cause stress?*

stress a physical or mental response to pressure

INTERNET ACTIVITY
For another activity related to this chapter, go to **go.hrw.com** and type in the keyword **HL5BD7W.**

Coping with Stress

You have a big soccer game tomorrow. Are you excited and ready for action? You got a low grade on your English paper. Are you upset or angry? The game and the test are causing you stress. **Stress** is the physical and mental response to pressure.

Some stress is a normal part of life. Stress stimulates your body to prepare for difficult or dangerous situations. However, sometimes you may have no outlet for the stress, and it builds up. Many things are causing stress for the girl shown in **Figure 4.** Excess stress is harmful to your health and can decrease your ability to carry out your daily activities.

You may not even realize you are stressed until your body reacts. Perhaps you get a headache, have an upset stomach, or lie awake at night. You might feel tired all the time or begin an old nervous habit, such as nail-biting. You may become irritable or resentful. All of these things can be signs of too much stress.

Dealing with Stress

Different people are stressed by different things. Once you identify the source of the stress, you can find ways to deal with it. If you cannot remove the cause of stress, here are some ideas for handling stress.

- Share your problems. Talk things over with someone you trust, such as a parent, friend, teacher, or school counselor.
- Make a list of all the things you would like to get done, and rank the things in order of importance. Do the most important things first.
- Exercise regularly, and get enough sleep.
- Pet a friendly animal.
- Spend some quiet time alone, or practice deep breathing or other relaxation techniques.

Homework ———— GENERAL

Stress Management Ask students, "What are the three things in your life that cause you the most stress?" Have students list the sources of stress in their life and come up with ways of eliminating, reducing, or coping with this stress. Keep in mind that some students are uncomfortable sharing personal information. **LS** Verbal

Injury Prevention

Have you ever fallen off your bike or sprained your ankle? Accidents happen, and they can cause injury and even death. It is impossible to prevent all accidents, but you can decrease your risk by using your common sense and following basic safety rules.

Safety Outdoors

Always dress appropriately for the weather and for the activity. Never hike or camp alone. Tell someone where you are going and when you expect to return. If you do not bring water from home, be sure to purify any water you drink in the wilderness.

Learn how to swim. It could save your life! Never swim alone, and do not dive into shallow water or water of unknown depth. When in a boat, wear a life jacket. If a storm threatens, get out of the water and seek shelter.

✔ **Reading Check** Name three safety tips for the outdoors.

Safety at Home

Many accidents can be avoided. **Figure 5** shows tips for safety around the house.

Figure 5 **Home Safety Tips**

• Have a parent install smoke detectors on every floor.

Bathroom
• Never touch electrical switches or appliances while touching water.
• Use nonslip mats in the shower and tub.
• Use a night light.

Kitchen
• Clean up spills quickly.
• Do not allow pot handles to extend over the edge of the stove.
• Use a stool to reach high shelves.
• Keep grease and drippings away from open flames.

Entrance and Stairs
• Use a railing.
• Never leave objects on stairs.

Living Room
• Keep electrical cords out of walkways.
• Do not plug too many electrical devices into one outlet.

Homework ——— GENERAL

Writing **Temperature Injuries** Have students research and write a report about the physical symptoms and emergency treatments for hypothermia and heatstroke. **LS** Verbal

Answer to Reading Check

Sample answers: Never hike or camp alone, dress for the weather, learn how to swim, wear a life jacket, and never drink unpurified water.

Discussion ——— GENERAL

Fatal Injuries Tell students that injuries cause more deaths among children between the ages of 1 and 19 than any major diseases. Point out that bicycle injuries alone cause the death of more than 500 children and teens in the United States each year. Most of these deaths involve head trauma. Remind students that many accidents can be prevented. Experts estimate that the simple act of wearing a bicycle helmet can reduce the risk of head injury by 85%, yet many children don't wear helmets. Ask students why they think people don't wear helmets. (Sample answers: Perhaps some people cannot afford helmets. Some people think that helmets are "funny-looking" or "uncool." Other people may think helmets are uncomfortable.) Ask students if there are other activities in which a helmet protects participants. (Sample answers: skating, snowboarding, football, and hockey) Ask students to brainstorm ways to get more children and teens to wear helmets during physical activity. **LS** Verbal

Group ACTIVITY — GENERAL

Poster Project Have students work in groups of four, and provide each group with poster board and markers. Have students create posters designed to educate the public about injury prevention. After students present their posters to the class, display the posters in the classroom. **LS** Visual

Close

Reteaching ——— BASIC

Taking Care Write the following headings on the board: "Healthy habits," "Coping with stress," and "Preventing injuries." Ask students to write examples of each under the headings. **LS Logical/Verbal**

Quiz ——— GENERAL

1. List three ways to deal with stress. (Sample answers: Share your problems. Make a list. Exercise regularly. Get enough sleep. Pet a friendly animal. Spend some quiet time alone. Practice relaxation techniques.)

2. What do bicycle helmets and seat belts have in common? (Sample answer: They both decrease the risk of injury from accidents.)

3. When you call for emergency help, what should you tell the operator? (the location of the emergency, the type of accident, the number of people injured, and the types of injuries)

Alternative Assessment ——— ADVANCED

Writing **Analyzing Habits** Have students write an analysis of their hygienic habits, exercise regimens, sleep patterns, and injury risks. Tell students to explain whether their activities and habits are encouraging good health and to describe what changes they might need to make to their routines. **LS Verbal**

Figure 6 *It is always important to use the appropriate safety equipment.*

Figure 7 *When calling 911, stay calm and listen carefully to what the dispatcher tells you.*

Safety on the Road

In the car, always wear a seat belt, even if you are traveling only a short distance. Never ride in a car with someone who has been drinking. Safety equipment and common sense are your best defense against injury. When riding a bicycle, always wear a helmet like those shown in **Figure 6.** Ride with traffic, and obey all traffic rules. Be sure to signal when stopping or turning.

Safety in Class

Accidents can happen in school, especially in a lab class or during woodworking class. To avoid hurting yourself and others, always follow your teacher's instructions, and wear the proper safety equipment at all times.

When Accidents Happen

No matter how well you practice safety measures, accidents can still happen. What should you do if a friend chokes on food and cannot breathe? What if a friend is stung by a bee and has a violent allergic reaction?

Call for Help

Once you've checked for other dangers, call for medical help immediately, as the person shown in **Figure 7** is doing. In most communities, you can dial 911. Speak slowly and clearly. Give the complete address and a description of the location. Describe the accident, the number of people injured, and the types of injuries. Ask what to do, and listen carefully to the instructions. Let the other person hang up first to be sure there are no more questions or instructions for you.

⬤ INCLUSION Strategies

• *Developmentally Delayed* • *Visually Impaired*
• *Learning Disabled*
Students often benefit from verbal activities. Give students a chance to participate by having the class role-play 911 calls. Tell students that the calls should include the following parts:

• slow, clear speech
• description of emergency

• complete address or description of location
• type of injury
• number of people injured
• what has been done to help the victim
• request for instructions
• careful listening
LS Kinesthetic/Verbal

Learn First Aid

If you want to learn more about what to do in an emergency, you can take a first-aid or CPR course, such as the one shown in **Figure 8.** *CPR* can revive a person who is not breathing and has no heartbeat. If you are over 12 years old, you can become certified in both CPR and first aid. Some baby-sitting classes also provide information on first aid. The American Red Cross, community organizations, and local hospitals offer these classes. However, you should not attempt any lifesaving procedure unless you have been trained.

✓ Reading Check What is CPR, and how can you learn it?

Figure 8 *These teenagers are taking a CPR course to prepare themselves for emergency situations.*

SECTION Review

Summary

- Good hygiene includes taking care of your skin, hair, and teeth.
- Good posture is important to health.
- Exercise keeps your heart, lungs, and bones healthy.
- Teenagers need more than 9 hours of sleep to stay rested and healthy.
- Coping with stress is an important part of staying physically and emotionally healthy.
- It is important to be aware of the possible hazards around your home, outdoors, and at school. Using the appropriate safety equipment can also help keep you safe.

Using Key Terms

Complete each of the following sentences by choosing the correct term from the word bank.

hygiene   aerobic exercise
sleep   stress

1. The science of protecting your health is called ___.

2. ___ strengthens your heart, lungs, and bones.

3. ___ is the physical and mental response to pressure.

Understanding Key Ideas

4. Which of the following is important for good health?
   a. irregular exercise
   b. getting your hair cut
   c. taking care of your teeth
   d. getting plenty of sun

5. List two things you should do when calling for help in a medical emergency.

6. List three ways to stay safe when you are outside, and three ways to stay safe at home.

7. How do seat belts and safety equipment protect you?

Math Skills

8. It is estimated that only 65% of adults wear their seat belts. If there are 10,000 people driving in your area right now, how many of them are wearing their seat belts?

Critical Thinking

9. **Applying Concepts** What situations cause you stress? What can you do to help relieve the stress you are feeling?

10. **Making Inferences** According to the newspaper, the temperature outside is 61°F right now. Later, it will be 90°F outside. If you and your friends want to play soccer in the park, what should you wear? What should you bring with you?

SCILINKS
Developed and maintained by the National Science Teachers Association

For a variety of links related to this chapter, go to www.scilinks.org

Topic: Safety
SciLinks code: HSM1339

Answer to Reading Check

CPR is a way to revive someone whose heart has stopped beating. CPR classes are available in many places in the community.

CHAPTER RESOURCES

Chapter Resource File

- Section Quiz **GENERAL**
- Section Review **GENERAL**
- Vocabulary and Section Summary **GENERAL**

Keep It Clean

Teacher's Notes

Time Required
One 45-minute class period

Lab Ratings

EASY ——————————————→ HARD

Teacher Prep 🔬🔬🔬
Student Set-Up 🔬
Concept Level 🔬🔬
Clean Up 🔬🔬

MATERIALS

You can reduce the number of materials needed by having students work in groups and having each group select a volunteer.

Safety Caution

Remind students to review all safety cautions and icons before beginning this lab activity. Check for known allergies to antibacterial soaps or other soaps before beginning the activity. If possible, use plastic Petri dishes.

Skills Practice Lab

OBJECTIVES

Investigate how well antibacterial soap works.

Practice counting bacterial colonies.

MATERIALS

- incubator
- pencil, wax
- Petri dishes, nutrient agar–filled, sterile (3)
- scrub brush, new
- soap, liquid antibacterial
- stopwatch
- tape, transparent

SAFETY

Keep It Clean

One of the best ways to prevent the spread of bacterial and viral infections is to frequently wash your hands with soap and water. Many companies advertise that their soap ingredients can destroy bacteria normally found on the body. In this activity, you will investigate how effective antibacterial soaps are at killing bacteria.

Procedure

1. Keeping the agar plates closed at all times, use the wax pencil to label the bottoms of three agar plates. Label one plate "Control," one plate "No soap," and one plate "Soap."

2. Without washing your hands, carefully press several surfaces of your hands on the agar plate marked "Control." Have your partner immediately put the cover back on the plate. After you touch the agar, do not touch anything with either hand.

3. Hold your right hand under running water for 2 min. Ask your partner to scrub all surfaces of your right hand with the scrub brush throughout these 2 min. Be sure that he or she scrubs under your fingernails. After scrubbing, your partner should turn off the water and open the plate marked "No soap." Touching only the agar, carefully press on the "No soap" plate with the same surfaces of your right hand that you used to press on the "Control" plate.

Elizabeth Rustad
Higley School District
Gilbert, Arizona

CHAPTER RESOURCES

Chapter Resource File

 • Datasheet for Chapter Lab
• Lab Notes and Answers

Technology

 Classroom Videos
• Lab Video

• To Diet or Not to Diet

④ Repeat step 3, but use your left hand instead of your right. This time, ask your partner to scrub your left hand with liquid antibacterial soap and the scrub brush. Use the plate marked "Soap" instead of the plate marked "No soap."

⑤ Secure the lid of each plate to its bottom half with transparent tape. Place the plates upside down in the incubator. Incubate all three plates overnight at 37°C.

⑥ Remove the plates from the incubator, and turn them right side up. Check each plate for the presence of bacterial colonies, and count the number of colonies present on each plate. Record this information. **Caution:** Do not remove the lids on any of the plates.

Analyze the Results

❶ Examining Data Compare the bacterial growth on the plates. Which plate contained the most growth? Which contained the least?

Draw Conclusions

❷ Drawing Conclusions Does water alone effectively kill bacteria? Explain.

Applying Your Data

Repeat this experiment, but scrub with regular, not antibacterial, liquid soap. Describe how the results of the two experiments differ.

Analyze the Results

1. Students should observe that the control dish shows the most bacterial growth. Ideally, the dish inoculated after scrubbing hands with antibacterial soap should show the least bacterial growth.

Draw Conclusions

2. Because of chlorine and other agents used to purify drinking water, water alone kills many bacteria. Washing with antibacterial soap for a short time may be only slightly better than washing with water alone.

Applying Your Data

On average, hands must be scrubbed with antibacterial soap for a minimum of 4 minutes to see a significant reduction or absence of bacterial growth in nutrient agar. Ask students if they know how long doctors scrub their hands before surgery. (4–5 min)

Chapter Review

Assignment Guide

SECTION	QUESTIONS
1	1–3, 14–15, 17–18
2	4–7, 9, 11–13
3	8, 10, 16, 19–21

ANSWERS

Using Key Terms

1. nutrients
2. Food Guide Pyramid
3. malnutrition
4. addiction
5. drug

Understanding Key Ideas

6. d
7. b
8. c
9. d
10. c
11. a

USING KEY TERMS

Complete each of the following sentences by choosing the correct term from the word bank.

nutrients   Food Guide
addiction   Pyramid
malnutrition drug

1 Carbohydrates, proteins, fats, vitamins, minerals, and water are the six categories of ___.

2 The ___ divides foods into six groups and gives a recommended number of servings for each group.

3 Both bulimia nervosa and anorexia nervosa cause ___.

4 A physical or psychological dependence on a drug can lead to ___.

5 A(n) ___ is any substance that causes a change in a person's physical or psychological state.

UNDERSTANDING KEY IDEAS

Multiple Choice

6 Which of the following statements about drugs is true?

  a. A child cannot become addicted to drugs.
  b. Smoking just one or two cigarettes is safe for anyone.
  c. Alcohol is not a drug.
  d. Withdrawal symptoms may be painful.

7 What does alcohol do to the central nervous system (CNS)?

  a. It speeds the CNS up.
  b. It slows the CNS down.
  c. It keeps the CNS regulated.
  d. It has no effect on the CNS.

8 To keep your teeth healthy,

  a. brush your teeth as hard as you can.
  b. use a toothbrush until it is worn out.
  c. brush at least twice a day.
  d. floss at least once a week.

9 According to the Food Guide Pyramid, what foods should you eat most?

  a. meats
  b. milk, yogurt, and cheese
  c. fruits and vegetables
  d. bread, cereal, rice, and pasta

10 Which of the following can help you deal with stress?

  a. ignoring your homework
  b. drinking a caffeinated drink
  c. talking to a friend
  d. watching television

11 Tobacco use increases the risk of

  a. lung cancer.
  b. car accidents.
  c. liver damage.
  d. depression.

Short Answer

12 Are all narcotics illegal? Explain.

13 What are three dangers of tobacco and alcohol use?

14 What are the three types of nutrients that provide energy in Calories, and what is the main function of each type in the body?

15 Name two conditions that can lead to malnutrition.

16 Explain why you should always wear safety equipment when you ride your bicycle.

CRITICAL THINKING

17 **Concept Mapping** Use the following terms to create a concept map: *carbohydrates, water, proteins, nutrients, fats, vitamins, minerals, saturated fats,* and *unsaturated fats.*

18 **Applying Concepts** You have recently become a vegetarian, and you worry that you are not getting enough protein. Name two foods that you could eat to get more protein.

19 **Analyzing Ideas** Your two-year-old cousin will be staying with your family. Name three things that you can do to make sure that the house is safe for a young child.

INTERPRETING GRAPHICS

Look at the photos below. The people in the photos are not practicing safe habits. List the unsafe habits shown in these photos. For each unsafe habit, tell what the corresponding safe habit is.

20

21

12. Sample answer: No, not all narcotics are illegal. Some narcotics are prescribed by doctors for the treatment of pain.

13. Sample answer: Alcohol use is a factor in car accidents, and it can cause liver damage. Tobacco use can damage the lungs.

14. Sample answer: Carbohydrates are the body's main source of energy. Fats are energy-storage nutrients. Proteins are used for building and repairing the body.

15. Sample answers: anorexia nervosa, bulimia nervosa, and obesity

16. Sample answer: Safety equipment, such as a helmet, can prevent a head injury if I fall off my bicycle or if I'm involved in an accident.

Critical Thinking

17. An answer to this exercise can be found at the end of this book.

18. Sample answers: nuts, beans, eggs, and dairy foods

19. Sample answer: Keep objects off the stairs, use a night light, and keep electrical cords out of walkways.

Interpreting Graphics

20. Sample answer: The girl is riding without her seat belt. She needs to fasten her seat belt.

21. Sample answer: A pot handle is hanging over the edge of the stove. The woman should use a pot holder to turn the handle of the pot so that it faces inward.

CHAPTER RESOURCES

Chapter Resource File

- **Chapter Review** GENERAL
- **Chapter Test A** GENERAL
- **Chapter Test B** ADVANCED
- **Chapter Test C** SPECIAL NEEDS
- **Vocabulary Activity** GENERAL

Workbooks

Study Guide
- Assessment resources are also available in Spanish.

Standardized Test Preparation

Teacher's Note

To provide practice under more realistic testing conditions, give students 20 minutes to answer all of the questions in this Standardized Test Preparation.

MISCONCEPTION ///ALERT\\\

Answers to the standardized test preparation can help you identify student misconceptions and misunderstandings.

READING

Passage 1

1. C
2. G
3. B

 TEST DOCTOR

Question 3: The passage states that holes in the air sacks of the lungs do not heal. Students may infer that cigarette smoking does not cause all cases of emphysema and bronchitis, but cigarette smoking does cause 80% of cases. Students may think that chronic bronchitis will go away if someone stopped smoking, but the passage states that a chronic disease is a disease that does not go away.

READING

Read each of the passages below. Then, answer the questions that follow each passage.

Passage 1 A <u>chronic</u> disease is a disease that, once developed, is always present and will not go away. Chronic bronchitis is a disease that causes the airways in the lungs to become swollen. This irritation causes a lot of mucus to form in the lungs. As a result, a person who has chronic bronchitis coughs a lot. Another chronic condition is emphysema. Emphysema destroys the tiny air sacs and the walls in the lungs. The holes in the air sacs cannot heal. Eventually, the lung tissue dies, and the lungs can no longer work. Cigarette smoking causes more than 80% of all cases of chronic bronchitis and emphysema.

1. In the passage, what does the word *chronic* mean?
   A disappearing
   B temporary
   C always present
   D mucus filled

2. According to the passage, what disease destroys the tiny air sacs and walls of the lungs?
   F chronic bronchitis
   G emphysema
   H chronic cough
   I cigarette smoking

3. Which of the following is a true statement according to the passage?
   A Holes in the air sacs of lungs heal very quickly.
   B Cigarette smoking causes more than 80% of all cases of chronic bronchitis and emphysema.
   C Cigarette smoking does not cause chronic bronchitis or emphysema.
   D Chronic bronchitis will go away after a person stops smoking cigarettes.

Passage 2 Each body reacts differently to alcohol. Several factors affect how a body reacts to alcohol. A person who has several drinks in a short time is likely to be affected more than a person who has a single drink in the same amount of time. Food in a drinker's stomach can also slow alcohol absorption into the blood. Finally, the way that women absorb and process alcohol differs from the way that men do. If a man and a woman drink the same amount of alcohol, the woman's blood alcohol content (BAC) will be higher than the man's. As BAC increases, mental and physical abilities decline. Muscle coordination, which is especially important for walking and driving, decreases. Vision becomes blurred. Speech and memory are impaired. A high BAC can cause a person to pass out or even die.

1. According to the passage, what does *BAC* stand for?
   A blood alcohol content
   B blood alcohol contaminant
   C blurred alcohol capacity
   D blood alcoholic coordination

2. According to the passage, which of the following factors can affect BAC?
   F time of day
   G food in the stomach
   H age
   I physical activity

3. Which of the following is a fact according to the passage?
   A Alcohol does not affect mood or mental abilities.
   B Men absorb alcohol in the same way that women do.
   C Alcohol decreases muscle coordination.
   D Everybody reacts to alcohol in the same way.

Passage 2

1. A
2. G
3. C

 TEST DOCTOR

Question 2: Each body reacts differently to alcohol. However, time of day, age, and physical activity are not mentioned as factors which affect how a person reacts to alcohol. The factors mentioned in the passage include how many drinks a person has over a period of time, whether a person has food in his or her stomach, and gender.

The figure below shows a sample prescription drug label. Use this figure to answer the questions that follow.

Patient's name

Directions for taking the medicine

Name of drug

Doctor's name

The People's Pharmacy
252 FIRST STREET
HOUSTON, TX 77077
(713) 242-2299
DEA# AS 3455

Rx 00674312C02/01/04   02/01/04

BAKER, RICHARD   CC

TAKE 1 TABLET BY MOUTH DAILY

TEQUIN   400MG TABS   (BMS)
DR. SANCHEZ, DAVID   QTY: 10   NO REFILL

CAUTION: FEDERAL LAW PROHIBITS THE TRANSFER OF THIS DRUG TO ANY PERSON OTHER THAN THE PATIENT TO WHOM IT WAS PRESCRIBED.

Keep out of reach of children

1. According to the label, what is the patient's name?
- **A** Richard Baker
- **B** Baker Richard
- **C** David Sanchez
- **D** James Beard

2. According to the label, how often should the medication be taken?
- **F** once a day
- **G** twice a day
- **H** three times a day
- **I** once a week

3. According to the label, how many refills remain on the prescription?
- **A** 0
- **B** 1
- **C** 2
- **D** 3

4. If this patient follows the directions exactly, how long will he need to take this medicine?
- **F** 1 day
- **G** 5 days
- **H** 10 days
- **I** There is not enough data to determine the answer.

MATH

Read each question below, and choose the best answer.

1. Which of the following ratios is equal to 2/4?
- **A** 1/2
- **B** 17/18
- **C** 5/2
- **D** 7/2

2. If 1 gal = 3.79 L, how many liters are in 3 gal?
- **F** 3.79 L
- **G** 7.58 L
- **H** 11.37 L
- **I** 15.16 L

3. Approximately how many liters are in 5 gal?
- **A** 5 L
- **B** 10 L
- **C** 20 L
- **D** 30 L

4. Ada has just built a car for a Pinewood Derby. She wants to find the average speed of her new car. During her first test run, she goes 5 mi/h. During her second run, she goes 4 mi/h, and in her third run, she goes 6 mi/h. What is her average speed?
- **F** 4 mi/h
- **G** 5 mi/h
- **H** 6 mi/h
- **I** 7 mi/h

5. Which of the following numbers is largest?
- **A** 1×10^2
- **B** 1×10^5
- **C** 3×10^5
- **D** 5×10^4

6. On Saturday, Mae won a goldfish at the school carnival. On the way home, Mae and her mother bought a fishbowl for $10.25, a container of fish food for $3.75, and a plastic coral for $8.15. How much money did Mae and her mother spend?
- **F** $11.90
- **G** $18.40
- **H** $22.15
- **I** $30.30

Standardized Test Preparation

1. A
2. F
3. A
4. H

 **TEST DOCTOR**

Question 1: Baker Richard is the reversed form of the patient's name. It starts with the patient's last name. David Sanchez is the doctor who prescribed the drug, and James Beard is not a name that appears on the label.

MATH

1. A
2. H
3. C
4. G
5. C
6. H

 **TEST DOCTOR**

Question 1: 2/4 can be simplified to 1/2, or one-half of the whole. 17/18 is almost equal to the whole and 5/2 and 7/2 are greater than the whole. Students struggling with fractions may benefit from working with visual aids, such as wooden blocks.

Question 5: 1×10^2 is the smallest number in the answer choices. Some students may base their answer on the power of ten alone and answer 1×10^5, not realizing that 3×10^5 is a larger number. Some students may answer 5×10^4 because 5 is larger than 1 and 3, which are used in the other answer choices. However, a higher power of ten is used in two of the other answer choices.

CHAPTER RESOURCES

Chapter Resource File

 • Standardized Test Preparation GENERAL

Workbooks

 North Carolina Standardized Test Preparation
• Provides practice for the EOG test.

State Resources

 For specific resources for your state, visit **go.hrw.com** and type in the keyword **HSMSTR.**

Science, Technology, and Society

Teaching Strategy—ADVANCED

Explain that a protein consists of a long chain of amino acids. Assign each student one of the 20 common amino acids to investigate. Tell students to find out what foods the amino acid can be found in and what function it serves in the body. Then, on a large index card, have students write information about the amino acid and make illustrations of food sources for the amino acid. Use the index cards to make a poster for the class.

Scientific Discoveries

Background

The female athlete triad is most likely to begin with an attempt to lose weight, which leads to disordered eating. Disordered eating ranges from moderate restriction of food intake to eating disorders, such as anorexia nervosa and bulimia nervosa. Signs that a girl may have disordered eating include a preoccupation with food and weight, a constant expression of being too fat, eating alone, use of laxatives, and trips to the bathroom immediately after eating.

Science in Action

Bones can become severely weakened by the female athlete triad.

Science, Technology, and Society

Meatless Munching

Recent studies suggest that a vegetarian diet may reduce the risk of heart disease, adult-onset diabetes, and some forms of cancer. However, a vegetarian diet takes careful planning. Vegetarians must ensure that they get the proper balance of protein and vitamins in their diet. New foods that can help vegetarians remain healthy are being developed constantly. Meat substitutes are now made from soybeans, textured vegetable protein, and tofu. One new food, which is shown above, is made of a fungus that is a relative of mushrooms and truffles.

Social Studies ACTIVITY

WRITING SKILL Research a culture that has a mostly vegetarian diet, such as Hindu or Buddhist. What kinds of food do the people eat? Why don't they eat animals? Write a short report on your findings.

Scientific Discoveries

Female Athlete Triad

Getting enough exercise is an important part of staying healthy. But in 1992, doctors learned that too much exercise can be harmful for women. When a girl or woman exercises too much, three things can happen. She may lose too much weight. She may stop having her period. And her bones may become very weak. These three symptoms form the female athlete triad. To prevent this condition, female athletes need to take in enough Calories. Women who exercise heavily and try to lose weight may have a reduction in estrogen. Estrogen is the hormone that helps regulate the menstrual cycle. Low levels of estrogen and inadequate nutrition can cause bones to become weak and brittle. The photo above shows bone that has been weakened greatly.

Math ACTIVITY

Some scientists recommend that teenagers get 1,200 to 1,500 mg of calcium every day. A cup of milk has 300 mg of calcium, and a serving of yogurt has 400 mg of calcium. Calculate two combinations of milk and yogurt that would give you the recommended 1,500 mg of calcium.

Answer to Social Studies Activity

Answers may vary. Students should identify some foods eaten by the people in the cultures that they research. Students should also identify reasons such as religious beliefs, cultural traditions, and the availability of meat as reasons why people in these cultures have vegetarian diets.

Answer to Math Activity

Sample answer: 1 serving of yogurt and 4 cups of milk (4 × 300 mg = 1200 mg calcium; 1200 mg + 400 mg = 1600 mg calcium), or 3 cups of milk and 2 servings of yogurt (3 × 300 mg = 900 mg calcium; 2 × 400 mg = 800 mg calcium; 900 mg + 800 mg = 1700 mg calcium)

Careers

Russell Selger

Guidance Counselor Guidance counselors help students think about their future by helping them discover their interests. After focusing their interests, a guidance counselor helps students plan a good academic schedule. A guidance counselor might talk to you about taking an art or computer science class that may help you discover a hidden talent. Many skills are vital to being a good guidance counselor. The job requires empathy, which is the ability to understand and sympathize with another person's feelings. Counselors also need patience, good listening skills, and a love of helping young people. Russell Selger, a guidance counselor at Timberlane Middle School, has a great respect for middle school students. "The kids are just alive. They want to learn. There's something about the spark that they have, and it's so much fun to guide them through all of this stuff," he explains.

Language Arts ACTIVITY

WRITING SKILL Visit the guidance counselor's office at your school. What services does your guidance counselor offer? Conduct an interview with a guidance counselor. Ask why he or she became a counselor. Write an article for the school paper about your findings.

go.hrw.com
To learn more about these Science in Action topics, visit **go.hrw.com** and type in the keyword **HL5BD7F**.

Current Science
Check out Current Science® articles related to this chapter by visiting **go.hrw.com**. **Just type in the keyword HL5CS28.**

Careers

Discussion ——— GENERAL

Ask students the following questions: "What do you think guidance counselors talk to students about?" (Many students will likely say grades and future career options. Help students understand that guidance counselors can also help them with other problems, such as stress management, conflict management, and mediation.) "What skills does a good guidance counselor need?" (Sample answers: good listening skills, patience, and empathy)

Answer to Language Arts Activity
Answers may vary.

Heredity and Genes

The differences and similarities between living things are the subject of this unit. You will learn how characteristics are passed from one generation to another, how living things are classified based on their characteristics, and how these characteristics help living things survive.

Scientists have not always understood these topics, and there is still much to be learned. This timeline will give you an idea of some things that have been learned so far.

1753

Carolus Linnaeus publishes the first of two volumes containing the classification of all known species.

1905

Nettie Stevens describes how human gender is determined by the X and Y chromosomes.

1930

The planet Pluto is discovered.

1969

Apollo 11 lands on the moon. Neil Armstrong becomes the first person to walk on the lunar surface.

1859
Charles Darwin suggests that natural selection is a mechanism of evolution.

1860
Abraham Lincoln is elected the 16th president of the United States.

1865
Gregor Mendel publishes the results of his studies of genetic inheritance in pea plants.

1951
Rosalind Franklin photographs DNA.

1953
James Watson and Francis Crick figure out the structure of DNA.

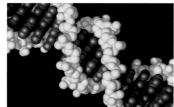

1960
Mary and Jonathan Leakey discover fossil bones of the human ancestor *Homo habilis* in Olduvai Gorge, Tanzania.

1974
Donald Johanson discovers a fossilized skeleton of one of the first hominids, *Australopithecus afarensis,* also called "Lucy."

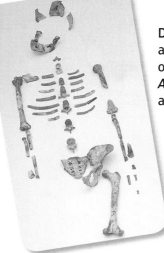

1990
Ashanti DeSilva's white blood cells are genetically engineered to treat her immune deficiency disease.

2003
The Human Genome Project is completed. Scientists spent 13 years mapping out the 3 billion DNA subunits of chromosomes.

12

It's Alive!! Or Is It?
Chapter Planning Guide

Compression guide:
To shorten instruction because of time limitations, omit the Chapter Lab.

OBJECTIVES	LABS, DEMONSTRATIONS, AND ACTIVITIES	TECHNOLOGY RESOURCES
PACING • 90 min pp. 330–335 **Chapter Opener**	SE **Start-up Activity,** p. 331 GENERAL	OSP **Parent Letter** GENERAL CD **Student Edition on CD-ROM** CD **Guided Reading Audio CD** TR **Chapter Starter Transparency*** VID **Brain Food Video Quiz**
Section 1 Characteristics of Living Things • Describe the six characteristics of living things. • Describe how organisms maintain stable internal conditions. • Explain how asexual reproduction differs from sexual reproduction.	SE **Connection to Physics** Temperature Regulation, p. 333 GENERAL TE **Activity** Poster Project, p. 333 GENERAL TE **Connection Activity** Math, p. 334 GENERAL SE **Skills Practice Lab** Roly-Poly Races, p. 342 ◆ GENERAL CRF **Datasheet for Chapter Lab***	CRF **Lesson Plans*** TR **Bellringer Transparency*** VID **Lab Videos for Life Science**
PACING • 45 min pp. 336–341 **Section 2 The Necessities of Life** • Explain why organisms need food, water, air, and living space. • Describe the chemical building blocks of cells.	TE **Demonstration** Fire and Life, p. 337 BASIC TE **Activity** Poster Project, p. 337 GENERAL SE **School-to-Home Activity** Pen a Menu, p. 338 GENERAL TE **Activity** Vocabulary Review, p. 338 BASIC SE **Quick Lab** Starch Search, p. 339 GENERAL CRF **Datasheet for Quick Lab*** SE **Connection to Social Studies** Whaling, p. 340 GENERAL SE **Skills Practice Lab** The Best-Bread Bakery Dilemma, p. 602 ◆ GENERAL CRF **Datasheet for LabBook*** LB **Labs You Can Eat** Say Cheese!* GENERAL LB **Long-Term Projects & Research Ideas** I Think, Therefore I Live* ADVANCED	CRF **Lesson Plans*** TR **Bellringer Transparency*** TR *LINK TO EARTH SCIENCE* The Earth's Land Biomes* TR Phospholipid Molecule and Cell Membrane* CRF **SciLinks Activity*** GENERAL TE **Internet Activity,** p. 337 GENERAL

PACING • 90 min

CHAPTER REVIEW, ASSESSMENT, AND STANDARDIZED TEST PREPARATION

CRF **Vocabulary Activity*** GENERAL
SE **Chapter Review,** pp. 344–345 GENERAL
CRF **Chapter Review*** ■ GENERAL
CRF **Chapter Tests A*** ■ GENERAL, **B*** ADVANCED, **C*** SPECIAL NEEDS
SE **Standardized Test Preparation,** pp. 346–347 GENERAL
CRF **Standardized Test Preparation*** GENERAL
CRF **Performance-Based Assessment*** GENERAL
OSP **Test Generator** GENERAL
CRF **Test Item Listing*** GENERAL

Online and Technology Resources

Visit **go.hrw.com** for a variety of free resources related to this textbook. Enter the keyword **HT5R7ALV.**

Students can access interactive problem-solving help and active visual concept development with the *Holt Science and Technology* Online Edition available at **www.hrw.com.**

 Guided Reading Audio CD

These CDs are designed to help auditory learners and reluctant readers.

 Science Tutor CD-ROM

Excellent for remediation and test practice.

SKILLS DEVELOPMENT RESOURCES	SECTION REVIEW AND ASSESSMENT	STANDARDS CORRELATIONS
SE **Pre-Reading Activity**, p. 330 (GENERAL) OSP **Science Puzzlers, Twisters & Teasers*** (GENERAL)		North Carolina Standard Course of Study
CRF **Directed Reading A*** (BASIC), **B*** (SPECIAL NEEDS) CRF **Vocabulary and Section Summary*** (GENERAL) SE **Reading Strategy** Prediction Guide, p. 332 (GENERAL) TE **Inclusion Strategies**, p. 333 MS **Math Skills for Science** A Shortcut for Multiplying Large Numbers* (GENERAL) MS **Math Skills for Science** Multiplying and Dividing in Scientific Notation* (GENERAL) MS **Math Skills for Science** Decimals and Fractions* (GENERAL) MS **Math Skills for Science** Percentages, Fractions, and Decimals* (GENERAL) CRF **Critical Thinking** Intergalactic Planetary Mission* (ADVANCED)	SE **Reading Checks**, pp. 333, 334 (GENERAL) TE **Reteaching**, p. 334 (BASIC) TE **Quiz**, p. 334 (GENERAL) TE **Alternative Assessment**, p. 334 (ADVANCED) SE **Section Review**,* p. 335 ■ (GENERAL) CRF **Section Quiz*** ■ (GENERAL)	4.04; *Chapter Lab:* 1.01, 1.02, 1.03, 1.05
CRF **Directed Reading A*** (BASIC), **B*** (SPECIAL NEEDS) CRF **Vocabulary and Section Summary*** (GENERAL) SE **Reading Strategy** Discussion, p. 336 (GENERAL) TE **Connection to Earth Science** Adaptation, p. 337 (GENERAL) SE **Math Practice** How Much Oxygen?, p. 339 (GENERAL) TE **Inclusion Strategies**, p. 340 CRF **Reinforcement Worksheet** Amazing Discovery* (BASIC) CRF **Reinforcement Worksheet** Building Blocks* (BASIC)	SE **Reading Checks**, pp. 336, 339, 340 (GENERAL) TE **Reteaching**, p. 340 (BASIC) TE **Quiz**, p. 340 (GENERAL) TE **Alternative Assessment**, p. 340 (ADVANCED) SE **Section Review**,* p. 341 ■ (GENERAL) CRF **Section Quiz*** ■ (GENERAL)	*LabBook:* 1.01, 1.02, 1.03, 1.05

One-Stop Planner® CD-ROM

This convenient CD-ROM includes:
- Lab Materials QuickList Software
- Holt Calendar Planner
- Customizable Lesson Plans
- Printable Worksheets
- ExamView® Test Generator

cnnstudentnews.com

Find the latest news, lesson plans, and activities related to important scientific events.

www.scilinks.org

Maintained by the **National Science Teachers Association.** See Chapter Enrichment pages for a complete list of topics.

Check out *Current Science* articles and activities by visiting the HRW Web site at **go.hrw.com.** Just type in the keyword **HL5CS02T.**

 Classroom Videos

- **Lab Videos** demonstrate the chapter lab.
- **Brain Food Video Quizzes** help students review the chapter material.
- **CNN Videos** bring science into your students' daily life.

Visual Resources

CHAPTER STARTER TRANSPARENCY

It's Alive!! Or Is It? CHAPTER STARTER

Imagine . . .

The Movile Cave, in Romania, is one of the spookiest, slimiest, and smelliest places on Earth. For more than 5 million years, the cave and its inhabitants were sealed off from the outside world. Many of the creepiest organisms known to science inhabit the Movile Cave.

Poisonous water scorpions lurk in murky pools and breathe through snorkels attached to their stomach. Predatory centipedes zero in on smaller bugs and inject them with a paralyzing toxin. Wolf spiders move on spindly legs in pursuit of millipedes, pill bugs, and even their own young!

Almost all living things get their energy either directly or indirectly from the sun. But what about the inhabitants of the Movile Cave, a place where sunlight never enters? The supply of energy that fuels life in the Movile Cave comes from organisms that can't be seen. These microorganisms don't feed on other creepy crawlies; they feed on hydrogen sulfide. This chemical, which smells like rotten eggs, is abundant in the cave. The hydrogen sulfide provides the microorganisms with the energy they need for life. When the microorganisms are eaten, their energy is transferred to other organisms.

Using energy is just one of the characteristics of life. Read on to find out what else all living things have in common.

BELLRINGER TRANSPARENCIES

It's Alive!! Or Is It? BELLRINGER TRANSPARENCY

Section: Characteristics of Living Things
What are four living and nonliving things that you interact with every day? How do you know whether each is living or nonliving? Do you know what the word *inanimate* means? If so, write out a definition. Does *nonliving* mean the same thing as *dead*? Explain your answer.

Write your answers in your **science journal.**

Section: The Necessities of Life
What do you think your mass would be if there were no water in your body? What else besides water is your body composed of? Where do you think you get the minerals that make up your body mass?

Record your answers in your **science journal.**

TEACHING TRANSPARENCIES

L4

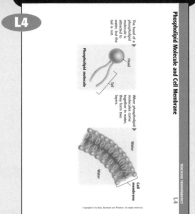

Phospholipid Molecule and Cell Membrane

TEACHING TRANSPARENCIES

E75

The Earth's Land Biomes

LINK TO EARTH SCIENCE

Chapter: Climate

CONCEPT MAPPING TRANSPARENCY

It's Alive!! Or Is It? CONCEPT MAPPING TRANSPARENCY

Use the following terms to complete the concept map below:
DNA, sugars, energy, enzymes, living cells, proteins, starches, carbohydrates

contain — use — which provides instructions for making — in the form of — simple — complex — such as — to provide

Planning Resources

LESSON PLANS

Lesson Plan SAMPLE

Section: Waves

Pacing
Regular Schedule: with lab(s):2 days   without lab(s)1 days
Block Schedule: with lab(s): 1 1/2 days   without lab(s)1 day

Objectives
1. Relate the seven properties of life to a living organism.
2. Describe some themes that can help you to organize what you learn about biology.
3. Identify the tiny structures that make up all living organisms.
4. Differentiate between reproduction and heredity and between metabolism and homeostasis.

National Science Education Standards Covered
LSInter6:Cells have particular structures that underlie their functions.
LSMat1:Most cell functions involve chemical reactions.
LSBeh1:Cells store and use information to guide their functions.
UCP1:Cell functions are regulated.
SI1: Cells can differentiate and form complete multicellular organisms.
PS1: Species evolve over time.
ESS1: The great diversity of organisms is the result of more than 3.5 billion years of evolution.
ESS2: Natural selection and its evolutionary consequences provide a scientific explanation for the fossil record of ancient life forms as well as for the striking molecular similarities observed among the diverse species of living organisms.
ST1: The millions of different species of plants, animals, and microorganisms that live on Earth today are related by descent from common ancestors.
ST2: The energy for life primarily comes from the sun.
SPSP1: The complexity and organization of organisms accommodates the need for obtaining, transforming, transporting, releasing, and eliminating the matter and energy used to sustain the organism.
SPSP6: As matter and energy flows through different levels of organization of living systems—cells, organs, communities—and between living systems and the physical environment, chemical elements are recombined in different ways.
HNS1: Organisms have behavioral responses to internal changes and to external stimuli.

PARENT LETTER

SAMPLE

Dear Parent,

Your son's or daughter's science class will soon begin exploring the chapter entitled "The World of Physical Science." In this chapter, students will learn about how the scientific method applies to the world of physical science and the role of physical science in the world. By the end of the chapter, students should demonstrate a clear understanding of the chapter's main ideas and be able to discuss the following topics:

1. physical science is the study of energy and matter (Section 1)
2. the role of physical science in the world around them (Section 1)
3. careers that rely on physical science (Section 1)
4. the steps used in the scientific method (Section 2)
5. examples of technology (Section 2)
6. how the scientific method is used to answer questions and solve problems (Section 2)
7. how our knowledge of science changes over time (Section 2)
8. how models represent real objects or systems (Section 3)
9. examples of different ways models are used in science (Section 3)
10. the importance of the International System of Units (Section 4)
11. the appropriate units to use for particular measurements (Section 4)
12. how area and density are derived quantities (Section 4)

Questions to Ask Along the Way
You can help your son or daughter learn about these topics by asking interesting questions such as the following:
• What are some surprising careers that use physical science?
• What is a characteristic of a good hypothesis?
• When is it a good idea to use a model?
• Why do Americans measure things in terms of inches and yards instead of centimeters and meters?

TEST ITEM LISTING

TEST ITEM LISTING
The World of Science SAMPLE

MULTIPLE CHOICE
1. A limitation of models is that
   a. they are large enough to see.
   b. they do not act exactly like the things that they model.
   c. they are smaller than the things that they model.
   d. they model unfamiliar things.
   Answer: B   Difficulty: 1   Section: 3   Objective: 2

2. The length 10 m is equal to
   a. 100 cm.   c. 10,000 mm.
   b. 1,000 cm.   d. Both (b) and (c)
   Answer: B   Difficulty: 1   Section: 3   Objective: 2

3. To be valid, a hypothesis must be
   a. testable.   c. made into a law
   b. supported by evidence.   d. Both (a) and (b)
   Answer: B   Difficulty: 1   Section: 3   Objective: 2   1

4. The statement "Sheila has a stain on her shirt" is an example of a(n)
   a. law.   c. observation.
   b. hypothesis.   d. prediction.
   Answer: B   Difficulty: 1   Section: 3   Objective: 2

5. A hypothesis is often developed out of
   a. observations.   c. laws.
   b. experiments.   d. Both (a) and (b)
   Answer: B   Difficulty: 1   Section: 3   Objective: 2

6. How many milliliters are in 3.5 kL?
   a. 3,500 mL.   c. 3,500, 000 mL.
   b. 0.035 mL.   d. 35,000 mL.
   Answer: B   Difficulty: 1   Section: 3   Objective: 2

7. A map of Seattle is an example of a
   a. law.   c. model
   b. theory.   d. unit.
   Answer: B   Difficulty: 1   Section: 3   Objective: 2

8. A lab has the safety icons shown below. These icons mean that you should wear
   a. only safety goggles.   c. safety goggles and a lab apron.
   b. only a lab apron.   d. safety goggles, a lab apron, and gloves.
   Answer: B   Difficulty: 1   Section: 3   Objective: 2

9. The law of conservation of mass says the tot al mass before a chemical change is
   a. more than the total mass after the change.
   b. less than the total mass after the change.
   c. the same as the total mass after the change.
   d. not the same as the total mass after the change.
   Answer: B   Difficulty: 1   Section: 3   Objective: 2

10. In which of the following areas might you find a geochemist at work?
   a. studying the chemistry of rocks   c. studying the atmosphere
   b. studying forestry   d. studying the atmosphere
   Answer: B   Difficulty: 1   Section: 3   Objective: 2

One-Stop Planner® CD-ROM

This CD-ROM includes all of the resources shown here and the following time-saving tools:

• *Lab Materials QuickList Software*
• *Customizable lesson plans*
• *Holt Calendar Planner*
• *The powerful ExamView® Test Generator*

Meeting Individual Needs

DIRECTED READING A
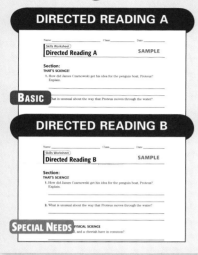
Skills Worksheet
Directed Reading A   SAMPLE

Section:
THAT'S SCIENCE!
1. How did James Czarnowski get his idea for the penguin boat, Proteus? Explain.

BASIC

DIRECTED READING B
Skills Worksheet
Directed Reading B   SAMPLE

Section:
THAT'S SCIENCE!
1. How did James Czarnowski get his idea for the penguin boat, Proteus? Explain.

2. What is unusual about the way that Proteus moves through the water?

SPECIAL NEEDS

VOCABULARY ACTIVITY
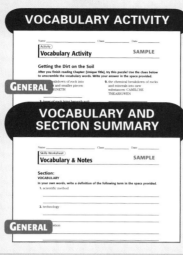
Activity
Vocabulary Activity   SAMPLE

Getting the Dirt on the Soil
After you finish reading Chapter: [Unique Title], try this puzzle! Use the clues below to unscramble the vocabulary words. Write your answer in the space provided.

GENERAL

VOCABULARY AND SECTION SUMMARY
Skills Worksheet
Vocabulary & Notes   SAMPLE

Section:
VOCABULARY
In your own words, write a definition of the following term in the space provided.
1. scientific method

2. technology

GENERAL

REINFORCEMENT
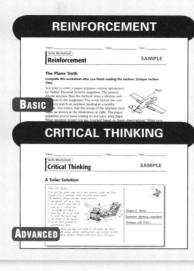
Skills Worksheet
Reinforcement   SAMPLE

The Plane Truth
Complete this worksheet after you finish reading the Section: [Unique Section Title]

BASIC

CRITICAL THINKING
Skills Worksheet
Critical Thinking   SAMPLE

A Solar Solution

ADVANCED

SCILINKS ACTIVITY
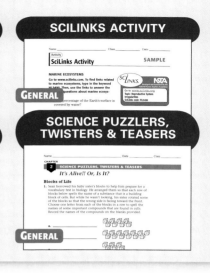
Activity
SciLinks Activity   SAMPLE

MARINE ECOSYSTEMS
Go to www.scilinks.com. To find links related to marine ecosystems, type in the keyword

GENERAL

SCIENCE PUZZLERS, TWISTERS & TEASERS
CHAPTER
SCIENCE PUZZLERS, TWISTERS & TEASERS
It's Alive!! Or, Is It?

Blocks of Life
1. Sean borrowed his baby sister's blocks to help him prepare for a vocabulary test in biology.

GENERAL

Labs and Activities

LONG-TERM PROJECTS & RESEARCH IDEAS

PROJECT
STUDENT WORKSHEET   DESIGN YOUR OWN
I Think, Therefore I Live

In May 1997, an IBM supercomputer called Deep Blue defeated the world chess champion, Gary Kasparov, in a highly publicized chess match.

INTERNET KEYWORDS
artificial intelligence
cybernetics
neural networks

Living Computers?
1. Can computers really think like people? Will future thinking machines force us to redefine living?

Other Research Ideas
2. Do you think you have too much fat in your diet?

ADVANCED

LABS YOU CAN EAT
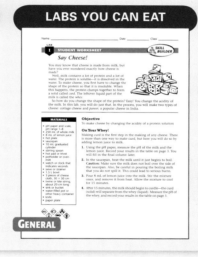
LAB
STUDENT WORKSHEET   SKILL BUILDER
Say Cheese!

You may know that cheese is made from milk, but have you ever wondered exactly how cheese is made?

MATERIALS

Objective
To make cheese by changing the acidity of a protein solution.

On Your Whey!

GENERAL

DATASHEETS FOR QUICK LABS

TEACHER RESOURCE PAGE
Quick Lab   DATASHEET FOR QUICK LAB
Reaction to Stress   SAMPLE

Background

DATASHEETS FOR CHAPTER LABS
TEACHER RESOURCE PAGE
Skills Practice Lab   DATASHEET FOR CHAPTER LAB
Using Scientific Methods   SAMPLE

Teacher's Notes
TIME REQUIRED
One 45-minute class period.

DATASHEETS FOR LABBOOK
TEACHER RESOURCE PAGE
Skills Practice Lab   DATASHEET FOR LABBOOK LAB
Does It All Add Up?   SAMPLE

Teacher's Notes
TIME REQUIRED
One 45-minute class period.

Review and Assessments

SECTION QUIZ
Assessment
Section Quiz   SAMPLE

Section:
In the space provided, write the letter of the description that best matches the term or phrase.

GENERAL   ALSO IN SPANISH

SECTION REVIEW

Skills Worksheet
Section Review   SAMPLE

Section:
KEY TERMS
1. What do paleontologists study?

2. How does a trace fossil differ from petrified wood?

GENERAL   ALSO IN SPANISH

CHAPTER REVIEW
Skills Worksheet
Chapter Review   SAMPLE

USING VOCABULARY
1. Define biome in your own words.

2. Describe the characteristics of a savanna and a desert.

GENERAL   ALSO IN SPANISH

CHAPTER TEST A

Assessment
Chapter Test A   SAMPLE

MULTIPLE CHOICE
In the space provided, write the letter of the term or phrase that best completes each statement or best answers each question.

GENERAL   ALSO IN SPANISH

CHAPTER TEST B
Assessment
Chapter Test B   SAMPLE

MULTIPLE CHOICE
In the space provided, write the letter of the term or phrase that best completes each statement or best answers each question.
1. Surface currents are formed by
   a. the moon's gravity.   c. wind.
   b. the sun's gravity.   d. increased water density.
When waves come near the shore,
   a. they speed up.   c. their wavelength increases.
   b. they maintain their speed.   d. their wave height increases.

ADVANCED

CHAPTER TEST C
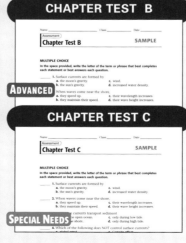
Assessment
Chapter Test C   SAMPLE

MULTIPLE CHOICE
In the space provided, write the letter of the term or phrase that best completes each statement or best answers each question.
1. Surface currents are formed by
   a. the moon's gravity.   c. wind.
   b. the sun's gravity.   d. increased water density.
2. When waves come near the shore,
   a. they speed up.   c. their wavelength decreases.
   b. they maintain their speed.   d. their wave height increases.

SPECIAL NEEDS

STANDARDIZED TEST PREPARATION
Assessment
Standardized Test Preparation   SAMPLE

READING
Read the passages below. Then, read each question that follows the passage. Decide which is the best answer to each question.

GENERAL

PERFORMANCE-BASED ASSESSMENT
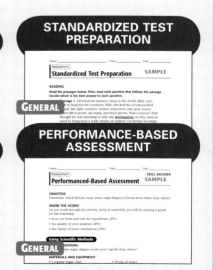
Assessment   SKILL BUILDER
Performanced-Based Assessment   SAMPLE

OBJECTIVE
Determine which factors cause some sugar shapes to break down faster than others.

KNOW THE SCORE!
As you work through the activity, keep in mind that you will be earning a grade for the following:
• how you form and test the hypothesis (30%)
• the quality of your analysis (40%)
• the clarity of your conclusions (30%)

Using Scientific Methods

GENERAL

This Chapter Enrichment provides relevant and interesting information to expand and enhance your presentation of the chapter material.

Section 1

Characteristics of Living Things

Biogenesis

- The theory of biogenesis states that living things come only from other living things. However, until the late 1600s, people generally believed in *spontaneous generation*, the theory that lower forms of life, such as insects, come from nonliving things.

- The first evidence disproving spontaneous generation came from controlled experiments conducted in 1667 by Italian scientist Francesco Redi. Redi showed that maggots will appear on meat in an uncovered jar but not on meat in a closed container. Why? The maggots came from eggs laid by flies that had access to the uncovered meat.

Robert Hooke

- Robert Hooke was one of the greatest scientists of his time. In 1665, he discovered cells with the compound microscope. Hooke was also involved in physics, astronomy, chemistry, geology, and architecture. Hooke applied his discovery of the law of elasticity (which states that the stretching of a solid material is proportional to the force applied to it) to the design of balance springs for watches and clocks. His sketches of Mars were used 200 years later to determine that planet's rate of rotation. In 1672, he developed the wave theory of light to explain diffraction, which he had also discovered. Hooke was the first person to examine fossils with a microscope and to recognize, 200 years before Charles Darwin was born, that fossils provide evidence of changes in organisms on Earth over millions of years.

Is That a Fact!

- Different cells in the human body have different life spans, which range from a few days for intestinal cells to about 120 days for red blood cells and years for brain cells.

Section 2

The Necessities of Life

A Place to Call Home

- Every organism needs a place to live, and the places where some organisms thrive are surprising.

- Antarctica is a harsh environment. Most of the subantarctic islands are solid rock, and 98% of the continent is covered with ice, but it is home to more than 400 types of lichens and 85 mosses. Lichens can tolerate low temperatures and little moisture. Moss grows on the few patches of soil that exist.

- In Death Valley National Park, summertime temperatures routinely reach 50°C (122°F), and rainfall averages 3.8 cm per year. Yet, more than 900 types of plants live there. More than 400 animal species, including bats, kangaroo rats, bighorn sheep, lizards, tortoises, snakes, spiders, scorpions, beetles, turkey vultures, and roadrunners, also live in this region

- Three to four kilometers into the ocean depths, the pressure is 275 times that at sea level, and it is cold and dark. Huge yellow jellyfish, giant clams, blind fish, and red worms that are 2 m long can be found here. These animals live near deep-sea vents. Water that is heated by volcanic activity to as much as 300°C escapes through these vents. The cold ocean cools the water around the vents to about 13°C. Because there is no sunlight at this depth, the animals use the chemicals in the water for energy through a process called *chemosynthesis*.

Is That a Fact!

◆ The sand grouse of Chad, in northern Africa, builds its nest many miles from water. When the chicks hatch, the parents fly to Lake Chad, where they soak their breast feathers before flying back to their chicks. The chicks then drink the water from their parents' feathers to both feed and cool themselves.

Chemical Menu

● Carbohydrates are the body's primary source of energy. Simple carbohydrates, or sugars, are found in fruits, some vegetables, and milk. Complex carbohydrates, which include starches, are obtained from pasta, seeds, nuts, and vegetables such as peas, beans, and potatoes.

 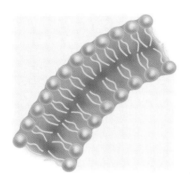

● Lipids include saturated and polyunsaturated fats. Saturated fats are present in greater amounts in animal products. Vegetable-based oils have more polyunsaturated fats.

● Nucleic acids are composed of thousands of nucleotides. The sequence of the nucleotides contains the information for the construction of proteins.

● Proteins are made of 20 different amino acids. Our cells arrange these amino acids in different sequences to make all the proteins in our body.

Is That a Fact!

◆ If stretched out end to end, the DNA in an average human body would measure 20 billion kilometers.

◆ For about 100 years, beginning in the late 1700s, sperm whales were a major source of oil for lubricants and fuel for lamps. These huge animals grow to 18 m long. Whaling made sperm whales nearly extinct.

Metabolism

● Biochemical reactions that take place within a cell are collectively known as *metabolism*. Enzymes, which are proteins, catalyze or accelerate most of the chemical reactions within a cell. Each type of reaction is catalyzed by a specific enzyme.

● A *metabolic pathway* is the sequence of chemical reactions needed to make a particular biological molecule. If a disruption occurs somewhere along the pathway, then the organism might develop an illness or suffer a deficiency.

Is That a Fact!

◆ When bears sleep in their dens during winter, their body temperature decreases several degrees. The lower body temperature reduces energy requirements, so bears can sleep for weeks or months without eating.

SCiLINKS®

NSTA
Developed and maintained by the
National Science Teachers Association

SciLinks is maintained by the National Science Teachers Association to provide you and your students with interesting, up-to-date links that will enrich your classroom presentation of the chapter.

Visit www.scilinks.org and enter the SciLinks code for more information about the topic listed.

Topic: Characteristics of Living Things
SciLinks code: HSM0258

Topic: The Necessities of Life
SciLinks code: HSM1018

Topic: Chemistry of Life
SciLinks code: HSM0278

Topic: Life on Other Planets?
SciLinks code: HSM0875

Overview

Tell students that this chapter will help them learn about the characteristics of living things. The chapter also describes the basic nutrient needs of living things and describes some of the molecules cells use for energy and for passing on information.

Assessing Prior Knowledge

Students should be familiar with the following topic:

• scientific methods

Identifying Misconceptions

As students learn the material in this chapter, some of them may be confused about the difference between living and nonliving things. For example, students may think that clouds are living because clouds move and change shape. Many students also mistakenly think that fire is alive. Students often assign intentions to nonliving things and phenomena. For example, students may think that the sun or sunshine *wants* to keep people warm. Students may also confuse cells and molecules. Help them understand that molecules are not alive, that molecules are much smaller than cells, and that cells are made of molecules.

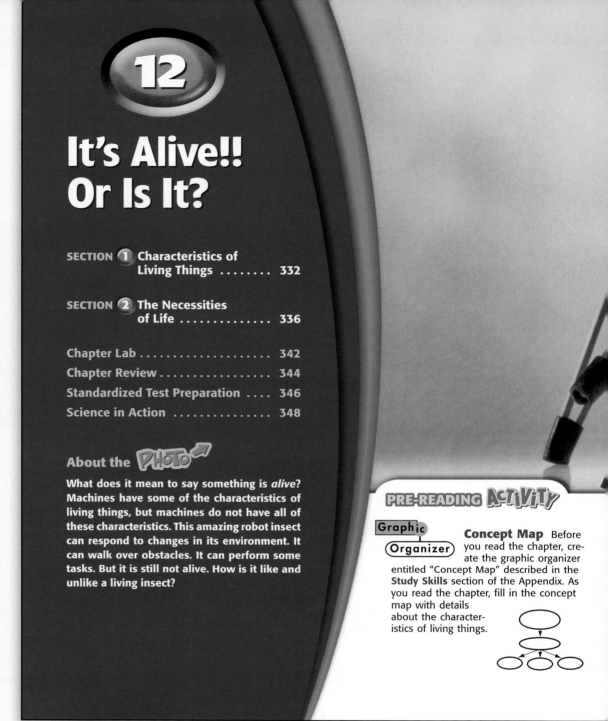

12

It's Alive!! Or Is It?

About the PHOTO

What does it mean to say something is *alive*? Machines have some of the characteristics of living things, but machines do not have all of these characteristics. This amazing robot insect can respond to changes in its environment. It can walk over obstacles. It can perform some tasks. But it is still not alive. How is it like and unlike a living insect?

PRE-READING ACTIVITY

Graphic Organizer

Concept Map Before you read the chapter, create the graphic organizer entitled "Concept Map" described in the **Study Skills** section of the Appendix. As you read the chapter, fill in the concept map with details about the characteristics of living things.

Standards Correlations

North Carolina Standard Course of Study

1.01 Identify and create questions and hypotheses that can be answered through scientific investigations. (Chapter Lab and LabBook)

1.02 (partial) Develop appropriate experimental procedures for: . . . Student generated questions. (Chapter Lab and LabBook)

1.03 Apply safety procedures in the laboratory and in field studies: Recognize potential hazards, Safely manipulate materials and equipment, [and] Conduct appropriate procedures. (Chapter Lab and LabBook)

1.05 Analyze evidence to: Explain observations, Make inferences and predictions, [and] Develop the relationship between evidence and explanation. (Chapter Lab and LabBook)

4.04 (partial) Evaluate how systems in the human body help regulate the internal environment. (Section 1)

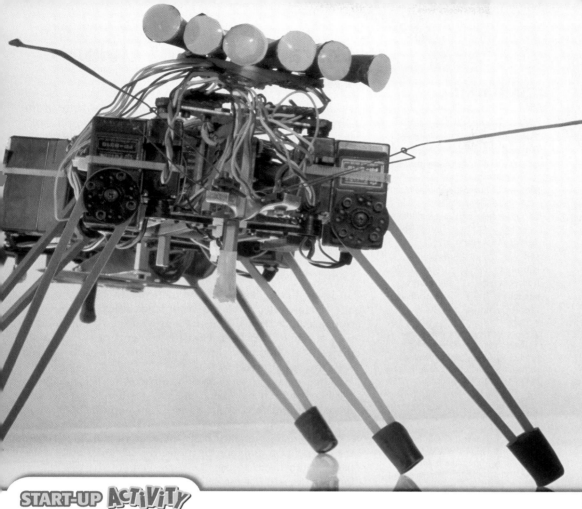

MATERIALS

FOR EACH GROUP
• flashlight

Safety Caution: Students must not use the sun as a source of light.

Answers

1. Sample answer: Pupils were smaller when exposed to light. Pupils became enlarged when light was taken away.

2. Sample answer: In a dark environment, pupils become larger, so more light enters the eye. The surroundings appear brighter and can be more easily seen. In a bright environment, the pupils become smaller, and less light enters the eye. The surroundings are clearly visible without extra light entering the eye. Otherwise, too much light might over-stimulate the eye.

START-UP **ACTIVITY**

Lights On!

In this activity, you will work with a partner to see how eyes react to changes in light.

Procedure

1. Observe a classmate's eyes in a lighted room. Note the size of your partner's pupils.

2. Have your partner keep both eyes open. Ask him or her to cover each one with a cupped hand. Wait about one minute.

3. Instruct your partner to pull away both hands quickly. Immediately, look at your partner's pupils. Record what happens.

4. Now, briefly shine a **flashlight** into your partner's eyes. Record how this affects your partner's pupils. **Caution:** Do not use the sun as the source of the light.

5. Change places with your partner, and repeat steps 1–4 so that your partner can observe your eyes.

Analysis

1. How did your partner's eyes respond to changes in the level of light?

2. How did changes in the size of your pupils affect your vision? What does this tell you about why pupils change size?

Chapter Starter Transparency
Use this transparency to help students begin thinking about how living things get energy.

CHAPTER RESOURCES

Technology

 Transparencies
• Chapter Starter Transparency

READING SKILLS

Student Edition on CD-ROM

Guided Reading Audio CD

Classroom Videos
• Brain Food Video Quiz

Workbooks

 Science Puzzlers, Twisters & Teasers
• It's Alive!! Or Is It? **GENERAL**

SECTION
1

Focus

Overview

This section describes the characteristics of living things. Students will learn that living things have cells, sense and respond to stimuli, reproduce, have DNA, use energy, and grow and develop.

Bellringer

Display this question on the board or an overhead projector: "What are four living and four nonliving things that you interact with or see every day?" (Sample answer: living: family members, pets, house plants, trees; nonliving: clothes, books, furniture, radio)

Motivate

Discussion ——— GENERAL

Stimuli Ask students what they do when they go outside and the air is cold. (They put on a jacket or go back inside.) Explain to students that feeling cold is a stimulus and that their reaction to the cold is a response. Ask students how people use technology to improve their ability to respond to environmental stimuli. (Sample answer: furnaces to heat buildings, air conditioners to cool buildings, and sunglasses to shield eyes from bright sunlight)

LS Verbal

READING WARM-UP

Objectives

● Describe the six characteristics of living things.

● Describe how organisms maintain stable internal conditions.

● Explain how asexual reproduction differs from sexual reproduction.

Terms to Learn

cell   asexual
stimulus   reproduction
homeostasis   heredity
sexual   metabolism
  reproduction

READING STRATEGY

Prediction Guide Before reading this section, write the title of each heading in this section. Next, under each heading, write what you think you will learn.

cell the smallest unit that can perform all life processes; cells are covered by a membrane and have DNA and cytoplasm

Characteristics of Living Things

While outside one day, you notice something strange in the grass. It's slimy, bright yellow, and about the size of a dime. You have no idea what it is. Is it a plant part that fell from a tree? Is it alive? How can you tell?

An amazing variety of living things exists on Earth. But living things are all alike in several ways. What does a dog have in common with a bacterium? What does a fish have in common with a mushroom? And what do *you* have in common with a slimy, yellow blob, known as a *slime mold*? Read on to find out about the six characteristics that all organisms share.

Living Things Have Cells

All living things, such as those in **Figure 1,** are composed of one or more cells. A **cell** is a membrane-covered structure that contains all of the materials necessary for life. The membrane that surrounds a cell separates the contents of the cell from the cell's environment. Most cells are too small to be seen with the naked eye.

Some organisms are made up of trillions of cells. In an organism with many cells, different kinds of cells perform specialized functions. For example, your nerve cells transport signals, and your muscle cells are specialized for movement.

In an organism made up of only one cell, different parts of the cell perform different functions. For example, a one-celled paramecium needs to eat. So, some parts of the cell take in food. Other parts of the cell break down the food. Still other parts of the cell excrete wastes.

Figure 1 *Some organisms, such as the protists on the right, are made of one cell or a few cells. The monkeys on the left are made up of trillions of cells.*

CHAPTER RESOURCES

Chapter Resource File

 • **Lesson Plan**
• **Directed Reading A** BASIC
• **Directed Reading B** SPECIAL NEEDS

Technology

 Transparencies
• Bellringer

WEIRD SCIENCE

An early indication that the pancreas was the organ that secreted insulin, the compound that regulates sugar levels in the blood, came when flies were noticed swarming over the urine of a dog whose pancreas was damaged. The flies were attracted to the excess sugar in the urine.

Figure 2 *The touch of an insect triggers the Venus' flytrap to close its leaves quickly.*

Living Things Sense and Respond to Change

All organisms have the ability to sense change in their environment and to respond to that change. When your pupils are exposed to light, they respond by becoming smaller. A change that affects the activity of the organism is called a **stimulus** (plural, *stimuli*).

Stimuli can be chemicals, gravity, light, sounds, hunger, or anything that causes organisms to respond in some way. A gentle touch causes a response in the plant shown in **Figure 2.**

stimulus anything that causes a reaction or change in an organism or any part of an organism

homeostasis the maintenance of a constant internal state in a changing environment

Homeostasis

Even though an organism's outside environment may change, conditions inside an organism's body must stay the same. Many chemical reactions keep an organism alive. These reactions can take place only when conditions are exactly right, so an organism must maintain stable internal conditions to survive. The maintenance of a stable internal environment is called **homeostasis** (HOH mee OH STAY sis).

Responding to External Changes

Your body maintains a temperature of about 37°C. When you get hot, your body responds by sweating. When you get cold, your muscles twitch in an attempt to warm you up. This twitching is called *shivering*. Whether you are sweating or shivering, your body is trying to return itself to normal.

Other animals also need to have stable internal conditions. But many cannot respond the way you do. They have to control their body temperature by moving from one environment to another. If they get too warm, they move to the shade. If they get too cool, they move out into the sunlight.

✓ **Reading Check** How do some animals maintain homeostasis? *(See the Appendix for answers to Reading Checks.)*

CONNECTION TO Physics

Temperature Regulation
Your body temperature does not change very much throughout the day. When you exercise, you sweat. Sweating helps keep your body temperature stable. As your sweat evaporates, your skin cools. Given this information, why do you think you feel cooler faster when you stand in front of a fan?

Answer to Reading Check
Sample answer: They control their body temperature by moving from one environment to another. If they get too warm, they move to the shade. If they get too cool, they move out into the sunlight.

Answer to Connection To Physics
Sample answer: When a fan is blowing on the skin, more air is passing over it per minute. So, the rate of evaporation increases, allowing more thermal energy to leave the body.

Section 1 • Characteristics of Living Things **333**

Asexual Reproduction Tell students to look at **Figure 4**. Ask them to find the buds that will become new hydras. (Students can find two buds forming close to the base of the hydra.) **LS** **Visual**

Quiz — GENERAL

1. Explain how you can tell that an apple tree is a living thing. (Apple trees have the six characteristics of living things: they have cells, they sense and respond to change, they have DNA, they can reproduce, they use energy, and they grow.)

2. What is the difference between growth and development? (Growth is an increase in size. Development is a change in the form of an organism that happens as it grows.)

3. Name three activities of an organism that require energy. (Sample answer: Organisms need energy to break down food, to move materials into and out of cells, and to build cell parts.)

Alternative Assessment — ADVANCED

Writing **Responding** Have students read a story of their choice and find five examples of stimuli and responses. Then, have students write an explanation of why the ability to respond to all of these stimuli is important. **LS** **Verbal**

Figure 3 *Like most animals, bears produce offspring by sexual reproduction.*

Figure 4 *The hydra can reproduce asexually by forming buds that break off and grow into new individuals.*

sexual reproduction reproduction in which the sex cells from two parents unite, producing offspring that share traits from both parents

asexual reproduction reproduction that does not involve the union of sex cells and in which one parent produces offspring identical to itself

heredity the passing of genetic traits from parent to offspring

metabolism the sum of all chemical processes that occur in an organism

Living Things Reproduce

Organisms make other organisms similar to themselves. They do so in one of two ways: by sexual reproduction or by asexual reproduction. In **sexual reproduction,** two parents produce offspring that will share characteristics of both parents. Most animals and plants reproduce in this way. The bear cubs in **Figure 3** were produced sexually by their parents.

In **asexual reproduction,** a single parent produces offspring that are identical to the parent. **Figure 4** shows an organism that reproduces asexually. Most single-celled organisms reproduce in this way.

Living Things Have DNA

The cells of all living things contain the molecule **d**eoxyribo**n**ucleic (dee AHKS uh RIE boh noo KLEE ik) **a**cid, or DNA. *DNA* controls the structure and function of cells. When organisms reproduce, they pass copies of their DNA to their offspring. Passing DNA ensures that offspring resemble parents. The passing of traits from one generation to the next is called **heredity.**

Living Things Use Energy

Organisms use energy to carry out the activities of life. These activities include such things as making food, breaking down food, moving materials into and out of cells, and building cells. An organism's **metabolism** (muh TAB uh LIZ uhm) is the total of all of the chemical activities that the organism performs.

✓ **Reading Check** Name four chemical activities in living things that require energy.

CONNECTION ACTIVITY
Math ———— GENERAL

Calculating Distance The red kangaroo can cover 12 m in a single jump. The African sharp-nosed frog can jump about 5.4 m. What percentage of the kangaroo's jump is the frog's leap? (5.4 ÷ 12 × 100 = 45%) **LS** **Logical**

Answer to Reading Check

making food, breaking down food, moving materials into and out of cells, and building cells

Living Things Grow and Develop

All living things, whether they are made of one cell or many cells, grow during periods of their lives. In a single-celled organism, the cell gets larger and divides, making other organisms. In organisms made of many cells, the number of cells gets larger, and the organism gets bigger.

In addition to getting larger, living things may develop and change as they grow. Just like the organisms in **Figure 5,** you will pass through different stages in your life as you develop into an adult.

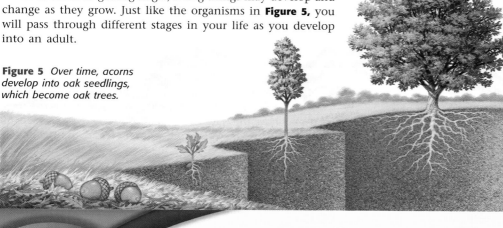

Figure 5 *Over time, acorns develop into oak seedlings, which become oak trees.*

SECTION Review

Summary

- Organisms are made of one or more cells.
- Organisms detect and respond to stimuli.
- Organisms make more organisms like themselves by reproducing either asexually or sexually.
- Organisms have DNA.
- Organisms use energy to carry out the chemical activities of life.
- Organisms grow and develop.

Using Key Terms

Complete each of the following sentences by choosing the correct term from the word bank.

cells	stimulus
homeostasis	metabolism

1. Sunlight can be a ___.

2. Living things are made of ___.

Understanding Key Ideas

3. Homeostasis means maintaining
   a. stable internal conditions.
   b. varied internal conditions.
   c. similar offspring.
   d. varied offspring.

4. Explain the difference between asexual and sexual reproduction.

5. Describe the six characteristics of living things.

Math Skills

6. Bacteria double every generation. One bacterium is in the first generation. How many are in the sixth generation?

Critical Thinking

7. **Applying Concepts** How do you respond to some stimuli in your environment?

8. **Identifying Relationships** What does the fur coat of a bear have to do with homeostasis?

Developed and maintained by the
National Science Teachers Association

For a variety of links related to this chapter, go to www.scilinks.org

Topic: Characteristics of Living Things
SciLinks code: HSM0258

Answers to Section Review

1. stimulus

2. cells

3. a

4. Sample answer: In asexual reproduction, there is one parent, and the offspring are identical to the parent. In sexual reproduction, there are two parents, and offspring share the characteristics of both parents.

5. Sample answer: Organisms are made of cells, detect and respond to stimuli, reproduce, have DNA, use energy, and grow and develop.

6. 64 bacteria

first generation:	1
second generation	2
third generation	4
fourth generation	8
fifth generation	16
sixth generation	32

7. Sample answer: I sweat or shiver to maintain a constant body temperature. I go inside or put on a coat if I get cold. I squint my eyes when the sun is too bright.

8. Sample answer: The fur coat of a bear helps keep the bear's body warm during cold weather. By keeping the bear warm, the coat helps the bear maintain homeostasis.

CHAPTER RESOURCES

Chapter Resource File

- Section Quiz GENERAL
- Section Review GENERAL
- Vocabulary and Section Summary GENERAL
- Critical Thinking ADVANCED

Focus

Overview

This section identifies the things that an organism needs to live. Students will learn the roles that food, water, and air play in an organism's survival. They will also learn that where an organism lives is related to its ability to obtain the necessities of life. Students will also learn about the chemical building blocks and processes necessary for life.

 Bellringer

Have students answer the following question in their **science journal:** "What do you think your mass would be if there were no water in your body?"
(Sample answer: If a student has a mass of 40 kg, the water's mass is 40 kg × 0.70 = 28 kg. The student's mass without water would be 40 kg − 28 kg = 12 kg.)

Answer to Reading Check

photosynthesis

READING WARM-UP

Objectives
- Explain why organisms need food, water, air, and living space.
- Describe the chemical building blocks of cells.

Terms to Learn

producer   lipid
consumer   phospholipid
decomposer   ATP
protein   nucleic acid
carbohydrate

READING STRATEGY

Discussion Read this section silently. Write down questions that you have about this section. Discuss your questions in a small group.

The Necessities of Life

Would it surprise you to learn that you have the same basic needs as a tree, a frog, and a fly?

In fact, almost every organism has the same basic needs: water, air, a place to live, and food.

Water

You may know that your body is made mostly of water. In fact, your cells and the cells of almost all living organisms are approximately 70% water. Most of the chemical reactions involved in metabolism require water.

Organisms differ greatly in terms of how much water they need and how they get it. You could survive for only about three days without water. You get water from the fluids you drink and the food you eat. The desert-dwelling kangaroo rat never drinks. It gets all of its water from its food.

Air

Air is a mixture of several different gases, including oxygen and carbon dioxide. Most living things use oxygen in the chemical process that releases energy from food. Organisms living on land get oxygen from the air. Organisms living in water either take in dissolved oxygen from the water or come to the water's surface to get oxygen from the air. The European diving spider in **Figure 1** goes to great lengths to get oxygen.

Green plants, algae, and some bacteria need carbon dioxide gas in addition to oxygen. These organisms produce food and oxygen by using photosynthesis (FOHT oh SIN thuh sis). In *photosynthesis*, green organisms convert the energy in sunlight to energy stored in food.

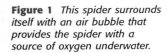 **Reading Check** What process do plants use to make food? (*See the Appendix for answers to Reading Checks.*)

Figure 1 *This spider surrounds itself with an air bubble that provides the spider with a source of oxygen underwater.*

CHAPTER RESOURCES

Chapter Resource File

- **Lesson Plan**
- **Directed Reading A** BASIC
- **Directed Reading B** SPECIAL NEEDS

Technology

- **Transparencies**
  - Bellringer
  - *LINK TO EARTH SCIENCE* The Earth's Land Biomes

Is That a Fact!

Camels in the Sahara don't need to drink water at all during the winter months. They get enough water from the plants they eat. During the hottest part of the summer, they can go a week without drinking water. When a water source is available, they can drink up to 190 L (50 gal) at a time!

A Place to Live

All organisms need a place to live that contains all of the things they need to survive. Some organisms, such as elephants, require a large amount of space. Other organisms may live their entire life in one place.

Space on Earth is limited. So, organisms often compete with each other for food, water, and other necessities. Many animals, including the warbler in **Figure 2,** will claim a particular space. After claiming a space, they try to keep other animals away.

Food

All living things need food. Food gives organisms energy and the raw materials needed to carry on life processes. Organisms use nutrients from food to replace cells and build body parts. But not all organisms get food in the same way. In fact, organisms can be grouped into three different groups based on how they get their food.

Making Food

Some organisms, such as plants, are called producers. **Producers** can make their own food. Like most producers, plants use energy from the sun to make food from water and carbon dioxide. Some producers get energy and food from the chemicals in their environment.

Taking Food

Other organisms are called **consumers** because they must eat (consume) other organisms to get food. The frog in **Figure 3** is an example of a consumer. It gets the energy it needs by eating insects and other organisms.

Some consumers are decomposers. **Decomposers** are organisms that get their food by breaking down the nutrients in dead organisms or animal wastes. The mushroom in **Figure 3** is a decomposer.

Figure 2 *A warbler's song is more than just a pretty tune. The warbler is protecting its home by telling other warblers to stay out of its territory.*

producer an organism that can make its own food by using energy from its surroundings

consumer an organism that eats other organisms or organic matter

decomposer an organism that gets energy by breaking down the remains of dead organisms or animal wastes and consuming or absorbing the nutrients

Figure 3 *The frog is a consumer. The mushroom is a decomposer. The green plants are producers.*

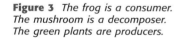

ACTIVITY ——— GENERAL

Writing **Poster Project** Have students collect pictures from magazines and create a poster that shows the home of a plant and the home of an animal with all the necessities of life that were discussed in this section. **LS** Visual

INTERNET ACTIVITY
Short Story ——— GENERAL

For an internet activity related to this chapter, have students go to **go.hrw.com** and type in the keyword **HL5ALVW.**

ACTIVITY — BASIC

Vocabulary Review Have students unscramble the following words and then use all four in a single sentence.

cdporesru (producers)
gnreey (energy)
dofo (food)
rwtea (water)

(Sample sentence: Producers use energy from the sun to make food from carbon dioxide and water.)

LS Logical/Verbal

Using the Figure — BASIC

Writing

Protein Structures
Have students discuss or describe in writing the characteristics of each of the protein structures illustrated in **Figure 4.** Ask students the following question: "How can all of these structures be proteins and have such different properties?" (Sample answer: Most proteins are made from different combinations of the same 20 amino acids. Different combinations of amino acids create proteins with different characteristics.)

LS Auditory/Verbal

SCHOOL to HOME

Pen a Menu

 WRITING SKILL With a parent, write a menu for a favorite meal. Using Nutrition Facts labels, find out which items on your menu include proteins, carbohydrates, and fats. Try making the meal.

ACTIVITY

protein a molecule that is made up of amino acids and that is needed to build and repair body structures and to regulate processes in the body

Figure 4 *Spider webs, hair, horns, and feathers are all made from proteins.*

Putting It All Together

Some organisms make their own food. Some organisms get food from eating other organisms. But all organisms need to break down that food in order to use the nutrients in it.

Nutrients are made up of molecules. A *molecule* is a substance made when two or more atoms combine. Molecules made of different kinds of atoms are *compounds*. Molecules found in living things are usually made of different combinations of six elements: carbon, hydrogen, nitrogen, oxygen, phosphorus, and sulfur. These elements combine to form proteins, carbohydrates, lipids, ATP, and nucleic acids.

Proteins

Almost all of the life processes of a cell involve proteins. **Proteins** are large molecules that are made up of smaller molecules called *amino acids.*

Making Proteins

Organisms break down the proteins in food to supply their cells with amino acids. These amino acids are then linked together to form new proteins. Some proteins are made up of only a few amino acids, but others contain more than 10,000 amino acids.

Proteins in Action

Proteins have many different functions. Some proteins form structures that are easy to see, such as those in **Figure 4.** Other proteins are very small and help cells do their jobs. Inside red blood cells, the protein hemoglobin (HEE moh GLOH bin) binds to oxygen to deliver and release oxygen throughout the body. Some proteins protect cells. Other proteins, called *enzymes* (EN ziEMZ), start or speed up chemical reactions in cells.

 **Cultural Awareness** GENERAL

Staple Crops Hunters and gatherers of all races historically required very large areas of land to sustain themselves. Most cultures later developed farming and herding techniques that made higher population densities possible. Staple crops vary around the world, but the millet and sorghum grains of Africans, the wheat and barley of Europeans, the corn and squash of Native Americans, and the rice and soybeans of Asians, in correct amounts and supplemented with other foods, are all equally nutritious. Have interested students research the diet of another culture and compose a menu representing the food of that culture. **LS** Verbal

Figure 5 *The extra sugar in a potato plant is stored in the potato as starch, a complex carbohydrate.*

Carbohydrates

Molecules made of sugars are called **carbohydrates.** Cells use carbohydrates as a source of energy and for energy storage. An organism's cells break down carbohydrates to release the energy stored in them. There are two kinds of carbohydrates—simple carbohydrates and complex carbohydrates.

Simple Carbohydrates

Simple carbohydrates are made up of one sugar molecule or a few sugar molecules linked together. Table sugar and the sugar in fruits are examples of simple carbohydrates.

Complex Carbohydrates

When an organism has more sugar than it needs, its extra sugar may be stored as complex carbohydrates. *Complex carbohydrates* are made of hundreds of sugar molecules linked together. Plants, such as the potato plant in **Figure 5,** store extra sugar as starch. When you eat mashed potatoes, you are eating a potato plant's stored starch. Your body then breaks down this complex carbohydrate to release the energy stored in the potato.

Reading Check What is the difference between simple carbohydrates and complex carbohydrates?

carbohydrate a class of energy-giving nutrients that includes sugars, starches, and fiber; contains carbon, hydrogen, and oxygen

How Much Oxygen?
Each red blood cell carries about 250 million molecules of hemoglobin. How many molecules of oxygen could a single red blood cell deliver throughout the body if every hemoglobin molecule attached to four oxygen molecules?

Starch Search

1. Obtain several **food samples** from your teacher.
2. Put **a few drops of iodine** on each sample. Record your observations. **Caution:** Iodine can stain clothing.
3. When iodine comes into contact with starch, a black substance appears. Which samples contain starch?

Answer to Reading Check
Simple carbohydrates are made of one sugar. Complex carbohydrates are made of many sugars linked together.

MATERIALS

FOR EACH GROUP
• aluminum foil to hold food samples, 25 cm × 3 cm × 25 cm
• eyedropper, plastic
• food samples (cracker, piece of bread, potato, chocolate, apple, broccoli, celery, piece of hot dog)
• iodine solution in small bottle

Safety Caution: Remind students to review all safety cautions and icons before beginning this lab activity.

Students should not eat any of the food samples. Iodine will stain and can be toxic. Dilute the iodine to prevent injury. Have a functioning eyewash available. Each student should wear safety goggles, an apron, and protective gloves.

Instruct students to use only a few drops of iodine on each sample.

Answer
3. Sample answer: cracker, bread, and potato

Answer to Math Practice
1 billion molecules of oxygen ($250,000,000 \times 4 = 1,000,000,000$)

Making Tables Have students make tables describing carbohydrates, proteins, and lipids.
LS Logical/Verbal

1. Give an example of a producer, consumer, and a decomposer. (Sample answer: producer: plants; consumer: animals; decomposer: fungi)

2. Name two functions of lipids. (Some lipids store energy, and others form the cell membrane.)

3. How are proteins used by an organism? (An organism breaks down proteins and uses their amino acids to build other proteins. These other proteins are used to carry out chemical reactions in cells, transport materials, and protect the cell.)

Alternative Assessment — **ADVANCED**

Writing **Job Description** Have students write a job description for one of the cell's basic chemical building blocks. Tell students to describe the required job responsibilities. Have them include a description of the expected workload by explaining whether the building block will have to work constantly or sporadically. Finally, indicate whether the building block will work independently or with other cell components.
LS Verbal

Figure 6 **Phospholipid Membranes**

The head of a phospholipid molecule is attracted to water, but the tail is not.

Head

Tail

Phospholipid molecule

When phospholipid molecules come together in water, they form two layers.

Water

Cell membrane

Water

lipid a type of biochemical that does not dissolve in water; fats and steroids are lipids

phospholipid a lipid that contains phosphorus and that is a structural component in cell membranes

ATP **a**denosine **tri**phosphate, a molecule that acts as the main energy source for cell processes

CONNECTION TO Social Studies

Whaling In the 1900s, whales were hunted and killed for their oil. Whale oil was often used as fuel for oil lamps. Most of the oil taken from whales was taken from their fat, or *blubber*. Some whales had blubber over 18 in. thick, producing over 40 barrels of oil per whale. Research whether anyone still hunts whales or uses whale oil. Make a presentation to the class on your findings.

Lipids

Lipids are compounds that cannot mix with water. Lipids have many important jobs in the cell. Like carbohydrates, some lipids store energy. Other lipids form the membranes of cells.

Phospholipids

All cells are surrounded by a cell membrane. The cell membrane helps protect the cell and keep the internal conditions of the cell stable. **Phospholipids** (FAHS foh LIP idz) are the molecules that form much of the cell membrane. The head of a phospholipid molecule is attracted to water. The tail is not. Cells are mostly water. When phospholipids are in water, the tails come together, and the heads face out into the water. **Figure 6** shows how phospholipid molecules form two layers in water.

Fats and Oils

Fats and oils are lipids that store energy. When an organism has used up most of its carbohydrates, it can get energy from these lipids. The structures of fats and oils are almost the same, but at room temperature, most fats are solid, and most oils are liquid. Most of the lipids stored in plants are oils. Most of the lipids stored in animals are fats.

✓ **Reading Check** What is one difference between oils and fats?

ATP

Adenosine **tri**phosphate (uh DEN uh SEEN trie FAHS FAYT), also called ATP, is another important molecule. **ATP** is the major energy-carrying molecule in the cell. The energy in carbohydrates and lipids must be transferred to ATP, which then provides fuel for cellular activities.

INCLUSION Strategies

• *Attention Deficit Disorder* • *Behavior Control Issues*
• *Developmentally Delayed*

Try this hands-on activity to help students understand that lipids cannot mix with water.

1. Pour a cup of water into each of three small bowls.
2. Pour 1/4 cup of cooking oil into one of the bowls.
3. Drop 2 tablespoons of butter into the second bowl.
4. Pour 1/4 cup of sugar into the third bowl.
5. Ask three volunteers to use spoons to stir the added ingredient.

After a couple of minutes, discuss that lipids, such as oil and butter, cannot be dissolved in water, but sugar can be dissolved, which explains why the sugar seems to have "disappeared" into the water. **LS** Kinesthetic/Visual

Nucleic Acids

Nucleic acids are sometimes called the blueprints of life because they have all the information needed for a cell to make proteins. **Nucleic acids** are large molecules made up of molecules called *nucleotides* (NOO klee oh TIEDZ). A nucleic acid may have thousands of nucleotides. The order of those nucleotides stores information. DNA is a nucleic acid. A DNA molecule is like a recipe book entitled *How to Make Proteins*. When a cell needs to make a certain protein, the cell gets information from the order of the nucleotides in DNA. This order of nucleotides tells the cell the order of the amino acids that are linked together to make that protein.

nucleic acid a molecule made up of subunits called *nucleotides*

SECTION Review

Summary

- Organisms need water for cellular processes.
- Organisms need oxygen to release the energy contained in their food.
- Organisms must have a place to live.
- Cells store energy in carbohydrates, which are made of sugars.
- Proteins are made up of amino acids. Some proteins are enzymes.
- Fats and oils store energy and make up cell membranes.
- Cells use molecules of ATP to fuel their activities.
- Nucleic acids, such as DNA, are made up of nucleotides.

Using Key Terms

For each pair of terms, explain how the meanings of the terms differ.

1. *producer* and *consumer*
2. *lipid* and *phospholipid*

Understanding Key Ideas

3. Plants store extra sugar as
   a. proteins.
   b. starch.
   c. nucleic acids.
   d. phospholipids.
4. Explain why organisms need food, water, air, and living space.
5. Describe the chemical building blocks of cells.
6. Why are decomposers categorized as consumers? How do they differ from producers?
7. What are the subunits of proteins?

Math Skills

8. Protein A is a chain of 660 amino acids. Protein B is a chain of 11 amino acids. How many times more amino acids does protein A have than protein B?

Critical Thinking

9. **Making Inferences** Could life as we know it exist on Earth if air contained only oxygen? Explain.
10. **Identifying Relationships** How might a cave, an ant, and a lake each meet the needs of an organism?
11. **Predicting Consequences** What would happen to the supply of ATP in your cells if you did not eat enough carbohydrates? How would this affect your cells?
12. **Applying Concepts** Which resource do you think is most important to your survival: water, air, a place to live, or food? Explain your answer.

For a variety of links related to this chapter, go to www.scilinks.org

Topic: The Necessities of Life
SciLinks code: HSM1018

Developed and maintained by the National Science Teachers Association

Answer to Reading Check

Most fats are solid, and most oils are liquid.

CHAPTER RESOURCES

Chapter Resource File

- Section Quiz `GENERAL`
- Section Review `GENERAL`
- Vocabulary and Section Summary `GENERAL`
- Reinforcement Worksheet `BASIC`
- SciLinks Activity `GENERAL`
- Datasheet for Quick Lab

Technology

Transparencies
- Phospholipid Molecule and Cell Membrane

Answers to Section Review

1. Sample answer: Producers can make their own food. Consumers must eat other organisms to get food.
2. Sample answer: A phospholipid contains phosphorous and forms cell membranes.
3. b
4. Sample answer: Most of the chemical reactions involved in metabolism require water. Most living things need oxygen from air to release energy from food. Plants and other organisms need carbon dioxide from air to make food. Food gives organisms the energy they need to carry out life processes. Organisms need a place to live that contains the things they need to survive.
5. Sample answer: Proteins contain amino acids, which are used to build other proteins. Carbohydrates provide energy. Lipids are energy-storage molecules and form cell membranes.
6. Sample answer: Decomposers cannot make their own food, as producers can, so decomposers consume dead organisms.
7. amino acids
8. $660 \div 11 = 60$ times
9. Sample answer: Green plants, algae, and some bacteria need carbon dioxide gas as well as oxygen. Without the carbon dioxide, these organisms could not survive, and other organisms could not rely on them as a food source.
10. Sample answer: A cave provides shelter. An ant could be food. A lake provides water.
11. Sample answer: The supply of ATP would decrease. A decrease in ATP would cause a cell to have less energy than it needs to carry out its activities. Your body would have to get ATP from other sources, such as lipids.
12. Sample answer: They are all equally important. An organism could not survive without any one resource.

Roly-Poly Races

Teacher's Notes

Time Required
One or two 45-minute class periods

Lab Ratings

EASY ——————————→ HARD

Teacher Prep 🧪🧪
Student Set-Up 🧪🧪
Concept Level 🧪
Clean Up 🧪

MATERIALS
The materials listed on the student page are enough for 1 or 2 students. Remind students that they are handling living things that should be treated with respect. The soil used in this lab should be sterilized potting soil to avoid causing allergic reactions among the students.

Safety Caution
Remind students to review all safety cautions and icons before beginning this lab activity.

Using Scientific Methods
Inquiry Lab

OBJECTIVES
Observe responses to stimuli.
Analyze responses to stimuli.

MATERIALS
- chalk (1 stick)
- container, plastic, small, with lid
- gloves, protective
- isopod (4)
- potato, raw (1 small slice)
- ruler, metric
- soil (8 oz)
- stopwatch

SAFETY

Roly-Poly Races

Have you ever watched a bug run? Did you wonder why it was running? The bug you saw running was probably reacting to a stimulus. In other words, something happened to make the bug run! One characteristic of living things is that they respond to stimuli. In this activity, you will study the movement of roly-polies. Roly-polies are also called *pill bugs*. But they are not really bugs; they are land-dwelling animals called *isopods*. Isopods live in dark, moist areas under rocks or wood. You will provide stimuli to determine how fast your isopod can move and what affects its speed and direction. Remember that isopods are living things and must be treated gently and respectfully.

Ask a Question
1. Ask a question such as, "Which stimuli cause pill bugs to run?"

Form a Hypothesis
2. Using your question as a guide, form a hypothesis. For example, you could form the following hypothesis: "Light, sound, and touch stimulate pill bugs to run."

Test the Hypothesis
3. Choose a partner, and decide together how you will run your roly-poly race. Discuss some gentle ways to stimulate your isopods to move. Choose five or six things that might cause movement, such as a gentle nudge or a change in temperature, sound, or light. Check your choices with your teacher.

4. Make a data table similar to the table below. Label the columns with the stimuli that you've chosen. Label the rows "Isopod 1," "Isopod 2," "Isopod 3," and "Isopod 4."

Isopod Responses			
	Stimulus 1	**Stimulus 2**	**Stimulus 3**
Isopod 1			
Isopod 2			
Isopod 3	DO NOT WRITE IN BOOK		
Isopod 4			

Lab Notes
Isopods were selected for this lab because they are very common in most areas and can be collected and released in natural areas. If you choose to use other animals that you can obtain at a pet store, such as mealworms, be sure to have a plan for appropriate disposal after the lab.

5. Place a layer of soil that is 1 cm or 2 cm deep in a small plastic container. Add a small slice of potato and a piece of chalk. Your isopods will eat these items.

6. Place four isopods in your container. Observe them for a minute or two before you perform your tests. Record your observations.

7. Decide which stimulus you want to test first. Carefully arrange the isopods at the "starting line." The starting line can be an imaginary line at one end of the container.

8. Gently stimulate each isopod at the same time and in the same way. In your data table, record the isopods' responses to the stimulus. Be sure to record the distance that each isopod travels. Don't forget to time the race.

9. Repeat steps 7–8 for each stimulus. Be sure to wait at least 2 min between trials.

Analyze the Results

1. **Describing Events** Describe the way that isopods move. Do their legs move together?

2. **Analyzing Results** Did your isopods move before or between the trials? Did the movement seem to have a purpose, or were the isopods responding to a stimulus? Explain.

Draw Conclusions

3. **Interpreting Information** Did any of the stimuli make the isopods move faster or go farther? Explain.

Applying Your Data

Like isopods and all other living things, humans react to stimuli. Describe three stimuli that might cause humans to run.

CHAPTER RESOURCES

Workbooks

 Labs You Can Eat
• Say Cheese! GENERAL

 Long-Term Projects & Research Ideas
• I Think, Therefore I Live ADVANCED

CLASSROOM TESTED & APPROVED

Gladys Cherniak
St. Paul's Episcopal School
Mobile, Alabama

Chapter Review

Assignment Guide

Section	Questions
1	1–2, 6–7, 9, 13, 17, 19–21
2	3–5, 8, 10–12, 14–16, 18

ANSWERS

Using Key Terms

1. homeostasis
2. heredity
3. consumer
4. carbohydrate
5. lipid

Understanding Key Ideas

6. d
7. b
8. a
9. b
10. c
11. c
12. a

USING KEY TERMS

Complete each of the following sentences by choosing the correct term from the word bank.

lipid   carbohydrate
consumer   heredity
homeostasis   producer

1 The process of maintaining a stable internal environment is known as ___.

2 Offspring resemble their parents because of ___.

3 A ___ obtains food by eating other organisms.

4 Starch is a ___ and is made up of sugars.

5 Fat is a ___ that stores energy for an organism.

UNDERSTANDING KEY IDEAS

Multiple Choice

6 Which of the following statements about cells is true?

a. Cells are the structures that contain all of the materials necessary for life.
b. Cells are found in all organisms.
c. Cells are sometimes specialized for particular functions.
d. All of the above

7 Which of the following statements about all living things is true?

a. All living things reproduce sexually.
b. All living things have one or more cells.
c. All living things must make their own food.
d. All living things reproduce asexually.

8 Organisms must have food because

a. food is a source of energy.
b. food supplies cells with oxygen.
c. organisms never make their own food.
d. All of the above

9 A change in an organism's environment that affects the organism's activities is a

a. response.   c. metabolism.
b. stimulus.   d. producer.

10 Organisms store energy in

a. nucleic acids.   c. lipids.
b. phospholipids.   d. water.

11 The molecule that contains the information about how to make proteins is

a. ATP.
b. a carbohydrate.
c. DNA.
d. a phospholipid.

12 The subunits of nucleic acids are

a. nucleotides.
b. oils.
c. sugars.
d. amino acids.

Short Answer

13 What is the difference between asexual reproduction and sexual reproduction?

14 In one or two sentences, explain why living things must have air.

15 What is ATP, and why is it important to a cell?

CRITICAL THINKING

16 **Concept Mapping** Use the following terms to create a concept map: *cell, carbohydrates, protein, enzymes, DNA, sugars, lipids, nucleotides, amino acids,* and *nucleic acid.*

17 **Analyzing Ideas** A flame can move, grow larger, and give off heat. Is a flame alive? Explain.

18 **Applying Concepts** Based on what you know about carbohydrates, lipids, and proteins, why is it important for you to eat a balanced diet?

19 **Evaluating Hypotheses** Your friend tells you that the stimulus of music makes his goldfish swim faster. How would you design a controlled experiment to test your friend's claim?

INTERPRETING GRAPHICS

The pictures below show the same plant over a period of 3 days. Use the pictures below to answer the questions that follow.

Day 1

Day 2

Day 3

20 What is the plant doing?

21 What characteristic(s) of living things is the plant exhibiting?

Critical Thinking

16. An answer to this exercise can be found at the end of this book.

17. Sample answer: The flame is not alive. Although a flame can move, grow, and give off heat, it does not have all of the characteristics of a living organism. For example, a flame is not made up of cells and does not contain DNA.

18. Sample answer: Cells use carbohydrates as a source of energy and for energy storage. Eating protein supplies the body with amino acids. The body uses these amino acids to make its own proteins. Proteins have many functions. For example, the protein hemoglobin helps deliver oxygen throughout the body. Other proteins called *enzymes* help speed up chemical reactions. Lipids store energy and form the membranes of cells. If you eat an unbalanced diet, you may lack one or more of these three nutrients, and your cells will not be able to function properly as a result.

19. Answers may vary. Sample answer: I could put the goldfish bowl in a box, making sure that the fish does not see anything outside the bowl. I would make sure that the fish gets light, air, and food in regulated amounts. Then, I would observe the fish without the stimulus of music and with the stimulus of music to see what happens.

Interpreting Graphics

20. The plant is bending toward the light coming through the window.

21. Sample answer: The plant is sensing a stimulus (the light) and is responding to it.

13. In sexual reproduction, two parents produce offspring that will share characteristics of both parents. In asexual reproduction, a single parent produces offspring that are identical to the parent.

14. Sample answer: Most organisms need oxygen from air to release energy from food. Green plants, algae, and some bacteria need carbon dioxide from air for photosynthesis.

15. ATP is the energy-containing molecule in a cell. It provides fuel for cellular activities.

Teacher's Note

To provide practice under more realistic testing conditions, give students 20 minutes to answer all of the questions in this Standardized Test Preparation.

MISCONCEPTION
////ALERT\\\\

Answers to the standardized test preparation can help you identify student misconceptions and misunderstandings.

READING

Passage 1
1. A
2. G
3. C
4. G

✚ TEST DOCTOR

Question 4: Some students may answer that the difference between sexual and asexual reproduction pertains to the number of offspring produced or the number that survive. However, the passage does not discuss either. Some students may infer that sexual reproduction produces more traits because two parents are involved rather than one parent as in asexual reproduction. Again, this idea is not discussed in the passage.

Standardized Test Preparation

READING

Read each of the passages below. Then, answer the questions that follow each passage.

Passage 1 Organisms make other organisms similar to themselves. They do so in one of two ways: by sexual reproduction or by <u>asexual reproduction</u>. In sexual reproduction, two parents produce offspring that will share characteristics of both parents. Most animals and plants reproduce in this way. In asexual reproduction, a single parent produces offspring that are identical to the parent. Most single-celled organisms reproduce in this way.

1. In the passage, what does the term *asexual reproduction* mean?
   A A single parent produces offspring.
   B Two parents make identical offspring.
   C Plants make offspring.
   D Animals make offspring.

2. What is characteristic of offspring produced by sexual reproduction?
   F They are identical to both parents.
   G They share the traits of both parents.
   H They are identical to one parent.
   I They are identical to each other.

3. What is characteristic of offspring produced by asexual reproduction?
   A They are identical to both parents.
   B They share the traits of both parents.
   C They are identical to one parent.
   D They are usually plants.

4. What is the difference between sexual and asexual reproduction?
   F the number of offspring produced
   G the number of parents needed to produce offspring
   H the number of traits produced
   I the number of offspring that survive

Passage 2 In 1996, a group of researchers led by NASA scientists studied a 3.8-billion-year-old meteorite named ALH84001. These scientists agree that ALH84001 is a potato-sized piece of the planet Mars. They also agree that it fell to Earth about 13,000 years ago. It was discovered in Antarctica in 1984. According to the NASA team, ALH84001 brought with it evidence that life once existed on Mars.

Scientists found certain kinds of organic molecules (molecules containing carbon) on the surface of ALH84001. These molecules are similar to those left behind when living things break down substances for food. When these scientists examined the interior of the meteorite, they found the same organic molecules throughout. Because these molecules were spread throughout the meteorite, scientists concluded that the molecules were not contamination from Earth. The NASA team believes that these organic compounds are strong evidence that tiny organisms similar to bacteria lived, ate, and died on Mars millions of years ago.

1. How old is the meteorite named ALH84001?
   A 13,000 years old
   B millions of years old
   C 3.8 billion years old
   D 3.8 trillion years old

2. Which of the following would best support a claim that life might have existed on Mars?
   F remains of organisms
   G water
   H meteorite temperatures similar to Earth temperatures
   I oxygen

Passage 2
1. C
2. F

✚ TEST DOCTOR

Question 1: Some students may answer 13,000 years old because the passage states that the meteorite fell to Earth about 13,000 years ago. Some students may answer millions of years old because the passage mentions life that lived millions of years ago, but the passage gives the meteorite's age as 3.8 billion years old. Students may answer 3.8 trillion years old if they misread the passage or the answers.

INTERPRETING GRAPHICS

The graph below shows an ill person's body temperature. Use the graph below to answer the questions that follow.

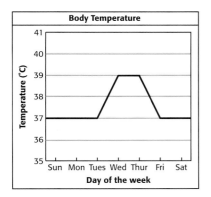

Body Temperature

1. A fever is a spike in temperature. On which day does this person have a fever?
   - **A** Sunday
   - **B** Monday
   - **C** Wednesday
   - **D** Saturday

2. A body with a fever is often fighting an infection. Fevers help eliminate the pathogens that cause the infection. According to the chart, when does this person probably have the highest fever?
   - **F** Sunday
   - **G** Monday
   - **H** Wednesday
   - **I** Saturday

3. What is the highest temperature that this fever reaches?
   - **A** 37°C
   - **B** 38°C
   - **C** 39°C
   - **D** 40°C

4. What is probably this person's normal body temperature?
   - **F** 37°C
   - **G** 38°C
   - **H** 39°C
   - **I** 40°C

MATH

Read each question below, and choose the best answer.

1. An aquarium is a place where fish can live. What is the volume of the aquarium shown below?

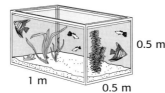

0.5 m

1 m   0.5 m

   - **A** 0.25 m
   - **B** 0.25 m^2
   - **C** 0.25 m^3
   - **D** 0.52 m^3

2. The cost of admission to a natural history museum is $7 per adult. What is the total cost of admission for a group of five adults?
   - **F** $25
   - **G** $35
   - **H** $45
   - **I** $55

3. Lee biked 25.3 km on Monday, 20.7 km on Tuesday, and 15.6 km on Wednesday. How many kilometers did Lee bike during those three days?
   - **A** 66.1 km
   - **B** 61.6 km
   - **C** 51.6 km
   - **D** 16.6 km

4. Laura collected 24 leaves. One-third of the leaves were oak leaves. How many oak leaves did Laura collect?
   - **F** 6
   - **G** 8
   - **H** 12
   - **I** 24

Standardized Test Preparation

INTERPRETING GRAPHICS

1. C
2. H
3. C
4. F

 TEST DOCTOR

Question 4: Students may answer 38°C if they find the value between 37°C and 39°C rather than observe that 37°C is the person's temperature when not feverish. Some students may answer 39°C if they don't realize that this temperature is the person's fever, not the person's normal body temperature. Finally, 40°C is above even the fever temperature, so this answer is incorrect.

MATH

1. C
2. G
3. B
4. G

 TEST DOCTOR

Question 1: Students may answer 0.25 m or 0.25 m^2 if they forget that the correct units for volume are m^3. If they transpose the 2 and the 5 in the answer, they will incorrectly answer 0.52 m^3. You may want to show students how to do this problem on the board so that they understand where m^3 comes from (m × m × m = m^3).

Question 3: Some students may answer 51.6 km if they forget to carry the 1 to the tens column. Some students may answer 66.1 or 16.6 km if they transpose numbers in the correct answer.

Science, Technology, and Society

Teaching Strategy—GENERAL

Students may not be familiar with the game of chess. Understanding how chess is played may assist students in understanding the complexity of chess playing computers. Encourage students who know how to play chess to demonstrate the game to the other students.

Students who are interested in the history of science may be interested in creating a timeline showing the achievements in the development of chess-playing computers.

Science Fiction

Background

Terry Bisson has written comic books, short stories, novels, plays, how-to articles about writing, and news editorials. In 1991, Bisson's short story "Bears Discover Fire" received the highest honors possible for science fiction writers—both the Nebula Award and the Hugo Award.

Science in Action

HOLT ANTHOLOGY OF
Science Fiction
HOLT, RINEHART AND WINSTON

Science, Technology, and Society

Chess-Playing Computers

Computers can help us explore how humans think. One way to explore how humans think is to study how people and computers play chess against each other.

A computer's approach to chess is straightforward. By calculating each piece's possible board position for the next few moves, a computer creates what is called a *position tree*. A position tree shows how each move can lead to other moves. This way of playing requires millions of calculations.

Human chess champions play differently. Humans calculate only three or four moves every minute. Even so, human champions are still a match for computer opponents. By studying the ways that people and computers play chess, scientists are learning how people think and make choices.

Math ACTIVITY

A chess-playing computer needs to evaluate 3 million positions before a move. If you could evaluate two positions in 1 min, how long would it take you to evaluate 3 million possible positions?

Science Fiction

"They're Made Out of Meat" by Terry Bisson

Two space explorers millions of light-years from home are visiting an uncharted sector of the universe to find signs of life. Their mission is to contact, welcome, and log any and all beings in this part of the universe.

During their mission, they encounter a life-form quite unlike anything they have ever seen before. It looked too strange and, well, disgusting. The explorers have very strong doubts about adding this new organism to the list. But the explorers' official duty is to contact and welcome all life-forms no matter how ugly they are. Can the explorers bring themselves to perform their duty?

You'll find out by reading "They're Made Out of Meat," a short story by Terry Bisson. This story is in the *Holt Anthology of Science Fiction*.

Language Arts ACTIVITY

WRITING SKILL Write a story about what happens when the explorers next meet the creatures on the star in G445 zone.

Answer to Math Activity

1,500,000 minutes

(3,000,000 ÷ 2 = 1,500,000 minutes)

Answer to Language Arts Activity

Answers may vary.

People in Science

Janis Davis-Street

NASA Nutritionist Do astronauts eat shrimp cocktail in space? Yes, they do! Shrimp cocktail is nutritious and tastes so good that it is one of the most popular foods in the space program. And eating a proper diet helps astronauts stay healthy while they are in space.

But who figures out what astronauts need to eat? Janis Davis-Street is a nutritionist and laboratory supervisor for the Nutritional Biochemistry Laboratory at the Johnson Space Center in Houston, Texas. She was born in Georgetown, Guyana, on the northeastern coast of South America. She was educated in Canada.

Davis-Street is part of a team that uses their knowledge of nutrition, biology, and chemistry to figure out the nutritional requirements for spaceflight. For example, they determine how many calories and other nutrients each astronaut needs per day during spaceflight.

The Nutritional Biochemistry Laboratory's work on the space shuttle missions and *Mir* space station developed into tests that allow NASA to help ensure astronaut health before, during, and after flight. These tests are important for understanding how the human body adapts to long space missions, and for determining whether treatments for preventing bone and muscle loss during spaceflight are working.

Social Studies ACTiViTY

Scientists from more than 30 countries have been on space missions. Research which countries have provided astronauts or cosmonauts for space missions. Using a map, place self-stick notes on countries that have provided scientists for space missions. Write the names of the appropriate scientists on the self-stick notes.

go.hrw.com

To learn more about these Science in Action topics, visit go.hrw.com and type in the keyword HL5ALVF.

Current Science

Check out Current Science® articles related to this chapter by visiting go.hrw.com. Just type in the keyword HL5CS02.

People in Science

Background

One of the reasons to conduct nutritional tests in space is to determine potential benefits for disease research and medicine on earth. One of Davis-Street's current tests is Experiment E381, "Calcium Kinetics During Space Flight." Experiment E381 addresses bone health and bone loss during space missions.

Calcium may be lost from bones during space flight partly as a result of insufficient levels of vitamin D in the body. Vitamin D is critical to calcium absorption and metabolism. Vitamin D is synthesized using sunlight and ultraviolet radiation, and spaceships are heavily shielded from any ultraviolet light. Calcium kinetics will track the movement of calcium tracers through an astronaut's body, from the absorption from food to the formation and breakdown of bones.

If the rate of bone loss during flight and the recovery rate on the ground are constant, scientists predict it will take 2.5 times the mission length to recover lost bone mass. Understanding bone and calcium dynamics in accelerated contexts such as space might help us to better understand earth bone diseases, such as osteoporosis.

Answer to Social Studies Activity

Answers may vary. Some of the countries from which astronauts or cosmonauts have come include the United States, Russia, Israel, India, Japan, Canada, Brazil, Germany, Italy, Switzerland, France, and Sweden.

Cells: The Basic Units of Life
Chapter Planning Guide

Compression guide:
To shorten instruction because of time limitations, omit the LabBook Lab.

OBJECTIVES	LABS, DEMONSTRATIONS, AND ACTIVITIES	TECHNOLOGY RESOURCES
PACING • 90 min pp. 350–359 **Chapter Opener**	SE **Start-up Activity,** p. 351 ◆ GENERAL	OSP **Parent Letter** GENERAL CD **Student Edition on CD-ROM** CD **Guided Reading Audio CD** TR **Chapter Starter Transparency*** VID **Brain Food Video Quiz**
Section 1 The Diversity of Cells • State the parts of the cell theory. • Explain why cells are so small. • Describe the parts of a cell. • Describe how eubacteria are different from archaebacteria. • Explain the difference between prokaryotic cells and eukaryotic cells.	TE **Activity** Modeling Cell Discovery, p. 352 ◆ GENERAL SE **Connection to Physics** Microscopes, p. 353 GENERAL SE **Quick Lab** Bacteria in Your Lunch?, p. 356 ◆ GENERAL CRF **Datasheet for Quick Lab*** TE **Group Activity** Archaebacteria, p. 356 ADVANCED SE **Connection to Social Studies** Where Do They Live?, p. 357 GENERAL SE **Skills Practice Labs** Elephant-Sized Amoebas?, p. 372 ◆ GENERAL CRF **Datasheet for Chapter Lab***	CRF **Lesson Plans*** TR **Bellringer Transparency*** TR Math Focus: Surface Area–to-Volume Ratio* TR A Typical Eukaryotic Cell* VID **Lab Videos for Life Science** TE **Internet Activity,** p. 358 GENERAL
PACING • 45 min pp. 360–367 **Section 2 Eukaryotic Cells** • Identify the different parts of a eukaryotic cell. • Explain the function of each part of a eukaryotic cell.	TE **Demonstration** Cell Walls and Cell Membranes, p. 361 BASIC TE **Activity** Cellular Sieve, p. 361 ◆ BASIC TE **Group Activity** Drawing Cells, p. 362 BASIC TE **Activity** Cell Models, p. 363 GENERAL TE **Activity** Vacuole Model, p. 366 ◆ BASIC SE **Skills Practice Lab** Cells Alive!, p. 604 ◆ GENERAL CRF **Datasheet for LabBook*** LB **Whiz-Bang Demonstrations** Grand Strand* ◆ GENERAL LB **Labs You Can Eat** The Incredible Edible Cell* ◆ ADVANCED LB **Long-Term Projects & Research Ideas** Ewe Again, Dolly?* ◆ ADVANCED	CRF **Lesson Plans*** TR **Bellringer Transparency*** TR *LINK TO PHYSICAL SCIENCE* Structural Formulas* TR Organelles and Their Functions* CRF **SciLinks Activity*** GENERAL
PACING • 45 min pp. 368–371 **Section 3 The Organization of Living Things** • List three advantages of being multicellular. • Describe the four levels of organization in living things. • Explain the relationship between the structure and function of a part of an organism.	TE **Activity** Concept Mapping, p. 368 ◆ GENERAL TE **Activity** Explain It to a Friend, p. 371 BASIC SE **Science in Action** Math, Social Studies, and Language Arts Activities, pp. 378–379 GENERAL	CRF **Lesson Plans*** TR **Bellringer Transparency*** TR Levels of Organization in the Cardiovascular System*

PACING • 90 min

CHAPTER REVIEW, ASSESSMENT, AND STANDARDIZED TEST PREPARATION

CRF **Vocabulary Activity*** GENERAL
SE **Chapter Review,** pp. 374–375 GENERAL
CRF **Chapter Review*** ■ GENERAL
CRF **Chapter Tests A*** ■ GENERAL, **B*** ADVANCED, **C*** SPECIAL NEEDS
SE **Standardized Test Preparation,** pp. 376–377 GENERAL
CRF **Standardized Test Preparation*** GENERAL
CRF **Performance-Based Assessment*** GENERAL
OSP **Test Generator** GENERAL
CRF **Test Item Listing*** GENERAL

Online and Technology Resources

Visit **go.hrw.com** for a variety of free resources related to this textbook. Enter the keyword **HT5R7CEL**.

Holt Online Learning

Students can access interactive problem-solving help and active visual concept development with the *Holt Science and Technology* Online Edition available at **www.hrw.com**.

 Guided Reading Audio CD

These CDs are designed to help auditory learners and reluctant readers.

 Science Tutor CD-ROM

Excellent for remediation and test practice.

KEY		CRF	Chapter Resource File	SS	Science Skills Worksheets	*	Also on One-Stop Planner
		OSP	One-Stop Planner	MS	Math Skills for Science Worksheets	◆	Requires advance prep
SE	Student Edition	LB	Lab Bank	CD	CD or CD-ROM	■	Also available in Spanish
TE	Teacher Edition	TR	Transparencies	VID	Classroom Video/DVD		

SKILLS DEVELOPMENT RESOURCES	SECTION REVIEW AND ASSESSMENT	STANDARDS CORRELATIONS
SE Pre-Reading Activity, p. 350 GENERAL **OSP** Science Puzzlers, Twisters & Teasers GENERAL		North Carolina Standard Course of Study
CRF Directed Reading A* BASIC, B* SPECIAL NEEDS **CRF** Vocabulary and Section Summary* GENERAL **SE** Reading Strategy Reading Organizer, p. 352 GENERAL **TE** Inclusion Strategies, p. 353 **SE** Math Focus Surface Area-to-Volume Ratio, p. 354 GENERAL **TE** Reading Strategy Prediction Guide, p. 354 GENERAL **TE** Reading Strategy Prediction Guide, p. 355 GENERAL **TE** Research Be a Good Host, p. 357 GENERAL **MS** Math Skills for Science What Is a Ratio?* GENERAL **MS** Math Skills for Science Finding Perimeter and Area* GENERAL **MS** Math Skills for Science Finding Volume* GENERAL	**SE** Reading Checks, pp. 353, 354, 355, 357, 358 GENERAL **TE** Reteaching, p. 358 BASIC **TE** Quiz, p. 358 GENERAL **TE** Alternative Assessment, p. 358 GENERAL **SE** Section Review,* p. 359 ■ GENERAL **CRF** Section Quiz* ■ GENERAL	Chapter Lab: 1.06
CRF Directed Reading A* BASIC, B* SPECIAL NEEDS **CRF** Vocabulary and Section Summary* GENERAL **SE** Reading Strategy Reading Organizer, p. 360 GENERAL **SE** Connection to Language Arts The Great Barrier, p. 361 GENERAL **TE** Inclusion Strategies, p. 362 **TE** Reading Strategy Prediction Guide, p. 364 GENERAL **CRF** Critical Thinking Cellular Construction* ADVANCED **CRF** Reinforcement Worksheet Building a Eukaryotic Cell* BASIC	**SE** Reading Checks, pp. 360, 361, 362, 364, 366 GENERAL **TE** Homework, p. 361 GENERAL **TE** Homework, p. 363 GENERAL **TE** Homework, p. 365 GENERAL **TE** Reteaching, p. 366 BASIC **TE** Quiz, p. 366 GENERAL **TE** Alternative Assessment, p. 366 GENERAL **SE** Section Review,* p. 367 ■ GENERAL **CRF** Section Quiz* ■ GENERAL	
CRF Directed Reading A* BASIC, B* SPECIAL NEEDS **CRF** Vocabulary and Section Summary* GENERAL **SE** Reading Strategy Paired Summarizing, p. 368 GENERAL **SE** Math Practice A Pet Protist, p. 369 GENERAL	**SE** Reading Checks, pp. 368, 369, 370 GENERAL **TE** Homework, p. 369 GENERAL **TE** Reteaching, p. 370 BASIC **TE** Quiz, p. 370 GENERAL **TE** Alternative Assessment, p. 370 GENERAL **SE** Section Review,* p. 371 ■ GENERAL **CRF** Section Quiz* ■ GENERAL	

One-Stop Planner® CD-ROM

This convenient CD-ROM includes:
- Lab Materials QuickList Software
- Holt Calendar Planner
- Customizable Lesson Plans
- Printable Worksheets
- ExamView® Test Generator

CNN Student News™

cnnstudentnews.com

Find the latest news, lesson plans, and activities related to important scientific events.

SCI LINKS NSTA

www.scilinks.org

Maintained by the **National Science Teachers Association**. See Chapter Enrichment pages for a complete list of topics.

Current Science®

Check out *Current Science* articles and activities by visiting the HRW Web site at go.hrw.com. Just type in the keyword **HL5CS03T**.

Classroom Videos

- **Lab Videos** demonstrate the chapter lab.
- **Brain Food Video Quizzes** help students review the chapter material.
- **CNN Videos** bring science into your students' daily life.

Visual Resources

CHAPTER STARTER TRANSPARENCY

Cells: The Basic Units of Life — CHAPTER STARTER

What If . . . ?

Imagine this scene from a horror film. A young man sits down to dinner to find that his mother has made asparagus again. The young man eats the dreaded asparagus stalks. Later, he finds out that instead of being digested, one of the stalks has taken up residence inside his body and is very much alive! Too horrifying to think about? What if the asparagus began to do wonderful things for the young man, such as giving him more energy than he ever dreamed possible? Lynn Margulis, a scientist, thinks that something similar may have happened to certain one-celled organisms that lived more than a billion years ago, giving rise to the kinds of cells that we are made of today.

According to Margulis's theory, about 1.2 billion years ago, some larger cells began eating smaller cells for dinner. Like the white blood cell on this page, these larger cells trapped the smaller cells with extensions of their cell body. But some of these smaller cells resisted being digested. In fact, they began to do very well in their new homes. The larger cells also benefited from their new guests. The smaller cells released large amounts of energy from food taken in by the larger cells. Other kinds of small cells used the energy in sunlight to make enough food to feed themselves and the larger cell. The energy-producing structures of most cells, including yours, are thought to have descended from these smaller cells. In this chapter, you will learn more about cells and their structures.

BELLRINGER TRANSPARENCIES

Cells: The Basic Units of Life — BELLRINGER TRANSPARENCY

Section: The Diversity of Cells
Why do you think cells weren't discovered until 1665? What invention do you think made their discovery possible? Do you think people can ever see cells with the naked eye? Explain your answer.

Write your responses in your **science journal.**

Section: Eukaryotic Cells
List three differences between *prokaryotic* and *eukaryotic* cells. Draw two diagrams illustrating the differences.

Write your responses in your **science journal.**

TEACHING TRANSPARENCIES

L6 — Math Focus: Surface Area-to-Volume Ratio

L7 — Organelles and Their Functions

TEACHING TRANSPARENCIES

L5 — A Typical Eukaryotic Cell

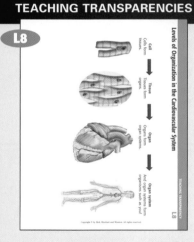

L8 — Levels of Organization in the Cardiovascular System

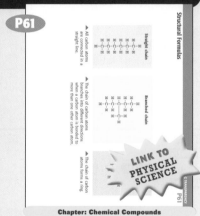

P61 — Structural Formulas

LINK TO PHYSICAL SCIENCE

Chapter: Chemical Compounds

CONCEPT MAPPING TRANSPARENCY

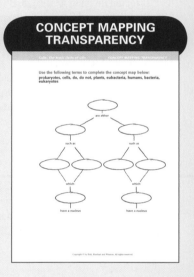

Cells: The Basic Units of Life — CONCEPT MAPPING TRANSPARENCY

Use the following terms to complete the concept map below: prokaryotes, cells, do, do not, plants, eubacteria, humans, bacteria, eukaryotes.

Planning Resources

LESSON PLANS

Lesson Plan — SAMPLE

Section: Waves

Pacing
Regular Schedule: with lab(s):2 days | without lab(s):2 days
Block Schedule: with lab(s):1 1/2 days | without lab(s):1 day

Objectives
1. Relate the seven properties of life to a living organism.
2. Describe seven themes that can help you to organize what you learn about biology.
3. Identify the tiny structures that make up all living organisms.
4. Differentiate between reproduction and heredity and between metabolism and homeostasis.

National Science Education Standards Covered
LSInter1:Cells have particular structures that underlie their functions.
LSMat1: Most cell functions involve chemical reactions.
LSBeh1:Cells store and use information to guide their functions.
UCP1:Cell functions are regulated.
SI1: Cells can differentiate and form complete multicellular organisms.
PS1: Species evolve over time.
ESS1: The great diversity of organisms is the result of more than 3.5 billion years of evolution.
ESS2: Natural selection and its evolutionary consequences provide a scientific explanation for the fossil record of ancient life forms as well as for the striking molecular similarities observed among the diverse species of living organisms.
ST1: The millions of different species of plants, animals, and microorganisms that live on Earth today are related by descent from common ancestors.
ST2: The energy for life primarily comes from the sun.
SPS1: The complexity and organization of organisms accommodates the need for obtaining, transforming, transporting, releasing, and eliminating the matter and energy used to sustain the organism.
SPS6: As matter and energy flows through different levels of organization of living systems—cells, organs, communities—and between living systems and the physical environment, chemical elements are recombined in different ways.
HNS1: Organisms have behavioral responses to internal changes and to external stimuli.

PARENT LETTER

SAMPLE

Dear Parent,

Your son's or daughter's science class will soon begin exploring the chapter entitled "The World of Physical Science." In this chapter, students will learn about how the scientific method applies to the world of physical science and the role of physical science in the world. By the end of the chapter, students should demonstrate a clear understanding of the chapter's main ideas and be able to discuss the following topics:

1. physical science as the study of energy and matter (Section 1)
2. the role of physical science in the world around them (Section 1)
3. careers that rely on physical science (Section 1)
4. the steps used in the scientific method (Section 2)
5. examples of technology (Section 2)
6. how the scientific method is used to answer questions and solve problems (Section 2)
7. how our knowledge of science changes over time (Section 2)
8. how models represent real objects or systems (Section 3)
9. examples of different ways models are used in science (Section 3)
10. the importance of the International System of Units (Section 4)
11. the appropriate units to use for particular measurements (Section 4)
12. how area and density are derived quantities (Section 4)

Questions to Ask Along the Way

You can help your son or daughter learn about these topics by asking interesting questions such as the following:

- What are some surprising careers that use physical science?
- What is a characteristic of a good hypothesis?
- When is it a good idea to use a model?
- Why do Americans measure things in terms of inches and yards instead of centimeters and meters?

TEST ITEM LISTING

TEST ITEM LISTING
The World of Science — SAMPLE

MULTIPLE CHOICE

1. A limitation of models is that
   a. they are large enough to see.
   b. they do not act exactly like the things that they model.
   c. they are smaller than the things that they model.
   d. they model unfamiliar things.
   Answer: B | Difficulty: 1 | Section: 3 | Objective: 2

2. The length 10 m is equal to
   a. 100 cm.   c. 10,000 mm.
   b. 1,000 cm.   d. Both (b) and (c)
   Answer: B | Difficulty: 1 | Section: 3 | Objective: 2

3. To be valid, a hypothesis must be
   a. testable.   c. made into a law.
   b. supported by evidence. d. Both (a) and (b)
   Answer: D | Difficulty: 1 | Section: 2 | Objective: 2

4. The statement "Stella has a stain on her shirt" is an example of a/n
   a. law.   c. observation.
   b. hypothesis.   d. prediction.
   Answer: B | Difficulty: 1 | Section: 2 | Objective: 2

5. A hypothesis is often developed out of
   a. observations.   c. laws.
   b. experiments.   d. Both (a) and (b)
   Answer: D | Difficulty: 1 | Section: 2 | Objective: 2

6. How many milliliters are in 3.5 kL?
   a. 3,500 mL   c. 3,500, 000 mL
   b. 0.0035 mL   d. 35,000 mL
   Answer: B | Difficulty: 1 | Section: 3 | Objective: 2

7. A map of Seattle is an example of a
   a. model.   c. theory.
   b. theory.   d. self.
   Answer: A | Difficulty: 1 | Section: 3 | Objective: 2

8. A lab has the safety icons shown below. These icons mean that you should wear
   a. only safety goggles.   c. safety goggles and a lab apron.
   b. only a lab apron.   d. safety goggles, a lab apron, and gloves.
   Answer: B | Difficulty: 1 | Section: 3 | Objective: 2

9. The law of conservation of mass says the list of mass before a chemical change is
   a. more than the total mass after the change.
   b. less than the total mass after the change.
   c. the same as the total mass after the change.
   d. not the same as the total mass after the change.
   Answer: B | Difficulty: 1 | Section: 3 | Objective: 2

10. In which of the following areas might you find a geochemist at work?
    a. studying the chemistry of rocks   c. studying the atmosphere
    b. studying forestry   d. studying the atmosphere
    Answer: B | Difficulty: 1 | Section: 3 | Objective: 2

One-Stop Planner® CD-ROM

This CD-ROM includes all of the resources shown here and the following time-saving tools:

- **Lab Materials QuickList Software**
- **Customizable lesson plans**
- **Holt Calendar Planner**
- **The powerful ExamView® Test Generator**

Meeting Individual Needs

DIRECTED READING A

BASIC

DIRECTED READING B

SPECIAL NEEDS

VOCABULARY ACTIVITY

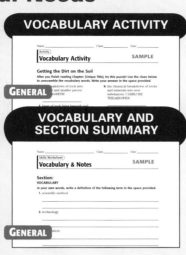

GENERAL

VOCABULARY AND SECTION SUMMARY

GENERAL

REINFORCEMENT

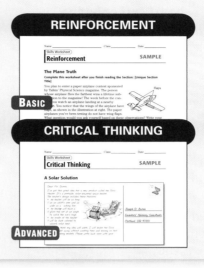

BASIC

CRITICAL THINKING

ADVANCED

SCILINKS ACTIVITY

GENERAL

SCIENCE PUZZLERS, TWISTERS & TEASERS

GENERAL

Labs and Activities

LONG-TERM PROJECTS & RESEARCH IDEAS

ADVANCED

WHIZ-BANG DEMONSTRATIONS

GENERAL

LABS YOU CAN EAT

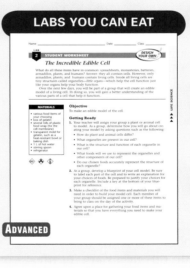

ADVANCED

DATASHEETS FOR QUICK LABS

DATASHEETS FOR CHAPTER LABS

DATASHEETS FOR LABBOOK

Review and Assessments

SECTION QUIZ

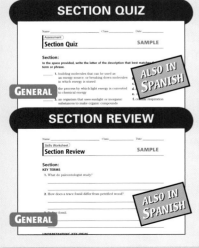

GENERAL

SECTION REVIEW

GENERAL

CHAPTER REVIEW

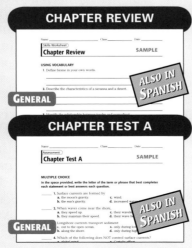

GENERAL

CHAPTER TEST A

GENERAL

CHAPTER TEST B

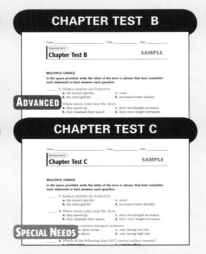

ADVANCED

CHAPTER TEST C

SPECIAL NEEDS

STANDARDIZED TEST PREPARATION

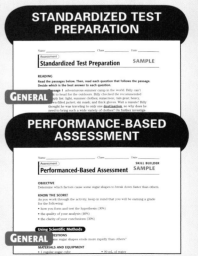

GENERAL

PERFORMANCE-BASED ASSESSMENT

GENERAL

This Chapter Enrichment provides relevant and interesting information to expand and enhance your presentation of the chapter material.

Section 1

The Diversity of Cells

Microtomy

- The development of high-magnification microscopes required that the preparation of specimens for viewing also become more sophisticated. Microtomy once referred only to specimen cutting, because a microtome is the instrument used to slice tissue sections. Today, microtomy refers collectively to the art of preparing specimens by any number of techniques.

- When microscopic organisms are viewed as whole- mounts, they are preserved, stained, dried (alcohol removes the water), and made transparent with clove or cedar oil. Then, the organism is mounted in a drop of resin on a glass slide and covered with a piece of glass only 0.005 mm thick.

Physiology and the Cell Theory

- The development of the cell theory aided research in other fields. In the mid-1800s, French physiologist Claude Bernard proposed that plants and animals are composed of sets of control mechanisms that work to maintain the internal conditions necessary for life. He recognized that a mammal can sustain a constant body temperature regardless of the outside temperature. Today, we recognize the ability of organisms to regulate their physiological processes to maintain specific conditions as *homeostasis*. But at the time, no one knew what the "organized sets of control mechanisms" were. The discovery of cells and the way their many components function to sustain life in an organism gave credence to Bernard's position.

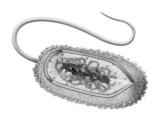

Is That a Fact!

- The Earth is 4.5 billion years old, and the oldest cell-like fossils are about 3.5 billion years old!

- Aeolid nudibranchs are mollusks that eat hydroids, small polyps that have protective stinging cells. The nudibranch's digestive system carefully sorts out the hydroid's stinging cells and sends them to the protective tentacles on the nudibranch's own back.

Section 2

Eukaryotic Cells

"Protein" Therapy

- Decades of investigation into cell biology have produced what scientists call *gene therapy*, which refers to the use of genetic material to cure disease. It might be more appropriate to call this rapidly expanding field of science *protein therapy*.

- The gene can be thought of as a recipe for the proteins essential to life. For example, people with Duchenne muscular dystrophy lack dystrophin, an essential muscle protein that maintains the structure of muscle cells. Researchers have been able to remove the harmful genetic components of a virus and replace them with the gene for dystrophin. Their plan is to inject the dystrophin gene (the gene that codes for the dystrophin protein) directly into the muscles of Duchenne muscular dystrophy patients. If the process is successful, the dystrophin gene in the virus will compensate for patients' faulty dystrophin gene.

Tiny Scientists?

- Microbiologists study the characteristics of bacteria and other microorganisms to understand how they interact with other organisms. Virologists investigate viruses, which are active only inside a living host cell. Mycologists study fungi, which include molds and yeasts. Environmental microbiologists inspect the water in rivers and lakes. Microbiologists in agriculture study organisms that affect soil quality and crops.

Is That a Fact!

◆ The oldest unquestionably eukaryotic fossil is about 2.1 billion years old.

Section 3

The Organization of Living Things

In a Heartbeat

● The heart will function properly only if the cells that form the connective tissue and muscle perform their jobs in coordination. Scientists can use an enzyme to dissolve an embryonic heart into its individual cells. When placed in a dish, these cells, called *myocytes,* will continue to beat, although they are out of sync with each other. After a couple of days, sheets of interconnected cells form, and the myocytes beat in unison. Why do these changes happen? Openings develop between cells that touch, and their cytoplasms connect, which allows the cells to communicate directly with each other.

Organs: Delicate Workhorses

● The most frequently transplanted organ is the kidney, followed by the liver, the heart, and the lung. Most transplants must be done within a few hours after the organ is removed from a donor because organs are too delicate to survive current long-term storage procedures.

● Cryobiologists, scientists who study how life systems tolerate low temperatures, are studying the possibility of storing organs and organ systems at subfreezing temperatures. They are investigating the fluids that keep insects and some frogs alive during subfreezing temperatures. Cryobiologists hope that this knowledge can be applied to human organs.

Development

● In a multicellular organism, almost every cell has the same set of genes. (Some specialized cells delete or duplicate sections of their DNA.) Yet, different cell types are structurally distinct and perform widely different functions. Part of the reason is that each cell expresses some genes but not others. Sometimes, genes can be expressed in tissues where they should not be. Doctors have occasionally operated on people and removed tumors that had hair and teeth!

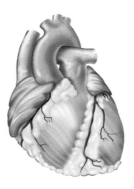

Is That a Fact!

◆ The oldest fossils of multicellular organisms are fossils of tiny algae approximately 1.2 billion years old.

◆ In 1931, a doctor removed a patient's parathyroid glands in error. These glands control the amount of calcium in the blood, which in turn regulates the heart. As a last-ditch effort to save the patient, a cow's parathyroid glands were ground up and injected into the patient. The patient recuperated and lived another 30 years with similar treatments.

SCiLINKS.

NSTA
Developed and maintained by the
National Science Teachers Association

SciLinks is maintained by the National Science Teachers Association to provide you and your students with interesting, up-to-date links that will enrich your classroom presentation of the chapter.

Visit www.scilinks.org and enter the SciLinks code for more information about the topic listed.

Topic: Prokaryotic Cells
SciLinks code: HSM1225

Topic: Eukaryotic Cells
SciLinks code: HSM0541

Topic: Cell Structures
SciLinks code: HSM0240

Topic: Archaebacteria
SciLinks code: HSM0091

Topic: Organization of Life
SciLinks code: HSM1080

Topic: Body Systems
SciLinks code: HSM0184

Overview

This chapter will help students understand the great diversity of cells. The chapter will take students from the time when cells were unknown through the discovery of cells to the understanding of the tremendous diversity of cells. Students will learn about cell structures and will also learn how cells, tissues, and organs form organisms.

Assessing Prior Knowledge

Students should be familiar with the following topic:

- characteristics of a living thing

Identifying Misconceptions

Students may not understand that all cells and organisms have the same basic structures. Also, students may not have a sense of scale. When asked to draw a molecule, most students will draw something that resembles a cell. Instruction should emphasize the relationship between molecules and cells. For example, many students believe that proteins and molecules are bigger than cells.

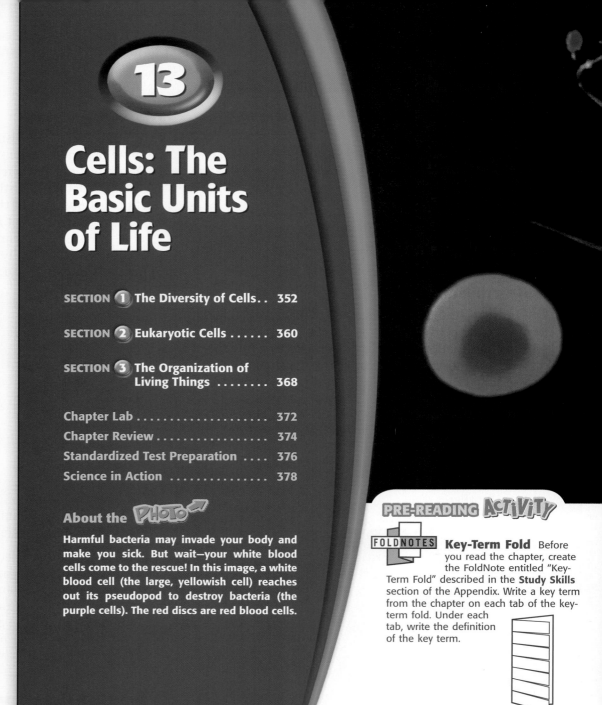

13

Cells: The Basic Units of Life

About the PHOTO

Harmful bacteria may invade your body and make you sick. But wait—your white blood cells come to the rescue! In this image, a white blood cell (the large, yellowish cell) reaches out its pseudopod to destroy bacteria (the purple cells). The red discs are red blood cells.

PRE-READING ACTIVITY

FOLDNOTES **Key-Term Fold** Before you read the chapter, create the FoldNote entitled "Key-Term Fold" described in the **Study Skills** section of the Appendix. Write a key term from the chapter on each tab of the key-term fold. Under each tab, write the definition of the key term.

Standards Correlations

North Carolina Standard Course of Study

1.06 (partial) Use mathematics to gather, organize, and present quantitative data resulting from scientific investigations: Measurement [and] Analysis of data . . . (Chapter Lab)

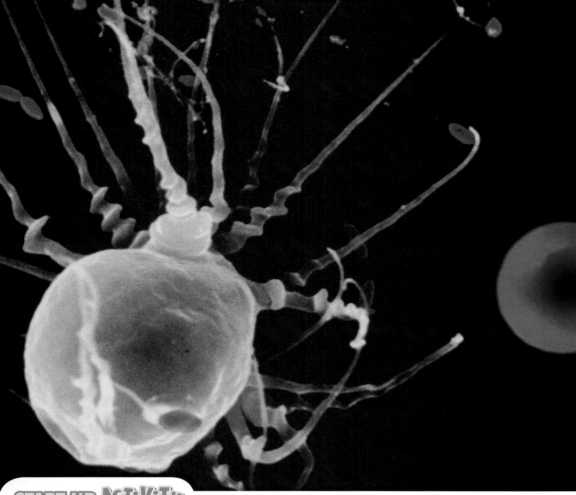

START-UP ACTIVITY

MATERIALS

FOR EACH STUDENT
- coverslip, plastic
- Elodea, small leaf
- forceps
- microscope
- microscope slide, plastic
- water

Safety Caution: Remind students to review all safety cautions and icons before beginning this activity.

Answers

1. Students should be able to describe accurately the cells that they see. Students should observe that all of the cells share similar structures but the cells may not be exactly the same.

2. Accept all reasonable responses. Students may note that plant cells differ from human body cells but that plant and animal cells share many of the same structures.

START-UP ACTIVITY

What Are Plants Made Of?

All living things, including plants, are made of cells. What do plant cells look like? Do this activity to find out.

Procedure

1. Tear off a **small leaf** from near the tip of an **Elodea sprig.**

2. Using **forceps,** place the whole leaf in a **drop of water** on a **microscope slide.**

3. Place a **coverslip** on top of the water drop by putting one edge of the coverslip on the slide near the water drop. Next, lower the coverslip slowly so that the coverslip does not trap air bubbles.

4. Place the slide on your **microscope.**

5. Using the lowest-powered lens first, find the plant cells. When you can see the cells under the lower-powered lens, switch to a higher-powered lens.

6. Draw a picture of what you see.

Analysis

1. Describe the shape of the *Elodea* cells. Are all of the cells in the *Elodea* the same?

2. Do you think human cells look like *Elodea* cells? How do you think they are different? How might they be similar?

What If . . . ?

Imagine this scene from a horror film. A young man sits down to dinner to find that his mother has made asparagus again. The young man eats the dreaded asparagus stalks. Later, he finds out that instead of being digested, one of the stalks has taken up residence inside his body and is very much alive! Too horrifying to think about? What if the asparagus began to do wonderful things for the young man, such as giving him more energy than he ever dreamed possible? Lynn Margulis, a scientist, thinks that something similar may have

According to Margulis's theory, about 1.2 billion years ago, some larger cells began eating smaller cells for dinner. Like the white blood cell on this page, these larger cells trapped the smaller cells with extensions of their cell body. But some of these smaller cells resisted being digested. In fact, they began to do very well in their new homes. The larger cells also benefited from these new guests. The smaller cells released large amounts of energy from food taken in by the larger cells. Other kinds of small cells used the energy in sunlight to make enough food to feed themselves and their larger cell

Chapter Starter Transparency
Use this transparency to help students begin thinking about cells, cell structures, and organisms.

CHAPTER RESOURCES

Technology

 **Transparencies**
- Chapter Starter Transparency

READING SKILLS

Student Edition on CD-ROM

Guided Reading Audio CD

Classroom Videos
- Brain Food Video Quiz

Workbooks

Science Puzzlers, Twisters & Teasers
- Cells: The Basic Units of Life **GENERAL**

Chapter 13 • Cells: The Basic Units of Life **351**

Focus

Overview

This section introduces students to cells, their discovery, and their diversity. Students will learn about the parts of a cell and the reason that cells are so small. Finally, students will learn about eubacterial, archaebacterial, and eukaryotic cells.

Bellringer

Write the following questions on the board:

Why weren't cells discovered until 1665? What invention made their discovery possible? (Cells weren't discovered until 1665 because almost all cells are too small to be seen with the naked eye. The microscope is the invention that made their discovery possible.)

Motivate

ACTIVITY ——————— GENERAL

Modeling Cell Discovery Before students begin this section, have them model Robert Hooke's discovery. Organize the class into small groups. Provide each group with a microscope and a prepared slide of cork cells. Have students describe and sketch their observations. **LS Visual**

The Diversity of Cells

Most cells are so small they can't be seen by the naked eye. So how did scientists find cells? By accident, that's how! The first person to see cells wasn't even looking for them.

All living things are made of tiny structures called cells. A **cell** is the smallest unit that can perform all the processes necessary for life. Because of their size, cells weren't discovered until microscopes were invented in the mid-1600s.

Cells and the Cell Theory

Robert Hooke was the first person to describe cells. In 1665, he built a microscope to look at tiny objects. One day, he looked at a thin slice of cork. Cork is found in the bark of cork trees. The cork looked like it was made of little boxes. Hooke named these boxes *cells,* which means "little rooms" in Latin. Hooke's cells were really the outer layers of dead cork cells. Hooke's microscope and his drawing of the cork cells are shown in **Figure 1.**

Hooke also looked at thin slices of living plants. He saw that they too were made of cells. Some cells were even filled with "juice." The "juicy" cells were living cells.

Hooke also looked at feathers, fish scales, and the eyes of houseflies. But he spent most of his time looking at plants and fungi. The cells of plants and fungi have cell walls. This makes them easy to see. Animal cells do not have cell walls. This absence of cell walls makes it harder to see the outline of animal cells. Because Hooke couldn't see their cells, he thought that animals weren't made of cells.

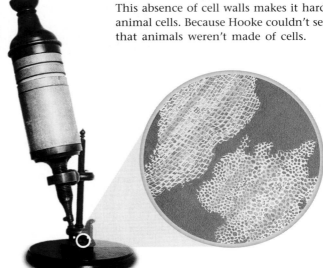

Figure 1 *Hooke discovered cells using this microscope. Hooke's drawing of cork cells is shown to the right of his microscope.*

CHAPTER RESOURCES

Chapter Resource File

- **Lesson Plan**
- **Directed Reading A** BASIC
- **Directed Reading B** SPECIAL NEEDS

Technology

- **Transparencies**
  - Bellringer

Cultural Awareness   GENERAL

Yeast Yeast is a fungus. Yeast used in baking is related to wild fungi living in the air around us. Strains of native yeasts vary regionally. For example, sourdough from San Francisco has its characteristic taste because bakers there use a yeast that is common in the air around that city. Not all breads require yeast. Many cultures have flat breads, such as tortillas from Mexico.

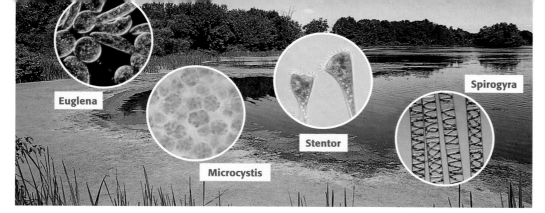

Euglena

Spirogyra

Stentor

Microcystis

Finding Cells in Other Organisms

In 1673, Anton van Leeuwenhoek (LAY vuhn HOOK), a Dutch merchant, made his own microscopes. Leeuwenhoek used one of his microscopes to look at pond scum. Leeuwenhoek saw small organisms in the water. He named these organisms *animalcules,* which means "little animals." Today, we call these single-celled organisms protists (PROH tists). Pond scum and some of the protists it contains are shown in **Figure 2.**

Leeuwenhoek also looked at animal blood. He saw differences in blood cells from different kinds of animals. For example, blood cells in fish, birds, and frogs are oval. Blood cells in humans and dogs are round and flat. Leeuwenhoek was also the first person to see bacteria. And he discovered that yeasts that make bread dough rise are single-celled organisms.

The Cell Theory

Almost 200 years passed before scientists concluded that cells are present in all living things. Scientist Matthias Schleiden (mah THEE uhs SHLIE duhn) studied plants. In 1838, he concluded that all plant parts were made of cells. Theodor Schwann (TAY oh dohr SHVAHN) studied animals. In 1839, Schwann concluded that all animal tissues were made of cells. Soon after that, Schwann wrote the first two parts of what is now known as the *cell theory.*

- All organisms are made of one or more cells.
- The cell is the basic unit of all living things.

Later, in 1858, Rudolf Virchow (ROO dawlf FIR koh), a doctor, stated that all cells could form only from other cells. Virchow then added the third part of the cell theory.

- All cells come from existing cells.

Reading Check What are the three parts of the cell theory? (*See the Appendix for answers to Reading Checks.*)

Figure 2 *The green area at the edge of the pond is a layer of pond scum. This pond scum contains organisms called* protists, *such as those shown above.*

cell in biology, the smallest unit that can perform all life processes; cells are covered by a membrane and have DNA and cytoplasm

CONNECTION TO Physics

Microscopes The microscope Hooke used to study cells was much different from microscopes today. Research different kinds of microscopes, such as light microscopes, scanning electron microscopes (SEMs), and transmission electron microscopes (TEMs). Select one type of microscope. Make a poster or other presentation to show to the class. Describe how the microscope works and how it is used. Be sure to include images.

ACTIVITY

Answer to Reading Check
All organisms are made of one or more cells, the cell is the basic unit of all living things, and all cells come from existing cells.

Prediction Guide Before students read this page, ask them to choose one of the following reasons for why they think cells are so small:

1. There isn't enough microscopic food available for them.

2. There isn't enough room in a multicellular organism.

3. another reason (ask for suggestions)

Have students evaluate their answer after they read the page. **LS Logical**

MISCONCEPTION ALERT

Molecular Mix-Up The physical relationship between molecules and cells may be confusing to students. Molecules are not alive and are much smaller than cells. Cells and cell structures are made of molecules.

Answer to Reading Check

If a cell's volume gets too large, the cell's surface area will not be able to take in enough nutrients or get rid of wastes fast enough to keep the cell alive.

Cell Size

Most cells are too small to be seen without a microscope. It would take 50 human cells to cover the dot on this letter *i*.

A Few Large Cells

Most cells are small. A few, however, are big. The yolk of a chicken egg, shown in **Figure 3,** is one big cell. The egg can be this large because it does not have to take in more nutrients.

Figure 3 *The white and yolk of this chicken egg provide nutrients for the development of a chick.*

Many Small Cells

There is a physical reason why most cells are so small. Cells take in food and get rid of wastes through their outer surface. As a cell gets larger, it needs more food and produces more waste. Therefore, more materials pass through its outer surface.

As the cell's volume increases, its surface area grows too. But the cell's volume grows faster than its surface area. If a cell gets too large, the cell's surface area will not be large enough to take in enough nutrients or pump out enough wastes. So, the area of a cell's surface—compared with the cell's volume—limits the cell's size. The ratio of the cell's outer surface area to the cell's volume is called the *surface area–to-volume ratio,* which can be calculated by using the following equation:

$$surface\ area\text{–}to\text{-}volume\ ratio = \frac{surface\ area}{volume}$$

✔ **Reading Check** Why are most cells small?

 **MATH FOCUS**

Surface Area-to-Volume Ratio Calculate the surface area–to-volume ratio of a cube whose sides measure 2 cm.

Step 1: Calculate the surface area.

$$surface\ area\ of\ cube = number\ of\ sides \times area\ of\ side$$

$$surface\ area\ of\ cube = 6 \times (2\ cm \times 2\ cm)$$

$$surface\ area\ of\ cube = 24\ cm^2$$

Step 2: Calculate the volume.

$$volume\ of\ cube = side \times side \times side$$

$$volume\ of\ cube = 2\ cm \times 2\ cm \times 2\ cm$$

$$volume\ of\ cube = 8\ cm^3$$

Step 3: Calculate the surface area–to-volume ratio.

$$surface\ area\text{–}to\text{-}volume\ ratio = \frac{surface\ area}{volume} = \frac{24}{8} = \frac{3}{1}$$

Now It's Your Turn

1. Calculate the surface area–to-volume ratio of a cube whose sides are 3 cm long.

2. Calculate the surface area–to-volume ratio of a cube whose sides are 4 cm long.

3. Of the cubes from questions 1 and 2, which has the greater surface area–to-volume ratio?

4. What is the relationship between the length of a side and the surface area–to-volume ratio of a cell?

CHAPTER RESOURCES

Technology

 Transparencies
• Math Focus: Surface Area–to-Volume Ratio

Answers to Math Focus

1. Surface area of cube (SA) =
   (3 cm × 3 cm) × 6 = 54 cm²
   Volume of cube (V) =
   3 cm × 3 cm × 3 cm = 27 cm³
   SA:V ratio = 54:27 or 2:1

2. SA = (4 cm × 4 cm) × 6 = 96 cm²
   V = 4 cm × 4 cm × 4 cm = 64 cm³
   SA:V = 96:64 or 1.5:1

3. the cube whose sides are 3 cm long

4. The larger the cell is, the smaller the surface-to-volume ratio is.

Parts of a Cell

Cells come in many shapes and sizes. Cells have many different functions. But all cells have the following parts in common.

The Cell Membrane and Cytoplasm

All cells are surrounded by a cell membrane. The **cell membrane** is a protective layer that covers the cell's surface and acts as a barrier. It separates the cell's contents from its environment. The cell membrane also controls materials going into and out of the cell. Inside the cell is a fluid. This fluid and almost all of its contents are called the *cytoplasm* (SIET oh PLAZ uhm).

Organelles

Cells have organelles that carry out various life processes. **Organelles** are structures that perform specific functions within the cell. Different types of cells have different organelles. Most organelles are surrounded by membranes. For example, the algal cell in **Figure 4** has membrane-bound organelles. Some organelles float in the cytoplasm. Other organelles are attached to membranes or other organelles.

✓ **Reading Check** What are organelles?

Genetic Material

All cells contain DNA (**d**eoxyribo**n**ucleic **a**cid) at some point in their life. *DNA* is the genetic material that carries information needed to make new cells and new organisms. DNA is passed on from parent cells to new cells and controls the activities of a cell. **Figure 5** shows the DNA of a bacterium.

In some cells, the DNA is enclosed inside an organelle called the **nucleus.** For example, your cells have a nucleus. In contrast, bacterial cells do not have a nucleus.

In humans, mature red blood cells lose their DNA. Red blood cells are made inside bones. When red blood cells are first made, they have a nucleus with DNA. But before they enter the bloodstream, red blood cells lose their nucleus and DNA. They survive with no new instructions from their DNA.

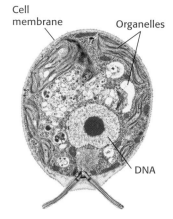

Cell membrane

Organelles

DNA

Figure 4 *This green alga has organelles. The organelles and the fluid surrounding them make up the cytoplasm.*

cell membrane a phospholipid layer that covers a cell's surface; acts as a barrier between the inside of a cell and the cell's environment

organelle one of the small bodies in a cell's cytoplasm that are specialized to perform a specific function

nucleus in a eukaryotic cell, a membrane-bound organelle that contains the cell's DNA and that has a role in processes such as growth, metabolism, and reproduction

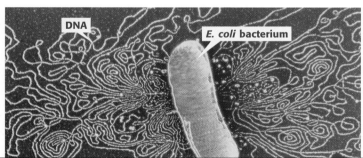

DNA

E. coli bacterium

Figure 5 *This photo shows an* Escherichia coli *bacterium. The bacterium's cell membrane has been treated so that the cell's DNA is released.*

CONNECTION to Earth Science — GENERAL

Subsurface Cells Astronomers are interested in the work of scientists who investigate bacteria and other microscopic organisms in Earth's crust. Microbiologists have drilled deep into the crust and found microbes nearly 3 km below the surface, where the temperature is 75°C (167°F). Because other planets have surface conditions similar to the harsh environment within the Earth's crust, astronomers believe that microbes may live elsewhere in the solar system. Have students research and write a brief report on the conditions in Earth's crust, and have students learn about the organisms that live there. **LS** Verbal

Bacteria in Your Lunch?

Most of the time, you don't want bacteria in your food. Many bacteria make toxins that will make you sick. However, some foods—such as yogurt—are supposed to have bacteria in them! The bacteria in these foods are not dangerous.

In yogurt, masses of rod-shaped bacteria feed on the sugar (lactose) in milk. The bacteria convert the sugar into lactic acid. Lactic acid causes milk to thicken. This thickened milk makes yogurt.

1. Using a **cotton swab,** put a **small dot of yogurt** on a **microscope slide.**
2. Add a **drop of water.** Use the cotton swab to stir.
3. Add a **coverslip.**
4. Use a **microscope** to examine the slide. Draw what you observe.

prokaryote an organism that consists of a single cell that does not have a nucleus

Two Kinds of Cells

All cells have cell membranes, organelles, cytoplasm, and DNA in common. But there are two basic types of cells—cells without a nucleus and cells with a nucleus. Cells with no nucleus are *prokaryotic* (proh KAR ee AHT ik) *cells.* Cells that have a nucleus are *eukaryotic* (yoo KAR ee AHT ik) *cells.* Prokaryotic cells are further classified into two groups: *eubacteria* (yoo bak TIR ee uh) and *archaebacteria* (AHR kee bak TIR ee uh).

Prokaryotes: Eubacteria and Archaebacteria

Eubacteria and archaebacteria are prokaryotes (pro KAR ee OHTS). **Prokaryotes** are single-celled organisms that do not have a nucleus or membrane-bound organelles.

Eubacteria

The most common prokaryotes are eubacteria (or just *bacteria*). Bacteria are the world's smallest cells. These tiny organisms live almost everywhere. Bacteria do not have a nucleus, but they do have DNA. A bacteria's DNA is a long, circular molecule, shaped sort of like a rubber band. Bacteria have no membrane-covered organelles. But they do have ribosomes. *Ribosomes* are tiny, round organelles made of protein and other material.

Bacteria also have a strong, weblike exterior cell wall. This wall helps the cell retain its shape. A bacterium's cell membrane is just inside the cell wall. Together, the cell wall and cell membrane allow materials into and out of the cell.

Some bacteria live in the soil and water. Others live in, or on, other organisms. For example, you have bacteria living on your skin and teeth. You also have bacteria living in your digestive system. These bacteria help the process of digestion. A typical bacterial cell is shown in **Figure 6.**

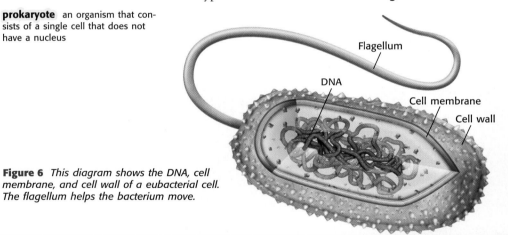

Figure 6 *This diagram shows the DNA, cell membrane, and cell wall of a eubacterial cell. The flagellum helps the bacterium move.*

Archaebacteria Have students work in pairs to find out if archaebacteria are more similar to eubacteria or eukaryotes. What kinds of evidence do scientists use to answer this question? Have students make a poster or other visual presentation of their results. **LS** Visual/Interpersonal

WEIRD SCIENCE

In 1969, the *Apollo 12* crew retrieved a space probe from the moon that had been launched nearly 3 years earlier. NASA scientists found a stowaway in the probe's camera. The bacterium *Streptococcus mitis* had traveled to the moon and back. Despite the rigors of space travel, more than 2.5 years of radiation exposure, and freezing temperatures, the *Streptococcus mitis* was successfully reconstituted.

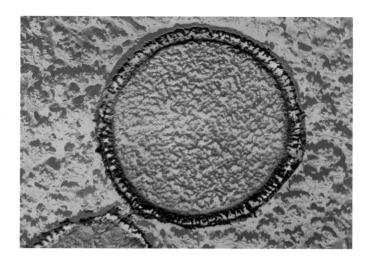

Figure 7 *This photograph, taken with an electron microscope, is of an archaebacterium that lives in the very high temperatures of deep-sea volcanic vents. The photograph has been colored so that the cell wall is green and the cell contents are pink.*

Archaebacteria

The second kind of prokaryote are the archaebacteria. These organisms are also called *archaea* (ahr KEE uh). Archaebacteria are similar to bacteria in some ways. For example, both are single-celled organisms. Both have ribosomes, a cell membrane, and circular DNA. And both lack a nucleus and membrane-bound organelles. But archaebacteria are different from bacteria. For example, archaebacterial ribosomes are different from eubacterial ribosomes.

Archaebacteria are similar to eukaryotic cells in some ways, too. For example, archaebacterial ribosomes are more like the ribosomes of eukaryotic cells. But archaebacteria also have some features that no other cells have. For example, the cell wall and cell membranes of archaebacteria are different from the cell walls of other organisms. And some archaebacteria live in places where no other organisms could live.

Three types of archaebacteria are *heat-loving, salt-loving,* and *methane-making.* Methane is a kind of gas frequently found in swamps. Heat-loving and salt-lovng archaebacteria are sometimes called extremophiles. *Extremophiles* live in places where conditions are extreme. They live in very hot water, such as in hot springs, or where the water is extremely salty. **Figure 7** shows one kind of methane-making archaebacteria that lives deep in the ocean near volcanic vents. The temperature of the water from those vents is extreme: it is above the boiling point of water at sea level.

Reading Check What is one difference between eubacteria and archaebacteria?

CONNECTION TO Social Studies

Where Do They Live?
While most archaebacteria live in extreme environments, scientists have found that archaebacteria live almost everywhere. Do research about archaebacteria. Select one kind of archaebacteria. Create a poster showing the geographical location where the organism lives, describing its physical environment, and explaining how it survives in its environment.

ACTIVITY

Answer to Reading Check
One difference between eubacteria and archaea is that bacterial ribosomes are different from archaebacterial ribosomes.

Reteaching — BASIC

Drawing Cells Ask students to create a short picture book. Have them draw a picture of a typical prokaryotic cell on one page. Have them draw a picture of a typical eukaryotic cell on the next page. Students should label all the parts of both cells.
LS Visual

Quiz — GENERAL

1. When Robert Hooke saw "juice" in some cells, what was he looking at? (cytoplasm)

2. Why did Hooke think that cells existed only in plants and fungi and not in animals? (Plant and fungal cells have cell walls. Hooke's microscope wasn't strong enough to view the more delicate cell membranes of animal cells.)

Alternative Assessment — GENERAL

Writing **Vocabulary Game**
Organize the students into groups, and assign two or three vocabulary words to each group. Ask students to write a descriptive statement about each word without using the vocabulary word in the sentence. Each group should challenge the other groups to guess the word described. For example, if "genetic material" is the definition, "What is DNA?" is the correct response. **LS** Verbal

eukaryote an organism made up of cells that have a nucleus enclosed by a membrane; eukaryotes include animals, plants, and fungi, but not archaebacteria or eubacteria

Eukaryotic Cells and Eukaryotes

Eukaryotic cells are the largest cells. Most eukaryotic cells are still microscopic, but they are about 10 times larger than most bacterial cells. A typical eukaryotic cell is shown in **Figure 8.**

Unlike bacteria and archaebacteria, eukaryotic cells have a nucleus. The nucleus is one kind of membrane-bound organelle. A cell's nucleus holds the cell's DNA. Eukaryotic cells have other membrane-bound organelles as well. Organelles are like the different organs in your body. Each kind of organelle has a specific job in the cell. Together, organelles, such as the ones shown in **Figure 8,** perform all the processes necessary for life.

All living things that are not bacteria or archaebacteria are made of one or more eukaryotic cells. Organisms made of eukaryotic cells are called **eukaryotes.** Many eukaryotes are multicellular. *Multicellular* means "many cells." Multicellular organisms are usually larger than single-cell organisms. So, most organisms you see with your naked eye are eukaryotes. There are many types of eukaryotes. Animals, including humans, are eukaryotes. So are plants. Some protists, such as amoebas, are single-celled eukaryotes. Other protists, including some types of green algae, are multicellular eukaryotes. Fungi are organisms such as mushrooms or yeasts. Mushrooms are multicellular eukaryotes. Yeasts are single-celled eukaryotes.

✓ *Reading Check* How are eukaryotes different from prokaryotes?

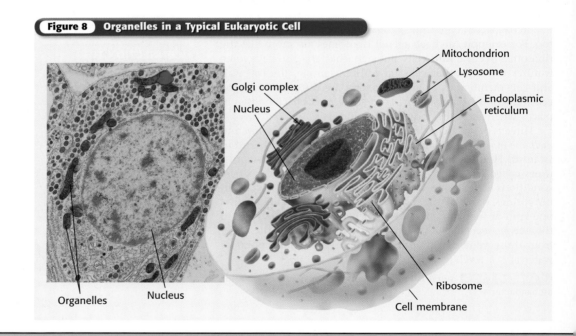

Figure 8 **Organelles in a Typical Eukaryotic Cell**

Golgi complex
Nucleus
Mitochondrion
Lysosome
Endoplasmic reticulum
Ribosome
Cell membrane
Organelles
Nucleus

Answer to Reading Check
The main difference between prokaryotes and eukaryotes is that eukaryotic cells have a nucleus and membrane-bound organelles and prokaryotic cells do not.

INTERNET ACTIVITY
Brochure — GENERAL

For an internet activity related to this chapter, have students go to **go.hrw.com** and type in the keyword **HL5CELW.**

Summary

- Cells were not discovered until microscopes were invented in the 1600s.
- Cell theory states that all organisms are made of cells, the cell is the basic unit of all living things, and all cells come from other cells.
- All cells have a cell membrane, cytoplasm, and DNA.
- Most cells are too small to be seen with the naked eye. A cell's surface area–to-volume ratio limits the size of a cell.

- The two basic kinds of cells are prokaryotic cells and eukaryotic cells. Eukaryotic cells have a nucleus and membrane-bound organelles. Prokaryotic cells do not.
- Prokaryotes are classified as archaebacteria and eubacteria.
- Archaebacterial cell walls and ribosomes are different from the cell walls and ribosomes of other organisms.
- Eukaryotes can be single-celled or multicellular.

Using Key Terms

1. In your own words, write a definition for the term *organelle*.

2. Use the following terms in the same sentence: *prokaryotic, nucleus,* and *eukaryotic.*

Understanding Key Ideas

3. Cell size is limited by the
   a. thickness of the cell wall.
   b. size of the cell's nucleus.
   c. cell's surface area–to-volume ratio.
   d. amount of cytoplasm in the cell.

4. What are the three parts of the cell theory?

5. Name three structures that every cell has.

6. Give two ways in which archaebacteria are different from bacteria.

Critical Thinking

7. **Applying Concepts** You have discovered a new single-celled organism. It has a cell wall, ribosomes, and long, circular DNA. Is it a eukaryote or a prokaryote cell? Explain.

8. **Identifying Relationships** One of your students brings you a cell about the size of the period at the end of this sentence. It is a single cell, but it also forms chains. What characteristics would this cell have if the organism is a eukaryote? If it is a prokaryote? What would you look for first?

Interpreting Graphics

The picture below shows a particular organism. Use the picture to answer the questions that follow.

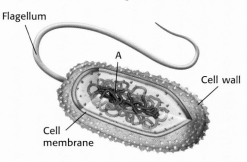

Flagellum

A

Cell wall

Cell membrane

9. What type of organism does the picture represent? How do you know?

10. Which structure helps the organism move?

11. What part of the organism does the letter *A* represent?

SCI LINKS®

NSTA
Developed and maintained by the
National Science Teachers Association

For a variety of links related to this chapter, go to www.scilinks.org
Topic: Prokaryotic Cells
SciLinks code: HSM1225

CHAPTER RESOURCES

Chapter Resource File

 • Section Quiz **GENERAL**
  • Section Review **GENERAL**
  • Vocabulary and Section Summary **GENERAL**
  • Reinforcement Worksheet **BASIC**

Technology

 Transparencies
  • A Typical Eukaryotic Cell

Answers to Section Review

1. Sample answer: An organelle is a structure inside a cell that performs a specific function for the cell.

2. Sample answer: Eukaryotic cells have a nucleus, but prokaryotic cells do not.

3. c

4. All organisms are made of one or more cells, the cell is the basic unit of all living things, and all cells come from existing cells.

5. Every cell has a cell membrane, DNA, and cytoplasm.

6. Sample answer: The cell walls and the ribosomes of archaebacteria are different from those structures in eubacteria.

7. Sample answer: The cell is probably a prokaryote; The key is that it does not appear to have a nucleus and its DNA is long and circular.

8. Sample answer: eukaryote: whether the chains were a multicellular organism or a collection of individual cells, membrane-bound organelles, certain types of ribosomes and certain materials in the cell membranes, where the DNA is located, and a nucleus; prokaryote: other types of ribosomes and cell membrane materials, the structure of the DNA, and a nucleus; The first thing I would look for is a nucleus.

9. a typical eubacterial cell; It has no nucleus, and its DNA is long and circular.

10. the flagellum

11. the cell's DNA

Focus

Overview

In this section, students will learn the names and functions of the cell structures, called *organelles,* in a eukaryotic cell.

◉ Bellringer

On the board, write the following:

List three differences between prokaryotic and eukaryotic cells. (Prokaryotic cells have circular DNA, no nucleus, and no membrane-covered organelles. Eukaryotic cells have linear DNA, a nucleus, and membrane-covered organelles.)

Motivate

Discussion —— GENERAL

Cellular Activity Ask students if they can feel the flurry of activity within their cells that keeps them alive. (no; But even though students can't feel activity in the cells, they can feel the heat produced by cellular activity. Students are not likely to know this.)

Ask students how they know their cells are working. (The students are alive: they can breathe, digest food, and move.) **LS** Logical/Intrapersonal

Answer to Reading Check

Plant, algae, and fungi cells have cell walls.

READING WARM-UP

Objectives
● Identify the different parts of a eukaryotic cell.
● Explain the function of each part of a eukaryotic cell.

Terms to Learn

cell wall   mitochondrion
ribosome   Golgi complex
endoplasmic   vesicle
  reticulum   lysosome

READING STRATEGY

Reading Organizer As you read this section, make a table comparing plant cells and animal cells.

cell wall a rigid structure that surrounds the cell membrane and provides support to the cell

Eukaryotic Cells

Most eukaryotic cells are small. For a long time after cells were discovered, scientists could not see what was going on inside cells. They did not know how complex cells are.

Now, scientists know a lot about eukaryotic cells. These cells have many parts that work together and keep the cell alive.

Cell Wall

Some eukaryotic cells have cell walls. A **cell wall** is a rigid structure that gives support to a cell. The cell wall is the outermost structure of a cell. Plants and algae have cell walls made of cellulose (SEL yoo LOHS) and other materials. *Cellulose* is a complex sugar that most animals can't digest.

The cell walls of plant cells allow plants to stand upright. In some plants, the cells must take in water for the cell walls to keep their shape. When such plants lack water, the cell walls collapse and the plant droops. **Figure 1** shows a cross section of a plant cell and a close-up of the cell wall.

Fungi, including yeasts and mushrooms, also have cell walls. Some fungi have cell walls made of *chitin* (KIE tin). Other fungi have cell walls made from a chemical similar to chitin. Eubacteria and archaebacteria also have cell walls, but those walls are different from plant or fungal cell walls.

✓ Reading Check What types of cells have cell walls? (*See the Appendix for answers to Reading Checks.*)

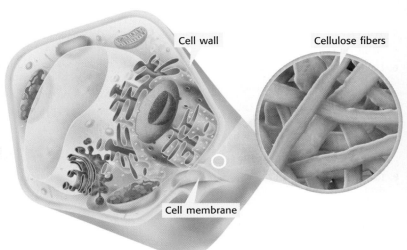

Figure 1 *The cell walls of plant cells help plants retain their shape. Plant cell walls are made of cellulose.*

Cell wall

Cellulose fibers

Cell membrane

CHAPTER RESOURCES

Chapter Resource File

• **Lesson Plan**
• **Directed Reading A** BASIC
• **Directed Reading B** SPECIAL NEEDS

Technology

Transparencies
• Bellringer

MISCONCEPTION /// ALERT \\\

Cells Are Three-Dimensional Students often think of cells as flat. Looking at pictures and even viewing cells in a microscope can reinforce that misconception. Make sure that students understand that even though most cells are very small, they do have three dimensions, and they do take up space.

Cell Membrane

All cells have a cell membrane. The *cell membrane* is a protective barrier that encloses a cell. It separates the cell's contents from the cell's environment. The cell membrane is the outermost structure in cells that lack a cell wall. In cells that have a cell wall, the cell membrane lies just inside the cell wall.

The cell membrane contains proteins, lipids, and phospholipids. *Lipids,* which include fats and cholesterol, are a group of compounds that do not dissolve in water. The cell membrane has two layers of phospholipids (FAHS foh LIP idz), shown in **Figure 2.** A *phospholipid* is a lipid that contains phosphorus. Lipids are "water fearing," or *hydrophobic.* Lipid ends of phospholipids form the inner part of the membrane. Phosphorus-containing ends of the phospholipids are "water loving," or *hydrophilic.* These ends form the outer part of the membrane.

Some of the proteins and lipids control the movement of materials into and out of the cell. Some of the proteins form passageways. Nutrients and water move into the cell, and wastes move out of the cell, through these protein passageways.

✓ **Reading Check** What are two functions of a cell membrane?

CONNECTION TO Language Arts

WRITING SKILL **The Great Barrier** In your **science journal,** write a science fiction story about tiny travelers inside a person's body. These little explorers need to find a way into or out of a cell to solve a problem. You may need to do research to find out more about how the cell membrane works. Illustrate your story.

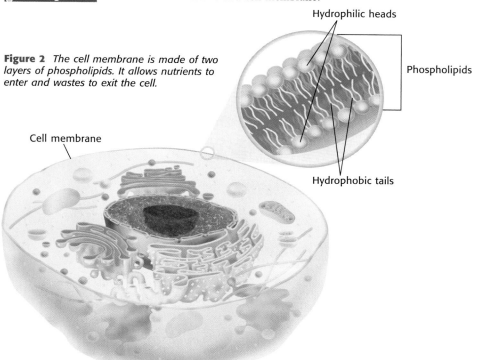

Figure 2 The cell membrane is made of two layers of phospholipids. It allows nutrients to enter and wastes to exit the cell.

Hydrophilic heads

Phospholipids

Hydrophobic tails

Cell membrane

Answer to Reading Check

A cell membrane encloses the cell and separates and protects the cell's contents from the cell's environment. The cell membrane also controls movement of materials into and out of the cell.

Group ACTIVITY — BASIC

Drawing Cells Arrange students in pairs. Tell each pair to draw a plant or animal cell based on information presented in the text. Instruct students not to label the cell's parts. Then, have students exchange drawings with another pair. Students should put the proper labels on their classmates' picture. Finally, have each group of two pairs compare and discuss each other's work. **LS** Visual/Interpersonal

Answer to Reading Check

The cytoskeleton is a web of proteins in the cytoplasm. It gives the cell support and structure.

CONNECTION to Physical Science — GENERAL

Studying Cells Biophysics uses tools and techniques of physics to study the life processes of cells. Biophysicists are interested in the relationship between a molecule's structure and its function. Sophisticated techniques, such as electron microscopy, X-ray diffraction, magnetic resonance spectroscopy, and electrophoresis, allow biophysicists to study the structure of proteins, nucleic acids, and even parts of cells, such as ribosomes. Use the teaching transparency "Structural Formulas" to illustrate molecular structure. **LS** Visual

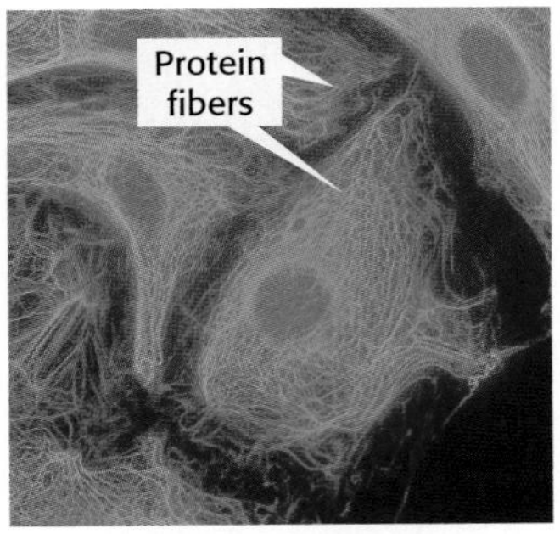

Figure 3 *The cytoskeleton, made of protein fibers, helps a cell retain its shape, move in its environment, and move its organelles.*

Figure 4 *The nucleus contains the cell's DNA. Pores allow materials to move between the nucleus and the cytoplasm.*

Cytoskeleton

The *cytoskeleton* (SIET oh SKEL uh tuhn) is a web of proteins in the cytoplasm. The cytoskeleton, shown in **Figure 3**, acts as both a muscle and a skeleton. It keeps the cell's membranes from collapsing. The cytoskeleton also helps some cells move.

The cytoskeleton is made of three types of protein. One protein is a hollow tube. The other two are long, stringy fibers. One of the stringy proteins is also found in muscle cells.

✓ **Reading Check** What is the cytoskeleton?

Nucleus

All eukaryotic cells have the same basic membrane-bound organelles, starting with the nucleus. The *nucleus* is a large organelle in a eukaryotic cell. It contains the cell's DNA, or genetic material. DNA contains the information on how to make a cell's proteins. Proteins control the chemical reactions in a cell. They also provide structural support for cells and tissues. But proteins are not made in the nucleus. Messages for how to make proteins are copied from the DNA. These messages are then sent out of the nucleus through the membranes.

The nucleus is covered by two membranes. Materials cross this double membrane by passing through pores. **Figure 4** shows a nucleus and nuclear pores. The nucleus of many cells has a dark area called the nucleolus (noo KLEE uh luhs). The *nucleolus* is where a cell begins to make its ribosomes.

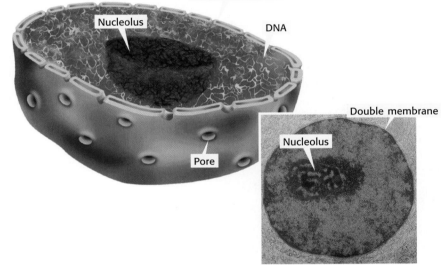

CHAPTER RESOURCES

Technology

📦 **Transparencies**
- *LINK TO* **PHYSICAL SCIENCE** Structural Formulas

⚙ INCLUSION Strategies

- *Developmentally Delayed*
- *Attention Deficit Disorder*
- *Behavior Control Issues*

Have six volunteers line up at the front of the room. Then, write "ABC order" on the board, and ask students to line up correctly. Next, add "by last letter of first name," and ask them to line up correctly. Discuss that having DNA in cells is like having complete, specific directions. **LS** Kinesthetic — English Language Learners

Ribosomes

Organelles that make proteins are called **ribosomes.** Ribosomes are the smallest of all organelles. And there are more ribosomes in a cell than there are any other organelles. Some ribosomes float freely in the cytoplasm. Others are attached to membranes or the cytoskeleton. Unlike most organelles, ribosomes are not covered by a membrane.

Proteins are made within the ribosomes. Proteins are made of amino acids. An *amino acid* is any one of about 20 different organic molecules that are used to make proteins. All cells need proteins to live. All cells have ribosomes.

Endoplasmic Reticulum

Many chemical reactions take place in a cell. Many of these reactions happen on or in the endoplasmic reticulum (EN doh PLAZ mik ri TIK yuh luhm). The **endoplasmic reticulum,** or ER, is a system of folded membranes in which proteins, lipids, and other materials are made. The ER is shown in **Figure 5.**

The ER is part of the internal delivery system of the cell. Its folded membrane contains many tubes and passageways. Substances move through the ER to different places in the cell.

Endoplasmic reticulum is either rough ER or smooth ER. The part of the ER covered in ribosomes is rough ER. Rough ER is usually found near the nucleus. Ribosomes on rough ER make many of the cell's proteins. The ER delivers these proteins throughout the cell. ER that lacks ribosomes is smooth ER. The functions of smooth ER include making lipids and breaking down toxic materials that could damage the cell.

ribosome cell organelle composed of RNA and protein; the site of protein synthesis

endoplasmic reticulum a system of membranes that is found in a cell's cytoplasm and that assists in the production, processing, and transport of proteins and in the production of lipids

Figure 5 *The endoplasmic reticulum (ER) is a system of membranes. Rough ER is covered with ribosomes. Smooth ER does not have ribosomes.*

Smooth ER
Rough ER
Endoplasmic reticulum
Ribosomes

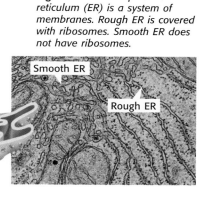
Smooth ER
Rough ER

Homework ——— **GENERAL**

Cell Search Have students search the Internet for images (photomicrographs) of cells. Encourage students to compare images of cells from different types of organisms. Also, have students compare images of the same type of cell made by different microscopes, such as light microscopes, scanning electron microscopes, and transmission electron microscopes. Have students describe the cells that they find. **LS** Logical/Visual

ACTiViTY ——— **GENERAL**

Cell Models Students will be making edible models of cells. Students can bring edible items for the cell wall or cell membrane, such as crackers or pita bread. They can also bring items to represent organelles within the cell, such as small pieces of different kinds of candy (the hard candy shell on some candies may represent an organelle's membrane), olives, or other items. Have students explain the way they have represented the cell's structure in food. Pictures of the edible cells can be displayed in the classroom. **English Language Learners**
LS Kinesthetic

CONNECTION to Chemistry ——— **ADVANCED**

Ribosome Structure Ribosomes make proteins. The structure of ribosomes has been intensely studied. Scientists now know how ribosome structure relates to ribosome function. Have students research and report on how ribosomes work. Their report should include a diagram of ribosome structure and its relationship to ribosome function. **LS** Verbal/Visual

CONNECTION to Language Arts ——— **ADVANCED**

No Energy? Mitochondrial diseases are a group of illnesses caused by malfunctioning mitochondria. These diseases can be caused by genes in the mitochondria or genes in the cell. Any activity or organ that requires energy is affected by these diseases. Have students conduct Internet or library research on mitochondrial diseases. Have them create a brochure or a pamphlet explaining one or more of these diseases. (Interested students may want to read *A Wind in the Door,* by Madeleine L'Engle, which is a story about a little boy with mitochondrial disease.) **LS** Verbal

Prediction Guide Before students read this page, ask them if the following statement is true or false: Animal cells are completely different from plant cells. (false; Animal cells and plant cells have many features in common, such as membrane-covered organelles and a cell membrane. The main difference between animal and plant cells is that animal cells do not have a cell wall and they do not have chloroplasts and chlorophyll.)

Have students explain their answer. Then, have them evaluate their answer after they read the page. **LS** Logical

Answer to Reading Check
Most of a cell's ATP is made in the cell's mitochondria.

CONNECTION to Language Arts — ADVANCED

Writing **Far-Out Fiction** Have students write a story about an animal whose cells are invaded by chloroplasts. Students should describe how the animal's life processes at the cellular level would be affected. Students may also describe how the animal might use this chloroplast invasion to its advantage. Encourage students to write about an animal other than a mammal (corals might be an interesting subject). **LS** Verbal/Logical

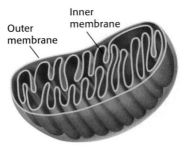
Outer membrane / Inner membrane

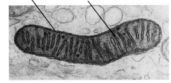
Outer membrane / Inner membrane

Figure 6 *Mitochondria break down sugar and make ATP. ATP is produced on the inner membrane.*

mitochondrion in eukaryotic cells, the cell organelle that is surrounded by two membranes and that is the site of cellular respiration

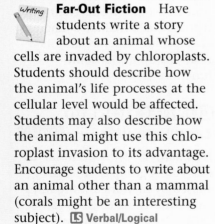

Figure 7 *Chloroplasts harness and use the energy of the sun to make sugar. A green pigment—chlorophyll—traps the sun's energy.*

Outer membrane / Inner membrane

Mitochondria

A mitochondrion (MIET oh KAHN dree uhn) is the main power source of a cell. A **mitochondrion** is the organelle in which sugar is broken down to produce energy. Mitochondria are covered by two membranes, as shown in **Figure 6.** Energy released by mitochondria is stored in a substance called *ATP* (**a**denosine **tri**phosphate). The cell then uses ATP to do work. ATP can be made at several places in a cell. But most of a cell's ATP is made in the inner membrane of the cell's mitochondria.

Most eukaryotic cells have mitochondria. Mitochondria are the size of some bacteria. Like bacteria, mitochondria have their own DNA, and mitochondria can divide within a cell.

✓ Reading Check Where is most of a cell's ATP made?

Chloroplasts

Animal cells cannot make their own food. Plants and algae are different. They have chloroplasts (KLAWR uh PLASTS) in some of their cells. *Chloroplasts* are organelles in plant and algae cells in which photosynthesis takes place. Like mitochondria, chloroplasts have two membranes and their own DNA. A chloroplast is shown in **Figure 7.** *Photosynthesis* is the process by which plants and algae use sunlight, carbon dioxide, and water to make sugar and oxygen.

Chloroplasts are green because they contain *chlorophyll*, a green pigment. Chlorophyll is found inside the inner membrane of a chloroplast. Chlorophyll traps the energy of sunlight, which is used to make sugar. The sugar produced by photosynthesis is then used by mitochondria to make ATP.

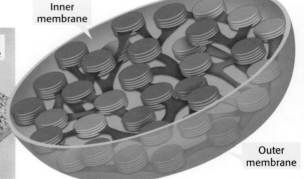
Inner membrane / Outer membrane

SCIENTISTS AT ODDS

Acquiring Genomes Dr. Lynn Margulis knew that mitochondria and chloroplasts have their own DNA and divide by binary fission. She proposed that these organelles were once bacteria that entered organisms and became parts of those cells. Other scientists disagreed, but research proved Dr. Margulis right. Now, Margulis proposes that all eukaryotes developed as a result of genetic mergers between different kinds of organisms. And other scientists disagree. Only more research will settle the debate.

Is That a Fact!

About 100 eukaryotic species do not have mitochondria. *Giardia* is a freshwater protist that lacks mitochondria. *Giardia* can make people sick if they drink water from an infected lake or stream.

Golgi Complex

The organelle that packages and distributes proteins is called the **Golgi complex** (GOHL jee KAHM PLEKS). It is named after Camillo Golgi, the Italian scientist who first identified the organelle.

The Golgi complex looks like smooth ER, as shown in **Figure 8.** Lipids and proteins from the ER are delivered to the Golgi complex. There, the lipids and proteins may be modified to do different jobs. The final products are enclosed in a piece of the Golgi complex's membrane. This membrane pinches off to form a small bubble. The bubble transports its contents to other parts of the cell or out of the cell.

Cell Compartments

The bubble that forms from the Golgi complex's membrane is a vesicle. A **vesicle** (VES i kuhl) is a small sac that surrounds material to be moved into or out of a cell. All eukaryotic cells have vesicles. Vesicles also move material within a cell. For example, vesicles carry new protein from the ER to the Golgi complex. Other vesicles distribute material from the Golgi complex to other parts of the cell. Some vesicles form when part of the cell membrane surrounds an object outside the cell.

Golgi complex cell organelle that helps make and package materials to be transported out of the cell

vesicle a small cavity or sac that contains materials in a eukaryotic cell

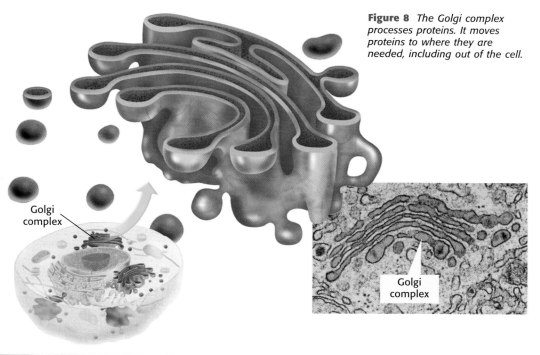

Golgi complex

Golgi complex

Figure 8 *The Golgi complex processes proteins. It moves proteins to where they are needed, including out of the cell.*

SCIENTISTS AT ODDS

Is It There or Not? Many scientists did not believe Golgi's claims about the organelle he observed and described. Those scientists thought that Golgi just saw tiny globs of the staining material. The existence of the organelle that was eventually named the *Golgi complex* was finally confirmed in the mid-1950s with the aid of the electron microscope.

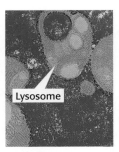
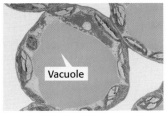

Figure 9 *Lysosomes digest materials inside a cell. In plant and fungal cells, vacuoles often perform the same function.*

Lysosome

Vacuole

lysosome a cell organelle that contains digestive enzymes

Cellular Digestion

Lysosomes (LIE suh SOHMZ) are vesicles that are responsible for digestion inside a cell. **Lysosomes** are organelles that contain digestive enzymes. They destroy worn-out or damaged organelles, get rid of waste materials, and protect the cell from foreign invaders. Lysosomes, which come in a wide variety of sizes and shapes, are shown in **Figure 9.**

Lysosomes are found mainly in animal cells. When eukaryotic cells engulf particles, they enclose the particles in vesicles. Lysosomes bump into these vesicles and pour enzymes into them. These enzymes digest the particles in the vesicles.

✓ **Reading Check** Why are lysosomes important?

Vacuoles

A *vacuole* (VAK yoo OHL) is a large vesicle. In plant and fungal cells, some vacuoles act like large lysosomes. They store digestive enzymes and aid in digestion within the cell. Other vacuoles in plant cells store water and other liquids. Vacuoles that are full of water, such as the one in **Figure 9,** help support the cell. Some plants wilt when their vacuoles lose water. **Table 1** shows some organelles and their functions.

Table 1   Organelles and Their Functions

	Nucleus the organelle that contains the cell's DNA and is the control center of the cell		**Chloroplast** the organelle that uses the energy of sunlight to make food
	Ribosome the organelle in which amino acids are hooked together to make proteins		**Golgi complex** the organelle that processes and transports proteins and other materials out of cell
	Endoplasmic reticulum the organelle that makes lipids, breaks down drugs and other substances, and packages proteins for Golgi complex		**Vacuole** the organelle that stores water and other materials
	Mitochondria the organelle that breaks down food molecules to make ATP		**Lysosome** the organelle that digests food particles, wastes, cell parts, and foreign invaders

Answer to Reading Check
Lysosomes destroy worn-out organelles, attack foreign invaders, and get rid of waste material from inside the cell.

ACTiViTY ——— BASIC

Vacuole Model You can make a demonstration model of a vacuole within a cell by filling a balloon with water or air and putting it inside a clear plastic storage bag. Show that the vacuole is part of the cell and is distinct within the cell. You can demonstrate that cells are full of motion and activity by moving the balloon around inside the bag. English Language Learners
LS Visual

Summary

- Eukaryotic cells have organelles that perform functions that help cells remain alive.
- All cells have a cell membrane. Some cells have a cell wall. Some cells have a cytoskeleton.
- The nucleus of a eukaryotic cell contains the cell's genetic material, DNA.
- Ribosomes are the organelles that make proteins. Ribosomes are not covered by a membrane.

- The endoplasmic reticulum (ER) and the Golgi complex make and process proteins before the proteins are transported to other parts of the cell or out of the cell.
- Mitochondria and chloroplasts are energy-producing organelles.
- Lysosomes are organelles responsible for digestion within a cell. In plant cells, organelles called *vacuoles* store cell materials and sometimes act like large lysosomes.

Using Key Terms

1. In your own words, write a definition for each of the following terms: *ribosome, lysosome,* and *cell wall.*

Understanding Key Ideas

2. Which of the following are found mainly in animal cells?
   a. mitochondria
   b. lysosomes
   c. ribosomes
   d. Golgi complexes

3. What is the function of a Golgi complex? What is the function of the endoplasmic reticulum?

Critical Thinking

4. **Making Comparisons** Describe three ways in which plant cells differ from animal cells.

5. **Applying Concepts** Every cell needs ribosomes. Explain why.

6. **Predicting Consequences** A certain virus attacks the mitochondria in cells. What would happen to a cell if all of its mitochondria were destroyed?

7. **Expressing Opinions** Do you think that having chloroplasts gives plant cells an advantage over animal cells? Support your opinion.

Interpreting Graphics

Use the diagram below to answer the questions that follow.

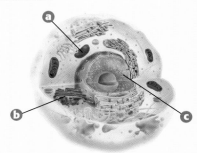

8. Is this a diagram of a plant cell or an animal cell? Explain how you know.

9. What organelle does the letter *b* refer to?

Developed and maintained by the
National Science Teachers Association

For a variety of links related to this chapter, go to www.scilinks.org

Topic: Eukaryotic Cells
SciLinks code: HSM0541

CHAPTER RESOURCES

Chapter Resource File

- Section Quiz (GENERAL)
- Section Review (GENERAL)
- Vocabulary and Section Summary (GENERAL)
- SciLinks Activity (GENERAL)

Technology

Transparencies
- Organelles and Their Functions

Answers to Section Review

1. Sample answer: Ribosomes are organelles where amino acids are joined together to make proteins. Lysosomes are organelles that carry out cellular digestion. The cell wall is the outermost structure in cells of plants, fungi, and algae.

2. b

3. Sample answer: Golgi complex: packages and distributes proteins within a cell; endoplasmic reticulum: a series of folded membranes on which lipids, proteins, and other materials are made, and through which those materials are delivered to other places in the cell

4. Sample answer: Plant cells have cell walls, but animal cells do not. Plant cells have chloroplasts, which animal cells do not have. Plant cells do not seem to have small lysosomes (they have large vacuoles instead), which animal cells do have.

5. Sample answer: Ribosomes are the organelles where proteins are made. All cells need protein in order to live.

6. Sample answer: Mitochondria are organelles that produce most of a cell's energy. If its mitochondria were destroyed, a cell would eventually die because it would not be able to produce enough energy to survive.

7. Sample answer: I think plants have an advantage over animals because plants can make their own food just by using sunlight and other nutrients. Animals have to wait for plants to grow in order to get food.

8. This diagram is of an animal cell; the first clue is that the cell has no cell wall.

9. the Golgi complex

Focus

Overview

In this section, students will learn that a cell is the smallest unit of life. In most multicellular organisms, groups of cells form tissues that compose organs. Two or more organs can interact to form an organ system.

 Bellringer

Write the following questions on the board for students to answer:

Why can't you use your teeth to breathe? Why can't you use your arm muscles to digest food?

Motivate

 GENERAL

Concept Mapping Organize the class into small groups. Provide each group with pictures of tissues, organs, and organ systems. Have students arrange the pictures into concept maps. Encourage students to notice similarities and differences between organs. For example, the stomach and the heart are very different organs, but both are made of muscle tissue, and both function by holding and moving substances through their cavities. **LS Intrapersonal/ Visual Co-op Learning**

READING WARM-UP

Objectives

● List three advantages of being multicellular.

● Describe the four levels of organization in living things.

● Explain the relationship between the structure and function of a part of an organism.

Terms to Learn

tissue	organism
organ	structure
organ system	function

READING STRATEGY

Paired Summarizing Read this section silently. In pairs, take turns summarizing the material. Stop to discuss ideas that seem confusing.

The Organization of Living Things

In some ways, organisms are like machines. Some machines have just one part. But most machines have many parts. Some organisms exist as a single cell. Other organisms have many—even trillions—of cells.

Most cells are smaller than the period that ends this sentence. Yet, every cell in every organism performs all the processes of life. So, are there any advantages to having many cells?

The Benefits of Being Multicellular

You are a *multicellular organism*. This means that you are made of many cells. Multicellular organisms grow by making more small cells, not by making their cells larger. For example, an elephant is bigger than you are, but its cells are about the same size as yours. An elephant just has more cells than you do. Some benefits of being multicellular are the following:

● **Larger Size** Many multicellular organisms are small. But they are usually larger than single-celled organisms. Larger organisms are prey for fewer predators. Larger predators can eat a wider variety of prey.

● **Longer Life** The life span of a multicellular organism is not limited to the life span of any single cell.

● **Specialization** Each type of cell has a particular job. Specialization makes the organism more efficient. For example, the cardiac muscle cell in **Figure 1** is a specialized muscle cell. Heart muscle cells contract and make the heart pump blood.

✓ Reading Check List three advantages of being multicellular. (See the Appendix for answers to Reading Checks.)

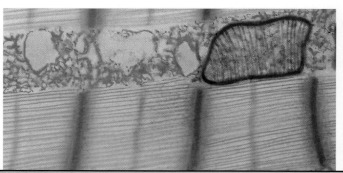

Figure 1 *This photomicrograph shows a small part of one heart muscle cell. The green line surrounds one of many mitochondria, the powerhouses of the cell. The pink areas are muscle filaments.*

Answer to Reading Check

Sample answer: larger size, longer life, cell specialization

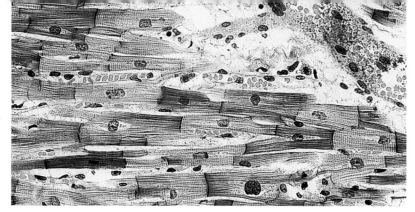

Figure 2 This photomicrograph shows cardiac muscle tissue. Cardiac muscle tissue is made up of many cardiac cells.

Cells Working Together

A **tissue** is a group of cells that work together to perform a specific job. The material around and between the cells is also part of the tissue. The cardiac muscle tissue, shown in **Figure 2,** is made of many cardiac muscle cells. Cardiac muscle tissue is just one type of tissue in a heart.

Animals have four basic types of tissues: nerve tissue, muscle tissue, connective tissue, and protective tissue. In contrast, plants have three types of tissues: transport tissue, protective tissue, and ground tissue. Transport tissue moves water and nutrients through a plant. Protective tissue covers the plant. It helps the plant retain water and protects the plant against damage. Photosynthesis takes place in ground tissue.

Tissues Working Together

A structure that is made up of two or more tissues working together to perform a specific function is called an **organ.** For example, your heart is an organ. It is made mostly of cardiac muscle tissue. But your heart also has nerve tissue and tissues of the blood vessels that all work together to make your heart the powerful pump that it is.

Another organ is your stomach. It also has several kinds of tissue. In the stomach, muscle tissue makes food move in and through the stomach. Special tissues make chemicals that help digest your food. Connective tissue holds the stomach together, and nervous tissue carries messages back and forth between the stomach and the brain. Other organs include the intestines, brain, and lungs.

Plants also have different kinds of tissues that work together as organs. A leaf is a plant organ that contains tissue that traps light energy to make food. Other examples of plant organs are stems and roots.

✔ **Reading Check** What is an organ?

tissue a group of similar cells that perform a common function

organ a collection of tissues that carry out a specialized function of the body

A Pet Protist

Imagine that you have a tiny box-shaped protist for a pet. To care for your pet protist properly, you have to figure out how much to feed it. The dimensions of your protist are roughly 25 μm × 20 μm × 2 μm. If seven food particles per second can enter through each square micrometer of surface area, how many particles can your protist eat in 1 min?

Is That a Fact!

In your lifetime, your body will shed about 18 kg (almost 40 lb) of dead skin.

MISCONCEPTION ALERT

Dead Cells Students may think that hair is alive: advertisements for shampoo create the impression that hair is living tissue. Hair, and fingernails, too, are dead. Hair and fingernails grow out of specialized skin cells. They grow continuously, but both are composed of dead cells and a protein called *keratin*. If hair and fingernails were alive and contained nerve cells, as the deep skin layers do, haircuts and manicures would be quite painful.

Teach

Discussion ——— GENERAL

Muscles Ask students to list all of the ways they use their muscles. Responses will probably include walking, riding a bike, swimming, and throwing or kicking a ball. Lead students to understand that muscles are also involved in swallowing food (tongue and esophagus), digestion (stomach and intestines), and blinking eyes (eyelids). Also, help students understand that sometimes muscles act voluntarily (jumping, writing), and sometimes they act involuntarily (heart beating). **LS** Auditory/Logical

Homework ——— GENERAL

Writing **Respiration Variations** Not all living things have the same kinds of tissues and organs. Yet, all must perform similar life processes. Have students do research in order to compare the structures a fish uses to breathe with those that a human uses. Students' reports should also answer the question, What parts of the human and fish respiratory systems are similar? (Even though a fish has gills and a human has lungs, both have cells that exchange and transport oxygen and carbon dioxide.) **LS** Logical

Answer to Math Practice

The surface area of the protist is [(25 μm × 20 μm) + (25 μm × 2 μm) + (20 μm × 2 μm)] × 2 = 1,180 μm^2, so it can eat 1,180 μm^2 × 7 particles per second = 8,260 particles of food every second, or 60 s/min × 8,260 particles/s = 495,600 particles of food per minute.

Answer to Reading Check

An organ is a structure of two or more tissues working together to perform a specific function in the body.

Levels of Organization Write the following headings on the board:

Cell, Tissue, Organ, Organ system, Organism

Have students write these headings on their paper and list at least two examples under each heading. English Language Learners
LS Verbal/Logical

Quiz ———— GENERAL

1. What is the relationship between your digestive system, stomach, and intestines? (The digestive system is an organ system. The stomach and intestines are organs that are parts of the digestive system.)

2. What is the main difference between a unicellular organism and a multicellular organism in the way life processes are carried out? (Sample answer: A unicellular organism must perform all life functions by itself. A multicellular organism may have specialized cells that work together to carry out each function.)

Alternative Assessment ———— GENERAL

Concept Mapping Have students choose an organ system and identify its component organs. Then, have students make a concept map describing the function of the organs and their relationship to one another. **LS** Logical/Visual

---

organ system a group of organs that work together to perform body functions

organism a living thing; anything that can carry out life processes independently

structure the arrangement of parts in an organism

function the special, normal, or proper activity of an organ or part

---

Organs Working Together

A group of organs working together to perform a particular function is called an **organ system.** Each organ system has a specific job to do in the body.

For example, the digestive system is made up of several organs, including the stomach and intestines. The digestive system's job is to break down food into small particles. Other parts of the body then use these small particles as fuel. In turn, the digestive system depends on the respiratory and cardiovascular systems for oxygen. The cardiovascular system, shown in **Figure 3,** includes organs and tissues such as the heart and blood vessels. Plants also have organ systems. They include leaf systems, root systems, and stem systems.

✓ **Reading Check** List the levels of organization in living things.

Organisms

Anything that can perform life processes by itself is an **organism.** An organism made of a single cell is called a *unicellular organism.* Bacteria, most protists, and some kinds of fungi are unicellular. Although some of these organisms live in colonies, they are still unicellular. They are unicellular organisms living together, and all of the cells in the colony are the same. Each cell must carry out all life processes in order for that cell to survive. In contrast, even the simplest multicellular organism has specialized cells that depend on each other for the organism to survive.

Figure 3 **Levels of Organization in the Cardiovascular System**

Cell	**Tissue**	**Organ**	**Organ system**
Cells form tissues.	Tissues form organs.	Organs form organ systems.	And organ systems form organisms such as you!

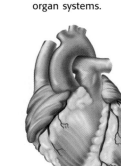
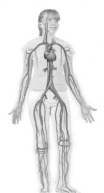

Is That a Fact!

An elephant's trunk is constructed of 135 kg (300 lb) of hair, skin, connective tissue, nerves, and muscles. The muscle tissue is composed of 150,000 tiny sub-units of muscle, each of which is coordinated with the others to enable an elephant to greet its friends, breathe, grab, and drink.

Answer to Reading Check

cell, tissue, organ, organ system, organism

Structure and Function

In organisms, structure and function are related. **Structure** is the arrangement of parts in an organism. It includes the shape of a part and the material of which the part is made. **Function** is the job the part does. For example, the structure of the lungs is a large, spongy sac. In the lungs, there are millions of tiny air sacs called *alveoli*. Blood vessels wrap around the alveoli, as shown in **Figure 4.** Oxygen from air in the alveoli enters the blood. Blood then brings oxygen to body tissues. Also, in the alveoli, carbon dioxide leaves the blood and is exhaled.

The structures of alveoli and blood vessels enable them to perform a function. Together, they bring oxygen to the body and get rid of its carbon dioxide.

Figure 4   The Structure and Function of Alveoli

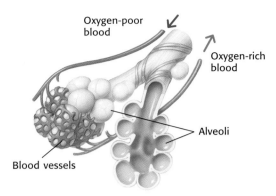

Oxygen-poor blood

Oxygen-rich blood

Alveoli

Blood vessels

SECTION Review

Summary

- Advantages of being multicellular are larger size, longer life, and cell specialization.
- Four levels of organization are cell, tissue, organ, and organ system.
- A *tissue* is a group of cells working together. An *organ* is two or more tissues working together. An *organ system* is two or more organs working together.
- In organisms, a part's structure and function are related.

Using Key Terms

1. Use each of the following terms in a separate sentence: *tissue, organ,* and *function*.

Understanding Key Ideas

2. What are the four levels of organization in living things?
   a. cell, multicellular, organ, organ system
   b. single cell, multicellular, tissue, organ
   c. larger size, longer life, specialized cells, organs
   d. cell, tissue, organ, organ system

Math Skills

3. One multicellular organism is a cube. Each of its sides is 3 cm long. Each of its cells is 1 cm³. How many cells does it have? If each side doubles in length, how many cells will it then have?

Critical Thinking

4. **Applying Concepts** Explain the relationship between structure and function. Use alveoli as an example. Be sure to include more than one level of organization.

5. **Making Inferences** Why can multicellular organisms be more complex than unicellular organisms? Use the three advantages of being multicellular to help explain your answer.

SCI LINKS

NSTA
Developed and maintained by the National Science Teachers Association

For a variety of links related to this chapter, go to www.scilinks.org

Topic: Organization of Life
SciLinks code: HSM1080

ACTIVITY — BASIC

Writing **Explain It to a Friend**   A great way to learn something is to teach it to someone else. Have students write a letter to a friend explaining how cells, tissues, organs, and organ systems are related.
LS Logical/Verbal   PORTFOLIO

CHAPTER RESOURCES

Chapter Resource File
- Section Quiz GENERAL
- Section Review GENERAL
- Vocabulary and Section Summary GENERAL
- Reinforcement Worksheet BASIC
- Critical Thinking ADVANCED

Elephant-Sized Amoebas?

Teacher's Notes

Time Required

Two 45-minute class periods

Lab Ratings

EASY ——————————→ HARD

Teacher Prep 🧪🧪
Student Set-Up 🧪🧪
Concept Level 🧪🧪🧪
Clean Up 🧪

Safety Caution

Remind students to review all safety cautions and icons before beginning this lab activity.

Preparation Notes

Some students may find it difficult to work with a nonspecific unit of measurement. If so, the cube models easily convert to centimeters. You may want to add some small items, such as peas, beans, popcorn, or peppercorns, to the sand to represent organelles floating in the cytoplasm. Some students may need to review what a ratio is and how ratios are used.

Model-Making Lab

OBJECTIVES

Explore why a single-celled organism cannot grow to the size of an elephant.

Create a model of a cell to illustrate the concept of surface area–to-volume ratio.

MATERIALS

- calculator (optional)
- cubic cell patterns
- heavy paper or poster board
- sand, fine
- scale or balance
- scissors
- tape, transparent

SAFETY

Elephant-Sized Amoebas?

An amoeba is a single-celled organism. Like most cells, amoebas are microscopic. Why can't amoebas grow as large as elephants? If an amoeba grew to the size of a quarter, the amoeba would starve to death. To understand how this can be true, build a model of a cell and see for yourself.

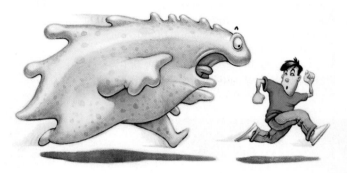

Procedure

1 Use heavy paper or poster board to make four cube-shaped cell models from the patterns supplied by your teacher. Cut out each cell model, fold the sides to make a cube, and tape the tabs on the sides. The smallest cell model has sides that are each one unit long. The next larger cell has sides of two units. The next cell has sides of three units, and the largest cell has sides of four units. These paper models represent the cell membrane, the part of a cell's exterior through which food and wastes pass.

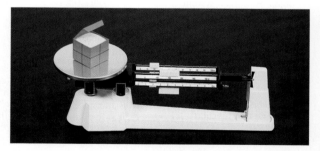

CHAPTER RESOURCES

Chapter Resource File

- 📁 • **Datasheet for Chapter Lab**
  - • **Lab Notes and Answers**

Technology

- 💿 **Classroom Videos**
  - • Lab Video

LabBook

• Cells Alive!

CHAPTER RESOURCES

Workbooks

- 📓 **Whiz-Bang Demonstrations**
  - • Grand Strand **GENERAL**
- 📓 **Labs You Can Eat**
  - • The Incredible Edible Cell **GENERAL**
- 📓 **Long-Term Projects & Research Ideas**
  - • Ewe Again, Dolly? **ADVANCED**

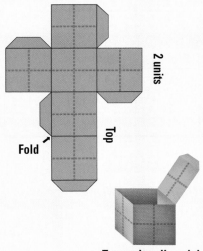

Two-unit cell model

Using the template above, prepare four patterns for students to use to make their cubes. Make one cube 1 unit wide, one cube 2 units wide, one cube 3 units wide, and one cube 4 units wide. The unit can be the size of your choosing.

Data Table for Measurements

Length of side	Area of one side (A = S × S)	Total surface area of cube cell (TA = S × S × 6)	Volume of cube cell (V = S × S × S)	Mass of filled cube cell
1 unit	1 unit²	6 unit²	1 unit³	
2 unit				
3 unit		DO NOT WRITE IN BOOK		
4 unit				

Key to Formula Symbols

S = the length of one side
A = area
6 = number of sides
V = volume
TA = total area

2 Copy the data table shown above. Use each formula to calculate the data about your cell models. Record your calculations in the table. Calculations for the smallest cell have been done for you.

3 Carefully fill each model with fine sand until the sand is level with the top edge of the model. Find the mass of the filled models by using a scale or a balance. What does the sand in your model represent?

4 Record the mass of each filled cell model in your Data Table for Measurements. (Always remember to use the appropriate mass unit.)

Analyze the Results

1 Constructing Tables Make a data table like the one shown at right.

2 Organizing Data Use the data from your Data Table for Measurements to find the ratios for each of your cell models. For each of the cell models, fill in the Data Table for Ratios .

Draw Conclusions

3 Interpreting Information As a cell grows larger, does the ratio of total surface area to volume increase, decrease, or stay the same?

4 Interpreting Information As a cell grows larger, does the total surface area–to-mass ratio increase, decrease, or stay the same?

5 Drawing Conclusions Which is better able to supply food to all the cytoplasm of the cell: the cell membrane of a small cell or the cell membrane of a large cell? Explain your answer.

6 Evaluating Data In the experiment, which is better able to feed all of the cytoplasm of the cell: the cell membrane of a cell that has high mass or the cell membrane of a cell that has low mass? You may explain your answer in a verbal presentation to the class, or you may choose to write a report and illustrate it with drawings of your models.

Data Table for Ratios

Length of side	Ratio of total surface area to volume	Ratio of total surface area to mass
1 unit		
2 unit		
3 unit		DO NOT WRITE IN BOOK
4 unit		

Procedure

3. The sand represents cytoplasm.

4. Masses may vary.

Analyze the Results

2. See the tables below.

Draw Conclusions

3. decreases

4. decreases

5. the cell membrane of a small cell. A small cell has a higher surface-area-to-volume ratio than a large cell has, so more nutrients per cubic unit of volume can enter a small cell.

6. the cell membrane of a cell with low mass

Data Table for Measurements

Length of side S	Area of one side (square units)	Total surface area of cube cell (square units)	Volume of cube cell (cubic units)	Mass of cube cell (sample answer, in grams)
1	1	6	1	4.5
2	4	24	8	30
3	9	54	27	105
4	16	96	64	230

Data Table for Ratios

Length of side S	Total surface area-to-volume ratio	Total surface area-to-mass ratio (sample answer)
1	6:1	6:4.5 = 1.33:1
2	24:8 = 3:1	24:30 = 0.80:1
3	54:27 = 2:1	54:105 = 0.51:1
4	96:64 = 1.5:1	96:230 = 0.42:1

Terry Rakes
Elmwood Junior High School
Rogers, Arkansas

Assignment Guide

SECTION	QUESTIONS
1	1, 4, 10–13, 23
2	3, 6, 9, 16–19, 22, 24–26
3	2, 5, 7–8, 14–15, 20–21

ANSWERS

Using Key Terms

1. cell
2. function
3. organelles
4. eukaryote
5. tissue
6. cell wall

Understanding Key Ideas

7. c
8. d
9. a
10. b
11. b
12. c

USING KEY TERMS

Complete each of the following sentences by choosing the correct term from the word bank.

cell   organ
cell membrane   prokaryote
organelles   eukaryote
cell wall   tissue
structure   function

1 A(n) ___ is the most basic unit of all living things.

2 The job that an organ does is the ___ of that organ.

3 Ribosomes and mitochondria are types of ___.

4 A(n) ___ is an organism whose cells have a nucleus.

5 A group of cells working together to perform a specific function is a(n) ___.

6 Only plant cells have a(n) ___.

UNDERSTANDING KEY IDEAS

Multiple Choice

7 Which of the following best describes an organ?

  a. a group of cells that work together to perform a specific job

  b. a group of tissues that belong to different systems

  c. a group of tissues that work together to perform a specific job

  d. a body structure, such as muscles or lungs

8 The benefits of being multicellular include

  a. small size, long life, and cell specialization.

  b. generalized cells, longer life, and ability to prey on small animals.

  c. larger size, more enemies, and specialized cells.

  d. longer life, larger size, and specialized cells.

9 In eukaryotic cells, which organelle contains the DNA?

  a. nucleus   **c.** smooth ER

  b. Golgi complex **d.** vacuole

10 Which of the following statements is part of the cell theory?

  a. All cells suddenly appear by themselves.

  b. All cells come from other cells.

  c. All organisms are multicellular.

  d. All cells have identical parts.

11 The surface area–to-volume ratio of a cell limits

  a. the number of organelles that the cell has.

  b. the size of the cell.

  c. where the cell lives.

  d. the types of nutrients that a cell needs.

12 Two types of organisms whose cells do not have a nucleus are

  a. prokaryotes and eukaryotes.

  b. plants and animals.

  c. eubacteria and archaebacteria.

  d. single-celled and multicellular organisms.

13. Cells must be small in order to have a large enough surface area–to-volume ratio to get sufficient nutrients to survive and to get rid of wastes.

14. Cells are the smallest unit of all living things. Cells combine to make tissues. Different tissues combine to make organs, which have specialized jobs in the body. Organs work together in organ systems, which perform body functions.

Short Answer

13 Explain why most cells are small.

14 Describe the four levels of organization in living things.

15 What is the difference between the structure of an organ and the function of the organ?

16 Name two functions of a cell membrane.

17 What are the structure and function of the cytoskeleton in a cell?

CRITICAL THINKING

18 **Concept Mapping** Use the following terms to create a concept map: *cells, organisms, Golgi complex, organ systems, organs, nucleus, organelle,* and *tissues.*

19 **Making Comparisons** Compare and contrast the functions of the endoplasmic reticulum and the Golgi complex.

20 **Identifying Relationships** Explain how the structure and function of an organism's parts are related. Give an example.

21 **Evaluating Hypotheses** One of your classmates states a hypothesis that all organisms must have organ systems. Is your classmate's hypothesis valid? Explain your answer.

22 **Predicting Consequences** What would happen if all of the ribosomes in your cells disappeared?

23 **Expressing Opinions** Scientists think that millions of years ago the surface of the Earth was very hot and that the atmosphere contained a lot of methane. In your opinion, which type of organism, a eubacterium or an archaebacterium, is the older form of life? Explain your reasoning.

INTERPRETING GRAPHICS

Use the diagram below to answer the questions that follow.

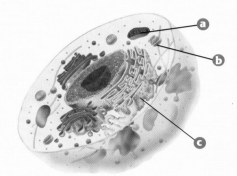

24 What is the name of the structure identified by the letter *a*?

25 Which letter identifies the structure that digests food particles and foreign invaders?

26 Which letter identifies the structure that makes proteins, lipids, and other materials and that contains tubes and passageways that enable substances to move to different places in the cell?

CHAPTER RESOURCES

Chapter Resource File

- **Chapter Review** GENERAL
- **Chapter Test A** GENERAL
- **Chapter Test B** ADVANCED
- **Chapter Test C** SPECIAL NEEDS
- **Vocabulary Activity** GENERAL

Workbooks

Study Guide
• Assessment resources are also available in Spanish.

Teacher's Note

To provide practice under more realistic testing conditions, give students 20 minutes to answer all of the questions in this Standardized Test Preparation.

MISCONCEPTION ALERT

Answers to the standardized test preparation can help you identify student misconceptions and misunderstandings.

READING

Passage 1

1. D
2. G
3. B

 TEST DOCTOR

Question 1: Students may select incorrect answer B if they misread the part of the passage about snottites eventually becoming rock. Snottites themselves are a mixture of bacteria, sticky fluids, and minerals.

Question 2: Students may select incorrect answer I if, again, they misread the part of the passage about snottites eventually hardening into rock structures. Snottites do not create other structures in caves. The best answer is that snottite bacteria do not need sunlight because snottites live deep underground and are acidophiles that do not depend on sunlight for food.

READING

Read each of the passages below. Then, answer the questions that follow each passage.

Passage 1 Exploring caves can be dangerous but can also lead to interesting discoveries. For example, deep in the darkness of Cueva de Villa Luz, a cave in Mexico, are slippery formations called *snottites*. They were named snottites because they look just like a two-year-old's runny nose. If you use an electron microscope to look at them, you see that snottites are bacteria; thick, sticky fluids; and small amounts of minerals produced by the bacteria. As tiny as they are, these bacteria can build up snottite structures that may eventually turn into rock. Formations in other caves look like hardened snottites. The bacteria in snottites are acidophiles. Acidophiles live in environments that are highly acidic. Snottite bacteria produce sulfuric acid and live in an environment that is similar to the inside of a car battery.

1. Which statement best describes snottites?
   A Snottites are bacteria that live in car batteries.
   B Snottites are rock formations found in caves.
   C Snottites were named for a cave in Mexico.
   D Snottites are made of bacteria, sticky fluids, and minerals.

2. Based on this passage, which conclusion about snottites is most likely to be correct?
   F Snottites are found in caves everywhere.
   G Snottite bacteria do not need sunlight.
   H You could grow snottites in a greenhouse.
   I Snottites create other bacteria in caves.

3. What is the main idea of this passage?
   A Acidophiles are unusual organisms.
   B Snottites are strange formations.
   C Exploring caves is dangerous.
   D Snottites are large, slippery bacteria.

Passage 2 The world's smallest mammal may be a bat about the size of a jelly bean. The scientific name for this tiny animal, which was unknown until 1974, is *Craseonycteris thonglongyai*. It is so small that it is sometimes called the *bumblebee bat*. Another name for this animal is the *hog-nosed bat*. Hog-nosed bats were given their name because one of their distinctive features is a piglike muzzle. Hog-nosed bats differ from other bats in another way: they do not have a tail. But, like other bats, hog-nosed bats do eat insects that they catch in mid-air. Scientists think that the bats eat small insects that live on the leaves at the tops of trees. Hog-nosed bats live deep in limestone caves and have been found in only one country, Thailand.

1. According to the passage, which statement about hog-nosed bats is most accurate?
   A They are the world's smallest animal.
   B They are about the size of a bumblebee.
   C They eat leaves at the tops of trees.
   D They live in hives near caves in Thailand.

2. Which of the following statements describes distinctive features of hog-nosed bats?
   F The bats are very small and eat leaves.
   G The bats live in caves and have a tail.
   H The bats live in Thailand and are birds.
   I The bats have a piglike muzzle and no tail.

3. From the information in this passage, which conclusion is most likely to be correct?
   A Hog-nosed bats are similar to other bats.
   B Hog-nosed bats are probably rare.
   C Hog-nosed bats can sting like a bumblebee.
   D Hog-nosed bats probably eat fruit.

Passage 2

1. B
2. I
3. B

 TEST DOCTOR

Question 1: Students may select incorrect answer A if they misread "world's smallest mammal" as being "world's smallest animal."

Question 3: Students may select incorrect answer A if they overlook information in the passage that describes how hog-nosed bats are both similar to and different from other bats.

The diagrams below show two kinds of cells. Use these cell diagrams to answer the questions that follow.

Cell 1

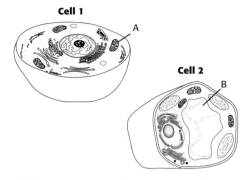

Cell 2

1. What is the name of the organelle labeled *A* in Cell 1?
   A endoplasmic reticulum
   B mitochondrion
   C vacuole
   D nucleus

2. What type of cell is Cell 1?
   F a bacterial cell
   G a plant cell
   H an animal cell
   I a prokaryotic cell

3. What is the name and function of the organelle labeled *B* in Cell 2?
   A The organelle is a vacuole, and it stores water and other materials.
   B The organelle is the nucleus, and it contains the DNA.
   C The organelle is the cell wall, and it gives shape to the cell.
   D The organelle is a ribosome, where proteins are put together.

4. What type of cell is Cell 2? How do you know?
   F prokaryotic; because it does not have a nucleus
   G eukaryotic; because it does not have a nucleus
   H prokaryotic; because it has a nucleus
   I eukaryotic; because it has a nucleus

Read each question below, and choose the best answer.

1. What is the surface area–to-volume ratio of the rectangular solid shown in the diagram below?

6 cm
3 cm   2 cm

   A 0.5:1
   B 2:1
   C 36:1
   D 72:1

2. Look at the diagram of the cell below. Three molecules of food per cubic unit of volume per minute are required for the cell to survive. One molecule of food can enter through each square unit of surface area per minute. What will happen to this cell?

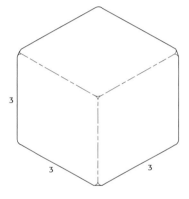

3

3   3

   F The cell is too small, and it will starve.
   G The cell is too large, and it will starve.
   H The cell is at a size that will allow it to survive.
   I There is not enough information to determine the answer.

Standardized Test Preparation

1. B
2. H
3. A
4. I

 **TEST DOCTOR**

Question 2: The cell is not a bacterium or a prokaryotic cell because it has a nucleus, and it is not a plant cell because it has no cell wall.

Question 4: The cell has a nucleus, and only eukaryotic cells have a nucleus. Answer I is the only answer that has that combination of facts.

1. B
2. G

TEST DOCTOR

Question 2: When students calculate the cell's surface area–to-volume ratio, they will find that it is 2.00:1. Therefore, only 2.00 food molecules can enter per minute. Because the cell needs 3 molecules of food per minute, the cell is too large, and it will starve. It may help students to understand how the surface area–to-volume ratio affects survival by showing students a variety of three-dimensional models.

CHAPTER RESOURCES

Chapter Resource File

• Standardized Test Preparation GENERAL

Workbooks

North Carolina Standardized Test Preparation
• Provides practice for the EOG test.

State Resources

For specific resources for your state, visit **go.hrw.com** and type in the keyword **HSMSTR**.

Weird Science

Background

Within the last 20 years, biologists' ideas of which environments would be suitable for life have increased dramatically. Discoveries of organisms that live under extreme conditions of temperature and pressure have led to the use of the word *extremophile* for these life-forms.

Scientific Discoveries

Background

It is important to note that stem cells are very different from other cells. All stem cells—embryonic or adult—have three unique characteristics. First, stem cells are unspecialized. So, a stem cell in its original form cannot perform the function of a muscle cell or a blood cell. But these unspecialized cells can give rise to specialized cells and then can perform these functions. Second, stem cells can divide and renew for long periods of time. Scientists have shown that as long as a stem cell remains unspecialized, it can continue to divide for an extended period of time. Third, stem cells can evolve into specialized cells through the process of differentiation.

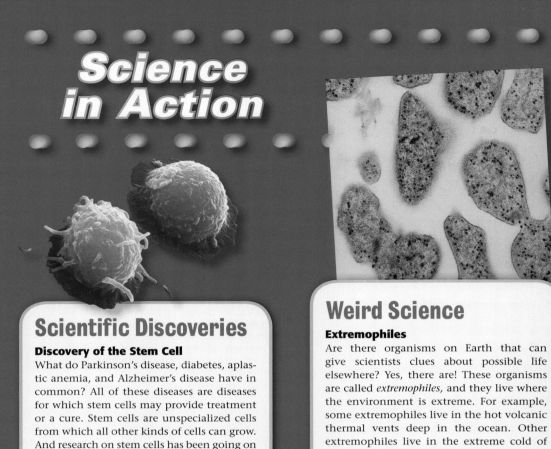

Science in Action

Scientific Discoveries

Discovery of the Stem Cell

What do Parkinson's disease, diabetes, aplastic anemia, and Alzheimer's disease have in common? All of these diseases are diseases for which stem cells may provide treatment or a cure. Stem cells are unspecialized cells from which all other kinds of cells can grow. And research on stem cells has been going on almost since microscopes were invented. But scientists have been able to culture, or grow, stem cells in laboratories for only about the last 20 years. Research during these 20 years has shown scientists that stem cells can be useful in treating—and possibly curing—a variety of diseases.

Language Arts ACTIVITY

WRITING SKILL Imagine that you are a doctor who treats diseases such as Parkinson's disease. Design and create a pamphlet or brochure that you could use to explain what stem cells are. Include in your pamphlet a description of how stem cells might be used to treat one of your patients who has Parkinson's disease. Be sure to include information about Parkinson's disease.

Weird Science

Extremophiles

Are there organisms on Earth that can give scientists clues about possible life elsewhere? Yes, there are! These organisms are called *extremophiles,* and they live where the environment is extreme. For example, some extremophiles live in the hot volcanic thermal vents deep in the ocean. Other extremophiles live in the extreme cold of Antarctica. But these organisms do not live only in extreme environments. Research shows that extremophiles may be abundant in plankton in the ocean. And not all extremophiles are archaebacteria; some extremophiles are eubacteria.

Social Studies ACTIVITY

Choose one of the four types of extremophiles. Do some research about the organism you have chosen and make a poster showing what you learned about it, including where it can be found, under what conditions it lives, how it survives, and how it is used.

Answer to Social Studies Activity

Students' posters should reflect the research they have done. For example, a student who chooses methanogens may show that these extremophiles live in a wide variety of places and in a large number of geographical locations. The poster may also include an explanation of how these organisms get nutrients and how the metabolism of methanogens is different from human metabolism. Students should also show any commercial, industrial, or medical uses of whichever organism they have chosen.

Answer to Language Arts Activity

Students' pamphlets or brochures should present a basic explanation of what stem cells are, where they come from, why they are useful, and how they may be used specifically to treat Parkinson's disease. So, the student will also have to include a little information about Parkinson's disease.

People in Science

Caroline Schooley

Microscopist Imagine that your assignment is the following: Go outside. Look at 1 ft² of the ground for 30 min. Make notes about what you observe. Be prepared to describe what you see. If you look at the ground with just your naked eyes, you may quickly run out of things to see. But what would happen if you used a microscope to look? How much more would you be able to see? And how much more would you have to talk about? Caroline Schooley could tell you.

Caroline Schooley joined a science club in middle school. That's when her interest in looking at things through a microscope began. Since then, Schooley has spent many years studying life through a microscope. She is a microscopist. A *microscopist* is someone who uses a microscope to look at small things. Microscopists use their tools to explore the world of small things that cannot be seen by the naked eye. And with today's powerful electron microscopes, microscopists can study things we could never see before, things as small as atoms.

Math ACTIVITY

An average bacterium is about 0.000002 m long. A pencil point is about 0.001 m wide. Approximately how many bacteria would fit on a pencil point?

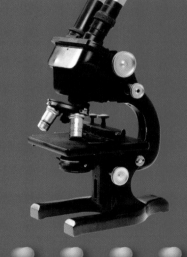

People in Science

Background

Caroline Schooley wants students to think about microscopes and microscopy. The field is changing. One of the newest uses of microscopy is in nanotechnology. *Nanotechnology* is the science of manipulating materials on an atomic or molecular level to build microscopic devices. To do so, scientists will develop tiny machines (called *assemblers*) that can manipulate atoms and molecules as directed. Tiny nanomachines (called *replicators*) will be then programmed to build more assemblers. Nanotechnology can be thought of as molecular manufacturing.

Answer to Math Activity

0.001 m (size of pencil point) ÷ 0.000002 m (size of bacteria) = 500

So, approximately 500 bacteria could fit on a pencil point.

The Cell in Action
Chapter Planning Guide

Compression guide:
To shorten instruction
because of time limitations,
omit the Chapter Lab.

OBJECTIVES	LABS, DEMONSTRATIONS, AND ACTIVITIES	TECHNOLOGY RESOURCES
PACING • 135 min pp. 380–385 **Chapter Opener**	SE **Start-up Activity**, p. 381 ◆ GENERAL	OSP **Parent Letter** GENERAL CD **Student Edition on CD-ROM** CD **Guided Reading Audio CD** TR **Chapter Starter Transparency*** VID **Brain Food Video Quiz**
Section 1 Exchange with the Environment • Explain the process of diffusion. • Describe how osmosis occurs. • Compare passive transport with active transport. • Explain how large particles get into and out of cells.	TE **Demonstration** Membrane Model, p. 382 ◆ GENERAL SE **Quick Lab** Bead Diffusion, p. 383 ◆ GENERAL CRF **Datasheet for Quick Lab*** TE **Demonstration** Crossing Membranes, p. 383 ◆ GENERAL SE **Inquiry Labs** The Perfect Taters Mystery, p. 394 ◆ GENERAL CRF **Datasheet for Chapter Lab*** LB **Inquiry Labs** Fish Farms in Space* ◆ GENERAL LB **Whiz-Bang Demonstrations** It's in the Bag!* ◆ BASIC	CRF **Lesson Plans*** TR **Bellringer Transparency*** TR Passive Transport and Active Transport* TR Endocytosis and Exocytosis* CRF **SciLinks Activity*** GENERAL VID **Lab Videos for Life Science** CD **Interactive Explorations CD-ROM** The Nose Knows GENERAL
PACING • 45 min pp. 386–389 **Section 2 Cell Energy** • Describe photosynthesis and cellular respiration. • Compare cellular respiration with fermentation.	TE **Demonstration** Leaves and Light, p. 386 GENERAL SE **Connection to Chemistry**, Earth's Early Atmosphere p. 387 GENERAL TE **Group Activity** Recycling Carbon, p. 387 GENERAL TE **Group Activity** Photosynthesis and Cellular Respiration, p. 388 GENERAL SE **Skills Practice Lab** Stayin' Alive!, p. 605 GENERAL CRF **Datasheet for LabBook***	CRF **Lesson Plans*** TR **Bellringer Transparency*** TR The Connection Between Photosynthesis and Respiration* TR **LINK TO PHYSICAL SCIENCE** Solar Heating Systems*
PACING • 45 min pp. 390–393 **Section 3 The Cell Cycle** • Explain how cells produce more cells. • Describe the process of mitosis. • Explain how cell division differs in animals and plants.	TE **Activity** Making Models, p. 390 GENERAL SE **Connection to Language Arts** Picking Apart Vocabulary, p. 391 GENERAL TE **Connection Activity** Math, p. 391 ADVANCED TE **Activity** Four Phases of Mitosis, p. 393 ADVANCED LB **Labs You Can Eat** The Mystery of the Runny Gelatin* ◆ GENERAL LB **Whiz-Bang Demonstrations** Stop Picking on My Enzyme* ◆ BASIC LB **Long-Term Projects & Research Ideas** Taming the Wild Yeast* ◆ ADVANCED SE **Science in Action** Math, Social Studies, and Language Arts Activities, pp. 400–401 GENERAL	CRF **Lesson Plans*** TR **Bellringer Transparency*** TR The Cell Cycle* TE **Internet Activity**, p. 392 GENERAL

PACING • 90 min

CHAPTER REVIEW, ASSESSMENT, AND STANDARDIZED TEST PREPARATION

CRF **Vocabulary Activity*** GENERAL
SE **Chapter Review**, pp. 396–397 GENERAL
CRF **Chapter Review*** ■ GENERAL
CRF **Chapter Tests A*** ■ GENERAL, **B*** ADVANCED, **C*** SPECIAL NEEDS
SE **Standardized Test Preparation**, pp. 398–399 GENERAL
CRF **Standardized Test Preparation*** GENERAL
CRF **Performance-Based Assessment*** GENERAL
OSP **Test Generator** GENERAL
CRF **Test Item Listing*** GENERAL

Online and Technology Resources

Visit **go.hrw.com** for a variety of free resources related to this textbook. Enter the keyword **HT5R7ACT.**

Holt Online Learning

Students can access interactive problem-solving help and active visual concept development with the *Holt Science and Technology* Online Edition available at **www.hrw.com.**

 Guided Reading Audio CD

These CDs are designed to help auditory learners and reluctant readers.

 Science Tutor CD-ROM

Excellent for remediation and test practice.

KEY		CRF Chapter Resource File	SS Science Skills Worksheets	* Also on One-Stop Planner
SE Student Edition		OSP One-Stop Planner	MS Math Skills for Science Worksheets	◆ Requires advance prep
TE Teacher Edition		LB Lab Bank	CD CD or CD-ROM	■ Also available in Spanish
		TR Transparencies	VID Classroom Video/DVD	

SKILLS DEVELOPMENT RESOURCES	SECTION REVIEW AND ASSESSMENT	STANDARDS CORRELATIONS
SE **Pre-Reading Activity,** p. 380 `GENERAL` OSP **Science Puzzlers, Twisters & Teasers** `GENERAL`		North Carolina Standard Course of Study
CRF **Directed Reading A*** `BASIC`, **B*** `SPECIAL NEEDS` CRF **Vocabulary and Section Summary*** `GENERAL` SE **Reading Strategy** Reading Organizer, p. 382 `GENERAL` TE **Inclusion Strategies,** p. 383 CRF **Reinforcement Worksheet** Into and Out of the Cell* `BASIC` SS **Science Skills** Doing a Lab Write-Up* `BASIC` SS **Science Skills** Taking Notes* `BASIC` MS **Math Skills for Science** Multiplying Whole Numbers* `BASIC` MS **Math Skills for Science** Dividing Whole Numbers with Long Division* `BASIC`	SE **Reading Checks,** pp. 383, 385 `GENERAL` TE **Reteaching,** p. 384 `BASIC` TE **Quiz,** p. 384 `GENERAL` TE **Alternative Assessment,** p. 384 `ADVANCED` TE **Homework,** p. 384 `GENERAL` SE **Section Review,*** p. 385 ■ `GENERAL` CRF **Section Quiz*** ■ `GENERAL`	*Chapter Lab:* 1.01, 1.02, 1.08
CRF **Directed Reading A*** `BASIC`, **B*** `SPECIAL NEEDS` CRF **Vocabulary and Section Summary*** `GENERAL` SE **Reading Strategy** Discussion, p. 386 `GENERAL` CRF **Reinforcement Worksheet** Activities of the Cell* `BASIC` CRF **Critical Thinking** A Celluloid Thriller* `ADVANCED` SS **Science Skills** Using Logic* `BASIC` SS **Science Skills** Identifying Bias* `GENERAL`	SE **Reading Checks,** pp. 387, 389 `GENERAL` TE **Reteaching,** p. 388 `BASIC` TE **Quiz,** p. 388 `GENERAL` TE **Alternative Assessment,** p. 388 `GENERAL` TE **Homework,** p. 388 `ADVANCED` SE **Section Review,*** p. 389 ■ `GENERAL` CRF **Section Quiz*** ■ `GENERAL`	*LabBook:* 1.06
CRF **Directed Reading A*** `BASIC`, **B*** `SPECIAL NEEDS` CRF **Vocabulary and Section Summary*** `GENERAL` SE **Reading Strategy** Paired Summarizing, p. 390 `GENERAL` TE **Connection to Math** Cell Multiplication, p. 390 `BASIC` TE **Reading Strategy** Prediction Guide, p. 391 `GENERAL` TE **Inclusion Strategies,** p. 392 MS **Math Skills for Science** Multiplying Whole Numbers* `GENERAL` MS **Math Skills for Science** Grasping Graphing* `GENERAL` SS **Science Skills** Organizing Your Research* `GENERAL` SS **Science Skills** Researching on the Web* `BASIC` CRF **Reinforcement Worksheet** This Is Radio KCEL* `BASIC`	SE **Reading Checks,** pp. 391, 392 `GENERAL` TE **Reteaching,** p. 392 `BASIC` TE **Quiz,** p. 392 `GENERAL` TE **Alternative Assessment,** p. 392 `GENERAL` SE **Section Review,*** p. 393 ■ `GENERAL` CRF **Section Quiz*** ■ `GENERAL`	

One-Stop Planner® CD-ROM

This convenient CD-ROM includes:
- **Lab Materials QuickList Software**
- **Holt Calendar Planner**
- **Customizable Lesson Plans**
- **Printable Worksheets**
- **ExamView® Test Generator**

cnnstudentnews.com

Find the latest news, lesson plans, and activities related to important scientific events.

www.scilinks.org

Maintained by the **National Science Teachers Association.** See Chapter Enrichment pages for a complete list of topics.

Check out *Current Science* articles and activities by visiting the HRW Web site at **go.hrw.com.** Just type in the keyword **HL5CS04T.**

Classroom Videos

- **Lab Videos** demonstrate the chapter lab.
- **Brain Food Video Quizzes** help students review the chapter material.
- **CNN Videos** bring science into your students' daily life.

Visual Resources

CHAPTER STARTER TRANSPARENCY

Happy 140th Birthday!

What If . . . ?

How long would you like to live? What if you could live to be 120 years old? Or 150 and beyond? Since ancient times, people have searched in vain for a magical fountain or potion that could give them eternal youth. No one has yet found the secret of immortality, but scientists have recently made a startling discovery that may help extend people's lives.

In January of 1998, researchers at the University of Texas reported that they had found an enzyme in the body that acts like a "cellular fountain of youth." In the laboratory, the enzyme enables human cells to stay young and multiply long

past the time when cells would normally stop dividing and die. Researchers hope that the enzyme can someday be used to understand and treat certain cancers and other incurable diseases. Although the so-called immortalizing enzyme won't help people live forever, it may help them live longer, healthier lives.

Every living thing is made of cells. In this chapter you will learn how cells grow and how they make more cells. You will also learn how cells transport materials and obtain the energy they need to survive.

BELLRINGER TRANSPARENCIES

Section: Exchange with the Environment
Which of the following best describes a living cell:
a) building block
b) a living organism
c) a complex factory
d) all of the above

Write a paragraph in your **science journal** defending your choice.

Section: Cell Energy
Make a list of all the different types of cells that you can think of and the jobs they do. Then make a list of all the reasons that a cell needs energy.

Write your answers in your **science journal.**

TEACHING TRANSPARENCIES

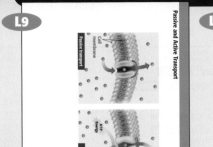

L9 Passive and Active Transport

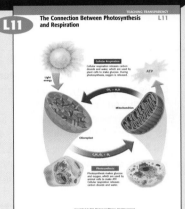

L11 The Connection Between Photosynthesis and Respiration

TEACHING TRANSPARENCIES

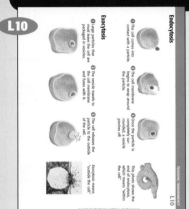

L10 Exocytosis / Endocytosis

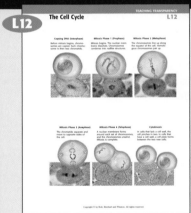

L12 The Cell Cycle

P44 Solar Heating Systems

LINK TO PHYSICAL SCIENCE

Chapter: Heat and Heat Technology

CONCEPT MAPPING TRANSPARENCY

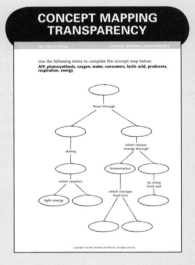

Use the following terms to complete the concept map below: ATP, photosynthesis, oxygen, water, consumers, lactic acid, producers, respiration, energy

Planning Resources

LESSON PLANS

Lesson Plan SAMPLE

Section: Waves

Pacing
Regular Schedule: with lab(s):2 days without lab(s):2 days
Block Schedule: with lab(s):1 1/2 days without lab(s):1 day

Objectives
1. Relate the seven properties of life to a living organism.
2. Describe seven themes that can help you to organize what you learn about biology.
3. Identify the tiny structures that make up all living organisms.
4. Differentiate between reproduction and heredity and between metabolism and homeostasis.

National Science Education Standards Covered
LSInter6:Cells have particular structures that underlie their functions.
LSMat1:Most cell functions involve chemical reactions.
LSBeh1:Cells store and use information to guide their functions.
UCP1:Cell functions are regulated.
SI1: Cells can differentiate and form complete multicellular organisms.
PS1: Species evolve over time.
ESS1: The great diversity of organisms is the result of more than 3.5 billion years of evolution.
ESS2: Natural selection and its evolutionary consequences provide a scientific explanation for the fossil record of ancient life forms as well as for the striking molecular similarities observed among the diverse species of living organisms.
ST1: The millions of different species of plants, animals, and microorganisms that live on Earth today are related by descent from common ancestors.
ST2: The energy for life primarily comes from the sun.
SPSP1: The complexity and organization of organisms accommodates the need for obtaining, transforming, transporting, releasing, and eliminating the matter and energy used to sustain the organism.
SPSP6: As matter and energy flows through different levels of organization of living systems—cells, organs, communities—and between living systems and the physical environment, chemical elements are recombined in different ways.
HNS1: Organisms have behavioral responses to internal changes and to external stimuli.

PARENT LETTER

SAMPLE

Dear Parent,

Your son's or daughter's science class will soon begin exploring the chapter entitled "The World of Physical Science." In this chapter, students will learn about how the scientific method applies to the world of physical science and the role of physical science in the world. By the end of the chapter, students should demonstrate a clear understanding of the chapter's main ideas and be able to discuss the following topics:

1. physical science as the study of energy and matter (Section 1)
2. the role of physical science in the world around them (Section 1)
3. careers that rely on physical science (Section 1)
4. the steps used in the scientific method (Section 2)
5. examples of technology (Section 2)
6. how the scientific method is used to answer questions and solve problems (Section 2)
7. how our knowledge of science changes over time (Section 2)
8. how models represent real objects or systems (Section 3)
9. examples of different ways models are used in science (Section 3)
10. the importance of the International System of Units (Section 4)
11. the appropriate units to use for particular measurements (Section 4)
12. how area and density are related quantities (Section 4)

Questions to Ask Along the Way

You can help your son or daughter learn about these topics by asking interesting questions such as the following:

• What are some surprising careers that use physical science?
• What is a characteristic of a good hypothesis?
• When is it a good idea to use a model?
• Why do Americans measure things in terms of inches and yards instead of centimeters and meters?

TEST ITEM LISTING

TEST ITEM LISTING
The World of Science SAMPLE

MULTIPLE CHOICE

1. A limitation of models is that
   a. they are large enough to see.
   b. they do not act exactly like the things that they model.
   c. they are smaller than the things that they model.
   d. they model unfamiliar things
   Answer: B   Difficulty: 1   Section: 3   Objective: 2

2. The length 10 m is equal to
   a. 100 cm.   c. 10,000 mm.
   b. 1,000 cm.   d. Both (b) and (c))
   Answer: B   Difficulty: 1   Section: 3   Objective: 2

3. To be valid, a hypothesis must be
   a. testable.   c. made into a law
   b. supported by evidence.   d. Both (a) and (b)
   Answer: B   Difficulty: 1   Section: 2   Objective: 2 1

4. The statement "Sheila has a stain on her shirt" is an example of a(n)
   a. law.   c. observation.
   b. hypothesis.   d. prediction.
   Answer: B   Difficulty: 1   Section: 3   Objective: 2

5. A hypothesis is often developed out of
   a. observations.   c. laws.
   b. experiments.   d. Both (a) and (b)
   Answer: B   Difficulty: 1   Section: 3   Objective: 2

6. How many milliliters are in 3.5 kL?
   a. 3,500 mL   c. 3,500, 000 mL
   b. 0.0035 mL.   d. 35,000 mL.
   Answer: B   Difficulty: 1   Section: 3   Objective: 2

7. A map of Seattle is an example of a
   a. law.   c. model.
   b. theory.   d. unit.
   Answer: B   Difficulty: 1   Section: 3   Objective: 2

8. A lab has the safety icons shown below. These icons mean that you should wear
   a. only safety goggles.   c. safety goggles and a lab apron.
   b. only a lab apron.   d. safety goggles, a lab apron, and gloves
   Answer: B   Difficulty: 1   Section: 3   Objective: 2

9. The law of conservation of mass says the tot al mass before a chemical change is
   a. more than the total mass after the change.
   b. less than the total mass after the change.
   c. the same as the total mass after the change.
   d. not the same as the total mass after the change.
   Answer: B   Difficulty: 1   Section: 3   Objective: 2

10. In which of the following areas might you find a geochemist at work?
    a. studying the chemistry of rocks   c. studying fishes
    b. studying forestry   d. studying the environment
    Answer: B   Difficulty: 1   Section: 3   Objective: 2

One-Stop Planner® CD-ROM

This CD-ROM includes all of the resources shown here and the following time-saving tools:

• **Lab Materials QuickList Software**
• **Customizable lesson plans**
• **Holt Calendar Planner**
• **The powerful ExamView® Test Generator**

For a preview of available worksheets covering math and science skills, see pages T26–T33. All of these resources are also on the One-Stop Planner®.

Meeting Individual Needs

DIRECTED READING A
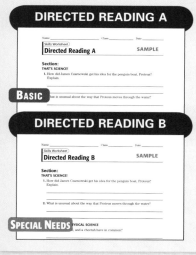
Skills Worksheet
Directed Reading A SAMPLE

Section:
THAT'S SCIENCE!
1. How did James Czarnowski get his idea for the penguin boat, Proteus? Explain.

_____ is unusual about the way that Proteus moves through the water?

BASIC

DIRECTED READING B
Skills Worksheet
Directed Reading B SAMPLE

Section:
THAT'S SCIENCE!
1. How did James Czarnowski get his idea for the penguin boat, Proteus? Explain.

2. What is unusual about the way that Proteus moves through the water?

SPECIAL NEEDS PHYSICAL SCIENCE
_____ and a cheetah have in common?

VOCABULARY ACTIVITY
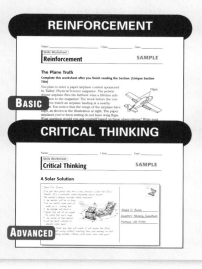
Skills Worksheet
Vocabulary Activity SAMPLE

Getting the Dirt on the Soil
After you finish reading Chapter: [Unique Title], try this puzzle! Use the clues below to unscramble the vocabulary words. Write your answer in the space provided.

_____ breakdown of rock into _____ and smaller pieces. ENGNETH
9. the chemical breakdown of rocks and minerals into new substances: CAMILCHE THEAIRGWEN

GENERAL

VOCABULARY AND SECTION SUMMARY
Skills Worksheet
Vocabulary & Notes SAMPLE

Section:
VOCABULARY
In your own words, write a definition of the following term in the space provided.
1. scientific method

2. technology

GENERAL

REINFORCEMENT
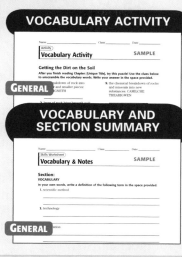
Skills Worksheet
Reinforcement SAMPLE

The Plane Truth
Complete this worksheet after you finish reading the Section: [Unique Section Title]

You plan to enter a paper airplane contest sponsored by Talkin' Physical Science magazine.

BASIC

CRITICAL THINKING
Skills Worksheet
Critical Thinking SAMPLE

A Solar Solution

ADVANCED

SCILINKS ACTIVITY

Activity
SciLinks Activity SAMPLE

MARINE ECOSYSTEMS
Go to www.scilinks.com. To find links related to marine ecosystems, type in the keyword HL5491. Then, use the links to answer the following questions about marine ecosystems.
_____ percentage of the Earth's surface is covered by water?

GENERAL

SCIENCE PUZZLERS, TWISTERS & TEASERS
CHAPTER 4 **SCIENCE PUZZLERS, TWISTERS & TEASERS**
The Cell in Action

Fractured Frames
1. Each frame represents a word from the chapter. If you read it in just the right way: Decipher each puzzle and write the answer in the space provided.

Fusion Fusion | taFIRMhun

2. Unravel these symbols to find a word from the chapter.

GENERAL

Labs and Activities

LONG-TERM PROJECTS & RESEARCH IDEAS

PROJECT 4 **STUDENT WORKSHEET**
Taming the Wild Yeast

If you have ever made bread, you probably used a packet of dried yeast that you bought at the grocery store.

Pet Yeast
1. Try your hand at raising yeast. Find a recipe for a sourdough starter in a bread cook book or on the Internet.

Another Long-Term Project Idea
2. How do you think different cells of different organisms look during mitosis?

Research Idea
3. How can you make salt water drinkable?

ADVANCED

WHIZ-BANG DEMONSTRATIONS
DEMO 5 **TEACHER-LED DEMONSTRATION** MAKING MODELS
It's in the Bag!

Purpose
Students are challenged to simulate the process of endocytosis in cells.

Time Required

materials. The bag represents the cell, and the candy represents food that the cell takes in.
Arrange the candy on the string and the scissors inside the bag. Keep your hands

BASIC

WHIZ-BANG DEMONSTRATIONS
DEMO 4 **TEACHER-LED DEMONSTRATION** MAKING MODELS
Stop Picking on My Enzyme

Purpose
This activity is a fun, simple way to familiarize students with the vocabulary and processes of enzyme action.

Time Required
10–15 minutes

Lab Ratings

What to Do
1. Ask students to imagine that your hand is an enzyme. Pinch your thumb and forefinger together, and tell students that the area between the tips of your fingers is the enzyme's active site.
2. Pick up a toothpick with one hand, and hold it in the "active site." Explain that the toothpick now represents the substrate. Break the toothpick. The break in the toothpick represents the place where the chemical bonds have been weakened by the enzyme and subsequently broken.

MATERIALS
_____ wooden toothpicks

Introduction

BASIC

INQUIRY LABS

LAB 2 **STUDENT WORKSHEET** DISCOVERY LAB
Fish Farms in Space

Dear Junior Researcher,
Frequent Fryer Fish Farms, in partnership with Universal Studios for Space Enterprises, is working to develop a sustainable food supply for an international space station.

Sincerely,

GENERAL LIFE SCIENCE

LABS YOU CAN EAT
LAB 3 **STUDENT WORKSHEET** DISCOVERY LAB
The Mystery of the Runny Gelatin

Chef Uva Plantana is famous for her magnificent molded fruit salads. A recent tour of the South Pacific inspired Uva to create a spectacular salad of fresh pineapples, papayas, apples, figs, oranges, kiwis, and bananas as an edible centerpiece for the Culinary Convention banquet.

GENERAL LIFE SCIENCE

DATASHEETS FOR QUICK LABS
TEACHER RESOURCE PAGE
Quick Lab
Reaction to Stress SAMPLE
DATASHEET FOR QUICK LAB

Background
The graph below illustrates changes that occur in the membrane potential of a neuron during an action potential. Use the graph to answer the following questions. Refer to Figure 3 as needed.

DATASHEETS FOR CHAPTER LABS
TEACHER RESOURCE PAGE
Skills Practice Lab
Using Scientific Methods SAMPLE
DATASHEET FOR CHAPTER LAB

Teacher's Notes
TIME REQUIRED
One 45-minute class period.

DATASHEETS FOR LABBOOK
TEACHER RESOURCE PAGE
Skills Practice Lab
Does It All Add Up? SAMPLE
DATASHEET FOR LABBOOK LAB

Teacher's Notes
TIME REQUIRED
One 45-minute class period.

Review and Assessments

SECTION QUIZ
Assessment
Section Quiz SAMPLE

Section:
In the space provided, write the letter of the description that best matches the term or phrase.
___ 1. building molecules that can be used as an energy source, or breaking down molecules in which energy is stored
___ 2. the process by which light energy is converted to chemical energy
___ 3. an organism that uses sunlight or inorganic substances to make organic compounds

GENERAL

ALSO IN SPANISH

SECTION REVIEW
Skills Worksheet
Section Review SAMPLE

Section:
KEY TERMS
1. What do paleontologists study?

2. How does a trace fossil differ from petrified wood?

GENERAL UNDERSTANDING KEY IDEAS
_____ fossil.

ALSO IN SPANISH

CHAPTER REVIEW
Skills Worksheet
Chapter Review SAMPLE

USING VOCABULARY
1. Define biome in your own words.

2. Describe the characteristics of a savanna and a desert.

GENERAL

ALSO IN SPANISH

CHAPTER TEST A
Assessment
Chapter Test A SAMPLE

MULTIPLE CHOICE
In the space provided, write the letter of the term or phrase that best completes each statement or best answers each question.
___ 1. Surface currents are formed by
  a. the moon's gravity. c. wind.
  b. the sun's gravity. d. increased water density.
___ 2. When waves come near the shore,
  a. they speed up. c. their wavelength increases.
  b. they maintain their speed. d. their wave height increases.
___ Longshore currents transport sediment
  a. out to the open ocean. c. only during low tide.
  b. along the shore. d. only during high tide.
___ 4. Which of the following does NOT control surface currents?

GENERAL

ALSO IN SPANISH

CHAPTER TEST B
Assessment
Chapter Test B SAMPLE

MULTIPLE CHOICE
In the space provided, write the letter of the term or phrase that best completes each statement or best answers each question.
___ 1. Surface currents are formed by
  a. the moon's gravity. c. wind.
  b. the sun's gravity. d. increased water density.
___ When waves come near the shore,
  a. they speed up. c. their wavelength increases.
  b. they maintain their speed. d. their wave height increases.

ADVANCED

CHAPTER TEST C
Assessment
Chapter Test C SAMPLE

MULTIPLE CHOICE
In the space provided, write the letter of the term or phrase that best completes each statement or best answers each question.
___ 1. Surface currents are formed by
  a. the moon's gravity. c. wind.
  b. the sun's gravity. d. increased water density.
___ 2. When waves come near the shore,
  a. they speed up. c. their wavelength increases.
  b. they maintain their speed. d. their wave height increases.
___ Longshore currents transport sediment
  a. out to the open ocean. c. only during low tide.
  b. along the shore. d. only during high tide.
___ 4. Which of the following does NOT control surface currents?

SPECIAL NEEDS

STANDARDIZED TEST PREPARATION
Assessment
Standardized Test Preparation SAMPLE

READING
Read the passages below. Then, read each question that follows the passage. Decide which is the best answer to each question.

Passage 1 adventure summer camp in the world. Billy can't wait to head for the outdoors. Billy checked the recommended supply list: light, summer clothes; sunscreen; rain gear; heavy, water-filled jacket; ski mask; and thick gloves. Wait a minute! Billy thought he was traveling to only one **destination**, so why does he need to bring such a wide variety of clothes? On further investiga-

GENERAL

PERFORMANCE-BASED ASSESSMENT
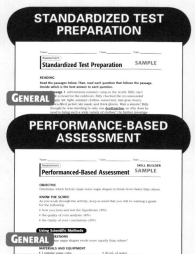
Assessment
Performanced-Based Assessment SKILL BUILDER SAMPLE

OBJECTIVE
Determine which factors cause water sugar shapes to break down faster than others.

KNOW THE SCORE!
Read all the way through the activity, keep in mind that you will be earning a grade for the following.
• how you form and test the hypothesis (30%)
• the quality of your analysis (40%)
• the clarity of your conclusions (30%)

Using Scientific Methods
QUESTIONS
MATERIALS AND EQUIPMENT
• 1 regular sugar cube • 90 mL of water

This Chapter Enrichment provides relevant and interesting information to expand and enhance your presentation of the chapter material.

Section 1

Exchange with the Environment

Endocytosis

- There are three different mechanisms of endocytosis: phagocytosis, receptor-mediated endocytosis, and pinocytosis. These processes allow a substance to enter a cell without passing through the cell membrane. The substance involved determines which method is used.

- Large particles such as bacteria enter the cell by phagocytosis. The host cell changes shape, and the membrane sends out projections called *pseudopods,* meaning "false feet," which surround the particle, bringing it inside the cell.

- In receptor-mediated endocytosis, receptors on the membrane that are specific for a given substance bind to the substance before the endocytotic process begins. This method is used during cholesterol metabolism.

- In pinocytosis, the cell membrane surrounds the substance and forms a vesicle to bring the material into the cell. Pinocytosis usually involves material that is dissolved in water.

Reverse Osmosis

- Reverse osmosis is a process that forces water across semipermeable membranes under high pressure. The high pressure reverses the natural tendency of the solutes on the more concentrated side of the membrane to pass through to the less-concentrated side. In this way, water passing through the membrane is purified.

Is That a Fact!

- ◆ The largest single-celled organism that ever lived was a protozoan that measured 20 cm in diameter. It is now extinct.

Section 2

Cell Energy

Early Plant Scientists

- Jan Baptista Van Helmont (1580–1644) was a Belgian chemist, physiologist, and physician who coined the word *gas.* Van Helmont was the first scientist to comprehend the existence of gases separate from the atmospheric air. Although he didn't know that it was carbon dioxide, van Helmont stated that the *spiritus sylvestre,* or "wild spirit," emitted by burning charcoal was the same as that given off by fermenting grape juice. He applied chemistry to the study of physiological processes, and for this he is known as the "father of biochemistry."

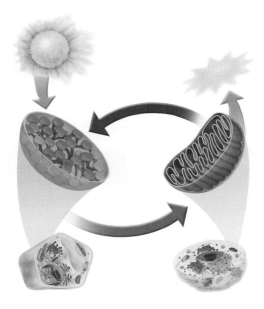

- Joseph Priestley (1733–1804) was an English clergyman and physical scientist who was one of the discoverers of oxygen. He also observed that light was vital for plant growth and that green leaves released oxygen.

- Jan Ingenhousz (1730–1799), a Dutch-born British physician and scientist, discovered photosynthesis.

Carotenoids and Photosynthesis

- Carotenoids are responsible for the orange colors in plants. Carotenoids are usually masked by chlorophyll which is more abundant until autumn. They are sensitive to wavelengths of light to which chlorophyll cannot respond. Carotenoids absorb wavelengths and transfer the energy to chlorophyll, which then incorporates that energy into the photosynthetic pathway.

Section 3

The Cell Cycle

Cytogenetics

- Cytogeneticists study the role of human chromosomes in health and disease. Chromosome studies can reveal abnormalities such as whether a person is carrying the genetic material for a genetically linked disease.

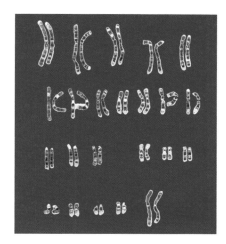

Cell Division

- The frequency of cell division varies a great deal. Fruit-fly embryo cells divide about every eight minutes. Human liver cells may not divide for up to one year. Scientists are still trying to determine what orchestrates growth and regulates cell division. This information would help scientists understand diseases of unregulated cell division, such as cancer.

- DNA and chromosomes are related but are not the same thing. A chromosome is made up of DNA that has been wound up and organized with proteins that hold it all together. For much of the cell cycle, DNA is loose and not very visible.

Is That a Fact!

◆ In an adult human body, cell division happens at least 10 million times every second.

Cell Adhesion

- Blood cells exist individually in the body, but most other cells are connected to each other. Usually this involves special adhesion proteins, such as adherins, cadherins, catenins, and integrins. These proteins connect adjoining cells by physically locking the cells together, fastening one cell to the next. Sometimes these junctions are outside the cell, and sometimes they are inside. Adhesion proteins can span the cell membranes and connect the inside of one cell to the inside of its neighbor cell.

Is That a Fact!

◆ In a healthy body, cells reproduce at exactly the same rate at which cells die. However, some agents make cells reproduce uncontrollably, causing a disease known as cancer. One of these carcinogenic agents is ultraviolet radiation, which is emitted by the sun and ultraviolet lamps. People who spend excessive amounts of time in the sun run the risk of developing skin cancer.

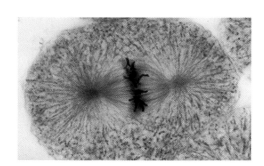

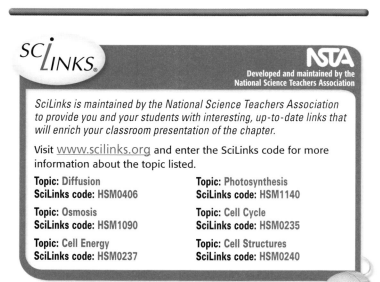

SCILINKS®

Developed and maintained by the National Science Teachers Association

SciLinks is maintained by the National Science Teachers Association to provide you and your students with interesting, up-to-date links that will enrich your classroom presentation of the chapter.

Visit www.scilinks.org and enter the SciLinks code for more information about the topic listed.

Topic: Diffusion
SciLinks code: HSM0406

Topic: Osmosis
SciLinks code: HSM1090

Topic: Cell Energy
SciLinks code: HSM0237

Topic: Photosynthesis
SciLinks code: HSM1140

Topic: Cell Cycle
SciLinks code: HSM0235

Topic: Cell Structures
SciLinks code: HSM0240

Overview

In this chapter, students will learn about how cells interact with their environment, how cells get nutrients and get rid of wastes, and where cells get the energy from to carry out all the activities of life. Students will also learn about how cells produce more cells.

Assessing Prior Knowledge

Students should be familiar with the following topic:
• cells as the basic units of life

Identifying Misconceptions

Students may not think of cells as self-contained units of life. It is important for students to realize that cells, just like multicellular organisms, live in an environment and must perform all the activities—such as taking in nutrients, producing energy, and getting rid of wastes—necessary to stay alive and reproduce. Students may also be confused about the difference between cells and molecules. Emphasize the relationship between cells and molecules, and that proteins, carbohydrates, and other substances are made of molecules. These molecules must be smaller than the cells they enter and leave. Many students believe that proteins and other molecules are bigger than cells.

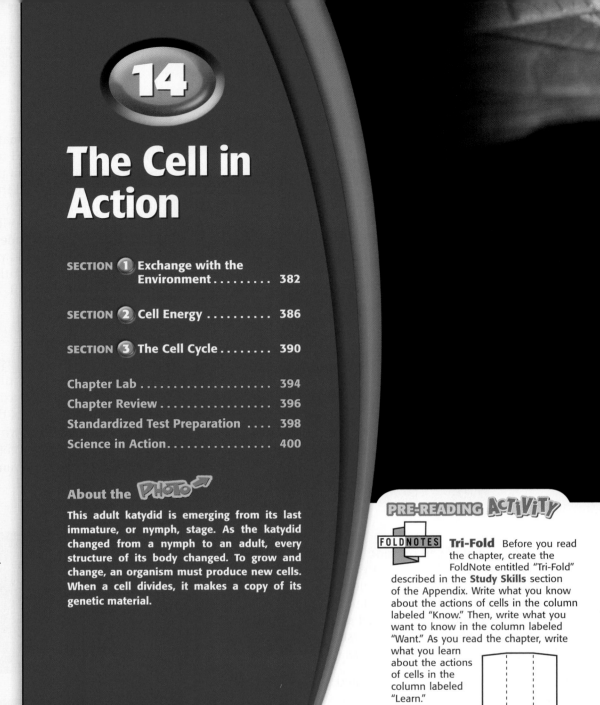

The Cell in Action

About the PHOTO

This adult katydid is emerging from its last immature, or nymph, stage. As the katydid changed from a nymph to an adult, every structure of its body changed. To grow and change, an organism must produce new cells. When a cell divides, it makes a copy of its genetic material.

PRE-READING ACTIVITY

FOLDNOTES **Tri-Fold** Before you read the chapter, create the FoldNote entitled "Tri-Fold" described in the **Study Skills** section of the Appendix. Write what you know about the actions of cells in the column labeled "Know." Then, write what you want to know in the column labeled "Want." As you read the chapter, write what you learn about the actions of cells in the column labeled "Learn."

Standards Correlations

North Carolina Standard Course of Study

1.01 Identify and create questions and hypotheses that can be answered through scientific investigations. (Chapter Lab)

1.02 (partial) Develop appropriate experimental procedures for: . . . Student generated questions. (Chapter Lab)

1.06 (partial) Use mathematics to gather, organize, and present quantitative data resulting from scientific investigations: Measurement [and] Analysis of data. (LabBook)

1.08 Use oral and written language to: Communicate findings [and] Defend conclusions of scientific investigations. (Chapter Lab)

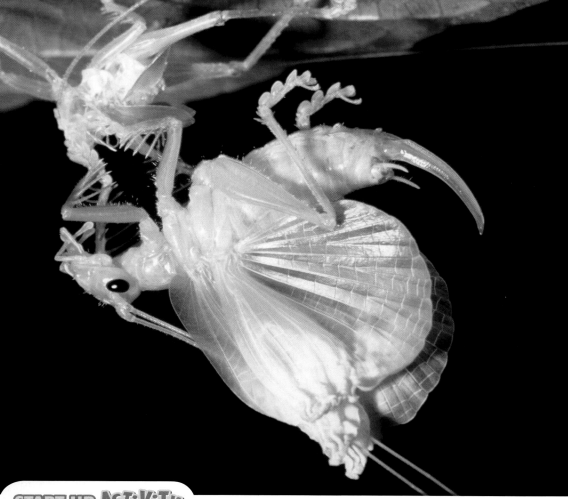

MATERIALS

FOR EACH STUDENT
- cup, small plastic
- ruler
- stirring rod
- sugar solution
- test tube, large plastic
- test-tube rack
- test tube, small plastic
- yeast-and-water mixture

Safety Caution: Remind students to review all safety cautions and icons before beginning this lab activity. Students should wear safety goggles at all times and wash their hands when they are finished. Students should not taste the solutions.

Teacher's Notes: The yeast suspension is prepared by mixing one package of dry yeast in 250 mL of water. The sugar solution is prepared by dissolving 30 mL (2 tbsp) of sugar in 100 mL of water.

Answers

1. Answers may vary. Students should subtract the first measurement from the second measurement.

2. When the yeast cells released the energy in sugar, the CO_2 that the cells produced increased the volume of air in the smaller tube and pushed more yeast-and-sugar mixture into the larger tube, increasing the height of the liquid in the larger tube.

START-UP ACTIVITY

Cells in Action

Yeast are single-celled fungi that are an important ingredient in bread. Yeast cells break down sugar molecules to release energy. In the process, carbon dioxide gas is produced, which causes bread dough to rise.

Procedure

1. Add **4 mL of a sugar solution** to **10 mL of a yeast-and-water mixture**. Use a **stirring rod** to thoroughly mix the two liquids.

2. Pour the stirred mixture into a small test tube.

3. Place a slightly **larger test tube** over the **small test tube**. The top of the small test tube should touch the bottom of the larger test tube.

4. Hold the test tubes together, and quickly turn both test tubes over. Place the test tubes in a test-tube rack.

5. Use a **ruler** to measure the height of the fluid in the large test tube. Wait 20 min, and then measure the height of the liquid again.

Analysis

1. What is the difference between the first height measurement and the second height measurement?

2. What do you think caused the change in the fluid's height?

Chapter Starter Transparency
Use this transparency to help students begin thinking about the relationship between cells and their environment.

CHAPTER RESOURCES

Technology

 Transparencies
- Chapter Starter Transparency

 READING SKILLS

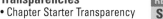 **Student Edition on CD-ROM**

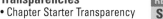 **Guided Reading Audio CD**

 Classroom Videos
- Brain Food Video Quiz

Workbooks

 Science Puzzlers, Twisters & Teasers
- The Cell in Action **GENERAL**

Overview

This section explains the processes of diffusion and osmosis. Students will compare the passive and active transport of particles into and out of cells.

🔊 Bellringer

Write the following on the board:

Which of the following best describes a living cell: a building block, a living organism, a complex factory, or all of the above? Explain your choice.

Motivate

Demonstration — GENERAL

Membrane Model Blow soap bubbles for the class. Explain that soap bubbles have properties, such as flexibility, that are similar to biological membranes. Components of soap film and of cell membranes move around freely. Soap bubbles and membranes are self-sealing. If two bubbles or membranes collide, they fuse. If one is cut in half, two smaller but whole bubbles or membranes form.

English Language Learners

LS Visual

READING WARM-UP

Objectives
- Explain the process of diffusion.
- Describe how osmosis occurs.
- Compare passive transport with active transport.
- Explain how large particles get into and out of cells.

Terms to Learn
diffusion
osmosis
passive transport
active transport
endocytosis
exocytosis

READING STRATEGY

Reading Organizer As you read this section, make a table comparing active transport and passive transport.

diffusion the movement of particles from regions of higher density to regions of lower density

---

Exchange with the Environment

What would happen to a factory if its power were shut off or its supply of raw materials never arrived? What would happen if the factory couldn't get rid of its garbage?

Like a factory, an organism must be able to obtain energy and raw materials and get rid of wastes. An organism's cells perform all of these functions. These functions keep cells healthy so that they can divide. Cell division allows organisms to grow and repair injuries.

The exchange of materials between a cell and its environment takes place at the cell's membrane. To understand how materials move into and out of the cell, you need to know about diffusion.

What Is Diffusion?

What happens if you pour dye on top of a layer of gelatin? At first, it is easy to see where the dye ends and the gelatin begins. But over time, the line between the two layers will blur, as shown in **Figure 1.** Why? Everything, including the gelatin and the dye, is made up of tiny moving particles. Particles travel from where they are crowded to where they are less crowded. This movement from areas of high concentration (crowded) to areas of low concentration (less crowded) is called **diffusion** (di FYOO zhuhn). Dye particles diffuse from where they are crowded (near the top of the glass) to where they are less crowded (in the gelatin). Diffusion also happens within and between living cells. Cells do not need to use energy for diffusion.

Figure 1 *The particles of the dye and the gelatin slowly mix by diffusion.*

CHAPTER RESOURCES

Chapter Resource File

- Lesson Plan
- Directed Reading A BASIC
- Directed Reading B SPECIAL NEEDS

Technology

- Transparencies
- Bellringer

Workbooks

- Science Skills
  - Doing a Lab Write-up GENERAL
  - Taking Notes GENERAL
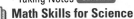
- Math Skills for Science
  - Multiplying Whole Numbers BASIC
  - Dividing Whole Numbers with Long Division BASIC

CONNECTION to Math — GENERAL

Gas Diffusion Have students solve the following problem in class or as part of their homework:

Gases diffuse about 10,000 times faster in air than in water. If a gas diffuses to fill a room completely in 6 min, how long would it take the gas to fill a similar volume of still water? (60,000 min) How many hours would that be? (1,000 h) How many days? (41.67 days) LS Logical

Figure 2   Osmosis

❶ The side that holds only pure water has the higher concentration of water particles.

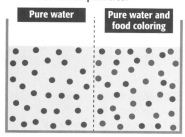
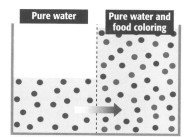

Pure water | **Pure water and food coloring**

❷ During osmosis, water particles move to where they are less concentrated.

Pure water | **Pure water and food coloring**

Diffusion of Water

The cells of organisms are surrounded by and filled with fluids that are made mostly of water. The diffusion of water through cell membranes is so important to life processes that it has been given a special name—**osmosis** (ahs MOH sis).

Water is made up of particles, called *molecules*. Pure water has the highest concentration of water molecules. When you mix something, such as food coloring, sugar, or salt, with water, you lower the concentration of water molecules. **Figure 2** shows how water molecules move through a membrane that is semipermeable (SEM i PUHR mee uh buhl). *Semipermeable* means that only certain substances can pass through. The picture on the left in **Figure 2** shows liquids that have different concentrations of water. Over time, the water molecules move from the liquid with the high concentration of water molecules to the liquid with the lower concentration of water molecules.

The Cell and Osmosis

Osmosis is important to cell functions. For example, red blood cells are surrounded by plasma. Plasma is made up of water, salts, sugars, and other particles. The concentration of these particles is kept in balance by osmosis. If red blood cells were in pure water, water molecules would flood into the cells and cause them to burst. When red blood cells are put into a salty solution, the concentration of water molecules inside the cell is higher than the concentration of water outside. This difference makes water move out of the cells, and the cells shrivel up. Osmosis also occurs in plant cells. When a wilted plant is watered, osmosis makes the plant firm again.

✓ **Reading Check**   Why would red blood cells burst if you placed them in pure water? (*See the Appendix for answers to Reading Checks.*)

osmosis   the diffusion of water through a semipermeable membrane

Quick Lab

Bead Diffusion

1. Put three groups of **colored beads** on the bottom of a **plastic bowl**. Each group should be made up of five beads of the same color.

2. Stretch some **clear plastic wrap** tightly over the top of the bowl. Gently shake the bowl for 10 seconds while watching the beads.

3. How is the scattering of the beads like the diffusion of particles? How is it different from the diffusion of particles?

Answer to Reading Check

Red blood cells would burst in pure water because water particles move from outside, where particles were dense, to inside the cell, where particles were less dense. This movement of water would cause red blood cells to fill up and burst.

Close

Reteaching ———— BASIC

Writing **Cell Transport Instructions** Have students write an instruction manual that tells a cell how to transport both a large molecule and a small molecule through the cell membrane. **LS Logical**

Quiz ———— GENERAL

1. What part of the cell do materials pass through to get into and out of the cell? (the cell membrane)

2. What is osmosis? (the diffusion of water through a semipermeable membrane)

Alternative Assessment ———— ADVANCED

Writing **Science Biography** Have students write a brief biography of Albert Claude (1898–1983), who used the electron microscope to study cells. (Claude shared the 1974 Nobel Prize for physiology with his student George Palade and with Christian de Duve.) **LS Verbal**

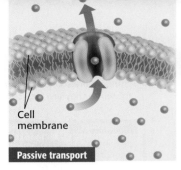
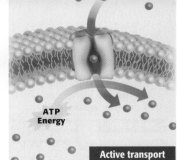

Figure 3 *In passive transport, particles travel through proteins to areas of lower concentration. In active transport, cells use energy to move particles, usually to areas of higher concentration.*

Cell membrane

Passive transport

ATP Energy

Active transport

passive transport the movement of substances across a cell membrane without the use of energy by the cell

active transport the movement of substances across the cell membrane that requires the cell to use energy

endocytosis the process by which a cell membrane surrounds a particle and encloses the particle in a vesicle to bring the particle into the cell

Moving Small Particles

Small particles, such as water and sugars, cross the cell membrane through passageways called *channels*. These channels are made up of proteins in the cell membrane. Particles travel through these channels by either passive or active transport. The movement of particles across a cell membrane without the use of energy by the cell is called **passive transport**, and is shown in **Figure 3**. During passive transport, particles move from an area of high concentration to an area of low concentration. Diffusion and osmosis are examples of passive transport.

A process of transporting particles that requires the cell to use energy is called **active transport.** Active transport usually involves the movement of particles from an area of low concentration to an area of high concentration.

Moving Large Particles

Small particles cross the cell membrane by diffusion, passive transport, and active transport. Large particles move into and out of the cell by processes called *endocytosis* and *exocytosis*.

Endocytosis

The active-transport process by which a cell surrounds a large particle, such as a large protein, and encloses the particle in a vesicle to bring the particle into the cell is called **endocytosis** (EN doh sie TOH sis). *Vesicles* are sacs formed from pieces of cell membrane. **Figure 4** shows endocytosis.

Figure 4   Endocytosis

❶ The cell comes into contact with a particle.

❷ The cell membrane begins to wrap around the particle.

❸ Once the particle is completely surrounded, a vesicle pinches off.

This photo shows the end of *endocytosis*, which means "within the cell."

CHAPTER RESOURCES

Technology

Transparencies
• Passive Transport and Active Transport
• Endocytosis/Exocytosis

Homework ———— GENERAL

Writing **Transport** Ask students to describe how each of the following materials would get through a cell membrane and into a cell.

a. pure water (osmosis)

b. sugar entering a cell that already contains a high concentration of particles (active transport)

c. sugar entering a cell that has a low concentration of particles (diffusion or passive transport)

d. a protein (active transport or endocytosis)

LS Logical

Figure 5 Exocytosis

1 Large particles that must leave the cell are packaged in vesicles.

2 The vesicle travels to the cell membrane and fuses with it.

3 The cell releases the particle to the outside of the cell.

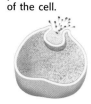

Exocytosis means "outside the cell."

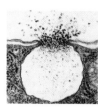

Exocytosis

When large particles, such as wastes, leave the cell, the cell uses an active-transport process called **exocytosis** (EK soh sie TOH sis). During exocytosis, a vesicle forms around a large particle within the cell. The vesicle carries the particle to the cell membrane. The vesicle fuses with the cell membrane and releases the particle to the outside of the cell. **Figure 5** shows exocytosis.

exocytosis the process in which a cell releases a particle by enclosing the particle in a vesicle that then moves to the cell surface and fuses with the cell membrane

✓ **Reading Check** What is exocytosis?

SECTION Review

Summary

- Diffusion is the movement of particles from an area of high concentration to an area of low concentration.
- Osmosis is the diffusion of water through a semipermeable membrane.
- Cells move small particles by diffusion, which is an example of passive transport, and by active transport.
- Large particles enter the cell by endocytosis, and exit the cell by exocytosis.

Using Key Terms

For each pair of terms, explain how the meanings of the terms differ.

1. *diffusion* and *osmosis*

2. *active transport* and *passive transport*

3. *endocytosis* and *exocytosis*

Understanding Key Ideas

4. The movement of particles from a less crowded area to a more crowded area requires
   a. sunlight.   c. a membrane.
   b. energy.   d. osmosis.

5. What structures allow small particles to cross cell membranes?

Math Skills

6. The area of particle 1 is 2.5 mm². The area of particle 2 is 0.5 mm². The area of particle 1 is how many times as big as the area of particle 2?

Critical Thinking

7. **Predicting Consequences** What would happen to a cell if its channel proteins were damaged and unable to transport particles? What would happen to the organism if many of its cells were damaged in this way? Explain your answer.

8. **Analyzing Ideas** Why does active transport require energy?

SCiLINKS **NSTA**
Developed and maintained by the National Science Teachers Association

For a variety of links related to this chapter, go to www.scilinks.org

Topics: Diffusion; Osmosis
SciLinks code: HSM0406; HSM1090

Answer to Reading Check

Exocytosis is the process by which a cell moves large particles to the outside of the cell.

CHAPTER RESOURCES

Chapter Resource File
- **Section Quiz** GENERAL
- **Section Review** GENERAL
- **Vocabulary and Section Summary** GENERAL
- **Reinforcement Worksheet** BASIC
- **SciLinks Activity** GENERAL
- **Datasheet for Quick Lab**

Technology
- **Interactive Explorations CD-ROM**
  - The Nose Knows GENERAL

Focus

Overview

This section introduces energy and the cell. Students learn about solar energy and the process of photosynthesis. Finally, students learn about cellular respiration and fermentation.

 Bellringer

Ask students to make a list of all the reasons why a cell might need energy. Remind students that there are many types of cells doing many different jobs.

Motivate

Demonstration — GENERAL

Leaves and Light Ask students what they think would happen if a plant could not get sunlight. A few days before teaching this section, cut out a square from black construction paper. Fold the square over a leaf of any common plant, such as a geranium. Affix the square with a paper clip. Be sure the leaf does not receive any sunlight. Leave the leaf covered for about one week. Remove the black square. The leaf will be paler than the other leaves. In the absence of sunlight, chlorophyll is depleted and not replenished. The leaf's green color will have faded.

LS Visual   **English Language Learners**

READING WARM-UP

Objectives
- Describe photosynthesis and cellular respiration.
- Compare cellular respiration with fermentation.

Terms to Learn
photosynthesis
cellular respiration
fermentation

READING STRATEGY

Discussion Read this section silently. Write down questions that you have about this section. Discuss your questions in a small group.

---

photosynthesis the process by which plants, algae, and some bacteria use sunlight, carbon dioxide, and water to make food

---

Cell Energy

Why do you get hungry? Feeling hungry is your body's way of telling you that your cells need energy.

All cells need energy to live, grow, and reproduce. Plant cells get their energy from the sun. Many animal cells get the energy they need from food.

From Sun to Cell

Nearly all of the energy that fuels life comes from the sun. Plants capture energy from the sun and change it into food through a process called **photosynthesis.** The food that plants make supplies them with energy. This food also becomes a source of energy for the organisms that eat the plants.

Photosynthesis

Plant cells have molecules that absorb light energy. These molecules are called *pigments*. Chlorophyll (KLAWR uh FIL), the main pigment used in photosynthesis, gives plants their green color. Chlorophyll is found in chloroplasts.

Plants use the energy captured by chlorophyll to change carbon dioxide and water into food. The food is in the form of the simple sugar glucose. Glucose is a carbohydrate. When plants make glucose, they convert the sun's energy into a form of energy that can be stored. The energy in glucose is used by the plant's cells. Photosynthesis also produces oxygen. Photosynthesis is summarized in **Figure 1.**

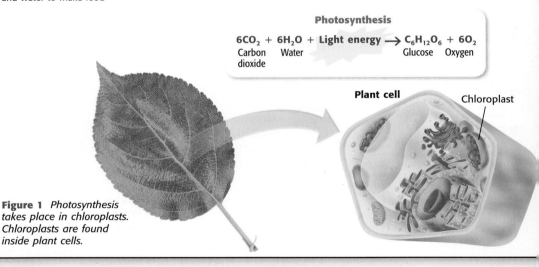

Photosynthesis

$$6CO_2 + 6H_2O + \text{Light energy} \rightarrow C_6H_{12}O_6 + 6O_2$$

Carbon dioxide   Water   Glucose   Oxygen

Plant cell

Chloroplast

Figure 1 *Photosynthesis takes place in chloroplasts. Chloroplasts are found inside plant cells.*

CHAPTER RESOURCES

Chapter Resource File
- **Lesson Plan**
- **Directed Reading A** BASIC
- **Directed Reading B** SPECIAL NEEDS

Technology
- **Transparencies**
  - Bellringer
  - *LINK TO PHYSICAL SCIENCE* Solar Heating Systems

Workbooks
- **Science Skills**
  - Using Logic GENERAL
  - Identifying Bias GENERAL

MISCONCEPTION ALERT

Not the Only Steps The processes of photosynthesis and respiration are complex chemical reactions that involve several steps shown by many chemical reactions. The much-simpler equations shown for the processes of respiration and photosynthesis in this chapter are the *net* equations for those reactions.

Getting Energy from Food

Animal cells have different ways of getting energy from food. One way, called **cellular respiration,** uses oxygen to break down food. Many cells can get energy without using oxygen through a process called **fermentation.** Cellular respiration will release more energy from a given food than fermentation will.

Cellular Respiration

The word *respiration* means "breathing," but cellular respiration is different from breathing. Breathing supplies the oxygen needed for cellular respiration. Breathing also removes carbon dioxide, which is a waste product of cellular respiration. But cellular respiration is a chemical process that occurs in cells.

Most complex organisms, such as the cow in **Figure 2,** obtain energy through cellular respiration. During cellular respiration, food (such as glucose) is broken down into CO_2 and H_2O, and energy is released. Most of the energy released maintains body temperature. Some of the energy is used to form adenosine triphosphate (ATP). ATP supplies energy that fuels cell activities.

Most of the process of cellular respiration takes place in the cell membrane of prokaryotic cells. But in the cells of eukaryotes, cellular respiration takes place mostly in the mitochondria. The process of cellular respiration is summarized in **Figure 2.** Does the equation in the figure remind you of the equation for photosynthesis? **Figure 3** on the next page shows how photosynthesis and respiration are related.

✔ Reading Check What is the difference between cellular respiration and breathing? (*See the Appendix for answers to Reading Checks.*)

cellular respiration the process by which cells use oxygen to produce energy from food

fermentation the breakdown of food without the use of oxygen

Figure 2 *The mitochondria in the cells of this cow will use cellular respiration to release the energy stored in the grass.*

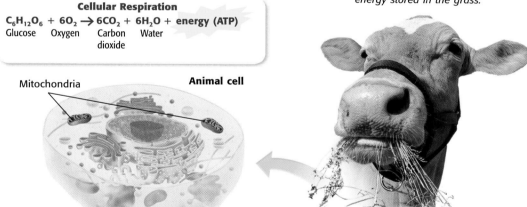

Cellular Respiration

$$C_6H_{12}O_6 + 6O_2 \rightarrow 6CO_2 + 6H_2O + energy\ (ATP)$$

Glucose Oxygen Carbon dioxide Water

Mitochondria

Animal cell

Q: How do cells communicate with each other?

A: by cell phone, of course

Answer to Reading Check

Cellular respiration is a chemical process by which cells produce energy from food. Breathing supplies oxygen for cellular respiration and removes the carbon dioxide produced by cellular respiration.

Close

Reteaching — BASIC

Concept Mapping Have students draw a concept map of energy transfer using the following images:

> sunshine; tree, for firewood; sugar cane; yeast consuming sugar, making bread rise; person chopping firewood, for baking oven; person eating bread

Students should note on their maps which organisms use photosynthesis, which use respiration, and which use fermentation. **LS** Visual

Quiz — GENERAL

Ask students whether the following statements are true or false.

1. Plants and animals capture their energy from the sun. (false)

2. Cellular respiration describes how a cell breathes. (false)

3. Fermentation in animals produces ATP and lactic acid. (true)

Alternative Assessment — GENERAL

Lungs of the Earth Tell students that plants are sometimes called the "lungs of the Earth." Ask students to think about this and to prepare an illustrated presentation for the class. Students may want to research the role that rain forests play as Earth's "lungs" and explain the contributions rain forests make to the health of the planet. **LS** Verbal/Visual

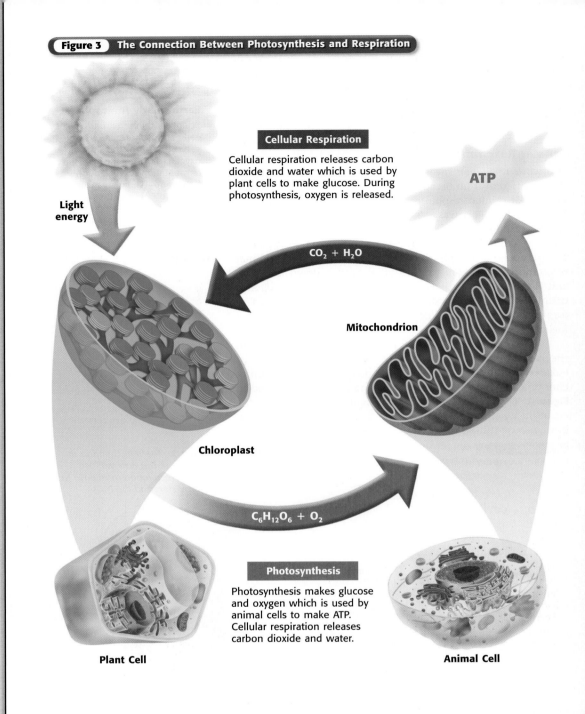

Figure 3 The Connection Between Photosynthesis and Respiration

Light energy

Cellular Respiration
Cellular respiration releases carbon dioxide and water which is used by plant cells to make glucose. During photosynthesis, oxygen is released.

ATP

$CO_2 + H_2O$

Mitochondrion

Chloroplast

$C_6H_{12}O_6 + O_2$

Photosynthesis
Photosynthesis makes glucose and oxygen which is used by animal cells to make ATP. Cellular respiration releases carbon dioxide and water.

Plant Cell

Animal Cell

Group Activity — GENERAL

Photosynthesis and Cellular Respiration Have students work in pairs and refer to the diagram on this page. Have each pair compare and contrast photosynthesis and respiration. Ask students to answer the following questions: "What happens to the ATP? Where does the ATP go? How is ATP used by the cell? How is the cell's use of CO_2 and H_2O similar to people's recycling of paper and glass bottles?" **LS** Interpersonal/Logical

Homework — ADVANCED

Comparing Cell Processes Newer kinds of solar cells simulate photosynthesis more closely than older solar cells do. Just as plant cells use energy from the sun to change water and carbon dioxide into energy-rich sugars, these new solar cells use the sun's energy to convert water into energy-rich hydrogen gas, which can be used as fuel. The byproduct of this process is oxygen. Have students research these newer solar cells and make a poster showing how they work. **LS** Visual

Connection Between Photosynthesis and Respiration

As shown in **Figure 3,** photosynthesis transforms energy from the sun into glucose. During photosynthesis, cells use CO_2 to make glucose, and the cells release O_2. During cellular respiration, cells use O_2 to break down glucose and release energy and CO_2. Each process makes the materials that are needed for the other process to occur elsewhere.

Fermentation

Have you ever felt a burning sensation in your leg muscles while you were running? When muscle cells can't get the oxygen needed for cellular respiration, they use the process of fermentation to get energy. One kind of fermentation happens in your muscles and produces lactic acid. The buildup of lactic acid contributes to muscle fatigue and causes a burning sensation. This kind of fermentation also happens in the muscle cells of other animals and in some fungi and bacteria. Another type of fermentation occurs in some types of bacteria and in yeast as described in **Figure 4.**

 Reading Check What are two kinds of fermentation?

Figure 4 *Yeast forms carbon dioxide during fermentation. The bubbles of CO_2 gas cause the dough to rise and leave small holes in bread after it is baked.*

SECTION Review

Summary

- Most of the energy that fuels life processes comes from the sun.
- The sun's energy is converted into food by the process of photosynthesis.
- Cellular respiration breaks down glucose into water, carbon dioxide, and energy.
- Fermentation is a way that cells get energy from their food without using oxygen.

Using Key Terms

1. In your own words, write a definition for the term *fermentation*.

Understanding Key Ideas

2. O_2 is released during
   a. cellular respiration.
   b. photosynthesis.
   c. breathing.
   d. fermentation.

3. How are photosynthesis and cellular respiration related?

4. How are respiration and fermentation similar? How are they different?

Math Skills

5. Cells of plant A make 120 molecules of glucose an hour. Cells of plant B make half as much glucose as plant A does. How much glucose does plant B make every minute?

Critical Thinking

6. **Analyzing Relationships** Why are plants important to the survival of all other organisms?

7. **Applying Concepts** You have been given the job of restoring life to a barren island. What types of organisms would you put on the island? If you want to have animals on the island, what other organisms must you bring? Explain your answer.

For a variety of links related to this chapter, go to www.scilinks.org

Topic: Cell Energy; Photosynthesis
SciLinks code: HSM0237; HSM1140

Answers to Section Review

1. Sample answer: Fermentation is how some organisms get energy from food without using oxygen.

2. b

3. Photosynthesis uses the waste materials of cellular respiration, CO_2 and H_2O, to generate glucose. Cellular respiration uses the waste material of photosynthesis, O_2, to break down glucose.

4. Cellular respiration and fermentation both release the energy stored in food. Fermentation does not use oxygen, and cellular respiration does use oxygen.

5. The cells of plant B make an average of 1 glucose molecule per minute.

6. Sample answer: Plants turn energy from the sun into chemical energy. Animals that eat the plants use the stored energy. Plants also produce O_2.

7. Sample answer: Animals such as birds, insects, and mammals would be good on the island. Plants must be on the island in order to provide a source of food for the animals.

Answer to Reading Check

One kind of fermentation produces CO_2, and the other kind produces lactic acid.

CHAPTER RESOURCES

Chapter Resource File

- **Section Quiz** GENERAL
- **Section Review** GENERAL
- **Vocabulary and Section Summary** GENERAL
- **Reinforcement Worksheet** BASIC
- **Critical Thinking** ADVANCED

Technology

Transparencies
- The Connection Between Photosynthesis and Respiration

Focus

Overview

This section introduces the life cycle of a cell. Students will learn how cells reproduce and how mitosis is important. Finally, students will learn how cell division differs in plants and animals.

Bellringer

On the board, write the following:

Biology is the only science in which multiplication means the same thing as division.

Have students write an explanation of this sentence. (When cells divide, they are multiplying. Some students may point out that multiplying a number by a fraction is the same as division.)

Motivate

ACTIVITY ———— GENERAL

Making Models Have pairs of students use string for the cell membrane and pieces of pipe cleaners for chromosomes to demonstrate the basic steps of mitosis, as described in this section. **LS** Visual/Interpersonal

---

READING WARM-UP

Objectives

● Explain how cells produce more cells.

● Describe the process of mitosis.

● Explain how cell division differs in animals and plants.

Terms to Learn

cell cycle
chromosome
homologous chromosomes
mitosis
cytokinesis

READING STRATEGY

Paired Summarizing Read this section silently. In pairs, take turns summarizing the material. Stop to discuss ideas that seem confusing.

---

cell cycle the life cycle of a cell

chromosome in a eukaryotic cell, one of the structures in the nucleus that are made up of DNA and protein; in a prokaryotic cell, the main ring of DNA

The Cell Cycle

In the time that it takes you to read this sentence, your body will have made millions of new cells! Making new cells allows you to grow and replace cells that have died.

The environment in your stomach is so acidic that the cells lining your stomach must be replaced every few days. Other cells are replaced less often, but your body is constantly making new cells.

The Life of a Cell

As you grow, you pass through different stages in life. Your cells also pass through different stages in their life cycle. The life cycle of a cell is called the **cell cycle.**

The cell cycle begins when the cell is formed and ends when the cell divides and forms new cells. Before a cell divides, it must make a copy of its deoxyribonucleic acid (DNA). DNA is the hereditary material that controls all cell activities, including the making of new cells. The DNA of a cell is organized into structures called **chromosomes.** Copying chromosomes ensures that each new cell will be an exact copy of its parent cell. How does a cell make more cells? It depends on whether the cell is prokaryotic (with no nucleus) or eukaryotic (with a nucleus).

Making More Prokaryotic Cells

Prokaryotic cells are less complex than eukaryotic cells are. Bacteria, which are prokaryotes, have ribosomes and a single, circular DNA molecule but don't have membrane-enclosed organelles. Cell division in bacteria is called *binary fission,* which means "splitting into two parts." Binary fission results in two cells that each contain one copy of the circle of DNA. A few of the bacteria in **Figure 1** are undergoing binary fission.

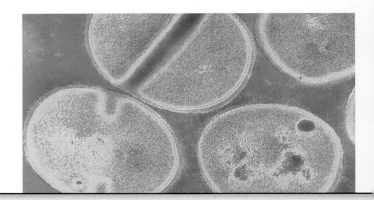

Figure 1 *Bacteria reproduce by binary fission.*

CHAPTER RESOURCES

Chapter Resource File

● **Lesson Plan**
● **Directed Reading A** BASIC
● **Directed Reading B** SPECIAL NEEDS

Technology

Transparencies
● Bellringer
● The Cell Cycle

Workbooks

Math Skills for Science
● Multiplying Whole Numbers BASIC
● Grasping Graphing GENERAL

CONNECTION to
Math ———— BASIC

Cell Multiplication It takes Cell A 1 h to complete its cell cycle and produce two cells. The cell cycle of Cell B takes 2 h. How many more cells would be formed from Cell A than from Cell B in 6 h?

(After 6 h, Cell A would have formed 64 cells, and Cell B would have formed 8 cells. Cell A would have formed 56 cells more than Cell B.)
LS Logical/Verbal

Eukaryotic Cells and Their DNA

Eukaryotic cells are more complex than prokaryotic cells are. The chromosomes of eukaryotic cells contain more DNA than those of prokaryotic cells do. Different kinds of eukaryotes have different numbers of chromosomes. More-complex eukaryotes do not necessarily have more chromosomes than simpler eukaryotes do. For example, fruit flies have 8 chromosomes, potatoes have 48, and humans have 46. **Figure 2** shows the 46 chromosomes of a human body cell lined up in pairs. These pairs are made up of similar chromosomes known as **homologous chromosomes** (hoh MAHL uh guhs KROH muh sOHMZ).

✓ **Reading Check** Do more-complex organisms always have more chromosomes than simpler organisms do? (*See the Appendix for answers to Reading Checks.*)

Figure 2 *Human body cells have 46 chromosomes, or 23 pairs of chromosomes.*

Making More Eukaryotic Cells

The eukaryotic cell cycle includes three stages. In the first stage, called *interphase,* the cell grows and copies its organelles and chromosomes. After each chromosome is duplicated, the two copies are called *chromatids.* Chromatids are held together at a region called the *centromere.* The joined chromatids twist and coil and condense into an X shape, as shown in **Figure 3.** After this step, the cell enters the second stage of the cell cycle.

In the second stage, the chromatids separate. The complicated process of chromosome separation is called **mitosis.** Mitosis ensures that each new cell receives a copy of each chromosome. Mitosis is divided into four phases, as shown on the following pages.

In the third stage, the cell splits into two cells. These cells are identical to each other and to the original cell.

homologous chromosomes chromosomes that have the same sequence of genes and the same structure

mitosis in eukaryotic cells, a process of cell division that forms two new nuclei, each of which has the same number of chromosomes

Figure 3 *This duplicated chromosome consists of two chromatids. The chromatids are joined at the centromere.*

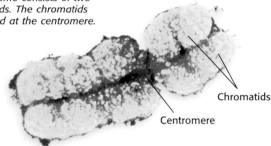

Chromatids

Centromere

CONNECTION TO Language Arts

Picking Apart Vocabulary

Brainstorm what words are similar to the parts of the term *homologous chromosome.* What can you guess about the meaning of the term's root words? Look up the roots of the words, and explain how they help describe the concept.

ᴬCᴛᵢᵥᵢᵀʏ

WEIRD SCIENCE

A fern called *Ophioglossum reticulatum* has 1,260 chromosomes per cell, more than any other organism.

Is That a Fact!

Before sophisticated microscopes were available, scientists could not see cells pinching and dividing. Many scientists believed that cells came into existence spontaneously—as though crystallizing out of bodily fluids.

Writing **Biography of a Cell**
Have students write and illustrate the biography of a cell. It can be humorous or serious, but it should include accurate descriptions of how materials are transported into and out of the cell and how cells reproduce. **LS** Visual/Verbal

Quiz ———————— GENERAL

1. What is cell division? (It is the process by which cells reproduce themselves.)

2. How do prokaryotic cells make more cells? (binary fission)

3. How do eukaryotic cells make more cells? (mitosis and cytokinesis)

Alternative Assessment ——— GENERAL

Writing **Mitosis and Cancer**
Have students research the role of mitosis in cancer and write a report or create a poster or other visual presentation on what they learn. Students' reports should include information about various cancer treatments, such as radiation, chemotherapy, and surgery. **LS** Verbal/Visual

Answer to Reading Check
During cytokinesis in plant cells, a cell plate is formed. During cytokinesis in animal cells, a cell plate does not form.

Figure 4 The Cell Cycle

Copying DNA (Interphase)	Mitosis Phase 1 (Prophase)	Mitosis Phase 2 (Metaphase)
Before mitosis begins, chromosomes are copied. Each chromosome is then two chromatids.	Mitosis begins. The nuclear membrane dissolves. Chromosomes condense into rodlike structures.	The chromosomes line up along the equator of the cell. Homologous chromosomes pair up.

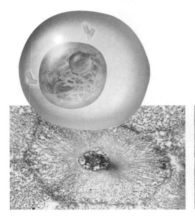 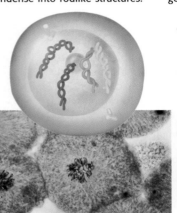 

cytokinesis the division of the cytoplasm of a cell

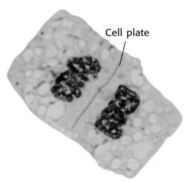

Cell plate

Figure 5 *When a plant cell divides, a cell plate forms and the cell splits into two cells.*

Mitosis and the Cell Cycle

Figure 4 shows the cell cycle and the phases of mitosis in an animal cell. Mitosis has four phases that are shown and described above. This diagram shows only four chromosomes to make it easy to see what's happening inside the cell.

Cytokinesis

In animal cells and other eukaryotes that do not have cell walls, division of the cytoplasm begins at the cell membrane. The cell membrane begins to pinch inward to form a groove, which eventually pinches all the way through the cell, and two daughter cells form. The division of cytoplasm is called **cytokinesis** and is shown at the last step of **Figure 4.**

Eukaryotic cells that have a cell wall, such as the cells of plants, algae, and fungi, reproduce differently. In these cells, a *cell plate* forms in the middle of the cell. The cell plate contains the materials for the new cell membranes and the new cell walls that will separate the new cells. After the cell splits into two, a new cell wall forms where the cell plate was. The cell plate and a late stage of cytokinesis in a plant cell are shown in **Figure 5.**

✓ **Reading Check** What is the difference between cytokinesis in an animal cell and cytokinesis in a plant cell?

INCLUSION Strategies

• *Developmentally Delayed* • *Hearing Impaired*
• *Learning Disabled*
Make a three-column table with these column headings: *Characteristics, Prokaryotic Cells,* and *Eukaryotic Cells.* Under Characteristics, use these five row headings: *Small or large?, Complex or simple?, More or less DNA?, Has organelles?,* and *Number of stages in cell division.* Have students copy the table and fill it in. **LS** Logical/Visual

INTERNET ACTIVITY
Sequence Board —— GENERAL

For an internet activity related to this chapter, have students go to **go.hrw.com** and type in the keyword **HL5ACTW.**

Mitosis Phase 3 (Anaphase)

The chromatids separate and move to opposite sides of the cell.

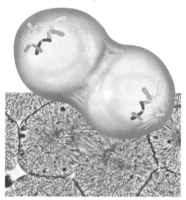

Mitosis Phase 4 (Telophase)

A nuclear membrane forms around each set of chromosomes, and the chromosomes unwind. Mitosis is complete.

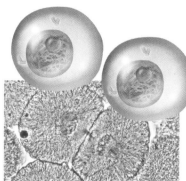

Cytokinesis

In cells that lack a cell wall, the cell pinches in two. In cells that have a cell wall, a cell plate forms between the two new cells.

SECTION Review

Summary

- A cell produces more cells by first copying its DNA.
- Eukaryotic cells produce more cells through the four phases of mitosis.
- Mitosis produces two cells that have the same number of chromosomes as the parent cell.
- At the end of mitosis, a cell divides the cytoplasm by cytokinesis.
- In plant cells, a cell plate forms between the two new cells during cytokinesis.

Using Key Terms

1. In your own words, write a definition for each of the following terms: *cell cycle* and *cytokinesis*.

Understanding Key Ideas

2. Eukaryotic cells
   a. do not divide.
   b. undergo binary fission.
   c. undergo mitosis.
   d. have cell walls.

3. Why is it important for chromosomes to be copied before cell division?

4. Describe mitosis.

Math Skills

5. Cell A takes 6 h to complete division. Cell B takes 8 h to complete division. After 24 h, how many more copies of cell A would there be than cell B?

Critical Thinking

6. **Predicting Consequences** What would happen if cytokinesis occurred without mitosis?

7. **Applying Concepts** How does mitosis ensure that a new cell is just like its parent cell?

8. **Making Comparisons** Compare the processes that animal cells and plant cells use to make new cells. How are the processes different?

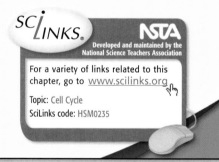

SCLINKS.

NSTA
Developed and maintained by the National Science Teachers Association

For a variety of links related to this chapter, go to www.scilinks.org

Topic: Cell Cycle
SciLinks code: HSM0235

The Perfect Taters Mystery

Teacher's Notes

Time Required
Two 45-minute class periods

Lab Ratings

EASY ———— HARD

Teacher Prep 🧪🧪
Student Set-Up 🧪🧪
Concept Level 🧪🧪🧪
Clean Up 🧪

MATERIALS

The materials listed on the student pages are enough for one class of students. You will need one or two potatoes per class. Do not allow students to cut or peel potatoes. You will need to do this ahead of time. Allow students to choose the number of containers they will need for the experiment. They may wish to test several salt concentrations.

Safety Caution

Remind students to review all safety cautions and icons before beginning this lab activity.

Avoid including green or discolored parts of the potato in the pieces students work with. These could cause illness.

OBJECTIVES

Examine osmosis in potato cells.

Design a procedure that will give the best results.

MATERIALS

- cups, clear plastic, small
- potato pieces, freshly cut
- potato samples (A, B, and C)
- salt
- water, distilled

SAFETY

The Perfect Taters Mystery

You are the chief food detective at Perfect Taters Food Company. The boss, Mr. Fries, wants you to find a way to keep his potatoes fresh and crisp before they are cooked. His workers have tried several methods, but these methods have not worked. Workers in Group A put the potatoes in very salty water, and something unexpected happened to the potatoes. Workers in Group B put the potatoes in water that did not contain any salt, and something else happened! Workers in Group C didn't put the potatoes in any water, and that didn't work either. Now, you must design an experiment to find out what can be done to make the potatoes stay crisp and fresh.

- Before you plan your experiment, review what you know. You know that potatoes are made of cells. Plant cells contain a large amount of water. Cells have membranes that hold water and other materials inside and keep some things out. Water and other materials must travel across cell membranes to get into and out of the cell.

- Mr. Fries has told you that you can obtain as many samples as you need from the workers in Groups A, B, and C. Your teacher will have these samples ready for you to observe.

- Make a data table like the one below. List your observations in the data table. Make as many observations as you can about the potatoes tested by workers in Groups A, B, and C.

Observations	
Group A	
Group B	
Group C	

Ask a Question

1 Now that you have made your observations, state Mr. Fries's problem in the form of a question that can be answered by your experiment.

Lab Notes

Osmosis is often a confusing and misunderstood concept in life science. Quite often, students can repeat the definition of the process but are unable to apply the concept to explain the movement of water in different osmotic environments. In this lab, students will have an opportunity to observe osmosis in a model and obtain measurable results. This lab can be done as a class demonstration if materials and space are limited. The purpose of this lab is to reinforce comprehension of osmosis and to practice the scientific method.

CHAPTER RESOURCES

Chapter Resource File
- Datasheet for Chapter Lab
- Lab Notes and Answers

Technology
- Classroom Videos
  - Lab Video

LabBook
- Stayin' Alive!

Form a Hypothesis

2 Form a hypothesis based on your observations and your questions. The hypothesis should be a statement about what causes the potatoes not to be crisp and fresh. Based on your hypothesis, make a prediction about the outcome of your experiment. State your prediction in an if-then format.

Test the Hypothesis

3 Once you have made a prediction, design your investigation. Check your experimental design with your teacher before you begin. Mr. Fries will give you potato pieces, water, salt, and no more than six containers.

4 Keep very accurate records. Write your plan and procedure. Make data tables. To be sure your data is accurate, measure all materials carefully and make drawings of the potato pieces before and after the experiment.

Analyze the Results

1 **Explaining Events** Explain what happened to the potato cells in Groups A, B, and C in your experiment. Include a discussion of the cell membrane and the process of osmosis.

Draw Conclusions

2 **Analyzing Results** Write a letter to Mr. Fries that explains your experimental method, results, and conclusion. Then, make a recommendation about how he should handle the potatoes so that they will stay fresh and crisp.

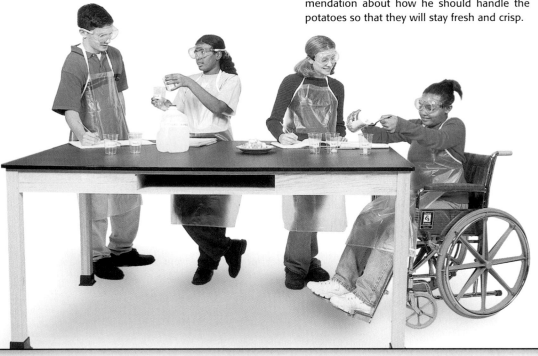

CLASSROOM TESTED & APPROVED

Susan Gorman
North Ridge Middle School
North Richland Hills, Texas

Analyze the Results

1. The potato cells in Group A were placed in very salty water. The potatoes shriveled up because water moved out of the cell and into the salty water (from an area of high concentration of water to an area of low concentration of water). This may be confusing to some students, who may think that because the concentration of salt is high outside the potato, the salt should move to the area of lower concentration. Explain that although water can move through a cell membrane by osmosis, salt must be moved across a cell membrane by a process that requires energy.

The potato cells in Group B were placed in water with no salt. The potatoes swelled because the concentration of water was lower inside the cell. (The concentration of salt and other molecules was higher inside the potato cell.)

The potato cells in Group C turned brown and dried up because the water concentration outside the cell was low. In fact, there wasn't any water at all. The water evaporated as soon as it left the cell membrane. The potato cells turned brown because of chemical reactions with the air.

Draw Conclusions

2. Letters to Mr. Fries will vary according to each student's results. However, all students should explain that through trial and error they found one salt concentration that was closest to the concentration of salt and other molecules inside the potato. This is the concentration that should be used to maintain an osmotic balance in the potato. Furthermore, some students will realize that the potatoes must be kept in water to prevent them from turning brown.

Chapter Review

Assignment Guide

SECTION	QUESTIONS
1	1, 2, 6, 8, 12, 16
2	3, 4, 7, 10, 13, 17
3	5, 9, 11, 14, 15, 18–22

ANSWERS

Using Key Terms

1. Sample answer: Osmosis is the diffusion of water through a semipermeable membrane.

2. Sample answer: Exocytosis is the process cells use to remove large particles; endocytosis is the process cells use to move large particles into a cell

3. photosynthesis

4. cellular respiration

5. Cytokinesis is the division of just the cytoplasm. Mitosis is the process in eukaryotic cells in which the nuclear material splits to form two new nuclei.

6. Active transport requires the cell to use energy to move substances. Passive transport does not require the cell to use any energy.

7. Cellular respiration releases stored energy by using oxygen. Fermentation releases stored energy without using oxygen.

Understanding Key Ideas

8. c
9. a
10. d
11. c

USING KEY TERMS

1 Use the following terms in the same sentence: *diffusion* and *osmosis*.

2 In your own words, write a definition for each of the following terms: *exocytosis* and *endocytosis*.

Complete each of the following sentences by choosing the correct term from the word bank.

cellular respiration
photosynthesis
fermentation

3 Plants use ___ to make glucose.

4 During ___, oxygen is used to break down food molecules releasing large amounts of energy.

For each pair of terms, explain how the meanings of the terms differ.

5 *cytokinesis* and *mitosis*

6 *active transport* and *passive transport*

7 *cellular respiration* and *fermentation*

UNDERSTANDING KEY IDEAS

Multiple Choice

8 The process in which particles move through a membrane from a region of low concentration to a region of high concentration is

a. diffusion.
b. passive transport.
c. active transport.
d. fermentation.

---

9 What is the result of mitosis and cytokinesis?

a. two identical cells
b. two nuclei
c. chloroplasts
d. two different cells

10 Before the energy in food can be used by a cell, the energy must first be transferred to molecules of

a. proteins.
b. carbohydrates.
c. DNA.
d. ATP.

11 Which of the following cells would form a cell plate during the cell cycle?

a. a human cell
b. a prokaryotic cell
c. a plant cell
d. All of the above

Short Answer

12 Are exocytosis and endocytosis examples of active or passive transport? Explain your answer.

13 Name the cell structures that are needed for photosynthesis and the cell structures that are needed for cellular respiration.

14 Describe the three stages of the cell cycle of a eukaryotic cell.

---

12. Endocytosis and exocytosis are examples of active transport. In both processes the cell must change shape, wrap around a particle, and make other movements that require the cell to use energy.

13. Chloroplasts are needed for photosynthesis. Cellular respiration requires mitochondria.

14. The first stage is cell growth and copying of DNA (duplication). The second stage is mitosis, which involves separating the duplicated chromosomes. The third stage is cytokinesis (cell division), which results in two separate, identical cells.

CRITICAL THINKING

15. Concept Mapping Use the following terms to create a concept map: *chromosome duplication, cytokinesis, prokaryote, mitosis, cell cycle, binary fission,* and *eukaryote.*

16. Making Inferences Which one of the plants pictured below was given water mixed with salt, and which one was given pure water? Explain how you know, and be sure to use the word *osmosis* in your answer.

17. Identifying Relationships Why would your muscle cells need to be supplied with more food when there is a lack of oxygen than when there is plenty of oxygen present?

18. Applying Concepts A parent cell has 10 chromosomes.

  a. Will the cell go through binary fission or mitosis and cytokinesis to produce new cells?

  b. How many chromosomes will each new cell have after the parent cell divides?

INTERPRETING GRAPHICS

The picture below shows a cell. Use the picture below to answer the questions that follow.

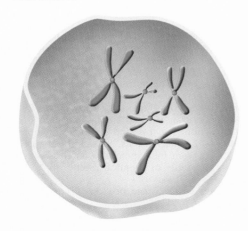

19. Is the cell prokaryotic or eukaryotic?

20. Which stage of the cell cycle is this cell in?

21. How many chromatids are present? How many pairs of homologous chromosomes are present?

22. How many chromosomes will be present in each of the new cells after the cell divides?

Critical Thinking

15. An answer to this exercise can be found at the end of this book.

16. The plant on the left was given pure water. The plant on the right was given salt water. Osmosis occurred in both plants. In the plant on the right, water moved into the plant because the concentration of water was lower in the plant than in the soil. So, the plant on the right did not wilt. In the plant on the left, the water in the plant moved into the soil, where the concentration of water was lower. The concentration of water in the soil was lower because the water contained salt. As a result, the plant on the left wilted.

17. When there is plenty of oxygen, the cells can get energy from cellular respiration. When there is a lack of oxygen, the cells must use fermentation, which doesn't produce as much energy. For fermentation to produce more energy, more food would be required.

18. a. The cell is a eukaryotic cell and will go through mitosis and cytokinesis. Prokaryotic cells have only one chromosome.

  b. Each new cell will receive a copy of each chromosome, so each new cell will have 10 chromosomes.

Interpreting Graphics

19. The cell is eukaryotic because it shows chromatids held together at a centromere. Prokaryotic cells do not have chromatids.

20. The cell is in mitosis because the chromosomes have already duplicated.

21. There are 12 chromatids. There are three pairs of homologous chromosomes.

22. There will be six chromosomes in each new cell.

Standardized Test Preparation

EOG Prep

READING

Passage 1

1. C
2. G
3. A

 TEST DOCTOR

Question 1: Students may choose wrong answers A and B if they mistakenly read the passage to say that burning a log is the same as the release of energy in a cell during cellular respiration.

Question 3: Students may choose wrong answer B if they already know that heat is released during cellular respiration. While this may be true, the information is not contained anywhere in this passage. The correct answer, based on the passage, is A.

READING

Read each of the passages below. Then, answer the questions that follow each passage.

Passage 1 Perhaps you have heard that jogging or some other kind of exercise "burns" a lot of Calories. The word *burn* is often used to describe what happens when your cells release stored energy from food. The burning of food in living cells is not the same as the burning of logs in a campfire. When logs burn, the energy stored in wood is released as thermal energy and light in a single reaction. But this kind of reaction is not the kind that happens in cells. Instead, the energy that cells get from food molecules is released at each step of a series of chemical reactions.

1. According to the passage, how do cells release energy from food?
   A in a single reaction
   B as thermal energy and light
   C in a series of reactions
   D by burning

2. Which of the following statements is a fact in the passage?
   F Wood burns better than food does.
   G Both food and wood have stored energy.
   H Food has more stored energy than wood does.
   I When it is burned, wood releases only thermal energy.

3. According to the passage, why might people be confused between what happens in a living cell and what happens in a campfire?
   A The word *burn* may describe both processes.
   B Thermal energy is released during both processes.
   C Wood can be burned and broken down by living cells.
   D Jogging and other exercises use energy.

Passage 2 The word *respiration* means "breathing," but cellular respiration is different from breathing. Breathing supplies your cells with the oxygen that they need for cellular respiration. Breathing also rids your body of carbon dioxide, which is a waste product of cellular respiration. Cellular respiration is the chemical process that releases energy from food. Most organisms obtain energy from food through cellular respiration. During cellular respiration, oxygen is used to break down food (glucose) into CO_2 and H_2O, and energy is released. In humans, most of the energy released is used to maintain body temperature.

1. According to the passage, what is glucose?
   A a type of chemical process
   B a type of waste product
   C a type of organism
   D a type of food

2. According to the passage, how does cellular respiration differ from breathing?
   F Breathing releases carbon dioxide, but cellular respiration releases oxygen.
   G Cellular respiration is a chemical process that uses oxygen to release energy from food, but breathing supplies cells with oxygen.
   H Cellular respiration requires oxygen, but breathing does not.
   I Breathing rids your body of waste products, but cellular respiration stores wastes.

3. According to the passage, how do humans use most of the energy released?
   A to break down food
   B to obtain oxygen
   C to maintain body temperature
   D to get rid of carbon dioxide

Passage 2

1. D
2. G
3. C

 TEST DOCTOR

Question 2: Students may choose wrong answer F if they mistakenly read the passage to say that cellular respiration "releases" oxygen instead of "requires" oxygen. Cellular respiration releases carbon dioxide and water.

Question 3: The passage talks about the release of energy from food. Students may choose wrong answer A if they mistakenly read the passage to say that most of the energy is used to break down food. Most of the food energy is used to maintain body temperature.

The graph below shows the cell cycle. Use this graph to answer the questions that follow.

The Cell Cycle

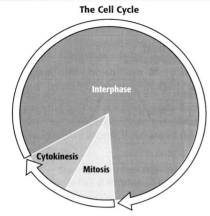

Interphase

Cytokinesis

Mitosis

1. Which part of the cell cycle lasts longest?

A interphase

B mitosis

C cytokinesis

D There is not enough information to determine the answer.

2. Which of the following lists the parts of the cell cycle in the proper order?

F mitosis, cytokinesis, mitosis

G interphase, cytokinesis, mitosis

H interphase, mitosis, interphase

I mitosis, cytokinesis, interphase

3. Which part of the cell cycle is the briefest?

A interphase

B cell division

C cytokinesis

D There is not enough information to determine the answer.

4. Why is the cell cycle represented by a circle?

F The cell cycle is a continuous process that begins again after it finishes.

G The cell cycle happens only in cells that are round.

H The cell cycle is a linear process.

I The cell is in interphase for more than half of the cell cycle.

MATH

Read each question below, and choose the best answer.

1. A normal cell spends 90% of its time in interphase. How is 90% expressed as a fraction?

A 3/4

B 4/5

C 85/100

D 9/10

2. If a cell lived for 3 weeks and 4 days, how many days did it live?

F 7

G 11

H 21

I 25

3. How is $2 \times 3 \times 3 \times 3 \times 3$ expressed in exponential notation?

A 3×2^4

B 2×3^3

C 3^4

D 2×3^4

4. Cell A has 3 times as many chromosomes as cell B has. After cell B's chromosomes double during mitosis, cell B has 6 chromosomes. How many chromosomes does cell A have?

F 3

G 6

H 9

I 18

5. If $x + 2 = 3$, what does $x + 1$ equal?

A 4

B 3

C 2

D 1

6. If $3x + 2 = 26$, what does $x + 1$ equal?

F 7

G 8

H 9

I 10

Standardized Test Preparation

1. A

2. I

3. D

4. F

 **TEST DOCTOR**

Question 2: Students may select incorrect answers F and H if they follow the arrow but skip a step on the graph. They may select incorrect answer G if they ignore the direction of the arrow. Only answer I has the steps of the cell cycle in proper sequence.

MATH

1. D

2. I

3. D

4. H

5. C

6. H

 **TEST DOCTOR**

Question 4: Students may have trouble converting this word problem into a numerical statement because they may confuse what is happening to cell B (its chromosomes are doubling in number to 6, which means that it starts with 3) with what is happening to cell A (nothing). Students may select incorrect answer I because 3 times 6 is 18. Students who are struggling may want to create a small data table that shows what they "know" (the information given in the word problem) and what they are trying to find out (what the question asks). Word problems are a challenge for many students, and often a table or chart will help them keep the information straight.

CHAPTER RESOURCES

Chapter Resource File

 • Standardized Test Preparation **GENERAL**

Workbooks

 North Carolina Standardized Test Preparation
• Provides practice for the EOG test.

State Resources

 For specific resources for your state, visit **go.hrw.com** and type in the keyword **HSMSTR**.

Scientific Discovery

Background

The release of energy from food is called *cellular respiration*. Cellular respiration takes place in two stages. The end result of the process is that energy is stored in the cell in the form of ATP (adenosine triphosphate) molecules.

In the microbial battery, scientists harvest some of this energy and transfer it into electricity that can be readily used.

One of the benefits of the microbial battery is its ability to make use of waste products. Ask students to consider the effect this might have on the energy demands of nations that have limited access to fossil fuels.

Science Fiction

Teaching Strategy— BASIC

This is a relatively long story, containing quite a few medical terms. Students may find it easier to read if the class discusses some of the unfamiliar terms before they start reading the story.

Science in Action

Scientific Discoveries

Electrifying News About Microbes

Your car is out of fuel, and there isn't a service station in sight. This is not a problem! Your car's motor runs on electricity supplied by trillions of microorganisms. Some chemists think that "living" batteries will someday operate everything from watches to entire cities. A group of scientists at King's College in London have demonstrated that microorganisms can convert food into usable electrical energy. The microorganisms convert foods such as table sugar and molasses most efficiently. An efficient microorganism can convert more than 90% of its food into compounds that will fuel an electric reaction. A less efficient microbe will only convert 50% of its food into these types of compounds.

Math ACTIVITY

An efficient microorganism converts 90% of its food into fuel compounds, and an inefficient microorganism converts only 50%. If the inefficient microorganism makes 60 g of fuel out of a possible 120 g of food, how much fuel would an efficient microorganism make out of the same amount of food?

Science Fiction

"Contagion" by Katherine MacLean

A quarter mile from their spaceship, the *Explorer*, a team of doctors walk carefully along a narrow forest trail. Around them, the forest looks like a forest on Earth in the fall—the leaves are green, copper, purple, and fiery red. But it isn't fall. And the team is not on Earth.

Minos is enough like Earth to be the home of another colony of humans. But Minos might also be home to unknown organisms that could cause severe illness or death among the crew of *Explorer*. These diseases might be enough like diseases on Earth to be contagious, but they might be different enough to be very difficult to treat.

Something large moves among the shadows—it looks like a man. What happens next? Read Katherine's MacLean's "Contagion" in the *Holt Anthology of Science Fiction* to find out.

Language Arts ACTIVITY

WRITING SKILL Write two to three paragraphs that describe what you think might happen next in the story.

Answer to Math Activity

An efficient microbe converts 90% of its food to fuel compounds; 90% of 120 g is 108 g of fuel compounds.

Answer to Language Arts Activity

Students' predictions will vary. Whatever a student predicts, the prediction should be reasonably related to the information that the student has from reading this introductory paragraph.

Jerry Yakel

Neuroscientist Jerry Yakel credits a sea slug for making him a neuroscientist. In a college class studying neurons, or nerve cells, Yakel got to see firsthand how ions move across the cell membrane of *Aplysia californica,* also known as a sea hare. He says, "I was totally hooked. I knew that I wanted to be a neurophysiologist then and there. I haven't wavered since."

Today, Yakel is a senior investigator for the National Institutes of Environmental Health Sciences, which is part of the U.S. government's National Institutes of Health. "We try to understand how the normal brain works," says Yakel of his team. "Then, when we look at a diseased brain, we train to understand where the deficits are. Eventually, someone will have an idea about a drug that will tweak the system in this or that way."

Yakel studies the ways in which nicotine affects the human brain. "It is one of the most prevalent and potent neurotoxins in the environment," says Yakel. "I'm amazed that it isn't higher on the list of worries for the general public."

Social Studies ActivITY

WRITING SKILL Research a famous or historical figure in science. Write a short report that outlines how he or she became interested in science.

go.hrw.com
To learn more about these Science in Action topics, visit go.hrw.com and type in the keyword **HL5ACTF.**

Current Science
Check out Current Science® articles related to this chapter by visiting go.hrw.com. Just type in the keyword **HL5CS04.**

Careers

Background

Jerry Yakel grew up in Ventura County, California. After graduating from high school, he attended a nearby community college "ostensibly to continue running track, figuring out life." Eventually, he relocated to Oregon State University, where he obtained a B.S. in 1982. He was accepted into UCLA in 1983 and received a Ph.D. in 1988.

Working for the NIH was not something Yakel originally expected to do. "Most of us trained in universities think we will work there," he says. He does enjoy some aspects of being outside the typical university setting. "In the NIH, we are supposed to take more risks in our research." He also enjoys the focus he is able to bring to his work. "I miss having students to teach, but then again I get to spend more time doing research," Yakel says. His choice of environment hasn't affected his passion. "Honestly, the type of research I [would] do actually is the same."

Answer to Social Studies Activity

Students may write about any historical figure in science. Some students may go back as far as Archimedes; others may choose Hypatia (the first woman to be a true astronomer), Benjamin Franklin, Marie Curie, Albert Einstein, Rosalind Franklin, or one of hundreds of other people. The important issues for the student are why the person is important to science and how the person became interested in science.

Heredity
Chapter Planning Guide

Compression guide:
To shorten instruction because of time limitations, omit the Chapter Lab.

OBJECTIVES	LABS, DEMONSTRATIONS, AND ACTIVITIES	TECHNOLOGY RESOURCES
PACING • 90 min pp. 402–409 **Chapter Opener**	**SE** Start-up Activity, p. 403 ◆ `GENERAL`	**OSP** Parent Letter `GENERAL` **CD** Student Edition on CD-ROM **CD** Guided Reading Audio CD **TR** Chapter Starter Transparency* **VID** Brain Food Video Quiz
Section 1 Mendel and His Peas • Explain the relationship between traits and heredity. • Describe the experiments of Gregor Mendel. • Explain the difference between dominant and recessive traits.	**TE** Activity Trait Trends, p. 404 `GENERAL` **SE** School-to-Home Activity Describing Traits, p. 405 `GENERAL` **TE** Demonstration Flower Dissection, p. 406 ◆ `BASIC` **TE** Activity Mendelian Crosses, p. 406 `ADVANCED` **SE** Science in Action Math, Science, and Social Studies Activities, pp. 430-431 `GENERAL`	**CRF** Lesson Plans* **TR** Bellringer Transparency* **CRF** SciLinks Activity* `GENERAL`
PACING • 90 min pp. 410–415 **Section 2 Traits and Inheritance** • Explain how genes and alleles are related to genotype and phenotype. • Use the information in a Punnett square. • Explain how probability can be used to predict possible genotypes in offspring. • Describe three exceptions to Mendel's observations.	**TE** Demonstration, p. 410 ◆ `BASIC` **SE** Quick Lab Making a Punnett Square, p. 411 `GENERAL` **CRF** Datasheet for Quick Lab* **SE** Quick Lab Taking Your Chances, p. 412 ◆ `GENERAL` **CRF** Datasheet for Quick Lab* **TE** Connection Activity Math, p. 412 `ADVANCED` **SE** Connection to Chemistry Round and Wrinkled, p. 413 `GENERAL` **SE** Model-Making Lab Bug Builders, Inc., p. 424 ◆ `GENERAL` **CRF** Datasheet for Chapter Lab*	**CRF** Lesson Plans* **TR** Bellringer Transparency* **TR** Punnett Squares **TR** *LINK TO PHYSICAL SCIENCE* The Periodic Table of the Elements* **VID** Lab Videos for Life Science
PACING • 45 min pp. 416–423 **Section 3 Meiosis** • Explain the difference between mitosis and meiosis. • Describe how chromosomes determine sex. • Explain why sex-linked disorders occur in one sex more often than in the other. • Interpret a pedigree.	**TE** Activity Crosses, p. 416 `GENERAL` **TE** Connection Activity Math, p. 416 `ADVANCED` **TE** Activity Describing Meiosis, p. 419 `BASIC` **TE** Connection Activity Math, p. 419 `GENERAL` **TE** Group Activity Comparing Mitosis and Meiosis, p. 420 `GENERAL` **TE** Connection Activity Language Arts, p. 421 `ADVANCED` **SE** Inquiry Lab Tracing Traits, p. 607 `GENERAL` **CRF** Datasheet for LabBook* **LB** Long-Term Projects & Research Ideas Portrait of a Dog* `ADVANCED`	**CRF** Lesson Plans* **TR** Bellringer Transparency* **TR** The Steps of Meiosis: A* **TR** The Steps of Meiosis: B* **TR** Meiosis and Dominance* **TE** Internet Activity, p.423 `GENERAL`

PACING • 90 min

CHAPTER REVIEW, ASSESSMENT, AND STANDARDIZED TEST PREPARATION

CRF Vocabulary Activity* `GENERAL`
SE Chapter Review, pp. 426–427 `GENERAL`
CRF Chapter Review* ■ `GENERAL`
CRF Chapter Tests A* ■ `GENERAL`, B* `ADVANCED`, C* `SPECIAL NEEDS`
SE Standardized Test Preparation, pp. 428–429 `GENERAL`
CRF Standardized Test Preparation* `GENERAL`
CRF Performance-Based Assessment* `GENERAL`
OSP Test Generator `GENERAL`
CRF Test Item Listing* `GENERAL`

Online and Technology Resources

Visit **go.hrw.com** for a variety of free resources related to this textbook. Enter the keyword **HT5R7HER.**

Holt Online Learning

Students can access interactive problem-solving help and active visual concept development with the *Holt Science and Technology* Online Edition available at **www.hrw.com**.

 Guided Reading Audio CD

These CDs are designed to help auditory learners and reluctant readers.

 Science Tutor CD-ROM

Excellent for remediation and test practice.

SKILLS DEVELOPMENT RESOURCES	SECTION REVIEW AND ASSESSMENT	STANDARDS CORRELATIONS
SE **Pre-Reading Activity,** p. 402 `GENERAL` OSP **Science Puzzlers, Twisters & Teasers*** `GENERAL`		North Carolina Standard Course of Study 5.02
CRF **Directed Reading A*** `BASIC`**, B*** `SPECIAL NEEDS` CRF **Vocabulary and Section Summary*** `GENERAL` SE **Reading Strategy** Brainstorming, p. 404 `GENERAL` SE **Math Practice** Understanding Ratios, p. 408 `GENERAL` TE **Reading Strategy** Paired Reading, p. 405 `BASIC` TE **Inclusion Strategies,** p. 407 ◆ MS **Math Skills for Science** What Is a Ratio?* `GENERAL` SS **Science Skills** Finding Useful Sources* `GENERAL` CRF **Critical Thinking** A Bittersweet Solution* `ADVANCED`	SE **Reading Checks,** pp. 404, 407, 408 `GENERAL` TE **Reteaching,** p. 408 `BASIC` TE **Quiz,** p. 408 `GENERAL` TE **Alternative Assessment,** p. 408 `ADVANCED` SE **Section Review,*** p. 409 ■ `GENERAL` TE **Homework,** p. 409 `GENERAL` CRF **Section Quiz*** ■ `GENERAL`	5.03; *Science in Action:* 5.05, 5.06
CRF **Directed Reading A*** `BASIC`**, B*** `SPECIAL NEEDS` CRF **Vocabulary and Section Summary*** `GENERAL` SE **Reading Strategy** Paired Summarizing, p. 410 `GENERAL` SE **Math Focus** Probability, p. 413 `GENERAL` MS **Math Skills for Science** Punnett Square Popcorn* `GENERAL` CRF **Reinforcement Worksheet** Dimples and DNA* `BASIC`	SE **Reading Checks,** pp. 410, 412, 414 `GENERAL` TE **Homework,** p. 413 `GENERAL` TE **Reteaching,** p. 414 `BASIC` TE **Quiz,** p. 414 `GENERAL` TE **Alternative Assessment,** p. 415 `GENERAL` SE **Section Review,*** p. 415 ■ `GENERAL` CRF **Section Quiz*** ■ `GENERAL`	5.01, 5.03, 5.04, 5.06; *Chapter Lab:* 1.07, 5.04
CRF **Directed Reading A*** `BASIC`**, B*** `SPECIAL NEEDS` CRF **Vocabulary and Section Summary*** `GENERAL` SE **Reading Strategy** Reading Organizer, p. 416 `GENERAL` TE **Reading Strategy** Prediction Guide, p. 418 `GENERAL` TE **Inclusion Strategies,** p. 420 CRF **Reinforcement Worksheet** Vocabulary Garden* `BASIC`	SE **Reading Checks,** pp. 417, 418 `GENERAL` TE **Reteaching,** p. 422 `BASIC` TE **Quiz,** p. 422 `GENERAL` TE **Alternative Assessment,** p. 422 `GENERAL` TE **Homework,** p. 422 `ADVANCED` SE **Section Review,*** p. 423 ■ `GENERAL` CRF **Section Quiz*** ■ `GENERAL`	5.01, 5.02. 5.04, 5.05, *LabBook:* 5.04

 **One-Stop Planner® CD-ROM**

This convenient CD-ROM includes:
- **Lab Materials QuickList Software**
- **Holt Calendar Planner**
- **Customizable Lesson Plans**
- **Printable Worksheets**
- **ExamView® Test Generator**

 **CNN student News™**

cnnstudentnews.com

Find the latest news, lesson plans, and activities related to important scientific events.

 SCLINKS. NSTA

www.scilinks.org

Maintained by the **National Science Teachers Association.** See Chapter Enrichment pages for a complete list of topics.

Current Science®

Check out *Current Science* articles and activities by visiting the HRW Web site at **go.hrw.com.** Just type in the keyword **HL5CS05T.**

 Classroom Videos

- **Lab Videos** demonstrate the chapter lab.
- **Brain Food Video Quizzes** help students review the chapter material.
- **CNN Videos** bring science into your students' daily life.

Visual Resources

CHAPTER STARTER TRANSPARENCY

BELLRINGER TRANSPARENCIES

Section: Mendel and His Peas

You have probably noticed that different people have different characteristics, such as eye color, hair color, or whether or not their ear lobes attach directly to their head or hang down loosely. These characteristics are called traits. Where do you think people get these different traits? How do you think they are passed from one generation to the next?

Write your answers in your **science journal.**

Section: Traits and Inheritance

If you flip a coin, what are the chances that it will land on heads? tails? Suppose that you flip the coin, get heads, and then flip again. What are the chances that you will get heads again? What are the chances you will get heads two times in a row? five times?

Record your answers in your **science journal.**

TEACHING TRANSPARENCIES

L14 — Steps of Meiosis: A

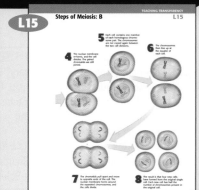

L15 — Steps of Meiosis: B

TEACHING TRANSPARENCIES

L13 — Punnett Squares

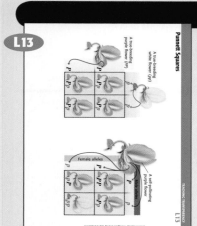

L16 — Meiosis and Dominance

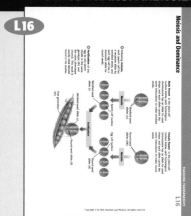

P49 — The Periodic Table of the Elements

LINK TO PHYSICAL SCIENCE

Chapter: The Periodic Table

CONCEPT MAPPING TRANSPARENCY

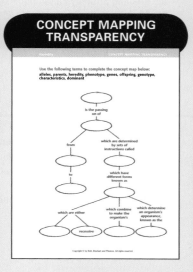

Use the following terms to complete the concept map below: alleles, parents, heredity, phenotype, genes, offspring, genotype, characteristics, dominant

Planning Resources

LESSON PLANS

Lesson Plan — SAMPLE

Section: Waves

Pacing
Regular Schedule: with lab(s):2 days   without lab(s):2 days
Block Schedule: with lab(s):1 1/2 days   without lab(s):1 day

Objectives
1. Relate the seven properties of life to a living organism.
2. Describe seven themes that can help you to organize what you learn about biology.
3. Identify the tiny structures that make up all living organisms.
4. Differentiate between reproduction and heredity and between metabolism and homeostasis.

National Science Education Standards Covered
LSInter6:Cells have particular structures that underlie their functions.
LSMat1:Most cell functions involve chemical reactions.
LSBeh1:Cells store and use information to guide their functions.
UCP1:Cell functions are regulated.
SI1: Cells can differentiate and form complete multicellular organisms.
PS1: Species evolve over time.
ESS1: The great diversity of organisms is the result of more than 3.5 billion years of evolution.
ESS2: Natural selection and its evolutionary consequences provide a scientific explanation for the fossil record of ancient life forms as well as for the striking molecular similarities observed among the diverse species of living organisms.
ST1: The millions of different species of plants, animals, and microorganisms that live on Earth today are related by descent from common ancestors.
ST2: The energy for life primarily comes from the sun.
SPSP1: The complexity and organization of organisms accommodates the need for obtaining, transforming, transporting, releasing, and eliminating the matter and energy used to sustain the organism.
SPSP6: As matter and energy flows through different levels of organization of living systems—cells, organs, communities—and between living systems and the physical environment, chemical elements are recombined in different ways.
HNS1: Organisms have behavioral responses to internal changes and to external stimuli.

PARENT LETTER

Dear Parent,

Your son's or daughter's science class will soon begin exploring the chapter entitled "The World of Physical Science." In this chapter, students will learn about how the scientific method applies to the world of physical science and the role of physical science in the world. By the end of the chapter, students should demonstrate a clear understanding of the chapter's main ideas and be able to discuss the following topics:

1. physical science is the study of energy and matter (Section 1)
2. the role of physical science in the world around them (Section 1)
3. careers that rely on physical science (Section 1)
4. the steps used in the scientific method (Section 2)
5. examples of technology (Section 2)
6. how the scientific method is used to answer questions and solve problems (Section 2)
7. how our knowledge of science changes over time (Section 2)
8. how models represent real objects or systems (Section 3)
9. examples of different ways models are used in science (Section 3)
10. the importance of the International System of Units (Section 4)
11. the appropriate units to use for particular measurements (Section 4)
12. how area and density are derived quantities (Section 4)

Questions to Ask Along the Way

You can help your son or daughter learn about these topics by asking interesting questions such as the following:

- What are some surprising careers that use physical science?
- What is a characteristic of a good hypothesis?
- When is it a good idea to use a model?
- Why do Americans measure things in terms of inches and yards instead of centimeters and meters?

TEST ITEM LISTING

TEST ITEM LISTING
The World of Science — SAMPLE

MULTIPLE CHOICE

1. A limitation of models is that
   a. they are large enough to see.
   b. they do not act exactly like the things that they model.
   c. they are smaller than the things that they model.
   d. they model unfamiliar things.
   Answer: B   Difficulty: 1   Section: 3   Objective: 1

2. The length 10 m is equal to
   a. 100 cm.   c. 10,000 mm.
   b. 1,000 cm.   d. Both (b) and (c)
   Answer: D   Difficulty: 1   Section: 3   Objective: 2

3. To be valid, a hypothesis must be
   a. testable.   c. made into a law.
   b. supported by evidence.   d. Both (a) and (b)
   Answer: B   Difficulty: 1   Section: 3   Objective: 2

4. The statement "Sheila has a stain on her shirt" is an example of a(n)
   a. law.   c. observation.
   b. hypothesis.   d. prediction.
   Answer: B   Difficulty: 1   Section: 3   Objective: 1

5. A hypothesis is often developed out of
   a. observations.   c. laws.
   b. experiments.   d. Both (a) and (b)
   Answer: B   Difficulty: 1   Section: 1   Objective: 2

6. How many milliliters are in 3.5 kL?
   a. 3,500 mL.   c. 3,500,000 mL.
   b. 0.0035 mL.   d. 35,000 mL.
   Answer: B   Difficulty: 1   Section: 3   Objective: 2

7. A map of Seattle is an example of a
   a. law.   c. model.
   b. theory.   d. unit.
   Answer: B   Difficulty: 1   Section: 3   Objective: 2

8. A lab has the safety icons shown below. These icons mean that you should wear
   a. only safety goggles.   c. safety goggles, a lab apron, and gloves.
   b. only a lab apron.   d. safety goggles, a lab apron, and a lab apron.
   Answer: B   Difficulty: 1   Section: 3   Objective: 2

9. The law of conservation of mass says that the total mass before a chemical change is
   a. more than the total mass after the change.
   b. less than the total mass after the change.
   c. the same as the total mass after the change.
   d. not the same as the total mass after the change.
   Answer: B   Difficulty: 1   Section: 3   Objective: 2

10. In which of the following areas might you find a geochemist at work?
    a. studying the chemistry of rocks   c. studying fabrics
    b. studying forestry   d. studying the atmosphere
    Answer: B   Difficulty: 1   Section: 3   Objective: 2

One-Stop Planner® CD-ROM

This CD-ROM includes all of the resources shown here and the following time-saving tools:

- *Lab Materials QuickList Software*
- *Customizable lesson plans*
- *Holt Calendar Planner*
- *The powerful ExamView® Test Generator*

Meeting Individual Needs

DIRECTED READING A

BASIC

DIRECTED READING B
SPECIAL NEEDS

VOCABULARY ACTIVITY
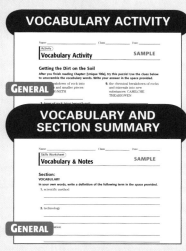
GENERAL

VOCABULARY AND SECTION SUMMARY
GENERAL

REINFORCEMENT
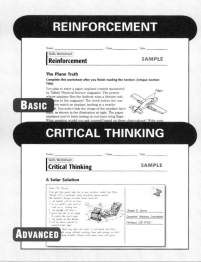
BASIC

CRITICAL THINKING
ADVANCED

SCILINKS ACTIVITY

GENERAL

SCIENCE PUZZLERS, TWISTERS & TEASERS
GENERAL

Labs and Activities

LONG-TERM PROJECTS & RESEARCH IDEAS
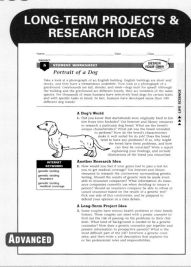
ADVANCED

DATASHEETS FOR QUICK LABS

DATASHEETS FOR CHAPTER LABS

DATASHEETS FOR LABBOOK

Review and Assessments

SECTION QUIZ

ALSO IN SPANISH
GENERAL

SECTION REVIEW
ALSO IN SPANISH
GENERAL

CHAPTER REVIEW
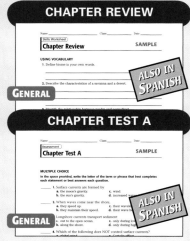
ALSO IN SPANISH
GENERAL

CHAPTER TEST A
ALSO IN SPANISH
GENERAL

CHAPTER TEST B
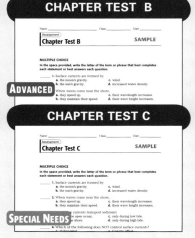
ADVANCED

CHAPTER TEST C
SPECIAL NEEDS

STANDARDIZED TEST PREPARATION
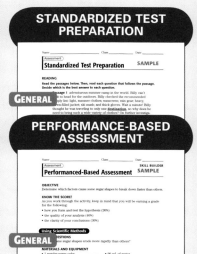
GENERAL

PERFORMANCE-BASED ASSESSMENT
GENERAL

This Chapter Enrichment provides relevant and interesting information to expand and enhance your presentation of the chapter material.

Section 1

Mendel and His Peas

Gregor Mendel

- In 1843, in the city of Brünn, Austria (which is now Brno, a city in the Czech Republic), Gregor Mendel (1822–1884) entered a monastery. In 1865, Mendel published the results of his garden-pea experiments. Although Mendel's ideas are widespread today, few scientists learned of his work during his lifetime because there were few ways to distribute information. Mendel presented his findings in two lectures, and only 40 copies of his work were printed in his lifetime.

- When Mendel was elected abbot of the monastery in 1868, his duties prevented him from visiting other scientists or attending conferences where he could have discussed his results. Not until 1900, when Mendel's work was rediscovered by scientists in Holland, Germany, and Austria-Hungary, were his theories spread through the scientific community.

- Mendel's work was used to support Darwin's theory of evolution by natural selection and is considered to be the foundation of modern genetics. Mendel also made contributions to beekeeping, horticulture, and meteorology. In 1877, Mendel became interested in weather and began issuing weather reports to local farmers.

Is That a Fact!

◆ From 1856 to 1863, while studying inheritance, Mendel grew almost 30,000 pea plants!

Section 2

Traits and Inheritance

Punnett and His Squares

- Punnett squares are named after their inventor, R. C. Punnett. Punnett explored inheritance by crossing different breeds of chickens in the early 1900s, soon after Mendel's work was rediscovered.

Pollination

- Pollen can be transferred between plants by wind, insects, and a variety of animals. Some common pollinators are bees, butterflies, moths, flies, bats, and birds. Animals are attracted to the color of the flower, the patterns found on the petals, or the flower's fragrance. Pollen is an excellent food for some animals.

Is That a Fact!

◆ Male bees have only half the number of chromosomes that female bees have.

Section 3

Meiosis

Chromosomes

- Chromosomes are composed of genes, the sequences of DNA that provide the instructions for making all the proteins in an organism. During cell division, the duplicated chromosomes separate so that one copy of each chromosome is present in the two new cells.

Walther Flemming

- Walther Flemming (1843–1905), a German physician and anatomist, was the first to use a microscope and special dyes to study cell division. Flemming used the term *mitosis* to describe the process he observed.

Mitosis

- In mitosis, a cell divides to form two identical cells. The steps of the process are similar in almost all living organisms. In addition to enabling growth, mitosis allows organisms to replace cells that have died or malfunctioned. Mitosis can take anywhere from a few minutes to a few hours, and it may be affected by characteristics of the environment, such as light and temperature.

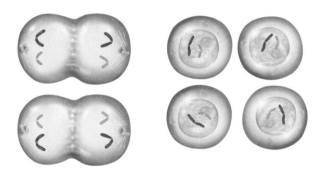

Meiosis

- Meiosis is not the same in all organisms. In humans, meiosis is very different in males and females. In males, meiosis results in four similar sperm cells. In females, however, only one functional egg is produced. The other resulting cells, which are known as *polar bodies,* are formed during the division of the original cell but do not mature.

Genetic Disorders

- A genetic disorder results from an inherited disruption in an organism's DNA. These inherited disruptions can take several forms, including a change in the number of chromosomes and the deletion or duplication of entire chromosomes or parts of chromosomes. Often, the change responsible for a disorder is the alteration of a single specific gene. However, some genetic disorders result from several of these genetic alterations occurring simultaneously. Diseases resulting from these alterations cause a wide variety of physical malfunctions and developmental problems.

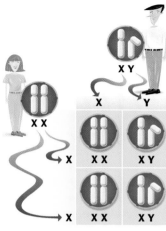

- Cystic fibrosis (CF) is a disease for which one in 31 Americans carries a recessive trait. If two of these people have children together, there is a 25% chance that any child born to them will have the disease. CF affects the intestinal, bronchial, and sweat glands. In people with CF, these glands secrete thick, sticky fluids that are difficult for the body to process, impeding breathing and digestion. Due to improvements in diagnosis and treatment, median life expectancy for those with CF has improved from under 10 years in 1960 to an estimated 40 years for those born in 1990.

- Rubinstein-Taybi syndrome (RTS) is a complex genetic disorder whose characteristics include broad thumbs and toes, mental retardation, and distinctive facial features. This wide range of characteristics is believed to be linked to any one of a number of mutations in a gene responsible for providing the body with a protein called *CBP.* CBP is thought to be vital to the body's delicate metabolism. Because CBP greatly influences body processes, people with a problem producing CBP have a wide range of difficulties. Children with RTS can benefit from proper nutrition and early intervention with therapies and special education.

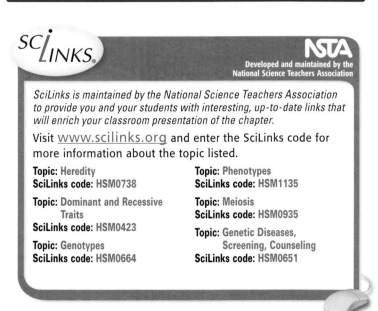

SciLinks is maintained by the National Science Teachers Association to provide you and your students with interesting, up-to-date links that will enrich your classroom presentation of the chapter.

Visit www.scilinks.org and enter the SciLinks code for more information about the topic listed.

Topic: Heredity
SciLinks code: HSM0738

Topic: Phenotypes
SciLinks code: HSM1135

Topic: Dominant and Recessive Traits
SciLinks code: HSM0423

Topic: Meiosis
SciLinks code: HSM0935

Topic: Genotypes
SciLinks code: HSM0664

Topic: Genetic Diseases, Screening, Counseling
SciLinks code: HSM0651

Overview

Tell students that this chapter will introduce heredity—the ways that traits are passed from parents to offspring. The chapter describes the ways scientists study heredity and the role of sexual reproduction.

Assessing Prior Knowledge

Students should be familiar with the following topics:

- scientific methods
- cells
- mitosis

Identifying Misconceptions

Students often hold onto misconceptions about inheritance, even after instruction. For example, they may believe that traits are inherited from only one parent or that environmentally caused characteristics may be passed on to offspring. Students tend to understand phenotype (physical traits) more easily than genotype. Finally, the process of meiosis, as it relates to the structure and location of chromosomes, is very complex. Most students require time and repeated exposure in order to comprehend all the parts and steps of meiosis. Assure students that the concepts of heredity are a foundation that will be built upon throughout their studies of life science.

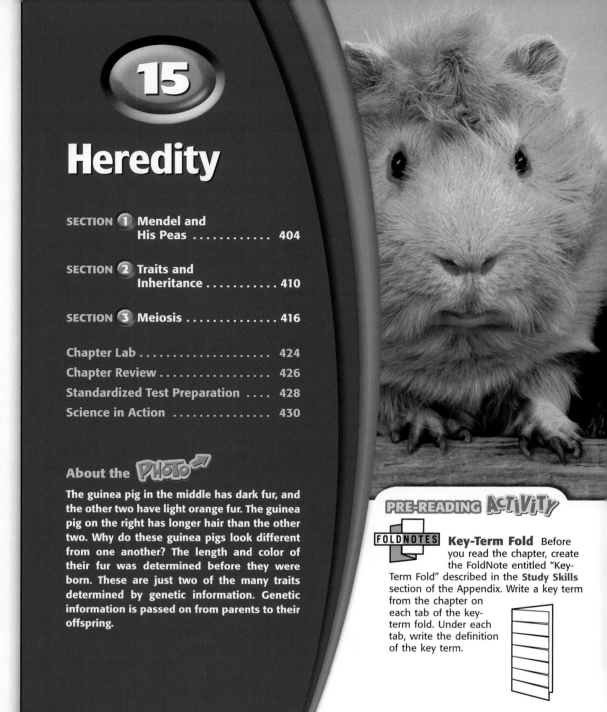

15
Heredity

About the PHOTO

The guinea pig in the middle has dark fur, and the other two have light orange fur. The guinea pig on the right has longer hair than the other two. Why do these guinea pigs look different from one another? The length and color of their fur was determined before they were born. These are just two of the many traits determined by genetic information. Genetic information is passed on from parents to their offspring.

PRE-READING ACTIVITY

FOLDNOTES **Key-Term Fold** Before you read the chapter, create the FoldNote entitled "Key-Term Fold" described in the **Study Skills** section of the Appendix. Write a key term from the chapter on each tab of the key-term fold. Under each tab, write the definition of the key term.

Standards Correlations

North Carolina Standard Course of Study

1.07 (partial) Prepare models and/or computer simulations to: Test hypotheses ... (Chapter Lab)

5.01 Explain the significance of genes to inherited characteristics: Genes are the units of information, Parents transmit genes to their offspring, [and] Some medical conditions and diseases are genetic. (Sections 2 and 3)

5.02 Explain the significance of reproduction: Sorting and recombination of parents' genetic material, [and] Potential variation among offspring. (Chapter Opener and Section 3)

5.03 Identify examples and patterns of human genetic traits: Dominant and recessive, [and] Incomplete dominance. (Sections 1 and 2)

5.04 Analyze the role of probability in the study of heredity: Role of each parent in transfer of genetic traits, [and] Analysis of pedigrees. (Sections 2 and 3, Chapter Lab, and LabBook)

5.05 Summarize the genetic transmittance of disease. (Section 3 and Science in Action)

5.06 Evaluate evidence that human characteristics are a product of: Inheritance, Environmental factors, [and] Lifestyle choices. (Section 2 and Science in Action)

START-UP **ACTIVITY**

Clothing Combos

How do the same parents have children with many different traits?

Procedure

1. Gather **three boxes**. Put **five hats** in the first box, **five gloves** in the second, and **five scarves** in the third.

2. Without looking in the boxes, select one item from each box. Repeat this process, five students at a time, until the entire class has picked "an outfit." Record what outfit each student chooses.

Analysis

1. Were any two outfits exactly alike? Did you see all possible combinations? Explain your answer.

2. Choose a partner. Using your outfits, how many different combinations could you make by giving a third person one hat, one glove, and one scarf? How is this process like parents passing traits to their children?

3. After completing this activity, why do you think parents often have children who look very different from each other?

START-UP **ACTIVITY**

MATERIALS

FOR EACH GROUP
- boxes large, (3)
- gloves different types, (5)
- hats different types, (5)
- scarves different types, (5)

Safety Caution: Infestations of head lice are a common problem in schools. Sharing hats should be avoided during such a period. Jackets or sweatshirts could be substituted for hats in this exercise.

Answers

1. Answers may vary. There should be many different combinations. It is not likely that students will see all of the possible combinations.

2. Sample answer: eight new combinations (taken from the outfits of the two "parents") would be possible for the third person ("offspring"). This process is like inheritance because you are choosing combinations of hats, scarves, and gloves randomly. Traits are also passed from parent to offspring randomly. By combining the traits (outfits) of two "parents" (partners), there are many possible combinations of traits in the "offspring" (third person).

3. Sample answer: The number of possible genetic combinations is huge because we have so many genes.

Chapter Starter Transparency
Use this transparency to help students begin thinking about heredity.

CHAPTER RESOURCES

Technology

 Transparencies
- Chapter Starter Transparency

READING **SKILLS**

 **Student Edition on CD-ROM**

Guided Reading Audio CD

 Classroom Videos
- Brain Food Video Quiz

Workbooks

 Science Puzzlers, Twisters & Teasers
- Heredity GENERAL

Overview

This section introduces the genetic experiments of Gregor Mendel. Students explore how crosses between different parent plants produce different offspring. Students are also introduced to genetic probability.

Bellringer

Present the following prompt to your students: "You have probably noticed that different people have different traits, such as eye color, hair color, and ear lobes that do or do not attach directly to their head. Where do people get these different traits?" (Many traits are inherited from parents and passed from parents to offspring through genes.)

ACTIVITY ——— GENERAL

Trait Trends Create a large table to record the number of students with the following traits: widow's peak, ability to roll tongue, and attached earlobes. Have pairs of students enter data for each other by adding tick marks on the table. Ask students if they can see any trends in the class data. If possible, compile data from several classes. **LS Kinesthetic/Interpersonal**

READING WARM-UP

Objectives
- Explain the relationship between traits and heredity.
- Describe the experiments of Gregor Mendel.
- Explain the difference between dominant and recessive traits.

Terms to Learn
heredity
dominant trait
recessive trait

READING STRATEGY

Brainstorming The key idea of this section is heredity. Brainstorm words and phrases related to heredity.

heredity the passing of genetic traits from parent to offspring

Figure 1 *Gregor Mendel discovered the principles of heredity while studying pea plants.*

Mendel and His Peas

Why don't you look like a rhinoceros? The answer to this question seems simple: Neither of your parents is a rhinoceros. But there is more to this answer than meets the eye.

As it turns out, **heredity,** or the passing of traits from parents to offspring, is more complicated than you might think. For example, you might have curly hair, while both of your parents have straight hair. You might have blue eyes even though both of your parents have brown eyes. How does this happen? People have investigated this question for a long time. About 150 years ago, Gregor Mendel performed important experiments. His discoveries helped scientists begin to find some answers to these questions.

✓ **Reading Check** What is heredity? (*See the Appendix for answers to Reading Checks.*)

Who Was Gregor Mendel?

Gregor Mendel, shown in **Figure 1,** was born in 1822 in Heinzendorf, Austria. Mendel grew up on a farm and learned a lot about flowers and fruit trees.

When he was 21 years old, Mendel entered a monastery. The monks taught science and performed many scientific experiments. From there, Mendel was sent to Vienna where he could receive training in teaching. However, Mendel had trouble taking tests. Although he did well in school, he was unable to pass the final exam. He returned to the monastery and put most of his energy into research. Mendel discovered the principles of heredity in the monastery garden.

Unraveling the Mystery

From working with plants, Mendel knew that the patterns of inheritance were not always clear. For example, sometimes a trait that appeared in one generation (parents) was not present in the next generation (offspring). In the generation after that, though, the trait showed up again. Mendel noticed these kinds of patterns in several other living things, too. Mendel wanted to learn more about what caused these patterns.

To keep his investigation simple, Mendel decided to study only one kind of organism. Because he had studied garden pea plants before, they seemed like a good choice.

CHAPTER RESOURCES

Chapter Resource File
- Lesson Plan
- Directed Reading A **BASIC**
- Directed Reading B **SPECIAL NEEDS**

Technology
- Transparencies
  - Bellringer

Answer to Reading Check

the passing of traits from parents to offspring

Self-Pollinating Peas

In fact, garden peas were a good choice for several reasons. Pea plants grow quickly, and there are many different kinds available. They are also able to self-pollinate. A *self-pollinating plant* has both male and female reproductive structures. So, pollen from one flower can fertilize the ovule of the same flower or the ovule of another flower on the same plant. The flower on the right side of **Figure 2** is self-pollinating.

Why is it important that pea plants can self-pollinate? Because eggs (in an ovule) and sperm (in pollen) from the same plant combine to make a new plant, Mendel was able to grow true-breeding plants. When a *true-breeding plant* self-pollinates, all of its offspring will have the same trait as the parent. For example, a true-breeding plant with purple flowers will always have offspring with purple flowers.

Pea plants can also cross-pollinate. In *cross-pollination,* pollen from one plant fertilizes the ovule of a flower on a different plant. There are several ways that this can happen. Pollen may be carried by insects to a flower on a different plant. Pollen can also be carried by the wind from one flower to another. The left side of **Figure 2** shows these kinds of cross-pollination.

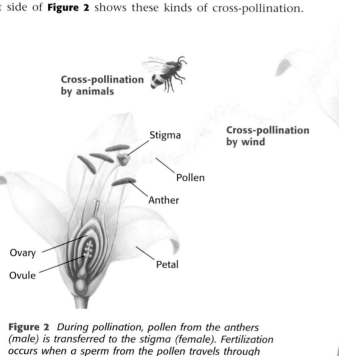

Cross-pollination by animals

Cross-pollination by wind

Self-pollination

Stigma

Pollen

Anther

Ovary

Ovule

Petal

Figure 2 *During pollination, pollen from the anthers (male) is transferred to the stigma (female). Fertilization occurs when a sperm from the pollen travels through the stigma and enters the egg in an ovule.*

Is That a Fact!

Although Mendel was brilliant, he had difficulty learning from scientific texts. In the monastery gardens, Mendel explored the scientific ideas he had trouble with in school. While trying to grow better peas, he discovered genetics, an entirely new field of science!

CONNECTION to Physical Science— GENERAL

Seeing Flower Color Flower color depends on which wavelength of light is reflected by the petals. For example, red absorbs all of the wavelengths except those for red. Display a color spectrum to illustrate that white light is composed of a "rainbow" gradient of colors. Show students different colors, and ask them which colors of light are being absorbed and which are being reflected to our eye. **LS** Visual

Discussion —————— GENERAL

Scientific Methods Have students identify the use of scientific methods in Mendel's work.

- **Ask a question:** How are traits inherited?
- **Form a hypothesis:** Inheritance has a pattern.
- **Test the hypothesis:** Cross true-breeding plants and offspring.
- **Analyze the results:** Identify patterns in inherited traits.
- **Draw conclusions:** Traits are inherited in predictable patterns.
- **Communicate the results:** Publish the results for peer review.

Ask students, "Why weren't Mendel's ideas accepted for so many years?" (because of problems with the last step—other scientists could not easily read or understand his findings)

LS Logical/Verbal

Demonstration —————— BASIC

Flower Dissection Obtain a flower that has anthers and a stigma, such as a pea flower, a tulip, or a lily. Be careful because pollen can stain clothing and cause allergic reactions. Dissect the flower, and show students the anthers and the stigma. Ask students if this flower could self-pollinate. (yes, because it has both anthers and a stigma) Demonstrate how Mendel removed the anthers of his flowers and then used a small brush to transfer pollen from plant to plant.

LS Kinesthetic   English Language Learners

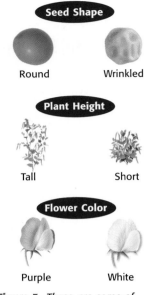

Seed Shape

Round   Wrinkled

Plant Height

Tall   Short

Flower Color

Purple   White

Figure 3 *These are some of the plant characteristics that Mendel studied.*

Characteristics

Mendel studied only one characteristic at a time. A *characteristic* is a feature that has different forms in a population. For example, hair color is a characteristic in humans. The different forms, such as brown or red hair, are called *traits*. Mendel used plants that had different traits for each of the characteristics he studied. For instance, for the characteristic of flower color, he chose plants that had purple flowers and plants that had white flowers. Three of the characteristics Mendel studied are shown in **Figure 3.**

Mix and Match

Mendel was careful to use plants that were true breeding for each of the traits he was studying. By doing so, he would know what to expect if his plants were to self-pollinate. He decided to find out what would happen if he bred, or crossed, two plants that had different traits of a single characteristic. To be sure the plants cross-pollinated, he removed the anthers of one plant so that the plant could not self-pollinate. Then, he used pollen from another plant to fertilize the plant, as shown in **Figure 4.** This step allowed Mendel to select which plants would be crossed to produce offspring.

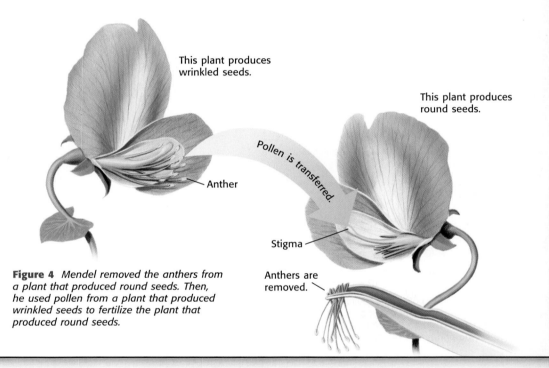

This plant produces wrinkled seeds.

This plant produces round seeds.

Pollen is transferred.

Anther

Stigma

Anthers are removed.

Figure 4 *Mendel removed the anthers from a plant that produced round seeds. Then, he used pollen from a plant that produced wrinkled seeds to fertilize the plant that produced round seeds.*

ACTIVITY —————— ADVANCED

Mendelian Crosses Give each student a purple bead (*P*) and a white bead (*p*), and ask students to perform a Mendelian cross. Tell students to begin the first generation with the allele combination *Pp*. Have students randomly "pollinate" with 10 other members of the class. To pollinate, one student should hide one bead in each hand. The partner should pick a hand. That hand holds the allele from one parent. Partners should switch roles and repeat this step to determine the allele from the second parent. Students should record the genotype for each pollination. Have students tally the results and determine the ratio of white-flowering plants to purple-flowering plants that results from the matches.

LS Kinesthetic/Interpersonal   Co-op Learning

Mendel's First Experiments

In his first experiments, Mendel crossed pea plants to study seven different characteristics. In each cross, Mendel used plants that were true breeding for different traits for each characteristic. For example, he crossed plants that had purple flowers with plants that had white flowers. This cross is shown in the first part of **Figure 5.** The offspring from such a cross are called *first-generation plants.* All of the first-generation plants in this cross had purple flowers. Are you surprised by the results? What happened to the trait for white flowers?

Mendel got similar results for each cross. One trait was always present in the first generation, and the other trait seemed to disappear. Mendel chose to call the trait that appeared the **dominant trait.** Because the other trait seemed to fade into the background, Mendel called it the **recessive trait.** (To *recede* means "to go away or back off.") Dominant and recessive traits appear in all organisms, including humans. For example, dark hair is a dominant trait and light hair is a recessive trait.

Mendel's Second Experiments

To find out what happens to recessive traits, Mendel did more experiments. He allowed the first-generation plants to self-pollinate. **Figure 5** shows what happened when a first-generation plant with purple flowers could self-pollinate. The recessive trait for white flowers reappeared in the second generation. Mendel did this same experiment on each of the seven characteristics. In each case, some of the second-generation plants had the recessive trait.

Reading Check Describe Mendel's second set of experiments.

dominant trait the trait observed in the first generation when parents that have different traits are bred

recessive trait a trait that reappears in the second generation after disappearing in the first generation when parents with different traits are bred

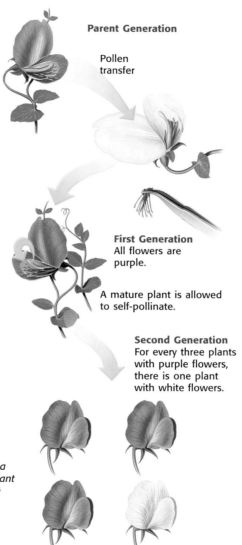

Parent Generation

Pollen transfer

First Generation All flowers are purple.

A mature plant is allowed to self-pollinate.

Second Generation For every three plants with purple flowers, there is one plant with white flowers.

Figure 5 *Mendel used the pollen from a plant with purple flowers to fertilize a plant with white flowers. Then, he allowed the offspring to self-pollinate.*

MISCONCEPTION ///**ALERT**\\\

Recessive Traits Students may believe that recessive traits are rare. Point out that either dominant *or* recessive traits may be more common in a population. For example, blond hair is a recessive trait, yet blond hair is very common in parts of Scandinavia. Conversely, dominant traits are not always the most common. For example, the trait of having six fingers on one hand is dominant!

Answer to Reading Check

During his second set of experiments, Mendel allowed the first-generation plants, which resulted from his first set of experiments, to self-pollinate. The recessive trait reappeared in the second generation.

• *Learning Disabled*
• *Attention Deficit Disorder*
• *Developmentally Delayed*

Use this activity to physically model the abstract concepts of *recessive* and *dominant*. To prepare, gather sheets of two kinds of transparent film: clear and purple. Cut the sheets into rectangles that are small enough to handle. Make one rectangle of each type for each student in the class.

1. Tell students that they are going to serve as models of Mendel's experiment in **Figure 5.** Give half of the students two purple rectangles each. Announce that these students have purple flowers. Give the other half of the students two clear rectangles each. Announce that these students have white flowers. Announce that the class now represents Mendel's parent generation.

2. Have each student trade one rectangle with another student. Announce that these new combinations represent Mendel's first generation. Tell students to hold the rectangles together in front of a light. Tell students that the purple gene is dominant and that those who see purple through the rectangles have purple flowers. This generation all has purple flowers.

3. Finally, have students trade one rectangle randomly with another student. Announce that the class now represents Mendel's second generation. Have students count the number of "flowers" of each type, and compare these results to Mendel's.

LS Kinesthetic

English Language Learners

Reteaching ——— BASIC

Mendel's Experiments Have students re-enact Mendel's experiments using cups (to represent a plant), colored buttons or chips (to represent various alleles or genotypes), and colored strips of paper (to represent visible traits or phenotypes). Have students perform crosses by taking alleles from "parent" cups and creating "offspring" cups, deciding which traits would then become visible. **LS** Kinesthetic/Logical

English Language Learners

Quiz ——— GENERAL

1. What did Mendel call the trait that appeared in all of his first-generation plants? (the dominant trait)

2. What is the probability of getting heads in a coin toss? (1/2)

Alternative Assessment ——— ADVANCED

Story of a Scientist Have students create a comic book or short video drama about Mendel's life and work. Tell students to highlight his use of the scientific method and his habits as a scientist. **LS** Interpersonal

MATH PRACTICE

Understanding Ratios

A ratio is a way to compare two numbers. Look at **Table 1.** The ratio of plants with purple flowers to plants with white flowers can be written as 705 to 224 or 705:224. This ratio can be reduced, or simplified, by dividing the first number by the second as follows:

$$\frac{705}{224} = \frac{3.15}{1}$$

which is the same thing as a ratio of 3.15:1.

For every 3 plants with purple flowers, there will be roughly 1 plant with white flowers. Try this problem:

In a box of chocolates, there are 18 nougat-filled chocolates and 6 caramel-filled chocolates. What is the ratio of nougat-filled chocolates to caramel-filled chocolates?

Ratios in Mendel's Experiments

Mendel then decided to count the number of plants with each trait that turned up in the second generation. He hoped that this might help him explain his results. Take a look at Mendel's results, shown in **Table 1.**

As you can see, the recessive trait did not show up as often as the dominant trait. Mendel decided to figure out the ratio of dominant traits to recessive traits. A *ratio* is a relationship between two different numbers that is often expressed as a fraction. Calculate the dominant-to-recessive ratio for each characteristic. (If you need help, look at the Math Practice at left.) Do you notice anything interesting about the ratios? Round to the nearest whole number. Are the ratios all the same, or are they different?

✓ **Reading Check** What is a ratio?

Table 1 Mendel's Results

Characteristic	Dominant traits	Recessive traits	Ratio
Flower color	705 purple	224 white	3.15:1
Seed color	6,002 yellow	2,001 green	?
Seed shape	5,474 round	1,850 wrinkled	?
Pod color	428 green	152 yellow	?
Pod shape	882 smooth	299 bumpy	?
Flower position	651 along stem	207 at tip	?
Plant height	787 tall	277 short	?

Answer to Math Practice

The ratio of nougat-filled chocolates to caramel-filled chocolates is 18:6, or 18/6, which can be reduced to 3/1. This fraction can be rewritten as 3:1 or 3 to 1.

Answers to questions on student page

All the ratios are about the same. They can be rounded to 3:1.

Answer to Reading Check

A ratio is a relationship between two different numbers that is often expressed as a fraction.

Gregor Mendel—Gone but Not Forgotten

Mendel realized that his results could be explained only if each plant had two sets of instructions for each characteristic. Each parent would then donate one set of instructions. In 1865, Mendel published his findings. But good ideas are sometimes overlooked or misunderstood at first. It wasn't until after his death, more than 30 years later, that Mendel's work was widely recognized. Once Mendel's ideas were rediscovered and understood, the door was opened to modern genetics. Genetic research, as shown in **Figure 6,** is one of the fastest changing fields in science today.

Figure 6 *This researcher is continuing the work started by Gregor Mendel more than 100 years ago.*

SECTION Review

Summary

- Heredity is the passing of traits from parents to offspring.
- Gregor Mendel made carefully planned experiments using pea plants that could self-pollinate.
- When parents with different traits are bred, dominant traits are always present in the first generation. Recessive traits are not visible in the first generation but reappear in the second generation.
- Mendel found a 3:1 ratio of dominant-to-recessive traits in the second generation.

Using Key Terms

1. Use each of the following terms in a separate sentence: *heredity, dominant trait,* and *recessive trait.*

Understanding Key Ideas

2. A plant that has both male and female reproductive structures is able to
   a. self-replicate.
   b. self-pollinate.
   c. change colors.
   d. None of the above

3. Explain the difference between self-pollination and cross-pollination.

4. What is the difference between a trait and a characteristic? Give one example of each.

5. Describe Mendel's first set of experiments.

6. Describe Mendel's second set of experiments.

Math Skills

7. In a bag of chocolate candies, there are 21 brown candies and 6 green candies. What is the ratio of brown to green? What is the ratio of green to brown?

Critical Thinking

8. **Predicting Consequences** Gregor Mendel used only true-breeding plants. If he had used plants that were not true breeding, do you think he would have discovered dominant and recessive traits? Explain.

9. **Applying Concepts** In cats, there are two types of ears: normal and curly. A curly-eared cat mated with a normal-eared cat, and all of the kittens had curly ears. Are curly ears a dominant or recessive trait? Explain.

10. **Identifying Relationships** List three other fields of study that use ratios.

Answers to Section Review

1. Sample answer: Heredity is the passing of traits from parents to their offspring. A dominant trait is a trait that is present in the first generation when parents with different traits produce offspring. A recessive trait is a trait that is not present in the first generation but often reappears in the second generation.

2. b

3. Self-pollination occurs when pollen from a particular plant is deposited on a stigma from the same plant. Cross-pollination occurs when the pollen and stigma are from two different plants.

4. Sample answer: A characteristic is something that has different forms in a population, and a trait is each one of the possible forms. For example, eye color is a characteristic in humans, and brown eyes, green eyes, and blue eyes are all possible traits.

5. Sample answer: During Mendel's first experiments, he crossed two plants that were true breeding for different traits. In each case, the offspring had the dominant trait.

6. During Mendel's second experiments, he allowed the plants that were the offspring from his first experiments to self-pollinate. In these cases, some of the second-generation plants had the recessive trait.

7. 7:2, or 3.5:1, brown to green; 2:7, or 1:3.5, green to brown

8. Sample answer: If Mendel had used plants that were not true breeding, the dominant trait would not have been as clear for each characteristic, and he would not have gotten such a clear 3:1 ratio. The concept of dominant and recessive may have stayed hidden for a longer period of time.

9. Curly ears are dominant because it is the trait that is represented in the first generation.

10. Sample answer: sociology, physics, and chemistry

Homework — GENERAL

Poster Project Have students create posters to illustrate Mendel's first and second experiments. Have each student demonstrate one of the seven traits that Mendel studied. Encourage students to use materials such as flowers, yellow and green seeds, or wrinkled and round peas. Each project should clearly identify the parents, the first generation, and the second generation. **LS Visual/Logical**

CHAPTER RESOURCES

Chapter Resource File
- Section Quiz GENERAL
- Section Review GENERAL
- Vocabulary and Section Summary GENERAL
- Critical Thinking Worksheet ADVANCED
- SciLinks Activity GENERAL

Workbooks

Science Skills
- Finding Useful Sources GENERAL

Math Skills for Science
- What is a Ratio? GENERAL

Focus

Overview

In this section, students distinguish between genotype and phenotype and use mathematical models to predict the results of genetic crosses. They also learn some exceptions to Mendel's rules of inheritance.

🔊 Bellringer

Have students respond to the following prompts: "If you flip a coin, what are the chances that it will land on heads?" (1/2 or 50%) "tails?" (same) "Suppose you flip the coin once, get heads, and then flip it again. What are the chances that you will get heads again?" (still 1/2 or 50%) "Explain." (Each flip of the coin is independent of the last. The chances are the same on each flip.)

Motivate

Demonstration —— BASIC

Ratios To review fractions and ratios, display three pennies and one nickel, and then ask students the following questions: "How many coins are there in all?" (4) "What fraction of the coins are pennies?" (3/4) "What fraction of the coins are nickels?" (1/4) "What is the ratio of pennies to nickels?" (3 to 1)
 Visual/Verbal

READING WARM-UP

Objectives
- Explain how genes and alleles are related to genotype and phenotype.
- Use the information in a Punnett square.
- Explain how probability can be used to predict possible genotypes in offspring.
- Describe three exceptions to Mendel's observations.

Terms to Learn
gene   genotype
allele   probability
phenotype

READING STRATEGY

Paired Summarizing Read this section silently. In pairs, take turns summarizing the material. Stop to discuss ideas that seem confusing.

---

gene one set of instructions for an inherited trait

allele one of the alternative forms of a gene that governs a characteristic, such as hair color

phenotype an organism's appearance or other detectable characteristic

Figure 1 Albinism is an inherited disorder that affects a person's phenotype in many ways.

CHAPTER RESOURCES

Chapter Resource File
- **Lesson Plan**
- **Directed Reading A** BASIC
- **Directed Reading B** SPECIAL NEEDS

Technology
Transparencies
- Bellringer
- Punnett Squares
- **LINK TO PHYSICAL SCIENCE** The Periodic Table of the Elements

Traits and Inheritance

Mendel calculated the ratio of dominant traits to recessive traits. He found a ratio of 3:1. What did this tell him about how traits are passed from parents to offspring?

A Great Idea

Mendel knew from his experiments with pea plants that there must be two sets of instructions for each characteristic. The first-generation plants carried the instructions for both the dominant trait and the recessive trait. Scientists now call these instructions for an inherited trait **genes.** Each parent gives one set of genes to the offspring. The offspring then has two forms of the same gene for every characteristic—one from each parent. The different forms (often dominant and recessive) of a gene are known as **alleles** (uh LEELZ). Dominant alleles are shown with a capital letter. Recessive alleles are shown with a lowercase letter.

✔ **Reading Check** What is the difference between a gene and an allele? (*See the Appendix for answers to Reading Checks.*)

Phenotype

Genes affect the traits of offspring. An organism's appearance is known as its **phenotype** (FEE noh TIEP). In pea plants, possible phenotypes for the characteristic of flower color would be purple flowers or white flowers. For seed color, yellow and green seeds are the different phenotypes.

Phenotypes of humans are much more complicated than those of peas. Look at **Figure 1** below. The man has an inherited condition called *albinism* (AL buh NIZ uhm). Albinism prevents hair, skin, and eyes from having normal coloring.

Answer to Reading Check

A gene contains the instructions for an inherited trait. the different versions of a gene are called *alleles.*

Genotype

Both inherited alleles together form an organism's **genotype.** Because the allele for purple flowers (*P*) is dominant, only one *P* allele is needed for the plant to have purple flowers. A plant with two dominant or two recessive alleles is said to be *homozygous* (HOH moh ZIE guhs). A plant that has the genotype *Pp* is said to be *heterozygous* (HET uhr OH ZIE guhs).

Punnett Squares

A Punnett square is used to organize all the possible combinations of offspring from particular parents. The alleles for a true-breeding, purple-flowered plant are written as *PP.* The alleles for a true-breeding, white-flowered plant are written as *pp.* The Punnett square for this cross is shown in **Figure 2.** All of the offspring have the same genotype: *Pp.* The dominant allele, *P,* in each genotype ensures that all of the offspring will be purple-flowered plants. The recessive allele, *p,* may be passed on to the next generation. This Punnett square shows the results of Mendel's first experiments.

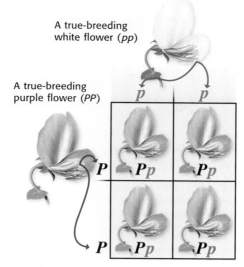

A true-breeding white flower (*pp*)

A true-breeding purple flower (*PP*)

Figure 2 *All of the offspring for this cross have the same genotype—Pp.*

genotype the entire genetic makeup of an organism; also the combination of genes for one or more specific traits

Making a Punnett Square

1. Draw a square, and divide it into four sections.
2. Write the letters that represent alleles from one parent along the top of the box.
3. Write the letters that represent alleles from the other parent along the side of the box.
4. The cross shown at right is between two plants that produce round seeds. The genotype for each is *Rr.* Round seeds are dominant, and wrinkled seeds are recessive. Follow the arrows to see how the inside of the box was filled. The resulting alleles inside the box show all the possible genotypes for the offspring from this cross. What would the phenotypes for these offspring be?

SCIENCE HUMOR

Q: What do you get when you cross a bridge with a bicycle?

A: to the other side

4. Students should get *bb* on average 1/4 or 25% of the time.

5. 1/4 or 25%

6. 1/4 (If brown fur results from genotype *Bb*, then brown fur is dominant, and white fur will result from the genotype *bb*.)

CONNECTION ACTIVITY
Math ——— ADVANCED

Probability of Independent Events The probability of two or more independent events is the product of the individual probabilities. For example, the probability of getting heads in a coin toss is 1/2, but the probability of getting heads twice in a row is $1/2 \times 1/2$, or 1/4. Have students consider the following parent genotypes for pea plants: *PpRr* and *Pprr*. Work out and discuss the probability of each possible combined phenotype. (For example, the probability of a plant with white flowers and round seeds is $1/4 \times 1/2 = 1/8$.) **LS** Logical

Answer to Reading Check
Probability is the mathematical chance that something will happen.

Quick Lab

Taking Your Chances

You have two guinea pigs. Each has brown fur and the genotype *Bb*. You want to predict what their offspring might look like. Try this to find out.

1. Stick a **piece of masking tape** on each side of **two quarters.**
2. Label one side with a capital *B* and the other side with a lowercase *b*.
3. Toss both coins 10 times, making note of your results each time.
4. How many times did you get the *bb* combination?
5. What is the probability that the next toss will result in *bb*?
6. What are the chances that the guinea pigs' offspring will have white fur (with the genotype *bb*)?

probability the likelihood that a possible future event will occur in any given instance of the event

---

A self-pollinating purple flower

Male alleles

Female alleles

	P	*p*
P	*PP*	*Pp*
p	*pP*	*pp*

Figure 3 *This Punnett square shows the possible results from the cross Pp × Pp.*

More Evidence for Inheritance

In Mendel's second experiments, he allowed the first generation plants to self-pollinate. **Figure 3** shows a self-pollination cross of a plant with the genotype *Pp.* What are the possible genotypes of the offspring?

Notice that one square shows the genotype *Pp,* while another shows *pP.* These are exactly the same genotype. The other possible genotypes of the offspring are *PP* and *pp.* The combinations *PP, Pp,* and *pP* have the same phenotype—purple flowers. This is because each contains at least one dominant allele (*P*).

Only one combination, *pp,* produces plants that have white flowers. The ratio of dominant to recessive is 3:1, just as Mendel calculated from his data.

What Are the Chances?

Each parent has two alleles for each gene. When these alleles are different, as in *Pp,* offspring are equally likely to receive either allele. Think of a coin toss. There is a 50% chance you'll get heads and a 50% chance you'll get tails. The chance of receiving one allele or another is as random as a coin toss.

Probability

The mathematical chance that something will happen is known as **probability.** Probability is most often written as a fraction or percentage. If you toss a coin, the probability of tossing tails is 1/2—you will get tails half the time.

✓ **Reading Check** What is probability?

MISCONCEPTION ALERT

The Role of Chance Students' lack of understanding of mathematical probability may block their understanding of the random and independent sorting of genes that occurs during meiosis. Be careful that students do not overextend mathematical probabilities to predict the outcome of single events. It is correct to predict that an average of many outcomes will be similar to, but not exactly match, a probability ratio.

SCIENCE HUMOR

Q: What do you get when you cross a crocodile with an abalone?

A: a crocabaloney

MATH FOCUS

Probability If you roll a pair of dice, what is the probability that you will roll 2 threes?

Step 1: Count the number of faces on a single die. Put this number in the denominator: 6.

Step 2: Count how many ways you can roll a three with one die. Put this number in the numerator: 1/6.

Step 3: To find the probability that you will throw 2 threes, multiply the probability of throwing the first three by the probability of throwing the second three: $1/6 \times 1/6 = 1/36$.

Now It's Your Turn
If you roll a single die, what is the probability that you will roll an even number?

Calculating Probabilities

To find the probability that you will toss two heads in a row, multiply the probability of tossing the first head (1/2) by the probability of tossing the second head (1/2). The probability of tossing two heads in a row is 1/4.

Genotype Probability

To have white flowers, a pea plant must receive a *p* allele from each parent. Each offspring of a *Pp* × *Pp* cross has a 50% chance of receiving either allele from either parent. So, the probability of inheriting two *p* alleles is $1/2 \times 1/2$, which equals 1/4, or 25%. Traits in pea plants are easy to predict because there are only two choices for each trait, such as purple or white flowers and round or wrinkled seeds. Look at **Figure 4.** Do you see only two distinct choices for fur color?

Figure 4 *These kittens inherited one allele from their mother for each trait.*

CONNECTION TO Chemistry

Round and Wrinkled Round seeds may look better, but wrinkled seeds taste sweeter. The dominant allele for seed shape, *R*, causes sugar to be changed into starch (which is a storage molecule for sugar). This change makes the seed round. Seeds with the genotype *rr* do not make or store this starch. Because the sugar has not been changed into starch, the seed tastes sweeter. If you had a pea plant with round seeds (*Rr*), what would you cross it with to get some offspring with wrinkled seeds? Draw a Punnett square showing your cross.

 ACTIVITY

Homework — GENERAL

Punnett Squares Have students create Punnett squares for each of the different crosses in Mendel's experiments. Students should include the genotype and phenotype of each parent and each set of possible offspring. **LS** Visual/Logical

WEIRD SCIENCE

Many ordinary fruits and vegetables carry recessive genes for bizarre traits. For instance, a recessive gene in tomatoes causes the skin to be covered with fuzzy hair!

MISCONCEPTION ALERT

Exception to Mendel's Rules Caution students not to assume that all inherited traits follow the examples studied by Mendel. For instance, a cross between a red-haired horse and a white-haired horse can produce a horse with both red and white hair. Such a horse is said to have a roan coat. This is an example of *codominance*—the expression of two phenotypes at the same time within the same organism. As in the case of incomplete dominance (which is when a heterozygote shows a phenotype that is intermediate between the homozygous traits), both alleles are visible in the offspring, and therefore neither allele is purely dominant.

More About Traits

Things are often more complicated than they first appear to be. Gregor Mendel uncovered the basic principles of how genes are passed from one generation to the next. But scientists have found exceptions to Mendel's principles.

Incomplete Dominance

Since Mendel's discoveries, researchers have found that sometimes one trait is not completely dominant over another. These traits do not blend together, but each allele has its own degree of influence. This is known as *incomplete dominance*. A curly-haired parent and a straight-haired parent have wavy-haired children because of incomplete dominance.

A classic example of incomplete dominance is found in the snapdragon flower. **Figure 5** shows a cross between a true-breeding red snapdragon (R^1R^1) and a true-breeding white snapdragon (R^2R^2). As you can see, all of the possible phenotypes for their offspring are pink because both alleles of the gene have some degree of influence.

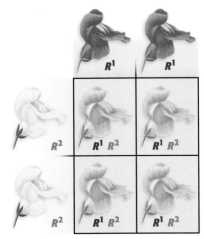

Figure 5 *Cross-breeding two true-breeding snapdragons provides a good example of incomplete dominance.*

✓ **Reading Check** What is incomplete dominance?

One Gene, Many Traits

Sometimes one gene influences more than one trait. An example of this phenomenon is shown by the white tiger in **Figure 6.** The white fur is caused by a single gene, but this gene influences more than just fur color. If you look closely, you'll see that the tiger has blue eyes. Here, the gene that controls fur color also influences eye color.

Many Genes, One Trait

Some traits, such as the color of your skin, hair, and eyes, are the result of several genes acting together. Therefore, it's difficult to tell if some traits are the result of a dominant or a recessive gene. Different combinations of alleles result in different eye-color shades.

Figure 6 *The gene that gave this tiger white fur also influenced its eye color.*

BRAIN FOOD

Round Peas Mendel found that round seeds were dominant over wrinkled seeds. However, at the microscopic level, this is a case of incomplete dominance. The *R* and *r* alleles actually seem to affect the amount of starch produced in the pea. *RR* seeds have many starch grains that give them a full, round shape, but *rr* seeds have few starch grains and a wrinkled shape. *Rr* seeds have an intermediate number of starch grains—but enough for the pea to be full and round.

The Importance of Environment

Genes aren't the only influences on traits. A guinea pig could have the genes for long fur, but its fur could be cut. In the same way, your environment influences how you grow. Your genes may make it possible that you will grow to be tall, but you need a healthy diet to reach your full potential height. Lifestyle choices can also affect a person's traits. The foods a person chooses to eat and the activities a person chooses to take part in affect how that person grows and develops. Choosing healthy foods and healthy activities can help you develop healthy traits. Together, the combination of genes, environmental factors, and lifestyle choices determine an individual's characteristics.

SECTION Review

Summary

- Instructions for an inherited trait are called *genes*. For each gene, there are two alleles, one inherited from each parent. Both alleles make up an organism's genotype. Phenotype is an organism's appearance.
- Punnett squares show all possible offspring genotypes.
- Probability can be used to describe possible outcomes in offspring and the likelihood of each outcome.
- Incomplete dominance occurs when one allele is not completely dominant over the other allele.
- Some genes influence more than one trait.

Using Key Terms

1. Use the following terms in the same sentence: *gene* and *allele*.

2. In your own words, write a definition for each of the following terms: *genotype* and *phenotype*.

Understanding Key Ideas

3. Use a Punnett square to determine the possible genotypes of the offspring of a *BB* × *Bb* cross.
   - **a.** all *BB*
   - **b.** *BB, Bb*
   - **c.** *BB, Bb, bb*
   - **d.** all *bb*

4. How are genes and alleles related to genotype and phenotype?

5. Describe three exceptions to Mendel's observations.

Math Skills

6. What is the probability that the offspring of a homozygous dominant parent and a heterozygous parent will show a recessive phenotype?

Critical Thinking

7. **Applying Concepts** The allele for a cleft chin, *C*, is dominant among humans. What are the results of a cross between parents with genotypes *Cc* and *cc*?

Interpreting Graphics

The Punnett square below shows the alleles for fur color in rabbits. Black fur, *B*, is dominant over white fur, *b*.

8. Given the combinations shown, what are the genotypes of the parents?

9. If black fur had incomplete dominance over white fur, what color would the offspring be?

For a variety of links related to this chapter, go to www.scilinks.org

Topic: Genotypes; Phenotypes
SciLinks code: HSM0664; HSM1135

Developed and maintained by the National Science Teachers Association

Answer to Reading Check

In incomplete dominance, one trait is not completely dominant over another.

Answers to Section Review

1. Sample answer: Alleles are different versions of the same gene.

2. Sample answer: Genotype is the set of alleles an organism has inherited from its parents. Phenotype is the way the genes are expressed physically.

3. b

4. The genotype of an organism contains the two alleles for each characteristic. One allele of each pair was inherited from each of the organism's parents. The phenotype of the organism is the way the genotype affects the organism physically. For example, if an organism inherits one dominant allele for brown fur and one recessive allele for white fur, its phenotype will be brown fur.

5. incomplete dominance, one gene influencing more than one trait, and one trait being influenced by many genes

6. 1/4

7. Approximately half of the offspring will have the phenotype of cleft chins (genotypes Cc), and half will not (genotypes cc).

8. BB, bb

9. Sample answer: a shade of gray

MISCONCEPTION ///ALERT\\\

Nature Versus Nurture Many students believe that characteristics acquired through the environment may be inherited, or believe that learned skills and behavioral similarities (perhaps learned from parents) are necessarily inherited. Although environment may influence the expression of genes, an organism may only pass on those genes that it was born with (unless there is a mutation in the genes of the sex cells).

CHAPTER RESOURCES

Chapter Resource File

- Section Quiz **GENERAL**
- Section Review **GENERAL**
- Vocabulary and Section Summary **GENERAL**
- Reinforcement Worksheet **BASIC**
- Datasheet for Quick Lab

Focus

Overview

In this section, students are introduced to meiosis and relate it to Mendel's findings. Students also learn about sex chromosomes and hereditary disorders.

💿 Bellringer

Ask students to write a sentence for each of the following terms: *heredity, genotype, phenotype.* (Sample answer: Heredity is the passing of traits from parents to offspring. The combination of an organism's alleles is its genotype. All of an organism's physical traits are its phenotype.)

Motivate

ACTIVITY ——— GENERAL

Crosses Have students model a cross between an organism with one pair of chromosomes and a member of the opposite sex of its species. Show the chromosomes in the cross as "$F_1F_2 \times M_1M_2$." Explain that F_1 and F_2 represent the father's chromosomes, and M_1 and M_2 represent the mother's chromosomes. Ask students, "If each parent contributes only one chromosome from his or her own pair to the offspring, what are the possible combinations in the offspring?" (F_1M_1, F_1M_2, F_2M_1, and F_2M_2) **Logical/Visual**

READING WARM-UP

Objectives
● Explain the difference between mitosis and meiosis.
● Describe how chromosomes determine sex.
● Explain why sex-linked disorders occur in one sex more often than in the other.
● Interpret a pedigree.

Terms to Learn
homologous chromosomes
meiosis
sex chromosome
pedigree

READING STRATEGY

Reading Organizer As you read this section, make a flowchart of the steps of meiosis.

---

homologous chromosomes chromosomes that have the same sequence of genes and the same structure

meiosis a process in cell division during which the number of chromosomes decreases to half the original number by two divisions of the nucleus, which results in the production of sex cells

---

Meiosis

Where are genes located? How do genes pass information? Understanding reproduction can provide some answers.

There are two kinds of reproduction: asexual and sexual. Asexual reproduction results in offspring with genotypes that are exact copies of their parent's genotype. Sexual reproduction produces offspring that share traits with their parents but are not exactly like either parent. In fact, offspring that share the same two parents vary a lot from each other, as well.

Asexual Reproduction

In *asexual reproduction,* only one parent cell is needed. The structures inside the cell are copied, and then the parent cell divides, making two exact copies. This type of cell reproduction is known as *mitosis.* Most of the cells in your body and most single-celled organisms reproduce in this way.

Sexual Reproduction

In sexual reproduction, two parent cells join together to form offspring that are different from both parents. The parent cells are called *sex cells.* Sex cells are different from ordinary body cells. Human body cells have 46, or 23 pairs of, chromosomes. One set of human chromosomes is shown in **Figure 1.** Chromosomes that carry the same sets of genes are called **homologous** (hoh MAHL uh guhs) **chromosomes.** Imagine a pair of shoes. Each shoe is like a homologous chromosome. The pair represents a homologous pair of chromosomes. But human sex cells are different. They have 23 chromosomes—half the usual number. Each sex cell has only one of the chromosomes from each homologous pair. Sex cells have only one "shoe."

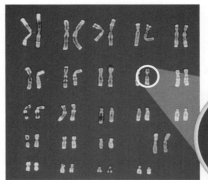

Figure 1 *Human body cells have 23 pairs of chromosomes. One member of a pair of homologous chromosomes is shown below.*

CHAPTER RESOURCES

Chapter Resource File

📁 • **Lesson Plan**
• **Directed Reading A** BASIC
• **Directed Reading B** SPECIAL NEEDS

Technology

🖥 **Transparencies**
• Bellringer

CONNECTION ACTIVITY
Math ——— ADVANCED

Crosses In algebraic multiplication, some students use the mnemonic device FOIL (**f**irst, **o**uter, **i**nner, **l**ast). This device can be used to calculate genotype crosses. For example, the cross $X_1X_2 \times Y_1Y_2$ yields:

First: X_1X_2

Outer: X_1Y_2

Inner: X_2Y_1

Last: Y_1Y_2

 Logical/Auditory

Meiosis

Sex cells are made during meiosis (mie OH sis). **Meiosis** is a copying process that produces cells with half the usual number of chromosomes. Each sex cell receives one-half of each homologous pair. For example, a human egg cell has 23 chromosomes, and a sperm cell has 23 chromosomes. The new cell that forms when an egg cell and a sperm cell join has 46 chromosomes.

Because the genes of the parents are sorted and recombined randomly in the offspring, the offspring is different from the parents. If the same parents have more offspring, the genes will be sorted again, and these offspring will be different from each other as well as from the parents.

✔ **Reading Check** How many chromosomes does a human egg cell have? (*See the Appendix for answers to Reading Checks.*)

Genes and Chromosomes

What does all of this have to do with the location of genes? Not long after Mendel's work was rediscovered, a graduate student named Walter Sutton made an important observation. Sutton was studying sperm cells in grasshoppers. Sutton knew of Mendel's studies, which showed that the egg and sperm must each contribute the same amount of information to the offspring. That was the only way the 3:1 ratio found in the second generation could be explained. Sutton also knew from his own studies that although eggs and sperm were different, they did have something in common: Their chromosomes were located inside a nucleus. Using his observations of meiosis, his understanding of Mendel's work, and some creative thinking, Sutton proposed something very important:

Genes are located on chromosomes!

Understanding meiosis was critical to finding the location of genes. Before you learn about meiosis, review mitosis, shown in **Figure 2**. Meiosis is outlined in **Figure 3** on the next two pages.

Figure 2 Mitosis Revisited

❶ Each chromosome is copied.

❷ The chromosomes thicken and shorten. Each chromosome consists of two identical copies, called *chromatids.*

❸ The nuclear membrane dissolves. The chromatids line up along the equator (center) of the cell.

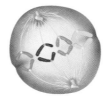
❹ The chromatids pull apart.

❺ The nuclear membrane forms around the separated chromatids. The chromosomes unwind, and the cell divides.

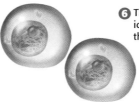
❻ The result is two identical copies of the original cell.

Science Bloopers

Wrong Number In 1918, a prominent scientist miscounted the number of chromosomes in a human cell. He counted 48. For almost 40 years, scientists thought this number was correct. In fact, not until 1956 were chromosomes counted correctly and found to number only 46.

Prediction Guide Before students read the passage about meiosis, ask them whether the following statements are true or false. Students will discover the answers as they explore the rest of the section.

• Mitosis is the only type of cell division. (false)

• Only cells that produce sex cells undergo meiosis. (true)

• Sex cells contain half the number of chromosomes that other body cells do. (true)

LS Verbal/Auditory

Answer to Reading Check
During meiosis, one parent cell makes four new cells.

Discussion ── GENERAL

Predicting Problems Ask students what they think would happen if something went wrong during cell division and the sperm or egg cell ended up with either too few or too many chromosomes? (The fertilized egg, with too few or too many chromosomes, may die, or the growing embryo may have birth defects. Down syndrome occurs in humans when the offspring receives an extra twenty-first chromosome.)

LS Verbal/Logical

The Steps of Meiosis

During mitosis, chromosomes are copied once, and then the nucleus divides once. During meiosis, chromosomes are copied once, and then the nucleus divides twice. The resulting sperm and eggs have half the number of chromosomes of a normal body cell. **Figure 3** shows all eight steps of meiosis. Read about each step as you look at the figure. Different types of living things have different numbers of chromosomes. In this illustration, only four chromosomes are shown.

✓ *Reading Check* How many cells are made from one parent cell during meiosis?

Figure 3 Steps of Meiosis

Read about each step as you look at the diagram. Different types of living things have different numbers of chromosomes. In this diagram, only four chromosomes are shown.

One pair of homologous chromosomes

Two chromatids

1 Before meiosis begins, the chromosomes are in a threadlike form. Each chromosome makes an exact copy of itself, forming two halves called *chromatids*. The chromosomes then thicken and shorten into a form that is visible under a microscope. The nuclear membrane disappears.

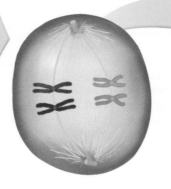

2 Each chromosome is now made up of two identical chromatids. Similar chromosomes pair with one another, and the paired homologous chromosomes line up at the equator of the cell.

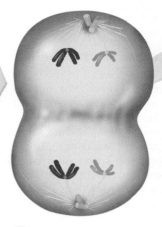

3 The chromosomes separate from their homologous partners and then move to opposite ends of the cell.

CHAPTER RESOURCES
Technology
💾 **Transparencies** • The Steps of Meiosis: A • The Steps of Meiosis: B

Is That a Fact!

There are many organisms that have more chromosomes than humans do.

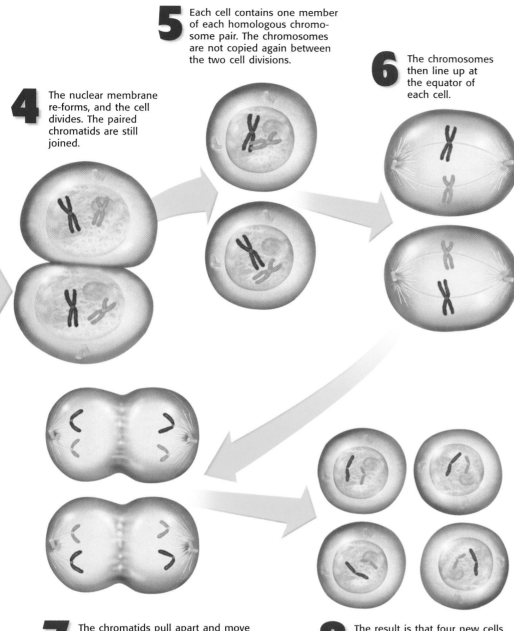

5 Each cell contains one member of each homologous chromosome pair. The chromosomes are not copied again between the two cell divisions.

6 The chromosomes then line up at the equator of each cell.

4 The nuclear membrane re-forms, and the cell divides. The paired chromatids are still joined.

7 The chromatids pull apart and move to opposite ends of the cell. The nuclear membrane forms around the separated chromosomes, and the cells divide.

8 The result is that four new cells have formed from the original single cell. Each new cell has half the number of chromosomes present in the original cell.

MISCONCEPTION ALERT

Chromatids and Chromosome Pairing Students often have difficulty keeping track of the differences between the way that chromatids and chromosome pairs move during mitosis as compared to meiosis. Caution students to note these differences as they compare mitosis and meiosis, and to analyze the ways that these differences are critical to each process.

ACTIVITY ——— **BASIC**

Describing Meiosis Have students write their own captions for the steps of meiosis illustrated here. They should use language and descriptions that will help them understand and remember the material.
LS Verbal/Visual

CONNECTION ACTIVITY
Math ——— **GENERAL**

Chromosome Number Meiosis and sexual reproduction have benefits for organisms because these processes maintain a variety of traits within a population. Meiosis and sexual recombination reshuffle the genetic material in each generation. Furthermore, the division of chromosomes during meiosis ensures that when the egg and sperm combine, the new organism has the same number of chromosomes as its parents. To explore these concepts, ask students the following questions:

• If the normal number of chromosomes for a certain organism is 30, how many chromosomes would be found in the egg or sperm cells? (15)

• What would happen if eggs and sperm were produced by mitosis instead of by meiosis? (The organism would produce sex cells with a full set of 30 chromosomes.)

• If the organism described above were to have offspring that also produced sex cells by mitosis, how many chromosomes would be found in the descendants after four generations? (first generation: 60; second generation: 120; third generation: 240; fourth generation: 480)
LS Verbal/Logical

INCLUSION *Strategies*

• *Learning Disabled*
• *Attention Deficit Disorder*

Have students make a flip book that animates the phases of meiosis. First, have students draw the events of meiosis in at least 15 sketches on sturdy cards. Explain that each drawing should vary only slightly from the one before it. When the book is flipped through quickly, the images should appear to be in motion, and students will be able to watch meiosis in action. This activity could be repeated to demonstrate mitosis.

English Language Learners

LS Visual

Group ACTIVITY—GENERAL

Comparing Mitosis and Meiosis Organize the class into small groups. Instruct each group to create a table listing the similarities and differences between mitosis and meiosis. Challenge groups to make the longest list possible in a limited time period. After their time is up, have groups report items from their lists. Discuss and correct items as you compile a single, large table for display in the classroom. **English Language Learners**

LS Visual/Verbal

Meiosis and Mendel

As Walter Sutton figured out, the steps in meiosis explained Mendel's results. **Figure 4** shows what happens to a pair of homologous chromosomes during meiosis and fertilization. The cross shown is between a plant that is true breeding for round seeds and a plant that is true breeding for wrinkled seeds.

Each fertilized egg in the first generation had one dominant allele and one recessive allele for seed shape. Only one genotype was possible because all sperm formed by the male parent during meiosis had the wrinkled-seed allele, and all of the female parent's eggs had the round-seed allele. Meiosis also helped explain other inherited characteristics.

Figure 4 **Meiosis and Dominance**

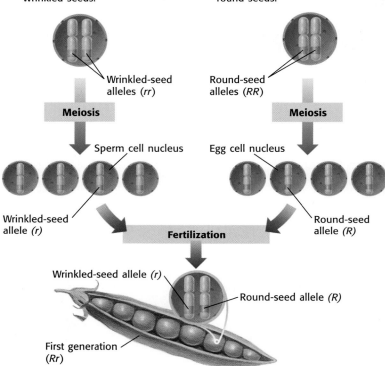

Male Parent In the plant-cell nucleus below, each homologous chromosome has an allele for seed shape, and each allele carries the same instructions: to make wrinkled seeds.

Female Parent In the plant-cell nucleus below, each homologous chromosome has an allele for seed shape, and each allele carries the same instructions: to make round seeds.

Wrinkled-seed alleles *(rr)*

Round-seed alleles *(RR)*

Meiosis

Meiosis

a Following **meiosis,** each sperm cell has a recessive allele for wrinkled seeds, and each egg cell has a dominant allele for round seeds.

Sperm cell nucleus

Egg cell nucleus

Wrinkled-seed allele *(r)*

Round-seed allele *(R)*

b **Fertilization** of any egg by any sperm results in the same genotype *(Rr)* and the same phenotype (round). This result is exactly what Mendel found in his studies.

Fertilization

Wrinkled-seed allele *(r)*

Round-seed allele *(R)*

First generation *(Rr)*

CHAPTER RESOURCES

Technology

Transparencies
• Meiosis and Dominance

Is That a Fact!

Martin-Bell syndrome is a genetic disorder also known as *Fragile X syndrome.* It is one of the most common forms of inherited mental retardation. This disorder is a genetic condition associated with mental retardation and autism. The disorder is identified by flaws apparent in the long arm of the X chromosome.

Sex Chromosomes

Information contained on chromosomes determines many of our traits. **Sex chromosomes** carry genes that determine sex. In humans, females have two X chromosomes. But human males have one X chromosome and one Y chromosome.

During meiosis, one of each of the chromosome pairs ends up in a sex cell. Females have two X chromosomes in each body cell. When meiosis produces the egg cells, each egg gets one X chromosome. Males have both an X chromosome and a Y chromosome in each body cell. Meiosis produces sperm with either an X or a Y chromosome. An egg fertilized by a sperm with an X chromosome will produce a female. If the sperm contains a Y chromosome, the offspring will be male, as shown in **Figure 5**.

Sex-Linked Disorders

The Y chromosome does not carry all of the genes of an X chromosome. Females have two X chromosomes, so they carry two copies of each gene found on the X chromosome. This makes a backup gene available if one becomes damaged. Males have only one copy of each gene on their one X chromosome. The genes for certain disorders, such as colorblindness, are carried on the X chromosome. These disorders are called *sex-linked disorders*. Because the gene for such disorders is recessive, men are more likely to have sex-linked disorders.

People who are colorblind can have trouble distinguishing between shades of red and green. To help the colorblind, some cities have added shapes to their street lights, as shown in **Figure 6**. Hemophilia (HEE moh FIL ee uh) is another sex-linked disorder. Hemophilia prevents blood from clotting, and people with hemophilia bleed for a long time after small cuts. Hemophilia can be fatal.

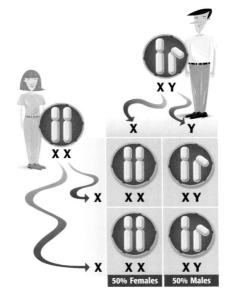

Figure 5 *Egg and sperm combine to form either the XX or XY combination.*

sex chromosome one of the pair of chromosomes that determine the sex of an individual

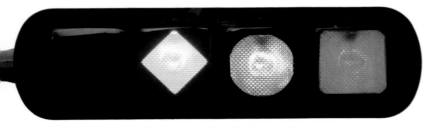

Figure 6 *This stoplight in Canada is designed to help the colorblind see signals easily. This photograph was taken over a few minutes to show all three shapes.*

BRAIN FOOD

In human males, meiosis and sperm production take about nine weeks and occur continuously after puberty begins. In females, meiosis and egg production begin before birth and then stop until puberty. From puberty until menopause, one egg each month resumes meiosis and finishes developing. So, production of a mature egg may take up to 50 years!

Modeling Mates Have students use Punnett squares to model several possible combinations of parents with sex-linked traits that are variously dominant and recessive.

LS Logical/Kinesthetic | English Language Learners

Are the following statements true or false?

1. Every one of the chromosomes is different between men and women. (false)

2. Men and women each have different numbers of chromosomes in their sex cells. (false)

3. If you looked inside a cell during mitosis and you could see the chromosomes lining up, you could tell whether the cell belongs to a man or a woman. (true)

Alternative Assessment ———— GENERAL

Writing **Meiosis versus Mitosis** Tell students that there will be a mock debate to decide whether mitosis or meiosis is "better." First, have the class discuss and agree upon a definition of "better." Then, have students choose a "side" and prepare a written argument that is supported by scientific facts. You may wish to allow volunteers to act out such a debate. **LS** Verbal

---

Figure 7 Pedigree for a Recessive Disease

☐ Males   ○ Females

●┬☐ Vertical lines connect
◐   children to their parents.

■ or ● A solid square or circle indicates that the person has a certain trait.

◨ or ◑ A half-filled square or circle indicates that the person is a carrier of the trait.

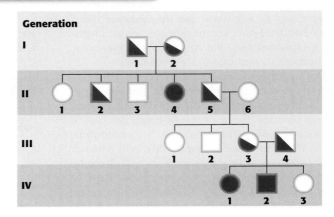

pedigree a diagram that shows the occurrence of a genetic trait in several generations of a family

Figure 8 *Roses have been selectively bred to create large, bright flowers.*

Genetic Counseling

Hemophilia and other genetic disorders can be traced through a family tree. If people are worried that they might pass a disease to their children, they may consult a genetic counselor. These counselors often make use of a diagram known as a **pedigree,** which is a tool for tracing a trait through generations of a family. By making a pedigree, a counselor can often predict whether a person is a carrier of a hereditary disease. The pedigree shown in **Figure 7** traces a disease called *cystic fibrosis* (SIS tik FIE broh sis). Cystic fibrosis causes serious lung problems. People with this disease have inherited two recessive alleles. Both parents need to be carriers of the gene for the disease to show up in their children.

Pedigrees can be drawn up to trace any trait through a family tree. You could even draw a pedigree that would show how you inherited your hair color. Many different pedigrees could be drawn for a typical family.

Selective Breeding

For thousands of years, humans have seen the benefits of the careful breeding of plants and animals. In *selective breeding,* organisms with desirable characteristics are mated. You have probably enjoyed the benefits of selective breeding, although you may not have realized it. For example, you have probably eaten an egg from a chicken that was bred to produce more eggs. Your pet dog may be a result of selective breeding. Roses, like the one shown in **Figure 8,** have been selectively bred to produce large flowers. Wild roses are much smaller and have fewer petals than roses that you could buy at a nursery.

WEIRD SCIENCE

Gene therapy is an experimental field of medical research in which defective genes are replaced with healthy genes. One way to insert healthy genes involves using a delivery system called a *gene gun* to inject microscopic gold bullets coated with genetic material.

Homework ———— ADVANCED

Pet Pedigrees Have students obtain a copy of the pedigree of a thoroughbred animal from a professional breeder of dogs, cats, horses, or other animals. Ask students to write a paragraph explaining what information the pedigree provides about the animal and its ancestors. **LS** Verbal/Interpersonal

SECTION Review

Summary

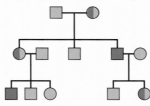

- In mitosis, chromosomes are copied once, and then the nucleus divides once. In meiosis, chromosomes are copied once, and then the nucleus divides twice.
- The process of meiosis produces sex cells, which have half the number of chromosomes. These two halves combine during reproduction.
- In humans, females have two X chromosomes. So, each egg contains one X chromosome. Males have both an X and a Y chromosome. So, each sperm cell contains either an X or a Y chromosome.
- Sex-linked disorders occur in males more often than in females. Colorblindness and hemophilia are examples of sex-linked disorders.
- A pedigree is a diagram used to trace a trait through many generations of a family.

Using Key Terms

In each of the following sentences, replace the incorrect term with the correct term from the word bank.

pedigree   homologous chromosomes

meiosis   mitosis

1. During fertilization, chromosomes are copied, and then the nucleus divides twice.

2. A Punnett square is used to show how inherited traits move through a family.

3. During meiosis, sex cells line up in the middle of the cell.

Understanding Key Ideas

4. Genes are found on
   a. chromosomes.
   b. proteins.
   c. alleles.
   d. sex cells.

5. If there are 14 chromosomes in pea plant cells, how many chromosomes are present in a sex cell of a pea plant?

6. Draw the eight steps of meiosis. Label one chromosome, and show its position in each step.

7. What alleles must be present in the parents of a child that is born with cystic fibrosis?

Interpreting Graphics

Use this pedigree to answer the question below.

8. Is this disorder sex linked? Explain your reasoning.

Critical Thinking

9. **Identifying Relationships** Put the following in order of smallest to largest: chromosome, gene, and cell.

10. **Applying Concepts** A pea plant has purple flowers. What alleles for flower color could the sex cells carry?

SCILINKS®

NSTA
Developed and maintained by the National Science Teachers Association

For a variety of links related to this chapter, go to www.scilinks.org

Topic: Meiosis; Genetic Diseases, Screening, Counseling
SciLinks code: HSM0935; HSM0651

Answers to Section Review

1. During meiosis, chromosomes are copied, and then the nucleus divides twice.

2. A pedigree is used to show how inherited traits move through a family.

3. During meiosis, homologous chromosomes line up in the middle of the cell.

4. a

5. 7

6. Answers may vary. Students' drawings should be similar to the diagram of meiosis in the student text.

7. Sample answer: The two parents must each carry the gene for cystic fibrosis, and the child must inherit two recessive alleles.

8. Sample answer: yes; The disorder seems to be sex linked because the females are carriers of the disease but only males have the disease itself.

9. gene, chromosome, cell

10. Sample answer: Because the purple gene (P) is dominant over the white gene (p), the genotype of the purple-flowered pea plant could be either PP or Pp. Thus, the possible alleles carried by the sex cells would be P or p.

INTERNET ACTiViTY

Essay ——————— GENERAL

For an internet activity related to this chapter, have students go to **go.hrw.com** and type in the keyword **HL5HERW.**

CHAPTER RESOURCES

Chapter Resource File

- **Section Quiz** GENERAL
- **Section Review** GENERAL
- **Vocabulary and Section Summary** GENERAL
- **Reinforcement Worksheet** BASIC

Bug Builders, Inc.

Teacher's Notes

Time Required
Two 45-minute class periods

Lab Ratings

EASY ——————————→ HARD

Teacher Prep 🧪🧪🧪
Student Set-Up 🧪🧪
Concept Level 🧪🧪🧪
Clean Up 🧪

MATERIALS

The materials listed on the student page are enough for a group of 3–4 students. For step 3, prepare 14 small paper sacks—representing paired parent alleles for each of seven characteristics—as follows:

1. Use the table in step 6 to decide the genotypes for each of the parent bugs' characteristics.
2. Cut 1 in. squares of paper to represent alleles. Use seven colors of paper—a different color for each characteristic. Cut enough squares so that each student will receive two alleles for each characteristic.
3. Label the alleles for each characteristic according to the genotypes you chose.
4. Label each pair of sacks with one of the seven characteristics. Place an equal number of alleles in each sack.
5. For each characteristic, label one sack "Mom" and the other sack "Dad." Have students draw one allele from each sack.

Safety Caution
Remind students to review all safety cautions and icons before beginning this lab activity. Students should use caution with toothpicks and should not eat any of the materials used.

Bug Builders, Inc.

Imagine that you are a designer for a toy company that makes toy alien bugs. The president of Bug Builders, Inc., wants new versions of the wildly popular Space Bugs, but he wants to use the bug parts that are already in the warehouse. It's your job to come up with a new bug design. You have studied how traits are passed from one generation to another. You will use this knowledge to come up with new combinations of traits and assemble the bug parts in new ways. Model A and Model B, shown below, will act as the "parent" bugs.

Ask a Question

1 If there are two forms of each of the seven traits, then how many possible combinations are there?

Form a Hypothesis

2 Write a hypothesis that is a possible answer to the question above. Explain your reasoning.

Test the Hypothesis

3 Your teacher will display 14 allele sacks. The sacks will contain slips of paper with capital or lowercase letters on them. Take one piece of paper from each sack. (Remember: Capital letters represent dominant alleles, and lowercase letters represent recessive alleles.) One allele is from "Mom," and one allele is from "Dad." After you have recorded the alleles you have drawn, place the slips of paper back into the sack.

OBJECTIVES

Build models to further your understanding of inheritance.

Examine the traits of a population of offspring.

MATERIALS

- allele sacks (14) (supplied by your teacher)
- gumdrops, green and black (feet)
- map pins (eyes)
- marshmallows, large (head and body segments)
- pipe cleaners (tails)
- pushpins, green and blue (noses)
- scissors
- toothpicks, red and green (antennae)

SAFETY

Model A ("Mom")
- red antennae
- 3 body segments
- curly tail
- 2 pairs of legs
- green nose
- black feet
- 3 eyes

Model B ("Dad")
- green antennae
- 2 body segments
- straight tail
- 3 pairs of legs
- blue nose
- green feet
- 2 eyes

Bug Family Traits				
Trait	Model A "Mom" allele	Model B "Dad" allele	New model "Baby" genotype	New model "Baby" phenotype
Antennae color				
Number of body segments				
Tail shape				
Number of leg pairs				
Nose color				
Foot color				
Number of eyes				

DO NOT WRITE IN BOOK

4 Create a table like the one above. Fill in the first two columns with the alleles that you selected from the sacks. Next, fill in the third column with the genotype of the new model ("Baby").

5 Use the information below to fill in the last column of the table.

Genotypes and Phenotypes	
RR or *Rr*—red antennae	*rr*—green antennae
SS or *Ss*—3 body segments	*ss*—2 body segments
CC or *Cc*—curly tail	*cc*—straight tail
LL or *Ll*—3 pairs of legs	*ll*—2 pairs of legs
BB or *Bb*—blue nose	*bb*—green nose
GG or *Gg*—green feet	*gg*—black feet
EE or *Ee*—2 eyes	*ee*—3 eyes

6 Now that you have filled out your table, you are ready to pick the parts you need to assemble your bug. (Toothpicks can be used to hold the head and body segments together and as legs to attach the feet to the body.)

Analyze the Results

1 **Organizing Data** Take a poll of the traits of the offspring. What are the ratios for each trait?

2 **Examining Data** Do any of the new models look exactly like the parents? Explain.

Draw Conclusions

3 **Interpreting Information** What are the possible genotypes of the parent bugs?

4 **Making Predictions** How many different genotypes are possible in the offspring?

> ### Applying Your Data
> Find a mate for your "Baby" bug. What are the possible genotypes and phenotypes of the offspring from this match?

Ask a Question
1. There are 128 possible combinations. (Calculation: There are two forms of each of seven characteristics, so, $2 \times 2 \times 2 \times 2 \times 2 \times 2 \times 2 = 2^7 = 128$)

Analyze the Results
1. Student ratios should be similar to the ratios determined when the alleles were selected by the teacher.

2. If any students have offspring bugs that look like one of the parents, have students compare the genotype of the offspring with the genotype of the parents. The offspring and parents look alike but still have different genotypes for some traits.

Draw Conclusions
3. Student answers should reflect the data on parent alleles that were recorded in step 6.

4. Students' answers should include Punnett squares based on the parental traits. Except for the results obtained by parental genotypes that are all homozygous recessive, students will see other possibilities for genotypes and phenotypes from the same parents.

Applying Your Data
Students should create Punnett squares to show the possible genotypes and describe phenotypes that follow the rules of dominance for each characteristic.

CHAPTER RESOURCES

Workbooks

 Long-Term Projects & Research Ideas
• Portrait of a Dog **ADVANCED**

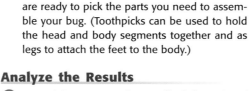

CLASSROOM TESTED & APPROVED

Kathy LaRoe
East Valley Middle School
East Helena, Montana

Assignment Guide

SECTION	QUESTIONS
1	7, 13, 18
2	2, 4, 5, 8, 9, 11, 19–23
3	1, 3, 6, 10, 12, 14–17

ANSWERS

Using Key Terms

1. sex cells

2. phenotype, genotype

3. Meiosis

4. alleles

Understanding Key Ideas

5. d

6. c

7. b

8. b

9. c

10. c

11. b

USING KEY TERMS

Complete each of the following sentences by choosing the correct term from the word bank.

sex cells   genotype
sex chromosomes   alleles
phenotype   meiosis

1 Sperm and eggs are known as _____.

2 The _____ is the expression of a trait and is determined by the combination of alleles called the _____.

3 _____ produces cells with half the normal number of chromosomes.

4 Different versions of the same genes are called _____.

UNDERSTANDING KEY IDEAS

Multiple Choice

5 Genes carry information that determines
  a. alleles.
  b. ribosomes.
  c. chromosomes.
  d. traits.

6 The process that produces sex cells is
  a. mitosis.
  b. photosynthesis.
  c. meiosis.
  d. probability.

7 The passing of traits from parents to offspring is called
  a. probability.
  b. heredity.
  c. recessive.
  d. meiosis.

8 If you cross a white flower with the genotype *pp* with a purple flower with the genotype *PP*, the possible genotypes in the offspring are
  a. *PP* and *pp*.
  b. all *Pp*.
  c. all *PP*.
  d. all *pp*.

9 For the cross in item 8, what would the phenotypes be?
  a. all white
  b. 3 purple and 1 white
  c. all purple
  d. half white, half purple

10 In meiosis,
  a. chromosomes are copied twice.
  b. the nucleus divides once.
  c. four cells are produced from a single cell.
  d. two cells are produced from a single cell.

11 When one trait is not completely dominant over another, it is called
  a. recessive.
  b. incomplete dominance.
  c. environmental factors.
  d. uncertain dominance.

Short Answer

12 Which sex chromosomes do females have? Which do males have?

13 In one or two sentences, define the term *recessive trait* in your own words.

14 How are sex cells different from other body cells?

15 What is a sex-linked disorder? Give one example of a sex-linked disorder that is found in humans.

CRITICAL THINKING

16 Concept Mapping Use the following terms to create a concept map: *meiosis, eggs, cell division, X chromosome, mitosis, Y chromosome, sperm,* and *sex cells.*

17 Identifying Relationships If you were a carrier of one allele for a certain recessive disorder, how could genetic counseling help you prepare for the future?

18 Applying Concepts If a child has blond hair and both of her parents have brown hair, what does that tell you about the allele for blond hair? Explain.

19 Applying Concepts What is the genotype of a pea plant that is true-breeding for purple flowers?

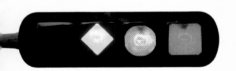

INTERPRETING GRAPHICS

Use the Punnett square below to answer the questions that follow.

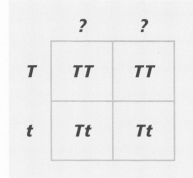

	?	**?**
T	**TT**	**TT**
t	**Tt**	**Tt**

20 What is the unknown genotype?

21 If *T* represents the allele for tall pea plants and *t* represents the allele for short pea plants, what is the phenotype of each parent and of the offspring?

22 If each of the offspring were allowed to self-fertilize, what are the possible genotypes in the next generation?

23 What is the probability of each genotype in item 22?

Standardized Test Preparation

Teacher's Note

To provide practice under more realistic testing conditions, give students 20 minutes to answer all of the questions in this Standardized Test Preparation.

MISCONCEPTION ALERT

Answers to the standardized test preparation can help you identify student misconceptions and misunderstandings.

READING

Passage 1

1. C
2. F
3. C

TEST DOCTOR

Question 2: This question primarily requires the reader to re-read the sentence in which the word is used, which clearly serves to define the word. Then, the reader must look among the possible answers for the one that most closely matches the meaning given in the sentence.

Question 3: This question requires a simple deduction from the final two sentences of the passage. The uses of "if," "then," and "therefore" are clear indicators of logical reasoning. Remind students to look for these kinds of indicators for these types of test questions.

READING

Read the passages below. Then, answer the questions that follow each passage.

Passage 1 The different versions of a gene are called *alleles*. When two different alleles occur together, one is often expressed while the other has no obvious effect on the organism's appearance. The expressed form of the trait is dominant. The trait that was not expressed when the dominant form of the trait was present is called *recessive*. Imagine a plant that has both purple and white alleles for flower color. If the plant blooms purple, then purple is the dominant form of the trait. Therefore, white is the recessive form.

1. According to the passage, which of the following statements is true?
   - A All alleles are expressed all of the time.
   - B All traits for flower color are dominant.
   - C When two alleles are present, the expressed form of the trait is dominant.
   - D A recessive form of a trait is always expressed.

2. According to the passage, a trait that is not expressed when the dominant form is present is called
   - F recessive.
   - G an allele.
   - H heredity.
   - I a gene.

3. According to the passage, which allele for flower color is dominant?
   - A white
   - B pink
   - C purple
   - D yellow

Passage 2 Sickle cell anemia is a recessive genetic disorder. People inherit this disorder only when they inherit the disease-causing recessive allele from both parents. The disease causes the body to make red blood cells that bend into a sickle (or crescent moon) shape. The sickle-shaped red blood cells break apart easily. Therefore, the blood of a person with sickle cell anemia carries less oxygen. Sickle-shaped blood cells also tend to get stuck in blood vessels. When a blood vessel is blocked, the blood supply to organs can be cut off. But the sickle-shaped blood cells can also protect a person from malaria. Malaria is a disease caused by an organism that invades red blood cells.

1. According to the passage, sickle cell anemia is a
   - A recessive genetic disorder.
   - B dominant genetic disorder.
   - C disease caused by an organism that invades red blood cells.
   - D disease also called *malaria*.

2. According to the passage, sickle cell anemia can help protect a person from
   - F blocked blood vessels.
   - G genetic disorders.
   - H malaria.
   - I low oxygen levels.

3. Which of the following is a fact in the passage?
   - A When blood vessels are blocked, vital organs lose their blood supply.
   - B When blood vessels are blocked, it causes the red blood cells to bend into sickle shapes.
   - C The blood of a person with sickle cell anemia carries more oxygen.
   - D Healthy red blood cells never get stuck in blood vessels.

Passage 2

1. A
2. H
3. A

TEST DOCTOR

Question 2: The answer to this question comes from the second-to-last sentence in the passage. Weak readers often miss details from the middle parts of passages, and standardized tests sometimes probe for this kind of mistake with such questions. One strategy for this type of question is to form a question such as "From what problem can sickle cell anemia protect a person?" and then re-read or skim the passage with this question in mind.

The Punnett square below shows a cross between two flowering plants. Use this Punnett square to answer the questions that follow.

	R	**r**
r		**rr**
r	**Rr**	

1. What is the genotype of the offspring represented in the upper left-hand box of the Punnett square?

A *RR*

B *Rr*

C *rr*

D *rrr*

2. What is the genotype of the offspring represented in the lower right-hand box of the Punnett square?

F *RR*

G *Rr*

H *rr*

I *rrr*

3. What is the ratio of *Rr* (purple-flowered plants) to *rr* (white-flowered plants) in the offspring?

A 1:3

B 2:2

C 3:1

D 4:0

Read each question below, and choose the best answer.

1. What is another way to write $4 \times 4 \times 4$?

A 4^2

B 4^3

C 3^3

D 3^4

2. Jane was making a design on top of her desk with pennies. She put 4 pennies in the first row, 7 pennies in the second row, and 13 pennies in the third row. If Jane continues this pattern, how many pennies will she put in the sixth row?

F 25

G 49

H 97

I 193

3. In which of the following lists are the numbers in order from smallest to greatest?

A 0.012, 0.120, 0.123, 1.012

B 1.012, 0.123, 0.120, 0.012

C 0.123, 0.120, 0.012, 1.012

D 0.123, 1.012, 0.120, 0.012

4. In which of the following lists are the numbers in order from smallest to greatest?

F $-12.0, -15.5, 2.2, 4.0$

G $-15.5, -12.0, 2.2, 4.0$

H $-12.0, -15.5, 4.0, 2.2$

I $2.2, 4.0, -12.0, -15.5$

5. Which of the following is equal to -11?

A $7 + 4$

B $-4 + 7$

C $-7 + 4$

D $-7 + -4$

6. Catherine earned $75 for working 8.5 h. How much did she earn per hour?

F $10.12

G $9.75

H $8.82

I $8.01

1. B

2. H

3. B

TEST DOCTOR

Questions 1 and 2: These questions require understanding of the term *genotype* and the ability to complete a Punnett square. Students who miss these questions may need to review these concepts.

Question 3: This question asks for the ratio of the genotype *Rr* to the genotype *rr*. If completed, the Punnett square would show 2 *Rr* and 2 *rr* genotypes. Thus, the ratio would be 2:2 (answer B). Students who miss this question may need to review the concept of ratios.

MATH

1. B

2. H

3. A

4. G

5. D

6. H

TEST DOCTOR

Question 6: This question is essentially a simple long-division problem, but students may get confused or discouraged by long division when the calculation extends for many decimal places. For this problem, students can save time if they recognize that they need only to find the answer in dollars and cents. Thus, they need to calculate to the thousandths place ($8.823) and then round their answer to the nearest cent.

Standardized Test Preparation

CHAPTER RESOURCES

Chapter Resource File

 • Standardized Test Preparation GENERAL

Workbooks

North Carolina Standardized Test Preparation
• Provides practice for the EOG test.

State Resources

For specific resources for your state, visit **go.hrw.com** and type in the keyword **HSMSTR**.

Science, Technology, and Society

Background

Genetic research has spawned a flurry of debate over ethical, social, and legal issues surrounding the use of genetic information. These issues include the privacy and ownership of personal genetic information and the possibility that people will selectively breed or control the birth of their children based on genetic knowledge.

Weird Science

Teaching Strategy—GENERAL

Offer the following analogies to help students grasp the concepts discussed in this article.

- Blueprints: Show students sample construction blueprints. Explain that genes are like these plans for a building and that mutations are like mistakes in copying, reading, or building from the blueprints.

- Recipes: Show students a book of cake recipes. Genes are like recipes, and an organism is like a cake made according to a recipe. A mutation is like using a different ingredient or a different amount of an ingredient. The mutation may or may not "ruin" the "cake."

Science in Action

This is a normal fruit fly under a scanning electron microscope.

This fruit fly has legs growing where its antennae should be.

Science, Technology, and Society

Mapping the Human Genome

In 2003, scientists finished one of the most ambitious research projects ever. Researchers with the Human Genome Project (HGP) mapped the human body's complete set of genetic instructions, which is called the *genome*. You might be wondering whose genome the scientists are decoding. Actually, it doesn't matter—only 0.1% of each person's genetic material is unique. The researchers' goals are to identify how tiny differences in that 0.1% make each of us who we are and to begin to understand how some differences can cause disease. Scientists are already using the map to think of new ways to treat genetic diseases, such as asthma, diabetes, and kidney disease.

Social Studies ACTIVITY

WRITING SKILL Research DNA fingerprinting. Write a short report describing how DNA fingerprinting has affected the way criminals are caught.

Weird Science

Lab Rats with Wings

Drosophila melanogaster (droh SAHF i luh muh LAN uh GAS tuhr) is the scientific name for the fruit fly. This tiny insect has played a big role in helping scientists understand many illnesses. Because fruit flies reproduce every 2 weeks, scientists can alter a fruit fly gene and see the results of the experiment very quickly. Another important reason for using these "lab rats with wings" is that their genetic code is simple and well understood. Fruit flies have 12,000 genes, but humans have more than 25,000. Scientists use fruit flies to find out about diseases like cancer, Alzheimer's, and muscular dystrophy.

Language Arts ACTIVITY

WRITING SKILL The mythical creature called the *Chimera* (kie MIR uh) was said to be part lion, part goat, and part serpent. According to legend, the Chimera terrorized people for years until it was killed by a brave hero. The word *chimera* now refers to any organism that has parts from many organisms. Write a short story about the Chimera that describes what it looks like and how it came to be.

Answer to Social Studies Activity

Sample answer: DNA fingerprinting has made it much easier to match genetic material (evidence) at a crime scene to the genetic information of one particular individual. DNA can be found in hair, saliva, blood, and small skin cells. The DNA is analyzed and then compared to the DNA fingerprint of particular individuals. When the DNA fingerprints match, police can be sure that the person was at the scene of the crime.

Answer to Language Arts Activity

The Chimera (or Chimaera) was said to be a savage beast that spat fire from its mouth. In classical Greco-Roman stories, it wreaked havoc on the ancient lands until it was killed by the hero Bellerophon, who rode his winged horse Pegasus. This basic story is among the most ancient myths and appears in many texts from Homer's *Iliad* to traditional fairy tales.

Stacey Wong

Genetic Counselor If your family had a history of a particular disease, what would you do? Would you eat healthier foods, get more exercise, or visit your doctor regularly? All of those are good ideas, but Stacey Wong went a step farther. Her family's history of cancer helped her decide to become a genetic counselor. "Genetic counselors are usually part of a team of health professionals," she says, which can include physicians, nurses, dieticians, social workers, laboratory personnel, and others. "If a diagnosis is made by the geneticist," says Wong, "then I provide genetic counseling." When a patient visits a genetic counselor, the counselor asks many questions and builds a family medical history. Although counseling involves discussing what it means to have a genetic condition, Wong says "the most important part is to get to know the patient or family we are working with, listen to their concerns, gain an understanding of their values, help them to make decisions, and be their advocate."

Careers

Background

Stacey Wong was born in Oakland, California, and grew up in the nearby suburb of Alameda. She received a B.S. in cell and molecular biology from UCLA and an M.S. in genetic counseling from California State University Northridge. More information about genetic-counseling careers can be obtained from the National Society of Genetic Counselors.

Math ACTIVITY

The probability of inheriting genetic disease *A* is 1/10,000. The probability of inheriting genetic disease *B* is also 1/10,000. What is the probability that one person would inherit both genetic diseases *A* and *B*?

go.hrw.com

To learn more about these Science in Action topics, visit go.hrw.com and type in the keyword **HL5HERF**.

Current Science

Check out Current Science® articles related to this chapter by visiting go.hrw.com. **Just type in the keyword HL5CS05.**

Answer to Math Activity

$1/10,000 \times 1/10,000 = 1/100,000,000$

Compression guide: To shorten instruction because of time limitations, omit the Chapter Lab.

OBJECTIVES	LABS, DEMONSTRATIONS, AND ACTIVITIES	TECHNOLOGY RESOURCES
PACING • 90 min pp. 432–437 **Chapter Opener**	**SE Start-up Activity,** p. 433 ◆ GENERAL	**OSP Parent Letter** GENERAL **CD Student Edition on CD-ROM** **CD Guided Reading Audio CD** **TR Chapter Starter Transparency*** **VID Brain Food Video Quiz**
Section 1 What Does DNA Look Like? • List three important events that led to understanding the structure of DNA. • Describe the basic structure of a DNA molecule. • Explain how DNA molecules can be copied.	**TE Activity** Modeling Code, p. 434 GENERAL **TE Group Activity** A Place in History, p. 435 GENERAL **SE Quick Lab** Making a Model of DNA, p. 436 ◆ GENERAL **CRF Datasheet for Quick Lab*** **SE Science in Action** Math, Social Studies, and Language Arts Activities, pp. 452–453 GENERAL **SE Model-Making Lab** Base-Pair Basics, p. 446 ◆ GENERAL **CRF Datasheet for Chapter Lab*** **LB Whiz-Bang Demonstrations** Grand Strand* GENERAL	**CRF Lesson Plans*** **TR Bellringer Transparency*** **TR DNA Structure*** **CRF SciLinks Activity*** GENERAL **VID Lab Videos for Life Science**
PACING • 45 min pp. 438–445 **Section 2 How DNA Works** • Explain the relationship between DNA, genes, and proteins. • Outline the basic steps in making a protein. • Describe three types of mutations, and provide an example of a gene mutation. • Describe two examples of uses of genetic knowledge.	**TE Demonstration** A Tight Fit, p. 438 ◆ GENERAL **TE Connection Activity** Chemistry, p. 440 ADVANCED **TE Group Activity** Skit, p. 440 GENERAL **TE Connection Activity** Math, p. 441 ◆ GENERAL **TE Activity** Complementary Code, p. 442 GENERAL **SE School-to-Home Activity** An Error in the Message, p. 443 GENERAL **TE Connection Activity** Social Studies, p. 444 ADVANCED **LB Long-Term Projects & Research Ideas** The Antifreeze Protein* ADVANCED **LB Long-Term Projects & Research Ideas** Ewe Again, Dolly?* ADVANCED	**CRF Lesson Plans*** **TR Bellringer Transparency*** **TR Unraveling DNA*** **TR The Making of a Protein: A*** **TR The Making of a Protein: B*** **TR LINK TO EARTH SCIENCE** The Formation of Smog*** **TR How Sickle Cell Anemia Results from a Mutation*** **SE Internet Activity,** p. 440 GENERAL **CD Interactive Explorations CD-ROM** DNA Pawprints GENERAL

PACING • 90 min

CHAPTER REVIEW, ASSESSMENT, AND STANDARDIZED TEST PREPARATION

CRF Vocabulary Activity* GENERAL
SE Chapter Review, pp. 448–449 GENERAL
CRF Chapter Review* ■ GENERAL
CRF Chapter Tests A* ■ GENERAL, **B*** ADVANCED, **C*** SPECIAL NEEDS
SE Standardized Test Preparation, pp. 450–451 GENERAL
CRF Standardized Test Preparation* GENERAL
CRF Performance-Based Assessment* GENERAL
OSP Test Generator GENERAL
CRF Test Item Listing* GENERAL

Online and Technology Resources

Visit **go.hrw.com** for a variety of free resources related to this textbook. Enter the keyword **HT5R7DNA.**

Holt Online Learning

Students can access interactive problem-solving help and active visual concept development with the *Holt Science and Technology* Online Edition available at **www.hrw.com.**

 Guided Reading Audio CD

These CDs are designed to help auditory learners and reluctant readers.

 Science Tutor CD-ROM

Excellent for remediation and test practice.

SKILLS DEVELOPMENT RESOURCES

SE Pre-Reading Activity, p. 432 `GENERAL`
OSP Science Puzzlers, Twisters & Teasers `GENERAL`

CRF Directed Reading A* `BASIC`, B* `SPECIAL NEEDS`
CRF Vocabulary and Section Summary* `GENERAL`
SE Reading Strategy Prediction Guide, p. 434 `GENERAL`
SE Connection to Chemistry Linus Pauling, p. 435 `GENERAL`
TE Reading Strategy Mnemonics, p. 435 `BASIC`
TE Inclusion Strategies, p. 435
MS Math Skills for Science A Shortcut for Multiplying Large Numbers* `GENERAL`
SS Science Skills Science Drawing* `GENERAL`

CRF Directed Reading A* `BASIC`, B* `SPECIAL NEEDS`
CRF Vocabulary and Section Summary* `GENERAL`
SE Reading Strategy Reading Organizer, p. 438 `GENERAL`
SE Math Practice Code Combinations, p. 441 `GENERAL`
TE Inclusion Strategies, p. 443
SE Connection to Social Studies Genetic Property, p. 444 `GENERAL`
CRF Reinforcement Worksheet DNA Mutations* `BASIC`
CRF Critical Thinking The Perfect Parrot* `ADVANCED`

SECTION REVIEW AND ASSESSMENT

SE Reading Checks, pp. 435, 437 `GENERAL`
TE Reteaching, p. 436 `BASIC`
SE Section Review,* p. 437 ■ `GENERAL`
TE Quiz, p. 437 `GENERAL`
TE Alternative Assessment, p. 437 `GENERAL`
CRF Section Quiz* ■ `GENERAL`

SE Reading Checks, pp. 438, 441, 442, 443, 444 `GENERAL`
TE Homework, p. 440 `GENERAL`
TE Homework, p. 443 `GENERAL`
TE Reteaching, p. 444 `BASIC`
SE Section Review,* p. 445 ■ `GENERAL`
TE Quiz, p. 444 `GENERAL`
TE Alternative Assessment, p. 444 `GENERAL`
CRF Section Quiz* ■ `GENERAL`

STANDARDS CORRELATIONS

North Carolina
Standard Course of Study

1.06; *Chapter Lab:* 1.07

5.01, 5.05

One-Stop Planner® CD-ROM

This convenient CD-ROM includes:
- **Lab Materials QuickList Software**
- **Holt Calendar Planner**
- **Customizable Lesson Plans**
- **Printable Worksheets**
- **ExamView® Test Generator**

cnnstudentnews.com

Find the latest news, lesson plans, and activities related to important scientific events.

SCiLINKS®
NSTA

www.scilinks.org

Maintained by the **National Science Teachers Association.** See Chapter Enrichment pages for a complete list of topics.

Check out *Current Science* articles and activities by visiting the HRW Web site at **go.hrw.com.** Just type in the keyword **HL5CS06T.**

Classroom Videos

- **Lab Videos** demonstrate the chapter lab.
- **Brain Food Video Quizzes** help students review the chapter material.
- **CNN Videos** bring science into your students' daily life.

Visual Resources

CHAPTER STARTER TRANSPARENCY

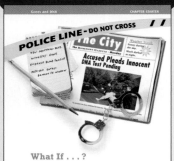

BELLRINGER TRANSPARENCIES

Section: What Does DNA Look Like?
Can you explain the difference between traits and characteristics? Which is more closely associated with DNA and genes? Where do you think DNA and genes are usually found?

Write your answers in your **science journal.**

Section: How DNA Works
Unscramble the following words:
tpsoneir
neesg
Now think of three words you associate with each of the above words and use them all in a paragraph that highlights what you know about DNA.

Write your paragraph in your **science journal.**

TEACHING TRANSPARENCIES

L17 DNA Structure

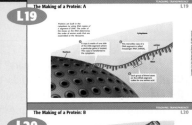

L19 The Making of a Protein: A

L20 The Making of a Protein: B

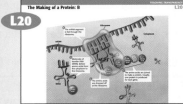

TEACHING TRANSPARENCIES

L21 How Sickle Cell Anemia Results from a Mutation

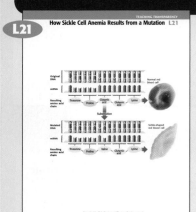

L18 Unraveling DNA

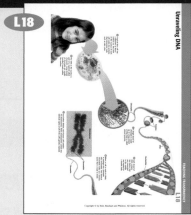

E66 The Formation of Smog

LINK TO EARTH SCIENCE

Chapter: The Atmosphere

CONCEPT MAPPING TRANSPARENCY

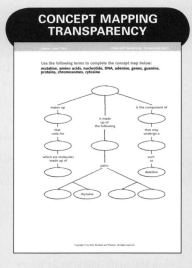

Use the following terms to complete the concept map below: mutation, amino acids, nucleotide, DNA, adenine, genes, guanine, proteins, chromosomes, cytosine

Planning Resources

LESSON PLANS

Lesson Plan SAMPLE

Section: Waves

Pacing
Regular Schedule: with lab(s):2 days   without lab(s)2 days
Block Schedule: with lab(s): 1 1/2 days   without lab(s)1 day

Objectives
1. Relate the seven properties of life to a living organism.
2. Describe seven themes that can help you to organize what you learn about biology.
3. Identify the tiny structures that make up all living organisms.
4. Differentiate between reproduction and heredity and between metabolism and homeostasis.

National Science Education Standards Covered
LSInter6:Cells have particular structures that underlie their functions.
LSMat1:Most cell functions involve chemical reactions.
LSBeh1:Cells store and use information to guide their functions.
UCP1:Cell functions are regulated.
SI1: Cells can differentiate and form complete multicellular organisms.
PS1: Species evolve over time.
ESS1: The great diversity of organisms is the result of more than 3.5 billion years of evolution.
ESS2: Natural selection and its evolutionary consequences provide a scientific explanation for the fossil record of ancient life forms as well as for the striking molecular similarities observed among the diverse species of living organisms.
ST1: The millions of different species of plants, animals, and microorganisms that live on Earth today are related by descent from common ancestors.
ST2: The energy for life primarily comes from the sun.
SPSP1: The complexity and organization of matter accommodates the need for obtaining, transforming, transporting, releasing, and eliminating the matter and energy used to sustain the organism.
SPSP6: As matter and energy flows through different levels of organization of living systems—cells, organs, communities—and between living systems and the physical environment, chemical elements are recombined in different ways.
HNS1: Organisms have behavioral responses to internal changes and to external stimuli.

PARENT LETTER

SAMPLE

Dear Parent,

Your son's or daughter's science class will soon begin exploring the chapter entitled "The World of Physical Science." In this chapter, students will learn about how the scientific method applies to the world of physical science and the role of physical science in the world. By the end of the chapter, students should demonstrate a clear understanding of the chapter's main ideas and be able to discuss the following topics:

1. physical science is the study of energy and matter (Section 1)
2. the role of physical science in the world around them (Section 1)
3. careers that rely on physical science (Section 1)
4. the steps used in the scientific method (Section 2)
5. examples of technology (Section 2)
6. how the scientific method is used to answer questions and solve problems (Section 2)
7. how our knowledge of science changes over time (Section 2)
8. how models represent real objects or systems (Section 3)
9. examples of different ways models are used in science (Section 3)
10. the importance of the International System of Units (Section 4)
11. the appropriate units to use for particular measurements (Section 4)
12. how area and density are derived quantities (Section 4)

Questions to Ask Along the Way

You can help your son or daughter learn about these topics by asking interesting questions such as the following:

• What are some surprising careers that use physical science?
• What is a characteristic of a good hypothesis?
• When is it a good idea to use a model?
• Why do Americans measure things in terms of inches and yards instead of centimeters and meters?

TEST ITEM LISTING

TEST ITEM LISTING
The World of Science SAMPLE

MULTIPLE CHOICE

1. A limitation of models is that
   a. they are large enough to see.
   b. they do not act exactly like the things that they model.
   c. they are smaller than the things that they model.
   d. they model unfamiliar things.
2. The length 10 m is equal to
   a. 100 cm.   c. 10,000 mm.
   b. 1,000 cm.   d. Both (b) and (c)
   Answer: B   Difficulty: 1   Section: 3   Objective: 2
3. To be valid, a hypothesis must be
   a. testable.   c. made into a law.
   b. supported by evidence.   d. Both (a) and (b)
   Answer: B   Difficulty: 1   Section: 3   Objective: 2
4. The statement "Sheila has a stain on her shirt" is an example of a(n)
   a. law.   c. observation.
   b. hypothesis.   d. prediction.
   Answer: B   Difficulty: 1   Section: 3   Objective: 2
5. A hypothesis is often developed out of
   a. observations.   c. laws.
   b. experiments.   d. Both (a) and (b).
   Answer: B   Difficulty: 1   Section: 3   Objective: 2
6. How many milliliters are in 3.5 kL?
   a. 3,500 mL.   c. 3,500, 000 mL.
   b. 0.0035 mL.   d. 35,000 mL.
   Answer: B   Difficulty: 1   Section: 3   Objective: 2
7. A map of Seattle is an example of a
   a. law.   c. model.
   b. theory.   d. unit.
   Answer: B   Difficulty: 1   Section: 3   Objective: 2
8. A lab has the safety icons shown below. These icons mean that you should wear
   a. only safety goggles.   c. safety goggles and a lab apron.
   b. only a lab apron.   d. safety goggles, a lab apron, and gloves
   Answer: B   Difficulty: 1   Section: 3   Objective: 2
9. The law of conservation of mass says the the total mass before a chemical change is
   a. more than the total mass after the change.
   b. less than the total mass after the change.
   c. the same as the total mass after the change.
   d. not the same as the total mass after the change.
   Answer: B   Difficulty: 1   Section: 3   Objective: 2
10. In which of the following areas might you find a geochemist at work?
    a. studying the chemistry of rocks   c. studying the atmosphere
    b. studying forestry   d. studying the atmosphere
    Answer: B   Difficulty: 1   Section: 3   Objective: 2

One-Stop Planner® CD-ROM

This CD-ROM includes all of the resources shown here and the following time-saving tools:

• *Lab Materials QuickList Software*
• *Customizable lesson plans*
• *Holt Calendar Planner*
• *The powerful ExamView® Test Generator*

Meeting Individual Needs

DIRECTED READING A

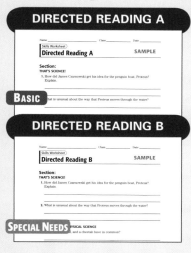

BASIC

DIRECTED READING B

Directed Reading B SAMPLE

SPECIAL NEEDS

VOCABULARY ACTIVITY

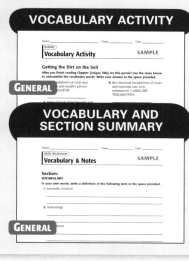

GENERAL

VOCABULARY AND SECTION SUMMARY

Vocabulary & Notes SAMPLE

GENERAL

REINFORCEMENT

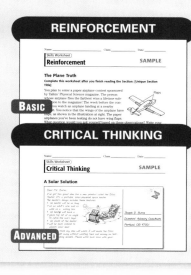

BASIC

CRITICAL THINKING

ADVANCED

SCILINKS ACTIVITY

GENERAL

SCIENCE PUZZLERS, TWISTERS & TEASERS

GENERAL

Labs and Activities

LONG-TERM PROJECTS & RESEARCH IDEAS

ADVANCED

LONG-TERM PROJECTS & RESEARCH IDEAS

ADVANCED

WHIZ-BANG DEMONSTRATIONS

GENERAL

DATASHEETS FOR QUICK LABS

DATASHEETS FOR CHAPTER LABS

DATASHEETS FOR LABBOOK

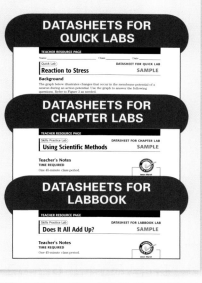

Review and Assessments

SECTION QUIZ

GENERAL — *ALSO IN SPANISH*

SECTION REVIEW

GENERAL — *ALSO IN SPANISH*

CHAPTER REVIEW

GENERAL — *ALSO IN SPANISH*

CHAPTER TEST A

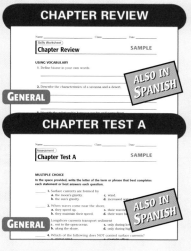

GENERAL — *ALSO IN SPANISH*

CHAPTER TEST B

ADVANCED

CHAPTER TEST C

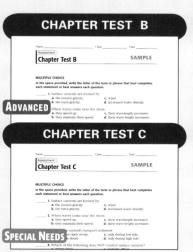

SPECIAL NEEDS

STANDARDIZED TEST PREPARATION

GENERAL

PERFORMANCE-BASED ASSESSMENT

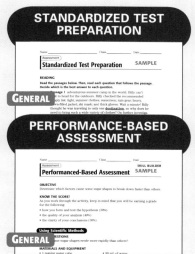

GENERAL

This Chapter Enrichment provides relevant and interesting information to expand and enhance your presentation of the chapter material.

Section 1

What Does DNA Look Like?

Discovering DNA

- In 1869, long before the time of Watson and Crick, a 22-year-old Swiss scientist isolated DNA from a cell nucleus. Unfortunately, he had no idea of its function, much less of its role in inheritance. It was not until 75 years later, in 1944, that an American geneticist named Oswald T. Avery found evidence that DNA is the carrier of genetic information.

Section 2

How DNA Works

Cracking the Genetic Code

- In the 1960s, scientists cracked the genetic code—the translation between codons (sequences of three bases) and amino acids. They have found that the genetic code is similar in all living organisms. If a codon aligns with a particular amino acid in humans, the same codon aligns with the same amino acid in bacteria. This similarity suggests that all life-forms have a common evolutionary ancestor.

Is That a Fact!

- ◆ Human DNA consists of about 3 billion base pairs. If you could print a book with all the genetic information carried in just one human cell, it would be 500,000 pages long.

Amino Acids

- All known organisms produce proteins using only 20 amino acids as building blocks (some use a rare 21st amino acid). The human body can manufacture 10 of these amino acids. The other 10 must be obtained from proteins in the diet and for this reason are called the *essential* amino acids. Foods that contain all the essential amino acids at once include eggs, milk, seafood, and meat. However, all amino acids can be obtained from a varied diet.

Protein Synthesis

- It took many years for scientists to determine how protein is synthesized in the cell. The discovery that DNA's nucleotide sequence corresponds to a certain amino acid sequence was a key step in unlocking this mystery. This link was conclusively proven by Charles Yanofsky and Sydney Brenner in 1964.

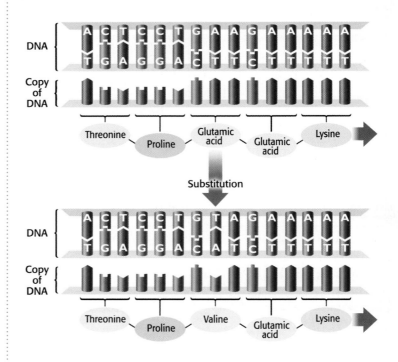

- The genetic sequences used to make proteins can be compared to sentences. Where each three-letter "word" in the genetic "sentence" starts and stops is very important for constructing a protein. For example, suppose the sentence to code for a particular protein read "PAT SAW THE FAT CAT." If you start just one base pair too late, the sentence would read "ATS AWT HEF ATC AT," which is meaningless.

Is That a Fact!

◆ If uncoiled, the DNA in the 46 chromosomes of a human body cell is about 2 m long. Within chromosomes, this DNA is so tightly coiled that if all 46 chromosomes were lined up end to end, they would span less than 0.5 cm.

Genetic Engineering

● Genetically engineered hybrid organisms are often called *chimeras*. The word *chimera* comes from Greek mythology, in which the Chimera was a fire-breathing monster, usually depicted as a composite of a lion, a goat, and a serpent.

● Scientists often disagree about the ethics of genetic engineering and about the safety risks involved. Dr. Maxine Frank Singer was one of the first scientists to warn the National Academy of Science of the potential hazards of genetic engineering. Because of the efforts of Dr. Singer and her colleagues, the National Institute of Health began to develop specific guidelines for genetic research as early as 1976. These guidelines, now regularly amended, continue to regulate the production and use of DNA and genetically engineered organisms.

The Human Genome Project

● The Human Genome Project (HGP) was started in 1990 as an international collaboration of scientists with the goal of mapping the entire sequence of DNA found in humans. In April 2003, in conjunction with the anniversary of the historic publication by Watson and Crick of DNA's molecular structure, the HGP announced that its work was mostly done. The HGP had completed mapping 99% of the human genetic code. Some mystery remained about the area of chromosomes called the *centromere*.

● Many potential benefits are predicted to result from the Human Genome Project, and some benefits have already been realized. Scientists working on the HGP have developed faster methods of determining the sequences within DNA samples. Also, scientists have improved methods of finding and tracking the functions of specific genes within cells. Such advances have made it easier to study the genetics of all kinds of organisms and to find the genetic indicators of specific kinds of cancer and other diseases.

DNA Fingerprints

● DNA fingerprints are frequently used in criminal investigations. The DNA can come from hair, skin cells, blood, or other body fluids left at the crime scene by the perpetrator. Scientists use enzymes to make copies of specific DNA sections from different locations on different chromosomes. The copied fragments are separated by size and other characteristics on a gel, and they are stained to yield a unique set of dark bands on the gel. This set of bands is known as a *DNA fingerprint*. The fingerprint is then compared with the DNA fingerprint of the suspect to help determine innocence or guilt.

NSTA
Developed and maintained by the
National Science Teachers Association

SciLinks is maintained by the National Science Teachers Association to provide you and your students with interesting, up-to-date links that will enrich your classroom presentation of the chapter.

Visit www.scilinks.org and enter the SciLinks code for more information about the topic listed.

Topic: DNA
SciLinks code: HSM0418

Topic: Genes and Traits
SciLinks code: HSM0647

Topic: Genetics
SciLinks code: HSM0659

Topic: Genetic Engineering
SciLinks code: HSM0654

Topic: DNA Fingerprinting
SciLinks code: HSM0419

Topic: Genetic Diseases, Screening, and Counseling
SciLinks code: HSM0651

Topic: Human Genome Project
SciLinks code: HSM0770

Overview

Tell students that this chapter is about DNA—the substance that makes up genes—and about how DNA works within cells to direct the growth and functioning of every organism.

Assessing Prior Knowledge

Students should be familiar with the following topics:

- cell structure
- mitosis and meiosis
- basic rules of heredity
- chromosomes

Identifying Misconceptions

The roles of DNA, RNA, and proteins in cells are very complex, and many puzzles remain. Students may tend to simplify their concept of the "rules" as they learn them. Students may remain unconvinced of the role of chance and probability in heredity. Also, students may have difficulty linking their knowledge of the functions of DNA at the cellular level to what they have learned and will learn about the functioning of tissues and organs within an entire organism.

16

Genes and DNA

About the PHOTO

These adult mice have no hair—not because their hair was shaved off but because these mice do not grow hair. In cells of these mice, the genes that normally cause hair to grow are not working. The genes were "turned off" by scientists who have learned to control the function of some genes. Scientists changed the genes of these mice to research medical problems such as cancer.

PRE-READING ACTIVITY

Graphic Organizer

Concept Map Before you read the chapter, create the graphic organizer entitled "Concept Map" described in the **Study Skills** section of the Appendix. As you read the chapter, fill in the concept map with details about DNA.

Standards Correlations

North Carolina Standard Course of Study

1.06 Use mathematics to gather, organize, and present quantitative data resulting from scientific investigations: . . . Analysis of data [and] Graphing . . . (Science in Action)

1.07 (partial) Prepare models and/or computer simulations to: . . . Evaluate how data fit. (Chapter Lab)

5.01 Explain the significance of genes to inherited characteristics: Genes are the units of information, Parents transmit genes to their offspring, [and] Some medical conditions and diseases are genetic. (Section 2)

5.05 (partial) Summarize the genetic transmittance of disease. (Section 2)

START-UP ACTIVITY

MATERIALS

FOR EACH GROUP
- magnifying lens
- paper, tracing (1 sheet)
- paper, white (1 sheet for each student)
- pencil or piece of charcoal
- tape, transparent

Safety Caution: Remind students to review all safety cautions and icons before beginning this lab activity. Charcoal is nontoxic, but it can stain clothes.

Teacher's Notes: The loop pattern is found in about 65% of the population, the whorl in about 30%, and the arch in about 5%.

Answers

1. The number of fingerprint types will vary for each class. No two students should have the same fingerprint (those of identical twins may be similar but still unique). Accept any reasonable explanation that incorporates variation in inherited traits among populations.

START-UP ACTIVITY

Fingerprint Your Friends

One way to identify people is by taking their fingerprints. Does it really work? Are everyone's fingerprints unique? Try this activity to find out.

Procedure

1. Rub the tip of a **pencil** back and forth across a **piece of tracing paper.** Make a large, dark mark.

2. Rub the tip of one of your fingers on the pencil mark. Then place a small **piece of transparent tape** over the darkened area on your finger.

3. Remove the tape, and stick it on **a piece of white paper.** Repeat steps 1–3 for the rest of your fingers.

4. Look at the fingerprints with a **magnifying lens.** What patterns do you see? Is the pattern the same on every finger?

Analysis

1. Compare your fingerprints with those of your classmates. Do any two people in your class have the same prints? Try to explain your findings.

Chapter Starter Transparency
Use this transparency to help students begin thinking about genes and DNA.

CHAPTER RESOURCES

Technology

 Transparencies
- Chapter Starter Transparency   **READING SKILLS**

 Student Edition on CD-ROM

 Guided Reading Audio CD

Classroom Videos
- Brain Food Video Quiz

Workbooks

Science Puzzlers, Twisters & Teasers
- Genes and DNA **GENERAL**

Focus

Overview

This section introduces students to the structure and function of DNA and to the process of DNA replication.

🔊 Bellringer

To test prior knowledge, have students answer the following questions:

1. Give an example of the difference between traits and characteristics. (Sample answer: Eye color is a characteristic, while having blue eyes is a trait.)

2. Where are genes found in cells? (in chromosomes; in cells that have nuclei, chromosomes are within the nucleus)

Motivate

ACTIVITY ———————— GENERAL

Modeling Code Create a code by pairing each letter of the alphabet with a numeral. For example, the numeral 1 could represent the letter *a*. Have students encode a brief message. Then, have students exchange and decode the message. Explain that a code is simply another way to represent information and that there are many types of codes. The genetic code is based on sequences of the four nucleotide bases of DNA. English Language Learners

LS Logical

READING WARM-UP

Objectives

● List three important events that led to understanding the structure of DNA.

● Describe the basic structure of a DNA molecule.

● Explain how DNA molecules can be copied.

Terms to Learn
DNA
nucleotide

READING STRATEGY

Prediction Guide Before reading this section, write the title of each heading in this section. Next, under each heading, write what you think you will learn.

DNA **d**eoxyribo**n**ucleic **a**cid, a molecule that is present in all living cells and that contains the information that determines the traits that a living thing inherits and needs to live

nucleotide in a nucleic-acid chain, a subunit that consists of a sugar, a phosphate, and a nitrogenous base

---

What Does DNA Look Like?

For many years, the structure of a DNA molecule was a puzzle to scientists. In the 1950s, two scientists deduced the structure while experimenting with chemical models. They later won a Nobel Prize for helping solve this puzzle!

Inherited characteristics are determined by genes, and genes are passed from one generation to the next. Genes are parts of chromosomes, which are structures in the nucleus of most cells. Chromosomes are made of protein and DNA. **DNA** stands for *deoxyribonucleic acid* (dee AHKS ee RIE boh noo KLEE ik AS id). DNA is the genetic material—the material that determines inherited characteristics. But what does DNA look like?

The Pieces of the Puzzle

Scientists knew that the material that makes up genes must be able to do two things. First, it must be able to give instructions for building and maintaining cells. Second, it must be able to be copied each time a cell divides, so that each cell contains identical genes. Scientists thought that these things could be done only by complex molecules, such as proteins. They were surprised to learn how much the DNA molecule could do.

Nucleotides: The Subunits of DNA

DNA is made of subunits called nucleotides. A **nucleotide** consists of a sugar, a phosphate, and a base. The nucleotides are identical except for the base. The four bases are *adenine, thymine, guanine,* and *cytosine.* Each base has a different shape. Scientists often refer to a base by the first letter of the base, *A, T, G,* and *C.* **Figure 1** shows models of the four nucleotides.

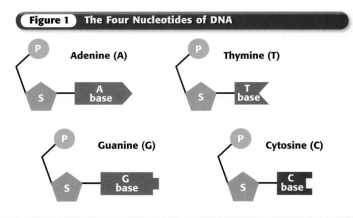

Figure 1 The Four Nucleotides of DNA

Adenine (A)

Thymine (T)

Guanine (G)

Cytosine (C)

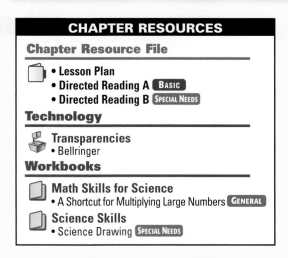

CHAPTER RESOURCES

Chapter Resource File

📁 • **Lesson Plan**
• **Directed Reading A** BASIC
• **Directed Reading B** SPECIAL NEEDS

Technology

💾 **Transparencies**
• Bellringer

Workbooks

📓 **Math Skills for Science**
• A Shortcut for Multiplying Large Numbers GENERAL

📓 **Science Skills**
• Science Drawing SPECIAL NEEDS

Chargaff's Rules

In the 1950s, a biochemist named Erwin Chargaff found that the amount of adenine in DNA always equals the amount of thymine. And he found that the amount of guanine always equals the amount of cytosine. His findings are known as *Chargaff's rules*. At the time of his discovery, no one knew the importance of these findings. But Chargaff's rules later helped scientists understand the structure of DNA.

Reading Check Summarize Chargaff's rules. (*See the Appendix for answers to Reading Checks.*)

Franklin's Discovery

More clues about the structure of DNA came from scientists in Britain. There, chemist Rosalind Franklin, shown in **Figure 2,** was able to make images of DNA molecules. She used a process known as *X-ray diffraction* to make these images. In this process, X rays are aimed at the DNA molecule. When an X ray hits a part of the molecule, the ray bounces off. The pattern made by the bouncing rays is captured on film. Franklin's images suggested that DNA has a spiral shape.

Watson and Crick's Model

At about the same time, two other scientists were also trying to solve the mystery of DNA's structure. They were James Watson and Francis Crick, shown in **Figure 3.** After seeing Franklin's X-ray images, Watson and Crick concluded that DNA must look like a long, twisted ladder. They were then able to build a model of DNA by using simple materials from their laboratory. Their model perfectly fit with both Chargaff's and Franklin's findings. The model eventually helped explain how DNA is copied and how it functions in the cell.

Figure 2 *Rosalind Franklin used X-ray diffraction to make images of DNA that helped reveal the structure of DNA.*

Figure 3 *This photo shows James Watson (left) and Francis Crick (right) with their model of DNA.*

Answer to Connection to Chemistry
Linus Pauling was an innovator in the use of models to deduce chemical behavior. Whereas some scientists belittled the practice of "playing" with chemical models, Pauling inspired other scientists, such as Watson and Crick, to try this strategy. Watson and Crick's deduction of DNA's ladder structure was partly brought about by manipulating models of nucleotides.

Reteaching — BASIC

DNA's Complementary Strands

To help students understand how the term *complementary* relates to the structure of DNA, point out that the term means "completing." Using **Figure 4** and **Figure 5,** explain that complementary base pairs join to *complete* each rung on the spiral-staircase structure of DNA. Then, point out that complementary strands of DNA join to complete one DNA molecule.
LS Visual/Verbal

Quiz — GENERAL

1. When is DNA copied? (every time a cell divides)

2. Name the four types of nucleotides. (adenine, thymine, guanine, and cytosine)

Alternative Assessment — GENERAL

Custom Code Have students create an alternative code that functions like DNA in the following ways:

• The code is based on four letters or symbols.

• Coded information can be split up and then reassembled.

Have students draw and explain their coding system. **LS** Logical

Making a Model of DNA

1. Gather assorted simple materials that you could use to build a basic model of DNA. You might use **clay, string, toothpicks, paper, tape, plastic foam,** or **pieces of food.**

2. Work with a partner or a small team to build your model. Use your book and other resources to check the details of your model.

3. Show your model to your classmates. Give your classmates feedback about the scientific aspects of their models.

DNA's Double Structure

The shape of DNA is shown in **Figure 4.** As you can see, a strand of DNA looks like a twisted ladder. This shape is known as a *double helix* (DUB uhl HEE LIKS). The two sides of the ladder are made of alternating sugar parts and phosphate parts. The rungs of the ladder are made of a pair of bases. Adenine on one side of a rung always pairs with thymine on the other side. Guanine always pairs with cytosine.

Notice how the double helix structure matches Chargaff's observations. When Chargaff separated the parts of a sample of DNA, he found that the matching bases were always present in equal amounts. To model how the bases pair, Watson and Crick tried to match Chargaff's observations. They also used information from chemists about the size and shape of each of the nucleotides. As it turned out, the width of the DNA ladder matches the combined width of the matching bases. Only the correct pairs of bases fit within the ladder's width.

Making Copies of DNA

The pairing of bases allows the cell to *replicate,* or make copies of, DNA. Each base always bonds with only one other base. Thus, pairs of bases are *complementary* to each other, and both sides of a DNA molecule are complementary. For example, the sequence CGAC will bond to the sequence GCTG.

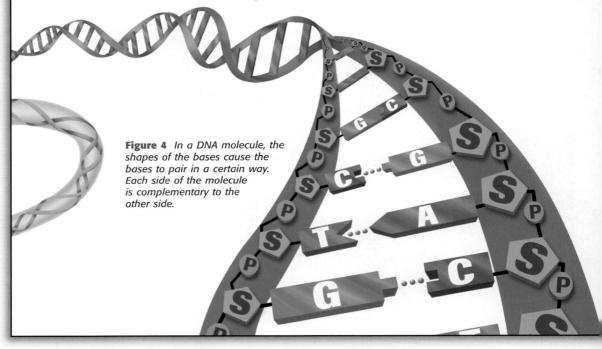

Figure 4 *In a DNA molecule, the shapes of the bases cause the bases to pair in a certain way. Each side of the molecule is complementary to the other side.*

MATERIALS

FOR EACH GROUP
• variety of materials, such as clay, string, toothpicks, paper, tape, plastic foam, beads or buttons and pipe cleaners or wire.
• food or candy items could be another option

Teacher's Note: Display student models within the school. Have students reevaluate or improve upon them later.

Safety Caution: Advise students to keep the area around them uncluttered. Students should exercise caution with sharp objects. Any food items used should not be eaten and should be disposed of.

Answers

2. Student models should resemble **Figure 4** in basic structure but may vary in size, color, and construction.

3. Students should suggest ways to make each model more accurate.

How Copies Are Made

During replication, as shown in **Figure 5,** a DNA molecule is split down the middle, where the bases meet. The bases on each side of the molecule are used as a pattern for a new strand. As the bases on the original molecule are exposed, complementary nucleotides are added to each side of the ladder. Two DNA molecules are formed. Half of each of the molecules is old DNA, and half is new DNA.

When Copies Are Made

DNA is copied every time a cell divides. Each new cell gets a complete copy of all the DNA. The job of unwinding, copying, and re-winding the DNA is done by proteins within the cell. So, DNA is usually found with several kinds of proteins. Other proteins help with the process of carrying out the instructions written in the code of the DNA.

Reading Check How often is DNA copied?

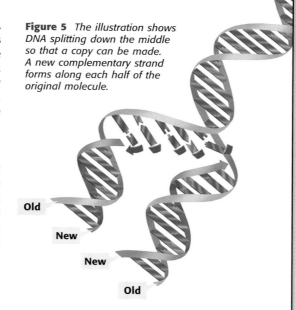

Figure 5 *The illustration shows DNA splitting down the middle so that a copy can be made. A new complementary strand forms along each half of the original molecule.*

Old

New

New

Old

SECTION Review

Summary

- DNA is the material that makes up genes. It carries coded information that is copied in each new cell.

- The DNA molecule looks like a twisted ladder. The two halves are long strings of nucleotides. The rungs are complementary pairs of bases.

- Because each base has a complementary base, DNA can be replicated accurately.

Using Key Terms

1. Use the term *DNA* in a sentence.

2. In your own words, write a definition for the term *nucleotide*.

Understanding Key Ideas

3. List three important events that led to understanding the structure of DNA.

4. Which of the following is NOT part of a nucleotide?
   a. base
   b. sugar
   c. fat
   d. phosphate

Math Skills

5. If a sample of DNA contained 20% cytosine, what percentage of guanine would be in this sample? What percentage of adenine would be in the sample? Explain.

Critical Thinking

6. **Making Inferences** Explain what is meant by the statement "DNA unites all organisms."

7. **Applying Concepts** What would the complementary strand of DNA be for the sequence of bases below?

   C T T A G G C T T A C C A

8. **Analyzing Processes** How are copies of DNA made? Draw a picture as part of your answer.

Developed and maintained by the National Science Teachers Association

For a variety of links related to this chapter, go to www.scilinks.org

Topic: DNA; Genes and Traits
SciLinks code: HSM0418; HSM0647

Answer to Reading Check

every time a cell divides

Answers to Section Review

1. Sample answer: DNA is the material that makes up genes and is found in all cells.

2. Sample answer: A nucleotide is a subunit of a DNA molecule and consists of a sugar, a phosphate, and a base; there are four kinds of bases and thus four kinds of nucleotides.

3. Sample answers: Scientists thought only complex materials such as proteins could make up genes; Erwin Chargaff discovered the rules of nucleotide base pairing; Rosalind Franklin made images of DNA molecules; Watson and Crick made a correct model of DNA's structure.

4. c

5. 20% guanine, because it should be equal to the amount of cytosine; 30% adenine, because the remaining 60% of the DNA should be made up of equal amounts of adenine and thymine

6. Sample answer: DNA is found in the cells of all organisms.

7. GAATCCGAATGGT

8. DNA copies are made by splitting the molecule down the middle and then adding new nucleotides to each side. (Students' drawings should resemble **Figure 5.**)

SECTION
2

How DNA Works

Almost every cell in your body contains about 2 m of DNA. How does all of the DNA fit in a cell? And how does the DNA hold a code that affects your traits?

DNA is found in the cells of all organisms, including bacteria, mosquitoes, and humans. Each organism has a unique set of DNA. But DNA functions the same way in all organisms.

Unraveling DNA

DNA is often wound around proteins, coiled into strands, and then bundled up even more. In a cell that lacks a nucleus, each strand of DNA forms a loose loop within the cell. In a cell that has a nucleus, the strands of DNA and proteins are bundled into chromosomes, as shown in **Figure 1.**

The structure of DNA allows DNA to hold information. The order of the bases on one side of the molecule is a code that carries information. A *gene* consists of a string of nucleotides that give the cell information about how to make a specific trait. There is an enormous amount of DNA, so there can be a large variety of genes.

✓ Reading Check What makes up a gene? (*See the Appendix for answers to Reading Checks.*)

Focus

Overview

This section shows how DNA is a part of chromosomes, how DNA is used as a template for making proteins, and how errors in DNA can lead to mutations and genetic disorders.

🎵 Bellringer

Have students unscramble the following words and use them both in one sentence:

tpsoneir (proteins)

neesg (genes)

(Sample answer: Genes contain instructions for making proteins.)

Motivate

Demonstration —— GENERAL

A Tight Fit To illustrate the way that DNA is *supercoiled* within chromosomes and cells, hold up a long rubber band or thick piece of string. Begin to twist each end in opposite directions until coils form. Continue twisting until the band is highly compacted. Then, challenge students to fit 2 m of fine thread into a thimble or an empty gelatin capsule. English Language Learners

LS Kinesthetic

Answer to Reading Check

a string of nucleotides that give the cell information about how to make a specific trait

Figure 1 **Unraveling DNA**

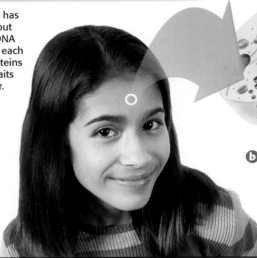

ⓐ A typical skin cell has a diameter of about 0.0025 cm. The DNA in the nucleus of each cell codes for proteins that determine traits such as skin color.

ⓑ The DNA in the nucleus is part of a material called *chromatin*. Long strands of chromatin are usually bundled loosely within the nucleus.

⚛WEIRD SCIENCE

In 2003, the Human Genome Project had successfully mapped 99% of the 3 billion base pairs that make up a set of human DNA. But the project has raised new questions as well. For example, only about 3% of those base pairs are used in making proteins; the other 97% are regulatory sequences, nonfunctioning genes, and sequences with no known function.

Additionally, scientists originally expected to find over 50,000 human genes because human cells produce at least that many proteins. Instead, latest estimates indicate that there are about 25,000 human genes, and many genes code for multiple proteins. In this and other ways, human genes appear to be unique among organisms.

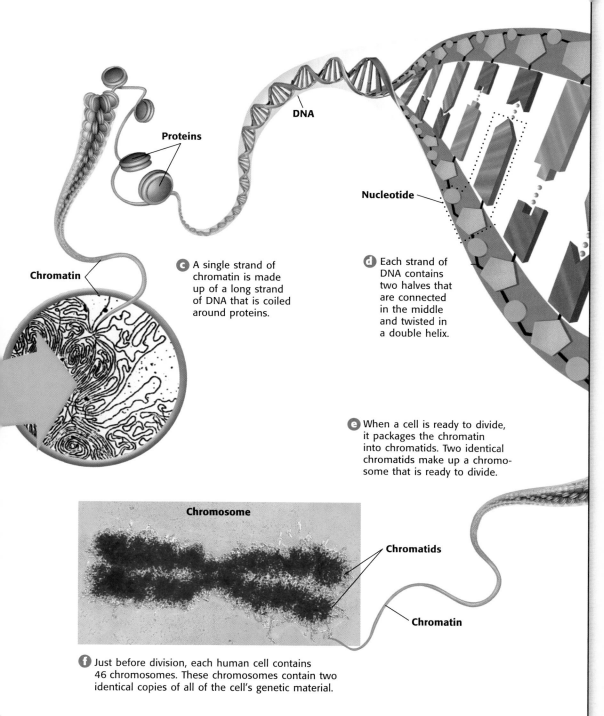

DNA

Proteins

Nucleotide

Chromatin

(c) A single strand of chromatin is made up of a long strand of DNA that is coiled around proteins.

(d) Each strand of DNA contains two halves that are connected in the middle and twisted in a double helix.

(e) When a cell is ready to divide, it packages the chromatin into chromatids. Two identical chromatids make up a chromosome that is ready to divide.

Chromosome

Chromatids

Chromatin

(f) Just before division, each human cell contains 46 chromosomes. These chromosomes contain two identical copies of all of the cell's genetic material.

DNA from the Dead Can ancient DNA be used to produce dinosaurs? In some science fiction, scientists make dinosaurs by combining fragments of ancient DNA with DNA from modern organisms. In reality, less-ancient fragments of DNA have indeed been found. However, a fragment of DNA is not enough information to make an entire organism. And identifying the owner of a given DNA fragment is difficult.

CHAPTER RESOURCES

Technology

📠 **Transparencies**
• Unraveling DNA

Teach

Using the Figure— BASIC

Unraveling DNA Have students carefully study **Figure 1**. Remind them that each chromosome is a pair of chromatids, and each chromatid is one long strand of DNA. This DNA strand is usually somewhat wound up around proteins in the form of chromatin. The chromatin may be tightly bundled (and visible) or loose (and not visible) within the nucleus. Most of the time, the chromatin is loose. Ask students the following questions:

• Where is the DNA in your cells? (in the nucleus)

• How does so much DNA fit into the nucleus? (It is coiled up tightly around proteins.)

• What is the name for strands of DNA wound around proteins? (chromatin)

• When do chromosomes become visible in cells? (when the cell is about to divide)

• What are chromatids? (two identical copies of a chromosome that is about to divide)

LS Visual/Auditory

BRAIN FOOD

Hereditary Hearing
Researchers are trying to find out if a gene is responsible for "perfect pitch," the ability to determine any musical note upon hearing it. It is a rare ability—possessed by one in every 2,000 people—found most often among musicians. People with perfect pitch can easily tell the musical note of a dial tone, the hum of a refrigerator, or of any sound they hear. The researchers think that people with perfect pitch may inherit the ability, but an early education in music may also be necessary.

RNA ribonucleic acid, a molecule that is present in all living cells and that plays a role in protein production

Figure 2 *Proteins are built in the cytoplasm by using RNA copies of a segment of DNA. The order of the bases on the RNA determines the order of amino acids that are assembled at the ribosome.*

Genes and Proteins

The DNA code is read like a book—from one end to the other and in one direction. The bases form the alphabet of the code. Groups of three bases are the codes for specific amino acids. For example, the three bases CCA form the code for the amino acid proline. The bases AGC form the code for the amino acid serine. A long string of amino acids forms a protein. Thus, each gene is usually a set of instructions for making a protein.

Proteins and Traits

How are proteins related to traits? Proteins are found throughout cells and cause most of the differences that you can see among organisms. Proteins act as chemical triggers and messengers for many of the processes within cells. Proteins help determine how tall you grow, what colors you can see, and whether your hair is curly or straight. Proteins exist in an almost limitless variety. A single organism may have thousands of genes that code for thousands of proteins.

Help from RNA

Another type of molecule that helps make proteins is called **RNA,** or *ribonucleic acid* (RIE boh noo KLEE ik AS id). RNA is so similar to DNA that RNA can serve as a temporary copy of a DNA sequence. Several forms of RNA help in the process of changing the DNA code into proteins, as shown in **Figure 2.**

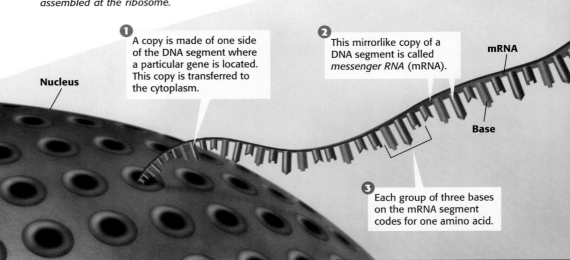

Cytoplasm

1 A copy is made of one side of the DNA segment where a particular gene is located. This copy is transferred to the cytoplasm.

Nucleus

2 This mirrorlike copy of a DNA segment is called *messenger RNA* (mRNA).

mRNA

Base

3 Each group of three bases on the mRNA segment codes for one amino acid.

SCIENCE HUMOR

Q: What happens when an amateur-tein gets paid?

A: It becomes a pro-tein.

The Making of a Protein

The first step in making a protein is to copy one side of the segment of DNA containing a gene. A mirrorlike copy of the DNA segment is made out of RNA. This copy of the DNA segment is called *messenger RNA* (mRNA). It moves out of the nucleus and into the cytoplasm of the cell.

In the cytoplasm, the messenger RNA is fed through a protein assembly line. The "factory" that runs this assembly line is known as a ribosome. A **ribosome** is a cell organelle composed of RNA and protein. The messenger RNA is fed through the ribosome three bases at a time. Then, molecules of *transfer RNA* (tRNA) translate the RNA message. Each transfer RNA molecule picks up a specific amino acid from the cytoplasm. Inside the ribosome, bases on the transfer RNA match up with bases on the messenger RNA like pieces of a puzzle. The transfer RNA molecules then release their amino acids. The amino acids become linked in a growing chain. As the entire segment of messenger RNA passes through the ribosome, the growing chain of amino acids folds up into a new protein molecule.

✓ **Reading Check** What do the transfer RNA molecules transfer?

ribosome a cell organelle composed of RNA and protein; the site of protein synthesis

CONNECTION ACTIVITY
Math ———————— GENERAL

Redundant Code Mathematics has a lot to do with how DNA codes for amino acids. Each combination of three nucleotides that codes for one amino acid is called a *codon*. Yet cells use only 20 different amino acids to build proteins. Thus, most amino acids have several, redundant corresponding codons. This redundancy is another reason that mutations in genes do not always result in changes in proteins. To physically model the possible base combinations that make up codons, organize the class into small groups. Give each group four pieces of paper, with one of the following four letters printed on each piece: *A, T, C,* or *G.* Ask students to come up with as many different three-letter "words" as possible by using the four different bases. (There are 4³, or 64, possible three-letter "words"—or codons. For example, the four possible combinations that would start with the bases AA are AAA, AAT, AAG, and AAC.) Check that students realize that the order of letters in each combination also matters. For example, *ATA* is not the same "word" as *AAT.* **LS Kinesthetic/Logical**

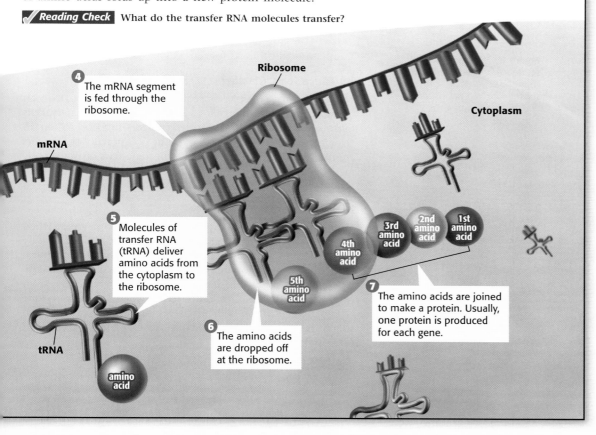

Ribosome

Cytoplasm

④ The mRNA segment is fed through the ribosome.

mRNA

⑤ Molecules of transfer RNA (tRNA) deliver amino acids from the cytoplasm to the ribosome.

tRNA

amino acid

⑥ The amino acids are dropped off at the ribosome.

5th amino acid

4th amino acid

3rd amino acid **2nd amino acid** **1st amino acid**

⑦ The amino acids are joined to make a protein. Usually, one protein is produced for each gene.

WEIRD SCIENCE

There is a gene located on the X chromosome that causes thick hair to grow on the upper body and face, including the ears, nose, cheeks, forehead, and even eyelids of people who have the gene. This condition is sometimes called *werewolf syndrome* because people who have the condition resemble fictional werewolves. This condition affects only appearance, however, not behavior.

Complementary Code Write a sequence of DNA bases, such as AACTACGGT, on the board. Ask students to write the complementary base sequence by using base-pairing rules. (TTGATGCCA) Then, ask students to give examples of deletions, insertions, and substitutions. **English Language Learners**

LS Visual/Verbal

MISCONCEPTION ALERT

Mutants Among Us? Students may think mutations occur rarely, because organisms that are visibly "mutated" appear infrequently. However, scientists estimate that mistakes are made during DNA replication in approximately one out of every 10,000 base pairs. With cellular proofing mechanisms, the final error rate is as low as one in a billion. Still, we inherit hundreds of mutations from our parents' gametes. Many mutations have no apparent effect. For example, a mutation may occur in a cell that does not produce a particular protein or in a "junk" region of DNA that does not code for anything.

Answer to Reading Check

a physical or chemical agent that can cause a mutation in DNA

Original sequence

a Base pair replaced

b Base pair added

c Base pair removed

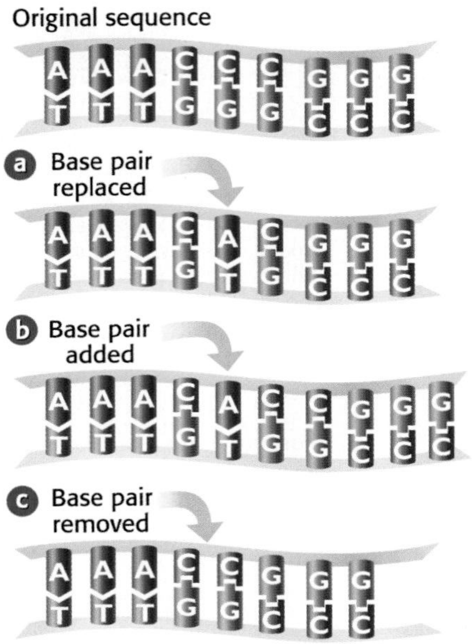

Figure 3 *The original base sequence on the top has been changed to illustrate (a) a substitution, (b) an insertion, and (c) a deletion.*

mutation a change in the nucleotide-base sequence of a gene or DNA molecule

---

Changes in Genes

Imagine that you have been invited to ride on a new roller coaster at the state fair. Before you climb into the front car, you are told that some of the metal parts on the coaster have been replaced by parts made of a different substance. Would you still want to ride this roller coaster? Perhaps a strong metal was used as a substitute. Or perhaps a material that is not strong enough was used. Imagine what would happen if cardboard were used instead of metal!

Mutations

Substitutions like the ones in the roller coaster can accidentally happen in DNA. Changes in the number, type, or order of bases on a piece of DNA are known as **mutations.** Sometimes, a base is left out. This kind of change is known as a *deletion.* Or an extra base might be added. This kind of change is known as an *insertion.* The most common change happens when the wrong base is used. This kind of change is known as a *substitution.* **Figure 3** illustrates these three types of mutations.

Do Mutations Matter?

There are three possible consequences to changes in DNA: an improved trait, no change, or a harmful trait. Fortunately, cells make some proteins that can detect errors in DNA. When an error is found, it is usually fixed. But occasionally the repairs are not accurate, and the mistakes become part of the genetic message. If the mutation occurs in the sex cells, the changed gene can be passed from one generation to the next.

How Do Mutations Happen?

Mutations happen regularly because of random errors when DNA is copied. In addition, damage to DNA can be caused by abnormal things that happen to cells. Any physical or chemical agent that can cause a mutation in DNA is called a *mutagen.* Examples of mutagens include high-energy radiation from X rays and ultraviolet radiation. Ultraviolet radiation is one type of energy in sunlight. It is responsible for suntans and sunburns. Other mutagens include asbestos and the chemicals in cigarette smoke.

✓ **Reading Check** What is a mutagen?

CHAPTER RESOURCES

Technology

Transparencies
- **LINK TO EARTH SCIENCE** The Formation of Smog
- How Sickle Cell Anemia Results from a Mutation

CONNECTION to Earth Science ——— GENERAL

Pollution and Ozone Ozone is a gas made of three oxygen atoms. High in the atmosphere, ozone absorbs dangerous ultraviolet radiation (the high-energy light that can cause DNA mutations). When produced near the surface of the Earth, however, ozone is a pollutant that affects plant growth and makes breathing more difficult. Use the teaching transparency entitled "The Formation of Smog" to illustrate the process of ozone production. LS Visual

---

An Example of a Substitution

A mutation, such as a substitution, can be harmful because it may cause a gene to produce the wrong protein. Consider the DNA sequence GAA. When copied as mRNA, this sequence gives the instructions to place the amino acid glutamic acid into the growing protein. If a mistake happens and the original DNA sequence is changed to GTA, the sequence will code for the amino acid valine instead.

This simple change in an amino acid can cause the disease *sickle cell disease*. Sickle cell disease affects red blood cells. When valine is substituted for glutamic acid in a blood protein, as shown in **Figure 4,** the red blood cells are changed into a sickle shape.

The sickle cells are not as good at carrying oxygen as normal red blood cells are. Sickle cells are also likely to get stuck in blood vessels and cause painful and dangerous clots.

✓ Reading Check What causes sickle cell disease?

SCHOOL to HOME

An Error in the Message

The sentence below is the result of an error similar to a DNA mutation. The original sentence was made up of three-letter words, but an error was made in this copy. Explain the idea of mutations to your parent. Then, work together to find the mutation, and write the sentence correctly.

THE IGB ADC ATA TET HEB IGR EDR AT.

ACTiViTY

Figure 4 How Sickle Cell Disease Results from a Mutation

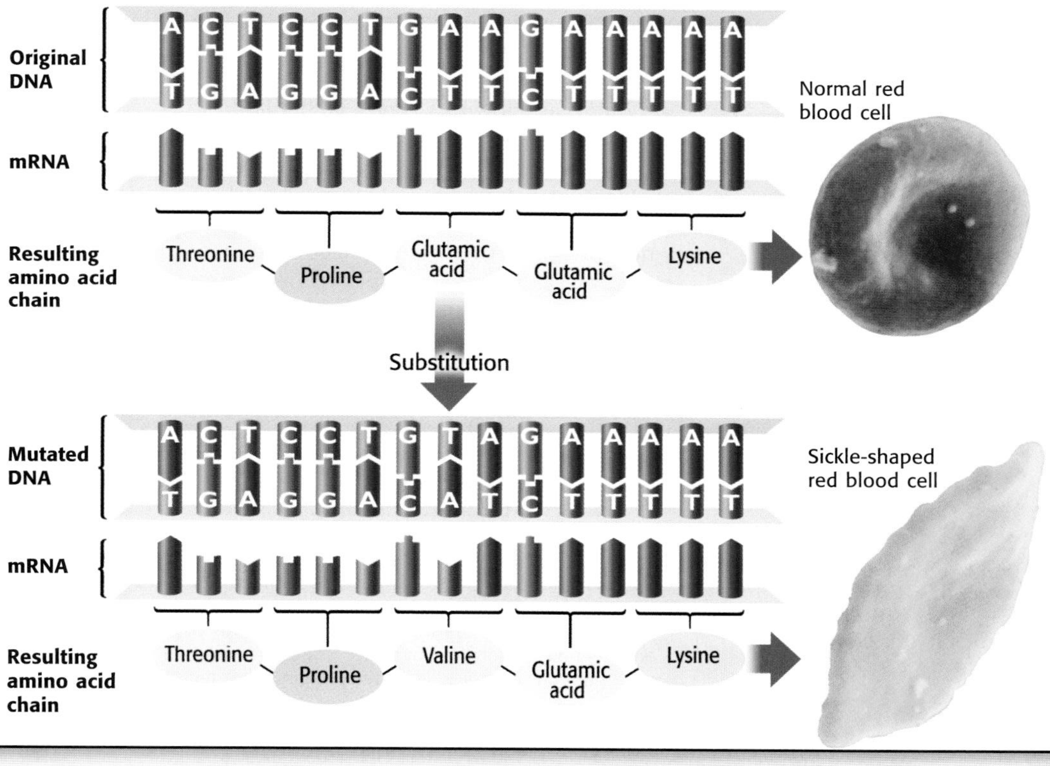

Original DNA: A C T C C T G A A G A A A A A / T G A G G A C T T C T T T T T

mRNA

Resulting amino acid chain: Threonine — Proline — Glutamic acid — Glutamic acid — Lysine → Normal red blood cell

Substitution

Mutated DNA: A C T C C T G T A G A A A A A / T G A G G A C A T C T T T T T

mRNA

Resulting amino acid chain: Threonine — Proline — Valine — Glutamic acid — Lysine → Sickle-shaped red blood cell

CONNECTION to Real Life — GENERAL

Misunderstood Disease A person who carries a single allele for sickle cell disease is said to have *sickle cell trait*. Only persons with two of these alleles usually develop the disease. In the past, many people did not understand that sickle cell trait and sickle cell disease are not contagious. In some areas, children with the trait were banned from public schools. **LS Verbal**

Answer to Reading Check

Sickle cell disease is caused by a mutation in a single nucleotide of DNA, which then causes the wrong amino acid to be assembled in a protein used in blood cells.

Answer to School-to-Home Activity

The mutation is a deletion. THE BIG BAD CAT ATE THE BIG RED RAT.

INCLUSION Strategies

- *Behavior Control Issues*
- *Attention Deficit Disorder*
- *Visually Impaired*

Many students benefit from small-group work and learn well when actively involved. Divide all but four students into groups of three. Assign a DNA combination to each team (AT, CG, TA, or GC). Have students identify their DNA pairs by taping construction paper to their shirts. Ask students to line up to create a "human" DNA chain. Assign each of the remaining four students one of the four combinations. Have the four "extras" move around to create the three types of mutations: deletions, insertions, and substitutions. **LS Intrapersonal**

Homework —— GENERAL

Writing **Genetic Diseases** Have students select a genetic disease about which to conduct research and write a report. Suggest diseases such as hemophilia, diabetes, Familial ALS (Amyotrophic Lateral Sclerosis, or Lou Gehrig's Disease), SCID (Severe Combined Immunodeficiency Syndrome, or "Plastic Bubble" syndrome), Huntington's disease, and neurofibromatosis ("elephantitis"). Suggest that their reports focus on historical occurrence of the disease, famous persons that had or have the disease, and treatments that have been tried. **LS Verbal** PORTFOLIO

Figure 5 *This genetically engineered tobacco plant contains firefly genes.*

Figure 6 *This scientist is gathering dead skin cells from a crime scene. DNA from the cells could be used as evidence of a criminal's identity.*

Uses of Genetic Knowledge

In the years since Watson and Crick made their model, scientists have learned a lot about genetics. This knowledge is often used in ways that benefit humans. But some uses of genetic knowledge also cause ethical and scientific debates.

Genetic Engineering

Scientists can manipulate individual genes within organisms. This kind of manipulation is called *genetic engineering*. In some cases, genes may be transferred from one type of organism to another. An example of a genetically engineered plant is shown in **Figure 5.** Scientists added a gene from fireflies to this plant. The gene produces a protein that causes the plant to glow.

Scientists may use genetic engineering to create new products, such as drugs, foods, or fabrics. For example, bacteria may be used to make the proteins found in spider's silk. Or cows may be used to produce human proteins. In some cases, this practice could produce a protein that is needed by a person who has a genetic disease. However, some scientists worry about the dangers of creating genetically engineered organisms.

Genetic Identification

Your DNA is unique, so it can be used like a fingerprint to identify you. *DNA fingerprinting* identifies the unique patterns in an individual's DNA. DNA samples are now used as evidence in crimes, as shown in **Figure 6.** Similarities between people's DNA can reveal other information, too. For example, DNA can be used to identify family relations or hereditary diseases.

Identical twins have truly identical DNA. Scientists are now able to create something like a twin, called a clone. A *clone* is a new organism that has an exact copy of another organism's genes. Clones of several types of organisms, including some mammals, have been developed by scientists. However, the possibility of cloning humans is still being debated among both scientists and politicians.

Reading Check What is a clone?

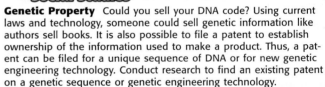

CONNECTION TO Social Studies

Genetic Property Could you sell your DNA code? Using current laws and technology, someone could sell genetic information like authors sell books. It is also possible to file a patent to establish ownership of the information used to make a product. Thus, a patent can be filed for a unique sequence of DNA or for new genetic engineering technology. Conduct research to find an existing patent on a genetic sequence or genetic engineering technology.

SECTION Review

Summary

- A gene is a set of instructions for assembling a protein. DNA is the molecular carrier of these genetic instructions.

- Every organism has DNA in its cells. Humans have about 2 m of DNA in each cell.

- Within a gene, each group of three bases codes for one amino acid. A sequence of amino acids is linked to make a protein.

- Proteins are fundamental to the function of cells and the expression of traits.

- Proteins are assembled within the cytoplasm through a multi-step process that is assisted by several forms of RNA.

- Genes can become mutated when the order of the bases is changed. Three main types of mutations are possible: insertion, deletion, and substitution.

- Genetic knowledge has many practical uses. Some applications of genetic knowledge are controversial.

Using Key Terms

1. Use each of the following terms in the same sentence: *ribosome* and *RNA*.

2. In your own words, write a definition for the term *mutation*.

Understanding Key Ideas

3. Explain the relationship between genes and proteins.

4. List three possible types of mutations.

5. Which type of mutation causes sickle cell anemia?
   a. substitution
   b. insertion
   c. deletion
   d. mutagen

Math Skills

6. A set of 23 chromosomes in a human cell contains 3.2 billion pairs of DNA bases in sequence. On average, about how many pairs of bases are in each chromosome?

Critical Thinking

7. **Applying Concepts** In which cell type might a mutation be passed from generation to generation? Explain.

8. **Making Comparisons** How is genetic engineering different from natural reproduction?

Interpreting Graphics

The illustration below shows a sequence of bases on one strand of a DNA molecule. Use the illustration below to answer the questions that follow.

 A C T C C T G A A

9. How many amino acids are coded for by the sequence on one side (A) of this DNA strand?

10. What is the order of bases on the complementary side of the strand (B), from left to right?

11. If a G were inserted as the first base on the top side (A), what would the order of bases be on the complementary side (B)?

For a variety of links related to this chapter, go to www.scilinks.org

Topic: Genetic Engineering
SciLinks code: HSM0654

WEIRD SCIENCE

Gene therapy is an experimental field of medical research in which defective genes are replaced with healthy genes. One way to insert healthy genes involves using a delivery system called a gene gun to inject microscopic gold bullets coated with genetic material.

CHAPTER RESOURCES

Chapter Resource File

- **Section Quiz** GENERAL
- **Section Review** GENERAL
- **Vocabulary and Section Summary** GENERAL
- **Reinforcement Worksheet** BASIC
- **Critical Thinking** ADVANCED

Technology

- **Interactive Explorations CD-ROM**
  - DNA Pawprints GENERAL

Model-Making Lab

Base-Pair Basics

Base-Pair Basics

Teacher's Notes

Time Required

One 45-minute class period

Lab Ratings

EASY ——————————————→ HARD

Teacher Prep 🧪

Student Set-Up 🧪🧪

Concept Level 🧪

Clean Up 🧪

MATERIALS

The materials listed on the student page are enough for a group of 4–5 students. You may want to provide additional materials for the Applying Your Data section.

Safety Caution

Remind students to review all safety cautions and icons before beginning this lab activity. Students should always exercise care when using scissors.

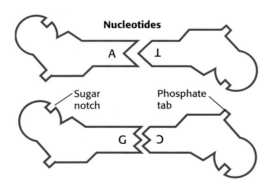

Nucleotides

A ⟨ T

Sugar notch   Phosphate tab

G ⟩ C

OBJECTIVES

Construct a model of a DNA strand.

Model the process of DNA replication.

MATERIALS

- bag, large paper
- paper, colored (4 colors)
- paper, white
- scissors

SAFETY

Base-Pair Basics

You have learned that DNA is shaped something like a twisted ladder. The side rails of the ladder are made of sugar parts and phosphate parts. The two side rails are connected to each other by parts called *bases*. The bases join in pairs to form the rungs of the ladder. Within DNA, each base can pair with only one other base. Each of these pairs is called a *base pair*. When DNA replicates, enzymes separate the base pairs, which breaks the rungs of the ladder in half. Then, each half of the DNA ladder can be used as a template for building a new half. In this activity, you will construct a paper model of DNA and use it to model the replication process.

Procedure

1 Trace the models of nucleotides below onto white paper. Label the pieces "A" (**a**denine), "T" (**t**hymine), "C" (**c**ytosine), and "G" (**g**uanine). Draw the pieces again on colored paper. Use a different color for each type of base. Draw the pieces as large as you want, and draw as many of the white pieces and as many of the colored pieces as time will allow.

2 Carefully cut out all of the pieces.

3 Put all of the colored pieces in the classroom into a large paper bag. Spread all of the white pieces in the classroom onto a large table.

4 Remove nine colored pieces from the bag. Arrange the colored pieces in any order in a straight column so that the letters *A, T, C,* and *G* are right side up. Be sure to fit the sugar notches to the phosphate tabs. Draw this arrangement.

5 Find the white bases that correctly pair with the nine colored bases. Remember the base-pairing rules, and pair the bases according to those rules.

6 Pair the pieces by fitting tabs to notches. The letters on the white pieces should be upside down. You now have a model of a double-stranded piece of DNA. The strand contains nine pairs of complementary nucleotides. Draw your model.

Lab Notes

You may wish to enlarge the nucleotide template for your students so that the models will be easier to cut out. Explain to students that the white pieces and the colored pieces represent the complementary sides of DNA strands. Also, suggest that students refer to the figure depicting DNA replication in their text. Remind students that this is a model of the parts of a DNA molecule and that the parts of real DNA molecules are three-dimensional and have a more complex shape.

CHAPTER RESOURCES

Chapter Resource File

📁 • **Datasheet for Chapter Lab**
  • **Lab Notes and Answers**

Technology

💿 **Classroom Videos**
  • Lab Video

Workbooks

📗 **Whiz-Bang Demonstrations**
  • Grand Strand **GENERAL**

📗 **Long-Term Projects & Research Ideas**
  • The Antifreeze Protein **ADVANCED**
  • Ewe Again, Dolly? **ADVANCED**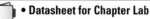

Analyze the Results

1 Identifying Patterns Now, separate the two halves of your DNA strand along the middle of the base pair rungs of the ladder. Keep the side rails together by keeping the sugar notches fitted to the phosphate tabs. Draw this arrangement.

2 Recognizing Patterns Look at the drawing made in the previous step. Along each strand in the drawing, write the letters of the bases that complement the bases in that strand.

3 Examining Data Find all of the bases that you need to complete replication. Find white pieces to pair with the bases on the left, and find colored pieces to pair with the bases on the right. Be sure that the tabs and notches fit and the sides are straight. You have now replicated your model of DNA. Are the two models identical? Draw your results.

Draw Conclusions

4 Interpreting Information State the correct base-pairing rules. How do these rules make DNA replication possible?

5 Evaluating Models What happens when you attempt to pair thymine with guanine? Do they fit together? Are the sides straight? Do all of the tabs and notches fit? Explain.

Applying Your Data

Construct a 3-D model of a DNA molecule that shows DNA's twisted-ladder structure. Use your imagination and creativity to select materials. You may want to use licorice, gum balls, and toothpicks or pipe cleaners and paper clips.

1. Display your model in your classroom.

2. Take a vote to decide which models are the most accurate and the most creative.

Debra Sampson
Booker T. Washington Middle School
Elgin, Texas

Analyze the Results

1. Student drawings should show an "unzipped" DNA strand.

2. Student responses should always show A matched with T and C matched with G.

3. The two new molecules should exactly match each other and match the original molecule.

Draw Conclusions

4. G and C always pair, and A and T always pair. These pairings allow the two halves of a DNA molecule to be separated and replicated and ensure that identical new molecules can be formed.

5. The joining areas of guanine and thymine don't match up. They don't fit together well. The sides of the DNA molecule would not be straight and the parts would not line up if the bases were forced together in this way.

Applying Your Data

1. Student models should be more accurate than any models of DNA that they have previously constructed. Check for the correct "right-handed" orientation of the double-helix spiral, representation of the four base types, correct matching of the base-pairs and subunits, and overall uniformity of the helix.

2. Before voting, have students brainstorm their criteria for "accurate" and "creative." Take a separate vote for each category.

Assignment Guide

Section	Questions
1	4, 5, 10, 13, 15, 16, 20–22
2	1–3, 6–9, 11, 12, 14, 17–19

ANSWERS

Using Key Terms

1. A mutagen is a substance that can cause a mutation in DNA.
2. nucelotides
3. ribosome

Understanding Key Ideas

4. d
5. b
6. b
7. b
8. a
9. b

USING KEY TERMS

1 Use the following terms in the same sentence: *mutation* and *mutagen*.

The statements below are false. For each statement, replace the underlined term to make a true statement.

2 The information in DNA is coded in the order of <u>amino acids</u> along one side of the DNA molecule.

3 The "factory" that assembles proteins based on the DNA code is called a <u>gene</u>.

UNDERSTANDING KEY IDEAS

Multiple Choice

4 James Watson and Francis Crick
  a. took X-ray pictures of DNA.
  b. discovered that genes are in chromosomes.
  c. bred pea plants to study heredity.
  d. made models to figure out DNA's shape.

5 In a DNA molecule, which of the following bases pair together?
  a. adenine and cytosine
  b. thymine and adenine
  c. thymine and guanine
  d. cytosine and thymine

6 A gene can be all of the following EXCEPT
  a. a set of instructions for a trait.
  b. a complete chromosome.
  c. instructions for making a protein.
  d. a portion of a strand of DNA.

7 Which of the following statements about DNA is NOT true?
  a. DNA is found in all organisms.
  b. DNA is made up of five subunits.
  c. DNA has a structure like a twisted ladder.
  d. Mistakes can be made when DNA is copied.

8 Within the cell, where are proteins assembled?
  a. the cytoplasm
  b. the nucleus
  c. the amino acids
  d. the chromosomes

9 Changes in the type or order of the bases in DNA are called
  a. nucleotides.
  b. mutations.
  c. RNA.
  d. genes.

Short Answer

10 What would be the complementary strand of DNA for the following sequence of bases?

C T T A G G C T T A C C A

11 If the DNA sequence TGAGCCATGA is changed to TGAGCACATGA, what kind of mutation has occurred?

12 Explain how the DNA in genes relates to the traits of an organism.

13 Why is DNA frequently found associated with proteins inside of cells?

14 What is the difference between DNA and RNA?

10. GAATCCGAATGGT
11. an insertion
12. The DNA in genes codes for specific proteins, and proteins control cells and result in traits.
13. because proteins do much of the work of copying and handling the DNA

14. DNA is deoxyribonucleic acid, and exact copies of a set of DNA are found in each cell of an organism. RNA is ribonucleic acid, which is similar to DNA but is used to carry copies of DNA code around the cell and to build proteins based on this code.

CRITICAL THINKING

15 **Concept Mapping** Use the following terms to create a concept map: *bases, adenine, thymine, nucleotides, guanine, DNA,* and *cytosine*.

16 **Analyzing Processes** Draw and label a picture that explains how DNA is copied.

17 **Analyzing Processes** Draw and label a picture that explains how proteins are made.

18 **Applying Concepts** The following DNA sequence codes for how many amino acids?

T C A G C C A C C T A T G G A

19 **Making Inferences** Why does the government make laws about the use of chemicals that are known to be mutagens?

INTERPRETING GRAPHICS

The illustration below shows the process of replication of a DNA strand. Use this illustration to answer the questions that follow.

20 Which strands are part of the original molecule?

a. A and B
b. A and C
c. A and D
d. None of the above

21 Which strands are new?

a. A and B
b. B and C
c. C and D
d. None of the above

22 Which strands are complementary?

a. A and C
b. B and C
c. All of the strands
d. None of the strands

Critical Thinking

15. An answer to this exercise can be found at the end of this book.

16. Student drawings should resemble the diagram of replication in their student text and should have appropriate labels.

17. Student drawings should resemble the diagram of protein assembly in their student text and should have appropriate labels.

18. This sequence codes for five amino acids.

19. Sample answer: The government is trying to protect people from the risk of mutagens causing harmful mutations in people's cells—mutations could cause a disease such as cancer.

Interpreting Graphics

20. c
21. b
22. b

Standardized Test Preparation

EOG Prep

Teacher's Note

To provide practice under more realistic testing conditions, give students 20 minutes to answer all of the questions in this Standardized Test Preparation.

MISCONCEPTION ALERT

Answers to the standardized test preparation can help you identify student misconceptions and misunderstandings.

READING

Passage 1

1. B
2. H

✚ TEST DOCTOR

Question 2: This question asks for the main idea of the second paragraph. Main ideas are often introduced or summarized in the first sentence of a paragraph, and sometimes summarized or rephrased in the last sentence of a paragraph. The first sentence of the second paragraph is closest in meaning to answer H. Students who chose answer I may have looked for clues in the last sentence of the paragraph but missed the contradiction indicated by the use of "however." For this type of question, advise students to reread the first and last sentences and check for contradictions before choosing an answer.

READING

Read each of the passages below. Then, answer the questions that follow each passage.

Passage 1 The tension in the courtroom was so thick that you could cut it with a knife. The prosecuting attorney presented this evidence: "DNA analysis indicates that blood found on the defendant's shoes matches the blood of the victim. The odds of this match happening by chance are 1 in 20 million." The jury members were stunned by these figures. Can there be any doubt that the defendant is guilty?

DNA is increasingly used as evidence in court cases. Traditional fingerprinting has been used for more than 100 years, and it has been an extremely important identification tool. Recently, DNA fingerprinting, also called *DNA profiling,* has started to replace traditional techniques. DNA profiling has been used to clear thousands of wrongly accused or convicted individuals. However, there is some controversy over whether DNA evidence should be used to prove a suspect's guilt.

1. What does the first sentence in this passage describe?
   A the air pollution in a particular place
   B the feeling that a person might experience during an event
   C the motion of an object
   D the reason that a person was probably guilty of a crime

2. Which of the following best describes the main idea of the second paragraph of this passage?
   F A defendant was proven guilty by DNA analysis.
   G Court battles involving DNA fingerprinting are very exciting.
   H The technique of DNA profiling is increasingly used in court cases.
   I The technique of DNA profiling is controversial.

Passage 2 Most of the biochemicals found in living things are proteins. In fact, other than water, proteins are the most abundant molecules in your cells. Proteins have many functions, including regulating chemical activities, transporting and storing materials, and providing structural support.

Every protein is composed of small "building blocks" called *amino acids.* Amino acids are molecules that are composed of carbon, hydrogen, oxygen, and nitrogen atoms. Some amino acids also include sulfur atoms. Amino acids chemically bond to form proteins of many shapes and sizes.

The function of a protein depends on the shape of the bonded amino acids. If even a single amino acid is missing or out of place, the protein may not function correctly or may not function. Foods such as meat, fish, cheese, and beans contain proteins, which are broken down into amino acids as the foods are digested. Your body can then use these amino acids to make new proteins.

1. In the passage, what does *biochemical* mean?
   A a chemical found in nonliving things
   B a chemical found in living things
   C a pair of chemicals
   D a protein

2. According to the passage, which of the following statements is true?
   F Amino acids contain carbon dioxide.
   G Amino acids contain proteins.
   H Proteins are made of living things.
   I Proteins are made of amino acids.

Passage 2

1. B
2. I

✚ TEST DOCTOR

Question 1: From the first sentence, one can infer that biochemicals are something found in living things and that proteins are one type of biochemical. Hence, the most likely meaning is answer B. Answer A is contradictory to the sentence. Answer C wrongly assumes that the "bi" in "biochemical" means "two." Answer D is a reasonable guess, but answer B best reflects the inference from the first sentence. Remind students to carefully read all answers and compare each with the question and the passage before deciding.

INTERPRETING GRAPHICS

The diagram below shows an original sequence of DNA and three possible mutations. Use the diagram to answer the questions that follow.

Original sequence

Mutation A

Mutation B

Mutation C

1. In which mutation was an original base pair replaced?
   A Mutation A
   B Mutation B
   C Mutation C
   D There is not enough information to determine the answer.

2. In which mutation was a new base pair added?
   F Mutation A
   G Mutation B
   H Mutation C
   I There is not enough information to determine the answer.

3. In which mutation was an original base pair removed?
   A Mutation A
   B Mutation B
   C Mutation C
   D There is not enough information to determine the answer.

MATH

Read each question below, and choose the best answer.

1. Mary was making a design on top of her desk with marbles. She put 3 marbles in the first row, 7 marbles in the second row, 15 marbles in the third row, and 31 marbles in the fourth row. If Mary continues this pattern, how many marbles will she put in the seventh row?
   A 46
   B 63
   C 127
   D 255

2. Bobby walked 3 1/2 km on Saturday, 2 1/3 km on Sunday, and 1 km on Monday. How many kilometers did Bobby walk on those 3 days?
   F 5 1/6
   G 5 5/6
   H 6 1/6
   I 6 5/6

3. Marie bought a new aquarium for her goldfish. The aquarium is 60 cm long, 20 cm wide, and 30 cm high. Which equation could be used to find the volume of water needed to fill the aquarium to 25 cm deep?

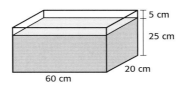

   A $V = 30 \times 60 \times 20$
   B $V = 25 \times 60 \times 20$
   C $V = 30 \times 60 \times 20 - 5$
   D $V = 30 \times 60 \times 25$

4. How is the product of $6 \times 6 \times 6 \times 4 \times 4 \times 4$ expressed in scientific notation?
   F $6^4 \times 3^6$
   G $6^3 \times 4^3$
   H $3^6 \times 3^4$
   I 24^6

Standardized Test Preparation

INTERPRETING GRAPHICS

1. B
2. F
3. C

 **TEST DOCTOR**

Question 1: The student must recognize that, in Mutation B, the only change from the original sequence is a different base-pair in the middle of the sequence—a replacement. Mutation A is an insertion, and Mutation C is a deletion.

MATH

1. D
2. I
3. B
4. G

TEST DOCTOR

Question 1: The problem requires students to predict the next three values in a patterned sequence of numbers. The pattern is as follows:

3, 7, 15, 31, . . .

The logic of the pattern is to multiply each number by 2 and then add 1 to get the next number. Thus,

1	3
2	$(3 \times 2) + 1 = 7$
3	$(7 \times 2) + 1 = 15$
4	$(15 \times 2) + 1 = 31$
5	$(31 \times 2) + 1 = 63$
6	$(63 \times 2) + 1 = 127$
7	$(127 \times 2) + 1 = 255$

Question 3: The problem asks for the equation to find the volume of water in the aquarium, which is a rectangular box. The equation for the volume of a rectangular box is *length × width × height* (in any order). The problem and the diagram indicate that the depth of water needed is only 25 cm, so the value to use for *height* is 25 cm. Answer B uses the correct values in the order *height × length × width*.

Science in Action

Scientific Debate

Background

The U.S. Food and Drug Administration began approving genetically modified organisms (GMOs) for consumer use in the 1990s. Some consumer groups have protested and boycotted such foods. Several countries around the world have banned the creation, sale, or importation of GMOs. Some consumer groups have asked that all GMO foods be clearly labeled. The majority of GMO foods being sold in the United States are made with corn or soybeans that contain bacterial genes.

Scientists have mixed opinions about GMOs. However, most scientists recognize that the potential to create new and unknown types of organisms should be undertaken with careful scientific scrutiny, should involve ethical considerations, and should be regulated by governments.

Science Fiction

ACTIVITY ——— ADVANCED

Further Reading If students liked this story, encourage them to read more of McKillip's stories, such as the following:

• *Fool's Run,* Warner, 1987

• *Something Rich and Strange,* Bantam, 1994

• *Winter Rose,* Ace, 1996

Scientific Debate

Supersquash or Frankenfruit?

Some food that you buy may have been developed in a new way. Food producers may use genetic engineering to make food crops easier to grow or sell, more nutritious, or resistant to pests and disease. More than half of the packaged foods sold in the United States are likely to contain ingredients from genetically modified organisms.

The U.S. government has stated that research shows that these foods are safe. But some scientists are concerned that genes introduced into crop plants could cause new environmental or health problems. For example, people who are allergic to peanuts might also be allergic to tomato plants that contain peanut genes.

Math ACTIVITY

Write a survey about genetically altered foods. Ask your teacher to approve your questions. Ask at least 15 people to answer your survey. Create graphs to summarize your results.

Science Fiction

"Moby James" by Patricia A. McKillip

Rob Trask and his family live on a space station. Rob thinks that his real brother was sent back to Earth. The person who claims to be his brother, James, is really either some sort of mutated plant or a mutant pair of dirty sweat socks.

Now, Rob has another problem—his class is reading Herman Melville's novel *Moby Dick.* As he reads the novel, Rob becomes convinced that his brother is a great white mutant whale—Moby James. To see how Rob solves his problems, read "Moby James" in the *Holt Anthology of Science Fiction.*

Language Arts ACTIVITY

WRITING SKILL Read "Moby James" by Patricia A. McKillip. Then, write your own short science-fiction story about a mutant organism. Be sure to incorporate some science into your science fiction.

Answer to Math Activity

Check that student surveys ask questions for which answers can be easily tallied, such as "Do you think that genetically modified foods should be labeled in the store?" Check that students have kept records and summarized their results accurately. Give them feedback about how well their graphs communicate the data they gathered.

Answer to Language Arts Activity

Instead of collecting and grading students' stories, you may want to have them read their stories to each other or to a family member, and then ask for feedback about how much science is included in their fiction.

People in Science

Lydia Villa-Komaroff

Genetic Researcher When Lydia Villa-Komaroff was young, science represented "a kind of refuge" for her. She grew up in a very large family that lived in a very small house. "I always wanted to find things out. I was one of those kids who took things apart."

In college, Villa-Komaroff became very interested in the process of embryonic development—how a simple egg grows into a complex animal. This interest led her to study genes and the way that genes code for proteins. For example, insulin is a protein that is normally produced by the human body. Often, people who suffer from diabetes lack the insulin gene, so their bodies can't make insulin. These people may need to inject insulin into their blood as a drug treatment.

Before the research by Villa-Komaroff's team was done, insulin was difficult to produce. Villa-Komaroff's team isolated the human gene that codes for insulin. Then, the scientists inserted the normal human insulin gene into the DNA of bacteria. This inserted gene caused the bacteria to produce insulin. This technique was a new and more efficient way to produce insulin. Now, most of the insulin used for diabetes treatment is made in this way. Many genetic researchers dream of making breakthroughs like the one that Villa-Komaroff made in her work with insulin.

Social Studies ACTiViTY

WRITING SKILL Do some research about several women, such as Marie Curie, Barbara McClintock, or Maxine Frank Singer, who have done important scientific research. Write a short biography about one of these women.

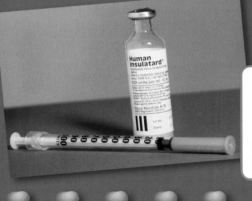

To learn more about these Science in Action topics, visit go.hrw.com and type in the keyword HL5DNAF.

Check out Current Science® articles related to this chapter by visiting go.hrw.com. Just type in the keyword HL5CS06.

Answer to Social Studies Activity

Suggest that students do research in the library or on the Internet for information. Additional women scientists to consider are as follows:

• Jewel Plummer Cobb
• Ruth Fulton Benedict
• Emma Perry Carr
• Rosalyn Yalow

Check student biographies for accuracy, and comment on any interesting facts.

People in Science

Background

Lydia Villa-Komaroff grew up in Santa Fe, New Mexico, in a household that loved to tell family stories. One favorite was the story of Villa-Komaroff's grandfather, Encarnacion Villa, and his brush with the Mexican revolutionary Pancho Villa. Encarnacion was going to be killed by Pancho Villa's soldiers when he refused to join their fight. But when Pancho Villa heard the captive's name, he ordered his release but told him he must have many sons. Pancho Villa probably could not imagine that a granddaughter of his former captive would someday become the third Mexican-American woman to earn a Ph.D. in the United States and would go on to make many important contributions to science.

When Lydia Villa-Komaroff and her colleagues inserted the human gene that directs the production of insulin into the DNA of bacteria, they were using recombinant DNA technology. In recombinant DNA technology, researchers identify which segment of DNA is the gene that directs the production of the desired substance, cut this section out of the DNA with special enzymes, and make copies, or clones. The researchers then take one of these clones and insert it, again using special enzymes, into the correct spot on the host DNA. The researchers look for a location on the host DNA that will ensure that the host organism will read the DNA and produce the substance.

Motion, Forces, and Work

It's hard to imagine a world where nothing ever moves or where there are no machines. In this unit, you will learn about the relationship between force and motion and explore the scientific meaning of *work.* You will learn how to describe the motion of objects, how forces affect motion, how fluids exert force, and how machines make work easier. This timeline shows some events and discoveries that have occurred as scientists have advanced their understanding of the motion of objects here on Earth and in space, of work, and of machines.

Around 250 BCE

Archimedes, a Greek mathematician, develops the principle that bears his name. The principle relates the buoyant force on an object in a fluid to the amount of fluid displaced by the object.

1764

In London, Wolfgang Amadeus Mozart composes his first symphony—at the age of 8.

1846

After determining that the orbit of Uranus is different from what is predicted from the law of universal gravitation, scientists discover Neptune whose gravitational force is causing Uranus's unusual orbit.

1947

While flying a Bell X-1 rocket-powered airplane, American pilot Chuck Yeager becomes the first human to travel faster than the speed of sound.

PHILOSOPHIÆ
NATURALIS
PRINCIPIA
MATHEMATICA.

Autore JS. NEWTON, Trin. Coll. Cantab. Soc. Matheseos
Professore Lucasiano, & Societatis Regalis Sodali.

Around 240 BCE

Chinese astronomers are the first to record a sighting of Halley's Comet.

1519

Portuguese explorer Ferdinand Magellan begins the first voyage around the world.

1687

Sir Isaac Newton, a British mathematician and scientist, publishes *Principia*, a book describing his laws of motion and the law of universal gravitation.

1905

While employed as a patent clerk, German physicist Albert Einstein publishes his special theory of relativity. The theory states that the speed of light is constant no matter what the reference frame is.

1921

Bessie Coleman becomes the first African American woman licensed to fly an airplane.

1971

American astronaut Alan Shepard takes a break from gathering lunar data to play golf on the moon during the *Apollo 14* mission.

1990

The *Magellan* spacecraft begins orbiting Venus for a four-year mission to map the planet. By using the sun's gravitational forces, it propels itself to Venus without burning much fuel.

2003

NASA launches *Spirit* and *Opportunity,* two Mars Exploration Rovers, to study Mars.

Motion, Forces, and Work   **455**

Compression guide:
To shorten instruction
because of time limitations,
omit the Chapter Lab.

OBJECTIVES	LABS, DEMONSTRATIONS, AND ACTIVITIES	TECHNOLOGY RESOURCES
PACING • 90 min pp. 456–463 **Chapter Opener**	**SE Start-up Activity,** p. 457 GENERAL	**OSP Parent Letter** GENERAL **CD Student Edition on CD-ROM** **CD Guided Reading Audio CD** **TR Chapter Starter Transparency*** **VID Brain Food Video Quiz**
Section 1 Measuring Motion • Describe the motion of an object by the position of the object in relation to a reference point. • Identify the two factors that determine speed. • Explain the difference between speed and velocity. • Analyze the relationship between velocity and acceleration. • Demonstrate that changes in motion can be measured and represented on a graph.	**TE Demonstration** Models, p. 458 GENERAL **SE School-to-Home Activity** What's Your Speed?, p. 459 GENERAL **TE Connection Activity** Math, p. 459 GENERAL **TE Activity** The Speed of Light, p. 460 ADVANCED **TE Activity** Diagramming Acceleration, p. 461 BASIC **SE Skills Practice Lab** Detecting Acceleration, p. 484 GENERAL **SE Skills Practice Lab** Built for Speed, p. 609 GENERAL **LB Calculator-Based Labs,** The Fast Track ADVANCED **LB Calculator-Based Labs,** Graphing Your Motion ADVANCED	**CRF Lesson Plans*** **TR Bellringer Transparency*** **TR** A Graph Showing Speed* **TR** Finding Resultant Velocity* **TR** Calculating Average Acceleration* **TR** A Graph Showing Acceleration* **CRF SciLinks Activity*** GENERAL **CD Interactive Explorations CD-ROM** Force in the Forest GENERAL **VID Lab Videos for Physical Science**
PACING • 45 min pp. 464–469 **Section 2 What Is a Force?** • Describe forces, and explain how forces act on objects. • Determine the net force when more than one force is acting on an object. • Compare balanced and unbalanced forces. • Describe ways that unbalanced forces cause changes in motion.	**TE Activity** Bridge Building, p. 464 GENERAL **SE Science in Action** Math, Social Studies, and Language Arts Activities, pp. 490–491 GENERAL	**CRF Lesson Plans*** **TR Bellringer Transparency*** **TR** Forces in the Same Direction/Forces in Opposite Directions*
PACING • 45 min pp. 470–475 **Section 3 Friction: A Force That Opposes Motion** • Explain why friction occurs. • List the two types of friction, and give examples of each type. • Explain how friction can be both harmful and helpful.	**TE Activity** Fingerprints, p. 470 GENERAL **SE Quick Lab** The Friction 500, p. 471 GENERAL **SE School-to-Home Activity** Comparing Friction, p. 472 GENERAL **TE Connection Activity** Real World, p. 472 ADVANCED **SE Quick Lab** Reducing Friction, p. 474 GENERAL **SE Skills Practice Lab** Science Friction, p. 611 GENERAL	**CRF Lesson Plans*** **TR Bellringer Transparency*** **TR** Force and Friction* **TR** Static Friction* **SE Internet Activity,** p. 473 GENERAL **CD Interactive Explorations CD-ROM** Stranger Than Friction GENERAL
PACING • 45 min pp. 476–483 **Section 4 Gravity: A Force of Attraction** • Describe gravity and its effect on matter. • Explain the law of universal gravitation. • Explain how an object's center of mass is used to determine gravitational force. • Describe the difference between mass and weight.	**TE Group Activity** Gravity Poster, p. 476 GENERAL **TE Demonstration** Modeling Gravity, p. 477 ◆ GENERAL **TE Connection Activity** Math, p. 478 ADVANCED **TE Activity** Story Analysis, p. 479 GENERAL **SE Skills Practice Lab** Relating Mass and Weight, p. 610 GENERAL **LB Long-Term Projects & Research Ideas** ADVANCED	**CRF Lesson Plans*** **TR Bellringer Transparency*** **TR** LINK TO EARTH SCIENCE Tidal Variations* **TR** Gravitational Force Depends on Mass/Gravitational Force Depends on Distance* **TR** Weight and Mass*

PACING • 90 min

CHAPTER REVIEW, ASSESSMENT, AND STANDARDIZED TEST PREPARATION

CRF Vocabulary Activity* GENERAL
SE Chapter Review, pp. 486–487 GENERAL
CRF Chapter Review* ■ GENERAL
CRF Chapter Tests A* ■ GENERAL, **B*** ADVANCED, **C*** SPECIAL NEEDS
SE Standardized Test Preparation, pp. 488–489 GENERAL
CRF Standardized Test Preparation* GENERAL
CRF Performance-Based Assessment* GENERAL
OSP Test Generator GENERAL
CRF Test Item Listing* GENERAL

Online and Technology Resources

Visit **go.hrw.com** for a variety of free resources related to this textbook. Enter the keyword **HT5R7MON.**

 Holt Online Learning

Students can access interactive problem-solving help and active visual concept development with the *Holt Science and Technology* Online Edition available at **www.hrw.com.**

 Guided Reading Audio CD

These CDs are designed to help auditory learners and reluctant readers.

 Science Tutor CD-ROM

Excellent for remediation and test practice.

SKILLS DEVELOPMENT RESOURCES	SECTION REVIEW AND ASSESSMENT	STANDARDS CORRELATIONS
SE Pre-Reading Activity, p. 456 `GENERAL` **OSP** Science Puzzlers, Twisters & Teasers `GENERAL`		North Carolina Standard Course of Study
CRF Directed Reading A* `BASIC`, B* `SPECIAL NEEDS` **CRF** Vocabulary and Section Summary* `GENERAL` **SE** Reading Strategy Discussion, p. 458 `GENERAL` **TE** Inclusion Strategies, p. 459 **SE** Math Focus Calculating Average Speed, p. 460 `GENERAL` **TE** Reading Strategy Writing Activity, p. 460 `GENERAL` **TE** Reading Strategy Prediction Guide, p. 461 `GENERAL` **SE** Math Practice Calculating Acceleration, p. 462 `GENERAL` **MS** Math Skills for Science The Unit Factor and Dimensional Analysis,* Average Speed in a Pinewood Derby* `GENERAL` **SS** Science Skills Organizing Your Research* `GENERAL` **CRF** Reinforcement Worksheet Bug Race* `BASIC`	**SE** Reading Checks, pp. 458, 460, 462 `GENERAL` **TE** Homework, p. 459 `ADVANCED` **TE** Homework, p. 461 `GENERAL` **TE** Reteaching, p. 462 `BASIC` **TE** Quiz, p. 462 `GENERAL` **TE** Alternative Assessment, p. 462 `GENERAL` **SE** Section Review,* p. 463 ■ `GENERAL` **CRF** Section Quiz* ■ `GENERAL`	6.04, 6.05; *Chapter Lab:* 1.03, 1.05, 6.05; *LabBook:* 1.02, 1.03
CRF Directed Reading A* `BASIC`, B* `SPECIAL NEEDS` **CRF** Vocabulary and Section Summary* `GENERAL` **SE** Reading Strategy Reading Organizer, p. 464 `GENERAL` **TE** Reading Strategy Prediction Guide, p. 465 `GENERAL`	**SE** Reading Checks, pp. 465, 466, 468 `GENERAL` **TE** Reteaching, p. 468 `BASIC` **TE** Quiz, p. 468 `GENERAL` **TE** Alternative Assessment, p. 468 `GENERAL` **SE** Section Review,* p. 469 ■ `GENERAL` **CRF** Section Quiz* ■ `GENERAL`	6.03, 6.06
CRF Directed Reading A* `BASIC`, B* `SPECIAL NEEDS` **CRF** Vocabulary and Section Summary* `GENERAL` **SE** Reading Strategy Brainstorming, p. 470 `GENERAL` **TE** Inclusion Strategies, p. 472 **SE** Connection to Social Studies Invention of the Wheel, p. 473 `GENERAL` **CRF** Reinforcement Worksheet Friction Action* `BASIC`	**SE** Reading Checks, pp. 471, 473, 474 `GENERAL` **TE** Homework, p. 473 `GENERAL` **TE** Reteaching, p. 474 `BASIC` **TE** Quiz, p. 474 `GENERAL` **TE** Alternative Assessment, p. 474 `GENERAL` **SE** Section Review,* p. 475 ■ `GENERAL` **CRF** Section Quiz* ■ `GENERAL`	1.03, 1.05, 6.03; *LabBook:* 1.01, 1.03
CRF Directed Reading A* `BASIC`, B* `SPECIAL NEEDS` **CRF** Vocabulary and Section Summary* `GENERAL` **SE** Reading Strategy Paired Summarizing, p. 476 `GENERAL` **TE** Reading Strategy Prediction Guide, p. 477 `GENERAL` **SE** Connection to Astronomy Black Holes, p. 478 `GENERAL` **SE** Connection to Language Arts Gravity Story, p. 481 `GENERAL` **CRF** Reinforcement Worksheet A Weighty Problem* `BASIC` **CRF** Critical Thinking A Mission in Motion* `ADVANCED`	**SE** Reading Checks, pp. 477, 478, 481, 482 `GENERAL` **TE** Reteaching, p. 482 `BASIC` **TE** Quiz, p. 482 `GENERAL` **TE** Alternative Assessment, p. 482 `GENERAL` **SE** Section Review,* p. 483 ■ `GENERAL` **CRF** Section Quiz* ■ `GENERAL`	6.05

One-Stop Planner® CD-ROM

This convenient CD-ROM includes:
- Lab Materials QuickList Software
- Holt Calendar Planner
- Customizable Lesson Plans
- Printable Worksheets
- ExamView® Test Generator

cnnstudentnews.com

Find the latest news, lesson plans, and activities related to important scientific events.

www.scilinks.org

Maintained by the **National Science Teachers Association.** See Chapter Enrichment pages for a complete list of topics.

Current Science®

Check out *Current Science* articles and activities by visiting the HRW Web site at **go.hrw.com**. Just type in the keyword **HP5CS05T.**

Classroom Videos

- **Lab Videos** demonstrate the chapter lab.
- **Brain Food Video Quizzes** help students review the chapter material.
- **CNN Videos** bring science into your students' daily life.

Visual Resources

TEACHING TRANSPARENCIES

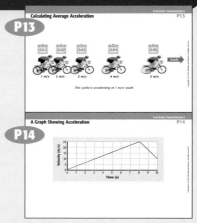

P19 — Weight and Mass

P11 — A Graph Showing Speed

P13 — Calculating Average Acceleration

P12 — Finding Resultant Velocity

P14 — A Graph Showing Acceleration

TEACHING TRANSPARENCIES

P15 — Forces in the Same Direction / Forces in Opposite Directions

P16 — Force and Friction

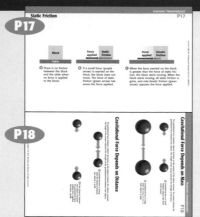

P17 — Static Friction

P18 — Gravitational Force Depends on Distance / Gravitational Force Depends on Mass

E57 — Tidal Variations: Spring Tides; Neap Tides

Spring Tides During spring tides, the gravitational forces of the sun and moon pull on the Earth either from the same direction (left) or from opposite directions (right).

Neap Tides During neap tides, the sun and moon are at right angles with respect to the Earth. This arrangement lessens their gravitational effect on the Earth.

LINK TO EARTH SCIENCE

Chapter: The Movement of Ocean Water

CONCEPT MAPPING TRANSPARENCY

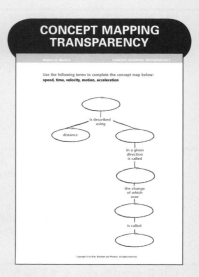

Use the following terms to complete the concept map below: speed, time, velocity, motion, acceleration

is described using · distance · in a given direction is called · the change of which over · is called

Planning Resources

LESSON PLANS

Lesson Plan SAMPLE

Section: Waves

Pacing
Regular Schedule: with lab(s):2 days without lab(s):2 days
Block Schedule: with lab(s):1 1/2 days without lab(s):1 day

Objectives
1. Relate the seven properties of a living organism.
2. Describe seven themes that can help you to organize what you learn about biology.
3. Identify the tiny structures that make up all living organisms.
4. Differentiate between reproduction and heredity and between metabolism and homeostasis.

National Science Education Standards Covered
LSInter4:Cells have particular structures that underlie their functions.
LSMat1:Most cell functions involve chemical reactions.
LSBeh1:Cells store and use information to guide their functions.
UCP1:Cell functions are regulated.
SI1: Cells can differentiate and form complete multicellular organisms.
PS1: Species evolve over time.
ESS1: The great diversity of organisms is the result of more than 3.5 billion years of evolution.
ESS2: Natural selection and its evolutionary consequences provide a scientific explanation for the fossil record of ancient life forms as well as for the striking molecular similarities observed among the diverse species of living organisms.
ST1: The millions of different species of plants, animals, and microorganisms that live on Earth today are related by descent from common ancestors.
ST2: The energy for life primarily comes from the sun.
SPSP1:The complexity and organization of organisms accommodates the need for obtaining, transforming, transporting, releasing, and eliminating the matter and energy used to sustain the organisms.
SPSP6: As matter and energy flows through different levels of organization of living systems—cells, organs, communities—and between living systems and the physical environment, chemical elements are recombined in different ways.
HNS1: Organisms have behavioral responses to internal changes and to external stimuli.

PARENT LETTER

SAMPLE

Dear Parent,

Your son's or daughter's science class will soon begin exploring the chapter entitled "The World of Physical Science." In this chapter, students will learn about how the scientific method applies to the world of physical science and the role of physical science in the world. By the end of the chapter, students should demonstrate a clear understanding of the chapter's main ideas and be able to discuss the following topics:

1. physical science as the study of energy and matter (Section 1)
2. the role of physical science in the world around them (Section 1)
3. careers that rely on physical science (Section 1)
4. the steps used in the scientific method (Section 2)
5. examples of technology (Section 2)
6. how the scientific method is used to answer questions and solve problems (Section 2)
7. how our knowledge of science changes over time (Section 2)
8. how models represent real objects or systems (Section 3)
9. examples of different ways models are used in science (Section 3)
10. the importance of the International System of Units (Section 4)
11. the appropriate units to use for particular measurements (Section 4)
12. how area and density are derived quantities (Section 4)

Questions to Ask Along the Way

You can help your son or daughter learn about these topics by asking interesting questions such as the following:

• What are some surprising careers that use physical science?
• What is a characteristic of a good hypothesis?
• When is it a good idea to use a model?
• Why do Americans measure things in terms of inches and yards instead of centimeters and meters ?

TEST ITEM LISTING

TEST ITEM LISTING
The World of Science SAMPLE

MULTIPLE CHOICE

1. A limitation of models is that
   a. they are large enough to see.
   b. they do not exactly like the things that they model.
   c. they are smaller than the things that they model.
   d. they model unfamiliar things.
   Answer: B Difficulty: 1 Section: 3 Objective: 2

2. The length 10 m is equal to
   a. 100 cm. c. 10,000 mm.
   b. 1,000 cm. d. Both (b) and (c)
   Answer: B Difficulty: 1 Section: 3 Objective: 2

3. To be valid, a hypothesis must be
   a. testable. c. made into a law.
   b. supported by evidence. d. Both (a) and (b)
   Answer: B Difficulty: 1 Section: 2 Objective: 2 · 1

4. The statement "Sheila has a stain on her shirt" is an example of a(n)
   a. law. c. observation.
   b. hypothesis. d. prediction.
   Answer: B Difficulty: 1 Section: 1 Objective: 2

5. A hypothesis is often developed out of
   a. observations. c. laws.
   b. experiments. d. Both (a) and (b)
   Answer: B Difficulty: 1 Section: 2 Objective: 2

6. How many milliliters are in 3.5 kL?
   a. 3,500 mL. c. 3,500, 000 mL.
   b. 0.0035 mL. d. 35,000 mL.
   Answer: B Difficulty: 1 Section: 3 Objective: 2

7. A map of Seattle is an example of a
   a. law. c. model.
   b. theory. d. unit.
   Answer: B Difficulty: 1 Section: 3 Objective: 2

8. A lab has the safety icons shown below. These icons mean that you should wear
   a. only safety goggles. c. safety goggles and a lab apron.
   b. only a lab apron. d. safety goggles, a lab apron, and gloves.
   Answer: B Difficulty: 3 Section: 3 Objective: 2

9. The law of conservation of mass says the lot of mass before a chemical change is
   a. more than the total mass after the change.
   b. less than the total mass after the change.
   c. the same as the total mass after the change.
   d. not the same as the total mass after the change.
   Answer: B Difficulty: 1 Section: 1 Objective: 2

10. In which of the following areas might you find a geochemist at work?
    a. studying the chemistry of rocks c. studying helm
    b. studying forestry d. studying the atmosphere
    Answer: B Difficulty: 1 Section: 3 Objective: 2

One-Stop Planner® CD-ROM

This CD-ROM includes all of the resources shown here and the following time-saving tools:

• *Lab Materials QuickList Software*
• *Customizable lesson plans*
• *Holt Calendar Planner*
• *The powerful ExamView® Test Generator*

Meeting Individual Needs

DIRECTED READING A
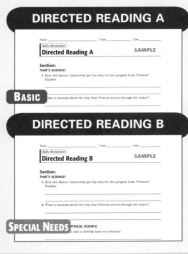

Name ___ Class ___ Date ___
Skills Worksheet
Directed Reading A   SAMPLE

Section:
THAT'S SCIENCE!
1. How did James Czarnowski get his idea for the penguin boat, Proteus? Explain.

that is unusual about the way that Proteus moves through the water?

BASIC

DIRECTED READING B

Name ___ Class ___ Date ___
Skills Worksheet
Directed Reading B   SAMPLE

Section:
THAT'S SCIENCE!
1. How did James Czarnowski get his idea for the penguin boat, Proteus? Explain.

2. What is unusual about the way that Proteus moves through the water?

PHYSICAL SCIENCE

SPECIAL NEEDS

VOCABULARY ACTIVITY
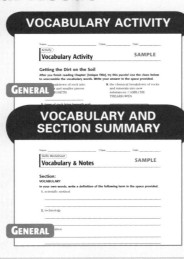

Name ___ Class ___ Date ___
Activity
Vocabulary Activity   SAMPLE

Getting the Dirt on the Soil
After you finish reading Chapter: [Unique Title], try this puzzle! Use the clues below to unscramble the vocabulary words. Write your answer in the space provided.

breakdown of rock into   9. the chemical breakdown of rocks
smaller pieces.   and minerals into new
GNETH   substances. CAMILCHE
   THEARIGWEN

GENERAL

VOCABULARY AND SECTION SUMMARY

Name ___ Class ___ Date ___
Skills Worksheet
Vocabulary & Notes   SAMPLE

Section:
VOCABULARY
In your own words, write a definition of the following term in the space provided.

1. scientific method

2. technology

GENERAL

REINFORCEMENT
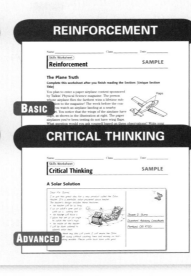

Name ___ Class ___ Date ___
Skills Worksheet
Reinforcement   SAMPLE

The Plane Truth
Complete this worksheet after you finish reading the Section: [Unique Section Title]

You plan to enter a paper airplane contest sponsored by Talkin' Physical Science magazine. The person whose airplane flies the farthest wins a lifetime subscription to the magazine! The week before the contest, you watch an airplane landing at a nearby airport. You notice that the wings of the airplane have flaps, as shown in the illustration at right. The paper airplanes you've been testing do not have wing flaps. What question would you ask yourself based on these observations? Write your own question now!

BASIC

CRITICAL THINKING

Name ___ Class ___ Date ___
Skills Worksheet
Critical Thinking   SAMPLE

A Solar Solution

ADVANCED

SCILINKS ACTIVITY

Name ___ Class ___ Date ___
Activity
SciLinks Activity   SAMPLE

MARINE ECOSYSTEMS
Go to www.scilinks.org. To find links related to marine ecosystems, type in the keyword HL5499. Then, use the links to answer the questions about marine ecosystems.

percentage of the Earth's surface is covered by water?

GENERAL

SCIENCE PUZZLERS, TWISTERS & TEASERS

CHAPTER
5   SCIENCE PUZZLERS, TWISTERS & TEASERS
Matter in Motion

Daffy Definitions
1. Below are some really silly definitions for words found in the chapter. The number after each word shows the number of letters in the answer. See how many you can solve!

a. A very weighty subject – (7) ___
b. Opposite of a lubrican (9) ___
c. Web propulsion (8) ___
d. Roman "fire," (new metropolis (8) ___
e. Presently falling forward, also (10)
___
f. light of 2,000 frecs (8) ___
g. Playground pastime, type of friction (7)

GENERAL

Labs and Activities

LONG-TERM PROJECTS & RESEARCH IDEAS

Name ___ Date ___ Class ___
PROJECT
55   STUDENT WORKSHEET   DESIGN YOUR OWN
Tiny Troubles

The evil Dr. Monnie Mizer has shrunk you to the size of a small mouse with her incredible shrink ray! She's left you on her desk, which is too high for you to climb down. The nearest piece of furniture is a bookshelf 25 cm away. On the shelf is a lamp with a cord that you are pretty certain you can climb down. You could easily escape if you could just reach that lamp. But, you are unable to make such a long jump. The only things on the desktop are a small bottle of glue and several boxes of toothpicks. Suddenly, you have an idea. If you can use the glue and the toothpicks to build a bridge across the gaping chasm, you could flee to safety. You better hurry, because Dr. Mizer's cat, Snacker, may show up any minute now!

Toothpick Task Force
1. Balanced forces are very important when it comes to bridge designs. Research how different kinds of bridges are made. What forces do engineers consider when designing a bridge? Build a bridge with toothpicks and glue. You may use craft sticks instead of toothpicks. The bridge should span 25 cm and should be strong enough to hold your textbook. For a challenge, build a contest to see whose bridge can support the most weight.

SUGGESTED
MATERIALS
• aluminum foil
• bamboo skewers
• drinking straws
• glue
• rubber bands
• masking tape
• plastic film canister
• pins
• jar lids
• sand paper
• tongue depression

Another Long-Term Project Idea
2. Design and construct a model of a motorless car that will move in a straight line. The car should accelerate to top speed by traveling down a ramp, and must continue traveling a distance of 3 m on a smooth surface. Build your car from scrap materials, like the materials listed at left. Calculate the speed of your car over a fixed distance and average it over three trials. Where should friction be minimized on the car? What materials can be used to reduce friction? Where does the force of friction help the car move faster? What materials can be used to increase friction? How does mass affect the car? How does the angle of the ramp affect the car's speed? Demonstrate for the class what your car can do. Be sure to explain which features of the car allow it to reach top speed.

Research Idea
3. You know that you use a scale to measure weight and a balance to measure mass. But, how are scales and balances constructed? What measurements are used in association with them? How do various types of scales or balances differ? Why are some types of scales or balances considered more reliable than others? Make a poster displaying what you have learned.

ADVANCED

CALCULATOR-BASED LABS

Name ___ Class ___ Date ___
LAB
3   STUDENT WORKSHEET   DISCOVERY LAB
The Fast Track

Speed and velocity are rates. They tell us how much distance is covered in a unit of time. What factors affect velocity? In this experiment, you will study the velocity of a car after it is released from different points on a ramp. You will use a motion detector to measure velocity.

MATERIALS
• LabPro or CBL 2 inter-
face
• TI graphing calculator
• DataMate program
• Vernier motion detector
• board 1.8 m long
• several books
• meterstick
• small toy car
• small index card

Procedure
1. To prepare the track, set up a ramp on books as shown in the illustration below. The high end of the ramp should be 45 cm above the floor.
2. Place a meterstick down the center of the ramp. The 0 cm mark on the meterstick should be at the very bottom of the ramp. Tape the meterstick to the ramp in two places. The meterstick will serve as a guide rail for your car.
3. Fasten the Vernier motion detector at the top and center of the ramp as shown in the illustration below.
4. Plug the motion detector into the DIG/SONIC 1 port of the LabPro or CBL 2 interface. Use the link cable to connect the TI graphing calculator to the interface. Firmly press in the cable ends.
5. Turn on the calculator, and start the DataMate program. Press [ENTER] to reset the program.
6. Set up the calculator and interface for data collection by completing the following steps.
   a. Use [◄] and [►] to select MODE.
   b. Press [ENTER] to change the mode to TIME GRAPH.
   c. Explore making Distance vs. Time graphs by completing the following steps.
     a. Stand at the 1.0 m mark, facing away from the motion detector.
     b. Signal your partner to select START.
     c. Slowly walk to the 2.5 m mark and stop.
     d. When data collection ends, select DISTANCE from the SELECT GRAPH menu.
     e. Plot your data on the graph on the next page.
     f. Press [2nd] to return to the SELECT GRAPH menu.
     g. Select RETURN TO MAIN SCREEN to return to the main screen.
7. Repeat step 6 while walking faster. Sketch your new line on the same graph.

motion detector

meterstick   dynamic cart

ramp   books

SCIENCE AND TECHNOLOGY

ADVANCED

CALCULATOR-BASED LABS

Name ___ Class ___ Date ___
LAB
9   STUDENT WORKSHEET   SKILL BUILDER
Graphing Your Motion

Graphs made using a motion detector can be used to study motion. In this experiment, you and a partner will use a motion detector to make graphs of your own motion.

MATERIALS
• LabPro or CBL 2 inter-
face
• TI graphing calculator
• DataMate program
• Vernier motion detector
• tape
• masking tape
• meter stick

Procedure
Part A: Distance vs. Time Graphs
1. Fasten a motion detector to a tabletop facing an area free of furniture and other objects. The motion detector should be at a height of about 15 cm above your waist level.
2. Use short strips of masking tape on the floor to mark 1 m, 2 m, 3 m, and 4 m distances from the motion detector.
3. Plug the motion detector into the DIG/SONIC 1 port of the LabPro or CBL 2 interface. Use the link cable to connect the TI graphing calculator to the interface. Firmly press in the cable ends.
4. Turn on the calculator and start the DataMate program. Press [ENTER] to reset the program.
5. Set up the calculator and interface for data collection by completing the following steps.

SCIENCE AND TECHNOLOGY

ADVANCED

DATASHEETS FOR QUICK LABS

TEACHER RESOURCE PAGE
Name ___ Class ___ Date ___
Quick Lab   DATASHEET FOR QUICK LAB
Reaction to Stress   SAMPLE

Background
The graph below illustrates changes that occur in the membrane potential of a neuron during an action potential. Use the graph to answer the following questions. Refer to Figure 3 as needed.

DATASHEETS FOR CHAPTER LABS

TEACHER RESOURCE PAGE
Name ___ Class ___ Date ___
Skills Practice Lab   DATASHEET FOR CHAPTER LAB
Using Scientific Methods   SAMPLE

Teacher's Notes
TIME REQUIRED
One 45-minute class period.

DATASHEETS FOR LABBOOK

TEACHER RESOURCE PAGE
Name ___ Class ___ Date ___
Skills Practice Lab   DATASHEET FOR LABBOOK LAB
Does It All Add Up?   SAMPLE

Teacher's Notes
TIME REQUIRED
One 45-minute class period.

Review and Assessments

SECTION QUIZ
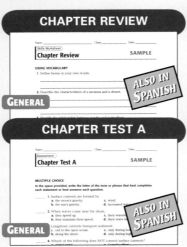

Name ___ Class ___ Date ___
Assessment
Section Quiz   SAMPLE

Section:
In the space provided, write the letter of the description that best matches the term or phrase.

1. building molecules that can be used as an energy source, or breaking down molecules in which energy is stored

the process by which light energy is converted to chemical energy

an organism that uses sunlight or inorganic substances to make organic compounds

ALSO IN SPANISH

GENERAL

SECTION REVIEW

Name ___ Class ___ Date ___
Skills Worksheet
Section Review   SAMPLE

Section:
KEY TERMS
1. What do paleontologists study?

2. How does a trace fossil differ from petrified wood?

fossil.

ALSO IN SPANISH

UNDERSTANDING KEY IDEAS

GENERAL

CHAPTER REVIEW
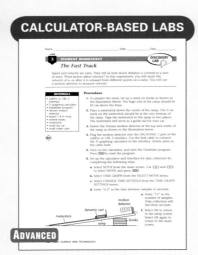

Name ___ Class ___ Date ___
Skills Worksheet
Chapter Review   SAMPLE

USING VOCABULARY
1. Define biome in your own words.

2. Describe the characteristics of a savanna and a desert.

ALSO IN SPANISH

GENERAL

CHAPTER TEST A

Name ___ Class ___ Date ___
Assessment
Chapter Test A   SAMPLE

MULTIPLE CHOICE
In the space provided, write the letter of the term or phrase that completes each statement or best answers each question.

1. Surface currents are formed by
   a. the moon's gravity.   c. wind.
   b. the sun's gravity.   d. increased water density.

2. When waves come near the shore,
   a. they speed up.   c. their wavelength increases.
   b. they maintain their speed.   d. their wave

out to the open ocean.   c. only during low tide.
along the shore.   d. only during high

4. Which of the following does NOT control surface currents?

ALSO IN SPANISH

GENERAL

CHAPTER TEST B
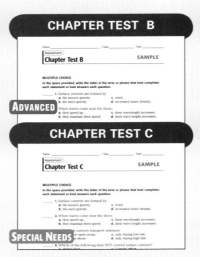

Name ___ Class ___ Date ___
Assessment
Chapter Test B   SAMPLE

MULTIPLE CHOICE
In the space provided, write the letter of the term or phrase that best completes each statement or best answers each question.

1. Surface currents are formed by
   a. the moon's gravity.   c. wind.
   b. the sun's gravity.   d. increased water density.

When waves come near the shore,
   a. they speed up.   c. their wavelength increases.
   b. they maintain their speed.   d. their wave height increases.

ADVANCED

CHAPTER TEST C

Name ___ Class ___ Date ___
Assessment
Chapter Test C   SAMPLE

MULTIPLE CHOICE
In the space provided, write the letter of the term or phrase that best completes each statement or best answers each question.

1. Surface currents are formed by
   a. the moon's gravity.   c. wind.
   b. the sun's gravity.   d. increased water density.

When waves come near the shore,
   a. they speed up.   c. their wavelength increases.
   b. they maintain their speed.   d. their wave height increases.

currents transport sediment
   out to the open ocean.   c. only during low tide.
   shore.   d. only during high tide.

4. Which of the following does NOT control surface currents?

SPECIAL NEEDS

STANDARDIZED TEST PREPARATION
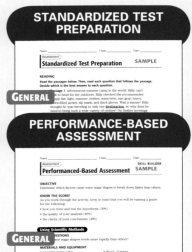

Name ___ Class ___ Date ___
Assessment
Standardized Test Preparation   SAMPLE

READING
Read the passages below. Then, read each question that follows the passage. Decide which is the best answer to each question.

Passage 1 Adventurous summer camp in the world: Billy can't wait to head for the outdoors. Billy checked the recommended supply list: light, summer clothes; sunscreen; rain gear; heavy, mud-filled jacket, ski mask; and much more. Wait a minute! Billy thought he was traveling to only one destination, so why does he need to bring such a wide variety of clothes? On further investiga-

GENERAL

PERFORMANCE-BASED ASSESSMENT

Name ___ Class ___ Date ___
Assessment
Performanced-Based Assessment   SKILL BUILDER

OBJECTIVE
Determine which factors cause some sugar shapes to break down faster than others.

KNOW THE SCORE!
As you work through the activity, keep in mind that you will be earning a grade for the following:
• how you form and test the hypothesis (30%)
• the quality of your analysis (40%)
• the clarity of your conclusions (30%)

Using Scientific Methods
QUESTIONS

MATERIALS AND EQUIPMENT
• 1 regular sugar cube   • 90 mL of water

GENERAL

This Chapter Enrichment provides relevant and interesting information to expand and enhance your presentation of the chapter material.

Section 1

Measuring Motion

The Scientific Revolution

● The movement now called the Scientific Revolution took place between the 16th and 18th centuries. Mainstream science of the time still taught the Aristotelian view of the universe. With the translation of Greek, Roman, and Arabic texts and the improvement of the printing press, ideas that are now the basis of modern science first became available to a large number of people.

● In astronomy, the theory that the sun is the center of the solar system was proposed by Copernicus. Galileo laid the foundations of the principles of mechanics (the study of motion) and first turned a telescope toward the sky. Philosophers such as Descartes began to develop the idea of nature as a complicated system of particles in motion.

● Sir Isaac Newton (1642–1727) was a central figure in the Scientific Revolution during the 17th century. He was born in 1642, the year Galileo died.

Acceleration

● Remember that acceleration, like velocity, always includes direction. However, the relationship between acceleration and motion is different from the relationship between velocity and motion. An object's motion is always in the same direction as its velocity. But an object's motion is not always in the same direction as its acceleration. For example, when an object is in circular motion its acceleration is toward the center of the circle, but its motion is not.

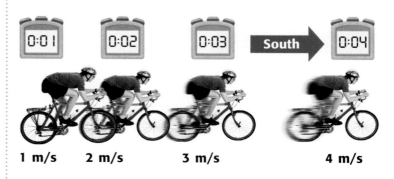

1 m/s   2 m/s   3 m/s   4 m/s

Is That a Fact!

◆ A fast runner can reach a speed of 32 km/h (about 20 mi/h). But the highest speed a person can attain when swimming is only about 8 km/h (about 5 mi/h).

Section 2

What Is a Force?

Basic Forces of Nature

● Scientists have found evidence that the interactions of only four basic forces can describe all physical properties and relationships in nature. These forces are:

• the gravitational force, which acts on all matter that has mass and on light, which has no mass

• the electromagnetic force, which is responsible for the attraction and repulsion of all kinds of matter that have electric or magnetic properties

• the strong nuclear force, which binds the protons and neutrons of atoms together in the nucleus

• the weak nuclear force, which describes some interactions between subatomic particles

Is That a Fact!

◆ Gravitational force and electromagnetic force were discovered long before nuclear forces because people can observe their effects on ordinary matter. The strong and weak nuclear forces were not discovered until the 20th century, when scientists were able to probe the structure of nuclei.

Tug-of-War and Force

● In a tug-of-war contest, both teams and the rope move in the direction of the net force.

Section 3

Friction: A Force That Opposes Motion

Sports and Friction

● Many sports participants want to reduce friction as much as possible. Downhill skiers wax their skis to reduce friction between the skis and the snow. Surfers wax their boards to reduce friction between the boards and the water. However, in some sports, increased friction is what the athlete wants. A runner in the 100 m dash wants maximum friction between his or her shoes and the running track.

Is That a Fact!

◆ Athletic shoes come in so many varieties because they are designed to provide the proper amount of friction for maximum performance in each sport.

Wheels

● A wheel makes movement easier by reducing friction. Yet without friction between the wheel and the ground, the wheel would just spin around and the object to which the wheel is attached would go nowhere.

Section 4

Gravity: A Force of Attraction

Gravity

● Every object in the universe is constantly subject to the pull of gravity from other objects. The net gravitational force acting on the object may be extremely small, but it is always present.

Newton's Universal Law of Gravitation

● The gravitational force exists between two objects anywhere in the universe. The gravitational force is purely attractive—each object is pulled by the other one. These two forces are equal and opposite.

● The magnitude of the gravitational force is related to the masses of the objects and the distance between them. The equation for Newton's universal law of gravitation is as follows:

$$F_g = G \frac{m_1 m_2}{d^2}$$

where F_g is the gravitational force, G is the constant of universal gravitation, m_1 is the mass of object 1, m_2 is the mass of object 2, and d is the distance between the centers of mass of objects 1 and 2. The value for G is 6.67×10^{-11} N•m^2/kg^2.

SCILINKS

NSTA

Developed and maintained by the
National Science Teachers Association

SciLinks is maintained by the National Science Teachers Association to provide you and your students with interesting, up-to-date links that will enrich your classroom presentation of the chapter.

Visit www.scilinks.org and enter the SciLinks code for more information about the topic listed.

Topic: Measuring Motion
SciLinks code: HSM0927

Topic: Matter and Gravity
SciLinks code: HSM0922

Topic: Forces
SciLinks code: HSM0604

Topic: Force of Gravity
SciLinks code: HSM0602

Topic: Force and Friction
SciLinks code: HSM0601

Overview

Tell students that this chapter is about measuring motion and about how forces affect motion. Students will learn how to calculate average speed and average acceleration. The chapter also explains balanced and unbalanced forces, friction, and gravity.

Assessing Prior Knowledge

Students should be familiar with the following topics:

• SI units

• mass

Identifying Misconceptions

As students learn the material in this chapter, some of them may be confused about the difference between mass and weight. Explain to students that the weight of an object depends on gravity, but the mass of the object does not. Also explain that the weight of an object will change if the object is moved to the moon or to other planets, but that the mass of the object will remain the same. However, because mass and weight are proportional and constant on Earth, people tend to confuse the two concepts and often use the terms *mass* and *weight* interchangeably in everyday usage.

17
Matter in Motion

About the PHOTO

Speed skaters are fast. In fact, some skaters can skate at a rate of 12 m/s! That's equal to a speed of 27 mi/h. To reach such a speed, skaters must exert large forces. They must also use friction to turn corners on the slippery surface of the ice.

PRE-READING ACTIVITY

FOLDNOTES **Four-Corner Fold**
Before you read the chapter, create the FoldNote entitled "Four-Corner Fold" described in the **Study Skills** section of the Appendix. Label the flaps of the four-corner fold with "Motion," "Forces," "Friction," and "Gravity." Write what you know about each topic under the appropriate flap. As you read the chapter, add other information that you learn.

Standards Correlations

North Carolina Standard Course of Study

1.01 Identify and create questions and hypotheses that can be answered through scientific investigations. (LabBook)

1.02 (partial) Develop appropriate experimental procedures for: Given questions. . . (LabBook)

1.03 Apply safety procedures in the laboratory and in field studies, Recognize potential hazards, Safely manipulate materials and equipment, [and] Conduct appropriate procedures. (Section 3, Chapter Lab, and LabBook)

1.05 (partial) Analyze evidence to: Explain observations, [and] Make inferences and predictions . . .(Section 3 and Chapter Lab)

1.06 (partial) Use mathematics to gather, organize, and present quantitative data resulting from scientific investigations: Measurement . . . [and] Graphing . . . (LabBook)

2.01 Explore evidence that "technology" has many definitions: Artifact or hardware . . . (Science in Action)

6.03 (partial) Evaluate motion in terms of Newton's Laws: The force of friction retards motion, . . . [and] An object's motion is the result of the combined effect of all forces acting on the object . . . (Sections 2 and 3)

START-UP ACTIVITY
MATERIALS
FOR EACH GROUP
- dominoes, 25
- meterstick
- stopwatch

Teacher's Notes: You might want to allow students to line up their dominoes along the side edge of a meterstick to ensure that the dominoes are in a straight line.

You may also wish to demonstrate how to line up the dominoes in case your students do not fully understand the instructions given.

Answers
1. Answers may vary.
2. Students should determine that putting dominoes very close together and putting them very far apart both lead to slower average speed. The average speed is fastest when the distance between the dominoes is about half the length of a domino. Accept all reasonable predictions. Students will likely find that the results do not confirm their predictions. They will probably predict that setting the dominoes very close together will reduce the time taken for all the dominoes to fall and thus will increase the average speed.

START-UP ACTIVITY
The Domino Derby
Speed is the distance traveled by an object in a certain amount of time. In this activity, you will observe one factor that affects the speed of falling dominoes.

Procedure
1. Set up **25 dominoes** in a straight line. Try to keep equal spacing between the dominoes.
2. Use a **meterstick** to measure the total length of your row of dominoes, and record the length.
3. Use a **stopwatch** to time how long it takes for the dominoes to fall. Record this measurement.
4. Predict what would happen to that amount of time if you changed the distance between the dominoes. Write your predictions.

5. Repeat steps 2 and 3 several times using distances between the dominoes that are smaller and larger than the distance used in your first setup. Use the same number of dominoes in each trial.

Analysis
1. Calculate the average speed for each trial by dividing the total distance (the length of the domino row) by the time the dominoes take to fall.
2. How did the spacing between dominoes affect the average speed? Is this result what you expected? If not, explain.

6.04 Analyze that an object's motion is always judged relative to some other object or point. (Section 1)

6.05 Describe and measure quantities that characterize moving objects and their interactions within a system: Time, Distance, Mass, Force, Velocity, Center of mass, [and] Acceleration. (Sections 1, 2, 3, and 4, Chapter Lab, and Chapter Review)

6.06 Investigate and analyze the real world interactions of balanced and unbalanced forces: Sports and recreation, Transportation, [and] The human body. (Section 2)

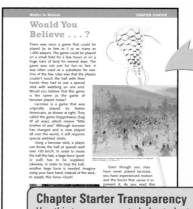

Chapter Starter Transparency
Use this transparency to help students begin thinking about motion, speed, and force.

CHAPTER RESOURCES
Technology
Transparencies
- Chapter Starter Transparency

READING SKILLS

Student Edition on CD-ROM

Guided Reading Audio CD

Classroom Videos
- Brain Food Video Quiz

Workbooks
Science Puzzlers, Twisters & Teasers
- Matter in Motion **GENERAL**

Focus

Overview

This section introduces students to the concept of motion. It introduces the idea of a *reference point* as a necessary starting point to observe motion. Students learn about average speed, velocity, and acceleration.

Bellringer

Have students describe their position in the classroom using a reference point and a set of reference directions. For example, a student might say, "I sit three desks behind Ahmed's desk," or "I sit 2 m east of the vent hood and 10 m north of the emergency shower."

Motivate

Demonstration — GENERAL

Models Place two identical wind-up toys on a table, one wound, the other not wound, so that one toy moves across the table while the other one remains motionless. Ask students to explain the difference between the toys. Help students understand that the difference is movement. Ask students to define motion in their own terms. Explain that in this section, they will learn how to identify and measure different quantities related to motion.
LS Visual

Measuring Motion

Look around you—you are likely to see something in motion. Your teacher may be walking across the room, or perhaps your friend is writing with a pencil.

Even if you don't see anything moving, motion is still occurring all around you. Air particles are moving, the Earth is circling the sun, and blood is traveling through your blood vessels!

Observing Motion by Using a Reference Point

You might think that the motion of an object is easy to detect—you just watch the object. But you are actually watching the object in relation to another object that appears to stay in place. The object that appears to stay in place is a *reference point.* When an object changes position over time relative to a reference point, the object is in **motion.** You can describe the direction of the object's motion with a reference direction, such as north, south, east, west, up, or down.

✓ Reading Check What is a reference point? (*See the Appendix for answers to Reading Checks.*)

Common Reference Points

The Earth's surface is a common reference point for determining motion, as shown in **Figure 1.** Nonmoving objects, such as trees and buildings, are also useful reference points.

A moving object can also be used as a reference point. For example, if you were on the hot-air balloon shown in **Figure 1,** you could watch a bird fly by and see that the bird was changing position in relation to your moving balloon.

Figure 1 *During the interval between the times that these pictures were taken, the hot-air balloon changed position relative to a reference point—the mountain.*

READING WARM-UP

Objectives

● Describe the motion of an object by the position of the object in relation to a reference point.

● Identify the two factors that determine speed.

● Explain the difference between speed and velocity.

● Analyze the relationship between velocity and acceleration.

● Demonstrate that changes in motion can be measured and represented on a graph.

Terms to Learn

motion	velocity
speed	acceleration

READING STRATEGY

Discussion Read this section silently. Write down questions that you have about this section. Discuss your questions in a small group.

CHAPTER RESOURCES

Chapter Resource File

- Lesson Plan
- Directed Reading A **BASIC**
- Directed Reading B **SPECIAL NEEDS**

Technology

Transparencies
- Bellringer
- A Graph Showing Speed

MISCONCEPTION ///ALERT\\\

Describing Position The text defines *motion* as an object's change in position over time when compared with a reference point. Remind students that an object's *position* can be described in terms of a reference point and a set of reference directions. Common reference directions are compass directions (such as south and west) and relative directions (such as left of, just beyond, and in front of).

Speed Depends on Distance and Time

Speed is the distance traveled by an object divided by the time taken to travel that distance. Look again at **Figure 1.** Suppose the time interval between the pictures was 10 s and that the balloon traveled 50 m in that time. The speed of the balloon is (50 m)/(10 s), or 5 m/s.

The SI unit for speed is meters per second (m/s). Kilometers per hour (km/h), feet per second (ft/s), and miles per hour (mi/h) are other units commonly used to express speed.

Determining Average Speed

Most of the time, objects do not travel at a constant speed. For example, you probably do not walk at a constant speed from one class to the next. So, it is very useful to calculate *average speed* using the following equation:

$$average\ speed = \frac{total\ distance}{total\ time}$$

Recognizing Speed on a Graph

Suppose a person drives from one city to another. The blue line in the graph in **Figure 2** shows the total distance traveled during a 4 h period. Notice that the distance traveled during each hour is different. The distance varies because the speed is not constant. The driver may change speed because of weather, traffic, or varying speed limits. The average speed for the entire trip can be calculated as follows:

$$average\ speed = \frac{360\ km}{4\ h} = 90\ km/h$$

The red line on the graph shows how far the driver must travel each hour to reach the same city if he or she moved at a constant speed. The slope of this line is the average speed.

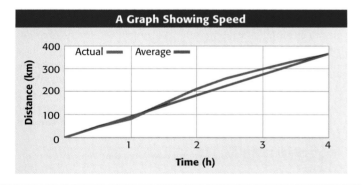

A Graph Showing Speed

Distance (km) vs. Time (h)
Actual ━━ Average ━━

motion an object's change in position relative to a reference point

speed the distance traveled divided by the time interval during which the motion occurred

SCHOOL to HOME

What's Your Speed?
Measure a distance of 5 m or a distance of 25 ft inside or outside. Ask an adult at home to use a stopwatch or a watch with a second hand to time you as you travel the distance you measured. Then, find your average speed. Find the average speed of other members of your family in the same way. **ACTIVITY**

Figure 2 *Speed can be shown on a graph of distance versus time.*

Homework ──── **ADVANCED**

Calculating Average Speed Obtain bus, train, or airplane schedules that list departure and arrival times. Help students plan a trip with at least four segments. Using a map of the route, have students estimate the distance between points on the route. Have them calculate the average speed of the vehicle between checkpoints and compare the average speed for each segment. Does the average speed remain constant or does it change? What might account for any differences? **LS Logical**

CHAPTER RESOURCES

Workbooks

Math Skills for Science
• The Unit Factor and Dimensional Analysis **GENERAL**
• Average Speed in a Pinewood Derby **GENERAL**

Writing Activity After students have read about velocity, have them write a paragraph in their **science journal** that gives examples of when it is sufficient to know only the speed of something and when it is important to know the velocity. **LS** Verbal

Answers to Math Focus

1. 2 m/s

2. 5 km/h

3. 360 km/h

ACTIVITY — ADVANCED

The Speed of Light Have students research the history of the measurement of the speed of light. Have them focus on the measurements involving distance and time. Ask students to write a short report that lists the difficulties in making these measurements and the factors that improved their accuracy. **LS** Verbal

Research — GENERAL

Navigational Terms Have students research navigational terms referring to speed and velocity. Ask students to list the terms that are used in sailing, aviation, and rocketry and to compare the usages. Tell students to focus on the importance placed on direction in the terms. **LS** Logical

---

MATH FOCUS

Calculating Average Speed An athlete swims a distance from one end of a 50 m pool to the other end in a time of 25 s. What is the athlete's average speed?

Step 1: Write the equation for average speed.

$$average\ speed = \frac{total\ distance}{total\ time}$$

Step 2: Replace the total distance and total time with the values given, and solve.

$$average\ speed = \frac{50\ m}{25\ s} = 2\ m/s$$

Now It's Your Turn

1. Kira jogs to a store 72 m away in a time of 36 s. What is Kira's average speed?

2. If you travel 7.5 km and walk for 1.5 h, what is your average speed?

3. An airplane traveling from San Francisco to Chicago travels 1,260 km in 3.5 h. What is the airplane's average speed?

Figure 3 *The speeds of these cars may be similar, but the velocities of the cars differ because the cars are going in different directions.*

Velocity: Direction Matters

Imagine that two birds leave the same tree at the same time. They both fly at 10 km/h for 5 min, 12 km/h for 8 min, and 5 km/h for 10 min. Why don't they end up at the same place?

Have you figured out the answer? The birds went in different directions. Their speeds were the same, but they had different velocities. **Velocity** (vuh LAHS uh tee) is the speed of an object in a particular direction.

Be careful not to confuse the terms *speed* and *velocity*. They do not have the same meaning. Velocity must include a reference direction. If you say that an airplane's velocity is 600 km/h, you would not be correct. But you could say the plane's velocity is 600 km/h south. **Figure 3** shows an example of the difference between speed and velocity.

Changing Velocity

You can think of velocity as the rate of change of an object's position. An object's velocity is constant only if its speed and direction don't change. Therefore, constant velocity is always motion along a straight line. An object's velocity changes if either its speed or direction changes. For example, as a bus traveling at 15 m/s south speeds up to 20 m/s south, its velocity changes. If the bus continues to travel at the same speed but changes direction to travel east, its velocity changes again. And if the bus slows down at the same time that it swerves north to avoid a cat, the velocity of the bus changes, too.

Reading Check What are the two ways that velocity can change?

Answer to Reading Check
Velocity can change by changing speed or changing direction.

CHAPTER RESOURCES
Technology
Transparencies • Finding Resultant Velocity
Workbooks
Science Skills • Organizing Your Research GENERAL

Figure 4 **Finding Resultant Velocity**

15 m/s east

1 m/s east

When you combine two velocities that are **in the same direction,** add them together to find the resultant velocity.

Person's resultant velocity
15 m/s east + 1 m/s east = 16 m/s east

1 m/s west

15 m/s east

When you combine two velocities that are **in opposite directions,** subtract the smaller velocity from the larger velocity to find the resultant velocity. The resultant velocity is in the direction of the larger velocity.

Person's resultant velocity
15 m/s east − 1 m/s west = 14 m/s east

Combining Velocities

Imagine that you are riding in a bus that is traveling east at 15 m/s. You and the other passengers are also traveling at a velocity of 15 m/s east. But suppose you stand up and walk down the bus's aisle while the bus is moving. Are you still moving at the same velocity as the bus? No! **Figure 4** shows how you can combine velocities to find the *resultant velocity.*

Acceleration

Although the word *accelerate* is commonly used to mean "speed up," the word means something else in science. **Acceleration** (ak SEL uhr AY shuhn) is the rate at which velocity changes. Velocity changes if speed changes, if direction changes, or if both change. So, an object accelerates if its speed, its direction, or both change.

An increase in velocity is commonly called *positive acceleration.* A decrease in velocity is commonly called *negative acceleration,* or *deceleration.* Keep in mind that acceleration is not only how much velocity changes but also how fast velocity changes. The faster the velocity changes, the greater the acceleration is.

velocity the speed of an object in a particular direction

acceleration the rate at which velocity changes over time; an object accelerates if its speed, direction, or both change

Reteaching — BASIC

Acceleration Chart Have students make a two-column chart. In the first column, students should list examples of acceleration. In the second column, students should write how the velocity changed in each example. For example, students could write "riding a bike around a corner" in the first column, and "change in direction" in the second column. **LS** Logical

Quiz — GENERAL

1. What distinguishes the measurement of speed from that of velocity and acceleration? (Speed does not involve direction. Both velocity and acceleration do include direction.)

2. What is centripetal acceleration? (acceleration that occurs in circular motion)

3. How do you calculate average speed? average acceleration? (divide the distance traveled by the time; subtract the starting velocity from the final velocity, and divide by the time it takes to change velocity)

Alternative Assessment — GENERAL

Visualizing Acceleration Ask students to draw two pictures of rolling balls as they would appear at 1 s intervals. The first picture should show a ball rolling at a constant speed and the second picture should show a ball that is accelerating. **LS** Visual

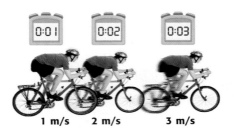
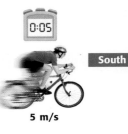

Figure 5 *This cyclist is accelerating at 1 m/s² south.*

Calculating Acceleration
Use the equation for average acceleration to do the following problem.

A plane passes over point A at a velocity of 240 m/s north. Forty seconds later, it passes over point B at a velocity of 260 m/s north. What is the plane's average acceleration?

Calculating Average Acceleration

You can find average acceleration by using the equation:

$$average\ acceleration = \frac{final\ velocity - starting\ velocity}{time\ it\ takes\ to\ change\ velocity}$$

Velocity is expressed in meters per second (m/s), and time is expressed in seconds (s). So acceleration is expressed in meters per second per second, or (m/s)/s, which equals m/s². For example, look at **Figure 5.** Every second, the cyclist's southward velocity increases by 1 m/s. His average acceleration can be calculated as follows:

$$average\ acceleration = \frac{5\ m/s - 1\ m/s}{4\ s} = 1\ m/s^2\ south$$

Reading Check What are the units of acceleration?

Recognizing Acceleration on a Graph

Suppose that you are riding a roller coaster. The roller-coaster car moves up a hill until it stops at the top. Then, you are off! The graph in **Figure 6** shows your acceleration for the next 10 s. During the first 8 s, you move down the hill. You can tell from the graph that your acceleration is positive for the first 8 s because your velocity increases as time passes. During the last 2 s, your car starts climbing the next hill. Your acceleration is negative because your velocity decreases as time passes.

Figure 6 *Acceleration can be shown on a graph of velocity versus time.*

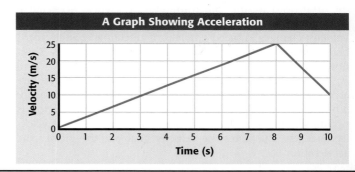

A Graph Showing Acceleration

Answer to Reading Check
The unit for acceleration is meters per second per second (m/s²).

Answer to Math Practice
0.5 m/s² north.

CHAPTER RESOURCES
Technology

Transparencies
• Calculating Acceleration
• A Graph Showing Acceleration

Circular Motion: Continuous Acceleration

You may be surprised to know that even when you are completely still, you are experiencing acceleration. You may not seem to be changing speed or direction, but you are! You are traveling in a circle as the Earth rotates. An object traveling in a circular motion is always changing its direction. Therefore, its velocity is always changing, so it is accelerating. The acceleration that occurs in circular motion is known as *centripetal acceleration* (sen TRIP uht uhl ak SEL uhr AY shuhn). Centripetal acceleration occurs on a Ferris wheel at an amusement park or as the moon orbits Earth. Another example of centripetal acceleration is shown in **Figure 7.**

Figure 7 *The blades of these windmills are constantly changing direction. Thus, centripetal acceleration is occurring.*

Using Key Terms

1. In your own words, write definitions for each of the following terms: *motion* and *acceleration*.

2. Use each of the following terms in a separate sentence: *speed* and *velocity*.

Understanding Key Ideas

3. Which of the following is NOT an example of acceleration?
   a. a person jogging at 3 m/s along a winding path
   b. a car stopping at a stop sign
   c. a cheetah running 27 m/s east
   d. a plane taking off

4. Which of the following would be a good reference point to describe the motion of a dog?
   a. the ground
   b. another dog running
   c. a tree
   d. All of the above

5. Explain the difference between speed and velocity.

6. What two things must you know to determine speed?

7. How are velocity and acceleration related?

Math Skills

8. Find the average speed of a person who swims 105 m in 70 s.

9. What is the average acceleration of a subway train that speeds up from 9.6 m/s to 12 m/s in 0.8 s on a straight section of track?

Critical Thinking

10. **Applying Concepts** Why is it more helpful to know a tornado's velocity rather than its speed?

11. **Evaluating Data** A wolf is chasing a rabbit. Graph the wolf's motion using the following data: 15 m/s at 0 s, 10 m/s at 1 s, 5 m/s at 2 s, 2.5 m/s at 3 s, 1 m/s at 4 s, and 0 m/s at 5 s. What does the graph tell you?

SCi_LINKS

NSTA

Developed and maintained by the
National Science Teachers Association

For a variety of links related to this chapter, go to www.scilinks.org

Topic: Measuring Motion
SciLinks code: HSM0927

Answers to Section Review

1. Sample answer: Motion is the change in position of an object relative to a reference point. Acceleration is the change in velocity over time.

2. Sample answer: The cat is moving with a speed of 1 m/s. The cat is moving with a velocity of 1 m/s to the east.

3. c

4. d

5. Speed does not include direction; velocity does.

6. the distance traveled and the time taken to travel that distance

7. Acceleration is the rate at which velocity changes.

8. 1.5 m/s

9. 3 m/s^2

10. It would be important to know the velocity because velocity includes direction. Knowing only the speed of a tornado would not tell the direction that the tornado is traveling. Knowing a tornado's direction of travel would allow people to avoid or escape its path.

11. The graph shows that the wolf has negative acceleration (slows down) until it comes to a stop.

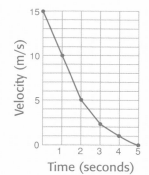

CHAPTER RESOURCES

Chapter Resource File

- Section Quiz **GENERAL**
- Section Review **GENERAL**
- Vocabulary and Section Summary **GENERAL**
- Reinforcement Worksheet **BASIC**
- SciLinks Activity **GENERAL**

Focus

Overview

This section defines *force* and describes how all forces act on objects. Students learn to determine the net force on an object and compare balanced and unbalanced forces.

Bellringer

Have students look around the room and think about the objects they see in terms of force. Tell them that a force is always exerted by one object on another object. Ask them the following questions:

Where do you see a force happening in the room right now? Which object is exerting the force, and which is receiving it?

Motivate

ACTiViTY ———————— GENERAL

Bridge Building Have students work in groups to build a bridge using toothpicks and glue. The bridge should span a 15 cm gap and be wide enough to hold a toy car. Students should identify the forces acting on their bridge. (An alternate and less time consuming activity would be to have students build a house of cards that can support a 500 g mass.) **Kinesthetic**

READING WARM-UP

Objectives

- Describe forces, and explain how forces act on objects.
- Determine the net force when more than one force is acting on an object.
- Compare balanced and unbalanced forces.
- Describe ways that unbalanced forces cause changes in motion.

Terms to Learn

force
newton
net force

READING STRATEGY

Reading Organizer As you read this section, make a table comparing balanced forces and unbalanced forces.

What Is a Force?

You have probably heard the word force *in everyday conversation. People say things such as "That storm had a lot of force" or "Our football team is a force to be reckoned with." But what, exactly, is a force?*

In science, a **force** is simply a push or a pull. All forces have both size and direction. A force can change the acceleration of an object. This acceleration can be a change in the speed or direction of the object. In fact, any time you see a change in an object's motion, you can be sure that the change in motion was created by a force. Scientists express force using a unit called the **newton** (N).

Forces Acting on Objects

All forces act on objects. For any push to occur, something has to receive the push. You can't push nothing! The same is true for any pull. When doing schoolwork, you use your fingers to pull open books or to push the buttons on a computer keyboard. In these examples, your fingers are exerting forces on the books and the keys. So, the forces act on the books and keys. Another example of a force acting on an object is shown in **Figure 1.**

However, just because a force acts on an object doesn't mean that motion will occur. For example, you are probably sitting on a chair. But the force you are exerting on the chair does not cause the chair to move. The chair doesn't move because the floor is also exerting a force on the chair.

Figure 1 *The bulldozer is exerting a force on the pile of soil. But the pile of soil also exerts a force by just sitting on the ground!*

CHAPTER RESOURCES

Chapter Resource File

- **Lesson Plan**
- **Directed Reading A** BASIC
- **Directed Reading B** SPECIAL NEEDS

Technology

- **Transparencies**
  - Bellringer
  - Forces in the Same Direction

Is That a Fact!

Some trains are too massive to be moved by one locomotive. To compensate for the larger mass, extra locomotives are added until the net force provided by all the locomotives is large enough to move the train.

Unseen Sources and Receivers of Forces

It is not always easy to tell what is exerting a force or what is receiving a force, as shown in **Figure 2.** You cannot see what exerts the force that pulls magnets to refrigerators. And you cannot see that the air around you is held near Earth's surface by a force called *gravity*.

Determining Net Force

Usually, more than one force is acting on an object. The **net force** is the combination all of the forces acting on an object. So, how do you determine the net force? The answer depends on the directions of the forces.

Forces in the Same Direction

Suppose the music teacher asks you and a friend to move a piano. You pull on one end and your friend pushes on the other end, as shown in **Figure 3.** The forces you and your friend exert on the piano act in the same direction. The two forces are added to determine the net force because the forces act in the same direction. In this case, the net force is 45 N. This net force is large enough to move the piano—if it is on wheels, that is!

✔ Reading Check How do you determine the net force on an object if all forces act in the same direction? (*See the Appendix for answers to Reading Checks.*)

Figure 2 *Something that you cannot see exerts a force that makes this cat's fur stand up.*

force a push or a pull exerted on an object in order to change the motion of the object; force has size and direction

newton the SI unit for force (symbol, N)

net force the combination of all of the forces acting on an object

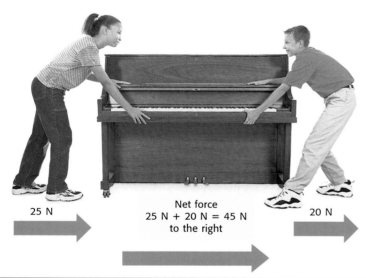

25 N

Net force
25 N + 20 N = 45 N
to the right

20 N

Figure 3 *When forces act in the same direction, you add the forces to determine the net force. The net force will be in the same direction as the individual forces.*

Answer to Reading Check

If all of the forces act in the same direction, you must add the forces to determine the net force.

📖 **READING STRATEGY** — GENERAL

Prediction Guide Before students read about determining net force, have them look at **Figures 3** and **4** in this section. While they are looking at these pictures, ask students to predict what happens when forces act in the same direction and when forces act in opposite directions. **LS** **Visual**

BRAIN FOOD

Force and Pressure Force and pressure are different from each other. Magicians depend on this difference when they lie down on a bed of nails. The **force**—the magician's weight—is fairly large, but because there are hundreds or even thousands of nails, the **pressure** (the amount of force exerted on a given area) from each nail is not enough to break the magician's skin.

Discussion ——— GENERAL

Everyday Forces Using objects in the room or situations with which students are familiar (like riding a bicycle), discuss with students the forces that are operating on them. Ask students in each case to identify which object is exerting the force and which is receiving it. (Sample answers for riding a bicycle: feet exert force on the pedals, the tires exert force on the ground, fingers exert force on the hand brakes, the brake pads exert force on the wheel rims) Continue the discussion by asking them to identify other types of daily activities that involve forces. **LS** **Verbal**

MATERIALS

- magnet, bar
- paper clip, wire
- shoe box
- tape
- thread, 20–40 cm

Floating Paper Clip Tape a strong magnet inside one end of a shoe box. Stand the box on end with the magnet side up. Tie a piece of thread to a paper clip, and tape the other end of the thread inside the bottom end of the box. Test how long the thread must be so that the magnet holds the paper clip in the air.

Before making your students aware of the magnet, show them the box and ask them to speculate why the paper clip stays suspended. Ask what forces might be holding the paper clip in the air and whether the forces are balanced or unbalanced. (Students will likely conclude that there must be a force pulling the paper clip up. Some students may correctly determine that there is a magnetic force acting on the paper clip. The forces on the paper clip are the magnetic force from the magnet, gravity, and tension from the string. Because the paper clip is not moving, all the forces on it are balanced.) Finally, ask students if this demonstration would work with a larger object. Have them explain their answers. If feasible, students can test their hypotheses. **LS** Visual/Logical

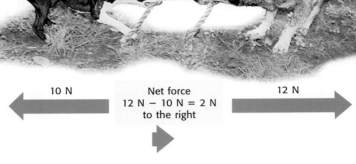

Figure 4 *When two forces act in opposite directions, you subtract the smaller force from the larger force to determine the net force. The net force will be in the same direction as the larger force.*

10 N

Net force
12 N − 10 N = 2 N
to the right

12 N

Forces in Different Directions

Look at the two dogs playing tug of war in **Figure 4.** Each dog is exerting a force on the rope. But the forces are in opposite directions. Which dog will win the tug of war?

Because the forces are in opposite directions, the net force on the rope is found by subtracting the smaller force from the larger one. In this case, the net force is 2 N in the direction of the dog on the right. Give that dog a dog biscuit!

✓ **Reading Check** What is the net force on an object when you combine a force of 7 N north with a force of 5 N south?

Balanced and Unbalanced Forces

If you know the net force on an object, you can determine the effect of the net force on the object's motion. Why? The net force tells you whether the forces on the object are balanced or unbalanced.

Balanced Forces

When the forces on an object produce a net force of 0 N, the forces are *balanced*. Balanced forces will not cause a change in the motion of a moving object. And balanced forces do not cause a nonmoving object to start moving.

Many objects around you have only balanced forces acting on them. For example, a light hanging from the ceiling does not move because the force of gravity pulling down on the light is balanced by the force of the cord pulling upward. A bird's nest in a tree and a hat resting on your head are also examples of objects that have only balanced forces acting on them. **Figure 5** shows another example of balanced forces.

Figure 5 *Because all the forces on this house of cards are balanced, none of the cards move.*

Answer to Reading Check

2 N north

CHAPTER RESOURCES
Technology
Transparencies   • Forces in Opposite Directions

Unbalanced Forces

When the net force on an object is not 0 N, the forces on the object are *unbalanced*. Unbalanced forces produce a change in motion, such as a change in speed or a change in direction. Unbalanced forces are necessary to cause a nonmoving object to start moving.

Unbalanced forces are also necessary to change the motion of moving objects. For example, consider the soccer game shown in **Figure 6**. The soccer ball is already moving when it is passed from one player to another. When the ball reaches another player, that player exerts an unbalanced force—a kick—on the ball. After the kick, the ball moves in a new direction and has a new speed.

An object can continue to move when the unbalanced forces are removed. For example, when it is kicked, a soccer ball receives an unbalanced force. The ball continues to roll on the ground long after the force of the kick has ended.

Balanced and Unbalanced Forces in Action

Balanced and unbalanced forces and the interactions between them are important in all parts of your life. Balanced and unbalanced forces help you enjoy your free time, play sports, travel, and move your body.

Forces in Recreation

How do you spend your free time? Perhaps you play board games, read, or ride a skateboard. Forces are important in all these recreational activities. Your game piece stays on a game board because all of the forces on it are balanced. But you exert unbalanced forces to lift and roll the dice. Balanced forces keep your book open so that you can read it. But unbalanced forces are needed to turn the pages. Balanced and unbalanced forces are also important for the skateboarder in **Figure 7**.

Figure 6 *The soccer ball moves because the players exert an unbalanced force on the ball each time they kick it.*

Figure 7 *A skateboarder stays on his skateboard when the forces on him are balanced. But unbalanced forces let him have fun going down a ramp.*

CONNECTION ACTIVITY
Chemistry ———— ADVANCED

Forces in Molecules Molecules are held together by balanced forces. If the forces weren't balanced, the atoms that make up molecules would move apart. Have students find out what kinds of forces hold molecules together. Ask students to make a poster of what they learn. **LS Visual**

CONNECTION to History ———— GENERAL

Aristotle's Theory of Force
Aristotle believed that a moving object must have a force acting on it or it would stop moving. His belief was suggested by everyday experiences. If you slide an object and then remove your hand, the object will stop sliding. What Aristotle did not realize was that when you remove your hand, you remove a force that is balancing an opposing force—the force of friction. So, the object stopped moving because friction is an unbalanced force that changed the object's motion. Students will learn about friction in the next section of this chapter.

Figure 8 *All the forces on this skater are balanced as she glides across the ice. But an unbalanced force was needed for her to start moving.*

Figure 9 *Balanced forces keep a cyclist on his bicycle, but unbalanced forces are needed for him to turn corners or accelerate.*

Forces in Sports

Athletes use balanced and unbalanced forces all the time—even if they don't realize it. The figure skater in **Figure 8** probably doesn't know that balanced forces are helping her look graceful on the ice.

Now, think about what has to happen for a football placekicker to kick a field goal. First, the center exerts an unbalanced force on the football to snap the ball to the holder. Next, the holder makes sure that all the forces on ball are balanced as he or she holds the ball steady for the kicker. The kicker then exerts an unbalanced force on the ball to send it sailing through the goal posts.

A swimmer also uses balanced and unbalanced forces. The upward and downward forces on a swimmer have to be balanced so that the swimmer will stay afloat. If they weren't balanced, the swimmer would sink! To move forward, a swimmer pushes on the water with his or her arms and legs. These pushes create unbalanced forces that move the swimmer forward.

Forces in Transportation

The purpose of transportation is to move. And you already know that unbalanced forces are needed to start motion. The engines in cars, buses, and trains exert forces that turn their wheels to move forward or backward. Propellers on motorboats exert forces on the water to move the boat, and wind exerts forces on a sail to move a sailboat forward.

But balanced forces are also important in transportation. For example, the cyclist in **Figure 9** doesn't fall off his bicycle because the forces on him are balanced. Also, airplanes stay at their cruising altitude only when the downward force of gravity is balanced with an upward force called *lift*. Lift is created as an airplane moves through the air. The shape of an airplane's wings helps create lift, so a pilot can change the amount of lift by moving the flaps on the wings. If the pilot of the plane wants to land the plane, he or she has to decrease lift so that the force of gravity is greater than the lift. When this happens, gravity and lift are no longer balanced and the plane starts moving downward.

✓ **Reading Check** What two forces must be balanced so that a plane can fly at a certain altitude?

Forces in the Human Body

Nod your head. Now, hold it still. You've just experienced unbalanced and balanced forces on your body. To move any part of your body, your muscles have to exert unbalanced forces. For example, your muscles have to exert a force on your arm if you want to raise your hand in class. To hold any part of your body still, the forces on it have to be balanced, as shown in **Figure 10.** But unbalanced forces are always acting in your body even when you are completely still. For example, your blood flows through your body because the muscles of the heart exert unbalanced forces to keep the heart beating.

Figure 10 *To keep her hand up, this girl's muscles have to continue exerting a force to balance the force of gravity.*

SECTION Review

Summary

● A force is a push or a pull. Forces have size and direction and are expressed in newtons.

● Force is always exerted by one object on another object.

● Net force is determined by combining forces. Forces in the same direction are added. Forces in opposite directions are subtracted.

● Balanced forces produce no change in motion. Unbalanced forces produce a change in motion.

● Interactions of balanced and unbalanced forces are useful in recreation, sports, transportation, and the human body.

Using Key Terms

1. In your own words, write a definition for each of the following terms: *force* and *net force*.

Understanding Key Ideas

2. Which of the following may happen when an object receives unbalanced forces?
   a. The object changes direction.
   b. The object changes speed.
   c. The object starts to move.
   d. All of the above

3. Explain the difference between balanced and unbalanced forces.

4. Give an example of an unbalanced force causing a change in motion.

5. Give an example of an object that has balanced forces acting on it.

6. Explain the meaning of the phrase "Forces act on objects."

Math Skills

7. A boy pulls a wagon with a force of 6 N east as another boy pushes it with a force of 4 N east. What is the net force?

Critical Thinking

8. **Making Inferences** When finding net force, why must you know the directions of the forces acting on an object?

9. **Applying Concepts** List three forces that you exert when riding a bicycle.

10. **Analyzing Processes** Think about an activity that you do in your free time. Analyze the interactions of balanced and unbalanced forces needed to do that activity.

11. **Applying Concepts** How does the interaction of balanced and unbalanced forces help you get from your home to school?

SCILINKS

NSTA
Developed and maintained by the National Science Teachers Association

For a variety of links related to this chapter, go to www.scilinks.org

Topic: Forces
SciLinks code: HSM0604

CHAPTER RESOURCES

Chapter Resource File

• Section Quiz `GENERAL`
• Section Review `GENERAL`
• Vocabulary and Section Summary `GENERAL`

Focus

Overview

This section introduces and describes friction. Students learn about the kinds of friction and about the role of friction in everyday life.

Bellringer

Have students answer the following question:

> Suppose you and a younger sister or brother are at a neighborhood pool. Your sister or brother asks why there are signs that say "NO RUNNING." What would be your answer?

Motivate

ACTIVITY ——— GENERAL

Fingerprints Humans have ridges in the skin of their hands. These ridges increase friction between the skin and objects the hands touch. Have students make a fingerprint to better see the ridges on one finger. Give students dark-colored, washable markers. Tell students to use the marker to color the pad of one finger, and to immediately press the finger to a sheet of paper 3 or 4 times. Show students pictures of different types of fingerprints and have them classify their fingerprints as arches, loops, or whorls. **Kinesthetic**

READING WARM-UP

Objectives

- Explain why friction occurs.
- List the two types of friction, and give examples of each type.
- Explain how friction can be both harmful and helpful.

Terms to Learn

friction

READING STRATEGY

Brainstorming The key idea of this section is friction. Brainstorm words and phrases related to friction.

friction a force that opposes motion between two surfaces that are in contact

Friction: A Force That Opposes Motion

While playing ball, your friend throws the ball out of your reach. Rather than running for the ball, you walk after it. You know that the ball will stop. But do you know why?

You know that the ball is slowing down. An unbalanced force is needed to change the speed of a moving object. So, what force is stopping the ball? The force is called friction. **Friction** is a force that opposes motion between two surfaces that are in contact. Friction retards motion, which means that it can cause a moving object to slow down and eventually stop.

The Source of Friction

Friction occurs because the surface of any object is rough. Even surfaces that feel smooth are covered with microscopic hills and valleys. When two surfaces are in contact, the hills and valleys of one surface stick to the hills and valleys of the other surface, as shown in **Figure 1.** This contact causes friction.

The amount of friction between two surfaces depends on many factors. Two factors include the force pushing the surfaces together and the roughness of the surfaces.

The Effect of Force on Friction

The amount of friction depends on the force pushing the surfaces together. If this force increases, the hills and valleys of the surfaces can come into closer contact. The close contact increases the friction between the surfaces. Objects that weigh less exert less downward force than objects that weigh more do, as shown in **Figure 2.** But changing how much of the surfaces come in contact does not change the amount of friction.

Figure 1 *When the hills and valleys of one surface stick to the hills and valleys of another surface, friction is created.*

CHAPTER RESOURCES

Chapter Resource File

- **Lesson Plan**
- **Directed Reading A** BASIC
- **Directed Reading B** SPECIAL NEEDS

Technology

- **Transparencies**
  - Bellringer
  - Force and Friction

MISCONCEPTION ALERT

The Cause of Friction Many people believe that friction is caused when the hills and valleys of one surface "climb" over the hills and valleys of another surface. In fact, friction is caused by chemical bonds that are formed and broken between the hills and valleys of two surfaces. Scientists call this phenomenon the "stick and slip" cause of friction.

Figure 2   Force and Friction

ⓐ There is more friction between the book with more weight and the table than there is between the book with less weight and the table. A harder push is needed to move the heavier book.

ⓑ Turning a book on its edge does not change the amount of friction between the table and the book.

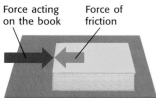

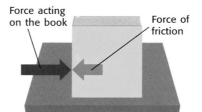

Force acting on the book   Force of friction

Force acting on the book   Force of friction

Force acting on the book   Force of friction

The Effect of Rougher Surfaces on Friction

Rough surfaces have more microscopic hills and valleys than smooth surfaces do. So, the rougher the surface is, the greater the friction is. For example, a ball rolling on the ground slows down because of the friction between the ball and the ground. A large amount of friction is produced because the ground has a rough surface. But imagine that you were playing ice hockey. If the puck passed out of your reach, it would slide across the ice for a long while before stopping. The reason the puck would continue to slide is that the ice is a smooth surface that has very little friction.

✔ Reading Check   Why is friction greater between surfaces that are rough? (*See the Appendix for answers to Reading Checks.*)

The Friction 500

1. Make a short ramp out of **a piece of cardboard** and **one or two books** on a table.
2. Put a **toy car** at the top of the ramp, and let go of the car. If necessary, adjust the ramp height so that your car does not roll off the table.
3. Put the car at the top of the ramp again, and let go of the car. Record the distance the car travels after leaving the ramp.

4. Repeat step 3 two more times, and calculate the average for your results.
5. Change the surface of the table by covering the table with **sandpaper.** Repeat steps 3 and 4.
6. Change the surface of the table one more time by covering the table with **cloth.** Repeat steps 3 and 4 again.
7. Which surface had the most friction? Why? What do you predict would happen if the car were heavier?

SCIENCE HUMOR

Tom: **This match won't light.**

Jerry: **What's the matter with it?**

Tom: **I don't know; it worked a minute ago.**

WEIRD SCIENCE

Air hockey is challenging because the puck floats on a very thin layer of air. Tiny holes in the table surface allow pressurized air to escape from underneath. The puck moves with very little friction.

Quick Lab

MATERIALS

FOR EACH GROUP
- books (2)
- cardboard, corrugated
- cloth, fuzzy or nappy
- meterstick
- sandpaper, very coarse
- toy car

Teacher's Notes: You can substitute pieces of plywood or several metersticks for the corrugated cardboard.

To keep the cars from rolling off the table, have students use one or two thin books. Students may also do the lab on the floor if they are having trouble keeping the car on the table.

If your classroom is carpeted, you can move the ramp to the floor for one of the trials.

To reduce cost, have students lay narrow strips of sandpaper and cloth in front of the ramp rather than covering the table top.

Answer

7. Answers may vary. Sample answer: The sandpaper surface had the most friction because it is the roughest. A heavier car would result in even more friction between the car and the surface because the force pushing the surfaces together would be increased. (**Note:** If students start the car from the same spot, the mass of the car will not affect the distance it travels on a given surface.)

Answer to Reading Check

Friction is greater between rough surfaces because rough surfaces have more microscopic hills and valleys.

Tires and Friction
Vehicle tires are designed to use friction to increase grip. Have students find information on as many different kinds of tires, tire compounds, and tread designs as they can. Have them do a poster or other project showing some of the types of tires and treads they have learned about. **LS** Visual

INCLUSION Strategies

- *Learning Disabled*
- *Attention Deficit Disorder*
- *Developmentally Delayed*

Let students experience the two kinds of friction. Choose several students to participate in the activity. Ask each student to try both options. Use the following situations to create each of the types of friction:

Static Friction—Gently push a school desk and feel the resistance before it starts moving.

Kinetic Friction—Push a school desk across the floor and feel the resistance to the movement. **LS** Kinesthetic *English Language Learners*

Comparing Friction
Ask an adult at home to sit on the floor. Try to push the adult across the room. Next, ask the adult to sit on a chair that has wheels and to keep his or her feet off the floor. Try pushing the adult and the chair across the room. If you do not have a chair that has wheels, try pushing the adult on different kinds of flooring. Explain why there was a difference between the two trials in your **science journal.**

Types of Friction

There are two types of friction. The friction you observe when sliding books across a tabletop is called *kinetic friction*. The other type of friction is *static friction*. You observe static friction when you push on a piece of furniture and it does not move.

Kinetic Friction

The word *kinetic* means "moving." So, kinetic friction is friction between moving surfaces. The amount of kinetic friction between two surfaces depends in part on how the surfaces move. Surfaces can slide past each other. Or a surface can roll over another surface. Usually, the force of sliding kinetic friction is greater than the force of rolling kinetic friction. Thus, it is usually easier to move objects on wheels than to slide the objects along the floor, as shown in **Figure 3.**

Kinetic friction is very useful in everyday life. You use sliding kinetic friction when you apply the brakes on a bicycle and when you write with a pencil or a piece of chalk. You also use sliding kinetic friction when you scratch a part of your body that is itchy!

Rolling kinetic friction is an important part of almost all means of transportation. Anything that has wheels—bicycles, in-line skates, cars, trains, and planes—uses rolling kinetic friction.

Figure 3 **Comparing Kinetic Friction**

a Moving a heavy piece of furniture in your room can be hard work because **the force of sliding kinetic friction is large.**

b Moving a heavy piece of furniture is easier if you put it on wheels. **The force of rolling kinetic friction is smaller** and easier to overcome.

MISCONCEPTION ///ALERT\\\

Rolling Versus Sliding   Rolling kinetic friction is usually smaller than sliding kinetic friction, but it depends on the situation. If both surfaces are hard, rolling friction is smaller. But if one of the surfaces is soft, such as deep snow, the sliding friction of skis or a sled might be a lot smaller than the rolling friction of a loaded wagon. Friction depends on several characteristics of both surfaces.

Answer to School-to-Home Activity
It is easier to push a person in a chair with wheels because rolling kinetic friction is less than sliding kinetic friction. Alternate answer: It is easier to push a person on a smooth floor because there is less friction between the person and the floor. (**Teacher's Notes:** Tell students that they can have their parents put on roller skates or roller blades or stand on a skateboard instead of sitting in a chair with wheels.)

Figure 4 ▶ Static Friction

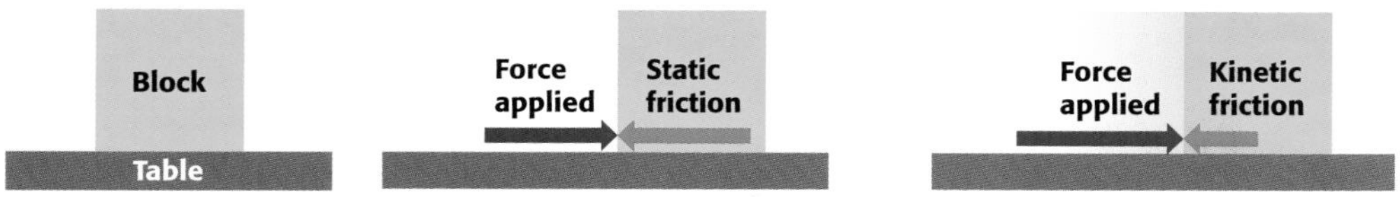

Block
Table

ⓐ There is no friction between the block and the table when no force is applied to the block.

Force applied →	← Static friction

ⓑ If a small force (purple arrow) is exerted on the block, the block does not move. The force of static friction (green arrow) balances the force applied.

Force applied →	← Kinetic friction

ⓒ When the force exerted on the block is greater than the force of static friction, the block starts moving. When the block starts moving, all static friction is gone, and only kinetic friction (green arrow) opposes the force applied.

Static Friction

When a force is applied to an object but does not cause the object to move, *static friction* occurs. The word *static* means "not moving." The object does not move because the force of static friction balances the force applied. Static friction can be overcome by applying a large enough force. Static friction disappears as soon as an object starts moving, and then kinetic friction immediately occurs. Look at **Figure 4** to understand under what conditions static friction affects an object.

✓ **Reading Check** What does the word *static* mean?

Friction: Harmful and Helpful

Think about how friction affects a car. Without friction, the tires could not push against the ground to move the car forward, and the brakes could not stop the car. Without friction, a car is useless. However, friction can also cause problems in a car. Friction between moving engine parts increases their temperature and causes the parts to wear down. A liquid coolant is added to the engine to keep the engine from overheating. And engine parts need to be changed as they wear out.

Friction is both harmful and helpful to you and the world around you. Friction can cause holes in your socks and in the knees of your jeans. Friction by wind and water can cause erosion of the topsoil that nourishes plants. On the other hand, friction between your pencil and your paper is necessary to allow the pencil to leave a mark. Without friction, you would just slip and fall when you tried to walk. Because friction can be both harmful and helpful, it is sometimes necessary to decrease or increase friction.

INTERNET ACTIVITY

For another activity related to this chapter, go to **go.hrw.com** and type in the keyword **HP5MOTW**.

CONNECTION TO Social Studies

WRITING SKILL **Invention of the Wheel** Archeologists have found evidence that the first vehicles with wheels were used in ancient Mesopotamia sometime between 3500 and 3000 BCE. Before wheels were invented, people used planks or sleds to carry loads. In your **science journal**, write a paragraph about how your life would be different if wheels did not exist.

SCIENCE HUMOR

An impatient young girl named Lenore
Tried to run on a freshly waxed floor.
Since the friction was less,
She made quite a mess
As she slid right under the door.

CHAPTER RESOURCES

Technology

Transparencies
• Static Friction

Close

Reteaching — BASIC

Helpful and Harmful Friction

Have half the class draw a comic strip showing a situation in which friction is helpful. Have the other half draw a comic strip showing a situation in which friction is harmful. Ask student volunteers to share their comic strips with the class. **LS** Visual

Quiz — GENERAL

1. Which of the following would NOT help you move a heavy object across a concrete floor? water, ball bearings, oil, liquid soap, steel rods, foam rubber (foam rubber)

2. Name three common items you might use to increase friction. (Sample answers: sticky tape, sand, work gloves)

Alternative Assessment — GENERAL

Designing a Bowling Alley

Ask students to imagine that they have been asked to design a bowling alley. Have them describe the areas where they would try to reduce friction and the areas where they would try to increase friction. Have them describe what materials they would use and why. **LS** Logical

Answer to Reading Check

Three common lubricants are oil, grease, and wax.

Reducing Friction

1. Stack **two or three heavy books** on a table. Use one finger to push the books across the table.

2. Place **five round pens or pencils** under the books, and push the books again.

3. Compare the force used in step 1 with the force used in step 2. Explain.

4. Open a **jar** with your hands, and close it again.

5. Spread a small amount of **liquid soap** on your hands.

6. Try to open the jar again. Was the jar easier or harder to open with the soap? Explain your observations.

7. In which situation was friction helpful? In which situation was friction harmful?

Figure 5 *When you work on a bicycle, watch out for the chain! You might get dirty from the grease or oil that keeps the chain moving freely. Without this lubricant, friction between the sections of the chain would quickly wear the chain out.*

Some Ways to Reduce Friction

One way to reduce friction is to use lubricants (LOO bri kuhnts). *Lubricants* are substances that are applied to surfaces to reduce the friction between the surfaces. Some examples of common lubricants are motor oil, wax, and grease. Lubricants are usually liquids, but they can be solids or gases. An example of a gas lubricant is the air that comes out of the tiny holes of an air-hockey table. **Figure 5** shows one use of a lubricant.

Friction can also be reduced by switching from sliding kinetic friction to rolling kinetic friction. Ball bearings placed between the wheels and axles of in-line skates and bicycles make it easier for the wheels to turn by reducing friction.

Another way to reduce friction is to make surfaces that rub against each other smoother. For example, rough wood on a park bench is painful to slide across because there is a large amount of friction between your leg and the bench. Rubbing the bench with sandpaper makes the bench smoother and more comfortable to sit on. The reason the bench is more comfortable is that the friction between your leg and the bench is reduced.

✓ Reading Check List three common lubricants.

MATERIALS

FOR EACH GROUP
- books, heavy (2–3)
- jar, with lid
- liquid soap
- pens or pencils, round (5)

Teacher's Note: To control the amount of soap used, you may wish to assign a single student to dispense the soap.

Answers

3. Less force was needed in step 2 because the friction was reduced by changing sliding kinetic friction to rolling kinetic friction.

6. The jar was harder to open with the soap. The soap was a lubricant that reduced the friction between my hands and the jar.

7. Friction is helpful when trying to open a jar. Friction is harmful when trying to push books across the table.

Some Ways to Increase Friction

One way to increase friction is to make surfaces rougher. For example, sand scattered on icy roads keeps cars from skidding. Baseball players sometimes wear textured batting gloves to increase the friction between their hands and the bat so that the bat does not fly out of their hands.

Another way to increase friction is to increase the force pushing the surfaces together. For example, if you are sanding a piece of wood, you can sand the wood faster by pressing harder on the sandpaper. Pressing harder increases the force pushing the sandpaper and wood together. So, the friction between the sandpaper and wood increases. **Figure 6** shows another example of friction increased by pushing on an object.

Figure 6 *No one likes cleaning dirty pans. To get this chore done quickly, press down with the scrubber to increase friction.*

SECTION Review

Summary

- Friction is a force that opposes motion.
- Friction is caused by hills and valleys on the surfaces of two objects touching each other.
- The amount of friction depends on factors such as the roughness of the surfaces and the force pushing the surfaces together.
- Two kinds of friction are kinetic friction and static friction.
- Friction can be helpful or harmful.

Using Key Terms

1. In your own words, write a definition for the term *friction*.

Understanding Key Ideas

2. Why is it easy to slip when there is water on the floor?
   a. The water is a lubricant and reduces the friction between your feet and the floor.
   b. The friction between your feet and the floor changes from kinetic to static friction.
   c. The water increases the friction between your feet and the floor.
   d. The friction between your feet and the floor changes from sliding kinetic friction to rolling kinetic friction.

3. Explain why friction occurs.

4. How does the roughness of surfaces that are touching affect the friction between the surfaces?

5. Describe how the amount of force pushing two surfaces together affects friction.

6. Name two ways in which friction can be increased.

7. List the two types of friction, and give an example of each.

Interpreting Graphics

8. Why do you think the sponge shown below has a layer of plastic bristles attached to it?

Critical Thinking

9. **Applying Concepts** Name two ways that friction is harmful and two ways that friction is helpful to you when riding a bicycle.

10. **Making Inferences** Describe a situation in which static friction is useful.

Developed and maintained by the National Science Teachers Association

For a variety of links related to this chapter, go to www.scilinks.org

Topic: Force and Friction
SciLinks code: HSM0601

Answers to Section Review

1. Sample answer: Friction is a force that works against the motion of an object.

2. a

3. Friction occurs because the microscopic hills and valleys of two touching surfaces stick to each other.

4. As the roughness of the surfaces increases, the friction between the surfaces increases.

5. As the force pushing two surfaces together increases, the friction between the surfaces increases.

6. Friction can be increased by making surfaces rougher and by increasing the force pushing the surfaces together.

7. The two kinds of friction are kinetic friction and static friction. Sample answer: An example of kinetic friction is the friction that happens when you slide a chair across the floor. An example of static friction is the friction that keeps an eraser sitting on a tilted book from sliding down.

8. The sponge has a layer of plastic bristles on it to make it rougher. The rough bristles increase the friction between the sponge and the surface being cleaned. The increased friction helps clean pots and pans.

9. Answers may vary. Sample answer: Friction is harmful because it causes tire tread to wear down and causes the brakes to wear down. Friction is helpful because it helps the wheels grip the road and helps your feet and hands stay on the pedals and handlebars.

10. Answers may vary. Sample answer: Static friction is useful when you lean against a table for support. The table doesn't move because of static friction between the feet of the table and the floor.

Focus

Overview

This section describes gravity and the relationship between gravitational force, mass, and distance. It also distinguishes between weight and mass.

Bellringer

Significantly decreased gravity gives astronauts the sensation of being weightless and forces astronauts to make many adjustments in their activities. Ask students to write a paragraph explaining what they would like and dislike about living with reduced gravity.

Motivate

Group ACTiViTy — GENERAL

Gravity Poster Before beginning this activity, lead a brief discussion about gravity. During this discussion, be sure your students understand that gravity pulls objects toward Earth. Then, have students work in small groups. Each group should pick a sport or an activity that is affected by gravity. Each group should identify examples from the sport or activity in which gravity is beneficial and examples of when gravity is harmful. Ask each group to make a poster illustrating their examples.
 Visual Co-op Learning

READING WARM-UP

Objectives

- Describe gravity and its effect on matter.
- Explain the law of universal gravitation.
- Explain how an object's center of mass is used to determine gravitational force.
- Describe the difference between mass and weight.

Terms to Learn

gravity
weight
mass

READING STRATEGY

Paired Summarizing Read this section silently. In pairs, take turns summarizing the material. Stop to discuss ideas that seem confusing.

gravity a force of attraction between objects that is due to their masses

Gravity: A Force of Attraction

Have you ever seen a video of astronauts on the moon? They bounce around like beach balls even though they wear big, bulky spacesuits. Why is leaping on the moon easier than leaping on Earth?

The answer is gravity. **Gravity** is a force of attraction between objects that is due to their masses. The force of gravity can change the motion of an object by changing its speed, direction, or both. In this section, you will learn about gravity and its effects on objects, such as the astronaut in **Figure 1.**

The Effects of Gravity on Matter

All matter has mass. Gravity is a result of mass. Therefore, all matter is affected by gravity. That is, all objects experience an attraction toward all other objects. This gravitational force pulls objects toward each other. Right now, because of gravity, you are being pulled toward this book, your pencil, and every other object around you.

These objects are also being pulled toward you and toward each other because of gravity. So why don't you see the effects of this attraction? In other words, why don't you notice objects moving toward each other? The reason is that the mass of most objects is too small to cause a force large enough to move objects toward each other. However, you are familiar with one object that is massive enough to cause a noticeable attraction—the Earth.

Figure 1 *Because the moon has less gravity than the Earth does, walking on the moon's surface was a very bouncy experience for the Apollo astronauts.*

CHAPTER RESOURCES

Chapter Resource File

- **Lesson Plan**
- **Directed Reading A** BASIC
- **Directed Reading B** SPECIAL NEEDS

Technology

Transparencies
- Bellringer
- *LINK TO EARTH SCIENCE* Tidal Variations

The Size of Earth's Gravitational Force

Compared with all objects around you, Earth has a huge mass. Therefore, Earth's gravitational force is very large. You must apply forces to overcome Earth's gravitational force any time you lift objects or even parts of your body.

Earth's gravitational force pulls everything toward the center of Earth. Because of this force, the books, tables, and chairs in the room stay in place, and dropped objects fall to Earth rather than moving together or toward you.

✓ Reading Check Why must you exert a force to pick up an object? (*See the Appendix for answers to Reading Checks.*)

Newton and the Study of Gravity

For thousands of years, people asked two very puzzling questions: Why do objects fall toward Earth, and what keeps the planets moving in the sky? The two questions were treated separately until 1665 when a British scientist named Sir Isaac Newton realized that they were two parts of the same question.

The Core of an Idea

The legend is that Newton made the connection between the two questions when he watched a falling apple, as shown in **Figure 2.** He knew that unbalanced forces are needed to change the motion of objects. He concluded that an unbalanced force on the apple made the apple fall. And he reasoned that an unbalanced force on the moon kept the moon moving circularly around Earth. He proposed that these two forces are actually the same force—a force of attraction called *gravity*.

The Birth of a Law

Newton summarized his ideas about gravity in a law now known as the *law of universal gravitation*. This law describes the relationships between gravitational force, mass, and distance. The law is called *universal* because it applies to all objects in the universe.

Figure 2 *Sir Isaac Newton realized that the same unbalanced force affected the motions of the apple and the moon.*

Is That a Fact!

In the reduced gravity of space, astronauts lose bone and muscle mass. Sleep patterns may be affected and so may cardiovascular strength and the immune response. These same effects happen more gradually as people age on Earth. Scientists are interested in studying the effects of microgravity so they can find ways to counteract them in space and here on Earth.

Answer to Reading Check

You must exert a force to overcome the gravitational force between the object and Earth.

📖 READING STRATEGY — GENERAL

Prediction Guide Before students read this section, ask them to predict whether the following statements are true or false:

- Objects of any size exert a gravitational force. (true)
- The moon is held in its orbit by unbalanced forces. (true)
- If you traveled to Jupiter and you neither gained nor lost mass, your weight on Jupiter would be much greater than your weight on Earth. (true)

LS Verbal

Demonstration — GENERAL

MATERIALS

- beanbag
- sock
- string
- toilet-paper tube

Safety Caution: Everyone should wear safety goggles during this demonstration.

Modeling Gravity Cut a length of string about 2 m long. Ball up the sock, and tie one end of the string around it. Pull the free end of the string through the tube, then tie it around the beanbag. Hold the tube, and twirl the beanbag in a circle. The sock represents the sun, and the beanbag represents Earth. Explain that the string represents the gravitational attraction between Earth and the sun. **LS** Visual

CONNECTION to Earth Science — GENERAL

Gravity and the Tides Use the teaching transparency titled "Tidal Variations" to help students understand the effects the moon's gravitational force has on Earth's tides. **LS** Visual

Jupiter's Moons Have students research the unusual characteristics of Io and Europa, two of the moons of Jupiter studied by the *Voyager* and *Galileo* spacecraft. Have students write a report that describes the effects of Jupiter's gravitational force on the moons and explains why scientists think Europa may have life forms. LS Verbal

The Law of Universal Gravitation Have students find the mathematical formula for the law of universal gravitation. Ask students to write the equation and write what each symbol means. Then, have students write a brief paragraph explaining the mathematical relationships between the variables in the equation. (The relationships between the variables are as follows: Gravitational force and the masses of the objects are directly proportional (gravitational force will increase if either mass increases). Gravitational force is inversely proportional to the square of the distance between the objects (gravitational force will decrease if the distance between the masses increases).) LS Logical

CONNECTION TO
Astronomy

WRITING **Black Holes** Black
SKILL holes are 4 times to 1 billion times as massive as our sun. So, the gravitational effects around a black hole are very large. The gravitational force of a black hole is so large that objects that enter a black hole can never get out. Even light cannot escape from a black hole. Because black holes do not emit light, they cannot be seen. Research how astronomers can detect black holes without seeing them. Write a one-page paper that details the results of your research.

The Law of Universal Gravitation

The law of universal gravitation is the following: All objects in the universe attract each other through gravitational force. The size of the force depends on the masses of the objects and the distance between the objects. Understanding the law is easier if you consider it in two parts.

Part 1: Gravitational Force Increases as Mass Increases

Imagine an elephant and a cat. Because an elephant has a larger mass than a cat does, the amount of gravity between an elephant and Earth is greater than the amount of gravity between a cat and Earth. So, a cat is much easier to pick up than an elephant! There is also gravity between the cat and the elephant, but that force is very small because the cat's mass and the elephant's mass are so much smaller than Earth's mass. **Figure 3** shows the relationship between mass and gravitational force.

This part of the law of universal gravitation also explains why the astronauts on the moon bounce when they walk. The moon has less mass than Earth does. Therefore, the moon's gravitational force is less than Earth's. The astronauts bounced around on the moon because they were not being pulled down with as much force as they would have been on Earth.

✓ **Reading Check** How does mass affect gravitational force?

Figure 3 **How Mass Affects Gravitational Force**

The gravitational force between objects increases as the masses of the objects increase. The arrows indicate the gravitational force between two objects. The length of the arrows indicates the strength of the force.

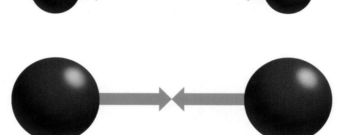

ⓐ Gravitational force is small between objects that have small masses.

ⓑ Gravitational force is large when the mass of one or both objects is large.

⚛ WEIRD SCIENCE

Black Holes and Gravity Black holes are more massive than the sun, but they are extremely small relative to other celestial objects. A black hole can be 10 times more massive than our sun and have a radius of only 30 km. The gravitational force exerted by a black hole is so powerful that it crushes any matter that falls into the black hole to a point of zero volume. This phenomenon of a mass occupying zero volume is called a *singularity* and is treated as the center of a black hole.

Part 2: Gravitational Force Decreases as Distance Increases

The gravitational force between you and Earth is large. Whenever you jump up, you are pulled back down by Earth's gravitational force. On the other hand, the sun is more than 300,000 times more massive than Earth. So why doesn't the sun's gravitational force affect you more than Earth's does? The reason is that the sun is so far away.

You are about 150 million kilometers (93 million miles) away from the sun. At this distance, the gravitational force between you and the sun is very small. If there were some way you could stand on the sun, you would find it impossible to move. The gravitational force acting on you would be so great that you could not move any part of your body!

Although the sun's gravitational force on your body is very small, the force is very large on Earth and the other planets, as shown in **Figure 4.** The gravity between the sun and the planets is large because the objects have large masses. If the sun's gravitational force did not have such an effect on the planets, the planets would not stay in orbit around the sun. **Figure 5** will help you understand the relationship between gravitational force and distance.

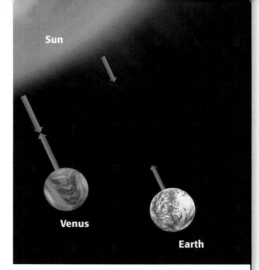

Figure 4 *Venus and Earth have approximately the same mass. But because Venus is closer to the sun, the gravitational force between Venus and the sun is greater than the gravitational force between Earth and the sun.*

Figure 5 **How Distance Affects Gravitational Force**

The gravitational force between objects decreases as the distance between the objects increases. The length of the arrows indicates the strength of the gravitational force between two objects.

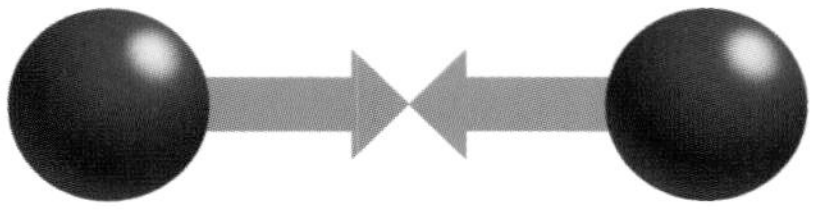

ⓐ Gravitational force is strong when the distance between two objects is small.

ⓑ If the distance between two objects increases, the gravitational force pulling them together decreases rapidly.

ACTIVITY — GENERAL

Story Analysis Have students read H. G. Wells's 1901 story "The First Men in the Moon." Take one class to discuss the story and Wells's use of "Cavorite." Discuss how well the story fits with current scientific knowledge of the moon and gravity. How might the story be different if it were written today?

LS Verbal

Research — ADVANCED

Gravitational Force on Other Planets Have students research and compare the gravitational force on other planets with the gravitational force on Earth. Then, have students write a short story or make a poster about what life would be like with different gravitational forces acting on their bodies. English Language Learners

LS Visual

Answer to Reading Check

Gravitational force increases as mass increases. (**Teacher's note:** Gravitational force increases as one or both of the masses increase.)

Science Bloopers

It's Not the Moon's Fault The moon used to be blamed for some strange behaviors in humans and animals (the word *lunatic* comes from the Latin word *luna,* meaning "moon"). Scientists once thought the moon affected the human body's fluids the same way it affects ocean tides. Women's menstrual cycles reinforced this belief. Today, scientists know that there is little evidence to support these beliefs.

CHAPTER RESOURCES

Technology

Transparencies
- Gravitational Force Depends on Mass
- Gravitational Force Depends on Distance

Demonstration — GENERAL

MATERIALS

- cardboard, thin
- corkboard
- hole punch
- pencil or pen
- pushpin
- ruler
- scissors
- string, 40 cm
- weight (such as a washer)

Use this demonstration to show students another way to find the center of mass of an object. If enough materials are available, students can do this demonstration as an activity. Cut out an irregular shape from a piece of thin cardboard. Use a hole punch to punch 3–5 holes around the edge of the shape. Put a pushpin through one of the holes, and tack the shape to a corkboard so that the shape can rotate freely. Attach a weight to the end of a string. Tie a loop on the other end of the string. Use the loop to hang the string from the pushpin. When the string stops moving, use a ruler to trace a line on the cardboard that follows the string. Repeat for each of the holes in the cardboard. The point where the lines intersect is the center of mass of the cardboard.

LS Visual/Kinesthetic

Figure 6 *The distance between a person standing on the ground and Earth is not 0 m! When finding distance to determine gravitational force, you always measure from the center of mass of each object.*

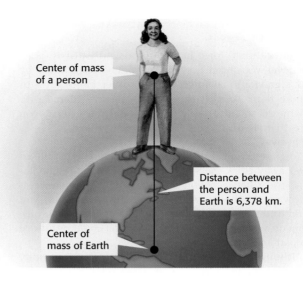

Center of mass of a person

Distance between the person and Earth is 6,378 km.

Center of mass of Earth

Gravitational Force and Center of Mass

You know that gravitational force depends on the distance between objects. But, how do you find the distance between objects? For example, if you need to know the distance between you and your friend, where would you measure? Would you measure from your nose to your friend's nose or from your foot to your friend's foot? When finding the distance between objects to determine gravitational force, scientists always measure from the center of mass of each object. The *center of mass* is the point at which all the mass of an object can be considered to be concentrated. **Figure 6** shows how the distance between a person and Earth is measured by using centers of mass.

Finding the Center of Mass

Finding the center of mass for regularly shaped objects, such as spheres and cubes, is easy. The center of mass is in the center of such objects. But finding the center of mass of an irregular object or an object that does not have a uniform density can be more difficult. However, one simple way to find the center of mass of an object is to spin the object. The point around which the object spins is its center of mass.

Scientists usually measure the motion of an object by the motion of its center of mass. Look at **Figure 7.** The hammer is spinning around its center of mass as it moves through the air. The line drawn on the photo shows how the center of mass moves. So, if you wanted to measure how far the hammer moved, you would measure from one end of the red line to the other end.

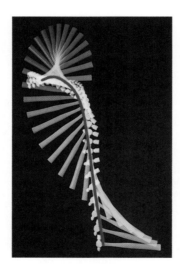

Figure 7 *Objects always spin around their center of mass. The motion of an object is usually described as the motion of its center of mass.*

CONNECTION ACTIVITY
Real World —— BASIC

Diving and Center of Mass The day before doing this activity, ask students to bring jointed dolls or action figures to class. Show students videos of competitive divers. Discuss how the divers spin around their centers of mass when somersaulting in the air. Then, have students find the centers of mass of their dolls. Encourage them to bend the dolls' arms and legs to see how the centers of mass change as the dolls' shapes change. **LS Visual/Kinesthetic**

Weight as a Measure of Gravitational Force

Gravity is a force of attraction between objects. **Weight** is a measure of the gravitational force on an object. When you see or hear the word *weight,* it usually refers to Earth's gravitational force on an object. But weight can also be a measure of the gravitational force exerted on objects by the moon or other planets.

The Differences Between Weight and Mass

Weight is related to mass, but they are not the same. Weight changes when gravitational force changes. **Mass** is the amount of matter in an object. An object's mass does not change. Imagine that an object is moved to a place that has a greater gravitational force—such as the planet Jupiter. The object's weight will increase, but its mass will remain the same. **Figure 8** shows the weight and mass of an astronaut on Earth and on the moon. The moon's gravitational force is about one-sixth of Earth's gravitational force.

Gravitational force is about the same everywhere on Earth. So, the weight of any object is about the same everywhere. Because mass and weight are constant on Earth, the terms *weight* and *mass* are often used to mean the same thing. This can be confusing. Be sure you understand the difference!

✓ Reading Check How is gravitational force related to the weight of an object?

weight a measure of the gravitational force exerted on an object; its value can change with the location of the object in the universe

mass a measure of the amount of matter in an object

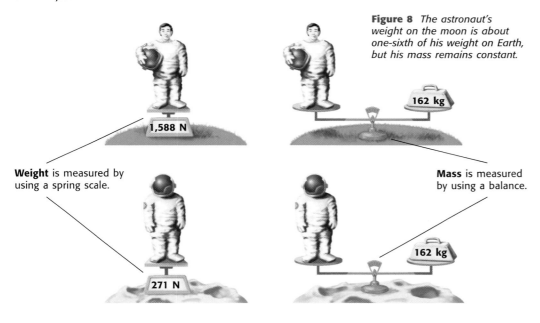

Figure 8 *The astronaut's weight on the moon is about one-sixth of his weight on Earth, but his mass remains constant.*

162 kg

1,588 N

Weight is measured by using a spring scale.

Mass is measured by using a balance.

271 N

162 kg

Discussion ——— **ADVANCED**

Weight and Position Ask students if they would weigh the same at sea level, on Mount Everest, and on the moon. Students should know from the information in this section that their weight would be less on the moon. However, some students may have difficulties understanding that their weight will be slightly less on Mount Everest than it will be at sea level. To help students understand this idea, remind them that gravitational force depends on distance. Then, remind them that the distance between Earth and a person on Earth is the distance between the centers of mass. Explain that a person on Mount Everest is farther away from Earth's center of mass, so there is less gravitational force on that person and he or she weighs less. **LS Logical**

Answer to Reading Check
The weight of an object is a measure of the gravitational force on the object.

Close

Reteaching ——— BASIC
Illustrating Mass and Weight
To reinforce the difference between mass and weight, have students make a poster similar to **Figure 8**. In the posters students should compare the mass and weight of an object on Earth and on another planet.
LS Visual

Quiz ——————— GENERAL

1. What is the difference between mass and weight?
(Mass is the amount of matter in an object. Weight is a measure of the gravitational force on an object.)

2. What must you know in order to calculate the gravitational force between two objects?
(their masses and the distance between them)

3. Where would you weigh the most, on a boat, on the space shuttle, or on the moon?
(on a boat)

Alternative Assessment ——— GENERAL

Gravity Improvisation Have small groups of students use objects they find in the classroom to explain the relationship between mass, distance, and gravitational force. Tell students that they may move around the classroom and move objects if needed. LS Kinesthetic

Figure 9 *A small apple weighs 1 N. The newton is the SI unit of weight.*

Figure 10 *Jellyfish look like flying saucers when gravity is balanced by the upward force of water but are only lumps when washed up on the beach.*

Units of Weight and Mass

You have learned that the SI unit of force is a newton (N). Gravity is a force, and weight is a measure of gravity. So, weight is also measured in newtons. The SI unit of mass is the kilogram (kg). Mass is often measured in grams (g) and milligrams (mg) as well. On Earth, a 100 g object, such as the apple shown in **Figure 9**, weighs about 1 N.

When you use a bathroom scale, you are measuring the gravitational force between your body and Earth. So, you are measuring your weight, which should be given in newtons. However, many bathroom scales have units of pounds and kilograms instead of newtons. Thus, people sometimes mistakenly think that the kilogram (like the pound) is a unit of weight.

✓ **Reading Check** What is the SI unit for force? What is the SI unit for mass?

The Influences of Weight on Shape

Gravitational force influences the shapes of living things. On land, large animals must have strong skeletons to support their mass against the force of gravity. For example, you would never see an elephant that has legs as thin as a person's legs! And the trunks of trees support the mass of the tree. For organisms that live in water, however, the downward force of gravity is balanced by the upward force of the water. For many of these creatures, strong skeletons are unnecessary. Jellyfish, such as the ones shown in **Figure 10**, have no skeleton. So, jellyfish drift gracefully through the water, but they collapse if they wash up on the beach.

Answer to Reading Check
The SI unit of force is the newton. The SI unit of mass is the kilogram.

Summary

- Gravity is a force of attraction between objects that is due to their masses.
- The law of universal gravitation states that all objects in the universe attract each other through gravitational force.
- Gravitational force increases as mass increases.
- Gravitational force decreases as distance increases.
- The distance between objects is measured between the centers of mass.
- Mass is the amount of matter in an object. Weight is a measure of the gravitational force on an object.

Using Key Terms

1. In your own words, write a definition for the term *gravity*.

2. Use each of the following terms in a separate sentence: *mass* and *weight*.

Understanding Key Ideas

3. If Earth's mass doubled without changing its size, your weight would
   a. increase because gravitational force increases.
   b. decrease because gravitational force increases.
   c. increase because gravitational force decreases.
   d. not change because you are still on Earth.

4. What is the law of universal gravitation?

5. How does the mass of an object relate to the gravitational force that the object exerts on other objects?

6. How does the distance between objects affect the gravitational force between them?

7. Why are mass and weight often confused?

8. How is an object's center of mass used to determine gravitational force?

Critical Thinking

9. **Applying Concepts** Your friend thinks that there is no gravity in space. How could you explain to your friend that there must be gravity in space?

10. **Making Comparisons** Explain why it is your weight and not your mass that would change if you landed on Mars.

Interpreting Graphics

A teacher placed four sets of objects around the classroom. A student measured the mass of each object and the distance between the two objects in each set. The data the student collected are shown in the table below. Use the table below to answer the questions that follow.

Data Collected			
Set	Mass A (g)	Mass B (g)	Distance (cm)
1	100	50	40
2	100	100	20
3	50	50	40
4	100	50	20

11. For which set of objects is the gravitational force between the two objects the greatest? Explain your answer.

12. Compare sets 1 and 4. For which set is the gravitational force smaller? Explain your answer.

SCiLINKS®
NSTA
Developed and maintained by the National Science Teachers Association

For a variety of links related to this chapter, go to www.scilinks.org

Topic: Matter and Gravity
SciLinks code: HSM0922

Answers to Section Review

1. Sample answer: Gravity is a force of attraction between objects that is due to their masses.

2. Sample answer: The mass of the astronaut is the same whether he is on Earth or in space. The weight of a small apple is about 1 N.

3. a

CHAPTER RESOURCES

Chapter Resource File

- **Section Quiz** GENERAL
- **Section Review** GENERAL
- **Vocabulary and Section Summary** GENERAL
- **Reinforcement Worksheet** BASIC
- **Critical Thinking** ADVANCED

---

4. The law of universal gravitation states that all objects attract each other through gravitational force and that the size of the gravitational force between objects depends on their masses and the distance between them.

5. The greater an object's mass, the larger the gravitational force it exerts on other objects.

6. As the distance between objects increases, the gravitational force between them decreases. As the distance between objects decreases, the gravitational force between them increases.

7. Mass and weight are often confused because they both are constant on Earth and because the terms *mass* and *weight* are sometimes used to mean the same thing.

8. The gravitational force between two objects depends on the distance between the objects. When finding the distance between objects, scientists always measure from the centers of mass of the objects.

9. Sample answer: You can tell your friend that there must be gravity in space because gravity holds the planets in orbit around the sun.

10. Your weight would change if you landed on Mars because the gravitational force on Mars is different from the gravitational force on Earth. But your mass would not change because the amount of matter in your body would not change.

11. Set 2; The masses of the objects is the greatest for all sets and the distance between the objects is one of the shortest distances in the data table.

12. Set 1; The objects in Sets 1 and 4 have the same mass, so the distance between the objects causes the difference in gravitational force. The objects in Set 1 are the farther apart, so the gravitational force between them is smaller.

Detecting Acceleration

Teacher's Notes

Time Required

One or two 45-minute class periods

Lab Ratings

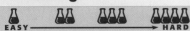

EASY — HARD

Teacher Prep 🧪
Student Set-Up 🧪🧪
Concept Level 🧪🧪🧪
Clean Up 🧪🧪

MATERIALS

The materials listed are for each student or each small group of 2–3 students. Instead of using modeling clay to secure the thread to the bottle cap, students can cut the thread long enough so that it hangs out while the lid is screwed on tightly.

Safety Caution

Remind students to review all safety cautions and icons before beginning this lab activity.

Preparation Notes

You may wish to build an accelerometer before class to show students. You may wish to have students make a chart to collect their data.

Skills Practice Lab

Detecting Acceleration

Have you ever noticed that you can "feel" acceleration? In a car or in an elevator, you may notice changes in speed or direction—even with your eyes closed! You are able to sense these changes because of tiny hair cells in your ears. These cells detect the movement of fluid in your inner ear. The fluid accelerates when you do, and the hair cells send a message about the acceleration to your brain. This message allows you to sense the acceleration. In this activity, you will build a device that detects acceleration. This device is called an *accelerometer* (ak SEL uhr AHM uht uhr).

Procedure

1 Cut a piece of string that reaches three-quarters of the way into the container.

2 Use a pushpin to attach one end of the string to the cork or plastic-foam ball.

3 Use modeling clay to attach the other end of the string to the center of the inside of the container lid. The cork or ball should hang no farther than three-quarters of the way into the container.

4 Fill the container with water.

5 Put the lid tightly on the container. The string and cork or ball should be inside the container.

6 Turn the container upside down. The cork should float about three-quarters of the way up inside the container, as shown at right. You are now ready to detect acceleration by using your accelerometer and completing the following steps.

7 Put the accelerometer on a tabletop. The container lid should touch the tabletop. Notice that the cork floats straight up in the water.

8 Now, gently push the accelerometer across the table at a constant speed. Notice that the cork quickly moves in the direction you are pushing and then swings backward. If you did not see this motion, repeat this step until you are sure you can see the first movement of the cork.

OBJECTIVES

Build an accelerometer.

Explain how an accelerometer works.

MATERIALS

- container, 1 L, with watertight lid
- cork or plastic-foam ball, small
- modeling clay
- pushpin
- scissors
- string
- water

SAFETY

Elsie Waynes
Terrell Junior High
Washington, D.C.

CHAPTER RESOURCES

Chapter Resource File

- Datasheet for Chapter Lab
- Lab Notes and Answers

Technology
- Classroom Videos
  - Lab Video

LabBook

- Built for Speed
- Science Friction
- Relating Mass and Weight

9 After you are familiar with how to use your accelerometer, try the following changes in motion. For each change, record your observations of the cork's first motion.

a. As you move the accelerometer across the table, gradually increase its speed.

b. As you move the accelerometer across the table, gradually decrease its speed.

c. While moving the accelerometer across the table, change the direction in which you are pushing.

d. Make any other changes in motion you can think of. You should make only one change to the motion for each trial.

Analyze the Results

1 **Analyzing Results** When you move the bottle at a constant speed, why does the cork quickly swing backward after it moves in the direction of acceleration?

2 **Explaining Events** The cork moves forward (in the direction you were moving the bottle) when you speed up but moves backward when you slow down. Explain why the cork moves this way. (Hint: Think about the direction of acceleration.)

Draw Conclusions

3 **Making Predictions** Imagine you are standing on a corner and watching a car that is waiting at a stoplight. A passenger inside the car is holding some helium balloons. Based on what you observed with your accelerometer, what do you think will happen to the balloons when the car begins moving?

Applying Your Data

If you move the bottle in a circle at a constant speed, what do you predict the cork will do? Try it, and check your answer.

Analyze the Results

1. The bottle stops accelerating (it is moving with a constant speed), so the cork shows zero acceleration.

2. The cork will move opposite to the motion of the water. As the bottle accelerates forward, the water sloshes backward, which makes the cork move forward. The cork will always move in the direction of acceleration.

Draw Conclusions

3. As the car begins accelerating forward, the balloons will move forward because the air in the car moves backward. When the car reaches a steady speed, the balloons will move back to stand straight up.

Applying Your Data

The cork will also travel in a circle, staying closest to the side of the bottle nearest the center of the circle.

Chapter Review

Assignment Guide

Section	Questions
1	4, 6, 10–11, 14–15, 17–19
2	2–3, 7, 20
3	1, 16
4	5, 8–9, 12–13

ANSWERS

Using Key Terms

1. Friction
2. newton
3. net force
4. velocity
5. weight

Understanding Key Ideas

6. b
7. d
8. c
9. c
10. Motion occurs when an object changes position over time when compared with a reference point (an object that appears to stay in place).
11. Acceleration can occur simply by a change in direction. Thus, no change in speed is necessary for acceleration.

USING KEY TERMS

Complete each of the following sentences by choosing the correct term from the word bank.

mass   gravity
friction   weight
speed   velocity
net force   newton

1. ___ opposes motion between surfaces that are touching.

2. The ___ is the unit of force.

3. ___ is determined by combining forces.

4. Acceleration is the rate at which ___ changes.

5. ___ is a measure of the gravitational force on an object.

UNDERSTANDING KEY IDEAS

Multiple Choice

6. If a student rides her bicycle on a straight road and does not speed up or slow down, she is traveling with a
   a. constant acceleration.
   b. constant velocity.
   c. positive acceleration.
   d. negative acceleration.

7. A force
   a. is expressed in newtons.
   b. can cause an object to speed up, slow down, or change direction.
   c. is a push or a pull.
   d. All of the above

8. If you are in a spacecraft that has been launched into space, your weight would
   a. increase because gravitational force is increasing.
   b. increase because gravitational force is decreasing.
   c. decrease because gravitational force is decreasing.
   d. decrease because gravitational force is increasing.

9. The gravitational force between 1 kg of lead and Earth is ___ the gravitational force between 1 kg of marshmallows and Earth.
   a. greater than   c. the same as
   b. less than   d. None of the above

Short Answer

10. Describe the relationship between motion and a reference point.

11. How is it possible to be accelerating but traveling at a constant speed?

12. What is the center of mass of an object? How can you find it?

13. Explain the difference between mass and weight.

12. The center of mass of an object is the point at which all the mass of the object can be considered to be concentrated. You can find the center of mass of an object by spinning it. The object will spin around its center of mass.

13. Mass is the amount of matter in an object, and its value does not change with the object's location. Weight measures the gravitational force on an object, so it can change as the amount of gravitational force changes.

Math Skills

14 A kangaroo hops 60 m to the east in 5 s. Use this information to answer the following questions.

a. What is the kangaroo's average speed?

b. What is the kangaroo's average velocity?

c. The kangaroo stops at a lake for a drink of water and then starts hopping again to the south. Each second, the kangaroo's velocity increases 2.5 m/s. What is the kangaroo's acceleration after 5 s?

CRITICAL THINKING

15 Concept Mapping Use the following terms to create a concept map: *speed, velocity, acceleration, force, direction,* and *motion.*

16 Applying Concepts Your family is moving, and you are asked to help move some boxes. One box is so heavy that you must push it across the room rather than lift it. What are some ways you could reduce friction to make moving the box easier?

17 Analyzing Ideas Considering the scientific meaning of the word *acceleration,* how could using the term *accelerator* when talking about a car's gas pedal lead to confusion?

18 Identifying Relationships Explain why it is important for airplane pilots to know wind velocity and not just wind speed during a flight.

INTERPRETING GRAPHICS

Use the figures below to answer the questions that follow.

19 Is the graph below showing positive acceleration or negative acceleration? How can you tell?

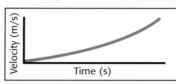

20 You know how to combine two forces that act in one or two directions. The same method can be used to combine several forces acting in several directions. Look at the diagrams, and calculate the net force in each diagram. Predict the direction each object will move.

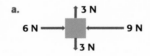

a.

3 N
6 N → ■ ← 9 N
3 N

b.

5 N → ■ ← 5 N
5 N

c.

4 N
8 N → ■
4 N

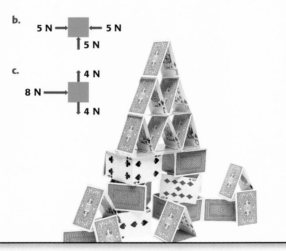

---

14. a. 12 m/s

b. 12 m/s east

c. 2.5 m/s² south

Critical Thinking

15. An answer to this exercise can be found at the end of this book.

16. Accept all reasonable answers. Sample answers: Use a hand-cart or dolly to take advantage of rolling kinetic friction. Polish the floor to reduce sliding kinetic friction.

17. The car's gas pedal is pressed by the driver to increase the car's speed. Since the scientific meaning of the term *acceleration* can include slowing down and even changing direction, *accelerator* is not an accurate term for this device.

18. It is helpful for pilots to know wind velocity because velocity includes direction. Pilots need to know the wind's speed and direction so that they will know whether the wind is blowing in the same direction as the plane (which could increase the plane's resultant velocity and lead to an earlier arrival time) or in a different direction than the plane (which might lead to a later arrival).

Interpreting Graphics

19. The graph shows positive acceleration. Velocity increases as time passes.

20. a. 3 N to the left

b. 5 N up

c. 8 N to the right

Standardized Test Preparation

Standardized Test Preparation

Teacher's Note

To provide practice under more realistic testing conditions, give students 20 minutes to answer all of the questions in this Standardized Test Preparation.

READING

Passage 1

1. C
2. I
3. B

 TEST DOCTOR

Question 3: A definition for *wind tunnel* is not given in the reading passage. However, students can infer from the passage that a wind tunnel is a place that can be used to test the speed of objects in the air. The passage states that DiTullio tested the dimpled bat in a wind tunnel and states that DiTullio learned from the results in the wind tunnel that the dimpled bat could be swung faster.

READING

Read each of the passages below. Then, answer the questions that follow each passage.

Passage 1 If you look closely at the surface of a golf ball, you'll see dozens of tiny dimples. When air flows past these dimples, the air is stirred up and stays near the surface of the ball. By keeping air moving near the surface of the ball, the dimples help the golf ball move faster and farther through the air. Jeff DiTullio, a teacher at MIT in Cambridge, Massachusetts, decided to apply this principle to a baseball bat. When DiTullio tested his dimpled bat in a <u>wind tunnel</u>, he found that the bat could be swung 3% to 5% faster than a bat without dimples. That increase may not seem like much, but the dimpled bat could add about 5 m of distance to a fly ball!

1. Who is Jeff DiTullio?
   A the inventor of the dimpled golf ball
   B a teacher at Cambridge University
   C the inventor of the dimpled bat
   D a professional baseball player

2. Which of the following ideas is NOT stated in the passage?
   F Dimples make DiTullio's bat move faster.
   G MIT is in Cambridge, Massachusetts.
   H Air that is stirred up near the surface of DiTullio's bat makes it easier to swing the bat faster.
   I DiTullio will make a lot of money from his invention.

3. In the passage, what does *wind tunnel* mean?
   A a place to practice batting
   B a place to test the speed of objects in the air
   C a baseball stadium
   D a passageway that is shielded from the wind

Passage 2 The Golden Gate Bridge in San Francisco, California, is one of the most famous <u>landmarks</u> in the world. Approximately 9 million people from around the world visit the bridge each year.

The Golden Gate Bridge is a suspension bridge. A suspension bridge is one in which the roadway is hung, or suspended, from huge cables that extend from one end of the bridge to the other. The main cables on the Golden Gate Bridge are 2.33 km long. Many forces act on the main cables. For example, smaller cables pull down on the main cables to connect the roadway to the main cables. And two towers that are 227 m tall push up on the main cables. The forces on the main cable must be balanced, or the bridge will collapse.

1. In this passage, what does *landmarks* mean?
   A large areas of land
   B well-known places
   C street signs
   D places where people meet

2. Which of the following statements is a fact from the passage?
   F The roadway of the Golden Gate Bridge is suspended from huge cables.
   G The towers of the Golden Gate Bridge are 2.33 km tall.
   H The main cables connect the roadway to the towers.
   I The forces on the cables are not balanced.

3. According to the passage, why do people from around the world visit the Golden Gate Bridge?
   A It is the longest bridge in the world.
   B It is a suspension bridge.
   C It is the only bridge that is painted orange.
   D It is a famous landmark.

Passage 2

1. B
2. F
3. D

 TEST DOCTOR

Question 2: Students may chose answer G because they see the number 2.33 in the passage. However, the number 2.33 refers to the length of the main cables of the Golden Gate Bridge and not to the height of the bridge's towers. Some students should be able to eliminate this answer because it would be impossible to build towers that are 2.33 km tall.

The graph below shows the data collected by a student as she watched a squirrel running on the ground. Use the graph below to answer the questions that follow.

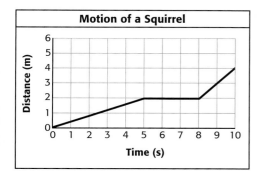

Motion of a Squirrel

1. Which of the following best describes the motion of the squirrel between 5 s and 8 s?
   A The squirrel's speed increased.
   B The squirrel's speed decreased.
   C The squirrel's speed did not change.
   D The squirrel moved backward.

2. Which of the following statements about the motion of the squirrel is true?
   F The squirrel moved with the greatest speed between 0 s and 5 s.
   G The squirrel moved with the greatest speed between 8 s and 10 s.
   H The squirrel moved with a constant speed between 0 s and 8 s.
   I The squirrel moved with a constant speed between 5 s and 10 s.

3. What is the average speed of the squirrel between 8 s and 10 s?
   A 0.4 m/s
   B 1 m/s
   C 2 m/s
   D 4 m/s

MATH

Read each question below, and choose the best answer.

1. The distance between Cedar Rapids, Iowa, and Sioux Falls, South Dakota, is about 660 km. How long will it take a car traveling with an average speed of 95 km/h to drive from Cedar Rapids to Sioux Falls?
   A less than 1 h
   B about 3 h
   C about 7 h
   D about 10 h

2. Martha counted the number of people in each group that walked into her school's cafeteria. In the first 10 groups, she counted the following numbers of people: 6, 4, 9, 6, 4, 10, 9, 5, 9, and 8. What is the mode of this set of data?
   F 6
   G 7
   H 9
   I 10

3. Which of the following terms describes the angle marked in the triangle below.

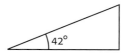

   A acute
   B obtuse
   C right
   D None of the above

4. Donnell collected money for a charity fundraiser. After one hour, he counted the money and found that he had raised $10.00 in bills and $3.74 in coins. Which of the following represents the number of coins he collected?
   F 4 pennies, 9 nickels, 18 dimes, and 6 quarters
   G 9 pennies, 7 nickels, 18 dimes, and 6 quarters
   H 6 pennies, 7 nickels, 15 dimes, and 8 quarters
   I 9 pennies, 8 nickels, 12 dimes, and 3 quarters

Standardized Test Preparation

INTERPRETING GRAPHICS

1. C
2. G
3. B

TEST DOCTOR

Question 1: Students may be confused about the motion of the squirrel between 5 s and 8 s. According to the graph, the distance the squirrel traveled between 5 s and 8 s did not change. In other words, the squirrel did not move. Because the squirrel did not move between 5 s and 8 s, its speed did not change. During that time interval the speed of the squirrel remained constant at 0 m/s.

MATH

1. C
2. H
3. A
4. G

TEST DOCTOR

Question 2: Some students may choose answer G because it is equal to the average of the numbers in the problem. Remind students that the *mode* of a set of numbers is the number that appears most frequently and that the *mean* of a set of numbers is the average.

CHAPTER RESOURCES

Chapter Resource File
 • Standardized Test Preparation GENERAL

Workbooks
 North Carolina Standardized Test Preparation
• Provides practice for the EOG test.

State Resources
 For specific resources for your state, visit **go.hrw.com** and type in the keyword **HSMSTR**.

Science in Action

Science, Technology, and Society

Background

The Global Positioning System (GPS) is a network of 27 human-made satellites that orbit Earth. At any given time, 24 of the satellites are in operation. The other three satellites are in place as a backup system. Each satellite continually transmits a unique radio signal that can be picked up by GPS receivers on Earth. A GPS receiver normally receives signals from at least four satellites at one time. The receiver uses the signals and a process called *triangulation* to determine its location on Earth. Encourage interested students to learn how triangulation works. Students may present what they learn in a report to the class.

Weird Science

Discussion ———— GENERAL

Tell students that some cities are considering limiting or banning the use of Segways on sidewalks. Lead a discussion about why Segways might be considered dangerous to pedestrians. Also discuss possible rules that may be used to avoid the danger yet still allow people to use Segways.

Science, Technology, and Society

GPS Watch System

Some athletes are concerned about knowing their speed during training. To calculate speed, they need to know distance and time. Finding time by using a watch is easy to do. But determining distance is more difficult. However, a GPS watch system is now available to help with this problem. *GPS* stands for *global positioning system*. A GPS unit, which is worn on an athlete's upper arm, monitors the athlete's position by using signals from satellites. As the athlete moves, the GPS unit calculates the distance traveled. The GPS unit sends a signal to the watch, which keeps the athlete's time, and the watch displays the athlete's speed.

Math ACTIVITY

Suppose an athlete wishes to finish a 5 K race in under 25 min. The distance of a 5 K is 5 km. (Remember that 1 km = 1,000 m.) If the athlete runs the race at a constant speed of 3.4 m/s, will she meet her goal?

Weird Science

The Segway™ Human Transporter

In November 2002, a new people-moving machine was introduced, and people have been fascinated by the odd-looking device ever since. The device is called the *Segway Human Transporter*. The Segway is a two-wheeled device that is powered by a rechargeable battery. To move forward, the rider simply leans forward. Sensors detect this motion and send signals to the onboard computer. The computer, in turn, tells the motor to start going. To slow down, the rider leans backward, and to stop, the rider stands straight up. The Segway has a top speed of 20 km/h (about 12.5 mi/h) and can travel up to 28 km (about 17.4 mi) on a single battery charge.

Language Arts ACTIVITY

WRITING SKILL The inventor of the Segway thinks that the machine will make a good alternative to walking and bicycle riding. Write a one-page essay explaining whether you think using a Segway is better or worse than riding a bicycle.

Answer to Math Activity

Yes, the athlete will meet her goal. She will finish the race in about 24.5 min (1470 s).

Answer to Language Arts Activity

Accept all reasonable answers. All essays should discuss the benefits or drawbacks of using a Segway instead of riding a bicycle.

People in Science

Victor Petrenko

Snowboard and Ski Brakes Have you ever wished for emergency brakes on your snowboard or skis? Thanks to Victor Petrenko and the Ice Research Lab of Dartmouth College, snowboards and skis that have braking systems may soon be available.

Not many people know more about the properties of ice and ice-related technologies than Victor Petrenko does. He has spent most of his career researching the electrical and mechanical properties of ice. Through his research, Petrenko learned that ice can hold an electric charge. He used this property to design a braking system for snowboards. The system is a form of electric friction control.

The power source for the brakes is a battery. The battery is connected to a network of wires embedded on the bottom surface of a snowboard. When the battery is activated, the bottom of the snowboard gains a negative charge. This negative charge creates a positive charge on the surface of the snow. Because opposite charges attract, the snowboard and the snow are pulled together. The force that pulls the surfaces together increases friction, and the snowboard slows down.

Social Studies ACTIVITY

Research the history of skiing. Make a poster that includes a timeline of significant dates in the history of skiing. Illustrate your poster with photos or drawings.

To learn more about these Science in Action topics, visit go.hrw.com and type in the keyword HP5MOTF.

Current Science

Check out Current Science® articles related to this chapter by visiting go.hrw.com. **Just type in the keyword** HP5CS05.

Answer to Social Studies Activity
Accept all reasonable answers. All posters should include a timeline that marks significant dates in the history of skiing.

People in Science

Teaching Strategy — GENERAL

Explain and demonstrate the effects of static electricity to help students understand how the electric brakes designed by Victor Petrenko work. Start by telling students that objects can be charged by gaining or losing electrons. Objects that gain electrons become negatively charged and objects that lose electrons become positively charged. Objects that have opposite charges attract each other. To demonstrate this attraction, rub a balloon on your hair. Tell students that the friction between your hair and the balloon causes electrons to be transferred from your hair to the balloon. Then, hold the balloon away from your head. Your hair should be attracted to the balloon. Ask students why the hair is pulled to the balloon. (The hair is positively charged and the balloon is negatively charged. Oppositely charged object attract each other.) Tell students that a snowboard with an electric braking system is pulled toward the snow for the same reasons.

Note: This demonstration may not work if the air is too humid. If your hair is not long enough to do this demonstration, ask a student with long hair to volunteer.

Forces and Motion
Chapter Planning Guide

Compression guide:
To shorten instruction because of time limitations, omit Section 3.

OBJECTIVES	LABS, DEMONSTRATIONS, AND ACTIVITIES	TECHNOLOGY RESOURCES
PACING • 90 min pp. 492–501 **Chapter Opener**	**SE** Start-up Activity, p. 493 GENERAL	**OSP** Parent Letter GENERAL **CD** Student Edition on CD-ROM **CD** Guided Reading Audio CD **TR** Chapter Starter Transparency* **VID** Brain Food Video Quiz
Section 1 Gravity and Motion • Explain the effect of gravity and air resistance on falling objects. • Explain why objects in orbit are in free fall and appear to be weightless. • Describe how projectile motion is affected by gravity.	**TE** Demonstration Falling Objects, p. 494 GENERAL **TE** Connection Activity Social Studies, p. 495 ADVANCED **TE** Connection Activity Math, p. 495 GENERAL **TE** Connection Activity Earth Science, p. 496 GENERAL **TE** Activity The Meaning of a Vacuum, p. 497 BASIC **TE** Connection Activity Astronomy, p. 498 ADVANCED **TE** Connection Activity Math, p. 499 ADVANCED **SE** Quick Lab Penny Projectile Motion, p. 500 GENERAL **SE** Skills Practice Lab A Marshmallow Catapult, p. 613 GENERAL **LB** Inquiry Lab On the Fast Track ADVANCED **LB** Calculator-Based Labs Falling Objects ADVANCED **LB** Calculator-Based Labs Graphing Your Motion ADVANCED	**CRF** Lesson Plans* **TR** Bellringer Transparency* **SE** Internet Activity, p. 500 GENERAL **TR** Falling Objects Accelerate at a Constant Rate* **TR** Effect of Air Resistance on a Falling Object* **TR** LINK TO EARTH SCIENCE Layers of the Atmosphere* **TR** How an Orbit Is Formed/Projectile Motion* **CD** Interactive Explorations CD-ROM Extreme Skiing GENERAL
PACING • 90 min pp. 502–509 **Section 2 Newton's Laws of Motion** • Describe Newton's first law of motion, and explain how it relates to objects at rest and objects in motion. • State Newton's second law of motion, and explain the relationship between force, mass, and acceleration. • State Newton's third law of motion, and give examples of force pairs.	**TE** Demonstration Egg in a Buggy, p. 502 GENERAL **SE** Quick Lab First Law Skateboard, p. 503 ◆ GENERAL **TE** Connection Activity Real World, p. 503 GENERAL **SE** Quick Lab First-Law Magic, p. 504 GENERAL **SE** Connection to Environmental Science Car Sizes and Pollution, p. 504 GENERAL **TE** Connection Activity Math, p. 506 GENERAL **SE** School-to-Home Activity Newton Ball, p. 507 GENERAL **TE** Connection Activity Life Science, p. 507 GENERAL **SE** Skills Practice Lab Inertia-Rama!, p. 514 GENERAL **SE** Model-Making Lab Blast Off!, p. 614 GENERAL **LB** Whiz-Bang Demonstrations Newton's Eggciting Experiment* BASIC **LB** Whiz-Bang Demonstrations Inertia Can Hurt Ya* GENERAL **LB** Whiz-Bang Demonstrations Fountain of Knowledge* BASIC **LB** Long-Term Projects & Research Ideas "Any Color You Want, so Long as It's Black"* ADVANCED	**CRF** Lesson Plans* **TR** Bellringer Transparency* **CRF** SciLinks Activity* GENERAL **TR** Acceleration, Mass, and Force* **VID** Lab Videos for Physical Science
PACING • 45 min pp. 510–513 **Section 3 Momentum** • Calculate the momentum of moving objects. • Explain the law of conservation of momentum.	**TE** Group Activity Testing Momentum, p. 510 GENERAL **TE** Demonstration Toy Car Momentum, p. 511 BASIC **SE** Science in Action Math, Social Studies, and Language Arts Activities, pp. 520–521 GENERAL **SE** Skills Practice Lab Quite a Reaction, p. 615 GENERAL	**CRF** Lesson Plans* **TR** Bellringer Transparency*

PACING • 90 min

CHAPTER REVIEW, ASSESSMENT, AND STANDARDIZED TEST PREPARATION

CRF Vocabulary Activity* GENERAL
SE Chapter Review, pp. 516–517 GENERAL
CRF Chapter Review* ■ GENERAL
CRF Chapter Tests A* ■ GENERAL, B* ADVANCED, C* SPECIAL NEEDS
SE Standardized Test Preparation, pp. 518–519 GENERAL
CRF Standardized Test Preparation* GENERAL
CRF Performance-Based Assessment* GENERAL
OSP Test Generator GENERAL
CRF Test Item Listing* GENERAL

Online and Technology Resources

Visit **go.hrw.com** for a variety of free resources related to this textbook. Enter the keyword **HT5R7FOR.**

 Holt Online Learning

Students can access interactive problem-solving help and active visual concept development with the *Holt Science and Technology* Online Edition available at **www.hrw.com.**

 Guided Reading Audio CD

These CDs are designed to help auditory learners and reluctant readers.

 Science Tutor CD-ROM

Excellent for remediation and test practice.

SKILLS DEVELOPMENT RESOURCES	SECTION REVIEW AND ASSESSMENT	STANDARDS CORRELATIONS
SE Pre-Reading Activity, p. 492 `GENERAL` **OSP** Science Puzzlers, Twisters & Teasers `GENERAL`		North Carolina Standard Course of Study
CRF Directed Reading A* `BASIC`, B* `SPECIAL NEEDS` **CRF** Vocabulary and Section Summary* `GENERAL` **SE** Reading Strategy Reading Organizer, p. 494 `GENERAL` **SE** Math Focus Calculating the Velocity of Falling Objects, p. 495 `GENERAL` **TE** Reading Strategy Prediction Guide, p. 496 `GENERAL` **TE** Inclusion Strategy, p. 497 **MS** Math Skills for Science Arithmetic with Decimals* `GENERAL` **CRF** Reinforcement Worksheet Falling Fast* `BASIC`	**SE** Reading Checks, pp. 495, 496, 498, 500 `GENERAL` **TE** Reteaching, p. 500 `BASIC` **TE** Quiz, p. 500 `GENERAL` **TE** Alternative Assessment, p. 500 `GENERAL` **SE** Section Review,* p. 501 ■ `GENERAL` **CRF** Section Quiz* ■ `GENERAL`	*LabBook:* 1.01, 1.05
CRF Directed Reading A* `BASIC`, B* `SPECIAL NEEDS` **CRF** Vocabulary and Section Summary* `GENERAL` **SE** Reading Strategy Paired Summarizing, p. 502 `GENERAL` **TE** Reading Strategy Prediction Guide, p. 505 `GENERAL` **TE** Inclusion Strategy, p. 505 **SE** Math Focus Second-Law Problems, p. 506 `GENERAL` **MS** Math Skills for Science Newton: Force and Motion* `GENERAL` **CRF** Critical Thinking Forces to Reckon With* `ADVANCED`	**SE** Reading Checks, pp. 503, 505, 507, 508 `GENERAL` **TE** Homework, p. 507 `BASIC` **TE** Reteaching, p. 508 `BASIC` **TE** Quiz, p. 508 `GENERAL` **TE** Alternative Assessment, p. 508 `GENERAL` **SE** Section Review,* p. 509 ■ `GENERAL` **CRF** Section Quiz* ■ `GENERAL`	6.03; *Chapter Lab:* 1.01, 1.02, 1.05; *LabBook:* 6.03
CRF Directed Reading A* `BASIC`, B* `SPECIAL NEEDS` **CRF** Vocabulary and Section Summary* `GENERAL` **SE** Reading Strategy Prediction Guide, p. 510 `GENERAL` **SE** Math Focus Momentum Calculations, p. 511 `GENERAL` **SE** Connection to Language Arts p. 512 `GENERAL` **MS** Math Skills for Science Momentum* `GENERAL`	**SE** Reading Checks, pp. 511, 512 `GENERAL` **TE** Reteaching, p. 512 `BASIC` **TE** Quiz, p. 512 `GENERAL` **TE** Alternative Assessment, p. 512 `ADVANCED` **SE** Section Review,* p. 513 ■ `GENERAL` **CRF** Section Quiz* ■ `GENERAL`	6.03; *LabBook:* 6.03

One-Stop Planner® CD-ROM

This convenient CD-ROM includes:
- Lab Materials QuickList Software
- Holt Calendar Planner
- Customizable Lesson Plans
- Printable Worksheets
- ExamView® Test Generator

cnnstudentnews.com

Find the latest news, lesson plans, and activities related to important scientific events.

SCiLINKS.
NSTA

www.scilinks.org

Maintained by the **National Science Teachers Association**. See Chapter Enrichment pages for a complete list of topics.

Current Science®

Check out *Current Science* articles and activities by visiting the HRW Web site at **go.hrw.com.** Just type in the keyword **HP5CS06T.**

Classroom Videos

- **Lab Videos** demonstrate the chapter lab.
- **Brain Food Video Quizzes** help students review the chapter material.
- **CNN Videos** bring science into your students' daily life.

Visual Resources

CHAPTER STARTER TRANSPARENCY

Imagine . . .

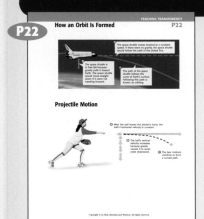

BELLRINGER TRANSPARENCIES

Section: Gravity and Motion
Answer the following questions in your **science journal:**

If Wile E. Coyote and a boulder fall off a cliff at the same time, which do you think will hit the ground first? Would it matter if the cliff were very high or particularly low? How could Mr. Coyote slow down his fall?

Section: Newton's Laws of Motion
Respond to the following question in your **science journal:**

If you are sitting still in your seat on a bus that is traveling 100 km/h on a highway, is your body at rest or in motion? Explain your answer. Use a diagram if it will help make your answer clear.

TEACHING TRANSPARENCIES

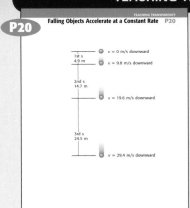

P20 Falling Objects Accelerate at a Constant Rate P20

P21 Effect of Air Resistance on a Falling Object

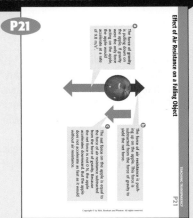

TEACHING TRANSPARENCIES

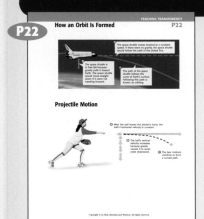

P22 How an Orbit Is Formed P22

Projectile Motion

P23 Mass, Force, and Acceleration

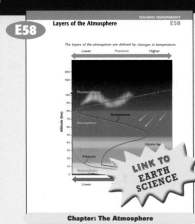

E58 Layers of the Atmosphere E58

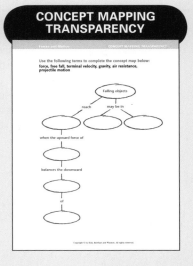

Chapter: The Atmosphere

CONCEPT MAPPING TRANSPARENCY

Use the following terms to complete the concept map below: force, free fall, terminal velocity, gravity, air resistance, projectile motion

Planning Resources

LESSON PLANS

Lesson Plan SAMPLE

Section: Waves

Pacing
Regular Schedule: with lab(s):2 days without lab(s):2 days
Block Schedule: with lab(s): 1 1/2 days without lab(s):1 day

Objectives
1. Relate the seven properties of life to a living organism.
2. Describe seven themes that can help you to organize what you learn about biology.
3. Identify the tiny structures that make up all living organisms.
4. Differentiate between reproduction and heredity and between metabolism and homeostasis.

National Science Education Standards Covered
LSInter6:Cells have particular structures that underlie their functions.
LSMat1:Most cell functions involve chemical reactions.
LSBeh1:Cells store and use information to guide their functions.
UCP1:Cell functions are regulated.
SI1: Cells can differentiate and form complete multicellular organisms.
PS1: Species evolve over time.
ESS1: The great diversity of organisms is the result of more than 3.5 billion years of evolution.
ESS2: Natural selection and its evolutionary consequences provide a scientific explanation for the fossil record of ancient life forms as well as for the striking molecular similarities observed among the diverse species of living organisms.
ST1: The millions of different species of plants, animals, and microorganisms that live on Earth today are related by descent from common ancestors.
ST2: The energy for life primarily comes from the sun.
SPSP1: The complexity and organization of organisms accommodates the need for obtaining, transforming, transporting, releasing, and eliminating the matter and energy used to sustain the organism.
SPSP6: As matter and energy flows through different levels of organization of living systems—cells, organs, communities—and between living systems and the physical environment, chemical elements are recombined in different ways.
HNS1: Organisms have behavioral responses to internal changes and to external stimuli.

PARENT LETTER

SAMPLE

Dear Parent,

Your son's or daughter's science class will soon begin exploring the chapter entitled "The World of Physical Science." In this chapter, students will learn about how the scientific method applies to the world of physical science and the role of physical science in the world. By the end of the chapter, students should demonstrate a clear understanding of the chapter's main ideas and be able to discuss the following topics:

1. physical science is the study of energy and matter (Section 1)
2. the role of physical science in the world around them (Section 1)
3. careers that rely on physical science (Section 1)
4. the steps used in the scientific method (Section 2)
5. examples of technology (Section 2)
6. how the scientific method is used to answer questions and solve problems (Section 2)
7. how our knowledge of science changes over time (Section 2)
8. how models represent real objects or systems (Section 3)
9. examples of different ways models are used in science (Section 3)
10. the importance of the International System of Units (Section 4)
11. the appropriate units to use for particular measurements (Section 4)
12. how area and density are derived quantities (Section 4)

Questions to Ask Along the Way

You can help your son or daughter learn about these topics by asking interesting questions such as the following:

• What are some surprising careers that use physical science?
• What is a characteristic of a good hypothesis?
• When is it a good idea to use a model?
• Why do Americans measure things in terms of inches and yards instead of centimeters and meters?

TEST ITEM LISTING

TEST ITEM LISTING
The World of Science SAMPLE

MULTIPLE CHOICE

1. A limitation of models is that
   a. they are large enough to see.
   b. they do not exactly like the things that they model.
   c. they are smaller than the things that they model.
   d. they model unfamiliar things.
   Answer: B Difficulty: 1 Section: 3 Objective: 2
2. The length 10 m is equal to
   a. 100 cm. c. 10,000 mm.
   b. 1,000 cm. d. Both (b) and (c)
   Answer: B Difficulty: 1 Section: 3 Objective: 2
3. To be valid, a hypothesis must be
   a. testable. c. made into a law.
   b. supported by evidence. d. Both (a) and (b)
   Answer: B Difficulty: 1 Section: 2 Objective: 2 1
4. The statement "Sheila has a stain on her shirt" is an example of a(n)
   a. law. c. observation.
   b. hypothesis. d. prediction.
   Answer: B Difficulty: 1 Section: 2 Objective: 1
5. A hypothesis is often developed out of
   a. observations. c. laws.
   b. experiments. d. Both (a) and (b)
   Answer: B Difficulty: 1 Section: 2 Objective: 2
6. How many milliliters are in 5.5 kL?
   a. 5,500 mL c. 5,500, 000 mL
   b. 0.0035 mL d. 35,000 mL
   Answer: B Difficulty: 1 Section: 3 Objective: 2
7. A map of Seattle is an example of a
   a. law. c. model.
   b. theory. d. unit.
   Answer: B Difficulty: 1 Section: 3 Objective: 2
8. A lab has the safety cones shown below. These icons mean that you should wear
   a. only safety goggles. c. safety goggles and a lab apron.
   b. only a lab apron. d. safety goggles, a lab apron, and gloves.
   Answer: B Difficulty: 1 Section: 3 Objective: 3
9. The law of conservation of mass says the test al mass before a chemical change is
   a. more than the total mass after the change.
   b. less than the total mass after the change.
   c. the same as the total mass after the change.
   d. not the same as the total mass after the change.
   Answer: B Difficulty: 1 Section: 3 Objective: 2
10. In which of the following areas might you find a geochemist at work?
    a. studying the chemistry of rocks c. studying fishes
    b. studying forestry d. studying the atmosphere
    Answer: B Difficulty: 1 Section: 3 Objective: 2

One-Stop Planner® CD-ROM

This CD-ROM includes all of the resources shown here and the following time-saving tools:

• *Lab Materials QuickList Software*
• *Customizable lesson plans*
• *Holt Calendar Planner*
• *The powerful ExamView® Test Generator*

Meeting Individual Needs

DIRECTED READING A

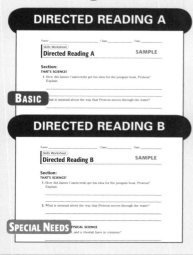

Skills Worksheet
Directed Reading A   SAMPLE

Section:
THAT'S SCIENCE!

1. How did James Czarnowski get his idea for the penguin boat, Proteus? Explain.

___ that is unusual about the way that Proteus moves through the water?

BASIC

DIRECTED READING B

Skills Worksheet
Directed Reading B   SAMPLE

Section:
THAT'S SCIENCE!

1. How did James Czarnowski get his idea for the penguin boat, Proteus? Explain.

2. What is unusual about the way that Proteus moves through the water?

SPECIAL NEEDS PHYSICAL SCIENCE

VOCABULARY ACTIVITY

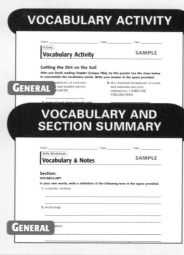

Activity
Vocabulary Activity   SAMPLE

Getting the Dirt on the Soil

After you finish reading Chapter [Unique Title], try this puzzle! Use the clues below to unscramble the vocabulary words. Write your answer in the space provided.

___ breakdown of rocks and ___ smaller pieces: ___GNETH

9. the chemical breakdown of rocks and minerals into new substances: CAMILCHE THEARIGWEN

GENERAL

VOCABULARY AND SECTION SUMMARY

Skills Worksheet
Vocabulary & Notes   SAMPLE

Section:
VOCABULARY

In your own words, write a definition of the following term in the space provided.

1. scientific method

2. technology

GENERAL

REINFORCEMENT

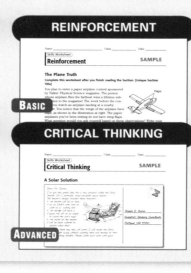

Skills Worksheet
Reinforcement   SAMPLE

The Plane Truth

Complete this worksheet after you finish reading the Section: [Unique Section Title]

You plan to enter a paper airplane content sponsored by Talkin' Physical Science magazine. The person whose airplane flies the farthest wins a lifetime subscription to the magazine! The week before the contest, you watch an airplane landing at a nearby airport. You notice that the wings of the airplane have flaps, as shown in the illustration at right. The paper airplanes you've been testing do not have any flaps. What question would you ask yourself based on these observations? Write your

BASIC

CRITICAL THINKING

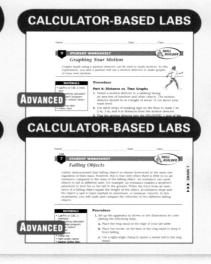

Skills Worksheet
Critical Thinking   SAMPLE

A Solar Solution

___ Joseph D. Burns ___ Portland, OR 97001

ADVANCED

SCILINKS ACTIVITY

Activity
SciLinks Activity   SAMPLE

MARINE ECOSYSTEMS

Go to www.scilinks.com. To find links related to marine ecosystems, type in the keyword HL5##. Then, use the links to answer the questions about marine ecosys-

___ percentage of the Earth's surface is covered by water?

GENERAL

SCIENCE PUZZLERS, TWISTERS & TEASERS

CHAPTER
6   SCIENCE PUZZLERS, TWISTERS & TEASERS
Forces in Motion

Letter Comet

1. Commander Eileen Collins was playing Scrabble® with her four-man crew on board the KC-135. In this game, new words are formed by adding wooden tiles, each with a letter and a point value, to a board. Each word must share at least one letter with the word it crosses. The numbers on the tiles are added to find the score for each word. When the crew of the KC-135 play, they use only words from their favorite chapter, "Forces in Motion."

Just after Commander Collins spelled *comet* on the board, the KC-135 tipped downward, throwing many of the tiles into free fall. Only the tiles that were sticky from yesterday's orange-juice spill didn't fly off. Help them figure out where the other tiles belong. (Each tile is used only once.) Write the correct letters on

E T R M R A E W
N T N N E E S Q A S

GENERAL

Labs and Activities

LONG-TERM PROJECTS & RESEARCH IDEAS

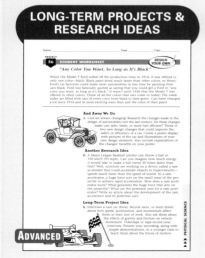

PROJECT
86 STUDENT WORKSHEET   DESIGN YOUR OWN
"Any Color You Want, So Long as It's Black"

When the Model T Ford rolled off the production lines in 1914, it was offered in only one color—black. Black paint dried much faster than other colors, so Henry Ford's car factories could make more automobiles in less time by painting their cars black. Ford was famously quoted as saying that you could get a Ford in "any color you want, so long as it's black." It wasn't until 1926 that the Model T was offered in other colors. Think of all the colors that cars come in today! The roads today are filled with cars of every color from black to lime green. Cars have changed a lot since 1914 and in more exciting ways than just the color of their paint.

And Away We Go

1. Cars are always changing! Research the changes made in the design of automobiles over the last century. Do these changes make cars safer, faster, or more fuel efficient? Think of two new design changes that could improve the safety or efficiency of a car. Create a poster display with pictures of the car and illustrations of your new design elements. Also include explanations of the changes' benefits on your poster.

Another Research Idea

2. A Major League Baseball pitcher can throw a ball at 150 km/h (93 mph). Can you imagine how much energy it would take to make a ball travel 20 times faster than that? Well, scientists are working on a device called a rare accelerate that could accelerate objects to hypervelocity— speeds much faster than the speed of sound. In a rail accelerator, a huge force acts on the small mass of the projectile to achieve rapid acceleration. How does a ram accel-erator work? What generates the huge force that acts on the projectile? What are the potential uses for a ram accel-erator? Write an article about the development of the ram accelerator and its potential uses.

Long-Term Project Idea

3. Interview a race car driver, bicycle racer, or stunt driver about how speed, acceleration, and momentum affect them in their line of work. Also ask them about the effects of gravity and friction on vehicle movement. Videotape or tape-record your interview. Present your recording, along with simple demonstrations, to a younger class to teach them about the forces of motion.

ADVANCED PHYSICAL SCIENCE

WHIZ-BANG DEMONSTRATIONS

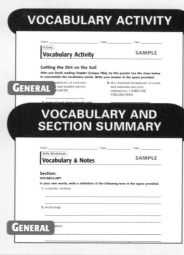

DEMO
43 TEACHER-LED DEMONSTRATION   DISCOVERY LAB
Newton's Eggciting Experiment

Purpose
Students are introduced to Newton's first law of motion.

Time Required
10–15 minutes

Lab Ratings

MATERIALS

glasses. Place a cardboard tube verti-cally over each glass. Then place an egg sideways on top of each tube.

1. Stand the broom at the edge of the table so that the handle touches the edge of the pie pan. Carefully step on the bristles of the broom to hold it in place.

2. Tell students that you will knock the edge of the pie pan with the broom. Challenge them to predict what will happen. (Accept all reasonable responses.)

3. Pull the broom handle toward you, and then release it.

BASIC

INQUIRY LABS

LAB
18 STUDENT WORKSHEET   DESIGN YOUR OWN
On the Fast Track

As the chief design engineer for a new theme park, you must ensure that all rides and attractions are the biggest, fastest, tallest, safest, and most thrilling in the world.

Your latest assignment is to design the world's fastest wooden roller coaster. The roller coaster must have one loop and two hills. Your first task is to build a model for the roller coaster. If the design is sound, the model will serve as the prototype for a new roller coaster called the Eliminator. The park owner and visitors expect the Eliminator to be the main attraction at the theme park's grand opening next year.

MATERIALS

Ask a Question

How do you build a model roller coaster to meet the following criteria?

• It includes a loop that is at least 50 cm in height.
• It includes two hills.
• It includes safety features to protect the rider ___

ADVANCED

CALCULATOR-BASED LABS

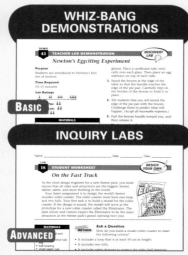

LAB
9 STUDENT WORKSHEET   SKILL BUILDER
Graphing Your Motion

Graphs made using a motion detector can be used to study motion. In this experiment, you and a partner will use a motion detector to make graphs of your own motion.

MATERIALS

Part A: Distance vs. Time Graphs

1. Fasten a motion detector to a tabletop facing an area free of furniture and other objects. The motion detector should be at a height of about 15 cm above the water level.

2. Use short strips of masking tape on the floor to mark 1 m, 2 m, 3 m, and 4 m distances from the motion detector.

3. Plug the motion detector into the DIG/SONIC 1 port of the ___

ADVANCED

CALCULATOR-BASED LABS

LAB
7 STUDENT WORKSHEET   SKILL BUILDER
Falling Objects

Galileo demonstrated that falling objects accelerate downward at the same rate regardless of their mass. However, this is true only when there is little to no air resistance compared to the mass of the falling object. Air resistance can cause objects to fall at different rates. For example, air resistance enables a skydiver's parachute to slow him or her fall to the ground. When the force from an resis-tance of a falling object equals the weight of the object, acceleration stops and the object is said to have reached its maximum, or terminal, velocity. In this experiment, you will study and compare the velocities of two different falling objects.

MATERIALS

Procedure

1. Set up the apparatus as shown in the illustration by com-pleting the following steps.

a. Place the ring stand at the edge of your lab table.

b. Place two books on the base of the ring stand to keep it from tipping.

c. Use a right-angle clamp to fasten a metal rod to the ring stand.

ADVANCED

DATASHEETS FOR QUICK LABS

TEACHER RESOURCE PAGE

Quick Lab   DATASHEET FOR QUICK LAB
Reaction to Stress   SAMPLE

Background

The graph below illustrates changes that occur in the membrane potential of a neuron during an action potential. Use the graph to answer the following questions. Refer to Figure 3 as needed.

DATASHEETS FOR CHAPTER LABS

TEACHER RESOURCE PAGE

Skills Practice Lab   DATASHEET FOR CHAPTER LAB
Using Scientific Methods SAMPLE

Teacher's Notes
TIME REQUIRED
One 45-minute class period.

DATASHEETS FOR LABBOOK

TEACHER RESOURCE PAGE

Skills Practice Lab   DATASHEET FOR LABBOOK LAB
Does It All Add Up?   SAMPLE

Teacher's Notes
TIME REQUIRED
One 45-minute class period.

Review and Assessments

SECTION QUIZ

Assessment
Section Quiz   SAMPLE

Section:

In the space provided, write the letter of the description that best matches the term or phrase.

___ 1. building molecules that can be used as an energy source, or breaking down molecules in which energy is stored

___ the process by which light energy is converted to chemical energy

___ an organism that uses inorganic or inorganic substances to make organic compounds

c. ___

d. ___ respiration

ALSO IN SPANISH

GENERAL

SECTION REVIEW

Skills Worksheet
Section Review   SAMPLE

Section:
KEY TERMS

1. What do paleontologists study?

2. How does a trace fossil differ from petrified wood?

___ fossil

ALSO IN SPANISH

GENERAL UNDERSTANDING KEY TERMS

CHAPTER REVIEW

Skills Worksheet
Chapter Review   SAMPLE

USING VOCABULARY

1. Define *biome* in your own words.

2. Describe the characteristics of a savanna and a desert.

___ Identify the relationship between an herb and a carnivore

ALSO IN SPANISH

GENERAL

CHAPTER TEST A

Assessment
Chapter Test A   SAMPLE

MULTIPLE CHOICE

In the space provided, write the letter of the term or phrase that best completes each statement or best answers each question.

___ 1. Surface currents are formed by
   a. the moon's gravity.   c. wind.
   b. the sun's gravity.   d. increased water ___

___ 2. When waves come near the shore,
   a. they speed up.   c. their wave ___
   b. they maintain their speed. d. their wave height ___

___ 3. Longshore currents transport sediment
   a. out to the open ocean.   c. only during low ___
   b. along the shore.   d. only during high tide.

___ 4. Which of the following does NOT control surface ___

ALSO IN SPANISH

GENERAL

CHAPTER TEST B

Assessment
Chapter Test B   SAMPLE

MULTIPLE CHOICE

In the space provided, write the letter of the term or phrase that best completes each statement or best answers each question.

___ 1. Surface currents are formed by
   a. the moon's gravity.   c. wind.
   b. the sun's gravity.   d. increased water density.

___ 2. When waves come near the shore,
   a. they speed up.   c. their wave height increases.
   b. they maintain their speed. d. their wave height increases.

ADVANCED

CHAPTER TEST C

Assessment
Chapter Test C   SAMPLE

MULTIPLE CHOICE

In the space provided, write the letter of the term or phrase that best completes each statement or best answers each question.

___ 1. Surface currents are formed by
   a. the moon's gravity.   c. wind.
   b. the sun's gravity.   d. increased water density.

___ 2. When waves come near the shore,
   a. they speed up.   c. their wavelength increases.
   b. they maintain their speed. d. their wave height increases.

___ 3. Longshore currents transport sediment
   a. out to the open ocean.   c. only during low tide.
   b. along the shore.   d. only during high tide.

___ 4. Which of the following does NOT control surface currents?

SPECIAL NEEDS

STANDARDIZED TEST PREPARATION

Assessment
Standardized Test Preparation SAMPLE

READING

Read the passages below. Then, read each question that follows the passage. Decide which is the best answer to each question.

Passage 1 ___ adventurous summer camp in the world. Billy ___ to head for the mountains. Billy checked the recommended ___ a rain-filled jacket, ski mask, and thick gloves. Wait a minute! Billy thought he was traveling to only one **destination**, so why does he need to bring such a wide variety of clothes? On further investiga-

GENERAL

PERFORMANCE-BASED ASSESSMENT

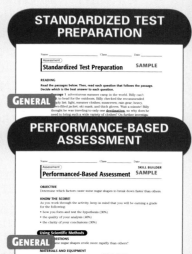

Assessment
Performance-Based Assessment SKILL BUILDER
SAMPLE

OBJECTIVE

Determine which factors cause some sugar shapes to break down faster than others.

KNOW THE SCORE!

As you work through the activity, keep in mind that you will be earning a grade based on the following:

• how you form and test the hypothesis (30%)
• the quality of your analysis (40%)
• the clarity of your conclusions (30%)

Using Scientific Methods

QUESTIONS

MATERIALS AND EQUIPMENT

• 1 regular sugar cube   • 30 mL of water

GENERAL

This Chapter Enrichment provides relevant and interesting information to expand and enhance your presentation of the chapter material.

Section 1

Gravity and Motion

The Apple and the Moon

- Galileo's theory that all objects fall with the same acceleration has been verified on Earth many times. It wasn't the same old proof, though, on July 30, 1971, when astronaut David Randolph Scott stood on the surface of the moon and dropped a feather and a hammer simultaneously. Just as Galileo's theory had predicted, in the absence of air resistance, the feather hit the ground at the same time as the hammer.

- Sir Isaac Newton is said to have realized the importance of gravitational force in 1666, when he watched an apple fall from a tree in his garden. John Conduitt, one of Newton's contemporaries, said of Newton, ". . . [I]t came into his thought that the power of gravity (which brought an apple from the tree to the ground) was not limited to a certain distance from the earth, but that this power must extend much further than was usually thought. Why not as high as the Moon though he said to himself & that if so, that must influence her motion & perhaps retain her in her orbit. [W]hereupon he fell a-calculating what would be the effect of that supposition. . ."

- Newton calculated the acceleration of the moon in a circular orbit around Earth and compared this with an apple's downward acceleration. He discovered that the acceleration of the moon was approximately 3,600 times smaller than the acceleration of an object

near the surface of Earth. Newton eventually accounted for this difference by assuming that the gravitational force was inversely proportional to the square of the distance from Earth.

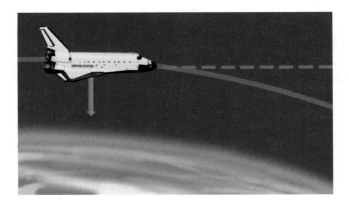

Air Resistance and Terminal Velocity

- Air resistance, a type of friction, limits the velocity of an object as it falls. As long as a falling object is somewhat streamlined and has not accelerated to high velocity, its acceleration due to gravity near the surface of Earth is a constant 9.8 m/s².

- As the velocity of a falling object increases, more air must be pushed out of the way each second. Eventually, the force of the air resistance pushing upward on the falling object is equal to Earth's gravitational force pulling downward on the object.

- When the upward and downward forces are equal, the net force on the falling object is 0 N. Then, the object falls with a constant velocity, called the *terminal velocity.*

Parachutes

- How do para-chutes work to increase air resistance? The parachute pro-vides a larger surface area to pull through the air. The larger sur-face area requires a much larger amount of air be moved out of the way each second as the parachute falls toward Earth.

Is That a Fact!

◆ Galileo timed the motion of balls rolling down an inclined plane to prove that all objects fall with the same acceleration.

Section 2

Newton's Laws of Motion

Sir Isaac Newton (1642–1727)

- In 1661, Isaac Newton went to study at Cambridge University. But Newton made many of his most important discoveries while spending time at the family home, Woolsthorpe Manor, near Grantham, in Lincolnshire, England, in 1665 and 1666.

Principia

- Newton's *Principia*, published in 1687, explains the three basic laws that govern the way objects move and Newton's theory of gravity. Newton explained how the force of gravity keeps the planets moving around the sun. Interestingly, Newton used his laws to predict that Earth must be a slightly flattened sphere and that comets orbit the sun in elongated elliptical paths. These predictions were later shown to be true.

Frogs and Fastballs

- What does a jumping frog have in common with a 42 m/s fastball? What does the space shuttle have in common with a sky diver? They are all affected by gravity, and their flights are governed by certain laws of motion. Although some observers in ancient China theorized about objects in motion and objects at rest, Newton is usually given credit for stating and testing the three basic laws that describe and predict motion.

Section 3

Momentum

Momentum and Martial Arts

- Momentum is the product of an object's mass and its velocity. Like velocity, momentum always includes a direction. The direction of an object's momentum is always in the direction of its motion.

- When a person (the attacker) kicks or throws a punch during a martial arts match, the attacker has momentum in the forward direction. The attacker's opponent can take advantage of this momentum when blocking the hit. Instead of trying to stop the hit, the opponent sweeps the attacker's arm or leg away with his or her own arm. This motion redirects the hit away from the opponent's body. The attacker's momentum continues in a generally forward direction, which can cause the attacker to lose his or her balance.

Developed and maintained by the National Science Teachers Association

SciLinks is maintained by the National Science Teachers Association to provide you and your students with interesting, up-to-date links that will enrich your classroom presentation of the chapter.

Visit www.scilinks.org and enter the SciLinks code for more information about the topic listed.

Topic: Force of Gravity
SciLinks code: HSM0602

Topic: Gravity and Orbiting Objects
SciLinks code: HSM0692

Topic: Projectile Motion
SciLinks code: HSM1223

Topic: Newton's Laws of Motion
SciLinks code: HSM1028

Topic: Momentum
SciLinks code: HSM0988

Overview

In this chapter, students will learn about gravity's role in the acceleration of falling objects, in orbiting, and in projectile motion. Students will also study Newton's laws of motion. Finally, students will learn how to calculate momentum and will study the law of conservation of momentum.

Assessing Prior Knowledge

Students should be familiar with the following topics:

- velocity and acceleration
- net force and balanced and unbalanced forces
- friction
- gravity

Identifying Misconceptions

Some students may think that an object will stay in motion only if a force continually acts on the object. Explain to students that a force is needed to start the motion of an object but that the object will continue to move if no other forces (such as friction) act on the object. Discuss an air hockey puck as an example of an object that moves with a (nearly) constant speed after the force causing its motion has ended.

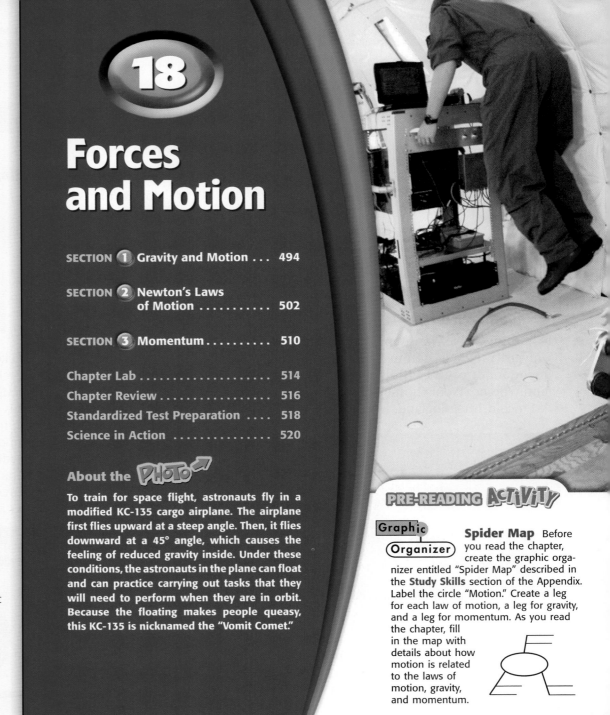

18

Forces and Motion

About the PHOTO

To train for space flight, astronauts fly in a modified KC-135 cargo airplane. The airplane first flies upward at a steep angle. Then, it flies downward at a 45° angle, which causes the feeling of reduced gravity inside. Under these conditions, the astronauts in the plane can float and can practice carrying out tasks that they will need to perform when they are in orbit. Because the floating makes people queasy, this KC-135 is nicknamed the "Vomit Comet."

PRE-READING ACTIVITY

Graphic Organizer

Spider Map Before you read the chapter, create the graphic organizer entitled "Spider Map" described in the **Study Skills** section of the Appendix. Label the circle "Motion." Create a leg for each law of motion, a leg for gravity, and a leg for momentum. As you read the chapter, fill in the map with details about how motion is related to the laws of motion, gravity, and momentum.

Standards Correlations

North Carolina Standard Course of Study

1.01 Identify and create questions and hypotheses that can be answered through scientific investigations. (Chapter Lab and LabBook)

1.02 (partial) Develop appropriate experimental procedures for: Given questions . . . (Chapter Lab)

1.05 Analyze evidence to: Explain observations, Make inferences and predictions, [and] Develop the relationship between evidence and explanation. (Chapter Lab and LabBook)

6.03 Evaluate motion in terms of Newton's Laws: The force of friction retards motion, For every action there is an equal and opposite reaction, The greater the force, the greater the change in motion, An object's motion is the result of the combined effect of all forces acting on the object, A moving object that is not subjected to a force will continue to move at a constant speed in a straight line, [and] An object at rest will remain at rest. (Sections 2 and 3 and LabBook)

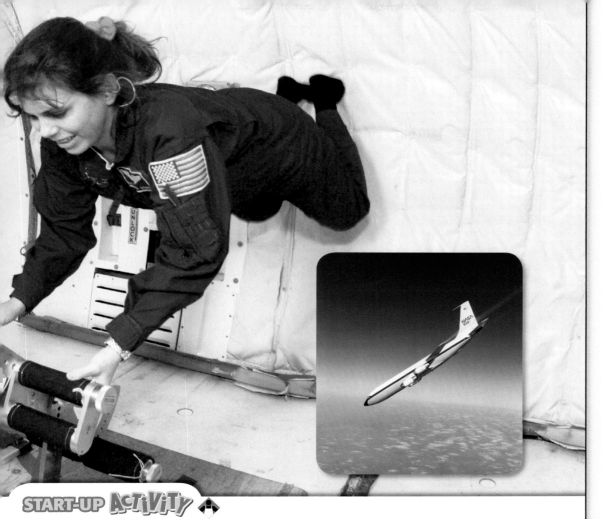

START-UP ACTIVITY

MATERIALS

FOR EACH GROUP
- cup, paper
- paper towels
- tub, wide plastic
- water

Teacher's Notes: Food coloring may be added to the water so that students will see the water better. Furthermore, the activity can be done outdoors to minimize cleanup.

To reduce the mess, have students fill the cups only half full. Spread plenty of newspapers on the floor.

Answers

1. In Trial 1, students should see the water coming out of the hole and falling to the ground. In Trial 2, they should not see any water coming out of the hole as the cup falls.

2. The cup and the water fall at the same rate. Students may not know that both are accelerating, and students may say that both fell with the same velocity, or speed.

3. Sample answer: My prediction was wrong because I thought the water would come out of the cup faster, but no water came out at all.

START-UP ACTIVITY

Falling Water

Gravity is one of the most important forces in your life. In this activity, you will observe the effect of gravity on a falling object.

Procedure

1. Place a **wide plastic tub** on the floor. Punch a small hole in the side of a **paper cup,** near the bottom.

2. Hold your finger over the hole, and fill the cup with **water.** Keep your finger over the hole, and hold the cup waist-high above the tub.

3. Uncover the hole. Record your observations as Trial 1.

4. Predict what will happen to the water if you drop the cup at the same time you uncover the hole.

5. Cover the hole, and refill the cup with water.

6. Uncover the hole, and drop the cup at the same time. Record your observations as Trial 2.

7. Clean up any spilled water with **paper towels.**

Analysis

1. What differences did you observe in the behavior of the water during the two trials?

2. In Trial 2, how fast did the cup fall compared with how fast the water fell?

3. How did the results of Trial 2 compare with your prediction?

Chapter Starter Transparency
Use this transparency to help students begin thinking about forces and motion.

CHAPTER RESOURCES

Technology

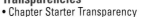 **Transparencies**
- Chapter Starter Transparency

READING SKILLS

 Student Edition on CD-ROM

Guided Reading Audio CD

Classroom Videos
- Brain Food Video Quiz

Workbooks

 **Science Puzzlers, Twisters & Teasers**
- Forces and Motion GENERAL

Focus

Overview

In this section, students learn how gravity and air resistance affect falling objects. Students also learn about orbiting and study the relationship between gravity and projectile motion. You may wish to review the concepts of velocity, acceleration, and net force with your students before starting this section.

Bellringer

Have students write an answer to the following question: "If Wile E. Coyote and a boulder fall off a cliff at the same time, which do you think will hit the ground first?"

Motivate

Demonstration— GENERAL

Falling Objects Have students examine a 12 in. softball and a women's sized shot. Then, discuss the objects' similar sizes and different masses. Place a protective board on the floor and stand on a sturdy table. Tell students that you will drop both objects from the same height. Hold the objects above the board, and ask students to predict which will land first. Drop the objects *at the same time*. Ask students for their observations, and repeat as necessary. **LS** Visual

READING WARM-UP

Objectives
- Explain the effect of gravity and air resistance on falling objects.
- Explain why objects in orbit are in free fall and appear to be weightless.
- Describe how projectile motion is affected by gravity.

Terms to Learn
terminal velocity
free fall
projectile motion

READING STRATEGY

Reading Organizer As you read this section, create an outline of the section. Use the headings from the section in your outline.

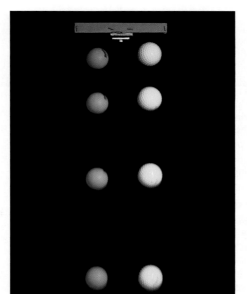

CHAPTER RESOURCES

Chapter Resource File
- Lesson Plan
- Directed Reading A BASIC
- Directed Reading B SPECIAL NEEDS

Technology
- Transparencies
  - Bellringer
  - Falling Objects Accelerate at a Constant Rate

Workbooks
- Math Skills for Science
  - Arithmetic with Decimals GENERAL

Gravity and Motion

Suppose you dropped a baseball and a marble at the same time from the top of a tall building. Which do you think would land on the ground first?

In ancient Greece around 400 BCE, a philosopher named Aristotle (AR is TAWT uhl) thought that the rate at which an object falls depended on the object's mass. If you asked Aristotle whether the baseball or the marble would land first, he would have said the baseball. But Aristotle never tried dropping objects with different masses to test his idea about falling objects.

Gravity and Falling Objects

In the late 1500s, a young Italian scientist named Galileo Galilei (GAL uh LAY oh GAL uh LAY) questioned Aristotle's idea about falling objects. Galileo argued that the mass of an object does not affect the time the object takes to fall to the ground. According to one story, Galileo proved his argument by dropping two cannonballs of different masses from the top of the Leaning Tower of Pisa in Italy. The people watching from the ground below were amazed to see the two cannonballs land at the same time. Whether or not this story is true, Galileo's work changed people's understanding of gravity and falling objects.

Gravity and Acceleration

Objects fall to the ground at the same rate because the acceleration due to gravity is the same for all objects. Why is this true? Acceleration depends on both force and mass. A heavier object experiences a greater gravitational force than a lighter object does. But a heavier object is also harder to accelerate because it has more mass. The extra mass of the heavy object exactly balances the additional gravitational force. **Figure 1** shows objects that have different masses falling with the same acceleration.

Figure 1 *This stop-action photo shows that a table-tennis ball and a golf ball fall at the same rate even though they have different masses.*

SCIENTISTS AT ODDS

Velocities of Falling Objects When Galileo attended the University of Pisa in the 1500s, scholars generally accepted Aristotle's theory that bodies fall to Earth at different velocities depending on their mass. It is said that Galileo questioned Aristotle's teachings after observing different-sized hailstones hitting the ground at the same time.

Acceleration Due to Gravity

Acceleration is the rate at which velocity changes over time. So, the acceleration of an object is the object's change in velocity divided by the amount of time during which the change occurs. All objects accelerate toward Earth at a rate of 9.8 meters per second per second. This rate is written as 9.8 m/s/s, or 9.8 m/s², So, for every second that an object falls, the object's downward velocity increases by 9.8 m/s, as shown in **Figure 2.**

✓ **Reading Check** What is the acceleration due to gravity? (*See the Appendix for answers to Reading Checks.*)

Velocity of Falling Objects

You can calculate the change in velocity (Δv) of a falling object by using the following equation:

$$\Delta v = g \times t$$

In this equation, *g* is the acceleration due to gravity on Earth (9.8 m/s²), and *t* is the time the object takes to fall (in seconds). The change in velocity is the difference between the final velocity and the starting velocity. If the object starts at rest, this equation yields the velocity of the object after a certain time period.

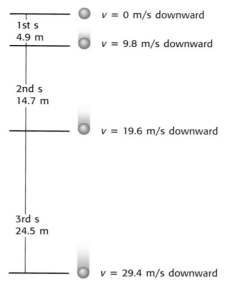

1st s
4.9 m
  v = 0 m/s downward
  v = 9.8 m/s downward

2nd s
14.7 m
  v = 19.6 m/s downward

3rd s
24.5 m
  v = 29.4 m/s downward

Figure 2 *A falling object accelerates at a constant rate. The object falls faster and farther each second than it did the second before.*

MATH FOCUS

Calculating the Velocity of Falling Objects A stone at rest is dropped from a cliff, and the stone hits the ground after a time of 3 s. What is the stone's velocity when it hits the ground?

Step 1: Write the equation for change in velocity.

$$\Delta v = g \times t$$

Step 2: Replace *g* with its value and *t* with the time given in the problem, and solve.

$$\Delta v = 9.8 \ \frac{m/s}{s} \times 3 \ s$$
$$= 29.4 \ m/s$$

To rearrange the equation to find time, divide by the acceleration due to gravity:

$$t = \frac{\Delta v}{g}$$

Now It's Your Turn

1. A penny at rest is dropped from the top of a tall stairwell. What is the penny's velocity after it has fallen for 2 s?
2. The same penny hits the ground in 4.5 s. What is the penny's velocity as it hits the ground?
3. A marble at rest is dropped from a tall building. The marble hits the ground with a velocity of 98 m/s. How long was the marble in the air?
4. An acorn at rest falls from an oak tree. The acorn hits the ground with a velocity of 14.7 m/s. How long did it take the acorn to land?

Answer to Reading Check

The acceleration due to gravity is 9.8 m/s².

CONNECTION ACTIVITY
Social Studies ——— ADVANCED

Greek Letters The triangle in the symbol for change in velocity is actually the Greek letter delta (Δ). In science, Δ often means "change in." When used in front of a variable, such as velocity, it indicates the result of subtracting the initial value of the variable from the final value of the variable. So, $\Delta v = v_{final} - v_{initial}$. Have students research how other Greek letters are used as symbols in science. Students should summarize their findings in a poster. **LS Verbal**

Prediction Guide Before students read about air resistance, ask them to explain whether a school bus or a racing car would be affected less by air resistance. (a racing car, because a racing car is built low to the ground, with smooth lines to reduce air resistance) **LS** Verbal

CONNECTION ᴀᴄᴛɪᴠɪᴛʏ
Earth Science ── GENERAL

Air Resistance and the Atmosphere Use the teaching transparency titled "Layers of the Atmosphere" to discuss how air pressure decreases as altitude increases. As air pressure decreases, the potential for air resistance also decreases. **LS** Visual

CONNECTION to
History ── GENERAL

First Parachutist The first person to use a parachute regularly was French aeronaut André-Jacques Garnerin. He gave his first demonstration of parachuting in Paris, France, in 1797. This first jump was from a balloon flying at height of about 1,000 m (3,200 ft). Garnerin traveled around Europe to demonstrate his parachuting technique. In fact, during one show in England, Garnerin made a jump from 2,440 m (8,000 ft)!

Figure 3 | **Effect of Air Resistance on a Falling Object**

a The **force of gravity** is pulling down on the apple. If gravity were the only force acting on the apple, the apple would accelerate at a rate of 9.8 m/s².

b The **force of air resistance** is pushing up on the apple. This force is subtracted from the force of gravity to yield the net force.

c The **net force** on the apple is equal to the force of air resistance subtracted from the force of gravity. Because the net force is not 0 N, the apple accelerates downward. But the apple does not accelerate as fast as it would without air resistance.

Air Resistance and Falling Objects

Try dropping two sheets of paper—one crumpled in a tight ball and the other kept flat. What happened? Does this simple experiment seem to contradict what you just learned about falling objects? The flat paper falls more slowly than the crumpled paper because of *air resistance*. Air resistance is the force that opposes the motion of objects through air.

The amount of air resistance acting on an object depends on the size, shape, and speed of the object. Air resistance affects the flat sheet of paper more than the crumpled one. The larger surface area of the flat sheet causes the flat sheet to fall slower than the crumpled one. **Figure 3** shows the effect of air resistance on the downward acceleration of a falling object.

✓ **Reading Check** Will air resistance have more effect on the acceleration of a falling leaf or the acceleration of a falling acorn?

Acceleration Stops at the Terminal Velocity

As the speed of a falling object increases, air resistance increases. The upward force of air resistance continues to increase until it is equal to the downward force of gravity. At this point, the net force is 0 N and the object stops accelerating. The object then falls at a constant velocity called the **terminal velocity.**

Terminal velocity can be a good thing. Every year, cars, buildings, and vegetation are severely damaged in hailstorms. The terminal velocity of hailstones is between 5 and 40 m/s, depending on their size. If there were no air resistance, hailstones would hit the Earth at velocities near 350 m/s! **Figure 4** shows another situation in which terminal velocity is helpful.

Figure 4 *The parachute increases the air resistance of this sky diver and slows him to a safe terminal velocity.*

terminal velocity the constant velocity of a falling object when the force of air resistance is equal in magnitude and opposite in direction to the force of gravity

---

Answer to Reading Check
Air resistance will have more of an effect on the acceleration of a falling leaf.

CHAPTER RESOURCES

Technology

 Transparencies
• Effect of Air Resistance on a Falling Object
• *LINK TO EARTH SCIENCE* Layers of the Atmosphere

Free Fall Occurs When There Is No Air Resistance

Sky divers are often described as being in free fall before they open their parachutes. However, that is an incorrect description, because air resistance is always acting on the sky diver.

An object is in **free fall** only if gravity is pulling it down and no other forces are acting on it. Because air resistance is a force, free fall can occur only where there is no air. Two places that have no air are in space and in a vacuum. A vacuum is a place in which there is no matter. **Figure 5** shows objects falling in a vacuum. Because there is no air resistance in a vacuum, the two objects are in free fall.

Orbiting Objects Are in Free Fall

Look at the astronaut in **Figure 6.** Why is the astronaut floating inside the space shuttle? You may be tempted to say that she is weightless in space. However, it is impossible for any object to be weightless anywhere in the universe.

Weight is a measure of gravitational force. The size of the force depends on the masses of objects and the distances between them. Suppose you traveled in space far away from all the stars and planets. The gravitational force acting on you would be very small because the distance between you and other objects would be very large. But you and all the other objects in the universe would still have mass. Therefore, gravity would attract you to other objects—even if just slightly—so you would still have weight.

Astronauts float in orbiting spacecrafts because of free fall. To better understand why astronauts float, you need to know what *orbiting* means.

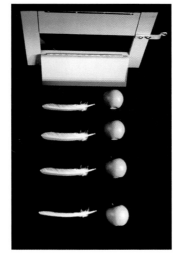

Figure 5 *Air resistance usually causes a feather to fall more slowly than an apple falls. But in a vacuum, a feather and an apple fall with the same acceleration because both are in free fall.*

free fall the motion of a body when only the force of gravity is acting on the body

Figure 6 *Astronauts appear to be weightless while they are floating inside the space shuttle— but they are not weightless!*

Using the Figure—GENERAL

How an Orbit is Formed Draw students' attention to **Figure 7.** Ask students why the shuttle does not fall to Earth if gravity is pulling downward on it. (The forward motion of the shuttle occurs together with free fall to produce a path that follows the curve of Earth's surface.) Ask what would happen if the shuttle started moving much faster or much slower. (If the shuttle moved fast enough, it would escape Earth's gravitational force and move off into space. If the shuttle moved more slowly, it would begin to fall toward Earth. **Note:** Tell students that the shuttle slows down to land in a controlled "fall" toward Earth. However, the shuttle continues to move forward so it spirals down toward Earth rather than falling straight down.)  **Visual**

Cultural Awareness GENERAL

An Astronaut First On September 12, 1992, Dr. Mae Jemison became the first African-American woman to orbit Earth. She was a science mission specialist on the space shuttle *Endeavour.* Dr. Jemison, who has degrees in chemical engineering and medicine, was in charge of many of the experiments conducted during the mission.

Answer to Reading Check

The word *centripetal* means "toward the center."

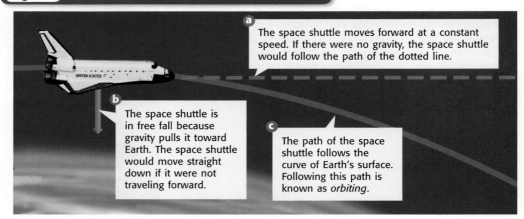

Figure 7 How an Orbit Is Formed

a The space shuttle moves forward at a constant speed. If there were no gravity, the space shuttle would follow the path of the dotted line.

b The space shuttle is in free fall because gravity pulls it toward Earth. The space shuttle would move straight down if it were not traveling forward.

c The path of the space shuttle follows the curve of Earth's surface. Following this path is known as *orbiting.*

Two Motions Combine to Cause Orbiting

An object is orbiting when it is traveling around another object in space. When a spacecraft orbits Earth, it is moving forward. But the spacecraft is also in free fall toward Earth. **Figure 7** shows how these two motions combine to cause orbiting.

As you can see in **Figure 7,** the space shuttle is always falling while it is in orbit. So why don't astronauts hit their heads on the ceiling of the falling shuttle? Because they are also in free fall—they are always falling, too. Because astronauts are in free fall, they float.

Orbiting and Centripetal Force

Besides spacecrafts and satellites, many other objects in the universe are in orbit. The moon orbits the Earth. Earth and the other planets orbit the sun. In addition, many stars orbit large masses in the center of galaxies. Many of these objects are traveling in a circular or nearly circular path. Any object in circular motion is constantly changing direction. Because an unbalanced force is necessary to change the motion of any object, there must be an unbalanced force working on any object in circular motion.

The unbalanced force that causes objects to move in a circular path is called a *centripetal force* (sen TRIP uht uhl FOHRS). Gravity provides the centripetal force that keeps objects in orbit. The word *centripetal* means "toward the center." As you can see in **Figure 8,** the centripetal force on the moon points toward the center of the moon's circular orbit.

✓ **Reading Check** What does the word *centripetal* mean?

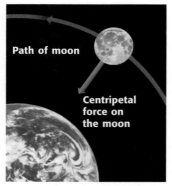

Path of moon

Centripetal force on the moon

Figure 8 *The moon stays in orbit around Earth because Earth's gravitational force provides a centripetal force on the moon.*

MISCONCEPTION ALERT

Shuttle Orbit The shuttle in **Figure 7** is shown in orbit facing forward and oriented right side up (called *airplane mode*). In orbit, the shuttle spends most of the time upside down and backward. It also orbits upside down and sideways (wing first), but it rarely orbits in airplane mode. It is only in airplane mode for landings.

CONNECTION ACTIVITY Astronomy——ADVANCED

Scale Drawing In **Figure 8,** the relative sizes of Earth and the moon and the distance between the two are not drawn to scale. Ask students to find average distance between Earth and the moon and the diameters of Earth and the moon. Then, have students use this information to make a poster of the moon in orbit around Earth that is drawn to scale.  **Logical/Visual**

Projectile Motion and Gravity

The motion of a hopping grasshopper is an example of projectile motion (proh JEK tuhl MOH shuhn). **Projectile motion** is the curved path an object follows when it is thrown or propelled near the surface of the Earth. Projectile motion has two components—horizontal motion and vertical motion. The two components are independent, so they have no effect on each other. When the two motions are combined, they form a curved path, as shown in **Figure 9.** Some examples of projectile motion include the following:

- a frog leaping
- water sprayed by a sprinkler
- a swimmer diving into water
- balls being juggled
- an arrow shot by an archer

Horizontal Motion

When you throw a ball, your hand exerts a force on the ball that makes the ball move forward. This force gives the ball its horizontal motion, which is motion parallel to the ground.

After you release the ball, no horizontal forces are acting on the ball (if you ignore air resistance). Even gravity does not affect the horizontal component of projectile motion. So, there are no forces to change the ball's horizontal motion. Thus, the horizontal velocity of the ball is constant after the ball leaves your hand, as shown in **Figure 9.**

projectile motion the curved path that an object follows when thrown, launched, or otherwise projected near the surface of Earth

---

Figure 9 | Projectile Motion

ⓐ After the ball leaves the pitcher's hand, the ball's horizontal velocity is constant.

ⓑ The ball's vertical velocity increases because gravity causes it to accelerate downward.

ⓒ The two motions combine to form a curved path.

CHAPTER RESOURCES

Technology

Transparencies
- How an Orbit is Formed
- Projectile Motion

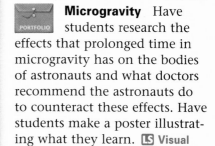

Reteaching ━━━━ BASIC

Horizontal Velocity Give students photocopies of **Figure 10** and ask them to use a ruler to draw vertical lines through the centers of the yellow balls. Then, have students measure the distance between the lines. Students should find that the distances are equal. Explain that this fact shows that the horizontal velocity is constant. **LS** Visual

Quiz ━━━━━━ GENERAL

1. Why do you have to aim above a target that you want to hit with a thrown object? (The thrown object will be in projectile motion and will therefore accelerate downward.)

2. When does an object reach its terminal velocity? (when the upward force of air resistance equals the downward force of gravity)

Alternative Assessment ━━━ GENERAL

Making Models Give each group a plastic bag, string, tape, a washer, scissors, and a stopwatch. Have each group design a parachute. Challenge the groups to make the parachute that descends the slowest. How does the design of a parachute affect its rate of fall? **LS** Kinesthetic

INTERNET ACTIVITY
For another activity related to this chapter, go to **go.hrw.com** and type in the keyword **HP5FORW**.

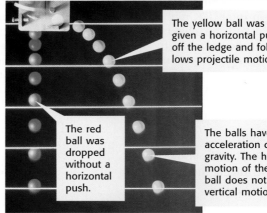

Figure 10 Projectile Motion and Acceleration Due to Gravity

The yellow ball was given a horizontal push off the ledge and follows projectile motion.

The red ball was dropped without a horizontal push.

The balls have the same acceleration due to gravity. The horizontal motion of the yellow ball does not affect its vertical motion.

Vertical Motion

Gravity pulls everything on Earth downward toward the center of Earth. A ball in your hand is prevented from falling by your hand. After you throw the ball, gravity pulls it downward and gives the ball vertical motion. Vertical motion is motion that is perpendicular to the ground. Gravity pulls objects in projectile motion down at an acceleration of 9.8 m/s² (if air resistance is ignored). This rate is the same for all falling objects. **Figure 10** shows that the downward acceleration of a thrown object and a falling object are the same.

Because objects in projectile motion accelerate downward, you always have to aim above a target if you want to hit it with a thrown or propelled object. That's why when you aim an arrow directly at a bull's-eye, your arrow strikes the bottom of the target rather than the middle of the target.

Reading Check What gives an object in projectile motion its vertical motion?

Penny Projectile Motion
1. Position a **flat ruler** and **two pennies** on a **desk or table** as shown below.

2. Hold the ruler by the end that is on the desk. Move the ruler quickly in the direction shown so that the ruler knocks the penny off the table and so that the other penny also drops. Repeat this step several times.

3. Which penny travels with projectile motion? In what order do the pennies hit the ground? Record and explain your answers.

MATERIALS

FOR EACH GROUP
• pennies (2)
• ruler, flat

Teacher's Notes: Make sure students have plenty of room. The penny in projectile motion may travel 1–2 m from its starting point. If the Quick Lab is done in a room without a carpet, students can listen for the sound of the pennies hitting the floor. Students should move the ruler quickly enough so that the penny on the ruler drops straight down.

Answers

3. The penny that was knocked off the table with the ruler was in projectile motion. The pennies should land at the same time because they have the same acceleration due to gravity. The horizontal motion does not affect the vertical motion.

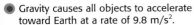
SECTION Review

Summary

- Gravity causes all objects to accelerate toward Earth at a rate of 9.8 m/s².
- Air resistance slows the acceleration of falling objects. An object falls at its terminal velocity when the upward force of air resistance equals the downward force of gravity.
- An object is in free fall if gravity is the only force acting on it.
- Objects in orbit appear to be weightless because they are in free fall.

- A centripetal force is needed to keep objects in circular motion. Gravity acts as a centripetal force to keep objects in orbit.
- Projectile motion is the curved path an object follows when thrown or propelled near the surface of Earth.
- Projectile motion has two components—horizontal motion and vertical motion. Gravity affects only the vertical motion of projectile motion.

Using Key Terms

1. Use each of the following terms in a separate sentence: *terminal velocity* and *free fall*.

Understanding Key Ideas

2. Which of the following is in projectile motion?
   a. a feather falling in a vacuum
   b. a cat leaping on a toy
   c. a car driving up a hill
   d. a book laying on a desk

3. How does air resistance affect the acceleration of falling objects?

4. How does gravity affect the two components of projectile motion?

5. How is the acceleration of falling objects affected by gravity?

6. Why is the acceleration due to gravity the same for all objects?

Math Skills

7. A rock at rest falls off a tall cliff and hits the valley below after 3.5 s. What is the rock's velocity as it hits the ground?

Critical Thinking

8. **Applying Concepts** Think about a sport that uses a ball. Identify four examples from that sport in which an object is in projectile motion.

9. **Making Inferences** The moon has no atmosphere. Predict what would happen if an astronaut on the moon dropped a hammer and a feather at the same time from the same height.

Interpreting Graphics

10. Whenever Jon delivers a newspaper to the Zapanta house, the newspaper lands in the bushes, as shown below. What should Jon do to make sure the newspaper lands on the porch?

For a variety of links related to this chapter, go to www.scilinks.org
Topic: Gravity and Orbiting Objects; Projectile Motion
SciLinks code: HSM0692; HSM1223

Section 1 • Gravity and Motion

Focus

Overview

This section introduces students to Newton's laws of motion. Before teaching this section, you may wish to review the concepts of acceleration, force, net force, friction, and balanced and unbalanced forces with your students.

 Bellringer

Have students respond to the following question:

If you are sitting still in your seat on a bus that is traveling on a highway, is your body at rest or in motion? (in motion with respect to the ground)

Explain your answer. Use a diagram if it will help make your answer clear.

Motivate

Demonstration — GENERAL

Egg in a Buggy Place a hard-boiled egg in a small, wheeled cart. Apply a strong force to the cart so that it strikes a wall. Ask students to draw a series of pictures that shows what happens to the egg as the cart moves across the floor and strikes the wall. Then, ask them to draw a picture of how the egg could be protected in the cart. Challenge students to explain what happened to the egg. LS Visual

Figure 1 *A golf ball will remain at rest on a tee until it is acted on by the unbalanced force of a moving club.*

Newton's Laws of Motion

Imagine that you are playing baseball. The pitch comes in, and—crack—you hit the ball hard! But instead of flying off the bat, the ball just drops to the ground. Is that normal?

You would probably say no. You know that force and motion are related. When you exert a force on a baseball by hitting it with a bat, the baseball should move. In 1686, Sir Isaac Newton explained this relationship between force and the motion of an object with his three laws of motion.

Newton's First Law of Motion

An object at rest remains at rest, and an object in motion remains in motion at constant speed and in a straight line unless acted on by an unbalanced force.

Newton's first law of motion describes the motion of an object that has a net force of 0 N acting on it. This law may seem complicated when you first read it. But, it is easy to understand when you consider its two parts separately.

Part 1: Objects at Rest

An object that is not moving is said to be at rest. A chair on the floor and a golf ball balanced on a tee are examples of objects at rest. Newton's first law says that objects at rest will stay at rest unless they are acted on by an unbalanced force. For example, objects will not start moving until a push or a pull is exerted on them. So, a chair won't slide across the room unless you push the chair. And, a golf ball won't move off the tee unless the ball is struck by a golf club, as shown in **Figure 1.**

Unbalanced force

Object at rest

Object in motion

CONNECTION to History — GENERAL

Sir Isaac Newton Long before Newton, others had observed relationships between forces and motion, rest, and acceleration. When Newton extended their work with his three laws of motion, he said, "If I have seen further it is by standing on the shoulders of Giants." Newton's genius was that he combined previous discoveries plus his own observations into a unified picture of how the universe worked.

Part 2: Objects in Motion

The second part of Newton's first law is about objects moving with a certain velocity. Such objects will continue to move forever with the same velocity unless an unbalanced force acts on them.

Think about driving a bumper car at an amusement park. Your ride is pleasant as long as you are driving in an open space. But the name of the game is bumper cars! Sooner or later you are likely to run into another car, as shown in **Figure 2.** Your bumper car stops when it hits another car. But, you continue to move forward until the force from your seat belt stops you.

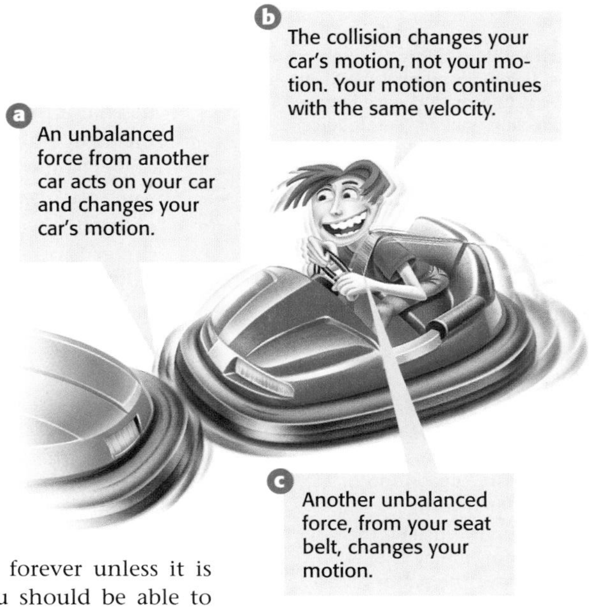

Friction and Newton's First Law

An object in motion will stay in motion forever unless it is acted on by an unbalanced force. So, you should be able to give your desk a push and send it sliding across the floor. If you push your desk, the desk quickly stops. Why?

There must be an unbalanced force that acts on the desk to stop its motion. That unbalanced force is friction. The friction between the desk and the floor works against the motion of the desk. Because of friction, observing the effects of Newton's first law is often difficult. For example, friction will cause a rolling ball to slow down and stop. Friction will also make a car slow down if the driver lets up on the gas pedal. Because of friction, the motion of objects changes.

✓ Reading Check When you ride a bus, why do you fall forward when the bus stops moving? (*See the Appendix for answers to Reading Checks.*)

ⓐ An unbalanced force from another car acts on your car and changes your car's motion.

ⓑ The collision changes your car's motion, not your motion. Your motion continues with the same velocity.

ⓒ Another unbalanced force, from your seat belt, changes your motion.

Figure 2 *Bumper cars let you have fun with Newton's first law.*

Quick Lab

First Law Skateboard

1. Place an **empty soda can** on top of a **skateboard.**

2. Ask a friend to catch the skateboard after you push it. Now, give the skateboard a quick, firm push. What happened to the soda can?

3. Put the can on the skateboard again. Push the skateboard gently so that the skateboard moves quickly but so that the can does not fall.

4. Ask your friend to stop the skateboard after he or she allows it to travel a short distance. What happened to the can?

5. Explain how Newton's first law applies to what happened.

Answer to Reading Check

When the bus is moving, both you and the bus are in motion. When the bus stops moving, no unbalanced force acts on your body, so your body continues to move forward.

Is That a Fact!

Antilock braking systems (ABS) controlled by a computer prevent skidding by sensing when the wheels are about to lock. They release and reapply the brakes up to 25 times a second. Instead of skidding out of control, the car slows down and stops safely.

MATERIALS

FOR EACH STUDENT
- paper towel or construction paper
- plastic cup, empty
- water

Teacher's Notes: Cups should be large (12 oz or more). 500 mL plastic beakers will also work.

Make sure students don't fill the cups more than half full of water. This will reduce spills, but it still makes the cup noticeably more massive.

Instruct students to keep the outer surfaces of the cups dry. A wet paper towel may break when pulled.

Beans or popcorn kernels can be substituted for the water, if desired.

Be sure to have extra paper towels on hand to clean up any spilled water

Answers

2. Students will quickly learn that they have to jerk the paper towel out from under the cup as in a magic trick.

5. It should be easier for students to do the trick with water in the cup because the cup has more mass and therefore more inertia. When the cup has more inertia, it is harder to move. It is therefore easier to move the paper towel out from under it.

inertia the tendency of an object to resist being moved or, if the object is moving, to resist a change in speed or direction until an outside force acts on the object

First-Law Magic

1. On a **table or desk**, place a **large, empty plastic cup** on top of a **paper towel.**
2. Without touching the cup or tipping it over, remove the paper towel from under the cup. How did you accomplish this? Repeat this step.
3. Fill the cup half full with **water,** and place the cup on the paper towel.
4. Once again, remove the paper towel from under the cup. Was it easier or harder to do this time?
5. Explain your observations in terms of mass, inertia, and Newton's first law of motion.

Inertia and Newton's First Law

Newton's first law of motion is sometimes called the *law of inertia.* **Inertia** (in UHR shuh) is the tendency of all objects to resist any change in motion. Because of inertia, an object at rest will remain at rest until a force makes it move. Likewise, inertia is the reason a moving object stays in motion with the same velocity unless a force changes its speed or direction. For example, because of inertia, you slide toward the side of a car when the driver turns a corner. Inertia is also why it is impossible for a plane, car, or bicycle to stop immediately.

Mass and Inertia

Mass is a measure of inertia. An object that has a small mass has less inertia than an object that has a large mass. So, changing the motion of an object that has a small mass is easier than changing the motion of an object that has a large mass. For example, a softball has less mass and therefore less inertia than a bowling ball. Because the softball has a small amount of inertia, it is easy to pitch a softball and to change its motion by hitting it with a bat. Imagine how difficult it would be to play softball with a bowling ball! **Figure 3** further shows the relationship between mass and inertia.

Figure 3 *Inertia makes it harder to accelerate a car than to accelerate a bicycle. Inertia also makes it easier to stop a moving bicycle than a car moving at the same speed.*

Newton's Second Law of Motion

The acceleration of an object depends on the mass of the object and the amount of force applied.

Newton's second law describes the motion of an object when an unbalanced force acts on the object. As with Newton's first law, you should consider the second law in two parts.

Part 1: Acceleration Depends on Mass

Suppose you are pushing an empty cart. You have to exert only a small force on the cart to accelerate it. But, the same amount of force will not accelerate the full cart as much as the empty cart. Look at the first two photos in **Figure 4.** They show that the acceleration of an object decreases as its mass increases and that its acceleration increases as its mass decreases.

Part 2: Acceleration Depends on Force

Suppose you give the cart a hard push, as shown in the third photo in **Figure 4.** The cart will start moving faster than if you gave it only a soft push. So, an object's acceleration increases as the force on the object increases. On the other hand, an object's acceleration decreases as the force on the object decreases.

The acceleration of an object is always in the same direction as the force applied. The cart in **Figure 4** moved forward because the push was in the forward direction.

✓ **Reading Check** What is the relationship between the force on an object and the object's acceleration?

CONNECTION TO Environmental Science

Car Sizes and Pollution

On average, newer cars pollute the air less than older cars do. One reason for this is that newer cars have less mass than older cars have. An object that has less mass requires less force to achieve the same acceleration as an object that has more mass. So, a small car can have a small engine and still have good acceleration. Because small engines use less fuel than large engines use, small engines create less pollution. Research three models of cars from the same year, and make a chart to compare the mass of the cars with the amount of fuel they use.

Figure 4 **Mass, Force, and Acceleration**

Acceleration **Acceleration** **Acceleration**

If the force applied to the carts is the same, the acceleration of the empty cart is greater than the acceleration of the loaded cart.

Acceleration will increase when a larger force is exerted.

Answer to Reading Check

The acceleration of an object increases as the force exerted on the object increases. (**Note:** this assumes that the mass of the object is constant.)

SCIENCE HUMOR

There once was a trucker from Nome,

Whose rig was loaded with foam.

Its very small mass

Made him able to pass

The other trucks all the way home.

Teach, *continued*

Discussion ——— ADVANCED

Rearranging Newton's Second Law Discuss with students how the equation $F = m \times a$ can be used to find the mass of an object. Have them imagine that they hit an object of unknown mass with a force of 15 N and that the object accelerates at 5 m/s². What is the mass of the object? (3 kg) **LS** Logical

CONNECTION to
Math ——————— BASIC

Evaluating the Equation When you introduce the equation for Newton's second law, point out to students that acceleration and force are directly proportional (as force increases, acceleration increases) and that acceleration and mass are inversely proportional (as mass increases, acceleration decreases). These relationships are explained qualitatively, but students may not see the connection on their own. Also remind students of the definition of a newton:

1 newton = 1 kilogram-meter per second per second

OR

$1 \text{ N} = 1 \text{ kg} \cdot \text{m/s}^2$

This is important for helping students through the unit cancellation in the Math Focus and in **Figure 5**.

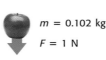 **Figure 5** Newton's Second Law and Acceleration Due to Gravity

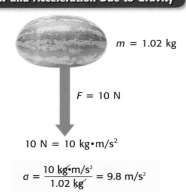

$m = 0.102$ kg
$F = 1$ N

$1 \text{ N} = 1 \text{ kg} \cdot \text{m/s}^2$

$a = \dfrac{1 \text{ kg} \cdot \text{m/s}^2}{0.102 \text{ kg}} = 9.8 \text{ m/s}^2$

$m = 1.02$ kg

$F = 10$ N

$10 \text{ N} = 10 \text{ kg} \cdot \text{m/s}^2$

$a = \dfrac{10 \text{ kg} \cdot \text{m/s}^2}{1.02 \text{ kg}} = 9.8 \text{ m/s}^2$

The apple has less mass than the watermelon does. So, less force is needed to give the apple the same acceleration that the watermelon has.

Expressing Newton's Second Law Mathematically

The relationship of acceleration (a) to mass (m) and force (F) can be expressed mathematically with the following equation:

$$a = \frac{F}{m}, \text{ or } F = m \times a$$

Notice that the equation can be rearranged to find the force applied. Both forms of the equation can be used to solve problems.

Newton's second law explains why objects fall to Earth with the same acceleration. In **Figure 5,** you can see how the large force of gravity on the watermelon is offset by its large mass. Thus, you find that the accelerations of the watermelon and the apple are the same when you solve for acceleration.

MATH FOCUS

Second-Law Problems What is the acceleration of a 3 kg mass if a force of 14.4 N is used to move the mass? (Note: 1 N is equal to $1 \text{ kg} \cdot \text{m/s}^2$)

Step 1: Write the equation for acceleration.

$$a = \frac{F}{m}$$

Step 2: Replace F and m with the values given in the problem, and solve.

$$a = \frac{14.4 \text{ kg} \cdot \text{m/s}^2}{3 \text{ kg}} = 4.8 \text{ m/s}^2$$

Now It's Your Turn

1. What is the acceleration of a 7 kg mass if a force of 68.6 N is used to move it toward Earth?
2. What force is necessary to accelerate a 1,250 kg car at a rate of 40 m/s²?
3. Zookeepers carry a stretcher that holds a sleeping lion. The total mass of the lion and the stretcher is 175 kg. The lion's forward acceleration is 2 m/s². What is the force necessary to produce this acceleration?

CONNECTION ACTIVITY
Math ——————— GENERAL

More Second Law Problems Have students do the following problems:

- Calculate the gravitational force acting on your 6 kg backpack. (This force is the weight of your backpack.)
 ($F = 6 \text{ kg} \times 9.8 \text{ m/s}^2 = 58.8 \text{ N}$)

- A 50 kg skater pushes off from a wall with a force of 200 N. What is the skater's acceleration? ($a = 200 \text{ N} \div 50 \text{ kg} = 200 \text{ kg} \cdot \text{m/s}^2 \div 50 \text{ kg} = 4 \text{ m/s}^2$)

LS Logical

Answers to Math Focus

1. $a = F \div m = 68.6 \text{ N} \div 7 \text{ kg} = 9.8 \text{ m/s}^2$ (This is acceleration due to gravity.)
2. $F = m \times a = 1{,}250 \text{ kg} \times 40 \text{ m/s}^2 = 50{,}000 \text{ N}$
3. $F = m \times a = 175 \text{ kg} \times 2 \text{ m/s}^2 = 350 \text{ N}$

Newton's Third Law of Motion

Whenever one object exerts a force on a second object, the second object exerts an equal and opposite force on the first.

Newton's third law can be simply stated as follows: All forces act in pairs. If a force is exerted, another force occurs that is equal in size and opposite in direction. The law itself addresses only forces. But the way that force pairs interact affects the motion of objects.

How do forces act in pairs? Study **Figure 6** to learn how one force pair helps propel a swimmer through water. Action and reaction force pairs are present even when there is no motion. For example, you exert a force on a chair when you sit on it. Your weight pushing down on the chair is the action force. The reaction force is the force exerted by the chair that pushes up on your body. The force is equal to your weight.

✓ Reading Check How are the forces in each force pair related?

Force Pairs Do Not Act on the Same Object

A force is always exerted by one object on another object. This rule is true for all forces, including action and reaction forces. However, action and reaction forces in a pair do not act on the same object. If they did, the net force would always be 0 N and nothing would ever move! To understand how action and reaction forces act on objects, look at **Figure 6** again. The action force was exerted on the water by the swimmer's hands. But the reaction force was exerted on the swimmer's hands by the water. The forces did not act on the same object.

Newton Ball

Play catch with an adult. As you play, discuss how Newton's laws of motion are involved in the game. After you finish your game, make a list in your **science journal** of what you discussed.

Figure 6 *The action force and reaction force are a pair. The two forces are equal in size but opposite in direction.*

The action force is the swimmer's hands pushing on the water.

The reaction force is the water pushing on the hands. The reaction force moves the swimmer forward.

CHAPTER RESOURCES

Workbooks

📖 **Math Skills for Science**
• Newton: Force and Motion **GENERAL**

CONNECTION to Real World — **GENERAL**

Artillery Recoil Newton's third law explains that when a shell is fired from an artillery piece, the force opposite to that which propels the shell forward causes the gun to recoil, or move backward. Because the mass of the gun is so much greater than the mass of the shell, the shell moves forward with a far greater velocity than the gun moves backward. This same law applies to the human cannonball at the circus!

Close

Figure 7 Examples of Action and Reaction Force Pairs

The space shuttle's thrusters push the exhaust gases downward as the gases push the shuttle upward with an equal force.

The rabbit's legs exert a force on Earth. Earth exerts an equal force on the rabbit's legs and causes the rabbit to accelerate upward.

The bat exerts a force on the ball and sends the ball flying. The ball exerts an equal force on the bat, but the bat does not move backward because the batter is exerting another force on the bat.

All Forces Act in Pairs—Action and Reaction

Newton's third law says that all forces act in pairs. When a force is exerted, there is always a reaction force. A force never acts by itself. **Figure 7** shows some examples of action and reaction force pairs. In each example, the action force is shown in yellow and the reaction force is shown in red.

The Effect of a Reaction Can Be Difficult to See

Another example of a force pair is shown in **Figure 8.** Gravity is a force of attraction between objects that is due to their masses. If you drop a ball, gravity pulls the ball toward Earth. This force is the action force exerted by Earth on the ball. But gravity also pulls Earth toward the ball. The force is the reaction force exerted by the ball on Earth.

It's easy to see the effect of the action force—the ball falls to Earth. Why don't you notice the effect of the reaction force—Earth being pulled upward? To find the answer to this question, think about Newton's second law. It states that the acceleration of an object depends on the force applied to it and on the mass of the object. The force on Earth is equal to the force on the ball. But the mass of Earth is much larger than the mass of the ball. Thus, the acceleration of Earth is much smaller than the acceleration of the ball. The acceleration of the Earth is so small that you can't see or feel the acceleration. So, it is difficult to observe the effect of Newton's third law on falling objects.

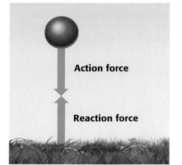

Action force

Reaction force

Figure 8 The force of gravity between Earth and a falling object is a force pair.

 **Reading Check** Why do objects fall toward Earth?

Summary

- Newton's first law of motion states that the motion of an object will not change if no unbalanced forces act on it.
- Objects at rest will not move unless acted upon by an unbalanced force.
- Objects in motion will continue to move at a constant speed and in a straight line unless acted upon by an unbalanced force.
- Inertia is the tendency of matter to resist a change in motion. Mass is a measure of inertia.

- Newton's second law of motion states that the acceleration of an object depends on its mass and on the force exerted on it.
- Newton's second law is represented by the following equation: $F = m \times a$.
- Newton's third law of motion states that whenever one object exerts a force on a second object, the second object exerts an equal and opposite force on the first object.

Using Key Terms

1. In your own words, write a definition for the term *inertia*.

Understanding Key Ideas

2. Which of the following will increase the acceleration of an object that is pushed by a force?
   a. decreasing the mass of the object
   b. increasing the mass of the object
   c. increasing the force pushing the object
   d. Both (a) and (c)

3. Give three examples of force pairs that occur when you do your homework.

4. What does Newton's first law of motion say about objects at rest and objects in motion?

5. Use Newton's second law to describe the relationship between force, mass, and acceleration.

Math Skills

6. What force is necessary to accelerate a 70 kg object at a rate of 4.2 m/s²?

Critical Thinking

7. **Applying Concepts** When a truck pulls a trailer, the trailer and truck accelerate forward even though the action and reaction forces are the same size but are in opposite directions. Why don't these forces balance each other?

8. **Making Inferences** Use Newton's first law of motion to explain why airbags in cars are important during head-on collisions.

Interpreting Graphics

9. Imagine you accidentally bumped your hand against a table, as shown in the photo below. Your hand hurts after it happens. Use Newton's third law of motion to explain what caused your hand to hurt.

SCiLINKS.

NSTA
Developed and maintained by the
National Science Teachers Association

For a variety of links related to this chapter, go to www.scilinks.org

Topic: Newton's Laws of Motion
SciLinks code: HSM1028

CHAPTER RESOURCES

Chapter Resource File
- Section Quiz GENERAL
- Section Review GENERAL
- Vocabulary and Section Summary GENERAL
- Critical Thinking ADVANCED
- SciLinks Activity GENERAL
- Datasheet for Quick Lab

Answers to Section Review

1. Sample answer: Inertia is the tendency of an object to resist changes in motion.

2. d

3. Accept all reasonable answers. Students should list three examples of force pairs. Partial sample answer: using a pencil or pen (action: hand pushing on pencil; reaction: pencil pushing back on hand OR action: pencil pushing on paper; reaction: paper pushing on pencil).

4. Newton's first law says that objects at rest tend to stay at rest and objects in motion tend to stay in motion unless acted on by an unbalanced force.

5. Newton's second law states that the acceleration of an object increases as the force acting on it increases, but the acceleration decreases as the mass of the object increases.

6. $F = 70 \text{ kg} \times 4.2 \text{ m/s}^2 = 294 \text{ N}$

7. The action and reaction forces do not balance each other because the forces are acting on two different objects. Because they act on two different objects, you cannot combine them to determine a net force.

8. Sample answer: During a head-on collision, an unbalanced force stops the motion of the car. But no unbalanced force immediately acts on the people inside the car. The people continue to move forward. Airbags are important because they provide unbalanced forces to stop the motion of the people in the car. The airbags prevent the people from hitting the dashboard or windshield of the car.

9. Your hand hit the table with a certain amount of force. According to Newton's third law of motion, the table exerts an equal and opposite force on your hand. The force exerted by the table causes your hand to hurt.

SECTION
3

Focus

Overview

In this section, students learn about momentum and perform calculations with the equation for momentum. Students also study the law of conservation of momentum and learn how it relates to Newton's third law of motion.

Bellringer

Tell students that this section is about momentum. Then, ask students to make a list of five things that they think have momentum and a list of five things that don't have momentum.

Motivate

Testing Momentum Give each group of students two balls that have different masses. Have students take turns rolling the balls to each other with the same velocity. Ask the students to compare the forces needed to stop the balls. (More force is needed to stop the ball with more mass.) Ask students to explain why different forces are needed. (The ball that has more mass has more momentum. Therefore, it is harder to stop.) **LS** Kinesthetic

READING WARM-UP

Objectives
 Calculate the momentum of moving objects.
 Explain the law of conservation of momentum.

Terms to Learn
momentum

READING STRATEGY

Prediction Guide Before reading this section, write the title of each heading in this section. Next, under each heading, write what you think you will learn.

---

momentum a quantity defined as the product of the mass and velocity of an object

Momentum

Imagine a compact car and a large truck traveling with the same velocity. The drivers of both vehicles put on the brakes at the same time. Which vehicle will stop first?

You would probably say that the compact car will stop first. You know that smaller objects are easier to stop than larger objects. But why? The answer is momentum (moh MEN tuhm).

Momentum, Mass, and Velocity

The **momentum** of an object depends on the object's mass and velocity. The more momentum an object has, the harder it is to stop the object or change its direction. In the example above, the truck has more mass and more momentum than the car has. So, a larger force is needed to stop the truck. Similarly, a fast-moving car has a greater velocity and thus more momentum than a slow-moving car of the same mass. So, a fast-moving car is harder to stop than a slow-moving car. **Figure 1** shows another example of an object that has momentum.

Calculating Momentum

Momentum (*p*) can be calculated with the equation below:

$$p = m \times v$$

In this equation, *m* is the mass of an object in kilograms and *v* is the object's velocity in meters per second. The units of momentum are kilograms multiplied by meters per second, or kg•m/s. Like velocity, momentum has a direction. Its direction is always the same as the direction of the object's velocity.

Figure 1 *The teen on the right has less mass than the teen on the left. But, the teen on the right can have a large momentum by moving quickly when she kicks.*

CHAPTER RESOURCES

Chapter Resource File

• Lesson Plan
• Directed Reading A **BASIC**
• Directed Reading B **SPECIAL NEEDS**

Technology

Transparencies
• Bellringer

Workbooks

Math Skills for Science
• Momentum **GENERAL**

MATH FOCUS

Momentum Calculations What is the momentum of an ostrich with a mass of 120 kg that runs with a velocity of 16 m/s north?

Step 1: Write the equation for momentum.

$$p = m \times v$$

Step 2: Replace m and v with the values given in the problem, and solve.

$$p = 120 \text{ kg} \times 16 \text{ m/s north}$$
$$p = 19{,}200 \text{ kg•m/s north}$$

Now It's Your Turn

1. What is the momentum of a 6 kg bowling ball that is moving at 10 m/s down the alley toward the pins?
2. An 85 kg man is jogging with a velocity of 2.6 m/s to the north. Nearby, a 65 kg person is skateboarding and is traveling with a velocity of 3 m/s north. Which person has greater momentum? Show your calculations.

The Law of Conservation of Momentum

When a moving object hits another object, some or all of the momentum of the first object is transferred to the object that is hit. If only some of the momentum is transferred, the rest of the momentum stays with the first object.

Imagine that a cue ball hits a billiard ball so that the billiard ball starts moving and the cue ball stops, as shown in **Figure 2.** The white cue ball had a certain amount of momentum before the collision. During the collision, all of the cue ball's momentum was transferred to the red billiard ball. After the collision, the billiard ball moved away with the same amount of momentum the cue ball had. This example shows the *law of conservation of momentum.* The law of conservation of momentum states that any time objects collide, the total amount of momentum stays the same. The law of conservation of momentum is true for any collision if no other forces act on the colliding objects. This law applies whether the objects stick together or bounce off each other after they collide.

✓ **Reading Check** What can happen to momentum when two objects collide? (*See the Appendix for answers to Reading Checks.*)

Figure 2 *The momentum before a collision is equal to the momentum after the collision.*

Answer to Reading Check

When two objects collide, some or all of the momentum of each object can be transferred to the other object.

Answers to Math Focus

1. $p = 6 \text{ kg} \times 10 \text{ m/s down the alley} = 60 \text{ kg•m/s down the alley}$
2. The man jogging has greater momentum.

   $p = 85 \text{ kg} \times 2.6 \text{ m/s north} = 221 \text{ kg•m/s north (man jogging)}$

   $p = 65 \text{ kg} \times 3 \text{ m/s north} = 195 \text{ kg•m/s north (person skateboarding)}$

Reteaching — BASIC

Velocity and Momentum Tell students that slow-moving objects that have large masses can have more momentum than fast-moving objects that have smaller masses. For example, a large cruise ship moving slowly into port has more momentum than a person running very fast. Have students describe other slow-moving objects that have a large momentum. [LS] Verbal

Quiz — GENERAL

1. What is the equation for momentum? ($p = m \times v$)

2. Give an example of an object with a small mass that has a large momentum. Explain your answer. (Sample answer: A fastball pitched by a baseball pitcher has a small mass, but a large velocity. Therefore, the ball has a large momentum.)

Alternative Assessment — ADVANCED

Writing **Momentum Analysis** Have students chose a sport that they participate in or that they can watch. Then, ask students to write a one-page paper describing how conservation of momentum affects the movement of the players or the objects used in the game. [LS] Verbal

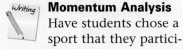

CONNECTION TO Language Arts

WRITING SKILL **Momentum and Language** The word *momentum* is often used in everyday language. For example, a sports announcer may say that the momentum of a game has changed. Or you may read that an idea is gaining momentum. In your **science journal**, write a paragraph that explains how the everyday use of the word *momentum* differs from momentum in science.

Objects Sticking Together

Sometimes, objects stick together after a collision. The football players shown in **Figure 3** are an example of such a collision. A dog leaping and catching a ball and a teen jumping on a skateboard are also examples. After two objects stick together, they move as one object. The mass of the combined objects is equal to the masses of the two objects added together. In a head-on collision, the combined objects move in the direction of the object that had the greater momentum before the collision. But together, the objects have a velocity that differs from the velocity of either object before the collision. The objects have a different velocity because momentum is conserved and depends on mass and velocity. So, when mass changes, the velocity must change, too.

Objects Bouncing Off Each Other

In some collisions, the objects bounce off each other. The bowling ball and bowling pins shown in **Figure 3** are examples of objects that bounce off each other after they collide. Billiard balls and bumper cars are other examples. During these types of collisions, momentum is usually transferred from one object to another object. The transfer of momentum causes the objects to move in different directions at different speeds. However, the total momentum of all the objects will remain the same before and after the collision.

✓ **Reading Check** What are two ways that objects may interact after a collision?

Figure 3 Examples of Conservation of Momentum

When football players tackle another player, they stick together. The velocity of each player changes after the collision because of conservation of momentum.

Although the bowling ball and bowling pins bounce off each other and move in different directions after a collision, momentum is neither gained nor lost.

Answer to Reading Check

After a collision, objects can stick together or can bounce off each other.

Conservation of Momentum and Newton's Third Law

Conservation of momentum can be explained by Newton's third law of motion. In the example of the billiard ball, the cue ball hit the billiard ball with a certain amount of force. This force was the action force. The reaction force was the equal but opposite force exerted by the billiard ball on the cue ball. The action force made the billiard ball start moving, and the reaction force made the cue ball stop moving, as shown in **Figure 4.** Because the action and reaction forces are equal and opposite, momentum is neither gained nor lost.

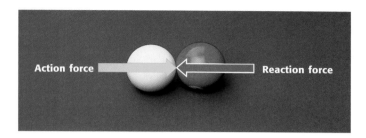

Action force   **Reaction force**

Figure 4 *The action force makes the billiard ball begin moving, and the reaction force stops the cue ball's motion.*

SECTION Review

Summary

- Momentum is a property of moving objects.
- Momentum is calculated by multiplying the mass of an object by the object's velocity.
- When two or more objects collide, momentum may be transferred, but the total amount of momentum does not change. This is the law of conservation of momentum.

Using Key Terms

1. Use the following term in a sentence: *momentum.*

Understanding Key Ideas

2. Which of the following has the smallest amount of momentum?
   a. a loaded truck driven at highway speeds
   b. a track athlete running a race
   c. a baby crawling on the floor
   d. a jet airplane being towed toward an airport

3. Explain the law of conservation of momentum.

4. How is Newton's third law of motion related to the law of conservation of momentum?

Math Skills

5. Calculate the momentum of a 2.5 kg puppy that is running with a velocity of 4.8 m/s south.

Critical Thinking

6. **Applying Concepts** A car and a train are traveling with the same velocity. Do the two objects have the same momentum? Explain your answer.

7. **Analyzing Ideas** When you catch a softball, your hand and glove move in the same direction that the ball is moving. Analyze the motion of your hand and glove in terms of momentum.

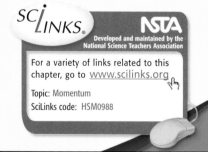

SCI LINKS.

NSTA

Developed and maintained by the
National Science Teachers Association

For a variety of links related to this chapter, go to  www.scilinks.org

Topic: Momentum
SciLinks code: HSM0988

CHAPTER RESOURCES

Chapter Resource File

- **Section Quiz** GENERAL
- **Section Review** GENERAL
- **Vocabulary and Section Summary** GENERAL

Answers to Section Review

1. Sample answer: To calculate the momentum of an object, multiply the mass of the object by its velocity.

2. c

3. The law of conservation of momentum states that any time objects collide, the total amount of momentum stays the same. The law of conservation of momentum is true when no other forces act on the objects.

4. Newton's third law can explain the law of conservation of momentum. Because the action and reaction forces are equal and opposite, momentum is neither gained nor lost.

5. $p = 2.5$ kg $\times 4.8$ m/s south $= 12$ kg•m/s south

6. No. Although the train and the car have the same velocity, the train has more mass than the car so the train has greater momentum.

7. The softball has momentum as it travels toward your glove. When the ball hits your glove, some of its momentum is transferred to your glove and your hand. As a result, your glove and hand move in the direction the ball was moving before the catch.

Inertia-Rama!

Teacher's Notes

Time Required
Two 45-minute class periods

Lab Ratings

EASY ———————→ HARD

Teacher Prep 🧪🧪
Student Set-Up 🧪
Concept Level 🧪🧪
Clean Up 🧪

MATERIALS

1. Be sure to have a few extra raw and hard-boiled eggs on hand. Having students spin their eggs in a box may reduce the chance that an egg will break.
2. Use a relatively large coin, such as a quarter or 50-cent piece. Or you may have students try the Station 2 procedure with coins of different sizes and compare the results.
3. The mass used at Station 3 should be at least 1 kg. A larger mass will give better results.

Safety Caution
Remind students to review all safety cautions and icons before beginning this lab activity.

Preparation Notes
This lab may be done in one class period if enough supplies are available to avoid changing stations.

Skills Practice Lab

OBJECTIVES

Observe several effects of inertia.

Describe the motion of objects in terms of inertia.

MATERIALS

Station 1
- egg, hard-boiled
- egg, raw

Station 2
- card, index
- coin
- cup

Station 3
- mass, hanging, 1 kg
- meterstick
- scissors
- thread, spool

SAFETY

Inertia-Rama!

Inertia is a property of all matter, from small particles of dust to enormous planets and stars. In this lab, you will investigate the inertia of various shapes and kinds of matter. Keep in mind that each investigation requires you to either overcome or use the object's inertia.

Station 1: Magic Eggs

Procedure

1. There are two eggs at this station—one is hard-boiled (solid all the way through) and the other is raw (liquid inside). The masses of the two eggs are about the same. The eggs are not marked. You should not be able to tell them apart by their appearance. Without breaking them open, how can you tell which egg is raw and which egg is hard-boiled?

2. Before you do anything to either egg, make some predictions. Will there be any difference in the way the two eggs spin? Which egg will be the easier to stop?

3. First, spin one egg. Then, place your finger on it gently to make it stop spinning. Record your observations.

4. Repeat step 3 with the second egg.

5. Compare your predictions with your observations. (Repeat steps 3 and 4 if necessary.)

6. Which egg is hard-boiled and which one is raw? Explain.

Analyze the Results

1. **Explaining Events** Explain why the eggs behave differently when you spin them even though they should have the same inertia. (Hint: Think about what happens to the liquid inside the raw egg.)

Draw Conclusions

2. **Drawing Conclusions** Explain why the eggs react differently when you try to stop them.

CHAPTER RESOURCES

Chapter Resource File
- Datasheet for Chapter Lab
- Lab Notes and Answers

Technology
- Classroom Videos
  - Lab Video

LabBook
- A Marshmallow Catapult
- Blast Off!
- Quite a Reaction

Station 2: Coin in a Cup

Procedure

1 At this station, you will find a coin, an index card, and a cup. Place the card over the cup. Then, place the coin on the card over the center of the cup, as shown below.

2 Write down a method for getting the coin into the cup without touching the coin and without lifting the card.

3 Try your method. If it doesn't work, try again until you find a method that does work.

Analyze the Results

1 **Describing Events** Use Newton's first law of motion to explain why the coin falls into the cup if you remove the card quickly.

Draw Conclusions

2 **Defending Conclusions** Explain why pulling on the card slowly will not work even though the coin has inertia. (Hint: Friction is a force.)

Station 3: The Magic Thread

Procedure

1 At this station, you will find a spool of thread and a mass hanging from a strong string. Cut a piece of thread about 40 cm long. Tie the thread around the bottom of the mass, as shown at right.

2 Pull gently on the end of the thread. Observe what happens, and record your observations.

3 Stop the mass from moving. Now hold the end of the thread so that there is a lot of slack between your fingers and the mass.

4 Give the thread a quick, hard pull. You should observe a very different event. Record your observations. Throw away the thread.

Analyze the Results

1 **Analyzing Results** Use Newton's first law of motion to explain why the result of a gentle pull is different from the result of a hard pull.

Draw Conclusions

2 **Applying Conclusions** Both moving and non-moving objects have inertia. Explain why throwing a bowling ball and catching a thrown bowling ball are hard.

3 **Drawing Conclusions** Why is it harder to run with a backpack full of books than to run with an empty backpack?

Station 2

Analyze the Results

1. The coin remains at rest, so when the card is removed quickly, there is not enough friction to move the coin. So, the coin falls into the cup when the card it removed.

Draw Conclusions

2. When you pull slowly, there is enough time for the friction between the card and the coin to move the coin. So, the coin remains on the card.

Station 3

Analyze the Results

1. The mass tends to stay at rest. A gentle pull exerts a small force over a longer time and moves the mass, but a hard pull breaks the thread before the mass moves.

Draw Conclusions

2. It is just as hard to catch the bowling ball as it is to throw the bowling ball because the bowling ball has the same inertia in both cases.

3. Accept all reasonable answers that take into account the added inertia of the objects in the backpack. Sample answer: Starting and stopping will be harder because the extra mass increases your inertia. In addition, the books in the backpack act like the liquid inside a raw egg. As you bounce up, they resist your upward movement. As you bounce down, they are still moving upward.

Station 1

Analyze the Results

1. The liquid inside the raw egg sloshes; it doesn't spin smoothly like the hard-boiled egg.

Draw Conclusions

2. When you stop the eggs, the hard-boiled egg stops as a whole, while the shell of the raw egg can be stopped and the liquid inside keeps spinning.

Assignment Guide

SECTION	QUESTIONS
1	2–3, 5, 7, 11–12, 15
2	1, 6, 8–9, 13, 16, 18
3	4, 10, 17, 19
1 and 3	14

ANSWERS

Using Key Terms
1. inertia
2. terminal velocity
3. Projectile motion
4. Momentum
5. Free fall

Understanding Key Ideas
6. b
7. d
8. d
9. b
10. b

USING KEY TERMS

Complete each of the following sentences by choosing the correct term from the word bank.

free fall projectile motion
inertia terminal velocity
momentum

1 An object in motion has ___, so it tends to stay in motion.

2 An object is falling at its ___ if it falls at a constant velocity.

3 ___ is the path that a thrown object follows.

4 ___ is a property of moving objects that depends on mass and velocity.

5 ___ occurs only when air resistance does not affect the motion of a falling object.

UNDERSTANDING KEY IDEAS

Multiple Choice

6 When a soccer ball is kicked, the action and reaction forces do not cancel each other out because
a. the forces are not equal in size.
b. the forces act on different objects.
c. the forces act at different times.
d. All of the above

7 An object is in projectile motion if it
a. is thrown with a horizontal push.
b. is accelerated downward by gravity.
c. does not accelerate horizontally.
d. All of the above

8 Newton's first law of motion applies to
a. moving objects.
b. objects that are not moving.
c. objects that are accelerating.
d. Both (a) and (b)

9 To accelerate two objects at the same rate, the force used to push the object that has more mass should be
a. smaller than the force used to push the object that has less mass.
b. larger than the force used to push the object that has less mass.
c. the same as the force used to push the object that has less mass.
d. equal to the object's weight.

10 A golf ball and a bowling ball are moving at the same velocity. Which of the two has more momentum?
a. The golf ball has more momentum because it has less mass.
b. The bowling ball has more momentum because it has more mass.
c. They have the same momentum because they have the same velocity.
d. There is not enough information to determine the answer.

Short Answer

⓫ Give an example of an object that is in free fall.

⓬ Describe how gravity and air resistance are related to an object's terminal velocity.

⓭ Why can friction make observing Newton's first law of motion difficult?

Math Skills

⓮ A 12 kg rock falls from rest off a cliff and hits the ground in 1.5 s.

a. Without considering air resistance, what is the rock's velocity just before it hits the ground?

b. What is the rock's momentum just before it hits the ground?

CRITICAL THINKING

⓯ **Concept Mapping** Use the following terms to create a concept map: *gravity, free fall, terminal velocity, projectile motion,* and *air resistance*.

⓰ **Identifying Relationships** During a space shuttle launch, about 830,000 kg of fuel is burned in 8 min. The fuel provides the shuttle with a constant thrust, or forward force. How does Newton's second law of motion explain why the shuttle's acceleration increases as the fuel is burned?

⓱ **Analyzing Processes** When using a hammer to drive a nail into wood, you have to swing the hammer through the air with a certain velocity. Because the hammer has both mass and velocity, it has momentum. Describe what happens to the hammer's momentum after the hammer hits the nail.

⓲ **Applying Concepts** Suppose you are standing on a skateboard or on in-line skates and you toss a backpack full of heavy books toward your friend. What do you think will happen to you? Explain your answer in terms of Newton's third law of motion.

INTERPRETING GRAPHICS

⓳ The picture below shows a common desk toy. If you pull one ball up and release it, it hits the balls at the bottom and comes to a stop. In the same instant, the ball on the other side swings up and repeats the cycle. How does conservation of momentum explain how this toy works?

CHAPTER RESOURCES

Chapter Resource File

- **Chapter Review** GENERAL
- **Chapter Test A** GENERAL
- **Chapter Test B** ADVANCED
- **Chapter Test C** SPECIAL NEEDS
- **Vocabulary Activity** GENERAL

Workbooks

 Study Guide
- Assessment resources are also available in Spanish.

EOG Prep

Teacher's Note

To provide practice under more realistic testing conditions, give students 20 minutes to answer all of the questions in this Standardized Test Preparation.

MISCONCEPTION ALERT

Answers to the standardized test preparation can help you identify student misconceptions and misunderstandings.

READING

Passage 1

1. A
2. H
3. D

TEST DOCTOR

Question 3: Some students may pick answer choice A because the passage states that astronauts train underwater. However, the passage also states that astronauts train in a modified KC-135 airplane. Students should recognize that the training on this airplane is not done underwater, so the statement that astronauts always have to train underwater is incorrect.

READING

Read each of the passages below. Then, answer the questions that follow each passage.

Passage 1 How do astronauts prepare for trips in the space shuttle? One method is to use simulations on Earth that mimic the conditions in space. For example, underwater training lets astronauts experience reduced gravity. They can also ride on NASA's modified KC-135 airplane. NASA's KC-135 simulates how it feels to be in a space shuttle. How does this airplane work? It flies upward at a steep angle and then flies downward at a 45° angle. When the airplane flies downward, the effect of reduced gravity is produced. As the plane falls, the astronauts inside the plane can float like astronauts in the space shuttle do!

1. What is the purpose of this passage?
   - **A** to explain how astronauts prepare for missions in space
   - **B** to convince people to become astronauts
   - **C** to show that space is similar to Earth
   - **D** to describe what it feels like to float in space

2. What can you conclude about NASA's KC-135 from the passage?
   - **F** NASA's KC-135 is just like other airplanes.
   - **G** All astronauts train in NASA's KC-135.
   - **H** NASA's KC-135 simulates the space shuttle by reducing the effects of gravity.
   - **I** Being in NASA's KC-135 is not very much like being in the space shuttle.

3. Based on the passage, which of the following statements is a fact?
   - **A** Astronauts always have to train underwater.
   - **B** Flying in airplanes is similar to riding in the space shuttle.
   - **C** People in NASA's KC-135 float at all times.
   - **D** Astronauts use simulations to learn what reduced gravity is like.

Passage 2 There once was a game that could be played by as few as 5 or as many as 1,000 players. The game could be played on a small field for a few hours or on a huge tract of land for several days. The game was not just for fun—in fact, it was often used as a <u>substitute</u> for war. One of the few rules was that the players couldn't touch the ball with their hands—they had to use a special stick with webbing on one end. Would you believe that this game is the same as the game of lacrosse that is played today?

Lacrosse is a game that was originally played by Native Americans. They called the game *baggataway*, which means "little brother of war." Although lacrosse has changed and is now played all over the world, it still requires special, webbed sticks.

1. What is the purpose of this passage?
   - **A** to explain the importance of rules in lacrosse
   - **B** to explain why sticks are used in lacrosse
   - **C** to describe the history of lacrosse
   - **D** to describe the rules of lacrosse

2. Based on the passage, what does the word *substitute* mean?
   - **F** something that occurs before war
   - **G** something that is needed to play lacrosse
   - **H** something that is of Native American origin
   - **I** something that takes the place of something else

Passage 2

1. C
2. I

TEST DOCTOR

Question 1: Although some of the rules of lacrosse are mentioned in the passage, the main purpose of the article is not to explain the importance of lacrosse rules or to describe lacrosse rules. Instead, the passage focuses on how and why the game that is now known as lacrosse was originally played. Therefore, the purpose of the passage is to describe the history of lacrosse.

Read each question below, and choose the best answer.

1. Which of the following images shows an object with no momentum that is about to be set in motion by an unbalanced force?

A

B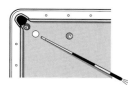

C

D

2. During a laboratory experiment, liquid was collected in a graduated cylinder. What is the volume of the liquid?

F 30 mL
G 35 mL
H 40 mL
I 45 mL

Read each question below, and choose the best answer.

1. The table below shows the accelerations produced by different forces for a 5 kg mass. Assuming that the pattern continues, use this data to predict what acceleration would be produced by a 100 N force.

Force	Acceleration
25 N	5 m/s^2
50 N	10 m/s^2
75 N	15 m/s^2

A 10 m/s^2
B 20 m/s^2
C 30 m/s^2
D 100 m/s^2

2. The average radius of the moon is 1.74×10^6 m. What is another way to express the radius of the moon?

F 0.00000174 m
G 0.000174 m
H 174,000 m
I 1,740,000 m

3. The half price bookstore is selling 4 paperback books for a total of $5.75. What would the price of 20 paperback books be?

A $23.00
B $24.75
C $28.75
D $51.75

4. A 75 kg speed skater is moving with a velocity of 16 m/s east. What is the speed skater's momentum? (Momentum is calculated with the equation: *momentum = mass × velocity*.)

F 91 kg•m/s
G 91 kg•m/s east
H 1,200 kg•m/s east
I 1,200 kg•m/s^2 east

Standardized Test Preparation

1. B
2. G

➕ **TEST DOCTOR**

Question 1: To answer this question, students must remember that momentum is equal to the product of mass and velocity. Because all objects have mass, the only way an object can have no momentum is if its velocity is 0 m/s. Only answer choices B and D have objects with no momentum. However, answer choice D does not show any impending unbalanced force. Answer choice B shows that the cue stick is moving and is about to exert an unbalanced force on the cue ball (that has no momentum). Therefore, B is the correct answer.

1. B
2. I
3. C
4. H

➕ **TEST DOCTOR**

Question 4: The product of 75 and 16 is 1,200. Some students may have difficulty selecting between answer choices H and I because both choices appear to have the correct answer. However, answer choice I has units of kilograms-meters per second squared (kg•m/s^2) and the correct units for momentum are kilograms-meters per second (kg•m/s). Answer choice H is correct.

CHAPTER RESOURCES

Chapter Resource File

📄 • Standardized Test Preparation GENERAL

Workbooks

📘 **North Carolina Standardized Test Preparation**
• Provides practice for the EOG test.

State Resources

 For specific resources for your state, visit **go.hrw.com** and type in the keyword **HSMSTR**.

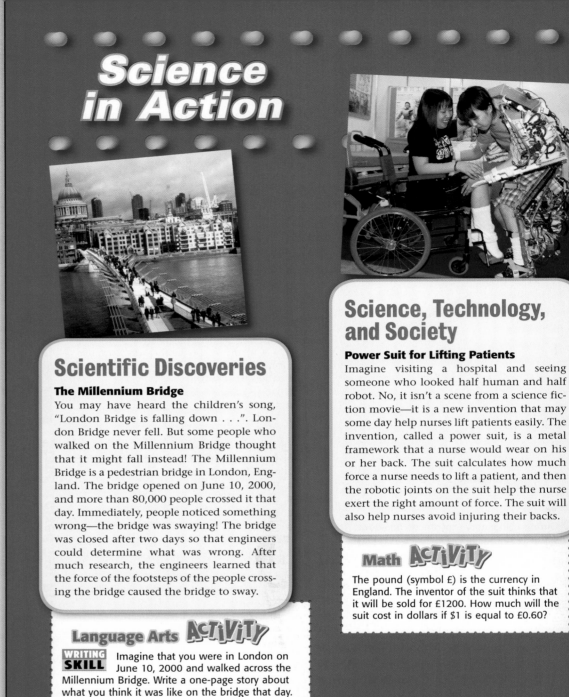

Science in Action

Scientific Discoveries

Background
The Millennium Bridge swayed because the people walking on the bridge subconsciously started to walk in-step. The steps of the people matched the resonant frequency of the bridge, which caused the bridge to sway even more. This phenomenon has been observed on a few other bridges. In fact, marching soldiers are often instructed to "break step" when crossing bridges to avoid the possibility of marching at the bridge's resonant frequency.

The engineers who built the Millennium Bridge installed dampers and shock absorbers to stop the swaying of the bridge. The bridge reopened on February 22, 2003.

Science, Technology, and Society

Discussion———GENERAL

Lead a discussion about the benefits of the power suit. (Sample answers: The power suit will make nurses' jobs easier. The power suit will prevent back injuries.) Ask students to describe other situations or jobs that may benefit from the use of the power suit. (Sample answer: Construction workers and people who move furniture could benefit from the power suit.)

Scientific Discoveries

The Millennium Bridge
You may have heard the children's song, "London Bridge is falling down . . .". London Bridge never fell. But some people who walked on the Millennium Bridge thought that it might fall instead! The Millennium Bridge is a pedestrian bridge in London, England. The bridge opened on June 10, 2000, and more than 80,000 people crossed it that day. Immediately, people noticed something wrong—the bridge was swaying! The bridge was closed after two days so that engineers could determine what was wrong. After much research, the engineers learned that the force of the footsteps of the people crossing the bridge caused the bridge to sway.

Language Arts ACTIVITY

WRITING SKILL Imagine that you were in London on June 10, 2000 and walked across the Millennium Bridge. Write a one-page story about what you think it was like on the bridge that day.

Science, Technology, and Society

Power Suit for Lifting Patients
Imagine visiting a hospital and seeing someone who looked half human and half robot. No, it isn't a scene from a science fiction movie—it is a new invention that may some day help nurses lift patients easily. The invention, called a power suit, is a metal framework that a nurse would wear on his or her back. The suit calculates how much force a nurse needs to lift a patient, and then the robotic joints on the suit help the nurse exert the right amount of force. The suit will also help nurses avoid injuring their backs.

Math ACTIVITY

The pound (symbol £) is the currency in England. The inventor of the suit thinks that it will be sold for £1200. How much will the suit cost in dollars if $1 is equal to £0.60?

Answer to Language Arts Activity
Accept all reasonable answers. Students may describe the motion of the bridge or how they felt when the bridge started to sway. Students may also describe the reaction of the other people on the bridge.

Answer to Math Activity
£1200 × $1 ÷ £0.60 = $2,000
The answer to this Math Activity may vary as the rate of exchange between the dollar and the pound changes. As an extension, you may ask your students to research the current exchange rate and find the current price of the power suit.

Steve Okamoto

Roller Coaster Designer Roller coasters have fascinated Steve Okamoto ever since his first ride on one. "I remember going to Disneyland as a kid. My mother was always upset with me because I kept looking over the sides of the rides, trying to figure out how they worked," he says. To satisfy his curiosity, Okamoto became a mechanical engineer. Today he uses his scientific knowledge to design and build machines, systems, and buildings. But his specialty is roller coasters.

Roller coasters really do coast along the track. A motor pulls the cars up a high hill to start the ride. After that, the cars are powered by only gravity. Designing a successful roller coaster is not a simple task. Okamoto has to calculate the cars' speed and acceleration on each part of the track. He must also consider the safety of the ride and the strength of the structure that supports the track.

Social Studies ACTiViTy

Research the history of roller coasters to learn how roller coaster design has changed over time. Make a poster to summarize your research.

To learn more about these Science in Action topics, visit **go.hrw.com** and type in the keyword **HP5FORF.**

Current Science

Check out Current Science® articles related to this chapter by visiting **go.hrw.com. Just type in the keyword HP5CS06.**

Background

Steve Okamoto has a degree in product design. He studied both mechanical engineering and studio art. Product designers consider an object's form as well as its function and take into account the interests and abilities of the product's consumer.

Two of Okamoto's first coasters were the Ninjas at Six Flags Over Mid-America, in St. Louis, Missouri, and Six Flags Magic Mountain, in Los Angeles, California.

When designing a ride, Okamoto studies site maps of the location, then goes to the amusement park to look at the actual site. Because most rides he designs are for older parks, fitting a coaster around, above, and between existing rides and buildings is one of his biggest challenges. Most rides and parks also have some kind of theme, so marketing goals and concerns figure into his designs as well. (As an example, Okamoto designed a roller coaster named the *Mamba*. The coaster is named for one of the fastest snakes in Africa and is designed around this theme.)

Answer to Social Studies Activity
Accept all reasonable answers. Student posters may show different types of roller coasters including old-fashioned wooden roller coasters and modern steel-tube roller coasters. You may wish to challenge students to learn when the first roller coaster was built or to learn when the first roller coaster with a loop was built.

19

Forces in Fluids
Chapter Planning Guide

Compression guide:
To shorten instruction
because of time limitations,
omit Section 3.

OBJECTIVES	LABS, DEMONSTRATIONS, AND ACTIVITIES	TECHNOLOGY RESOURCES
PACING • 90 min pp. 522–529 **Chapter Opener**	**SE** Start-up Activity, p. 523 `GENERAL`	**OSP** Parent Letter `GENERAL` **CD** Student Edition on CD-ROM **CD** Guided Reading Audio CD **TR** Chapter Starter Transparency* **VID** Brain Food Video Quiz
Section 1 Fluids and Pressure • Describe how fluids exert pressure. • Analyze how atmospheric pressure varies with depth. • Explain how depth and density affect water pressure. • Give examples of fluids flowing from high to low pressure.	**TE** Demonstration Building Pressure, p. 525 `GENERAL` **TE** Connection Activity Language Arts, p. 525 `ADVANCED` **TE** Connection Activity Earth Science, p. 526 `GENERAL` **SE** Quick Lab Blown Away, p. 528 `GENERAL` **CRF** Datasheet for Quick Lab* **LB** Whiz-Bang Demonstrations The Rise and Fall of Raisins,* Going Against the Flow* `GENERAL`	**CRF** Lesson Plans* **TR** Bellringer Transparency* **TR** *LINK TO LIFE SCIENCE* Math Focus: Surface Area-to-Volume Ratio* **TR** Exhaling Pressure; Fluid Flow*
PACING • 90 min pp. 530–535 **Section 2 Buoyant Force** • Explain the relationship between fluid pressure and buoyant force. • Predict whether an object will float or sink in a fluid. • Analyze the role of density in an object's ability to float. • Explain how the overall density of an object can be changed.	**TE** Demonstration Density Layers, p. 530 `GENERAL` **SE** School-to-Home Activity Floating Fun, p. 531 `GENERAL` **TE** Connection Activity Math, p. 531 `ADVANCED` **TE** Activity Making Models, p. 532 `GENERAL` **TE** Connection Activity Math, p. 532 `ADVANCED` **SE** Connection to Geology Floating Rocks, p. 533 `GENERAL` **TE** Group Activity Buoyancy and Scuba Diving, p. 533 `GENERAL` **TE** Demonstration Sinking and Floating, p. 533 `GENERAL` **SE** Quick Lab Ship Shape, p. 534 `GENERAL` **CRF** Datasheet for Quick Lab* **SE** Skills Practice Lab Fluids, Force, and Floating, p. 542 `GENERAL` **CRF** Datasheet for Chapter Lab* **SE** Skills Practice Lab Density Diver, p. 617 `GENERAL` **CRF** Datasheet for LabBook*	**CRF** Lesson Plans* **TR** Bellringer Transparency* **TR** Shape and Overall Density* **TR** Controlling Density by Using Ballast Tanks* **SE** Internet Activity, p. 533 `GENERAL` **CRF** SciLinks Activity* `GENERAL` **VID** Lab Videos for Physical Science **CD** Interactive Explorations CD-ROM Sea the Light `GENERAL`
PACING • 45 min pp. 536–541 **Section 3 Fluids and Motion** • Describe the relationship between pressure and fluid speed. • Analyze the roles of lift, thrust, and wing size in flight. • Explain Pascal's principle. • Describe drag, and explain how it affects lift.	**TE** Demonstration Magic Water, p. 536 `GENERAL` **TE** Activity Pressure Analogy, p. 537 `BASIC` **TE** Activity Wing Shape, p. 537 `ADVANCED` **TE** Demonstration Flying Ball, p. 537 `GENERAL` **SE** Connection to Social Studies The First Flight, p. 538 `GENERAL` **TE** Activity Wind Tunnels, p. 538 `ADVANCED` **TE** Connection Activity Language Arts, p. 539 `GENERAL` **TE** Group Activity Floating Bubbles, p. 539 ◆ `GENERAL` **SE** Science in Action Math, Social Studies, and Language Arts Activities, pp. 548–549 `GENERAL` **LB** EcoLabs & Field Activities What's the Flap All About?* `BASIC` **LB** Long-Term Projects & Research Ideas Scuba Dive* `ADVANCED`	**CRF** Lesson Plans* **TR** Bellringer Transparency* **TR** Wing Design and Lift* **TR** Bernoulli's Principle and the Curveball*

PACING • 90 min

CHAPTER REVIEW, ASSESSMENT, AND STANDARDIZED TEST PREPARATION

CRF Vocabulary Activity* `GENERAL`
SE Chapter Review, pp. 544–545 `GENERAL`
CRF Chapter Review* ■ `GENERAL`
CRF Chapter Tests A* ■ `GENERAL`, B* `ADVANCED`, C* `SPECIAL NEEDS`
SE Standardized Test Preparation, pp. 546–547 `GENERAL`
CRF Standardized Test Preparation* `GENERAL`
CRF Performance-Based Assessment* `GENERAL`
OSP Test Generator `GENERAL`
CRF Test Item Listing* `GENERAL`

Online and Technology Resources

Visit **go.hrw.com** for a variety of free resources related to this textbook. Enter the keyword **HT5R7FLU.**

Students can access interactive problem-solving help and active visual concept development with the *Holt Science and Technology* Online Edition available at **www.hrw.com.**

 Guided Reading Audio CD

These CDs are designed to help auditory learners and reluctant readers.

 Science Tutor CD-ROM

Excellent for remediation and test practice.

KEY

SE Student Edition	**CRF** Chapter Resource File	**SS** Science Skills Worksheets
TE Teacher Edition	**OSP** One-Stop Planner	**MS** Math Skills for Science Worksheets
	LB Lab Bank	**CD** CD or CD-ROM
	TR Transparencies	**VID** Classroom Video/DVD

* Also on One-Stop Planner
◆ Requires advance prep
■ Also available in Spanish

SKILLS DEVELOPMENT RESOURCES	SECTION REVIEW AND ASSESSMENT	STANDARDS CORRELATIONS
SE Pre-Reading Activity, p. 522 `GENERAL` **OSP** Science Puzzlers, Twisters & Teasers `GENERAL`		North Carolina Standard Course of Study
CRF Directed Reading A* `BASIC`, B* `SPECIAL NEEDS` **CRF** Vocabulary and Section Summary* `GENERAL` **SE** Reading Strategy Brainstorming, p. 524 `GENERAL` **SE** Math Focus Pressure, Force, and Area, p. 525 `GENERAL` **TE** Inclusion Strategies, p. 527 **MS** Math Skills for Science The Pressure Is On!* `GENERAL` **MS** Math Skills for Science Density* `GENERAL`	**SE** Reading Checks, pp. 525, 526, 528 `GENERAL` **TE** Homework, p. 525 `ADVANCED` **TE** Homework, p. 526 `GENERAL` **TE** Reteaching, p. 528 `BASIC` **TE** Quiz, p. 528 `GENERAL` **TE** Alternative Assessment, p. 528 `ADVANCED` **SE** Section Review,* p. 529 ■ `GENERAL` **CRF** Section Quiz* ■ `GENERAL`	
CRF Directed Reading A* `BASIC`, B* `SPECIAL NEEDS` **CRF** Vocabulary and Section Summary* `GENERAL` **SE** Reading Strategy Discussion, p. 530 `GENERAL` **TE** Reading Strategy Prediction Guide, p. 531 `GENERAL` **SE** Math Focus Finding Density, p. 532 `GENERAL`	**SE** Reading Checks, pp. 531, 532, 534 `GENERAL` **TE** Homework, p. 531 `GENERAL` **TE** Reteaching, p. 534 `BASIC` **TE** Quiz, p. 534 `GENERAL` **TE** Alternative Assessment, p. 535 `GENERAL` **SE** Section Review,* p. 535 ■ `GENERAL` **CRF** Section Quiz* ■ `GENERAL`	6.03; *Chapter Lab:* 1.05, 1.06; *LabBook:* 1.01
CRF Directed Reading A* `BASIC`, B* `SPECIAL NEEDS` **CRF** Vocabulary and Section Summary* `GENERAL` **SE** Reading Strategy Reading Organizer, p. 536 `GENERAL` **TE** Inclusion Strategies, p. 538 **CRF** Critical Thinking Build a Better Submarine* `ADVANCED` **CRF** Reinforcement Worksheet Building Up Pressure* `BASIC`	**SE** Reading Checks, pp. 537, 539, 540 `GENERAL` **TE** Homework, p. 539 `GENERAL` **TE** Reteaching, p. 540 `BASIC` **TE** Quiz, p. 540 `GENERAL` **TE** Alternative Assessment, p. 540 `GENERAL` **SE** Section Review,* p. 541 ■ `GENERAL` **CRF** Section Quiz* ■ `GENERAL`	

One-Stop Planner® CD-ROM

This convenient CD-ROM includes:
• Lab Materials QuickList Software
• Holt Calendar Planner
• Customizable Lesson Plans
• Printable Worksheets
• ExamView® Test Generator

cnnstudentnews.com

Find the latest news, lesson plans, and activities related to important scientific events.

www.scilinks.org

Maintained by the **National Science Teachers Association.** See Chapter Enrichment pages for a complete list of topics.

Check out *Current Science* articles and activities by visiting the HRW Web site at **go.hrw.com.** Just type in the keyword **HP5CS07T.**

Classroom Videos

• **Lab Videos** demonstrate the chapter lab.
• **Brain Food Video Quizzes** help students review the chapter material.
• **CNN Videos** bring science into your students' daily life.

Visual Resources

CHAPTER STARTER TRANSPARENCY

BELLRINGER TRANSPARENCIES

Section: Fluids and Pressure
Imagine the following situation:
One afternoon, you go outside to find your younger sister standing by her bike with a nail in her hand. The bike has a flat tire. She wants to know why the air came out of the tire when she pulled the nail out.

Write a few sentences in your **science journal** to explain why air rushes out of a hole in a tire.

Section: Buoyant Force
Identify which of the following objects will float in water: a rock, an orange, a screw, a quarter, a candle, a plastic-foam "peanut," and a chalkboard eraser.

Write a hypothesis in your **science journal** about why an aircraft carrier, which weighs thousands of tons, does not sink.

TEACHING TRANSPARENCIES

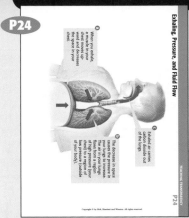

P24 Exhaling, Pressure, and Fluid Flow

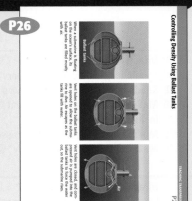

P26 Controlling Density Using Ballast Tanks

TEACHING TRANSPARENCIES

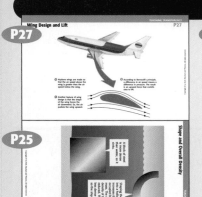

P27 Wing Design and Lift

P25 Shape and Overall Density

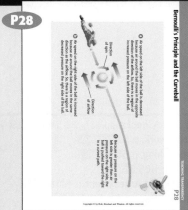

P28 Bernoulli's Principle and the Curveball

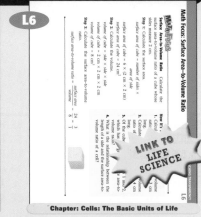

L6 Math Focus: Surface Area-to-Volume Ratio

LINK TO LIFE SCIENCE

Chapter: Cells: The Basic Units of Life

CONCEPT MAPPING TRANSPARENCY

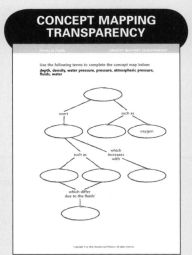

Use the following terms to complete the concept map below:
depth, density, water pressure, pressure, atmospheric pressure, fluids, water

Planning Resources

LESSON PLANS

Lesson Plan   SAMPLE

Section: Waves

Pacing
Regular Schedule: with lab(s):2 days   without lab(s):3 days
Block Schedule: with lab(s): 1 1/2 days   without lab(s):1 day

Objectives
1. Relate the seven properties of life to a living organism.
2. Describe seven themes that can help you to organize what you learn about biology.
3. Identify the tiny structures that make up all living organisms.
4. Differentiate between reproduction and heredity and between metabolism and homeostasis.

National Science Education Standards Covered
LSInter6:Cells have particular structures that underlie their functions.
LSMat1:Most cell functions involve chemical reactions.
LSBeh1:Cells store and use information to guide their functions.
UCP1:Cell functions are regulated.
ST1: Cells can differentiate and form complete multicellular organisms.
ESS1: Species evolve over time.
ESS1: The great diversity of organisms is the result of more than 3.5 billion years of evolution.
ESS2: Natural selection and its evolutionary consequences provide a scientific explanation for the fossil record of ancient life forms as well as for the striking molecular similarities observed among the diverse species of living organisms.
ST1: The millions of different species of plants, animals, and microorganisms that live on Earth today are related by descent from common ancestors.
ST2: The energy for life primarily comes from the sun.
SPSP1: The complexity and organization of organisms accommodates the need for obtaining, transforming, transporting, releasing, and eliminating the matter and energy used to sustain the organism.
SPSP6: As matter and energy flows through different levels of organization of living systems—cells, organs, communities—and between living systems and the physical environment, chemical elements are recombined in different ways.
HNS1: Organisms have behavioral responses to internal changes and to external stimuli.

PARENT LETTER

Dear Parent,   SAMPLE

Your son's or daughter's science class will soon begin exploring the chapter entitled "The World of Physical Science." In this chapter, students will learn about how the scientific method applies to the world of physical science and the role of physical science in the world. By the end of the chapter, students should demonstrate a clear understanding of the chapter's main ideas and be able to discuss the following topics:

1. physical science is the study of energy and matter (Section 1)
2. the role of physical science in the world around them (Section 1)
3. careers that rely on physical science (Section 1)
4. the steps used in the scientific method (Section 2)
5. examples of technology (Section 2)
6. how the scientific method is used to answer questions and solve problems (Section 2)
7. how our knowledge of science changes over time (Section 2)
8. how models represent real objects or systems (Section 3)
9. examples of different ways models are used in science (Section 3)
10. the importance of the International System of Units (Section 4)
11. the appropriate units to use for particular measurements (Section 4)
12. how area and density are derived quantities (Section 4)

Questions to Ask Along the Way

You can help your son or daughter learn about these topics by asking interesting questions such as the following:

- What are some surprising careers that use physical science?
- What is a characteristic of a good hypothesis?
- When is it a good idea to use a model?
- Why do Americans measure things in terms of inches and yards instead of centimeters and meters?

TEST ITEM LISTING

TEST ITEM LISTING
The World of Science   SAMPLE

MULTIPLE CHOICE

1. A limitation of models is that
   a. they are large enough to see.
   b. they do not act exactly like the things that they model.
   c. they are smaller than the things that they model.
   d. they model unfamiliar things.
   Answer: B   Difficulty: I   Section: 3   Objective: 2

2. The length 10 m is equal to
   a. 100 cm.   c. 10,000 mm.
   b. 1,000 cm.   d. Both (b) and (c)
   Answer: B   Difficulty: I   Section: 3   Objective: 2

3. To be valid, a hypothesis must be
   a. testable.   c. made into a law.
   b. supported by evidence.   d. Both (a) and (b)
   Answer: D   Difficulty: I   Section: 2   Objective: 3

4. The statement "Sheila has a stain on her shirt" is an example of a(n)
   a. law.   c. observation.
   b. hypothesis.   d. prediction.
   Answer: C   Difficulty: I   Section: 2   Objective: 2

5. A hypothesis is often developed out of
   a. observations.   c. laws.
   b. experiments.   d. Both (a) and (b)
   Answer: B   Difficulty: I   Section: 2   Objective: 3

6. How many milliliters are in 3.5 kL?
   a. 3,500 mL.   c. 3,500,000 mL.
   b. 0.0035 mL.   d. 35,000 mL.
   Answer: B   Difficulty: I   Section: 3   Objective: 2

7. A map of Seattle is an example of a
   a. law.   c. model.
   b. theory.   d. unit.
   Answer: C   Difficulty: I   Section: 3   Objective: 2

8. A lab has the safety rules shown below. These icons mean that you should wear
   a. only safety goggles.   c. safety goggles and a lab apron.
   b. only a lab apron.   d. safety goggles, a lab apron, and gloves
   Answer: D   Difficulty: I   Section: 3   Objective: 2

9. The law of conservation of mass says that the sci al mass before a chemical change is
   a. more than the total mass after the change.
   b. less than the total mass after the change.
   c. the same as the total mass before the change.
   d. not the same as the total mass after the change.
   Answer: C   Difficulty: I   Section: 3   Objective: 3

10. In which of the following areas might you find a geochemist at work?
    a. studying the chemistry of rocks   c. studying insects
    b. studying forestry   d. studying the atmosphere

One-Stop Planner® CD-ROM

This CD-ROM includes all of the resources shown here and the following time-saving tools:

- *Lab Materials QuickList Software*
- *Customizable lesson plans*
- *Holt Calendar Planner*
- *The powerful ExamView® Test Generator*

Meeting Individual Needs

DIRECTED READING A
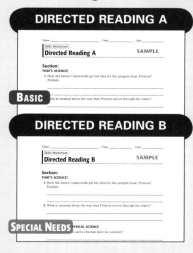
BASIC

DIRECTED READING B
SPECIAL NEEDS

VOCABULARY ACTIVITY
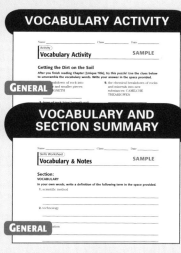
GENERAL

VOCABULARY AND SECTION SUMMARY
GENERAL

REINFORCEMENT
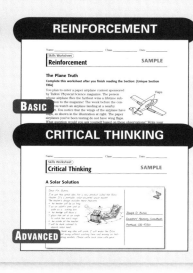
BASIC

CRITICAL THINKING
ADVANCED

SCILINKS ACTIVITY

GENERAL

SCIENCE PUZZLERS, TWISTERS & TEASERS
GENERAL

Labs and Activities

ECOLABS & FIELD ACTIVITIES

BASIC

LONG-TERM PROJECTS & RESEARCH IDEAS

ADVANCED

WHIZ-BANG DEMONSTRATIONS

WHIZ-BANG DEMONSTRATIONS
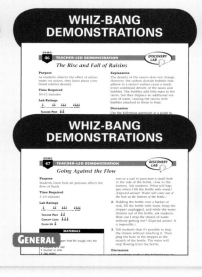
GENERAL

DATASHEETS FOR QUICK LABS

DATASHEETS FOR CHAPTER LABS

DATASHEETS FOR LABBOOK

Review and Assessments

SECTION QUIZ
GENERAL

SECTION REVIEW

GENERAL

CHAPTER REVIEW
GENERAL

CHAPTER TEST A
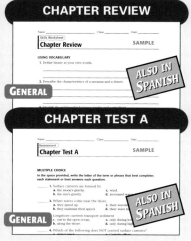
GENERAL

CHAPTER TEST B
ADVANCED

CHAPTER TEST C
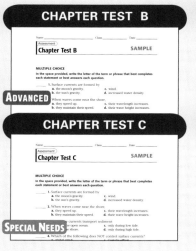
SPECIAL NEEDS

STANDARDIZED TEST PREPARATION
GENERAL

PERFORMANCE-BASED ASSESSMENT
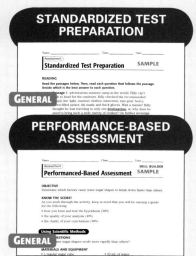
GENERAL

This Chapter Enrichment provides relevant and interesting information to expand and enhance your presentation of the chapter material.

Section 1

Fluids and Pressure

Refresher on Gas Laws

- Nearly all materials expand when they are heated and contract when they are cooled. Gases are not an exception. A gas expands as it gets hotter because the kinetic energy of its particles increases. When the kinetic energy increases, the particles move faster and bounce against each other harder. This movement causes the gas particles to move farther apart, and the gas expands. If the pressure does not change, the volume of the gas will increase as the temperature increases. This property of gases is known as *Charles's law.*

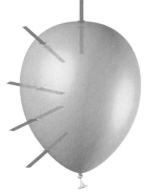

- The air pressure inside the tires of an automobile can be much greater than the pressure outside the tires. The pressure can be greater inside an enclosed container because air, like all gases, is compressible. If the temperature does not change, the pressure of a gas will increase as the volume decreases. This property of gases is known as *Boyle's law.*

Is That a Fact!

◆ The water pressure at the bottom of a small, deep pond is greater than the pressure at the bottom of a large, shallow lake because water pressure is determined by the depth of the water, not the volume of the water.

Section 2

Buoyant Force

Archimedes (287–212 BCE)

- Archimedes, a Greek mathematician, inventor, and physicist, lived in the ancient city of Syracuse from 287 to 212 BCE. He is famous for his work in geometry, physics, mechanics, and water pressure.

Diving and Water Pressure

- Scuba diving relies in part on the principles of buoyancy and fluid pressure. Some of the effects of water pressure can be felt even in a swimming pool. Just a few meters under water, your ears begin to hurt from the pressure of the water on your eardrums.

- As a diver descends deeper into the water with scuba gear, the diver's lungs hold more air because the air is compressed by the water pressure. As a diver rises to the surface, the air expands again. Under certain circumstances, the air in a diver's lungs could expand enough to rupture the air sacs in the diver's lungs.

Is That a Fact!

◆ Humans have built underwater vessels for hundreds of years. In 1620, the Dutch inventor Cornelis Drebbel built what is thought to be the first submarine. His vessel was not much more than a rowboat covered with greased leather. It traveled at a depth of 4 to 5 m under water in the Thames River, in London, England. King James I of England is said to have taken a short ride in this vessel.

Neutral Buoyancy

- Scuba divers use weights to compensate for the buoyancy of their body and diving gear. When a diver weighs exactly the same as an equal volume of the surrounding water, the diver can swim to any depth and remain there effortlessly. This state is called *neutral buoyancy.*

Section 3

Fluids and Motion

Daniel Bernoulli (1700–1782)

- Daniel Bernoulli was born in the Netherlands in 1700. For most of his life, he lived in Basel, Switzerland.

- Bernoulli was born into a family distinguished for accomplishments in science and mathematics. His father, Johann, was famous for his work in calculus, trigonometry, and the study of geodesics. Bernoulli's uncle Jacob was integral in the development of calculus. Bernoulli's brothers, Nicolaus and Johann II, were also noted mathematicians and physicists.

- Bernoulli's greatest work was *Hydrodynamica,* which was published in 1738. It included the concept now known as Bernoulli's principle. He also made important contributions to probability theory and studied astronomy, botany, physiology, gravity, and magnetism.

Examples of Bernoulli's Principle

- Even on a calm night, air moves across the top of a chimney. This air movement causes the pressure at the top of the chimney to be lower than the pressure in the house. According to Bernoulli's principle, the smoke in the fireplace is pushed up the chimney by the greater air pressure in the house.

- Bernoulli's principle also explains why a soft convertible top on a car bulges when the car travels at high speeds. The air moving over the top causes an area of low pressure, and the higher pressure inside the car pushes the soft top up.

Is That a Fact!

- ◆ Water flowing in a stream speeds up when it flows through a narrow part of the stream bed. According to Bernoulli's principle, the water pressure decreases as the speed increases.

Blaise Pascal

- Blaise Pascal (1623–1662) was a famous French scientist, mathematician, philosopher, and writer of prose. He had no formal schooling but pursued his interests under his father's guidance. Pascal's father forbade him to study mathematics until he was 15 years old, but Pascal's curiosity led him to begin studying geometry in secret at the age of 12. By the time he was 14, Pascal was regularly attending sessions with the leading geometricians of his time. Pascal presented his first mathematics paper at the age of 16. The SI unit for pressure, the pascal, is named after Blaise Pascal.

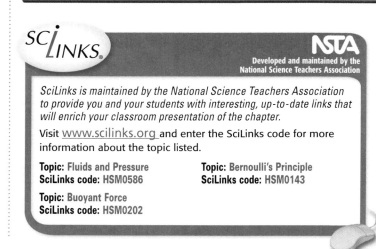

SciLinks is maintained by the National Science Teachers Association to provide you and your students with interesting, up-to-date links that will enrich your classroom presentation of the chapter.

Visit www.scilinks.org and enter the SciLinks code for more information about the topic listed.

Topic: Fluids and Pressure
SciLinks code: HSM0586

Topic: Bernoulli's Principle
SciLinks code: HSM0143

Topic: Buoyant Force
SciLinks code: HSM0202

19

Overview

Tell students that this chapter will help them learn about fluids and the forces caused by fluids, including buoyant force, lift, and drag. Students also learn about pressure and the factors that affect flight.

Assessing Prior Knowledge

Students should be familiar with the following topics:

• forces and net force
• motion and speed
• SI units

Identifying Misconceptions

As students learn the material in this chapter, some of them may have difficulties understanding that gases, such as oxygen and air, are fluids. This confusion may result from the common usage of the word *fluid*. In everyday language, fluids usually refer to liquids only.

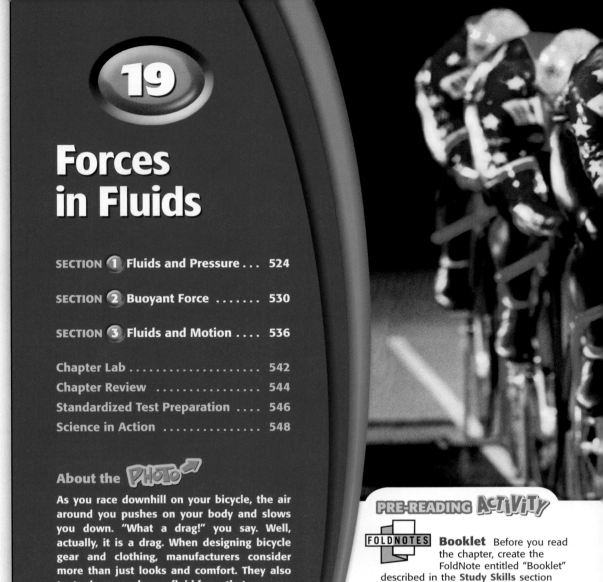

19

Forces in Fluids

About the PHOTO

As you race downhill on your bicycle, the air around you pushes on your body and slows you down. "What a drag!" you say. Well, actually, it is a drag. When designing bicycle gear and clothing, manufacturers consider more than just looks and comfort. They also try to decrease drag, a fluid force that opposes motion. This photo shows cyclists riding their bikes in a wind tunnel in a study of how a fluid—air—affects their ride.

PRE-READING ACTIVITY

FOLDNOTES **Booklet** Before you read the chapter, create the FoldNote entitled "Booklet" described in the **Study Skills** section of the Appendix. Label each page of the booklet with a main idea from the chapter. As you read the chapter, write what you learn about each main idea on the appropriate page of the booklet.

Standards Correlations

North Carolina Standard Course of Study

1.01 Identify and create questions and hypotheses that can be answered through scientific investigations. (LabBook)

1.05 (partial) Analyze evidence to: Explain observations [and] Make inferences and predictions . . . (Chapter Lab)

1.06 (partial) Use mathematics to gather, organize, and present quantitative data resulting from scientific investigations: Measurement [and] Analysis of data . . . (Chapter Lab)

6.03 (partial) Evaluate motion in terms of Newton's Laws: . . . An object's motion is the result of the combined effect of all forces acting on the object . . . (Section 2)

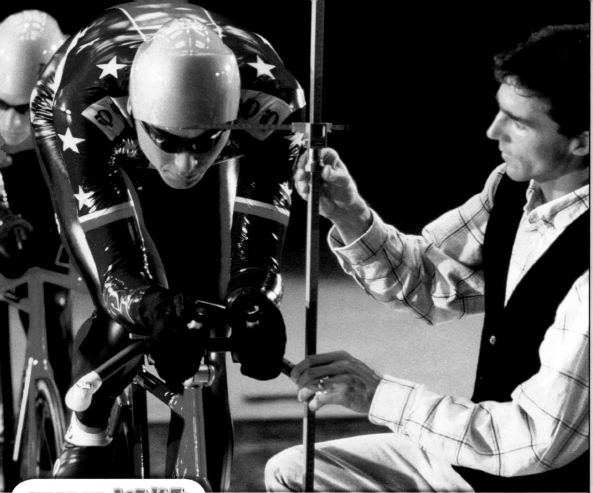

Teacher's Notes: Tell students that this activity is an exception to the usual rules about flying paper planes in class.

Answers

1. Sample answer: The plane did not stay in the air as long. To get a longer flight, I had to throw much harder.

2. Sample answer: I gave the plane its forward motion when I threw the plane.

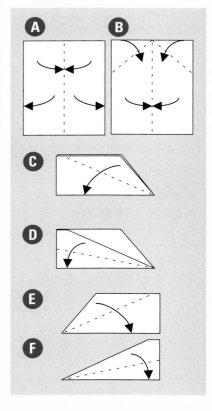

START-UP ACTiViTY

Taking Flight

In this activity, you will build a model airplane to learn how wing size affects flight.

Procedure

1. Fold a **sheet of paper** in half lengthwise. Then, open it. Fold the top corners toward the center crease. Keep the corners folded down, and fold the entire sheet in half along the center crease.

2. With the plane on its side, fold the top front edge down so that it meets the bottom edge. Fold the top edge down again so that it meets the bottom edge. Turn the plane over, and repeat.

3. Raise the wings so that they are perpendicular to the body.

4. Point the plane slightly upward, and gently throw it. Repeat several times. Describe what you see.

5. Make the wings smaller by folding them one more time. Gently throw the plane. Repeat several times. Describe what you see.

6. Using the smaller wings, try to achieve the same flight path you saw when the wings were bigger.

Analysis

1. What happened to the plane's flight when you reduced the size of its wings? What did you have to do to achieve the same flight path as when the wings were bigger?

2. What gave your plane its forward motion?

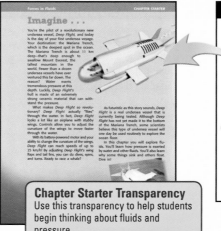

Imagine . . .

You're the pilot of a revolutionary new undersea vessel, *Deep Flight*, and today is the day of your first undersea voyage. Your destination: the Mariana Trench, which is the deepest spot in the ocean. The Mariana Trench is about 11 km deep—that's deep enough to swallow Mount Everest, the tallest mountain in the world. Fewer than a dozen undersea vessels have ever ventured this far down. The reason? Water exerts tremendous pressure at this depth. Luckily, *Deep Flight's* hull is made of an extremely strong ceramic material that can withstand the pressure.

What makes *Deep Flight* so revolutionary? *Deep Flight* actually "flies" through the water. In fact, *Deep Flight* looks a lot like an airplane with stubby wings. Controls allow you to adjust the curvature of the wings to move faster through the water.

With its battery-powered motor and your ability to change the curvature of the wings, *Deep Flight* can reach speeds of up to 25 km/h! By adjusting *Deep Flight's* wing flaps and tail fins, you can do dives, spins, and turns. Ready to race a whale?

As futuristic as this story sounds, *Deep Flight* is a real undersea vessel that is currently being tested. Although *Deep Flight* has not yet made it to the bottom of the Mariana Trench, some scientists believe this type of undersea vessel will one day be used routinely to explore the ocean floor.

In this chapter you will explore fluids. You'll learn how pressure is exerted by water and other fluids. You'll also learn why some things sink and others float. Dive in!

Chapter Starter Transparency
Use this transparency to help students begin thinking about fluids and pressure.

CHAPTER RESOURCES

Technology

Transparencies
• Chapter Starter Transparency

READING SKILLS

Student Edition on CD-ROM

Guided Reading Audio CD

Classroom Videos
• Brain Food Video Quiz

Workbooks

Science Puzzlers, Twisters & Teasers
• Forces in Fluids GENERAL

Focus

Overview

In this section, students learn about the properties of fluids. Students also learn how pressure is related to depth and density and how fluids flow from areas of high pressure to areas of low pressure.

 Bellringer

Have your students imagine the following situation: "One afternoon, you go outside to find your younger sister standing by her bike holding a nail in her hand. The bike has a flat tire. She wants to know why the air came out of the tire when she pulled the nail out." Have students write a few sentences to explain why air rushes out of a hole in a tire.

MISCONCEPTION
///// **ALERT** \\\\\

Pressure and Weight
Students might assume that pressure calculations will always involve the force of a fluid. Explain that because weight is a measure of gravitational force, anything that has weight exerts pressure. Thus, a crate on a floor exerts pressure on the floor.

READING WARM-UP

Objectives
- Describe how fluids exert pressure.
- Analyze how atmospheric pressure varies with depth.
- Explain how depth and density affect water pressure.
- Give examples of fluids flowing from high to low pressure.

Terms to Learn
fluid
pressure
pascal
atmospheric pressure

READING STRATEGY

Brainstorming The key idea of this section is pressure. Brainstorm words and phrases related to pressure.

fluid a nonsolid state of matter in which the atoms or molecules are free to move past each other, as in a gas or liquid

pressure the amount of force exerted per unit area of a surface

pascal the SI unit of pressure (symbol, Pa)

atmospheric pressure the pressure caused by the weight of the atmosphere

Fluids and Pressure

What does a dolphin have in common with a sea gull? What does a dog have in common with a fly? What do you have in common with all these living things?

One answer to these questions is that you and all these other living things spend a lifetime moving through fluids. A **fluid** is any material that can flow and that takes the shape of its container. Fluids include liquids and gases. Fluids can flow because the particles in fluids move easily past each other.

Fluids Exert Pressure

You probably have heard the terms *air pressure* and *water pressure*. Air and water are fluids. All fluids exert pressure. So, what is pressure? Think about this example. When you pump up a bicycle tire, you push air into the tire. And like all matter, air is made of tiny particles that are constantly moving.

Look at **Figure 1.** Inside the tire, the air particles collide with each other and with the walls of the tire. Together, these collisions create a force on the tire. The amount of force exerted on a given area is **pressure.**

Calculating Pressure

Pressure can be calculated by using the following equation:

$$pressure = \frac{force}{area}$$

The SI unit for pressure is the **pascal.** One pascal (1 Pa) is the force of one newton exerted over an area of one square meter (1 N/m^2).

Figure 1 *The force of the air particles hitting the inner surface of the tire creates pressure, which keeps the tire inflated.*

CHAPTER RESOURCES

Chapter Resource File

 • **Lesson Plan**
• **Directed Reading A** BASIC
• **Directed Reading B** SPECIAL NEEDS

Technology

 Transparencies
• Bellringer
• *LINK TO LIFE SCIENCE* Math Focus: Surface Area-to-Volume Ratio

Workbooks

 Math Skills for Science
• The Pressure Is On! GENERAL

Is That a Fact!

The air in a large room in your house weighs about as much as an average adult male (about 736 N)!

Pressure, Force, and Area What is the pressure exerted by a book that has an area of 0.2 m² and a weight of 10 N?

Step 1: Write the equation for pressure.

$$pressure = \frac{force}{area}$$

Step 2: Replace *force* and *area* with the values given, and solve. (Hint: Weight is a measure of gravitational force.)

$$pressure = \frac{10 \text{ N}}{0.2 \text{ m}^2} = 50 \text{ N/m}^2 = 50 \text{ Pa}$$

The equation for pressure can be rearranged to find force or area, as shown below.

$force = pressure \times area$ *(Rearrange by multiplying by area.)*

$area = \dfrac{force}{pressure}$ *(Rearrange by multiplying by area and then dividing by pressure.)*

Now It's Your Turn

1. Find the pressure exerted by a 3,000 N crate that has an area of 2 m².
2. Find the weight of a rock that has an area of 10 m² and that exerts a pressure of 250 Pa.

Pressure and Bubbles

When you blow a soap bubble, you blow in only one direction. So, why does the bubble get rounder instead of longer as you blow? The shape of the bubble partly depends on an important property of fluids: Fluids exert pressure evenly in all directions. The air you blow into the bubble exerts pressure evenly in all directions. So, the bubble expands in all directions to create a sphere.

Atmospheric Pressure

The *atmosphere* is the layer of nitrogen, oxygen, and other gases that surrounds Earth. Earth's atmosphere is held in place by gravity, which pulls the gases toward Earth. The pressure caused by the weight of the atmosphere is called **atmospheric pressure.**

Atmospheric pressure is exerted on everything on Earth, including you. At sea level, the atmosphere exerts a pressure of about 101,300 N on every square meter, or 101,300 Pa. So, there is a weight of about 10 N (about 2 lbs) on every square centimeter of your body. Why don't you feel this crushing pressure? Like the air inside a balloon, the fluids inside your body exert pressure. **Figure 2** can help you understand why you don't feel the pressure.

Reading Check Name two gases in the atmosphere. *(See the Appendix for answers to Reading Checks.)*

Atmospheric pressure

Air pressure inside the balloon

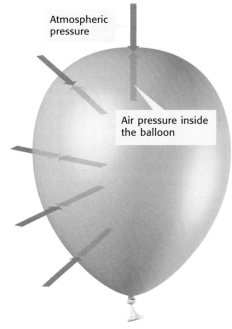

Figure 2 *The air inside a balloon exerts pressure that keeps the balloon inflated against atmospheric pressure. Similarly, fluid inside your body exerts pressure that works against atmospheric pressure.*

Answer to Math Focus
1. *pressure* = 3,000 N ÷ 2 m² = 1,500 Pa
2. *force* = 250 Pa × 10 m² = 2,500 N

Answer to Reading Check
Two gases in the atmosphere are nitrogen and oxygen.

CONNECTION to Life Science — GENERAL

Surface Area-to-Volume Ratio Use the teaching transparency titled "Math Focus: Surface Area-to-Volume Ratio" to help students understand how objects, including human bodies, can withstand atmospheric pressure.

Weather and Pressure Have students research the effects of atmospheric pressure on weather. Have students make a poster or concept map to display their results. **LS** Visual

BRAIN FOOD

Mount Everest The high altitude of Mount Everest can be hazardous to visitors' health. Most of the mountain's base camps are more than 4,000 m above sea level. Altitude sickness can affect people who reach that elevation. Climbers must use oxygen masks above 5,500 m because there is not enough oxygen to sustain normal body functions.

Homework — GENERAL

Pressure Essay Have students write an essay describing how they are affected by fluid pressure on a typical day. Students should include examples such as weather, transportation, plumbing, breathing, and so on. **LS** Verbal

Answer to Reading Check
Pressure increases as depth increases.

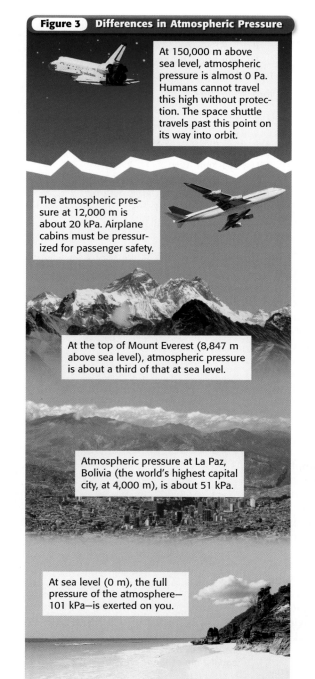

Figure 3   Differences in Atmospheric Pressure

At 150,000 m above sea level, atmospheric pressure is almost 0 Pa. Humans cannot travel this high without protection. The space shuttle travels past this point on its way into orbit.

The atmospheric pressure at 12,000 m is about 20 kPa. Airplane cabins must be pressurized for passenger safety.

At the top of Mount Everest (8,847 m above sea level), atmospheric pressure is about a third of that at sea level.

Atmospheric pressure at La Paz, Bolivia (the world's highest capital city, at 4,000 m), is about 51 kPa.

At sea level (0 m), the full pressure of the atmosphere—101 kPa—is exerted on you.

Variation of Atmospheric Pressure

The atmosphere stretches about 150 km above Earth's surface. However, about 80% of the atmosphere's gases are found within 10 km of Earth's surface. At the top of the atmosphere, pressure is almost nonexistent. The pressure is close to 0 Pa because the gas particles are far apart and rarely collide. Mount Everest in south-central Asia is the highest point on Earth. At the top of Mount Everest, atmospheric pressure is about 33,000 Pa, or 33 kilopascals (33 kPa). (Remember that the prefix *kilo-* means 1,000. So, 1 kPa is equal to 1,000 Pa.) At sea level, atmospheric pressure is about 101 kPa.

Atmospheric Pressure and Depth

Take a look at **Figure 3**. Notice how atmospheric pressure changes as you travel through the atmosphere. The further down through the atmosphere you go, the greater the pressure is. In other words, the pressure increases as the atmosphere gets "deeper." An important point to remember about fluids is that pressure varies depending on depth. At lower levels of the atmosphere, there is more fluid above that is being pulled by Earth's gravitational force. So, there is more pressure at lower levels of the atmosphere.

✓ **Reading Check** Describe how pressure changes with depth.

Pressure Changes and Your Body

So, what happens to your body when atmospheric pressure changes? If you travel to higher or lower points in the atmosphere, the fluids in your body have to adjust to maintain equal pressure. You may have experienced this adjustment if your ears have "popped" when you were in a plane taking off or in a car traveling down a steep mountain road. The "pop" happens because of pressure changes in pockets of air behind your eardrums.

MISCONCEPTION /// ALERT \\\

Variation of Air Density The relationship between pressure and depth in the atmosphere is not the same as in the ocean. Air is less dense at higher altitudes. So, the pressure in the upper atmosphere varies less with depth than pressure in the lower atmosphere does. But water density in the ocean remains approximately constant with depth. So, pressure variations with depth are about the same near the surface of the ocean or farther below.

Water Pressure

Water is a fluid. So, it exerts pressure like the atmosphere does. Water pressure also increases as depth increases, as shown in **Figure 4.** The deeper a diver goes in the water, the greater the pressure is. The pressure increases because more water above the diver is being pulled by Earth's gravitational force. In addition, the atmosphere presses down on the water, so the total pressure on the diver includes water pressure and atmospheric pressure.

Water Pressure and Depth

Like atmospheric pressure, water pressure depends on depth. Water pressure does not depend on the total amount of fluid present. A swimmer would feel the same pressure swimming at 3 m below the surface of a small pond and at 3 m below the surface of an ocean. Even though there is more water in the ocean than in the pond, the pressure on the swimmer in the pond would be the same as the pressure on the swimmer in the ocean.

Density Making a Difference

Water is about 1,000 times more dense than air. *Density* is the amount of matter in a given volume, or mass per unit volume. Because water is more dense than air, a certain volume of water has more mass—and weighs more—than the same volume of air. So, water exerts more pressure than air.

For example, if you climb a 10 m tree, the decrease in atmospheric pressure is too small to notice. But if you dive 10 m underwater, the pressure on you increases to 201 kPa, which is almost twice the atmospheric pressure at the surface!

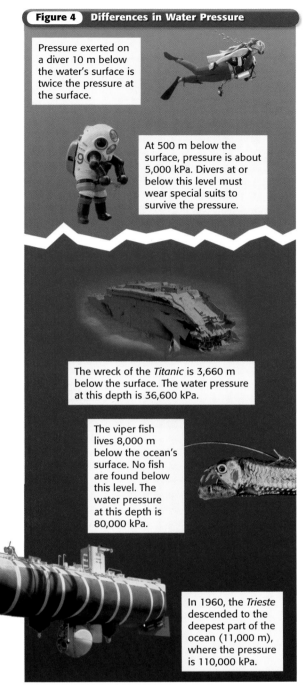

Figure 4   Differences in Water Pressure

Pressure exerted on a diver 10 m below the water's surface is twice the pressure at the surface.

At 500 m below the surface, pressure is about 5,000 kPa. Divers at or below this level must wear special suits to survive the pressure.

The wreck of the *Titanic* is 3,660 m below the surface. The water pressure at this depth is 36,600 kPa.

The viper fish lives 8,000 m below the ocean's surface. No fish are found below this level. The water pressure at this depth is 80,000 kPa.

In 1960, the *Trieste* descended to the deepest part of the ocean (11,000 m), where the pressure is 110,000 kPa.

SCIENCE HUMOR

Q: What do you call a pod of whales on a deep dive?

A: grays under pressure

Reteaching — BASIC

How Droppers Work Give each pair of students a plastic dropper and a small cup of water. Ask students to write a paragraph describing how the dropper works. Students should address why water goes up into the dropper and why the water can be forced out. Students may experiment with the droppers as they write their paragraphs. (Both events can be explained by the fact that fluids flow from areas of high pressure to areas of low pressure.) **LS** Verbal/Kinesthetic

Quiz — GENERAL

1. What do liquids and gases have in common? (They are both fluids.)

2. Why does pressure increase with depth? (As depth increases, the weight of the fluid above increases, which increases pressure.)

Alternative Assessment — ADVANCED

Airflow Tracking Have students make a poster showing the airflow in their home. Have them write a short description of the circulation of the air by using the concept of fluid pressure. Students should also describe how they tracked the airflow in their home. **LS** Visual

Answer to Reading Check

You decrease pressure inside a straw by removing some of the air inside the straw.

Blown Away

1. Lay an **empty plastic soda bottle** on its side.
2. Wad a **small piece of paper** (about 4 × 4 cm) into a ball.
3. Place the paper ball just inside the bottle's opening.
4. Blow straight into the opening.
5. Record your observations.
6. Explain your results in terms of high and low fluid pressures.

Pressure Differences and Fluid Flow

When you drink through a straw, you remove some of the air in the straw. Because there is less air inside the straw, the pressure in the straw is reduced. But the atmospheric pressure on the surface of the liquid remains the same. Thus, there is a difference between the pressure inside the straw and the pressure outside the straw. The outside pressure forces the liquid up the straw and into your mouth. So, just by drinking through a straw, you can observe an important property of fluids: Fluids flow from areas of high pressure to areas of low pressure.

✓ **Reading Check** When drinking through a straw, how do you decrease the pressure inside the straw?

Pressure Differences and Breathing

Take a deep breath—fluid is flowing from high to low pressure! When you inhale, a muscle increases the space in your chest and gives your lungs room to expand. This expansion decreases the pressure in your lungs. The pressure in your lungs becomes lower than the air pressure outside your lungs. Air then flows into your lungs—from high to low pressure. This air carries oxygen that you need to live. **Figure 5** shows how exhaling also causes fluids to flow from high to low pressure. You can see a similar flow of fluid when you open a carbonated beverage or squeeze toothpaste onto your toothbrush.

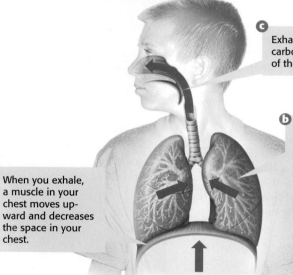

Figure 5 Exhaling, Pressure, and Fluid Flow

a When you exhale, a muscle in your chest moves upward and decreases the space in your chest.

b The decrease in space causes the pressure in your lungs to increase. The air in your lungs flows from a region of high pressure (your chest) to a region of low pressure (outside of your body).

c Exhaled air carries carbon dioxide out of the lungs.

MATERIALS

FOR EACH STUDENT
• bottle, soda, plastic
• paper, 4 × 4 cm square

Answers

5. Students should observe that the paper wad flies out of the bottle.

6. By blowing into the bottle, the air pressure inside the bottle is increased. Fluids flow from high pressure to low pressure, so the air inside flows out of the bottle, carrying the paper wad with it.

Pressure Differences and Tornadoes

Look at the tornado in **Figure 6.** Some of the damaging winds caused by tornadoes are the result of pressure differences. The air pressure inside a tornado is very low. Because the air pressure outside of the tornado is higher than the pressure inside, air rushes into the tornado. The rushing air causes the tornado to be like a giant vacuum cleaner—objects are pushed into the tornado. The winds created are usually very strong and affect the area around the tornado. So, objects, such as trees and buildings, can be severely damaged by wind even if they are not in the direct path of a tornado.

Figure 6 *Tornadoes are like giant vacuum cleaners because of pressure differences.*

SECTION Review

Summary

- A fluid is any material that flows and takes the shape of its container.
- Pressure is force exerted on a given area.
- Moving particles of matter create pressure by colliding with one another and with the walls of their container.
- The pressure caused by the weight of the atmosphere is called *atmospheric pressure.*
- Fluid pressure increases as depth increases.
- As depth increases, water pressure increases faster than atmospheric pressure does because water is denser than air.
- Fluids flow from areas of high pressure to areas of low pressure.

Using Key Terms

1. In your own words, write a definition for each of the following terms: *fluid* and *atmospheric pressure.*

2. Use the following terms in the same sentence: *pressure* and *pascal.*

Understanding Key Ideas

3. Which of the following statements about fluids is true?
   a. Fluids rarely take the shape of their container.
   b. Fluids include liquids and gases.
   c. Fluids flow from low pressure to high pressure.
   d. Fluids exert the most pressure in the downward direction.

4. How do fluids exert pressure on a container?

5. Why are you not crushed by atmospheric pressure?

6. Explain why atmospheric pressure changes as depth changes.

7. Give three examples of fluids flowing from high pressure to low pressure in everyday life.

Math Skills

8. The water in a glass has a weight of 2.4 N. The bottom of the glass has an area of 0.012 m². What is the pressure exerted by the water on the bottom of the glass?

Critical Thinking

9. **Identifying Relationships** Mercury is a liquid that has a density of 13.5 g/mL. Water has a density of 1.0 g/mL. Equal volumes of mercury and water are in identical containers. Explain why the pressures exerted on the bottoms of the containers are different.

10. **Making Inferences** Why do airplanes need to be pressurized for passenger safety when flying high in the atmosphere?

For a variety of links related to this chapter, go to www.scilinks.org

Topic: Fluids and Pressure
SciLinks code: HSM0586

CHAPTER RESOURCES

Chapter Resource File

- Section Quiz GENERAL
- Section Review GENERAL
- Vocabulary and Section Summary GENERAL
- Datasheet for Quick Lab

Technology

Transparencies
- Exhaling, Pressure, and Fluid Flow

Answers to Section Review

1. Sample answer: A fluid is a gas or a liquid. Atmospheric pressure is the pressure caused by the weight of the gases in the atmosphere.

2. Sample answer: A pascal is a unit of pressure.

3. b

4. Particles in the fluid collide with the side of the container. The force of the collisions creates pressure on the container.

5. You aren't crushed by atmospheric pressure because the fluids inside your body exert pressure that works against atmospheric pressure.

6. Atmospheric pressure increases as depth increases because at lower levels of the atmosphere, there is more air above that is being pulled down by gravitational force.

7. Sample answer: Examples of fluids flowing from high pressure to low pressure are drinking through a straw, breathing, and squeezing toothpaste from a tube.

8. *pressure* = 2.4 N ÷ 0.012 m² = 200 Pa

9. Mercury has a higher density than water. So, a given volume of mercury will weigh more than the same volume of water. Because pressure depends on force (weight) and area, mercury will exert more pressure than water will on the bottoms of identical containers.

10. As an airplane travels higher in the atmosphere, the atmospheric pressure becomes much lower than it is on the ground. At lower pressures, gas particles, including oxygen particles, are farther apart. As a result, people have a difficulty breathing at low pressures. Airplanes are pressurized so that there is enough oxygen for people to breathe comfortably.

Focus

Overview

This section describes how differences in fluid pressure create buoyant force. Students are introduced to Archimedes' principle and learn how to find the buoyant force on an object. Finally, students learn the factors that determine whether an object floats or sinks in a fluid.

 Bellringer

Ask your students to identify which of the following objects will float in water: a rock, an orange, a screw, a quarter, a candle, a plastic-foam "peanut," and a chalkboard eraser. Ask students to write a hypothesis about why an aircraft carrier, which weighs thousands of tons, does not sink.

Motivate

Demonstration —— GENERAL

Density Layers Layer 20 mL each of corn syrup, water, and cooking oil in a 100 mL graduated cylinder. Have students observe as you drop in objects that will float on the different layers. You might also try adding droplets of alcohol. Use the results of the demonstration to launch a discussion about buoyant force. **LS** Visual

---

READING WARM-UP

Objectives

● Explain the relationship between fluid pressure and buoyant force.

● Predict whether an object will float or sink in a fluid.

● Analyze the role of density in an object's ability to float.

● Explain how the overall density of an object can be changed.

Terms to Learn

buoyant force
Archimedes' principle

READING STRATEGY

Discussion Read this section silently. Write down questions that you have about this section. Discuss your questions in a small group.

buoyant force the upward force that keeps an object immersed in or floating on a liquid

Archimedes' principle the principle that states that the buoyant force on an object in a fluid is an upward force equal to the weight of the volume of fluid that the object displaces

Figure 1 *There is more pressure at the bottom of an object because pressure increases with depth. This results in an upward buoyant force on the object.*

Buoyant Force

Why does an ice cube float on water? Why doesn't it sink to the bottom of your glass?

Imagine that you use a straw to push an ice cube under water. Then, you release the cube. A force pushes the ice back to the water's surface. The force, called **buoyant force** (BOY uhnt FAWRS), is the upward force that fluids exert on all matter.

Buoyant Force and Fluid Pressure

Look at **Figure 1.** Water exerts fluid pressure on all sides of an object. The pressure exerted horizontally on one side of the object is equal to the pressure exerted on the opposite side. These equal pressures cancel one another. So, the only fluid pressures affecting the net force on the object are at the top and at the bottom. Pressure increases as depth increases. So, the pressure at the bottom of the object is greater than the pressure at the top. The water exerts a net upward force on the object. This upward force is buoyant force.

Determining Buoyant Force

Archimedes (AHR kuh MEE deez), a Greek mathematician who lived in the third century BCE, discovered how to determine buoyant force. **Archimedes' principle** states that the buoyant force on an object in a fluid is an upward force equal to the weight of the fluid that the object takes the place of, or displaces. Suppose the object in **Figure 1** displaces 250 mL of water. The weight of that volume of displaced water is about 2.5 N. So, the buoyant force on the object is 2.5 N. Notice that only the weight of the displaced fluid determines the buoyant force on an object. The weight of the object does not affect buoyant force.

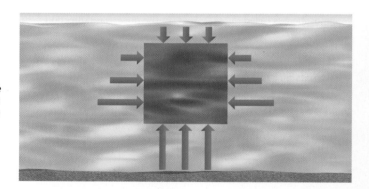

CHAPTER RESOURCES

Chapter Resource File

- Lesson Plan
- Directed Reading A BASIC
- Directed Reading B SPECIAL NEEDS

Technology

- Transparencies
  - Bellringer

 SCIENCE
 HUMOR

Q: Why did the banker jump into the swimming pool?

A: He needed to float a loan.

Weight Versus Buoyant Force

An object in a fluid will sink if its weight is greater than the buoyant force (the weight of the fluid it displaces). An object floats only when the buoyant force on the object is equal to the object's weight.

Sinking

The rock in **Figure 2** weighs 75 N. It displaces 5 L of water. Archimedes' principle says that the buoyant force is equal to the weight of the displaced water—about 50 N. The rock's weight is greater than the buoyant force. So, the rock sinks.

Floating

The fish in **Figure 2** weighs 12 N. It displaces a volume of water that weighs 12 N. Because the fish's weight is equal to the buoyant force, the fish floats in the water. In fact, the fish is suspended in the water as it floats. Now, look at the duck. The duck does not sink. So, the buoyant force on the duck must be equal to the duck's weight. But the duck isn't all the way underwater! Only the duck's feet, legs, and stomach have to be underwater to displace 9 N of water, which is equal to the duck's weight. So, the duck floats on the surface of the water.

Buoying Up

If the duck dove underwater, it would displace more than 9 N of water. So, the buoyant force on the duck would be greater than the duck's weight. When the buoyant force on an object is greater than the object's weight, the object is *buoyed up* (pushed up) in water. An object is buoyed up until the part of the object underwater displaces an amount of water that equals the object's entire weight. Thus, an ice cube pops to the surface when it is pushed to the bottom of a glass of water.

Reading Check What causes an object to buoy up? (*See the Appendix for answers to Reading Checks.*)

Figure 2 *Will an object sink or float? That depends on whether the buoyant force is less than or equal to the object's weight.*

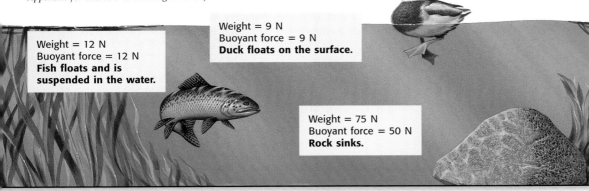

Weight = 12 N
Buoyant force = 12 N
Fish floats and is suspended in the water.

Weight = 9 N
Buoyant force = 9 N
Duck floats on the surface.

Weight = 75 N
Buoyant force = 50 N
Rock sinks.

📖 READING STRATEGY —— GENERAL

Prediction Guide Before students read the next three pages, ask them to predict whether the following statements are true or false:

1. The shape of an object helps determine whether it will float. (true)

2. Something made of steel cannot float in water. (false)

3. Whether an object floats depends on its weight. (true)

Have students evaluate their answers after they read the next three pages. **LS** Logical

CONNECTION ACTIVITY
Math —————— ADVANCED

Determining Weight Ask students to solve the following problem: "A force of 15 N is required to lift an object that is underwater. The object displaces 2 L of water (1 L of water weighs 10 N). What is the weight of the object out of water?" (*force required to lift object in water = weight of object out of water − buoyant force*

15 N = weight of object out of water − 20 N

weight of object out of water = 20 N + 15 N = 35 N) **LS** Logical

---

Homework —————— GENERAL

Concept Mapping Have students create a buoyant force concept map and discuss objects that float on the surface of water, objects that float between the surface and the bottom, and objects that sink to the bottom. **LS** Verbal

Answer to Reading Check

An object is buoyed up if the buoyant force on the object is greater than the object's weight.

Teach, continued

ACTIVITY — GENERAL

Making Models Have students make a model of a hot-air balloon. Before they begin, discuss how heating the air inside the balloon changes the balloon's overall density and therefore changes its buoyancy. Provide students with tissue paper, tape, glue, string, and other materials to make a model balloon. Fill the completed models with hot air from a hair dryer. Release the model to see if it floats. Have students evaluate their balloon's performance.

LS Kinesthetic

CONNECTION ACTIVITY
Math — ADVANCED

Rearranging the Density Equation Have students rearrange the equation for density to solve for mass and volume. (*mass = density × volume*; *volume = mass ÷ density*) Then, have students solve the following problems:

1. The density of the liquid mercury is 13.5 g/mL. What is the mass of a 2.4 mL sample of mercury? (32.4 g)

2. The density of aluminum is 2.7 g/cm³. What is the volume of a 9.45 g sample of aluminum? (3.5 cm³)

LS Logical

Figure 3 *Helium in a balloon floats in air for the same reason an ice cube floats on water—helium is less dense than the surrounding fluid.*

Floating, Sinking, and Density

Think again about the rock in the lake. The rock displaces 5 L of water. But volumes of solids are measured in cubic centimeters (cm^3). Because 1 mL is equal to 1 cm^3, the volume of the rock is 5,000 cm^3. But 5,000 cm^3 of rock weighs more than an equal volume of water. So, the rock sinks.

Because mass is proportional to weight, you can say that the rock has more mass per volume than water has. Mass per unit volume is density. The rock sinks because it is more dense than water is. The duck floats because it is less dense than water is. The density of the fish is equal to the density of the water.

More Dense Than Air

Why does an ice cube float on water but not in air? An ice cube floats on water because it is less dense than water. But most substances are *more* dense than air. So, there are few substances that float in air. The ice cube is more dense than air, so the ice cube doesn't float in air.

Less Dense Than Air

One substance that is less dense than air is helium, a gas. In fact, helium has one-seventh the density of air under normal conditions. A given volume of helium displaces an equal volume of air that is much heavier than itself. So, helium floats in air. Because helium floats in air, it is used in parade balloons, such as the one shown in **Figure 3**.

✓ **Reading Check** Name a substance that is less dense than air.

MATH FOCUS

Finding Density Find the density of a rock that has a mass of 10 g and a volume of 2 cm^3.

Step 1: Write the equation for density. Density is calculated by using this equation:

$$density = \frac{mass}{volume}$$

Step 2: Replace *mass* and *volume* with the values in the problem, and solve.

$$density = \frac{10 \text{ g}}{2 \text{ cm}^3} = 5 \text{ g/cm}^3$$

Now It's Your Turn

1. What is the density of a 20 cm^3 object that has a mass of 25 g?

2. A 546 g fish displaces 420 mL of water. What is the density of the fish? (Note: 1 mL = 1 cm^3)

3. A beaker holds 50 mL of a slimy green liquid. The mass of the liquid is 163 g. What is the density of the liquid?

Answer to Reading Check

Helium is less dense than air.

Answers to Math Focus

1. 1.25 g/cm³
2. 1.3 g/cm³
3. 3.26 g/mL

Is That a Fact!

Before plastics can be recycled, they must first be separated by type. Most containers display a number that identifies the type of plastic used. Containers that do not display number codes can be separated by density by being floated in liquids of different densities.

Changing Overall Density

Steel is almost 8 times denser than water. And yet huge steel ships cruise the oceans with ease. But hold on! You just learned that substances that are more dense than water will sink in water. So, how does a steel ship float?

Changing Shape

The secret of how a ship floats is in the shape of the ship. What if a ship were just a big block of steel, as shown in **Figure 4**? If you put that block into water, the block would sink because it is more dense than water. So, ships are built with a hollow shape. The amount of steel in the ship is the same as in the block. But the hollow shape increases the volume of the ship. Remember that density is mass per unit volume. So, an increase in the ship's volume leads to a decrease in its density. Thus, ships made of steel float because their *overall density* is less than the density of water.

Most ships are built to displace more water than is necessary for the ship to float. Ships are made this way so that they won't sink when people and cargo are loaded on the ship.

Floating Rocks The rock that makes up Earth's continents is about 15% less dense than the molten (melted) mantle rock below it. Because of this difference in density, the continents are floating on the mantle. Research the structure of Earth, and make a poster that shows Earth's interior layers.

Figure 4   Shape and Overall Density

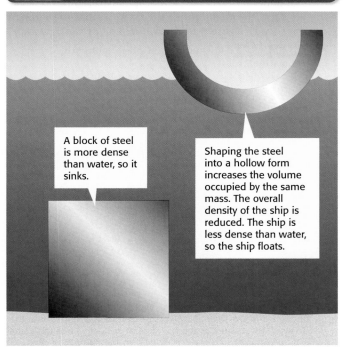

A block of steel is more dense than water, so it sinks.

Shaping the steel into a hollow form increases the volume occupied by the same mass. The overall density of the ship is reduced. The ship is less dense than water, so the ship floats.

For another activity related to this chapter, go to **go.hrw.com** and type in the keyword **HP5FLUW**.

Close

Reteaching — BASIC

Rubber Ducky Place a rubber duck in a large, clear container of water. Explain to students that the overall density of the rubber and the air allows the duck to float. Then, cut the duck in two and put the pieces in the water. Explain that the pieces sink because there is no air trapped inside the duck and the rubber is more dense than water. **LS** Visual

Quiz — GENERAL

1. How can you determine the buoyant force acting on an object? (Determine the weight of the volume of fluid displaced by the object.)

2. Who discovered how to determine buoyant force? (Archimedes)

3. How can a scuba diver keep from floating back to the surface of the water? (The diver can add weights.)

Answer to Reading Check

Crew members control the density of a submarine by controlling the amount of water in the ballast tanks.

Ship Shape

1. Roll a **piece of clay** into a ball the size of a golf ball, and drop it into a **container of water.** Record your observations.

2. With your hands, flatten the ball of clay until it is a bit thinner than your little finger, and press it into the shape of a bowl or canoe.

3. Place the clay boat gently in the water. How does the change of shape affect the buoyant force on the clay? How is that change related to the overall density of the clay boat? Record your answers.

Changing Mass

A submarine is a special kind of ship that can travel both on the surface of the water and underwater. Submarines have *ballast tanks* that can be opened to allow sea water to flow in. As water is added, the submarine's mass increases, but its volume stays the same. The submarine's overall density increases so that it can dive under the surface. Crew members control the amount of water taken in. In this way, they control how dense the submarine is and how deep it dives. Compressed air is used to blow the water out of the tanks so that the submarine can rise. Study **Figure 5** to learn how ballast tanks work.

✓ **Reading Check** How do crew members control the density of a submarine?

Figure 5 Controlling Density Using Ballast Tanks

When a submarine is floating on the ocean's surface, its ballast tanks are filled mostly with air.

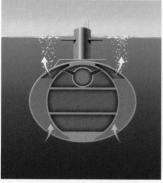

Vent holes on the ballast tanks are opened to allow the submarine to dive. Air escapes as the tanks fill with water.

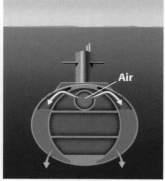

Vent holes are closed, and compressed air is pumped into the ballast tanks to force the water out, so the submarine rises.

MATERIALS

FOR EACH STUDENT
- bowl or pail, medium, one for every two or three students
- clay, modeling, golf-ball-sized piece
- water

Answer

3. Forming the clay into a boat shape causes the clay to displace more water, which increases the buoyant force. The change in shape causes the overall density of the clay boat to decrease so that the clay boat is less dense than the water. Therefore, the clay boat floats.

Changing Volume

Like a submarine, some fish adjust their overall density to stay at a certain depth in the water. Most bony fishes have an organ called a *swim bladder,* shown in **Figure 6.** This swim bladder is filled with gases produced in a fish's blood. The inflated swim bladder increases the fish's volume and thereby decreases the fish's overall density, which keeps the fish from sinking in the water. The fish's nervous system controls the amount of gas in the bladder. Some fish, such as sharks, do not have a swim bladder. These fish must swim constantly to keep from sinking.

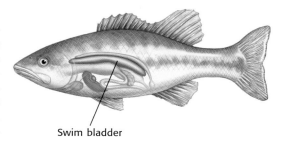
Swim bladder

Figure 6 *Most bony fishes have an organ called a* swim bladder *that allows them to adjust their overall density.*

SECTION Review

Summary

- All fluids exert an upward force called *buoyant force.*
- Buoyant force is caused by differences in fluid pressure.
- Archimedes' principle states that the buoyant force on an object is equal to the weight of the fluid displaced by the object.
- Any object that is more dense than the surrounding fluid will sink. An object that is less dense than the surrounding fluid will float.
- The overall density of an object can be changed by changing the object's shape, mass, or volume.

Using Key Terms

1. Use the following terms in the same sentence: *buoyant force* and *Archimedes' principle.*

Understanding Key Ideas

2. Which of the following changes increases the overall density of the object?
   a. A block of iron is formed into a hollow shape.
   b. A submarine fills its ballast tanks with water.
   c. A submarine fills its ballast tanks with air.
   d. A fish increases the amount of gas in its swim bladder.

3. Explain how differences in fluid pressure create buoyant force on an object.

4. How does an object's density determine whether the object will sink or float in water?

5. Name three methods that can be used to change the overall density of an object.

Math Skills

6. What is the density of an object that has a mass of 184 g and a volume of 50 cm³?

Critical Thinking

7. **Applying Concepts** An object weighs 20 N. It displaces a volume of water that weighs 15 N.
   a. What is the buoyant force on the object?
   b. Will this object float or sink? Explain your answer.

8. **Predicting Consequences** Iron has a density of 7.9 g/cm³. Mercury is a liquid that has a density of 13.5 g/cm³. Will iron float or sink in mercury? Explain your answer.

9. **Evaluating Hypotheses** Imagine that your brother tells you that all heavy objects sink in water. Explain why you agree or disagree with his statement.

SCILINKS®

NSTA
Developed and maintained by the National Science Teachers Association

For a variety of links related to this chapter, go to www.scilinks.org

Topic: Buoyant Force
SciLinks code: HSM0202

Alternative Assessment — GENERAL

Life Jackets Ask students to make a poster that explains how a life jacket helps a person float. (Most life jackets are made from porous material filled with air.) (A life jacket keeps a person from sinking because the air inside the life jacket increases the person's volume but does not increase his or her weight by very much. The person's overall density decreases, and the person floats.) **LS** Visual

Answers to Section Review

1. Sample answer: Archimedes' principle is about the relationship between the buoyant force of an object and the amount of water the object displaces.

2. b

3. Water pressure is exerted on all sides of an object. The pressures exerted horizontally on the sides cancel each other out. The pressure exerted at the bottom is greater than that exerted at the top because pressure increases with depth. This creates an overall upward force on the object—the buoyant force.

4. An object will float in water if its density is less than the density of water. An object will sink in water if its density is greater than the density of water.

5. The density of an object can be changed by changing its shape, changing its mass, or changing its volume.

6. 184 g ÷ 50 cm³ = 3.68 g/cm³

7. **a.** 15 N
   b. It will sink because its weight is greater than the buoyant force acting on it.

8. Iron will float in mercury because iron is less dense than mercury.

9. Sample answer: I disagree with this statement because steel ships are heavy but they float in water. The ships float because the overall density of the steel and the air inside the ship is less than the density of water.

Focus

Overview

In this section, students learn about Bernoulli's principle. They then explore how heavier-than-air objects can achieve flight. Students also learn about the basic aspects of flight. Finally, students learn about Pascal's principle.

Bellringer

Pose the following problem to your students: "You have been asked to design two kites. One kite will be flown in areas where there is almost always a good breeze. The other kite will be flown in areas with very little wind." What differences in design and materials are there between your two kites?

Motivate

Demonstration —— GENERAL

Magic Water Place a straw upright in a glass of water. Hold a second straw at a right angle at the top of the first so that the straws are just touching. Blow very hard through the horizontal straw. Water will rise up in the vertical straw and form a spray. Tell students they will learn why this occurs after reading this section. **LS** Visual

---

READING WARM-UP

Objectives

- Describe the relationship between pressure and fluid speed.
- Analyze the roles of lift, thrust, and wing size in flight.
- Explain Pascal's principle.
- Describe drag, and explain how it affects lift.

Terms to Learn

Bernoulli's principle
lift
thrust
drag
Pascal's principle

READING STRATEGY

Reading Organizer As you read this section, create an outline of the section. Use the headings from the section in your outline.

Bernoulli's principle the principle that states that the pressure in a fluid decreases as the fluid's velocity increases

Figure 1 *This ball is pushed by the higher pressure of the air into an area of reduced pressure— the water stream.*

Fluids and Motion

Hold two sheets of paper so that the edges are hanging in front of your face about 4 cm apart. The flat faces of the paper should be parallel to each other. Now, blow as hard as you can between the two sheets of paper.

What's going on? You can't separate the sheets by blowing between them. In fact, the sheets move closer together the harder you blow. You may be surprised that the explanation for this unusual occurrence also includes how wings help birds and planes fly and how pitchers throw curve balls.

Fluid Speed and Pressure

The strange reaction of the paper is caused by a property of moving fluids. This property was first described in the 18th century by Daniel Bernoulli (ber NOO lee), a Swiss mathematician. **Bernoulli's principle** states that as the speed of a moving fluid increases, the fluid's pressure decreases. In the case of the paper, air speed between the two sheets increased when you blew air between them. Because air speed increased, the pressure between the sheets decreased. Thus, the higher pressure on the outside of the sheets pushed them together.

Science in a Sink

Bernoulli's principle is at work in **Figure 1.** A table-tennis ball is attached to a string and swung into a stream of water. Instead of being pushed out of the water, the ball is held in the water. Why? The water is moving faster than the air around it, so the water has a lower pressure than the surrounding air. The higher air pressure pushes the ball into the area of lower pressure—the water stream. Try this at home to see for yourself!

CHAPTER RESOURCES

Chapter Resource File

- **Lesson Plan**
- **Directed Reading A** BASIC
- **Directed Reading B** SPECIAL NEEDS

Technology

Transparencies
- Bellringer
- Wing Design and Lift

Figure 2 Wing Design and Lift

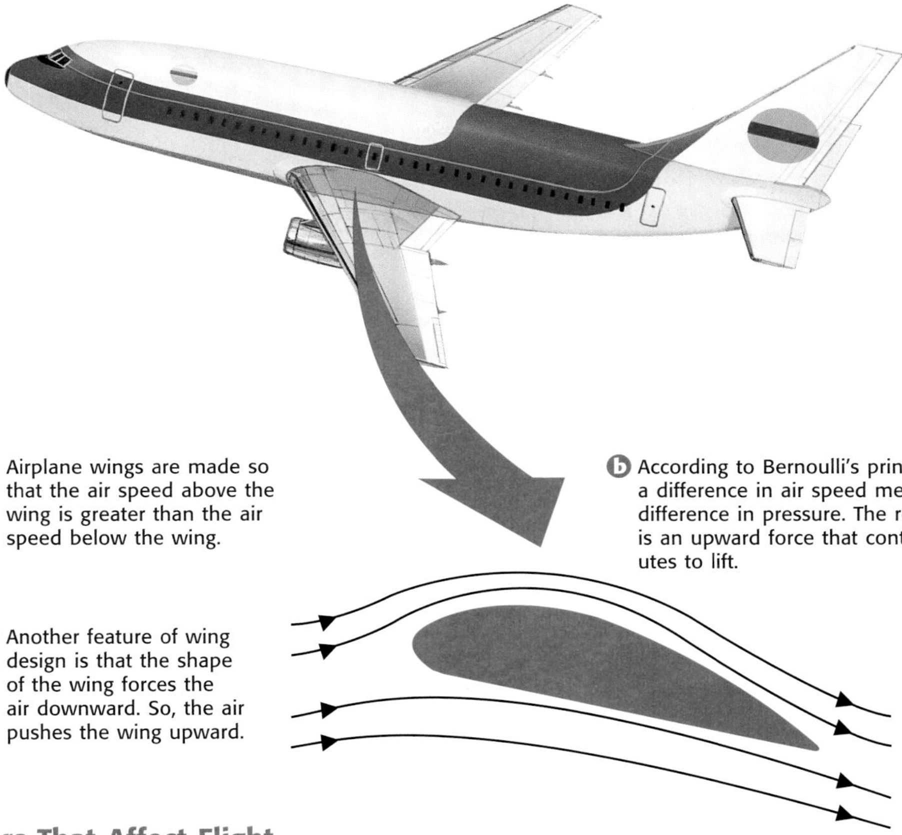

ⓐ Airplane wings are made so that the air speed above the wing is greater than the air speed below the wing.

ⓑ According to Bernoulli's principle, a difference in air speed means a difference in pressure. The result is an upward force that contributes to lift.

ⓒ Another feature of wing design is that the shape of the wing forces the air downward. So, the air pushes the wing upward.

Factors That Affect Flight

A common commercial airplane in the skies today is the Boeing 737 jet. Even without passengers, the plane weighs 350,000 N. How can something so big and heavy get off the ground and fly? Wing shape plays a role in helping these big planes—as well as smaller planes and birds—achieve flight, as shown in **Figure 2.**

According to Bernoulli's principle, the fast-moving air above the wing exerts less pressure than the slow-moving air below the wing. The greater pressure below the wing exerts an upward force. This upward force, known as **lift,** pushes the wings (and the rest of the airplane or bird) upward against the downward pull of gravity.

lift an upward force on an object that moves in a fluid

✓ **Reading Check** What is lift? (*See the Appendix for answers to Reading Checks.*)

MISCONCEPTION ALERT

More Than Bernoulli When teaching about airplane flight, emphasize that there is more to understanding lift than can be explained by Bernoulli's principle. Newton's third law also plays a part. A tilted wing deflects horizontal airflow downward (the action force exerted by the wing on the air). The reaction force is the upward force the air exerts on the wing. This force also contributes to lift.

Answer to Reading Check
Lift is an upward force on an object that is moving in a fluid.

Teach

ACTIVITY ————— BASIC

Pressure Analogy Before you discuss Bernoulli's principle, it may help some students to imagine the pressure of a fluid as the combined pressure of many particles striking a surface. Have students imagine a swarm of bees trapped in a short section of a long piece of pipe. As the bees fly around inside the pipe, they bounce off each other and off the walls of the pipe, creating pressure. Then, have students imagine that the bees are suddenly able to fly the entire length of the pipe. Explain that, because the bees have more room, they bounce against the walls of the pipe much less frequently, creating less pressure inside the pipe. **LS** Verbal/Logical

ACTIVITY ————— ADVANCED

Wing Shape Ask students to examine the wing shape shown in **Figure 2.** Have students use their knowledge of Bernoulli's principle to hypothesize about what type of wings might work in flight. Does the wing have to be curved? Is flight possible without wings? **LS** Logical/Visual

Demonstration ——— GENERAL

Flying Ball Point the airflow of a portable hair dryer straight up, and suspend a table-tennis ball in the airstream. Change the direction of the airflow slightly to maneuver the ball. Have students speculate on the forces that are at work in this demonstration. **LS** Visual

- *Hearing Impaired*
- *Learning Disabled*
- *Developmentally Delayed*

The concept of airplane lift is complicated for students with language delays to understand. Use this experiment to give them a chance to experience the idea of lift. Organize the students into small groups. Give each group an 8 1/2 in. × 11 in. sheet of paper and an 11 in. × 17 in. sheet of paper. Ask each team to make two paper airplanes that are alike except that one has much larger wings. Ask students to note the lift of each plane as they do the following: Throw the two planes with the same force. Throw the short-winged plane with light force and then with heavy force. Throw the long-winged plane with light force and then with heavy force.

LS Kinesthetic   English Language Learners

ACTIVITY ———— ADVANCED

Wind Tunnels Have students research how engineers use wind tunnels to test the design of airplane wings. Then, have students use what they have learned to build their own wings and wind tunnel, and show the class how to test the wing designs.

LS Kinesthetic

Figure 3 Increased Thrust Versus Increased Wing Size

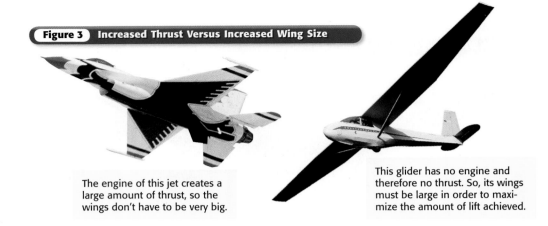

The engine of this jet creates a large amount of thrust, so the wings don't have to be very big.

This glider has no engine and therefore no thrust. So, its wings must be large in order to maximize the amount of lift achieved.

thrust the pushing or pulling force exerted by the engine of an aircraft or rocket

CONNECTION TO Social Studies

The First Flight The first successful flight of an engine-driven machine that was heavier than air happened in Kitty Hawk, North Carolina, in 1903. Orville Wright was the pilot. The plane flew only 37 m (about the length of a 737 jet) before landing, and the entire flight lasted only 12 s. Research another famous pilot in the history of flight. Make a poster that includes information about the pilot as well as pictures of the pilot and his or her airplane.

ACTIVITY

Thrust and Lift

The amount of lift created by a plane's wing is determined partly by the speed at which air travels around the wing. The speed of a plane is determined mostly by its thrust. **Thrust** is the forward force produced by the plane's engine. In general, a plane with a large amount of thrust moves faster than a plane that has less thrust does. This faster speed means air travels around the wing at a higher speed, which increases lift.

Wing Size, Speed, and Lift

The amount of lift also depends partly on the size of a plane's wings. Look at the jet plane in **Figure 3.** This plane can fly with a relatively small wing size because its engine gives a large amount of thrust. This thrust pushes the plane through the sky at great speeds. So, the jet creates a large amount of lift with small wings by moving quickly through the air. Smaller wings keep a plane's weight low, which also helps it move faster.

Compared with the jet, the glider in **Figure 3** has a large wing area. A glider is an engineless plane. It rides rising air currents to stay in flight. Without engines, gliders produce no thrust and move more slowly than many other kinds of planes. Thus, a glider must have large wings to create the lift it needs to stay in the air.

Bernoulli and Birds

Birds don't have engines, so birds must flap their wings to push themselves through the air. A small bird must flap its wings at a fast pace to stay in the air. But a hawk flaps its wings only occasionally because it has larger wings than the small bird has. A hawk uses its large wings to fly with very little effort. Fully extended, a hawk's wings allow the hawk to glide on wind currents and still have enough lift to stay in the air.

Cultural Awareness   GENERAL

Boomerangs More than 8,000 years ago, Australian aborigines discovered the aerodynamic qualities of a type of hunting stick called a boomerang. Have students research boomerangs and compare a boomerang's flight with an airplane's flight. Ask students to present their findings in a poster. **LS Visual**

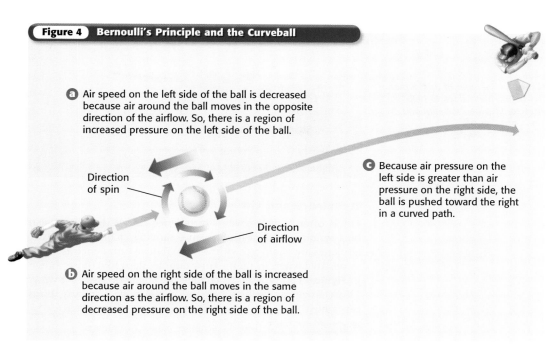

Figure 4 Bernoulli's Principle and the Curveball

a Air speed on the left side of the ball is decreased because air around the ball moves in the opposite direction of the airflow. So, there is a region of increased pressure on the left side of the ball.

Direction of spin

Direction of airflow

c Because air pressure on the left side is greater than air pressure on the right side, the ball is pushed toward the right in a curved path.

b Air speed on the right side of the ball is increased because air around the ball moves in the same direction as the airflow. So, there is a region of decreased pressure on the right side of the ball.

Bernoulli and Baseball

You don't have to look up at a bird or a plane flying through the sky to see Bernoulli's principle in your world. Any time fluids are moving, Bernoulli's principle is at work. **Figure 4** shows how a baseball pitcher can take advantage of Bernoulli's principle to throw a confusing curveball that is difficult for a batter to hit.

Drag and Motion in Fluids

Have you ever walked into a strong wind and noticed that the wind seemed to slow you down? It may have felt like the wind was pushing you backward. Fluids exert a force that opposes the motion of objects moving through the fluids. The force that opposes or restricts motion in a fluid is called **drag.**

In a strong wind, air "drags" on your body and makes it difficult for you to move forward. Drag also works against the forward motion of a plane or bird in flight. Drag is usually caused by an irregular flow of air. An irregular or unpredictable flow of fluids is known as *turbulence.*

Reading Check What is turbulence?

drag a force parallel to the velocity of the flow; it opposes the direction of an aircraft and, in combination with thrust, determines the speed of the aircraft

SCIENTISTS AT ODDS

Traveling Faster Than Sound In the 1940s, pilots of high-speed airplanes reported that as they approached the speed of sound (343 m/s at 20°C), their planes began to shake and the controls did not function properly. At these speeds, shock waves formed a cone of turbulence around the plane, interrupting the airflow over the wings. Some scientists thought that an airplane could not go faster than the speed of sound because the turbulence from shock waves would tear the wings apart. Other scientists thought that with better designs, planes could exceed this speed. Jet planes with swept-back wings and stronger frames eventually exceeded the speed of sound.

Reteaching — BASIC

Seeing Turbulence Give pairs of students a shallow pan of water and an index card. Tell students to slowly drag the index card through the water and to watch the water behind the card. Tell students that the ripples behind the card and the swirls that come off the edge of the card are examples of turbulence. **LS** Visual

Quiz — GENERAL

1. What forces act on an aircraft? (lift, thrust, drag, and gravity)

2. When an airplane is flying, how does the air pressure above a wing compare with that below the wing? (Air pressure above the wing is lower.)

3. How is thrust related to the speed of an airplane? (The speed of an airplane increases as its thrust increases.)

Alternative Assessment — GENERAL

Aircraft Chart Display two or three photographs or models of different types of aircraft, such as a glider, a jet, a biplane, or even an airship. Ask students to select two of the aircraft and to make a chart that compares and contrasts the aircraft in terms of lift, drag, thrust, and gravity. **LS** Verbal

Figure 5 *The pilot of this airplane can adjust these flaps to help increase lift when the airplane lands or takes off.*

Turbulence and Lift

Lift is often reduced when turbulence causes drag. Drag can be a serious problem for airplanes moving at high speeds. So, airplanes are equipped with ways to reduce turbulence as much as possible when in flight. For example, flaps like those shown in **Figure 5** can be used to change the shape or area of a wing. This change can reduce drag and increase lift. Similarly, birds can adjust their wing feathers in response to turbulence.

✓ **Reading Check** How do airplanes reduce turbulence?

Pascal's Principle

Imagine that the water-pumping station in your town increases the water pressure by 20 Pa. Will the water pressure be increased more at a store two blocks away or at a home 2 km away?

Believe it or not, the increase in water pressure will be the same at both locations. This equal change in water pressure is explained by Pascal's principle. **Pascal's principle** states that a change in pressure at any point in an enclosed fluid will be transmitted equally to all parts of that fluid. This principle was discovered by the 17th-century French scientist Blaise Pascal.

Pascal's principle the principle that states that a fluid in equilibrium contained in a vessel exerts a pressure of equal intensity in all directions

Pascal's Principle and Motion

Hydraulic (hie DRAW lik) devices use Pascal's principle to move or lift objects. Liquids are used in hydraulic devices because liquids cannot be easily compressed, or squeezed, into a smaller space. Cranes, forklifts, and bulldozers have hydraulic devices that help them lift heavy objects.

Hydraulic devices can multiply forces. Car brakes are a good example. In **Figure 6,** a driver's foot exerts pressure on a cylinder of liquid. This pressure is transmitted to all parts of the liquid-filled brake system. The liquid moves the brake pads. The pads press against the wheels, and friction stops the car. The force is multiplied because the pistons that push the brake pads are larger than the piston that is pushed by the brake pedal.

Answer to Reading Check
Airplanes can reduce turbulence by changing the shape or area of the wings.

Figure 6 *Because of Pascal's principle, the touch of a foot can stop tons of moving metal.*

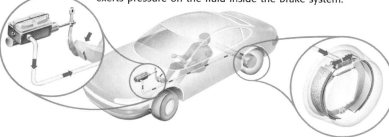

❶ When the driver pushes the brake pedal, a small piston exerts pressure on the fluid inside the brake system.

❷ The change in pressure is transmitted to the large pistons that push on the brake pads.

SECTION Review

Summary

● Bernoulli's principle states that fluid pressure decreases as the speed of the fluid increases.

● Wing shape allows airplanes to take advantage of Bernoulli's principle to achieve flight.

● Lift on an airplane is determined by wing size and thrust.

● Drag opposes motion through fluids.

● Pascal's principle states that a change in pressure in an enclosed fluid is transmitted equally to all parts of the fluid.

Using Key Terms

For each pair of terms, explain how the meanings of the terms differ.

1. *Bernoulli's principle* and *Pascal's principle*

2. *thrust* and *drag*

Understanding Key Ideas

3. The shape of an airplane's wing helps it gain
   a. drag.   c. thrust.
   b. lift.   d. turbulence.

4. What is the relationship between pressure and fluid speed?

5. What is Pascal's principle?

6. What force opposes motion through a fluid? How does this force affect lift?

7. How do thrust and lift help an airplane achieve flight?

Critical Thinking

8. **Applying Concepts** Air moving around a speeding race car can create lift. Upside-down wings, or spoilers, are mounted on the rear of race cars. Use Bernoulli's principle to explain how spoilers reduce the danger of accidents.

9. **Making Inferences** When you squeeze a balloon, where is the pressure inside the balloon increased the most? Explain.

Interpreting Graphics

10. Look at the image below. When the space through which a fluid flows becomes narrow, fluid speed increases. Using this information, explain how the two boats could collide.

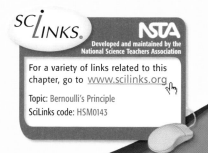

For a variety of links related to this chapter, go to www.scilinks.org

Topic: Bernoulli's Principle
SciLinks code: HSM0143

CHAPTER RESOURCES

Chapter Resource File

- **Section Quiz** GENERAL
- **Section Review** GENERAL
- **Vocabulary and Section Summary** GENERAL
- **Reinforcement Worksheet** BASIC
- **Critical Thinking** ADVANCED

Answers to Section Review

1. Bernoulli's principle states that the pressure in a fluid decreases as the fluid's velocity increases. Pascal's principle states that a fluid in an enclosed container exerts pressure equally in all directions.

2. Thrust is the pushing or pulling force exerted by the engine of an airplane that moves the airplane forward. Drag is a force that opposes motion in a fluid.

3. b

4. As fluid speed increases, the pressure exerted by the fluid decreases.

5. Pascal's principle states that an enclosed fluid exerts pressure equally in all directions.

6. Drag is a force that opposes motion through a fluid. Lift is often reduced when turbulence causes drag.

7. Lift helps an airplane achieve flight by pushing the airplane up. Thrust helps an airplane achieve flight by causing the airplane to move faster through the air. The faster speed means that air travels faster around the wings, which increases lift.

8. Sample answer: Air traveling around the spoiler produces a downward force. This downward force pushes down on the rear of the car and helps keep the rear wheels of the cars in contact with the road. The cars travel more safely because the rear wheels stay in contact with the road.

9. The pressure inside the balloon increases equally in all directions. Squeezing a balloon demonstrates Pascal's principle.

10. As the fluid speed between the boats increases, the fluid pressure decreases. The pressure on the outer sides of the boats then becomes greater than the pressure between them. This increased pressure from the outside can push the boats together, causing them to collide.

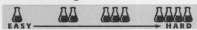
Fluids, Force, and Floating

Teacher's Notes

Time Required

One to two 45-minute class periods

Lab Ratings

🧪 —— 🧪🧪 🧪🧪🧪 🧪🧪🧪🧪
EASY —————————→ HARD

Teacher Prep 🧪
Student Set-Up 🧪🧪
Concept Level 🧪🧪🧪
Clean Up 🧪

MATERIALS

The supplies listed are for one group of 3–4 students. The tank or tub should have vertical sides. A small or medium-sized tub works best because changes in volume can be observed easily. Masses should be added near the center of the baking pan. A fish tank or aquarium works well for this activity.

Preparation Notes

If you use a tub or pan without vertical sides, the buoyant force and the weight of the pan and masses will not be equal. In most cases, the buoyant force will be greater than the weight. Have students measure the side of the baking pan and mark the one-quarter, one-half, and three-quarter levels.

Lab Notes

Volumes of liquids are usually expressed in milliliters (mL). Here, the volume measurements for the water displaced are based on a rectangular container (the tank or tub), so cubic centimeters (cm³) are used.

Skills Practice Lab

OBJECTIVES

Calculate the buoyant force on an object.

Compare the buoyant force on an object with its weight.

MATERIALS

- balance
- mass set
- pan, rectangular baking
- paper towels
- ruler, metric
- tub, plastic, large rectangular
- water

SAFETY

Fluids, Force, and Floating

Why do some objects sink in fluids but others float? In this lab, you'll get a sinking feeling as you determine that an object floats when its weight equals the buoyant force exerted by the surrounding fluid.

Procedure

① Copy the table shown below.

Measurement	Trial 1	Trial 2
Length (l), cm		
Width (w), cm		
Initial height (h_1), cm		
Initial volume (V_1), cm³ $V_1 = l \times w \times h_1$		
New height (h_2), cm		
New total volume (V_2), cm³ $V_2 = l \times w \times h_2$		
Displaced volume (ΔV), cm³ $\Delta V = V_2 - V_1$		
Mass of displaced water, g $m = \Delta V \times 1\ \text{g/cm}^3$		
Weight of displaced water, N (buoyant force)		
Weight of pan and masses, N		

DO NOT WRITE IN BOOK

② Fill the tub half full with water. Measure (in centimeters) the length, width, and initial height of the water. Record your measurements in the table.

③ Using the equation given in the table, determine the initial volume of water in the tub. Record your results in the table.

④ Place the pan in the water, and place masses in the pan, as shown on the next page. Keep adding masses until the pan sinks to about three-quarters of its height. Record the new height of the water in the table. Then, use this value to determine and record the new total volume of water plus the volume of water displaced by the pan.

CHAPTER RESOURCES

Chapter Resource File

 • **Datasheet for Chapter Lab**
• **Lab Notes and Answers**

Technology

 Classroom Videos
• Lab Video

LabBook

• Density Diver

5. Determine the volume of the water that was displaced by the pan and masses, and record this value in the table. The displaced volume is equal to the new total volume minus the initial volume.

6. Determine the mass of the displaced water by multiplying the displaced volume by its density (1 g/cm^3). Record the mass in the table.

7. Divide the mass by 100. The value you get is the weight of the displaced water in newtons (N). This is equal to the buoyant force. Record the weight of the displaced water in the table.

8. Remove the pan and masses, and determine their total mass (in grams) using the balance. Convert the mass to weight (N), as you did in step 7. Record the weight of the masses and pan in the table.

9. Place the empty pan back in the tub. Perform a second trial by repeating steps 4–8. This time, add masses until the pan is just about to sink.

Analyze the Results

1. **Identifying Patterns** Compare the buoyant force (the weight of the displaced water) with the weight of the pan and masses for both trials.

2. **Examining Data** How did the buoyant force differ between the two trials? Explain.

Draw Conclusions

3. **Drawing Conclusions** Based on your observations, what would happen if you were to add even more mass to the pan than you did in the second trial? Explain your answer in terms of the buoyant force.

4. **Making Predictions** What would happen if you put the masses in the water without the pan? What difference does the pan's shape make?

Analyze the Results

1. In each trial, the buoyant force and the weight should be the same.

2. The buoyant force is larger in the second trial because more water is displaced.

Draw Conclusions

3. The pan would sink because its weight would be greater but the buoyant force (the weight of the water displaced) would be about the same.

4. The masses would sink. The shape of the pan allows the masses to displace more water than the masses alone displace.

CLASSROOM TESTED & APPROVED

Sharon L. Woolf
Langston Hughes Middle School
Reston, Virginia

Chapter Review

Assignment Guide

Section	Questions
1	1, 3, 7, 11–15, 20–21
2	5, 8–10, 18, 22–24
3	2, 4, 6, 17, 19
1 and 2	16

ANSWERS

Using Key Terms

1. replace *lift* with *pressure*
2. replace *drag* with *thrust*
3. replace *pascal* with *fluid*
4. replace *Archimedes' principle* with *Pascal's principle*
5. replace *Atmospheric pressure* with *Buoyant force*

Understanding Key Ideas

6. d
7. d
8. a
9. d
10. b
11. c

USING KEY TERMS

In each of the following sentences, replace the incorrect term with the correct term from the word bank.

thrust pressure
drag lift
buoyant force fluid
Pascal's principle
Bernoulli's principle

1. Lift increases with the depth of a fluid.

2. A plane's engines produce drag to push the plane forward.

3. A pascal can be a liquid or a gas.

4. A hydraulic device uses Archimedes' principle to lift or move objects.

5. Atmospheric pressure is the upward force exerted on objects by fluids.

UNDERSTANDING KEY IDEAS

Multiple Choice

6. The design of a wing
   a. causes the air above the wing to travel faster than the air below the wing.
   b. helps create lift.
   c. creates a low-pressure zone above the wing.
   d. All of the above

7. Fluid pressure is always directed
   a. up.   c. sideways.
   b. down.   d. in all directions.

8. An object surrounded by a fluid will displace a volume of fluid that is
   a. equal to its own volume.
   b. less than its own volume.
   c. greater than its own volume.
   d. denser than itself.

9. If an object weighing 50 N displaces a volume of water that weighs 10 N, what is the buoyant force on the object?
   a. 60 N   c. 40 N
   b. 50 N   d. 10 N

10. A helium-filled balloon will float in air because
    a. there is more air than helium.
    b. helium is less dense than air.
    c. helium is as dense as air.
    d. helium is more dense than air.

11. Materials that can flow to fit their containers include
    a. gases.
    b. liquids.
    c. both gases and liquids.
    d. gases, liquids, and solids.

Short Answer

12 Where is water pressure greater, at a depth of 1 m in a large lake or at a depth of 2 m in a small pond? Explain your answer.

13 Why are bubbles round?

14 Why are tornadoes like giant vacuum cleaners?

Math Skills

15 Calculate the area of a 1,500 N object that exerts a pressure of 500 Pa (500 N/m²). Then, calculate the pressure exerted by the same object over twice that area.

CRITICAL THINKING

16 **Concept Mapping** Use the following terms to create a concept map: *fluid, pressure, depth, density,* and *buoyant force.*

17 **Forming Hypotheses** Gases can be easily compressed into smaller spaces. Why would this property of gases make gases less useful than liquids in hydraulic brakes?

18 **Making Comparisons** Will a ship loaded with beach balls float higher or lower in the water than an empty ship? Explain your reasoning.

19 **Applying Concepts** Inside all vacuum cleaners is a high-speed fan. Explain how this fan causes the vacuum cleaner to pick up dirt.

20 **Evaluating Hypotheses** A 600 N girl on stilts says to two 600 N boys sitting on the ground, "I am exerting over twice as much pressure as the two of you are exerting together!" Could this statement be true? Explain your reasoning.

INTERPRETING GRAPHICS

Use the diagram of an iceberg below to answer the questions that follow.

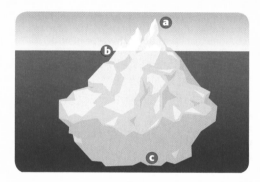

21 At what point (a, b, or c) is water pressure greatest on the iceberg?

22 How much of the iceberg has a weight equal to the buoyant force?
   a. all of it
   b. the section from a to b
   c. the section from b to c
   d. None of the above

23 How does the density of ice compare with the density of water?

24 Why do you think icebergs are dangerous to passing ships?

CHAPTER RESOURCES

Chapter Resource File

- Chapter Review **GENERAL**
- Chapter Test A **GENERAL**
- Chapter Test B **ADVANCED**
- Chapter Test C **SPECIAL NEEDS**
- Vocabulary Activity **GENERAL**

Workbooks

 Study Guide
- Assessment resources are also available in Spanish.

Teacher's Note

To provide practice under more realistic testing conditions, give students 20 minutes to answer all of the questions in this Standardized Test Preparation.

MISCONCEPTION ///ALERT

Answers to the standardized test preparation can help you identify student misconceptions and misunderstandings.

READING

Passage 1

1. C
2. I
3. B

 **TEST DOCTOR**

Question 1: Although "overthrowing the government" is a meaning of the word *revolutionary*, it is not the correct meaning of the word in the passage. There is no mention of government in the passage. "Radically different" is also a meaning of the word *revolutionary* and is the correct answer.

READING

Read each of the passages below. Then, answer the questions that follow each passage.

Passage 1 The Mariana Trench is about 11 km deep—that's deep enough to swallow Mount Everest, the tallest mountain in the world. Fewer than a dozen undersea vessels have ever ventured this deep into the ocean. Why? Water exerts tremendous pressure at this depth. A <u>revolutionary</u> new undersea vessel, *Deep Flight,* has a hull made of an extremely strong ceramic material that can withstand such pressure. Although *Deep Flight* has not made it to the bottom of the Mariana Trench, some scientists think this type of undersea vessel will one day be used routinely to explore the ocean floor.

1. What is the meaning of the word *revolutionary* in this passage?
   - **A** strange
   - **B** overthrowing the government
   - **C** radically different
   - **D** disgusting

2. Based on the name of the undersea vessel described in this passage, what does the vessel look like?
   - **F** a robot
   - **G** a house
   - **H** a car
   - **I** an airplane

3. Based on the passage, which of the following statements is a fact?
   - **A** Scientists hope to fly *Deep Flight* to the top of Mount Everest.
   - **B** *Deep Flight* can withstand very high pressures.
   - **C** Scientists cannot explore the ocean without using *Deep Flight.*
   - **D** *Deep Flight* has gone to the bottom of the Mariana Trench a dozen times.

Passage 2 Buoyancy is an object's ability to float. An object will float if the water it displaces has a mass greater than the object's mass. It will sink if the water it displaces has a mass less than its own mass. But if an object displaces its own mass in water, it will neither float nor sink. Instead, it will remain <u>suspended</u> in the water because of what is called *neutral buoyancy.*

A goldfish has neutral buoyancy. A goldfish has a sac in its body called a *swim bladder.* Gases from blood vessels can diffuse into and out of the swim bladder. When the goldfish needs to rise in the water, for example, gases diffuse into the swim bladder and cause it to inflate. The swim bladder helps the goldfish maintain neutral buoyancy.

1. What is the purpose of this passage?
   - **A** to explain how a goldfish maintains neutral buoyancy
   - **B** to explain how to change the buoyancy of an object
   - **C** to convince people to buy goldfish
   - **D** to describe objects that float and sink

2. What is the meaning of the word *suspended* in this passage?
   - **F** not allowed to attend school
   - **G** stopped for a period of time
   - **H** weighed down
   - **I** supported from sinking

3. What is buoyancy?
   - **A** a sac in a goldfish's body
   - **B** the ability to float
   - **C** the mass of an object
   - **D** an inflated balloon

Passage 2

1. A
2. I
3. B

 **TEST DOCTOR**

Question 2: Answer choices F, G, and I are all correct meanings of the word *suspended.* However, both answer choices F and G can be eliminated because the passage does not discuss school attendance or mention stopping any activity for a period of time. The passage does discuss sinking and floating, and I is the correct answer.

The graph below shows the water pressure measured by a scientist at different depths in the ocean. Use the graph below to answer the questions that follow.

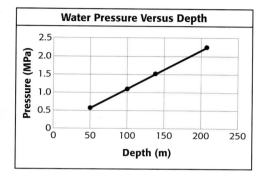

Water Pressure Versus Depth

1. What is the pressure on the object when it is 100 m underwater?

A 1.0 MPa
B 1.1 MPa
C 1.5 MPa
D 2.0 MPa

2. Based on the data in the graph, which of the following is the best estimate of the pressure at 250 m below the surface of the ocean?

F 1.7 MPa
G 2.2 MPa
H 2.6 MPa
I 5.0 MPa

3. Which of the following statements best describes the relationship between the water pressure on an object and the depth of the object in the ocean?

A Water pressure increases as the depth increases.
B Water pressure decreases as the depth increases.
C Water pressure does not change as the depth increases.
D Water pressure has no predictable relationship to the depth.

Read each question below, and choose the best answer.

1. Anna-Marie has a coil of wire. She uses a balance to find that the wire has a mass of 17.8 g. She uses water displacement to find that the volume of the wire is 2.0 cm³. Density is equal to mass divided by volume. What is the density of the wire?

A 0.11 g/cm³
B 8.9 g/cm³
C 19.8 g/cm³
D 35.6 g/cm³

2. Hussain rode his bike 30 km this weekend. What is this distance expressed in meters?

F 0.3 m
G 300 m
H 30,000 m
I 300,000 m

3. Olivia purchased 21 tubes of oil paint at $3.95 per tube, which includes tax. What was the total cost of the 21 tubes of paint?

A $65.15
B $82.95
C $89.10
D $93.50

4. Javi filled a container halfway full with water. The container measures 2 m wide, 3 m long, and 1 m high. How many cubic meters of water are in the container?

F 2 m³
G 3 m³
H 5 m³
I 6 m³

5. Pressure is equal to force divided by area. Jenny pushes a door with a force of 12 N. The area of her hand is 96 cm². What is the pressure exerted by Jenny's hand on the door?

A 0.125 N/cm
B 0.125 N/cm²
C 8 N/cm
D 8 N/cm²

Standardized Test Preparation

1. B
2. H
3. A

TEST DOCTOR

Question 2: To answer this question, students must extrapolate (or imagine) that the line in the graph continues up and to the right. Students should determine that the extrapolated line will cross the 250 m point somewhere just above 2.5 MPa. The only answer choice that is above and close to 2.5 MPa is H.

1. B
2. H
3. B
4. G
5. B

TEST DOCTOR

Question 4: Students may be tempted to multiply the dimensions of the container to find the total volume of the container. However, the problem clearly states that the container is only halfway full with water. Therefore, students must multiply 2 m, 3 m, and 0.5 m to find the number of cubic meters in the container. The correct choice is G.

CHAPTER RESOURCES

Chapter Resource File

 • Standardized Test Preparation **GENERAL**

Workbooks

North Carolina Standardized Test Preparation
• Provides practice for the EOG test.

State Resources

 For specific resources for your state, visit **go.hrw.com** and type in the keyword **HSMSTR**.

Science in Action

Science, Technology, and Society

Teaching Strategy—GENERAL

Go to an open area with your students. Have students throw a Frisbee® with different amounts of thrust, or have them vary the angle of attack when they throw their disk. Discuss Bernoulli's principle and other aspects of lift. Have students attempt to throw a Frisbee without any spin (eliminating the angular momentum that gives the disk stability in flight). Compare a spinning Frisbee with a spinning top or a moving bicycle.

Science Fiction

Background

Sports and science fiction may seem like an unlikely combination, but Jack C. Haldeman II enjoys both. He has written science fiction stories, sports stories, and stories such as "Wet Behind the Ears," which is a bit of both! Before becoming a writer, Haldeman received a college degree in life science and worked as a research assistant, a medical technician, a statistician, a photographer, and an apprentice in a print shop.

Science in Action

Science, Technology, and Society

Stayin' Aloft—The Story of the Frisbee®

In the late 1800s, a few fun-loving college students invented a game that involved tossing an empty tin pie plate. The pie plate was stamped with the name of a bakery: Frisbie's Pies. So, the game of Frisbie was created. Unfortunately, the metal pie plates tended to develop sharp edges that caused injuries. In 1947, plastic disks were made to replace the metal pie plates. These plastic disks were called Frisbees. How do Frisbees stay in the air? When you throw a Frisbee, you give it thrust. And as it moves through the air, lift is created because of Bernoulli's principle. But you don't have to think about the science behind Frisbees to have fun with them!

Math ACTIVITY

A Frisbee landed 10 m away from where it is thrown. The Frisbee was in the air for 2.5 s. What was the average speed of the Frisbee?

Science Fiction

"Wet Behind the Ears" by Jack C. Haldeman II

Willie Joe Thomas cheated to get a swimming scholarship. Now, he is faced with a major swim meet, and his coach told him that he has to swim or be kicked off the team. Willie Joe could lose his scholarship.

One day, Willie Joe's roommate, Frank, announces that he has developed a new "sliding compound." And Frank also said something about using the compound to make ships go faster. So, Willie Joe thought, if it works for ships, it might work for swimming.

See what happens when Willie Joe tries to save his scholarship by using Frank's compound at the swim meet. Read "Wet Behind the Ears," by Jack C. Haldeman II in the *Holt Anthology of Science Fiction*.

Language Arts ACTIVITY

Analyze the story structure of "Wet Behind the Ears." In your analysis, identify the introduction, the rising action, the climax, and the denouement. Summarize your analysis in a chart.

Answer to Math Activity

The equation for average speed is:

average speed = distance ÷ time

average speed = 10 m ÷ 2.5 s = 4 m/s

Answer to Language Arts Activity

Accept all reasonable answers. Students should make a chart that analyzes the story structure of "Wet Behind the Ears." The first column of their chart should list the parts of the story (introduction, rising action, climax, and denouement). The second column should have a brief summary of what occurred in each part of the story.

Alisha Bracken

Scuba Instructor Alisha Bracken first started scuba diving in her freshman year of college. Her first dives were in a saltwater hot spring near Salt Lake City, Utah. "It was awesome," Bracken says. "There were nurse sharks, angelfish, puffer fish and brine shrimp!" Bracken enjoyed her experience so much that she wanted to share it with other people. The best way to do that was to become an instructor and teach other people to dive.

Bracken says one of the biggest challenges of being a scuba instructor is teaching people to adapt and function in a foreign environment. She believes that learning to dive properly is important not only for the safety of the diver but also for the protection of the underwater environment. She relies on science principles to help teach people how to control their movements and protect the natural environment. "Buoyancy is the foundation of teaching people to dive comfortably," she explains. "Without it, we cannot float on the surface or stay off the bottom. Underwater life can be damaged if students do not learn and apply the concepts of buoyancy."

Social Studies ACTIVITY

Scuba divers and other underwater explorers sometimes investigate shipwrecks on the bottom of the ocean. Research the exploration of a specific shipwreck. Make a poster showing what artifacts were retrieved from the shipwreck and what was learned from the exploration.

go.hrw.com
To learn more about these Science in Action topics, visit go.hrw.com and type in the keyword **HP5FLUF**.

Current Science
Check out Current Science® articles related to this chapter by visiting go.hrw.com. Just type in the keyword **HP5CS07**.

Background

The word *scuba* is an acronym that stands for *self-contained underwater breathing apparatus*. The first scuba breathing device, known as the aqualung, was invented by Jacques Cousteau and Emile Gagnan in 1943. This invention allowed divers to move freely underwater for long periods of time.

Scuba diving has become a popular form of recreation, with about one million people becoming certified divers every year. To rent scuba equipment, divers must be certified by an organization such as the Professional Association of Diving Instructors (PADI) or the National Association of Underwater Instructors (NAUI). Some organizations certify divers as young as 10 years old, while other groups have an age requirement of 12 years. In order to receive a certification, divers must take an open water diving course, which can last from three days to six weeks.

Answer to Social Studies Activity
Accept all reasonable answers. All students' posters should identify a shipwreck, list or show some of the artifacts collected from the shipwreck, and summarize what was learned by the exploration of the shipwreck.

Compression guide:
To shorten instruction because of time limitations, omit Section 3.

OBJECTIVES	LABS, DEMONSTRATIONS, AND ACTIVITIES	TECHNOLOGY RESOURCES
PACING • 90 min pp. 550–557 **Chapter Opener**	SE **Start-up Activity,** p. 551 GENERAL	OSP **Parent Letter** GENERAL CD **Student Edition on CD-ROM** CD **Guided Reading Audio CD** TR **Chapter Starter Transparency*** VID **Brain Food Video Quiz**
Section 1 Work and Power • Determine when work is being done on an object. • Calculate the amount of work done on an object. • Explain the difference between work and power.	TE **Activity** Work in Sports, p. 552 GENERAL TE **Activity** Work Done on a Spring Scale, p. 554 GENERAL SE **Quick Lab** Get to Work!, p. 555 ◆ GENERAL CRF **Datasheet for Quick Lab*** SE **Skills Practice Lab** A Powerful Workout, p. 572 GENERAL CRF **Datasheet for Chapter Lab*** LB **Inquiry Lab** Get an Arm and an Egg Up* ADVANCED SE **Science in Action** Math, Social Studies, and Language Arts Activities, pp. 578–579 GENERAL	CRF **Lesson Plans*** TR **Bellringer Transparency*** TR Work or Not Work?* TR Force Times Distance* TR *LINK TO LIFE SCIENCE* A Pair of Muscles in the Arm* CRF **SciLinks Activity*** GENERAL VID **Lab Videos for Physical Science**
PACING • 45 min pp. 558–563 **Section 2 What Is a Machine?** • Explain how a machine makes work easier. • Describe and give examples of the force-distance trade-off that occurs when a machine is used. • Calculate mechanical advantage. • Explain why machines are not 100% efficient.	TE **Connection Activity** Home Economics, p. 558 GENERAL TE **Activity** Machines as Solutions to Problems, p. 560 ADVANCED TE **Connection Activity** Graphing, p. 560 GENERAL TE **Connection Activity** Life Science, p. 561 GENERAL TE **Connection Activity** History, p. 561 GENERAL SE **School-to-Home Activity** Useful Friction, p. 562 GENERAL LB **Whiz-Bang Demonstrations** Pull-Ease, Please!* BASIC LB **Whiz-Bang Demonstrations** A Clever Lever* BASIC	CRF **Lesson Plans*** TR **Bellringer Transparency*** TR Input Force and Distance* TR Machines Change the Size and/or Direction of a Force* SE **Internet Activity,** p. 560 GENERAL
PACING • 45 min pp. 564–571 **Section 3 Types of Machines** • Identify and give examples of the six types of simple machines. • Analyze the mechanical advantage provided by each simple machine. • Identify the simple machines that make up a compound machine.	TE **Activity** Loads on a First-Class Level, p. 564 GENERAL TE **Activity** Classifying Tools, p. 565 GENERAL TE **Connection Activity** Real World, p. 566 GENERAL TE **Activity** Wheels and Axles, p. 567 BASIC TE **Activity** Gears, p. 567 ADVANCED TE **Activity** Zippers, p. 569 GENERAL TE **Activity** Screws, p. 569 BASIC TE **Connection Activity** Math, p. 569 GENERAL SE **School-to-Home Activity** Everyday Machines, p. 570 GENERAL SE **Skills Practice Lab** Inclined to Move, p. 618 GENERAL SE **Skills Practice Lab** Wheeling and Dealing, p. 619 ADVANCED SE **Inquiry Lab** Building Machines, p. 621 BASIC LB **Long-Term Projects & Research Ideas** To Complicate Things* ADVANCED CRF **Datasheet for LabBook***	CRF **Lesson Plans*** TR **Bellringer Transparency***

PACING • 90 min

CHAPTER REVIEW, ASSESSMENT, AND STANDARDIZED TEST PREPARATION

CRF **Vocabulary Activity*** GENERAL
SE **Chapter Review,** pp. 574–575 GENERAL
CRF **Chapter Review*** ■ GENERAL
CRF **Chapter Tests A*** ■ GENERAL, **B*** ADVANCED, **C*** SPECIAL NEEDS
SE **Standardized Test Preparation,** pp. 576–577 GENERAL
CRF **Standardized Test Preparation*** GENERAL
CRF **Performance-Based Assessment*** GENERAL
OSP **Test Generator** GENERAL
CRF **Test Item Listing*** GENERAL

Online and Technology Resources

Visit **go.hrw.com** for a variety of free resources related to this textbook. Enter the keyword **HT5R7WRK.**

Students can access interactive problem-solving help and active visual concept development with the *Holt Science and Technology* Online Edition available at **www.hrw.com.**

 Guided Reading Audio CD

These CDs are designed to help auditory learners and reluctant readers.

 Science Tutor CD-ROM

Excellent for remediation and test practice.

SKILLS DEVELOPMENT RESOURCES	SECTION REVIEW AND ASSESSMENT	STANDARDS CORRELATIONS
SE Pre-Reading Activity, p. 550 GENERAL **OSP** Science Puzzlers, Twisters & Teasers GENERAL		North Carolina Standard Course of Study 6.01
CRF Directed Reading A* BASIC, B* SPECIAL NEEDS **CRF** Vocabulary and Section Summary* GENERAL **SE** Reading Strategy Reading Organizer, p. 552 GENERAL **TE** Reading Strategy Prediction Guide, p. 553 GENERAL **TE** Inclusion Strategies, p. 554 **SE** Math Focus More Power to You, p. 556 GENERAL **MS** Math Skills for Science Work and Power* GENERAL	**SE** Reading Checks, pp. 552, 555, 556 GENERAL **TE** Reteaching, p. 556 BASIC **TE** Quiz, p. 556 GENERAL **TE** Alternative Assessment, p. 556 GENERAL **SE** Section Review,* p. 557 ■ GENERAL **CRF** Section Quiz* ■ GENERAL	1.05; *Chapter Lab:* 1.01, 1.06
CRF Directed Reading A* BASIC, B* SPECIAL NEEDS **CRF** Vocabulary and Section Summary* GENERAL **SE** Reading Strategy Prediction Guide, p. 558 GENERAL **TE** Reading Strategy Concept Mapping, p. 559 BASIC **SE** Math Practice Finding the Advantage, p. 561 GENERAL **MS** Math Skills for Science Mechanical Advantage* GENERAL	**SE** Reading Checks, pp. 559, 560, 562 GENERAL **TE** Homework, p. 560 GENERAL **TE** Homework, p. 561 GENERAL **TE** Reteaching, p. 562 BASIC **TE** Quiz, p. 562 GENERAL **TE** Alternative Assessment, p. 562 GENERAL **SE** Section Review,* p. 563 GENERAL **CRF** Section Quiz* ■ GENERAL	6.01, 6.02
CRF Directed Reading A* BASIC, B* SPECIAL NEEDS **CRF** Vocabulary and Section Summary* GENERAL **SE** Reading Strategy Mnemonics, p. 564 GENERAL **TE** Inclusion Strategies, p. 567 **SE** Math Focus Mechanical Advantage of an Inclined Plane, p. 568 GENERAL **CRF** Reinforcement Worksheet Finding Machines in Everyday Life* BASIC **CRF** Reinforcement Worksheet Mechanical Advantage and Efficiency* BASIC **CRF** Critical Thinking Building Works of Art* ADVANCED	**SE** Reading Checks, pp. 565, 567, 568, 570 GENERAL **TE** Reteaching, p. 570 BASIC **TE** Quiz, p. 570 GENERAL **TE** Alternative Assessment, p. 570 GENERAL **SE** Section Review,* p. 571 ■ GENERAL **CRF** Section Quiz* ■ GENERAL	6.01, 6.02; *LabBook:* 1.01, 1.04, 1.06, 2.03, 6.02

One-Stop Planner® CD-ROM

This convenient CD-ROM includes:
• Lab Materials QuickList Software
• Holt Calendar Planner
• Customizable Lesson Plans
• Printable Worksheets
• ExamView® Test Generator

cnnstudentnews.com

Find the latest news, lesson plans, and activities related to important scientific events.

www.scilinks.org

Maintained by the **National Science Teachers Association.** See Chapter Enrichment pages for a complete list of topics.

Current Science®

Check out *Current Science* articles and activities by visiting the HRW Web site at **go.hrw.com.** Just type in the keyword **HP5CS08T.**

 Classroom Videos

• **Lab Videos** demonstrate the chapter lab.
• **Brain Food Video Quizzes** help students review the chapter material.
• **CNN Videos** bring science into your students' daily life.

Visual Resources

CHAPTER STARTER TRANSPARENCY

Work and Machines — CHAPTER STARTER

Would You Believe . . . ?

The Great Pyramid, located in Giza (GEE zuh), Egypt, could be called the largest tombstone ever created. A monument and tomb for the pharaoh King Khufu (KOO foo), it covers an area the size of seven city blocks and rises about 40 stories high. The Great Pyramid is the largest of the three pyramids of Giza. It was built around 2600 BCE and took less than 30 years to complete—a relatively short period of time considering that construction equipment didn't exist 4,000 years ago. So how did the Egyptians do it?

To build the Great Pyramid, the Egyptians cut and moved more than 2 million stone blocks, most averaging 2,000 kg (probably over 40 times your own mass). The blocks were cut from a stone quarry, moved near the pyramid, and then lifted into place. To finish in less than 30 years, the Egyptians would

have had to cut, move, and lift about 200 blocks per day! The Egyptians did not have cranes, bulldozers, or any other heavy-duty machines. What they had were two simple machines—the inclined plane and the lever.

Archaeologists have found the remains of inclined planes, or ramps, made from mud, stone, and wood. The Egyptians pushed or pulled the blocks along these ramps to raise them to the proper height. Using ramps required less force than lifting the blocks straight up. In addition, notches in many blocks indicate that huge levers were used like giant crowbars to lift and move the heavy blocks. The workers pushed down on the lever, and the lever pushed up a stone block, lifting it into place.

The Egyptians used simple machines to create something truly amazing. In this chapter, you'll learn about work and how machines can help make work easier.

The Great Pyramid was built over 4,000 years ago and remains one of the Seven Wonders of the World.

BELLRINGER TRANSPARENCIES

Work and Machines — BELLRINGER TRANSPARENCY

Section: Work and Power

First, in your **science journal,** define what specific kind of work is being done in each activity below. Then, select the activities that require the least amount of work.

- carrying heavy books home
- reading a 300-page novel
- skiing for 1 hour
- lifting a 45 kg mass
- holding a steel beam in place for 3 hours
- jacking up a car

Section: What Is a Machine?

Write a one-paragraph answer in your **science journal** to the following question:

Why do we use machines?

TEACHING TRANSPARENCIES

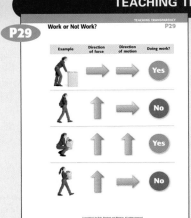

P29 — Work or Not Work?

TEACHING TRANSPARENCY — P29

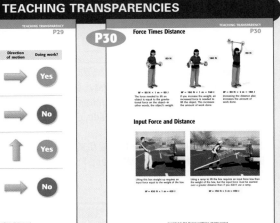

P30 — Force Times Distance

TEACHING TRANSPARENCY — P30

Input Force and Distance

TEACHING TRANSPARENCIES

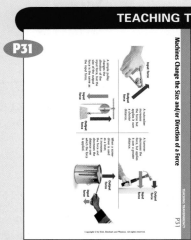

P31 — Machines Change the Size and/or Direction of a Force

TEACHING TRANSPARENCY — P31

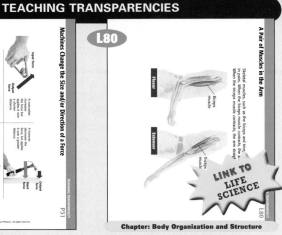

L80 — A Pair of Muscles in the Arm

LINK TO LIFE SCIENCE

Chapter: Body Organization and Structure

CONCEPT MAPPING TRANSPARENCY

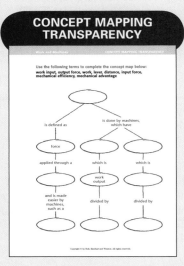

Work and Machines — CONCEPT MAPPING TRANSPARENCY

Use the following terms to complete the concept map below:

work input, output force, work, lever, distance, input force, mechanical efficiency, mechanical advantage

Planning Resources

LESSON PLANS

Lesson Plan — SAMPLE

Section: Waves

Pacing

Regular Schedule: with lab(s):2 days   without lab(s):2 days
Block Schedule: with lab(s):1 1/2 days   without lab(s):1 day

Objectives

1. Relate the seven properties of life to a living organism.
2. Describe seven themes that can help you to organize what you learn about biology.
3. Identify the tiny structures that make up all living organisms.
4. Differentiate between reproduction and heredity and between metabolism and homeostasis.

National Science Education Standards Covered

LSInter6:Cells have particular structures that underlie their functions.
LSMat1:Most cell functions involve chemical reactions.
LSBeh1:Cells store and use information to guide their functions.
UCP1:Cell functions are regulated.
SI1: Cells can differentiate and form complete multicellular organisms.
PS1: Species evolve over time.
ESS1: The great diversity of organisms is the result of more than 3.5 billion years of evolution.
ESS2: Natural selection and its evolutionary consequences provide a scientific explanation for the fossil record of ancient life forms as well as for the striking molecular similarities observed among the diverse species of living organisms.
ST1: The millions of different species of plants, animals, and microorganisms that live on Earth today are related by descent from common ancestors.
ST2: The energy for life primarily comes from the sun.
SPSP1: The complexity and organization of organisms accommodates the need for obtaining, transforming, transporting, releasing, and eliminating the matter and energy used to sustain the organism.
SPSP6: As matter and energy flows through different levels of organization of living systems—cells, organs, communities—and between living systems and the physical environment, chemical elements are used in science in different ways.
HNS1: Organisms have behavioral responses to internal changes and to external stimuli.

PARENT LETTER

SAMPLE

Dear Parent,

Your son's or daughter's science class will soon begin exploring the chapter entitled "The World of Physical Science." In this chapter, students will learn about how the scientific method applies to the world of physical science and the role of physical science in the world. By the end of the chapter, students should demonstrate a clear understanding of the chapter's main ideas and be able to discuss the following topics:

1. physical science as the study of energy and matter (Section 1)
2. the role of physical science in the world around them (Section 1)
3. careers that rely on physical science (Section 1)
4. the steps used in the scientific method (Section 2)
5. examples of technology (Section 2)
6. how the scientific method is used to answer questions and solve problems (Section 2)
7. how our knowledge of science changes over time (Section 3)
8. how models represent real objects or systems (Section 3)
9. examples of different ways models are used in science (Section 3)
10. the importance of the International System of Units (Section 4)
11. the appropriate units to use for particular measurements (Section 4)
12. how area and density are derived quantities (Section 4)

Questions to Ask Along the Way

You can help your son or daughter learn about these topics by asking interesting questions such as the following:

- What are some surprising careers that use physical science?
- What is a characteristic of a good hypothesis?
- When is it a good idea to use a model?
- Why do Americans measure things in terms of inches and yards instead of centimeters and meters.?

TEST ITEM LISTING

TEST ITEM LISTING
The World of Science — SAMPLE

MULTIPLE CHOICE

1. A limitation of models is that
   a. they are large enough to see.
   b. they do not act exactly like the things that they model.
   c. they are smaller than the things that they model.
   d. they model unfamiliar things.
   Answer: B   Difficulty: 1   Section: 3   Objective: 2

2. The length 10 m is equal to
   a. 100 cm.   c. 10,000 mm.
   b. 1,000 cm.   d. Both (b) and (c)
   Answer: B   Difficulty: 1   Section: 1

3. To be valid, a hypothesis must be
   a. testable.   c. made into a law.
   b. supported by evidence.   d. Both (a) and (b)
   Answer: B   Difficulty: 1   Section: 2

4. The statement "Sheila has a stain on her shirt" is an example of a(n)
   a. law.   c. observation.
   b. hypothesis.   d. prediction.
   Answer: A   Difficulty: 1   Section: 2   Objective: 2 1

5. A hypothesis is often developed out of
   a. observations.   c. laws.
   b. experiments.   d. Both (a) and (b)
   Answer: B   Difficulty: 1   Section: 3   Objective: 2

6. How many milliliters are in 3.5 kL?
   a. 3,500 mL   c. 3,500, 000 mL
   b. 0.0035 mL   d. 35,000 mL
   Answer: B   Difficulty: 1   Section: 1   Objective: 2

7. A map of Seattle is an example of a
   a. law.   c. model.
   b. theory.   d. unit.
   Answer: B   Difficulty: 1   Section: 3   Objective: 2

8. A lab has the safety icons shown below. These icons mean that you should wear
   a. only safety goggles.   c. safety goggles and a lab apron.
   b. only a lab apron.   d. safety goggles, a lab apron, and gloves.
   Answer: B   Difficulty: 1   Section: 1   Objective: 2

9. The law of conservation of mass says the total mass before a chemical change is
   a. less than the total mass after the change.
   b. less than the total mass after the change.
   c. the same as the total mass after the change.
   d. not the same as the total mass after the change.
   Answer: B   Difficulty: 1   Section: 3   Objective: 2

10. In which of the following areas might you find a geochemist at work?
    a. studying the chemistry of rocks   c. studying Earth
    b. studying forestry   d. studying the atmosphere
    Answer: B   Difficulty: 1   Section: 3

One-Stop Planner® CD-ROM

This CD-ROM includes all of the resources shown here and the following time-saving tools:

- **Lab Materials QuickList Software**
- **Customizable lesson plans**
- **Holt Calendar Planner**
- **The powerful ExamView® Test Generator**

Meeting Individual Needs

DIRECTED READING A
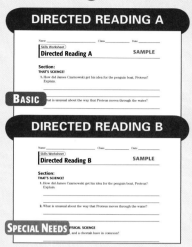
BASIC

VOCABULARY ACTIVITY
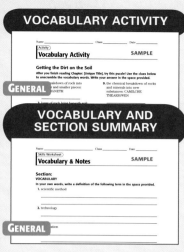

Getting the Dirt on the Soil
GENERAL

REINFORCEMENT
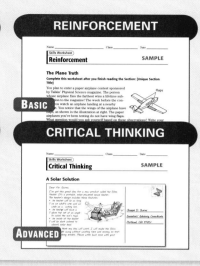

The Plane Truth
BASIC

SCILINKS ACTIVITY

GENERAL

DIRECTED READING B
Directed Reading B

Section:
THAT'S SCIENCE!

SPECIAL NEEDS

VOCABULARY AND SECTION SUMMARY
Vocabulary & Notes

Section:
VOCABULARY

GENERAL

CRITICAL THINKING
Critical Thinking

A Solar Solution
ADVANCED

SCIENCE PUZZLERS, TWISTERS & TEASERS
Work and Machines

Parallel Puzzle
GENERAL

Labs and Activities

LONG-TERM PROJECTS & RESEARCH IDEAS

To Complicate Things
ADVANCED

WHIZ-BANG DEMONSTRATIONS
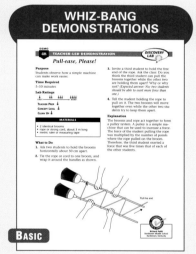

Pull-ease, Please!
BASIC

INQUIRY LABS
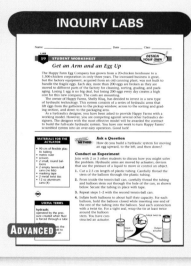

Get an Arm and an Egg Up
ADVANCED

DATASHEETS FOR QUICK LABS

Reaction to Stress

DATASHEETS FOR CHAPTER LABS

Using Scientific Methods

DATASHEETS FOR LABBOOK

Does It All Add Up?

Review and Assessments

SECTION QUIZ

Section Quiz

GENERAL

CHAPTER REVIEW
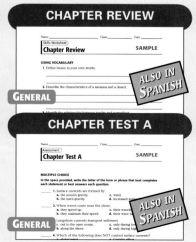

Chapter Review

USING VOCABULARY
GENERAL

CHAPTER TEST B
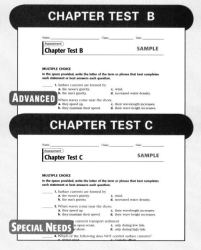

Chapter Test B

MULTIPLE CHOICE
ADVANCED

STANDARDIZED TEST PREPARATION
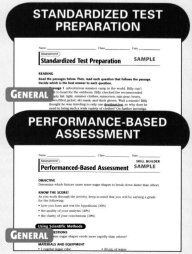

Standardized Test Preparation

READING
GENERAL

SECTION REVIEW
Section Review

Section:
KEY TERMS

GENERAL

CHAPTER TEST A
Chapter Test A

MULTIPLE CHOICE
GENERAL

CHAPTER TEST C
Chapter Test C

MULTIPLE CHOICE
SPECIAL NEEDS

PERFORMANCE-BASED ASSESSMENT
Performance-Based Assessment

OBJECTIVE
GENERAL

This Chapter Enrichment provides relevant and interesting information to expand and enhance your presentation of the chapter material.

Section 1

Work and Power

James Prescott Joule (1818–1889)

- James Joule was an English physicist who established that mechanical energy, electrical energy, and thermal energy are basically the same and that one type of energy can be converted into another. This principle is the basis of the first law of thermodynamics, the conservation of energy. It states that the total energy in any closed system remains the same, even when the energy is converted from one type to another.

- Joule developed mathematical equations that described the thermal energy of current in electrical wire and the amount of work needed to produce a unit of thermal energy. The standard unit of work and energy is called the *joule,* named in his honor.

Converting Energy

- In physics, *energy* is the ability to do work. Energy can exist in different forms, such as thermal, electrical, nuclear, potential, kinetic, and chemical. All forms of energy have to do with motion or position. Energy can be converted from one form to another. For example, electrical energy is usually converted from chemical, nuclear, or mechanical energy.

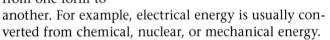

Is That a Fact!

◆ The term *horsepower* was coined in the late 18th century by Scottish engineer James Watt, who used horses as a measure of power in his experiments. In the English system, 1 horsepower can accomplish 33,000 foot-pounds of work per minute, or allow one to exert the force necessary to lift 33,000 lb 1 ft in 1 min. This unit was based on the dray horse, a horse adapted for pulling heavy loads.

Section 2

What Is a Machine?

Leonardo da Vinci (1452–1519)

- Leonardo da Vinci was an Italian painter, sculptor, and inventor. The motivating interest behind all of his work was the appearance of everyday things and the way they operated. He studied the flight of birds, the movement of water, the growth of plants, and the anatomy of the human body.

- One of da Vinci's interests was the mechanical advantage that could be obtained with gears. Da Vinci made drawings of complex machines that were centuries ahead of their time. Among his drawings were plans for tanks, a helicopter, and other aircraft. He was especially concerned with the problems of friction and resistance. He described and drew screws, gears, hydraulic jacks, transmission gears, and swiveling devices.

- Da Vinci thought that the basic laws of mechanics operated the same way in all aspects of the world and were the keys to understanding the world and reproducing it through art.

Is That a Fact!

◆ Many industrial towns in early America were located where water flow could be assured all year. Water and wind were the primary sources of mechanical energy until the end of the 18th century, when steam power was developed. Steam-powered mechanical devices launched the Industrial Revolution.

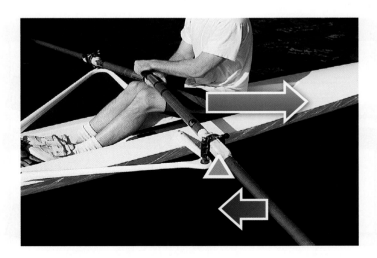

Perpetual Motion

- For centuries, inventors have tried to build a perpetual-motion machine—a device that would run forever once it is set in motion. However, no such machines can work because the laws of thermodynamics would be violated.

- A perpetual-motion machine would have to deliver as much or more energy than is put into it. The first law of thermodynamics states that the total energy of a closed system is constant. The second law states that some energy is always lost as thermal energy from a closed system when energy is used to do work. The practical effect of these two laws is that the output energy from any machine will never be as great as the energy put into it.

- Friction—in which kinetic energy is converted to thermal energy—can be reduced but never eliminated. Although some machines can be made to run very efficiently, they will always need a source of energy to operate, and they will never be able to produce more energy than is put into them.

Section 3

Types of Machines

The Invention of Machines

- The first machines were tools used by prehistoric people to help them hunt and gather food. A wedge shaped out of stone made an excellent cutting tool. Early axes were wedges made of stone. Levers were used in hoes, oars, and slings. Because simple machines multiply force or distance, they provided our early ancestors with a tremendous survival advantage.

The Plow

- The plow was one of the first agricultural machines to be invented, and it is still one of the most important. Evidence shows that plows first appeared more than 6,000 years ago. The first plow was not much more than a digging stick drawn by a person or an animal. As primitive as it was, the plow allowed people to dig deeper to turn over and loosen the soil. This simple machine magnified the effort of a single person enough to produce food for many people.

Is That a Fact!

◆ Tiny machines are being built with gears and levers so small they can be seen only under a powerful microscope. Scientists are learning how to make even tinier machines out of molecules. Tiny gears have been shaped out of strands of DNA molecules, and hydrogen molecules may one day control microscopic computers.

Overview

In this chapter, students will learn about the relationship between energy and work, the way machines do work, and the different types of simple and compound machines.

Assessing Prior Knowledge

Students should be familiar with the following topics:
- matter
- forces
- motion

Identifying Misconceptions

As students learn the concepts in this chapter, they will encounter the scientific usage of the word *work*. Students will need to relearn the meaning of *work* in terms of force applied over a distance, instead of simply effort expended. Students may also have to overcome the common usage of the word *machine*, which connotes a large and complicated apparatus such as a car engine. Students may be slow to consider a simple device such as a lever a machine.

20
Work and Machines

About the PHOTO

"One, two, stroke!" shouts the coach as the team races to the finish line. This paddling team is competing in Hong Kong's annual Dragon Boat Races. The Dragon Boat Festival is a 2,000-year-old Chinese tradition that commemorates Qu Yuan, a national hero. The paddlers that you see here are using the paddles to move the boat forward. Even though they are celebrating by racing their dragon boat, in scientific terms, this team is doing work.

PRE-READING ACTIVITY

FOLDNOTES **Booklet** Before you read the chapter, create the FoldNote entitled "Booklet" described in the **Study Skills** section of the Appendix. Label each page of the booklet with a main idea from the chapter. As you read the chapter, write what you learn about each main idea on the appropriate page of the booklet.

Standards Correlations

North Carolina Standard Course of Study

1.01 Identify and create questions and hypotheses that can be answered through scientific investigations. (Chapter Lab and LabBook)

1.04 (partial) Analyze variables in scientific investigations: ... Use of a Control [and] Manipulate ... (LabBook)

1.05 Analyze evidence to: Explain observations, Make inferences and predictions, [and] Develop the relationship between evidence and explanation. (Section 1)

1.06 (partial) Use mathematics to gather, organize, and present quantitative data resulting from scientific investiga-

tions: Measurement, Analysis of data, [and] Graphing ... (Chapter Lab and LabBook)

2.03 (partial) Evaluate technological designs for: Application of scientific principles ... [and] Constraints of design ... (LabBook)

6.01 Demonstrate ways that simple machines can change force. (Chapter Opener, Sections 2 and 3, Chapter Review, and Standardized Test Preparation)

6.02 Analyze simple machines for mechanical advantage and efficiency. (Sections 2 and 3, Chapter Review, Standardized Test Preparation, and LabBook)

START-UP ACTIVITY

MATERIALS

FOR EACH GROUP
• books (2)
• ruler, wooden
• pencil eraser, large
• table

Safety Caution: The rulers should be fairly stiff and sturdy. Use lightweight books if necessary. If the books are not too heavy and the activity is done carefully, the rulers should not get broken.

Teacher's Notes: The word *lever* comes from the Latin word *levare*, meaning "to lift." The lever was one of the first simple machines to be developed. It is thought that tree limbs may have been used by early humans as pry bars to move heavy rocks.

Answers

1. Students should find that lifting the books with the ruler was easier because it required less effort (force).

2. The direction of the force applied by students' fingers on the books was up, and the direction of the force applied on the ruler was down. Using the ruler changed the direction of the force.

START-UP ACTIVITY

C'mon, Lever a Little!

In this activity, you will use a simple machine, a lever, to make your task a little easier.

Procedure

1. Stack **two books,** one on top of the other, on a **table.**

2. Slide your index finger underneath the edge of the bottom book. Using only the force of your finger, try to lift one side of the books 2 or 3 cm off the table. Is it hard to do so? Write your observations.

3. Slide the end of a **wooden ruler** underneath the edge of the bottom book. Then, slip a **large pencil eraser** or similar object under the ruler.

4. Again, using only your index finger, push down on the edge of the ruler and try to lift the books. Record your observations. **Caution:** Push down slowly to keep the ruler and eraser from flipping.

Analysis

1. Which was easier: lifting the books with your finger or lifting the books with the ruler? Explain your answer.

2. In what way did the direction of the force that your finger applied on the books differ from the direction of the force that your finger applied on the ruler?

Chapter Starter Transparency
Use this transparency to help students begin thinking about concepts of work and machines.

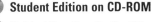

Chapter 20 • Work and Machines **551**

Focus

Overview

This section introduces the scientific definitions of *work* and *power*. Students learn how to calculate work and power.

Bellringer

Write the following task for students on the board:

Select the activities below that require the least amount of work.

- carrying heavy books home
- reading a 300-page novel
- skiing for 1 h
- lifting a 45 kg mass
- holding a steel beam in place for 3 h
- jacking up a car

Remind students to explain what work is being done in each of their selected activities.

Motivate

ACTIVITY — GENERAL

Work in Sports Have students, in groups of three or four, select a sport and discuss the different ways work is done in that sport. Have them estimate how much work is done in an average game. **LS Kinesthetic**

READING WARM-UP

Objectives

- Determine when work is being done on an object.
- Calculate the amount of work done on an object.
- Explain the difference between work and power.

Terms to Learn

work	power
joule	watt

READING STRATEGY

Reading Organizer As you read this section, make a table comparing work and power.

Figure 1
You might be surprised to find out that bowling is work!

Work and Power

Your science teacher has just given you tonight's homework assignment. You have to read an entire chapter by tomorrow! That sounds like a lot of work!

Actually, in the scientific sense, you won't be doing much work at all! How can that be? In science, **work** is done when a force causes an object to move in the direction of the force. In the example above, you may have to put a lot of mental effort into doing your homework, but you won't be using force to move anything. So, in the scientific sense, you will not be doing work—except the work to turn the pages of your book!

What Is Work?

The student in **Figure 1** is having a lot of fun, isn't she? But she is doing work, even though she is having fun. She is doing work because she is applying a force to the bowling ball and making the ball move through a distance. However, she is doing work on the ball only as long as she is touching it. The ball will keep moving away from her after she releases it. But she will no longer be doing work on the ball because she will no longer be applying a force to it.

Transfer of Energy

One way you can tell that the bowler in **Figure 1** has done work on the bowling ball is that the ball now has *kinetic energy.* This means that the ball is now moving. The bowler has transferred energy to the ball.

Differences Between Force and Work

Applying a force doesn't always result in work being done. Suppose that you help push a stalled car. You push and push, but the car doesn't budge. The pushing may have made you tired. But you haven't done any work on the car, because the car hasn't moved.

You do work on the car as soon as the car moves. Whenever you apply a force to an object and the object moves in the direction of the force, you have done work on the object.

✓ **Reading Check** Is work done every time a force is applied to an object? Explain. (*See the Appendix for answers to Reading Checks.*)

CHAPTER RESOURCES

Chapter Resource File

- Lesson Plan
- Directed Reading A **BASIC**
- Directed Reading B **SPECIAL NEEDS**

Technology

Transparencies
- Bellringer
- Work or Not Work?
- **LINK TO LIFE SCIENCE** A Pair of Muscles in the Arm

Answer to Reading Check

No, work is done on an object only if force makes the object move in a direction that is parallel to the force.

Force and Motion in the Same Direction

Suppose you are in the airport and late for a flight. You have to run through the airport carrying a heavy suitcase. Because you are making the suitcase move, you are doing work on it, right? Wrong! For work to be done on an object, the object must move in the *same direction* as the force. You are applying a force to hold the suitcase up, but the suitcase is moving forward. So, no work is done on the suitcase. But work *is* done on the suitcase when you lift it off the ground.

Work is done on an object if two things happen: (1) the object moves as a force is applied and (2) the direction of the object's motion is the same as the direction of the force. The pictures and arrows in **Figure 2** will help you understand when work is being done on an object.

work the transfer of energy to an object by using a force that causes the object to move in the direction of the force

Figure 2 · Work or Not Work?

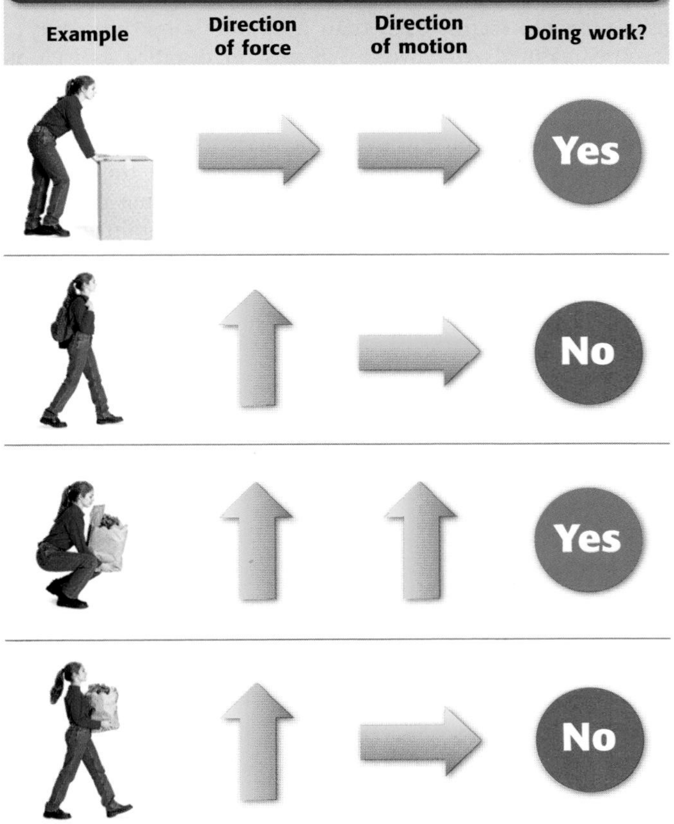

Example	Direction of force	Direction of motion	Doing work?
	→	→	Yes
	↑	→	No
	↑	↑	Yes
	↑	→	No

CONNECTION TO Biology

WRITING SKILL **Work in the Human Body**

You may not be doing any work on a suitcase if you are just holding it in your hands, but your body will still get tired from the effort because you are doing work on the muscles inside your body. Your muscles can contract thousands of times in just a few seconds while you try to keep the suitcase from falling. What other situations can you think of that might involve work being done somewhere inside your body? Describe these situations in your **science journal.**

MISCONCEPTION ALERT

Work and Force The text states that the girl does work on the bowling ball only when she is touching it. The ball continues to move when she lets go of it, but she's no longer applying a force to it. Disregarding friction, once the ball is moving, no additional force is needed to keep it moving at constant speed because of Newton's first law of motion.

📖 READING STRATEGY — GENERAL

Prediction Guide Before students read this section, ask them whether they agree with the following statements:

1. Any time a force is applied to an object, work is being done.
2. Power, work, and force are the same.
3. More power means doing work faster.

LS Logical

Using the Figure— GENERAL

Work and the Direction of Force Have students develop their own charts similar to the one on this pages using activities from their everyday lives, including sports and games. When their charts are completed, have students exchange charts and look for misconceptions about work. Discuss these in class. Throughout this chapter, the length of the force arrows represents the magnitude of the force. **LS** Visual

CONNECTION to Life Science — GENERAL

The Arm as a Lever A good example of a lever in the body is the arm, which is used as a third-class lever when lifting a load. A diagram of the arm as a lever can be found in the Teaching Transparency "A Pair of Muscles in the Arm."

- *Learning Disabled*
- *Developmentally Delayed*
- *Visually Impaired*

Create a working example of the "Work or Not Work" chart. Draw a thick arrow on a piece of paper, and make 10 copies. Write a large "Yes" and a large "No," and make 5 copies of each. Divide the class into five teams.

Give each team two arrows, a Yes, a No, and one of the following tasks:

Shut the door. (both arrows to right) Erase the board. (force arrow up, motion arrow sideways) Ride in a chair on wheels. (both arrows to the right) Do push-ups. (both arrows up) Ask each team to determine whether their tasks are work. Then, have each team demonstrate the task, show direction of force arrow and say "force," show direction of motion arrow and say "motion," and show Yes or No.

LS Interpersonal   English Language Learners

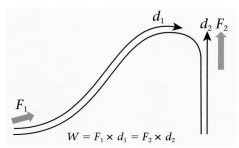

$$W = F_1 \times d_1 = F_2 \times d_2$$

Figure 3 *For each path, the same work is done to move the car to the top of the hill, although distance and force along the two paths differ.*

How Much Work?

Would you do more work on a car by pushing it up a long road to reach the top of a hill or by using a cable to raise the car up the side of a cliff to the top of the same hill? You would certainly need a different amount of force. Common use of the word *work* may make it seem that there would be a difference in the amount of work done in the two cases as well.

Same Work, Different Forces

You may be surprised to learn that the same amount of work is being done to push the car up a road as to raise it up the cliff. Look at **Figure 3.** A certain amount of energy is needed to move the car from the bottom to the top of the hill. Because the car ends up at the same place either way, the work done on the car is the same. However, pushing the car along the road up a hill seems easier than lifting it straight up. Why?

The reason is that work depends on distance as well as force. Consider a mountain climber who reaches the top of a mountain by climbing straight up a cliff, as in **Figure 4.** She must use enough force to overcome her entire weight. But the distance she travels up the cliff is shorter than the distance traveled by hikers who reach the top of the same mountain by walking up a slope. Either way, the same amount of work is done. But the hikers going up a slope don't need to use as much force as if they were going straight up the side of the cliff. This shows how you can use less force to do the same amount of work.

Figure 4 *Climbers going to the top of a mountain do the same amount of work whether they hike up a slope or go straight up a cliff.*

ACTIVITY ———— GENERAL

Work Done on a Spring Scale Obtain a meter stick, string, a spring scale, and various objects to lift. Organize students into pairs. Have each pair attach each object in turn to the spring scale and slowly lift or pull it and then record how much force was used. Next, have them measure the distance the object moved and record it in meters. Have them calculate how much work was done. **LS** Kinesthetic

Calculating Work

The amount of work (W) done in moving an object, such as the barbell in **Figure 5,** can be calculated by multiplying the force (F) applied to the object by the distance (d) through which the force is applied, as shown in the following equation:

$$W = F \times d$$

Force is expressed in newtons, and the meter is the basic SI unit for length or distance. Therefore, the unit used to express work is the newton-meter (N × m), which is more simply called the **joule.** Because work is the transfer of energy to an object, the joule (J) is also the unit used to measure energy.

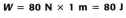 **Reading Check** How is work calculated?

joule the unit used to express energy; equivalent to the amount of work done by a force of 1 N acting through a distance of 1 m in the direction of the force (symbol, J)

 **Figure 5** **Force Times Distance**

80 N

$W = 80\ N \times 1\ m = 80\ J$

The force needed to lift an object is equal to the gravitational force on the object—in other words, the object's weight.

160 N

$W = 160\ N \times 1\ m = 160\ J$

If you increase the weight, an increased force is needed to lift the object. This increases the amount of work done.

80 N

$W = 80\ N \times 2\ m = 160\ J$

Increasing the distance also increases the amount of work done.

Get to Work!

1. Use a **loop of string** to attach a **spring scale** to a **weight.**

2. Slowly pull the weight across a **table** by dragging the spring scale. Record the amount of force that you exerted on the weight.

3. Use a **metric ruler** to measure the distance that you pulled the weight.

4. Now, use the spring scale to slowly pull the weight up a **ramp.** Pull the weight the same distance that you pulled it across the table.

5. Calculate the work you did on the weight for both trials.

6. How were the amounts of work and force affected by the way you pulled the weight? What other ways of pulling the weight could you test?

MATERIALS

FOR EACH STUDENT
• ramp
• ruler, metric
• scale, spring
• string, loop
• table
• weight

Teacher's Note: Be sure that students pull the weight with a constant speed. They should also keep the spring scale parallel to the tabletop or ramp when pulling.

Answer

6. Sample answer: More force was needed to pull the weight across the ramp than to pull it across the table. Therefore, more work was done when pulling the weight across the ramp. Other ways of pulling the weight might include using a much steeper ramp or pulling the weight straight up a vertical surface.

Answer to Reading Check

Work is calculated as force times distance.

SCIENCE HUMOR

Q: Did you hear about the criminals who never had to do any work?

A: They were joule thieves.

CHAPTER RESOURCES

Technology

Transparencies
• Force and Distance

Workbooks

Math Skills for Science
• Work and Power **GENERAL**

Reteaching — BASIC

Work and Power After students read the section on work and power, discuss with students the use of the words *work* and *power* in everyday language. Identify usages that do not match the scientific definition of work, and discuss why they are different.

English Language Learners

LS Verbal

Quiz — GENERAL

1. What are the two things that must happen for work to be done? (A force must be exerted on an object, and the object must move in the direction of the force.)

2. You use 75 N of force to push a box 3 m across the floor. How much work has been done? (225 J)

3. What is the power of a small motor that can do 4,500 J of work in 25 s? (180 W)

Alternative Assessment — GENERAL

Concept Mapping Have students create a concept map using the words *work, force, distance, power,* and *time* in a way that matches their scientific definitions. **LS** Visual

power the rate at which work is done or energy is transformed

watt the unit used to express power; equivalent to joules per second (symbol, W)

Power: How Fast Work Is Done

Like the term *work,* the term *power* is used a lot in everyday language but has a very specific meaning in science. **Power** is the rate at which energy is transferred.

Calculating Power

To calculate power (*P*), you divide the amount of work done (*W*) by the time (*t*) it takes to do that work, as shown in the following equation:

$$P = \frac{W}{t}$$

The unit used to express power is joules per second (J/s), also called the **watt.** One watt (W) is equal to 1 J/s. So if you do 50 J of work in 5 s, your power is 10 J/s, or 10 W.

Power measures how fast work happens, or how quickly energy is transferred. When more work is done in a given amount of time, the power output is greater. Power output is also greater when the time it takes to do a certain amount of work is decreased, as shown in **Figure 6.**

Reading Check How is power calculated?

Figure 6 *No matter how fast you can sand by hand, an electric sander can do the same amount of work faster. Therefore, the electric sander has more power.*

MATH FOCUS

More Power to You A stage manager at a play raises the curtain by doing 5,976 J of work on the curtain in 12 s. What is the power output of the stage manager?

Step 1: Write the equation for power.

$$P = \frac{W}{t}$$

Step 2: Replace *W* and *t* with work and time.

$$P = \frac{5,976\,\text{J}}{12\,\text{s}} = 498\,\text{W}$$

Now It's Your Turn
1. If it takes you 10 s to do 150 J of work on a box to move it up a ramp, what is your power output?
2. A light bulb is on for 12 s, and during that time it uses 1,200 J of electrical energy. What is the wattage (power) of the light bulb?

SCIENCE HUMOR

Q: What is the unit of power?

A: Watt.

Q: I said, What is the unit of power?

A: Watt!

Q: I SAID . . .

Answer to Reading Check
Power is calculated as work done (in joules) divided by the time (in seconds) in which the work was done.

Answers to Math Focus
1. 150 J ÷ 10 s = 15 W
2. 1,200 J ÷ 12 s = 100 W

Increasing Power

It may take you longer to sand a wooden shelf by hand than by an electric sander, but the amount of energy needed is the same either way. Only the power output is lower when you sand the shelf by hand (although your hand may get more tired). You could also dry your hair with a fan, but it would take a long time! A hair dryer is more powerful. It can give off energy more quickly than a fan does, so your hair dries faster.

Car engines are usually rated with a certain power output. The more powerful the engine is, the more quickly the engine can move a car. And for a given speed, a more powerful engine can move a heavier car than a less powerful engine can.

CONNECTION TO Language Arts

WRITING SKILL **Horsepower** The unit of power most commonly used to rate car engines is the *horsepower* (hp). Look up the word *horsepower* in a dictionary. How many watts is equal to 1 hp? Do you think all horses output exactly 1 hp? Why or why not? Write your answers in your **science journal**.

SECTION Review

Summary

- In scientific terms, *work* is done when a force causes an object to move in the direction of the force.
- Work is calculated as force times distance. The unit of work is the newton-meter, or joule.
- *Power* is a measure of how fast work is done.
- Power is calculated as work divided by time. The unit of power is the joule per second, or watt.

Using Key Terms

For each pair of terms, explain how the meanings of the terms differ.

1. *work* and *joule*
2. *power* and *watt*

Understanding Key Ideas

3. How is work calculated?
   a. force times distance
   b. force divided by distance
   c. power times distance
   d. power divided by distance

4. What is the difference between work and power?

Math Skills

5. Using a force of 10 N, you push a shopping cart 10 m. How much work did you do?

6. If you did 100 J of work in 5 s, what was your power output?

Critical Thinking

7. **Analyzing Processes** Work is done on a ball when a pitcher throws it. Is the pitcher still doing work on the ball as it flies through the air? Explain.

8. **Applying Concepts** You lift a chair that weighs 50 N to a height of 0.5 m and carry it 10 m across the room. How much work do you do on the chair?

Interpreting Graphics

9. What idea about work and force does the following diagram describe? Explain your answer.

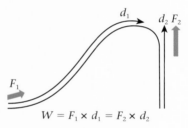

 $W = F_1 \times d_1 = F_2 \times d_2$

Developed and maintained by the National Science Teachers Association

For a variety of links related to this chapter, go to www.scilinks.org

Topic: Work and Power
SciLinks code: HSM1675

CHAPTER RESOURCES

Chapter Resource File

- Section Quiz **GENERAL**
- Section Review **GENERAL**
- Vocabulary and Section Summary **GENERAL**
- SciLinks Activity **GENERAL**
- Datasheet for Quick Lab

Overview

This section explains how machines make work easier. Students learn to calculate and compare the mechanical advantage of machines and their mechanical efficiency.

🎙 Bellringer

Pose the following question to your students, and have them write a one-paragraph answer in their **science journal:** "Why do we use machines?"

Discussion ——— GENERAL

Examples of Machines Show students a selection of pictures of familiar objects that represent simple machines either alone or in combination. Discuss with students how each of the objects can be used to make work easier. Later, when simple machines are introduced, you can have students identify the simple machines in each picture.
LS Visual

READING WARM-UP

Objectives

● Explain how a machine makes work easier.
● Describe and give examples of the force-distance trade-off that occurs when a machine is used.
● Calculate mechanical advantage.
● Explain why machines are not 100% efficient.

Terms to Learn

machine
work input
work output
mechanical advantage
mechanical efficiency

READING STRATEGY

Prediction Guide Before reading this section, write the title of each heading in this section. Next, under each heading, write what you think you will learn.

What Is a Machine?

You are in the car with your mom on the way to a party when suddenly—KABLOOM hissssss—a tire blows out. "Now I'm going to be late!" you think as your mom pulls over to the side of the road.

You watch as she opens the trunk and gets out a jack and a tire iron. Using the tire iron, she pries the hubcap off and begins to unscrew the lug nuts from the wheel. She then puts the jack under the car and turns the jack's handle several times until the flat tire no longer touches the ground. After exchanging the flat tire with the spare, she lowers the jack and puts the lug nuts and hubcap back on the wheel.

"Wow!" you think, "That wasn't as hard as I thought it would be." As your mom drops you off at the party, you think how lucky it was that she had the right equipment to change the tire.

Machines: Making Work Easier

Now, imagine changing a tire without the jack and the tire iron. Would it have been easy? No, you would have needed several people just to hold up the car! Sometimes, you need the help of machines to do work. A **machine** is a device that makes work easier by changing the size or direction of a force.

When you think of machines, you might think of things such as cars, big construction equipment, or even computers. But not all machines are complicated. In fact, you use many simple machines in your everyday life. **Figure 1** shows some examples of machines.

Figure 1 Some Everyday Machines

Wheelchair

Chopsticks

Scissors

CHAPTER RESOURCES

Chapter Resource File

 • Lesson Plan
• Directed Reading A **BASIC**
• Directed Reading B **SPECIAL NEEDS**

Technology

 Transparencies
• Bellringer
• Everyday Transparencies

CONNECTION ACTIVITY
Home Economics— GENERAL

Kitchen Utensils as Machines Show students some common kitchen utensils, such as knives, forks, can and bottle openers, nutcrackers, and manual eggbeaters. Allow students to examine the utensils and discuss their uses. Then, have students speculate about how each machine makes work easier. **LS** Visual

---

Work In, Work Out

Suppose that you need to get the lid off a can of paint. What do you do? One way to pry the lid off is to use a common machine known as a *lever*. **Figure 2** shows a screwdriver being used as a lever. You place the tip of the screwdriver under the edge of the lid and then push down on the screwdriver's handle. The tip of the screwdriver lifts the lid as you push down. In other words, you do work on the screwdriver, and the screwdriver does work on the lid.

Work is done when a force is applied through a distance. Look again at **Figure 2.** The work that you do on a machine is called **work input.** You apply a force, called the *input force,* to the machine through a distance. The work done by the machine on an object is called **work output.** The machine applies a force, called the *output force,* through a distance.

How Machines Help

You might think that machines help you because they increase the amount of work done. But that's not true. If you multiplied the forces by the distances through which the forces are applied in **Figure 2** (remember that $W = F \times d$), you would find that the screwdriver does not do more work on the lid than you do on the screwdriver. Work output can never be greater than work input. Machines allow force to be applied over a greater distance, which means that less force will be needed for the same amount of work.

> ✔ **Reading Check** How do machines make work easier? (*See the Appendix for answers to Reading Checks.*)

machine a device that helps do work by either overcoming a force or changing the direction of the applied force

work input the work done on a machine; the product of the input force and the distance through which the force is exerted

work output the work done by a machine; the product of the output force and the distance through which the force is exerted

Output force

Input force

Figure 2 *When you use a machine, you do work on the machine, and the machine does work on something else.*

Answer to Reading Check
Machines make work easier by allowing force to be applied over a greater distance.

Teach

📖 READING STRATEGY — BASIC

Concept Mapping Have students begin constructing a concept map of this section and continue it as they progress through the section. They should illustrate at least half the bubbles with their own drawings or photographs from magazines. The illustrations should elaborate on or relate to the ideas included in the map. **LS** Visual

Discussion — GENERAL

Benefits and Drawbacks of Machines Encourage a student debate about the benefits and drawbacks of machines since the Industrial Revolution. Students should understand that although machines have many benefits, machines may bring problems (pollution, workplace injury). **LS** Interpersonal

Using Science Fiction — ADVANCED

Have students read the story "Clean Up Your Room!" by Laura Anne Gilman in the *Holt Anthology of Science Fiction.* As you discuss the story, ask students to compare the positive and negative aspects of technology in our lives. **LS** Verbal

ACTIVITY ADVANCED

Machines as Solutions to Problems Have students think of a problem that has no apparent solution. The problem may also be something that students think may become a problem in the future. Challenge them to invent a machine that solves that problem. Have them describe it as carefully as possible and illustrate it with their own artwork. **LS** Logical

CONNECTION ACTIVITY
Math ——— GENERAL

Graphing Force and Distance
A certain task takes 480 J of work. Remind students that many combinations of $F \times d$ result in 480 J of work (480 N × 1 m; or 64 N × 7.5 m). Help students find combinations of forces and distances whose products are 480 J. Have them use these number pairs to plot and connect points on a graph (with F on the x-axis and d on the y-axis). Discuss the graphs and what they show about the relationship between force and distance. (*F* and *d* are inversely related.) (Students can start with any two of the quantities, calculate the third, and then do the graph.) **LS** Visual

INTERNET ACTIVITY
For another activity related to this chapter, go to **go.hrw.com** and type in the keyword **HP5WRKW**.

Same Work, Different Force

Machines make work easier by changing the size or direction (or both) of the input force. When a screwdriver is used as a lever to open a paint can, both the size and direction of the input force change. Remember that using a machine does not change the amount of work you will do. As **Figure 3** shows, the same amount of work is done with or without the ramp. The ramp decreases the size of the input force needed to lift the box but increases the distance over which the force is exerted. So, the machine allows a smaller force to be applied over a longer distance.

The Force-Distance Trade-Off

When a machine changes the size of the force, the distance through which the force is exerted must also change. Force or distance can increase, but both cannot increase. When one increases, the other must decrease.

Figure 4 shows how machines change force and distance. Whenever a machine changes the size of a force, the machine also changes the distance through which the force is applied. **Figure 4** also shows that some machines change only the direction of the force, not the size of the force or the distance through which the force is exerted.

✓ **Reading Check** What are the two things that a machine can change about how work is done?

Figure 3 **Input Force and Distance**

Lifting this box straight up requires an input force equal to the weight of the box.

$W = 450 \text{ N} \times 1 \text{ m} = 450 \text{ J}$

Using a ramp to lift the box requires an input force less than the weight of the box, but the input force must be exerted over a greater distance than if you didn't use a ramp.

$W = 150 \text{ N} \times 3 \text{ m} = 450 \text{ J}$

Homework ——— GENERAL

Everyday Use of Machines Have students keep a "machine diary" for a week. Each day, they should describe the machines they used or came into contact with over the course of the day. Have them expand their ideas of what a machine is by examining ordinary actions such as writing or playing and deciding whether a machine is involved. **LS** Intrapersonal

Answer to Reading Check
Machines can change the force or the distance through which force is applied.

| Figure 4 | Machines Change the Size and/or Direction of a Force |

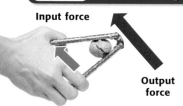

Input force

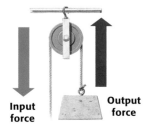

Output force

A nutcracker *increases* the force but applies it over a *shorter* distance.

A hammer *decreases* the force, but applies it over a *greater* distance.

Output force

Input force

A simple pulley changes the *direction* of the input force, but the size of the output force is the same as the input force.

Input force

Output force

When a screw-driver is used as a lever, it *increases* the force and *decreases* the distance over which the force is applied.

Output force

Input force

Mechanical Advantage

Some machines make work easier than others do because they can increase force more than other machines can. A machine's **mechanical advantage** is the number of times the machine multiplies force. In other words, the mechanical advantage compares the input force with the output force.

Calculating Mechanical Advantage

You can find mechanical advantage by using the following equation:

$$\text{mechanical advantage (MA)} = \frac{\text{output force}}{\text{input force}}$$

For example, imagine that you had to push a 500 N weight up a ramp and only needed to push with 50 N of force the entire time. The mechanical advantage of the ramp would be calculated as follows:

$$MA = \frac{500 \text{ N}}{50 \text{ N}} = 10$$

A machine that has a mechanical advantage that is greater than 1 can help move or lift heavy objects because the output force is greater than the input force. A machine that has a mechanical advantage that is less than 1 will reduce the output force but can increase the distance an object moves. **Figure 4** shows an example of such a machine—a hammer.

mechanical advantage a number that tells how many times a machine multiplies force

Finding the Advantage

A grocer uses a handcart to lift a heavy stack of canned food. Suppose that he applies an input force of 40 N to the handcart. The cart applies an output force of 320 N to the stack of canned food. What is the mechanical advantage of the handcart?

Guided Practice—GENERAL

Concept Mapping Give students examples of several different types of machines, such as those used in construction or industry. Have them analyze whether each machine changes the size or direction (or both) of a force. When they have finished their analysis, have students make a concept map showing their results. **LS** Visual

Homework——GENERAL

Writing **Machines in the Home** Have students go through their homes and select five machines that they find there. Encourage them to find unusual examples, things they might not use every day. Have them write one-paragraph descriptions of these machines in terms of the mechanical advantage they offer. **LS** Verbal

CONNECTION ACTIVITY
History——GENERAL

PORTFOLIO **Prehistoric Machines** Have students research prehistoric uses of machines, especially the earliest occurrences of machines that change the size or direction of force in the same ways as the examples in **Figure 4**. **LS** Logical

Answer to Math Practice
$MA = 320 \text{ N} \div 40 \text{ N} = 8$

CONNECTION ACTIVITY
Life Science——GENERAL

Animals Using Tools Humans aren't the only animals that use tools. Chimpanzees fashion specialized twigs to snare termites from inside their mounds, and some otters use carefully selected rocks to crack open shellfish. There are examples of other species using tools—a distinct evolutionary advantage. Have students find information about such tool use and make some creative presentations to the class. **LS** Verbal

CHAPTER RESOURCES

Technology

Transparencies
• Input Force and Distance
• Machines Change the Size and/or Direction of a Force

Workbooks

Math Skills for Science
• Mechanical Advantage GENERAL

Design of Machines For each of the examples of machines in **Figure 4** on the previous page, have students design a different machine that would accomplish the same job. The machine can be as simple or as elaborate as desired. Does the new machine change force in the same way as the original? **LS** Visual

1. How does a machine make work easier? (by changing the size or direction (or both) of a force)

2. What two things do you need to know in order to calculate mechanical efficiency? (work input and work output)

3. If the mechanical advantage of a machine is 5, how does the output force compare with the input force? (The output force is 5 times greater than the input force.)

Rube Goldberg Machines Show students one of Rube Goldberg's cartoons. Ask them to decipher what is happening in the cartoon. Focus students' attention on the action in each step and the results of the action. Challenge students to design and draw their own machine that uses multiple steps to perform a simple task. **LS** Logical

mechanical efficiency a quantity, usually expressed as a percentage, that measures the ratio of work output to work input; it can be calculated by dividing work output by work input

SCHOOL to HOME

Useful Friction

Friction is always present when two objects touch or rub together, and friction usually slows down moving parts in a machine and heats them up. In some cases, parts in a machine are designed to increase friction. While at home, observe three situations in which friction is useful. Describe them in your **science journal.**

ACTiViTY

Figure 5 *In this machine, some of the work input is converted into sound and heat energy.*

Mechanical Efficiency

The work output of a machine can never be greater than the work input. In fact, the work output of a machine is always less than the work input. Why? Some of the work done by the machine is used to overcome the friction created by the use of the machine. But keep in mind that no work is lost. The work output plus the work done to overcome friction is equal to the work input.

The less work a machine has to do to overcome friction, the more efficient the machine is. **Mechanical efficiency** (muh KAN i kuhl e FISH uhn see) is a comparison of a machine's work output with the work input.

Calculating Efficiency

A machine's mechanical efficiency is calculated using the following equation:

$$mechanical\ efficiency = \frac{work\ output}{work\ input} \times 100$$

The 100 in this equation means that mechanical efficiency is expressed as a percentage. Mechanical efficiency tells you what percentage of the work input gets converted into work output.

Figure 5 shows a machine that is used to drill holes in metal. Some of the work input is used to overcome the friction between the metal and the drill. This energy cannot be used to do work on the steel block. Instead, it heats up the steel and the machine itself.

✓ **Reading Check** How is mechanical efficiency calculated?

Answer to Reading Check

mechanical efficiency = (work output ÷ work input) × 100

Perfect Efficiency?

An *ideal machine* would be a machine that had 100% mechanical efficiency. An ideal machine's useful work output would equal the work done on the machine. Ideal machines are impossible to build, because every machine has moving parts. Moving parts always use some of the work input to overcome friction. But new technologies help increase efficiency so that more energy is available to do useful work. The train in **Figure 6** is floating on magnets, so there is almost no friction between the train and the tracks. Other machines use lubricants, such as oil or grease, to lower the friction between their moving parts, which makes the machines more efficient.

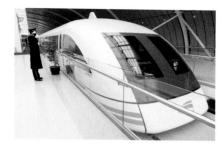

Figure 6 *There is very little friction between this magnetic levitation train and its tracks, so it is highly efficient.*

SECTION Review

Summary

- A machine makes work easier by changing the size or direction (or both) of a force.
- A machine can increase force or distance, but not both.
- Mechanical advantage tells how many times a machine multiplies force.
- Mechanical efficiency is a comparison of a machine's work output with work input.
- Machines are not 100% efficient because some of the work done is used to overcome friction.

Using Key Terms

For each pair of terms, explain how the meanings of the terms differ.

1. *work input* and *work output*

2. *mechanical advantage* and *mechanical efficiency*

Understanding Key Ideas

3. Which of the following is the correct way to calculate mechanical advantage?
   a. input force ÷ output force
   b. output force ÷ input force
   c. work input ÷ work output
   d. work output ÷ work input

4. Explain how using a ramp makes work easier.

5. Give a specific example of a machine, and describe how its mechanical efficiency might be calculated.

6. Why can't a machine be 100% efficient?

Math Skills

7. Suppose that you exert 60 N on a machine and the machine exerts 300 N on another object. What is the machine's mechanical advantage?

8. What is the mechanical efficiency of a machine whose work input is 100 J and work output is 30 J?

Critical Thinking

9. **Making Inferences** For a machine with a mechanical advantage of 3, how does the distance through which the output force is exerted differ from the distance through which the input force is exerted?

10. **Analyzing Processes** Describe the effect that friction has on a machine's mechanical efficiency. How do lubricants increase a machine's mechanical efficiency?

For a variety of links related to this chapter, go to www.scilinks.org

Topic: Mechanical Efficiency
SciLinks code: HSM0929

CHAPTER RESOURCES

Chapter Resource File

- Section Quiz **GENERAL**
- Section Review **GENERAL**
- Vocabulary and Section Summary **GENERAL**

Answers to Section Review

1. Sample answer: Work input is the work done on a machine. Work output is the work done by a machine.

2. Sample answer: Mechanical advantage is the number of times a machine multiplies force. Mechanical efficiency is the ratio of work output to work input of a machine.

3. b

4. A ramp allows you to lift something by pushing it a longer distance using less force.

5. Sample answer: an elevator; Its work output could be measured by the weight and distance a load is carried upward, and its work input could be measured by the electrical energy it uses to do that work. You would then divide the output work by the input work and multiply by 100 to get a percentage: the mechanical efficiency.

6. Machines have moving parts in which friction causes energy input to be lost as heat.

7. $MA = 300 \text{ N} \div 60 \text{ N} = 5$

8. $ME = (30 \text{ J} \div 100 \text{ J}) \times 100 = 30 \%$

9. Sample answer: The output force would be applied through a distance one-third that of the distance that the input force is applied.

10. Sample answer: Lubricants decrease the friction in a machine, thereby allowing more of the input work to be converted to output work.

SECTION
3

Focus

Overview

This section describes the six simple machines and explains how to determine the mechanical advantage of each. Students learn about compound machines (combinations of simple machines) they commonly encounter, and they learn how combining simple machines affects efficiency.

🔊 Bellringer

Pose the following question: "What type of machine can be found on at least half the students in this room right now?" (zipper)

Motivate

ActiVity ——————— GENERAL

Loads on a First-Class Lever
Organize the class into small groups. Have each group use a string to hang a meterstick from a ring. The meterstick should be balanced (hangs level). Then, ask the groups to tie five large metal washers (tied together) to the meterstick at the 2 cm mark. Challenge them to find a way to again balance the meterstick without adding any weights to the opposite end. Discuss the students' solutions to the problem. **LS Kinesthetic**

Types of Machines

Imagine that it's a hot summer day. You have a whole ice-cold watermelon in front of you. It would taste cool and delicious—if only you had a machine that could cut it!

The machine you need is a knife. But how is a knife a machine? A knife is actually a very sharp wedge, which is one of the six simple machines. The six simple machines are the lever, the inclined plane, the wedge, the screw, the pulley, and the wheel and axle. All machines are made from one or more of these simple machines.

Levers

Have you ever used the claw end of a hammer to remove a nail from a piece of wood? If so, you were using the hammer as a lever. A **lever** is a simple machine that has a bar that pivots at a fixed point, called a *fulcrum*. Levers are used to apply a force to a load. There are three classes of levers, which are based on the locations of the fulcrum, the load, and the input force.

First-Class Levers

With a first-class lever, the fulcrum is between the input force and the load, as shown in **Figure 1**. First-class levers always change the direction of the input force. And depending on the location of the fulcrum, first-class levers can be used to increase force or to increase distance.

Figure 1   **Examples of First-Class Levers**

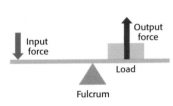
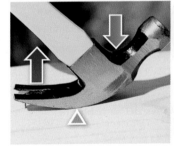
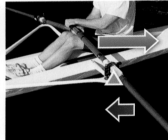

When the fulcrum is closer to the load than to the input force, the lever has a **mechanical advantage of greater than 1.** The output force is increased because it is exerted over a shorter distance.

When the fulcrum is exactly in the middle, the lever has a **mechanical advantage of 1.** The output force is not increased because the input force's distance is not increased.

When the fulcrum is closer to the input force than to the load, the lever has a **mechanical advantage of less than 1.** Although the output force is less than the input force, distance increases.

Figure 2 Examples of Second-Class Levers

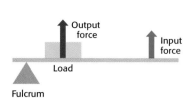

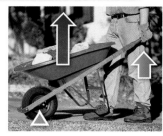

In a **second-class lever,** the output force, or load, is between the input force and the fulcrum.

Using a second-class lever results in a **mechanical advantage of greater than 1.** The closer the load is to the fulcrum, the more the force is increased and the greater the mechanical advantage is.

Second-Class Levers

The load of a second-class lever is between the fulcrum and the input force, as shown in **Figure 2.** Second-class levers do not change the direction of the input force. But they allow you to apply less force than the force exerted by the load. Because the output force is greater than the input force, you must exert the input force over a greater distance.

Third-Class Levers

The input force in a third-class lever is between the fulcrum and the load, as shown in **Figure 3.** Third-class levers do not change the direction of the input force. In addition, they do not increase the input force. Therefore, the output force is always less than the input force.

lever a simple machine that consists of a bar that pivots at a fixed point called a *fulcrum*

✔ *Reading Check* **How do the three types of levers differ from one another?** (*See the Appendix for answers to Reading Checks.*)

Figure 3 Examples of Third-Class Levers

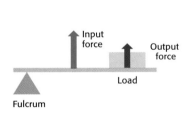

In a **third-class lever,** the input force is between the fulcrum and the load.

Using a third-class lever results in a **mechanical advantage of less than 1** because force is decreased. But third-class levers increase the distance through which the output force is exerted.

Teach

Making Models— BASIC

Seesaws as First-Class Levers
Provide students with triangular blocks and long pieces of wood so they can make small seesaws. Have students experiment with the position and size of the weights and the placement of the fulcrum. Have them write their observations and descriptions in their **science journal.** LS Kinesthetic

ACTiViTy ———— GENERAL

Classifying Tools Gather a selection of levers, such as brooms, shovels, crowbars, fishing poles, ice or sugar-cube tongs, pliers, scissors, baseball bats, tennis rackets, hockey sticks, golf clubs, canoe paddles, boat oars, wheelbarrows, nutcrackers, tweezers, and bottle openers. Divide the class into groups, and assign each group several tools. Have each group work together to locate the fulcrum, load, location of input force, and location of output force in each lever. Then, have each group share its information with other groups. LS Interpersonal

Answer to Reading Check
Each class of lever involves a different set of mechanical-advantage possibilities.

BRAIN FOOD

Levers Besides their obvious uses in bottle openers and nail pullers, levers are also used in devices such as fishing rods, cranes, typewriters, pianos, parking meters, and scales.

Is That a Fact!

The human body uses simple machines. Muscles and bones form first-class and third-class levers. When you look up, the skull pivots on the neck vertebrae, forming a first-class lever. When you kick a soccer ball, the contracting muscle pulls your leg upward, acting as a third-class lever.

Figure 4 The mechanical advantage of a pulley is equal to the number of rope segments that support the load. Each of these supporting rope segments applies a force equal to the input force to do the work of lifting the load. For this reason, the movable pulley has two input force arrows. The combined distance through which those input forces are exerted is the input distance, which is twice the distance that the load is actually lifted. **LS** Visual

Guided Practice— GENERAL

Simple Machines Collage Collect some old magazines. After students have read the section on simple machines, have them look through the magazines for pictures of different types of simple machines. Have students make a collage that classifies the pictures according to the type of simple machine they represent. **LS** Visual

pulley a simple machine that consists of a wheel over which a rope, chain, or wire passes

Pulleys

When you open window blinds by pulling on a cord, you're using a pulley. A **pulley** is a simple machine that has a grooved wheel that holds a rope or a cable. A load is attached to one end of the rope, and an input force is applied to the other end. Types of pulleys are shown in **Figure 4.**

Fixed Pulleys

A fixed pulley is attached to something that does not move. By using a fixed pulley, you can pull down on the rope to lift the load up. The pulley changes the direction of the force. Elevators make use of fixed pulleys.

Movable Pulleys

Unlike fixed pulleys, movable pulleys are attached to the object being moved. A movable pulley does not change a force's direction. Movable pulleys do increase force, but they also increase the distance over which the input force must be exerted.

Block and Tackles

When a fixed pulley and a movable pulley are used together, the pulley system is called a *block and tackle*. The mechanical advantage of a block and tackle depends on the number of rope segments.

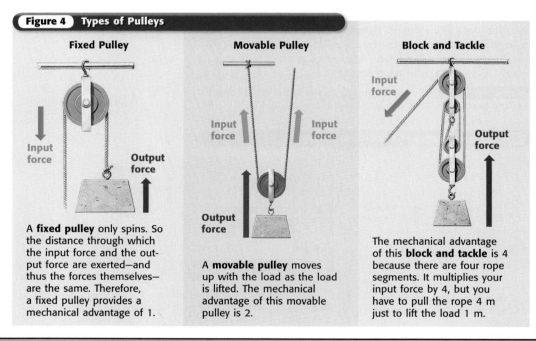

Figure 4 Types of Pulleys

Fixed Pulley

Input force

Output force

A **fixed pulley** only spins. So the distance through which the input force and the output force are exerted—and thus the forces themselves—are the same. Therefore, a fixed pulley provides a mechanical advantage of 1.

Movable Pulley

Input force

Input force

Output force

A **movable pulley** moves up with the load as the load is lifted. The mechanical advantage of this movable pulley is 2.

Block and Tackle

Input force

Output force

The mechanical advantage of this **block and tackle** is 4 because there are four rope segments. It multiplies your input force by 4, but you have to pull the rope 4 m just to lift the load 1 m.

CONNECTION ACTIVITY
Real World —— GENERAL

Machines in Your School Take students to visit the custodian's area in the school building. Have the custodian demonstrate the uses of different machines, and discuss how they make the necessary tasks of maintaining the school building easier. **LS** Interpersonal

Figure 5 **How a Wheel and Axle Works**

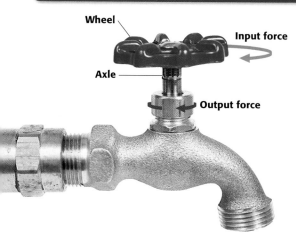

Wheel

Input force

Axle

Output force

a When a small input force is applied to the wheel, the wheel rotates through a circular distance.

b As the wheel turns, so does the axle. But because the axle is smaller than the wheel, it rotates through a smaller distance, which makes the output force larger than the input force

Wheel and Axle

Did you know that a faucet is a machine? The faucet shown in **Figure 5** is an example of a **wheel and axle,** a simple machine consisting of two circular objects of different sizes. Doorknobs, wrenches, and steering wheels all use a wheel and axle. **Figure 5** shows how a wheel and axle works.

wheel and axle a simple machine consisting of two circular objects of different sizes; the wheel is the larger of the two circular objects

Mechanical Advantage of a Wheel and Axle

The mechanical advantage of a wheel and axle can be found by dividing the *radius* (the distance from the center to the edge) of the wheel by the radius of the axle, as shown in **Figure 6.** Turning the wheel results in a mechanical advantage of greater than 1 because the radius of the wheel is larger than the radius of the axle.

✓ Reading Check How is the mechanical advantage of a wheel and axle calculated?

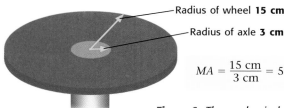

Radius of wheel **15 cm**

Radius of axle **3 cm**

$$MA = \frac{15 \text{ cm}}{3 \text{ cm}} = 5$$

Figure 6 *The mechanical advantage of a wheel and axle is the radius of the wheel divided by the radius of the axle.*

ACTiViTy ────── **BASIC**

Wheels and Axles Brainstorm with students to generate a list of everyday objects that contain wheels and axles. Write the list on the board, and then ask students to point out the wheel and the axle in each one.
LS Interpersonal

ACTiViTy ────── **ADVANCED**

Gears Set up a small gear station in the classroom. Obtain several gears of different sizes, a Pegboard, and some pins to secure the gears. Also, provide stickers or pens to mark the gears. Explain that a gear is a wheel with teeth around its edge. Have students experiment with the gears and try to calculate the mechanical advantage of a series of gears by using the equation for the wheel and axle. **LS** Kinesthetic

Answer to Reading Check

the radius of the wheel divided by the radius of the axle

Using the Figure—GENERAL

Inclined Planes Use **Figure 7** and the diagram below it to explain how you can determine mechanical advantage of an inclined plane by using distances. Explain the process as follows:

$$work\ input = work\ output$$

$$F\ (input) \times d\ (input) =$$
$$F\ (output) \times d\ (output)$$

This equation can be rearranged into ratios to show

$$\frac{F\ (input)}{F\ (output)} = \frac{d\ (output)}{d\ (input)}$$

The force ratio can be used to determine mechanical advantage. Because the distance ratio is equivalent to the force ratio, it can also be used to determine mechanical advantage. **LS** Visual

Answer to Reading Check

A slanted surface that makes the raising of loads easier, such as a ramp.

Answers to Math Focus

1. $MA = 9\ m \div 1.5\ m = 6$
2. $MA = 120\ m \div 20\ m = 6$
3. $MA = 2\ m \div 8\ m = 0.25$

Figure 7 *The work you do on the piano to roll it up the ramp is the same as the work you would do to lift it straight up. An inclined plane simply allows you to apply a smaller force over a greater distance.*

inclined plane a simple machine that is a straight, slanted surface, which facilitates the raising of loads; a ramp

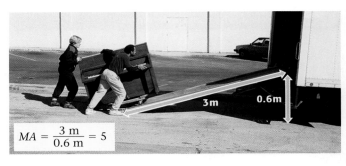

$$MA = \frac{3\ m}{0.6\ m} = 5$$

Inclined Planes

Do you remember the story about how the Egyptians built the Great Pyramid? One of the machines they used was the **inclined plane.** An *inclined plane* is a simple machine that is a straight, slanted surface. A ramp is an inclined plane.

Using an inclined plane to load a piano into a truck, as **Figure 7** shows, is easier than lifting the piano into the truck. Rolling the piano along an inclined plane requires a smaller input force than is needed to lift the piano into the truck. The same work is done on the piano, just over a longer distance.

✓ Reading Check What is an inclined plane?

Mechanical Advantage of Inclined Planes

The greater the ratio of an inclined plane's length to its height is, the greater the mechanical advantage is. The mechanical advantage (*MA*) of an inclined plane can be calculated by dividing the *length* of the inclined plane by the *height* to which the load is lifted. The inclined plane in **Figure 7** has a mechanical advantage of 3 m/0.6 m = 5.

 **MATH FOCUS**

Mechanical Advantage of an Inclined Plane A heavy box is pushed up a ramp that has an incline of 4.8 m long and 1.2 m high. What is the mechanical advantage of the ramp?

Step 1: Write the equation for the mechanical advantage of an inclined plane.

$$MA = \frac{l}{h}$$

Step 2: Replace *l* and *h* with length and height.

$$MA = \frac{4.8\ m}{1.2\ m} = 4$$

Now It's Your Turn

1. A wheelchair ramp is 9 m long and 1.5 m high. What is the mechanical advantage of the ramp?
2. As a pyramid is built, a stone block is dragged up a ramp that is 120 m long and 20 m high. What is the mechanical advantage of the ramp?
3. If an inclined plane were 2 m long and 8 m high, what would be its mechanical advantage?

 INCLUSION Strategies

- **Behavior Control Issues**
- **Attention Deficit Disorder**
- **Hearing Impaired**

Apply the concept of mechanical advantage in a concrete setting. Measure the mechanical advantage of two or three wheelchair ramps at your school. Use this formula: *mechanical advantage = ramp length ÷ ramp height.*

If the ramps have different slants, which of the ramps is easiest to use?
LS Logical/Kinesthetic

 **SCIENCE HUMOR**

Q: Why didn't the ramp help out when the piano was being loaded onto the truck?

A: It didn't have the inclination.

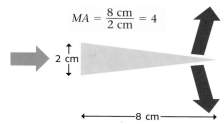

$$MA = \frac{8 \text{ cm}}{2 \text{ cm}} = 4$$

2 cm

←——— 8 cm ———→

Figure 8 *A knife is a common example of a wedge, a simple machine consisting of two inclined planes back to back.*

Wedges

Imagine trying to cut a melon in half with a spoon. It wouldn't be easy, would it? A knife is much more useful for cutting because it is a **wedge.** A *wedge* is a pair of inclined planes that move. A wedge applies an output force that is greater than your input force, but you apply the input force over a greater distance. For example, a knife is a common wedge that can easily cut into a melon and push apart its two halves, as shown in **Figure 8.** Other useful wedges include doorstops, plows, ax heads, and chisels.

Mechanical Advantage of Wedges

The longer and thinner the wedge is, the greater its mechanical advantage is. That's why axes and knives cut better when you sharpen them—you are making the wedge thinner. Therefore, less input force is required. The mechanical advantage of a wedge can be found by dividing the length of the wedge by its greatest thickness, as shown in **Figure 8.**

Screws

A **screw** is an inclined plane that is wrapped in a spiral around a cylinder, as you can see in **Figure 9.** When a screw is turned, a small force is applied over the long distance along the inclined plane of the screw. Meanwhile, the screw applies a large force through the short distance it is pushed. Screws are used most commonly as fasteners.

Mechanical Advantage of Screws

If you could unwind the inclined plane of a screw, you would see that the plane is very long and has a gentle slope. Recall that the longer an inclined plane is compared with its height, the greater its mechanical advantage. Similarly, the longer the spiral on a screw is and the closer together the threads are, the greater the screw's mechanical advantage is. A jar lid is a screw that has a large mechanical advantage.

wedge a simple machine that is made up of two inclined planes and that moves; often used for cutting

screw a simple machine that consists of an inclined plane wrapped around a cylinder

Figure 9 *If you could unwind a screw, you would see that it is actually a very long inclined plane.*

ACTIVITY ———— GENERAL

MATERIALS

FOR EACH PAIR
• cardboard
• magnifying lenses
• zippers, new or old

Zippers Have pairs of students examine a zipper. Have them discuss how the slide on the zipper works and write two or three paragraphs describing the parts of the slide in terms of simple machines. **LS** Verbal

Homework ———— ADVANCED

The Archimedes Screw Have students research the invention of the Archimedes screw and its use through the centuries up to the present day. Have them describe as many different applications of the screw as they can. **LS** Logical

Using the Figure — GENERAL

Wedges Using **Figure 8** and the drawing of a wedge, help students understand that the output force from the wedge is applied perpendicularly to the input force. For instance, when you slide a doorstop under a door (a horizontal input force), the wedge pushes up on the door (a vertical output force). **LS** Visual

ACTIVITY ———— BASIC

PORTFOLIO **Screws** To help students better understand the concept of a screw, have them make a screw by cutting out the shape of an inclined plane. Have them color the sloping edge of the plane with a marker. Then, have them wrap the inclined plane around a pencil, starting with the tallest end of the plane. Point out that the colored edge of the inclined plane forms the thread of a screw. **LS** Kinesthetic

CONNECTION ACTIVITY
Math ———— GENERAL

Mechanical Advantages of Screws Provide three or four screws for each student. Have students calculate and compare the mechanical advantage for each screw by dividing the length of the inclined plane by the height. To measure the length of the screw threads, students should wrap a piece of string around five turns of the screw and then unwind and measure the string. By counting the total number of screw threads over the entire length of the screw, they can estimate the total length. This total length should be used for the length of the inclined plane. To determine the height, students should measure the screw from the top screw thread to the bottom. **LS** Logical

Simple Versus Compound Machines Review the types of simple machines and the ways in which each changes size or direction of force. Then, ask students for examples of compound machines and the simple machines that compose them.
LS Logical

Quiz ──────── GENERAL

1. Why are simple machines so useful? (They make work easier.)

2. Identify types of simple machines you might find on a playground. Describe how each of them modifies work. (Sample answer: seesaw: lever changes direction of input force; merry-go-round: wheel and axle makes the input force on the axle cause the wheel to move in a circle)

3. How does reducing friction increase the mechanical efficiency of a compound machine? (Less work input is used to overcome friction, so work output is higher, and mechanical efficiency is higher.)

Alternative Assessment ───── GENERAL

Machines in a Story Have each student write a story that incorporates six simple or compound machines. The machines must operate in some way appropriate to the story line. Suggest that students illustrate their stories. **LS** Verbal

compound machine a machine made of more than one simple machine

Everyday Machines
With a parent, think of five simple or compound machines that you encounter each day. List them In your **science journal,** and indicate what type of machine each is. Include at least one compound machine and one machine that is part of your body.

Compound Machines

You are surrounded by machines. You even have machines in your body! But most of the machines in your world are **compound machines,** machines that are made of two or more simple machines. You have already seen one example of a compound machine: a block and tackle. A block and tackle consists of two or more pulleys.

Figure 10 shows a common example of a compound machine. A can opener may seem simple, but it is actually three machines combined. It consists of a second-class lever, a wheel and axle, and a wedge. When you squeeze the handle, you are making use of a second-class lever. The blade of the can opener acts as a wedge as it cuts into the can's top. The knob that you turn to open the can is a wheel and axle.

Mechanical Efficiency of Compound Machines

The mechanical efficiency of most compound machines is low. The efficiency is low because compound machines have more moving parts than simple machines do, thus there is more friction to overcome. Compound machines, such as automobiles and airplanes, can involve many simple machines. It is very important to reduce friction as much as possible, because too much friction can damage the simple machines that make up the compound machine. Friction can be lowered by using lubrication and other techniques.

✓ **Reading Check** What special disadvantage do compound machines have?

Figure 10 A can opener is a compound machine. The handle is a second-class lever, the knob is a wheel and axle, and a wedge is used to open the can.

Wheel and axle

Wedge

Second class lever

Answer to Reading Check
They have more moving parts than simple machines do, so they tend to be less efficient than simple machines.

Summary

- In a first-class lever, the fulcrum is between the force and the load. In a second-class lever, the load is between the force and the fulcrum. In a third-class lever, the force is between the fulcrum and the load.
- The mechanical advantage of an inclined plane is length divided by height. Wedges and screws are types of inclined planes.
- A wedge is a type of inclined plane. Its mechanical advantage is its length divided by its greatest thickness.

- The mechanical advantage of a wheel and axle is the radius of the wheel divided by the radius of the axle.
- Types of pulleys include fixed pulleys, movable pulleys, and block and tackles.
- Compound machines consist of two or more simple machines.
- Compound machines have low mechanical efficiencies because they have more moving parts and therefore more friction to overcome.

Using Key Terms

1. In your own words, write a definition for the term *lever*.

2. Use the following terms in the same sentence: *inclined plane*, *wedge*, and *screw*.

Understanding Key Ideas

3. Which class of lever always has a mechanical advantage of greater than 1?
   a. first-class
   b. second-class
   c. third-class
   d. None of the above

4. Give an example of each of the following simple machines: first-class lever, second-class lever, third-class lever, inclined plane, wedge, and screw.

Math Skills

5. A ramp is 0.5 m high and has a slope that is 4 m long. What is its mechanical advantage?

6. The radius of the wheel of a wheel and axle is 4 times the radius of the axle. What is the mechanical advantage of the wheel and axle?

Critical Thinking

7. **Applying Concepts** A third-class lever has a mechanical advantage of less than 1. Explain why it is useful for some tasks.

8. **Making Inferences** Which compound machine would you expect to have the lowest mechanical efficiency: a can opener or a pair of scissors? Explain your answer.

Interpreting Graphics

9. Indicate two simple machines being used in the picture below.

SCI*LINKS*. NSTA
Developed and maintained by the National Science Teachers Association

For a variety of links related to this chapter, go to www.scilinks.org
Topic: Simple Machines; Compound Machines
SciLinks code: HSM1395; HSM0331

Answers to Section Review

1. Sample answer: A lever is a simple machine consisting of a bar that pivots at a fulcrum, acting to lift a load.

2. Sample answer: Wedges and screws are two special types of inclined planes.

3. b

4. Sample answer: first-class lever: seesaw; second-class lever: bottle opener; third-class lever: hammer; inclined plane: ramp; wedge: doorstop; screw: jar lid

5. $MA = 4\,m \div 0.5\,m = 8$

6. $MA = 4 \div 1 = 4$

7. A third-class lever increases the distance through which force is output.

8. Sample answer: a can opener; It is a compound machine that consists of three simple machines, whereas a pair of scissors is a compound machine consisting of two simple machines. A complex machine can be expected to have greater mechanical efficiency the fewer simple machines it consists of, because there will be fewer moving parts with fewer machines.

9. The door on its hinge is a lever (second-class); the knob is a wheel and axle.

CHAPTER RESOURCES

Chapter Resource File

- **Section Quiz** GENERAL
- **Section Review** GENERAL
- **Vocabulary and Section Summary** GENERAL
- **Reinforcement Worksheet** BASIC
- **Critical Thinking** ADVANCED

A Powerful Workout

Teacher's Notes

Time Required

One or two 45-minute class periods

Lab Ratings

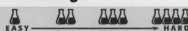

EASY ——————————— HARD

Teacher Prep 🧪
Student Set-Up 🧪
Concept Level 🧪🧪
Clean Up 🧪

MATERIALS

The materials listed for this lab are for the entire class or for smaller groups. Students in wheelchairs can use a ramp instead of a flight of stairs.

Safety Caution

Students with asthma or any other respiratory problems should not do this lab. Any student who becomes winded should sit down and take deep breaths. Caution students that this is not a race to see who can get the fastest time.

Answer

2. Sample answer: Climbing up a flight of stairs takes less than 100 W of power. This amount of energy doesn't seem to be as much energy as a light bulb gives off.

Lab Notes

To help students calculate averages, set up a class data table on the board. The table should have four columns: "Student"; "Power S" (for power for slow walk); "Power Q" (for power for quick walk); and "Average" (each student's average power). An individual average power is the power for a slow walk plus the power for a quick walk divided by 2. The class average power is all the individual averages together divided by the number of students in the class.

A Powerful Workout

Does the amount of work that you do depend on how fast you do it? No! But the amount of time in which you do work does affect your power—the rate of work done. In this lab, you'll calculate your work and power for climbing a flight of stairs at different speeds. Then you'll compare your power with that of an ordinary household object—a 100 W light bulb.

OBJECTIVES

Calculate the work and power used to climb a flight of stairs.

Compare your work and power with that of a 100 W light bulb.

MATERIALS

- flight of stairs
- ruler, metric
- stopwatch

Ask a Question

1. How does your power in climbing a flight of stairs compare with the power of a 100 W light bulb?

Form a Hypothesis

2. Write a hypothesis that answers the question in step 1. Explain your reasoning.

Data Collection Table

Height of step (cm)	Number of steps	Height of stairs (m)	Time for slow walk (s)	Time for quick walk (s)
		DO NOT WRITE IN BOOK		

Test the Hypothesis

3. Copy the Data Collection Table onto a separate sheet of paper.

4. Use a metric ruler to measure the height of one stair step. Record the measurement in your Data Collection Table. Be sure to include units for all measurements.

5. Count the number of stairs, including the top step, and record this number in your Data Collection Table.

6. Calculate the height of the climb by multiplying the number of steps by the height of one step. Record your answer in meters. (You will need to convert your answer from centimeters to meters.)

7. Use a stopwatch to measure how many seconds it takes you to walk slowly up a flight of stairs. Record your measurement in your Data Collection Table.

CHAPTER RESOURCES

Chapter Resource File

- Datasheet for Chapter Lab
- Lab Notes and Answers

Technology

Classroom Videos
- Lab Video

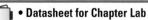

- Inclined to Move
- Building Machines
- Wheeling and Dealing

8 Now measure how many seconds it takes you to walk quickly up a flight of stairs. Be careful not to overexert yourself. This is not a race to see who can get the fastest time!

Analyze the Results

1 **Constructing Tables** Copy the Calculations Table below onto a separate sheet of paper.

Calculations Table			
Weight (N)	Work (J)	Power for slow walk (W)	Power for quick walk (W)
	DO NOT WRITE IN BOOK		

2 **Examining Data** Determine your weight in newtons, and record it in your Calculations Table. Your weight in newtons is your weight in pounds (lb) multiplied by 4.45 N/lb.

3 **Examining Data** Calculate and record your work done in climbing the stairs by using the following equation:

$$work = force \times distance$$

(Hint: If you are having trouble determining the force exerted, remember that force is measured in newtons.)

4 **Examining Data** Calculate and record your power output by using the following equation:

$$power = \frac{work}{time}$$

The unit for power is the watt (1 watt = 1 joule/second).

Draw Conclusions

5 **Evaluating Methods** In step 3 of "Analyze the Results," you were asked to calculate your work done in climbing the stairs. Why weren't you asked to calculate your work for each trial (slow walk and quick walk)?

6 **Drawing Conclusions** Look at your hypothesis. Was your hypothesis correct? Now that you have measured your power, write a statement that describes how your power compares with that of a 100 W light bulb.

7 **Applying Conclusions** The work done to move one electron in a light bulb is very small. Write down two reasons why the power used is large. (Hint: How many electrons are in the filament of a light bulb? How did you use more power in trial 2?)

Communicating Your Data

Your teacher will provide a class data table on the board. Add your average power to the table. Then calculate the average power from the class data. How many students would it take to create power equal to the power of a 100 W bulb?

Chapter Review

Assignment Guide

SECTION	QUESTIONS
1	1, 4–5, 8–9, 11,
2	7, 12, 15–16, 18, 20, 22
3	2–3, 6, 10, 13, 17, 19, 21, 23–24

ANSWERS

Using Key Terms

1. Sample answer: Work is a measure of the energy required to exert force over a distance. Power is a measure of the rate at which work is done.

2. Sample answer: A lever is a simple machine that consists of a bar that pivots on a fulcrum. An inclined plane is a simple machine that consists of a straight, slanted surface.

3. Sample answer: A wheel and axle is a simple machine that consists of two attached circular objects of different sizes. A pulley is a simple machine consisting of a grooved wheel that holds a rope or a cable.

Understanding Key Ideas

4. c
5. a
6. b
7. d
8. d
9. c
10. first-class levers and wedges

USING KEY TERMS

For each pair of terms, explain how the meanings of the terms differ.

1. *work* and *power*

2. *lever* and *inclined plane*

3. *wheel and axle* and *pulley*

UNDERSTANDING KEY IDEAS

Multiple Choice

4. Work is being done when
   a. you apply a force to an object.
   b. an object is moving after you applied a force to it.
   c. you exert a force that moves an object in the direction of the force.
   d. you do something that is difficult.

5. What is the unit for work?
   a. joule
   b. joule per second
   c. newton
   d. watt

6. Which of the following is a simple machine?
   a. a bicycle
   b. a jar lid
   c. a pair of scissors
   d. a can opener

7. A machine can increase
   a. distance by decreasing force.
   b. force by decreasing distance.
   c. neither distance nor force.
   d. Either (a) or (b)

---

8. What is power?
   a. the strength of someone or something
   b. the force that is used
   c. the work that is done
   d. the rate at which work is done

9. What is the unit for power?
   a. newton
   b. kilogram
   c. watt
   d. joule

Short Answer

10. Identify the two simple machines that make up a pair of scissors.

11. Explain why you do work on a bag of groceries when you pick it up but not when you carry it.

12. Why is the work output of a machine always less than the work input?

13. What does the mechanical advantage of a first-class lever depend upon? Describe how it can be changed.

Math Skills

14. You and a friend together apply a force of 1,000 N to a car, which makes the car roll 10 m in 1 min and 40 s.
    a. How much work did you and your friend do together?
    b. What was the power output?

15. A lever allows a 35 N load to be lifted with a force of 7 N. What is the mechanical advantage of the lever?

---

11. Sample answer: When you pick up a bag of groceries, the bag moves in the direction of the force. While you are holding the bag and walking, your forward motion is perpendicular to the upward force you are using to carry the bag, so you are not doing work on the bag.

12. Friction involved in the operation of the machine's moving parts causes some of the input energy to be lost as heat.

13. Sample answer: The mechanical advantage of a first-class lever depends upon the placement of the fulcrum. If the fulcrum is closer to the load than to the input force, the lever has a mechanical advantage of greater than 1. If the fulcrum is exactly in the middle of the load and the input force, the mechanical advantage of the lever is 1. If the fulcrum is closer to the input force than to the load, the lever has a mechanical advantage of less than 1.

14. a. $W = 1,000 \text{ N} \times 10 \text{ m} = 10,000 \text{ J}$
    b. $P = 10,000 \text{ J} \div 100 \text{ s} = 100 \text{ W}$

15. $MA = 35 \text{ N} \div 7 \text{ N} = 5$

CRITICAL THINKING

16 Concept Mapping Use the following terms to create a concept map: *work, force, distance, machine,* and *mechanical advantage*.

17 Analyzing Ideas Explain why levers usually have a greater mechanical efficiency than other simple machines do.

18 Making Inferences The amount of work done on a machine is 300 J, and the machine does 50 J of work. What can you say about the amount of friction that the machine has while operating?

19 Applying Concepts The winding road shown below is a series of inclined planes. Describe how a winding road makes it easier for vehicles to travel up a hill.

20 Predicting Consequences Why wouldn't you want to reduce the friction involved in using a winding road?

21 Making Comparisons How does the way that a wedge's mechanical advantage is determined differ from the way that a screw's mechanical advantage is determined?

22 Identifying Relationships If the mechanical advantage of a certain machine is greater than 1, what does that tell you about the relationship between the input force and distance and output force and distance?

INTERPRETING GRAPHICS

For each of the images below, identify the class of lever used and calculate the mechanical advantage of the lever.

23

Output force 120 N

Input force 40 N

Fulcrum

24

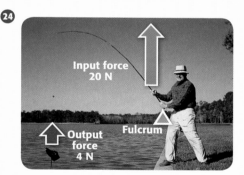

Input force 20 N

Output force 4 N

Fulcrum

Critical Thinking

16. An answer to this exercise can be found at the end of this book.

17. Levers don't have a lot of moving parts, so they don't generate as much friction as other machines do.

18. Sample answer: The work output of the machine is quite low compared to the work input. Presumably, the machine operates with a lot of friction.

19. It allows the work needed to climb up the hill to be spread out over a long distance, thereby requiring less force.

20. Sample answer: This is a case in which friction is useful. It increases the traction of the cars' tires on the road and keeps them from slipping as they make turns. Reducing the friction on the winding road would make the road more dangerous to drive on.

21. A wedge's mechanical advantage is its length divided by greatest width. A screw's mechanical advantage is determined by the comparison of its spiral thread length with its vertical length.

22. The input force will be less than the output force, and the input distance will be greater than the output distance.

Interpreting Graphics

23. second-class lever;
$MA = 120 \text{ N} \div 40 \text{ N} = 3$

24. third-class lever;
$MA = 4 \text{ N} \div 20 \text{ N} = 0.2$

Standardized Test Preparation

Teacher's Note

To provide practice under more realistic testing conditions, give students 20 minutes to answer all of the questions in this Standardized Test Preparation.

Answers to the standardized test preparation can help you identify student misconceptions and misunderstandings.

READING

Passage 1

1. D
2. F

Question 1: The information stated in answers A, B, and C is true, but those answers do not encompass the main idea of the passage as answer D does.

READING

Read each of the passages below. Then, answer the questions that follow each passage.

Passage 1   The Great Pyramid, located in Giza, Egypt, covers an area the size of 7 city blocks and rises about 40 stories high. The Great Pyramid was built around 2600 BCE and took less than 30 years to complete. During this time, the Egyptians cut and moved more than 2 million stone blocks, most of which average 2,000 kg. The workers did not have cranes, bulldozers, or any other heavy-duty machines. What they did have were two simple machines—the inclined plane and the lever. Archeologists have found the remains of inclined planes, or ramps, made from mud, stone, and wood. The Egyptians pushed or pulled the blocks along ramps to raise the blocks to the proper height. Notches in many blocks indicate that huge levers were used as giant crowbars to lift and move the heavy blocks.

1. What is the main idea of the passage?
   A Archeologists have found the remains of inclined planes near the pyramids.
   B The Great Pyramid at Giza was built in less than 30 years.
   C The Egyptians cut and moved more than 2 million stone blocks.
   D The Egyptians used simple machines to build the Great Pyramid at Giza.

2. Which of the following is a fact stated in the passage?
   F The Great Pyramid was made using more than 2 million stone blocks.
   G Each of the stone blocks used to build the Great Pyramid was exactly 2,000 kg.
   H Ancient Egyptians used cranes to build the Great Pyramid.
   I The Great Pyramid at Giza has a mass of about 2 million kg.

Passage 2   While riding a bicycle, you have probably experienced vibrations when the wheels of the bicycle hit bumps in the road. The force of the vibrations travels up through the frame to the rider. Slight vibrations can cause discomfort. Large ones can cause you to lose control of the bike and crash. Early bicycle designs made no attempt to dampen the <u>shock</u> of vibrations. Later designs used air-filled rubber tires and softer seats with springs to absorb some of the vibrations. Today's bike designs provide a safer, more comfortable ride. Various new materials—titanium, for example—absorb shock better than traditional steel and aluminum do. More important, designers are putting a variety of shock absorbers—devices that absorb energy—into bike designs.

1. In the passage, what does the term *shock* mean?
   A a medical emergency that can be caused by blood loss
   B a dry material used in early bicycles
   C a feeling of being stunned and surprised
   D a jolt or impact

2. Which of the following is a fact stated in the passage?
   F You have experienced vibrations while bicycle riding.
   G Slight vibrations can cause severe discomfort.
   H Titanium absorbs shock better than aluminum does.
   I Today's bike designs provide a more fashionable ride.

Passage 2

1. D
2. H

Question 1: A and C may be true alternative definitions of the word *shock,* but D states the meaning of the word given in the passage. This question tests students' ability to read for meaning in context.

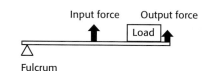

INTERPRETING GRAPHICS

Use the diagram below to answer the questions that follow.

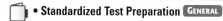

Input force   Output force

Load

Fulcrum

1. How does this lever make work easier?

A by changing the direction of the force

B by increasing both force and distance

C by increasing force and decreasing distance

D by decreasing force and increasing distance

2. What would the mechanical advantage of this lever be?

F less than 1

G 1

H greater than 1

I There is not enough information to determine the answer.

3. What type of lever is the lever in the diagram?

A a first-class lever

B a second-class lever

C a third-class lever

D There is not enough information to determine the answer.

4. Which of the following items is the same type of lever as the lever in the diagram?

F a seesaw

G a wheelbarrow

H a bottle opener

I an arm lifting a barbell

MATH

Read each question below, and choose the best answer.

1. For a special musical number during a school choir concert, 6 students stood in the first row, 10 students stood in the second row, and 14 students stood in the third row. If the pattern continued, how many students stood in the fifth row?

A 18

B 22

C 26

D 30

2. Michael baked some bread for his friends. He put 2½ cups of flour in each loaf. Altogether, he used 12½ cups of flour. How many loaves did he make?

F 2 loaves

G 4 loaves

H 5 loaves

I 15 loaves

3. A force of 15 N is exerted over a distance of 6 m. How much work was done? (Use the equation $W = F \times d$.)

A 21 J

B 21 N

C 90 J

D 90 N

4. If 350 J of work was done in 50 s, what was the power output? (Use the equation $P = W/t$.)

F 7 W

G 70 W

H 1,750 W

I 17,500 W

INTERPRETING GRAPHICS

1. D

2. F

3. C

4. I

 **TEST DOCTOR**

Question 1: The difference in sizes between the input force and output force arrows in the diagram indicates that the output force is smaller than the input force. This information alone is enough to point to answer D. You can tell by the directions of the arrows that the direction of the force is not changed.

MATH

1. B

2. H

3. C

4. F

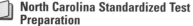 **TEST DOCTOR**

Question 3: The unit of work and energy is joules, so B and D can be ruled out. A would be selected by a student mistakenly adding force and distance instead of multiplying them.

Standardized Test Preparation

CHAPTER RESOURCES

Chapter Resource File

 • Standardized Test Preparation GENERAL

Workbooks

North Carolina Standardized Test Preparation
• Provides practice for the EOG test.

State Resources

For specific resources for your state, visit **go.hrw.com** and type in the keyword **HSMSTR**.

Science, Technology, and Society

Background
The kinetic sculpture pictured was built by Alexander Calder, who is best known for inventing the mobile. He died at the age of 78, after creating 16,000 works of art.

Weird Science

Background
Advances in microtechnology have allowed scientists to achieve impressive results in many fields. For example, medical researchers are working on special pills equipped with sensors, tiny pumps, and drug reservoirs.

Other technological advances include microscopic filters and air turbines for controlling the temperature of microchip arrays. One team of scientists has created a molecular "on-off switch" that could be used to store information in computers.

Science in Action

Science, Technology, and Society

Kinetic Sculpture
The collection of tubes, tracks, balls, and blocks of wood shown in the photo is an audio-kinetic sculpture. A conveyor belt lifts the balls to a point high on the track, and the balls wind their way down as they are pulled by the force of gravity and pushed by various other forces. They twist through spirals, drop straight down tubes, and sometimes go up and around loops as if on a roller coaster. All this is made possible by the artist's applications of principles of kinetic energy, the energy of motion.

Math ACTiViTY
A conveyor belt on a kinetic sculpture lifts a ball to a point 0.8 m high. It exerts 0.05 N of force as it does so. How much work does the conveyor belt do on the ball?

Weird Science

Nanomachines
The technology of making things smaller and smaller keeps growing and growing. Powerful computers can now be held in the palm of your hand. But what can motors that are smaller than grains of pepper do? How can gnat-sized robots that can swim through the bloodstream be used? One possible field in which very small machines, *nanomachines,* can be used is in medicine.

Some scientists are looking into the possibility of creating cell-sized machines called *nanobots.* These tiny robots may have many uses in medicine if they can be injected into a person's bloodstream.

Language Arts ACTiViTY
WRITING SKILL Write a short story in which nanobots are used to save someone's life. Describe the machines the nanobots use in destroying deadly bacteria, clearing blood clots, or delivering medicine.

Answer to Math Activity
$W = 0.05 \text{ N} \times 0.8 \text{ m} = 0.04 \text{ J}$

Answer to Language Arts Activity
Encourage creativity and scientific accuracy by providing students with a body atlas or similar reference work. Suggest the idea of specialized nanobots who can travel through only certain systems of the body (such as the circulatory, endocrine, or nervous system). What common problems might occur in that environment, and what could they do to help? For example, a nanobot inside a lung would see bronchial tubes, alveoli, and capillaries. The nanobot could break down contaminants in the air sacs, help fight off infections, or remove fluids in patients who have pneumonia.

People in Science

Mike Hensler

The Surf Chair Mike Hensler was a lifeguard at Daytona Beach, Florida, when he realized that it was next to impossible for someone in a wheelchair to come onto the beach. Although he had never invented a machine before, Hensler decided to build a wheelchair that could be driven across sand without getting stuck. He began spending many evenings in his driveway with a pile of lawn-chair parts, designing the chair by trial and error.

The result of Hensler's efforts looks very different from a conventional wheelchair. With huge rubber wheels and a thick frame of white PVC pipe, the Surf Chair not only moves easily over sandy terrain but also is weather resistant and easy to clean. The newest models of the Surf Chair come with optional attachments, such as a variety of umbrellas, detachable armrests and footrests, and even places to attach fishing rods.

Social Studies Activity

List some simple and compound machines that are used as access devices for people who are disabled. Research how these machines came to be in common use.

go.hrw.com
To learn more about these Science in Action topics, visit go.hrw.com and type in the keyword **HP5WRKF.**

Current Science
Check out Current Science® articles related to this chapter by visiting go.hrw.com. Just type in the keyword **HP5CS08.**

Contents

Skills Practice Lab

Go Fly a Bike!

Teacher's Notes

Time Required

One 45-minute class period

Lab Ratings

△	△△	△△△	△△△△
EASY			HARD

Teacher Prep △
Student Set-Up △△△
Concept Level △△
Clean Up △△

MATERIALS

The materials listed on the student page are enough for a group of 3 to 4 students.

Safety Caution

Remind students to review all safety cautions and icons before beginning this lab activity.

Preparation Notes

Conduct this activity on a day when the wind is blowing but not when the wind speed is greater than 50 km/h. Use straight, plastic straws. Before the activity, explain that an *anemometer* is a device that measures wind speed. It works because the wind pushes the cups at the same speed that the wind is moving.

Skills Practice Lab

Go Fly a Bike!

Your friend Daniel just invented a bicycle that can fly! Trouble is, the bike can fly only when the wind speed is between 3 m/s and 10 m/s. If the wind is not blowing hard enough, the bike won't get enough lift to rise into the air, and if the wind is blowing too hard, the bike is difficult to control. Daniel needs to know if he can fly his bike today. Can you build a device that can estimate how fast the wind is blowing?

Ask a Question

1. How can I construct a device to measure wind speed?

Form a Hypothesis

2. Write a possible answer for the question above. Explain your reasoning.

Test the Hypothesis

3. Cut off the rolled edges of all five paper cups. They will then be lighter so that they can spin more easily.

4. Measure and place four equally spaced markings 1 cm below the rim of one of the paper cups.

5. Use the hole punch to punch a hole at each mark so that the cup has four equally spaced holes. Use the sharp pencil to carefully punch a hole in the center of the bottom of the cup.

6. Push a straw through two opposite holes in the side of the cup.

7. Repeat step 5 for the other two holes. The straws should form an X.

8. Measure 3 cm from the bottom of the remaining paper cups, and mark each spot with a dot.

9. At each dot, punch a hole in the paper cups with the hole punch.

10. Color the outside of one of the four cups.

MATERIALS

- clay, modeling
- cups, paper, small (5)
- hole punch
- marker, colored
- pencil, sharp, with an eraser
- ruler, metric
- scissors
- stapler, small
- straws, straight plastic (2)
- tape, masking
- thumbtack
- watch (or clock) that indicates seconds

SAFETY

Terry J. Rakes
Elmwood Jr. High
Rogers, Arkansas

11. Slide a cup on one of the straws by pushing the straw through the punched hole. Rotate the cup so that the bottom faces to the right.

12. Fold the end of the straw, and staple it to the inside of the cup directly across from the hole.

13. Repeat steps 11–12 for each of the remaining cups.

14. Push the tack through the intersection of the two straws.

15. Push the eraser end of a pencil through the bottom hole in the center cup. Push the tack as far as it will go into the end of the eraser.

16. Push the sharpened end of the pencil into some modeling clay to form a base. The device will then be able to stand up without being knocked over, as shown at right.

17. Blow into the cups so that they spin. Adjust the tack so that the cups can freely spin without wobbling or falling apart. Congratulations! You have just constructed an anemometer.

18. Find a suitable area outside to place the anemometer vertically on a surface away from objects that would obstruct the wind, such as buildings and trees.

19. Mark the surface at the base of the anemometer with masking tape. Label the tape "starting point."

20. Hold the colored cup over the starting point while your partner holds the watch.

21. Release the colored cup. At the same time, your partner should look at the watch or clock. As the cups spin, count the number of times the colored cup crosses the starting point in 10 s.

Analyze the Results

1. How many times did the colored cup cross the starting point in 10 s?

2. Divide your answer in step 21 by 10 to get the number of revolutions in 1 s.

3. Measure the diameter of your anemometer (the distance between the outside edges of two opposite cups) in centimeters. Multiply this number by 3.14 to get the circumference of the circle made by the cups of your anemometer.

4. Multiply your answer from step 3 by the number of revolutions per second (step 2). Divide that answer by 100 to get wind speed in meters per second.

5. Compare your results with those of your classmates. Did you get the same results? What could account for any slight differences in your results?

Draw Conclusions

6. Could Daniel fly his bicycle today? Why or why not?

CHAPTER RESOURCES

Chapter Resource File

- Datasheet for LabBook
- Lab Notes and Answers

Skills Practice Lab

Watching the Weather

Teacher's Notes

Time Required

One 45-minute class period

Lab Ratings

EASY —————————— HARD

Teacher Prep ⚗
Student Set-Up ⚗
Concept Level ⚗⚗
Clean Up ⚗

MATERIALS

The only material required in this lab is a pencil. Have students complete the lab individually.

Skills Practice Lab

Watching the Weather

Imagine that you own a private consulting firm that helps people plan for big occasions, such as weddings, parties, and celebrity events. One of your duties is making sure the weather doesn't put a damper on your clients' plans. In order to provide the best service possible, you have taken a crash course in reading weather maps. Will the celebrity golf match have to be delayed on account of rain? Will the wedding ceremony have to be moved inside so the blushing bride doesn't get soaked? It is your job to say yea or nay.

MATERIALS

- pencil

Procedure

1. Study the station model and legend shown on the next page. You will use the legend to interpret the weather map on the final page of this activity.

2. Weather data is represented on a weather map by a station model. A station model is a small circle that shows the location of the weather station along with a set of symbols and numbers around the circle that represent the data collected at the weather station. Study the table below.

Weather-Map Symbols					
Weather conditions		**Cloud cover**		**Wind speed (mph)**	
••	Light rain	○	No clouds	◎	Calm
∴	Moderate rain	◑	One-tenth or less	—— ∕	3–8
⋮	Heavy rain	◔	Two- to three-tenths	——— ∕	9–14
,	Drizzle	◑	Broken	——— ∕∕	15–20
∗ ∗	Light snow	◕	Nine-tenths	——— ∕∕	21–25
∗ ∗ ∗	Moderate snow	●	Overcast	——— ∕∕∕	32–37
⚡	Thunderstorm	⊗	Sky obscured	——— ∕∕∕∕	44–48
∿	Freezing rain	**Special Symbols**		——— ◢	55–60
∞	Haze	▲▲▲▲	Cold front	——— ◢◢	66–71
≡	Fog	●●●●	Warm front		
		H	High pressure		
		L	Low pressure		
		ᔐ	Hurricane		

Gordon Zibelman
Drexel Hill Middle School
Drexel Hill, Pennsylvania

Station Model

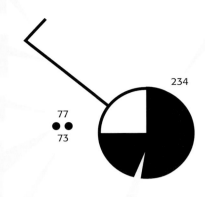

Wind speed is represented by whole and half tails.

A line indicates the direction the wind is coming from.

Air temperature

A symbol represents the current weather conditions. If there is no symbol, there is no precipitation.

Dew point temperature

Shading indicates the cloud coverage.

234

77

73

Atmospheric pressure in millibars (mbar). This number has been shortened on the station model. To read the number properly you must follow a few simple rules.

- If the first number is greater than 5, place a 9 in front of the number and a decimal point between the last two digits.

- If the first number is less than or equal to 5, place a 10 in front of the number and a decimal point between the last two digits.

Lab Notes

You may want to go over the different weather symbols with students and discuss how to convert the abbreviated form of atmospheric pressure to its actual measure. Before the lab, have students review the different kinds of fronts. Students may enjoy creating a weather report based on the weather report provided in this lab. Students can present this report to the class as a "live" studio show or through a videotape they create in their own time.

Interpreting Station Models

The station model below is for Boston, Massachusetts. The current temperature in Boston is 42°F, and the dew point is 39°F. The barometric pressure is 1011.0 mbar. The sky is overcast, and there is moderate rainfall. The wind is coming from the southwest at 15–20 mph.

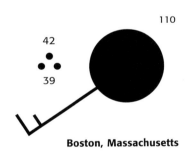

110

42

39

Boston, Massachusetts

CHAPTER RESOURCES

Chapter Resource File

- Datasheet for LabBook
- Lab Notes and Answers

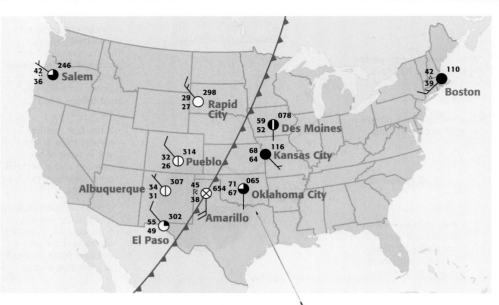

Analyze the Results

1. It's the winter. A cold front is coming through. Temperatures are low where the cold front has passed.

2. The temperature is 42°F. The dewpoint is 36°F. There is broken cloud cover, the wind is from the northwest at 3–8 mph, and the barometric pressure is 1,024.6 mb.

3. As the cold front approaches, the wind is generally from the south, temperatures are warmer and the barometric pressure is low. As the cold front passes, the wind is from the northwest, temperatures are much cooler, and the pressure rises.

Draw Conclusions

4. The temperature is 45°F. The barometric pressure is 965.4 mb, the dewpoint is 38°F, the sky is obscured, there is a thunderstorm, and the wind is from the south at 21–25 mph.

Analyze the Results

1. Based on the weather for the entire United States, what time of year is it? Explain your answer.

2. Interpret the station model for Salem, Oregon. What is the temperature, dew point, cloud coverage, wind direction, wind speed, and atmospheric pressure? Is there any precipitation? If so, what kind?

3. What is happening to wind direction, temperature, and pressure as the cold front approaches? as it passes?

Draw Conclusions

4. Interpret the station model for Amarillo, Texas.

Skills Practice Lab

Let It Snow!

Although an inch of rain might be good for your garden, 7 cm or 8 cm could cause an unwelcome flood. But what about snow? How much snow is too much? A blizzard might drop 40 cm of snow overnight. Sure it's up to your knees, but how does this much snow compare with rain? This activity will help you find out.

MATERIALS

- beaker, 100 mL
- gloves, heat-resistant
- graduated cylinder
- hot plate
- ice, shaved, 150 mL
- ruler, metric

SAFETY

Procedure

1. Pour 50 mL of shaved ice into your beaker. Do not pack the ice into the beaker. This ice will represent your snowfall.

2. Use the ruler to measure the height of the snow in the beaker.

3. Turn on the hot plate to a low setting. **Caution:** Wear heat-resistant gloves and goggles when working with the hot plate.

4. Place the beaker on the hot plate, and leave it there until all of the snow melts.

5. Pour the water into the graduated cylinder, and record the height and volume of the water.

6. Repeat steps 1–5 two more times.

Analysis

1. What was the difference in height before and after the snow melted in each of your three trials? What was the average difference?

2. Why did the volume change after the ice melted?

3. What was the ratio of snow height to water height?

4. Use the ratio you found in step 3 of the Analysis to calculate how much water 50 cm of this snow would produce. Use the following equation to help.

$$\frac{\text{measured height of snow}}{\text{measured height of water}} = \frac{50 \text{ cm of snow}}{? \text{ cm of water}}$$

5. Why is it important to know the water content of a snowfall?

Applying Your Data

Shaved ice isn't really snow. Research to find out how much water real snow would produce. Does every snowfall produce the same ratio of snow height to water depth?

CHAPTER RESOURCES

Chapter Resource File

- Datasheet for LabBook
- Lab Notes and Answers

Walter Woolbaugh
Manhattan School System
Manhattan, Montana

Applying Your Data

Every snowfall does not produce the same ratio of snow height to water depth. The ratio of snow height to water depth is dependent on several variables, including whether the snow is wet or dry.

Let It Snow!

Teacher's Notes

Time Required

One 45-minute class period

Lab Ratings

EASY ———————————→ HARD

Teacher Prep 🧪
Student Set-Up 🧪🧪
Concept Level 🧪
Clean Up 🧪

MATERIALS

The materials listed on the student page are enough for a group of 3 to 4 students.

Safety Caution

Remind students to review all safety cautions and icons before beginning this lab activity.

Analyze the Results

1. Answers may vary according to the water content of the ice or snow sample.

2. The volume changed because the water changed from a solid to a liquid.

3. Answers may vary.

4. Answers may vary

5. Sample answer: The water content of a snowfall—whether it is relatively wet or relatively dry—affects how much flooding may occur as the snow melts. A "wetter" snow has more water per volume and may cause more flooding than a "drier" snow.

Gone with the Wind

Teacher's Notes

Time Required
One 45-minute class period

Lab Ratings

EASY ——————————→ HARD

Teacher Prep 🧪🧪
Student Set-Up 🧪🧪
Concept Level 🧪🧪
Clean Up 🧪

MATERIALS
The materials listed on the student page are enough for a group of 2 to 3 students.

Safety Caution
Remind students to review all safety cautions and icons before beginning this lab activity.

Preparation Notes
You might want to watch your local weather station in order to schedule this experiment on a windy day. Use a magnetic compass to find magnetic north. Then, use masking tape or chalk to mark the sidewalk or parking lot with an arrow pointing toward magnetic north. Before the activity, ask students if they have ever seen a weather vane. Also, have them list several reasons why knowing the wind direction might be helpful.

Gone with the Wind

Pilots at the Fly Away Airport need your help—fast! Last night, lightning destroyed the orange windsock. This windsock helped pilots measure which direction the wind was blowing. But now the windsock is gone with the wind, and an incoming airplane needs to land. The pilot must know which direction the wind is blowing and is counting on you to make a device that can measure wind direction.

MATERIALS
- card, index
- compass, drawing
- compass, magnetic
- pencil, sharpened
- plate, paper
- protractor
- rock, small
- ruler, metric
- scissors
- stapler
- straw, straight plastic
- thumbtack (or pushpin)

SAFETY

Ask a Question

1. How can I measure wind direction?

Form a Hypothesis

2. Write a possible answer to the question above.

Test the Hypothesis

3. Find the center of the plate by tracing around its edge with a drawing compass. The pointed end of the compass should poke a small hole in the center of the plate.

4. Use a ruler to draw a line across the center of the plate.

5. Use a protractor to help you draw a second line through the center of the plate. This new line should be at a 90° angle to the line you drew in step 4.

6. Moving clockwise, label each line "N," "E," "S," and "W."

7. Use a protractor to help you draw two more lines through the center of the plate. These lines should be at a 45° angle to the lines you drew in steps 4 and 5.

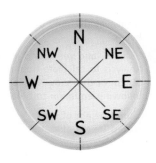

Walter Woolbaugh
Manhattan School System
Manhattan, Montana

8. Moving clockwise from *N*, label these new lines "NE," "SE," "SW," and "NW." The plate now resembles the face of a magnetic compass. The plate will be the base of your wind-direction indicator. It will help you read the direction of the wind at a glance.

9. Measure and mark a 5 cm × 5 cm square on an index card, and cut out the square. Fold the square in half to form a triangle.

10. Staple an open edge of the triangle to the straw so that one point of the triangle touches the end of the straw.

11. Hold the pencil at a 90° angle to the straw. The eraser should touch the balance point of the straw. Push a thumbtack or pushpin through the straw and into the eraser. The straw should spin without falling off.

12. Find a suitable area outside to measure the wind direction. The area should be clear of trees and buildings.

13. Press the sharpened end of the pencil through the center hole of the plate and into the ground. The labels on your paper plate should be facing the sky, as shown on this page.

14. Use a compass to find magnetic north. Rotate the plate so that the *N* on the plate points north. Place a small rock on top of the plate so that the plate does not turn.

15. Watch the straw as it rotates. The triangle will point in the direction the wind is blowing.

Analyze the Results

1. From which direction is the wind coming?

2. In which direction is the wind blowing?

Draw Conclusions

3. Would this be an effective way for pilots to measure wind direction? Why or why not?

4. What improvements would you suggest to Fly Away Airport to measure wind direction more accurately?

Applying Your Data

Use this tool to measure and record wind direction for several days. What changes in wind direction occur as a front approaches? as a front passes?
Review magnetic declination in the chapter entitled "Maps as Models of the Earth." How might magnetic declination affect your design for a tool to measure wind direction?

CHAPTER RESOURCES

Chapter Resource File

- **Datasheet for LabBook**
- **Lab Notes and Answers**

Global Impact

Teacher's Notes

Time Required
One 45-minute class period

Lab Ratings

EASY ———————→ HARD

Teacher Prep 🧪
Student Set-Up 🧪🧪🧪
Concept Level 🧪🧪
Clean Up 🧪

MATERIALS
The materials listed on the student page are enough for 1 student.

Preparation Notes

This activity requires graphing skills. Students may need a review of graphing, analyzing data from a graph, and calculating the slope of a graph.

Analyze the Results

1. Students will notice that temperatures fluctuated over the last 100 years but have increased in the last 30 years.

2. Sample answer: The larger the sample size, the more precise your analysis will be. The average temperature for a certain year might not be representative for the entire decade. There were very few similarities among the graphs.

Skills Practice Lab

Global Impact

For years, scientists have debated the topic of global warming. Is the temperature of the Earth actually getting warmer? In this activity, you will examine a table to determine if the data indicate any trends. Be sure to notice how much the trends seem to change as you analyze different sets of data.

MATERIALS
- pencils, colored (4)
- ruler, metric

Procedure

1. The table below shows average global temperatures recorded over the last 100 years.

2. Draw a graph. Label the horizontal axis "Time." Mark the grid in 5-year intervals. Label the vertical axis "Temperature (°C)," with values ranging from 13°C to 15°C.

3. Starting with 1900, use the numbers in red to plot the temperature in 20-year intervals. Connect the dots with straight lines.

4. Using a ruler, estimate the average slope for the temperatures. Draw a red line to represent the slope.

5. Using different colors, plot the temperatures at 10-year intervals and 5-year intervals on the same graph. Connect each set of dots, and draw the average slope for each set.

Analyze the Results

1. Examine your completed graph, and explain any trends you see in the graphed data. Was there an increase or a decrease in average temperature over the last 100 years?

2. What similarities and differences did you see between each set of graphed data?

Draw Conclusions

3. What conclusions can you draw from the data you graphed in this activity?

4. What would happen if your graph were plotted in 1-year intervals? Try it!

Average Global Temperatures

Year	°C	Year	°C	Year	°C	Year	°C	Year	°C	Year	°C
1900	14.0	1917	13.6	1934	14.0	1951	14.0	1968	13.9	1985	14.1
1901	13.9	1918	13.6	1935	13.9	1952	14.0	1969	14.0	1986	14.2
1902	13.8	1919	13.8	1936	14.0	1953	14.1	1970	14.0	1987	14.3
1903	13.6	1920	13.8	1937	14.1	1954	13.9	1971	13.9	1988	14.4
1904	13.5	1921	13.9	1938	14.1	1955	13.9	1972	13.9	1989	14.2
1905	13.7	1922	13.9	1939	14.0	1956	13.8	1973	14.2	1990	14.5
1906	13.8	1923	13.8	1940	14.1	1957	14.1	1974	13.9	1991	14.4
1907	13.6	1924	13.8	1941	14.1	1958	14.1	1975	14.0	1992	14.1
1908	13.7	1925	13.8	1942	14.1	1959	14.0	1976	13.8	1993	14.2
1909	13.7	1926	14.1	1943	14.0	1960	14.0	1977	14.2	1994	14.3
1910	13.7	1927	14.0	1944	14.1	1961	14.1	1978	14.1	1995	14.5
1911	13.7	1928	14.0	1945	14.0	1962	14.0	1979	14.1	1996	14.4
1912	13.7	1929	13.8	1946	14.0	1963	14.0	1980	14.3	1997	14.4
1913	13.8	1930	13.9	1947	14.1	1964	13.7	1981	14.4	1998	14.5
1914	14.0	1931	14.0	1948	14.0	1965	13.8	1982	14.1	1999	14.5
1915	14.0	1932	14.0	1949	13.9	1966	13.9	1983	14.3	2000	14.5
1916	13.8	1933	13.9	1950	13.8	1967	14.0	1984	14.1	2001	14.5

CHAPTER RESOURCES

Chapter Resource File

- Datasheet for LabBook
- Lab Notes and Answers

CLASSROOM TESTED & APPROVED

Janel Guse
West Central Middle School
Hartford, South Dakota

Draw Conclusions

3. Sample answer: You can conclude that a larger data set gives you a more complete picture of what is happening. Global temperatures have gradually increased in the last 100 years.

4. Sample answer: Global temperatures would appear to fluctuate more.

Skills Practice Lab

For the Birds

You and a partner have a new business building birdhouses. But your first clients have told you that birds do not want to live in the birdhouses you have made. The clients want their money back unless you can solve the problem. You need to come up with a solution right away!

You remember reading an article about microclimates in a science magazine. Cities often heat up because the pavement and buildings absorb so much solar radiation. Maybe the houses are too warm! How can the houses be kept cooler?

You decide to investigate the roofs; after all, changing the roofs would be a lot easier than building new houses. In order to help your clients and the birds, you decide to test different roof colors and materials to see how these variables affect a roof's ability to absorb the sun's rays.

One partner will test the color, and the other partner will test the materials. You will then share your results and make a recommendation together.

MATERIALS

- cardboard (4 pieces)
- paint, black, white, and light blue tempera
- rubber, beige or tan
- thermometers, Celsius (4)
- watch (or clock)
- wood, beige or tan

SAFETY

Part A: Color Test

Ask a Question

❶ What color would be the best choice for the roof of a birdhouse?

Form a Hypothesis

❷ Write down the color you think will keep a birdhouse coolest.

Test the Hypothesis

❸ Paint one piece of cardboard black, another piece white, and a third light blue.

❹ After the paint has dried, take the three pieces of cardboard outside, and place a thermometer on each piece.

❺ In an area where there is no shade, place each piece at the same height so that all three receive the same amount of sunlight. Leave the pieces in the sunlight for 15 min.

❻ Leave a fourth thermometer outside in the shade to measure the temperature of the air.

❼ Record the reading of the thermometer on each piece of cardboard. Also, record the outside temperature.

For the Birds

Teacher's Notes

Time Required

One 45-minute class period

Lab Ratings

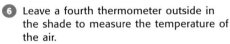

EASY ————————➤ HARD

Teacher Prep 🧪
Student Set-Up 🧪🧪
Concept Level 🧪🧪
Clean Up 🧪🧪

MATERIALS

The materials listed on the student page are enough for a group of 4 to 5 students.

Safety Caution

Remind students to review all safety cautions and icons before beginning this lab activity.

Part A
Analyze the Results

1. Sample answer: no, The thermometers recorded different temperatures. The black and blue pieces of cardboard, particularly the black one, caused the temperature to increase.

2. Sample answer: The temperature of the black cardboard was much higher than the outside temperature. Students should find that the temperature of the other colors was also different from the outside temperature.

Part A
Draw Conclusions

3. Answers may vary. Accept all reasonable responses.

Analyze the Results

1. Did each of the three thermometers record the same temperature after 15 min? Explain.

2. Were the temperature readings on each of the three pieces of cardboard the same as the reading for the outside temperature? Explain.

Draw Conclusions

3. How do your observations compare with your hypothesis?

Part B: Material Test

Ask a Question

1. Which material would be the best choice for the roof of a birdhouse?

Form a Hypothesis

2. Write down the material you think will keep a birdhouse coolest.

Test the Hypothesis

3. Take the rubber, wood, and the fourth piece of cardboard outside, and place a thermometer on each.

4. In an area where there is no shade, place each material at the same height so that they all receive the same amount of sunlight. Leave the materials in the sunlight for 15 min.

5. Leave a fourth thermometer outside in the shade to measure the temperature of the air.

6. Record the temperature of each material. Also, record the outside temperature. After you and your partner have finished your investigations, take a few minutes to share your results.

Analyze the Results

1 Did each of the thermometers on the three materials record the same temperature after 15 min? Explain.

2 Were the temperature readings on the rubber, wood, and cardboard the same as the reading for the outside temperature? Explain.

Draw Conclusions

3 How do your observations compare with your hypothesis?

4 Which material would you use to build the roofs for your birdhouses? Why?

5 Which color would you use to paint the new roofs? Why?

Applying Your Data

Make three different-colored samples for each of the three materials. When you measure the temperatures for each sample, how do the colors compare for each material? Is the same color best for all three materials? How do your results compare with what you concluded in steps 4 and 5 under Draw Conclusions of this activity? What's more important, color or material?

Part B
Analyze the Results

1. Sample answer: no, The temperatures were different. The temperature of the rubber was higher than that of the other two materials.

2. Sample answer: no, The temperature of the rubber was higher than the outside temperature. Accept all other reasonable answers for the other materials.

Part B
Draw Conclusions

3. Answers may vary. Accept all reasonable answers.

4. Sample answer: The wood would be the coolest. The cardboard would be a possible alternative.

5. Sample answer: The white roof would be the coolest. A light blue roof would be a possible alternative.

Applying Your Data

Answers may vary. Accept all reasonable interpretations of the data collected.

Muscles at Work

Teacher's Notes

Time Required
One 45-minute class period

Lab Ratings

EASY ———————————— HARD

Teacher Prep 🧪
Student Set-Up 🧪🧪
Concept Level 🧪🧪
Clean Up 🧪

Safety Caution

A digital thermometer that measures temperature from the ear is recommended.

Because of the vigorous nature of the exercise, you may want to ask for volunteers to do the exercising. Also, you should be aware of any health concerns your students have.

Muscles at Work

Have you ever exercised outside on a cold fall day wearing only a thin warm-up suit or shorts? How did you stay warm? The answer is that your muscle cells contracted, and when contraction takes place, some energy is used to do work, and the rest is converted to thermal energy. This process helps your body maintain a constant temperature in cold conditions. In this activity, you will learn how the release of energy can cause a change in your body temperature.

MATERIALS

- clock (or watch) with a second hand
- thermometer, small, hand held
- other materials as approved by your teacher

Ask a Question

1 Write a question that you can test about how activity affects body temperature.

Form a Hypothesis

2 Form a group of four students. In your group, discuss several exercises that can produce a change in body temperature. Write a hypothesis that could answer the question you asked.

Test the Hypothesis

3 Develop an experimental procedure that includes the steps necessary to test your hypothesis. Be sure to get your teacher's approval before you begin.

4 Assign tasks to individuals in the group, such as note taking, data recording, and timing. What observations and data will you be recording? Design your data tables accordingly.

5 Perform your experiment as planned by your group. Be sure to record all observations in your data tables.

Analyze the Results

1 How did you determine if muscle contractions cause the release of thermal energy? Was your hypothesis supported by your data? Explain your results in a written report. Describe how you could improve your experimental method.

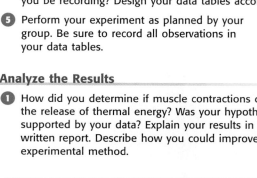

Applying Your Data

Why do humans shiver in the cold? Do all animals shiver? Find out why shivering is one of the first signs that your body is becoming too cold.

Analyze the Results

1. All answers will depend on the students' observations and their own hypotheses.

Applying Your Data

Sample answer: In a process known as *shivering thermogenesis,* muscle tone is gradually increased. Shivering increases the workload of the muscles and elevates oxygen and energy consumption. The heat that is produced warms the deep vessels. Shivering can elevate body temperature effectively. It can increase the rate of heat generation by as much as 400%. Endothermic animals have the capacity to shiver. Shivering is an automatic response of the body to cold.

CHAPTER RESOURCES

Chapter Resource File
- Datasheet for LabBook
- Lab Notes and Answers

Kathy LaRoe
East Valley Middle School
East Helena, Montana

Model-Making Lab

Build a Lung

When you breathe, you actually pull air into your lungs because your diaphragm muscle causes your chest to expand. You can see this is true by placing your hands on your ribs and inhaling slowly. Did you feel your chest expand?

In this activity, you will build a model of a lung by using some common materials. You will see how the diaphragm muscle works to inflate your lungs. Refer to the diagrams at right as you construct your model.

MATERIALS

- bag, trash, small plastic
- balloon, small
- bottle, top half, 2 L
- clay, golf-ball-sized piece
- rubber bands (2)
- ruler, metric
- straw, plastic
- tape, transparent

Procedure

1. Attach the balloon to the end of the straw with a rubber band. Make a hole through the clay, and insert the other end of the straw through the hole. Be sure at least 8 cm of the straw extends beyond the clay. Squeeze the ball of clay gently to seal the clay around the straw.

2. Insert the balloon end of the straw into the neck of the bottle. Use the ball of clay to seal the straw and balloon into the bottle.

3. Turn the bottle gently on its side. Place the trash bag over the cut end of the bottle. Expand a rubber band around the bottom of the bottle to secure the bag. You may wish to reinforce the seal with tape. Before the plastic is completely sealed, gather the excess material of the bag into your hand, and press toward the inside of the bottle slightly. (You may need to tie a knot about halfway up from the bottom of the bag to take up excess material.) Use tape to finish sealing the bag to the bottle with the bag in this position. The excess air will be pushed out of the bottle.

Analyze the Results

1. What can you do with your model to make the "lung" inflate?

2. What do the balloon, the plastic wrap, and the straw represent in your model?

3. Using your model, demonstrate to the class how air enters the lung and how air exits the lung.

> #### Applying Your Data
>
> Do some research to find out what an "iron lung" is and why it was used in the past. Research and write a report about what is used today to help people who have difficulty breathing.

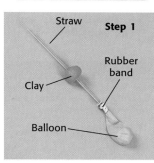

Step 1

Straw, Rubber band, Clay, Balloon

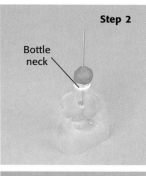

Step 2

Bottle neck

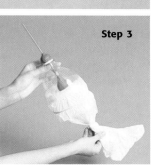

Step 3

Applying Your Data

From the late 1920s to the 1950s, iron lungs were used to treat respiratory paralysis due to poliomyelitis. The patient was encased within an airtight chamber from the neck down. A large set of leather bellows mounted in a separate pumping unit expanded, causing pressure changes inside the chamber. This, in turn, caused the chest of the patient to expand, drawing fresh air into the lungs through the mouth. Now, several models of portable ventilators allow patients much more freedom to move about.

Build a Lung

Teacher's Notes

Time Required
One 45-minute class period

Lab Ratings

EASY ——————————→ HARD

Teacher Prep 🧪🧪
Student Set-Up 🧪🧪
Concept Level 🧪
Clean Up 🧪🧪

MATERIALS

You may want to build a model first to use as a reference for students. If so, you may want to substitute a bag smaller than the one that students use to model the diaphragm.

Analyze the Results

1. The balloon will inflate when the plastic bag is pulled down.

2. The balloon represents a lung, the plastic wrap represents a diaphragm, and the straw represents a trachea. (Students may also note that the bottle represents the part of the body in which the lungs are located.)

3. Air enters the lungs when the diaphragm moves down and creates more space inside the chest cavity. Air is forced out of the lungs when the diaphragm moves up. Students should demonstrate this process by moving the plastic bag up and down.

Enzymes in Action

Teacher's Notes

Time Required
One 45-minute class period

Lab Ratings

EASY ——————————————→ HARD

Teacher Prep 🧪🧪
Student Set-Up 🧪🧪
Concept Level 🧪🧪🧪
Clean Up 🧪🧪

MATERIALS

The materials listed on the student page are enough for 1 student or a group of 2–4 students. If you do not have enough mortar and pestles or small plates, you may have students use any small container to mash the liver with a fork. Beef liver is readily obtained at the grocery store.

Safety Caution

Remind students to review all safety cautions and icons before beginning this lab activity. Use a dilute solution of hydrogen peroxide. Hydrogen peroxide can be harmful to skin and clothing. Caution students to be careful not to spill or splatter the solution while pouring. If hydrogen peroxide comes into contact with skin, wash the skin immediately with plenty of running water.

Skills Practice Lab

Enzymes in Action

You know how important enzymes are in the process of diges-tion. This lab will help you see enzymes at work. Hydrogen peroxide is continuously produced by your cells. If it is not quickly broken down, hydrogen peroxide will kill your cells. Luckily, your cells contain an enzyme that converts hydrogen peroxide into two nonpoisonous substances. This enzyme is also present in the cells of beef liver. In this lab, you will observe the action of this enzyme on hydrogen peroxide.

Procedure

① Draw a data table similar to the one below. Be sure to leave enough space to write your observations.

Data Table		
Size and condition of liver	**Experimental liquid**	**Observations**
1 cm cube beef liver	2 mL water	*DO NOT WRITE IN BOOK*
1 cm cube beef liver	2 mL hydrogen peroxide	
1 cm cube beef liver (mashed)	2 mL hydrogen peroxide	

CLASSROOM TESTED & APPROVED

James Chin
Frank A. Day Middle School
Newtonville, Massachusetts

CHAPTER RESOURCES

Chapter Resource File

- **Datasheet for LabBook**
- **Lab Notes and Answers**

2 Get three equal-sized pieces of beef liver from your teacher, and use your forceps to place them on your plate.

3 Pour 2 mL of water into a test tube labeled "Water and liver."

4 Using the tweezers, carefully place one piece of liver in the test tube. Record your observations in your data table.

5 Pour 2 mL of hydrogen peroxide into a second test tube labeled "Liver and hydrogen peroxide."
Caution: Do not splash hydrogen peroxide on your skin. If you do get hydrogen peroxide on your skin, rinse the affected area with running water immediately, and tell your teacher.

6 Using the tweezers, carefully place one piece of liver in the test tube. Record your observations of the second test tube in your data table.

7 Pour another 2 mL of hydrogen peroxide into a third test tube labeled "Ground liver and hydrogen peroxide."

8 Using a mortar and pestle (or fork and watch glass), carefully grind the third piece of liver.

9 Using the spatula, scrape the ground liver into the third test tube. Record your observations of the third test tube in your data table.

Analyze the Results

1 What was the purpose of putting the first piece of liver in water? Why was this a necessary step?

2 Describe the difference you observed between the liver and the ground liver when each was placed in the hydrogen peroxide. How can you account for this difference?

Applying Your Data

Do plant cells contain enzymes that break down hydrogen peroxide? Try this experiment using potato cubes instead of liver to find out.

Analyze the Results

1. Sample answer: The piece of liver in water is the control. A control is necessary so that differences in reactions to other substances can be observed.

2. Students should observe that the cube of liver produced a quick, foaming reaction to the hydrogen peroxide as the solution came into contact with the cells and destroyed them. The mashed liver should also produce a very quick reaction; however, students should observe that the effervescence subsides faster with the mashed liver than with the cube. The reason is that the mashed liver has a greater surface area than the cube, exposing more liver enzymes to the hydrogen peroxide. There should be no reaction in water.

Applying Your Data

Students will discover that plant cells do contain enzymes that will break down hydrogen peroxide. Have them experiment with different types of plants and vegetables so they can observe the different rates of reaction.

Skills Practice Lab

My, How You've Grown!

Teacher's Notes

Time Required

One 45-minute class period

Lab Ratings

EASY ——————————————→ HARD

Teacher Prep 🧪
Student Set-Up 🧪
Concept Level 🧪🧪
Clean Up 🧪

Procedure

2. Students' graphs should look like those below.

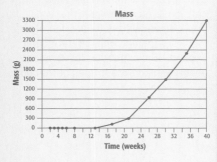

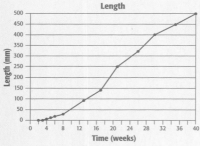

Skills Practice Lab

My, How You've Grown!

In humans, the process of development that takes place between fertilization and birth lasts about 266 days. In 4 weeks, the new individual grows from a single fertilized cell to an embryo whose heart is beating and pumping blood. All of the organ systems and body parts are completely formed by the end of the seventh month. During the last 2 months before birth, the baby grows, and its organ systems mature. At birth, the average mass of a baby is about 33,000 times as much as that of an embryo at 2 weeks of development! In this activity, you will discover just how fast a fetus grows.

MATERIALS

- paper, graph
- pencils, colored

Procedure

1. Using graph paper, make two graphs—one entitled "Length" and one entitled "Mass." On the length graph, use intervals of 25 mm on the *y*-axis. Extend the *y*-axis to 500 mm. On the mass graph, use intervals of 100 g on the *y*-axis. Extend this *y*-axis to 3,300 g. Use 2-week intervals for time on the *x*-axes for both graphs. Both *x*-axes should extend to 40 weeks.

2. Examine the data table at right. Plot the data in the table on your graphs. Use a colored pencil to draw the curved line that joins the points on each graph.

Analyze the Results

1. Describe the change in mass of a developing fetus. How can you explain this change?

2. Describe the change in length of a developing fetus. How does the change in mass compare to the change in length?

Increase of Mass and Length of Average Human Fetus		
Time (weeks)	Mass (g)	Length (mm)
2	0.1	1.5
3	0.3	2.3
4	0.5	5.0
5	0.6	10.0
6	0.8	15.0
8	1.0	30.0
13	15.0	90.0
17	115.0	140.0
21	300.0	250.0
26	950.0	320.0
30	1,500.0	400.0
35	2,300.0	450.0
40	3,300.0	500.0

Applying Your Data

Using the information in your graphs, estimate how tall a child would be at age 3 if he or she continued to grow at the same average rate that a fetus grows.

Analyze the Results

1. The change in mass of a developing fetus is steadily increasing, approximately tripling each month of the first and second trimesters. This period is one of rapid cell division.

2. Fetal length steadily increases, doubling and even tripling each month in the first two trimesters. In the third trimester, the rate of lengthening slows. Mass continues to increase, even in the last trimester.

Applying Your Data

The child would be 2.45 m (8.04 ft) tall!

CHAPTER RESOURCES

Chapter Resource File

- Datasheet for LabBook
- Lab Notes and Answers

Randy Christian
Stovall Junior High School
Houston, Texas

Model-Making Lab

Antibodies to the Rescue

Some cells of the immune system, called *B cells,* make antibodies that attack and kill invading viruses and microorganisms. These antibodies help make you immune to disease. Have you ever had chickenpox? If you have, your body has built up antibodies that can recognize that particular virus. Antibodies will attach themselves to the virus, tagging it for destruction. If you are exposed to the same disease again, the antibodies remember that virus. They will attack the virus even quicker and in greater number than they did the first time. This is the reason that you will probably never have chickenpox more than once.

In this activity, you will construct simple models of viruses and their antibodies. You will see how antibodies are specific for a particular virus.

MATERIALS

- craft materials, such as buttons, fabric scraps, pipe cleaners, and recycled materials
- paper, colored
- scissors
- tape (or glue)

Procedure

1. Draw the virus patterns shown on this page on a separate piece of paper, or design your own virus models from the craft supplies. Remember to design different receptors on each of your virus models.

2. Write a few sentences describing how your viruses are different.

3. Cut out the viruses, and attach them to a piece of colored paper with tape or glue.

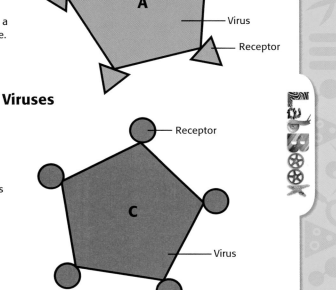

Viruses

Martha Kisiah
Fairview Middle School
Tallahassee, Florida

Model-Making Lab

Antibodies to the Rescue

Teacher's Notes

Time Required
One 45-minute class period

Lab Ratings

EASY ———————→ HARD

Teacher Prep
Student Set-Up
Concept Level
Clean Up

MATERIALS

You will be able to expand this activity from very simple to a grand art project! Have students bring craft supplies from home. You may want to include poster paper in the materials list.

Preparation Notes

Encourage students to be imaginative in this exercise. Have them come up with interesting shapes for the viruses and the antibodies that fit them. Remind students that the main lesson of this exercise is that the antibodies can fit only a specific pathogen and in only one specific way, just as a key fits only one lock.

Analyze the Results

1. Sample answer: Antibodies recognize and bind to specific pathogens because antibodies are shaped to match the specific three-dimensional shape of the antigen.

2. Sample answer: Antibodies bind to specific pathogens and either inactivate the pathogen or trigger its destruction by macrophages.

3. Sample answer: Vaccines produce immunity because they contain antigens that stimulate an immune response in which memory cells are produced. Students can use their models to demonstrate or give examples.

Draw Conclusions

4. Sample answer: The antibodies that are specific to a pathogen will be ineffective when the pathogen changes its receptors. Students can show this mutation by slightly changing their model so that the virus and the antibody no longer fit as a lock and key do.

4. Select the antibodies drawn below, or design your own antibodies that will exactly fit on the receptors on your virus models. Draw or create each antibody enough times to attach one to each receptor site on the virus.

Antibodies

5. Cut out the antibodies you have drawn. Arrange the antibodies so that they bind to the virus at the appropriate receptor. Attach them to the virus with tape or glue.

Analyze the Results

1. Explain how an antibody "recognizes" a particular virus.

2. After the attachment of antibodies to the receptors, what would be the next step in the immune response?

3. Many vaccines use weakened copies of the virus to protect the body. Use the model of a virus and its specific antibody to explain how vaccines work.

Draw Conclusions

4. Use your model of a virus to demonstrate to the class how a receptor might change or mutate so that a vaccine would no longer be effective.

Applying Your Data

Research in the library or on the Internet to find information about the discovery of the Salk vaccine for polio. Include information on how polio affects people today.

Research in the library or on the Internet to find information and write a report about filoviruses. What do they look like? What diseases do they cause? Why are they especially dangerous? Is there an effective vaccine against any filovirus? Explain.

Applying Your Data

Dr. Jonas Edward Salk (1914–1995) was trying to develop an anti-influenza vaccine. This work led him and his colleagues to develop an inactivated vaccine against polio in 1952. Wide-scale testing in 1954 was successful, and the vaccine was distributed nationally. The vaccine greatly reduced the incidence of the polio. Partly because of the Salk vaccine, the number of cases of polio have decreased year after year—the Western Hemisphere was declared polio-free in 1994, and only 4,000 polio cases were reported worldwide in 1996. The World Health Organization is planning to end routine polio vaccination around the year 2005. Filoviruses belong to the family Filoviridae, one of several groups of viruses that can cause hemorrhagic fever, such as Ebola, in animals and humans. When magnified many thousands of times by an electron microscope, filoviruses resemble long filaments or threads. Because filoviruses can be extremely hazardous, laboratory studies of these viruses must be conducted in special maximum-containment facilities. The reservoir and natural history of filoviruses remain unknown. Filoviruses have the highest fatality rates (as high as 90% for epidemics of hemorrhagic fever caused by Ebola-Zaire virus). No vaccine exists to protect against filovirus infection, and no specific treatment is available for diseases caused by these viruses.

Skills Practice Lab

To Diet or Not to Diet

There are six main classes of foods that we need in order to keep our bodies functioning properly: water, vitamins, minerals, carbohydrates, fats, and proteins. In this activity you will investigate the importance of a well-balanced diet in maintaining a healthy body. Then you will create a poster or picture that illustrates the importance of one of the three energy-producing nutrients—carbohydrates, fats, and proteins.

MATERIALS

- crayons (or markers), assorted colors
- diet books
- menus, fast-food (optional)
- nutrition reference books
- paper, white unlined

Procedure

1 Draw a table like the one below. Research in the library, on nutrition labels, in nutrition or diet books, or on the Internet to find the information you need to fill out the chart.

Nutrition Data Table			
	Fats	**Carbohydrates**	**Proteins**
Found in which foods			
Functions in the body	DO NOT WRITE IN BOOK		
Consequences of deficiency			

2 Choose one of the foods you have learned about in your research, and create a poster or picture that describes its importance in a well-balanced diet.

Analyze the Results

1 Based on what you have learned in this lab, how might you change your eating habits to have a well-balanced diet? Does the nutritional value of foods concern you? Why or why not? Write down your answers, and explain your reasoning.

Communicating Your Data

Write a paragraph explaining why water is a nutrient. Analyze a typical fast-food meal, and determine its overall nutritional value.

Communicating Your Data

Sample answer: Without water, most of the reactions that maintain life could not take place. Water carries the other essential nutrients to all parts of the body and is the medium in which waste products are dissolved and carried away from body tissues.

Answers will vary depending on the type of meal a student chooses. Fast-food restaurants usually post Nutrition Facts in public view. Have students obtain this information and evaluate a fast-food meal based on those Nutrition Facts and daily recommended amounts. Examining the Nutrition Facts labels on food packaging is helpful before beginning this activity.

To Diet or Not to Diet

Teacher's Notes

Time Required

Two 45-minute class periods

Lab Ratings

EASY ———————→ HARD

Teacher Prep 🧪🧪
Student Set-Up 🧪
Concept Level 🧪🧪
Clean Up 🧪🧪

MATERIALS

A copy of a chart that fast-food restaurants post in their dining rooms outlining the nutritional information of the food they serve would be very helpful in analyzing a fast-food meal.

Analyze the Results

1. Answers may vary. Students may say they might try to eat fewer fatty foods. The nutritional value of foods is a subject that may be new to many students.

CHAPTER RESOURCES

Chapter Resource File

- **Datasheet for LabBook**
- **Lab Notes and Answers**

CLASSROOM TESTED & APPROVED

Ivora Washington
Hyattsville Middle School
Hyattsville, Maryland

The Best-Bread Bakery Dilemma

Teacher's Notes

Time Required

Two 45-minute class periods

Lab Ratings

EASY ————————— HARD

Teacher Prep 🔺🔺
Student Set-Up 🔺
Concept Level 🔺
Clean Up 🔺

MATERIALS

The materials listed on the student page are enough for a group of 3–4 students. Yeast is easily obtained from the local grocery store. The school cafeteria may be willing to donate the amount you need.

You may wish to add other materials in anticipation of students' experimental design. For example, some students may recognize that they could collect CO_2 in a balloon attached to the top of a test tube containing live yeast.

Skills Practice Lab

The Best-Bread Bakery Dilemma

The chief baker at the Best-Bread Bakery thinks that the yeast the bakery received may be dead. Yeast is a central ingredient in bread. Yeast is a living organism, a member of the kingdom Fungi, and it undergoes the same life processes as other living organisms. When yeast grows in the presence of oxygen and other nutrients, yeast produces carbon dioxide. The gas forms bubbles that cause bread dough to rise. Thousands of dollars may be lost if the yeast is dead.

The Best-Bread Bakery has requested that you test the yeast. The bakery has furnished samples of live yeast and some samples of the yeast in question.

Procedure

1. Make a data table similar to the one below. Leave plenty of room to write your observations.

2. Examine each yeast sample with a magnifying lens. You may want to sniff the samples to determine the presence of an odor. (Your teacher will demonstrate the appropriate way to detect odors in this lab.) Record your observations in the data table.

3. Label three test tubes or plastic cups "Live Yeast," "Sample A Yeast," and "Sample B Yeast."

4. Fill a beaker with 125 mL of water, and place the beaker on a hot plate. Use a thermometer to be sure the water does not get warmer than 32°C. Attach the thermometer to the side of the beaker with a clip so the thermometer doesn't touch the bottom of the beaker. Turn off the hot plate when the water temperature reaches 32°C.

MATERIALS

- beaker, 250 mL
- flour
- gloves, heat-resistant
- graduated cylinder
- hot plate
- magnifying lens
- scoopula (or small spoon)
- stirring sticks, wooden (3)
- sugar
- test-tube rack
- test tubes (3) (or clear plastic cups)
- thermometer, Celsius, with clip
- water, 125 mL
- yeast samples (live, A, and B)

SAFETY

Yeast sample	Observations	0 min	5 min	10 min	15 min	20 min	25 min	Dead or alive?
Live								
Sample A		DO NOT WRITE IN BOOK						
Sample B								

Safety Caution

Remind students to review all safety cautions and icons before beginning this lab activity.

Caution students to be careful of the hot plate and the cord. You should demonstrate the proper lab technique for determining the presence of an odor. Hold the container away from your face about 25 cm and just below your nose. Use the other hand to "waft" the odor toward your face. Caution students NEVER to put their noses directly in a container and inhale.

CHAPTER RESOURCES

Chapter Resource File

- Datasheet for LabBook
- Lab Notes and Answers

Susan Gorman
North Ridge Middle School
North Richland Hills, Texas

5 Add a small scoop (about 1/2 tsp) of each yeast sample to the correctly labeled container. Add a small scoop of sugar to each container.

6 Add 10 mL of the warm water to each container, and stir.

7 Add a small scoop of flour to each container, and stir again. The flour will help make the process more visible but is not necessary as food for the yeast.

8 Observe the samples carefully. Look for bubbles. Make observations at 5 min intervals. Write your observations in the data table.

9 In the last column of the data table, write "alive" or "dead" based on your observations during the experiment.

Analyze the Results

1 Describe any differences in the yeast samples before the experiment.

2 Describe the appearance of the yeast samples at the conclusion of the experiment.

3 Why was a sample of live yeast included in the experiment?

4 Why was sugar added to the samples?

5 Based on your observations, is either Sample A or Sample B alive?

Draw Conclusions

6 Write a letter to the Best-Bread Bakery stating your recommendation to use or not use the yeast samples. Give reasons for your recommendation.

> #### Applying Your Data
>
> Based on your observations of the nutrient requirements of yeast, design an experiment to determine the ideal combination of nutrients. Vary the amount of nutrients, or examine different energy sources.

Preparation Notes

At least one of the suspect samples should be killed yeast. To kill the yeast, place the yeast in an oven at 400°F for 10 min or in a microwave oven for a few minutes at high power. Do not allow yeast to become moist before use. Toothpicks, coffee stirrers and so on, may be used for stirring. The amounts of each ingredient used are not definite, and you may wish to vary amounts, depending on the results desired.

Lab Notes

To help students prepare for this activity, you may wish to review cellular respiration and fermentation. The equation for respiration follows: $C_6H_{12}O_6 + 6O_2 \rightarrow 6CO_2 + 6H_2O +$ energy.

Analyze Results

1. Answers are based on students' observations and may vary.

2. Answers may vary.

3. Sample answer: Live yeast was included so that bubble formation from the respiration of living organisms could be observed.

4. Sugar was added as a nutrient for the living yeast.

5. Answers may vary according to students' experimental protocol.

Draw Conclusions

6. Student letters may vary but should recommend the optimal samples they determined in their experiment.

Cells Alive!

Teacher's Notes

Time Required
One 45-minute class period

Lab Ratings

EASY ———————→ HARD

Teacher Prep 🧪
Student Set-Up 🧪
Concept Level 🧪
Clean Up 🧪

MATERIALS
The materials listed on the student page are enough for a group of 3–4 students. Be sure to keep the algae in a warm, damp place out of direct sunlight; a closed plastic bag with water sprayed into it is ideal.

Procedure
4. Chloroplasts are the parts of the cell that are responsible for photosynthesis.

5. The nucleus of a cell controls most of the activities that take place in that cell and contains the hereditary information.

6. The cytoplasm is a clear gel-like substance that fills the cell and surrounds the organelles. The organelles are floating around in the cytoplasm.

Skills Practice Lab

Cells Alive!
You have probably used a microscope to look at single-celled organisms such as those shown below. They can be found in pond water. In the following exercise, you will look at *Protococcus*—algae that form a greenish stain on tree trunks, wooden fences, flowerpots, and buildings.

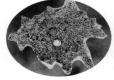
Euglena

Amoeba

Paramecium

Procedure

1. Locate some *Protococcus*. Scrape a small sample into a container. Bring the sample to the classroom, and make a wet mount of it as directed by your teacher. If you can't find *Protococcus* outdoors, look for algae on the glass in an aquarium. Such algae may not be *Protococcus,* but it will be a very good substitute.

2. Set the microscope on low power to examine the algae. On a separate sheet of paper, draw the cells that you see.

3. Switch to high power to examine a single cell. Draw the cell.

4. You will probably notice that each cell contains several chloroplasts. Label a chloroplast on your drawing. What is the function of the chloroplast?

5. Another structure that should be clearly visible in all the algae cells is the nucleus. Find the nucleus in one of your cells, and label it on your drawing. What is the function of the nucleus?

6. What does the cytoplasm look like? Describe any movement you see inside the cells.

Analyze the Results

1. Are *Protococcus* single-celled organisms or multicellular organisms?

2. How are *Protococcus* different from amoebas?

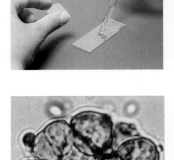
Protococcus

Analyze the Results
1. *Protococcus* is a genus composed of single-celled algae.

2. Many answers are possible, but the following are most likely: *Protococcus* cannot move about as amoebas can; unlike amoebas, they are green and photosynthesize.

CHAPTER RESOURCES

Chapter Resource File
- Datasheet for LabBook
- Lab Notes and Answers

Terry Rakes
Elmwood Junior High School
Rogers, Arkansas

Skills Practice Lab

Stayin' Alive!

Every second of your life, your body's trillions of cells take in, use, and store energy. They repair themselves, reproduce, and get rid of waste. Together, these processes are called *metabolism.* Your cells use the food that you eat to provide the energy you need to stay alive.

Your Basal Metabolic Rate (BMR) is a measurement of the energy that your body needs to carry out all the basic life processes while you are at rest. These processes include breathing, keeping your heart beating, and keeping your body's temperature stable. Your BMR is influenced by your gender, your age, and many other things. Your BMR may be different from everyone else's, but it is normal for you. In this activity, you will find the amount of energy, measured in Calories, you need every day in order to stay alive.

MATERIALS

- bathroom scale
- tape measure

Procedure

1. Find your weight on a bathroom scale. If the scale measures in pounds, you must convert your weight in pounds to your mass in kilograms. To convert your weight in pounds (lb) to mass in kilograms (kg), multiply the number of pounds by 0.454.

Example: If Carlos weighs 125 lb, his mass in kilograms is:	125 lb $\times$ 0.454 56.75 kg

2. Use a tape measure to find your height. If the tape measures in inches, convert your height in inches to height in centimeters. To convert your height in inches (in.) to your height in centimeters (cm), multiply the number of inches by 2.54.

If Carlos is 62 in. tall, his height in centimeters is:	62 in. $\times$ 2.54 157.48 cm

---

CHAPTER RESOURCES

Chapter Resource File

- Datasheet for LabBook
- Lab Notes and Answers

Kathy LaRoe
East Valley Middle School
East Helena, Montana

Stayin' Alive!

Teacher's Notes

Time Required
One 45-minute class period

Lab Ratings

EASY			HARD

Teacher Prep 🧪
Student Set-Up 🧪
Concept Level 🧪
Clean Up 🧪

MATERIALS

The materials listed on the student page are enough for each group of 5–6 students. You may wish to have your students use a calculator to complete this activity.

Preparation Notes

Some students may consider their height and weight to be personal and won't want to weigh and measure themselves with the others in the class. Give these students the option of using the data of a fictional person, such as one of the following:

Jenny	80 lb	4 ft	age 11
Ben	65 lb	3 ft	age 12
Carlos	110 lb	5 ft 2 in.	age 11
Alexa	120 lb	4 ft 6 in.	age 12
Tasheika	90 lb	4 ft 6 in.	age 13

Lab Notes

Some students will think that their basal metabolic rate, or BMR, is impossibly low. Emphasize that the BMR is the number of Calories a body needs just to keep the heart beating, the lungs breathing, and the cells respiring. The BMR is not the number of Calories a person needs for an active lifestyle.

Of course, a person can consume fewer than that number of Calories for a day, or even for a few days, without dying. Explain that the Calories required to live during starvation conditions are obtained from stored fat. When there is no more fat, then the energy comes from muscle tissue. Under extreme conditions of starvation, the body even begins to shut down some organ functions that use energy but that are not required for survival, such as the uterine cycle in women.

Some students may ask why the BMR numbers are so much higher in males than in females. Explain that before puberty, the numbers are much closer together. But as boys approach puberty, they generally develop a higher muscle-to-fat ratio than girls do. Cellular respiration for muscle tissue requires more energy than for fat tissue.

③ Now that you know your height and mass, use the appropriate formula below to get a close estimate of your BMR. Your answer will give you an estimate of the number of Calories your body needs each day just to stay alive.

Calculating Your BMR	
Females	**Males**
65 + (10 × your mass in kilograms)	66 + (13.5 × your mass in kilograms)
+ (1.8 × your height in centimeters)	+ (5 × your height in centimeters)
− (4.7 × your age in years)	− (6.8 × your age in years)

④ Your metabolism is also influenced by how active you are. Talking, walking, and playing games all take more energy than being at rest. To get an idea of how many Calories your body needs each day to stay healthy, select the lifestyle that best describes yours from the table at right. Then multiply your BMR by the activity factor.

Activity Factors	
Activity lifestyle	**Activity factor**
Moderately inactive (normal, everyday activities)	1.3
Moderately active (exercise 3 to 4 times a week)	1.4
Very active (exercise 4 to 6 times a week)	1.6
Extremely active (exercise 6 to 7 times a week)	1.8

Analyze the Results

① In what way could you compare your whole body to a single cell? Explain.

② Does an increase in activity increase your BMR? Does an increase in activity increase your need for Calories? Explain your answers.

Draw Conclusions

③ If you are moderately inactive, how many more Calories would you need if you began to exercise every day?

Applying Your Data

The best energy sources are those that supply the correct amount of Calories for your lifestyle and also provide the nutrients you need. Research in the library or on the Internet to find out which kinds of foods are the best energy sources for you. How does your list of best energy sources compare with your diet?

List everything you eat and drink in 1 day. Find out how many Calories are in each item, and find the total number of Calories you have consumed. How does this number of Calories compare with the number of Calories you need each day for all your activities?

Analyze the Results

1. Sample answer: Just as each cell needs energy on a small scale, your body requires energy on a much larger scale.

2. Sample answer: Technically, the BMR does not change with activity. The BMR is the minimum amount of energy a person needs to stay alive. Activity requires that more energy be added to the BMR, thereby increasing the need for Calories.

Draw Conclusions

3. Students should multiply their own BMR by 1.3 and then multiply their BMR by 1.8. Students should subtract the smaller number from the larger number. This number represents the additional Calories per day the student would expend shifting from a moderately inactive state to an extremely active one.

Inquiry Lab

Tracing Traits

Have you ever wondered about the traits you inherited from your parents? Do you have a trait that neither of your parents has? In this project, you will develop a family tree, or pedigree, similar to the one shown in the diagram below. You will trace an inherited trait through a family to determine how it has passed from generation to generation.

Procedure

1. The diagram at right shows a family history. On a separate piece of paper, draw a similar diagram of the family you have chosen. Include as many family members as possible, such as grandparents, parents, children, and grandchildren. Use circles to represent females and squares to represent males. You may include other information, such as the family member's name, birth date, or picture.

2. Draw a table similar to the one on the next page. Survey each of the family members shown in your family tree. Ask them if they have hair on the middle segment of their fingers. Write each person's name in the appropriate square. Explain to each person that it is normal to have either trait. The presence of hair on the middle segment is the dominant form of this trait.

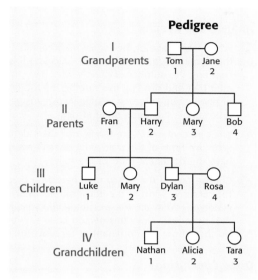

Pedigree

I Grandparents — Tom 1, Jane 2

II Parents — Fran 1, Harry 2, Mary 3, Bob 4

III Children — Luke 1, Mary 2, Dylan 3, Rosa 4

IV Grandchildren — Nathan 1, Alicia 2, Tara 3

CHAPTER RESOURCES

Chapter Resource File

- Datasheet for LabBook
- Lab Notes and Answers

CLASSROOM TESTED & APPROVED

Kerry Johnson
Isbell Middle School
Santa Paula, California

Tracing Traits

Teacher's Notes

Time Required

Two 45-minute class periods, separated by several days so students have time to complete their surveys

Lab Ratings

EASY ————————————→ HARD

Teacher Prep △

Student Set-Up △

Concept Level △△

Clean Up △

Lab Notes

Family histories will vary. Encourage students to include at least three generations in their histories.

Survey results will vary. Make sure that students actually surveyed each family member who was available. Responses will vary. You may check family members with shaded symbols against the survey results for accuracy.

Percentages will vary. A family member may receive a recessive allele from the father and a recessive allele from the mother. In such a case, this family member will exhibit the recessive form of the trait rather than the dominant form.

Because so many children are adopted or live in foster homes or group homes, please emphasize to your students that they may choose any family to study.

Analyze the Results

1. Answers may vary.

2. Answers may vary.

3. The genotype of the recessive form of the characteristic must be *hh* (homozygous recessive). Each allele came from one of the individual's parents; Possible genotypes for the parents of the individual expressing the recessive form are *Hh* and *hh*; Does the student know whether either of the parents expresses the recessive form of the trait? Does the student know if the individual chosen has brothers or sisters? Are their genotypes known? If so, have the student decide if each of them has a dominant or recessive genotype. If a dominant genotype is found among the siblings and one of the parents is known to have the recessive form, ask the student what the genotype of the other parent must be (*Hh*).

Draw Conclusions

4. The Punnett square should show *hh* in the bottom right-hand corner. One of the parents must have the genotype *hh*. The other parent must have either *hh* or *Hh*. If any sibling has the dominant trait, the genotype of the other parent must be *Hh*.

---

3 Trace this trait throughout the family tree you diagrammed in step 1. Shade or color the symbols of the family members who demonstrate the dominant form of this trait.

Analyze the Results

1 What percentage of the family members demonstrate the dominant form of the trait? Calculate this by counting the number of people who have the dominant trait and dividing this number by the total number of people you surveyed. Multiply your answer by 100. An example has been done at right.

Example: Calculating percentage

$$\frac{10 \text{ people with trait}}{20 \text{ people surveyed}} = \frac{1}{2}$$

$$\frac{1}{2} = 0.50 \times 100 = 50\%$$

2 What percentage of the family members demonstrate the recessive form of the trait? Why doesn't every family member have the dominant form of the trait?

3 Choose one of the family members who demonstrates the recessive form of the chosen trait. What is this person's genotype? What are the possible genotypes for the parents of this individual? Does this person have any brothers or sisters? Do they show the dominant or recessive trait?

Draw Conclusions

4 Draw a Punnett square like the one at right. Use this to determine the genotypes of the parents of the person you chose in step 3. Write this person's genotype in the bottom right-hand corner of your Punnett square. **Hint:** There may be more than one possible genotype for the parents. Don't forget to consider the genotypes of the person's brothers and sisters.

Father

	?	?
?		
?		

Mother

Skills Practice Lab

Built for Speed

Imagine that you are an engineer at GoCarCo, a toy-vehicle company. GoCarCo is trying to beat the competition by building a new toy vehicle. Several new designs are being tested. Your boss has given you one of the new toy vehicles and instructed you to measure its speed as accurately as possible with the tools you have. Other engineers (your classmates) are testing the other designs. Your results could decide the fate of the company!

MATERIALS

- meterstick
- stopwatch
- tape, masking
- toy vehicle

SAFETY

Procedure

① How will you accomplish your goal? Write a paragraph to describe your goal and your procedure for this experiment. Be sure that your procedure includes several trials.

② Show your plan to your boss (teacher). Get his or her approval to carry out your procedure.

③ Perform your stated procedure. Record all data. Be sure to express all data in the correct units.

Analyze the Results

① What was the average speed of your vehicle? How does your result compare with the results of the other engineers?

② Compare your technique for determining the speed of your vehicle with the techniques of the other engineers. Which technique do you think is the most effective?

③ Was your toy vehicle the fastest? Explain why or why not.

Applying Your Data

Think of several conditions that could affect your vehicle's speed. Design an experiment to test your vehicle under one of those conditions. Write a paragraph to explain your procedure. Be sure to include an explanation of how that condition changes your vehicle's speed.

CHAPTER RESOURCES

Chapter Resource File

 • Datasheet for LabBook
• Lab Notes and Answers

Elsie Waynes
Terrell Junior High
Washington, D.C.

Built for Speed

Teacher's Notes

Time Required
One or two 45-minute class periods

Lab Ratings

EASY ————————→ HARD

Teacher Prep 🜊
Student Set-Up 🜊
Concept Level 🜊🜊
Clean Up 🜊

MATERIALS
Students may be able to supply toy vehicles from home. The toy vehicles should be self-propelled, either battery operated or windup.

Preparation Notes
If you are using battery-operated cars, ensure that the batteries are fresh and that spare batteries are available. Discuss the correct units (m/s) before students begin.

Analyze the Results
1. Answers may vary.
2. Answers may vary. Students should analyze their procedure and that of others.
3. Answers may vary. Students may consider factors such as battery life, the age of the spring in wind-up vehicles, the testing surface, or the wheels of the vehicle.

Applying Your Data
Procedures may vary but should show a clear understanding of how the condition could affect the vehicle's speed.

Relating Mass and Weight

Teacher's Notes

Time Required

One 45-minute class period

Lab Ratings

EASY ———————————→ HARD

Teacher Prep 🧪
Student Set-Up 🧪
Concept Level 🧪🧪
Clean Up 🧪

MATERIALS

The materials listed are for each group of 2–3 students. A set of metric masses may be used as objects, but at least one random object should be included. Objects must be measurable with the spring scales and metric balances.

Safety Caution

Remind students to review all safety cautions and icons before beginning this lab activity.

Preparation Notes

If metric masses are used, put a small piece of opaque tape over the stamped value for mass. Ensure all objects are easily picked up with the spring scales. Use string to create a "handle." Choose at least five objects for each group.

Barry L. Bishop
San Rafael Junior High
Ferron, Utah

Skills Practice Lab

Relating Mass and Weight

Why do objects with more mass weigh more than objects with less mass? All objects have weight on Earth because their mass is affected by Earth's gravitational force. Because the mass of an object on Earth is constant, the relationship between the mass of an object and its weight is also constant. You will measure the mass and weight of several objects to verify the relationship between mass and weight on the surface of Earth.

Procedure

1 Copy the table below.

Mass and Weight Measurements		
Object	**Mass (g)**	**Weight (N)**
	~~DO NOT WRITE IN BOOK~~	

2 Using the metric balance, find the mass of five or six small classroom objects designated by your teacher. Record the masses.

3 Using the spring scale, find the weight of each object. Record the weights. (You may need to use the string to create a hook with which to hang some objects from the spring scale, as shown at right.)

Analyze the Results

1 Using your data, construct a graph of weight (y-axis) versus mass (x-axis). Draw a line that best fits all your data points.

2 Does the graph confirm the relationship between mass and weight on Earth? Explain your answer.

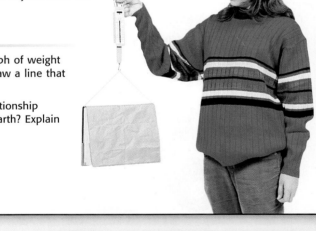

CHAPTER RESOURCES

Chapter Resource File

- **Datasheet for LabBook**
- **Lab Notes and Answers**

Skills Practice Lab

Science Friction

In this experiment, you will investigate three types of friction—static, sliding, and rolling—to determine which is the largest force and which is the smallest force.

Ask a Question

1 Which type of friction is the largest force—static, sliding, or rolling? Which is the smallest?

Form a Hypothesis

2 Write a statement or statements that answer the questions above. Explain your reasoning.

Test the Hypothesis

3 Cut a piece of string, and tie it in a loop that fits in the textbook, as shown on the next page. Hook the string to the spring scale.

4 Practice the next three steps several times before you collect data.

5 To measure the static friction between the book and the table, pull the spring scale very slowly. Record the largest force on the scale before the book starts to move.

6 After the book begins to move, you can determine the sliding friction. Record the force required to keep the book sliding at a slow, constant speed.

7 Place two or three rods under the book to act as rollers. Make sure the rollers are evenly spaced. Place another roller in front of the book so that the book will roll onto it. Pull the force meter slowly. Measure the force needed to keep the book rolling at a constant speed.

  MATERIALS

- rods, wood or metal (3–4)
- scissors
- spring scale (force meter)
- string
- textbook (covered)

 SAFETY

Science Friction

Teacher's Notes

Time Required

One 45-minute class period

Lab Ratings

EASY ———————————————→ HARD

Teacher Prep ⚗
Student Set-Up ⚗
Concept Level ⚗⚗
Clean Up ⚗

MATERIALS

The rollers may be made from ring-stand poles or wooden dowels.

Safety Caution

Remind students to review all safety cautions and icons before beginning this lab activity.

Preparation Notes

If the spring scale is not very sensitive, students may record a force of zero for rolling friction. Encourage students to discuss whether this is realistic and what could be causing them to get such a result. For best results, students should keep the spring scale parallel to the table and should pull gradually. A quick pull will give an incorrect reading.

CHAPTER RESOURCES

Chapter Resource File

- **Datasheet for LabBook**
- **Lab Notes and Answers**

CLASSROOM TESTED & APPROVED

Barry L. Bishop
San Rafael Junior High
Ferron, Utah

Analyze the Results

1. Static friction was the largest. Rolling friction was the smallest.

2. Answers may vary. Students may mention conducting more trials, using different objects or surfaces, or using the spring scale more carefully.

Draw Conclusions

3. Answers may vary but should show consideration of the experimental procedure.

Analyze the Results

1. Which type of friction was the largest? Which was the smallest?

2. Do the results support your hypothesis? If not, how would you revise or retest your hypothesis?

Draw Conclusions

3. Compare your results with those of another group. Are there any differences? Working together, design a way to improve the experiment and resolve possible differences.

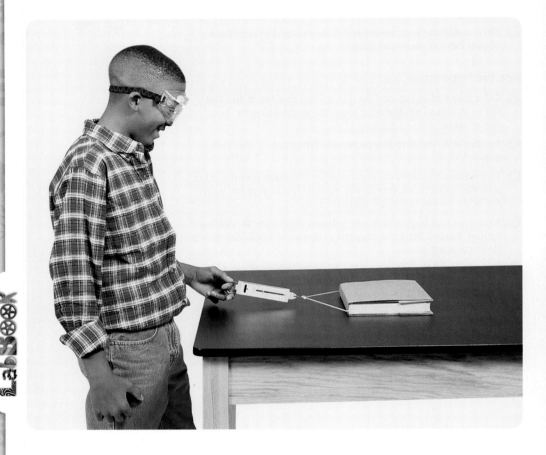

Skills Practice Lab

A Marshmallow Catapult

Catapults use projectile motion to launch objects. In this lab, you will build a simple catapult and determine the angle at which the catapult will launch an object the farthest.

Ask a Question

1. At what angle, from 10° to 90°, will a catapult launch a marshmallow the farthest?

Form a Hypothesis

2. Write a hypothesis that is a possible answer to your question.

Angle	Distance 1 (cm)	Distance 2 (cm)	Average distance	Data Collection
10°	DO NOT WRITE IN BOOK			

Test the Hypothesis

3. Copy the table above. In your table, add one row each for 20°, 30°, 40°, 50°, 60°, 70°, 80°, and 90° angles.

4. Using duct tape, attach the plastic spoon to the 1 cm side of the block. Use enough tape to attach the spoon securely.

5. Place one marshmallow in the center of the spoon, and tape it to the spoon. This marshmallow serves as a ledge to hold the marshmallow that will be launched.

6. Line up the bottom corner of the block with the bottom center of the protractor, as shown in the photograph. Start with the block at 10°.

7. Place a marshmallow in the spoon, on top of the taped marshmallow. Pull the spoon back lightly, and let go. Measure and record the distance from the catapult that the marshmallow lands. Repeat the measurement, and calculate an average.

8. Repeat step 7 for each angle up to 90°.

MATERIALS

- marshmallows, miniature (2)
- meterstick
- protractor
- spoon, plastic
- tape, duct
- wood block, 3.5 cm × 3.5 cm × 1 cm

SAFETY

Analyze the Results

1. At what angle did the catapult launch the marshmallow the farthest? Explain any differences from your hypothesis.

Draw Conclusions

2. At what angle should you throw a ball or shoot an arrow so that it will fly the farthest? Why? Support your answer with your data.

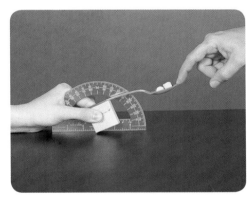

CHAPTER RESOURCES

Chapter Resource File

- Datasheet for LabBook
- Lab Notes and Answers

CLASSROOM TESTED & APPROVED

Vicky Farland
Crane Junior High
Yuma, Arizona

LabBook

Skills Practice Lab

A Marshmallow Catapult

Teacher's Notes

Time Required

One or two 45-minute class periods

Lab Ratings

⚗	⚗⚗	⚗⚗⚗	⚗⚗⚗⚗
EASY			HARD

Teacher Prep ⚗⚗
Student Set-Up ⚗
Concept Level ⚗⚗
Clean Up ⚗

MATERIALS

The materials listed are for each group of 1–3 students. Marshmallows may be dusted with alum (a harmless but bitter kitchen spice) to discourage students from eating all the materials. You may wish to leave the marshmallows out overnight to harden so they will be easier to launch.

Preparation Notes

Some ceilings may be too low and some classrooms too crowded for this lab. Move to the hallway or outdoors to give students plenty of room.

Analyze the Results

1. The catapult should launch farthest at a 40°–50° angle. Explanations may vary.

Draw Conclusions

2. Sample answer: An angle of about 45° is best because it gives the best combination of distance and height. The evidence is that the marshmallow traveled farthest at a 40°–50° angle.

Model-Making Lab

Blast Off!

Teacher's Notes

Time Required

One or two 45-minute class periods

Lab Ratings

EASY ———————→ HARD

Teacher Prep 🧪🧪
Student Set-Up 🧪🧪🧪
Concept Level 🧪🧪🧪🧪
Clean Up 🧪

MATERIALS

You need 100 pennies per group. Use 2 balloons for more force.

Analyze the Results

1. Sample answer: Newton's first law: The rocket remains at rest until a force is exerted on it. Newton's second law: The rocket's acceleration depends on the force (which is constant) and the mass (which increases with each penny). Newton's third law: The force of the air leaving the balloon on the rocket is equal and opposite to the force of the balloon on the air.

Draw Conclusions

2. See the sample diagram at left. You may wish to point out the less obvious force pairs.

Applying Your Data

Answers may vary but should show a clear understanding of how the variable affects the rocket's flight.

Model-Making Lab

Blast Off!

You have been hired as a rocket scientist for NASA. Your job is to design a rocket that will have a controlled flight while carrying a payload. Keep in mind that Newton's laws will have a powerful influence on your rocket.

Model-Making Lab

MATERIALS

- balloon, long, thin
- cup, paper, small
- fishing line, 3 m
- meterstick
- pencil
- pennies
- straw, straight plastic
- string, 15 cm (2)
- tape, masking
- twist tie

SAFETY

Procedure

1 When you begin your experiment, your teacher will tape one end of the fishing line to the ceiling.

2 Use a pencil to poke a small hole in each side of the cup near the top. Place a 15 cm piece of string through each hole, and tape down the ends inside.

3 Inflate the balloon, and use the twist tie to hold it closed.

4 Tape the free ends of the strings to the sides of the balloon near the bottom. The cup should hang below the balloon. Your model rocket should look like a hot-air balloon.

5 Thread the fishing line that is hanging from the ceiling through the straw. Tape the balloon securely to the straw. Tape the loose end of the fishing line to the floor.

6 Untie the twist tie while holding the end of the balloon closed. When you are ready, release the end of the balloon. Mark and record the maximum height of the rocket.

7 Repeat the procedure, adding a penny to the cup each time until your rocket cannot lift any more pennies.

Analyze the Results

1 In a paragraph, describe how all three of Newton's laws influenced the flight of your rocket.

Draw Conclusions

2 Draw a diagram of your rocket. Label the action and reaction forces.

> #### Applying Your Data
>
> Brainstorm ways to modify your rocket so that it will carry the most pennies to the maximum height. Select the best design. When your teacher has approved all the designs, build and launch your rocket. Which variable did you modify? How did this variable affect your rocket's flight?

Action: downward force of pennies

Reaction: upward force of balloon

Reaction: upward force of released air pushing balloon

Action: downward force of air being squeezed out of balloon

Action: downward gravitational force of the Earth on the rocket (rocket's weight)

Reaction: upward gravitational force of the rocket on Earth.

CHAPTER RESOURCES

Chapter Resource File

- Datasheet for LabBook
- Lab Notes and Answers

CLASSROOM
TESTED & APPROVED

Vicky Farland
Crane Junior High
Yuma, Arizona

Skills Practice Lab

Quite a Reaction

Catapults have been used for centuries to throw objects great distances. According to Newton's third law of motion (whenever one object exerts a force on a second object, the second object exerts an equal and opposite force on the first), when an object is launched, something must also happen to the catapult. In this activity, you will build a kind of catapult that will allow you to observe the effects of Newton's third law of motion and the law of conservation of momentum.

Procedure

1 Glue the cardboard rectangles together to make a stack of three.

2 Push two of the pushpins into the cardboard stack near the corners at one end, as shown below. These pushpins will be the anchors for the rubber band.

3 Make a small loop of string.

4 Put the rubber band through the loop of string, and then place the rubber band over the two pushpin anchors. The rubber band should be stretched between the two anchors with the string loop in the middle.

5 Pull the string loop toward the end of the cardboard stack opposite the end with the anchors, and fasten the loop in place with the third pushpin.

6 Place the six straws about 1 cm apart on a tabletop or on the floor. Then, carefully center the catapult on top of the straws.

7 Put the marble in the closed end of the V formed by the rubber band.

8 Use scissors to cut the string holding the rubber band, and observe what happens. (Be careful not to let the scissors touch the cardboard catapult when you cut the string.)

- cardboard rectangles, 10 cm × 15 cm (3)
- glue
- marble
- meterstick
- pushpins (3)
- rubber band
- scissors
- straws, plastic (6)
- string

SAFETY

Quite a Reaction

Teacher's Notes

Time Required

One to two 45-minute class periods

Lab Ratings

EASY			HARD

Teacher Prep 🧪🧪
Student Set-Up 🧪🧪
Concept Level 🧪🧪🧪
Clean Up 🧪

MATERIALS

The materials listed are for groups of 1–3 students. Thick pieces of poster board work well. One piece of corrugated cardboard will work as a substitute. A large marble will produce more-dramatic results than a small marble. Also, be sure to give students enough time for the glue to dry.

Safety Caution

Remind students to review all safety cautions and icons before beginning this lab activity.

Pick up any marbles, pins, or other materials that fall on uncarpeted floors immediately. This helps prevent slips and falls. Give students plenty of space to do this lab.

CHAPTER RESOURCES

Chapter Resource File

 • Datasheet for LabBook
• Lab Notes and Answers

Vicky Farland
Crane Junior High
Yuma, Arizona

Analyze the Results

1. Answers will depend on the type of marble and the type of cardboard. It is likely that the catapult will have more mass.

2. The catapult moved backward.

3. Answers may vary, depending on the mass of the marble, the type of cardboard, and the size of the straws.

4. Answers may vary, but the marble will likely go farther than the catapult.

Draw Conclusions

5. The catapult moved backward as a result of Newton's third law. The catapult exerted a force on the marble that made it move forward. The marble exerted an equal and opposite force on the catapult, making it move backward.

6. More friction acts on the cardboard because it is in contact with the straws. Some students may also note that the marble and the cardboard have different masses. The acceleration of each is different as a result of Newton's second law, $F = m \times a$.

7. The momentum of both the marble and the catapult is 0 kg•m/s because both have a velocity of 0 m/s before the marble is launched.

8. Because the initial momentum of the system is 0 kg•m/s, the catapult has to move backward with a momentum equal to that of the marble moving forward. The momenta of the catapult and marble have to be in opposite directions so they will cancel out.

Applying Your Data

Accept all reasonable designs.

---

9 Reset the catapult with a new piece of string. Try launching the marble several times to be sure that you have observed everything that happens during a launch. Record all your observations.

Analyze the Results

1 Which has more mass, the marble or the catapult?

2 What happened to the catapult when the marble was launched?

3 How far did the marble fly before it landed?

4 Did the catapult move as far as the marble did?

Draw Conclusions

5 Explain why the catapult moved backward.

6 If the forces that made the marble and the catapult move apart are equal, why didn't the marble and the catapult move apart the same distance? (Hint: The fact that the marble can roll after it lands is not the answer.)

---

7 The momentum of an object depends on the mass and velocity of the object. What is the momentum of the marble before it is launched? What is the momentum of the catapult? Explain your answers.

8 Using the law of conservation of momentum, explain why the marble and the catapult move in opposite directions after the launch.

Applying Your Data

How would you modify the catapult if you wanted to keep it from moving backward as far as it did? (It still has to rest on the straws.) Using items that you can find in the classroom, design a catapult that will move backward less than the one originally designed.

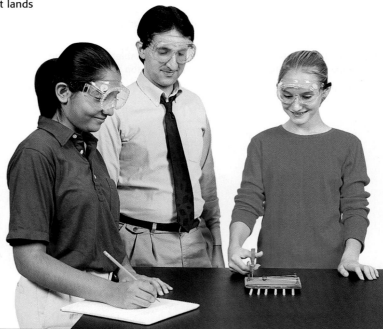

Density Diver

Crew members of a submarine can control the submarine's density underwater by allowing water to flow into and out of special tanks. These changes in density affect the submarine's position in the water. In this lab, you'll control a "density diver" to learn for yourself how the density of an object affects its position in a fluid.

Ask a Question

1 How does the density of an object determine whether the object floats, sinks, or maintains its position in a fluid?

Form a Hypothesis

2 Write a possible answer to the question above.

Test the Hypothesis

3 Completely fill the 2 L plastic bottle with water.

4 Fill the diver (medicine dropper) approximately halfway with water, and place it in the bottle. The diver should float with only part of the rubber bulb above the surface of the water. If the diver floats too high, carefully remove it from the bottle, and add a small amount of water to the diver. Place the diver back in the bottle. If you add too much water and the diver sinks, empty out the bottle and diver, and go back to step 3.

5 Put the cap on the bottle tightly so that no water leaks out.

6 Apply various pressures to the bottle. Carefully watch the water level inside the diver as you squeeze and release the bottle. Record what happens.

7 Try to make the diver rise, sink, or stop at any level. Record your technique and your results.

Analyze the Results

1 How do the changes inside the diver affect its position in the surrounding fluid?

2 What relationship did you observe between the diver's density and the diver's position in the fluid?

Draw Conclusions

3 Explain how your density diver is like a submarine.

4 Explain how pressure on the bottle is related to the diver's density. Be sure to include Pascal's principle in your explanation.

MATERIALS

- bottle, plastic, with screw-on cap, 2 L
- dropper, medicine
- water

SAFETY

Density Diver

Teacher's Notes

Time Required

One 45-minute class period

Lab Ratings

EASY —————————→ HARD

Teacher Prep 🧪
Student Set-Up 🧪🧪
Concept Level 🧪🧪
Clean Up 🧪

Lab Notes

If there is any air in the bottle, students will have to squeeze harder to make the diver move.

Analyze the Results

1. When the water level inside the diver rises, the diver starts sinking. When the level decreases, the diver floats.

2. Sample answer: Higher water level corresponds to higher density. Adding more water to the diver results in more mass in the same volume, so the density is greater.

Draw Conclusions

3. Controlling the water level inside the diver is similar to controlling the water level inside a submarine by using ballast tanks.

4. Sample answer: Squeezing the bottle increases the water pressure. This increase is transmitted equally throughout the bottle to the diver (Pascal's principle). The air inside the diver is compressed, and water enters the diver. This increases the density of the diver.

Skills Practice Lab

Inclined to Move

Teacher's Notes

Time Required
One 45-minute class period

Lab Ratings

EASY ——————→ HARD

Teacher Prep 🧪🧪
Student Set-Up 🧪🧪
Concept Level 🧪🧪🧪
Clean Up 🧪

Safety Caution

Remind students to review all safety cautions and icons before beginning this lab activity.

Ask a Question

1. Accept all clearly formulated questions.

Form a Hypothesis

2. Accept all testable hypotheses.

Analyze the Results

1. The amount of work done should increase as ramp height increases (line A).
2. The amount of work done should increase as ramp height increases (line B).

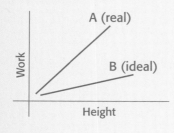

Draw Conclusions

3. It requires less force but more work to raise the book using the ramp. At each height, more work must be done to overcome friction.
4. The greater the height is, the greater the input force is.

Skills Practice Lab

Inclined to Move

In this lab, you will examine a simple machine—an inclined plane. Your task is to compare the work done with and without the inclined plane and to analyze the effects of friction.

Ask a Question

1. Write a question that you can test regarding inclined planes.

Form a Hypothesis

2. Write a possible answer to the question you wrote.

Test the Hypothesis

3. Copy the table at right.

4. Tie a piece of string around a book. Attach the spring scale to the string. Use the spring scale to slowly lift the book to a height of 50 cm. Record the output force (the force needed to lift the book). The output force is constant throughout the lab.

5. Use the board and blocks to make a ramp 10 cm high at the highest point. Measure and record the ramp length.

6. Keeping the spring scale parallel to the ramp, as shown, slowly raise the book. Record the input force (the force needed to pull the book up the ramp).

7. Increase the height of the ramp by 10 cm. Repeat step 6. Repeat this step for each ramp height up to 50 cm.

Analyze the Results

1. The real work done includes the work done to overcome friction. Calculate the real work at each height by multiplying the ramp length (converted to meters) by the input force. Graph your results, plotting work (*y*-axis) versus height (*x*-axis).

MATERIALS

- board, wooden
- blocks
- book, small
- meterstick
- paper, graph
- spring scale
- string

SAFETY

Force Versus Height			
Ramp height (cm)	Output force (N)	Ramp length (cm)	Input force (N)
10			
20			
30	DO NOT WRITE IN BOOK		
40			
50			

2. The ideal work is the work you would do if there were no friction. Calculate the ideal work at each height by multiplying the ramp height (cm) by the output force. Plot the data on your graph.

Draw Conclusions

3. Does it require more or less force and work to raise the book by using the ramp? Explain, using your calculations.

4. What is the relationship between the height of the inclined plane and the input force?

CHAPTER RESOURCES

Chapter Resource File

- 📁 • Datasheet for LabBook
- • Lab Notes and Answers

CLASSROOM TESTED & APPROVED

Jennifer Ford
North Ridge Middle School
North Richland Hills, Texas

Skills Practice Lab

Wheeling and Dealing

A crank handle, such as that used in pencil sharpeners, ice-cream makers, and water wells, is one kind of wheel and axle. In this lab, you will use a crank handle to find out how a wheel and axle helps you do work. You will also determine what effect the length of the handle has on the operation of the machine.

Ask a Question

1 What effect does the length of a handle have on the operation of a crank?

Form a Hypothesis

2 Write a possible answer to the question above.

Test the Hypothesis

3 Copy Table 1.

4 Measure the radius (in meters) of the large dowel in the wheel-and-axle assembly. Record this in Table 1 as the axle radius, which remains constant throughout the lab. (Hint: Measure the diameter, and divide by 2.)

5 Using the spring scale, measure the weight of the large mass. Record this in Table 1 as the output force, which remains constant throughout the lab.

6 Use two C-clamps to secure the wheel-and-axle assembly to the table, as shown.

7 Measure the length (in meters) of handle 1. Record this length as a wheel radius in Table 1.

8 Insert the handle into the hole in the axle. Attach one end of the string to the large mass and the other end to the screw in the axle. The mass should hang down, and the handle should turn freely.

9 Turn the handle to lift the mass off the floor. Hold the spring scale upside down, and attach it to the end of the handle. Measure the force (in newtons) as the handle pulls up on the spring scale. Record this as the input force.

MATERIALS

- C-clamps (2)
- handles(4)
- mass, large
- meterstick
- spring scale
- string, 0.5 m
- wheel-and-axle assembly

SAFETY

Table 1 Data Collection

Handle	Axle radius (m)	Output force (N)	Wheel radius (m)	Input force (N)
1				
2		DO NOT WRITE IN BOOK		
3				
4				

Lab Notes

Use a marker to number the handles 1 through 4 (shortest to longest). Drill a 0.5 in. diameter hole halfway through the large dowel near one end. The handles will be inserted into the hole. A small screw should be inserted into the large dowel near the handle attachment point, on the side away from the end. The string will attach to this point. The 1.5 in. PVC pipe should have an inside diameter slightly larger than that of the large dowel. The clamps are the most expensive pieces and are optional. If students work in groups, one student may act as the clamp and hold the PVC pipe firmly against the tabletop. Use a 500 g or 1 kg mass for the large mass. It takes a fair amount of time and materials to build the wheel-and-axle assemblies, but once you have built them, they will be available to use in subsequent years. Students should review the sections on work input, work output, mechanical efficiency, mechanical advantage, and a wheel and axle before beginning this lab. Demonstrate the assembly for students. Remind students that they can measure the axle radius and the wheel radius in centimeters and then convert to meters.

LabBook

Skills Practice Lab

Wheeling and Dealing

Teacher's Notes

Time Required

Two 45-minute class periods

Lab Ratings

EASY ————————————→ HARD

Teacher Prep 🧪🧪🧪🧪
Student Set-Up 🧪🧪
Concept Level 🧪🧪🧪🧪
Clean Up 🧪

MATERIALS

The materials listed in this lab are for each group of 2–4 students. The materials listed below are what you will need in order to prepare each wheel-and-axle assembly.

- 30 cm of 1 in. dowel
- 70 cm of 0.5 in. dowel for handles (cut into 4 pieces of 10 cm, 15 cm, 20 cm, and 25 cm)
- wheel
- small screw
- 1.5 in. PVC pipe

Safety Caution

Remind students to review all safety cautions and icons before beginning this lab activity.

Preparation Notes

The wheel-and-axle assembly must be constructed before class.

Form a Hypothesis

2. Accept all testable hypotheses.

Analyze the Results

2. **a.** Axle distance = 2π ×
   (0.012 m) = 0.075 m
   Wheel distance = 2π ×
   (handle length: 0.10 m, 0.15 m, 0.20 m, 0.25 m) = 0.63 m, 0.94 m, 1.3 m, 1.6 m

   b. Answers will depend on the mass used. Check calculations for accuracy.

   c. Mechanical efficiency will depend on the materials used. Check calculations for accuracy.

   d. Mechanical advantages are 8.3, 12.5, 16.7, and 20.8 for the handles (10 cm, 15 cm, 20 cm, and 25 cm).

Draw Conclusions

3. As the handle length increases, work output stays the same, but work input gets slightly larger because the machine becomes less efficient.

4. The mechanical efficiency decreases as the handle length increases because the large dowel rotates within the PVC pipe more, creating more friction. More friction leads to lower mechanical efficiency.

5. Mechanical advantage increases as handle length increases because the input force for a large handle (wheel) is less.

6. The mechanical advantage will decrease.

7. Controlled factors include the axle radius and the mass used. The variable was the wheel radius (the length of the handle).

---

10 Remove the spring scale, and lower the mass to the floor. Remove the handle.

11 Repeat steps 7 through 10 with the other three handles. Record all data in Table 1.

Analyze the Results

1 Copy Table 2.

Table 2 Calculations						
Handle	Axle distance (m)	Wheel distance (m)	Work input (J)	Work output (J)	Mechanical efficiency (%)	Mechanical advantage
1						
2						
3						
4						

DO NOT WRITE IN BOOK

2 Calculate the following for each handle, using the equations given. Record your answers in Table 2.

   a. *Distance axle rotates =*
   2 × π × *axle radius*

   Distance wheel rotates =
   2 × π × *wheel radius*

   (Use 3.14 for the value of π.)

   b. *Work input =*
   input force × wheel distance

   Work output =
   output force × axle distance

   c. *Mechanical efficiency =*
   $\frac{work\ output}{work\ input} \times 100$

   d. *Mechanical advantage =*
   $\frac{wheel\ radius}{axle\ radius}$

Draw Conclusions

3 What happens to work output and work input as the handle length increases? Why?

4 What happens to mechanical efficiency as the handle length increases? Why?

5 What happens to mechanical advantage as the handle length increases? Why?

6 What will happen to mechanical advantage if the handle length is kept constant and the axle radius gets larger?

7 What factors were controlled in this experiment? What was the variable?

Larry Tackett
Andrew Jackson Middle School
Cross Lanes, West Virginia

CHAPTER RESOURCES
Chapter Resource File
• Datasheet for LabBook
• Lab Notes and Answers

Building Machines

You are surrounded by machines. Some are simple machines, such as ramps for wheelchair access to a building. Others are compound machines, such as elevators and escalators, that are made of two or more simple machines. In this lab, you will design and build several simple machines and a compound machine.

Ask a Question

1 How can simple machines be combined to make compound machines?

Form a Hypothesis

2 Write a possible answer to the question above.

Test the Hypothesis

3 Use the listed materials to build a model of each simple machine: inclined plane, lever, wheel and axle, pulley, screw, and wedge. Describe and draw each model.

4 Design a compound machine by using the materials listed. You may design a machine that already exists, or you may invent your own machine. Be creative!

5 After your teacher approves your design, build your compound machine.

Analyze the Results

1 List a possible use for each of your simple machines.

2 How many simple machines are in your compound machine? List them.

3 Compare your compound machine with those created by your classmates.

4 What is a possible use for your compound machine? Why did you design it as you did?

5 A compound machine is listed in the materials list. What is it?

Applying Your Data

Design a compound machine that has all the simple machines in it. Explain what the machine will do and how it will make work easier. With your teacher's approval, build your machine.

MATERIALS

- bottle caps
- cardboard
- clay, modeling
- craft sticks
- glue
- paper
- pencils
- rubber bands
- scissors
- shoe boxes
- stones
- straws
- string
- tape
- thread spools, empty
- other materials available in your classroom that are approved by your teacher

SAFETY

Building Machines

Teacher's Notes

Time Required

One or two 45-minute class periods

Lab Ratings

EASY ———————————→ HARD

Teacher Prep 🧪🧪
Student Set-Up 🧪🧪
Concept Level 🧪🧪
Clean Up 🧪

MATERIALS

The materials listed for this lab should be available in quantities sufficient for the entire class. You may provide different materials for students to use. Be sure students work carefully with the supplied materials. Students should work in groups of 2–4. Be sure to approve designs before students begin building their compound machines.

Safety Caution

Remind students to review all safety cautions and icons before beginning this lab activity.

Analyze the Results

1–4. Accept all reasonable answers.

5. the pair of scissors

Applying Your Data

Accept all reasonable designs. Check all materials for safety and availability.

Norman Holcomb
Marion Elementary School
Maria Stein, Ohio

CLASSROOM TESTED & APPROVED

Contents

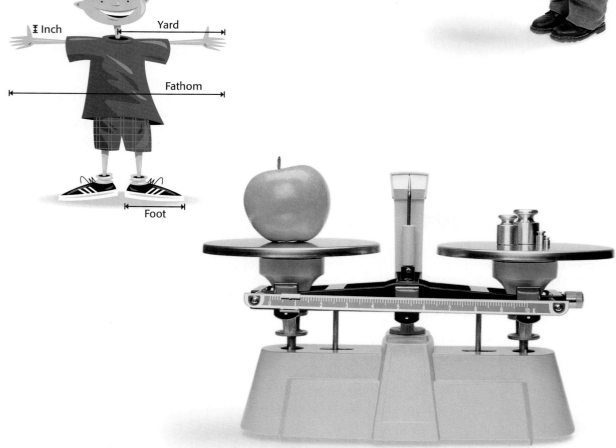

Appendix

✓ *Reading Check* Answers

Chapter 1 Science in Our World

Section 1
Page 4: Science is the knowledge obtained by observing natural events and conditions in order to discover facts and formulate laws or principles that can be verified or tested.

Page 7: Society can influence technology development by identifying important problems that need technological solutions.

Page 9: A volcanologist studies volcanoes and their products, such as lava and gases.

Section 2
Page 10: a series of steps used by scientists to solve problems

Page 12: A hypothesis is testable if an experiment can be designed to test the hypothesis.

Page 14: only one

Page 16: because the scientist has learned something

Section 3
Page 19: a mathematical model

Page 20: to explain a broad range of observations, facts, and tested hypotheses, to predict what might happen, and to organize scientific thinking

Section 4
Page 22: stopwatch, graduated cylinder, meterstick, spring scale, balance, and thermometer

Page 25: the kilogram

Page 27: Safety symbols alert you to particular safety concerns or specific dangers in a lab.

Chapter 2 The Atmosphere

Section 1
Page 40: Water can be liquid (rain), solid (snow or ice), or gas (water vapor).

Page 42: The troposphere is the layer of turning or change. The stratosphere is the layer in which gases are layered and do not mix vertically. The mesosphere is the middle layer. The thermosphere is the layer in which temperatures are highest.

Page 44: The thermosphere does not feel hot because air molecules are spaced far apart and cannot collide to transfer much thermal energy.

Section 2
Page 47: Cold air is more dense than warm air, so cold air sinks and warm air rises. This produces convection currents.

Page 49: A greenhouse gas is a gas that absorbs thermal energy in the atmosphere.

Section 3
Page 51: Sinking air causes areas of high pressure because sinking air presses down on the air beneath it.

Page 52: the westerlies

Page 55: At night, the air along the mountain slopes cools. This cool air moves down the slopes into the valley and produces a mountain breeze.

Section 4
Page 56: Sample answer: smoke, dust and sea salt

Page 59: Answers may vary. Acid precipitation may decrease the soil nutrients that are available to plants.

Page 60: Powdered limestone is used to counteract the effects of acidic snowmelt from snow that accumulated during the winter.

Section 5
Page 62: Sample answer: coughing, headaches, and irritation to the eyes

Page 65: Sample answer: One way to reduce air pollution is to walk or bike to your destination instead of driving.

Chapter 3 Understanding Weather

Section 1
Page 76: The water cycle is the continuous movement of water from Earth's oceans and rivers into the atmosphere, into the ground, and back into the oceans and rivers.

Page 78: A psychrometer is used to measure relative humidity.

Page 79: The bulb of a wet-bulb thermometer is covered with moistened material. The bulb cools as water evaporates from the material. If the air is dry, more water will evaporate from the material, and the temperature recorded by the thermometer will be low. If the air is humid, less water will evaporate from the material, and the temperature recorded by the thermometer will be higher.

Page 81: Altostratus clouds form at middle altitudes.

Section 2
Page 85: A maritime tropical air mass causes hot and humid summer weather in the midwestern United States.

Page 87: An occluded front produces cool temperatures and large amounts of rain.

Page 89: An anticyclone can produce dry, clear weather.

Section 3
Page 91: A severe thunderstorm is a thunderstorm that produces high winds, hail, flash floods, or tornadoes.

Page 93: Hurricanes are also called *typhoons* or *cyclones.*

Page 94: Hurricanes get their energy from the condensation of water vapor.

Section 4
Page 98: Meteorologists use weather balloons to collect atmospheric data above Earth's surface.

Chapter 4 Climate

Section 1
Page 112: Climate is the average weather condition in an area over a long period of time. Weather is the condition of the atmosphere at a particular time.

Page 114: Locations near the equator have less seasonal variation because the tilt of the Earth does not change the amount of energy these locations receive from the sun.

Page 116: The atmosphere becomes less dense and loses its ability to absorb and hold thermal energy, at higher elevations.

Page 117: The Gulf Stream current carries warm water past Iceland, which heats the air and causes milder temperatures.

Page 118: Each biome has a different climate and different plant and animals communities.

Section 2
Page 120: You would find the tropical zone from 23.5° north latitude to 23.5° south latitude.

Page 123: Answers may vary. Sample answer: rats, lizards, snakes, and scorpions.

Section 3
Page 124: The temperate zone is located between the Tropics and the polar zone.

Page 126: Temperate deserts are cold at night because low humidity and cloudless skies allow energy to escape.

Page 129: Cities have higher temperatures than the surrounding rural areas because buildings and pavement absorb solar radiation instead of reflecting it.

Section 4
Page 131: Changes in the Earth's orbit and the tilt of the Earth's axis are the two things that Milankovitch says cause ice ages.

Page 132: Dust, ash, and smoke from volcanic eruptions block the sun's rays, which causes the Earth to cool.

Page 135: The deserts would receive less rainfall, making it harder for plants and animals in the desert to survive.

Chapter 5 Body Organization and Structure

Section 1
Page 149: Cells need nutrients moved into the cells and wastes moved out of the cells in order to maintain homeostasis.

Page 150: A group of similar cells that work together form tissues.

Page 151: The stomach works with other organs, such as the small and large intestines, to digest food.

Page 152: Sample answer: The cardiovascular system includes the heart and blood vessels. These organs are also part of the circulatory system, which includes blood. Together, these systems deliver the materials cells need to survive.

Section 2
Page 155: Sample answer: As people grow, most of the cartilage that they start out with is replaced with bone.

Page 156: Sample answer: Joints are held together by ligaments. Cartilage cushions the area in a joint where bones meet.

Section 3
Page 159: Sample answer: One muscle, the flexor, bends part of the body. Another muscle, the extensor, straightens part of the body.

Page 161: Sample answer: Anabolic steroids can damage the heart, liver, and kidneys. They can also cause high blood pressure. Anabolic steroids can cause bones to stop growing.

Section 4
Page 163: The dermis is the layer of skin that lies beneath the epidermis. It is composed of a protein called *collagen,* while the epidermis contains keratin.

Page 164: Sample answer: A nail grows from living cells in the nail root at the base of the nail. As new cells form, the nail grows longer.

Chapter 6 Circulation and Respiration

Section 1
Page 176: The four main parts of the cardiovascular system are the heart and the arteries, capillaries, and veins.

Page 178: Arteries have thick, stretchy walls and carry blood away from the heart. Capillaries are tiny blood vessels that allow the exchange of oxygen, carbon dioxide, and nutrients between cells and blood. Veins are blood vessels that carry blood back to the heart.

Page 180: Atherosclerosis is dangerous because it is the buildup of material inside an artery. When the artery becomes blocked, blood can't flow and can't reach the cells. In some cases, a person can have a heart attack from a blocked artery.

Section 2
Page 182: plasma, red blood cells, white blood cells, and platelets

Page 183: White blood cells identify and attack pathogens that may make you sick.

Page 184: Systolic pressure is the pressure inside arteries when the ventricles contract. Diastolic pressure is the pressure inside the arteries when the ventricles are relaxed.

Page 185: The red blood cells of a person who has type O blood have no A or B antigens. The A or B antibodies in another person's blood will not react to the type O cells. It is safe for anyone to receive type O blood.

Section 3
Page 186: The lymphatic system is a secondary circulatory system in the body. The lymphatic system collects fluid and particles from between the cells and returns them to the cardiovascular system.

Page 188: The white pulp of the spleen is part of the lymphatic system. It helps fight infections by storing and producing lymphocytes. The red pulp of the spleen removes unwanted material, such as defective red blood cells, from the circulatory system.

Section 4
Page 191: Sample answer: In the lungs, each bronchiole branches to form thousands of alveoli. These small sacs allow for the exchange of oxygen and carbon dioxide. The alveoli provide a large amount of surface area, which allows gases to be exchanged efficiently.

Page 192: Cellular respiration is the process inside a cell in which oxygen is used to release energy stored in molecules of glucose. During the process, carbon dioxide (CO_2) and water are released.

Chapter 7   The Digestive and Urinary Systems
Section 1
Page 205   The digestive system works with the circulatory system to deliver the materials cells need to function. The digestive system breaks down food into a form that can be carried by the circulatory system.

Page 207   The stomach is a muscular, saclike organ with tiny glands that release enzymes and acids. This structure helps the stomach break down food mechanically and chemically.

Page 209   Bile breaks large fat droplets into very small droplets. This process allows more fat molecules to be exposed to digestive enzymes.

Page 210   Fiber keeps the stool soft and keeps material moving through the large intestine.

Section 2
Page 213   The function of kidneys is to filter blood. Nephrons are microscopic filters inside the kidneys that make this possible.

Page 214   Diuretics are chemicals that cause the kidneys to make more urine.

Chapter 8   Communication and Control
Section 1
Page 226: The CNS is the brain and the spinal cord. The PNS is all of the parts of the nervous system except the brain and the spinal cord.

Page 227: A neuron is a cell that has a cell body and a nucleus. A neuron also has dendrites that receive signals from other neurons and axons that send signals to other neurons.

Page 228: A nerve is a collection of nerve fibers, or axons, bundled together with blood vessels through which impulses travel between the central nervous system and other parts of the body.

Page 229: The PNS connects your CNS to the rest of your body, controls voluntary movements, and keeps your body's functions in balance.

Page 230: A voluntary action is an action over which you have conscious control. Voluntary activities include throwing a ball, playing a video game, talking to your friends, taking a bite of food, and raising your hand to answer a question in class. An involuntary action is an action that happens automatically. It is an action or process over which you have no conscious control.

Page 231: The medulla is important because it controls your heart rate, blood pressure, and ordinary breathing.

Page 232: When someone touches your skin, an impulse that travels along a sensory neuron to your spinal cord and then to your brain is created. The response travels back from your brain to your spinal cord and then along a motor neuron to a muscle.

Section 2
Page 234: Skin can detect pressure, temperature, pain, and vibration.

Page 235: Reflexes are important because they can protect you from injury.

Page 238: Neurons in the cochlea convert waves into electrical impulses that the brain interprets as sound.

Section 3
Page 241: Sample answer: The thyroid gland increases the rate at which the body uses energy. The thymus gland regulates the immune system, which helps your body fight disease.

Page 242: Insulin helps regulate the amount of glucose in the blood.

Chapter 9   Reproduction and Development
Section 1
Page 255: Sexual reproduction is reproduction in which the sex cells (egg and sperm) of two parents unite to form a new individual.

Page 256: External fertilization happens when the sex cells unite outside of the female's body. Internal fertilization happens when the sex cells unite inside the female's body.

Page 257: All mammals reproduce sexually and nurture their young with milk.

Section 2
Page 258: testes, epididymis, vas deferens, urethra, penis

Page 260: Twins happen about 30 times in every 1,000 births.

Section 3
Page 262: Fertilization happens when the nucleus of a sperm unites with the nucleus of an egg. Implantation happens after the fertilized egg travels down the fallopian tube to the uterus and embeds itself in the wall of the uterus.

Page 263: The placenta is important because it provides the embryo with oxygen and nutrients from the mother's blood. Wastes from the embryo also travel to the placenta, where they are carried to the mother so that she can excrete them.

Page 264: The embryo is now called a *fetus.* The fetus's face begins to look more human, and the fetus can swallow, grows rapidly (triples in size), and begins to make movements that the mother can feel.

Page 696: A person's reproductive system becomes mature.

Chapter 10 Body Defenses and Disease

Section 1

Page 281: Cooking kills dangerous bacteria or parasites living in meat, fish, and eggs.

Page 283: Frank's doctor did not prescribe antibiotics because Frank had a cold. Colds are caused by viruses. Antibiotics can't stop viruses.

Section 2

Page 285: Macrophages engulf, or eat, any microorganisms or viruses that enter your body.

Page 286: If a virus particle enters the body, it may pass into body cells and begin to replicate. Or it may be engulfed and broken up by macrophages.

Page 289: rheumatoid arthritis, diabetes, multiple sclerosis, and lupus

Page 290: HIV causes AIDS.

Chapter 11 Staying Healthy

Section 1

Page 303: An incomplete protein does not contain all of the essential amino acids.

Page 305: Sample answer: a peanut butter sandwich, a glass of milk, and fresh fruit and vegetable slices

Page 306: One serving of chicken noodle soup provides more than 10% of the daily recommended allowance of vitamin A and sodium.

Section 2

Page 309: Over-the-counter drugs can be bought without a prescription. Prescription drugs can be bought only with a prescription from a doctor or other medical professional.

Page 311: First-time use of cocaine can cause a heart attack or can cause a person to become addicted.

Page 312: Drug use is the proper use of a legal drug. Drug abuse is either the use of an illegal drug or the improper use of a legal drug.

Section 3

Page 315: Aerobic exercise strengthens the heart, lungs, and bones and reduces stress. Regular exercise also burns Calories and can give you more energy.

Page 317: Sample answers: Never hike or camp alone, dress for the weather, learn how to swim, wear a life jacket, and never drink unpurified water.

Page 319: CPR is a way to revive someone whose heart has stopped beating. CPR classes are available in many places in the community.

Chapter 12 It's Alive!! Or Is It?

Section 1

Page 333: Sample answer: They control their body temperature by moving from one environment to another. If they get too warm, they move to the shade. If they get too cool, they move out into the sunlight.

Page 334: making food, breaking down food, moving materials into and out of cells, and building cells

Section 2

Page 336: photosynthesis

Page 339: Simple carbohydrates are made of one sugar molecule. Complex carbohydrates are made of many sugar molecules linked together.

Page 340: Most fats are solid, and most oils are liquid.

Chapter 13 Cells: The Basic Units of Life

Section 1

Page 353: Sample answer: All organisms are made of one or more cells, the cell is the basic unit of all living things, and all cells come from existing cells.

Page 354: If a cell's volume gets too large, the cell's surface area will not be able to take in enough nutrients or get rid of wastes fast enough to keep the cell alive.

Page 355: Organelles are structures within a cell that perform specific functions for the cell.

Page 357: One difference between eubacteria and archaea is that bacterial ribosomes are different from archaebacterial ribosomes.

Page 358: The main difference between prokaryotes and eukaryotes is that eukaryotic cells have a nucleus and membrane-bound organelles and prokaryotic cells do not.

Section 2

Page 360: Plant, algae, and fungi cells have cell walls.

Page 361: A cell membrane encloses the cell and separates and protects the cell's contents from the cell's environment. The cell wall also controls the movement of materials into and out of the cell.

Page 362: The cytoskeleton is a web of proteins in the cytoplasm. It gives the cell support and structure.

Page 364: Most of a cell's ATP is made in the cell's mitochondria.

Page 366: Lysosomes destroy worn-out organelles, attack foreign invaders, and get rid of waste material from inside the cell.

Section 3

Page 368: Sample answer: larger size, longer life, and cell specialization

Page 369: An organ is a structure of two or more tissues working together to perform a specific function in the body.

Page 370: cell, tissue, organ, organ system

Chapter 14   The Cell in Action

Section 1
Page 383: Red blood cells would burst in pure water because water particles move from outside, where particles were dense, to inside the cell, where particles were less dense. This movement of water would cause red blood cells to fill up and burst.

Page 385: Exocytosis is the process by which a cell moves large particles to the outside of the cell.

Section 2
Page 387: Cellular respiration is a chemical process by which cells produce energy from food. Breathing supplies oxygen for cellular respiration and removes the carbon dioxide produced by cellular respiration.

Page 389: One kind of fermentation produces CO_2, and the other kind produces lactic acid.

Section 3
Page 391: No, the number of chromosomes is not always related to the complexity of organisms.

Page 392: During cytokinesis in plant cells, a cell plate is formed. During cytokinesis in animal cells, a cell plate does not form.

Chapter 15   Heredity

Section 1
Page 404: the passing of traits from parents to off-spring

Page 407: During his second set of experiments, Mendel allowed the first-generation plants, which resulted from his first set of experiments, to self-pollinate.

Page 408: A ratio is a relationship between two different numbers that is often expressed as a fraction.

Section 2
Page 410: A gene contains the instructions for an inherited trait. The different versions of a gene are called *alleles*.

Page 412: Probability is the mathematical chance that something will happen.

Page 414: In incomplete dominance, one trait is not completely dominant over another.

Section 3
Page 417: 23 chromosomes

Page 418: During meiosis, one parent cell makes four new cells.

Chapter 16   Genes and DNA

Section 1
Page 435: Guanine and cytosine are always found in DNA in equal amounts, as are adenine and thymine.

Page 437: every time a cell divides

Section 2
Page 438: a string of nucleotides that give the cell information about how to make a specific trait

Page 441: They transfer amino acids to the ribosome.

Page 442: a physical or chemical agent that can cause a mutation in DNA

Page 443: Sickle cell disease is caused by a mutation in a single nucleotide of DNA, which then causes a different amino acid to be assembled in a protein used in blood cells.

Page 444: a near-identical copy of another organism, created with the original organism's genes

Chapter 17   Matter in Motion

Section 1
Page 458: A reference point is an object that appears to stay in place.

Page 460: Velocity can change by changing speed or changing direction.

Page 462: The unit for acceleration is meters per second per second (m/s^2).

Section 2
Page 465: If all of the forces act in the same direction, you must add the forces to determine the net force.

Page 466: 2 N north

Page 468: The force of gravity and the force of lift must be balanced for an airplane to stay at a certain altitude.

Section 3
Page 471: Friction is greater between rough surfaces because rough surfaces have more microscopic hills and valleys.

Page 473: *Static* means "not moving."

Page 474: Three common lubricants are oil, grease, and wax.

Section 4
Page 477: You must exert a force to overcome the gravitational force between the object and Earth.

Page 478: Gravitational force increases as mass increases.

Page 481: The weight of an object is a measure of the gravitational force on the object.

Page 482: The SI unit of force is the newton. The SI unit of mass is the kilogram.

Chapter 18   Forces and Motion

Section 1
Page 495: The acceleration due to gravity is 9.8 m/s^2.

Page 496: Air resistance will have more of an effect on the acceleration of a falling leaf.

Page 498: The word *centripetal* means "toward the center."

Page 500: Gravity gives vertical motion to an object in projectile motion.

Section 2
Page 503: When the bus is moving, both you and the bus are in motion. When the bus stops moving, no unbalanced force acts on your body, so your body continues to move forward.

Page 505: The acceleration of an object increases as the force exerted on the object increases.

Page 507: The forces in a force pair are equal in size and opposite in direction.

Page 508: Objects accelerate toward Earth because the force of gravity pulls them toward Earth.

Section 3

Page 511: When two objects collide, some or all of the momentum of each object can be transferred to the other object.

Page 512: After a collision, objects can stick together or can bounce off each other.

Chapter 19   Forces in Fluids

Section 1

Page 525: Two gases in the atmosphere are nitrogen and oxygen.

Page 526: Pressure increases as depth increases.

Page 528: You decrease pressure inside a straw by removing some of the air inside the straw.

Section 2

Page 531: An object is buoyed up if the buoyant force on the object is greater than the object's weight.

Page 532: Helium is less dense than air.

Page 534: Crew members control the density of a submarine by controlling the amount of water in the ballast tanks.

Section 3

Page 537: Lift is an upward force on an object that is moving in a fluid.

Page 539: An irregular or unpredictable flow of fluids is known as *turbulence.*

Page 540: Airplanes can reduce turbulence by changing the shape or area of the wings.

Chapter 20   Work and Machines

Section 1

Page 552: No, work is done on an object only if force causes the object to move in a direction that is parallel to the force.

Page 555: Work is calculated as force times distance.

Page 556: Power is calculated as work done (in joules) divided by the time (in seconds) in which the work was done.

Section 2

Page 559: Machines make work easier by allowing a decreased force to be applied over a greater distance.

Page 560: Machines can change the force or the distance through which force is applied.

Page 562: *mechanical efficiency = (work output − work input) × 100*

Section 3

Page 565: Each class of lever has a different set of mechanical advantage possibilities.

Page 567: the radius of the wheel divided by the radius of the axle

Page 568: a slanted surface that makes the raising of loads easier, such as a ramp

Page 570: They have more moving parts than simple machines do, so they tend to be less efficient than simple machines are.

Study Skills

FoldNote Instructions

Have you ever tried to study for a test or quiz but didn't know where to start? Or have you read a chapter and found that you can remember only a few ideas? Well, FoldNotes are a fun and exciting way to help you learn and remember the ideas you encounter as you learn science!

FoldNotes are tools that you can use to organize concepts. By focusing on a few main concepts, FoldNotes help you learn and remember how the concepts fit together. They can help you see the "big picture." Below you will find instructions for building 10 different FoldNotes.

Pyramid

1. Place a sheet of paper in front of you. Fold the lower left-hand corner of the paper diagonally to the opposite edge of the paper.

2. Cut off the tab of paper created by the fold (at the top).

3. Open the paper so that it is a square. Fold the lower right-hand corner of the paper diagonally to the opposite corner to form a triangle.

4. Open the paper. The creases of the two folds will have created an X.

5. Using scissors, cut along one of the creases. Start from any corner, and stop at the center point to create two flaps. Use tape or glue to attach one of the flaps on top of the other flap.

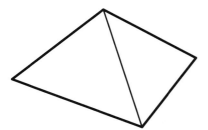

Double Door

1. Fold a sheet of paper in half from the top to the bottom. Then, unfold the paper.

2. Fold the top and bottom edges of the paper to the crease.

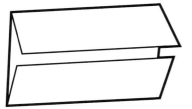

Booklet

1. Fold a sheet of paper in half from left to right. Then, unfold the paper.

2. Fold the sheet of paper in half again from the top to the bottom. Then, unfold the paper.

3. Refold the sheet of paper in half from left to right.

4. Fold the top and bottom edges to the center crease.

5. Completely unfold the paper.

6. Refold the paper from top to bottom.

7. Using scissors, cut a slit along the center crease of the sheet from the folded edge to the creases made in step 4. Do not cut the entire sheet in half.

8. Fold the sheet of paper in half from left to right. While holding the bottom and top edges of the paper, push the bottom and top edges together so that the center collapses at the center slit. Fold the four flaps to form a four-page book.

Layered Book

1. Lay one sheet of paper on top of another sheet. Slide the top sheet up so that 2 cm of the bottom sheet is showing.

2. Hold the two sheets together, fold down the top of the two sheets so that you see four 2 cm tabs along the bottom.

3. Using a stapler, staple the top of the FoldNote.

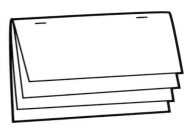

Key-Term Fold

1. Fold a sheet of lined notebook paper in half from left to right.

2. Using scissors, cut along every third line from the right edge of the paper to the center fold to make tabs.

Four-Corner Fold

1. Fold a sheet of paper in half from left to right. Then, unfold the paper.

2. Fold each side of the paper to the crease in the center of the paper.

3. Fold the paper in half from the top to the bottom. Then, unfold the paper.

4. Using scissors, cut the top flap creases made in step 3 to form four flaps.

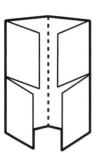

Three-Panel Flip Chart

1. Fold a piece of paper in half from the top to the bottom.

2. Fold the paper in thirds from side to side. Then, unfold the paper so that you can see the three sections.

3. From the top of the paper, cut along each of the vertical fold lines to the fold in the middle of the paper. You will now have three flaps.

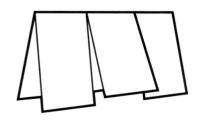

Table Fold

1. Fold a piece of paper in half from the top to the bottom. Then, fold the paper in half again.

2. Fold the paper in thirds from side to side.

3. Unfold the paper completely. Carefully trace the fold lines by using a pen or pencil.

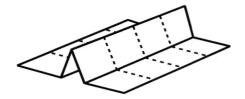

Two-Panel Flip Chart

1. Fold a piece of paper in half from the top to the bottom.

2. Fold the paper in half from side to side. Then, unfold the paper so that you can see the two sections.

3. From the top of the paper, cut along the vertical fold line to the fold in the middle of the paper. You will now have two flaps.

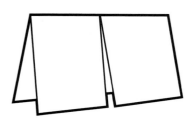

Tri-Fold

1. Fold a piece a paper in thirds from the top to the bottom.

2. Unfold the paper so that you can see the three sections. Then, turn the paper sideways so that the three sections form vertical columns.

3. Trace the fold lines by using a pen or pencil. Label the columns "Know," "Want," and "Learn."

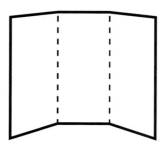

Graphic Organizer Instructions

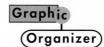 **Graphic Organizer** Have you ever wished that you could "draw out" the many concepts you learn in your science class? Sometimes, being able to *see* how concepts are related really helps you remember what you've learned. Graphic Organizers do just that! They give you a way to draw or map out concepts.

All you need to make a Graphic Organizer is a piece of paper and a pencil. Below you will find instructions for four different Graphic Organizers designed to help you organize the concepts you'll learn in this book.

Spider Map

1. Draw a diagram like the one shown. In the circle, write the main topic.

2. From the circle, draw legs to represent different categories of the main topic. You can have as many categories as you want.

3. From the category legs, draw horizontal lines. As you read the chapter, write details about each category on the horizontal lines.

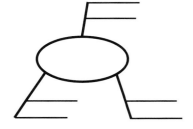

Comparison Table

1. Draw a chart like the one shown. Your chart can have as many columns and rows as you want.

2. In the top row, write the topics that you want to compare.

3. In the left column, write characteristics of the topics that you want to compare. As you read the chapter, fill in the characteristics for each topic in the appropriate boxes.

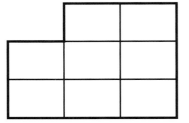

Chain-of-Events-Chart

1. Draw a box. In the box, write the first step of a process or the first event of a timeline.

2. Under the box, draw another box, and use an arrow to connect the two boxes. In the second box, write the next step of the process or the next event in the timeline.

3. Continue adding boxes until the process or timeline is finished.

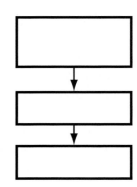

Concept Map

1. Draw a circle in the center of a piece of paper. Write the main idea of the chapter in the center of the circle.

2. From the circle, draw other circles. In those circles, write characteristics of the main idea. Draw arrows from the center circle to the circles that contain the characteristics.

3. From each circle that contains a characteristic, draw other circles. In those circles, write specific details about the characteristic. Draw arrows from each circle that contains a characteristic to the circles that contain specific details. You may draw as many circles as you want.

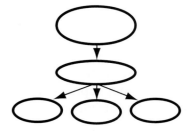

Appendix

SI Measurement

The International System of Units, or SI, is the standard system of measurement used by many scientists. Using the same standards of measurement makes it easier for scientists to communicate with one another.

SI works by combining prefixes and base units. Each base unit can be used with different prefixes to define smaller and larger quantities. The table below lists common SI prefixes.

SI Prefixes

Prefix	Symbol	Factor	Example
kilo-	k	1,000	kilogram, 1 kg = 1,000 g
hecto-	h	100	hectoliter, 1 hL = 100 L
deka-	da	10	dekameter, 1 dam = 10 m
		1	meter, liter, gram
deci-	d	0.1	decigram, 1 dg = 0.1 g
centi-	c	0.01	centimeter, 1 cm = 0.01 m
milli-	m	0.001	milliliter, 1 mL = 0.001 L
micro-	μ	0.000 001	micrometer, 1 μm = 0.000 001 m

SI Conversion Table

SI units	From SI to English	From English to SI
Length		
kilometer (km) = 1,000 m	1 km = 0.621 mi	1 mi = 1.609 km
meter (m) = 100 cm	1 m = 3.281 ft	1 ft = 0.305 m
centimeter (cm) = 0.01 m	1 cm = 0.394 in.	1 in. = 2.540 cm
millimeter (mm) = 0.001 m	1 mm = 0.039 in.	
micrometer (μm) = 0.000 001 m		
nanometer (nm) = 0.000 000 001 m		
Area		
square kilometer (km^2) = 100 hectares	1 km^2 = 0.386 mi^2	1 mi^2 = 2.590 km^2
hectare (ha) = 10,000 m^2	1 ha = 2.471 acres	1 acre = 0.405 ha
square meter (m^2) = 10,000 cm^2	1 m^2 = 10.764 ft^2	1 ft^2 = 0.093 m^2
square centimeter (cm^2) = 100 mm^2	1 cm^2 = 0.155 $in.^2$	1 $in.^2$ = 6.452 cm^2
Volume		
liter (L) = 1,000 mL = 1 dm^3	1 L = 1.057 fl qt	1 fl qt = 0.946 L
milliliter (mL) = 0.001 L = 1 cm^3	1 mL = 0.034 fl oz	1 fl oz = 29.574 mL
microliter (μL) = 0.000 001 L		
Mass		
kilogram (kg) = 1,000 g	1 kg = 2.205 lb	1 lb = 0.454 kg
gram (g) = 1,000 mg	1 g = 0.035 oz	1 oz = 28.350 g
milligram (mg) = 0.001 g		
microgram (μg) = 0.000 001 g		

Appendix

Temperature Scales

Temperature can be expressed by using three different scales: Fahrenheit, Celsius, and Kelvin. The SI unit for temperature is the kelvin (K).

Although 0 K is much colder than 0°C, a change of 1 K is equal to a change of 1°C.

Three Temperature Scales

	Fahrenheit	Celsius	Kelvin
Water boils	212°	100°	373
Body temperature	98.6°	37°	310
Room temperature	68°	20°	293
Water freezes	32°	0°	273

Temperature Conversions Table

To convert	Use this equation:	Example
Celsius to Fahrenheit °C → °F	$°F = \left(\dfrac{9}{5} \times °C\right) + 32$	Convert 45°C to °F. $°F = \left(\dfrac{9}{5} \times 45°C\right) + 32 = 113°F$
Fahrenheit to Celsius °F → °C	$°C = \dfrac{5}{9} \times (°F - 32)$	Convert 68°F to °C. $°C = \dfrac{5}{9} \times (68°F - 32) = 20°C$
Celsius to Kelvin °C → K	$K = °C + 273$	Convert 45°C to K. $K = 45°C + 273 = 318\ K$
Kelvin to Celsius K → °C	$°C = K - 273$	Convert 32 K to °C. $°C = 32K - 273 = -241°C$

Measuring Skills

Using a Graduated Cylinder

When using a graduated cylinder to measure volume, keep the following procedures in mind:

1 Place the cylinder on a flat, level surface before measuring liquid.

2 Move your head so that your eye is level with the surface of the liquid.

3 Read the mark closest to the liquid level. On glass graduated cylinders, read the mark closest to the center of the curve in the liquid's surface.

Using a Meterstick or Metric Ruler

When using a meterstick or metric ruler to measure length, keep the following procedures in mind:

1 Place the ruler firmly against the object that you are measuring.

2 Align one edge of the object exactly with the 0 end of the ruler.

3 Look at the other edge of the object to see which of the marks on the ruler is closest to that edge. (Note: Each small slash between the centimeters represents a millimeter, which is one-tenth of a centimeter.)

Using a Triple-Beam Balance

When using a triple-beam balance to measure mass, keep the following procedures in mind:

1 Make sure the balance is on a level surface.

2 Place all of the countermasses at 0. Adjust the balancing knob until the pointer rests at 0.

3 Place the object you wish to measure on the pan. **Caution:** Do not place hot objects or chemicals directly on the balance pan.

4 Move the largest countermass along the beam to the right until it is at the last notch that does not tip the balance. Follow the same procedure with the next-largest countermass. Then, move the smallest countermass until the pointer rests at 0.

5 Add the readings from the three beams together to determine the mass of the object.

6 When determining the mass of crystals or powders, first find the mass of a piece of filter paper. Then, add the crystals or powder to the paper, and remeasure. The actual mass of the crystals or powder is the total mass minus the mass of the paper. When finding the mass of liquids, first find the mass of the empty container. Then, find the combined mass of the liquid and container. The mass of the liquid is the total mass minus the mass of the container.

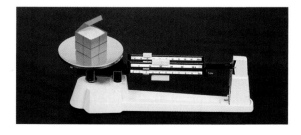

Scientific Methods

The ways in which scientists answer questions and solve problems are called **scientific methods.** The same steps are often used by scientists as they look for answers. However, there is more than one way to use these steps. Scientists may use all of the steps or just some of the steps during an investigation. They may even repeat some of the steps. The goal of using scientific methods is to come up with reliable answers and solutions.

Six Steps of Scientific Methods

Ask a Question Good questions come from careful **observations.** You make observations by using your senses to gather information. Sometimes, you may use instruments, such as microscopes and telescopes, to extend the range of your senses. As you observe the natural world, you will discover that you have many more questions than answers. These questions drive investigations.

Questions beginning with *what, why, how,* and *when* are important in focusing an investigation. Here is an example of a question that could lead to an investigation.

Question: How does acid rain affect plant growth?

Form a Hypothesis After you ask a question, you need to form a **hypothesis.** A hypothesis is a clear statement of what you expect the answer to your question to be. Your hypothesis will represent your best "educated guess" based on what you have observed and what you already know. A good hypothesis is testable. Otherwise, the investigation can go no further. Here is a hypothesis based on the question, "How does acid rain affect plant growth?"

Hypothesis: Acid rain slows plant growth.

The hypothesis can lead to predictions. A prediction is what you think the outcome of your experiment or data collection will be. Predictions are usually stated in an if-then format. Here is a sample prediction for the hypothesis that acid rain slows plant growth.

Prediction: If a plant is watered with only acid rain (which has a pH of 4), then the plant will grow at half its normal rate.

Test the Hypothesis After you have formed a hypothesis and made a prediction, your hypothesis should be tested. One way to test a hypothesis is with a controlled experiment. A **controlled experiment** tests only one factor at a time. In an experiment to test the effect of acid rain on plant growth, the **control group** would be watered with normal rain water. The **experimental group** would be watered with acid rain. All of the plants should receive the same amount of sunlight and water each day. The air temperature should be the same for all groups. However, the acidity of the water will be a variable. In fact, any factor that is different from one group to another is a **variable.** If your hypothesis is correct, then the acidity of the water and plant growth are *dependant variables.* The amount a plant grows is dependent on the acidity of the water. However, the amount of water each plant receives and the amount of sunlight each plant receives are *independent variables.* Either of these factors could change without affecting the other factor.

Sometimes, the nature of an investigation makes a controlled experiment impossible. For example, the Earth's core is surrounded by thousands of meters of rock. Under such circumstances, a hypothesis may be tested by making detailed observations.

Analyze the Results After you have completed your experiments, made your observations, and collected your data, you must analyze all the information you have gathered. Tables and graphs are often used in this step to organize the data.

5 Draw Conclusions

After analyzing your data, you can determine if your results support your hypothesis. If your hypothesis is supported, you (or others) might want to repeat the observations or experiments to verify your results. If your hypothesis is not supported by the data, you may have to check your procedure for errors. You may even have to reject your hypothesis and make a new one. If you cannot draw a conclusion from your results, you may have to try the investigation again or carry out further observations or experiments.

6 Communicate Results

After any scientific investigation, you should report your results. By preparing a written or oral report, you let others know what you have learned. They may repeat your investigation to see if they get the same results. Your report may even lead to another question and then to another investigation.

Scientific Methods in Action

Scientific methods contain loops in which several steps may be repeated over and over again. In some cases, certain steps are unnecessary. Thus, there is not a "straight line" of steps. For example, sometimes scientists find that testing one hypothesis raises new questions and new hypotheses to be tested. And sometimes, testing the hypothesis leads directly to a conclusion. Furthermore, the steps in scientific methods are not always used in the same order. Follow the steps in the diagram, and see how many different directions scientific methods can take you.

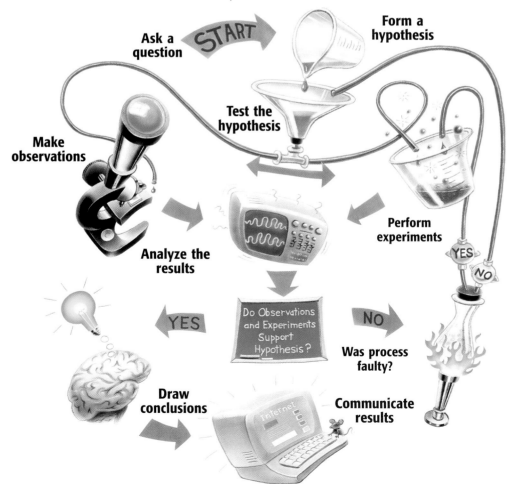

Using the Microscope

Parts of the Compound Light Microscope

- The **ocular lens** magnifies the image 10×.
- The **low-power objective** magnifies the image 10×.
- The **high-power objective** magnifies the image either 40× or 43×.
- The **revolving nosepiece** holds the objectives and can be turned to change from one magnification to the other.
- The **body tube** maintains the correct distance between the ocular lens and objectives.
- The **coarse-adjustment knob** moves the body tube up and down to allow focusing of the image.

- The **fine-adjustment knob** moves the body tube slightly to bring the image into sharper focus.
- The **stage** supports a slide.
- **Stage clips** hold the slide in place for viewing.
- The **diaphragm** controls the amount of light coming through the stage.
- The light source provides a **light** for viewing the slide.
- The **arm** supports the body tube.
- The **base** supports the microscope.

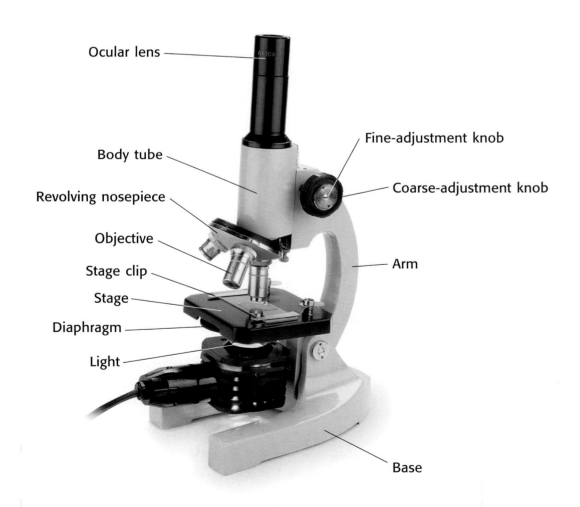

Ocular lens

Body tube

Revolving nosepiece

Objective

Stage clip

Stage

Diaphragm

Light

Fine-adjustment knob

Coarse-adjustment knob

Arm

Base

Appendix

Proper Use of the Compound Light Microscope

1. Use both hands to carry the microscope to your lab table. Place one hand beneath the base, and use the other hand to hold the arm of the microscope. Hold the microscope close to your body while carrying it to your lab table.

2. Place the microscope on the lab table at least 5 cm from the edge of the table.

3. Check to see what type of light source is used by your microscope. If the microscope has a lamp, plug it in and make sure that the cord is out of the way. If the microscope has a mirror, adjust the mirror to reflect light through the hole in the stage. **Caution:** If your microscope has a mirror, do not use direct sunlight as a light source. Direct sunlight can damage your eyes.

4. Always begin work with the low-power objective in line with the body tube. Adjust the revolving nosepiece.

5. Place a prepared slide over the hole in the stage. Secure the slide with the stage clips.

6. Look through the ocular lens. Move the diaphragm to adjust the amount of light coming through the stage.

7. Look at the stage from eye level. Slowly turn the coarse adjustment to lower the objective until the objective almost touches the slide. Do not allow the objective to touch the slide.

8. Look through the ocular lens. Turn the coarse adjustment to raise the low-power objective until the image is in focus. Always focus by raising the objective away from the slide. Never focus the objective downward. Use the fine adjustment to sharpen the focus. Keep both eyes open while viewing a slide.

9. Make sure that the image is exactly in the center of your field of vision. Then, switch to the high-power objective. Focus the image by using only the fine adjustment. Never use the coarse adjustment at high power.

10. When you are finished using the microscope, remove the slide. Clean the ocular lens and objectives with lens paper. Return the microscope to its storage area. Remember to use both hands when carrying the microscope.

Making a Wet Mount

1. Use lens paper to clean a glass slide and a coverslip.

2. Place the specimen that you wish to observe in the center of the slide.

3. Using a medicine dropper, place one drop of water on the specimen.

4. Hold the coverslip at the edge of the water and at a 45° angle to the slide. Make sure that the water runs along the edge of the coverslip.

5. Lower the coverslip slowly to avoid trapping air bubbles.

6. Water might evaporate from the slide as you work. Add more water to keep the specimen fresh. Place the tip of the medicine dropper next to the edge of the coverslip. Add a drop of water. (You can also use this method to add stain or solutions to a wet mount.) Remove excess water from the slide by using the corner of a paper towel as a blotter. Do not lift the coverslip to add or remove water.

Periodic Table of the Elements

Each square on the table includes an element's name, chemical symbol, atomic number, and atomic mass.

The color of the chemical symbol indicates the physical state at room temperature. Carbon is a solid.

6	Atomic number
C	Chemical symbol
Carbon	Element name
12.0	Atomic mass

The background color indicates the type of element. Carbon is a nonmetal.

Period 1

1
H
Hydrogen
1.0

Background

- Metals
- Metalloids
- Nonmetals

Chemical symbol

- Solid
- Liquid
- Gas

	Group 1	Group 2
Period 2	3 **Li** Lithium 6.9	4 **Be** Beryllium 9.0
Period 3	11 **Na** Sodium 23.0	12 **Mg** Magnesium 24.3

	Group 1	Group 2	Group 3	Group 4	Group 5	Group 6	Group 7	Group 8	Group 9
Period 4	19 **K** Potassium 39.1	20 **Ca** Calcium 40.1	21 **Sc** Scandium 45.0	22 **Ti** Titanium 47.9	23 **V** Vanadium 50.9	24 **Cr** Chromium 52.0	25 **Mn** Manganese 54.9	26 **Fe** Iron 55.8	27 **Co** Cobalt 58.9
Period 5	37 **Rb** Rubidium 85.5	38 **Sr** Strontium 87.6	39 **Y** Yttrium 88.9	40 **Zr** Zirconium 91.2	41 **Nb** Niobium 92.9	42 **Mo** Molybdenum 95.9	43 **Tc** Technetium (98)	44 **Ru** Ruthenium 101.1	45 **Rh** Rhodium 102.9
Period 6	55 **Cs** Cesium 132.9	56 **Ba** Barium 137.3	57 **La** Lanthanum 138.9	72 **Hf** Hafnium 178.5	73 **Ta** Tantalum 180.9	74 **W** Tungsten 183.8	75 **Re** Rhenium 186.2	76 **Os** Osmium 190.2	77 **Ir** Iridium 192.2
Period 7	87 **Fr** Francium (223)	88 **Ra** Radium (226)	89 **Ac** Actinium (227)	104 **Rf** Rutherfordium (261)	105 **Db** Dubnium (262)	106 **Sg** Seaborgium (263)	107 **Bh** Bohrium (264)	108 **Hs** Hassium (265)†	109 **Mt** Meitnerium (268)†

A row of elements is called a *period*.

A column of elements is called a *group* or *family*.

Values in parentheses are of the most stable isotope of the element.

† Estimated from currently available IUPAC data.

These elements are placed below the table to allow the table to be narrower.

Lanthanides	58 **Ce** Cerium 140.1	59 **Pr** Praseodymium 140.9	60 **Nd** Neodymium 144.2	61 **Pm** Promethium (145)	62 **Sm** Samarium 150.4
Actinides	90 **Th** Thorium 232.0	91 **Pa** Protactinium 231.0	92 **U** Uranium 238.0	93 **Np** Neptunium (237)	94 **Pu** Plutonium (244)

Topic: **Periodic Table**
Go To: **go.hrw.com**
Keyword: **HN0 PERIODIC**
Visit the HRW Web site for updates on the periodic table.

This zigzag line reminds you where the metals, nonmetals, and metalloids are.

Group 18

| 2 |
| **He** |
| Helium |
| 4.0 |

Group 13	Group 14	Group 15	Group 16	Group 17
5	6	7	8	9
B	**C**	**N**	**O**	**F**
Boron	Carbon	Nitrogen	Oxygen	Fluorine
10.8	12.0	14.0	16.0	19.0

| 10 |
| **Ne** |
| Neon |
| 20.2 |

13	14	15	16	17	18
Al	**Si**	**P**	**S**	**Cl**	**Ar**
Aluminum	Silicon	Phosphorus	Sulfur	Chlorine	Argon
27.0	28.1	31.0	32.1	35.5	39.9

Group 10	Group 11	Group 12
28	29	30
Ni	**Cu**	**Zn**
Nickel	Copper	Zinc
58.7	63.5	65.4

31	32	33	34	35	36
Ga	**Ge**	**As**	**Se**	**Br**	**Kr**
Gallium	Germanium	Arsenic	Selenium	Bromine	Krypton
69.7	72.6	74.9	79.0	79.9	83.8

46	47	48	49	50	51	52	53	54
Pd	**Ag**	**Cd**	**In**	**Sn**	**Sb**	**Te**	**I**	**Xe**
Palladium	Silver	Cadmium	Indium	Tin	Antimony	Tellurium	Iodine	Xenon
106.4	107.9	112.4	114.8	118.7	121.8	127.6	126.9	131.3

78	79	80	81	82	83	84	85	86
Pt	**Au**	**Hg**	**Tl**	**Pb**	**Bi**	**Po**	**At**	**Rn**
Platinum	Gold	Mercury	Thallium	Lead	Bismuth	Polonium	Astatine	Radon
195.1	197.0	200.6	204.4	207.2	209.0	(209)	(210)	(222)

110	111	112		114
Ds	**Uuu**	**Uub**		**Uuq**
Darmstadtium	Unununium	Ununbium		Ununquadium
(269)[†]	(272)[†]	(277)[†]		(285)[†]

The names and three-letter symbols of elements are temporary. They are based on the atomic numbers of the elements. Official names and symbols will be approved by an international committee of scientists.

63	64	65	66	67	68	69	70	71
Eu	**Gd**	**Tb**	**Dy**	**Ho**	**Er**	**Tm**	**Yb**	**Lu**
Europium	Gadolinium	Terbium	Dysprosium	Holmium	Erbium	Thulium	Ytterbium	Lutetium
152.0	157.2	158.9	162.5	164.9	167.3	168.9	173.0	175.0

95	96	97	98	99	100	101	102	103
Am	**Cm**	**Bk**	**Cf**	**Es**	**Fm**	**Md**	**No**	**Lr**
Americium	Curium	Berkelium	Californium	Einsteinium	Fermium	Mendelevium	Nobelium	Lawrencium
(243)	(247)	(247)	(251)	(252)	(257)	(258)	(259)	(262)

Appendix

Making Charts and Graphs

Pie Charts

A pie chart shows how each group of data relates to all of the data. Each part of the circle forming the chart represents a category of the data. The entire circle represents all of the data. For example, a biologist studying a hardwood forest in Wisconsin found that there were five different types of trees. The data table at right summarizes the biologist's findings.

Wisconsin Hardwood Trees	
Type of tree	Number found
Oak	600
Maple	750
Beech	300
Birch	1,200
Hickory	150
Total	3,000

How to Make a Pie Chart

1 To make a pie chart of these data, first find the percentage of each type of tree. Divide the number of trees of each type by the total number of trees, and multiply by 100.

$$\frac{600 \text{ oak}}{3,000 \text{ trees}} \times 100 = 20\%$$

$$\frac{750 \text{ maple}}{3,000 \text{ trees}} \times 100 = 25\%$$

$$\frac{300 \text{ beech}}{3,000 \text{ trees}} \times 100 = 10\%$$

$$\frac{1,200 \text{ birch}}{3,000 \text{ trees}} \times 100 = 40\%$$

$$\frac{150 \text{ hickory}}{3,000 \text{ trees}} \times 100 = 5\%$$

2 Now, determine the size of the wedges that make up the pie chart. Multiply each percentage by 360°. Remember that a circle contains 360°.

$20\% \times 360° = 72°$ $25\% \times 360° = 90°$

$10\% \times 360° = 36°$ $40\% \times 360° = 144°$

$5\% \times 360° = 18°$

3 Check that the sum of the percentages is 100 and the sum of the degrees is 360.

$20\% + 25\% + 10\% + 40\% + 5\% = 100\%$

$72° + 90° + 36° + 144° + 18° = 360°$

4 Use a compass to draw a circle and mark the center of the circle.

5 Then, use a protractor to draw angles of 72°, 90°, 36°, 144°, and 18° in the circle.

6 Finally, label each part of the chart, and choose an appropriate title.

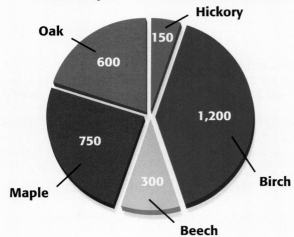

A Community of Wisconsin Hardwood Trees

Line Graphs

Line graphs are most often used to demonstrate continuous change. For example, Mr. Smith's students analyzed the population records for their hometown, Appleton, between 1900 and 2000. Examine the data at right.

Because the year and the population change, they are the *variables*. The population is determined by, or dependent on, the year. Therefore, the population is called the **dependent variable,** and the year is called the **independent variable.** Each set of data is called a **data pair.** To prepare a line graph, you must first organize data pairs into a table like the one at right.

Population of Appleton, 1900–2000	
Year	**Population**
1900	1,800
1920	2,500
1940	3,200
1960	3,900
1980	4,600
2000	5,300

How to Make a Line Graph

1 Place the independent variable along the horizontal (*x*) axis. Place the dependent variable along the vertical (*y*) axis.

2 Label the *x*-axis "Year" and the *y*-axis "Population." Look at your largest and smallest values for the population. For the *y*-axis, determine a scale that will provide enough space to show these values. You must use the same scale for the entire length of the axis. Next, find an appropriate scale for the *x*-axis.

3 Choose reasonable starting points for each axis.

4 Plot the data pairs as accurately as possible.

5 Choose a title that accurately represents the data.

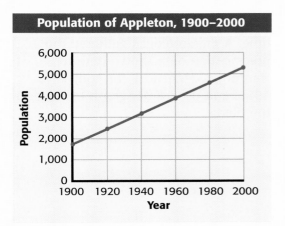

Population of Appleton, 1900–2000

How to Determine Slope

Slope is the ratio of the change in the *y*-value to the change in the *x*-value, or "rise over run."

1 Choose two points on the line graph. For example, the population of Appleton in 2000 was 5,300 people. Therefore, you can define point *a* as (2000, 5,300). In 1900, the population was 1,800 people. You can define point *b* as (1900, 1,800).

2 Find the change in the *y*-value.
(*y* at point *a*) − (*y* at point *b*) =
5,300 people − 1,800 people =
3,500 people

3 Find the change in the *x*-value.
(*x* at point *a*) − (*x* at point *b*) =
2000 − 1900 = 100 years

4 Calculate the slope of the graph by dividing the change in *y* by the change in *x*.

$$slope = \frac{change\ in\ y}{change\ in\ x}$$

$$slope = \frac{3,500\ people}{100\ years}$$

$$slope = 35\ people\ per\ year$$

In this example, the population in Appleton increased by a fixed amount each year. The graph of these data is a straight line. Therefore, the relationship is **linear.** When the graph of a set of data is not a straight line, the relationship is **nonlinear.**

Appendix

Using Algebra to Determine Slope

The equation in step 4 may also be arranged to be

$$y = kx$$

where y represents the change in the y-value, k represents the slope, and x represents the change in the x-value.

$$slope = \frac{change\ in\ y}{change\ in\ x}$$

$$k = \frac{y}{x}$$

$$k \times x = \frac{y \times x}{x}$$

$$kx = y$$

Bar Graphs

Bar graphs are used to demonstrate change that is not continuous. These graphs can be used to indicate trends when the data cover a long period of time. A meteorologist gathered the precipitation data shown here for Hartford, Connecticut, for April 1–15, 1996, and used a bar graph to represent the data.

Precipitation in Hartford, Connecticut April 1–15, 1996			
Date	Precipitation (cm)	Date	Precipitation (cm)
April 1	0.5	April 9	0.25
April 2	1.25	April 10	0.0
April 3	0.0	April 11	1.0
April 4	0.0	April 12	0.0
April 5	0.0	April 13	0.25
April 6	0.0	April 14	0.0
April 7	0.0	April 15	6.50
April 8	1.75		

How to Make a Bar Graph

1 Use an appropriate scale and a reasonable starting point for each axis.

2 Label the axes, and plot the data.

3 Choose a title that accurately represents the data.

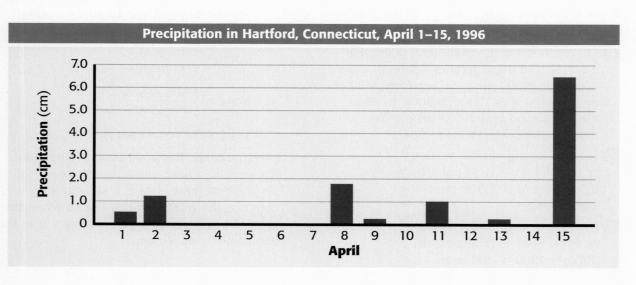

Math Refresher

Science requires an understanding of many math concepts. The following pages will help you review some important math skills.

Averages

An **average,** or **mean,** simplifies a set of numbers into a single number that *approximates* the value of the set.

> **Example:** Find the average of the following set of numbers: 5, 4, 7, and 8.

Step 1: Find the sum.

$$5 + 4 + 7 + 8 = 24$$

Step 2: Divide the sum by the number of numbers in your set. Because there are four numbers in this example, divide the sum by 4.

$$\frac{24}{4} = 6$$

The average, or mean, is **6.**

Ratios

A **ratio** is a comparison between numbers, and it is usually written as a fraction.

> **Example:** Find the ratio of thermometers to students if you have 36 thermometers and 48 students in your class.

Step 1: Make the ratio.

$$\frac{36 \text{ thermometers}}{48 \text{ students}}$$

Step 2: Reduce the fraction to its simplest form.

$$\frac{36}{48} = \frac{36 \div 12}{48 \div 12} = \frac{3}{4}$$

The ratio of thermometers to students is **3 to 4,** or $\frac{3}{4}$. The ratio may also be written in the form 3:4.

Proportions

A **proportion** is an equation that states that two ratios are equal.

$$\frac{3}{1} = \frac{12}{4}$$

To solve a proportion, first multiply across the equal sign. This is called *cross-multiplication.* If you know three of the quantities in a proportion, you can use cross-multiplication to find the fourth.

> **Example:** Imagine that you are making a scale model of the solar system for your science project. The diameter of Jupiter is 11.2 times the diameter of the Earth. If you are using a plastic-foam ball that has a diameter of 2 cm to represent the Earth, what must the diameter of the ball representing Jupiter be?

$$\frac{11.2}{1} = \frac{x}{2 \text{ cm}}$$

Step 1: Cross-multiply.

$$\frac{11.2}{1} \diagup\!\!\!\!\diagdown \frac{x}{2}$$

$$11.2 \times 2 = x \times 1$$

Step 2: Multiply.

$$22.4 = x \times 1$$

Step 3: Isolate the variable by dividing both sides by 1.

$$x = \frac{22.4}{1}$$

$$x = 22.4 \text{ cm}$$

You will need to use a ball that has a diameter of **22.4** cm to represent Jupiter.

Percentages

A **percentage** is a ratio of a given number to 100.

> **Example:** What is 85% of 40?

Step 1: Rewrite the percentage by moving the decimal point two places to the left.

0.85

Step 2: Multiply the decimal by the number that you are calculating the percentage of.

0.85 × 40 = 34

85% of 40 is **34.**

Decimals

To **add** or **subtract decimals,** line up the digits vertically so that the decimal points line up. Then, add or subtract the columns from right to left. Carry or borrow numbers as necessary.

> **Example:** Add the following numbers: 3.1415 and 2.96.

Step 1: Line up the digits vertically so that the decimal points line up.

```
  3.1415
+ 2.96
```

Step 2: Add the columns from right to left, and carry when necessary.

```
 1 1
  3.1415
+ 2.96
  _____
  6.1015
```

The sum is **6.1015.**

Fractions

Numbers tell you how many; **fractions** tell you *how much of a whole*.

> **Example:** Your class has 24 plants. Your teacher instructs you to put 5 plants in a shady spot. What fraction of the plants in your class will you put in a shady spot?

Step 1: In the denominator, write the total number of parts in the whole.

$$\frac{?}{24}$$

Step 2: In the numerator, write the number of parts of the whole that are being considered.

$$\frac{5}{24}$$

So, $\frac{5}{24}$ of the plants will be in the shade.

Reducing Fractions

It is usually best to express a fraction in its simplest form. Expressing a fraction in its simplest form is called *reducing* a fraction.

> **Example:** Reduce the fraction $\frac{30}{45}$ to its simplest form.

Step 1: Find the largest whole number that will divide evenly into both the numerator and denominator. This number is called the *greatest common factor* (GCF).

Factors of the numerator 30:

1, 2, 3, 5, 6, 10, **15,** 30

Factors of the denominator 45:

1, 3, 5, 9, **15,** 45

Step 2: Divide both the numerator and the denominator by the GCF, which in this case is 15.

$$\frac{30}{45} = \frac{30 \div 15}{45 \div 15} = \frac{2}{3}$$

Thus, $\frac{30}{45}$ reduced to its simplest form is $\frac{2}{3}$.

Appendix

Adding and Subtracting Fractions

To **add** or **subtract fractions** that have the **same denominator,** simply add or subtract the numerators.

Examples:
$$\frac{3}{5} + \frac{1}{5} = ? \text{ and } \frac{3}{4} - \frac{1}{4} = ?$$

Step 1: Add or subtract the numerators.
$$\frac{3}{5} + \frac{1}{5} = \frac{4}{\ } \text{ and } \frac{3}{4} - \frac{1}{4} = \frac{2}{\ }$$

Step 2: Write the sum or difference over the denominator.
$$\frac{3}{5} + \frac{1}{5} = \frac{4}{5} \text{ and } \frac{3}{4} - \frac{1}{4} = \frac{2}{4}$$

Step 3: If necessary, reduce the fraction to its simplest form.

$\frac{4}{5}$ cannot be reduced, and $\frac{2}{4} = \frac{1}{2}$.

To **add** or **subtract fractions** that have **different denominators,** first find the least common denominator (LCD).

Examples:
$$\frac{1}{2} + \frac{1}{6} = ? \text{ and } \frac{3}{4} - \frac{2}{3} = ?$$

Step 1: Write the equivalent fractions that have a common denominator.
$$\frac{3}{6} + \frac{1}{6} = ? \text{ and } \frac{9}{12} - \frac{8}{12} = ?$$

Step 2: Add or subtract the fractions.
$$\frac{3}{6} + \frac{1}{6} = \frac{4}{6} \text{ and } \frac{9}{12} - \frac{8}{12} = \frac{1}{12}$$

Step 3: If necessary, reduce the fraction to its simplest form.

The fraction $\frac{4}{6} = \frac{2}{3}$, and $\frac{1}{12}$ cannot be reduced.

Multiplying Fractions

To **multiply fractions,** multiply the numerators and the denominators together, and then reduce the fraction to its simplest form.

Example:
$$\frac{5}{9} \times \frac{7}{10} = ?$$

Step 1: Multiply the numerators and denominators.
$$\frac{5}{9} \times \frac{7}{10} = \frac{5 \times 7}{9 \times 10} = \frac{35}{90}$$

Step 2: Reduce the fraction.
$$\frac{35}{90} = \frac{35 \div 5}{90 \div 5} = \frac{7}{18}$$

Dividing Fractions

To **divide fractions,** first rewrite the divisor (the number you divide by) upside down. This number is called the *reciprocal* of the divisor. Then multiply and reduce if necessary.

Example:
$$\frac{5}{8} \div \frac{3}{2} = ?$$

Step 1: Rewrite the divisor as its reciprocal.
$$\frac{3}{2} \rightarrow \frac{2}{3}$$

Step 2: Multiply the fractions.
$$\frac{5}{8} \times \frac{2}{3} = \frac{5 \times 2}{8 \times 3} = \frac{10}{24}$$

Step 3: Reduce the fraction.
$$\frac{10}{24} = \frac{10 \div 2}{24 \div 2} = \frac{5}{12}$$

Appendix

Scientific Notation

Scientific notation is a short way of representing very large and very small numbers without writing all of the place-holding zeros.

> **Example:** Write 653,000,000 in scientific notation.

Step 1: Write the number without the place-holding zeros.

$$653$$

Step 2: Place the decimal point after the first digit.

$$6.53$$

Step 3: Find the exponent by counting the number of places that you moved the decimal point.

$$6.53000000$$

The decimal point was moved eight places to the left. Therefore, the exponent of 10 is positive 8. If you had moved the decimal point to the right, the exponent would be negative.

Step 4: Write the number in scientific notation.

$$\mathbf{6.53 \times 10^8}$$

Area

Area is the number of square units needed to cover the surface of an object.

Formulas:

area of a square = side × side
area of a rectangle = length × width
area of a triangle = $\frac{1}{2}$ × base × height

Examples: Find the areas.

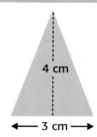

Triangle

$area = \frac{1}{2} \times base \times height$

$area = \frac{1}{2} \times 3 \text{ cm} \times 4 \text{ cm}$

$area = \mathbf{6 \text{ cm}^2}$

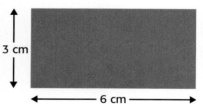

Rectangle

$area = length \times width$
$area = 6 \text{ cm} \times 3 \text{ cm}$
$area = \mathbf{18 \text{ cm}^2}$

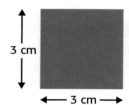

Square

$area = side \times side$
$area = 3 \text{ cm} \times 3 \text{ cm}$
$area = \mathbf{9 \text{ cm}^2}$

Volume

Volume is the amount of space that something occupies.

Formulas:

volume of a cube =
side × side × side

volume of a prism =
area of base × height

Examples:

Find the volume of the solids.

Cube

volume = side × side × side
volume = 4 cm × 4 cm × 4 cm
*volume = **64 cm³***

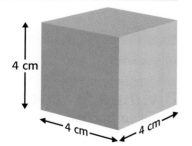

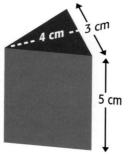

Prism

volume = area of base × height
volume = (area of triangle) × height
volume = ($\frac{1}{2}$ × 3 cm × 4 cm) × 5 cm
volume = 6 cm² × 5 cm
*volume = **30 cm³***

Physical Science Refresher

Atoms and Elements

Every object in the universe is made up of particles of some kind of matter. **Matter** is anything that takes up space and has mass. All matter is made up of elements. An **element** is a substance that cannot be separated into simpler components by ordinary chemical means. This is because each element consists of only one kind of atom. An **atom** is the smallest unit of an element that has all of the properties of that element.

Atomic Structure

Atoms are made up of small particles called subatomic particles. The three major types of subatomic particles are **electrons, protons,** and **neutrons.** Electrons have a negative electric charge, protons have a positive charge, and neutrons have no electric charge. The protons and neutrons are packed close to one another to form the **nucleus.** The protons give the nucleus a positive charge. Electrons are most likely to be found in regions around the nucleus called **electron clouds.** The negatively charged electrons are attracted to the positively charged nucleus. An atom may have several energy levels in which electrons are located.

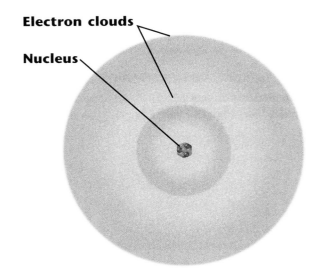

Electron clouds

Nucleus

Atomic Number

To help in the identification of elements, scientists have assigned an **atomic number** to each kind of atom. The atomic number is the number of protons in the atom. Atoms with the same number of protons are all the same kind of element. In an uncharged, or electrically neutral, atom there are an equal number of protons and electrons. Therefore, the atomic number equals the number of electrons in an uncharged atom. The number of neutrons, however, can vary for a given element. Atoms of the same element that have different numbers of neutrons are called **isotopes.**

Periodic Table of the Elements

In the periodic table, the elements are arranged from left to right in order of increasing atomic number. Each element in the table is in a separate box. An uncharged atom of each element has one more electron and one more proton than an uncharged atom of the element to its left. Each horizontal row of the table is called a **period.** Changes in chemical properties of elements across a period correspond to changes in the electron arrangements of their atoms. Each vertical column of the table, known as a **group,** lists elements with similar properties. The elements in a group have similar chemical properties because their atoms have the same number of electrons in their outer energy level. For example, the elements helium, neon, argon, krypton, xenon, and radon all have similar properties and are known as the noble gases.

Molecules and Compounds

When two or more elements are joined chemically, the resulting substance is called a **compound.** A compound is a new substance with properties different from those of the elements that compose it. For example, water, H_2O, is a compound formed when hydrogen (H) and oxygen (O) combine. The smallest complete unit of a compound that has the properties of that compound is called a **molecule.** A chemical formula indicates the elements in a compound. It also indicates the relative number of atoms of each element present. The chemical formula for water is H_2O, which indicates that each water molecule consists of two atoms of hydrogen and one atom of oxygen. The subscript number after the symbol for an element indicates how many atoms of that element are in a single molecule of the compound.

Acids, Bases, and pH

An ion is an atom or group of atoms that has an electric charge because it has lost or gained one or more electrons. When an acid, such as hydrochloric acid, HCl, is mixed with water, it separates into ions. An **acid** is a compound that produces hydrogen ions, H+, in water. The hydrogen ions then combine with a water molecule to form a hydronium ion, H_3O^+. A **base,** on the other hand, is a substance that produces hydroxide ions, OH^-, in water.

To determine whether a solution is acidic or basic, scientists use pH. The **pH** is a measure of the hydronium ion concentration in a solution. The pH scale ranges from 0 to 14. The middle point, pH = 7, is neutral, neither acidic nor basic. Acids have a pH less than 7; bases have a pH greater than 7. The lower the number is, the more acidic the solution. The higher the number is, the more basic the solution.

Chemical Equations

A chemical reaction occurs when a chemical change takes place. (In a chemical change, new substances with new properties are formed.) A chemical equation is a useful way of describing a chemical reaction by means of chemical formulas. The equation indicates what substances react and what the products are. For example, when carbon and oxygen combine, they can form carbon dioxide. The equation for the reaction is as follows: $C + O_2 \rightarrow CO_2$.

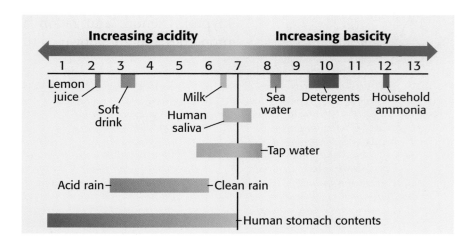

Physical Science Laws and Principles

Law of Conservation of Energy

The law of conservation of energy states that energy can be neither created nor destroyed.

The total amount of energy in a closed system is always the same. Energy can be changed from one form to another, but all of the different forms of energy in a system always add up to the same total amount of energy no matter how many energy conversions occur.

Law of Universal Gravitation

The law of universal gravitation states that all objects in the universe attract each other by a force called *gravity*. The size of the force depends on the masses of the objects and the distance between objects.

The first part of the law explains why a bowling ball is much harder to lift than a table-tennis ball. Because the bowling ball has a much larger mass than the table-tennis ball does, the amount of gravity between the Earth and the bowling ball is greater than the amount of gravity between the Earth and the table-tennis ball.

The second part of the law explains why a satellite can remain in orbit around the Earth. The satellite is carefully placed at a distance great enough to prevent the Earth's gravity from immediately pulling the satellite down but small enough to prevent the satellite from completely escaping the Earth's gravity and wandering off into space.

Newton's Laws of Motion

Newton's first law of motion states that an object at rest remains at rest and an object in motion remains in motion at constant speed and in a straight line unless acted on by an unbalanced force.

The first part of the law explains why a football will remain on a tee until it is kicked off or until a gust of wind blows it off.

The second part of the law explains why a bike rider will continue moving forward after the bike comes to an abrupt stop. Gravity and the friction of the sidewalk will eventually stop the rider.

Newton's second law of motion states that the acceleration of an object depends on the mass of the object and the amount of force applied.

The first part of the law explains why the acceleration of a 4 kg bowling ball will be greater than the acceleration of a 6 kg bowling ball if the same force is applied to both.

The second part of the law explains why the acceleration of a bowling ball will be larger if a larger force is applied to the bowling ball.

The relationship of acceleration (a) to mass (m) and force (F) can be expressed mathematically by the following equation:

$$acceleration = \frac{force}{mass}, \text{ or } a = \frac{F}{m}$$

This equation is often rearranged to the form

$$force = mass \times acceleration$$
$$\text{or}$$
$$F = m \times a$$

Newton's third law of motion states that whenever one object exerts a force on a second object, the second object exerts an equal and opposite force on the first.

This law explains that a runner is able to move forward because of the equal and opposite force that the ground exerts on the runner's foot after each step.

Law of Reflection

The law of reflection states that the angle of incidence is equal to the angle of reflection. This law explains why light reflects off a surface at the same angle that the light strikes the surface.

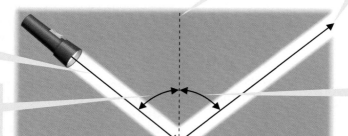

A line perpendicular to the mirror's surface is called the *normal.*

The beam of light reflected off the mirror is called the *reflected beam.*

The beam of light traveling toward the mirror is called the *incident beam.*

The angle between the incident beam and the normal is called the *angle of incidence.*

The angle between the reflected beam and the normal is called the *angle of reflection.*

Charles's Law

Charles's law states that for a fixed amount of gas at a constant pressure, the volume of the gas increases as the temperature of the gas increases. Likewise, the volume of the gas decreases as the temperature of the gas decreases.

If a basketball that was inflated indoors is left outside on a cold winter day, the air particles inside the ball will move more slowly. They will hit the sides of the basketball less often and with less force. The ball will get smaller as the volume of the air decreases.

Boyle's Law

Boyle's law states that for a fixed amount of gas at a constant temperature, the volume of a gas increases as the pressure of the gas decreases. Likewise, the volume of a gas decreases as its pressure increases.

If an inflated balloon is pulled down to the bottom of a swimming pool, the pressure of the water on the balloon increases. The pressure of the air particles inside the balloon must increase to match that of the water outside, so the volume of the air inside the balloon decreases.

Pascal's Principle

Pascal's principle states that a change in pressure at any point in an enclosed fluid will be transmitted equally to all parts of that fluid.

When a mechanic uses a hydraulic jack to raise an automobile off the ground, he or she increases the pressure on the fluid in the jack by pushing on the jack handle. The pressure is transmitted equally to all parts of the fluid-filled jacking system. As fluid presses the jack plate against the frame of the car, the car is lifed off the ground.

Archimedes' Principle

Archimedes' principle states that the buoyant force on an object in a fluid is equal to the weight of the volume of fluid that the object displaces.

A person floating in a swimming pool displaces 20 L of water. The weight of that volume of water is about 200 N. Therefore, the buoyant force on the person is 200 N.

Bernoulli's Principle

Bernoulli's principle states that as the speed of a moving fluid increases, the fluid's pressure decreases.

The lift on an airplane wing or on a Frisbee® can be explained in part by using Bernoulli's principle. Because of the shape of the Frisbee, the air moving over the top of the Frisbee must travel farther than the air below the Frisbee in the same amount of time. In other words, the air above the Frisbee is moving faster than the air below it. This faster-moving air above the Frisbee exerts less pressure than the slower-moving air below it does. The resulting increased pressure below exerts an upward force and pushes the Frisbee up.

Useful Equations

Average speed

$$\text{average speed} = \frac{\text{total distance}}{\text{total time}}$$

Example: A bicycle messenger traveled a distance of 136 km in 8 h. What was the messenger's average speed?

$$\frac{136 \text{ km}}{8 \text{ h}} = 17 \text{ km/h}$$

The messenger's average speed was **17 km/h.**

Average acceleration

$$\frac{\text{average}}{\text{acceleration}} = \frac{\text{final velocity} - \text{starting velocity}}{\text{time it takes to change velocity}}$$

Example: Calculate the average acceleration of an Olympic 100 m dash sprinter who reaches a velocity of 20 m/s south at the finish line. The race was in a straight line and lasted 10 s.

$$\frac{20 \text{ m/s} - 0 \text{ m/s}}{10 \text{s}} = 2 \text{ m/s/s}$$

The sprinter's average acceleration is **2 m/s/s south.**

Net force

Forces in the Same Direction

When forces are in the same direction, add the forces together to determine the net force.

Example: Calculate the net force on a stalled car that is being pushed by two people. One person is pushing with a force of 13 N northwest, and the other person is pushing with a force of 8 N in the same direction.

$$13 \text{ N} + 8 \text{ N} = 21 \text{ N}$$

The net force is **21 N northwest.**

Forces in Opposite Directions

When forces are in opposite directions, subtract the smaller force from the larger force to determine the net force. The net force will be in the direction of the larger force.

Example: Calculate the net force on a rope that is being pulled on each end. One person is pulling on one end of the rope with a force of 12 N south. Another person is pulling on the opposite end of the rope with a force of 7 N north.

$$12 \text{ N} - 7 \text{ N} = 5 \text{ N}$$

The net force is **5 N south.**

Work

Work is done by exerting a force through a distance. Work has units of joules (J), which are equivalent to Newton-meters.

$$\textbf{Work} = \textbf{\textit{F}} \times \textbf{\textit{d}}$$

Example: Calculate the amount of work done by a man who lifts a 100 N toddler 1.5 m off the floor.

$Work = 100 \text{ N} \times 1.5 \text{ m} = 150 \text{ N•m} = 150 \text{ J}$

The man did **150 J** of work.

Power

Power is the rate at which work is done. Power is measured in watts (W), which are equivalent to joules per second.

$$P = \frac{Work}{t}$$

Example: Calculate the power of a weightlifter who raises a 300 N barbell 2.1 m off the floor in 1.25 s.

$Work = 300 \text{ N} \times 2.1 \text{ m} = 630 \text{ N•m} = 630 \text{ J}$

$P = \dfrac{630 \text{ J}}{1.25 \text{ s}} = \dfrac{504 \text{ J}}{\text{s}} = 504 \text{ W}$

The weightlifter has **504 W** of power.

Pressure

Pressure is the force exerted over a given area. The SI unit for pressure is the pascal (Pa).

$$pressure = \frac{force}{area}$$

Example: Calculate the pressure of the air in a soccer ball if the air exerts a force of 25,000 N over an area of 0.15 m^2.

$pressure = \dfrac{25,000 \text{ N}}{0.15 \text{ m}^2} = \dfrac{167,000 \text{ N}}{\text{m}^2} = 167,000 \text{ Pa}$

The pressure of the air inside the soccer ball is **167,000 Pa.**

Density

$$density = \frac{mass}{volume}$$

Example: Calculate the density of a sponge that has a mass of 10 g and a volume of 40 cm^3.

$\dfrac{10 \text{ g}}{40 \text{ cm}^3} = \dfrac{0.25 \text{ g}}{\text{cm}^3}$

The density of the sponge is $\dfrac{0.25 \text{ g}}{\text{cm}^3}$.

Concentration

$$concentration = \frac{mass \ of \ solute}{volume \ of \ solvent}$$

Example: Calculate the concentration of a solution in which 10 g of sugar is dissolved in 125 mL of water.

$\dfrac{10 \text{ g of sugar}}{125 \text{ mL of water}} = \dfrac{0.08 \text{ g}}{\text{mL}}$

The concentration of this solution is $\dfrac{0.08 \text{ g}}{\text{mL}}$.

Glossary

A

acceleration (ak SEL uhr AY shuhn) the rate at which velocity changes over time; an object accelerates if its speed, direction, or both change (461)

acid precipitation rain, sleet, or snow that contains a high concentration of acids (59)

active transport the movement of substances across the cell membrane that requires the cell to use energy (384)

addiction a dependence on a substance, such as alcohol or drugs (308)

aerobic exercise physical exercise intended to increase the activity of the heart and lungs to promote the body's use of oxygen (315)

air mass a large body of air where temperature and moisture content are similar throughout (84)

air pollution the contamination of the atmosphere by the introduction of pollutants from human and natural sources (56)

air pressure the measure of the force with which air molecules push on a surface (41)

alcoholism a disorder in which a person repeatedly drinks alcoholic beverages in an amount that interferes with the person's health and activities (310)

allele (uh LEEL) one of the alternative forms of a gene that governs a characteristic, such as hair color (410)

allergy a reaction to a harmless or common substance by the body's immune system (289)

alveoli (al VEE uh LIE) any of the tiny air sacs of the lungs where oxygen and carbon dioxide are exchanged (191)

anemometer an instrument used to measure wind speed (99)

antibody a protein made by B cells that binds to a specific antigen (285)

anticyclone the rotation of air around a high-pressure center in the direction opposite to Earth's rotation (88)

Archimedes' principle (AHR kuh MEE DEEZ PRIN suh puhl) the principle that states that the buoyant force on an object in a fluid is an upward force equal to the weight of the volume of fluid that the object displaces (530)

area a measure of the size of a surface or a region (24)

artery a blood vessel that carries blood away from the heart to the body's organs (178)

asexual reproduction reproduction that does not involve the union of sex cells and in which a single parent produces offspring that are genetically identical to the parent (254, 334)

atmosphere a mixture of gases that surrounds a planet or moon (40)

atmospheric pressure the pressure caused by the weight of the atmosphere (525)

ATP **a**denosine **trip**hosphate, a molecule that acts as the main energy source for cell processes (340)

autoimmune disease a disease in which the immune system attacks the organism's own cells (289)

B

barometer an instrument that measures atmospheric pressure (99)

B cell a white blood cell that makes antibodies (285)

Bernoulli's principle (ber NOO leez PRIN suh puhl) the principle that states that the pressure in a fluid decreases as the fluid's velocity increases (536)

biome a large region characterized by a specific type of climate and certain types of plant and animal communities (118)

blood the fluid that carries gases, nutrients, and wastes through the body and that is made up of platelets, white blood cells, red blood cells, and plasma (182)

blood pressure the force that blood exerts on the walls of the arteries (184)

brain the mass of nerve tissue that is the main control center of the nervous system (230)

bronchus (BRAHNG kuhs) one of the two tubes that connect the lungs with the trachea (191)

buoyant force (BOY uhnt FAWRS) the upward force that keeps an object immersed in or floating on a liquid (530)

C

cancer a tumor in which the cells begin dividing at an uncontrolled rate and become invasive (290)

capillary a tiny blood vessel that allows an exchange between blood and cells in tissue (178)

carbohydrate a class of energy-giving nutrients that includes sugars, starches, and fiber; contains carbon, hydrogen, and oxygen (302, 339)

cardiovascular system a collection of organs that transport blood throughout the body (176)

cell in biology, the smallest unit that can perform all life processes; cells are covered by a membrane and contain DNA and cytoplasm (332, 352)

cell cycle the life cycle of a cell (390)

cell membrane a phospholipid layer that covers a cell's surface and acts as a barrier between the inside of a cell and the cell's environment (355)

cellular respiration the process by which cells use oxygen to produce energy from food (387)

cell wall a rigid structure that surrounds the cell membrane and provides support to the cell (360)

central nervous system the brain and the spinal cord; its main function is to control the flow of information in the body (226)

chromosome in a eukaryotic cell, one of the structures in the nucleus that are made up of DNA and protein; in a prokaryotic cell, the main ring of DNA (390)

climate the average weather conditions in an area over a long period of time (112)

cloud a collection of small water droplets or ice crystals suspended in the air, which forms when the air is cooled and condensation occurs (80)

cochlea (KAHK lee uh) a coiled tube that is found in the inner ear and that is essential to hearing (238)

compound machine a machine made of more than one simple machine (570)

condensation the change of state from a gas to a liquid (79)

consumer an organism that eats other organisms or organic matter (337)

controlled experiment an experiment that tests only one factor at a time by using a comparison of a control group with an experimental group (14)

convection the transfer of thermal energy by the circulation or movement of a liquid or gas (47)

Coriolis effect the apparent curving of the path of a moving object from an otherwise straight path due to the Earth's rotation (52)

cyclone an area in the atmosphere that has lower pressure than the surrounding areas and has winds that spiral toward the center (88)

cytokinesis the division of the cytoplasm of a cell (392)

D

decomposer an organism that gets energy by breaking down the remains of dead organisms or animal wastes and consuming or absorbing the nutrients (337)

density the ratio of the mass of a substance to the volume of a substance (26)

dermis the layer of skin below the epidermis (163)

diffusion (di FYOO zhuhn) the movement of particles from regions of higher density to regions of lower density (382)

digestive system the organs that break down food so that it can be used by the body (204)

DNA **d**eoxyribo**n**ucleic **a**cid, a molecule that is present in all living cells and that contains the information that determines the traits that a living thing inherits and needs to live (434)

dominant trait the trait observed in the first generation when parents that have different traits are bred (407)

drag a force parallel to the velocity of the flow; it opposes the direction of an aircraft and, in combination with thrust, determines the speed of the aircraft (539)

drug any substance that causes a change in a person's physical or psychological state (308)

E

egg a sex cell produced by a female (255)

elevation the height of an object above sea level (116)

embryo (EM bree OH) a developing human, from fertilization through the first 8 weeks of development (the 10th week of pregnancy) (262)

endocrine system a collection of glands and groups of cells that secrete hormones that regulate growth, development, and homeostasis; includes the pituitary, thyroid, parathyroid, and adrenal glands, the hypothalamus, the pineal body, and the gonads (240)

endocytosis (EN doh sie TOH sis) the process by which a cell membrane surrounds a particle and encloses the particle in a vesicle to bring the particle into the cell (384)

endoplasmic reticulum (EN doh PLAZ mik ri TIK yuh luhm) a system of membranes that is found in a cell's cytoplasm and that assists in the production, processing, and transport of proteins and in the production of lipids (363)

epidermis (EP uh DUHR mis) the surface layer of cells on a plant or animal (163)

esophagus (i SAHF uh guhs) a long, straight tube that connects the pharynx to the stomach (206)

eukaryote an organism made up of cells that have a nucleus enclosed by a membrane; eukaryotes include animals, plants, and fungi but not archaebacteria or eubacteria (358)

exocytosis (EK soh sie TOH sis) the process in which a cell releases a particle by enclosing the particle in a vesicle that then moves to the cell surface and fuses with the cell membrane (385)

external fertilization the union of sex cells outside the bodies of the parents (256)

F

fat an energy-storage nutrient that helps the body store some vitamins (303)

feedback mechanism a cycle of events in which information from one step controls or affects a previous step (235)

fermentation the breakdown of food without the use of oxygen (387)

fetus (FEET uhs) a developing human from seven or eight weeks after fertilization until birth (264)

fluid a nonsolid state of matter in which the atoms or molecules are free to move past each other, as in a gas or liquid (524)

force a push or a pull exerted on an object in order to change the motion of the object; force has size and direction (464)

free fall the motion of a body when only the force of gravity is acting on the body (497)

friction a force that opposes motion between two surfaces that are in contact (470)

front the boundary between air masses of different densities and usually different temperatures (86)

function the special, normal, or proper activity of an organ or part (371)

G

gallbladder a sac-shaped organ that stores bile produced by the liver (209)

gene one set of instructions for an inherited trait (410)

genotype the entire genetic makeup of an organism; also the combination of genes for one or more specific traits (411)

gland a group of cells that make special chemicals for the body (240)

global warming a gradual increase in average global temperature (49, 134)

Golgi complex (GOHL jee KAHM PLEKS) cell organelle that helps make and package materials to be transported out of the cell (365)

gravity a force of attraction between objects that is due to their masses (476)

greenhouse effect the warming of the surface and lower atmosphere of Earth that occurs when water vapor, carbon dioxide, and other gases absorb and reradiate thermal energy (48, 134)

H

heredity the passing of genetic traits from parent to offspring (334, 404)

homeostasis (HOH mee OH STAY sis) the maintenance of a constant internal state in a changing environment (148, 333)

homologous chromosomes (hoh MAHL uh guhs KROH muh SOHMZ) chromosomes that have the same sequence of genes and the same structure (391, 416)

hormone a substance that is made in one cell or tissue and that causes a change in another cell or tissue in a different part of the body (240)

humidity the amount of water vapor in the air (77)

hurricane a severe storm that develops over tropical oceans and whose strong winds of more than 120 km/h spiral in toward the intensely low-pressure storm center (93)

hygiene the science of health and ways to preserve health (314)

hypothesis (hie PAHTH uh sis) an explanation that is based on prior scientific research or observations and that can be tested (12)

I

ice age a long period of climate cooling during which ice sheets cover large areas of Earth's surface; also known as a *glacial period* (130)

immune system the cells and tissues that recognize and attack foreign substances in the body (285)

immunity the ability to resist an infectious disease (282)

inclined plane a simple machine that is a straight, slanted surface, which facilitates the raising of loads; a ramp (568)

inertia (in UHR shuh) the tendency of an object to resist being moved or, if the object is moving, to resist a change in speed or direction until an outside force acts on the object (504)

infectious disease a disease that is caused by a pathogen and that can be spread from one individual to another (280)

integumentary system (in TEG yoo MEN tuhr ee SIS tuhm) the organ system that forms a protective covering on the outside of the body (162, 234)

internal fertilization fertilization of an egg by sperm that occurs inside the body of a female (256)

J

jet stream a narrow belt of strong winds that blow in the upper troposphere (54)

joint a place where two or more bones meet (156)

joule the unit used to express energy; equivalent to the amount of work done by a force of 1 N acting through a distance of 1 m in the direction of the force (symbol, J) (555)

K

kidney one of the pair of organs that filter water and wastes from the blood and that excrete products as urine (213)

L

large intestine the wider and shorter portion of the intestine that removes water from mostly digested food and that turns the waste into semisolid feces, or stool (210)

larynx (LAR ingks) the area of the throat that contains the vocal cords and produces vocal sounds (191)

latitude the distance north or south from the equator; expressed in degrees (113)

law a summary of many experimental results and observations; a law tells how things work (21)

lever a simple machine that consists of a bar that pivots at a fixed point called a *fulcrum* (564)

lift an upward force on an object that moves in a fluid (537)

lightning an electric discharge that takes place between two oppositely charged surfaces, such as between a cloud and the ground, between two clouds, or between two parts of the same cloud (91)

lipid a type of biochemical that does not dissolve in water; fats and steroids are lipids (340)

liver the largest organ in the body; it makes bile, stores and filters blood, and stores excess sugars as glycogen (209)

lymph the fluid that is collected by the lymphatic vessels and nodes (186)

lymphatic system (lim FAT ik SIS tuhm) a collection of organs whose primary function is to collect extracellular fluid and return it to the blood; the organs in this system include the lymph nodes and the lymphatic vessels (186)

lymph node an organ that filters lymph and that is found along the lymphatic vessels (187)

lysosome (LIE suh SOHM) a cell organelle that contains digestive enzymes (366)

M

machine a device that helps do work by either overcoming a force or changing the direction of the applied force (558)

macrophage (MAK roh FAYJ) an immune system cell that engulfs pathogens and other materials (285)

malnutrition a disorder of nutrition that results when a person does not consume enough of each of the nutrients that are needed by the human body (306)

mass a measure of the amount of matter in an object (25, 481)

mechanical advantage a number that tells how many times a machine multiplies force (561)

mechanical efficiency (muh KAN i kuhl e FISH uhn see) the ratio of output to input of energy or of power; it can be calculated by dividing work output by work input (562)

meiosis (mie OH sis) a process in cell division during which the number of chromosomes decreases to half the original number by two divisions of the nucleus, which results in the production of sex cells (gametes or spores) (417)

memory B cell a B cell that responds to an antigen more strongly when the body is reinfected with an antigen than it does during its first encounter with the antigen (288)

mesosphere the layer of the atmosphere between the stratosphere and the thermosphere and in which temperature decreases as altitude increases (43)

metabolism (muh TAB uh LIZ uhm) the sum of all chemical processes that occur in an organism (334)

meter the basic unit of length in the SI (symbol, m) (24)

microclimate the climate of a small area (128)

mineral a class of nutrients that are chemical elements that are needed for certain body processes (304)

mitochondrion (MIET oh KAHN dree uhn) in eukaryotic cells, the cell organelle that is surrounded by two membranes and that is the site of cellular respiration (364)

mitosis in eukaryotic cells, a process of cell division that forms two new nuclei, each of which has the same number of chromosomes (391)

model a pattern, plan, representation, or description designed to show the structure or workings of an object, system, or concept (18)

momentum (moh MEN tuhm) a quantity defined as the product of the mass and velocity of an object (510)

motion an object's change in position relative to a reference point (458)

muscular system the organ system whose primary function is movement and flexibility (158)

mutation a change in the nucleotide-base sequence of a gene or DNA molecule (442)

N

narcotic a drug that is derived from opium and that relieves pain and induces sleep; examples include heroine, morphine, and codeine (311)

nephron the unit in the kidney that filters blood (213)

nerve a collection of nerve fibers through which impulses travel between the central nervous system and other parts of the body (228)

net force the combination of all of the forces acting on an object (465)

neuron (NOO RAHN) a nerve cell that is specialized to receive and conduct electrical impulses (227)

newton the SI unit for force (symbol, N) (464)

nicotine (NIK uh TEEN) a toxic, addictive chemical that is found in tobacco and that is one of the major contributors to the harmful effects of smoking (310)

noninfectious disease a disease that cannot spread from one individual to another (280)

nucleic acid a molecule made up of subunits called *nucleotides* (341)

nucleotide in a nucleic-acid chain, a subunit that consists of a sugar, a phosphate, and a nitrogenous base (434)

nucleus in a eukaryotic cell, a membrane-bound organelle that contains the cell's DNA and that has a role in processes such as growth, metabolism, and reproduction (355)

nutrient a substance in food that provides energy or helps form body tissues and that is necessary for life and growth (302)

O

organ a collection of tissues that carry out a specialized function of the body (151, 369)

organelle one of the small bodies in a cell's cytoplasm that are specialized to perform a specific function (355)

organism a living thing; anything that can carry out life processes independently (370)

organ system a group of organs that work together to perform body functions (370)

osmosis (ahs MOH sis) the diffusion of water through a semipermeable membrane (383)

ovary in the female reproductive system of animals, an organ that produces eggs (259)

P

pancreas the organ that lies behind the stomach and that makes digestive enzymes and hormones that regulate sugar levels (208)

pascal the SI unit of pressure (symbol, Pa) (524)

Pascal's principle the principle that states that a fluid in equilibrium contained in a vessel exerts a pressure of equal intensity in all directions (540)

passive transport the movement of substances across a cell membrane without the use of energy by the cell (384)

pathogen a virus, microorganism, or other organism that causes disease (280)

pedigree a diagram that shows the occurrence of a genetic trait in several generations of a family (422)

penis the male organ that transfers sperm to a female and that carries urine out of the body (258)

peripheral nervous system (puh RIF uhr uhl NUHR vuhs SIS tuhm) all of the parts of the nervous system except for the brain and the spinal cord (226)

pharynx (FAR ingks) the passage from the mouth to the larynx and esophagus (191)

phenotype (FEE noh TIEP) an organism's appearance or other detectable characteristic (410)

phospholipid (FAHS foh LIP id) a lipid that contains phosphorus and that is a structural component in cell membranes (340)

photosynthesis (FOHT oh SIN thuh sis) the process by which plants, algae, and some bacteria use sunlight, carbon dioxide, and water to make food (386)

placenta (pluh SEN tuh) the partly fetal and partly maternal organ by which materials are exchanged between a fetus and the mother (263)

polar easterlies prevailing winds that blow from east to west between 60° and 90° latitude in both hemispheres (52)

polar zone the North or South Pole and the surrounding region (127)

power the rate at which work is done or energy is transformed (556)

precipitation any form of water that falls to the Earth's surface from the clouds (82)

pressure the amount of force exerted per unit area of a surface (524)

prevailing winds winds that blow mainly from one direction during a given period (115)

probability the likelihood that a possible future event will occur in any given instance of the event (412)

producer an organism that can make its own food by using energy from its surroundings (337)

projectile motion (proh JEK tuhl MOH shuhn) the curved path that an object follows when thrown, launched, or otherwise projected near the surface of Earth (499)

prokaryote (pro KAR ee OHT) an organism that consists of a single cell that does not have a nucleus (356)

protein a molecule that is made up of amino acids and that is needed to build and repair body structures and to regulate processes in the body (303, 338)

pulley a simple machine that consists of a wheel over which a rope, chain, or wire passes (566)

pulmonary circulation (PUL muh NER ee SUHR kyoo LAY shuhn) the flow of blood from the heart to the lungs and back to the heart through the pulmonary arteries, capillaries, and veins (179)

R

radiation the transfer of energy as electromagnetic waves (46)

recessive trait a trait that is apparent only when two recessive alleles for the same characteristic are inherited (407)

reflex an involuntary and almost immediate movement in response to a stimulus (235)

relative humidity the ratio of the amount of water vapor in the air to the maximum amount of water vapor the air can hold at a set temperature (77)

respiration in biology, the exchange of oxygen and carbon dioxide between living cells and their environment; includes breathing and cellular respiration (190)

respiratory system a collection of organs whose primary function is to take in oxygen and expel carbon dioxide; the organs of this system include the lungs, the throat, and the passageways that lead to the lungs (190)

retina the light-sensitive inner layer of the eye, which receives images formed by the lens and transmits them through the optic nerve to the brain (236)

ribosome a cell organelle composed of RNA and protein; the site of protein synthesis (363, 441)

RNA ribonucleic acid, a molecule that is present in all living cells and that plays a role in protein production (440)

S

science the knowledge obtained by observing natural events and conditions in order to discover facts and formulate laws or principles that can be verified or tested (4)

scientific methods a series of steps followed to solve problems (10)

screw a simple machine that consists of an inclined plane wrapped around a cylinder (569)

sex chromosome one of the pair of chromosomes that determine the sex of an individual (421)

sexual reproduction reproduction in which the sex cells from two parents unite to produce offspring that share traits from both parents (255, 334)

skeletal system the organ system whose primary function is to support and protect the body and to allow the body to move (154)

small intestine the organ between the stomach and the large intestine where most of the breakdown of food happens and most of the nutrients from food are absorbed (208)

speed the distance traveled divided by the time interval during which the motion occurred (459)

sperm the male sex cell (255)

spleen the largest lymphatic organ in the body; serves as a blood reservoir, disintegrates old red blood cells, and produces lymphocytes and plasmids (188)

stimulus anything that causes a reaction or change in an organism or any part of an organism (333)

stomach the saclike, digestive organ between the esophagus and the small intestine that breaks down food by the action of muscles, enzymes, and acids (207)

stratosphere the layer of the atmosphere that is above the troposphere and in which temperature increases as altitude increases (43)

stress a physical or mental response to pressure (316)

structure the arrangement of parts in an organism (371)

surface current a horizontal movement of ocean water that is caused by wind and that occurs at or near the ocean's surface (117)

systemic circulation (sis TEM ik SUHR kyoo LAY shuhn) the flow of blood from the heart to all parts of the body and back to the heart (179)

T

T cell an immune system cell that coordinates the immune system and attacks many infected cells (285)

temperate zone the climate zone between the Tropics and the polar zone (124)

temperature a measure of how hot (or cold) something is; specifically, a measure of the average kinetic energy of the particles in an object (26)

terminal velocity the constant velocity of a falling object when the force of air resistance is equal in magnitude and opposite in direction to the force of gravity (496)

testes the primary male reproductive organs, which produce sperm cells and testosterone (singular, *testis*) (258)

theory an explanation that ties together many hypotheses and observations (20)

thermal conduction the transfer of as heat through a material (47)

thermometer an instrument that measures and indicates temperature (99)

thermosphere the uppermost layer of the atmosphere, in which temperature increases as altitude increases (44)

thrust the pushing or pulling force exerted by the engine of an aircraft or rocket (538)

thunder the sound caused by the rapid expansion of air along an electrical strike (91)

thunderstorm a usually brief, heavy storm that consists of rain, strong winds, lightning, and thunder (90)

thymus the main gland of the lymphatic system; it releases mature T lymphocytes (187)

tissue a group of similar cells that perform a common function (150, 369)

tonsils small, rounded masses of lymphatic tissue located in the pharynx and in the passage from the mouth to the pharynx (189)

tornado a destructive, rotating column of air that has very high wind speeds, is visible as a funnel-shaped cloud, and touches the ground (92)

trachea (TRAY kee uh) in insects, myriapods, and spiders, one of a network of air tubes; in vertebrates, the tube that connects the larynx to the lungs (191)

trade winds prevailing winds that blow from east to west from 30° latitude to the equator in both hemispheres (52)

tropical zone the region that surrounds the equator and that extends from about 23° north latitude to 23° south latitude (120)

troposphere the lowest layer of the atmosphere, in which temperature decreases at a constant rate as altitude increases (43)

U

umbilical cord (uhm BIL i kuhl KAWRD) the structure that connects an embryo and then the fetus to the placenta and through which blood vessels pass (263)

urinary system the organs that make, store, and eliminate urine (212)

uterus in female mammals, the hollow, muscular organ in which a fertilized egg is embedded and in which the embryo and fetus develop (259)

V

vagina the female reproductive organ that connects the outside of the body to the uterus (259)

variable a factor that changes in an experiment in order to test a hypothesis (14)

vein in biology, a vessel that carries blood to the heart (178)

velocity (vuh LAHS uh tee) the speed of an object in a particular direction (460)

vesicle (VES i kuhl) a small cavity or sac that contains materials in a eukaryotic cell; forms when part of the cell membrane surrounds the materials to be taken into the cell or transported within the cell (365)

vitamin a class of nutrients that contain carbon and that are needed in small amounts to maintain health and allow growth (304)

volume a measure of the size of a body or region in three-dimensional space (25)

W

watt the unit used to express power; equivalent to joules per second (symbol, W) (556)

weather the short-term state of the atmosphere, including temperature, humidity, precipitation, wind, and visibility (76, 112)

wedge a simple machine that is made up of two inclined planes and that moves; often used for cutting (569)

weight a measure of the gravitational force exerted on an object; its value can change with the location of the object in the universe (481)

westerlies prevailing winds that blow from west to east between 30° and 60° latitude in both hemispheres (52)

wheel and axle a simple machine consisting of two circular objects of different sizes; the wheel is the larger of the two circular objects (567)

wind the movement of air caused by differences in air pressure (50)

work the transfer of energy to an object by using a force that causes the object to move in the direction of the force (552)

work input the work done on a machine; the product of the input force and the distance through which the force is exerted (559)

work output the work done by a machine; the product of the output force and the distance through which the force is exerted (559)

Spanish Glossary

A

acceleration/aceleración la tasa a la que la velocidad cambia con el tiempo; un objeto acelera si su rapidez cambia, si su dirección cambia, o si tanto su rapidez como su dirección cambian (461)

acid precipitation/precipitación ácida lluvia, aguanieve o nieve que contiene una alta concentración de ácidos (59)

active transport/transporte activo el movimiento de substancias a través de la membrana celular que requiere que la célula gaste energía (384)

addiction/adicción una dependencia de una substancia, tal como el alcohol o las drogas (308)

aerobic exercise/ejercicio aeróbico ejercicio físico cuyo objetivo es aumentar la actividad del corazón y los pulmones para hacer que el cuerpo use más oxígeno (315)

air mass/masa de aire un gran volumen de aire que tiene una temperatura y contenido de humedad similar en toda su extensión (84)

air pollution/contaminación del aire la contaminación de la atmósfera debido a la introducción de contaminantes provenientes de fuentes humanas y naturales (56)

air pressure/presión del aire la medida de la fuerza con la que las moléculas del aire empujan contra una superficie (41)

alcoholism/alcoholismo un trastorno en el cual una persona consume bebidas alcohólicas repetidamente en una cantidad tal que interfiere con su salud y sus actividades (310)

allele/alelo una de las formas alternativas de un gene que rige un carácter, como por ejemplo, el color del cabello (410)

allergy/alergia una reacción del sistema inmunológico del cuerpo a una substancia inofensiva o común (289)

alveoli/alveolo cualquiera de las diminutas bolsas de aire de los pulmones, en donde ocurre el intercambio de oxígeno y dióxido de carbono (191)

anemometer/anemómetro un instrumento que se usa para medir la rapidez del viento (99)

antibody/anticuerpo una proteína producida por las células B que se une a un antígeno específico (285)

anticyclone/anticiclón la rotación del aire alrededor de un centro de alta presión en dirección opuesta a la rotación de la Tierra (88)

Archimedes' principle/principio de Arquímedes el principio que establece que la fuerza flotante de un objeto que está en un fluido es una fuerza ascendente cuya magnitud es igual al peso del volumen del fluido que el objeto desplaza (530)

area/área una medida del tamaño de una superficie o región (24)

artery/arteria un vaso sanguíneo que transporta sangre del corazón a los órganos del cuerpo (178)

asexual reproduction/reproducción asexual reproducción que no involucra la unión de células sexuales, en la que un solo progenitor produce descendencia que es genéticamente igual al progenitor (254, 334)

atmosphere/atmósfera una mezcla de gases que rodea un planeta o una luna (40)

atmospheric pressure/presión atmosférica la presión producida por el peso de la atmósfera (525)

ATP/ATP adenosín trifosfato, una molécula orgánica que funciona como la fuente principal de energía para los procesos celulares (340)

autoimmune disease/enfermedad autoinmune una enfermedad en la que el sistema inmunológico ataca las células del propio organismo (289)

B

barometer/barómetro un instrumento que mide la presión atmosférica (99)

B cell/célula B un glóbulo blanco de la sangre que fabrica anticuerpos (285)

Bernoulli's principle/principio de Bernoulli el principio que establece que la presión de un fluido disminuye a medida que la velocidad del fluido aumenta (536)

biome/bioma una región extensa caracterizada por un tipo de clima específico y ciertos tipos de comunidades de plantas y animales (118)

blood/sangre el líquido que lleva gases, nutrientes y desechos por el cuerpo y que está formado por plaquetas, glóbulos blancos, glóbulos rojos y plasma (182)

blood pressure/presión sanguínea la fuerza que la sangre ejerce en las paredes de las arterias (184)

brain/encéfalo la masa de tejido nervioso que es el centro principal de control del sistema nervioso (230)

bronchus/bronquio uno de los dos tubos que conectan los pulmones con la tráquea (191)

buoyant force/fuerza boyante la fuerza ascendente que hace que un objeto se mantenga sumergido en un líquido o flotando en él (530)

C

cancer/cáncer un tumor en el cual las células comienzan a dividirse a una tasa incontrolable y se vuelven invasivas (290)

capillary/capilar diminuto vaso sanguíneo que permite el intercambio entre la sangre y las células de los tejidos (178)

carbohydrate/carbohidrato una clase de nutrientes que proporcionan energía; incluye los azúcares, los almidones y las fibras; contiene carbono, hidrógeno y oxígeno (302, 339)

cardiovascular system/aparato cardiovascular un conjunto de órganos que transportan la sangre a través del cuerpo (176)

cell/célula en biología, la unidad más pequeña que puede realizar todos los procesos vitales; las células están cubiertas por una membrana y tienen ADN y citoplasma (332, 352)

cell cycle/ciclo celular el ciclo de vida de una célula (390)

cell membrane/membrana celular una capa de fosfolípidos que cubre la superficie de la célula y funciona como una barrera entre el interior de la célula y el ambiente de la célula (355)

cellular respiration/respiración celular el proceso por medio del cual las células utilizan oxígeno para producir energía a partir de los alimentos (387)

cell wall/pared celular una estructura rígida que rodea la membrana celular y le brinda soporte a la célula (360)

central nervous system/sistema nervioso central el cerebro y la médula espinal; su principal función es controlar el flujo de información en el cuerpo (226)

chromosome/cromosoma en una célula eucariótica, una de las estructuras del núcleo que está hecha de ADN y proteína; en una célula procariótica, el anillo principal de ADN (390)

climate/clima las condiciones promedio del tiempo en un área durante un largo período de tiempo (112)

cloud/nube un conjunto de pequeñas gotitas de agua o cristales de hielo suspendidos en el aire, que se forma cuando el aire se enfría y ocurre condensación (80)

cochlea/cóclea un tubo enrollado que se encuentra en el oído interno y es esencial para poder oír (238)

compound machine/máquina compuesta una máquina hecha de más de una máquina simple (570)

condensation/condensación el cambio de estado de gas a líquido (79)

consumer/consumidor un organismo que se alimenta de otros organismos o de materia orgánica (337)

controlled experiment/experimento controlado un experimento que prueba sólo un factor a la vez, comparando un grupo de control con un grupo experimental (14)

convection/convección la transferencia de energía térmica mediante la circulación o el movimiento de un líquido o gas (47)

Coriolis effect/efecto de Coriolis la desviación aparente de la trayectoria recta que experimentan los objetos en movimiento debido a la rotación de la Tierra (52)

cyclone/ciclón un área de la atmósfera que tiene una presión menor que la de las áreas circundantes y que tiene vientos que giran en espiral hacia el centro (88)

cytokinesis/citoquinesis la división del citoplasma de una célula (392)

D

decomposer/descomponedor un organismo que, para obtener energía, desintegra los restos de organismos muertos o los desechos de animales y consume o absorbe los nutrientes (337)

density/densidad la relación entre la masa de una substancia y su volumen (26)

dermis/dermis la capa de piel que está debajo de la epidermis (163)

diffusion/difusión el movimiento de partículas de regiones de mayor densidad a regiones de menor densidad (382)

digestive system/aparato digestivo los órganos que descomponen la comida de modo que el cuerpo la pueda usar (204)

DNA/ADN ácido desoxirribonucleico, una molécula que está presente en todas las células vivas y que contiene la información que determina los caracteres que un ser vivo hereda y necesita para vivir (434)

dominant trait/carácter dominante el carácter que se observa en la primera generación cuando se cruzan progenitores que tienen caracteres diferentes (407)

drag/resistencia aerodinámica una fuerza paralela a la velocidad del flujo; se opone a la dirección de un avión y, en combinación con el empuje, determina la velocidad del avión (539)

drug/droga cualquier substancia que produce un cambio en el estado físico o psicológico de una persona (308)

E

egg/óvulo una célula sexual producida por una hembra (255)

elevation/elevación la altura de un objeto sobre el nivel del mar (116)

embryo/embrión un ser humano desde la fecundación hasta las primeras 8 semanas de desarrollo (décima semana del embarazo) (262)

endocrine system/sistema endocrino un conjunto de glándulas y grupos de células que secretan hormonas que regulan el crecimiento, el desarrollo y la homeostasis; incluye las glándulas pituitaria, tiroides, paratiroides y suprarrenal, el hipotálamo, el cuerpo pineal y las gónadas (240)

endocytosis/endocitosis el proceso por medio del cual la membrana celular rodea una partícula y la encierra en una vesícula para llevarla al interior de la célula (384)

endoplasmic reticulum/retículo endoplásmico un sistema de membranas que se encuentra en el citoplasma de la célula y que tiene una función en la producción, procesamiento y transporte de proteínas y en la producción de lípidos (363)

epidermis/epidermis la superficie externa de las células de una planta o animal (163)

esophagus/esófago un conducto largo y recto que conecta la faringe con el estómago (206)

eukaryote/eucariote un organismo cuyas células tienen un núcleo rodeado por una membrana; entre los eucariotes se encuentran los animales, las plantas y los hongos, pero no las arqueobacterias (358)

exocytosis/exocitosis el proceso por medio del cual una célula libera una partícula encerrándola en una vesícula que luego se traslada a la superficie de la célula y se fusiona con la membrana celular (385)

external fertilization/fecundación externa la unión de células sexuales fuera del cuerpo de los progenitores (256)

F

fat/grasa un nutriente que almacena energía y ayuda al cuerpo a almacenar algunas vitaminas (303)

feedback mechanism/mecanismo de retroalimentación un ciclo de sucesos en el que la información de una etapa controla o afecta a una etapa anterior (235)

fermentation/fermentación la descomposición de los alimentos sin utilizar oxígeno (387)

fetus/feto un ser humano en desarrollo de las semanas siete a ocho después de la fecundación hasta el nacimiento (264)

fluid/fluido un estado no sólido de la materia en el que los átomos o moléculas tienen libertad de movimiento, como en el caso de un gas o un líquido (524)

force/fuerza una acción de empuje o atracción que se ejerce sobre un objeto con el fin de cambiar su movimiento; la fuerza tiene magnitud y dirección (464)

free fall/caída libre el movimiento de un cuerpo cuando la única fuerza que actúa sobre él es la fuerza de gravedad (497)

friction/fricción una fuerza que se opone al movimiento entre dos superficies que están en contacto (470)

front/frente el límite entre masas de aire de diferentes desidades y, normalmente, diferentes temperaturas (86)

function/función la actividad especial, normal o adecuada de un órgano o parte (371)

G

gallbladder/vesícula biliar un órgano que tiene la forma de una bolsa y que almacena la bilis producida por el hígado (209)

gene/gene un conjunto de instrucciones para un carácter heredado (410)

genotype/genotipo la constitución genética completa de un organismo; *también* la combinación genes para uno o más caracteres específicos (411)

gland/glándula un grupo de células que elaboran ciertas substancias químicas para el cuerpo (240)

global warming/calentamiento global un aumento gradual de la temperatura global promedio (49, 134)

Golgi complex/aparato de Golgi un organelo celular que ayuda a hacer y a empacar los materiales que serán transportados al exterior de la célula (365)

gravity/gravedad una fuerza de atracción entre dos objetos debido a sus masas (476)

greenhouse effect/efecto de invernadero el calentamiento de la superficie y de la parte más baja de la atmósfera, el cual se produce cuando el vapor de agua, el dióxido de carbono y otros gases absorben y vuelven a irradiar la energía térmica (48, 134)

H

heredity/herencia la transmisión de caracteres genéticos de padres a hijos (334, 404)

homeostasis/homeostasis la capacidad de mantener un estado interno constante en un ambiente en cambio (148, 333)

homologous chromosomes/cromosomas homólogos cromosomas con la misma secuencia de genes y la misma estructura (391, 416)

hormone/hormona una substancia que es producida en una célula o tejido, la cual causa un cambio en otra célula o tejido ubicado en una parte diferente del cuerpo (240)

humidity/humedad la cantidad de vapor de agua que hay en el aire (77)

hurricane/huracán tormenta severa que se desarrolla sobre océanos tropicales, con vientos fuertes que soplan a más de 120 km/h y que se mueven en espiral hacia el centro de presión extremadamente baja de la tormenta (93)

hygiene/higiene la ciencia de la salud y las formas de preservar la salud (314)

hypothesis/hipótesis una explicación que se basa en observaciones o investigaciones científicas previas y que se puede probar (12)

I

ice age/edad de hielo un largo período de tiempo frío durante el cual grandes áreas de la superficie terrestre están cubiertas por capas de hielo; también conocido como período glacial (130)

immune system/sistema inmunológico las células y tejidos que reconocen y atacan substancias extrañas en el cuerpo (285)

immunity/inmunidad la capacidad de resistir una enfermedad infecciosa (282)

inclined plane/plano inclinado una máquina simple que es una superficie recta e inclinada, que facilita el levantamiento de cargas; una rampa (568)

inertia/inercia la tendencia de un objeto a no moverse o, si el objeto se está moviendo, la tendencia a resistir un cambio en su rapidez o dirección hasta que una fuerza externa actúe en el objeto (504)

infectious disease/enfermedad infecciosa una enfermedad que es causada por un patógeno y que puede transmitirse de un individuo a otro (280)

integumentary system/sistema integumentario el sistema de órganos que forma una cubierta de protección en la parte exterior del cuerpo (162, 234)

internal fertilization/fecundación interna fecundación de un óvulo por un espermatozoide, la cual ocurre dentro del cuerpo de la hembra (256)

J

jet stream/corriente en chorro un cinturón delgado de vientos fuertes que soplan en la parte superior de la troposfera (54)

joint/articulación un lugar donde se unen dos o más huesos (156)

joule/joule la unidad que se usa para expresar energía; equivale a la cantidad de trabajo realizada por una fuerza de 1 N que actúa a través de una distancia de 1 m en la dirección de la fuerza (símbolo: J) (555)

K

kidney/riñón uno de los dos órganos que filtran el agua y los desechos de la sangre y excretan productos en fomra de orina (213)

L

large intestine/intestino grueso la porción más ancha y más corta del intestino, que elimina el agua de los alimentos casi totalmente digeridos y convierte los desechos en heces semisólidas o excremento (210)

larynx/laringe el área de la garganta que contiene las cuerdas vocales y que produce sonidos vocales (191)

latitude/latitud la distancia hacia el norte o hacia el sur del ecuador; se expresa en grados (113)

law/ley un resumen de muchos resultados y observaciones experimentales; una ley dice cómo funcionan las cosas (21)

lever/palanca una máquina simple formada por una barra que gira en un punto fijo llamado *fulcro* (564)

lift/propulsión una fuerza hacia arriba en un objeto que se mueve en un fluido (537)

lightning/relámpago una descarga eléctrica que ocurre entre dos superficies que tienen carga opuesta, como por ejemplo, entre una nube y el suelo, entre dos nubes o entres dos partes de la misma nube (91)

lipid/lípido un tipo de substancia bioquímica que no se disuelve en agua; las grasas y los esteroides son lípidos (340)

liver/hígado el órgano más grande del cuerpo; produce bilis, almacena y filtra la sangre, y almacena el exceso de azúcares en forma de glucógeno (209)

lymph/linfa el fluido que es recolectado por los vasos y nodos linfáticos (186)

lymphatic system/sistema linfático un conjunto de órganos cuya función principal es recolectar el fluido extracelular y regresarlo a la sangre; los órganos de este sistema incluyen los nodos linfáticos y los vasos linfáticos (186)

lymph nodes/nodos linfáticos masas ovaladas de tejido linfático que se encuentran en los vasos linfáticos y filtran la linfa (187)

lysosome/lisosoma un organelo celular que contiene enzimas digestivas (366)

M

machine/máquina un aparato que ayuda a realizar un trabajo, ya sea venciendo una fuerza o cambiando la dirección de la fuerza aplicada (558)

macrophage/macrófago una célula del sistema inmunológico que envuelve a los patógenos y otros materiales (285)

malnutrition/desnutrición un trastorno de nutrición que resulta cuando una persona no consume una cantidad suficiente de cada nutriente que el cuerpo humano necesita (306)

mass/masa una medida de la cantidad de materia que tiene un objeto (25, 481)

mechanical advantage/ventaja mecánica un número que dice cuántas veces una máquina multiplica una fuerza (561)

mechanical efficiency/eficiencia mecánica la relación entre la entrada y la salida de energía o potencia; se calcula dividiendo la salida de trabajo por la entrada de trabajo (562)

meiosis/meiosis un proceso de división celular durante el cual el número de cromosomas disminuye a la mitad del número original por medio de dos divisiones del núcleo, lo cual resulta en la producción de células sexuales (gametos o esporas) (417)

memory B cell/célula B de memoria una célula B que responde con mayor eficacia a un antígeno cuando el cuerpo vuelve a infectarse con él que cuando lo encuentra por primera vez (288)

mesosphere/mesosfera la capa de la atmósfera que se encuentra entre la estratosfera y la termosfera, en la cual la temperatura disminuye al aumentar la altitud (43)

metabolism/metabolismo la suma de todos los procesos químicos que ocurren en un organismo (334)

meter/metro la unidad fundamental de longitud en el sistema internacional de unidades (símbolo: m) (24)

microclimate/microclima el clima de un área pequeña (128)

mineral/mineral una clase de nutrientes que son elementos químicos necesarios para ciertos procesos del cuerpo (304)

mitochondrion/mitocondria en las células eucarióticas, el organelo celular rodeado por dos membranas que es el lugar donde se lleva a cabo la respiración celular (364)

mitosis/mitosis en las células eucarióticas, un proceso de división celular que forma dos núcleos nuevos, cada uno de los cuales posee el mismo número de cromosomas (391)

model/modelo un diseño, plan, representación o descripción cuyo objetivo es mostrar la estructura o funcionamiento de un objeto, sistema o concepto (18)

momentum/momento una cantidad que se define como el producto de la masa de un objeto por su velocidad (510)

motion/movimiento el cambio en la posición de un objeto respecto a un punto de referencia (458)

muscular system/sistema muscular el sistema de órganos cuya función principal es permitir el movimiento y la flexibilidad (158)

mutation/mutación un cambio en la secuencia de la base de nucleótidos de un gene o de una molécula de ADN (442)

N

narcotic/narcótico una droga que proviene del opio, la cual alivia el dolor e induce el sueño; entre los ejemplos se encuentran la heroína, morfina y codeína (311)

nephron/nefrona la unidad del riñón que filtra la sangre (213)

nerve/nervio un conjunto de fibras nerviosas a través de las cuales se desplazan los impulsos entre el sistema nervioso central y otras partes del cuerpo (228)

net force/fuerza neta la combinación de todas las fuerzas que actúan sobre un objeto (465)

neuron/neurona una célula nerviosa que está especializada en recibir y transmitir impulsos eléctricos (227)

newton/newton la unidad de fuerza del sistema internacional de unidades (símbolo: N) (464)

nicotine/nicotina una substancia química tóxica y adictiva que se encuentra en el tabaco y que es una de las principales causas de los efectos dañinos de fumar (310)

noninfectious disease/enfermedad no infecciosa una enfermedad que no se contagia de una persona a otra (280)

nucleic acid/ácido nucleico una molécula formada por subunidades llamadas *nucleótidos* (341)

nucleotide/nucleótido en una cadena de ácidos nucleicos, una subunidad formada por un azúcar, un fosfato y una base nitrogenada (434)

nucleus/núcleo en una célula eucariótica, un organelo cubierto por una membrana, el cual contiene el ADN de la célula y participa en procesos tales como el crecimiento, metabolismo y reproducción (355)

nutrient/nutriente una substancia de los alimentos que proporciona energía o ayuda a formar tejidos corporales y que es necesaria para la vida y el crecimiento (302)

O

organ/órgano un conjunto de tejidos que desempeñan una función especializada en el cuerpo (151, 369)

organelle/organelo uno de los cuerpos pequeños del citoplasma de una célula que están especializados para llevar a cabo una función específica (355)

organism/organismo un ser vivo; cualquier cosa que pueda llevar a cabo procesos vitales independientemente (370)

organ system/aparato (o sistema) de órganos un grupo de órganos que trabajan en conjunto para desempeñar funciones corporales (370)

osmosis/ósmosis la difusión del agua a través de una membrana semipermeable (383)

ovary/ovario en el aparato reproductor femenino de los animales, un órgano que produce óvulos (259)

P

pancreas/páncreas el órgano que se encuentra detrás del estómago y que produce las enzimas digestivas y las hormonas que regulan los niveles de azúcar (208)

pascal/pascal la unidad de presión del sistema internacional de unidades (símbolo: Pa) (524)

Pascal's principle/principio de Pascal el principio que establece que un fluido en equilibro que esté contenido en un recipiente ejerce una presión de igual intensidad en todas las direcciones (540)

passive transport/transporte pasivo el movimiento de substancias a través de una membrana celular sin que la célula tenga que usar energía (384)

pathogen/patógeno un virus, microorganismo u otra substancia que causa enfermedades (280)

pedigree/pedigrí un diagrama que muestra la incidencia de un carácter genético en varias generaciones de una familia (422)

penis/pene el órgano masculino que transfiere espermatozoides a una hembra y que lleva la orina hacia el exterior del cuerpo (258)

peripheral nervous system/sistema nervioso periférico todas las partes del sistema nervioso, excepto el encéfalo y la médula espinal (226)

pharynx/faringe en los gusanos planos, el tubo muscular que va de la boca a la cavidad gastrovascular; en los animales que tienen tracto digestivo, el conducto que va de la boca a la laringe y al esófago (191)

phenotype/fenotipo la apariencia de un organismo u otra característica perceptible (410)

phospholipid/fosfolípido un lípido que contiene fósforo y que es un componente estructural de la membrana celular (340)

photosynthesis/fotosíntesis el proceso por medio del cual las plantas, las algas y algunas bacterias utilizan la luz solar, el dióxido de carbono y el agua para producir alimento (386)

placenta/placenta el órgano parcialmente fetal y parcialmente materno por medio del cual se intercambian materiales entre el feto y la madre (263)

polar easterlies/vientos polares del este vientos preponderantes que soplan de este a oeste entre los 60° y los 90° de latitud en ambos hemisferios (52)

polar zone/zona polar el Polo Norte y el Polo Sur y la región circundante (127)

power/potencia la tasa a la que se realiza un trabajo o a la que se transforma la energía (556)

precipitation/precipitación cualquier forma de agua que cae de las nubes a la superficie de la Tierra (82)

pressure/presión la cantidad de fuerza ejercida en una superficie por unidad de área (524)

prevailing winds/vientos prevalecientes vientos que soplan principalmente de una dirección durante un período de tiempo determinado (115)

probability/probabilidad la probabilidad de que ocurra un posible suceso futuro en cualquier caso dado del suceso (412)

producer/productor un organismo que puede elaborar sus propios alimentos utilizando la energía de su entorno (337)

projectile motion/movimiento proyectil la trayectoria curva que sigue un objeto cuando es aventado, lanzado o proyectado de cualquier otra manera cerca de la superficie de la Tierra (499)

prokaryote/procariote un organismo que está formado por una sola célula y que no tiene núcleo (356)

protein/proteína una molécula formada por aminoácidos que es necesaria para construir y reparar estructuras corporales y para regular procesos del cuerpo (303, 338)

pulley/polea una máquina simple formada por una rueda sobre la cual pasa una cuerda, cadena o cable (566)

pulmonary circulation/circulación pulmonar el flujo de sangre del corazón a los pulmones y de vuelta al corazón a través de las arterias, los capilares y las venas pulmonares (179)

R

radiation/radiación la transferencia de energía en forma de ondas electromagnéticas (46)

recessive trait/carácter recesivo un carácter que se hace aparente sólo cuando se heredan dos alelos recesivos de la misma característica (407)

reflex/reflejo un movimiento involuntario y prácticamente inmediato en respuesta a un estímulo (235)

relative humidity/humedad relativa la proporción de la cantidad de vapor de agua que hay en el aire respecto a la cantidad máxima de vapor de agua que el aire puede contener a una temperatura dada (77)

respiration/respiración en biología, el intercambio de oxígeno y dióxido de carbono entre células vivas y su ambiente; incluye la respiración y la respiración celular (190)

respiratory system/aparato respiratorio un conjunto de órganos cuya función principal es tomar oxígeno y expulsar dióxido de carbono; los órganos de este aparato incluyen a los pulmones, la garganta y las vías que llevan a los pulmones (190)

retina/retina la capa interna del ojo, sensible a la luz, que recibe imágenes formadas por el lente ocular y las transmite al cerebro por medio del nervio óptico (236)

ribosome/ribosoma un organelo celular compuesto de ARN y proteína; el sitio donde ocurre la síntesis de proteínas (363, 441)

RNA/ARN ácido ribonucleico, una molécula que está presente en todas las células vivas y que juega un papel en la producción de proteínas (440)

S

science/ciencia el conocimiento que se obtiene por medio de la observación natural de acontecimientos y condiciones con el fin de descubrir hechos y formular leyes o principios que puedan ser verificados o probados (4)

scientific methods/métodos científicos una serie de pasos que se siguen para solucionar problemas (10)

screw/tornillo una máquina simple formada por un plano inclinado enrollado a un cilindro (569)

sex chromosome/cromosoma sexual uno de los dos cromosomas que determinan el sexo de un individuo (421)

sexual reproduction/reproducción sexual reproducción en la que se unen las células sexuales de los dos progenitores para producir descendencia que comparte caracteres de ambos progenitores (255, 334)

skeletal system/sistema esquelético el sistema de órganos cuya función principal es sostener y proteger el cuerpo y permitir que se mueva (154)

small intestine/intestino delgado el órgano que se encuentra entre el estómago y el intestino grueso en el cual se produce la mayor parte de la descomposición de los alimentos y se absorben la mayoría de los nutrientes (208)

speed/rapidez la distancia que un objeto se desplaza dividida entre el intervalo de tiempo durante el cual ocurrió el movimiento (459)

sperm/espermatozoide la célula sexual masculina (255)

spleen/bazo el órgano linfático más grande del cuerpo; funciona como depósito para la sangre, desintegra los glóbulos rojos viejos y produce linfocitos y plásmidos (188)

stimulus/estímulo cualquier cosa que causa una reacción o cambio en un organismo o cualquier parte de un organismo (333)

stomach/estómago el órgano digestivo con forma de bolsa ubicado entre el esófago y el intestino delgado, que descompone los alimentos por la acción de músculos, enzimas y ácidos (207)

stratosphere/estratosfera la capa de la atmósfera que se encuentra encima de la troposfera y en la que la temperatura aumenta al aumentar la altitud (43)

stress/estrés una respuesta física o mental a la presión (316)

structure/estructura el orden y distribución de las partes de un organismo (371)

surface current/corriente superficial un movimiento horizontal del agua del océano que es producido por el viento y que ocurre en la superficie del océano o cerca de ella (117)

systemic circulation/circulación sistémica el flujo de sangre del corazón a todas las partes del cuerpo y de vuelta al corazón (179)

T

T cell/célula T una célula del sistema inmunológico que coordina el sistema inmunológico y ataca a muchas células infectadas (285)

temperate zone/zona templada la zona climática ubicada entre los trópicos y la zona polar (124)

temperature/temperatura una medida de qué tan caliente (o frío) está algo; específicamente, una medida de la energía cinética promedio de las partículas de un objeto (26)

terminal velocity/velocidad terminal la velocidad constante de un objeto en caída cuando la fuerza de resistencia del aire es igual en magnitud y opuesta en dirección a la fuerza de gravedad (496)

testes/testículos los principales órganos reproductores masculinos, los cuales producen espermatozoides y testosterona (258)

theory/teoría una explicación que relaciona muchas hipótesis y observaciones (20)

thermal conduction/conducción térmica la transferencia de energía en forma de calor a través de un material (47)

thermometer/termómetro un instrumento que mide e indica la temperatura (99)

thermosphere/termosfera la capa más alta de la atmósfera, en la cual la temperatura aumenta a medida que la altitud aumenta (44)

thrust/empuje la fuerza de empuje o arrastre ejercida por el motor de un avión o cohete (538)

thunder/trueno el sonido producido por la expansión rápida del aire a lo largo de una descarga eléctrica (91)

thunderstorm/tormenta eléctrica una tormenta fuerte y normalmente breve que consiste en lluvia, vientos fuertes, relámpagos y truenos (90)

thymus/timo la glándula principal del sistema linfático; libera linfocitos T maduros (187)

tissue/tejido un grupo de células similares que llevan a cabo una función común (150, 369)

tonsils/amígdalas masas pequeñas y redondas de tejido linfático, ubicadas en la faringe y en el paso de la boca a la faringe (189)

tornado/tornado una columna destructiva de aire en rotación cuyos vientos se mueven a velocidades muy altas; se ve como una nube con forma de embudo y toca el suelo (92)

trachea/tráquea en los insectos, miriápodos y arañas, uno de los conductos de una red de conductos de aire; en los vertebrados, el conducto que une la laringe con los pulmones (191)

trade winds/vientos alisios vientos prevalecientes que soplan de este a oeste desde los 30° de latitud hacia el ecuador en ambos hemisferios (52)

tropical zone/zona tropical la región que rodea el ecuador y se extiende desde aproximadamente 23° de latitud norte hasta 23° de latitud sur (120)

troposphere/troposfera la capa inferior de la atmósfera, en la que la temperatura disminuye a una tasa constante a medida que la altitud aumenta (43)

U

umbilical cord/cordón umbilical la estructura que une al embrión y después al feto con la placenta, a través de la cual pasan vasos sanguíneos (263)

urinary system/sistema urinario los órganos que producen, almacenan y eliminan la orina (212)

uterus/útero en los mamíferos hembras, el órgano hueco y muscular en el que se incrusta el óvulo fecundado y en el que se desarrollan el embrión y el feto (259)

V

vagina/vagina el órgano reproductivo femenino que conecta la parte exterior del cuerpo con el útero (259)

variable/variable un factor que se modifica en un experimento con el fin de probar una hipótesis (14)

vein/vena en biología, un vaso que lleva sangre al corazón (178)

velocity/velocidad la rapidez de un objeto en una dirección dada (460)

vesicle/vesícula una cavidad o bolsa pequeña que contiene materiales en una célula eucariótica; se forma cuando parte de la membrana celular rodea los materiales que van a ser llevados al interior la célula o transportados dentro de ella (365)

vitamin/vitamina una clase de nutrientes que contiene carbono y que es necesaria en pequeñas cantidades para mantener la salud y permitir el crecimiento (304)

volume/volumen una medida del tamaño de un cuerpo o región en un espacio de tres dimensiones (25)

W

watt/watt (o vatio) la unidad que se usa para expresar potencia; es equivalente a un joule por segundo (símbolo: W) (556)

weather/tiempo el estado de la atmósfera a corto plazo que incluye la temperatura, la humedad, la precipitación, el viento y la visibilidad (76, 112)

wedge/cuña una máquina simple que está formada por dos planos inclinados y que se mueve; normalmente se usa para cortar (569)

weight/peso una medida de la fuerza gravitacional ejercida sobre un objeto; su valor puede cambiar en función de la ubicación del objeto en el universo (481)

westerlies/vientos del oeste vientos preponderantes que soplan de oeste a este entre 30° y 60° de latitud en ambos hemisferios (52)

wheel and axle/eje y rueda una máquina simple que está formada por dos objetos circulares de diferente tamaño; la rueda es el mayor de los dos objetos circulares (567)

wind/viento el movimiento de aire producido por diferencias en la presión barométrica (50)

work/trabajo la transferencia de energía a un objeto mediante una fuerza que hace que el objeto se mueva en la dirección de la fuerza (552)

work input/trabajo de entrada el trabajo realizado en una máquina; el producto de la fuerza de entrada por la distancia a través de la que se ejerce la fuerza (559)

work output/trabajo producido el trabajo realizado por una máquina; el producto de la fuerza de salida por la distancia a través de la que se ejerce la fuerza (559)

Spanish Glossary

Index

Boldface page numbers refer to illustrative material, such as figures, tables, margin elements, photographs, and illustrations.

A

arteries, 178, **178, 179, 180**
arthritis, 157, 289, **289**
artificial blood, 200
artificial satellites, 100
artificial vision, **250**
asexual reproduction, 254, **254,**
  334, **334**
  in bacteria, 390, **390**
  by binary fission, 390, **390**
  by budding, 254, **254, 334**
  by fragmentation, 254
  in hydras, 254, **254**
  mitosis in, 416
asteroids, climate change and,
  133, **133**
asthma, 193, 201
asthma camp counselors, 201
atherosclerosis, 180, **180**
atmosphere, 40–55, **40**
  acid precipitation, 59–60, **59**
  anticyclones and, 88–89, **88, 89**
  atmospheric pressure, 41, **41,**
    524, 525–526, **526**
  causes of winds, 50–52, **51, 52**
  composition of, 40, **40**
  cyclones and, 88–89, **88, 89**
  energy in, 46–49, **46, 47, 48, 49**
  global warming, 49
  greenhouse effect, 48–49, **48,**
    49, 134, **134**
  heating of, 46–49
  labs on, **59,** 66–67
  layers of, 42–45, **42, 43, 44, 45**
  pressure belts in, 51, **51**
  primary and secondary pollut-
    ants in, 56–57, **56, 57**
  relative humidity in, 77–78,
    77, 78
atmospheric pressure, 41, **41, 524,**
  525–526, **526**
atomic nucleus, 651
atomic number, 651
atoms, 651
ATP (adenosine triphosphate), 340,
  364, **364,** 387
atrium (plural, *atria*), 177, **177**
attention deficit hyperactivity disorder (ADHD), 251
auroras, 45, **45**
autoimmune diseases, 289, **289**
autonomic nervous system,
  229, **229**
average acceleration, 462, 652, 655
averages, **16,** 647
average speed, 459, **460,** 652, 655
axis of Earth, 114, **114,** 131, **131**
axons, 227, **227, 228**
axon terminals, 227, **227, 228**

Index

Index

Index

Index

Index

R

radar zoology, 72
radiation, 43, 46, **46–47**, 48, **48**
radiation balance, **46–47**, 48
radius, 567
rain, 82, **82** (*see also* precipitation)
    acid, 59–60, **59, 60**
    prevailing winds and, 115, **115**
    in rain shadows, **116, 126**
    in temperate biomes, **125, 126**
    in tropical biomes, **121, 122, 123**
    types of, 82, **82**
    in the water cycle, **76**
rain bands, **94**
rain shadows, **116, 126**
ramps, **560**, 568, **568**
ratios, 408, **408**, 647
RBCs (red blood cells), 182, **182**
receptors, 228, 234, **234**, 244–245
recessive diseases, 422, **422**
recessive traits, 407, **407, 408**, 411
recommended daily values, **306**
rectangle, area of, 650
rectum, 210, **210**
recycling, 6, **6,** 111
red blood cells (RBCs), 182, **182**
    blood types and, 184–185, **184, 185**
    hemoglobin in, 182, 338, **339**
    loss of DNA in, 355
    oxygen transport by, 182, **182, 339**
    platelets in, **183**
    in the spleen, 188, **188**
red marrow, 155, **155**
red pulp, 188, **188**
reducing fractions, 648
reference points, 458, **458**
reflection, law of, 654
reflexes, 235, **235**
regeneration, 254, **254**
registered nurses (RNs), 299
rehabilitation, 173
relative humidity, 77–78, **77, 78**
replication, 391–393, **392–393,** 436–437, **437**
reproduction, 254–261. *See also* asexual reproduction; human reproduction; sexual reproduction
    in animals, 254–257, **254, 255**
    in bacteria, 390, **390**
    by binary fission, 390, **390**
    as characteristic of life, 334
    in humans, 258–261
    in mammals, 255–257, **255, 256, 257**

mitosis, 391–393, **392–393**
    in plants, 405, 412, **412**
    by pollination, 405, **405**
    by regeneration, 254, **254**
resistance exercise, 160, **160**
respiration, 190–193, **190.** *See also* breathing; respiratory system
    cellular, 387–389, **387, 388**
    lab on, 194–195
    role of blood in, 192, **192**
respiratory system, **152,** 190–193, **190**
    bronchi and alveoli, 191, **191, 192**
    disorders of, 193, **193**
    nose, pharynx, and larynx, 191, **191**
    trachea, 191, **191**
resultant velocity, 461, **461**
retina, 236, **236**
retinitis pigmentosa, 250
revolving nosepiece, in a microscope, 640, **640**
rheumatoid arthritis, 289, **289**
ribonucleic acid (RNA), 440–441, **440–441**
ribosomes, 356–357, 363, **363, 440–441,** 441
ringworm, 281
RNA (ribonucleic acid), 440–441, **440–441**
RNs (registered nurses), 299
Roberts, Anthony, Jr., 201
Rocky Mountain spotted fever, 281
roller coasters, 521
rolling kinetic friction, 472, **472,** 474
roly-polies (pill bugs), 342–343
room temperature, **636**
rough ER, 363, **363**
roundworms, **208**
rulers, metric, 637, **637**
runoff, **76**

S

safety, 95–96, **96,** 317, **317**
safety symbols, 27, **27**
Sahara Desert, **115,** 123
saliva, 206
Salmonella, 281
Samoa, **121**
sample size, **19**
Santa Ana wind, **55**
SARS (severe acute respiratory syndrome), 193
satellites, weather, 100
saturated air, 77
saturated fats, 303
Schleiden, Matthias, 353

Schooley, Caroline, 379, **379**
Schwann, Theodor, 353
science, 4–7, **4, 5, 6**
scientific change, 21
scientific laws, **20,** 21, 653–655
scientific methods, 10–16, **10,** 638–639, **639**
    analyzing results, 15, **15,** 639
    asking questions, 11
    building knowledge through, 20
    communicating results, 639
    drawing conclusions, 16, **16,** 639
    forming hypotheses, 12, **12,** 638
    labs on, 28–29, 394–395
    making predictions, 13, **13,** 638
    testing hypotheses, 14–15, **14, 15,** 639
    theories and laws, 20–21
scientific models, 18–21, **18, 19, 20**
scientific notation, 650
scientific theories, 20, **20**
screws, 569, **569**
scrotum, **258**
scrubbers, 64
scuba instructors, 549
sea breezes, 54, **54**
sea hares, 401
sea level, atmospheric pressure at, 526, **526**
seasons, 114, **114**
sea stars, 254, **254**
seat belts, 232
seaweeds, **304**
secondary pollutants, 57, **57**
second-class levers, 565, **565**
secondhand smoke, 310
second law of motion, Newton's, 505–506, **505, 506**
seed shape, **413, 420**
Segway™ Human Transporter, 490, **490**
selective breeding, 422
self-pollination, 405, **405,** 412, **412**
Selger, Russell, 327
semen, 258, **258**
semipermeable membranes, 383, **383**
senses
    hearing, 238, **238,** 526
    responses to, 235, **235**
    sight, 236–237, **236, 237,** 250
    smell, 239, **239**
    taste, 238
    touch, 234, **234**
sensory neurons, 228, 229
severe acute respiratory syndrome (SARS), 193
sex cells, 416, **416,** 418, **418–419**
sex chromosomes, 421, **421**
sex hormones, 258, 259

T cells, 187, 285, **285, 287,** 288, **288**
teeth, 206, **206,** 207, **207**
temperate deserts, **124,** 126, **126**
temperate forests, **124,** 125, **125**
temperate grasslands, **124,** 125, **125**
temperate zone, 124–126, **124, 125, 126**
temperature
    in the atmosphere, 41, **41, 42,** 44
    body, 149, 184, 235, 333, **636**
    labs on, 115
    measurement of, **22, 26,** 78–79, 99, 102–103
    regulation of, **333**
    relative humidity and, 77–78, **77**
    in temperate biomes, **125, 126**
    in tropical biomes, **121, 122, 123**
    units of, **23,** 26, **26,** 636, **636**
temperature scales, 636, **636**
tendinitis, 161
tendons, 159, 161
terminal velocity, 496
testes (singular, *testis*), **241,** 258, **258**
testicular cancer, 261
testosterone, 258
theories, scientific, 20, **20**
thermal energy, 44, **44,** 47, **47**
thermal vents, **357**
thermometers, **22, 26,** 99, **99**
    labs on, 102–103, **115**
    temperature scales, 636, **636**
    use in weather forecasting, 99, **99**
    water, 102–103
    wet-bulb, 78–79, **78**
thermosphere, **42,** 44, **44**
"They're Made Out of Meat," 348
third-class levers, 565, **565**
third law of motion, Newton's, 507–508, **507, 508,** 513
three-panel flip chart instructions (FoldNote), 632, **632**
thrust, 538, **538,** 548
thunder, 91, **91**
thunderstorms, 85, **85,** 90–91, **90**
    air masses and, 85, **85**
    cumulus clouds and, 80
    lightning in, 91, **91,** 95
    safety during, 95
    severe, 90–91, **90, 91**
thymine, 434, **434,** 446
thymus glands, 187, **187,** 241, **241**
thyroid glands, 241, **241**
tires, air pressure in, 524, **524**
tissues, 150, **150,** 369, **369**
Titanic, **527**

TNX-901, 298
tobacco, 310, **310**
tolerance, drug, 308
tonsils, 189, **189**
tornadoes, 92, **92,** 529, **529**
    damage from, 93, **93**
    formation of, 92, **92**
    safety during, 96, **96**
touch, 234, **234**
trachea, 191, **191**
trade winds, 52, **52, 53**
traits, **406,** 410–415
    environment and, 415
    examples of, **405**
    genes and multiple, 414, **414**
    genotype probability, 411, **411**
    incomplete dominance, 414, **414**
    lab on, 424–425
    Mendel's experiments on, 406–407, **406, 407**
    selective breeding and, 422
transfer RNA (tRNA), **441**
transfusions, 185, **185**
transport tissue, 369
trees, 125, **125,** 128. *See also* forests
triangle, area of, 650
triceps muscles, 159, **159**
Trieste, **527**
tri-fold instructions (FoldNote), 633, **633**
triple-beam balances, 637, **637**
triplets, 260
tRNA (transfer RNA), **441**
tropical deserts, **120,** 123, **123**
tropical rain forests, 120–121, **120, 121**
tropical savannas, **120,** 122, **122**
tropical zone, 120–123, **120, 121, 122, 123**
the Tropics, 120–121
troposphere, **42,** 43, **43, 44**
tundra, 127, **127**
turbulence, 539–540, **540**
twins, 260
two-panel flip chart instructions (FoldNote), 633, **633**
typhoons, 93

U

ultrasound, 271
ultraviolet (UV) radiation
    effects on frogs, 14–16, **14, 15**
    mutations from, 442
    ozone layer and, 43
    for pathogen control, 282
    skin cancer and, 162

umbilical cords, 263, **263**
unbalanced forces, 467, **467,** 477
unicellular organisms, 370
units
    of area, **23,** 24, **24**
    conversion table, **635**
    of density, 26, **26**
    of force, 464
    of length, **23,** 24, **24**
    of mass, **23,** 25, **25,** 482
    of power, 556, **557**
    prefixes, **635**
    of pressure, 524, **524**
    SI, 23–26, 635, **635**
    of speed, 459
    of temperature, **23,** 26, **26**
    of volume, **23,** 25, **25**
    of weight, 482
    of work, 555, 656
universal gravitation, law of, 477–479, **478, 479,** 653
unsaturated fats, 303
urea, 213
ureters, 213, **213**
urethra, 213, 258, **258, 259**
urinary bladder, 213, **258, 259**
urinary system, **152,** 212–215, **212**
    function of, 212
    kidneys, 213–214, **213**
    problems in, 215, **215,** 270
    water balance, 214, **214**
urination, 213
urine, 213
uterus, 259, **259,** 262, **262**
UV (ultraviolet) radiation
    effects on frogs, 14–16, **14, 15**
    mutations from, 442
    ozone layer and, 43
    for pathogen control, 282
    skin cancer and, 162

V

vaccines, 282
vacuoles, 366, **366**
vacuum, free fall in a, 497, **497**
vagina, 259, **259**
valley breezes, 55
valves, heart, 177, **177**
vanes, wind, 99
variables, 14, **14**
vas deferens, 258, **258**
vegetables, **305**
vegetarian diets, 326
veins, 178, **178, 179**

Index

velocity, 460, **460**
  combining velocities, 461, **461**
  of falling objects, 495–496, **495**
  horizontal, 499, **499**
  speed and, 460, **460**
  terminal, 496
  vertical, 500, **500**
ventilation, 58
ventricles, 177, **177**
Venus flytraps, **333**
vertebrae, 232, **232**
vertical motion, 500, **500**
vesicles, 365, **365**, 384–385, **384,**
  385
Villa-Komaroff, Lydia, 451
villi, 208, **208**
viper fish, **527**
Virchow, Rudolf, 353
viruses
  controlling, 283
  diseases from, 292–293
  immune system response to,
    285–286, **285, 286–287**
  rabies, **280**
vision, 236–237, **236, 237, 250**
vitamins, 304, **304**
vocal cords, 191
volcanoes, climate change and,
  132, **132**
volcanologists, 9, **9**
volume
  buoyant force and, 535, **535**
  of a cube, 641
  formulas for, **354,** 650
  of a gas, 654
  measuring, 637
  units of, **23,** 25, **25, 635**
voluntary muscles, 158

W

warm air masses, 85, **85, 86–87**
warm fronts, 86, **86**
wastewater treatment, **210**
water
  climate and, 117
  diffusion into cells, 383, **383**
  diseases from, 281
  drinking, 214, **214,** 281, 303
  freezing and boiling points, **636**
  importance to humans, 214,
    214, 303, 336
  as necessity of life, 336
  pressure, 527, **527,** 540
  in thermometers, 102–103
  vapor, 40, 77, **77**
  water cycle, 76, **76**
water cycle, 76, **76**
water pressure, 527, **527,** 540
water thermometers, 102–103

water vapor, 40, 77, **77**
Watson, James, 435–436, **435**
watts (W), 556, **556**
waves, ocean, 95, **95**
WBCs (white blood cells), 183, **183,**
  187–188, **188**
weather, 76–101, **77,** 112, **113.** *See*
    also climate
  air masses and, 84–85, **84, 85**
  anticyclones, 88–89, **88, 89**
  birds and, 108
  clouds and, 80–81, **80, 81**
  condensation and, **76,** 79, **79**
  cyclones, 88–89, **88, 89**
  forecasting, 98–101, **98, 99, 100,**
    101, 108
  fronts and, 86–87, **86–87, 101**
  humidity, 77–79, **77, 78**
  hurricanes, 93–95, **93, 94, 95**
  labs on, **79,** 102–103
  precipitation, **76,** 82, **82**
  safety during severe, 95–96, **96**
  thunderstorms, 80, 85, **85,** 90–
    91, **90, 91**
  tornadoes, 92–93, **92, 93**
  water cycle and, 76, **76**
weather balloons, 98, **98**
weather forecasting
  animal and plant signs in, **100,**
    108
  meteorologists, 98, 109
  station models in, 100
  technology for, 98–99, **98, 99**
  weather maps, 100–101, **100,**
    101
  weather satellites in, 100
weather maps, 100–101, **100, 101**
weather satellites, 100
Webb, Gene, 8, **8**
wedges, 569, **569**
weighing procedures, 637
weight, 481, **481**
  from atmospheric pressure, 525
  buoyant force and, 531, **531**
  calculating, **525**
  influence on shape, 482, **482**
  mass and, 481, **481**
  as measure of gravitational force,
    481–482, **481, 482,** 497
  on the moon, **476,** 481, **481**
  units of, 482
weightlessness, **497**
westerlies, 52, **52, 53**
"Wet Behind the Ears," 548
wet-bulb thermometers, 78–79, **78**
wet mounts, 641
whaling, **340**
wheel and axle, 567, **567**
wheelchairs, for beaches, 579, **579**
wheels, invention of, **473**
white blood cells (WBCs), 183, **183,**
  187–188, **188**

white pulp, 188, **188**
winds, 50–55, **50**
  causes of, 50–52, **50, 51, 52**
  Coriolis effect on, 52, **52**
  direction measurement, 99, **99**
  global, 52–53, **53**
  in hurricanes, **94,** 95
  in jet streams, 54, **54**
  local, 54–55, **54, 55**
  prevailing, 115, **115**
  from storms, **50**
  trade, 52, **52, 53**
wind socks, 99, **99**
wind vanes, 99
wing shape, 537–538, **537, 538**
withdrawal symptoms, 308, 313
Wong, Stacey, 431
work, 552–570, **552**
  amount of, 554–555, **554, 555**
  calculating, 555, **555,** 656
  examples of, 552, **553,** 573
  force compared with, 552–553,
    553
  force-distance trade-off, 560, **560**
  in the human body, **553**
  by machines, 558–559, **559**
  power and, 556–557, 572–573
  units of, 555, 656
  work input/work output, 559–
    560, **559, 560, 561**
work input, 559–560, **559, 560,**
  561
work output, 559, **559**
worms, **208,** 222
Wright, Orville, **538**

X

X chromosomes, 421, **421**
X-ray diffraction, 435

Y

Yakel, Jerry, 401
Y chromosomes, 421, **421**
yeasts, 358
yellow fever, **281**
yellow marrow, 155, **155**
yogurt, **356**

Z

Zasloff, Michael, 298
zebras, 256, **256**
zoologists, 7, **7**
zoology, radar, 72
zygotes, 255, 259

Acknowledgments
continued from page ii

Academic Reviewers
continued

Simonetta Frittelli, Ph.D.
Associate Professor
Department of Physics
Duquesne University
Pittsburgh, Pennsylvania

William Grisham, Ph.D.
Lecturer
Psychology Department
University of California,
  Los Angeles
Los Angeles, California

David Haig, Ph.D.
Professor of Biology
Organismic and
  Evolutionary Biology
Harvard University
Cambridge, Massachusetts

David S. Hall, Ph.D.
*Assistant Professor
  of Physics*
Department of Physics
Amherst College
Amherst, Massachusetts

Deborah Hanley, Ph.D.
Meteorologist
State of Florida
Department of Agriculture
  and Consumer Services
Division of Forestry
Tallahassee, Florida

William H. Ingham, Ph.D.
Professor of Physics
James Madison University
Harrisonburg, Virginia

**Ping H. Johnson, M.D.,
  Ph.D., CHES**
*Assistant Professor of
  Health Education*
Department of Health,
  Physical Education
  and Sport Science
Kennesaw State University
Kennesaw, Georgia

Linda Jones
Program Manager
Texas Department
  of Public Health
Austin, Texas

David Lamp, Ph.D.
*Associate Professor
  of Physics*
Physics Department
Texas Tech University
Lubbock, Texas

Joel S. Leventhal, Ph.D.
Emeritus Scientist
United States Geological
  Survey (USGS)
Lakewood, Colorado

Mark Mattson, Ph.D.
Assistant Professor
Physics Department
James Madison University
Harrisonburg, Virginia

Nancy L. McQueen, Ph.D.
Professor of Microbiology
Department of Biological
  Sciences
California State University,
  Los Angeles
Los Angeles, California

**Madeline Micceri
  Mignone, Ph.D.**
Assistant Professor
Natural Science
Dominican College
Orangeburg, New York

Eva Oberdoerster, Ph.D.
Lecturer
Department of Biology
Southern Methodist
  University
Dallas, Texas

Dork Sahagian, Ph.D.
Research Professor
Department of Earth
  Sciences
Institute for the Study of
  Earth, Oceans, and Space
University of New
  Hampshire
Durham, New Hampshire

Laurie Santos, Ph.D.
Assistant Professor
Department of Psychology
Yale University
New Haven, Connecticut

Patrick K. Schoff, Ph.D.
Research Associate
Natural Resources Research
  Institute
University of Minnesota—
  Duluth
Duluth, Minnesota

**H. Michael Sommermann,
  Ph.D.**
Professor of Physics
Physics Department
Westmont College
Santa Barbara, California

Daniel Z. Sui, Ph.D.
Professor
Department of Geography
Texas A&M University
College Station, Texas

Dwight L. Whitaker, Ph.D.
Assistant Professor of Physics
Department of Physics
Williams College
Williamstown,
  Massachusetts

Lab Testing

Barry L. Bishop
*Science Teacher and
  Department Chair*
San Rafael Junior High
Ferron, Utah

Yvonne Brannum
*Science Teacher and
  Department Chair*
Hine Junior High School
Washington, D.C.

Daniel Bugenhagen
*Science Teacher and
  Department Chair*
Yutan Junior–Senior High
Yutan, Nebraska

Gladys Cherniak
Science Teacher
St. Paul's Episcopal School
Mobile, Alabama

James Chin
Science Teacher
Frank A. Day Middle School
Newtonville, Massachusetts

Randy Christian
Science Teacher
Stovall Junior High School
Houston, Texas

Vicky Farland
*Science Teacher and
  Department Chair*
Centennial Middle School
Yuma, Arizona

Susan Gorman
Science Teacher
North Ridge Middle School
North Richmond Hills,
  Texas

C. John Graves
Science Teacher
Monforton Middle School
Bozeman, Montana

Janel Guse
*Science Teacher and
  Department Chair*
West Central Middle School
Hartford, South Dakota

Norman Holcomb
Science Teacher
Marion Local Schools
Maria Stein, Ohio

Kerry A. Johnson
Science Teacher
Isbell Middle School
Santa Paula, California

M. R. Penny Kisiah
*Science Teacher and
  Department Chair*
Fairview Middle School
Tallahassee, Florida

Kathy LaRoe
Science Teacher
East Valley Middle School
East Helena, Montana

Edith C. McAlanis
*Science Teacher and
  Department Chair*
Socorro Middle School
El Paso, Texas

Jan Nelson
Science Teacher
East Valley Middle School
East Helena, Montana

Terry J. Rakes
Science Teacher
Elmwood Junior High
Rogers, Arkansas

Elizabeth Rustad
Science Teacher
Higley School District
Gilbert, Arizona

Debra A. Sampson
Science Teacher
Booker T. Washington
  Middle School
Elgin, Texas

David M. Sparks
Science Teacher
Redwater Junior High
  School
Redwater, Texas

Larry Tackett
*Science Teacher and
  Department Chair*
Andrew Jackson Middle
  School
Cross Lanes, West Virginia

Ivora Washington
*Science Teacher and
  Department Chair*
Hyattsville Middle School
Washington, D.C.

Elsie N. Waynes
*Science Teacher and
  Department Chair*
R. H. Terrell Junior High
  School
Washington, D.C.

Christopher Wood
Science Teacher
Western Rockingham
  Middle School
Madison, North Carolina

Sharon L. Woolf
Science Teacher
Langston Hughes Middle
  School
Reston, Virginia

Walter Woolbaugh
Science Teacher
Manhattan School System
Manhattan, Montana

Gordon Zibelman
Science Teacher
Drexel Hill Middle School
Drexel Hill, Pennsylvania

Teacher Reviewers

Laura Buchanan
*Science Teacher and
    Department Chairperson*
Corkran Middle School
Glen Burnie, Maryland

Sarah Carver
Science Teacher
Jackson Creek Middle
    School
Bloomington, Indiana

Robin K. Clanton
Science Department Head
Berrien Middle School
Nashville, Georgia

Karen Dietrich, S.S.J., Ph.D.
*Principal and Biology
    Instructor*
Mount Saint Joseph
    Academy
Flourtown, Pennsylvania

Meredith Hanson
Science Teacher
Westside Middle School
Rocky Face, Georgia

Denise Hulette
Teacher
Conway Middle School
Orlando, Florida

Debra S. Kogelman, MAed.
Science Teacher
University of Chicago
    Laboratory Schools
Chicago, Illinois

Deborah L. Kronsteiner
Teacher
Science Department
Spring Grove Area Middle
    School
Spring Grove, Pennsylvania

Jennifer L. Lamkie
Science Teacher
Thomas Jefferson Middle
    School
Edison, New Jersey

Augie Maldonado
Science Teacher
Grisham Middle School
Round Rock, Texas

Bill Martin
Science Teacher
Southeast Middle School
Kernersville, North
    Carolina

Maureen Martin
Science Teacher
Jackson Creek Middle
    School
Bloomington, Indiana

Alyson Mike
Science Teacher
East Valley Middle School
East Helena, Montana

Jean Pletchette
Health Educator
Winterset Community
    Schools
Winterset, Iowa

Susan H. Robinson
Science Teacher
Oglethorpe County Middle
    School
Lexington, Georgia

Elizabeth Rustad
Science Teacher
Higley School District
Gilbert, Arizona

Helen Schiller
Instructional Coach
Greenville County Schools
Greenville, South Carolina

Mark Schnably
Science Instructor
Thomas Jefferson Middle
    School
Winston-Salem, North
    Carolina

Stephanie Snowden
Science Teacher
Canyon Vista Middle
    School
Round Rock, Texas

Martha Tedrow
Science Teacher
Thomas Jefferson
    Middle School
Winston-Salem,
    North Carolina

Martha B. Trisler
Science Teacher
Rising Starr Middle School
Fayetteville, Georgia

Sherrye Valenti
Curriculum Leader
Science Department
Wildwood Middle School,
Wildwood, Missouri

Florence Vaughan
Science Teacher
University of Chicago
    Laboratory Schools
Chicago, Illinois

Angie Williams
Teacher
Riversprings Middle School
Crawfordville, Florida

Roberta Young
Science Teacher
Gunn Junior High School
Arlington, Texas

Answer Checking

Hatim Belyamani
Austin, Texas

John A. Benner
Austin, Texas

Catherine Podeszwa
Duluth, Minnesota

Staff Credits

Editorial

Leigh Ann García,
Executive Editor
Kelly Rizk,
Senior Editor
David Westerberg,
Senior Editor
Laura Zapanta,
Senior Editor

Editorial Development Team

Karin Akre
Monica Brown
Jen Driscoll
Shari Husain
Michael Mazza
Karl Pallmeyer
Laura Prescott
Bill Rader
Jim Ratcliffe
Dennis Rathnaw
Betsy Roll
Kenneth Shepardson

Copyeditors

Dawn Marie Spinozza,
Copyediting Manager
Simon Key
Jane A. Kirschman
Kira J. Watkins

Editorial Support Staff

Debbie Starr,
Managing Editor
Kristina Bigelow
Suzanne Krejci
Shannon Oehler

Online Products

Bob Tucek,
Executive Editor
Wesley M. Bain

Design

Book Design

Kay Selke,
Director of Book Design
Lisa Woods,
Page Designer
Holly Whittaker, *Project Administrator*

Media Design

Richard Metzger,
Design Director
Chris Smith,
Developmental Designer

Image Acquisitions

Curtis Riker, *Director*
Jeannie Taylor,
Photo Research Manager
Diana Goetting,
Senior Photo Researcher
Elaine Tate,
Art Buyer Supervisor
Angela Boehm,
Senior Art Buyer

Publishing Services

Carol Martin, *Director*

Graphic Services

Bruce Bond, *Director*
Jeff Bowers, *Graphic Services Manager*

Katrina Gnader,
Graphics Specialist
Cathy Murphy, *Senior Graphics Specialist*
Nanda Patel,
Graphics Specialist
JoAnn Stringer, *Senior Graphics Specialist II*

Technology Services

Laura Likon, *Director*
Juan Baquera, *Technology Services Manager*
Lana Kaupp,
Senior Technology Services Analyst
Margaret Sanchez, *Senior Technology Services Analyst*
Sara Buller, *Technology Services Analyst*
Patty Zepeda, *Technology Services Analyst*
Jeff Robinson, *Ancillary Design Manager*

New Media

Armin Gutzmer, *Director*
Melanie Baccus,
New Media Coordinator
Lydia Doty,
Senior Project Manager
Cathy Kuhles, *Technical Assistant*
Marsh Flournoy, *Quality Assurance Analyst*
Tara F. Ross, *Senior Project Manager*

Design New Media

Ed Blake, *Director*
Kimberly Cammerata, *Design Manager*
Michael Rinella,
Senior Designer

Production

Eddie Dawson,
Production Manager
Sherry Sprague,
Project Manager
Suzanne Brooks, *Production Coordinator*

Teacher Edition

Alicia Sullivan
David Hernandez
April Litz

Manufacturing and Inventory

Jevara Jackson
Ivania Quant Lee
Wilonda Ieans

Ancillary Development and Production

General Learning Communications,
Northbrook, Illinois

Credits

Abbreviations used: (t) top, (c) center, (b) bottom, (l) left, (r) right, (bkgd) background

PHOTOGRAPHY

Front Cover (tl) Mike Powell/Getty images; (bl) Daryl Benson/Masterfile; (r) Andrew Syred/Getty Images; (DNA strand) David Mack/Science Photo Library

Skills Practice Lab Teens Sam Dudgeon/HRW

Connection to Astrology Corbis Images; **Connection to Biology** David M. Phillips/Visuals Unlimited; **Connection to Chemistry** Digital Image copyright ©2005 PhotoDisc; **Connection to Environment** Digital Image copyright © 2005 PhotoDisc; **Connection to Geology** Letraset Phototone; **Connection to Language Arts** Digital Image copyright © 2005 PhotoDisc; **Connection to Meteorology** Digital Image copyright © 2005 PhotoDisc; **Connection to Oceanography** © ICONOTEC; **Connection to Physics** Digital Image copyright © 2005 PhotoDisc

Chapter One 2-3 Craig Line/AP/Wide World Photos; 4 Peter Van Steen/HRW Photo; 5 (t) Peter Van Steen/HRW Photo; 5 (b) Sam Dudgeon/HRW Photo; 6 (b) Peter Van Steen/HRW Photo; 6 (t) Hank Morgan/Photo Researchers, Inc.; 7 Dale Miquelle/National Geographic Society Image Collection; 8 (b) John Langford/HRW Photo; 8 (t) NC: Science VU/PNNL/Visuals Unlimited; 9 Jeremy Bishop/Science Photo Library/Photo Researchers, Inc.; 11 (t) Peter Van Steen/HRW Photo; 12 Sam Dudgeon/HRW Photo; 14 John Mitchell/Photo Researchers; 16 Sam Dudgeon/HRW Photo; 17 (t) John Mitchell/Photo Researchers; 18 (l) © Fujifotos/The Image Works; 18 (r) © Fujifotos/The Image Works; 20 Art by Christopher Sloan/Photograph by Mark Thiessen both National Geographic_Image Collection/© National Geographic Image Collection; 24 David Austen/Publishers Network, Inc.; 25 (l) Peter Van Steen/HRW Photo; 25(r) Peter Van Steen/HRW Photo; 26 (tl) Tony Freeman/PhotoEdit; 26 (tr) Victoria Smith/HRW; 26 (bl) Corbis Images; 34 (l), Craig Fugii/©1988 The Seattle Times; 35 (r), Bettman/CORBIS; 35 (bl), Layne Kennedy/CORBIS

Unit One 36 (t), Ronald Sheridan/Ancient Art & Architecture Collection; 36 (c), The Huntington Library, Art Collections, and Botanical Gardens, San Marino, California/SuperStock; 37 (tl), NASA; 37 (tr), Sam Dudgeon/HRW; 37 (cr), SuperStock; 37 (bc), Lawrence Livermore Laboratory/Photo Researchers, Inc.; 37, S.Feval/Le Matin/Corbis Sygma

Chapter Two 38-39, Robert Holmes/CORBIS; 41, Peter Van Steen/HRW; 43 (t), SuperStock; 43 (b), NASA; 44, Image Copyright ©2005 PhotoDisc, Inc.; 45, Patrick J. Endres/Alaskaphotographics.com; 50, Terry Renna/AP/Wide World Photos; 51 (b), Moredun Animal Health Ltd./Science Photo Library/Photo Researchers, Inc.; 54 (t), NASA/Science Photo Library/Photo Researchers, Inc.; 56 (c), Argus Fotoarchiv/Peter Arnold, Inc.; 56 (r), David Weintraub/Photo Researchers, Inc; 56 (l), Digital Image copyright © 2005 PhotoDisc/Getty Images; 57 CORBIS; 59, Simon Fraser/SPL/Photo Researchers, Inc.; 60 David R. Frazier Photolibrary; 62 (l), Goddard Space Flight Center Scientific Visualization Studio/NASA; 62 ©UNEP/Peter Arnold, Inc.; 64, (b) AP Wide World/ Joe Giblin; 64, (t) Tampa Electric; 65 Francis Dean/The Image Works; 66-67, Sam Dudgeon/HRW; 69 (t), Goddard Space Flight Center Scientific Visualization Studio/NASA; 72 (b), James McInnis/Los Alamos National Laboratories; 72 (t), Jonathan Blair/CORBIS; 73 (r), Fred Hirschmann; 73 (bl), Fred Hirschmann

Chapter Three 74-75, Tim Chapman/Miami Herald/NewsCom; 78, Sam Dudgeon/HRW; 79, Victoria Smith/HRW; 80 (tc), NOAA; 80 (tr), Joyce Photographics/Photo Researchers, Inc.; 80 (tl), Corbis Images; 82, Gene E. Moore; 82 (tl), Gerben Oppermans/Getty Images/Stone; 83 (c), Corbis Images; 83 (t), Victoria Smith/HRW; 85, Image Copyright ©2005 PhotoDisc, Inc.; 85 (t), Reuters/Gary Wiepert/NewsCom; 88, NASA; 90, William H. Edwards/Getty Images/The Image Bank; 91 (br), Jean-Loup Charmet/Science Photo Library/Photo Researchers, Inc.; 92 (all), Howard B. Bluestein/Photo Researchers, Inc.; 93 (t), Red Huber/Orlando Sentinel/SYGMA/CORBIS; 93 (b), NASA; 94 (tl), NASA/Science Photo Library/Photo Researchers, Inc.; 95, Dave Martin/AP/Wide World Photos; 96 (b), Joe Raedle/NewsCom; 97 (t), Will Chandler/Anderson Independent-Mail/AP/Wide World Photos; 97 (t), Jean-Loup Charmet/Science Photo Library/Photo Researchers, Inc.; 98 (c), NASA/Science Photo Library/Photo Researchers, Inc.; 98, Graham Neden/Ecoscene/CORBIS; 99, Sam Dudgeon/HRW; 99 (br), G.R. Roberts Photo Library; 99 (t), Guido Alberto Rossi/Getty Images/The Image Bank; 100, National Weather Service/NOAA; 104, Sam Dudgeon/HRW; 105 (tl), Corbis Images; 108 (tr), Lightscapes Photography, Inc./CORBIS; 105 (b), Joyce Photographics/Photo Researchers, Inc.; 109 (t), Michael Lyon; 109 (bl), Corbis Images

Chapter Four 110-111, Steve Bloom Images; 112 (bkgd), Tom Van Sant, Geosphere Project/Planetary Visions/Science Photo Library/Photo Researchers, Inc.; 112 (tl), G.R. Roberts Photo Library; 112 (tr), Index Stock; 112 (c), Yva Momatiuk & John Eastcott; 112 (bl), Gary Retherford/Photo Researchers, Inc.; 112 (br), SuperStock; 113 (t), CALLER-TIMES/AP/Wide World Photos; 113 (b), Chase Jarvis/CORBIS; 114 (t) Duomo/CORBIS; 115 Will & Deni McIntyre/CORBIS; 116 (bl), Larry Ulrich Photography; 116 (br), Paul Wakefield/Getty Images/Stone; 119, Index Stock; 120 ©Harold & Esther Edgerton Foundation, 2003, Courtesy of Palm Press, Inc.; 121 (tl), Carlos Navajas/Getty Images/The Image Bank; 121 (tr), Michael Fogden/Bruce Coleman, Inc.; 122,(l) Kevin Schafer/CORBIS, (r) Peter Johnson/CORBIS; 123, Larry Ulrich Photography; 124 (br), Tom Van Sant/Geosphere Project, Santa Monica/Science Photo Library/Photo Researchers, Inc.; 125 (b), Tom Bean/Getty Images/Stone; 125 (t), CORBIS Images/HRW; 126 (b), Steven Simpson/Getty Images/FPG International; 126 (t), Fred Hirschmann; 127 (b), Harry Walker/Alaska Stock; 127 (tr), Tom Van Sant/Geosphere Project, Santa Monica/Science Photo Library/Photo Researchers, Inc.; 128, SuperStock; 132 (br), Roger Werth/Woodfin Camp & Associates; 133, D. Van Ravenswaay/Photo Researchers, Inc.; 138, Gunter Ziesler/Peter Arnold, Inc.; 139, SuperStock; 142, Roger Ressmeyer/CORBIS; 142 (b), Terry Brandt/Grant Heilman Photography, Inc.; 143 (t), Courtesy of The University of Michigan

Unit Two 144 (t), Geoffrey Clifford/Woodfin Camp; 144 (c), J & L Weber/Peter Arnold; 144 (b), AP/Wide World Photos; 145 (cl), Brown Brothers; 145 (cr), SuperStock; 145 (tl), Gamma-Liaison/Getty News Images; 145 (bl), Enrico Ferorelli; 145 (tr), Sheila Terry/Science Photo Library/Photo Researchers, Inc.; 145 (br), © CORBIS

Chapter Five 146-147 AFP/CORBIS; 148 © Kevin Schafer/Getty Images/Stone; 149 Bob Daemmrich/Stock Boston; 150-151 © David Madison/Getty Images/Stone; 152 SamDudgeon/HRW; 157 Scott Camazine/Photo Researchers, Inc.; 158 (bkgd), © Bob Torrez/Getty Images/Stone; 158 (bl-inset), Dr. E.R. Degginger; 158 (r-inset), Manfred Kage/Peter Arnold, Inc. ; 158 (tl-inset), © G.W. Willis/Biological Photo Service; 160 (r), Sam Dudgeon/HRW; 160 (l), Chris Hamilton; 162 Sam Dudgeon/HRW; 164 (bkgd), Peter Van Steen/HRW; 164 (l), Dr. Robert Becker/Custom Medical Stock Photo; 164 (r), Peter Van Steen/HRW; 169 (t), Sam Dudgeon/HRW; 169 (b), Peter Van Steen/HRW; 172 (l), © Dan McCoy/Rainbow; 172 (r), Reuters/David Gray/NewsCom; 173 (t), Photo courtesy of Dr. Zahra Beheshti; 173 (b), Creatas/PictureQuest

Chapter Six 174-175 © Nih/Science Source/Photo Researchers, Inc.; 178 (l), O. Meckes/Nicole Ottawa/Photo Researchers; 178 (r), O. Meckes/Nicole Ottawa/Photo Researchers; 610 © John Bavosi/Photo Researchers, Inc.; 182 Susumu Nishinaga/Science Photo Library/Photo Researchers, Inc.; 183 (b), Don Fawcett/Photo Researchers; 185 © Getty Images/The Image Bank; 188 © Collection CNRI/Phototake Inc./Alamy Photos; 193 (l), Matt Meadows/Peter Arnold, Inc.; 193 (r), Matt Meadows/Peter Arnold, Inc.; 194 (b), Sam Dudgeon/HRW; 200 (l), Richard T. Nowitz/Phototake; 200 (r), © Paul A. Souders/CORBIS; 201 Courtesy of the Boggy Creek Gang Camp

Chapter Seven 202-203 © ISM/Phototake; 211 (t), Victoria Smith/HRW; 214 Getty Images/The Image Bank; 215 Stephen J. Krasemann/DRK Photo; 216 (b), Sam Dudgeon/HRW; 222 (l), J.H. Robinson/Photo Researchers; 222 (r), REUTERS/David Gray/NewsCom; 223 (t), Peter Van Steen/HRW

Chapter Eight 224-225 Omikron/Photo Researchers, Inc.; 231 (t), Sam Dudgeon/HRW; 235 Sam Dudgeon/HRW; 242 (c), Sam Dudgeon/HRW; 243 Will & Deni McIntyre/Photo Researchers; 244 (r), Sam Dudgeon/HRW; 244 (l), Sam Dudgeon/HRW; 245 Sam Dudgeon/HRW; 247 (t), Sam Dudgeon/HRW; 250 (l), Victoria Smith/HRW; 250 (r), Mike Derer/AP/Wide World Photos; 251 (t), Photo courtesy of Dr. Bertha Madras; 251 (b), SPL/Photo Researchers, Inc.

Chapter Eighteen 492-493 (all), NASA; 493 (br), NASA; 494 (bl), Richard Megna/Fundamental Photographs; 496 (cl), Toby Rankin/Masterfile; 497 (tr), James Sugar/Black Star; 497 (bl), NASA; 499 (bl), Michelle Bridwell/Frontera Fotos; 499 (br), Image copyright © 2005 PhotoDisc, Inc.; 500 (tc), Richard Megna/Fundamental Photographs; 501 (tr), Toby Rankin/Masterfile; 502 (b), John Langford/HRW; 504 (br), Mavournea Hay/HRW; 504 (bc), Michelle Bridwell/Frontera Fotos; 505 (all), Victoria Smith/HRW; 506 (all), Image copyright © 2005 PhotoDisc, Inc.; 507 (b), David Madison; 508 (tc), Gerard Lacz/Animals Animals/Earth Scenes; 508 (tr), Sam Dudgeon/HRW; 508 (tr), Image copyright © 2005 PhotoDisc, Inc.; 508 (tl), NASA; 509 (br), Lance Schriner/HRW; 509 (tr), Victoria Smith/HRW; 511 (all), Michelle Bridwell/HRW; 512 (br), Zigy Kaluzny/Getty Images; 512 (bl), © SuperStock; 513 (cl), Michelle Bridwell/HRW; 514 (bl), Image ©2001 PhotoDisc, Inc.; 515 (all), Sam Dudgeon/HRW; 516 (tc), Gerard Lacz/Animals Animals/Earth Scenes; 517 (all), Sam Dudgeon/HRW; 520 (tl), AP Photo/Martyn Hayhow; 520 (tr), Junko Kimura/Getty Images/NewsCom; 521 (tr), Steve Okamoto; 521 (br), Lee Schwabe

Chapter Nineteen 522-523 (all), © Nicholas Pinturas/Getty Images; 526 (tl), © I.M. House/Getty Images; 526 (tcl), David R. Frazier Photolibrary; 526 (cl), Dieter and Mary Plage/Bruce Coleman, Inc.; 526 (bcl), Wolfgang Kaehler/CORBIS; 526 (bl), © Martin Barraud/Getty Images; 527 (tr), © SuperStock; 527 (tcr), Daniel A. Nord; 527 (cr), © Ken Marschall/Madison Press Books; 527 (bcr), Dr. Paul A. Zahl/Photo Researchers, Inc.; 527 (br), CORBIS/Bettman; 529 (tr), © Charles Doswell III/Getty Images; 532 (tl), Bruno P. Zehnder/Peter Arnold, Inc.; 536 (br), Richard Megna/Fundamental Photographs/HRW Photo; 538 (tl), Larry L. Miller/Photo Researchers, Inc.; 538 (tr), Richard Neville/Check Six; 540 (tr), John Neubauer/PhotoEdit; 541 (br), Check Six; 543 (b), Sam Dudgeon/HRW; 544 (tr), © SuperStock; 548 (tc), © Victor Malafronte; 548 (tl), Sam Dudgeon/HRW; 549 (bl), Corbis Images; 549 (tr), Courtesy of Alisha Bracken

Chapter Twenty 550-551 (all), age fotostock/Photographer, Year; 552 (bl), John Langford/HRW; 553 (all), John Langford/HRW; 554 (all), © Galen Rowell/CORBIS; 555 (all), Sam Dudgeon/HRW; 556 (all), John Langford/HRW; 558 (cr), Scott Van Osdol/HRW; 558 (br), Robert Wolf/HRW; 558 (bc), Digital Image copyright © 2005 Artville; 559 (br), Sam Dudgeon/HRW; 560 (all), Scott Van Osdol/HRW; 561 (tr, cr), Sam Dudgeon/HRW; 561(tl), John Langford/HRW; 562 (br), CC Studio/Science Photo Library/Photo Researchers, Inc.; 563 (tr), © Reuters NewMedia Inc./CORBIS; 564 (all), Robert Wolf/HRW; 565 (tr), Robert Wolf/HRW; 565 (br), Scott Van Osdol/HRW; 565 (bc), Sam Dudgeon/HRW; 565 (tc), John Langford/HRW; 567 (t), Robert Wolf/HRW; 568 (tr), Lisa Davis/HRW; 569 (tl, cr), Sam Dudgeon/HRW; 569 (br), Peter Van Steen/HRW ; 570 (b), Robert Wolf/HRW; 571 (tr), Robert Wolf/HRW; 571 (br), John Langford/HRW; 572 (bl), Stephanie Morris/HRW; 573 (br), Paul Dance/Getty Images; 574 (tl), John Langford/HRW; 575 (cl), Helmut Gritscher/Peter Arnold, Inc.; 575 (tr), Robert Wolf/HRW; 575(cr), John Langford/HRW; 575 (br), Stephanie Morris/HRW; 576 (tr), © Visuals Unlimited; 578 (tl), Wayne Sorce; 579 (cr), A.W. Stegmeyer/Upstream; 579 (bl), Digital Image copyright © 2005 PhotoDisc

Lab Book 582, Sam Dudgeon/HRW; 585, Kuni Stringer/AP/Wide World Photos; 586, Victoria Smith/HRW; 587, Jay Malonson/AP/Wide World Photos; 589, 592, Sam Dudgeon/HRW; 593, Andy Christiansen/HRW; 594 Sam Dudgeon/HRW; 595 (t), Sam Dudgeon/HRW; 595 (c), Sam Dudgeon/HRW; 595 (b), Sam Dudgeon/HRW; 596 (tc), Sam Dudgeon/HRW; 597 Sam Dudgeon/HRW; 601 Peter Van Steen/HRW; 603 Sam Dudgeon/HRW; 604 (tl), Runk/Schoenberger/Grant Heilman; 604 (tc), Runk/Schoenberger/Grant Heilman; 604 (tr), Michael Abbey/Photo Researchers, Inc.; 604 (tr), Sam Dudgeon/HRW; 604 (br), Runk/Schoenberger/Grant Heilman; 605 (b), Sam Dudgeon/HRW; 605 (c), Sam Dudgeon/HRW; 606 Sam Dudgeon/HRW; 609 (all), Sam Dudgeon/HRW; 610 (br), Sam Dudgeon/HRW; 612 (c), Sam Dudgeon/HRW; 617 (br), Sam Dudgeon/HRW; 618 (b), Sam Dudgeon/HRW; 619 (br), John Langford/HRW; 612 (tr, cr), Robert Wolf; 621 (br), John Langford/HRW; 623 (l), Matt Meadows/Peter Arnold, Inc.; 623 (r), Matt Meadows/Peter Arnold, Inc.; 624 (b), Sam Dudgeon/HRW; 630 (br), Victoria Smith; 631 (br), Victoria Smith; 637 (tr), Peter Van Steen/HRW; 637 (br), Sam Dudgeon/HRW, 640 CENCO; 655 (tr), Sam Dudgeon/HRW

TEACHER EDITION CREDITS

1E (cl) Craig Line/AP/Wide World Photos; 1E (l) John Mitchell/Photo Researchers; 1F (l) Art by Christopher Sloan/Photograph by Mark Thiessen both National Geographic Image Collection/© National Geographic Image Collection; 1F (r) HRW; 37E (br) NASA; 37E (t) NASA/Science Photo Library/Photo Researchers, Inc.; 37E (r) Steve Starr/CORBIS; 73E (l), Gene E. Moore; 479E (br), Howard B. Bluestein/Photo Researchers, Inc.; 73F (t), NASA; 73F (br), Graham Neden/Ecoscene/CORBIS; 110E (tl), CALLER-TIMES/AP/Wide World Photos; 110E(tr), Doug Mills/AP/Wide World Photos; 110E (b), Tom Van Sant, Geosphere Project/Planetary Visions/Science Photo Library/Photo Researchers, Inc.; 145F (tr) Dr. Robert Becker/Custom Medical Stock Photo; 173E (r), SUSUMU NISHINAGA/SCIENCE PHOTO LIBRARY/Photo Researchers, Inc.; 173E (l), John Bavosi/Photo Researchers, Inc.; 251E (tl), Innerspace Visions; 251E (bl), Charles Phillip/CORBIS; 251F (r), Photo Lennart Nilsson/Albert Bonniers Forlag AB, A Child Is Born, Dell Publishing Company; 277E (l), Tektoff-RM/CNRI/Science Photo Library/Photo Researchers; 277E (r), Kent Wood/Photo Researchers, Inc.; 277F (l), Peter Van Steen/HRW Photo; 277F (r), SuperStock; 299E (l), Peter Van Steen/HRW Photo; 299E (r), John Kelly/Stone/Getty Images; 299F (r), Spencer Grant/Photo Researchers, Inc.; 299F (l), Peter Van Steen/HRW Photo; 329E (l), Visuals Unlimited/Science Visuals Unlimited; 329E (r), Visuals Unlimited/Stanley Flegler; 329F (r), SuperStock; 349E (tl), Visuals Unlimited/Kevin Collins; 349F (l), Quest/Science Photo Library/Photo Researchers, Inc.; 379E (t), Photo Researchers, Inc.; 379F (tl), L. Willatt, East Anglian Regional Genetics Service/Science Photo Library/Photo Researchers, Inc.; 379F (r), Ed Reschke/Peter Arnold, Inc.; 401E Ned M. Seidler/National Geographic Society Image Collection; 431E (l), Hulton Archive/Getty Images; 431F (l), Visuals Unlimited/Science Visuals Unlimited/Keith Wood; 431F (r), Volker Steger/Peter Arnold, Inc.; 455E (br) © Roger Ressmeyer/CORBIS; 455F (l) © Annie Griffiths Belt/CORBIS; 455F (r) NASA; 491E (br), Toby Rankin/Masterfile; 491F (br), © Zigy Kaluzny/Getty Images/Stone; 491F (tr), Index Stock Imagery, Inc.; 521F (tr), Larry L. Miller/Photo Researchers, Inc.; 521F (cl), © Charles Doswell III/Getty Images; 549F (tl), © Reuters NewMedia Inc./CORBIS

Answers to Concept Mapping Questions

The following pages contain sample answers to all of the concept mapping questions that appear in the Chapter Reviews. Because there is more than one way to do a concept map, your students' answers may vary.

CHAPTER 1   Science in Our World

19.

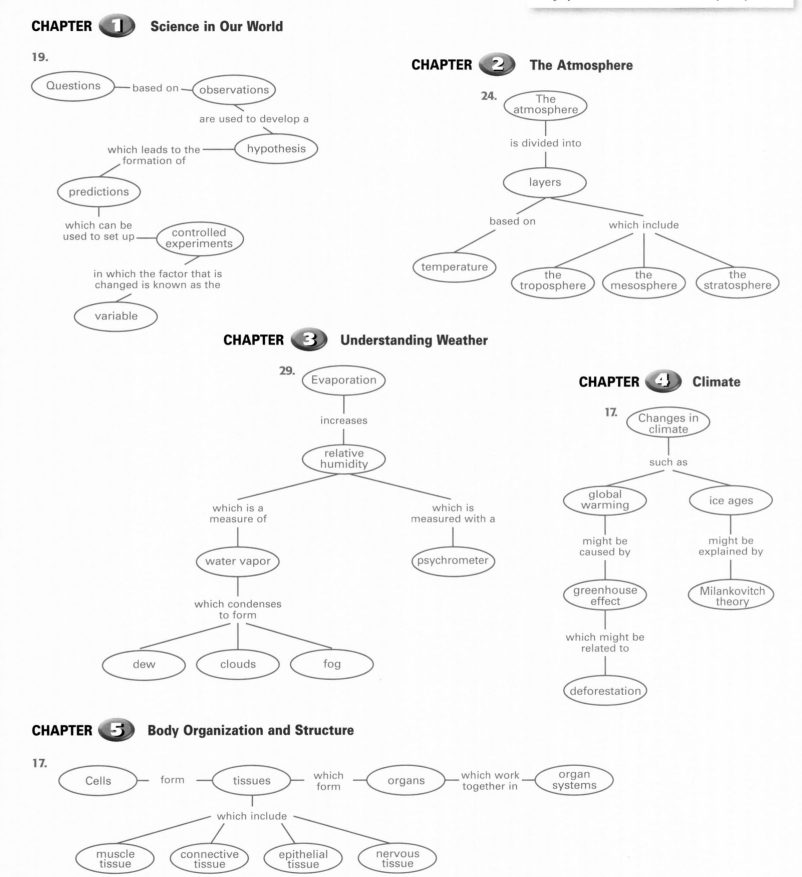

CHAPTER 2   The Atmosphere

24.

CHAPTER 3   Understanding Weather

29.

CHAPTER 4   Climate

17.

CHAPTER 5   Body Organization and Structure

17.

CHAPTER 6 Circulation and Respiration

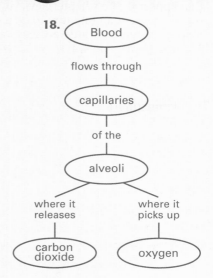

18.
- Blood
- flows through
- capillaries
- of the
- alveoli
  - where it releases → carbon dioxide
  - where it picks up → oxygen

CHAPTER 7 The Digestive and Urinary Systems

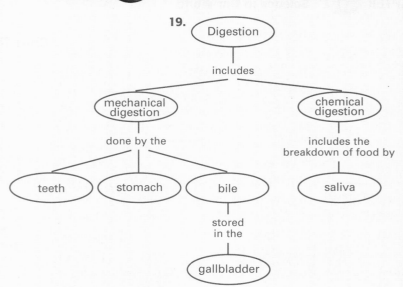

19.
- Digestion
- includes
  - mechanical digestion
    - done by the
      - teeth
      - stomach
      - bile
        - stored in the
          - gallbladder
  - chemical digestion
    - includes the breakdown of food by
      - saliva

CHAPTER 8 Communication and Control

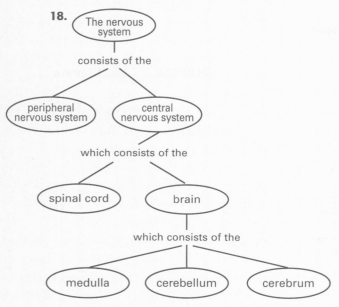

18.
- The nervous system
- consists of the
  - peripheral nervous system
  - central nervous system
    - which consists of the
      - spinal cord
      - brain
        - which consists of the
          - medulla
          - cerebellum
          - cerebrum

CHAPTER 9 Reproduction and Development

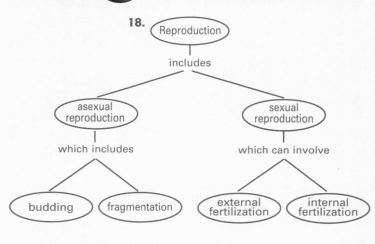

18.
- Reproduction
- includes
  - asexual reproduction
    - which includes
      - budding
      - fragmentation
  - sexual reproduction
    - which can involve
      - external fertilization
      - internal fertilization

CHAPTER 10 Body Defenses and Disease

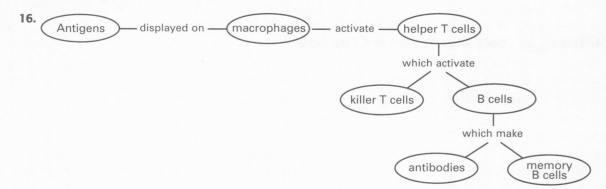

16.
- Antigens — displayed on — macrophages — activate — helper T cells
  - which activate
    - killer T cells
    - B cells
      - which make
        - antibodies
        - memory B cells

CHAPTER 11 Staying Healthy

17.

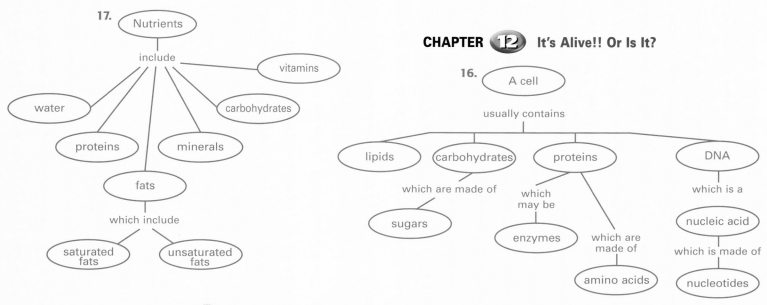

Nutrients — include — vitamins, water, carbohydrates, proteins, minerals, fats — which include — saturated fats, unsaturated fats

CHAPTER 12 It's Alive!! Or Is It?

16.

A cell — usually contains — lipids, carbohydrates, proteins, DNA

carbohydrates — which are made of — sugars

proteins — which may be — enzymes; which are made of — amino acids

DNA — which is a — nucleic acid — which is made of — nucleotides

CHAPTER 13 Cells: The Basic Units of Life

18.

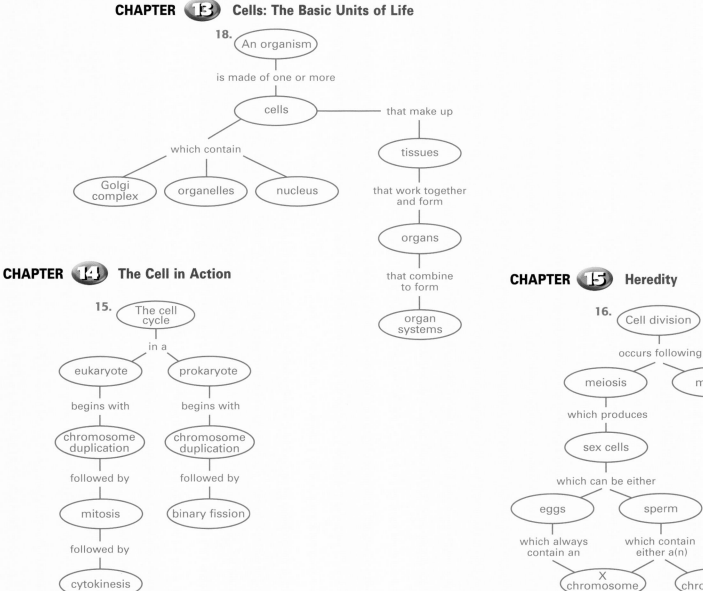

An organism — is made of one or more — cells

cells — which contain — Golgi complex, organelles, nucleus

cells — that make up — tissues — that work together and form — organs — that combine to form — organ systems

CHAPTER 14 The Cell in Action

15.

The cell cycle — in a — eukaryote, prokaryote

eukaryote — begins with — chromosome duplication — followed by — mitosis — followed by — cytokinesis

prokaryote — begins with — chromosome duplication — followed by — binary fission

CHAPTER 15 Heredity

16.

Cell division — occurs following — meiosis, mitosis

meiosis — which produces — sex cells — which can be either — eggs, sperm

eggs — which always contain an — X chromosome

sperm — which contain either a(n) — X chromosome, Y chromosome

CHAPTER 16 Genes and DNA

16.

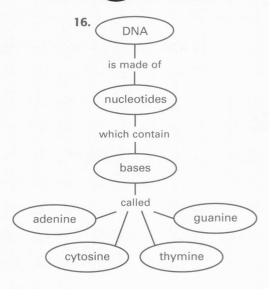

DNA
↓ is made of
nucleotides
↓ which contain
bases
called
adenine — cytosine — thymine — guanine

CHAPTER 17 Matter in Motion

15.

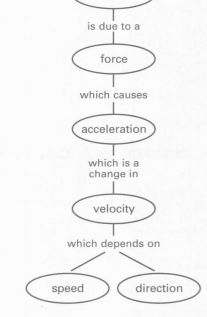

Motion
↓ is due to a
force
↓ which causes
acceleration
↓ which is a change in
velocity
↓ which depends on
speed — direction

CHAPTER 18 Forces and Motion

15.

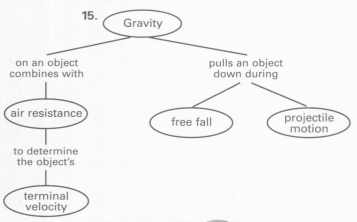

Gravity

on an object combines with
air resistance
↓ to determine the object's
terminal velocity

pulls an object down during
free fall — projectile motion

CHAPTER 19 Forces in Fluids

16.

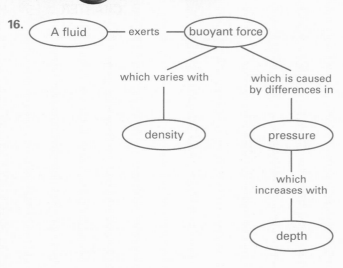

A fluid — exerts — buoyant force

which varies with
density

which is caused by differences in
pressure
↓ which increases with
depth

CHAPTER 20 Work and Machines

16.

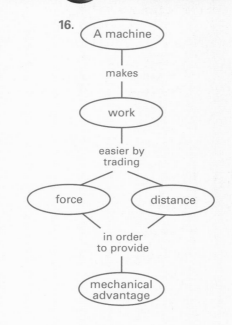

A machine
↓ makes
work
↓ easier by trading
force — distance
in order to provide
mechanical advantage